MAGNETIC RESONANCE
IMAGING OF THE PELVIS

MAGNETIC RESONANCE IMAGING OF THE PELVIS

A Practical Approach

Edited by

NEERAJ LALWANI, MBBS, DABR, FSAR

Professor of Radiology, Virginia Commonwealth University School of Medicine and Health System, Richmond, VA, United States

ACADEMIC PRESS

An imprint of Elsevier

elsevier.com/books-and-journals

ELSEVIER

Academic Press is an imprint of Elsevier
125 London Wall, London EC2Y 5AS, United Kingdom
525 B Street, Suite 1650, San Diego, CA 92101, United States
50 Hampshire Street, 5th Floor, Cambridge, MA 02139, United States
The Boulevard, Langford Lane, Kidlington, Oxford OX5 1GB, United Kingdom

Notices
Knowledge and best practice in this field are constantly changing. As new research and experience broaden our understanding, changes in research methods, professional practices, or medical treatment may become necessary.

Practitioners and researchers must always rely on their own experience and knowledge in evaluating and using any information, methods, compounds, or experiments described herein. In using such information or methods they should be mindful of their own safety and the safety of others, including parties for whom they have a professional responsibility.

To the fullest extent of the law, neither the Publisher nor the authors, contributors, or editors, assume any liability for any injury and/or damage to persons or property as a matter of products liability, negligence or otherwise, or from any use or operation of any methods, products, instructions, or ideas contained in the material herein.

ISBN: 978-0-323-89854-6

For Information on all Academic Press publications visit our website at
https://www.elsevier.com/books-and-journals

Publisher: Stacy Masucci
Acquisitions Editor: Rafael E Teixeira
Editorial Project Manager: Tracy I. Tufaga
Production Project Manager: Sajana Devasi PK
Cover Designer: Miles Hitchen

Working together
to grow libraries in
developing countries

www.elsevier.com • www.bookaid.org

Typeset by Aptara, New Delhi, India

To my wife, Yogita, and my son, Karthik,
for their patience, love, and unwavering support.

Contents

10. MRI of penis and penile prostheses

RYAN CLAYTON

11. MRI of female infertility

MARK D. SUGI, LIINA PÕDER, MARGARET HOUSER, JOANNA RIESS, NADIA J. KHATI

12. MRI of benign uterine pathologies

JILL BRUNO, CHRISTINA MILLER

13. MRI of malignant uterine tumors

RAJ MOHAN PASPULATI

Contributors

Ersan Altun Department of Radiology, The University of North Carolina at Chapel Hill, Chapel Hill, NC, United States

Pamela Argiriadi Department of Diagnostic, Molecular, & Interventional Radiology, Icahn School of Medicine at Mount Sinai, New York, NY, United States

Sandeep Arora Department of Radiology and Biomedical Imaging, Yale University, New Haven, CT, United States

Hannah Barnard Cleveland Clinic Imaging Institute, Cleveland, OH, United States

Candice A. Bookwalter Department of Radiology, Mayo Clinic, Rochester, MN, United States

Jill Bruno Department of Radiology, Virginia Commonwealth University/VCU Health, Richmond, VA, United States

Alex Chan Department of Radiology, Mayo Clinic Radiology, Rochester, MN, United States

Ryan Clayton Department of Radiology, VCU School of Medicine and Health System, Richmond, VA, United States

Teresa M. Cunha Department of Radiology, Instituto Português de Oncologia de Lisboa Francisco Gentil, Lisboa Codex, Portugal

Jacob Davis Professor of Radiology, Virginia Commonwealth University School of Medicine and Health System, Richmond, VA, United States

Myra K Feldman Cleveland Clinic Imaging Institute, Cleveland, OH, United States

Rakhee S. Gawande Russell H. Morgan Department of Radiology, Johns Hopkins School of Medicine, Baltimore, MD, United States

Luke Ginocchio Department of Radiology, NYU Langone Health, Grossman School of Medicine, New York, NY

Margaret Houser Department of Radiology, The George Washington University Hospital, Washington, DC, United States

Venkata S. Katabathina Department of Radiology, University of Texas Health Science Center, San Antonio

Lokesh Khanna Department of Radiology, University of Texas Health Science Center, San Antonio

Nadia J. Khati Department of Radiology, The George Washington University Hospital, Washington, DC, United States

Neeraj Lalwani Professor of Radiology, Virginia Commonwealth University School of Medicine and Health System, Richmond, VA, United States

Christine O. Menias Department of Radiology, Mayo Clinic in Arizona, Scottsdale, AZ, United States

Christina Miller Department of Radiology, Women's Imaging, Augusta Health, Fishersville, VA, United States

Pardeep Mittal Department of Radiology and Imaging: Diagnostic, Medical College of Georgia, Augusta University Medical Center, Augusta, GA, United States

Courtney Moreno Department of Radiology and Imaging Sciences, Emory University, Atlanta, GA, United States

Stephanie Nougaret IRCM, Montpellier Cancer Research institute, Montpellier, France; Department of Radiology, Montpellier Cancer institute, INSERM, University of Montpellier, Montpellier, France

Raj Mohan Paspulati Department of Radiology, Moffitt Cancer Center, Tampa, FL, United States

Marika A. Pitot Department of Radiology, Mayo Clinic, Rochester, MN, United States

Janardhana Ponnatapura Department of Radiology, Wake Forest University School of Medicine, Winston Salem, NC, United States

Srinivasa R. Prasad Department of Radiology, MD Anderson Cancer Center, Houston, TX, United States

Liina Põder Department of Radiology & Biomedical Imaging, Division of Abdominal Imaging and Ultrasound, University of California, San Francisco, CA, United States

Roopa Ram Department of Radiology, University of Arkansas Medical Center, Little Rock, AR, United States

Joanna Riess Department of Radiology, The George Washington University Hospital, Washington, DC, United States

Martina Sbarra Departmental Faculty of Medicine and Surgery, Unit of Diagnostic Imaging and Interventional Radiology, Università Campus Bio-Medico di Roma, Rome, Italy

Krishna Shanbhogue Department of Radiology, NYU Langone Health, Grossman School of Medicine, New York, NY

Clifford Shin Department of Radiology and Biomedical Imaging, Yale University, New Haven, CT, United States

Mark D. Sugi Department of Radiology & Biomedical Imaging, Division of Abdominal Imaging and Ultrasound, University of California, San Francisco, CA, United States

Karthik Sundaram Department of Radiology, University of Pennsylvania, Philadelphia, PA, United States

Bachir Taouli Department of Diagnostic, Molecular, & Interventional Radiology, Icahn School of Medicine at Mount Sinai, New York, NY, United States

Jacqueline Urbine Department of Radiology, Children's Hospital of Richmond, Virginia Commonwealth University Health System, Richmond, VA, United States

Gregory Vorona Department of Radiology, Children's Hospital of Richmond, Virginia Commonwealth University Health System, Richmond, VA, United States

Sarah G. Winks Department of Radiology, Virginia Commonwealth University Health System, Richmond, VA, United States

Jinxing Yu Department of Radiology, Virginia Commonwealth University Health System, Richmond, VA, United States

Atif Zaheer Russell H. Morgan Department of Radiology, Johns Hopkins School of Medicine, Baltimore, MD, United States

Foreword

The pelvis harbors many vital organs in a compact space and is a frequent site of complex pathologies. Imaging options for evaluating pelvic pathologies are limited, and magnetic resonance imaging (MRI) plays a critical role because of its high natural soft-tissue resolution and multiplanar capabilities.

Pelvic MRI has evolved profoundly in the last decade, and many radiologists rely on continuous medical education courses, online content, lectures, workshops, and hands-on training offered by various professional societies to learn pelvic MRI and related subjects. While some of these formats are informative, none promise quality content or always suit one's pace, area of interest, or clinical need. Moreover, some of the resources are very expensive. A conventional textbook provides an excellent solution to these problems.

This textbook serves as a comprehensive review of pelvic imaging, and all the contributors in this book are passionate educators and are known for their expertise in pelvic MR imaging. All chapters provide image-rich and case-based content that includes key clinical "teaching pearls" gained from the experience of the contributors. Each chapter is akin to personalized teaching. It is like doing a *mini fellowship* in pelvic MRI at your own pace (via a book).

Each chapter covers pertinent anatomy, cutting-edge MRI techniques, and practical tips. All the most common, clinically encountered male and female pelvic pathologies are covered in this book and the content is well presented and easy to understand. If you are a trainee or practicing radiologist, the content is equally helpful for learning new skills. This knowledge may also help radiologists start and establish a new service line in their practices.

In addition, the book includes a broad spectrum of diseases and pathologies. Therefore, it may also target a wide range of readers from different fields of medicine, including surgery, urology, obstetrics, gynecology, or urogynecology.

Edited by Neeraj Lalwani, MD, a renowned expert and educator in body MRI, this textbook serves as a single, comprehensive, and practical resource for learning about cutting-edge pelvic MRI covering commonly encountered pelvic conditions. I am honored to write this Foreword in support of this work as I have known him since the beginning of his career and have seen him grow to the clinical radiology expert that he is.

Christine O. (Cooky) Menias, M.D.
Professor of Radiology, Mayo Clinic in Arizona
Editor-in-chief, RadioGraphics, RSNA

Foreword

It is an honor for me to write this Foreword for *Magnetic Resonance Imaging of the Pelvis: A Practical Approach*. The title itself is extremely appealing to me, as a practical approach to radiologic interpretation is needed in today's busy clinical environment. Too often textbooks are filled with interesting but not clinically actionable information that can dissuade a reader from tackling the Herculean task of reading a tome. This is not the case with this textbook, as every chapter is clinically relevant, efficiently written and state-of-the-art. As Editor-in-Chief of *Abdominal Radiology* I have come to know and respect Dr. Lalwani. The rapid growth of pelvic imaging using magnetic resonance imaging (MRI) is challenging even for the subspecialized abdominal radiologist. The addition of advanced MR equipment, techniques and expanding applications for addressing a variety of pelvic conditions requires a lot of time and effort to keep up in this ever-evolving field. There is a need for a single, up-to-date, comprehensive but practical source. As practicing radiologists encounter these examinations, it will be most welcome to have a single textbook that they can rely for both protocoling their examinations and interpreting the MR images.

This book covers the breath of pelvic imaging as we know it today using MRI. The range of subject matter varies from staging of rectal, uterine, cervical, and prostate cancer to fetal and placental MR and everything in between. The depth of coverage is just right. Dr. Lalwani has steered the various chapter experts to follow a clear and useful structure. Most often the anatomy of the organ is explained, followed by current MR technique (protocol considerations), common disorders and their appearance, and finally a pearls and pitfalls section. All these sections are extremely useful, and I believe the pearls and pitfalls section is very innovative and helpful as a quick guide and summary of the key concepts from each chapter. I commend the various authors as their work is of high quality and clinically relevant.

I am personally excited to own a copy of this book. It addresses a practice need that I have, and I suspect most abdominal radiologists will benefit from having a copy in their reading rooms. Until now we did not have a single source to recommend to our residents and fellows. This book is a wonderful gift to trainees at all levels. It will be wonderful to have this resource at my fingertips the next time a challenging case or question comes my way. Thank you, Dr. Lalwani and co-authors, for filling a practice gap, and doing it in such an exemplary fashion.

C. Dan Johnson, MD, MMM, FACR, FSAR
Editor-in-Chief, Abdominal Radiology
Chair Emeritus, Department of Radiology,
Mayo Clinic Arizona

Preface

Magnetic resonance imaging (MRI) plays an essential role in diagnosing pelvic disease in both males and females. Pelvic MRI is a complex and evolving subject, but many qualified radiologists lack expertise in this area. It is interesting to note that even most current body imaging fellowships lack an adequate and comprehensive training in advanced pelvic MRI.

Although pelvic MRIs have increased exponentially over the last decade due to their implications in rectal and prostate cancers, they are still underutilized. MRI has enormous potential for the accurate diagnosis of complex pelvic conditions. Its popularity is increasing in gynecological, obstetric, and pelvic floor conditions. Advances in fetal MRI have made it a complementary modality for assessing complex fetal and placental conditions effectively. MRI has enormous potential to carry out critical diagnoses in the pathologies of the scrotum and penis, but there is a lack of awareness and expertise.

The number of pelvic MRIs ordered for certain pathologies remains low. With limited experience, low number of investigations, and deficient training, many practicing radiologists are not comfortable reading these studies. There are no comprehensive educational resources that can be referenced for pelvic MRI. Specifically, no reference book provides a detailed account of the relevant anatomy, cutting-edge techniques, the role of MRI in making diagnoses, and the depiction and staging of distinct pelvic pathologies. We need a book that can equally assist radiology trainees and radiology practitioners and serve as a quick reference for any complex pelvic MRI case encountered in real-world practice.

My aim is providing a comprehensive textbook focusing on MRI of pelvic pathologies with a "practical approach." This book has years of experience shared by all contributors and co-authors. I thank all the contributors and co-authors for their outstanding efforts in preparing this book. Without their endurance, patience and support, my vision of each chapter would have been very hard to realize. I hope that all audiences will find these efforts useful in their daily practice.

Finally, I want to thank my wife and son for their steadfast support. Finishing this work was not possible without both of you.

CHAPTER

1

MRI of mesorectum and rectal cancer staging

Neeraj Lalwani[a], *Christine O. Menias*[b]

[a]Professor of Radiology, Virginia Commonwealth University School of Medicine and Health System, Richmond, VA, United States [b]Department of Radiology, Mayo Clinic in Arizona, Scottsdale, AZ, United States

1.1 Introduction

Colorectal cancer (CRC) is the third leading cause of cancer mortality in the United States. The American Cancer Society projects an estimated 106,180 new cases of colon cancer and 44,850 new cases of rectal cancer to be diagnosed in 2022.[1] The lifetime risk of CRC is approximately 1 in 23 (4.3%) for men and 1 in 25 (4.0%) for women. CRC is projected to cause an estimated 52,580 deaths in 2022.[1] An interesting trend in CRC over the past few years has been a decrease in the number of cases among seniors accompanied by an increase in the number of cases among individuals younger than 50. This trend may be attributed to environmental factors and modern lifestyles, in addition to diet and obesity. Notwithstanding the absence of a family history of the disease among many young patients, genetics obviously plays a crucial role in the pathogenesis of CRC.

The mesorectum is a natural boundary for the spread of rectal cancer. Total mesorectal excision (TME) is the universally accepted standard surgical treatment for rectal cancer and involves en bloc resection of the mesorectum. A high-quality TME procedure can significantly reduce local recurrence from 20–30% to 8–10%, as well as increase the 5-year survival rate from 48% to 68%.[2,3] A negative circumferential resection margin (CRM) remains the key prognostic factor.

Locally infiltrative tumors within the mesorectum may require neoadjuvant chemotherapy (nCRT) before a TME is performed. The treatment decision is often based on factors unique to the tumor and the patient. Histological classification and TNM staging of the tumor are the two key attributes considered when making an evidence-based treatment decision. A personalized treatment approach can provide a balanced treatment plan that is neither too aggressive nor too conservative, allowing for a low propensity for recurrence and preserving quality of life.

Magnetic resonance imaging (MRI) allows surgeons to develop a tailored treatment plan based on accurate staging. Rectal cancer MRI staging is believed to be reliable with a diagnostic accuracy, sensitivity, and specificity of 85%, 87%, and 75%, respectively.[4] Using MRI during baseline staging, surgeons can identify patients who may need nCRT before a TME is planned. MRI may also facilitate the detection of poor prognostic factors, such as extramural vascular invasion (EMVI), mucinous component, and the status of the mesorectal fascia (MRF). MRI can also detect sphincteric involvement in low rectal cancers. Post nCRT, MRI can be used to assess treatment response, residual or viable tumors, and mucinous conversion.[5] During follow-up, MRI is also vital for detecting local recurrence after completion of therapy. The current role of MRI in the staging of rectal cancer and related issues is discussed in this chapter.

1.2 Anatomy of the rectum

The surgical and anatomic extent of the rectum is unique. Surgically, the rectum extends from the anorectal junction (ARJ) to the rectosigmoid junction (RSJ) (Fig. 1.1). The ARJ is defined as the area where the levator ani muscle joins the external sphincter, and the RSJ corresponds more or less to the sacral promontory.[6] Surgically, the segment below the ARJ is defined as the anal canal, although anatomically, it comprises both the anatomical anal canal (below the dentate line) and a portion of the lower rectum above the dentate line (Figs. 1.1 and 1.2).

Anatomically, the rectum measures 12–13 cm, but is measured as 15 cm when measuring from the anal verge (lowermost edge of the anal canal) because a portion of the lower rectum also comprises the surgical anal canal (Figs. 1.1 and 1.2). Surgically, the rectum is arbitrarily divided into three equal-sized segments (upper segment, middle segment, and lower third segment),[7] each measuring 5 cm (Fig. 1.1).

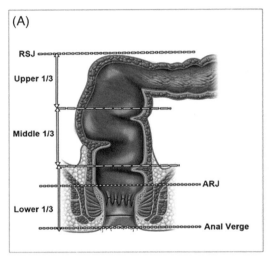
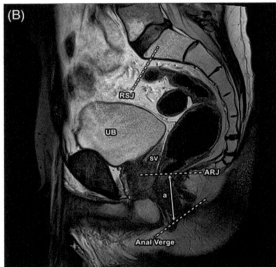

FIG. 1.1   **Anatomy of the rectum.** (A) The rectum is arbitrarily divided into three segments of equal size, each measuring 5 cm from the anal verge to the rectosigmoid junction (RSJ). The lower segment consists of a portion of the lower rectum and the surgical anal canal below the ARJ. (B) In MRI imaging, the ARJ corresponds to the point where the puborectalis joins the external sphincter. The surgical canal (a) extends from between the anal verge to the ARJ. The RSJ broadly corresponds to the sacral promontory. The rectum must be measured along its long axis in sagittal view. *SV*, seminal vesicles; *UB*, urinary bladder.

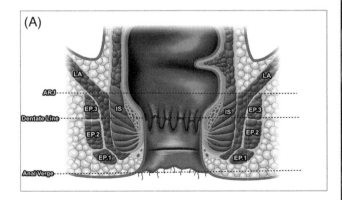
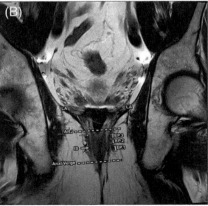

FIG. 1.2   **Anatomy of the anal canal.** The dentate line demarcates the anatomical anal canal, but this is not visualized on the MRI. The levator ani (LA) joins with the puborectalis and external sphincter (EP) to form the surgical ARJ. The skeletal muscle of the external sphincter has three components: subcutaneous (EP1), superficial (EP2), and deep (EP3). The internal sphincter (IS) is an involuntary smooth muscle formed by a thickening of the circular muscle layer of the surgical anal canal. (A) A visual representation of the anal canal and its muscular components. (B) Coronal MRI through the anal canal corresponding to the illustration (a).

The inferior mesenteric artery (IMA), a direct branch of the abdominal aorta, continues as the superior rectal artery and primarily supplies the rectum. Additionally, the middle and lower rectal arteries from the internal iliac arteries also supply the lower rectum and middle rectum, respectively. A similar pattern exists for venous drainage. The rectal venous drainage pattern may explain why individuals with superior rectal cancers exhibit a high propensity for developing hepatic metastasis (interior mesenteric vein drains via the portal venous system), and middle or lower rectal tumors tend to metastasize mostly to the lungs (via the systemic venous system).[8]

The upper one-third of the rectum is covered, along its anterior and lateral aspects, by the peritoneum (Fig. 1.3).

The middle third of the rectum is covered along the anterior aspect, while the lower third is not lined with peritoneum, making it an extraperitoneal aspect of the organ. Hence, there is a high probability that a tumor involving the anterior upper or middle third of the rectum will invade the peritoneum.[7]

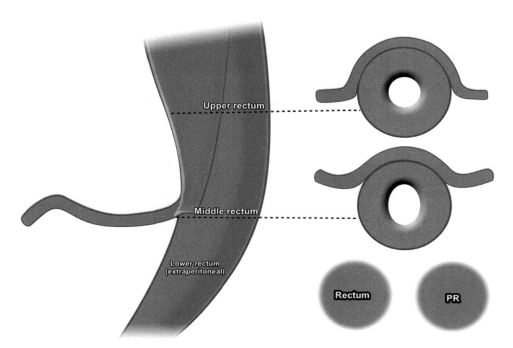

FIG. 1.3 **Illustration of the relationship between the rectum and its peritoneal reflection (PR).** The upper rectum has anterolateral coverage by the peritoneum, while the middle rectum has anterior coverage. The lower rectum is fully extraperitoneal. Because of this relationship, the mesorectum completely encloses only the lower rectum. The upper rectum does not have the mesorectum along its anterior and lateral aspect, while the middle rectum does not have the mesorectum along its anterior aspect. Tumors along the peritoneal surface of the rectum can often invade the peritoneal reflection and advance to the T4a stage.

1.3 MR technique and protocol

High-resolution, multiplanar, non–fat-suppressed T2-weighted (T2W) images are key to evaluating the rectum. Axial images taken perpendicular to the longitudinal axis of the rectum (Fig. 1.4) provide precise information on the spread of cancer in the mesorectum, which might otherwise be misinterpreted because of partial volume effects.

Furthermore, the entire pelvis is also imaged (with and without fat suppression) with T2W sequences. Diffusion-weighted imaging (DWI) and apparent diffusion coefficient (ADC) imaging are also recommended as standard MRI techniques for rectal imaging. Luminal ultrasound gels and antispasmodic agents are optional and may be used depending on institutional policies. Postcontrast fat-suppressed dynamic T1-weighted (T1W) sequences are optional but are recommended for both pretreatment and posttreatment studies. A proposed magnetic resonance (MR) protocol is summarized in Table 1.1.

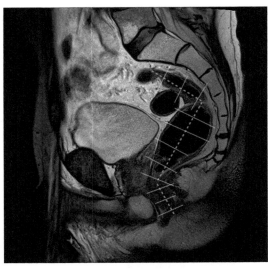

FIG. 1.4 How to obtain true axial images of the rectum: An accurate assessment of tumor extent is only possible on true axial images of the rectum taken perpendicular to the rectal longitudinal axis (yellow dotted line). As a result of the rectal curve, some images may overlap.

TABLE 1.1   MR protocol for rectal cancer staging.

Sequence	Plane(s)	Clinical relevance	Recommendation
High-resolution T2W (2–3 mm or 3–4 mm)	Sagittal plane, axial plane (perpendicular to the longitudinal axis of the tumor), and coronal plane (parallel to the tumor)	TN staging. Tumor location, morphology, and measurement. MRF or CRM assessment. EMVI and tumor deposits. Involvement of peritoneal reflection and adjacent structures.	Backbone of the staging; mandatory
	Plus, an additional plane parallel to the anal canal; for low rectal tumors	Assessment of the integrity and involvement of the sphincteric complex and intersphincteric plane.	Recommended; as needed.
T2W, whole pelvis	Axial plane	Evaluate entire pelvis and nonlocoregional lymph nodes. Mucinous tumors: Accurate assessment of the border between mucin and mesorectal fat.	Recommended
DWI	Axial plane	Baseline scan: TN staging. Restaging scan: Assessment of residual tumors and viable tumors.	Mandatory for (re)staging; recommended for baseline assessment
T1W, whole pelvis	Axial plane	Evaluation of bone findings.	Recommended
Postcontrast T1W fat-suppressed, dynamic sequences (DCE-MRI)	Axial plus, sagittal plane (perpendicular to tumor) and coronal plane (parallel to tumor); as needed	EMVI assessment. Assessment of fibrosis in posttreatment scans. Assessment of the involvement of neighboring structures in T4 tumors.	Can be helpful, more so in posttreatment scans

1.4 MR anatomy of the rectum

With cross-sectional MRI, three layers of the rectal wall (mucosa, submucosa, and muscularis propria) are discernible in axial T2W images.[9] The thinnest hypointense layer around the rectal lumen is mucosa, and the low-intensity outer layer in the T2W signal is the muscularis propria.[10] The relatively thick band with high T2W signal intensity interposed between the two hypointense layers is submucosa (Fig. 1.5).

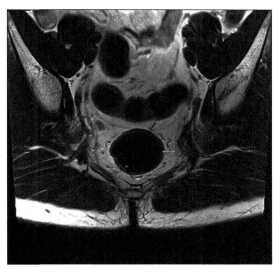

FIG. 1.5 An axial T2W image showing the three layers of the rectal wall. Mucosa (arrow head) forms the thinnest hypointense layer around the rectal lumen, and the muscularis propria forms the outermost T2W hypointense layer (large arrow). The submucosa is a relatively thick band of high-T2W-signal intensity (white arrow).

1.5 Concept of TME and the mesorectum

All pelvic organs are supported by two layers of endopelvic fascia: a visceral layer and a parietal layer. The visceral layer surrounds the pelvic organ, and the parietal layer covers the pelvic musculature and skeletal system. The visceral layer of the endopelvic fascia surrounding the rectum is referred to as the MRF, and the parietal layer is the presacral fascia. The MRF is not truly circumferential except in the lower rectum (Fig. 1.3). The space between the presacral fascia and the sacrum is called the presacral space, and it encloses the sacral veins (Figs. 1.6 and 1.7).[11]

The space between the MRF and the rectal surface is called the mesorectum (Figs. 1.7 and 1.8). The mesorectum forms a natural boundary to a rectal tumor and is comprised of adipose and connective tissue, lymphatics, and vasculature.[12] The mesorectum extends from the level of the peritoneal reflection down to the point of insertion of the levator ani at the ARJ (Figs. 1.7 and 1.8).

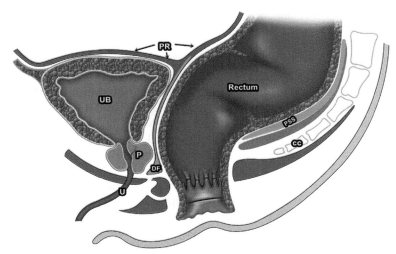

FIG. 1.6 Illustration showing the relationship between the rectal peritoneal reflection (PR) and the urinary bladder (UB) and Denonvilliers' fascia (DF). The posterior layer of the mesorectal fascia is closely bound to the presacral space (PSS) containing the presacral vessels. *CC*, coccyx; *P*, prostate; *U*, urethra.

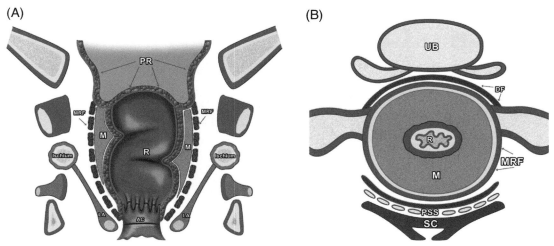

FIG. 1.7   The mesorectum (M). The mesorectum extends from the peritoneal reflection (PR) to the insertion of the levator ani (LA) muscle or the surgical anorectal junction and is surrounded by the visceral layer of the endopelvic fascia (or mesorectal fascia [MRF]). The posterior layer of the MRF is tightly connected to the presacral space (PSS) containing the presacral vessels. Denonvilliers fascia (DF) is a distinct layer of the fascia anterior to the MRF that cannot always be distinguished by MRI. *AC*, anal canal; *R*, rectum; and *SC*, sacrum.

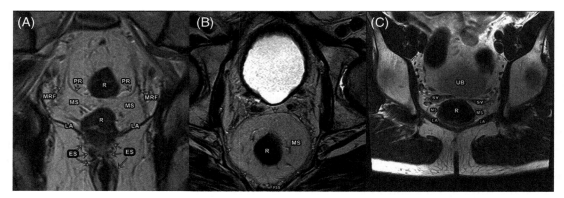

FIG. 1.8   MRI anatomy of the mesorectum (MS). (A) High-resolution coronal T2W image through the mesorectum. The mesorectum extends from the peritoneal reflection (PR) to the insertion of the levator ani (LA) muscle and is surrounded by the mesorectal fascia (MRF). (B) High-resolution axial T2W image through the lower rectum. The mesorectum forms a confined space along the lower rectum. The mesorectal fascia (arrows) is a thin, hypointense T2W layer surrounding the mesorectal fat and rectum. The presacral space (PSS) is comprised of presacral vessels, which are seen as T2W flow voids or hypointense dots. (C) High-resolution axial T2W image taken near the surgical anorectal junction. The thickness of the MS decreases in the craniocaudal direction barely noticeable near the LA insertion. Tumors involving the lower rectum are more likely to invade neighboring pelvic structures and upgrading to stage T4b. *ES*, external sphincter; *SV*, seminal vesicles; and *UB*, urinary bladder.

The MRF appears as a fine linear T2W hypointense structure enveloping the rectum, and is best viewed in axial and coronal images (Fig. 1.8).[10] The posterior layer of the MRF is closely bound to the presacral space containing presacral vessels and is best captured in T2W sagittal images (Figs. 1.7 and 1.8).[10] The parietal fascia located along the periosteum is not discernible as a distinctive structure on an MRI.

The thickness of the mesorectum decreases in the craniocaudal direction, disappearing completely close to the ARJ. Notably, the anterior and caudal mesorectum are barely perceptible due to a lack of adipose and connective tissue in these parts (Figs. 1.8C and 1.9).

Tumors in this area can therefore easily invade the neighboring structure (stage T4b). Similarly, neoplasms in the middle/anterior rectum have a relatively small cushion of adipose tissue within the anterior mesorectum (Fig. 1.3).

Along its caudal aspect, the anterior surface of the mesorectum is draped by Denonvilliers' fascia (rectoprostatic or rectovaginal) (Fig. 1.6), which contains hypogastric nerves responsible for maintaining genitourinary functions. The Denonvilliers' fascia also appears as a thin T2W structure clinging tightly to the anterior surface of the MRF and is best viewed in the sagittal plane.[13]

TME involves en bloc excision of the mesorectum, along with all its contents, and this procedure is associated with a significantly low likelihood of cell spillage, residual tumors, and tumor recurrence.[13] Conventionally, in the United States, TME does not include excision of pelvic side wall nodes.

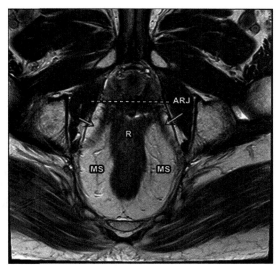

FIG. 1.9 High-resolution axial oblique T2W image of the lower rectum (R) showing decrease in the size of the mesorectum (MS) and the mesorectal fat near the insertion of the ani levator (LA). The anorectal junction (ARJ) is the point at which the LA joins the puborectalis and external sphincter.

1.6 Treatment approaches

Early rectal cancer (Tis N0 and T1 N0) with no high-risk traits can be treated via transanal resection, which has the best prognosis. All high-risk T1 N0 or T2 N0 and early T3 N0 tumors are treated via TME.[14] N+ diseases and all advanced T3 or T4 tumors are initially treated via nCRT until a regression is achieved, which is required to qualify for TME.

Tumors with a distal margin at least 1 cm above the ARJ are treated via low anterior resection (LAR). LAR is a sphincter-preserving surgery involving rectal anastomosis below the peritoneal reflection. Low rectal tumors, with their inferior edge below the ARJ and/or involving the intersphincteric plane or external sphincters, are conventionally treated via abdominoperineal resection (APR). APR is a debilitating sphincter compromising surgery with permanent colostomy (Fig. 1.10).[15] However, with recent advances in surgical techniques that enable deep dissection in the intersphincteric plane, an ultralow LAR can be performed to preserve natural continence.[16]

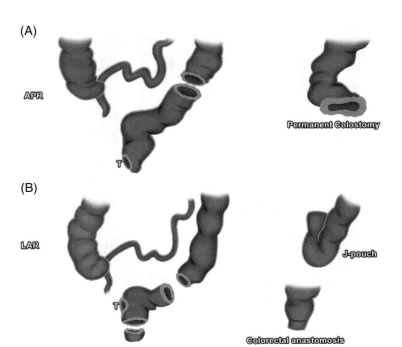

FIG. 1.10 Illustrations showing the differences in the two surgical options. (A) Abdominal resection (APR): APR is commonly performed for a tumor (T) with its lower margin below the anorectal junction and/or the involvement of sphincters or the intersphincteric plane. APR involves extensive sphincter resection as well as permanent colostomy. (B) Low anterior resection (LAR): Tumors (T) with a distal edge at least 1 cm above the anorectal juncture are treated with LAR. The procedure involves creating a temporary J-pouch formation and a subsequent colorectal anastomosis below the peritoneal reflection while preserving the natural sphincters.

1.7 Role of MRI

The role of MRI in rectal cancer staging includes the following[13]:

  i. distinguishing T1 and T2 tumors from T3 tumors,
  ii. differentiating between T3 and T4 tumors,
  iii. determining the depth of the mesorectal invasion or subclassifying T3 tumors as good or bad T3, (described below)
  iv. determining whether mesorectal node involvement is present, and
  v. detecting suspicious nonlocoregional lymph nodes.[18,19]

This information may help the clinician decide whether nCRT is required before a TME is attempted. MRI cannot detect Tis and T1 diseases, and we cannot confidently differentiate T1 and T2 diseases using MR images. With MRI, T1 and T2 diseases are grouped together for practicality (Figs. 1.11 and 1.12). If T1 and T2 diseases need to be differentiated to facilitate surgical decisions, an endoscopic rectal ultrasound should be performed.

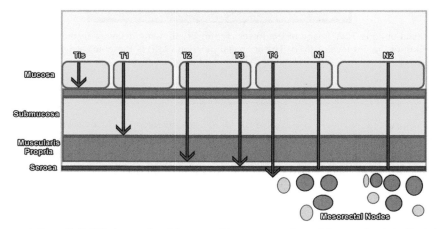

FIG. 1.11   **Schematic presentation of all TN stages of rectal cancer.** The presence of suspicious nodes is indicated in red.

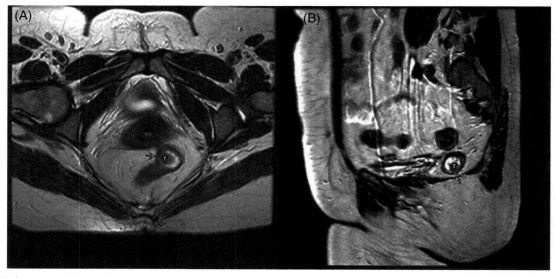

FIG. 1.12   **T1/T2 tumor.** (A) Axial T2W image showing an intraluminal polypoid tumor (T) with an intact overlying muscularis propria (arrow). (B) T2W sagittal image in same area of rectum showing intraluminal tumor (T). MRI cannot confidently differentiate between T1 and T2 tumors, and the two are grouped together for convenience.

1.8 MRI interpretation and reporting

A structured reporting of rectal cancer staging is essential for patient management. The disease-focused panel of the Society of Abdominal Radiology (SAR) has developed a comprehensive reporting model that covers all areas that are of interest to surgeons, and the model can be used for synoptic reporting.[20]

1.8.1 Clinical background

Ideally, colonoscopy results and pathology reports must be made available prior to MR interpretation. A colonoscopy may provide an approximate idea of the projected location of the tumor, while the pathology report confirms the diagnosis. A colonoscopy is essential because the tumor is sometimes poorly imaged in an MR image due to its size or shape or was detected in a resected adenoma with no residue tissue seen on MRI. A histopathologically proven adenocarcinoma is also critical because the description, reporting format, and staging system may not necessarily apply to other types of tumors, such as squamous cell carcinomas (SSCs) or inflammatory conditions. An SSC in the distal rectum should be staged as an anal cancer rather than a rectal cancer. Occasionally, nonmalignant pathologies such as Crohn's disease may mimic malignancy in an MR image.

In real-life situations, MRI may be performed even before pathology reports or colonoscopy results are available. In such a situation, it must be made clear that interpretation and staging may not apply if the cancer is subsequently not proven. Similarly, in the case of dysplasia or carcinoma incidentally discovered in a resected polyp, it may be difficult to find a tumor. Hence, the radiologist must point out this fact and not use the synoptic report.

1.8.2 Primary tumor

The description of a primary tumor should include its size, location, morphology, and distance from the anal verge. Tumor morphology may be localized, exophytic, polypoid, annular, or semiannular. However, the distance from the anal verge is critical, as it may affect surgical decisions. The craniocaudal length can be measured in the sagittal plane, and an additional plane (axial or coronal) can be included to determine the exact extent. Tumor location may be in the lower, mid, or upper rectum depending on the distance of the tumor from the anal verge, which is practically the transition zone between the anal mucosa and the perianal skin, and in MR images it is denoted by the fatty plane between the internal and external sphincter (Figs. 1.1 and 1.2). These measurements are made from the inferior aspect of the internal sphincter and follow the curvature of the long axis of the rectum for accuracy (Fig. 1.4).[21]

For a low rectal tumor, the shortest distance between the lowest margin of the tumor and the ARJ is also measured. This measurement can be made on the sagittal and coronal planes and is vital to surgical decision-making (Fig. 1.1). Typically, to perform a complete TME, surgeons prefer at least 1 cm between the lower margin of the tumor and the ARJ.[22,23]

1.8.3 Relation of the tumor to the peritoneum

The peritoneal reflection is imaged as a low-intensity linear structure in T2W images.[9,24] It is best viewed in sagittal images and stretches from the upper and posterior surface of the bladder dome to the anterior surface of the upper two-thirds of the rectum; the lower one-third of the rectum is extraperitoneal. The anterior peritoneal reflection at the junction of the upper two-thirds and the lower one-third of the rectum can usually be identified in T2W sagittal images (Fig. 1.13A). This point is located close to the tip of the seminal vesicle in males and the uterocervical junction in females—although the site of attachment may vary in females. The anterior peritoneal reflection delineates the lowest point in the peritoneal cavity and is the point at which the rectum transforms into a proximal intraperitoneal structure.

Furthermore, the peritoneum attaches to the anterior aspect of the rectum in the form of a *V* (the *seagull* sign) when viewed in axial T2W images (Fig. 1.13B).[10,13] This area should be carefully examined, as any tumor invasion of the peritoneal reflection may upgrade the T-staging to stage T4a, which is linked to a high incidence of peritoneal and distant metastasis.[18]

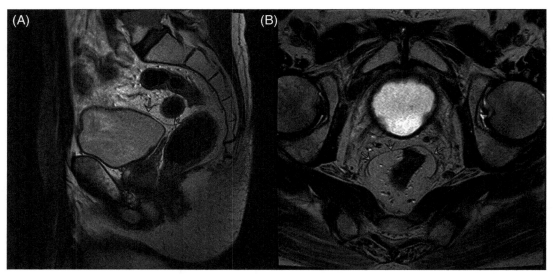

FIG. 1.13   Peritoneal reflection as seen on MRI. (A) Sagittal T2W image through the mid-pelvis. The peritoneum is identified by thin T2W structures at the junction of the upper two-thirds and the lower one-third of the rectum (arrows). The tip of the seminal vesicle in males acts as a landmark to identify peritoneal reflection. (B) Axial T2W image showing the seagull sign. The seagull sign demarcates the area where the peritoneum (arrows) attaches to the anterior aspect of the rectum in the form of a V or the wings of a seagull.

1.8.4 TNM staging

TNM staging of the rectal tumor remains one of the most critical features influencing treatment approach and final prognosis. TNM staging is summarized in Table 1.2.[25]

1.8.4.1 *Tumor (T) staging*

Fig. 1.11 depicts all T stages of the various rectal cancers. Once a tumor extends beyond the muscularis propria, it qualifies as stage T3. Such a tumor can be further subclassified based on its extension into the mesorectum: a T3a tumor extends less than 1 mm, a T3b tumor extends by 1.1–5 mm, T3c tumors extend by 5.1–15 mm, and T3d tumors extend by more than 15 mm.[10] Tumors with a >5 mm extension into the mesorectum are labeled *bad* T3 (Fig. 1.14), as they are associated with low 5-year survival rates.[26] Similarly, tumors with a less than 5 mm extension into the mesorectum are categorized as *good* T3 (Fig. 1.15) because of their association with high survival rates.[27]

An assessment of T3 diseases should be made strictly on the axial plane perpendicular to the tumor axis (Fig. 1.1B). Sometimes, feeding vessels may traverse through the muscularis propria, creating discontinuity in the outline, thus masking a T3 disease.

For an accurate assessment of T3 disease, a true extension of the actual tumor into the mesorectum fat needs to be evaluated,[28] as the desmoplastic reaction surrounding the tumor margin may overstage the disease.[29] An actual tumor may exhibit intermediate signal intensity and nodular bands on T2W images. Desmoplastic response appears as thin, low-intensity linear spicules on T2W images.[17,27] A reduced slice thickness may be useful to differentiate the desmoplastic reaction from the T3 stage tumor.

Tumoral invasion of the peritoneum is classified as T4a (Fig. 1.16), which is linked to an increased probability of intraperitoneal disease, and invasion of any pelvic structure, including the pelvic floor musculature or the levator ani, is classified as T4b disease.[18]

Invasion of any pelvic structure is indicative of T4 disease (Fig. 1.17). The invasion of a structure can be assessed by examining the fat plane between the tumor margin and the structure. Loss of the fat plane and altered T2 signal intensity of the underlying structure suggest an invasion. A preserved fat plane practically rules out an invasion. Loss of the fat plane, with the underlying structure exhibiting a normal T2 signal intensity, suggests a possible invasion.

TABLE 1.2 TNM staging of rectal cancer.

Primary tumor

TX	Primary tumor cannot be assessed.
T0	No evidence of a primary tumor.
Tis	Carcinoma in situ, intramucosal carcinoma (no extension through muscularis mucosae).
T1	Tumor invades submucosa (through the muscularis mucosa but not into the muscularis propria).
T2	Tumor invades muscularis propria.
T3	Tumor invades through the muscularis propria into the pericolorectal tissues.
T4	
T4a	Tumor invades through the visceral peritoneum (including gross perforation of the bowel through tumor and continuous invasion of tumor through areas of inflammation to the surface of the visceral peritoneum).
T4b	Tumor directly invades or adheres to other adjacent organs or structures.

Lymph nodes

NX	Regional lymph nodes cannot be assessed.
N0	No regional lymph node metastasis.
N1	Metastasis in 1–3 regional lymph nodes.
N1a	Metastasis in 1 regional lymph node.
N1b	Metastasis in 2–3 regional lymph nodes.
N1c	No regional lymph nodes are positive but there are tumor deposits in the subserosa, mesentery, or nonperitonealized pericolic or perirectal/mesorectal tissues.
N2	Metastasis in 4 or more regional lymph nodes.
N2a	Metastasis in 4–6 regional lymph nodes.
N2b	Metastasis in 7 or more regional lymph nodes.

Distant metastasis

M0	No distant metastasis
M1	Distant metastasis
M1a	Metastasis confined to one organ or site without peritoneal metastasis.
M1b	Metastasis to two or more sites or organs is identified without peritoneal metastasis.
M1c	Metastasis to the peritoneal surface is identified alone or with other site or organ metastases.

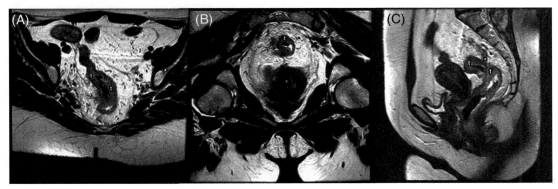

FIG. 1.14 High rectal cancer in stage T3C and with positive extramural vascular invasion. (A) T2W axial image: Semicircumferential tumor (t) involving the upper rectum with nodular extension to mesorectal fat (arrow). (B) Coronal T2W image: The mesorectal extension (>5.1 mm but <15 mm) of the tumor (t) is best depicted in this projection (arrow). (C) The sagittal T2W image of the mid-pelvis shows the exact location of the tumor (t) and its distance from the anal verge. There is an extension of the tumor to the superior rectal artery (*), which is expanded and shows the tumor extension as an increased T2W intensity.

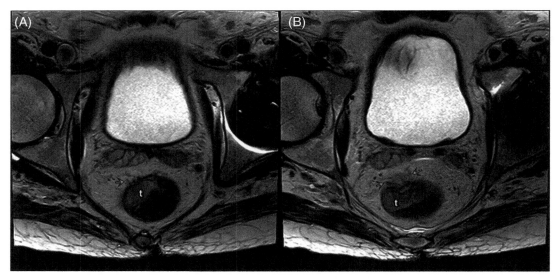

FIG. 1.15   Good T3 tumor. (A–B) T2W axial images of the rectum showing a localized and eccentric tumor (t). The overlying muscularis propria shows slight discontinuity and tumor extension to the mesorectal fat (arrows) measuring <5 mm.

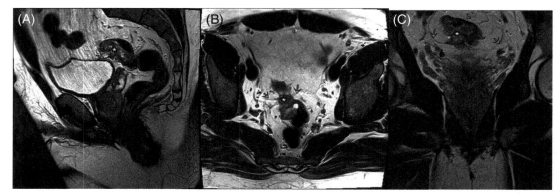

FIG. 1.16   T4a tumor. (A) Sagittal T2W image through the mid-pelvis shows an eccentric and localized tumor (*) within the high rectum. There is an anterior extension of the tumor beyond the rectal boundaries involving peritoneal reflection (arrow). (B) T2W axial image of the same segment shows similar findings. (C) T2W coronal image clearly shows tumor (*) above the peritoneal reflection (arrows). T4a disease is best assessed using T2W sagittal images.

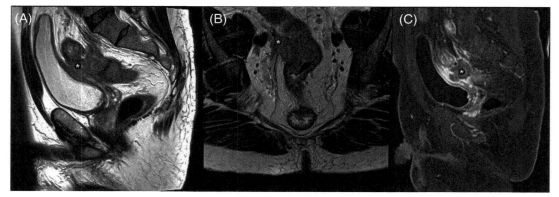

FIG. 1.17   T4b tumor. (A) T2W sagittal image through the upper rectum shows an infiltrative tumor along the anterior aspect (*) involving the bladder dome. The underlying bladder wall is thickened and shows increased T2W signal intensity similar to the tumor, which confirms tumor invasion of the bladder wall. (B) T2W axial image through the upper pelvis shows mesorectal extension of the tumor along the right side (*). There is tumor involvement of the mesorectal fascia, which is irregular, thickened, and demonstrates tumor-like intensity (arrow). (C) Post-contrast T1W sagittal image through the tumor shows relatively hypoenhancing (*) and involvement of the bladder dome.

1.8.4.2 Nodal staging (N)

Rectal lymphatics follow vascular supply and drain into the territories of the internal iliac, the IMA or superior rectal arteries, and lymph nodes in the immediate vicinity (Fig. 1.18). The perirectal or mesorectal, sigmoid mesocolic, lateral sacral, presacral, and internal pudendal nodes are categorized as proximal nodes. All nodes draining naturally rectum are considered *locoregional nodes* (Fig. 1.18). All other pelvic nodes, excluding the obturator lymph nodes, are described as *nonlocoregional* (Fig. 1.18A). Obturator nodes are given a special status because they are often found to be nonmetastatic on postsurgical pathology examination.[19,24]

Nodal staging applies exclusively to mesorectal lymph nodes, with N1 diseases having three or fewer nodes involved and the involvement of four or more nodes receiving N2 categorization (Fig. 1.11).[9] An N stage disease can simply be classified as N+ or N− as the presence of any node may necessitate nCRT. For reporting purposes: (i) N0: no lymph nodes involved; (ii) N+: any number of lymph nodes >9 mm in short axis diameter, or any number of lymph nodes 5–9 mm in short axis diameter that meet at least two morphological criteria, or any number of lymph nodes about 5 mm in short axis diameter that meet three morphological criteria; (iii) Nx: nodes are involved but do not meet the aforementioned criteria. The three morphological criteria for a suspicious node include a round shape, heterogeneously increased T2W intensity, and irregular borders (Fig. 1.18B).

Identification of nodes with mucinous deposits in non–fat-suppressed T2W images can be challenging. Such nodes can be identified in either fat-suppressed T2W images or low *b*-value DWI images. However, nodes should not be evaluated based on their DWI/ADC characteristics because DWI/ADC does not distinguish between the markers of inflammatory and malignant diseases.[30] All T2W hyperintense nodes associated with mucinous tumors should be considered suspicious, regardless of size (Fig. 1.19).[27]

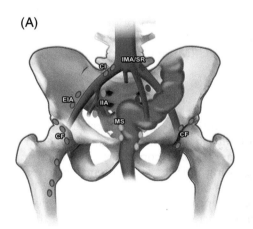
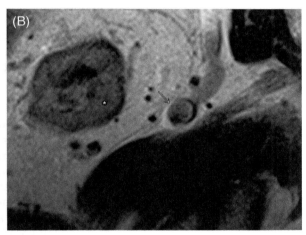

FIG. 1.18 Suspicious lymph nodes. (A) Involvement of the nonlocoregional lymph nodes (red) is taken as distant metastasis (M1 disease). Nonlocoregional nodes may include common iliac (CI), external iliac (EIA), common femoral (CF), and inguinal territories. Mesorectal nodes (MS) are assessed for TNM staging and taken as locoregional. Inferior mesenteric (IMA) or superior rectal (SR) nodes are also taken as locoregional. (B) T2W axial image through a circumferential rectal tumor (*) shows presence of a suspicious lymph node in left lateral mesorectum (arrow). This node meets all three criteria to be considered suspicious on MRI: round shape, heterogeneously increased T2W intensity, and irregular borders.

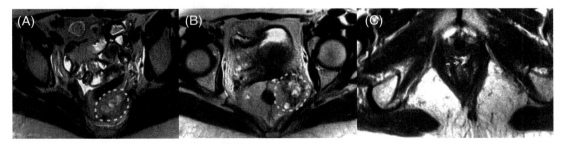

FIG. 1.19 Mucinous deposits within the pelvic side wall lymph nodes and anovaginal fistula. Status post transanal resection of an anterior rectal polyp. Postresection pathology consistent with an invasive mucinous adenocarcinoma. Patient had been treated with adjuvant chemoradiotherapy and given a follow-up surveillance scan. (A–B) T2W axial images through the pelvis show multiple left internal iliac lymph nodes (circle) with increased T2W intensity compared to the mesorectal fat. Findings are consistent with mucinous nodal deposits. (C) T2W axial image through the lower pelvis shows communication between the anal canal and vagina (arrow); this is likely a sequala of prior resection and/or radiation therapy.

Based on morphological criteria, calcified nodes in T2W images may also be erroneously considered suspicious if the size is acceptable. However, a correlation with DWI and postcontrast images (if available) may be helpful in such situations and can differentiate it as a nonsuspicious node. In addition, comparison with computerized tomography (CT) scan images (if available) can prove useful for troubleshooting.

1.8.4.3 *Metastasis (M) staging*

In general, the involvement of nonlocoregional nodes (inguinal, external iliac, common iliac, and para-aortic nodes located above the takeoff of the IMA) is considered indicative of a metastatic (M1) disease state in TNM staging.[19] However, because the segment below the dentate line (anatomical anal canal) normally drains into the inguinal region, a low rectal tumor with an extension below the dentate line may drain into both the external and inguinal lymph nodes. Such nodes are considered N diseased (and not M diseased) for that tumor.

1.8.5 Circumferential resection margin

Because of the peritoneal reflections, there is no anterior or lateral mesorectum along the upper rectum and no anterior mesorectum along the middle rectum. CRM refers to the surgically dissected surface of the *nonperitonealized* portion of the rectum and is a pathological term. Although technically incorrect, CRM and the MRF seen in an MR image are used interchangeably. CRM assessment is not applicable in T1, T2, and T4 tumors but should be assessed in all cases of T3 tumors. When the definitive tumor (not the desmoplastic response) extends into the MRF by less than 1 mm, the CRM is considered invaded (Figs. 1.17 and 1.20).

Similarly, an extension of the tumor within the 1–2 mm of the MRF indicates a *threatened* CRM.[31-33]

Because mesorectal fat is sparsely distributed along the anterior aspect, and the mesorectum becomes smaller in caliber near the insertion point of the levator ani, a threatened or invaded CRM may or may not be the most penetrating portion of the tumor. Even a less penetrating portion of the tumor within the anterior and lower mesorectum (compared to posterior) may have CRM involvement. Consequently, CRM involvement should be defined as the distance between the closest portion of the tumor and the MRF.

1.8.6 Extramural venous invasion and tumor deposits

EMVI is defined as the tumoral invasion of perirectal vessels and is indicative of an underlying T3 disease.[27] EMVI is a poor prognostic factor and has been linked to synchronous or subsequent distant metastasis, even after surgery and recurrence.[27,34] Contrary to common belief, EMVI may or may not occur in contiguity with the primary tumor.[27]

MRI has a sensitivity of 62%, with a specificity of 88%, for diagnosing EMVI.[35] The presence of an expanded vessel with tumoral signal intensity within the vessel should raise suspicions of EMVI (Fig. 1.14). The EMVI of a mucinous tumor will be distinctly T2W hyperintense, like the primary tumor. The primary tumor may or may not be contiguous with a major vessel. A disrupted border of the involved vessel and an irregular, nodular border of the vessel further enhance the level of diagnostic confidence.[10,33,36] Assessing EMVI in a vessel measuring <3 mm is usually not possible.

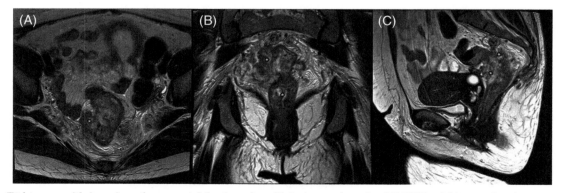

FIG. 1.20 **T3d tumor with invasion of mesorectal fascia and multiple tumor deposits.** (A) T2W axial image showing extra mural tumor extension (*) within the mesorectum involving the mesorectal fascia (arrow). About 50% of the tumor shows increased T2W intensity compared to the mesorectal fat, hence consistent with mucinous component. (B) Coronal T2W image shows the tumor's (*) distribution within the mesorectum. On close inspection, multiple tumor deposits (circles) are seen within the mesorectum. (C) Sagittal T2W image through the mid-pelvis shows tumor (*) extension to the presacral mesorectum and tumor deposits within the anticipated course of the superior rectal artery (circle). Tumor deposits may coexist with extra mural vascular invasion.

EMVI may coexist with a tumor deposit (TD) (or a satellite nodule), which may sometimes mimic lymph node (Fig. 1.20).[37] An assessment on all three planes may detect TD tapering within the vessel, a very low signal intensity in T2W images, and a shaggy margin. Lymph nodes are typically separate from vessels, and TDs form an acute angle with the vessel wall.[37] The presence of TDs indicates a poor prognosis.[38] Although TDs lack lymphoid tissue, the eight edition of the American Joint Cancer Commission (AJCC) classified TDs as an N1c disease (on a different classification scale that is not yet popular among radiologists).[39] The presence of TDs or EMVI within 1 mm (or 1.1–2 mm) of an MRF should be considered as constituting an invaded (or threatened) CRM. Contrary to prior belief, a suspicious lymph node within a stipulated CRM distance need not be assessed, as it does not increase the risk of recurrence.[40]

1.8.7 Mucinous rectal adenocarcinoma

Mucinous rectal adenocarcinoma (MRC) has a high incidence among the younger population (average age: 52.7–54.2 years) and often presents at advanced stages (stages III–IV). MRCs have a higher incidence of nodal and peritoneal metastatic diseases, with a poor 3-year disease-free survival rate (57%). Mucinous tumors are linked to an overall poor prognosis and a high risk of spillover during surgery.[41] Two subtypes of MRC have been identified: (i) mucinous adenocarcinoma (MAC) (10–15%), and (ii) signet ring cell carcinoma (SRCC) (<2%).

MACs comprise over 50% of the tumor volume, consisting of extracellular mucin pools lined with malignant epithelium. Classic intracytoplasmic mucin with *signet ring cell* morphology remains the characteristic feature of SRCC, and signet ring cells comprise >50% of tumor cells. In general, MRC is predictive of a poor response to traditional nCRT.

Classically, rectal adenocarcinoma exhibits an intermediary T2W signal, which is slightly higher than that of muscle (i.e., muscularis propria). MRC should be suspected if more than 50% of the tumor presents an increase in T2W intensity in relation to mesorectal fat (Figs. 1.20 and 1.21).

A lesion can be described as follows: with no mucin, with some mucin, or mostly mucinous. In postcontrast images, MRC appears as modest lacelike enhancements in the dense cellular portions (Fig. 1.22). Mucin may infiltrate beyond an otherwise intact rectal wall.

The interface between infiltrating mucin within the mesorectum and adjacent fat (mucin pseudocapsule) may sometimes be mistaken for an intact muscularis propria because it may appear as a thin T2W line (Fig. 1.22). Assessment of T2W fat-suppressed images and DWI images may aid in correct diagnosis. In addition, a perforated tumor with T2W perirectal fluid is better depicted on post contrast images (Fig. 1.23).

SRCC is rare but may present with a unique concentric ring pattern in T2W images. Signet ring cells within the submucosal layer give rise to a heightened T2W intensity bounded by relatively T2W hypointense outer and inner layers (primary linitis plastica of the rectum). Unfortunately, this morphology of the tumor may mimic inflammatory or ischemic conditions. Furthermore, SRCC is predominant among the younger population, among whom suspicion of malignancy remains low. The only key finding is the involvement of a short segment of the rectum versus a long segment in benign pathologies. Higher ADC values are noted for mucinous tumors compared to nonmucinous tumors due to its inherent T2W hyperintensity and lower cellular density.[42]

1.8.8 Low rectal tumor

Low rectal tumors arise within 5 cm of the anal verge. They are unique due to their relation to the pelvic floor musculature and anal sphincters. Furthermore, the mesorectum tapers near the ARJ. Consequently, low rectal tumors exhibit a high tendency to invade the MRF and the levator ani. In addition, they also have a high recurrence rate and an unfavorable prognosis. [43,44] The risk for MRF in low rectal tumors is much higher; surgical margins can be up to 30% positive.[45]

Sphincter invasion can practically be ruled out if the inferior edge of the tumor is located above the ARJ. When the tumor extends below the ARJ, the position of the tumor should be evaluated relative to the internal or external sphincters and the intersphincteric plane (Fig. 1.24).

High-resolution T2W imaging in the coronal plane is essential for assessing the relation of a tumor to the sphincter complex and the levator ani muscle (Fig. 1.2). It is critical to describe the extent of the tumor in relation to intersphincteric plane and external sphincter. A tumor confined to the rectal wall and internal sphincter is classified as stage T1–2. Involvement of the intersphincteric plane receives T3 disease categorization. Tumor invasion of the external sphincter or extension within 1 mm of the levator ani is qualified as a T4 disease (Figs. 1.25 and 1.26).[46,47] This staging is reserved only for adenocarcinomas. If a low rectal tumor exhibits nonadenocarcinoma (often an SSC) histology, staging should be performed as if it is an anal cancer.

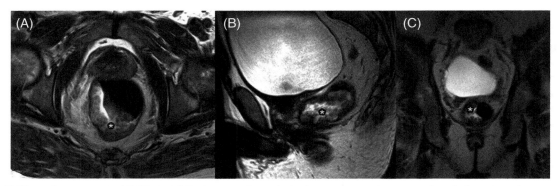

FIG. 1.21 T2W mucinous tumor. (A) The axial T2W image through the lower rectum shows a right-sided semiannular tumor (*) ranging from 3 o'clock to 11 o'clock. The overlying muscular propria remains intact. The tumor shows an increased intensity compared to the mesorectal fat, suggesting a mucinous component. (B) The sagittal T2W image on the right edge of the rectum shows an intraluminal extension of the tumor (*). Intact muscular is again noted along the superior and inferior aspect. (C) The coronal T2W image through the tumor (*) shows its caudocephalic extension in the lumen and its location in the lower rectum.

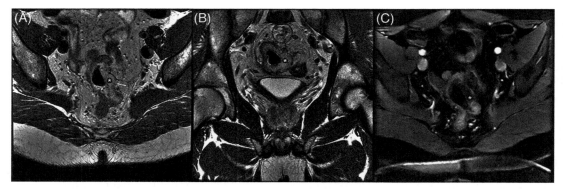

FIG. 1.22 T3 mucinous tumor with tumor deposits. (A) The axial T2W image shows a primarily hyperintense neoplasm along the left rectum (*) compatible with a mucinous tumor. Note the ill-defined interface (arrow) between the invasive edge of the tumor and the mesorectal fat (pseudomucin capsule). Although no intact muscularis propria can be seen overlying the tumor, a mucin pseudocapsule may be mistaken for an intact muscularis propria. (B) Coronal T2W image across the tumor (*) shows similar findings and mucin pseudocapsule. Tumor deposits are noted within the mesorectum at 12 o'clock (circle). (C) Postcontrast T1W axial image shows lace like hypoenhancement within the mucinous component (*).

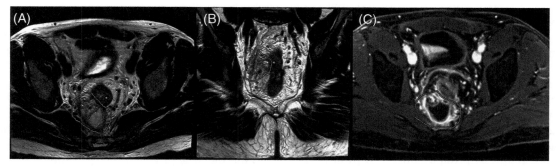

FIG. 1.23 Perforated tumor with perirectal abscess. (A) The axial T2W image across the pelvis shows a focal perirectal collection in the right mesorectum (uneven circle). The underlying rectum shows a subtle increase in submucosal intensity (*) consistent with a biopsy-proven cancer. (B) The T2W coronal image across the same rectal segment shows the full extent of mesorectal collection (uneven circle). The known tumor shows increased submucosal intensity (*). (C) The postcontrast T1W image with fat suppression delineates the extent and definition of unenhancing collection (uneven circle). Spontaneous perforation of a tumor signifies a T3 disease.

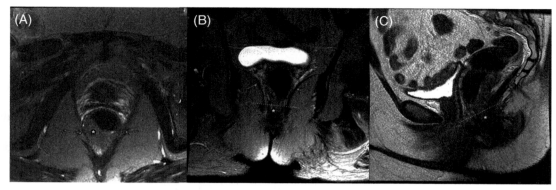

FIG. 1.24   Low rectal T2 tumor. (A) The axial T2W image through the lower rectum shows a localized tumor (*) along the right and posterior internal sphincter. The insertion of the puborectalis along the levator ani (arrows) demarcates the surgical anorectal junction. (B) The coronal T2W image across the tumor (*) clearly shows its extent below the anorectal junction (line). Bilateral levator ani is shown with arrows. (C) The sagittal T2W image through the tumor (*) also confirms its extent beneath the anorectal junction (line). The tumor is confined to the internal sphincter and qualifies as a T2 tumor.

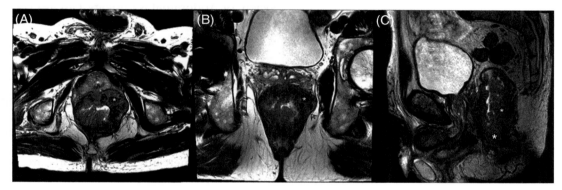

FIG. 1.25   T4b low-rectal tumor with involvement of intersphincteric plane. (A) The axial T2W image through the lower rectum shows a tumor on the left extending beyond the internal sphincter (*). The bulging component of the tumor is displacing the levator ani (arrow), which is thinned out at 1–2 o'clock. (B) The coronal T2W image through the lower rectum shows the extension of the tumor (*) within the intersphincteric space and closely abutting the levator ani (arrow). Note a well-maintained intersphincteric space on the right side. A tumor extension within 1 mm of the levator ani is consistent with a level T4b disease. (C) The sagittal T2W image through the tumor (*) shows its entire extent and distance from the anal verge.

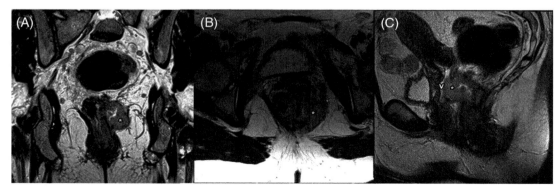

FIG. 1.26   T4 low-rectal squamous cell carcinoma. (A) The T2W coronal image shows a low exophytic rectal tumor (*) invading the levator ani (arrow) and the deep component of the external sphincter. (B) The axial T2W image also shows the anterior extension of the tumor (*) and the involvement of the left levator ani (arrow). (C) The sagittal image shows the anterior exophytic component of the tumor (*) and the invasion of the posterior vaginal wall (v). The pathology was consistent with squamous cell carcinoma. Such low rectal tumors are staged as anal cancer. Invasion of the levator ani and vagina makes it a T4 tumor irrespective of its size.

1.9 Standardized reporting

There are numerous advantages of standardized reports, including:

- A standardized report may provide great clarity, quality, and coherence.
- It may also reduce diagnostic, grammatical, and nongrammatical errors from using digital voice recognition technologies.
- It can ensure completeness of the documentation (enhances radiological reimbursement) and facilitate data mining and research (QA/QI projects).
- It can promote evidence-based medicine through the inclusion of clinical decision support tools in radiology reports.

A standardized rectal cancer staging report must contain the following information[48]:

1. The distance of the tumor to the anal verge and the length of the rectum involved.
2. Morphology of tumor with o'clock positioning.
3. TN staging (M staging may require CT/MRI of the abdomen).
4. Status of CRM involvement (if applicable).
5. Documentation of the distance of T3 tumors, TDs or EMVI within 0–5 mm of the CRM.
6. EMVI (number of invaded vessels and their location).
7. Status of the levator ani and sphincters (if applicable). Society of Abdominal Radiology Disease Focused Panel's reporting template v.2020 is reproduced in Fig. 1.27.

1.10 Posttreatment evaluation of rectal cancers

For restaging, a follow-up MRI is performed approximately 6–8 weeks after nCRT.[49] Ideally, pretreatment and posttreatment MRI should be performed using the same technique.[50] The pretreatment scan must be available for comparison.

In general, a decrease in tumor volume is a good marker indicative of positive treatment response for nonmucinous tumors (Fig. 1.27).[51,52] A more than 70% reduction in tumor volume is required to improve the chances of disease-free survival.[53,54] The tumor volume can be calculated using commercially available software, or the tumor can be measured in three comparable dimensions to assess tumor response on T2W sequences.[55,56]

In addition to volume, morphological changes in the tumor appearance are also critical for the assessment of the treatment response—the most important of which is fibrosis.[57] Fibrosis appears to be more T2W hypointense than the muscularis propria and exhibits no significant enhancement in the early postcontrast phase (Figs. 1.28 and 1.29).[50]

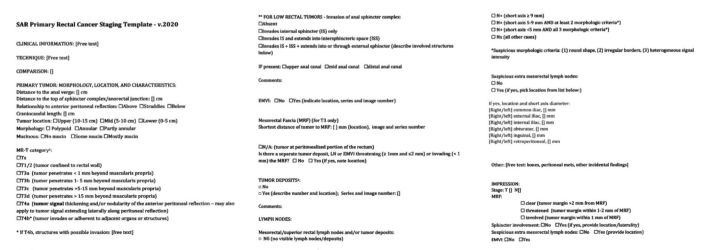

FIG. 1.27   Society of Abdominal Radiology Disease Focused Panel's reporting template for baseline staging (with permission from the panel).

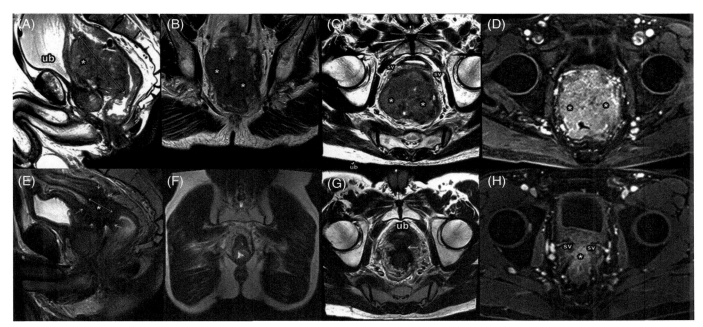

FIG. 1.28 Posttreatment assessment of a mid-to-low-rectal tumor; pretreatment images (A–D) and posttreatment images (E–H). (A) The sagittal T2W image shows the caudocephalic extent (arrow) of the pretreatment tumor (*). Note the heterogenous T2W intermediate intensity of the tumor. The fat plane between the posterior wall of the urinary bladder (ub) and tumor is lost, and the bladder wall shows altered T2W intensity with irregular outline. Findings are suggestive of bladder involvement. (B) The coronal T2W image shows the left lateral extent of the tumor (*) within the mesorectum. The tumor can be seen to invade the left mesorectal fascia. (C) Corresponding axial T2W image shows anterior extent of the mass closely abutting the seminal vesicles (sv). (D) The postcontrast axial T1W fat-suppressed image shows homogenous enhancement of the tumor (*). (E) The sagittal T2W image shows significantly decreased caudocephalic dimension of the posttreatment tumor. The tumor appears to be mostly T2W hypointense along the periphery, suggesting posttreatment fibrosis. The central portion of the tumor (*) retains T2W intermediate signal intensity. Involvement of the posterior bladder is clearly evident, as tumor is now mostly replaced with fibrosis. (F) The coronal T2W image shows a significant decrease in tumor dimensions. (G) Corresponding axial T2W image depicts fibrosis (arrow) along the posterior aspect of the urinary bladder (ub). Note the T2W intermediate signal intensity of the residual tumor. (H) The corresponding delayed postcontrast axial image shows enhancement of the fibrotic tissue (*). Overall, findings are consistent with partial response (grade 3 mTRG) in a T4b tumor.

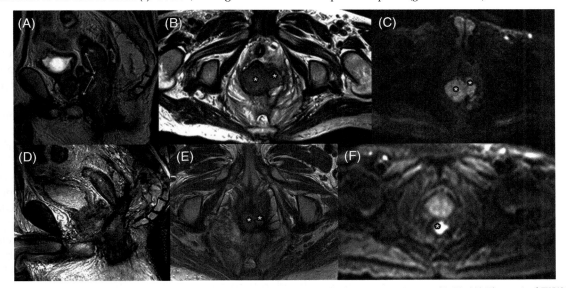

FIG. 1.29 Posttreatment assessment of the tumor; pretreatment images (A–C) and posttreatment images (D–F). (A) The sagittal T2W image shows the caudocephalic extent of the pretreatment tumor (arrows). The tumor anteriorly involves the posterior aspect of the prostate, which demonstrates T2W hypointensity and suggests the presence of desmoplastic reaction or fibrosis. (B) The axial T2W image shows the lower and left lateral extent (*) of the tumor and involvement of the left levator ani. Note the heterogenous T2W intermediate intensity of the tumor. (C) The corresponding axial high b-value DWI image shows the presence of diffusion restriction. (D) The sagittal T2W image shows significantly decreased posttreatment tumor bulk. The tumor along the posterior and superior aspect now shows T2W hypointensity, suggesting posttreatment fibrosis. (E) The axial T2W image shows decreased dimensions of the tumor but persistent involvement of the left levator ani. Again, the residual tumor at this location shows heterogenous T2W of intermediate intensity, suggestive of viable tumor. (F) Corresponding axial high b-value DWI image shows persistent diffusion restriction, which also suggests viable residual tumor. Overall, findings are consistent with partial response in a T4b tumor.

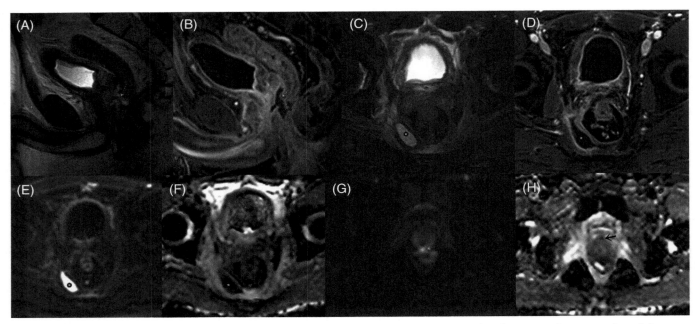

FIG. 1.30 **Mucinous conversion of a nonmucinous tumor.** A low rectal adenocarcinoma treated with rectorectal anastomosis and chemora-diation therapy for an anastomotic recurrence and right pelvic side wall deposit. Follow-up MRI was performed to assess treatment response and integrity of the anastomosis. (A) The T2W sagittal image shows presence of a T2W fat suppressed hyperintense area (arrow) and potential dehiscence along the anterior aspect of the anastomotic site. (B) The postcontrast T1W image confirms the anastomotic dehiscence (arrow) com-municating to a prerectal cavity. (C) The axial T2W fat-suppressed image through the pelvis shows a well circumscribed T2W hyperintense lesion (*) along the right pelvic side wall corresponding to previously reported deposit. (D) The postcontrast T1W fat-suppressed image shows an internal enhancement within the pelvic side wall lesion (*). (E–F) The axial high b-value DWI and corresponding ADC images through the pelvic side wall lesion demonstrate the presence of diffusion restriction (hyperintensity on DWI and hypointensity on ADC) within the lesion. (G–H) The axial high b-value DWI and corresponding ADC images through the anastomotic site show a focus of diffusion restriction (arrows). These findings are consistent with a posttreatment mucinous conversion of a nonmucinous primary tumor. Such a transformation is generally thought to be a good prognostic sign.

A more pronounced enhancement is rather visible in the delayed phase. Reactive posttreatment fibrosis is seen as linear T2W hypointense spiculations radiating into the mesorectum. Sometimes, tumors may develop mucinous changes after treatment, which is consistent with a form of treatment response—and is not associated with poor outcome or aggressiveness (as seen in pretreatment tumors) (Fig. 1.30).[50,57]

The normal rectal wall adjacent to the tumor may show wall thickening and/or salient mucosal edema, giving rise to a pseudotumor like appearance.[58]

The posttreatment tumor can be staged like the pretreatment tumor using the criteria described earlier. The y prefix can be used to determine posttreatment staging and to differentiate it from pretreatment staging.[50,59] The prefix yc means clinical and yp means posttreatment pathological stages. MRI can differentiate ypT0–T2 tumors from ypT3 tumors at high confidence levels. All essential imaging features, such as CRM involvement, EMVI, TDs, and involve-ment of the peritoneal reflections or sphincters, should be assessed during posttreatment MRI. Persistent CRM involvement after nCRT is associated with high recurrence rates.[60,61] EMVI may either completely disappear or be replaced by fibrotic bands after treatment. Contrast-enhanced imaging may increase EMVI detection accuracy.[62]

Some of the studies have demonstrated that DWI/ADC imaging is useful for assessing residual or viable tumors. DWI volumetric analysis has shown promising results in assessing treatment response.[63] Lower mean ADC values (0.981–1.053) are often linked to relatively aggressive (moderate to poor moderate differentiation) tumor profiles.[64] Higher mean ADC values (1.177–1.316) are associated with less aggressive (good to moderately good differentiation) tumor profiles. A universally accepted cutoff ADC is often limited by the lack of standard imaging and measure-ment techniques. Further studies are needed to determine the exact role of ADC values as an imaging biomarker of tumor aggressiveness and to determine accurate sensitivity and specificity.

DWI/ADC imaging has a limited role in the assessment of MRC, owing to the intrinsically high ADC values of mucinous tumors.[65]

1.10.1 Posttreatment nodal assessment

Generally, a decrease in the size and number of lymph nodes is an indicator of treatment response. However, small amounts of residual tumor within nodes cannot be completely ruled out with MRI, especially when relying wholly on size criteria.[50] Therefore, morphological criteria described in pretreatment baseline staging play a crucial role in postcontrast assessment of the lymph nodes.[50] Similar to the primary tumor, when the lymph node appears densely hypointense in T2W images, exhibits a fibrotic or spiculated outline, or develops posttreatment mucinous changes, these indicate treatment response.[50] Lack of nodal hyperintensity in DWI is suggestive of a node negative status, which is reliable predictor.[66] However, the presence of nodal intensity in DWI remains nonspecific and should not be relied upon. Overstaging typically occurs through misinterpretation of inflammation, edema, and mucinous data.[67]

1.10.2 Evaluation of posttreatment mucinous tumors

Posttreatment assessment of MRC and MAC poses unique challenges. The imaging extent of the mucin remains largely unchanged after nCRT, even if no tumor cells are present in the mucin pool.[68,69] Sometimes, an increase in the proportion of mucin after nCRT may actually be indicative of a positive treatment response.[42,70] Modest lacelike postcontrast enhancement in the soft tissue component of the MAC or MRC may not significantly change on visual inspection, despite a positive treatment response in the background. These shortcomings may lead to difficulty in evaluating the post-nCRT MRC/MAC treatment response, and the presence of acellular mucin can cause overestimation of both the T and N stages.[69] A reduction in volume, even if only modest, may be related to a reduction in the size of the soft tissue component.[69] For accurate assessment, it is best to concentrate efforts on the solid soft tissue component and ignore the mucin pool.[42] The DWI/ADC sequences have been shown to be limited in the evaluation of the therapeutic response of mucinous tumors and are not reliable.

1.10.3 Categorization of treatment responses

Posttreatment responses in MRI can be categorized as follows:

1. Near/complete response (only 4–31% of cases)
   - Fibrosis showing dense T2W hypointensity in T2W images and delayed enhancement.
   - No DWI restriction.
2. Partial response
   - Mixed signal intensity, with some parts of the tumor having fibrosis.[71]
   - Nodular DWI restriction in some areas.
3. Poor response
   - The tumor exhibits imaging characteristics similar to those in pretreatment scans.
   - No fibrosis.
   - Remarkable DWI restriction.

The histological tumor regression grade (TRG) can be used for a semiquantitative assessment of tumor response to treatment, and correlates well with disease-free survival.[72] Likewise, the MR tumor regression grade (mrTRG) has been developed and can be used as a prognostic predictor, but further validation with histopathology results is required[50,60] (Table 1.3).

TABLE 1.3 Tumor regression grades (TRG).

mrTRG	TRG (AJCC)
Grade 1: Complete radiologic response	Grade 0: No viable cancer cells
Grade 2: Dense (>75%) fibrosis	Grade 1: Single or small groups of tumor cells
Grade 3: >50% fibrosis or mucin	Grade 2: Residual cancer outgrown by fibrosis
Grade 4: <50% fibrosis or mucin	Grade 3: Minimal or no tumor cells killed
Grade 5: No posttreatment changes	

AJCC, American Joint Committee on Cancer; mrTRG, MR tumor regression grade.

MRI pelvis Rectal Cancer RESTAGING (12/2020)

CLINICAL INFORMATION: Rectal Cancer RESTAGING.
   Pretreatment Tumor staging: [pretreatment TN stage]
   Prior treatment: [induction chemotherapy/CRT/TNT/transanal excision/surveillance etc]

TECHNIQUE: Multiplanar, multisequence imaging of the pelvis.
   Magnet strength: [ ]
   IV gadolinium contrast: [ ]

COMPARISON: [ ]

TREATED PRIMARY TUMOR CHARACTERISTICS (compare to pre-treatment):

DWI (with associated low ADC) – restricted diffusion and low ADC in tumor or tumor bed
   ❑ Present [(if yes, is it regressed from prior?)]
   ❑ Absent
   ❑ Artifact/equivocal or N/A

MRI-T2W:
   ❑ Intermediate signal intensity, no dark T2/scar
   ❑ Mixed dark T2/scar and intermediate signal
   ❑ Entirely dark T2 signal/scar
   ❑ nearly normalized appearance of rectal wall
   ❑ T2 bright mucin (cannot distinguish between cellular and acellular mucin)
   [free text to describe above findings]

Distance of the inferior margin of treated tumor to the anal verge: [ ] cm
Distance of inferior margin to the top of the sphincter complex/anorectal junction: [ ] cm
Relationship of treated tumor to the anterior peritoneal reflection:
   [ ]Above   [ ]Straddles   [ ]Below
Craniocaudal length: [ ] cm   Pretreatment craniocaudal length: [ ] cm
Maximal wall thickness: [ ] cm   Previous wall thickness [ ] cm

[** FOR LOW RECTAL TUMORS - Invasion of anal sphincter complex:
   ❑ Absent
   ❑ Invades internal sphincter (IS) only
   ❑ Invades IS and extends into intersphincteric space (ISS)
   ❑ Invades IS + ISS + extends into or through external sphincter (describe)
   [IF present: ❑upper anal canal ❑mid anal canal ❑distal anal canal]]

Extramural Vascular Invasion (EMVI):
   ❑ No (none evident pre-treatment)
   ❑ No, complete regression
   ❑ Yes, partial regression
   ❑ Yes, present and unchanged from baseline

[Mesorectal Fascia (MRF), for T3 disease only:
   Shortest distance of tumor/fibrosis to the Mesorectal Fascia: [ ] mm (location)
   ❑ N/A if tumor above the peritoneal reflection
   Tumor deposit, LN or EMVI threatening (≥ 1mm and ≤2 mm) or invading (< 1 mm) the MRF?
   ❑ No
   ❑ Yes (if yes, note location)]

[For T4 disease, comment on interval change]

LYMPH NODES:

Mesorectal/superior rectal lymph nodes and/or tumor deposits:
   ❑ N0 (no visible lymph nodes/deposits or only < 5 mm short axis)
   ❑ N+ (any lymph nodes ≥ 5 mm short axis)

Extra-mesorectal lymph nodes: any suspicious?
   ❑ No
   ❑ Yes [if yes, location and change from prior]

Other: [free text: bones, peritoneal mets, other incidental findings]

IMPRESSION:

Since [date of prior], post treatment primary tumor assessment:
   ❑ Complete/near complete response
   ❑ Incomplete response (likely residual tumor)
   ❑ No response (tumor stable or increased from baseline)
[free text summary of relevant findings/interval change]

Suspicious Mesorectal lymph nodes: ❑No ❑Yes
Suspicious Extramesorectal lymph nodes: ❑No ❑Yes (provide location)

FIG. 1.31   Society of Abdominal Radiology Disease Focused Panel's reporting template for restaging (with permission from the panel).

What to report:

1. Treatment response based on tumor volume and imaging characteristics.
2. Measure residual tumor (if any).
3. Morphology and position of the residual tumor (o'clock), and distance from the anal verge.
4. yT/N stage in MRI. If yT3, then describe the depth within the mesorectum.
5. State of CRM.
6. TDs, EMVI.

Society of Abdominal Radiology Disease Focused Panel's reporting template for posttreatment restaging v.2020 is reproduced in Fig. 1.31.

1.11 Anal cancer

Anal cancers are rare, but their incidence has been increasing in recent years.[73] It is commonly seen in the elderly (60 years or older) population, with females having a greater predisposition to the disease. The American Cancer Society estimates that about 9440 new cases (3150 men and 6290 women) will be diagnosed in the United States in 2022.[74]

Eighty-five percent of the anal cancers are SSCs, and they either arise from the anal margin (Fig. 1.32) or anatomical anal canal.[75] The remaining tumors consist of adenocarcinoma, basal cell carcinoma, and melanoma.

Occasionally, an anal canal cancer may grow above the dentate line and mimic low rectal cancer. The dentate line demarcates a watershed between the intestinal columnar epithelium and the squamous cell epithelium of the skin.[76] Tumors arising below the dentate line drain into the external iliac and inguinal nodes (Fig. 1.33).

Tumors arising above the dentate line drain into the internal iliac and mesorectal lymph nodes. The 5-year survival rate is 81% if the cancer is localized, but decreases to 64% if there is regional nodal metastasis.[73]

Conventionally, anal cancers are preoperatively treated with chemoradiation; hence, imaging plays a crucial role in the staging and posttreatment assessment. Endoanal ultrasound (EAUS) and MRI are both used to evaluate the local spread of anal cancers.[75] MRI is superior to EAUS for evaluating nodal metastasis and invasion of local structures, while EAUS is better for superficial lesions. The National Comprehensive Cancer Network (NCCN) advocates FDG PET or CT for radiation treatment planning and determine metastasis.

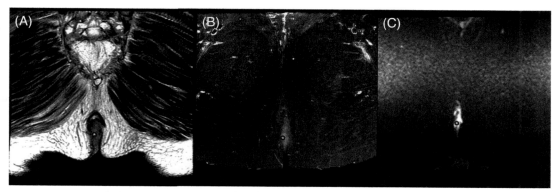

FIG. 1.32 **Adenocarcinoma arising from a pre-existing anal condyloma.** (A) The coronal T2W image through the right anal canal shows a >5 cm intermediate signal intensity lesion along the anal verge, which likely involves a portion of superficial external sphincter. (B) A corresponding T2W fat-suppressed image shows T2W hyperintensity within the lesion (*). (C) The lesion (*) shows a corresponding hyperintensity on the axial high *b*-value DWI. The size of the tumor qualifies it as T3-level disease. Note that an involvement of the external sphincters does not upgrade the staging. The postsurgical pathology was consistent with adenocarcinoma arising from a pre-existing anal condyloma with Paget's disease.

FIG. 1.33 **Anal squamous cell carcinoma with inguinal node.** (A) The axial T2W image through the lower anal canal shows a T2W intermediate lesion (*) along the anal verge. The lesion measures more than 2 cm but less than 5 cm. (B) The lesion (*) demonstrates corresponding diffusion restriction on a high *b*-value DWI. (C) Another axial T2W image through the lower pelvis shows extension of the tumor (*) along the left internal sphincter. Additionally, a suspicious right inguinal node is identified (uneven circle). Due to its size and the presence of an inguinal node, the tumor is staged as T2/N1a.

The staging of anal cancer is size dependent. Tumors measuring >5 cm (stage T3) denote a poor prognosis. The involvement of adjacent organs, such as the vagina, urethra, or bladder, may upgrade the staging to T4, irrespective of the size of the tumor.[75] Interestingly, the involvement of the external or internal sphincters, the levator ani, or the puborectalis does not upgrade the staging; however, such involvement has prognostic significance. The TNM staging of anal cancers is summarized in Table 1.4.

Nodal involvement cannot be predicted using size criteria on imaging. Although nodes >1 cm in short axis diameter in the external and common iliac regions should raise suspicions of nodal involvement, similar nodes in the inguinal region can be reactive.[76] Internal iliac nodes measuring >5 mm in short axis diameter should raise suspicions. Nodal assessment based on size criteria may yield high errors. Specific features such as the presence of nodal necrosis, heterogeneity on T2W sequences, a spiculated border, and avid enhancement, may further increase diagnostic confidence on MRI.[77-81] Furthermore, mesorectal nodes can be assessed in a similar manner as rectal cancer. PET, CT, and thoracoabdominal CT remain the mainstay for diagnosing distant metastasis.

1.12 Pearls and pitfalls

A ready reckoner of important points that may assist in real-world practice is summarized in Table 1.5. Knowledge and understanding of these pearls, pitfalls, and challenges can enable a lucid interpretation of rectal cancer MRI images.

TABLE 1.4 TNM staging of anal cancer.

Primary tumor	
TX	Primary tumor cannot be assessed
T0	No evidence of a primary tumor
Tis	High-grade squamous intraepithelial lesion (previously termed carcinoma in situ, Bowen disease, anal intraepithelial neoplasia II–III, and high-grade anal intraepithelial neoplasia)
T1	Tumor ≤2 cm
T2	Tumor >2 cm and ≤5 cm
T3	Tumor >5 cm
T4	Tumor of any size invading adjacent organ(s), such as the vagina, urethra, or bladder
Lymph nodes	
NX	Regional lymph nodes cannot be assessed
N0	No regional lymph node metastasis
N1	Metastasis in inguinal, mesorectal, internal iliac, or external iliac nodes
N1a	Metastasis in inguinal, mesorectal, or internal iliac lymph nodes
N1b	Metastasis in external iliac lymph nodes
N1c	Metastasis in external iliac with any N1a nodes
Distant metastasis	
MX	Distant metastasis cannot be assessed
cM0	No distant metastasis
cM1	Distant metastasis
pM1	Distant metastasis, microscopically confirmed

TABLE 1.5 Pearls and pitfalls.

MRI anatomy and technique

High-resolution T2W images perpendicular the longitudinal axis of the rectum are critical for evaluating T3 diseases. The findings may otherwise be misinterpreted because of the partial volume effect.

Locoregional lymph nodes: internal iliac, mesorectal, and IMA/superior rectal nodes.

Nonlocoregional nodes: inguinal, external/common iliac, periaortic (above the takeoff of IMA) nodes.

Involvement of nonlocoregional nodes = M1 disease.

MRF is absent along the peritonealized surface of the rectum.

The landmark for finding peritoneal reflections corresponds to the tip of the seminal vesicle in males and the uterocervical junction in females.

MR interpretation

Tumors involving the anterior mid-third or upper-third of the rectum have a greater propensity to invade the peritoneum due to unique peritoneal reflections involving these segments.

Tumor that involves or extends beyond the peritoneal reflection is defined as a T4a tumor.

T3 tumors with >5 mm mesorectal invasion are labeled *bad* T3. Tumoral invasion <5 mm within the mesorectum is regarded as *good* T3.

Presence of the primary tumor, TDs, and EMVI within 1 mm of the MRF is indicative of CRM invasion (or, within 1.1–2 mm = threatened CRM).

EMVI is seen only in a T3 (or higher) disease.

EMVI may or may not be contiguous with the tumor.

EMVI is a poor prognostic factor and has been linked to synchronous or subsequent distant metastasis even after surgery and recurrence.

Any mesorectal nodes >9 mm in short axis diameter should be considered suspicious.

Any pelvic sidewall node >1 cm in short axis diameter should be considered suspicious.

Morphological features are highly reliable for predicting nodal involvement.

Invasion of any pelvic structure (including the musculature or sphincters) should be regarded as T4 disease.

If the fat plane between the tumor and the pelvic organ is maintained, a T4 disease (invasion) can be ruled out.

If more than 50% of the tumor presents T2-weighted hyperintensity compared to the mesorectal fat, a mucinous tumor should be suspected.

N+ disease, irrespective of T stage, may require neoadjuvant therapy.

TME is the treatment of choice for all high-risk T1/T2, N0, and early T3 N0 tumors.

Posttreatment assessment

Interval decrease in the volume of tumors with development of fibrosis is a reliable indicator of treatment response. DWI may further increase diagnostic confidence levels.

Post-nCRT mucinous conversion or increase in the mucinous component is a sign of treatment response and not an indicator of poor prognosis despite the absence of change in the tumor volume.

Post-nCRT assessment of mucinous tumor can be challenging and measuring the volume of nonmucin soft tissue may help yield an accurate assessment.

Low rectal tumor

Low rectal tumor with squamous cell pathology should be treated as anal cancers.

Low rectal tumors have a high recurrence rate and poor prognosis.

Lower edge of tumor above anorectal junction practically rules out the sphincteric involvement.

Anal cancer

Anal cancer staging is based on the size of tumor: size of >5 cm = stage 3 tumor.

Involvement of adjacent organs such as the vagina, urethra, or bladder is indicative of stage T4 irrespective of the size of the tumor.

Involvement of the sphincters, the levator ani, or the puborectalis does not upgrade the staging.

1.13 Miscellaneous rectal cancers

In addition to adenocarcinoma, there are a variety of less frequent rectal malignancies, including carcinoids (0.4%), lymphoma (0.1–0.4%), and sarcoma (leiomyosarcoma or angiosarcoma) (0.3%).[82] Squamous cell carcinoma may develop in the transition zone of the dentate line and is practically considered an anal carcinoma. Melanoma is usually an extension of a primary anal neoplasm; consequently, the term anorectal melanoma is preferred when it occurs in this location (Fig. 1.34).[83] Approximately 3–5% of gastrointestinal stromal tumors (GISTs) tend to occur in the rectum (Fig. 1.35).[82] GISTs are the most common rectal mesenchymal tumors and may be malignant or benign.[84] GIST can be treated with tyrosine kinase inhibitors (Imatinib).

Metastases from the stomach, ovary, and cervix to the rectum have been documented.[85,86] The specifics of these unusual tumors are beyond the scope of this chapter.

1.14 Ultrasmall superparamagnetic iron oxide

Ultrasmall superparamagnetic iron oxide (USPIO)-enhanced MRI, though currently under investigation, may accurately differentiate benign from malignant nodes. USPIO consists of low-molecular weight iron oxide, which is administered to the patient 24–36 hours before analysis. Iron deposition in a normal node will be visualized as decreased signal intensity due to susceptibility artifacts on T2W sequences. No iron deposit in malignant nodes will be seen as high signal intensity on T2W images.[13,87] Larger hyperintense nodal component means a higher likelihood of malignancy.[14]

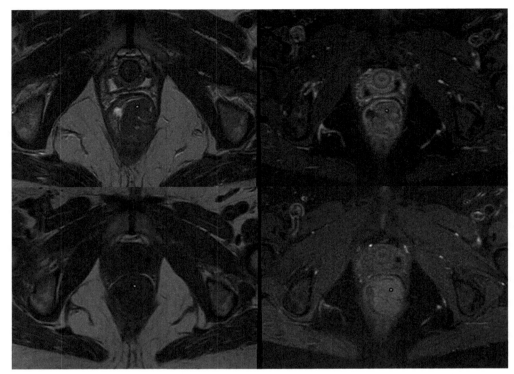

FIG. 1.34   Anorectal melanoma. (A–B) Axial T2W images without (A) and with fat suppression (B) show a multilobulated mass (*) in the left anorectum, which shows an intermediate intensity. (C–D) Axial T1W images without (C) and with fat suppression (D) show the mass which appears isointense to slightly hyperintense compared to the pelvic muscles. Contrary to popular belief, melanoma does not exhibit overt T1 hyperintensity.

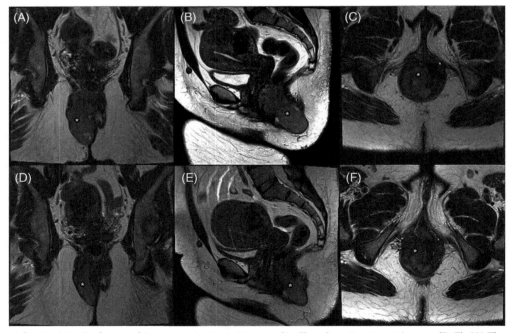

FIG. 1.35   Anorectal gastrointestinal stromal tumor; pretreatment images (A–C) and posttreatment images (D–F). (A) The coronal T2W image shows an elongated, well-circumscribed tumor (*) within the intersphincteric plane of intermediate intensity. The external sphincter is displaced peripherally. The tumor likely arises from the lower internal sphincter. (B) The sagittal T2W image demonstrates the relationship of the tumor (*) to the external sphincter and its caudocephalic extent. (C) The axial T2W image through the anorectal junction shows its origin from the internal sphincter and extension to the intersphincteric plane. Note that, despite its size and the extent of the tumor, it displays locally nonaggressive behavior. A diagnosis of a low-grade gastrointestinal stromal tumor was made based on imaging. Biopsy confirmed the diagnosis, and it was treated with tyrosine kinase inhibitor (imatinib mesylate). (D–F) Corresponding posttreatment images show interval decrease in the size of the tumor (*). Interval development of T2W hypointensity along the right anterolateral aspect of the tumor is suggestive of the development of posttreatment fibrosis (arrows).

1.15 Conclusion

MRI has become the investigative tool of choice for rectal cancer staging and follow-up after nCRT. A radiologist should have in-depth knowledge of the MRI anatomy of the mesorectum and rectal cancer staging.

References

1. Key Statistics for Colorectal Cancer, American Cancer Society, https://www.cancer.org/cancer/colon-rectal-cancer/about/key-statistics.html. Date Accessed 1st March 2022.
2. Kapiteijn E, Marijnen CA, Nagtegaal ID, et al. Preoperative radiotherapy combined with total mesorectal excision for resectable rectal cancer. *N Engl J Med.* 2001;345(9):638–646. doi:10.1056/NEJMoa010580.
3. Friedman K. Pathologist's perspective on primary rectal cancer. *Abdom Radiol.* 2019;44(11):3751–3754. doi:10.1007/s00261-019-02134-9.
4. Al-Sukhni E, Milot L, Fruitman M, et al. Diagnostic accuracy of MRI for assessment of T category, lymph node metastases, and circumferential resection margin involvement in patients with rectal cancer: a systematic review and meta-analysis. *Ann Surg Oncol.* 2012;19(7):2212–2223. doi:10.1245/s10434-011-2210-5.
5. Lambregts DMJ, Boellaard TN, Beets-Tan RGH. Response evaluation after neoadjuvant treatment for rectal cancer using modern mr imaging: a pictorial review. *Insights Imaging.* 2019;10(1):15. doi:10.1186/s13244-019-0706-x.
6. Jorge JM, Wexner SD. Anatomy and physiology of the rectum and anus. *Eur J Surg.* 1997;163(10):723–731.
7. Salerno G, Daniels IR, Brown G. Magnetic resonance imaging of the low rectum: defining the radiological anatomy. *Colorectal Dis.* 2006;8(Suppl 3):10–13. doi:10.1111/j.1463-1318.2006.01063.x.
8. Sakorafas GH, Zouros E, Peros G. Applied vascular anatomy of the colon and rectum: clinical implications for the surgical oncologist. *Surg Oncol.* 2006;15(4):243–255. doi:10.1016/j.suronc.2007.03.002.
9. Brown G, Kirkham A, Williams GT, et al. High-resolution MRI of the anatomy important in total mesorectal excision of the rectum. *Am J Roentgenol.* 2004;182(2):431–439. doi:10.2214/ajr.182.2.1820431.
10. Taylor FGM, Swift RI, Blomqvist L, Brown G. A systematic approach to the interpretation of preoperative staging MRI for rectal cancer. *Am J Roentgenol.* 2008;191(6):1827–1835. doi:10.2214/AJR.08.1004.
11. Kaiser AM, Ortega AE. Anorectal anatomy. *Surg Clin North Am.* 2002;82(6):1125–1138. doi:10.1016/s0039-6109(02)00056-7.
12. Heald RJ, Moran BJ. Embryology and anatomy of the rectum. *Semin Surg Oncol.* 1998;15(2):66–71. doi:10.1002/(sici)1098-2388(199809)15:2<66::aid-ssu2>3.0.co;2-3.
13. Langer A-OSaM. 1st ed. vol XII, MRI of Rectal Cancer. Berlin, Heidelberg: Springer-Verlag; 2010:215.
14. Merkel S, Klossek D, Gohl J, Papadopoulos T, Hohenberger W, Hermanek P. Quality management in rectal carcinoma: what is feasible? *Int J Colorectal Dis.* 2009;24(8):931–942. doi:10.1007/s00384-009-0736-9.
15. Seo N, Kim H, Cho MS, Lim JS. Response assessment with MRI after chemoradiotherapy in rectal cancer: current evidences. *Korean J Radiol.* 2019;20(7):1003–1018. doi:10.3348/kjr.2018.0611.
16. Ross HM, Mahmoud N, Fry RD. The current management of rectal cancer. *Curr Probl Surg.* 2005;42(2):72–131. doi:10.1067/j.cpsurg.2004.11.004.
17. Taylor FG, Swift RI, Blomqvist L, Brown G. A systematic approach to the interpretation of preoperative staging MRI for rectal cancer. *AJR Am J Roentgenol.* 2008;191(6):1827–1835. doi:10.2214/ajr.08.1004.
18. Jhaveri KS, Hosseini-Nik H. MRI of rectal cancer: an overview and update on recent advances. *Am J Roentgenol.* 2015;205(1):W42–W55. doi:10.2214/AJR.14.14201.
19. Hope TA, Gollub MJ, Arya S, et al. Rectal cancer lexicon: consensus statement from the Society of Abdominal Radiology Rectal & Anal Cancer Disease-Focused Panel. *Abdom Radiol (NY).* 2019;44(11):3508–3517. doi:10.1007/s00261-019-02170-5.
20. Members SD. *User's Guide for the Synoptic MRI Report for Pre-Operative Staging of Rectal Cancer*: Society of Abdominal Radiology, Diasease Focused Panel on Colorectal Cancer; 2022.
21. Bates DDB, Fuqua JL, Zheng J, et al. Measurement of rectal tumor height from the anal verge on MRI: a comparison of internal versus external anal sphincter. *Abdom Radiol (NY).* 2021;46(3):867–872. doi:10.1007/s00261-020-02757-3.
22. Monson JR, Weiser MR, Buie WD, et al. Practice parameters for the management of rectal cancer (revised). *Dis Colon Rectum.* 2013;56(5):535–550. doi:10.1097/DCR.0b013e31828cb66c.
23. Fitzgerald TL, Brinkley J, Zervos EE. Pushing the envelope beyond a centimeter in rectal cancer: oncologic implications of close, but negative margins. *J Am Coll Surg.* 2011;213(5):589–595. doi:10.1016/j.jamcollsurg.2011.07.020.
24. Radjindrin A. S.V. Does lateral pelvic lymph node matters in rectal cancer. *Glob Surg.* 2018;4(4): 3-3. doi:10.15761/GOS.1000196.
25. Amin MB, Greene FL, Byrd DR, et al. AJCC Cancer Staging Manual *American College of Surgeons 2017.* 8th ed. Springer Cham, Switzerland; 2017 Corr. 3rd printing 2018 Edition. 2018.
26. Rao S-X, Zeng M-S, Xu J-M, et al. Assessment of T staging and mesorectal fascia status using high-resolution MRI in rectal cancer with rectal distention. *World J Gastroenterol.* 2007;13(30):4141–4146. doi:10.3748/wjg.v13.i30.4141.
27. Nougaret S, Jhaveri K, Kassam Z, Lall C, Kim DH. Rectal cancer MR staging: pearls and pitfalls at baseline examination. *Abdom Radiol.* 2019;44(11):3536–3548. doi:10.1007/s00261-019-02024-0.
28. Extramural depth of tumor invasion at thin-section MR in patients with rectal cancer: results of the mercury study. *Radiology.* 2007;243(1):132–139. doi:10.1148/radiol.2431051825.
29. Beets-Tan RG, Beets GL, Vliegen RF, et al. Accuracy of magnetic resonance imaging in prediction of tumour-free resection margin in rectal cancer surgery. *Lancet.* 2001;357(9255):497–504. doi:10.1016/s0140-6736(00)04040-x.
30. Mizukami Y, Ueda S, Mizumoto A, et al. Diffusion-weighted magnetic resonance imaging for detecting lymph node metastasis of rectal cancer. *World J Surg.* 2011;35(4):895–899. doi:10.1007/s00268-011-0986-x.
31. Taylor FG, Quirke P, Heald RJ, et al. Preoperative high-resolution magnetic resonance imaging can identify good prognosis stage I, II, and III rectal cancer best managed by surgery alone: a prospective, multicenter, european study. *Ann Surg.* 2011;253(4):711–719. doi:10.1097/SLA.0b013e31820b8d52.

32. Park JS, Huh JW, Park YA, et al. A circumferential resection margin of 1 mm is a negative prognostic factor in rectal cancer patients with and without neoadjuvant chemoradiotherapy. *Dis Colon Rectum.* 2014;57(8):933–940. doi:10.1097/dcr.0000000000000171.

33. Brown G, Radcliffe AG, Newcombe RG, Dallimore NS, Bourne MW, Williams GT. Preoperative assessment of prognostic factors in rectal cancer using high-resolution magnetic resonance imaging. *BJS (Br J Surg).* 2003;90(3):355–364. doi:10.1002/bjs.4034.

34. Bokey EL, Chapuis PH, Dent OF, et al. Factors affecting survival after excision of the rectum for cancer: a multivariate analysis. *Dis Colon Rectum.* 1997;40(1):3–10. doi:10.1007/bf02055674.

35. Bipat S, Glas AS, Slors FJ, Zwinderman AH, Bossuyt PM, Stoker J. Rectal cancer: local staging and assessment of lymph node involvement with endoluminal US, CT, and MR imaging—a meta-analysis. *Radiology.* 2004;232(3):773–783. doi:10.1148/radiol.2323031368.

36. Smith NJ, Shihab O, Arnaout A, Swift RI, Brown G. MRI for detection of extramural vascular invasion in rectal cancer. *Am J Roentgenol.* 2008;191(5):1517–1522. doi:10.2214/AJR.08.1298.

37. Lord AC, Graham Martínez C, D'Souza N, Pucher PH, Brown G, Nagtegaal ID. The significance of tumour deposits in rectal cancer after neoadjuvant therapy: a systematic review and meta-analysis. *Eur J Cancer.* 2019;122:1–8. doi:10.1016/j.ejca.2019.08.020.

38. Lord AC, D'Souza N, Shaw A, et al. MRI-diagnosed tumour deposits and EMVI status have superior prognostic accuracy to current clinical TNM staging in rectal cancer. *Ann Surg.* 2020; 276(2):334–344. doi:10.1097/sla.0000000000004499.

39. Tong G-J, Zhang G-Y, Liu J, et al. Comparison of the eighth version of the American Joint Committee on cancer manual to the seventh version for colorectal cancer: a retrospective review of our data. *World J Clin Oncol.* 2018;9(7):148–161. doi:10.5306/wjco.v9.i7.148.

40. Nagtegaal ID, Quirke P. What is the role for the circumferential margin in the modern treatment of rectal cancer? *J Clin Oncol.* 2008;26(2):303–312. doi:10.1200/JCO.2007.12.7027.

41. McCawley N, Clancy C, O'Neill BDP, Deasy J, McNamara DA, Burke JP. Mucinous rectal adenocarcinoma is associated with a poor response to neoadjuvant chemoradiotherapy: a systematic review and meta-analysis. *Dis Colon Rectum.* 2016;59(12): 1200–1208 doi: 10.1097/DCR.0000000000000635.

42. Childs DD, Rocha Lima C, Zhou Y. Mucin-containing rectal cancer: a review of unique imaging, pathology, and therapeutic response features. *Semin Roentgenol.* 2021;56(2):186–200. doi:10.1053/j.ro.2020.07.010.

43. Taylor FG, Quirke P, Heald RJ, et al. Preoperative high-resolution magnetic resonance imaging can identify good prognosis stage I, II, and III rectal cancer best managed by surgery alone: a prospective, multicenter, european study. *Ann Surg.* 2011;253(4):711–719. doi:10.1097/SLA.0b013e31820b8d52.

44. Chamlou R, Parc Y, Simon T, et al. Long-term results of intersphincteric resection for low rectal cancer. *Ann Surg.* 2007;246(6): 916–922 doi: 10.1097/SLA.0b013e31815c29ff.

45. Shihab OC, Brown G, Daniels IR, Heald RJ, Quirke P, Moran BJ. Patients with low rectal cancer treated by abdominoperineal excision have worse tumors and higher involved margin rates compared with patients treated by anterior resection. *Dis Colon Rectum.* 2010;53(1):53–56. doi:10.1007/DCR.0b013e3181c70465.

46. Shihab OC, How P, West N, et al. Can a novel MRI staging system for low rectal cancer aid surgical planning? *Dis Colon Rectum.* 2011;54(10): 1260–1264 doi: 10.1097/DCR.0b013e31822abd78.

47. Shihab OC, Moran BJ, Heald RJ, Quirke P, Brown G. MRI staging of low rectal cancer. *Eur Radiol.* 2009;19(3):643–650. doi:10.1007/s00330-008-1184-6.

48. Gollub MJ, Arya S, Beets-Tan RG, et al. Use of magnetic resonance imaging in rectal cancer patients: Society of Abdominal Radiology (Sar) Rectal Cancer Disease-Focused Panel (DFP) recommendations 2017. *Abdom Radiol (NY).* 2018;43(11):2893–2902. doi:10.1007/s00261-018-1642-9.

49. Maliske S, Chau J, Ginader T, et al. Timing of surgery following neoadjuvant chemoradiation in rectal cancer: a retrospective analysis from an academic medical center. *J Gastrointest Oncol.* 2019;10(4):597–604. doi:10.21037/jgo.2019.02.02.

50. Kalisz KR, Enzerra MD, Paspulati RM. MRI evaluation of the response of rectal cancer to neoadjuvant chemoradiation therapy. *Radiographics.* 2019;39(2):538–556. doi:10.1148/rg.2019180075.

51. Barbaro B, Fiorucci C, Tebala C, et al. Locally advanced rectal cancer: MR imaging in prediction of response after preoperative chemotherapy and radiation therapy. *Radiology.* 2009;250(3):730–739. doi:10.1148/radiol.2503080310.

52. Schurink NW, Min LA, Berbee M, et al. Value of combined multiparametric MRI and FDG-PET/CT to identify well-responding rectal cancer patients before the start of neoadjuvant chemoradiation. *Eur Radiol.* 2020;30(5):2945–2954. doi:10.1007/s00330-019-06638-2.

53. Yeo SG, Kim DY, Kim TH, et al. Tumor volume reduction rate measured by magnetic resonance volumetry correlated with pathologic tumor response of preoperative chemoradiotherapy for rectal cancer. *Int J Radiat Oncol Biol Phys.* 2010;78(1):164–171. doi:10.1016/j.ijrobp.2009.07.1682.

54. Nougaret S, Rouanet P, Molinari N, et al. MR volumetric measurement of low rectal cancer helps predict tumor response and outcome after combined chemotherapy and radiation therapy. *Radiology.* 2012;263(2):409–418. doi:10.1148/radiol.12111263.

55. Nougaret S, Reinhold C, Mikhael HW, Rouanet P, Bibeau F, Brown G. The use of mr imaging in treatment planning for patients with rectal carcinoma: have you checked the "DISTANCE"? *Radiology.* 2013;268(2):330–344. doi:10.1148/radiol.13121361.

56. Therasse P, Arbuck SG, Eisenhauer EA, et al. New guidelines to evaluate the response to treatment in solid tumors. European Organization for Research and Treatment of Cancer, National Cancer Institute of the United States, National Cancer Institute of Canada. *J Natl Cancer Inst.* 2000;92(3):205–216. doi:10.1093/jnci/92.3.205.

57. Shia J, Guillem JG, Moore HG, et al. Patterns of morphologic alteration in residual rectal carcinoma following preoperative chemoradiation and their association with long-term outcome. *Am J Surg Pathol.* 2004;28(2):215–223. doi:10.1097/00000478-200402000-00009.

58. Bates DDB, Homsi ME, Chang KJ, Lalwani N, Horvat N, Sheedy SP. MRI for rectal cancer: staging, mrCRM, EMVI, lymph node staging and post-treatment response. *Clin Colorectal Cancer.* 2022;21(1):10–18. https://doi.org/10.1016/j.clcc.2021.10.007.

59. Amin MB, Greene FL, Edge SB, et al. The eighth edition AJCC cancer staging manual: continuing to build a bridge from a population-based to a more "personalized" approach to cancer staging. *CA Cancer J Clin.* 2017;67(2):93–99. doi:10.3322/caac.21388.

60. Patel UB, Taylor F, Blomqvist L, et al. Magnetic resonance imaging-detected tumor response for locally advanced rectal cancer predicts survival outcomes: mercury experience. *J Clin Oncol.* 2011;29(28):3753–3760. doi:10.1200/jco.2011.34.9068.

61. Agger EA, Jörgren FH, Lydrup MA, Buchwald PL. Risk of local recurrence of rectal cancer and circumferential resection margin: population-based cohort study. *Br J Surg.* 2020;107(5):580–585. doi:10.1002/bjs.11478.

62. Jhaveri KS, Hosseini-Nik H, Thipphavong S, et al. MRI detection of extramural venous invasion in rectal cancer: correlation with histopathology using elastin stain. *AJR Am J Roentgenol*. 2016;206(4):747–755. doi:10.2214/ajr.15.15568.

63. Lambregts DMJ, Rao S-X, Sassen S, et al. MRI and diffusion-weighted MRI volumetry for identification of complete tumor responders after preoperative chemoradiotherapy in patients with rectal cancer: a bi-institutional validation study. *Ann Surg*. 2015;262(6): 1034–1039 doi: 10.1097/SLA.0000000000000909.

64. Curvo-Semedo L, Lambregts DMJ, Maas M, Beets GL, Caseiro-Alves F, Beets-Tan RGH. Diffusion-weighted MRI in rectal cancer: apparent diffusion coefficient as a potential noninvasive marker of tumor aggressiveness. *J Magn Reson Imaging*. 2012;35(6):1365–1371. doi: https://doi.org/10.1002/jmri.23589.

65. Allen SD, Padhani AR, Dzik-Jurasz AS, Glynne-Jones R. Rectal carcinoma: MRI with histologic correlation before and after chemoradiation therapy. *Am J Roentgenol*. 2007;188(2):442–451. doi:10.2214/AJR.05.1967.

66. van Heeswijk MM, Lambregts DM, Palm WM, et al. DWI for assessment of rectal cancer nodes after chemoradiotherapy: is the absence of nodes at dwi proof of a negative nodal status? *AJR Am J Roentgenol*. 2017;208(3):W79–W84. doi:10.2214/ajr.16.17117.

67. Jia X, Zhang Y, Wang Y, et al. MRI for restaging locally advanced rectal cancer: detailed analysis of discrepancies with the pathologic reference standard. *AJR Am J Roentgenol*. 2019;213(5):1081–1090. doi:10.2214/ajr.19.21383.

68. Miyakita H, Sadahiro S, Ogimi T, et al. Mucinous components assessed by magnetic resonance imaging in primary rectal cancer tissue before and after chemoradiotherapy and tumor response. *Int J Colorectal Dis*. 2018;33(8):1135–1138. doi:10.1007/s00384-018-3047-1.

69. Park SH, Lim JS, Lee J, et al. Rectal mucinous adenocarcinoma: MR imaging assessment of response to concurrent chemotherapy and radiation therapy—a hypothesis-generating study. *Radiology*. 2017;285(1):124–133. doi:10.1148/radiol.2017162657.

70. Patel UB, Blomqvist LK, Taylor F, et al. MRI after treatment of locally advanced rectal cancer: how to report tumor response--the mercury experience. *AJR Am J Roentgenol*. 2012;199(4):W486–W495. doi:10.2214/ajr.11.8210.

71. Rullier A, Laurent C, Vendrely V, Le Bail B, Bioulac-Sage P, Rullier E. Impact of colloid response on survival after preoperative radiotherapy in locally advanced rectal carcinoma. *Am J Surg Pathol*. 2005;29(5):602–606. doi:10.1097/01.pas.0000153120.80385.29.

72. Rödel C, Martus P, Papadoupolos T, et al. Prognostic significance of tumor regression after preoperative chemoradiotherapy for rectal cancer. *J Clin Oncol*. 2005;23(34):8688–8696. doi:10.1200/jco.2005.02.1329.

73. NIH. Surveillance EAERP seer stat fact sheets: anal cancer.

74. Society AC. Key statistics for anal cancer. 2022.

75. Golia Pernicka JS, Sheedy SP, Ernst RD, Minsky BD, Ganeshan D, Rauch GM. MR staging of anal cancer: what the radiologist needs to know. *Abdom Radiol*. 2019;44(11):3726–3739. doi:10.1007/s00261-019-02020-4.

76. Golia Pernicka JS, Sheedy SP, Ernst RD, Minsky BD, Ganeshan D, Rauch GM. MR staging of anal cancer: what the radiologist needs to know. *Abdom Radiol (NY)*. 2019;44(11):3726–3739. doi:10.1007/s00261-019-02020-4.

77. Ciombor KK, Ernst RD, Brown G. Diagnosis and diagnostic imaging of anal canal cancer. *Surg Oncol Clin N Am*. 2017;26(1):45–55. doi:10.1016/j.soc.2016.07.002.

78. Parikh J, Shaw A, Grant LA, et al. Anal carcinomas: the role of endoanal ultrasound and magnetic resonance imaging in staging, response evaluation and follow-up. *Eur Radiol*. 2011;21(4):776–785. doi:10.1007/s00330-010-1980-7.

79. Roach SC, Hulse PA, Moulding FJ, Wilson R, Carrington BM. Magnetic resonance imaging of anal cancer. *Clin Radiol*. 2005;60(10):1111–1119. https://doi.org/10.1016/j.crad.2005.05.008.

80. Durot C, Dohan A, Boudiaf M, Servois V, Soyer P, Hoeffel C. Cancer of the anal canal: diagnosis, staging and follow-up with MRI. *Korean J Radiol*. 18(6):946-956.

81. Torkzad MR, Kamel I, Halappa VG, Beets-Tan RGH. Magnetic resonance imaging of rectal and anal cancer. *Magn Reson Imaging Clin N Am*. 2014;22(1):85–112. https://doi.org/10.1016/j.mric.2013.07.007.

82. Bates DDB, de Paula MCF, Horvat N, et al. Beyond adenocarcinoma: MRI of uncommon rectal neoplasms and mimickers. *Abdom Radiol (New York)*. 2019;44(11):3581–3594. doi:10.1007/s00261-019-02045-9.

83. Purysko AS, Coppa CP, Kalady MF, et al. Benign and malignant tumors of the rectum and perirectal region. *Abdom Imaging*. 2014;39(4):824–852. doi:10.1007/s00261-014-0119-8.

84. Kim H, Kim JH, Lim JS, et al. MRI findings of rectal submucosal tumors. *Korean J Radiol*. 2011;12(4):487–498. doi:10.3348/kjr.2011.12.4.487.

85. Derin D, Eralp Y, Guney N, Ozlük Y, Topuz E. Ovarian carcinoma with simultaneous breast and rectum metastases. *Onkologie*. 2008;31(4):200–202. doi:10.1159/000119121.

86. Wu YC, Yang CF, Hsu CN, Hsieh TC. Intramural metastases of rectum from carcinosarcoma (malignant Müllerian mixed tumor) of uterine cervix. *Clin Nucl Med*. 2013;38(2):137–139. doi:10.1097/RLU.0b013e318266d4bd.

87. Lahaye MJ, Engelen SME, Kessels AGH, et al. USPIO-enhanced MR imaging for nodal staging in patients with primary rectal cancer: predictive criteria. *Radiology*. 2008;246(3):804–811. doi:10.1148/radiol.2463070221.

2

MRI defecography

Neeraj Lalwani[a], Roopa Ram[b], Christine O. Menias[c]

[a]Professor of Radiology, Virginia Commonwealth University School of Medicine and Health System, Richmond, VA, United States [b]Department of Radiology, University of Arkansas Medical Center, Little Rock, AR, United States [c]Department of Radiology, Mayo Clinic in Arizona, Scottsdale, AZ, United States

2.1 Introduction

Pelvic floor dysfunction (PFD) is a complex problem that more commonly affects multiparous and postmenopausal women. Occasionally, premenopausal women and men are also affected. PFD may affect approximately 50% of women over the age of 50.[1] Approximately 10–20% of multiparous women require medical attention for some form of evacuation disorder.[2] Approximately 11% of these women undergo surgery, and 30% of these patients may require repeat surgery.[3]

The Pelvic Organ Prolapse Quantification (POP-Q) offered by the International Continence Society is one of the most acceptable clinical assessment and staging systems for assessing PFD. Clinical staging systems do not directly assess anatomy and may underestimate the magnitude of dysfunction or misdiagnose the prolapse sites.[4] As a result, the evaluation of PFD requires a combination of clinical evaluation and other functional investigations. These investigations include a broad spectrum, ranging from video urodynamic imaging to evacuation proctography and dynamic cystoproctography. With recent advancements in magnetic resonance imaging (MRI), MR defecography (MRD) has become the preferred modality for preoperative planning in patients with PFD and chronic constipation.[5]

2.2 Pathophysiology

A variety of factors can contribute to the pathogenesis of PFD. The most important reasons include prior vaginal delivery and/or pelvic surgery, advancing age, and declining estrogen levels. Other conditions, including connective tissue disorders, smoking, chronic obstructive pulmonary disease, obesity/being overweight, and excessive straining, such as the Valsalva maneuver, have also been implicated in the pathogenesis.

Although PFD is multifactorial, the main pathophysiology involves stretching and disruption of the components of the levator ani muscle, tears in the endopelvic fascia and/or ligaments, and subsequent denervation of the pudendal nerve. A pelvic floor descent of only 1.35 cm is sufficient to cause a 15% stretching of the pudendal nerve, which is sufficient to initiate demyelination of the nerve.[6] The pudendal mono neuropathy caused by this mechanical demyelination is often responsible for the prolapse of pelvic organs.[3] These events result in pelvic floor descent, which further exacerbates injuries to the muscles and fascia, triggering a vicious cycle.

2.3 Pelvic floor anatomy

Pelvic organs can be separated into three compartments in a female (Fig. 2.1). The anterior compartment comprises the bladder and the urethra. The middle compartment includes the reproductive organs (vagina, cervix, and uterus). The posterior compartment consists of the rectum and the anal canal.

Magnetic Resonance Imaging of The Pelvis.
DOI: https://doi.org/10.1016/B978-0-323-89854-6.00019-3

The pelvic floor is formed by intricate musculofascial layers that support the three pelvic compartments. Anatomically, three horizontal layers form the pelvic floor. The pubovesical, uterosacral, and cardinal ligaments form the most cephalic fascial layer (Fig. 2.1). These ligaments are constituted by the thickening of the endopelvic fascia and peritoneal reflections. The fascial layer is attached to the pelvic side wall and to the underlying muscle layers and is primarily responsible for supporting the anterior and the middle compartments.

The middle layer consists of the levator ani muscle and its components, which support all three pelvic floor compartments (Figs. 2.2 and 2.3). The levator ani is composed of three individual muscles—pubococcygeus, iliococcygeus, and puborectalis, which form a sling. The interlaced posterior fibers of the levator ani that attach to the coccyx form the levator plate.

The caudal muscular layer is formed by the urogenital diaphragm, which supports the urogenital structures (Fig. 2.1). The superficial and the deep transverse perineal muscles of the urogenital diaphragm mainly support the anterior compartment (Fig. 2.2).

All three musculofascial layers are tightly interwoven, and visual separation of individual layers may be difficult to assess surgically.

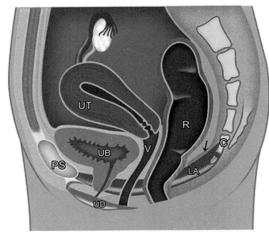

FIG. 2.1 **Anatomy of the pelvic floor.** The pelvic floor consists of complex musculofascial layers that support the three pelvic compartments. The cephalic layer (arrow) comprises thickened endopelvic fascia and peritoneal reflection. The middle layer is composed of all components of the levator ani (LA) muscle. The caudal layer is made up of the small muscles of the urogenital diaphragm (UD), which supports the anterior and the central compartments. C, coccyx; PS, pubic symphysis; R, rectum; UB, urinary bladder; UT, uterus.

(A)

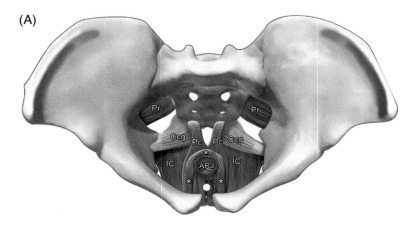

(B)

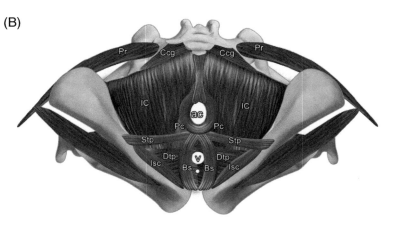

FIG. 2.2 (A–B) Anatomy of the pelvic floor muscles (A) from above and (B) from below. The levator ani (LA) is the main support of the entire pelvic floor and consists of three components: (1) Pubococcygeus (Pc) arises from the posterior aspect of the pubic bone and the anterior part of the obturator fascia and inserts to the sacrococcyx. (2) Iliococcygeus (IC) originates from the posterior half of the fascial line over the obturator internus and the ischial spine and inserts to the anococcygeal body. The anococcygeal body is a fibrous median raphe that extends between the coccyx and the margin of the anus and is not visualized on the MRI. (3) Puborectalis (*) arises from the posterior aspect of the lower pubic symphysis and adjacent fascia of the urogenital diaphragm to form a U-shaped sling around the rectum and demarcates the surgical anorectal junction (ARJ). The urogenital diaphragm (or triangular ligament) occupies the triangular area between the pubic symphysis and ischial tuberosity and overlies the pelvic diaphragm (refer to Fig. 2.3) externally and inferiorly. The urogenital diaphragm mainly consists of the urethral external sphincter and deep transverse perineal (Dtp) muscles. ac, anal canal; Bs, bulbospongiosus; Ccg, coccygeus; Isc, ischiococcygeus; Pr, piriformis; Stp, superficial transverse perineal; v, vagina.

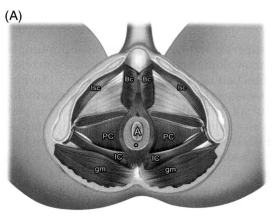
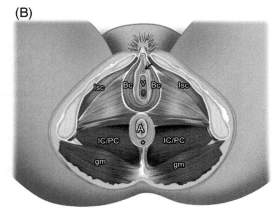

FIG. 2.3 (A–B) Myology of the pelvic floor: (A) male and (B) female. A layer of four small muscles is arranged along the inferior aspect of the urogenital diaphragm and additionally supports the pelvic floor structures. These muscles consist of bulbocavernosus (Bc), ischiocavernosus (Isc), superficial transverse perineal (refer to Fig. 2.2), and external anal sphincter (*). Bulbocavernosus (also called bulbospongiosus) surrounds the bulb of the penis and urethra in men. In females, it is divided into halves that lie just behind the clitoris to surround the vagina and aid in its constriction. Ischiocavernosus extends between the ischium and the crura of the penis (males) or the clitoris (females). The external anal sphincter is responsible for the closure of the anal orifice and surrounds the anal canal. The widest funnel-shaped musculofascial layer of the pelvic floor is called the pelvic diaphragm and forms the inferior border of the abdominopelvic cavity. The pelvic diaphragm extends from the symphysis pubis to the coccyx. Components of the levator ani (IC, iliococcygeus; Pc, pubococcygeus) form most of the bulk of the pelvic diaphragm in addition to the piriformis, coccygeus, and obturator internus (refer to Fig. 2.2). A, anus; arrow, urethra; gm, gluteus maximus; v, vagina; *demarcates anal sphincter.

2.4 Clinical presentation

Based on the pelvic floor compartment involved, patients may present with nonspecific symptoms, such as urinary or fecal incontinence, chronic constipation, pelvic pain, and organ prolapse. In the United States, approximately 23.7–25% of women report at least one symptom of PFD.[7,8] Urinary incontinence is the most commonly encountered symptom (15.7–17.1%), followed by fecal incontinence (9.0–9.4%) and pelvic organ prolapse (2.9%).[7,8] Abnormalities of the anterior and the middle compartments are more often diagnosed clinically, with imaging reserved for complex cases or when multicompartmental involvement is suspected. However, imaging plays a key role in the diagnosis of posterior compartmental abnormalities, which often involve problems with defecation.

Normal defecation involves a complex interplay of involuntary and voluntary muscles. Defecation is initiated by a strong propellant colonic wave that raises intracolonic and intrarectal pressure. The simultaneous relaxation of the anal sphincter complex and contraction of the musculature of the pelvic floor then complete the process. The sling-like contour of the puborectalis muscle gives a smooth posterior rectal impression, is responsible for voluntary fecal continence, and delineates the surgical anorectal junction (ARJ) (Fig. 2.4).

The angle between the posterior wall of the rectum and the longitudinal axis of the anal canal is called an anorectal angle (ARA) (Figs. 2.5 and 2.6). During defecation, the puborectalis sling relaxes and allows the anal canal to open and facilitate evacuation. Next, external sphincters also relax and allow the rectum to empty without significant pelvic floor descent. Consequently, the ARA becomes obtuse (Figs. 2.5 and 2.6) from the baseline during defecation. After defecation, the puborectalis, pelvic floor muscles, and anal sphincters return to their resting state, and the ARA regains its normal resting state.

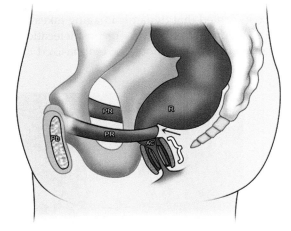

FIG. 2.4 Anatomy of the puborectalis (PR). The puborectalis is a U-shaped muscle that wraps around the rectum and demarcates the surgical anorectal junction (arrow). The puborectalis contributes to anal continence, usually remains contracted, and signifies a normal anorectal angle. Although the puborectalis is anatomically a part of the levator ani, it constitutes a synergistic functional unit with the external anal sphincter (depicted by }). The functional unit of the puborectalis and the external anal sphincter plays a critical and complex role in continence and defecation. AC, anal canal; Pb, pubic symphysis; R, rectum.

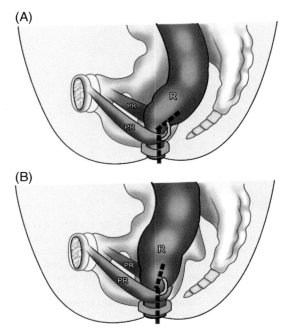

FIG. 2.5 (A–B) Normal defecation. (A) The puborectalis (PR) is contracted at rest, and its impression along the posterior aspect of the anorectal junction corresponds to the anorectal angle. The anorectal angle is the angle between the long axis of the anal canal and a line drawn parallel to the posterior rectal wall. (B) The PR relaxes during defecation, and the anorectal angle opens to becomes obtuse. R, rectum.

2.5 Imaging protocol

Due to its superior soft-tissue resolution and multiplanar capability, MRD can evaluate both the anatomy of the pelvic floor and the dynamic functioning of the pelvic organs during defecation. Dynamic assessment is crucial because certain pathologies are only revealed during defecation.[9] Dynamic imaging is performed with a rapid balanced steady-state gradient echo sequence (TrueFISP—Siemens, FIESTA—GE, and BFFE—Philips). A mid-sagittal image of the pelvis through the rectum is selected and repeated multiple times to generate a cine loop as the patient performs various maneuvers (contraction, squeezing, and defecation). The mid-sagittal image should include the entire coccyx and symphysis pubis (Fig. 2.7). Additional three-plane (axial, sagittal, and coronal) T2W images and optional axial T1W of the pelvis at rest are also included for a complete anatomical assessment of other pelvic structures. Refer to Table 2.1 for a comprehensive MRI protocol.

Approximately 120–200 cc of ultrasound (US) gel is instilled in the rectum to achieve distention. US gel is preferred over other available options, such as potato starch, because of its easy availability, inert nature, high water content, semisolid consistency, and patient tolerance. However, short episodes of diarrhea have been reported in patients after US gel instillation in the rectum, probably due to mucosal irritation.[3] Instillation of US gel in the vagina is optional to highlight its outline.[10] Approximately 30–50 cc of gel can be used for vaginal distention.[10]

2.5.1 Patient preparation and positioning

No prior bowel preparation is necessary.[11] Ideally, the urinary bladder should be emptied approximately 30 minutes before the study. An overdistended bladder may undermine the accurate assessment of PFD. Preprocedure counseling with a detailed explanation of the maneuvers that need to be performed during the study is crucial for the success of the study.[11] This not only helps relieve the apprehension of the patient but also leads to a high-quality study. Patients should be informed that dynamic imaging takes place during squeezing and defecation. Dynamic imaging during the Valsalva maneuver at either pre- or postdefecation is optional and performed in some institutions.[12] As patients may be hesitant to defecate, it should be emphasized to them that the defecation phase is important in detecting and quan-

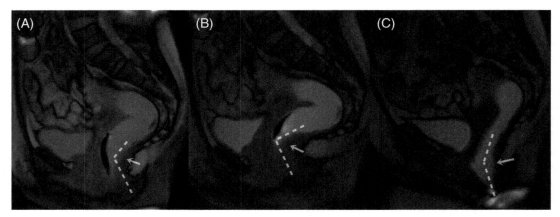

FIG. 2.6 (A–C) Anorectal angle. The angle between the posterior wall of the rectum and the longitudinal axis of the anal canal (dotted lines) is the anorectal angle. The posterior impression of the puborectalis regulates the anorectal angle (arrows). (A) The anorectal angle at rest is the baseline measurement for an individual. (B) The anorectal angle during the Kegel exercise (squeezing) becomes acute to the baseline due to the contraction of the puborectalis. (C) The anorectal angle becomes obtuse during defecation due to the relaxation of the puborectalis.

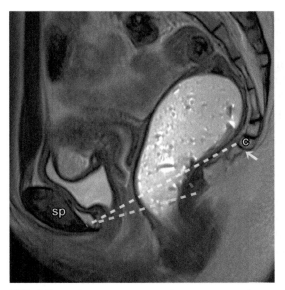

FIG. 2.7 Reference lines. The reference lines are drawn in a midline sagittal image and help detect and grade pelvic floor dysfunction in MR defecography studies. The pubococcygeal line (white line) joins the inferior border of the symphysis pubis to the first visible coccygeal joint (arrow). The H line (yellow line) corresponds to the diameter of the levator hiatus and extends from the inferior margin of the pubic symphysis to the posterior aspect of the anorectal junction. The M line (red line) is drawn perpendicularly to the pubococcygeal line to the posterior aspect of the H line. The M line follows the 2-cm rule and signifies the descent of the posterior compartment or the levator hiatus. c, coccyx; Sp, symphysis pubis.

tifying organ prolapse. Instructions should be provided in simple words for better compliance. For instance, squeezing may be better explained as a Kegel exercise or as if one is trying to withhold bowel movement, and defecation is better explained as if one is relaxing the pelvic floor and letting go of bowel contents. Conveying complex instructions in simple language that the patient can comprehend is crucial for the success of the study because patients often have no understanding of what the procedure entails and may be embarrassed. Having an experienced technologist who can deliver clear instructions and coach patients along the way is thus key to the success of the study. Providing patients with disposable safety pads is another way to ensure better patient compliance in case any fecal spillage occurs during the defecation maneuver.

The patient is placed feet first and in the lateral decubitus position in order to instill the US gel; 120–200 cc of warm, inert US gel is used. The gel can be instilled through the placement of a 30 Fr Foley catheter or a caulking gun. The gel should be instilled cautiously as its leakage may pose a potential electrical risk or damage to the instrument.[3]

The study is performed in on a patient in a supine position within a closed-configuration magnet. A pelvic phased-array coil is used for signal transmission and reception. Although in theory, a study performed on a seated patient with an open-bore magnet may be more physiological, open-configuration magnets are not widely available and have lower strength (0.5 T). Moreover, research data show that imaging in the supine position with a closed magnet is equally effective in diagnosing clinically relevant abnormalities of the pelvic floor.[13]

2.6 Image interpretation

Image interpretation is twofold, consisting of functional and anatomic evaluations. Steady-state mid-sagittal cine sequences are best suited for assessing the dynamic excursion of the pelvic organs, while high-resolution T2W images are useful for delineating the integrity of pelvic floor support structures, such as ligaments and muscles, as well as for identifying secondary signs of laxity of the endopelvic fascia.

Certain landmarks and reference lines facilitate the identification and quantification of suspected pelvic floor pathology. Additionally, a visual impression of organ motion remains decisive in most cases.[14] The most important

TABLE 2.1 Magnetic resonance imaging (MRI) protocol to evaluate pelvic floor dysfunction.

	At rest	Dynamic imaging
Sequence	T2W TSE	bSSFP (True FISP, bFFE, FIESTA)
Plane	Axial, coronal, sagittal	Mid-sagittal; single slice repeated 15–30 times at the same slice position
Maneuver	None	Squeezing and defecation*
Slice thickness	4 mm	8 mm
TR	4230–6940 ms	3.73–4.3 ms
TE	112 ms	1.87–2.15 ms
Matrix	512 × 205 or 512 × 154	256 × 123 or 128
FOV	275 mm	350–380 mm

bFFE, balanced fast field echo; *bSSFP*, balanced steady-state free precision; *FIESTA*, fast imaging employing steady-state acquisition; *FISP*, fast imaging with SSFP; *TSE*, turbo spin echo.
120–200-cc ultrasound gel instilled in the rectal lumen.

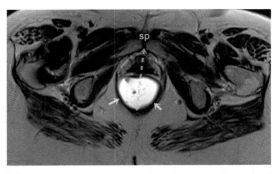

FIG. 2.8 Levator hiatus. An axial T2W image along the inferior aspect of the pubic symphysis demonstrates the levator hiatus (yellow line). The levator hiatus is traversed by the three compartments of the female pelvis. The hiatus is demarcated by the sling of the puborectalis muscle (arrows), which delineates the surgical anorectal junction. The rectum is filled with ultrasound gel and appears hyperintense.

reference line is the pubococcygeal line (PCL), which extends from the inferior margin of the pubic symphysis to the last visible coccygeal joint[15] (Fig. 2.7).

This represents the plane of the pelvic floor.

The H line, which denotes the anteroposterior diameter of the levator hiatus, extends from the inferior border of the symphysis pubis to the surgical ARJ (Figs. 2.7 and 2.8). The ARJ roughly corresponds to the posterior impression of the puborectalis.[15] The H line measures less than 6 cm in normal individuals.[16]

The M line, which is a vertical line drawn at a right angle from the PCL to the ARJ, indicates the vertical descent of the pelvic floor[15] (Fig. 2.7). The M line must not be longer than 2 cm in normal individuals.[16]

The levator hiatus is graded using the H line–M line-Organ Prolapse (HMO) classification criteria, as shown in Table 2.2.[17,18] The H line is classified as follows: mild hiatal enlargement (6–8 cm), moderate (8–10 cm), or severe (>10 cm).[16] The M line is classified similarly: mild pelvic floor descent (2–4 cm), moderate (4–6 cm), or severe (>6 cm). Organ descent is diagnosed by measuring the descent of certain reference points relative to the PCL. The bladder neck, the posterior cervix (or the posterior fornix of the vagina, if the uterus is absent), and the ARJ form the reference points in their respective compartments (Fig. 2.9).

The distances between the PCL and the bladder neck, the uterine cervix, and the ARJ are measured at rest and during defecation, and the evaluation of organ descent is determined. Most studies have suggested using the 2-cm or 3-cm rule as a system for classifying organ prolapse.[13,15,18,19]

The 3-cm rule categorizes pathology as follows: mild (<3 cm), moderate (3–6 cm), or severe (>6 cm). Similarly, the 2-cm rule classifies pathology as follows: benign (<2 cm), moderate (2–4 cm), or severe (>4 cm). Only rectocele and M lines are assessed with the 2-cm rule.

TABLE 2.2 HMO classification: diagnostic criteria.

	Mild	Moderate	Severe
H line	6–8 cm	8–10 cm	>10 cm
M line	2–4 cm	4–6 cm	>6 cm
Organ prolapse	<3 cm	3–6 cm	>6 cm

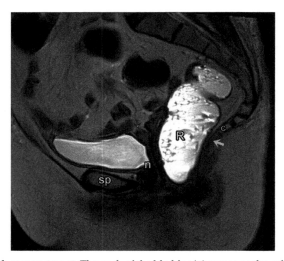

FIG. 2.9 The points of reference in each compartment. The neck of the bladder (n) serves as the reference point for the anterior compartment. The descent of the bladder neck >1 cm below the pubococcygeal line signifies a cystocele. The vaginal fornix (small arrow) is the reference point for the middle compartment in a posthysterectomy state. If the uterus is present, the posterior cervix is the point of reference. The anorectal junction bounded by the puborectalis sling is the reference point for the posterior compartment. The levator plate (arrow) consists of posterior fibers of the levator ani that attach to the coccyx (c). R, rectum; sp, symphysis pubis.

2.7 HMO: H line, M line, and organ prolapse

H line represents the diameter of levator hiatus, and M line represents the pelvic floor descent.

The ARA is measured as an angle between the central long axis of the anal canal and the posterior border of the rectum at the ARJ. No consensus about the normal range of ARA exists. Some authorities think that ARA measures 94–114° at rest[20,21]; others believe that its range is 108–127°.[15] The ARA should decrease or increase by 15–20° during squeezing or defecation, respectively (Figs. 2.5 and 2.6).[6,22,23]

Paradoxical contraction of the puborectalis can be seen as persistent posterior indentation along the ARJ during the defecatory attempt (Fig. 2.10). If the ARA stays the same or becomes acute rather than obtuse, the findings suggest dyssynergia. Dyssynergia has been linked to prior pelvic surgeries, sexual abuse, anxiety, and other psychological

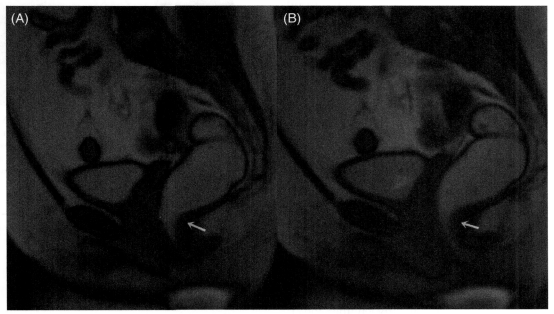

FIG. 2.10 (A–B) Spastic puborectalis at (A) rest and (B) during defecation. A nonrelaxing puborectalis (or the paradoxical contraction of the puborectalis) during defecation is compatible with dyssynergia. No change in the anorectal angle or the posterior impression of the puborectalis (arrow) means a nonrelaxing muscle (b). An acute anorectal angle during defecation vis-à-vis the baseline suggests a paradoxical contraction.

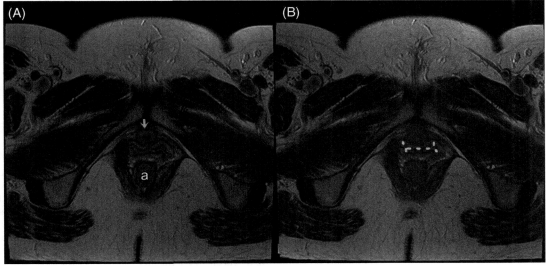

FIG. 2.11 (A–B) Normal vagina. Axial T2W images (A and B) through the vagina demonstrate a normal H shape (dotted line in B). A preserved H shape signifies intact paravaginal fascial support. Urethra (arrow) and anal canal (a).

factors.[24] The angle between the levator plate and the PCL must be <10°. An angle >10° indicates pelvic floor descent or loss of pelvic floor support (Fig. 2.9).[25]

The periurethral, paraurethral, suburethral, and pubourethral ligaments can be assessed on axial or reformatted axial images and help maintain the vertical orientation, midline position of the urethra. The vagina displays a typical H shape on axial images (Fig. 2.11). A maintained H shape, without drooping of the vaginal walls, indicates intact paravaginal fascial support. Similarly, when supported well by the endopelvic fascia, the posterior wall of the bladder appears flat, without drooping in the central or paracentral portions. The components of the levator ani can be better assessed on axial and coronal images (Fig. 2.12).[3] The iliococcygeus muscle's atrophy is seen as the loss of superior convexity on coronal images, and the muscle appears as either flat or concave.[3] An asymmetric loss of the muscular thickness of any of the components also indicates pathology. In patients with fecal incontinence, it is important to assess the integrity of the external and internal anal sphincter complex as well.

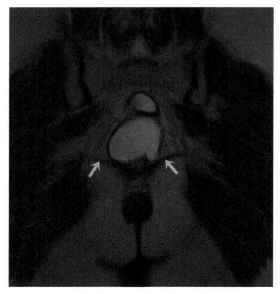

FIG. 2.12   **Assessment of the levator ani on MRI.** A coronal T2W image across the mid-pelvis shows the iliococcygeus component of the levator ani (arrows). The muscle exhibits superior convexity. Muscular atrophy may be observed as a decrease in thickness or an infiltration of fat. Loss of superior convexity signifies pelvic floor weakness.

2.8 Abnormalities of the anterior compartment

Cystocele. Cystocele is the most frequent pathology of the anterior compartment and indicates a stretched or torn pubocervical fascia. A cystocele is defined as >1-cm descent of the bladder neck below the PCL (Fig. 2.13). Cystocele is graded by the 3-cm rule[14] and may occupy the space within the levator hiatus and consequently lengthen the H line. As a result, cystocele can potentially interfere with the prolapse of other pelvic structures and mask other underlying conditions, such as enterocele, peritoneocele, or rectocele. It is necessary to repeat imaging with an empty bladder in order to fully assess pathology in other compartments. Cystocele can also displace the uterus and the ARJ posteroinferiorly, causing the M line to stretch.

Recurrent cystocele after retropubic and vaginal surgeries is clinically challenging but can be diagnosed on MRD. In this subset of patients, despite the bladder neck and proximal urethra maintaining their normal position above the PCL, the posterior wall of the bladder bulges into the anterior vagina (Fig. 2.14).

Urethral hypermobility. Urethral hypermobility is present when the urethra rotates abnormally about its axis with an increase in intra-abdominal pressure, due to the loss of intrinsic integrity of the urethral sphincter complex. The urethra may move horizontally or tilt downward. A urethral movement along the long axis measuring <60° is considered mild, 60–120° is moderate, and >120° is severe hypermobility (Fig. 2.15). A horizontal urethra during defecation roughly corresponds to moderate hypermobility, while an inferiorly slanting urethra indicates severe hypermobility.

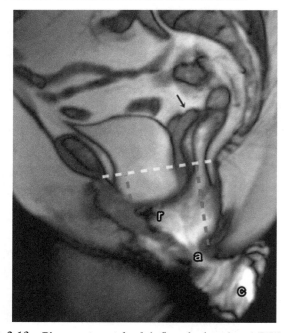

FIG. 2.13   **Bicompartmental pelvic floor dysfunction.** A T2W sagittal image through the mid-pelvis during defecation shows the descent of the bladder neck (green line) and the anorectal junction (red line) below the pubococcygeal line (white line). There is also an anterior protrusion of the rectum (r). The vaginal fornix (arrow) is above the pubococcygeal line. The findings suggest cystocele, posterior compartmental descent, and anterior rectocele. Note the open anal canal (a) and evacuated contrast (c).

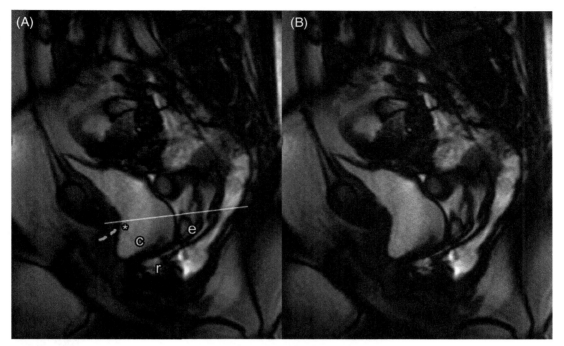

FIG. 2.14 (A–B) Posturethropexy recurrent cystocele. Sagittal T2W images through the mid-pelvis during defecation (A) with annotations and (B) without annotation. The bladder neck (*) and the proximal urethra (dotted line) relatively maintain their position near the pubococcygeal line (white line) due to prior urethropexy. However, the descending and bulging posterior wall of the bladder forms a cystocele (c). Note the coexisting anterior rectocele (r) and enterocele (e).

Diagnosing urethral hypermobility in patients with stress incontinence is clinically critical as correction of hypermobility may require a pubovaginal sling procedure. Uncomplicated stress incontinence can be treated with retropubic urethropexy without a sling.[15] Occasionally, kinking of the urethral–vesical junction may occur because of the prolapse of the base of the bladder and lead to urinary retention and infection.[15]

2.9 Abnormalities of the middle compartment

Uterovaginal descent and prolapse. Uterovaginal descent can be diagnosed upon clinical examination. Descent of the cervix or the posterior fornix inferior to the PCL is compatible with uterovaginal descent on MRD (Fig. 2.16). A prolapse is a more severe descent when the cervix is observed inside the vaginal cavity or outside the vaginal introitus. In the case of full uterine prolapse, the uterus is seen as domed out of the external genitalia, and the vaginal walls are everted. Uterovaginal prolapse is more noticeable when the rectum has been emptied. Therefore, the defecatory attempt should be repeated after the rectum is emptied. Uterovaginal descent is categorized by the 3-cm rule.[15]

Cul-de-sac hernias (peritoneocele, enterocele, and sigmoidocele). Uterine descent and/or prolapse can disrupt the rectovaginal fascia, which can cause enlargement of the cul-de-sac. Such enlargement results in herniation of abdominal contents in 17–37% of patients.[26,27] Patients with a history of hysterectomy are generally predisposed to developing these cul-de-sac hernias.[28] The hernia is named according to the contents; peritoneocele contains peritoneal fat without the intestine, enterocele contains bowel loops, and sigmoidocele contains the sigmoid colon (Figs. 2.17–2.19). These hernias can be classified per the 3-cm rule as mild (<3 cm), moderate (3–6 cm), or severe (>6 cm).[14,15] Interestingly, these disorders are frequently undiagnosed or misdiagnosed during clinical examination. As MRD can noninvasively and accurately diagnose the contents of these hernias, it is superior to traditional defecography.[29]

Cul-de-sac hernias are typically detected in the mid-sagittal plane at the end of defecation or rectal emptying (Figs. 2.18 and 2.19); for this reason, it is important to encourage patients to perform multiple defecatory attempts. Notably, large enteroceles can also mask small rectoceles or cystoceles.[26,29]

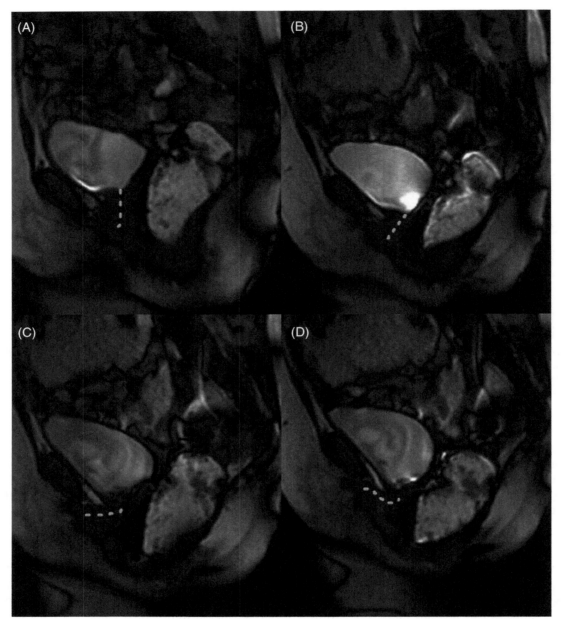

FIG. 2.15 (A–D) Urethral hypermobility. Sagittal T2W images through the mid-pelvis (A) at rest and (B–D) during defecation. The urethra (dotted line) is vertical at rest. A laxity of the suburethral supporting ligaments results in the rotation of the urethral axis from the vertical to the horizontal direction (B–C). Initially, the entire urethra rotates away from the pubis (B) as a single unit. Afterward, as a critical level is reached, the rotational descent of the anterior wall is arrested, but the posterior wall continuously rotates away (C–D). The urethra eventually becomes inferiorly slanting (D). Early urethral rotation (B) can roughly correspond to mild hypermobility. A horizontal urethra (B) stands for moderate hypermobility. An inclined urethra signifies severe hypermobility (D). Urethral hypermobility is common among patients suffering from stress incontinence.

2.10 Abnormalities of the posterior compartment

Rectocele. Rectocele is defined as abnormal bulging of the rectal wall beyond the intended normal contour (Figs. 2.13 and 2.20). While most rectoceles are anterior, they may sometimes be lateral or posterior and are best seen during defecation (Fig. 2.21).[30] Though rectoceles do not always cause obstructed defecation, they may be responsible for an incomplete emptying sensation. Rectocele can also be a result of obstructed defecation due to the misdirected vector of defecatory force (Fig. 2.22). The key factors for determining the clinical relevance of a rectocele are size, retention of contrast, and the need for digital manipulation to evacuate with a dimension >2 cm and retention of

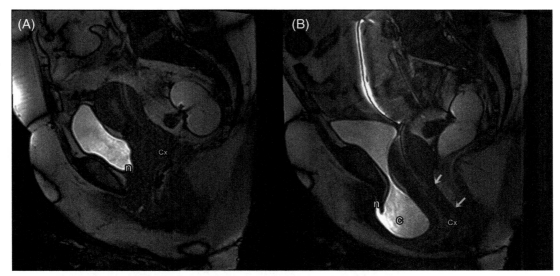

FIG. 2.16 (A–B) Uterine prolapse. Sagittal T2W images through the mid-pelvis. Note the reference points in the anterior and the middle compartments: bladder neck (n) and posterior uterine cervix (Cx) (A) at rest and (B) during defecation. There is a significant uterine descent while defecating, and the cervix is seen inside the vaginal cavity. The descending uterus prevents rectal emptying due to its mass effect over the lower rectum (arrows). There is a large coexisting cystocele (c), and the urethra is directed inferiorly.

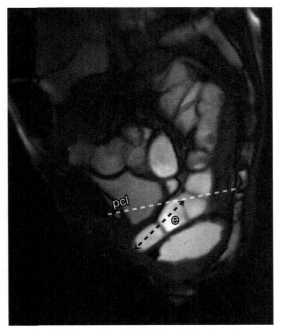

FIG. 2.17 **Enterocele.** A sagittal T2W image through the mid-pelvis during defecation. An outpouching containing small bowel loops (e) is seen below the pubococcygeal line. The outpouching occupies the rectovaginal space, and its size can be measured as its length in relation to the pubococcygeal line. The findings are consistent with an enterocele.

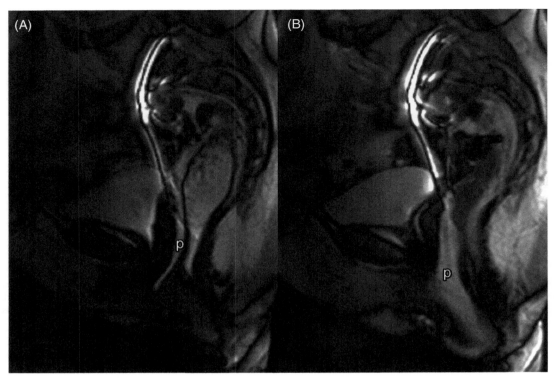

FIG. 2.18 (A–B) Peritoneocele. T2W sagittal images from the mid-pelvis (A) at rest and (B) during defecation. A small cul-de-sac hernia containing peritoneal fat (p) is observed at rest (A), suggesting a disrupted rectovaginal fascia. The patient is status posthysterectomy. The findings are most pronounced after rectal emptying and the delayed stage of defecation (B). Note that the peritoneocele is now herniating through the perineum, which the patient was able to palpate.

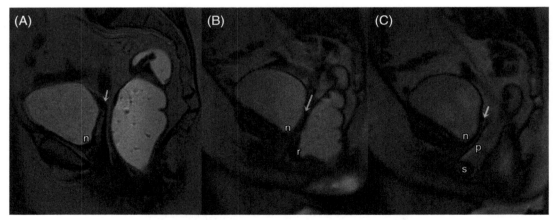

FIG. 2.19 (A–C) Sigmoidocele. A patient reporting perineal swelling during defecation. History of retropubic and vaginal support surgery. T2W sagittal images from the mid-pelvis: (A) a normally situated bladder neck (n) and vaginal fornix (arrow); (B) early defecation shows the formation of an anterior rectocele (r); (C) delayed defecation after rectal emptying shows a cul-de-sac hernia containing a sigmoid colon (s) and peritoneal fat (p). The position of the bladder neck and the vaginal fornix was maintained throughout the examination because of the surgical supports. Repeated defecatory attempts after rectal emptying are essential to unmask cul-de-sac hernias.

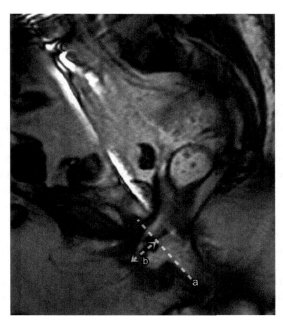

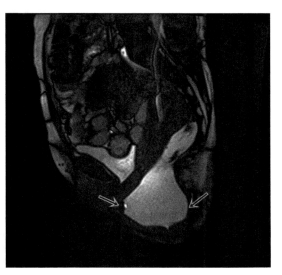

FIG. 2.20 **Grading a rectocele.** A T2W sagittal image from the mid-pelvis during defecation. The extent of a rectocele can be measured as the most bulging point of the outpouching (B) from a reference line drawn through the corresponding wall of the anal canal. For an anterior rectocele, the reference line passes through the anterior wall of the anal canal (A), as in this instance.

FIG. 2.21 **Bulging rectum.** A T2W sagittal image from the mid-pelvis during defecation shows a balloon-like bulging rectum (arrows). The findings are due to coexisting anterior and posterior rectoceles. Anterior rectoceles result from the loss of integrity of the rectovaginal fascia and the protrusion of the rectum through the posterior vaginal wall. Similarly, posterior rectoceles occur due to the loss of perirectal fascial supports.

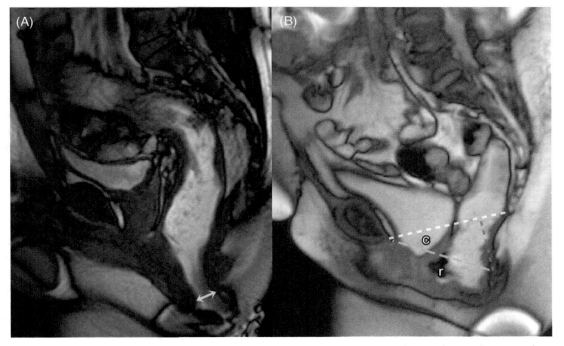

FIG. 2.22 (A–B) **Anal canal diameter.** (A) A T2W sagittal image from the mid-pelvis during defecation by a male patient shows an open anal canal (bidirectional arrow). The anal diameter is a rough indicator of a relaxing external anal sphincter. (B) A T2W sagittal image from the mid-pelvis during defecation by a female patient shows a closed anal canal. The vector of the force of defecation is exerted against nonrelaxing external anal sphincters and leads to posterior compartmental descent (red line) and anterior rectocele (r) formation. Blue line, levator hiatus; c, cystocele; white line, pubococcygeal line.

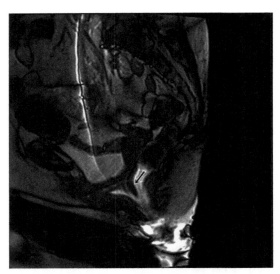

FIG. 2.23 **Rectoanal intussusception.** A T2W sagittal image from the mid-pelvis during delayed defecation shows focal thickening of the anterior rectal wall invaginating within the rectoanal lumen (arrow).

contrast being considered abnormal.[31] Rectoceles follow the 2-cm rule and are graded as mild (<2 cm), moderate (2–4 cm), or severe (>4 cm).[14] An ideal method of measuring a rectocele is depicted in Fig. 2.20.[32]

Rectal intussusception and prolapse. Rectal intussusception is invagination of the rectal wall into itself and can be partially mucosal or involve the full thickness of the rectal wall. The former is treated with transanal excision, while the latter requires rectopexy.[15,33,34] MRD can help differentiate between mucosal and full-thickness intussusception.[35] A full-thickness intussusception is seen as circumferential or focal anterior or posterior invagination during defecation (Fig. 2.23). Full-thickness intussusception can be intrarectal (upper 1/3, middle 1/3, or lower 1/3), intra-anal, or extra-anal. Rectal prolapse or extra-anal intussusception is an advanced condition where the rectal wall protrudes outside the anus. It is identified as a U-shaped rectal wall (double rectal wall) on the exterior of the anus on the mid-sagittal plane. In 30% of the cases, organ descent of the anterior or the middle compartment coexists.[35]

Anal canal diameter. The anal diameter corresponds to a partial relaxation of the external anal sphincter. The contrast column through the anal channel, measured during defecation, determines the anal diameter; a diameter <15 mm is pathological.[36] However, there is no consensus on the usefulness of measuring the anal diameter (Fig. 2.22).

Dyssynergia. Dyssynergia, also known as anismus or spastic pelvic floor syndrome, occurs due to the paradoxical contraction of the puborectalis or nonrelaxing external anal sphincter (Figs. 2.10 and 2.22). Attention should be paid to both the ARA and the anal canal width during defecation. The ARA should become more obtuse by >15–20° and the anal canal should open >15 mm during normal defecation.[36] The absence of one or both may signify dyssynergia.

Incomplete rectal emptying. Rectal emptying may be evaluated by visual inspection or by measuring the volume of the rectal contrast before and after defecation.[37] In general, no contrast evacuation for the duration of the entire study or evacuation of <2/3 contrast within 60 seconds is considered impaired evacuation.[37] Retention of >50% rectal content after defecation is clinically significant (Fig. 2.24).

2.10.1 Pelvic floor relaxation (descending perineum syndrome)

The perineum broadly signifies area between the anus and genitalia. Descending perineum syndrome signifies a widespread descent of the entire pelvic floor inferior to the PCL and occurs as secondary to the loss of muscle tone at rest and/or during evacuation. Often, it may be more pronounced in the posterior compartment (Fig. 2.25).[14] On MRD, descending perineum syndrome can be quantified by increased width and descent of the hiatus, caudal angulation of the levator plate, and low-lying ARJ even at rest.

2.11 Functional defecation disorders

Chronic constipation is a common clinical disorder that can affect as much as 3% of all adults and 20% of the elderly population.[38] Constipation can typically be classified as primary or secondary. Secondary constipation is caused by an identifiable organic or systemic condition. Primary constipation is diagnosed when no identifiable organic or systemic cause is found. Primary constipation is subdivided into four subcategories: normal transit, slow transit, outlet obstruction (defecation disorder), and mixed types.[39]

Some patients may misperceive their intestinal frequency and complain of constipation despite a normal colon transit time. These patients are classified as *normal transit* and remain unresponsive to fiber and laxative supplements.[39] Some patients have constipation as secondary to motor (autonomic and enteric) neuron disorders, leading to *slow transit*. Slow transit may affect the entire gastrointestinal tract or entire/segment of the colon (colon inertia). Slow-transit constipation does not respond to intestinal stimulators because the problem lies with the motor neurons.

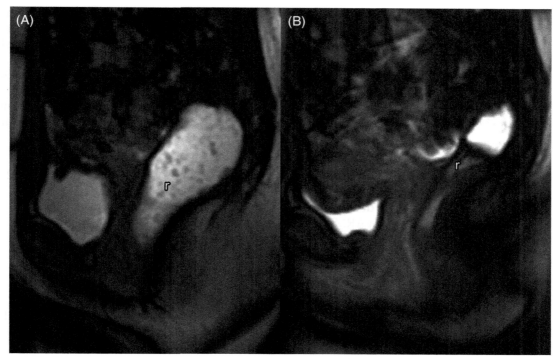

FIG. 2.24 (A–B) Assessment of rectal emptying. T2W sagittal images from the mid-pelvis at (A) pre- and (B) postdefecation. Hyperintense contrast within the rectal lumen (r) can be visually assessed before and after defecation. Retention of more than 50% contrast after the completion of the entire study is abnormal. An ideal study involves at least three defecation attempts.

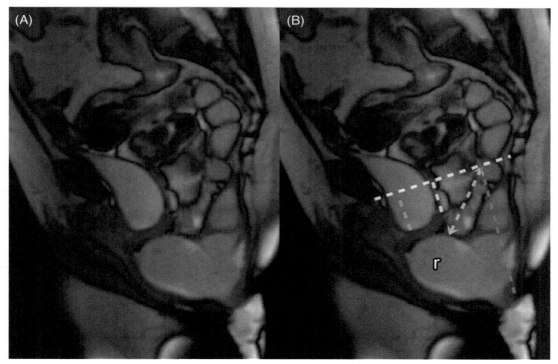

FIG. 2.25 (A–B) Descending perineum. T2W sagittal images from the mid-pelvis (A) without annotation and (B) with annotations. A widespread descent of the entire pelvic floor inferior to the pubococcygeal line (white line) signifies a descending perineum (or tricompartmental descent). Note the descent of the bladder neck (green line), vaginal fornix (blue line), and anorectal junction (red line). A large anterior rectocele (r) is also evident.

Functional and anatomical abnormalities of the anorectum that prohibit evacuation are classified as outlet-obstruction type constipation. This subset of constipation occurs as a result of a pelvic floor malfunction.[40] Most of such cases can be attributed to dyssynergia. Sometimes, outlet-obstruction constipation may coexist with slow transit (mixed type).[41]

The outlet-obstruction type constipation (with or without slow transit) is classified as functional defecation disorders (FDDs).

FDDs can be diagnosed by a combination of clinical symptoms and investigations, such as anorectal manometry (ARM), balloon expulsion test (BET), electromyography (EMG) during attempted defecation, defecography, and a colonic transit study.[42-44]

FDDs are diagnosed if the following criteria are met:

1. A clinical evaluation meets the diagnostic criteria for constipation (Rome IV criteria, Tables 2.3 and 2.4).[45,46]
2. A minimum of two of the following findings are present during an attempt to defecate:
   i. Inadequate evacuation on BET or defecography
   ii. Presence of dyssynergia proven on ARM, defecography, or EMG
   iii. Inadequate defecatory propulsion seen on ARM, defecography, or EMG.

2.11.1 Anorectal manometry and balloon expulsion test

The physiology of the rectum and the anal sphincter can be assessed with ARM. A high-definition ARM probe is placed in the rectum. Approximately 5 minutes are given for the anal sphincter tone to return to its basal level after insertion. Next, sphincter pressure is measured for 20 seconds.[47] The patient is then prompted to press the anal sphincter up to 30 seconds, and this maneuver is repeated three times.[47] Lastly, Valsalva maneuvers are performed, with and without distension of the rectal balloon. Approximately 50 mL of water is used to inflate the balloon.[47] Anorectal pressures are assessed each time with respect to normal pressure values stratified by age and gender. The rectoanal inhibitor reflex and rectal sensation are also evaluated during the procedure. The rectal balloon is initially distended in 10-mL increments until the patient reports an initial sensation. After this, the balloon is inflated in 20-mL increments, up to 400 mL. Each distension is sustained for a minimum of 30 seconds.[47] The volume of the balloon corresponding to the first sensation, the first desire to defecate, the urgency to defecate, and the maximum

TABLE 2.3 Diagnostic criteria* for functional defecation disorders (FDDs) (Rome IV).

1) The patient should meet diagnostic criteria for constipation and/or irritable bowel syndrome with constipation.
2) Two of the following three tests must demonstrate im paired evacuation on repeated defecatory attempts:
   a. Abnormal balloon expulsion test
   b. Abnormal anorectal evacuation pattern with manometry or anal surface EMG
   c. Impaired rectal evacuation by imaging
3) Subcategories F3a and F3b apply to patients who satisfy criteria for FDDs.
   F3a: Diagnostic criteria for inadequate defecatory propulsion
   Inadequate propulsive forces, as measured with manometry, with or without inappropriate contraction of the anal sphincter and/or pelvic floor muscles**
   F3b: Diagnostic criteria for dyssynergic defecationInappropriate contraction of the pelvic floor, as measured with anal survey EMG or manometry, with adequate propulsive forces during attempted defecation**

Criteria fulfilled for the last 3 months, with symptom onset at least 6 months before diagnosis.
**These criteria are defined by age- and sex-appropriate normal values for the technique.*

TABLE 2.4 Diagnostic criteria for constipation (Rome IV)*.

1) Must include two or more of the following:
   a) Straining during more than 25% of defecation,
   b) Lumpy or hard stools in more than 25% of defecation,
   c) Sensation of incomplete evacuation in more than 25% of defecation,
   d) Sensation of anorectal obstruction/blockage in more than 25% of defecation,
   e) Manual maneuvers to facilitate more than 25% of defecation (e.g., digital evacuation, support of the pelvic floor),
   f) Fewer than three spontaneous bowel movements per week.
2) Loose stools are rarely present without the use of laxatives.
3) Insufficient criteria for irritable bowel syndrome.

Criteria fulfilled for the last 3 months, with symptom onset at least 6 months before diagnosis.

TABLE 2.5 Types of dyssynergia diagnosed on anorectal manometry/balloon expulsion test.

Type	Rectal pressure	Anal pressure
I	Adequately increased (>40 mm Hg)	Paradoxically and simultaneously increased
II	Insufficiently increased (<40 mm Hg)	Paradoxically and simultaneously increased
III	Adequately increased (> 40 mm Hg)	Failure of reduction (< 20% baseline pressure)
IV	Insufficiently increased (<40 mm Hg)	Failure of reduction (<20% baseline pressure)

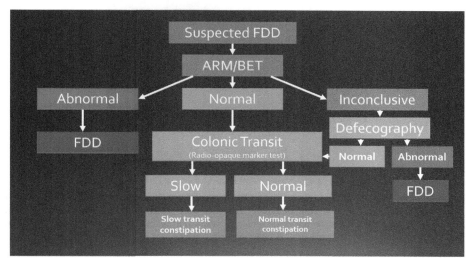

FIG. 2.26 **Making a diagnosis of functional defecatory disorder.**

tolerable sensation are registered. A transient relaxation of the internal anal sphincter in response to rectal distention is defined as a rectoanal inhibitory reflex. The rectoanal inhibitory reflex is also assessed as the balloon is inflated during the ARM. Usually, the reflex should be observed in the range of 10–30 mL. An absence of rectoanal reflex is seen with the loss of innervation or motor neuron conditions, such as Hirschsprung's disease, dysganglionosis, postcircular myotomy, and lower anterior resections.[47]

The BET simulates defecation and is performed in conjunction with the ARM.[48] The BET has a negative predictive value of 97%.[49] During the BET, an inflated balloon with approximately 50 mL of water (or a volume corresponding to the urge to defecate) is expelled by the patient while sitting on the toilet.[50] The test can also be carried out in the lateral decubitus position. Three to five minutes are allotted to expel the balloon.

Under normal circumstances, the rectal pressure is higher than the anal pressure during the BET.[47] An anal canal pressure that either fails to decrease or paradoxically increases during defecation suggests a diagnosis of dyssynergia.[51]

Four types of dyssynergia can be identified on the ARM/BET, based on changes in pressures measured in the rectum and the anal canal[52] (Table 2.5).

The presence of dyssynergy on the ARM and the inability to expel the balloon within 5 minutes on the BET may identify patients who may benefit from biofeedback therapy.[51] Typically, the BET and the ARM are adequate for diagnosing or ruling out an FDD diagnosis.[45] Defecography may be a tiebreaker if the tests are inconclusive (Fig. 2.26). MRD can diagnose dyssynergia, incomplete emptying of the rectum, and inadequate rectal propulsion.[38]

Assessment of rectal retention alone has low specificity for making an accurate diagnosis of FDD (23%) because retention can also be observed in asymptomatic individuals.[37] Dyssynergia is commonly treated with anorectal coordination training and behavioral modification (biofeedback training). Surgical interventions are reserved for the morphological pelvic floor abnormalities or the descending perineum syndrome.

2.12 Pearls, pitfalls, and challenges

The urinary bladder should be emptied 30 minutes before the investigation. An overdistended bladder may occupy excessive space at the levator hiatus and mask middle or posterior compartmental pathologies.

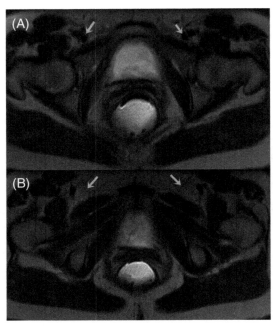

FIG. 2.27 (A–B) Assessing the adequacy of patient effort. Axial T2W images through femoral veins (arrows) (A) at rest and (B) during the Valsalva maneuver (or defecation) may help in assessing patient compliance and effort. Femoral veins become dilated and engorged with increased intra-abdominal pressure. Note the size of the femoral veins (arrows) (A) at rest and (B) during the Valsalva maneuver. A slow transit into the engorged veins during the Valsalva maneuver leads to T2W hyperintensity.

Assessment of femoral veins, with and without the Valsalva maneuver, may help in estimating the patient's efforts. Alteration in the signal intensity and increased caliber of the femoral vein suggest adequate patient effort (this technique can differentiate true dyssynergic defecation from inappropriate or feeble straining effort) (Fig. 2.27).

The importance of multiple (at least three) defecatory attempts should be emphasized during MRD. A false positive diagnosis of dyssynergia can be made due to incomplete evacuation, caused by the patient's anxiety or inability to understand and follow commands.

If the patient is unable to defecate after three attempts, he/she has to be sent to the rest room to evacuate in privacy using the maneuvers (e.g., digital evacuation) that they employ at home. Additional postevacuation baseline and dynamic imaging should be performed. This may reveal additional pathology and confirm whether or not the patient has been able to evacuate >50% contrast.

Cul-de-sac/Pouch of Douglas hernias (peritoneocele, enterocele, and sigmoidocele) are better assessed after rectal emptying (Figs. 2.18 and 2.19). Often, middle and anterior compartmental pathologies may manifest better after rectal emptying due to greater available room within the tightly spaced pelvic floor.

Tarlov cysts are extradural spinal meningeal cysts and contain cerebrospinal fluid and nerve tissue. They are seen as cystic dilation of the nerve root sheath at the dorsal root ganglia.

Tarlov cysts >1 cm and located at the S2–3 level may cause pelvic symptoms and should be evaluated and reported in all MRD studies (Fig. 2.28). Pelvic pain and lumbosacral discomfort are the most common symptoms. Symptoms of urinary dysfunction, including incontinence, urgency, and incomplete voiding, are uncommon. Bowel symptoms such as constipation have also been reported. See Table 2.6 for a quick reference regarding pearls and pitfalls.

2.13 Fluoroscopic versus magnetic resonance defecography

Although MRD is performed on a patient in a supine position, no significant differences between the clinically relevant results of MRD and fluoroscopic examination have been reported.[53] The current literature fully supports the fact that MRD can provide more information in many ways. A comprehensive comparison of the two modalities is presented in Table 2.7.[54-56]

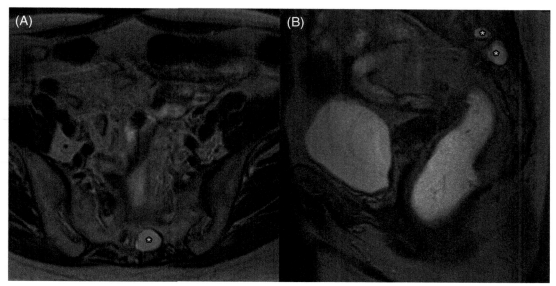

FIG. 2.28 (A–B) Tarlov (or extradural spinal meningeal) cysts. (A) An axial T2W image through the sacrum shows fluid intensity lesion containing cerebrospinal fluid at the S2 level on the left side (*). (B) A sagittal T2W image through the sacrum shows corresponding cystic lesions filled with cerebrospinal fluid at the S2–3 levels. Tarlov cysts represent cystic dilation of the nerve root sheath at the dorsal root ganglia.

TABLE 2.6 Pearls and pitfalls.

Protocol and technique

No prior preparation is necessary for magnetic resonance defecography (MRD).

Approximately 120–200 cc of ultrasound (US) gel is instilled into the rectum.

Approximately 30–50 cc of gel can be used for the vagina, but it is optional.

An overdistended bladder may undermine the accurate assessment of the pelvic floor pathologies in the other compartments. Therefore, it is recommended that patients empty their urinary bladder approximately 30 minutes before the study.

Preprocedure counseling with a detailed explanation of the instructions provided during the investigation is critical. This can help relieve the patient's apprehension, as well as lead to a high-quality study.

The importance of multiple (at least three) defecatory attempts should be stressed during MRD. Some findings are better assessed in the delayed phase of defecation or after rectal emptying.

Assessment of femoral veins, with and without the Valsalva maneuver in axial T2W sequences, may help in estimating the patient's efforts.

Interpretation

The anorectal angle should decrease or increase by 15–20° during squeezing or defecation, respectively.

Paradoxical contraction of the puborectalis can be seen as persistent posterior indentation along the anorectal junction (ARJ) during the defecatory attempt. The anorectal angle stays the same or becomes acute rather than obtuse.

Distances between the pubococcygeal line and the bladder neck, uterine cervix, and ARJ are measured at rest and during defecation, and organ descent is evaluated.

The 3-cm or 2-cm rule is implemented to quantify or classify an organ prolapse. Most of the pathologies follow the 3-cm rule, except rectocele, which follows the 2-cm rule.

3-cm rule: mild (1–3 cm), moderate (3–6 cm), or severe (>6 cm)

2-cm rule: mild (1–2 cm), moderate (2–4 cm), or severe (>4 cm)

Cystocele <1 cm should be ignored as it may not have any clinical relevance.

Recurrent cystocele after retropubic and vaginal surgeries is challenging and identified as a bulge of the posterior urinary bladder, despite the urethra and the bladder neck remaining stable.

A defecatory attempt after rectal emptying may reveal otherwise undetected pathologies, such as uterovaginal descent, cul-de-sac hernias, and cystocele.

A full-thickness intussusception is seen as circumferential or anterior or posterior focal thickening during defecation.

(Continued)

TABLE 2.6 *(Cont'd)*

Retention of >50% rectal content after defecation is clinically significant.

Tarlov cysts >1 cm and located at the S2–3 level may cause pelvic symptoms and should be evaluated and reported in all MRD studies.

Functional defecation disorder (FDD)

The combination of the balloon expulsion test and anorectal manometry is adequate for an FDD diagnosis or ruling it out. A defecography may be a tiebreaker if the tests are inconclusive.

TABLE 2.7   Comparison of magnetic resonance and fluoroscopic defecography.

	Magnetic resonance defecography	Fluoroscopic defecography
Diagnostic reliability	Equal or more	Equal or less
Overall sensitivity and specificity	Higher	Lower
Middle compartment pathology	Better seen, preferred modality	Not sensitive
Content of cul-de-sac hernia	Identifies peritoneocele, enterocele, and sigmoidocele. No additional preparation needed	Identifies enterocele or sigmoidocele after small bowel opacification and wait time of 1–2 hours
Rectal intussusception	Identifies, measures, and classifies full thickness versus mucosal intussusception	Intussusceptions are not seen, just inferred, based on indirect findings
Impact on final surgical plan	Significant, can demonstrate pathology in all three compartments	Not applicable
Radiation exposure	None	Present
Patient compliance	Better, patient in a quiet and closed room	Less/awkward, defecation occurs in the presence of technologists
Other pelvic pathology	Tarlov cysts, other causes of pelvic pain can be diagnosed	Not well characterized

2.14 What the referring physician needs to know

Every patient with PFD is unique and may require an individualized treatment plan. Most patients with pelvic floor disorders are treated by a multidisciplinary team, including gastroenterologists, colorectal surgeons, and urogynecologists. The referring physician would like to know relevant anatomical and functional results for each compartment to create an individual treatment plan. The clinicians are looking for:

a. Anterior compartment: Presence or absence of weakness of both endopelvic fascia and urethral ligament support system, presence or absence of cystocele (with size and grade), and documentation of urethral hypermobility

b. Middle compartment: Presence or absence of middle compartmental descent (with size and grade) and cul-de-sac hernias (contents and grade)

c. Posterior compartment: Presence or absence of sphincter defects; integrity of levator ani components; presence or absence of posterior compartmental descent, dyssynergia, rectal intussusception (full thickness or mucosal, intrarectal, intra-anal, or extra-anal), rectocele and its grade; comment on rectal retention with possible cause

d. Other related or unrelated incidental findings.

A template of a comprehensive MRD report is presented in Fig. 2.29.

2.15 Setting up and sustaining a successful MRD service

Before a new MRD practice is established in any institution, it must be clearly defined and communicated to the hospital management. A new range of services cannot be established unless the hospital management understands the new service's impact on patient care. The communication should clearly indicate if the service will be provided locally or regionally, how many locations are targeted, and what resources and workforce are needed.[57]

Anatomic imaging:

Central or lateral drooping of bladder wall– Present/ Absent
Normal H shape of the vagina – Maintained / Not maintained
Urethral support ligaments – Present/ Absent
Levator ani components – (Pubococcygeus, Puborectalis) - Symmetric/ Asymmetric, Avulsed
Iliococcygeus – Symmetric/ Asymmetric, Upward convexity maintained/ Not maintained

Dynamic imaging:
H line: Measured during rest, squeezing, and defecation
M line: Measured during rest, squeezing, and defecation
Anorectal angle: Measured during rest, squeezing <u>and</u> defecation

Anterior compartment:
Cystocele – Present/ Absent – Grade:
Urethral hypermobility: Present/ Absent

Middle compartment
Cervical/ vaginal apical descent- Present/ Absent – Grade:
Cul-de-sac hernia – (Peritoneocele, Enterocele, Sigmoidocele) – Grade:

Posterior compartment:
Levator plate angle during rest, squeezing, and defecation
Rectocele – Size, location, and % of retained contrast
Intussusception – Partial/Full thickness, Location
Dyssynergia – Present/ Absent

Post defecation: Is there rectal emptying (> 50% retention of contrast is abnormal)

Other pelvic organs:
Small bowel and colon
Lymph nodes
Bladder
Reproductive organs
Free fluid
Vascular structures:
Skeletal structures:

IMPRESSION:

Global assessment of pelvic floor descent and compartments involved
Cystocele and hypermobility (if any, with grading)
Cervical/vaginal descent (if any, with grading)
Cul-de-sac hernia (if any, with grading)
Rectocele (if any, with grading, and % contrast retained)
Intussusception (if any, with location)
Dyssynergia (if any)
Other pertinent findings (previous surgery, descending perineum, etc.)

FIG. 2.29 **Sample reporting template for MR defecography.**

Once approved by the management, the next step is to form a team. Since a learning curve is required, involving an existing enthusiastic early or mid-career-level staff is recommended rather than bringing in new members. Having an experienced MRI technologist to serve as the lead technologist of the team is a good way to maintain image quality and consistency. An ideal lead technologist should be interested in learning new ideas and be willing to experiment with the protocols.

Once a lead technologist is identified, he or she must be taught the MRI protocol and made to understand the significance of each sequence. The lead technologist should also be taught how to provide instructions to patients in easily understandable language. The lead technologist must be educated about the importance of emptying the bladder beforehand, performing repeated defecation sequences during the study, assessing the adequacy of patient's effort, and repeating imaging after maneuvers by patients who are unable to completely evacuate. It is also preferable to have practical hands-on training during the insertion of the rectal tube and gel instillation. A trained radiologist can participate in at least 10–15 initial studies. Training technologists at the control panel while the procedure is underway is vital during the first few studies. Once the lead technologist is comfortable with the imaging service in one location, he or she can then mentor and train more technologists to extend services to other locations. In addition to MRI technologists, it is important to train nurses (to place rectal tubes) and schedulers (to counsel patients beforehand about what to expect). Delivering a didactic educational lecture and having frequent check in/ Question and Answer sessions with involved team members are other strategies to ensure quality.

Once an established imaging service is in place, the next step is to educate clinicians. The main referral services for MRD include those of gastroenterologists, colorectal surgeons, gynecologists, and urogynecologists. Trust in and support from referring clinical services are crucial for success. Organizing formal grand rounds or casual lunch-time lectures/case review sessions with the concerned departments is an effective way to engage clinicians. These sessions should focus on the impact of MRD on patient care, discuss strengths and limitations, stress the importance of patient preparation, share case examples, and provide time for questions. Similar strategies with lunch-and-learn sessions in community physician offices can also be implemented. It is essential to be receptive to comments and feedback from clinicians while a practice is being set up.

At the institutional level, another recommendation is to establish a multispecialty pelvic floor clinic, where all specialties and investigations are available under one roof. Since clinical care can be streamlined and patients can be scheduled for multiple appointments on the same day, this will result in improved patient satisfaction and fewer missed appointments. Participating in regularly scheduled interdisciplinary conferences, authoring publications, and promoting the MRD service on social media are additional ways to remain engaged. As with any imaging service, there is no alternative to providing high-quality scans, producing clinically pertinent reports, and meeting the highest standards of patient satisfaction.[57] The entire process requires dedication, determination, and persistence, but once established, it is highly rewarding, and it functions as a problem-solving tool to serve a complex subset of patients.

2.16 Conclusion

PFD is a complex clinical disorder, and MRD has emerged as the preferred method of imaging to assess the pelvic floor anatomy and function. In contrast to fluoroscopic defecography, it does not involve radiation and has higher patient compliance. Furthermore, incidental diseases in the remainder of the pelvis and pathology involving multiple compartments are assessed at once. A well-established MRD imaging service can assist clinicians in developing individualized treatment plans and can have a significant beneficial impact on patient care.

References

1. Law YM, Fielding JR. MRI of pelvic floor dysfunction: review. *AJR Am J Roentgenol*. 2008;191(6 Suppl):S45–S53. doi:10.2214/AJR.07.7096.
2. Drossman DA, Li Z, Andruzzi E, et al. U.S. householder survey of functional gastrointestinal disorders. Prevalence, sociodemography, and health impact. *Dig Dis Sci*. 1993;38(9):1569–1580.
3. Seynaeve R, Billiet I, Vossaert P, Verleyen P, Steegmans A. MR imaging of the pelvic floor. *JBR-BTR*. 2006;89(4):182–189.
4. Maglinte DD, Kelvin FM, Fitzgerald K, Hale DS, Benson JT. Association of compartment defects in pelvic floor dysfunction. *AJR Am J Roentgenol*. 1999;172(2):439–444. doi:10.2214/ajr.172.2.9930799.
5. El Sayed RF, Alt CD, Maccioni F, et al. Magnetic resonance imaging of pelvic floor dysfunction - joint recommendations of the ESUR and ESGAR pelvic floor working group. *Eur Radiol*. 2017;27(5):2067–2085. doi:10.1007/s00330-016-4471-7.
6. Lalwani N, Moshiri M, Lee JH, Bhargava P, Dighe MK. Magnetic resonance imaging of pelvic floor dysfunction. *Radiol Clin North Am*. 2013;51(6):1127–1139. doi:10.1016/j.rcl.2013.07.004.
7. Wu JM, Vaughan CP, Goode PS, et al. Prevalence and trends of symptomatic pelvic floor disorders in U.S. women. *Obstet Gynecol*. 2014;123(1):141–148. doi:10.1097/AOG.0000000000000057.
8. Nygaard I, Barber MD, Burgio KL, et al. Prevalence of symptomatic pelvic floor disorders in us women. *JAMA*. 2008;300(11):1311–1316. doi:10.1001/jama.300.11.1311.
9. Lienemann A, Fischer T. Functional imaging of the pelvic floor. *Eur J Radiol*. 2003;47(2):117–122.
10. Flusberg M, Xi Y, Jambhekar K, et al. Variability in utilization and techniques of pelvic floor imaging: findings of the SAR pelvic floor dysfunction disease-focused panel. *Abdom Radiol (NY)*. 2021;46(4):1294–1301. doi:10.1007/s00261-021-02957-5.
11. Lalwani N, Khatri G, El Sayed RF, et al. MR defecography technique: recommendations of the Society of Abdominal Radiology's Disease-Focused Panel on pelvic floor imaging. *Abdom Radiol*. 2021;46(4):1351–1361. doi:10.1007/s00261-019-02160-7.
12. Khatri G, Kumar NM, Xi Y, et al. Defecation versus pre- and post-defecation valsalva maneuvers for dynamic MR assessment of pelvic floor dysfunction. *Abdom Radiol (NY)*. 2021;46(4):1362–1372. doi:10.1007/s00261-019-02208-8.
13. Bertschinger KM, Hetzer FH, Roos JE, Treiber K, Marincek B, Hilfiker PR. Dynamic MR imaging of the pelvic floor performed with patient sitting in an open-magnet unit versus with patient supine in a closed-magnet unit. *Radiology*. 2002;223(2):501–508.
14. Roos JE, Weishaupt D, Wildermuth S, Willmann JK, Marincek B, Hilfiker PR. Experience of 4 years with open MR defecography: pictorial review of anorectal anatomy and disease. *Radiographics*. 2002;22(4):817–832.
15. Colaiacomo MC, Masselli G, Polettini E, et al. Dynamic MR imaging of the pelvic floor: a pictorial review. *Radiographics*. 2009;29(3):e35. doi:10.1148/rg.e35.
16. Boyadzhyan L, Raman SS, Raz S. Role of static and dynamic mr imaging in surgical pelvic floor dysfunction. *Radiographics*. 2008;28(4):949–967. doi:10.1148/rg.284075139.
17. Barbaric ZL, Marumoto AK, Raz S. Magnetic resonance imaging of the perineum and pelvic floor. *Top Magn Reson Imaging*. 2001;12(2):83–92.

18. Comiter CV, Vasavada SP, Barbaric ZL, Gousse AE, Raz S. Grading pelvic prolapse and pelvic floor relaxation using dynamic magnetic resonance imaging. *Urology*. 1999;54(3):454–457.

19. Goh V, Halligan S, Kaplan G, Healy JC, Bartram CI. Dynamic MR imaging of the pelvic floor in asymptomatic subjects. *AJR Am J Roentgenol*. 2000;174(3):661–666. doi:10.2214/ajr.174.3.1740661.

20. Bartram CI, Turnbull GK, JE Lennard-Jones. Evacuation proctography: an investigation of rectal expulsion in 20 subjects without defecatory disturbance. *Gastrointest Radiol*. 1988;13(1):72–80. doi:10.1007/BF01889028.

21. Ekberg O, Nylander G, Fork FT. Defecography. *Radiology*. 1985;155(1):45–48.

22. Healy JC, Halligan S, Reznek RH, et al. Dynamic MR imaging compared with evacuation proctography when evaluating anorectal configuration and pelvic floor movement. *AJR Am J Roentgenol*. 1997;169(3):775–779. doi:10.2214/ajr.169.3.9275895.

23. Fielding JR, Griffiths DJ, Versi E, Mulkern RV, Lee ML, Jolesz FA. MR imaging of pelvic floor continence mechanisms in the supine and sitting positions. *AJR Am J Roentgenol*. 1998;171(6):1607–1610. doi:10.2214/ajr.171.6.9843296.

24. Bolog N, Weishaupt D. Dynamic MR imaging of outlet obstruction. *Rom J Gastroenterol*. 2005;14(3):293–302.

25. Macura KJ. Magnetic resonance imaging of pelvic floor defects in women. *Top Magn Reson Imaging*. 2006;17(6):417–426. doi:10.1097/RMR.0b013e3180417dc8.

26. Kelvin FM, Maglinte DD, Hale DS, Benson JT. Female pelvic organ prolapse: a comparison of triphasic dynamic mr imaging and triphasic fluoroscopic cystocolpoproctography. *AJR Am J Roentgenol*. 2000;174(1):81–88. doi:10.2214/ajr.174.1.1740081.

27. Hock D, Lombard R, Jehaes C, et al. Colpocystodefecography. *Dis Colon Rectum*. 1993;36(11):1015–1021.

28. Karasick S, Karasick D, Karasick SR. Functional disorders of the anus and rectum: findings on defecography. *AJR Am J Roentgenol*. 1993;160(4):777–782. doi:10.2214/ajr.160.4.8456664.

29. Lienemann A, Anthuber C, Baron A, Reiser M. Diagnosing enteroceles using dynamic magnetic resonance imaging. *Dis Colon Rectum*. 2000;43(2):205–212; discussion 212-213.

30. Mahieu P, Pringot J, Bodart P. Defecography: II. Contribution to the diagnosis of defecation disorders. *Gastrointest Radiol*. 1984;9(3):253–261.

31. Shorvon PJ, McHugh S, Diamant NE, Somers S, Stevenson GW. Defecography in normal volunteers: results and implications. *Gut*. 1989;30(12):1737–1749.

32. Yoshioka K, Takada H, Hioki K. Rectocele. *Nihon rinsho Jpn J Clin Med*. 1994(Suppl 6):602–604, doi: 10.1016/S0149-7944(01)00562-1.

33. McCue JL, Thomson JP. Rectopexy for internal rectal intussusception. *Br J Surg*. 1990;77(6):632–634.

34. Tsiaoussis J, Chrysos E, Glynos M, Vassilakis JS, Xynos E. Pathophysiology and treatment of anterior rectal mucosal prolapse syndrome. *Br J Surg*. 1998;85(12):1699–1702. doi:10.1046/j.1365-2168.1998.00914.x.

35. Dvorkin LS, Hetzer F, Scott SM, Williams NS, Gedroyc W, Lunniss PJ. Open-magnet MR defaecography compared with evacuation proctography in the diagnosis and management of patients with rectal intussusception. *Colorectal Dis*. 2004;6(1):45–53.

36. Lee TH, Lee JS, Hong SJ, et al. Rectal hyposensitivity and functional anorectal outlet obstruction are common entities in patients with functional constipation but are not significantly associated. *Korean J Intern Med*. 2013;28(1):54–61. doi:10.3904/kjim.2013.28.1.54.

37. Reiner CS, Tutuian R, Solopova AE, Pohl D, Marincek B, Weishaupt D. MR defecography in patients with dyssynergic defecation: spectrum of imaging findings and diagnostic value. *Br J Radiol*. 2011;84(998):136–144. doi:10.1259/bjr/28989463.

38. Lalwani N, El Sayed RF, Kamath A, Lewis S, Arif H, Chernyak V. Imaging and clinical assessment of functional defecatory disorders with emphasis on defecography. *Abdom Radiol*. 2021;46(4):1323–1333. doi:10.1007/s00261-019-02142-9.

39. Park K-S, Choi S-C, Park M-I, et al. Practical treatments for constipation in Korea. *Korean J Intern Med*. 2012;27(3):262–270. doi:10.3904/kjim.2012.27.3.262.

40. Ratuapli SK, Bharucha AE, Noelting J, Harvey DM, Zinsmeister AR. Phenotypic identification and classification of functional defecatory disorders using high-resolution anorectal manometry. *Gastroenterology*. 2013;144(2):314–322. e2. doi:10.1053/j.gastro.2012.10.049.

41. Feyen BJ, Rao SS. Functional disorders of defecation: evaluation and treatment. *Curr Treat Options Gastroenterol*. 2007;10(3):221–230.

42. Kobi M, Flusberg M, Paroder V, Chernyak V. Practical guide to dynamic pelvic floor MRI. *J Magn Reson Imaging: JMRI*. 2018;47(5):1155–1170. doi:10.1002/jmri.25998.

43. Bharucha AE, Pemberton JH, Locke GR. American Gastroenterological Association technical review on constipation. *Gastroenterology*. 2013;144(1):218–238. doi:10.1053/j.gastro.2012.10.028.

44. Patcharatrakul T, Rao SSC. Update on the pathophysiology and management of anorectal disorders. *Gut Liver*. 2018;12(4):375–384. doi:10.5009/gnl17172.

45. Rao SS, Bharucha AE, Chiarioni G, et al. Functional anorectal disorders. *Gastroenterology*. 2016;150(6), 1430–1442.e4, ISSN 0016-5085. doi:10.1053/j.gastro.2016.02.009.

46. Wong RK, Palsson OS, Turner MJ, et al. Inability of the Rome III criteria to distinguish functional constipation from constipation-subtype irritable bowel syndrome. *Am J Gastroenterol*. 2010;105(10):2228–2234. doi:10.1038/ajg.2010.200.

47. Lee TH, Bharucha AE. How to perform and interpret a high-resolution anorectal manometry test. *J Neurogastroenterol Motil*. 2016;22(1):46–59. doi:10.5056/jnm15168.

48. Lee BE, Kim GH. How to perform and interpret balloon expulsion test. *J Neurogastroenterol Motil*. 2014;20(3):407–409. doi:10.5056/jnm14068.

49. Minguez M, Herreros B, Sanchiz V, et al. Predictive value of the balloon expulsion test for excluding the diagnosis of pelvic floor dyssynergia in constipation. *Gastroenterology*. 2004;126(1):57–62.

50. Rao SS, Kavlock R, Rao S. Influence of body position and stool characteristics on defecation in humans. *Am J Gastroenterol*. 2006;101(12):2790–2796. doi:10.1111/j.1572-0241.2006.00827.x.

51. Chiarioni G, Salandini L, Whitehead WE. Biofeedback benefits only patients with outlet dysfunction, not patients with isolated slow transit constipation. *Gastroenterology*. 2005;129(1):86–97.

52. Grossi U, Carrington EV, Bharucha AE, Horrocks EJ, Scott SM, Knowles CH. Diagnostic accuracy study of anorectal manometry for diagnosis of dyssynergic defecation. *Gut*. 2016;65(3):447–455. doi:10.1136/gutjnl-2014-308835.

53. Gufler H, Ohde A, Grau G, Grossmann A. Colpocystoproctography in the upright and supine positions correlated with dynamic MRI of the pelvic floor. *Eur J Radiol*. 2004;51(1):41–47. doi:10.1016/S0720-048X(03)00133-5.

54. Lienemann A, Anthuber C, Baron A, Kohz P, Reiser M. Dynamic MR colpocystorectography assessing pelvic-floor descent. *Eur Radiol.* 1997;7(8):1309–1317.

55. Pannu HK, Scatarige JC, Eng J. Comparison of supine magnetic resonance imaging with and without rectal contrast to fluoroscopic cysto-colpoproctography for the diagnosis of pelvic organ prolapse. *J Comput Assist Tomogr.* 2009;33(1):125–130. doi:10.1097/RCT.0b013e318161d739.

56. Gufler H, Laubenberger J, DeGregorio G, Dohnicht S, Langer M. Pelvic floor descent: dynamic mr imaging using a half-Fourier rare sequence. *J Magn Reson Imaging: JMRI.* 1999;9(3):378–383.

57. Steiner A, Marks R, Bahrami S, Arif-Tiwari H. How to develop and sustain a successful pelvic floor mri practice. *Abdom Radiol (NY).* 2021;46(4):1443–1450. doi:10.1007/s00261-019-02204-y.

3

MRI evaluation of perianal fistulas and pelvic pain

Rakhee S. Gawande, Atif Zaheer

Russell H. Morgan Department of Radiology, Johns Hopkins School of Medicine, Baltimore, MD, United States

3.1 Introduction

Pelvic pain is a common presenting symptom in the acute and primary care setting with broad differential diagnosis depending on age, sex, and reproductive status.[1] Furthermore, the diagnosis also depends upon the organ of origin such as bowel, genitourinary tract, musculoskeletal system, etc. Ultrasound is the first line of imaging tests when gynecologic pathology is suspected while CT remains the workhorse for bowel pathology. MRI is reserved for diagnosis' requiring better anatomic delineation such as complications associated with inflammatory bowel disease (IBD) including perianal fistulas and to avoid radiation exposure in pregnant and young patients. Noncontrast MRI is considered a safe low risk and radiation free imaging modality for the evaluation of abdominal and pelvic pain particularly in young and pregnant patients. In this chapter we will discuss imaging findings of pelvic pain related to IBD, perianal fistula, and nongynecologic pathologies, focusing on techniques, tailored imaging protocols, guidelines for indications, and descriptions of important differential diagnoses and pitfalls that could be encountered in real-life scenarios.

3.2 General imaging technique for pelvic pain

CT of abdomen and pelvis with intravenous contrast remains mainstay for the evaluation of pelvic pain in the acute emergency setting. CT with oral contrast and intravenous contrast is usually performed for nonemergent outpatient imaging of pelvic pain. Pelvic ultrasound performed via a transabdominal and endovaginal approach is performed in female patients presenting with pelvic pain and is the modality of choice in young females to avoid ionizing radiation. MRI of the pelvis in the acute emergency setting is considered as a problem-solving modality. MRI imaging protocols for the evaluation of pelvic pain have to be tailored according to specific indication. MRI field strength of 1.5 or 3T are recommended along with use of dedicated phase array coil for improving signal-to-noise ratio (SNR). Use of vaginal and rectal gel depends on specific indications and is recommended for the evaluation of rectovaginal fistulas, vaginal and rectal lesions. Antiperistaltic agent glucagon can be given while evaluating bowel and rectum to minimize artifacts from bowel motion. However, role of antiperistatlic agents remains controversial and varies with institutions. Following MRI sequences are commonly obtained: T2-weighted imaging in axial and sagittal plane with and without fat suppression (FS), T1-weighted imaging in the axial plane, diffusion-weighted imaging (DWI) in axial plane with apparent diffusion coefficient (ADC) maps and postcontrast T1-weighted images in the axial and sagittal plane (Table 3.1). A general pelvic MRI protocol for imaging of male or female pelvis will include a field of view (FOV) from the iliac crest to perineum for females and inclusion of bulbous urethra for males. High-resolution protocols for specific indications will be discussed in the following sections.

TABLE 3.1 General MRI pelvis protocol.

Name	Slice thickness mm	FOV	Matrix	TR	TE	Averages	Flip angle
T2 SAG FS	3	440 × 230	320 × 256	7300	90	3	160
T1 AX	3	440 × 230	320 × 256	645	20	4	180
T2 AX	3	440 × 230	320 × 256	3900	85	4	160
DWI AX	6	500 × 250	160 × 120	5200	55	3	90
T1 SAG PRE	5	545 × 280	320 × 200	350	2.19	2	70
T1 AX PRE	5	470 × 245	320 × 210	398	2.19	2	70
T1 AX POST	5	470 × 245	320 × 210	398	2.19	2	70
T1 SAG POST	5	545 × 280	320 × 200	350	2.19	2	70

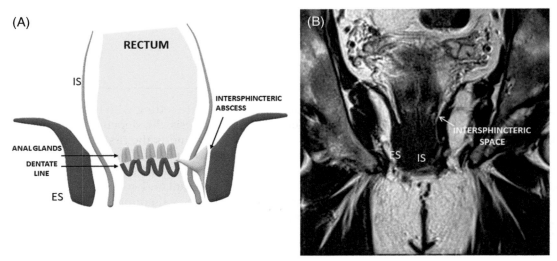

FIG. 3.1 (A) Cryptoglandular hypothesis: Intersphincteric abscess formation secondary to blockage of anal glands. *ES*, external sphincter; *IS*, internal sphincter. (B) Coronal high-resolution T2-weighted image showing anatomy of anal canal. IS is formed by continuation of circular smooth muscle of anal canal and is responsible for resting involuntary continence. ES is composed of striated muscles which are responsible for voluntary continence. Injury to ES can lead to loss of continence. The space between the sphincters is the intersphincteric space which is the path of least resistance for development of abscess.

3.3 Perianal fistula

Perianal fistula is defined as a connection between anal canal and skin of the perineum. It is an uncommon process with prevalence of only 0.01% but causes significant morbidity.[2,3] Perianal fistulas are frequently seen in patients with Crohn's disease with a cumulative incidence of 13–27% which increases with disease duration. The cumulative probability of developing perianal disease in patients with Crohn's disease is approximately 29.5% and 42.7% at 10 and 20 years after diagnosis, respectively.[4] MRI is considered as a gold standard for diagnosis and management of the disease with sensitivity of 100% and specificity of 86% for depiction of primary tract and sensitivity of 96% and specificity of 97% for the detection of abscess.

Most accepted theory for development of anal fistula is cryptoglandular hypotheses which states that approximately 90% fistula develop due to impaired drainage of anal glands (Fig. 3.1). Blocked duct openings lead to development of a tract or abscess in the intersphincteric space which is the path for least resistance. This leads to formation of an intersphincteric fistula. The tract can traverse both internal and external sphincters and become transphincteric fistula. The fistula can extend to the ischioanal or ischiorectal fossa and develop a tract or abscess.[2]

Approximately 10% perianal fistula develop secondary to underlying inflammatory conditions like Crohn's disease, tuberculosis, diverticulitis, trauma, pelvic infection, malignancy, or radiation therapy. These fistulas are generally more complex with abscesses and secondary tracts involving adjacent organs and have high chances for recurrences.

Treatment of perianal fistula is by surgery but frequently complicated by recurrence, with rates as high as 25%.[5] Successful surgical management requires accurate preoperative assessment of the course of the primary fistulous track and the site of any secondary extension or abscesses. MR imaging allows identification of infected tracks and abscesses that would otherwise remain undetected and helps in risk stratification by classifying disease severity. It also depicts anatomic relationships of the fistula to predict the likelihood of postoperative fecal incontinence by assessing sphincter involvement. Management aims of perianal fistula include eradication of the fistula or abscess, prevent recurrence, and maintain continence.

3.3.1 Imaging modalities for perianal fistulas

Prior to advent of cross-sectional imaging, fistulograms were a common imaging modality for diagnosis of perianal fistula and are very rarely performed in current age. This is a very painful procedure and involves catherization of external fistula opening and injection of water-soluble contrast medium with subsequent visualization via fluoroscopy or radiography. There is difficulty in assessing secondary tracts and relationships with anal sphincters. CT fistulography involves injection of nonionic iodinated contrast material into the external orifice and can show the fistula tract and internal opening, but is limited by several factors including invasive technique, pain during injection, difficulty in locating external opening, low spatial resolution for the detection of subtle fistulas and relationship to anal sphincter, and lastly risk for spread of infection.[6,7] Anal endosonogarphy (AES) can depict the internal opening and anal anatomy highly accurately, but is highly operator dependent and limited by small FOV which makes visualization of complex extrasphincteric and supralevator tracts very difficult. MRI is noninvasive technique that is highly accurate for depiction of fistula tract and its relationship to the adjacent structures including the musculature and adjacent organs.

3.3.2 MRI imaging technique for perianal fistula

Indications of perianal fistula MRI include confirmation of the presence of disease, characterization of fistula tracts, differentiation of active from chronic fistulas, identification of complex tracts, and the presence of complications like abscess formation or disease extension to adjacent organs, preoperative planning, and posttreatment disease monitoring. MRI should ideally be performed on 3T MRI if available which provides good quality high-resolution images with high SNR. Rectal gel, bowel preparation, or antiperistaltic agents are not routinely required. Vaginal gel can be used when rectovaginal fistulas are suspected. Pelvic phased array coil can be used with scout images obtained from the mid-sacrum to inferior fold of buttock and FOV centered over the anal canal. A large FOV T2-weighted sagittal images are obtained to determine plane of the anal canal and plan subsequent high-resolution images. Oblique axial high-resolution images of the anal canal should be obtained perpendicular to the anal canal and oblique coronal images parallel to the anal canal (Fig. 3.2).[8] Typical perianal fistula MRI protocol performed at our institution is shown in Table 3.2. High-resolution T2-weighted images can be obtained ideally with FS to depict fluid and inflammation within the tract indicative of active disease and differentiate these from chronic tracts which typically have fibrous tissue and hypointense signal on T2. A potential drawback of fat-suppressed images is poor depiction of anal sphincters which can be overcome by adding non-FS high-resolution T2-weighted images (Fig. 3.3) or a three-dimensional T2-weighted sequence like T2-SPACE. However, the later two sequences can substantially increase the imaging time and can be omitted in uncooperative patients or in busy imaging centers. Contrast-enhanced images are essential for confirming active inflammation and abscess and depicting complex fistula tract and are obtained in the axial and coronal plane. If scan timing is not an issue, DWI and ADC maps can be obtained particularly in patients who cannot get contrast-enhanced images. DWI can confirm the presence of abscess owing to restricted diffusion. DWI and ADC maps are not routinely performed at our institution in view of imaging time constraints. Typical perianal fistula MRI can be obtained with scan timing under 30 minutes.

3.3.3 Classification of perianal fistula

Parks classification of perianal fistula is based on surgical anatomy and is described in the coronal plane.[2,9] Four types of perianal fistulas are described according to their relationship to the sphincter complex: A, intersphincteric, B, transphincteric, C, suprasphincteric, and D, extrasphincteric. Based on the surgical classification, St. James's University Hospitals classification incorporates MRI imaging findings to provide a strong diagnostic tool for pre-surgical evaluation.[10] This classification system relates the Park surgical classification to MR anatomy in axial and coronal plane. We use the St. James's University Hospital classification system for describing perianal fistulas at our Institution (Fig. 3.4). It consists of five grades as follows:

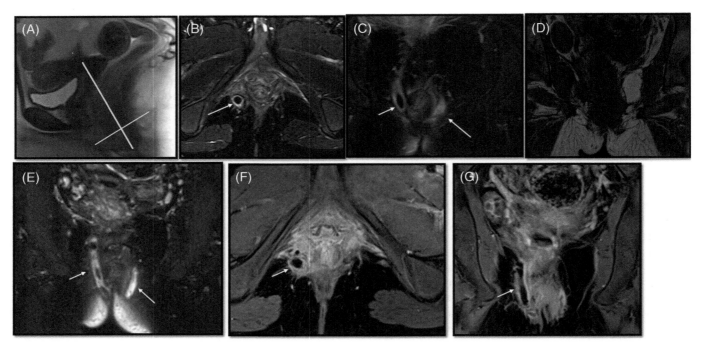

FIG. 3.2   Perianal fistula protocol: T2 sagittal scout (A), high-resolution T2 FS axial (B), and coronal (C), T1 coronal (D), T2 space coronal (E), and post gadolinium VIBE axial (F) and (G). Note complex grade 4 transsphincteric horseshoe fistula with abscess in bilateral ischioanal fossa (white arrows in B, C, E, F, and G).

TABLE 3.2   Perianal fistula MRI protocol.

Name	Slice thickness mm	FOV	Matrix	TR	TE	Averages	Flip angle
T2 SAG	5	300 × 300	320 × 256	1400	90	1	180
T2 SPACE COR	1	250 × 250	256 × 233	1700	120	2	120
T2 AX HIGH RES FS	3	180 × 180	256 × 179	6100	87	3	160
T2 COR HIGH RES FS	3	180 × 180	256 × 161	5400	86	5	160
T1 COR	4	200 × 200	384 × 346	600	10	4	160
PRE GD AX VIBE	2	200 × 200	320 × 240	4	7.8	2	9
POST GD AX VIBE	2	200 × 200	320 × 240	4	7.8	2	9
POST GD COR VIBE	2.5	250 × 250	320 × 240	4	7.8	2	9

Grade 1: Simple intersphincteric fistula: A simple linear tract seen in the intersphincteric space and entirely confined by the external sphincter (Fig. 3.5). It extends from the anal canal to skin of the perineum or natal cleft. No branches are seen within the sphincter complex.

Grade 2: Intersphincteric fistula with abscess or secondary track: A secondary tract or abscess is seen with an intersphincteric fistula and is limited by the external sphincter (Figs. 3.6 and 3.7). The secondary tract may extend or ramify on the ipsilateral side or may cross the midline and even form a horseshoe tract.

Intersphincteric fistula is the most common type of perianal fistula and can represent approximately 54% of perianal fistulas.[8]

Grade 3: Transsphincteric fistula: This type of fistula penetrates both the internal and external sphincters and extends via the ischiorectal or ischioanal fossa to the perineal skin surface (Fig. 3.8). These account for approximately 21% of perianal fistulas.

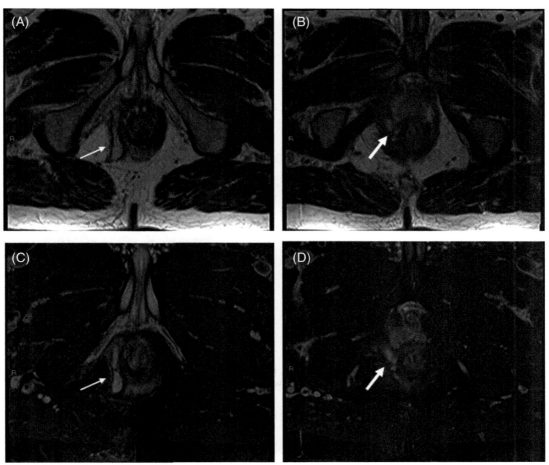

FIG. 3.3 High-resolution T2-weighted images without fat suppression (A and B) and with fat suppression (C and D) showing an intersphincteric fistula tract (thick arrow in B and D) and an abscess in the ischioanal fossa (A and C). Note that the abscess and tract with surrounding inflammation are easy to detect on the fat-suppressed images (C and D) while the anal sphincters are easy to see on the non–fat-suppressed images (A and B).

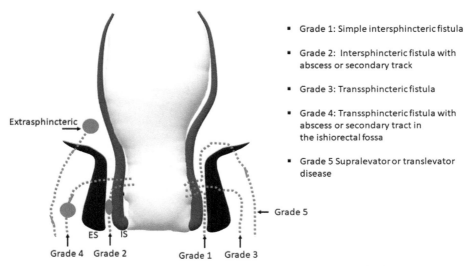

St. James's University Hospital classification system

- Grade 1: Simple intersphincteric fistula

- Grade 2: Intersphincteric fistula with abscess or secondary track

- Grade 3: Transsphincteric fistula

- Grade 4: Transsphincteric fistula with abscess or secondary tract in the ishiorectal fossa

- Grade 5 Supralevator or translevator disease

Extrasphincteric

Grade 5

ES   IS

Grade 4   Grade 2   Grade 1   Grade 3

FIG. 3.4 St. James's University Hospital classification system. *ES*, external sphincter; *IS*, internal sphincter.

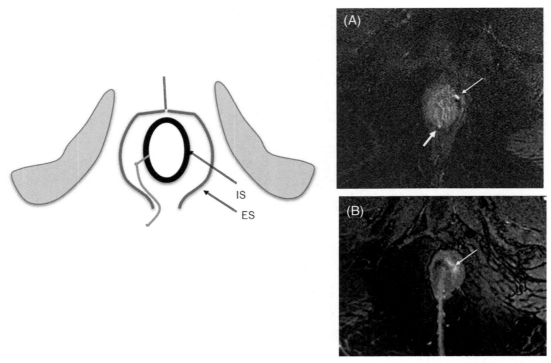

FIG. 3.5 Grade 1: Intersphincteric fistula. *ES*, external sphincter; *IS*, internal sphincter. Axial high-resolution T2 FS images (A and B) show a small linear tract at 2 o'clock position in intersphincteric space (thin white arrow). Another intersphincteric tract is seen at 6 o'clock position (thick arrow).

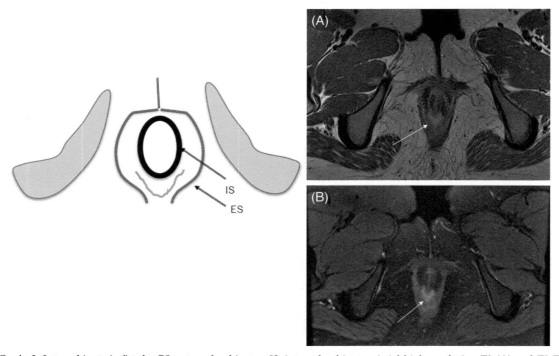

FIG. 3.6 Grade 2: Intersphincteric fistula. *ES*, external sphincter; *IS*, internal sphincter. Axial high-resolution T2 (A) and T2 FS (B) images show a small linear tract at 6 o'clock position in intersphincteric space which extends across the midline (arrow).

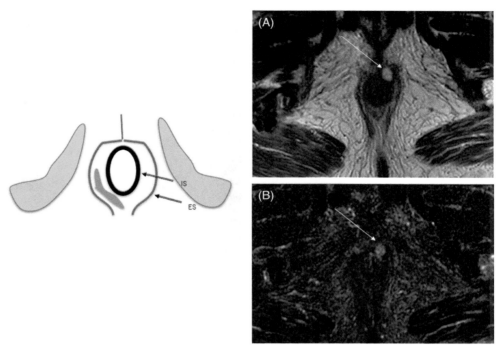

FIG. 3.7 Grade 2: Intersphincteric fistula with abscess: *ES*, external sphincter; *IS*, internal sphincter. Axial high-resolution T2 (A) and T2 FS images (B) small intersphincteric abscess is seen at 1 o'clock position bounded by the external sphincter.

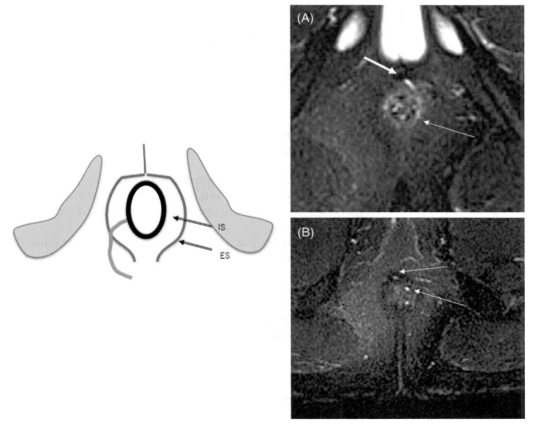

FIG. 3.8 Grade 3: Transsphincteric fistula: *ES*, external sphincter; *IS*, internal sphincter. Axial high-resolution T2 (A) and T2 FS (B) images show a fistula tract at 2 o'clock position traverses the external sphincter anteriorly (thick arrow on A).

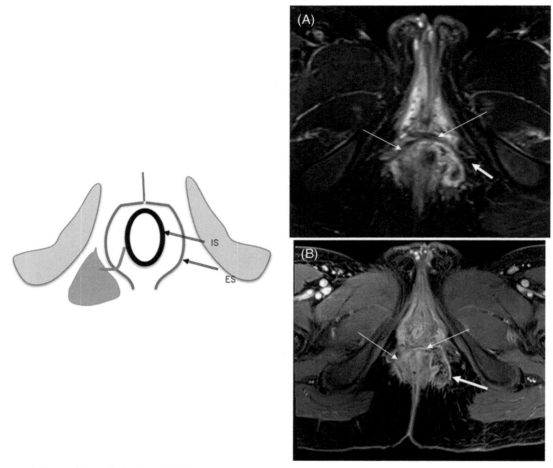

FIG. 3.9   Grade 4: Transsphincteric fistula with abscess or secondary tract: *ES*, external sphincter; *IS*, internal sphincter. Axial high-resolution T2 (A) and postcontrast (B) images show a horseshoe fistula tract (thin arrow) with abscess in the left ischiorectal fossa (thick arrow).

Grade 4: Transsphincteric fistula with abscess or secondary tract in the ischiorectal fossa: The fistula crosses the external sphincter and forms an abscess in the ischioanal or ischiorectal fossa. The fistula can be associated with secondary tracts (Figs. 3.9 and 3.10).

Grade 5: Supralevator and translevator disease: These are rare and complex fistula tracts and account for approximately 3% of perianal fistulas. Supralevator fistulas traverses the internal sphincter and then ascend upward in the intersphincteric space. The fistulas then traverses the levator ani muscle and descends into the ischiorectal fossa (Fig. 3.11).

Extrasphincteric fistulas do not affect the sphincter complex, but begin higher up in the rectum above the levator ani muscle. They then traverse the levator ani and extend to the ischiorectal fossa. These are also very rare types and account for approximately 3% of cases.

Recently, a new and unique type of fistula along the roof of ischiorectal fossa and inside the levator ani muscle (RIFIL) has been described.[11] These fistulas are more complex and have worse prognosis and cannot be diagnosed without MRI. The fistula track runs between the lateral muscle fibers of the external anal sphincters and its fascial covering and continues along the inferior border of puborectalis muscle and ascends under the levator ani muscle.

3.3.4 MR imaging features of perianal fistulas

A stepwise approach for the detection and characterization of perianal fistula should be ideally employed. T1-weighted noncontrast images in axial or coronal plane are utilized for defining anatomy of the anal sphincter complex, the supralevator and infralevator space, the perirectal and pararectal spaces, and the ischioanal and ischiorectal fossa. Perianal fistula appears as T1 hypointense or intermediate signal tracts, similar to surrounding muscular

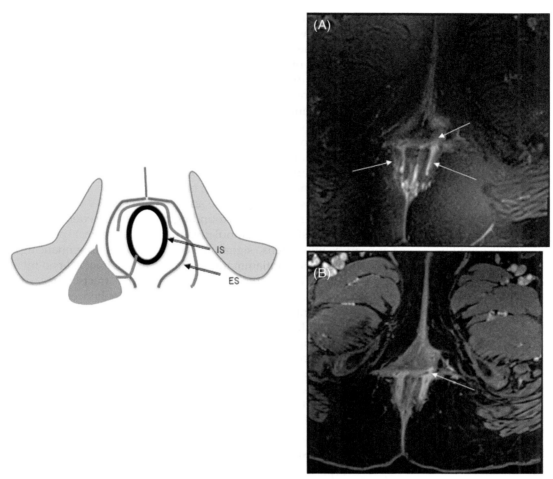

FIG. 3.10 Grade 4: Transsphincteric fistula with abscess or secondary tract: *ES*, external sphincter; *IS*, internal sphincter. Axial high-resolution T2 (A) and postcontrast (B) images show a horseshoe tract crossing the midline and extending to bilateral ischioanal fossa (arrow). A linear hypointense seton is seen with the tract on postcontrast images (thin arrow on B).

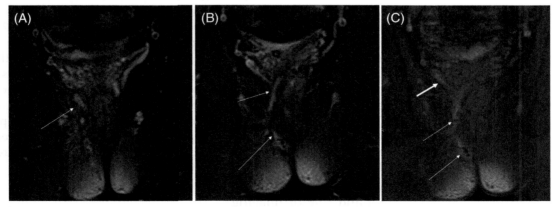

FIG. 3.11 Grade 5: Complex branching fistula with transsphincteric and supralevator branches. A 42-year-old man with history of Crohn's disease. Coronal T2 FS (A and B) and coronal postcontrast (C) images show a linear fluid-filled tract on the right side with multiple branches and extension to supralevator space (thick arrow on C).

structures, but can be well delineated against the T1 hyperintense fat in the ischiorectal and ischioanal fossa. After treatment, hemorrhage within the tracts can appear as T1 hyperintense signal. Furthermore, if the fistula is treated with seton placement, T1-weighted images best delineate the wire due to the gradient echo acquisition. Next, axial T2-weighted images are utilized to define the internal opening of the fistula tract within the anal canal in a clockwise direction. Distance of the internal anal opening from the anal verge can be obtained on the oblique coronal images. Oblique coronal T1- and T2-weighted images and postcontrast T1-weighted images are used to identify extent of fistula tract, presence of secondary tracts, abscesses, and fistula classification. It is imperative to define relationship of fistula tract with sphincter complex for preoperative planning and to prognosticate postoperative continence. A simple fistula is seen as a linear tract connecting to an internal opening within the anal canal and external opening on the skin surface. A sinus tract can sometimes be identified as a blind ending structure communicating with an internal anal opening. Complex fistulas are seen as multiple tracts branching from the primary tract and may either end blindly or communicate with skin surface or extend to surrounding organs, mostly vagina (Fig. 3.11). Horseshoe tracts can be seen extending across the midline and wrap around the anal canal (Figs. 3.9 and 3.10).

Active fistulas appear as T2-weighted hyperintense tracts with surrounding hyperintense edema and are particularly well identified on fat-suppressed images. On postcontrast images granulation tissue of active tract shows intense enhancement and fluid and surrounding edema appears as hypointense signal. Abscess present as rim-enhancing collections on postcontrast images and can be associated with edema and inflammation. Chronic fistula tract is lined by fibrous tissues and appear hypointense on T2-weighted sequences, differentiating them from active tracts. They show mild contrast enhancement and lack surrounding inflammatory changes. Decreasing postcontrast enhancement can help in evaluating fistula healing and treatment response. It is important to differentiate active from chronic fistulas to guide management of the disease. In practice, most fistulas can be well evaluated by combining T2 and postcontrast-weighted images.

Functional MRI sequences like DWI and ADC maps can improve the diagnostic confidence of detecting active tracts and inflammation, especially if contrast-enhanced images are not available. Lower ADC values can be found in fistulas with high inflammatory activity in comparison to fistulas with mild inflammation.[12] Role of dynamic contrast-enhanced imaging of perianal fistula has been proposed with promising results showing correlation of disease activity with maximum enhancement and initial slope of increase. A pilot study has found that K-trans can be an indicator of effect of therapy.[13]

3.3.5 Structured MRI reporting of perianal fistula

Structured reporting helps communicate relevant information and details to referring clinicians and surgeons which provide a uniformity in terminology and tremendously aids in guiding therapy and disease monitoring.[14] An example of structured MRI report is provided in Table 3.3.

3.3.6 Perianal fistula in inflammatory bowel disease

Perianal disease manifestations in patients with Crohn's disease include hemorrhoids, anal fissures, perianal fistulas and abscess, and rectal ulcers.[15] A frequent complication of Crohn's disease is perianal fistulas with a cumulative incidence of approximately 13–27% and present a major clinical challenge in the management of the disease.[15] These are often complex fistulas with multiple tracts and abscesses and do not close spontaneously (Fig. 3.12). They also heal slowly and are complicated by multiple relapses with postsurgical relapse rates of 30–50%.[16] Patients presenting with perianal disease frequently have colonic and rectal involvement of Crohn's disease seen in up to 92% patients with colonic involvement.[17] Complex fistulas in Crohn's disease are composed of primary tract with secondary branches anywhere along the tract but mostly in the ischiorectal or ischioanal fossa. Tracts can cross the midline and wrap around bilateral internal fissures either in the intersphincteric space or along the puborectalis muscle to form horseshoe tracts[16] (Fig. 3.10). Chronic inflammation along the horseshoe tracts can penetrate the sphincter complex and lead to spread of inflammation and abscess in the supralevator space and posterior to anal canal which are difficult to detect clinically (Fig. 3.11). Careful scrutiny of MRI images should be performed for the presence of supralevator disease and extra sphincteric fistulas. Complications of complex fistulas like anovaginal or rectovaginal fistulas can be seen in 9% of patients with Crohn's disease and are difficult to treat and prone to recurrences (Fig. 3.12).[16] Peripouch fistulas can develop in patients after proctocolectomy.

3.3.7 Management of perianal fistula and role of imaging

Medical management is the mainstay for perianal fistula in Crohn's disease with combined medical and surgical management reserved for complex fistulas. Monitoring of perianal disease is usually performed clinically and

TABLE 3.3 Structured reporting template for perianal fistula.

Number of fistulas	
Fistula #	
Point of origin	—o'clock
Distance from anal verge	–cm
Classification	Intersphincteric
	Trans sphincteric
	Supra sphincteric
	Extra sphincteric
Maximum tract diameter	–mm
Abscesses	Yes/No
Secondary branches	
Exit site	Gluteal
	Scrotal
	Vagina
	Labia
	Blind ending
T2 hyperintensity	
Enhancement within the tract	None: Tract is fluid-filled
	Yes with T2 hyperintensity: Granulation tissues
	Yes with T2 hypointensity; fibrosis
Rectal and sigmoid wall inflammation	
Presence of setons, drains, or prior surgery	
Grade	Grade 1 (simple linear intersphincteric fistula)
	Grade 2 (intersphincteric fistula with an abscess or secondary track)
	Grade 3 (transsphincteric fistula)
	Grade 4 (transsphincteric fistula with an abscess or secondary track in the ischiorectal or ischioanal fossa)
	Grade 5 (supralevator and translevator disease)
Other findings	Free fluid
	Lymphadenopathy

imaging follow-up is not part of standard of care in most institutions. Optimal timing for posttreatment MRI has not yet been well established and in general posttreatment MRI are reserved for cases with unfavorable clinical response.[4] Indications of posttreatment MRI include evaluation for the treatment response and fistula healing, detection of persistent disease, and the presence of complications like abscesses and extension to surrounding organs.

Medical management approaches include antibiotics (metronidazole) which help to control pelvic sepsis, alleviate symptoms, and contribute to healing. Immunosuppressant drugs like azathioprine and mercaptopurine and biologic therapy with tumor necrosis factor (TNF) inhibitors like infliximab have improved fistula healing with cessation of fistula drainage.[4] Posttreatment MRI performed after induction therapy with infliximab can show persistent fistula tracts with inflammation despite clinical response. These persistent tracts are implicated to produce disease recurrence which can be seen in up to 40% cases at 5 years.[16] With healing the fistula tracts are replaced by fibrous tissue which appears hypointense on T1- and T2-weighted images and also shows decreasing gadolinium enhancement. MRI-based activity score for determining disease activity has been proposed by van Assche et al. which included anatomic characteristics provided by Parks classification (location, branching, and extension of fistula) with MRI findings related to inflammation provided by T2-weighted images (T2 hyperintensity) and the presence of collections and rectal wall involvement.[18] Decrease in van Assche score reflects fistula healing.

Various surgical approaches have been employed for the treatment of pelvic sepsis and fistula tracts. Abscess drainage can be performed as complimentary to medical therapy to aid in fistula healing. MRI can accurately identify the presence and site of abscess and relation to sphincter complex.

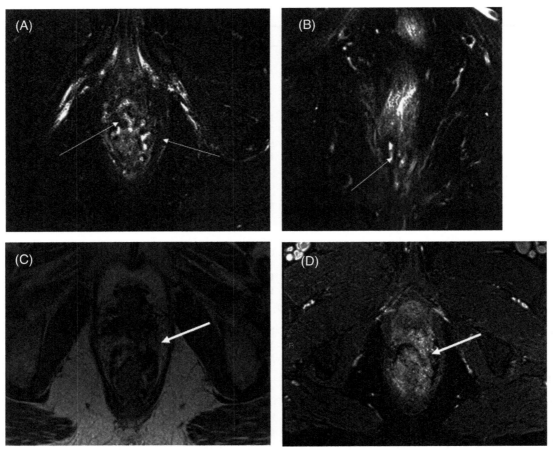

FIG. 3.12   **A 51-year-old female with Crohn's disease.** High-resolution T2 FS axial (A) and coronal (B) images show multiple bilateral intersphincteric and transsphincteric tracts (thin arrow). High-resolution T2 (C) and postcontrast images (D) show the presence of anovaginal fistula at 1 o'clock position (thick arrow).

Placement of noncutting seton is a main component of combined surgical and medical therapy. Loose setons are surgical sutures placed within the fistula tract which prevent premature closure of external opening and promote drainage and healing of fistula tract and also limit abscess formation.[4] Recurrence of fistula after removal of seton can be seen in 39% of cases.[8] Setons are easily identified as linear hypointense sutures on gradient echo and/or T2-weighted MRI sequences (Fig. 3.10).

Surgical approaches for the management of perianal fistulas include fistulotomy, insertion of biomaterials like fibrin glue or bioprosthetic plugs to promote healing, mucosal advancement flap and ligation of intersphincteric fistula tract. MRI provides vital information regarding the fistula tract and relation to sphincters which can aid in surgical planning and preserving continence. It also helps to identify secondary tracts or collections which can lead to disease recurrence. Specialized techniques and equipment's like video-assisted anal fistula treatment (VAAFT) and fistula laser closure (FiLac) are now available and require high-quality preoperative MRI for appropriate patient selection.[19] MRI helps in preoperative tract delineation, detection of complex tracts, and diameter of tract as well as internal opening which can aid in patient selection for the procedure.

Lastly fecal diversion surgeries are reserved for refractory cases and failure of conservative and surgical treatments. A diverting loop ileostomy temporarily diverts fecal stream with stoma reversal rates of 10–47%. Approximately 10–49% patients of Crohn's disease with complex fistulas ultimately require proctectomy with permanent colostomy.[16] Proctectomy is frequently complicated by poor wound healing and development of perineal sinus in approximately 25–50% cases.[17]

3.4 Pelvic pain in inflammatory bowel disease

MR enterography (MRE) is commonly used for the detection and characterization of IBD within the abdomen and pelvis and requires administration of neutral contrast agent VoLumen which is good for bowel distension without obscuring bowel wall details. Antiperistaltic agent glucagon (0.5–1 mg IM route) is commonly utilized to reduce bowel peristalsis. MRE sequences obtained include axial and coronal single shot fast spin echo, axial, and coronal steady state free precession (TruFISP), T2-weighted axial with FS, pre- and postcontrast T1-weighted images in axial and coronal plane and axial DWI with ADC maps (Table 3.4). MRI findings of active bowel inflammation in Crohn's disease include asymmetric bowel wall thickening more than 3 mm with mucosal hyperenhancement and mural stratification on postcontrast images, intramural T2 hyperintensity, engorgement of vasa recta, and mesenteric fat stranding and lymphadenopathy. MRE is also useful in detecting complications of Crohn's disease including strictures (fibrostenosing disease) and fistulas and abscess (penetrating disease) (Fig. 3.13). MRE also helps to differentiate reversible acute inflammatory strictures from irreversible fibrotic strictures which appear as T2 hypointense signal within the bowel wall showing progressive enhancement on delayed images. DWI and postcontrast images can help to distinguish active from chronic inflammation (Fig. 3.14). DWI is particularly helpful in patients who cannot receive intravenous contrast or are pregnant.

Within the pelvis, proctocolitis is a common manifestation of ulcerative colitis and Crohn's disease. Colonic involvement can be seen in up to 20% of cases with Crohn's disease. Proctocolitis is seen as diffuse rectal wall thickening with pericolonic inflammation (Figs. 3.14 and 3.15). Enterocolic and colocolic fistulas can be seen as a complication of penetrating disease (Fig. 3.13). Pelvic abscess can be seen in patients with active inflammation.

TABLE 3.4 Advantage and disadvantage of MRE sequences.

Sequence	Advantage	Pitfall
Coronal single shot fast spin echo (HASTE)	-Fast, insensitive to motion -Quick overview -Wall thickening, fold pattern seen	-Low spatial resolution -Prone to artifact from flow phenomenon from bowel peristalsis
Steady state free precession sequence (true FISP) axial and coronal -Give glucagon before	-High SNR provides sharp contrast between bowel wall and fluid -Assess motility in thickened areas -Fixed vs. transient narrowing	-Black border artifact can mask wall lesions
T2 W with FS axial	-Bowel wall edema in active vs. bowel wall fat in chronic disease -Mesenteric inflammation	-Long acquisition time -Motion artifact
Postcontrast T1 W axial and coronal	Mural enhancement, active vs. chronic disease	
DWI axial with ADC	-Good for active disease, abscess, LN -Useful for noncontrast MRI and pregnant patients	-Prone to artifacts due to respiratory motion, peristalsis, and susceptibility from air within the bowel lumen

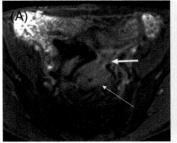 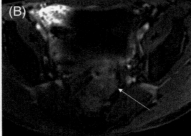 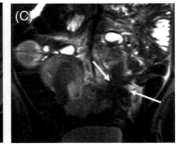

FIG. 3.13 **A 20-year-old man with active Crohn's disease and enterocolic and colocolic fistulas noted on MRE.** T2 FS axial (A and B) and T2 HASTE coronal (C) images show marked thickening and enhancement of bowel loops in the pelvis (thin arrow A and B) consistent with active inflammation. Colocolic fistula (thick arrow, A) and complex bowel thickening with adhesions in left lower quadrant suggestive of enterocolic fistula (thick arrow, C).

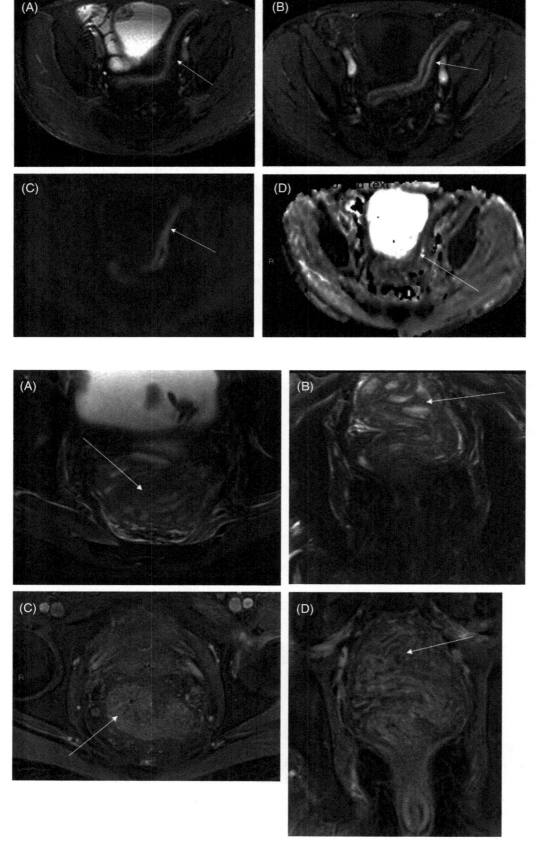

FIG. 3.14 A 43-year-old man with ulcerative colitis. T2 FS axial (A) and postcontrast T1 axial (B) images show wall thickening and mucosal enhancement of rectosigmoid colon with prominent pericolonic fat stranding indicating active colonic inflammation (arrow). Axial DWI (C) and ADC maps (D) show restricted diffusion in the colon consistent with active inflammation.

FIG. 3.15 A 26-year-old male with 3-month history of bloody diarrhea and pelvic pain with concern for infectious versus inflammatory colitis. Recent colonoscopy demonstrating multiple segments of severe colitis throughout the rectum and sigmoid colon, with biopsy-proven acute ulcerative colitis. T2 FS axial (A) and coronal (B) images show marked bowel wall thickening and edema of the rectosigmoid colon. Postcontrast axial (A) and coronal (B) images show marked bowel wall thickening and enhancement with perirectal fat stranding and fluid consistent with active inflammation.

3.5 Other causes of acute pelvic pain

Several acute pathologies of the bowel, pelvic musculature, or pelvic organs can present with pain and typically undergo CT of the abdomen and pelvis with intravenous contrast in the emergency setting. American College of Radiology's (ACR) appropriateness criteria recommend contrast-enhanced CT as diagnostic modality of choice for imaging of adults presenting in the emergency setting with right lower quadrant pain not related to gynecological pathology. MRI of pelvis in the emergency setting is generally reserved for pediatric and young patients and pregnant females as a radiation free modality or can be obtained in problem-solving situations. Historically, MRI is thought to be more expensive, time consuming, and needs technical expertise with limited availability of MRI in the emergency setting. However, with more widespread availability and reduction in imaging time due to technical advances in fast imaging and abbreviated protocols, MRI is now becoming popular in the emergency setting.

3.6 Diverticulitis

Acute colonic diverticulitis is a common cause of pelvic and abdominal pain. CT with intravenous and oral contrast is considered as gold standard for suspected cases of acute diverticulitis. MRI can serve as a radiation free alternative to CT for the detection and follow-up of patients with diverticulitis, particularly in young patients. MRI can accurately diagnose acute diverticulitis with sensitivity of 86–94% and specificity of 88–92%.[20] MRI findings of acute diverticulitis are similar to CT and include bowel wall thickening, pericolonic fat standing and fluid, and the presence of complications like perforation and abscess formations. Diverticulitis is often incidentally detected on MRI obtained for the evaluation of pelvic pain or pelvic inflammatory disease. An initial US may show an adnexal mass or abscess and MRI may be performed for further clarification (Figs. 3.16 and 3.17). General MRI pelvis protocol with T1- and T2-weighted sequences, T2-weighted sequence with FS, DWI and contrast-enhanced sequences (Table 3.1) can be obtained for the evaluation of acute diverticulitis and abscess formation. Rapidly acquired T2 HASTE sequences can be obtained to reduce motion artifacts and provide good delineation of diverticular outpouching. Contrast-enhanced sequences are essential to detect bowel wall thickening and enhancement of active inflammation and also aid in the detection of pelvic abscess and differentiation of colonic cancer from diverticular disease.[21] Complex bowel wall thickening and abscess should undergo follow-up imaging or colonoscopy to exclude underlying colonic malignancy. Differentiating malignancy from acute diverticulitis can be challenging due to similar

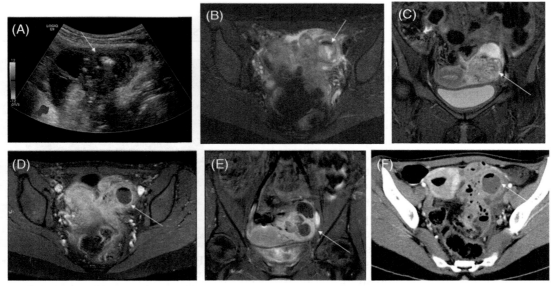

FIG. 3.16   A 26-year-old woman with pelvic pain. Pelvic ultrasound showed a complex cystic lesion in left adnexa with debris and air suspicious for tubo-ovarian abscess on US. MRI was performed for further characterization. T2 FS axial (B) and coronal (C) images showed a complex thick-walled collection in the left adnexa arising from sigmoid colon (thin arrow). Axial (D) and coronal (E) postcontrast images showed complex collection with peripheral enhancement and air communicating with sigmoid colon suggestive of diverticulitis with abscess. CT scan with intravenous contrast (F) performed next day confirmed perforated sigmoid diverticulitis. Subsequent sigmoidectomy showed low-grade sigmoid adenocarcinoma with perforation.

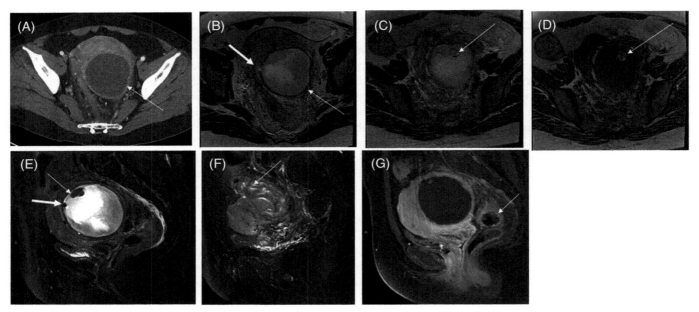

FIG. 3.17   **A 58-year-old woman with pelvic pain and rectal bleeding.** CT scan with contrast (A) showed a cystic mass in left adnexa with proctocolitis. T2 axial MRI image (B and C) shows a thick walled cystic lesion in the left adnexa with a mural nodule (thin arrow on C). T1 axial (D) shows fat within the nodule suggestive of a dermoid cyst. T2 FS sagittal (E) shows air loculus within the cyst (thick arrow) and fat suppression with the mural nodule (thin arrow). Fistulous communication of lesion with the adjacent rectum is noted (thick arrow on B). Note marked thickening of rectosigmoid colon and pericolonic inflammation on T2 FS sagittal (F) and postcontrast T1 sagittal images (G). Findings suggestive of dermoid cyst with rectal fistula.

imaging features of both pathologies. MRI has a higher sensitivity and specificity than CT for differentiating cancer from acute colonic diverticulitis due to excellent soft tissue contrast resolution of MRI. Tumors are seen as T2 hyperintense eccentric wall thickening with abrupt transition to normal bowel wall and relative lack of surrounding fat stranding. DWI can aid in the detection of colonic malignancy.

3.7 Epiploic appendagitis

Epiploic appendagitis is a rare cause of right or left lower quadrant pain and symptomatology often mimics acute diverticulitis or appendicitis. It is a benign self-limiting inflammation of appendices epiploicae which are fat containing peritoneal outpouchings arising from serosa of the colon parallel to taenia coli and contain a vascular stalk. Epiploic appendages can undergo torsion and become inflamed and infarcted giving rise to acute abdominal pain.[22] Common sites of acute epiploic appendagitis include sigmoid colon, descending colon, and right hemicolon.[23] CT scan of the abdomen and pelvis is modality of choice for investigating acute abdominal and pelvis pain and can detect acute epiploic appendagitis as an oval lesion with central fat density containing an engorged central vessel and surrounding inflammation. Associated peritoneal thickening and bowel wall thickening can be seen in some cases. MRI findings are similar to CT findings and more frequently seen on pelvic MRI obtained for pelvic pain in young patients or pregnant females (Fig. 3.18).[24]

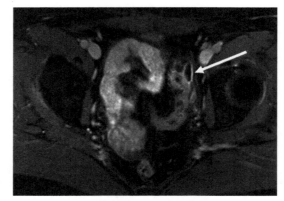

FIG. 3.18   **Epiploic appendagitis.** Postcontrast T1 axial image shows focal thickening of sigmoid colon with adjacent oval shaped fatty area with mild peripheral enhancement and fat stranding (thick arrow).

3.8 Appendicitis

Acute appendicitis is a common cause of right lower quadrant pain in the emergency setting. As with other causes of abdominal or pelvic pain, CT scan with intravenous contrast is imaging modality of choice with ultrasound commonly employed in pediatric setting. MRI can serve as a radiation free alternative particularly in young and pregnant patients and has recently gained popularity due to increasing availably and technological advances of fast MRI sequences.[25] Recently, abbreviated MRI protocols of lower abdomen and pelvis have been proposed which employ ultrafast T2-weighted single shot fast spin echo (SSFSE) or steady state free procession (TrueFISP) sequences in axial and coronal plane and axial diffusion-weighted images. Use of gadolinium contrast is contraindicated in pregnancy. MRI can be performed at 1.5T or 3T in pregnant patients. 3T MRI has advantage of increased SNR, however can be affected by increased dielectric effect in third trimester pregnant patients due to large abdomen and amniotic fluid of gravid uterus. Diagnostic accuracy of MRI for the detection of acute appendicitis is similar to CT with sensitivity of 96–100% and specificity of 81–96%.[26] MRI features of acute appendicitis include dilated appendix more than 7 mm with wall thickening, intraluminal fluid signal, and surrounding periappendiceal inflammation. Restricted diffusion signal within the dilated appendix can help in equivocal cases and serves as a surrogate marker of inflammation.

3.9 Pearls and pitfalls

Focused high-resolution small FOV T2-weighted and postcontrast images are essential for adequate delineation of perianal fistula.

T2-weighted images with FS are essential to identify fluid and inflammation in active tracts and differentiate these from chronic perianal fistulas.

Imaging plane for perianal fistula MRI should be parallel and perpendicular to anal canal for depiction of relationship of fistula to the sphincters.

Rectal gel or antiperistaltic agents are not required for perianal fistula MRI.

St. James's University Hospitals classification may be considered for description of fistulas.

A standardized reporting template is extremely useful to communicate imaging findings with referring physicians.

Complex perianal fistulas with multiple tracts, horseshoe tracts, and abscess are commonly seen in patients with Crohn's disease.

Medical management is the mainstay for perianal fistula in Crohn's disease with combined medical and surgical management reserved for complex fistulas.

MRI of pelvis in the emergency setting is generally reserved for pediatric and young patients and pregnant females as a radiation free modality or can be obtained in problem-solving situations.

MRI has a higher sensitivity and specificity than CT for differentiating cancer from acute colonic diverticulitis due to excellent soft tissue contrast resolution of MRI and colonoscopy with/without MRI should be considered in patients demonstrating complex bowel wall thickening or abscess on CT.

3.10 Conclusion

Pelvic MRI is generally reserved as a problem-solving tool for adult patients presenting with pelvic pain and can serve as a modality of choice in young adults and pregnant patients. Perianal fistula MRI is the gold standard modality for the detection of fistula, secondary tracts and abscess, and determine disease activity. T2-weighted images are essential for the detection of fluid in active tracts. Contrast-enhanced images are essential for delineating fistula tracts, differentiating fluid from granulation tissue, detection of abscesses, and differentiating active from chronic fistula tracts.

References

1. Bhavsar AK, Gelner EJ, Shorma T. Common questions about the evaluation of acute pelvic pain. *Am Fam Phys.* 2016;93(1):41–48.
2. de Miguel Criado J, del Salto LG, Rivas PF, et al. MR imaging evaluation of perianal fistulas: spectrum of imaging features. *Radiogr Rev Publ Radiol Soc North Am Inc.* 2012;32(1):175–194.
3. Jhaveri KS, Thipphavong S, Guo L, Harisinghani MG. MR imaging of perianal fistulas. *Radiol Clin North Am [Internet].* 2018;56(5):775–789. Available from: https://www.sciencedirect.com/science/article/pii/S0033838918300459.

4. Panés J, Rimola J. Perianal fistulizing Crohn's disease: pathogenesis, diagnosis and therapy. *Nat Rev Gastroenterol Hepatol.* 2017;14(11):652–664.

5. Buchanan GN, Halligan S, Bartram CI, Williams AB, Tarroni D, Cohen CRG. Clinical examination, endosonography, and MR imaging in preoperative assessment of fistula in ano: comparison with outcome-based reference standard. *Radiology [Internet].* 2004;233(3):674–681. Available from: https://doi.org/10.1148/radiol.2333031724.

6. Soker G, Gulek B, Yilmaz C, et al. The comparison of CT fistulography and MR imaging of perianal fistulae with surgical findings: a case-control study. *Abdom Radiol (New York).* 2016;41(8):1474–1483.

7. Liang C, Jiang W, Zhao B, Zhang Y, Du Y, Lu Y. CT imaging with fistulography for perianal fistula: does it really help the surgeon? *Clin Imaging.* 2013;37(6):1069–1076.

8. Gage KL, Deshmukh S, Macura KJ, Kamel IR, Zaheer A. MRI of perianal fistulas: bridging the radiological-surgical divide. *Abdom Imaging.* 2013 Oct;38(5):1033–1042.

9. Parks AG, Gordon PH, Hardcastle JD. A classification of fistula-in-ano. *Br J Surg [Internet].* 2005;63(1):1–12. Available from: https://doi.org/10.1002/bjs.1800630102.

10. Morris J, Spencer JA, Ambrose NS. MR imaging classification of perianal fistulas and its implications for patient management. *RadioGraphics [Internet].* 2000;20(3):623–635. Available from: https://doi.org/10.1148/radiographics.20.3.g00mc15623.

11. Garg P, Dawka S, Yagnik VD, Kaur B, Menon GR. Anal fistula at roof of ischiorectal fossa inside levator-ani muscle (RIFIL): a new highly complex anal fistula diagnosed on mri. *Abdom Radiol [Internet].* 2021;46(12):5550–5563. Available from: https://doi.org/10.1007/s00261-021-03261-y.

12. Pouillon L, Laurent V, Pouillon M, et al. Diffusion-weighted MRI in inflammatory bowel disease. *Lancet Gastroenterol Hepatol [Internet].* 2018;3(6):433–443. Available from: https://www.sciencedirect.com/science/article/pii/S2468125318300542.

13. Ziech MLW, Lavini C, Bipat S, et al. Dynamic contrast-enhanced MRI in determining disease activity in perianal fistulizing crohn disease: a pilot study. *AJR Am J Roentgenol.* 2013;200(2):W170–W177.

14. Thipphavong S, Costa AF, Ali HA, Wang DC, Brar MS, Jhaveri KS. Structured reporting of MRI for perianal fistula. *Abdom Radiol [Internet].* 2019;44(4):1295–1305. Available from: https://doi.org/10.1007/s00261-018-1839-y.

15. Reginelli A, Vacca G, Giovine S, et al. MRI of perianal fistulas in Crohn's disease. *Acta Biomed.* 2020;91(8-S):27–33.

16. Sheedy SP, Bruining DH, Dozois EJ, Faubion WA, Fletcher JG. MR imaging of perianal crohn disease. *Radiology.* 2017;282(3):628–645.

17. Lewis RT, Maron DJ. Anorectal Crohn's disease. *Surg Clin North Am [Internet].* 2010;90(1):83–97. Available from: https://www.sciencedirect.com/science/article/pii/S0039610909001224.

18. Van Assche G, Vanbeckevoort D, Bielen D, et al. Magnetic resonance imaging of the effects of infliximab on perianal fistulizing Crohn's disease. *Am J Gastroenterol [Internet].* 2003;98(2):332–339. Available from: https://www.sciencedirect.com/science/article/pii/S0002927002059099.

19. Iqbal N, Tozer PJ, Fletcher J, et al. Getting the most out of MRI in perianal fistula: update on surgical techniques and radiological features that define surgical options. *Clin Radiol.* 2021Oct;76(10):784.

20. Liu B, Ramalho M, AlObaidy M, et al. Gastrointestinal imaging—practical magnetic resonance imaging approach. *World J Radiol.* 2014;6(8):544–566.

21. Jerjen F, Zaidi T, Chan S, et al. Magnetic resonance imaging for the diagnosis and management of acute colonic diverticulitis: a review of current and future use. *J Med Radiat Sci.* 2021;68(3):310–319.

22. Chu EA, Kaminer E. Epiploic appendagitis: a rare cause of acute abdomen. *Radiol Case Rep.* 2018;13:599–601.

23. Eberhardt SC, Strickland CD, Epstein KN. Radiology of epiploic appendages: acute appendagitis, post-infarcted appendages, and imaging natural history. *Abdom Radiol [Internet].* 2016;41(8):1653–1665. Available from: https://doi.org/10.1007/s00261-016-0757-0.

24. Öistämö E, Hjern F, Blomqvist L, Von Heijne A, Abraham-Nordling M. Cancer and diverticulitis of the sigmoid colon. Differentiation with computed tomography versus magnetic resonance imaging: preliminary experiences. *Acta Radiol.* 2013;54(3):237–241.

25. Islam GMN, Yadav T, Khera PS, et al. Abbreviated MRI in patients with suspected acute appendicitis in emergency: a prospective study. *Abdom Radiol (NY).* 2021;46(11):5114–5124. Available from: https://doi.org/10.1007/s00261-021-03222-5.

26. Mervak BM, Wilson SB, Handly BD, Altun E, Burke LM. MRI of acute appendicitis. *J Magn Reson Imaging.* 2019;50(5):1367–1376.

CHAPTER

4

MRI of urinary bladder

Ersan Altun

Department of Radiology,
The University of North Carolina at Chapel Hill,
Chapel Hill, NC, United States

4.1 Introduction

Cystoscopy has been the essential diagnostic technique for bladder pathologies since it has also the potential to guide the biopsy under direct visualization. Although imaging techniques have been significantly improved during the last two decades, cystoscopy is still the gold standard for the identification and characterization of bladder pathologies despite its invasive nature.[1]

However, magnetic resonance imaging (MRI) has been focus of attention for the assessment of urinary bladder due to its intrinsic high contrast resolution. The use of high spatial resolution imaging techniques recently also contributed its diagnostic role, which have also played role in the development of newly proposed staging algorithms for bladder cancer.[2] Additionally, the use of high spatial resolution may also play role in the diagnosis of benign pathologies of the bladder. The artificial intelligence using radiomics of bladder pathologies may have potential role in MRI applications and assessments of bladder pathologies.[3]

4.2 Practical comprehensive MRI technique

MRI of the bladder can be performed at 1.5 T or 3.0 T with phased-array body coils. No patient preparation is required unless the patient needs premedication due to history of moderate allergic reaction to gadolinium-based contrast media.

MRI of the bladder can be performed specifically if the patient is instructed to void 60 minutes before the examination and given 500–1000 mL of fluid to drink subsequently 30–60 minutes before the examination to distend the bladder. Additionally, the use of antiperistaltic agents can improve the image quality, and glucagon can be used for this purpose if there is no contraindication. Glucagon should be administered particularly to increase the image quality of high resolution T2-weighted turbo spin echo (TSE) sequences. The effect of glucagon can be maximized if it is administered particularly before the acquisition of small field of view high-resolution T2-weighted TSE sequences and diffusion-weighted sequences (diffusion-weighted imaging [DWI]).

Precontrast and postcontrast sequences for the assessment of the pelvis including T2-weighted single shot echo train sequences with and without fat-suppression (SS-ETSE), in-phase and out-of-phase T1-weighted two- or three-dimensional (2D or 3D) gradient echo (GE), DWI sequence, precontrast T1-weighted fat-suppressed 3D-GE and dynamic postgadolinium T1-weighted fat-suppressed 3D-GE sequences are acquired. This is particularly important for the assessment of lymph node involvement, complications, and any additional chronic and incidental pathology or findings. A sample MRI protocol for bladder cancer staging is given in Table 4.1.

The key sequences for bladder assessment include high-resolution T2-weighted TSE in three planes, DWI and postgadolinium dynamic contrast-enhanced (DCE) 3D-GE imaging of the bladder. These examinations should be performed with small field of view, thinner slices (3–4 mm) without any intersection gap and with high image matrix. DCE imaging is performed at arterial phase, venous phase, interstitial phase, and excretory phase. Multiple repeated acquisitions through the bladder could be very helpful to assess the enhancement patterns of focal lesions during the arterial (25 seconds after the injection), venous (60 seconds after the injection), interstitial phases

TABLE 4.1 MR technique for bladder assessment at 1.5 T.

Sequence	Plane	TR*	TE**	Flip angle	Thickness/gap	FOV***	Matrix
Localizer	3-plane						
SS-ETSE#	Coronal	1500$^\Psi$	85	170	6 mm/20%	350–400	192 × 256
SS-ETSE	Axial	1500$^\Psi$	85	170	6 mm/20%	350–400	192 × 256
SS-ETSE	Sagittal	1500$^\Psi$	85	170	6 mm/20%	350	192 × 256
SS-ETSE fat-suppressed	Axial	1500$^\Psi$	85	170	8–10 mm/20%	350–400	192 × 256
T1 SGE& in/out-of-phase	Axial	170	2.2/4.4	70	7 mm/20%	350–400	192 × 320
T2 3D TSE+	Axial	1200	120	150	1.5 mm	250	256 × 256
T2 TSE	Axial/coronal/sagittal	5000	80	90	3–4 mm	230	256 × 256
Diffusion-weighted imaging	Axial	4500	88	90	3–4 mm	270	128 × 128
T1 3D GE$ FS pre	Axial	3.8	1.7	10	3 mm	350–400	160 × 256
Postgadolinium sequences							
T1 3D GE fat-suppressed@	Axial/coronal/sagittal	3.8	1.7	10	3 mm	250/350–400	160 × 256

*TR, repetition time.
**TE, echo time.
***FOV, field of view.
#SS-ETSE, single shot echo train spin echo.
$^\Psi$TR between slice acquisitions.
&SGE, spoiled gradient echo.
$3D GE, three-dimensional gradient echo.
@Axial imaging should be first performed at 25 seconds after the contrast administration with a small FOV for the bladder. This sequence should be repeated 4–6 times every 25 seconds for the bladder in the axial and coronal planes consecutively after the first acquisition. Larger FOV images covering the pelvis should be acquired in three planes following the acquisition of small FOV images. IV contrast is administered at 2 mL/s with the help of power injector.

(120 seconds after the injection), and excretory phase (360 seconds after the injection). Additionally, DCE with low spatial resolution and high temporal resolution could also be used alternatively.

4.3 Benign pathologies of the urinary bladder

4.3.1 Bladder stones

The majority of bladder stones are due to the migration of urinary stones from the upper urinary tract into the bladder (Fig. 4.1).

The minority of bladder stones develop in the bladder due to urinary stasis, foreign body such as stents and Foley catheters and recurrent infections. Urinary stasis can be due to bladder outlet obstruction, neurogenic bladder, cystocele, and diverticulum. Bladder outlet obstruction is most commonly due to enlarged prostate.[4,5]

A subtype of urinary stone which is composed of calcium oxalate dihydrate is almost always seen in the bladder with spiculated edges and is known as Jackstone. Additionally, the presence of infection also predisposes to the development of bladder stones and presence of infected stone may result in the development of recurrent infections.

The presence of bladder stones is also associated with the development of squamous cell carcinoma of the bladder.

Overall urinary stones are radiopaque stones including calcium stones (80%), struvite stones (15%), and nonradiopaque stones including uric acid stones (8%), ammonium urate stones (1%), medication-related stones (1%). Cystine (1%) stones could be radiopaque and radiolucent.[4,5]

The bladder stones are mobile and show low T1-weighted and T2-weighted signal in the bladder lumen on MRI[4,5] (Fig. 4.1). Intermediate signal on T1-weighted sequences can also be seen.

4.3.2 Pseuododiverticula and diverticula of the bladder

Neurogenic bladder can demonstrate trabeculated bladder wall with associated pseudodiverticula. Hydronephrosis can be seen with neurogenic bladder (Fig. 4.2).

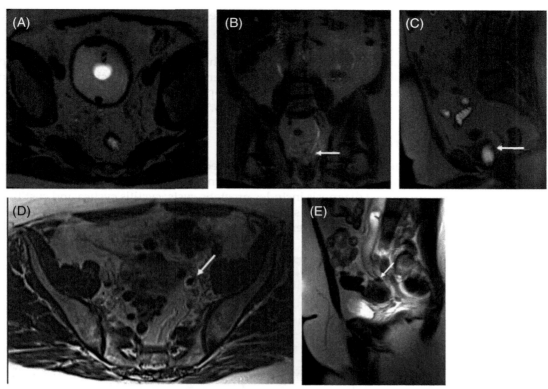

FIG. 4.1 Bladder and distal ureter stones. Transverse T2-weighted turbo spin echo (A) images show a moderate sized bladder stone with low T2 signal. A Foley and resultant nondependent air is seen along the anterior bladder wall. Coronal (B) and sagittal (C) T2-weighted single shot echo train spin echo images show an obstructing stone at the left ureterovesical junction (arrows, B, C). Transverse T2-weighted turbo spin echo (D) and single shot echo train spin echo (E) images show a small stone in the left distal ureter (arrows, D–E).

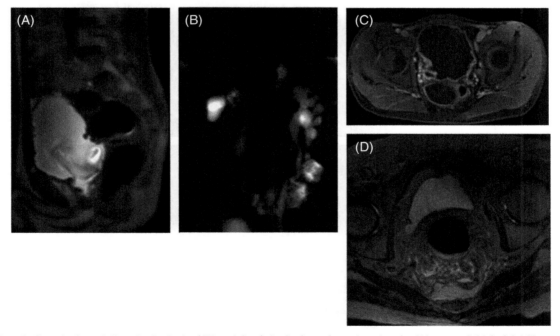

FIG. 4.2 Pseudodiverticula and diverticula. Sagittal T2-weighted single shot echo train spin echo (A), coronal thick slab MR urography image (B), transverse T1-weighted fat-suppressed postgadolinium three-dimensional gradient echo (C) demonstrate prominently trabeculated wall with associated pseudodiverticula due to neurogenic bladder. There is also nondependent air along the anterior bladder wall secondary to catheterization. Transverse T2-weighted turbo spin echo (D) image also show a small size diverticulum along the right posterolateral wall in another patient.

Real bladder diverticulum is the mucosal outpouching from the bladder wall and is usually associated with bladder outlet obstruction and high intraluminal pressure (Fig. 4.2). The bladder diverticulum increases the likelihood of development bladder stones and urothelial carcinoma.

Hutch diverticulum is the congenital diverticulum developing at the ureterovesical junction and these periureteric diverticula are secondary to congenital weakness or deficiency adjacent to the ureterovesical junction in an otherwise normal bladder. Hutch diverticulum is seen in 1.7% of the general population and its association with vesicourethral reflux is often due to the position change of normal ureter insertion.[6,7]

4.3.3 Bladder cyst and urachal remnants

Brunn's cyst arises from the von Brunn's nests which are considered to be the result of pinching off of epithelial nests from urothelial buds.[8,9] These cysts are most commonly seen in the bladder neck and trigone and may cause urinary tract obstruction.[8,9] The differential diagnosis includes prostatic cysts; cystitis cystica and cystitis glandularis which are caused by inflammatory processes. Brunn's cyst shows typical features of a cyst with low T1-weighted signal, high T2-weighted signal and no or mild wall enhancement on postgadolinium sequences (Fig. 4.3).

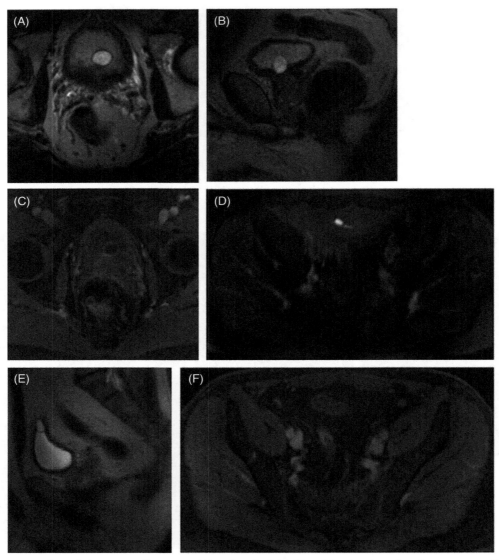

FIG. 4.3   Bladder cyst and urachal remnant. Transverse (A) and sagittal (B) T2-weighted turbo spin echo, transverse T1-weighted fat-suppressed three-dimensional gradient echo postgadolinium (C) images show a Brunn's cyst at the level of bladder neck with homogeneous internal fluid content and mild rim enhancement. Transverse fat-suppressed (D) and sagittal (E) T2-weighted single shot echo train spin echo, and transverse T1-weighted fat-suppressed three-dimensional gradient echo postgadolinium image (F) show a cystic lesion without obvious wall enhancement at the bladder dome and this lesion represents an intravesical urachal cyst.

Urachal remnant develops secondary to the failure of allantois to obliterate.[6,7] These remnants are located at the midline between the anterior bladder dome and umbilicus located between the anterior abdominal wall and peritoneum in the space of Retzius. There are four types of remnants including (i) patent urachus (persistent patent urachus from the level of bladder to the umbilicus), (ii) vesicourachal diverticulum (patent urachus at the level of bladder but closed at the level of umbilicus), (iii) urachal sinus (patent urachus at the level of umbilicus but closed at the level of bladder), (iv) urachal cyst (urachus is patent at the center but closed at both ends). Although the patent urachus is the most symptomatic variant in children, the remaining types are more common in adults and are usually asymptomatic. Infection and malignancy are the most common complications of urachal remnants. Urachal adenocarcinoma constitutes 0.5% of all bladder cancers and 34% of all bladder adenocarcinomas.[6,8,10]

Urachal remnants demonstrate show high T2 signal depending on the patency of the lumen/lumen size and morphologic features. Urachal cyst shows typical features of a cyst with low T1-weighted signal, high T2-weighted signal, and no or mild wall enhancement on postgadolinium sequences (Fig. 4.3).

Urachal carcinoma (Fig. 4.4) shows intermediate to high T2 signal, low T1 signal, high DWI signal with variable ADC signal and heterogeneous enhancement. It is usually exophytic and located along the anterior bladder dome and may extend toward the umbilicus. The tumor may also extend into the bladder lumen.

Infected urachal remnants may show complex heterogeneous signal and prominent rim enhancement.

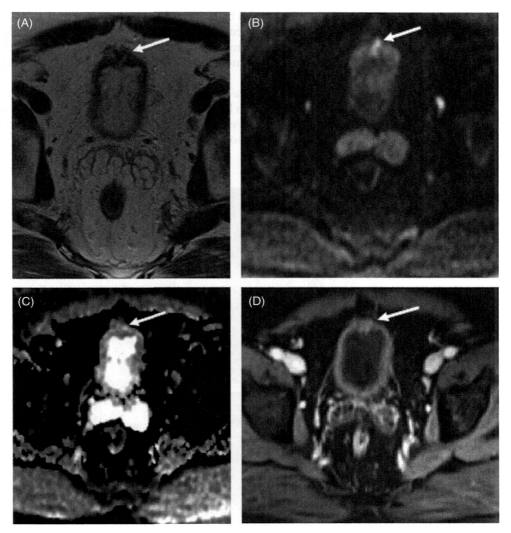

FIG. 4.4 Urachal adenocarcinoma. Transverse T2-weighted turbo spin echo (A), diffusion-weighted sequence (B), apparent diffusion coefficient map (C), and T1-weighted fat-suppressed postgadolinium three-dimensional gradient echo (D) sequences show a small urachal adenocarcinoma (arrow, A–D) with mildly high heterogeneous T2 signal (A), mildly high diffusion signal on high *b*-value set (B), isointense signal to the bladder wall on the apparent diffusion coefficient map (C), and mildly increased enhancement (D).

4.3.4 Ureterocele

Ureterocele is saccular dilatation of intramural portion of distal ureter and develops secondary to failure of recanalization of Chwalla membrane which is located between the urogenital sinus and developing ureteral bud.[6,7]

Ureteroceles are more commonly seen in females and can be seen bilaterally in 10% of cases. Most ureteroceles are congenital and usually associated with duplicated collecting system and ectopic insertion of the ureter. Ureteroceles can be seen as isolated abnormality, usually in adults.[6]

Ureteroceles can be intravesical (20% of cases) and extravesical (80% of cases).[6] Intravesical ureteroceles are orthotopic and occur at normally positioned ureteral orifices and are more commonly seen in adults with herniation of the distal ureter into the bladder lumen. Extravesical ureteroceles are associated with ectopic location of ureters which are more inferiorly and medially located close to the bladder neck and urethra including vagina. Extravesical ureteroceles are associated with a duplicated collecting system and causes obstruction. According to Weigert–Meyer rule, the upper moiety is obstructed with associated ectopic insertion of ureter with ureterocele, and the lower moiety is associated with orthotopic insertion of the ureter and vesicourethral reflux.[6]

Ureteroceles are best seen on T2-weighted sequences as high signal intensity structures in the bladder or adjacent to the bladder or ectopic ureter insertion sites (Fig. 4.5).

4.3.5 Endometriosis

Involvement of bladder is seen 1–15% of endometriosis.[10,11] The bladder involvement can be seen due to superficial endometriosis or deep infiltrating endometriosis. The most common locations for the superficial endometriosis are along the peritoneal surfaces of bladder and is most common along the vesicouterine pouch. Deep infiltrating endometriosis can involve the bladder wall and is most commonly seen along the vesicouterine pouch and posterior bladder and trigone.[10-13]

MRI findings include the presence of ill-defined soft tissue lesions along the bladder wall and these lesions may show T1 high signal and T2 high signal with shading due to blood products. However, due to the recurrent bleeding episodes with associated inflammatory changes and development of fibrosis, the lesions may commonly show low T1 and T2 signal intensity (Fig. 4.6). The lesions may show mild progressive enhancement.[10-13]

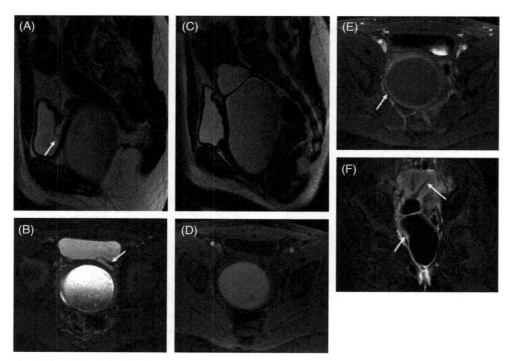

FIG. 4.5 Ureterocele. Sagittal T2-weighted turbo spin echo (A and C); transverse T2-weighted fat-suppressed single shot echo train spin echo (B); T1-weighted fat-suppressed precontrast transverse (D), postgadolinium transverse (E) and coronal (F) three-dimensional gradient echo images show a left-sided ureterocele (arrows, A and B). Please note the presence of septated uterus and hematocolpos without enhancement (arrows, E and F).

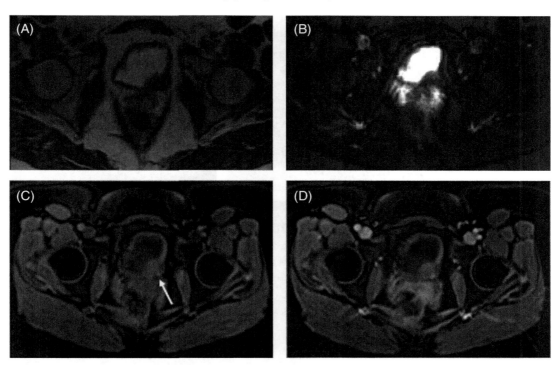

FIG. 4.6 **Endometriosis.** Transverse T2-weighted non–fat-suppressed (A) and fat-suppressed (B) single shot echo train spin echo, transverse T1-weighted fat-suppressed precontrast (C), and postgadolinium (D) three-dimensional gradient echo images show a T2 hypointense infiltrative mass with hypoenhancement along the left posterolateral wall. The findings are not specific but secondary to endometriosis in this patient. A tiny hyperintense focus on precontrast T1-weighted image is likely related to endometriosis (arrow, C).

4.3.6 Leiomyoma

Leiomyomas constitute 0.5% of bladder tumors and are the most common mesenchymal tumor of the bladder.[10] Most leiomyomas are incidental and asymptomatic. Leiomyomas can be located in the wall, intraluminal or exophytic extending toward the extravesical soft tissues. They may also demonstrate cystic degenerative changes although most of them are relatively homogeneous.

On MRI, leiomyomas demonstrate low T1 and low T2 signal on MRI with relatively low enhancement ion postgadolinium series (Fig. 4.7).[10]

4.3.7 Placenta percreta with bladder involvement

Placenta percreta is described as the placental invasion of adjacent periuterine structures beyond the wall of uterus. This is the result of abnormal placentation and lead to placental separation during the delivery.[14,15]

The border between the uterus and bladder should be clear on MRI. The presence of bulging of uterus and placenta toward the bladder, tenting of the bladder, abnormal vessels along the bladder wall, dark intraplacental bands on T2-weighted images, disorganized intraplacental vascularity, focal myometrial disruption or thinning on MRI are suggestive of placenta percreta with bladder involvement (Fig. 4.8). DWI has also been reported to be helpful for the identification of myometrium and placenta.[14,15]

4.3.8 Cystocele

Cystocele (Fig. 4.9) is the prolapse of bladder with or without adjacent additional organs below the level of pelvic diaphragm. Cystocele is characterized by the descent of the bladder below the level of pubococcygeal line.[16] The urethra is usually hypermobilized and appears angulated. Dynamic pelvic floor imaging with MRI (MR defecography) is the technique which should be used to assess pelvic floor dysfunction and associated organ prolapse.[16] MR defecography is beyond the scope of this review.

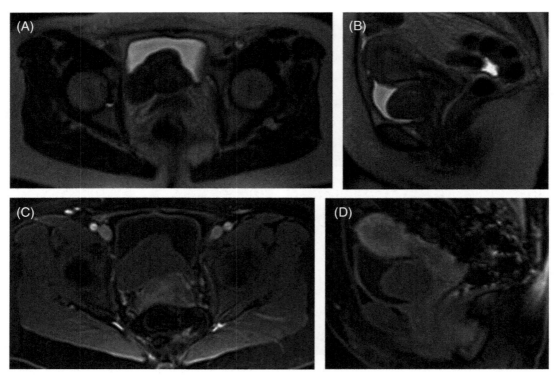

FIG. 4.7 **Leiomyoma.** Transverse (A) and sagittal (B) single shot echo train spin echo, transverse (C) and sagittal (D) fat-suppressed three-dimensional gradient echo postgadolinium images show a focal mass along the posterior wall of the bladder wall with low T2 signal and mild heterogeneous enhancement which represents a leiomyoma.

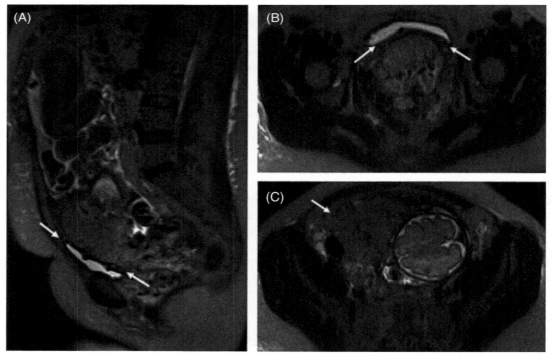

FIG. 4.8 **Placenta percreta.** Sagittal (A), transverse (B and C) T2-weighted single shot echo train spin echo images show lobulated placenta along the lower uterine segment anteriorly with prominent vessels with bulging of posterior bladder wall (arrows, A–C). Prominent vessels are noted along the posterior bladder wall. These findings are suggestive of abnormal placentation with the lack of myometrium anteriorly and presence of placenta percreta. There was involvement of the bladder wall during the surgery.

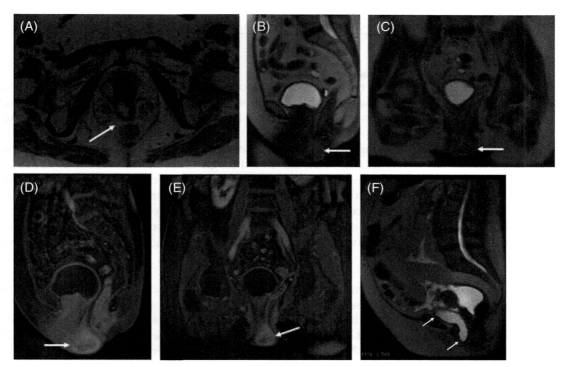

FIG. 4.9 **Cystocele.** Transverse T2-weighted turbo spin echo (A), sagittal (B), and coronal (C) T2-weighted single shot echo train spin echo; sagittal (D) and coronal (E) postgadolinium fat-suppressed three-dimensional gradient echo images show pelvic floor relaxation with a defect between vagina and rectum. There is a small cystocele (arrow, A) and complete uterus prolapse with inversion of uterus through the pelvic floor defect (arrows, B–E). Please note the endometrium (arrows, D and E) and presence of intramural fibroid. Sagittal T2-weighted single shot echo train spin echo (F) image shows a small cystocele and the bladder extends inferior to the symphysis pubis with horizontal orientation of urethra (arrows, F).

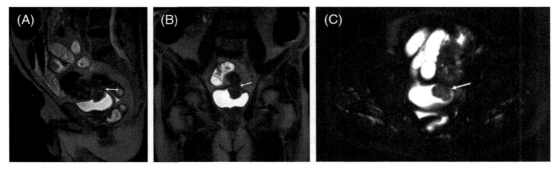

FIG. 4.10 **Sigmoid diverticulitis to bladder fistulization.** Sagittal (A), coronal (B), and transverse fat-suppressed (C) single shot echo train spin echo sequences show fistulization between the sigmoid colon and bladder (arrows, A–C) due to sigmoid diverticulitis.

4.3.9 Enterovesical fistula

Colovesicular fistula can develop secondary to diverticulitis, Crohn's disease, and rectal cancer.[11] Ileovesicular or ileocolovesicular fistula can develop in patients with Crohn's disease.[11] The bladder dome or left lateral wall are most commonly involved with fistulas secondary diverticulitis. Ileovesicular fistulas are the most common bladder fistulas secondary to Crohn's disease. MRI can detect these fistulas successfully due to its high contrast resolution (Fig. 4.10).

4.4 Malignant pathologies of the bladder

4.4.1 Bladder cancer

Urothelial carcinoma is the most common type of bladder cancer constituting 90% of the bladder cancers in the Western world.[17-20] Squamous cell carcinomas and adenocarcinomas forming 6–8% and 2% of the bladder cancers are rare in the Western world.[17-20] Squamous cell bladder cancer is the major type seen in the developing countries where schistosomiasis is endemic.[17, 20]

MRI has particularly been used for staging of the pelvic malignancies due to its high contrast resolution and relatively high spatial resolution in the last decade. Although initial diagnosis of bladder cancer is usually done with cystoscopy and initial assessment for concurrent upper tract cancers is usually done with CT urogram (or with MR urogram if there is contraindication to CT urogram) per the guidelines, bladder cancer staging (Tables 4.2 and 4.3) can also be performed particularly for advanced tumors with the help of MRI by using T2-weighted high-resolution TSE sequences, DWI sequence, and DCE sequence.[21] The evaluation of lymph node involvement and possible distant metastases is also possible with MRI. Additional chronic and incidental findings can also be assessed with MRI.

4.4.1.1 *T staging*

T staging is performed based on the assessment of involvement of detrusor muscle, which is muscularis propria. The muscularis propria of the bladder is hypointense on T2-weighted TSE, mildly hyperintense on high-value DWI showing intermediate signal intensity on ADC map and hypointense on T1-weighted images. The mucosa and submucosa cannot be visualized reliably on T2-weighted TSE and DWI images and show enhancement on the arterial phase DCE images while muscularis propria demonstrates late enhancement on the venous and interstitial phase DCE images.[2,20-28]

Bladder cancers demonstrate intermediate signal on T2-weighted TSE images compared to background hypointense muscularis propria which enables the differentiation of tumors from the normal bladder wall. High DWI signal

TABLE 4.2   TNM staging of bladder cancer based on AJCC 8th edition.*

T staging	Extent of disease
Tx	Primary tumor cannot be evaluated
T0	No evidence of primary tumor
Ta	Noninvasive papillary carcinoma
Tis	Carcinoma in situ
T1	Tumor has spread to the lamina propria
T2a	Tumor has spread to the inner half of the muscular wall of bladder
T2b	Tumor has spread to the outer half of the muscular wall of bladder
T3a	Tumor has spread into the extravesicle fat tissue as seen through a microscope
T3b	Tumor has spread into the extravesicle fat tissue macroscopically
T4a	Tumor has spread to the prostate, seminal vesicles, uterus, or vagina
T4b	Tumor has spread to the pelvic or abdominal wall
N staging	**Extent of disease**
Nx	Regional lymph nodes cannot be evaluated
N0	Cancer has not spread to the regional lymph nodes
N1	Cancer has spread to 1 regional lymph node
N2	Cancer has spread to 2 or more regional lymph nodes
N3	Cancer has spread to the common iliac lymph nodes
M staging	**Extent of disease**
M0	No evidence of distant metastases.
M1a	Cancer has spread only to lymph nodes outside of the pelvis
M1b	Cancer has spread other parts of the body

Reference.[21]

TABLE 4.3 TNM staging* of bladder cancer with associated corresponding most commonly used and recommended management options.

TNM staging	T staging	N staging	M staging	Nonmuscle invasive or muscle invasive tumors	Most commonly used and recommended management options
Stage 0	Ta or Tis	N0	M0	Nonmuscle invasive	TURBT
Stage 1	T1	N0	M0		Intravesical Chemotherapy
					Intravesical BCG
					Immunotherapy in patients with BCG failure
Stage 2	T2a or T2b	N0	M0	Muscle invasive	Neoadjuvant systemic chemotherapy followed by radical cystectomy
Stage 3a	T3a, T3b, T4a	N0 or N1	M0		
Stage 3b	T1-T4	N2 or N3	M0		Trimodal bladder sparing therapy with TURBT and concurrent chemoradiation
Stage 4a	T4b	Any N	M0		
Stage 4a	Any T	Any N	M1a		Systemic chemotherapy
					Followed by immunotherapy in refractory cases
Stage 4b	Any T	Any N	M1b		Systemic chemotherapy
					Followed by immunotherapy in refractory cases

*References.[17,21]

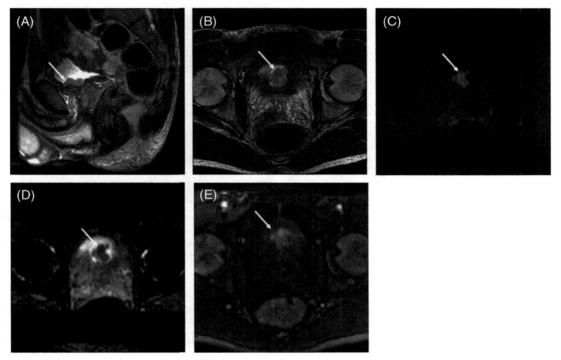

FIG. 4.11 **Bladder cancer.** T1 tumor. Sagittal (A) and transverse (B) T2-weighted turbo spin echo, transverse diffusion-weighted sequence (C), apparent coefficient map (D), and transverse T1-weighted dynamic contrast-enhanced image (E) acquired on the arterial phase demonstrate a polypoid mass at the level of bladder neck without evidence of bladder wall invasion (arrows, A–E). The lesion shows diffusion restriction and increased enhancement. VI-RADS 2. Histopathologically, these lesions are T1 urothelial carcinomas.

intensity of the tumor with corresponding low signal intensity on ADC compared to the muscularis propria and prominent enhancement of the tumor compared to nonenhancing or minimally enhancing muscularis propria on the arterial phase of DCE imaging differentiates the tumor from the bladder wall.[2,20-28] The extension of tumor into the muscularis propria and extravesical fat tissue differentiates T1 versus T2, and T2 versus T3, respectively.

Ta and T1 tumors (Figs. 4.11 and 4.12) are usually associated with fibrotic and/or inflammatory stalks, and the stalk usually shows intermediate to low in signal intensity on T2 TSE images although the signal can be variable.[2,20-28]

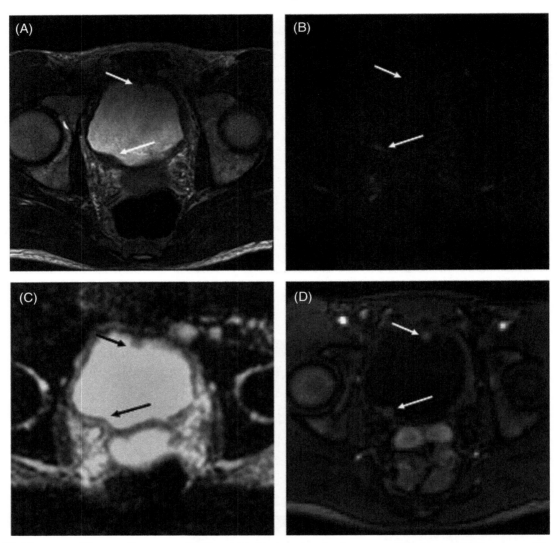

FIG. 4.12   Bladder cancer. T1 tumor. Transverse (A) T2-weighted turbo spin echo, transverse diffusion-weighted sequence (B), apparent coefficient map (C), and transverse T1-weighted dynamic contrast-enhanced image (D) acquired on the arterial phase demonstrate two polypoid masses at the anterior and right posterolateral walls without evidence of bladder wall invasion (arrows, A–D). The lesion shows diffusion restriction and increased enhancement. VI-RADS 2. Histopathologically, these lesions are T1 urothelial carcinomas.

Low signal on high *b*-value images with associated high signal on ADC map without diffusion restriction, and early enhancement on DCE similar to the tumor are also seen at the stalk.[2,20-28] The tumor containing stalk is usually a nonmuscle invasive tumor with "inchworm sign" and the tumor signal does not extend to the muscularis propria.[29] Tenting of the bladder wall and uninterrupted submucosal enhancement just beneath the tumor are additional findings which usually suggest nonmuscle invasive tumors.[2,20-28] The submucosa sometimes is seen as a thickened layer under the tumor with lack of diffusion restriction which is suggestive of inflammation and/or fibrosis (inchworm sign). T1 tumors may also invade the submucosa without the presence of stalk, and the stalk may occasionally show diffusion restriction without evidence of malignancy.[2,20-28] If the findings of T2 TSE, DWI or DCE are discordant, DWI should be the dominant sequence in staging due to the potential to differentiate the tumor tissue from inflammation and/or fibrosis.[28]

T2 tumors (Fig. 4.13) show intermediate signal which does not extend through the dark signal of muscularis propria completely on T2-weighted TSE images.[2,20-28] High DWI sign with corresponding low ADC signal, and increased arterial phase enhancement confined to the wall without any extension to extravesical fat are seen on T2 tumors.[2,20-28] Due to the potential to differentiate the tumor tissue from inflammation and/or fibrosis, DWI should be the dominant sequence in staging when there is particularly extravesical inflammation and fibrosis due to

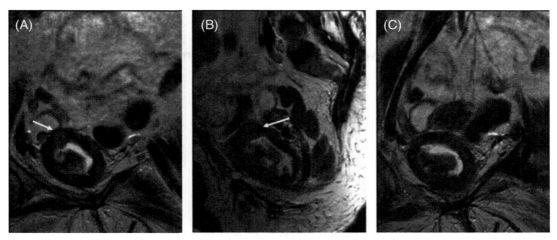

FIG. 4.13   **Bladder cancer.** T2 tumor. Coronal T2-weighted turbo spin echo sequences (A and C) and sagittal T2-weighted turbo spin echo sequence (B) demonstrate a squamous cell carcinoma of the bladder with muscular wall invasion (arrows, A and B). Note the presence of circumferential bladder wall thickening and heterogeneous intraluminal debris/blood products. VI-RADS 4. The lesion shows definite invasion of the bladder wall.

treatment or postprocedural changes which may demonstrate similar signal to the tumor on T2-weighted images or similar enhancement to the tumor on DCE.[28]

Vesicle Imaging-Reporting and Data System (VI-RADS) has been reported to have high accuracy with sensitivity of 74–97.3% and specificity 77–100% and this system depends on the determination of tumor extension through the bladder wall on T2-weighted TSE, DWI, and DCE sequences.[2,20-30] However, VI-RADS is at its early stages of development and there is still scarce information for the validation of this system in the literature. If the tumor is less than 1 cm with no evidence of extension of intermediate soft tissue tumor signal on T2 TSE, corresponding signal on DWI/ADC signal and early enhancement on DCE into the muscularis propria, VI-RADS category is 1 and the muscle invasion is highly unlikely.[2] If the tumor is larger than 1 cm with no evidence of extension of intermediate soft tissue tumor signal on T2 TSE, corresponding signal on DWI/ADC signal and early enhancement on DCE into the muscularis propria, VI-RADS category is 2 and the muscle invasion is unlikely.[2] If there is exophytic intraluminal tumor without stalk or sessile tumor without evidence of nonenhancing T2 high signal intensity inner lining and without disruption of muscularis propria, VI-RADS category is 3 and the muscle invasion is equivocal.[2] If there is evidence of interruption of normal signal intensity of muscularis propria with tumor extension on T2 TSE with associated corresponding abnormal DWI/ADC signal and early enhancement on DCE, VI-RADS category is 4 and the muscle invasion is likely.[2] If there is evidence of complete interruption of normal signal intensity of muscularis propria with tumor extension into the extravesical fat on T2 TSE with associated corresponding abnormal DWI/ADC signal and early enhancement on DCE through the whole muscularis propria, VI-RADS category is 5 and the muscle invasion is likely.[2]

T3 tumors (Fig. 4.14) demonstrate extension of the tumor to the extravesical fat with the intermediate tumor signal disrupting the muscularis propria on T2-weigted TSE images.[2,20-28] High DWI signal with corresponding low ADC signal, and increased enhancement of the tumor on the arterial phase extending into the extravesical fat beyond the confines of the bladder wall are noted.[2,20-28] Mild extension into the extravesical fat could still be present histopathologically, when the tumor involves the whole bladder wall without obvious disruption on MRI.[2,20-28]

The involvement of peritoneum, prostate, uterus, vagina, rectum, colon, small bowel loops and pelvic sidewalls, and abdominal wall represents T4 tumor (Figs. 4.15–4.17). T2 TSE is the dominant sequence for the evaluation of invasion of adjacent organs.

MRI is limited in the detection of small tumors including the small flat or sessile lesions which are usually Tis, or tumors less than 1 cm.[20]

DWI has also been reported to be helpful for the differentiation of noninvasive bladder cancers from muscle invasive bladder cancers or low-grade cancers from high-grade cancers although the data are very limited on the literature. It has been reported that a ADC cut-off value of 0.80×10^{-3} mm^2/s can differentiate noninvasive bladder cancers from muscle invasive bladder cancers with 96.7% accuracy; and ADC cut-off value of 0.9×10^{-3} mm^2/s can differentiate high-grade from low-grade tumors with 91.7% sensitivity and 60% specificity.[31]

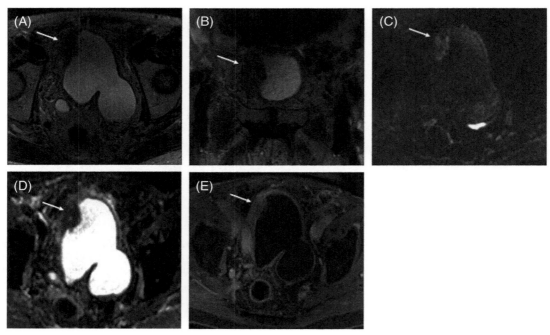

FIG. 4.14 **Bladder cancer.** T3 tumor. Transverse (A) and coronal (B) T2-weighted turbo spin echo, transverse diffusion-weighted sequence (C), apparent coefficient map (D), and transverse T1-weighted fat-suppressed there-dimensional gradient echo (E) images show a lesion invading the bladder wall and extending into perivesicle fat (arrows, A–E). The lesion shows diffusion restriction and increased enhancement. VI-RADS 5. This lesion represents a T3 urothelial carcinoma.

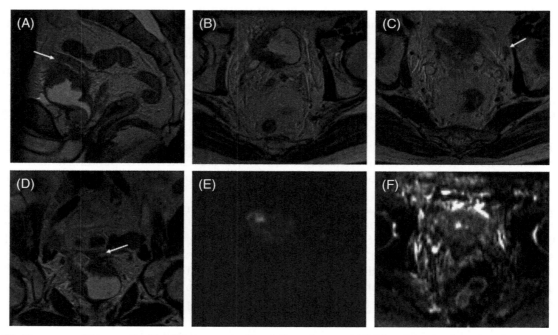

FIG. 4.15 **Bladder cancer.** T4 tumor. Sagittal (A), transverse (B and C), and coronal (D) T2-weighted turbo spin echo, transverse diffusion-weighted sequence (E), and apparent diffusion coefficient map (F) show T4 urothelial carcinoma with invasion to the perivesicle fat and peritoneal reflection (arrows, A and D). VI-RADS 5. The lesion shows diffusion restriction and bilateral hydroureter due to obstruction at the level of ureterovesicle junctions. A mildly enlarged left-sided obturator lymph node with low T2 signal is suggestive of metastasis.

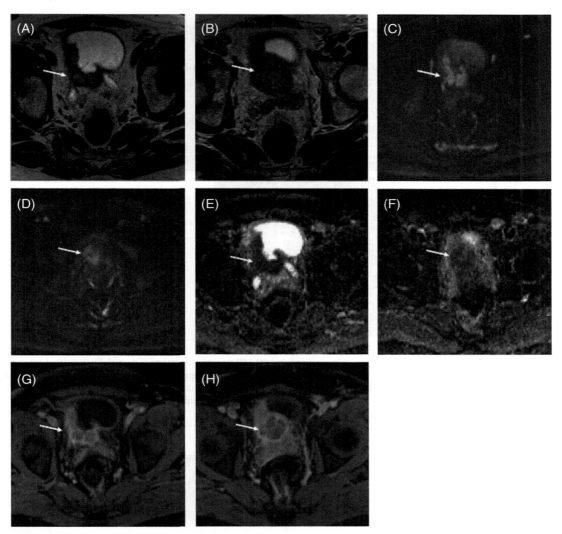

FIG. 4.16   **Bladder cancer.** T4 tumor. Transverse T2-weighted turbo spin echo (A and B) transverse diffusion-weighted sequence (C and D) and associated apparent diffusion coefficient map (E and F) and transverse T1-weighted postgadolinium fat-suppressed images (G, H) show a T4 urothelial carcinoma with invasion into the prostate gland (arrows, A–H). VI-RADS 5. Please note that bilateral hydroureters due to involvement of ureterovesical junctions.

Variable signal intensity changes including high, intermediate, and low signal changes representing edema, inflammation, and fibrosis following postbiopsy and posttreatment changes can be seen on T2-weighted TSE images.[2,20,22] Since these changes usually do not demonstrate diffusion restriction but show either high to intermediate signal on DWI and ADC map, or low to intermediate signal on DWI and ADC map, DWI can be helpful for the differentiation of postbiopsy and posttreatment changes from the tumor.[2,20,22]

MRI is also very successful for the identification of recurrent disease in the pelvis (Fig. 4.18).

4.4.1.2 N staging

Internal iliac, external iliac, obturator, and presacral lymph nodes can be involved with N1–N2 lymph node positive bladder cancer.[32] The common iliac chain lymph nodes are involved in N3 lymph node positive bladder cancer.[32] More extensive retroperitoneal lymph node involvement above the level of common iliac chains is regarded as distant metastatic disease and staged as M1.[32]

The accuracy of metastatic lymph node disease detection is limited due to the inability to differentiate reactive lymph node changes with enlarged size or heterogeneous enhancement from metastatic disease or inability to detect micrometastasis in morphologically normal lymph nodes seen on MRI. DWI and ultrasmall super paramagnetic iron oxide particles have not improved the accuracy.

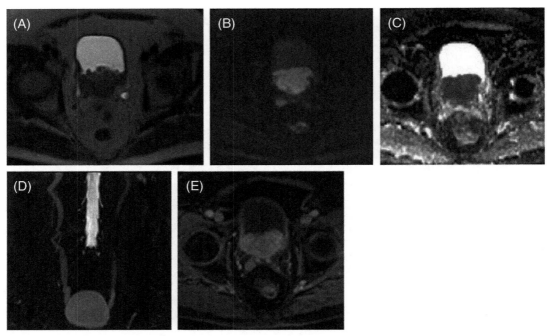

FIG. 4.17 **Bladder cancer.** T4 tumor. Transverse T2-weighted single shot echo train spin echo (A), transverse diffusion-weighted sequence (B), and associated apparent diffusion coefficient map (C), three-dimensional MR urography image (D), and T1-weighted fat-suppressed there-dimensional postgadolinium gradient echo image (E) show a large mass involving the trigone and posterior bladder wall with associated diffusion restriction and abnormal enhancement. Please note that the ureters are dilated due to obstruction secondary to urothelial carcinoma involving the trigone; and invasion of the seminal vesicles. Therefore, the lesion is a T4 tumor. VI-RADS 5.

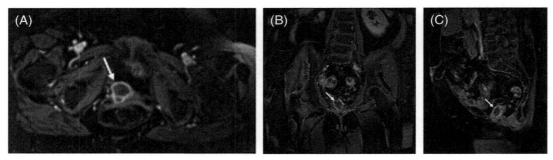

FIG. 4.18 **Vaginal recurrence after cystectomy for bladder cancer.** Transverse (A), coronal (B), and sagittal (C) T1-weighted fat-suppressed three-dimensional gradient echo postgadolinium images demonstrate peripherally enhancing mass at the vaginal cuff, suggestive of recurrence (arrows, A–C) in this patient with history of radical cystectomy and bladder cancer.

4.4.1.3 *Role of MRI in assessment of posttreatment changes and surveillance strategies following treatment*

MRI can be used for the assessment of posttreatment changes following TURBT and chemoradiation therapy (Fig. 4.19). MRI can demonstrate the size changes following the treatment; however, it is also able to differentiate the residual tumor from inflammation and fibrosis. Therefore, MRI has significant advantage over CT due to its different types of contrast resolution including T2 contrast, DWI contrast, and DCE contrast. Although there is scarce information about the performance of MRI, particularly VIRADS assessment, in posttreatment patients, MRI with VIRADS assessment has been reported to be performing similarly in posttreatment patients to pretreatment patients.[33] DWI has been reported to differentiate edema and fibrosis from the residual tumors since diffusion restriction is typically seen with residual tumors.[27] It has been reported that ADC cut-off value of 0.911×10^{-3} mm^2/s which has the ability to differentiate pathologic complete response from noncomplete response has sensitivity of 95.4–96.0%, specificity of 97.0–97.7%, and area under the curve of 0.971–0.981.[34] Regarding the use of ADC and DCE parameters

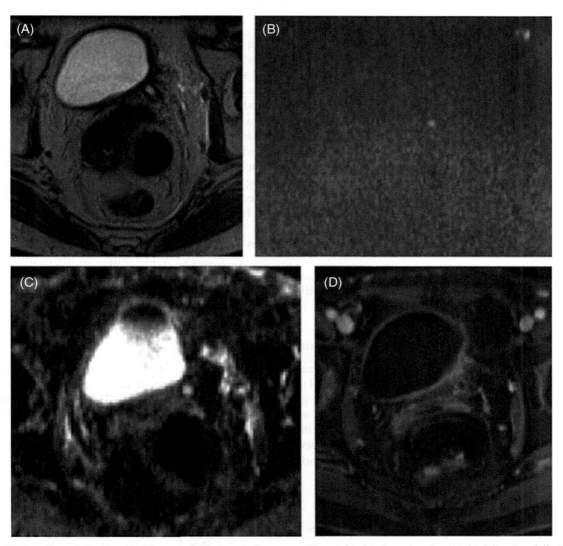

FIG. 4.19   MRI findings following bladder cancer treatment. Transverse T2-weighted turbo spin echo (A), high b-value diffusion-weighted sequence (B), apparent diffusion coefficient map (C) and T1-weighted fat-suppressed postgadolinium three-dimensional gradient echo (D) sequences show no evidence of residual tumor along the left bladder wall and left side of the trigone. Diffuse low T2 signal of the thickened bladder wall with extension into the extravesical fat is seen with associated left hydroureter. However, although there is evidence of increased enhancement along the left bladder wall and left side of trigone with the extravesical enhancement, there is no evidence of high diffusion signal or diffusion restriction. The findings are suggestive of fibrosis without evidence of residual or recurrent bladder cancer.

such as wash-out times to differentiate residual tumors, the data in the literature are still very limited but MRI has significant potential for the evaluation of posttreatment changes.

MRI can be used in the surveillance of muscle invasive bladder cancer according to current guidelines following the treatment in 3–6 months interval for the first 2 years and annually for 3–5 years.[17] However, the role of VIRADS in posttreatment assessment of noninvasive and muscle invasive bladder cancer has not been determined.

The role of PET-MRI has not also been determined yet and there is very limited information about the use of PET/MRI particularly in posttreatment muscle invasive bladder cancer patients. PET is limited for local T staging of bladder cancer due to the presence of residual radioactivity preventing the assessment of bladder wall and therefore MRI component of PET/MRI is particularly used for T staging.[35] It has been reported that PET-MRI is able to demonstrate metastatic disease burden comparable or better than PET/CT.[36] Additionally, PET/MRI has the potential to show metastatic lymph nodes better than MRI.

4.4.1.4 *Radiomics of bladder cancer*

Radiomics is a developing translational field of imaging trying to find associations between extracted quantitative information obtained from imaging studies, and clinical, laboratory, or histopathologic data with or without associated gene expression.[3,37,38] Quantitative information is extracted and analyzed by dedicated software and this process is affected by image acquisition, postprocessing, and segmentation.[3,37,38]

The role of radiomics analysis, its features, and individual parameters in the diagnosis and assessment of tumor response has not been still determined due to lack sufficient data in the literature and limitations of this technique.[37,38] A significant limitation for the use of radiomics features is the inability to have reproducible robust results without variability due to the dependence to acquisition technique and parameters.[37] Since the acquisition technique and parameters are very heterogeneous in the routine clinical practice and radiomics analysis are also affected by patient factors, contrast injection or enhancement changes or scanning factors such as magnetic field inhomogeneities on MRI or imaging artifacts, the results of radiomics analysis are adversely affected.[37] Additionally, the lack of fully automated postprocessing and segmentation techniques with high accuracy also lead to variable results with low reproducibility.[37]

Initial specific studies demonstrated that radiomics features may play role and may have high accuracy in the determination of tumor recurrence following TURBT[39]; pathologic grade of tumor based on MRI[40] muscle invasive status of the tumor or extension of tumor to extravesical fat[41]; and tumor volume changes following treatment.[42,43] Due to limited number of studies, more research studies are needed to determine to role of radiomics in the assessment of bladder cancer.

4.4.2 Invasion of the bladder by pelvic malignancies

Local malignant invasion of the bladder is most commonly seen secondary to rectal or sigmoid colon cancer, prostate cancer, and cervical cancer (Figs. 4.20 and 4.21). Local staging of rectal cancer and cervical cancer can be successfully performed with MRI, and bladder and distal ureter involvement can be determined. The role of MRI for prostate cancer staging has not been determined yet and the role of MRI for the identification of bladder neck involvement is limited due to the lack of sufficient contrast resolution.

Additionally, malignant invasion of the bladder secondary metastatic implants can also be seen (Fig. 4.22). The tumors may invade the bladder wall and even extend into the bladder lumen in some cases.

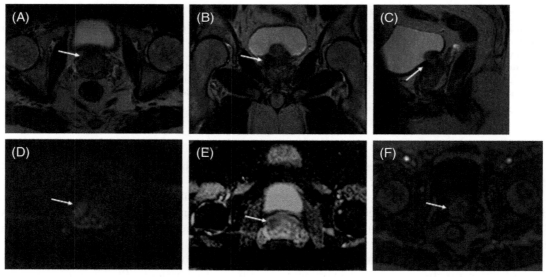

FIG. 4.20   **Prostate cancer with bladder involvement.** Transverse (A), coronal (B), sagittal (c) turbo spin echo, transverse diffusion-weighted sequence (D), apparent diffusion coefficient map (E) and transverse T1-weighted postgadolinium three-dimensional gradient echo dynamic contrast-enhanced sequence (F) show a PIRADS 5 lesion in the right transitional zone abutting the bladder neck. Although the invasion of the bladder wall is difficult to visualize in this case, the presence of bladder neck abutment should raise the suspicion for invasion. There was evidence of bladder neck invasion in this case histopathologically.

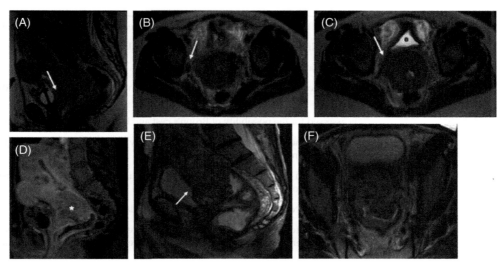

FIG. 4.21   Bladder invasion due to cervical cancer. Sagittal T2-weighted turbo spin echo (A), transverse T2-weighted single shot echo train spin echo (B and C), sagittal T1-weighted fat-suppressed three-dimensional gradient echo postgadolinium (D) images show a large infiltrative cervical cancer (asterisk, D) invading the posterior bladder wall (arrow, A) and upper vagina. The mass shows parametrial invasion and right ureter involvement (arrow, C). There is an associated right obturator enlarged lymph node with low T2 signal suggestive of metastatic disease (arrow, B). Please note that multiple fibroids are also present in the uterus. Sagittal (E) and transverse (F) T2-weighted turbo spin echo images show a large rectosigmoid junction tumor invading the posterior bladder wall with fistulization (arrow, E).

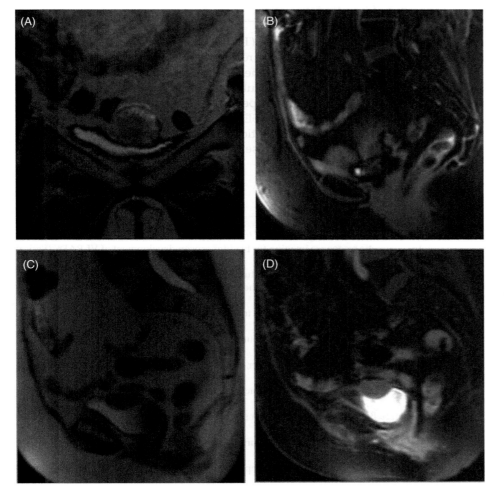

FIG. 4.22   Metastatic implants along the bladder dome. Metastatic implants along the coronal T2-weighted turbo spin echo (A), sagittal T1-weighted fat-suppressed three-dimensional gradient echo postgadolinium (B) sequences demonstrate an enhancing peritoneal implant along the bladder wall due to metastatic ovarian cancer. Sagittal T2-weighted single shot echo train spin echo (C) and T1-weighted fat-suppressed postgadolinium three-dimensional gradient echo (D) sequences show a metastatic implant along the bladder dome secondary to colon cancer metastasis.

TABLE 4.4 Pearl and pitfalls of MRI of bladder.

High-resolution three plane orthogonal T2-TSE imaging of the bladder with 3–4 mm slice thickness without gap should be performed.

High-resolution DWI should be performed with 3–4 mm slice thickness on transverse plane similar to high-resolution T2-TSE.

Antiperistaltic agents could be helpful to decrease motion artifacts due to peristalsis.

Voiding 60 minutes before the examination and consumption of 500–1000 mL of water subsequently 30–60 minutes before the examination is critical for optimal bladder distension.

Cysts located at the bladder neck should be carefully assessed for the possibility of Brunn's cyst and be differentiated from cystic changes of BPH.

Urachal remnants should always be carefully assessed for the possibility of any solid tissue with high T2 and DWI signal and increased enhancement which could be suggestive of urachal carcinoma.

Differential diagnosis of focal mass lesions of the bladder with low T2 signal includes leiomyoma, endometriosis, and metastases. Metastases tend to show more enhancement than leiomyomas and endometriosis.

Vessels along the bladder wall in a patient with abnormal placental location could be a sign of placenta percreta.

The bladder cancers demonstrate intermediate soft tissue intensity with associated diffusion restriction and increased early enhancement compared to the background normal bladder wall and therefore it is possible to differentiate noninvasive bladder cancers from muscle invasive cancers.

The presence of stalk at the base of tumor (inchworm sign) without diffusion restriction is suggestive of noninvasive bladder cancer.

VIRADS still needs to be validated for the accuracy of detection of bladder cancer in multicenter prospective trials.

The accuracy of MRI is limited for the detection of metastatic lymph nodes in patients with bladder cancer.

4.5 Conclusion

MRI is able to detect and diagnose various pathologic processes of bladder (Table 4.4). Although imaging is essential for the diagnosis and staging of bladder cancer and assessment of tumor response, it is still limited and therefore direct visualization with cystoscopy and histopathologic assessment are the preferred standard methods for initial diagnosis and assessment of bladder wall involvement. High spatial resolution MR imaging of the bladder cancer could be a promising technique for bladder cancer staging although its specific role has not been determined yet and this technique still needs validation. Therefore; development of T2-TSE, DWI, and DCE sequences with ultra-high spatial resolution, higher contrast resolution, higher signal-to-noise ratio combined with motion/artifact resistant techniques in the near future may have higher potential to diagnose and stage bladder cancer and assess treatment response.

References

1. Barocas DA, Boorjian SA, Alvarez RD, et al. Microhematuria: AUA/SUFU guideline. *J Urol.* 2020;204:778.
2. Panebianco V, Narumi Y, Altun E, et al. Multiparametric magnetic resonance imaging for bladder cancer: development of VI-RADS (Vesical Imaging-Reporting and Data System). *Eur Urol.* 2018;74:294–306.
3. Cacciamani GE, Nassiri N, Varghese B, et al. Radiomics and bladder cancer: current status. *Bladder Cancer.* 2020;6:343–362.
4. Kambadakone AR, Eisner BH, Catalano OA, Sahani DV. New and evolving concepts in the imaging and management of urolithiasis: urologists' perspective. *Radiographics.* 2010;30:603–623.
5. Cheng PM, Moin P, Dunn MD, Boswell WD, Duddalwar VA. What the radiologist needs to know about urolithiasis: part 1 – pathogenesis, types, assessment, and variant anatomy. *Am J Roentgenol.* 2021;198:W540–W547.
6. Rowell AC, Sangster GP, Caraway JD, Walker PW, Elmajian DA, Heldmann MG. Genitourinary imaging: part 1, congenital anomalies and their management. *Am J Roentgenol.* 2012;199:W545–W553.
7. Berrocal T, Lopez-Pereira P, Arjonilla A, Gutierrez J. Anomalies of the distal ureter, bladder, and urethra in children: embryologic, radiologic, and pathologic features. *Radiographics.* 2002;22:1139–1164.
8. Grimsby GM, Tyson MD, Salevitz B, Smith ML, Castle EP. Bladder outlet obstruction secondary to a Brunn's cyst. *Curr Urol.* 2012;6:50–52.
9. Baarimah A, Alsayed A, Yamani A, Aldawsari M, Soliman S. Bladder outlet obstruction secondary to Brunn's cyst: a rare presentation in young man. *Urol Case Rep.* 2021;38:101683.
10. Wong-You-Cheong JJ, Woodward PJ, Manning MA, Sesterhenn IA. Neoplasms of the urinary bladder: radiologic-pathologic correlation. *Radiographics.* 2006;26:553–580.
11. Wong-You-Cheong JJ, Woodward PJ, Manning MA, Davis CJ. Inflammatory and nonneoplastic bladder masses: radiologic-pathologic correlation. *Radiographics.* 2006;26:1847–1868.

12. Siegelman ES, Oliver ER. MR imaging of endometriosis: ten imaging pearls. *Radiographics*. 2012;32:1675–1691.

13. Coutinho A, Bittencourt LK, Pires CE, et al. MR imaging in deep pelvic endometriosis: a pictorial essay. *Radiographics*. 2011;31:549–567.

14. Kilcoyne A, Shenoy-Bhangle AS, Roberts DJ, Sisodia RC, Gervais DA, Lee SI. MRI of the placenta accrete, placenta increta, and placenta percreta: pearls and pitfalls. *Am J Roentgenol*. 2017;208:214–221.

15. Fadl S, Moshiri M, Fligner CL, Katz DS, Dighe M. Placental imaging: normal appearance with review of pathologic findings. *Radiographics*. 2017;37:979–998.

16. del Salto LG, Criado JM, del Hoyo L. MR imaging-based assessment of the female pelvic floor. *Radiographics*. 2014;34:1417–1439.

17. Lenis AT, Lec PM, Chamie K. Bladder cancer: a review. *JAMA*. 2020;324:1980–1991.

18. Lee CH, Tan CH, de Castro Faria S, Kundra V. Role of imaging in the local staging of urothelial carcinoma of the bladder. *Am J Roentgenol*. 2017;208:1193–1205.

19. Mirmomen SM, Shinagare AB, Williams KE, Silverman SG, Malayeri AA. Preoperative imaging for locoregional staging of bladder cancer. *Abdom Radiol*. 2019;44:3843–3857.

20. Altun E. MR imaging of the urinary bladder: added value of PET-MR imaging. *Magn Reson Imaging Clin N Am*. 2019;27:105–115.

21. Paner GP, Stadler WM, Hansel DE, Montironi R, Lin DW, Amin MB. Updates in the eighth edition of the tumor-node-metastasis staging classification for urologic cancers. *Eur Urol*. 2018;73:560–569.

22. Pecoraro M, Takeuchi M, Vargas HA, et al. Overview of VI-RADS in bladder cancer. *Am J Roentgenol*. 2020;214:1259–1268.

23. Rosenkrantz AB, Mussi TC, Melamed J, Taneja SS, Huang WC. Bladder cancer: utility of MRI in detection of occult muscle-invasive disease. *Acta Radiol*. 2012;53:695–699.

24. Wang H, Luo C, Zhang F, et al. Multiparametric MRI for bladder cancer: validation of VI-RADS for the detection of detrusor muscle invasion. *Radiology*. 2019;291:668–674.

25. Uneo Y, Takeuchi M, Tamada T, et al. Diagnostic accuracy and interobserver agreement for the Vesicle Imaging-Reporting and Data System for muscle-invasive bladder cancer: a multireader validation study. *Eur Urol*. 2019;76:54–56.

26. Panebianco V, Narumi Y, Barchetti G, Montironi R, Catto JWF. Should we perform multiparametric magnetic resonance imaging of the bladder? Time to reconsider the rules. *Eur Urol*. 2019;76:57–58.

27. Del Giudice F, Barchetti G, De Berardinis E, et al. Prospective assessment of Vesical Imaging Reporting and Data System (VI-RADS) and its clinical impact on the management of high-risk non-muscle-invasive bladder cancer patients candidate for repeated transurethral resection. *Eur Urol*. 2020;77:101–109.

28. Takeuchi M, Sasaki S, Naiki T, et al. MR imaging of urinary bladder cancer for T-staging: a review and a pictorial essay of diffusion-weighted imaging. *J Magn Reson Imaging*. 2013;38:1299–1309.

29. Yoshida S, Takahara T, Kwee TC, Waseda Y, Kobayashi S, Fujii Y. DWI as an imaging biomarker for bladder cancer. *Am J Roentgenol*. 2017;208:1218–1228.

30. Seguier D, Puech P, Kool R, et al. Multiparametric magnetic resonance imaging for bladder cancer: a comprehensive systematic review of the Vesical Imaging – Reporting and Data System (VI-RADS) performance and potential clinical applications. *Ther Adv Urol*. 2021;13:1–17.

31. Al Johi RS, Seifeldein GS, Moeen AM, et al. Diffusion weighted magnetic resonance imaging in bladder cancer, is it time to replace biopsy? *Cent Eur J Urol*. 2018;71:31–37.

32. Cornejo KM, Rice-Stitt T, Wu C-L. Updates in staging and reporting of genitourinary malignancies. *Arch Pathol Lab Med*. 2020;144:305–319.

33. Cao B, Li Q, Xu P, et al. Preliminary exploration of the application of vesical imaging-reporting and data system (VI-RADS) in post-treatment patients with bladder cancer: a prospective single-center study. *J Magn Reson Imaging*. 2022;55(1):275–286.

34. Ahmed SA, Taher MGA, Ali WA, Ebrahem M. Diagnostic performance of contrast-enhanced dynamic and diffusion-weighted MR imaging in the assessment of tumor response to neoadjuvant therapy in muscle-invasive bladder cancer. *Abdom Radiol*. 2021;46:2712–2721.

35. Eulitt PJ, Altun E, Sheikh A, et al. Pilot study [18F] fluorodeoxyglucose positron emission tomography (FDG-PET)/magnetic resonance imaging (MRI) for staging of muscle invasive bladder cancer (MIBC). *Clin Genitourin Cancer*. 2020;18:278–386.

36. Civelek AC, Niglio SA, Malayeri AA, et al. Clinical value of 18FDG PET/MRI in muscle-invasive, locally advanced, and metastatic bladder canceer. *Urol Oncol*. 2021;39(11):787.e17–787.e21.

37. Rizzo S, Botta F, Raimondi S, et al. Radiomics: the facts and the challenges of image analysis. *Eur Radiol Exp*. 2018;2:36.

38. van Timmeren J, Cester D, Tanadini-Lang S, Alkadhi H, Baessler B. Radiomics in medical imaging – "how-to" guide and critical reflection. *Insights Imaging*. 2020;11:91.

39. Xu X, Wang H, Du P, et al. A predictive nomogram for individualized recurrence stratification of bladder cancer using multiparametric MRI and clinical risk factors. *J Magn Reson Imaging*. 2019;50:1893–1904.

40. Wang H, Hu D, Yao H, et al. Radiomics analysis of multiparametric MRI for the preoperative evaluation of pathological grade in bladder cancer tumors. *Eur Radiol*. 2019;29:6182–6190.

41. Xu S, Yao Q, Liu G, et al. Combining DWI radiomics features with transurethral resection promotes the differentiation between muscle-invasive bladder cancer and non-muscle-invasive bladder cancer. *Eur Radiol*. 2020;30:1804–1812.

42. Cha KH, Hadjiiski LM, Samala RK, et al. Bladder cancer segmentation in CT for treatment response assessment: application of deep-learning convolution neural network – a pilot study. *Tomography*. 2016;2:421–429.

43. Cha KH, Hadjiiski L, Chan R, et al. Bladder cancer treatment response assessment in CT using radiomics with deep-learning. *Sci Rep*. 2017;7:1–12.

5

MRI of pelvic vessels

Marika A. Pitot, Candice A. Bookwalter

Department of Radiology, Mayo Clinic, Rochester, MN, United States

5.1 Introduction

Magnetic resonance imaging (MRI) is an important and versatile diagnostic tool in the anatomic and dynamic evaluation of vascular diseases and entities. Advantages of MRI and magnetic resonance angiography include lack of nonionizing radiation, exquisite soft tissue contrast, multiple contrast mechanisms, and the ability to acquire dynamic images. Both contrast-enhanced and noncontrast MR angiographic techniques are available from all major vendors. Additionally, magnetic resonance (MR) contrast agents are generally considered safer than iodinated contrast agents used in CT angiography for patients with renal dysfunction. When indicated, flow quantification with 2D and 3D phase contrast imaging is also possible with MRI/MRA.

Given the versatility of MR, it is important to tailor pelvic vascular MR imaging protocols to answer a specific clinical question to avoid intolerably long examination times. A fundamental imaging protocol for pelvic vascular findings should typically include high-quality, high spatial resolution contrast-enhanced MRA (CE-MRA) with multiple phases. CE-MRA is excellent for anatomic and structural vascular evaluation. Optional sequences for a standard protocol include axial T2W fat saturated and nonfat saturated as well as pre- and postcontrast axial fat saturated 3D T1W images to evaluate surrounding soft tissue structures and associated findings. Axial balance steady state free procession (bSSFP) with T2/T1W may be used in addition to or replacing standard T2W fat saturated images, while keeping in mind its characteristic artifacts and limitations (i.e., inhomogeneity artifacts).

Some vascular indications, such as assessment of vascular malformations, require dynamic high time-resolved MRA (TR-MRA). This technique is widely available on different vendor platforms (TWIST (Siemens, Erlangen, Germany), TRICKS (General Electric, Chicago, IL, USA), 4D-TRAK (Philips, Best, Netherlands), TRAQ (Hitachi, Tokyo, Japan), and Freeze Frame (Toshiba, Otawara, Japan). Other indications, such as pelvic venous congestion syndrome, require more comprehensive evaluation of pelvic soft tissue findings. Vascular findings may also be incidental on abdominopelvic or musculoskeletal MR. Therefore, recognition of pathology on nonangiographic sequences is important. The purpose of this article is to describe MR imaging protocols, findings, and pitfalls for common pelvic vascular diseases and related entities.

5.2 Contrast agents

CE-MRA is the most common MR method for vascular imaging, and typically uses a rapid 3D T1W spoiled gradient echo (GRE) pulse sequence with a short repetition time (TR) and echo time (TE).

5.2.1 Gadolinium-based contrast agents

Gadolinium-based contrast agents (GBCAs) are the most commonly used MR contrast agents. They are reportedly employed in 30–45% of all MRI examinations.[1] GBCAs are paramagnetic, causing T1 shortening and blood to appear bright on postcontrast T1-weighted images (Fig. 5.1A and B). The plasma half-life of GBCAs is 91 minutes in healthy volunteers, with primarily renal excretion.[2] In patients with renal insufficiency, the plasma half-life is lengthened, placing these patients at increased risk for nephrogenic systemic fibrosis (NSF). According to the current guidelines from the American College of Radiology (ACR), the risk of NSF is low or nonexistent with group II agents (e.g., gadobenate dimeglumine, gadobutrol, gadoteric acid, and gadoteridol).[3] Routine screening and laboratory testing of GFR prior to administration of Group 2 GBCAs is not considered necessary. In patients with known renal failure (i.e., GFR <30), the supervising radiologist should determine necessity of type 2 GBCAs. Routine screening and laboratory testing is still recommended prior to administration of Group 1 and 3 GBCAs, which are typically not used in patients with GFR <30. Although gadolinium deposition remains a concern, particularly with multiple doses, there are no known adverse health effects associated with this phenomenon.[4]

There are multiple methods for bolus timing including fixed delay, test bolus, and bolus tracking (fluoroscopic triggering). Fixed delay methods are not typically used due to wide variability in optimal scan time delay. At our institution, we use a test bolus method for bolus timing, where a portion of the contrast dose (typically 1–2 mL) is injected while obtaining multiphase high time-resolution single slice image through the heart or vascular structure of interest. Optimal scan time delay is calculated as

$$Scantime\ delay = Peaktime - \frac{scantime}{2} + \frac{contrast\,volume}{2*injection\,rate}.$$

where peak time is the time of peak contrast enhancement on test bolus images and scan time is the duration of CE-MRA acquisition. Following determination of the scan time delay, a weight-appropriate dose of GBCA is power injected at a rate of 1.5 mL/s followed by 20 mL of 0.9% NaCl. Imaging is set to start at the calculated scan time delay. Alternatively, bolus tracking methods inject the entire contrast bolus (approximately 20 mL) and simultaneously obtain 20–40 seconds of 2D single slice gradient echo images through the heart or vascular structure of interest. Optimal scan time is determined in real time by visual inspection or by vendor automatic detection. From personal experience, test bolus and bolus tracking methods work equally well and exact timing is not necessary. An example of arterial phase MRA with GBCA is shown in Fig. 5.1A and B for a patient with abdominal aortic dissection. Notice good filling of the aorta with some contrast in the portal vein, but no contrast in the inferior vena cava (IVC).

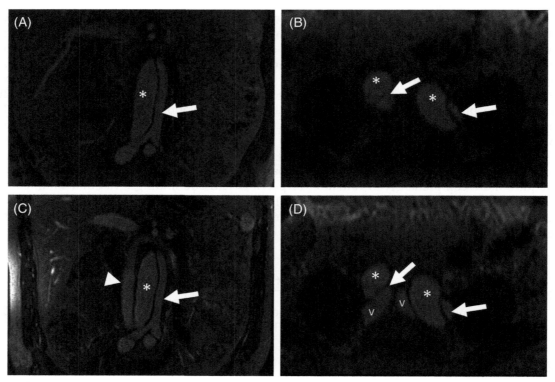

FIG. 5.1 **Aortoiliac dissection.** Arterial phase coronal CE-MRA image with GBCA (A) showing a dissection flap in the infrarenal aorta separating the true lumen (arrow) and false lumen (asterisk) and extending into the bilateral common iliac arteries. Reformatted axial arterial phase CE-MRA image with GBCA (B) at the level of the common iliac arteries showing the dissection flap as a thin dark line. Notice excellent enhancement of both the true and false lumens. Corresponding coronal and reformatted axial CE-MRA images from the same patient at subsequent follow-up several years later performed with ferumoxytol (C and D). Notice contrast filling the IVC (arrowhead) and iliac veins (V) for vascular steady state imaging with ferumoxytol.

Multiphase imaging even with some venous contamination is typically diagnostic for most indications. Note that TR-MRA uses a fixed delay, as images are acquired every 2–5 seconds for a designated period (typically 2 minutes).

5.2.2 Nongadolinium-based contrast agents

Ultrasmall paramagnetic iron oxide (USPIO) agents such as ferumoxytol are approved by the FDA for iron replacement therapy for anemia in adult patients with chronic kidney disease. Ferumoxytol has also been described as an intravenous MRI contrast agent due to its regional T1 and T2* shortening effects.[5,6] Ferumoxytol has a long intravascular half-life of 14–15 hours and no active excretory pathway, which makes it an excellent blood pool agent. As an MR contrast agent, it can be given as a rapid bolus for arterial phase images or as a long infusion for steady state vascular imaging. Fewer adverse reactions have been seen with long infusion and FDA labeling consequently recommends against bolus injections.[7] The disadvantage of slow infusion is that it does not allow for dynamic images. With slow infusion, images are "steady state," with contrast filling both arterial and venous structures, for example in Fig. 5.1C and D. Use of Ferumoxytol as an MR contrast agent is considered off-label use, however a multicenter registry has shown no serious adverse events and few contrast reactions at the time of writing.[8]

With no active excretory pathway, ferumoxytol is cleared by the reticuloendothelial system and macrophage uptake. This clearance mechanism causes T2* shortening in the liver and spleen for 3–11 months after contrast administration, which can affect the appearance of the liver and spleen in future MR examinations.[9] A primate study suggests that ferumoxytol does not cross the placental barrier and therefore may be a safe alternative to GBCA during pregnancy, although the practical and safe use in human pregnancy has not yet been determined.[10] Similar to techniques reported in the literature, at our institution, we infuse ferumoxytol via gravity flow or via an IV pump injected over 5 minutes prior to entering the scanner in order to obtain steady state vascular enhancement of both the arteries and veins (Fig. 5.1CC and D).[6] Because the dose given for IV contrast is much lower than the therapeutic dose for iron replacement, the 15-minute infusion length recommended by the FDA is not used. We use adult dosing of 4 mg/kg at 1.5T diluted in 60 mL 0.9% NaCl or 2 mg/kg at 3T diluted in 30 mL 0.9 NaCl (maximum 17 mL).[11] Blood pressure, heart rate, and respiratory rate are monitored during and for 30 minutes after the injection.

5.3 Noncontrast MRA techniques

MR angiography (MRA) can also be performed without IV contrast. Noncontrast MRA is performed at less cost and less risk to the patient, i.e., those associated with contrast reactions and other contrast-related issues. Noncontrast MR sequences can also be repeated if necessary, as there is no concern with contrast bolus timing.

Time of flight (TOF) imaging is a nonsubtractive, inflow-dependent MRA technique which can be performed 2D or 3D. This technique is commonly used in the evaluation of the carotid arteries, but can also be used to evaluate pelvic vessels (Fig. 5.2). TOF techniques perform best when the vessel is perpendicular to the plane of imaging, which is not always the case with vessels in the pelvis. 3D bSSFP has been shown to accurately identify thrombus in the IVC[12] and lower extremities.[13] bSSFP is widely available, with rapid acquisition that enables high blood signal, but is susceptible to signal loss due to field inhomogeneity and flow turbulence. Fig. 5.3 shows an example of acute

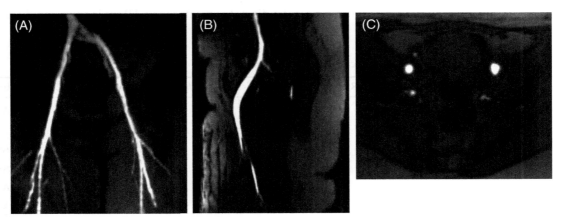

FIG. 5.2   Time of flight noncontrast MRV. Coronal MIP (A), double oblique (B), and axial (C) noncontrast MRV images of the iliac veins using time of flight MRA technique showing patent iliac veins in a 25-year-old female with a history of prior deep vein thrombosis.

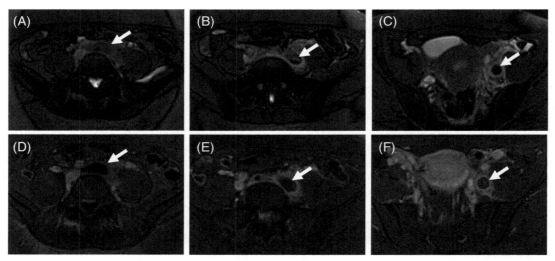

FIG. 5.3   Variable signal intensity of left iliac vein thrombus (arrows) on bSSFP images (A–C) with comparison postcontrast T1W images (D–F).

thrombus in the left common and external iliac veins with variable signal on bSSFP images at different level (A–C) compared to postcontrast images (D–F). Quiescent-interval slice-selective (QISS) MRA has also been shown to be useful in the evaluation of arterial vasculature from the infrarenal aorta through the ankle.[14] Unfortunately, QISS MRA technique is not available across all vendors.

5.4 Pelvic vascular diseases

MR protocols for the evaluation of pelvic vascular diseases should be tailored for the indication. Essential sequences for common pelvic vascular indications are summarized in Table 5.1. Specific sequence parameters are given in Table 5.2.

5.5 Aortoiliac aneurysm and acute aortic syndrome

Two common indications for aortoiliac MR angiographic evaluation are aneurysm and/or acute aortic syndrome. High-quality CE-MRA is sufficient for visualization of the entire abdominal aorta and iliac vessels. This section will focus on findings in the infrarenal aorta and bilateral iliac arteries.

By definition, an aneurysm is a focal dilatation of an artery which is increased more than 50% compared to the normal diameter of the artery. Aneurysms are described by location, for example, infrarenal abdominal aortic aneurysms are defined as involving the abdominal aorta distal to the renal arteries. Specifically for the infrarenal aorta, a diameter greater than 2 cm is considered ectatic, whereas a diameter greater than 3.0 cm is considered aneurysmal.[15]

TABLE 5.1   Summary of tailored MR imaging protocols for pelvic vascular diseases.

	CE-MRA	TR-MRA	T2	Pre/post-T1	MRV	DWI	bSSFP
Aneurysm, dissection, etc.	Cor		Ax	Ax			Ax
FMD	Cor		Ax	Ax			
May–Thurner	Cor		Ax	Ax	Cor		Ax, Cor
PVCS		Cor	Ax, Cor, Sag				Ax
Vascular malformation		Cor	FS Ax	Ax	Cor		Ax, Cor
Fibroid	Cor		Ax, Cor, Sag	Ax, Sag		Ax	Ax

Ax, axial; *bSSFP*, balance steady state free procession; *Cor*, coronal; *DWI*, diffusion-weighted imaging; *FMD*, fibromuscular dysplasia; *MRA*, MR angiogram; *MRV*, MR venogram; *PVCS*, pelvic venous congestion syndrome; *Sag*, sagittal; *SSFSE*, single shot fast spin echo; *TR-MRA*, time-resolved MR angiogram.

TABLE 5.2 MR imaging parameters for pelvic vascular sequences (at 3T):

	TR/TE (ms)	FOV (mm)	FA	ST (mm)	Matrix	NEX
SSFSE	Min/85	440	90	5	384 × 288	1
3D dual echo	6/min	300–360	15	3.4	256 × 224	1
T2 RTr Dixon	Resp/85	240	111	4	416 × 224	2
DWI (*b*-value = 50/100/800)	2000/min	280	90	5	128 × 128	
CE-MRA	min	360	25	2	320 × 224	0.75
TR-MRA	4.3/min	440	30	2.4	416 × 320	0.75
MRV	4.3/min	440	25	2	320 × 224	0.75
Lava-Flex +C	5.5/min	360	12	2.2	320 × 320	2
Lava-Flex +C	5/min	280–360	15	4–5	256 × 224	1
bSSFP	3.2/min	360	12	5	224 × 256	1

bSSFP, balanced steady state free procession; *+C*, postcontrast; *DWI*, diffusion-weighted imaging; *FA*, flip angle; *FOV*, field of view; *min*, minimum possible; *MRV*, MR venogram; *RTr*, respiratory triggered; *SSFSE*, single shot fast spin echo; *ST*, slice/slab thickness; *TE*, echo time; *TR*, repetition time; *TR-MRA*, time-resolved magnetic resonance angiography.

TABLE 5.3 Normal and aneurysmal aortoiliac artery diameter criteria.

	Normal	Ectasia	Aneurysmal
Infrarenal aorta	<2.0 cm	2.5–3.0 cm	>3.0 cm
Common iliac	Male <1.9 cm	1.9–2.5 cm	>2.5 cm
	Female <1.5 cm	1.5–2.5 cm	
Internal iliac			>0.8 cm

The common iliac artery is considered ectatic when its diameter is greater than 1.7 cm in men and 1.5 cm in women. When the diameter exceeds 2.5 cm for both men and women, the common ilac artery is considered aneurysmal. The internal iliac artery is considered aneurysmal when its diameter exceeds 0.8 cm.[16] A summary of these measurements can be found in Table 5.3.

Aortic aneurysms tend to grow over time and therefore require regular follow-up as the risk of complications (e.g., rupture) rises as aneurysms increase in size. Surgical or endovascular repair will typically be pursued when the diameter is greater than 5.5 cm, or 4.5 cm and increased 0.5 cm in the prior 6 months.[17-19] Iliac artery aneurysms are frequently associated with abdominal aortic aneurysm, however can also be an isolated finding.[20]

When measuring the diameter of a vessel, it is recommended to measure in double oblique cross-sectional diameter on source images. Fig. 5.4 demonstrates the method of measuring in double oblique cross-sectional diameter where the planes chosen are perpendicular to the vessel walls in two planes (dashed red lines in A and B) which give the plane for measurement (Fig. 5.3C). Measurements should include the vessel wall, including mural thrombus and atherosclerotic plaque if present. Mural thrombus will be hypointense on CE-MRA images (Figs. 5.4 and 5.5), whereas calcified atherosclerotic plaque will be very hypointense on all sequences. Of note, measuring on a MIP has been shown to cause underestimation of aneurysm size.[21]

5.5.1 Acute aortic syndrome

Acute aortic syndrome is defined as aortic dissection, intramural hematoma, and penetrating atherosclerotic ulcer. MRA can be used in the acute setting, however largely due to availability and perceived increased complexity of MRA, CTA is the preferred modality for rapid workup. Still, chronic dissection follow-up of these patients may be performed with either CTA or MRA. For both acute evaluation and chronic dissection follow-up, the extent, branch vessel involvement, and dimensions should be reported.

At our institution, the imaging protocol for aortic aneurysm and acute aortic syndrome includes SSFSE coronal, pre- and post-LAVA, and high-quality, breath-held isotropic resolution CE-MRA. CE-MRA for this purpose can be performed with either GBCA or ferumoxytol as shown in Fig. 5.1. Acquiring two or three phases of high spatial

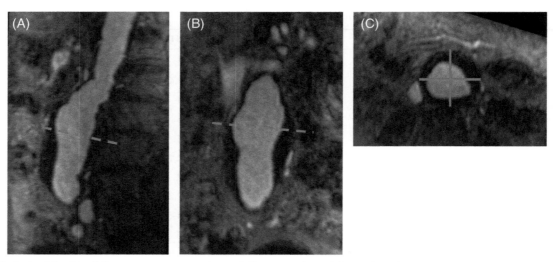

FIG. 5.4   Method of double oblique measurement of vessel diameter. The red dotted line shows proper orientation perpendicular to the vessel walls in two planes (A and B) giving image (C). Double oblique cross-sectional diameter measurement includes vessel lumen and vessel wall (solid red lines).

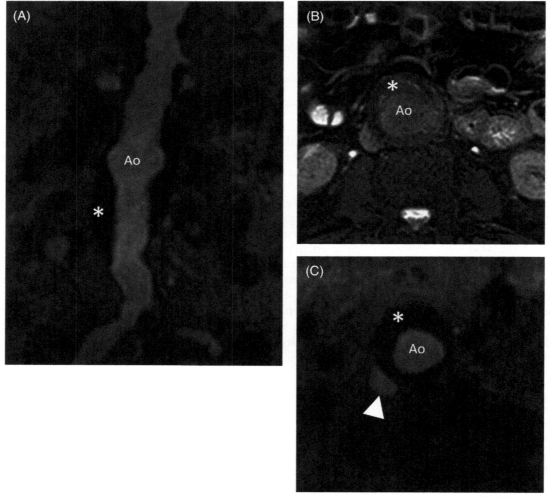

FIG. 5.5   Aortoiliac aneurysm. Curved planar reformat of the infrarenal aorta and right common iliac artery (A), axial bSSFP (B) and axial reformat MRA images of an 82-year-old male dilatation of the abdominal aorta and right common iliac artery. Mural thrombus is seen in the infrarenal aorta (*). This study was performed with ferumoxytol, contrast-filled IVC (arrowhead).

resolution dynamic CE-MRA with GBCA typically ensures compete contrast filling in the presence of slow flow. Later CE-MRA phases have been shown to benefit from lower flip angle due to decreased GBCA concentration with the vessels.[22] Black blood imaging techniques have been described, but these techniques take more time and are not included in our standard protocol.[16]

5.5.2 Fibromuscular dysplasia (iliac arteries)

Fibromuscular dysplasia (FMD) is an idiopathic, noninflammatory, and nonatherosclerotic angiopathy affecting medium- and large-caliber arteries. The most commonly involved arteries are the carotid and renal arteries, however, the disease process can also include mesenteric, iliac, subclavian, axillary, and coronary arteries. A typical imaging finding is a beaded appearance of the vessel with short segments of alternating dilatation and stenosis. Arterial dissection, aneurysms, and ectasia are less common. The mid portion of the artery is most often affected, with sparing of the origin. This is in contrast to atherosclerotic disease, which often involves the vessel origin. FMD most commonly affects women ages 30–50, but can been seen in a wide range of ages.[23,24] Diagnosis can be made based on typical imaging appearance and distribution.

MRA has been shown to have high specificity for differentiating renal artery stenosis from FMD (92%), compared to CTA with a specificity of 84% but relatively low sensitivity (62% and 64%, respectively).[25] In a study of 100 FMD patients, imaging of the pelvis and lower extremities revealed that 62% had findings of FMD in the lower extremity arteries (including common iliac, external iliac, internal iliac, common femoral, and tibioperoneal trunk), most commonly the external iliac (54/62 patients) and common iliac arteries (12/62 patients).[26] In the same study, all patients with findings of FMD in the iliac arteries also had changes of FMD in the renal or carotid artery distributions. This suggests that incidentally found FMD in the iliac system should prompt evaluation of other vascular territories. The same study reported that symptoms from FMD of the iliac arteries are uncommon and rarely require intervention.

Findings of FMD can be subtle, and therefore a high-quality, high spatial resolution arterial phase CE-MRA is essential. Fig. 5.6 shows two examples, the first of a patient with the classic beaded appearance in the external iliac artery (Fig. 5.6A), and the other of a patient with very subtle irregularity in the left external iliac artery (Fig. 5.6B). When evaluating MRA findings, it is important to review the source images and note that multiplanar reformatted (MPR) images and maximum intensity projection (MIP) images may both accentuate and obscure fine detail.[27,28] The field of view should include the iliac and renal arteries to evaluate multiple vascular distributions. Although additional imaging sequences are not necessary, T2W and/or pre/post-T1W images could be included for evaluation of incidental findings.

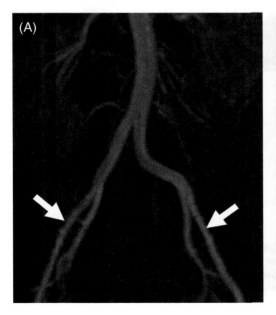
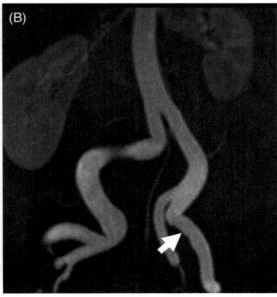

FIG. 5.6 **Fibromuscular dysplasia.** Coronal MIP image (A) showing classic beaded appearance in the bilateral external iliac arteries (arrows) of a 44-year-old female. Coronal MIP image (B) from a different patient showing a more subtle irregularity of the left external iliac artery (arrowhead) of a 55-year-old female.

5.5.3 Iliac vein compression (May–Thurner syndrome)

May–Thurner (MT) configuration is defined as extrinsic compression of iliocaval venous anatomy between an artery and bony structure. Most commonly, this presents as narrowing of the left common iliac vein by extrinsic compression between the right common iliac artery and the fifth lumbar vertebral body. There are no standardized imaging criteria for diagnosis, and hence a known tendency to overdiagnose compression by CT venography in a dehydrated patient.[29] Incidence of significant compression (greater than 50% narrowing) has been reported in as high as a third of the population, but most individuals with MT configuration are asymptomatic and require no treatment.[30,31] In symptomatic patients, left iliac vein thrombus is a common presentation. Other symptoms may include venous claudication, leg swelling, pain, and/or sequela of venous insufficiency (e.g., skin discoloration or ulceration). Hemodynamically significant narrowing can be treated with endovascular stenting.[32-34]

MRI/MRA has been shown to have a high sensitivity (>95%) for detecting iliac vein compression. MR imaging protocols should include high spatial resolution CE-MRA with both arterial and venous phases for vascular structural evaluation (Table 5.1). Degree of stenosis, presence of thrombus, venous collaterals, and anatomic variants should be evaluated. Additionally, axial T2W and T1W images should be included to aid in ruling out other causes of extrinsic compression such as pelvic mass, abscess, hematoma, retroperitoneal fibrosis, osteophytes, or aortoiliac aneurysm. Dynamic imaging has been described[35] but as symptoms rather than quantitative results usually drive treatment decisions for this configuration, the addition of this protocol would be clinically inconsequential.

CE-MRA will show the structural narrowing of the left common iliac vein. In Fig. 5.7, multiplanar reformatted axial images from a data set 4 mm and 2 mm thick illustrate how a high spatial resolution MRA will better depict narrowing of the iliac vein. Cine bSSFP oblique images may be useful to evaluate for flow turbulence at the level of the iliac vein narrowing (e.g., Fig. 5.8), which would suggest that the narrowing is significant. Significant narrowing is also suggested by the presence of venous collaterals (Fig. 5.8).

Evaluation for thromboembolic disease is important both in the setting of iliac vein compression while imaging for other indications, where a thrombus may present as an incidental finding. On CE-MRA, thrombus appears as a

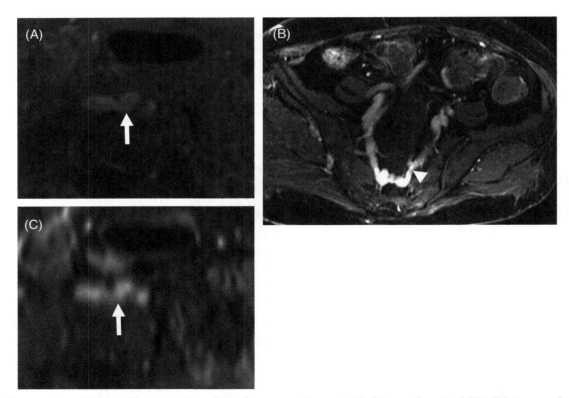

FIG. 5.7 **Compression of the left iliac vein with collateral venous pathway.** Axial oblique reformatted CE-MRA images of a 63-year-old female presenting with lower extremity edema. CE-MRA source slice thickness was 2 mm (A) and 4 mm (B). Notice better depiction of the narrowing of the left iliac vein (arrow) with small slice thickness. Axial oblique MIP postcontrast fat saturated T1W image (C) showing a collateral venous pathway in the posterior pelvis draining the left lower extremity through branches to the right internal iliac vein indicating a significant left common iliac vein narrowing.

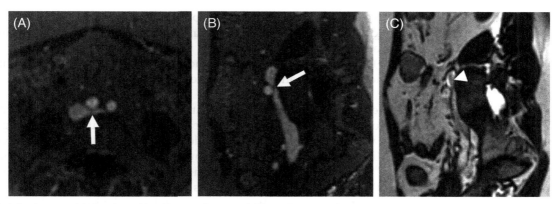

FIG. 5.8 Axial reformatted (A) and double oblique reformatted (B) MRA images showing narrowing of the left common iliac vein by the right common iliac artery (arrows) in a 61-year-old female presenting with deep vein thrombosis. The double oblique image is oriented along the axis of the left common iliac vein. Double oblique cine bSSFP image (C) showing flow acceleration beyond the narrowing (arrowhead).

hypointense filling defect within a vessel (Fig. 5.9A and C). Thrombus can also be seen on noncontrast images. For example, on noncontrast bSSFP, acute thrombus appears as a solid filling defect with uniform signal which will be seen in adjacent slices (Fig. 5.9B and D). Expansion of the vessel and surrounding edema are also features of acute thrombus. Postthrombotic change (i.e., chronic thrombus) will typically manifest as eccentric wall thickening or narrowing/occlusion of a vein.

5.5.4 Pelvic venous congestion from pelvic venous insufficiency

Pelvic venous congestion syndrome (PVCS) is defined as chronic pelvic pain caused by dilated pelvic varices. Specifically, pelvic venous insufficiency (PVI) is pelvic venous congestion in the setting of incompetent gonadal vein valves.[36] Valvular incompetence may be primary or be caused by structural phenomena such as chronically occluded inferior vena cava (IVC), congenital absence of the IVC, or arteriovenous malformations. Patients are typically premenopausal and multiparous females. Pain is often described as dull pelvic pain, pressure, and heaviness that is worse with prolonged standing and relieved in the supine position. Symptoms may also be aggravated by pregnancy. Although the presence of dilated pelvic veins is common in the general population, with a reported incidence of up to 10%, only a portion of these will develop symptomatic PVI.[37,38] Therefore, it is important to interpret imaging findings in the context of clinical symptoms.

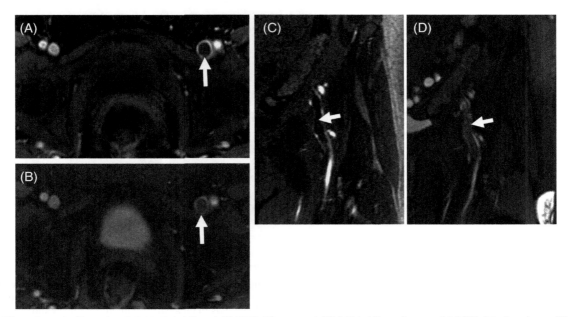

FIG. 5.9 **Thromboembolism.** Axial CE LAVA (A), axial bSSFP (B), coronal CE-MRA (C), and coronal bSSFP (D) showing a filling defect in the external iliac and common femoral veins.

Venous drainage of the pelvis is complex and interconnected but typically drain via the internal iliac veins and gonadal veins. The left gonadal vein typically drains to the left renal vein and the right gonadal vein drains directly to the IVC. Rarely seen is an anatomic variant where the right gonadal vein drains directly to the right renal vein. Other anatomic variants that may affect treatment approach and/or success include duplicated IVC, internal iliac veins draining to the contralateral common iliac vein, and reverse angle renal veins with variant left gonadal vein drainage pathways.[39]

MRI is ideally suited for noninvasive evaluation of PVI with its ability to obtain dynamic vascular imaging and exquisite soft tissue contrast. Protocols should be optimized for both vascular and soft tissue findings. High dynamic TR-MRA is essential for detecting gonadal vein reflux, as it shows caudal flow from the renal vein to the pelvis typically via a dilated gonadal vein (Fig. 5.8). TR-MRA is widely available across multiple vendors and has been shown to have high specificity, sensitivity, and accuracy.[40-42] Detection of retrograde gonadal vein flow has also been shown with 2D phase contrast MRI with a sensitivity of 100%,[43] however this technique is not routinely used in our protocol.

At our institution, TR-MRA is performed with coverage from the upper poles of the kidneys through the upper thigh in a coronal plane. Dynamic TR-MRA imaging is started 8 seconds following contrast injection with a time resolution of 3–5 seconds over 2 minutes. TR-MRA is performed during quiet free breathing. Additionally, high-resolution, small field of view T2-weighted images in three planes as well as pre- and postcontrast T1-weighted images in two planes are acquired to evaluate for alternative causes of chronic pelvic pain (e.g., endometriosis, inflammatory bowel disease, urinary tract causes and orthopedic conditions). Polycystic ovary configuration can also be evaluated on T2-weighted images and has been shown to be associated with PVCS.[44,45] A complete protocol for PVCS evaluation is given in Table 5.2.

There are no standardized diagnostic imaging criteria for the diagnosis of PVCS/PVI. At our institution, the presence of retrograde flow in one or both gonadal veins is considered the most important diagnostic findings for PVI, and is best evaluated with TR-MRA (Fig. 5.10A–D). Parauterine veins are dilated tubular structures with

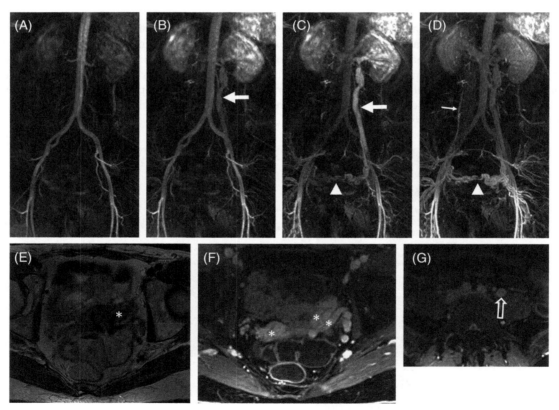

FIG. 5.10 **Pelvic venous congestion.** Sequential MIP images from TR-MRA of a 55-year-old female presenting with chronic pelvic pain showing retrograde flow in the left renal vein (arrow), arcuate uterine vein (arrowhead) and later filling of the right renal vein (small arrow). Pelvic venous congestion. Dilated parauterine varices (asterisks) are seen as flow voids in on axial T2 without fat sat (E) and as contract-filled, serpiginous structures on axial postcontrast T1 fat saturated (F) images. A more superior axial postcontrast T1 fat saturated slice (G) shows a contrast-filled, dilated left gonadal vein (open arrow).

variable but often dark T2W signal (flow voids) and postcontrast enhancement on T1W images (Fig. 5.10E and F). The size of the gonadal veins is well evaluated on MR venogram images or postcontrast axial 3D T1W images (Fig. 5.10G). At conventional venography, a diameter of less than 5 mm is considered normal and greater than 8 mm is considered abnormal for the gonadal vein.[46,47] The most specific finding of PVC/PVI by ultrasound is the presence of a dilated vein crossing midline in the uterine body which is also seen on MRA/TR-MRA (Fig. 5.10D).[45] Concurrent vulvar and thigh varices are also common.

5.5.5 Vascular malformations

Vascular malformations are congenital anomalies which encompass a variety of vascular lesions. They are classified by the type of vessel involved. The 2018 update from the ISSVA Classification System for Vascular Anomalies categorizes simple vascular malformations into either venous, capillary, lymphatic, or arteriovenous malformations with combined malformations expressing mixed features.[48,49] Vascular malformations may be associated with other anomalies (i.e., those with a genetic origin), such as those associated with Kippel–Trelauny and CLOVES syndromes. Noninvasive imaging with MRI is helpful in determining the type and extent of the lesion for treatment planning.

Venous malformations are the most common type of vascular malformations. They are thin walled, dilated vascular channels that are typically T2 hyperintense, best seen on fat sat T2W images. Venous malformations may be focal (Fig. 5.11) or more diffuse, infiltrating skin, bones, joints, muscles, and/or viscera (Fig. 5.12). Variable signal intensity is seen on T1W imaging due to thrombosis, hemorrhage or prior treatments. Phleboliths are common but difficult to see on MR. If seen on MRI, phleboliths are low signal intensity on all imaging sequences. TR-MRA will show gradual filling on postcontrast images, which is sometimes best seen on very delayed postcontrast images (5-minute delay). Contrast rise time of 90 seconds (time from onset of enhancement to peak enhancement) has been shown to differentiate from arteriovenous malformations.[50]

Capillary and lymphatic malformations are most frequently seen in the head and neck. Capillary malformations are typically diagnosed clinically and do not require MR evaluation. Lymphatic malformations may be macrocystic or microcystic. For the purpose of pelvic evaluation, combined vascular malformations such as capillary-venous or

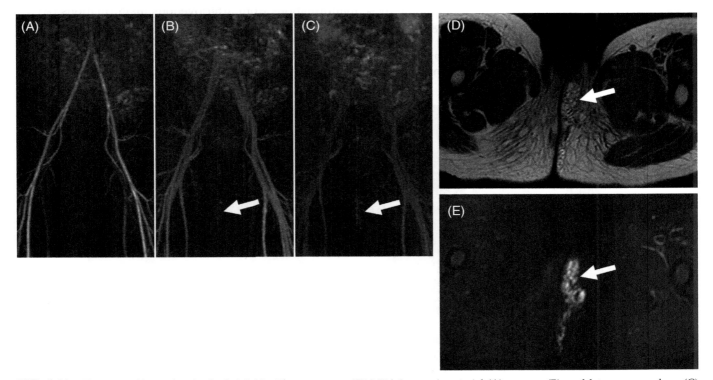

FIG. 5.11 **Venous malformation in the left labia.** Three coronary TR-MRA images in arterial (A), venous (B), and later venous phase (C) showing very minimal enhancement of a venous malformation in the left labia (arrow) of a 4-year-old female. Corresponding T2W nonfat sat (D) and fat sat (E) images showing the increased conspicuity of the venous malformation on T2W fat saturated images.

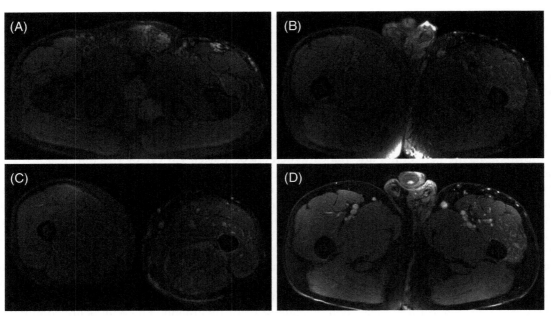

FIG. 5.12   **Venous malformation.** Extensive venous malformation shown as T2-weighted hyperintense serpiginous or mass-like structures in the left ischiorectal fossa (A), left scrotum (B), and infiltrating soft tissue and muscle in the left thigh (C) in a 43-year-old male patient. The venous malformation demonstrates enhancement on delayed postcontrast images (D).

venolymphatic malformations may also be seen. That being said, treatment options are similar for these "low flow" malformations and it may not clinically important to differentiate between them. We obtain a T1W series through the area of interest 20 minutes postcontrast to aid in differentiating venolymphatic and pure lymphatic malformations. Pure lymphatic malformations will show no enhancement on any postcontrast phases, while venolymphatic malformations may show some enhancement on delayed images.

Conversely, it is very important to differentiate these malformations from arteriovenous malformations (AVM) and arteriovenous fistulas (AVF) due to significant differences in treatment options.[51] In comparison to venous malformations, AVMs are typically seen as a serpiginous tangle of blood vessels with prominent flow voids on T2W images. These flow voids are much more apparent on nonfat sat T2W images. On TR-MRA, AVMs will rapidly fill a tangle or nidus of vessels that usually connects to an early filling, large draining vein (Fig. 5.13). An AVF will have

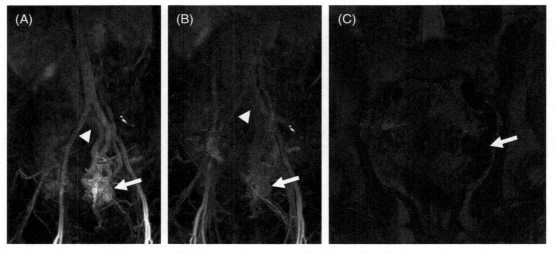

FIG. 5.13   **Pelvic arteriovenous malformation.** 3D oblique MIPs from TR-MRA (A and B) of a 38-year-old female with a tangle of vessels in the left hemipelvis (arrow) with rapid filling and near immediate filling of the IVC via a large internal iliac vein (arrowhead). Coronal T2W image (C) showing dilated vessels as signal voids in the left hemipelvis (arrow).

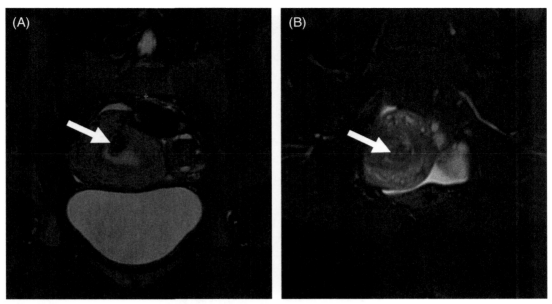

FIG. 5.14 **Acquired uterine arteriovenous malformation versus retained products of conception.** Tangle of vessels seen as serpiginous flow voids protruding into the endometrial canal (A) in a 28-year-old female with a history of second trimester pregnancy loss presenting with high volume vaginal bleeding. Heterogeneous T2W mass protruding into the endometrial canal (B) in a 31-year-old female presenting with vaginal bleeding after first trimester pregnancy loss.

a similar appearance, but will lack a tangle of intervening vessels. Reports describing AVMs should include a description of extent, involvement, arterial supply, and venous drainage.

Acquired uterine AVMs can present as uterine bleeding that can be massive and life threatening. By definition, these AVMs are acquired rather than congenital and occur after trauma, surgical intervention, or in the setting of a preexisting pathologic uterine process (e.g., infection, trophoblastic disease, or malignancy).[52] An acquired uterine AVM is characterized by a single communication between the branches of the uterine artery and the myometrial plexus. Acquired uterine AVMs must be differentiated from retained products of conception where the latter involves an enhancing soft tissue mass in the endometrial canal (Fig. 5.14).[53]

5.6 Retroperitoneal fibrosis

Retroperitoneal fibrosis is a condition characterized by abnormal soft tissue in the retroperitoneum, typically encasing the infrarenal aorta, common iliac arteries, IVC, and often the ureters. Two thirds of cases are idopathic whereas the remainder are attributed to secondary factors (e.g., drug use, malignancies, and infection). Patients present in their 40s–60s with some studies showing a male predominance. Lower back, flank, or abdominal pain are the most common presenting symptoms.

CT and MR demonstrate equal accuracy for diagnosis of retroperitoneal fibrosis.[54] The abnormal soft tissue may encircle the aorta, displacing it anteriorly from the spine. The ureters may be displaced medially with associated hydronephrosis of the affected side, which is sometimes bilateral. The soft tissue mass is usually dark on T1W with progressive enhancement, most obvious on delayed (5 minutes) images. T2-weighted signal intensity is variable with mild hyperintensity in the presence of active inflammation or mild T2-weighted hypointensity in the absence of active inflammation.

MR protocols should include CE-MRA, T2-weighted, pre/post-T1-weighted images. Diffusion images and delayed postcontrast T1-weighted images should also be considered. Reports should include description of the involved structures, any evidence of vascular narrowing, collateral pathways, and ureteral involvement. Fig. 5.15 shows a patient with retroperitoneal fibrosis encircling the infrarenal aorta and proximal common iliac arteries.

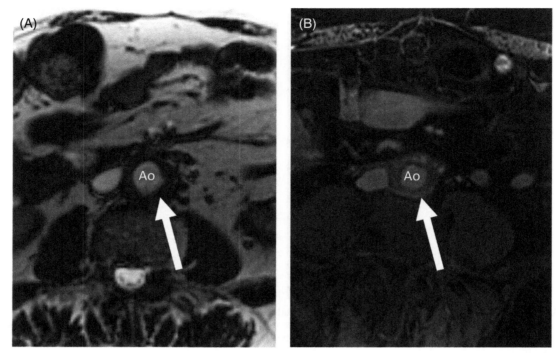

FIG. 5.15   Retroperitoneal fibrosis. A 73-year-old male presenting with right flank pain. Axial T2W (A) and axial postcontrast T1W (B) images show circumferential T2-weighted hypointense and mildly enhancing soft tissue thickening (arrow) surrounding the infrarenal aorta (Ao). This soft tissue extended inferiorly, surrounding the bilateral common iliac arteries, and also involved the right ureter (not shown).

TABLE 5.4   Reporting template for MRI preuterine artery embolization for fibroid.

Items to report	
Uterus	Size, volume
Fibroid	Total number size, volume, location, enhancement, stalk diameter (if applicable)—for each fibroid
Uterine arteries	Number, origin, and size
Ovarian arteries	Number, origin, and size
Suggested projection angle	For each uterine artery
Common femoral arteries	Patency, size
Coexistence of adenomyosis	Focal or diffuse
Other pelvic findings	Adnexal masses, endometriosis, etc.

5.6.1 Fibroid (uterine artery embolization)

Uterine artery embolization is a common minimally invasive treatment for uterine fibroids.[55] MRI/MRA has been described for preprocedural planning and fibroid characterization. This imaging technique can identify vascular anatomic variants, enlarged ovarian arteries, extrauterine collateral supply of fibroids, and important concurrent pelvic pathologies.[56,57]

The anatomy of the iliac, uterine, and ovarian arteries should be included in every preprocedural report. A table of suggested report content for pre-UAE is summarized in Table 5.4. Procedural vascular access is via the common femoral artery, so variants and patency of the bilateral common femoral arteries should also be included.

Recognition of normal vascular uterine artery variants is important for planning superselective catheterization and avoiding nontarget embolization. The uterine artery has a variable origin but most often arises from the anterior division of the internal iliac artery. Gomez-Jorge et al. describe a classification system for the uterine artery origin as arising as the first branch of the inferior gluteal artery (type 1), as the second or third branch of the inferior gluteal artery (type II), as a trifurcation with the inferior and superior gluteal arteries (type III), or as a direct offshoot from the internal iliac artery.[58] Unilateral congenital absence of the uterine artery is much more frequent than bilateral congenital absence.[59,60] When congenitally absent, the uterine artery is replaced by the ipsilateral ovarian artery or small arterial pelvic branches.

The ovarian arteries are not always seen on MRA due to small size (usually less than 1 mm in diameter), although they typically arise from the abdominal aorta typically a few centimeters inferior to the renal arteries.[61] That being said, the presence of enlarged ovarian arteries can be helpful in predicting the need for adjunct ovarian artery embolization for complete fibroid infarction.[62]

A high spatial resolution, arterial phase MRA is the most useful for anatomic evaluation of small arteries. There has also been discussion of using 4D flow for uterine artery evaluation.[63]

In addition to vascular findings, MRI is ideal for characterization of uterine fibroids. Reports should include the size, number, volume, location, and enhancement of each fibroid. Any atypical features of the uterine fibroids, such as T2W hyperintensity, T1-weighted hyperintensity, or atypical location should also be mentioned.[64] Other uterine and ovarian findings may be incidental, but are typically important as well.[57] The example in Fig. 5.16 shows two T2W hypointense fibroids arising from the uterus on T2-weighted imaging. In this case, the left ovarian vein is dilated with a tortuous "corkscrew" configuration, contributing to fibroid arterial supply and indicative of parasitization of the left ovarian artery.

5.7 Conclusion

MRI/MRA is well-suited for the evaluation of pelvic vascular pathologies. This imaging modality provides excellent soft tissue contrast, multiple contrast mechanisms, and high time-resolution dynamic imaging. Tailored protocols for clinical indications are essential to keep exam times tolerable for patients. It is also important to be able to recognize incidental vascular findings on nonvascular exams, as they may be either clinically significant and/or reveal the dominant pathology behind a patient's presenting symptom(s). Important pearls and pitfalls of pelvic vascular imaging are listed in Table 5.5.

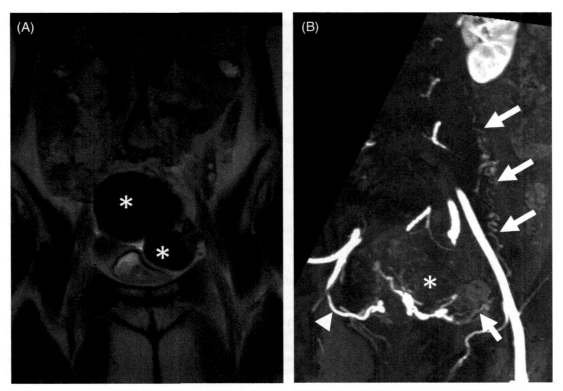

FIG. 5.16   Preprocedural uterine artery embolization MRI/MRA. Coronal T2W (A) and multiplanar reformatted MIP MRA (B) images of a 33-year-old female for preprocedural evaluation for uterine artery embolization. Two uterine fibroids (asterisks) with a prominent, corkscrew left ovarian artery (arrows) supplying the more inferior exophytic fibroid. The anterior divisions of the bilateral internal iliac artery also supply both fibroids, shown on the right (arrow head).

TABLE 5.5   Pelvic vascular imaging: pearls and pitfalls.

Multiple bolus timing methods may be used for contrast bolus MRA including fixed delay, test bolus, or bolus tracking.

An aneurysm is a focal dilatation of an artery which is increased more than 50% compared to the normal diameter of the artery.

Measuring on a MIP has been shown to cause underestimation of aneurysm size.

The mid portion of the artery is most often affected by fibromuscular dysplasia, with sparing of the origin, in contrast to atherosclerotic disease, which often involves the vessel origin.

There are no standardized imaging criteria for diagnosis of May–Thurner configuration, and there a known tendency to overdiagnose compression by CT venography in a dehydrated patient.

Pelvic venous insufficiency (PVI) is pelvic venous congestion in the setting of incompetent gonadal vein valves.

Although the presence of dilated pelvic veins is common in the general population, only a portion of these will develop symptomatic PVI.

The most specific finding of PVC/PVI by ultrasound is the presence of a dilated vein crossing midline in the uterine body which is also seen by MRA.

It is very important to differentiate venous malformations, lymphatic malformations, arteriovenous malformations, and arteriovenous fistulas due to significant differences in treatment options.

Presence of one or bilaterally enlarged ovarian arteries can be helpful in predicting the need for adjunct ovarian artery embolization for complete fibroid infarction.

References

1. Kanal E. Gadolinium based contrast agents (GBCA): safety overview after 3 decades of clinical experience. *Magn Reson Imaging*. 2016;34(10):1341–1345.
2. Le Mignon MM, Chambon C, Warrington S, Davies R, Bonnemain B. Gd-DOTA. Pharmacokinetics and tolerability after intravenous injection into healthy volunteers. *Invest Radiol*. 1990;25(8):933–937.
3. Radiology ACo. *ACR Manual on Contrast Media*; 2021.
4. McDonald JS, McDonald RJ. MR imaging safety considerations of gadolinium-based contrast agents: gadolinium retention and nephrogenic systemic fibrosis. *Magn Reson Imaging Clin N Am*. 2020;28(4):497–507.
5. Bashir MR, Bhatti L, Marin D, Nelson RC. Emerging applications for ferumoxytol as a contrast agent in MRI. *J Magn Reson Imaging*. 2015;41(4):884–898.
6. Vasanawala SS, Nguyen KL, Hope MD, et al. Safety and technique of ferumoxytol administration for MRI. *Magn Reson Med*. 2016;75(5):2107–2111.
7. Administration UFaD. Highlight of Prescribing Information: Fereheme (Ferumoxytol Injection). 2018.
8. Nguyen KL, Yoshida T, Kathuria-Prakash N, et al. Multicenter safety and practice for off-label diagnostic use of ferumoxytol in MRI. *Radiology*. 2019;293(3):554–564.
9. Storey P, Lim RP, Chandarana H, et al. MRI assessment of hepatic iron clearance rates after USPIO administration in healthy adults. *Invest Radiol*. 2012;47(12):717–724.
10. Zhu A, Reeder SB, Johnson KM, et al. Quantitative ferumoxytol-enhanced MRI in pregnancy: a feasibility study in the nonhuman primate. *Magn Reson Imaging*. 2020;65:100–108.
11. Stoumpos S, Hennessy M, Vesey AT, et al. Ferumoxytol magnetic resonance angiography: a dose-finding study in patients with chronic kidney disease. *Eur Radiol*. 2019;29(7):3543–3552.
12. Adams LC, Ralla B, Engel G, et al. Assessing venous thrombus in renal cell carcinoma: preliminary results for unenhanced 3D-SSFP MRI. *Clin Radiol*. 2018;73(8) 757 e759-757 e719.
13. Lindquist CM, Karlicki F, Lawrence P, Strzelczyk J, Pawlyshyn N, Kirkpatrick ID. Utility of balanced steady-state free precession MR venography in the diagnosis of lower extremity deep venous thrombosis. *AJR Am J Roentgenol*. 2010;194(5):1357–1364.
14. Edelman RR, Koktzoglou I. Noncontrast MR angiography: an update. *J Magn Reson Imaging*. 2019;49(2):355–373.
15. Khosa F, Krinsky G, Macari M, Yucel EK, Berland LL. Managing incidental findings on abdominal and pelvic CT and MRI, Part 2: white paper of the ACR Incidental Findings Committee II on vascular findings. *J Am Coll Radiol*. 2013;10(10):789–794.
16. Litmanovich D, Bankier AA, Cantin L, Raptopoulos V, Boiselle PM. CT and MRI in diseases of the aorta. *AJR Am J Roentgenol*. 2009;193(4):928–940.
17. Hirsch AT, Haskal ZJ, Hertzer NR, et al. ACC/AHA 2005 practice guidelines for the management of patients with peripheral arterial disease (lower extremity, renal, mesenteric, and abdominal aortic): a collaborative report from the American Association for Vascular Surgery/Society for Vascular Surgery, Society for Cardiovascular Angiography and Interventions, Society for Vascular Medicine and Biology, Society of Interventional Radiology, and the ACC/AHA Task Force on Practice Guidelines (Writing Committee to Develop Guidelines for the Management of Patients with Peripheral Arterial Disease): endorsed by the American Association of Cardiovascular and Pulmonary Rehabilitation; National Heart, Lung, and Blood Institute; Society for Vascular Nursing; Transatlantic Inter-Society Consensus; and Vascular Disease Foundation. *Circulation*. 2006;113(11):e463–e654.
18. Johnston KW, Rutherford RB, Tilson MD, Shah DM, Hollier L, Stanley JC Suggested standards for reporting on arterial aneurysms. Subcommittee on Reporting Standards for Arterial Aneurysms, Ad Hoc Committee on Reporting Standards, Society for Vascular Surgery and North American Chapter, International Society for Cardiovascular Surgery. J Vasc Surg.1991;13(3):452-458.
19. DeMartino RR, Huang Y, Mandrekar J, et al. External validation of a 5-year survival prediction model after elective abdominal aortic aneurysm repair. *J Vasc Surg*. 2018;67(1):151–156 e153.

20. Santilli SM, Wernsing SE, Lee ES. Expansion rates and outcomes for iliac artery aneurysms. *J Vasc Surg*. 2000;31(1 Pt 1):114–121.
21. Sakamoto I, Sueyoshi E, Uetani M. MR imaging of the aorta. *Radiol Clin North Am*. 2007;45(3):485–497 viii.
22. Benson DG, Schiebler ML, Repplinger MD, et al. Contrast-enhanced pulmonary MRA for the primary diagnosis of pulmonary embolism: current state of the art and future directions. *Br J Radiol*. 2017;90(1074):20160901.
23. Plouin PF, Perdu J, La Batide-Alanore A, Boutouyrie P, Gimenez-Roqueplo AP, Jeunemaitre X. Fibromuscular dysplasia. *Orphanet J Rare Dis*. 2007;2:28.
24. Shivapour DM, Erwin P, Kim E. Epidemiology of fibromuscular dysplasia: a review of the literature. *Vasc Med*. 2016;21(4):376–381.
25. Vasbinder GB, Nelemans PJ, Kessels AG, et al. Accuracy of computed tomographic angiography and magnetic resonance angiography for diagnosing renal artery stenosis. *Ann Intern Med*. 2004;141(9):674–682 discussion 682.
26. Brinza E, Grabinski V, Durga S, et al. Lower extremity fibromuscular dysplasia: clinical manifestations, diagnostic testing, and approach to management. *Angiology*. 2017;68(8):722–727.
27. Fishman EK, Ney DR, Heath DG, Corl FM, Horton KM, Johnson PT. Volume rendering versus maximum intensity projection in CT angiography: what works best, when, and why. *Radiographics*. 2006;26(3):905–922.
28. Mallouhi A, Schocke M, Judmaier W, et al. 3D MR angiography of renal arteries: comparison of volume rendering and maximum intensity projection algorithms. *Radiology*. 2002;223(2):509–516.
29. Ibrahim W, Al Safran Z, Hasan H, Zeid WA. Endovascular management of May-Thurner syndrome. *Ann Vasc Dis*. 2012;5(2):217–221.
30. Kibbe MR, Ujiki M, Goodwin AL, Eskandari M, Yao J, Matsumura J. Iliac vein compression in an asymptomatic patient population. *J Vasc Surg*. 2004;39(5):937–943.
31. Raju S, Neglen P. High prevalence of nonthrombotic iliac vein lesions in chronic venous disease: a permissive role in pathogenicity. *J Vasc Surg*. 2006;44(1):136–143 discussion 144.
32. Knuttinen MG, Naidu S, Oklu R, et al. May-Thurner: diagnosis and endovascular management. *Cardiovasc Diagn Ther*. 2017;7(Suppl 3):S159–S164.
33. Meissner MH, Gloviczki P, Comerota AJ, et al. Early thrombus removal strategies for acute deep venous thrombosis: clinical practice guidelines of the Society for Vascular Surgery and the American Venous Forum. *J Vasc Surg*. 2012;55(5):1449–1462.
34. Vedantham S, Millward SF, Cardella JF, et al. Society of Interventional Radiology position statement: treatment of acute iliofemoral deep vein thrombosis with use of adjunctive catheter-directed intrathrombus thrombolysis. *J Vasc Interv Radiol*. 2006;17(4):613–616.
35. Duran C, Abboud L, Karmonik C, Shah D, Lumsden AB, Bismuth J. The utility of dynamic magnetic resonance venography in the setting of pelvic venous pathology. *J Vasc Surg Venous Lymphat Disord*. 2013;1(1):78–81 e71.
36. Black CM, Thorpe K, Venrbux A, et al. Research reporting standards for endovascular treatment of pelvic venous insufficiency. *J Vasc Interv Radiol*. 2010;21(6):796–803.
37. Belenky A, Bartal G, Atar E, Cohen M, Bachar GN. Ovarian varices in healthy female kidney donors: incidence, morbidity, and clinical outcome. *AJR Am J Roentgenol*. 2002;179(3):625–627.
38. Mathias SD, Kuppermann M, Liberman RF, Lipschutz RC, Steege JF. Chronic pelvic pain: prevalence, health-related quality of life, and economic correlates. *Obstet Gynecol*. 1996;87(3):321–327.
39. Beckett D, Dos Santos SJ, Dabbs EB, Shiangoli I, Price BA, Whiteley MS. Anatomical abnormalities of the pelvic venous system and their implications for endovascular management of pelvic venous reflux. *Phlebology*. 2018;33(8):567–574. doi:10.1177/0268355517735727. PMID: 29059022.
40. Kim CY, Miller Jr MJ, Merkle EM. Time-resolved MR angiography as a useful sequence for assessment of ovarian vein reflux. *AJR Am J Roentgenol*. 2009;193(5):W458–W463.
41. Pandey T, Shaikh R, Viswamitra S, Jambhekar K. Use of time resolved magnetic resonance imaging in the diagnosis of pelvic congestion syndrome. *J Magn Reson Imaging*. 2010;32(3):700–704.
42. Yang DM, Kim HC, Nam DH, Jahng GH, Huh CY, Lim JW. Time-resolved MR angiography for detecting and grading ovarian venous reflux: comparison with conventional venography. *Br J Radiol*. 2012;85(1014):e117–e122.
43. Meneses LQ, Uribe S, Tejos C, Andia ME, Fava M, Irarrazaval P. Using magnetic resonance phase-contrast velocity mapping for diagnosing pelvic congestion syndrome. *Phlebology*. 2011;26(4):157–161.
44. Durham JD, Machan L. Pelvic congestion syndrome. *Semin Intervent Radiol*. 2013;30(4):372–380.
45. Park SJ, Lim JW, Ko YT, et al. Diagnosis of pelvic congestion syndrome using transabdominal and transvaginal sonography. *AJR Am J Roentgenol*. 2004;182(3):683–688.
46. Dos Santos SJ, Holdstock JM, Harrison CC, Lopez AJ, Whiteley MS. Ovarian vein diameter cannot be used as an indicator of ovarian venous reflux. *Eur J Vasc Endovasc Surg*. 2015;49(1):90–94.
47. Kennedy A, Hemingway A. Radiology of ovarian varices. *Br J Hosp Med*. 1990;44(1):38–43.
48. Anomalies ISftSoV. *ISSVA Classification of Vascular Anomalies*; 2018.
49. Zhang B, Ma L. Updated classification and therapy of vascular malformations in pediatric patients. *Pediatr Investig*. 2018;2(2):119–123.
50. Ohgiya Y, Hashimoto T, Gokan T, et al. Dynamic MRI for distinguishing high-flow from low-flow peripheral vascular malformations. *AJR Am J Roentgenol*. 2005;185(5):1131–1137.
51. Flors L, Leiva-Salinas C, Maged IM, et al. MR imaging of soft-tissue vascular malformations: diagnosis, classification, and therapy follow-up. *Radiographics*. 2011;31(5):1321–1340 discussion 1340-1321.
52. Yoon DJ, Jones M, Taani JA, Buhimschi C, Dowell JD. A systematic review of acquired uterine arteriovenous malformations: pathophysiology, diagnosis, and transcatheter treatment. *AJP Rep*. 2016;6(1):e6–e14.
53. Sellmyer MA, Desser TS, Maturen KE, Jeffrey Jr RB, Kamaya A. Physiologic, histologic, and imaging features of retained products of conception. *Radiographics*. 2013;33(3):781–796.
54. Arrive L, Hricak H, Tavares NJ, Miller TR. Malignant versus nonmalignant retroperitoneal fibrosis: differentiation with MR imaging. *Radiology*. 1989;172(1):139–143.
55. Keung JJ, Spies JB, Caridi TM. Uterine artery embolization: a review of current concepts. *Best Pract Res Clin Obstet Gynaecol*. 2018;46:66–73.

56. Maciel C, Tang YZ, Sahdev A, Madureira AM, Vilares Morgado P. Preprocedural MRI and MRA in planning fibroid embolization. *Diagn Interv Radiol*. 2017;23(2):163–171.

57. Williams PL, Coote JM, Watkinson AF. Pre-uterine artery embolization MRI: beyond fibroids. *Cardiovasc Intervent Radiol*. 2011;34(6):1143–1150.

58. Gomez-Jorge J, Keyoung A, Levy EB, Spies JB. Uterine artery anatomy relevant to uterine leiomyomata embolization. *Cardiovasc Intervent Radiol*. 2003;26(6):522–527.

59. Bratby MJ, Hussain FF, Walker WJ. Outcomes after unilateral uterine artery embolization: a retrospective review. *Cardiovasc Intervent Radiol*. 2008;31(2):254–259.

60. McLucas B, Reed RA, Goodwin S, et al. Outcomes following unilateral uterine artery embolisation. *Br J Radiol*. 2002;75(890):122–126.

61. Pelage JP, Cazejust J, Pluot E, et al. Uterine fibroid vascularization and clinical relevance to uterine fibroid embolization. *Radiographics*. 2005;25(Suppl 1):S99–117.

62. Lee MS, Kim MD, Lee M, et al. Contrast-enhanced MR angiography of uterine arteries for the prediction of ovarian artery embolization in 349 patients. *J Vasc Interv Radiol*. 2012;23(9):1174–1179.

63. Malone CD, Banerjee A, Alley MT, Vasanawala SS, Roberts AC, Hsiao A. Pelvic blood flow predicts fibroid volume and embolic required for uterine fibroid embolization: a pilot study with 4D flow mr angiography. *AJR Am J Roentgenol*. 2018;210(1):189–200.

64. Bolan C, Caserta MP. MR imaging of atypical fibroids. *Abdom Radiol (NY)*. 2016;41(12):2332–2349.

6

MRI of the prostate: technique, anatomy, and noncancerous disease processes

Clifford Shin[a], Karthik Sundaram[b], Sandeep Arora[a]

[a]Department of Radiology and Biomedical Imaging, Yale University, New Haven, CT, United States
[b]Department of Radiology, University of Pennsylvania, Philadelphia, PA, United States

6.1 Anatomy of the prostate

The prostate is an organ composed of three glandular (peripheral, transition, and central) and one stromal regions (anterior fibromuscular).[1] The peripheral zone represents nearly 75% of normal prostate glandular tissue and is the site of the majority of prostatic carcinomas. It surrounds the central zone and displays hyperintensity on T2-weighted MR (T2w) images (Fig. 6.1A).[2] The peripheral zone increases in size from the base (near the urinary bladder) to the apex of the prostate gland. The transition zone comprises less than 5% of prostatic glandular tissue and is the primary site for benign prostatic hyperplasia (BPH) as well as the secondary site for prostatic carcinomas.[1] It surrounds the anterior and lateral parts of the proximal urethra and demonstrates hypointensity on T2w images (Fig. 6.1B).[2,3] The central zone constitutes approximately 25% of the prostatic glandular tissue and surrounds the ejaculatory ducts and is posterior to the transition zone.[1] As the central zone also demonstrates low T2 signal due to compact muscle fiber bundles, it was often previously combined with the transition zone and referred as the "central gland" although this terminology is now discouraged.[4] Based on its orientation to the ejaculatory ducts, symmetric appearance on either side of the verumontanum and homogenous T2 hypointensity, the central zone can be distinguished from the transition zone in about 81–84% of patients.[5] The central zone is also most easily identified at the prostatic base (Fig. 6.1C). In addition to being T2 hypointense, the central zone can be hypointense on ADC and may mimic prostate cancer.[5,6] Often, it is distinguished based on its symmetrical appearance and expected location. Unusually it can be asymmetrical on T2w images but normal central gland neither demonstrates early enhancement nor asymmetric increased signal intensity on high b-value DWI. The anterior fibromuscular stroma composes the anterior surface of the prostate and contains no glandular tissue with marked hypointensity on T2w images due to dense fibromuscular tissue (Fig. 6.1A). The prominence of the anterior fibromuscular stroma varies between people. It is less prominent in older men and low gland size. The distinctive feature of normal anterior fibromuscular stroma is its midline and symmetrical position as well as hypovascularity due to its fibrous nature. It can usually be differentiated from cancer using its symmetric low signal intensity (similar to that of levator ani muscles) on T2w, ADC, and high b-value DWI images along with the absence of early enhancement.[1,2] The prostatic pseudocapsule, also known as the "surgical capsule," is seen on T2w images as a thin, dark rim at the interface of the transition zone with the peripheral zone (Fig. 6.1A). It can mimic a small tumor that grows within the limits of the lateral peripheral area however a tumor will be more mass-like than linear. A thin, dark rim partially surrounding the entire prostate on T2w is often referred to as the "prostate capsule" (Fig. 6.1A). It is not a true capsule as it contains an outer band of concentric fibromuscular tissue that is inseparable from prostatic stroma. It is incomplete along the anterior and apical aspects of prostate. This landmark is important for extraprostatic extension of tumor. A path for extraprostatic tumor extension is the neurovascular bundles seen posterolateral to the prostate at the 5 o'clock and 7 o'clock positions in the axial plane.[7] Neurovascular bundles comprise of nerves that supply the corpora cavernosa which are intimately associated with arterial branches from the

Magnetic Resonance Imaging of The Pelvis.
DOI: https://doi.org/10.1016/B978-0-323-89854-6.00015-6

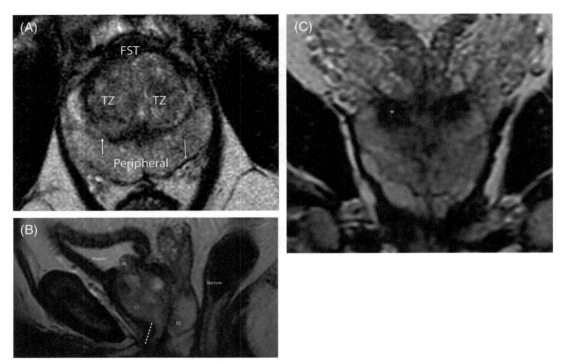

FIG. 6.1 (A) Axial, (B) Sagittal, and (C) Coronal T2w images showing normal anatomy structures annotated. White arrow in A is the pseudocapsule or surgical capsule, yellow arrow in A is the "capsule," dotted line in B is the membranous urethra, asterisk in C is the right central zone with left being visually symmetric. *FST*, fibromuscular stroma; *ML*, median lobe; *PZ*, peripheral zone; *SV*, seminal vesicles; *TZ*, transition zone.

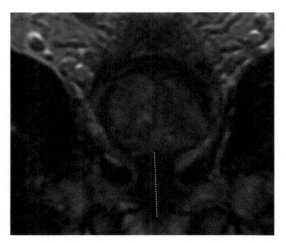

FIG. 6.2 **Coronal T2w image with annotation of the membranous urethra/external urethral sphincter which is T2 hypointense.** Length of the membranous urethra is important for predicting postprostatectomy incontinence. Every millimeter loss of membranous urethra correlates with higher incontinence.

inferior vesicle artery and accompanying veins.[4] Strong grasp of the zonal anatomy is important for interpreting MRI as different MRI sequences are used for different zones to characterize lesions.

The part of the urethra which traverses the prostate gland is termed the prostatic urethra.[8] The membranous segment of the urethra is located between the apex of the prostate and the bulb of the corpus spongiosum, extending through the urogenital diaphragm. The most proximal membranous urethra may actually be intraprostatic. The external urethral sphincter (EUS), which is composed of striated circular muscle fibers, surrounds the whole length of the membranous urethra.[9] The membranous urethra/ EUS appear T2 hypointense. The length of the membranous urethra which is usually measured on the coronal images is an important prognostic factor for postprostatectomy continence (Fig. 6.2). The periprostatic structures/spaces which are evaluated for prostate cancer local staging include: bladder, rectum, seminal vesicles, rectoprostatic angle, and prostate-seminal vesicle angle. The fascia between the prostate and rectum is known as the rectovesical septum or the Denonvillier's fascia. Its primary function is to form a barrier to the spread of disease between the perirectal and periprostatic spaces. This fascia is important for prostate and rectal surgeries with implications for negative margins, continence, and erectile function. During hydrogel injection for separation of rectum and prostate, prior to external beam radiotherapy with the purpose of reducing GI toxicity, the needle is placed between the anterior rectal wall and the fascia (Fig. 6.3A and B). If the needle traverses the fascia, there is risk of inadvertent injection into the periprostatic vessels. Injection in

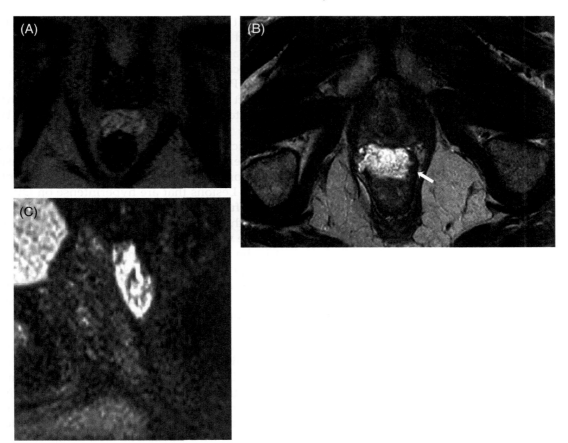

FIG. 6.3 (A) T2w axial image demonstrating correct preradiation injection of the Space-OAR gel between the rectum and prostate. (B) A T2w sagittal image with fat saturation in the same patient. The rectal wall is annotated by the white arrow. (C) Axial T2w image status post-SPACE-OAR injection in a different patient with prostate cancer demonstrating collection of space-oar inside the rectal wall.

the rectal wall can lead to increased radiation toxicity (Fig. 6.3C). The Denonvillier's fascia also provides some structural support to the male pelvic floor and there is increased incidence of anterior rectocele after prostatectomy. We have focused on few of the important MR visible prostate structures with special relevance for prostate cancer imaging. There are other details about pelvic fasciae, puboprostatic, and pubourethral ligaments and prostatic neurovascular supply, especially related to surgical approaches, which are beyond the purview of this chapter but can be easily found in the referred articles.[10–16]

6.2 Prostate MRI technique

Since its development in the early 1980s, MRI has become a widely accepted modality for noninvasive assessment of the prostate.[17] The wide range of imaging techniques, interpretation methods, and reporting styles of prostate MRI prompted the development of standardized guidelines called PI-RADS (Prostate Imaging-Reporting and Data System) with the most current iteration version 2.1.[4,18,19] Four sequences are recommended for the standard multiparametric prostate MRI including T1-weighted (T1w), T2-weighted (T2w), diffusion-weighted (DWI), and dynamic–contrast-enhanced (DCE) images. T2w imaging is recommended in at least two orthogonal planes. PI-RADS also defines basic minimum technical criteria for these sequences. T1w images are important for the detection of prostate hemorrhage especially in the setting of biopsy. Hemorrhage can appear striated either localized or diffuse with hyperintensity on T1w images and iso- to hypointensity on T2w.[20,21] A larger field of view (FOV) T1w acquisition, usually postcontrast, is also beneficial to detect lymphadenopathy and suspicious osseous lesions and is currently done at our institution.[22] For T1w and DCE images, fat suppression and/or subtraction can be done to improve lesion contrast, especially in the presence of background blood products.

T2w images are the sequence of choice to evaluate prostate anatomy due to high soft tissue contrast.[2] These images are also critical to evaluate extraprostatic extension for local cancer staging.[23] T2w sequences are the dominant parameter to characterize lesions in the transition zone for PI-RADS.[4,19] While 3D acquisition using isotropic voxels allows for more detail, this should be used as an adjunct to 2D acquisitions due to lower signal-to-noise ratio.[23] Additionally, there is no significant difference in lesion detection with 2D and 3D acquisitions.[24] We employ both 2D and 3D T2w acquisitions at our institution.

DWI measures the Brownian motion of water in tissues which is altered with changes in tissue density and organization.[25] These parameters are altered in carcinoma where there is restriction of water diffusion in the tissues. However DWI signal is dependent also on T2 relaxation time which can lead to errors in interpreting DWI, requiring an apparent diffusion coefficient (ADC) map.[26] Lesions that are hyperintense on DWI with corresponding hypointensity on ADC can be attributed to true diffusion restriction rather than intrinsic T2 relaxation time.[27] DWI is reliant on the magnitude and duration of the magnetic gradient quantified as b-values. At least two b-values are required to create an ADC map, with one value between 50 and 100 s/mm^2 and the other value between 800 and 1000 s/mm^2.[28] In PI-RADS, DWI is the dominant parameter to characterize lesions in the peripheral zone.[4,19] It is recommended to also have a high b-value above 1400 s/mm^2 as more diffusion weighing allows for better contrast between normal prostate and lesions.[29] This high b-value can either be obtained separately or extrapolated from previously acquired b-values.[30] Our institution employs extrapolated high b-values primarily to save examination time. The ADC map and high B-value DWI acquisitions are interpreted in concert with one another.

DCE measures vascularity, which is increased in prostatic carcinoma compared to surrounding tissue.[31] This is thought to be due to increased density, quantity, and permeability of vasculature in tumors.[32] However, benign processes in the prostate such as prostatitis can also demonstrate increased signal on DCE, thus DCE has a limited role compared to DWI and T2w sequences for lesion characterization with some suggesting a shorter biparametric protocol.[33] PI-RADS recommends a temporal resolution of less than 15 seconds with qualitative analysis rather than quantitative analysis.[4,19] In posttreatment cases, DCE actually becomes the most important sequence to detect recurrent or remnant disease. Other MRI sequences including MR spectroscopy can also be used to differentiate between cancerous and noncancerous MRI disease but are currently not a part of PI-RADS.

Prostate MRI can be adequately performed both on 1.5T and 3T systems as endorsed in PI-RADS.[4,19] 3T systems have the advantage of decreased acquisition times, increased spatial resolution and increased signal to noise. 3T is however, due to higher magnetic strength, more sensitive to inhomogeneities leading to artifacts.[34,35] This difference in image quality with 3T is seen more for DWI than for T2w images.[36] At our institution, we preferentially scan patients with 3T except in cases of implanted hardware when 1.5T is used. In addition to the magnetic strength, the choice of coil is also important. Pelvic surface phase-array coil is standard for prostate MRI. The addition of an endorectal coil can increase signal significantly[37]; however with improvements of surface coils with increased coil elements and radiofrequency channels, satisfactory images can also be obtained without an endorectal coil.[38,39] Endorectal coils can also increase patient discomfort, examination time, and has been shown to cause anatomic distortion of the prostate which can affect interpretation.[40] Carcinoma detection and staging accuracy was found to be similar using an endorectal coil in a 1.5T system compared to a 3T system without endorectal coil.[39] In patients with large body habitus, an endorectal coil may still provide sufficient benefit; however, it is not a requirement per PI-RADS.[4,19] As advanced surface coils provide excellent diagnostic images on newer scanners and especially at 3T, our institution does not use endorectal coils.

In addition to hardware, patient preparation plays an important role for a successful prostate MRI. As DWI is particularly susceptible to local magnetic field inhomogeneity from air, it is important that patients evacuate their bowel of as much stool and gas as possible.[41] Removal of stool is also important if an endorectal coil is to be placed. An enema prior to imaging has not been shown to significantly reduce artifacts.[42] All localizers are screened at our institution to look for significant amounts of air. If volume of gas cannot be decreased with evacuation or prone positioning, then patient would benefit from rescheduling rather than continuing with a subpar examination. Theoretically bowel peristalsis can introduce artifacts; however, the use of antispasmodic agents prior to scans to significantly improve image quality remains controversial.[43,44] Due to possible drug reaction and possible incremental benefit, our institution does not employ antispasmodic agents. In addition, abstinence from ejaculation up to 3 days prior to imaging can augment seminal vesicle evaluation for staging but it is not routinely used as it is not beneficial for lesion detection.[45]

6.3 Benign disease processes of the prostrate

6.3.1 Benign prostatic hyperplasia

BPH occurs in the transition zone of the prostate with proliferation of the smooth muscle and epithelial cells.[46] Incidence of BPH increases with age and its exact etiology is poorly understood but it is likely related to dihydrotestosterone regulation.[47] BPH clinical manifestations include lower urinary tract symptoms (LUTS) such as hesitancy, straining, urinary obstruction, and overflow incontinence as well as recurrent urinary tract infections and renal impairment.[46,47] Benign BPH nodules have well-defined margins and are rounded in contour.[48] On T2w images, BPH has a heterogeneous appearance with hypointense areas of smooth muscle stromal proliferation and hyperintense areas of epithelial glandular proliferation.[48,49] Some BPH nodules can mimic carcinoma with hypointensity on T2w, hyperintensity on DWI, and enhancement on DCE; however, margins and morphology can usually distinguish the two entities.[49] Extruded BPH nodules into the peripheral zone are sometimes very hard to differentiate from prostate carcinoma. BPH causes increase in prostatic gland volume which has been shown to correlate with LUTS.[50] There are various methods to determine prostatic tumor volume however PI-RADS recommends the ellipsoid volume method (Length × Width × Height × $\pi/6$).[4,19] This can sometimes lead to underestimation if the prostate has irregular contours. The "bullet" volume may be a better representation of prostate volume for prostate glands smaller than 55 mL.[51] "Bullet" (cylinder + half ellipsoid) volume is Length × Width × Height × $5\pi/24$. Manual and automated 3D segmentation may also be done.[52] BPH can be classified into types 0 through 7 depending on the distribution of prostate enlargement (Fig. 6.4). Median lobe hypertrophy (MLH) is a form of BPH readily appreciated on imaging due to its extension superiorly into the bladder trigone and can be related to significant bladder outlet obstruction.[53] Intravesical prostatic protrusion (IPP) has been used to evaluate BPH symptoms. Men with LUTS from bladder outlet obstruction with IPP exceeding 10 mm (Fig. 6.5) are frequently poor responders to medical treatment with tamsulosin. Some other MRI measurements for BPH severity include: puboprostatic angle (PPA) and prostate urethral angle (PUA). PPA is the angle between the pubic symphysis and the axis of the bladder neck. Under normal circumstances, micturition in men comprises five stages: relaxation of the pelvic floor, descent of the bladder neck, widening of the PPA, contraction of the ventral prostate and micturition. Prostate size can affect PPA and its widening. PUA is the acute angle between the proximal and distal prostatic urethra. An increased PUA at rest (greater than 34°) in patients with BPH has been shown to correlate with LUTS.[8]

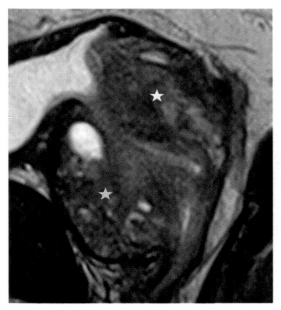

FIG. 6.4   Sagittal T2w image demonstrates type 3 BPH in a 71-year-old man. Type 3 BPH is the most common subcategory of BPH signifying involvement of bilateral TZ (partially shown, yellow star) and retrourethral area (white star) with BPH.

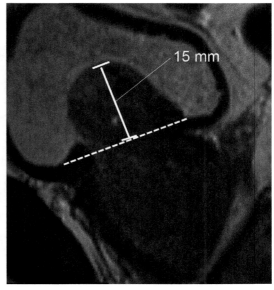

FIG. 6.5   Sagittal T2w image demonstrating method for measuring intravesical prostate protrusion.

15 mm

Although MRI is not routinely used in preprocedural evaluation of BPH, there is some evidence that preprocedural MRI variables can be useful in predicting postprocedure outcomes. MRI can also be used in evaluation of pre- and posttreatment postprostatectomy incontinence. Treatment options for postprostatectomy incontinence include urethral slings and artificial urinary sphincters.

Lower urinary tract symptoms from BPH can lead to significant decrease in quality of life with initial treatment consisting of medical therapy such as alpha-adrenergic and 5-alpha reductase inhibitors.[47] When medical therapy options are exhausted, BPH can also be treated procedurally, classically with transurethral resection of the prostate (TURP). After TURP, imaging can show widening of the upper portion of the prostatic urethra as well as a thin rim of T2 hypointensity at the resection site seen in about 50% of patients.[54] Prostate artery embolism has also emerged as a minimally invasive alternative for symptomatic BPH for which MRI can help to delineate prostate volume size decrease and infarction volume. Postprocedural MRI demonstrates areas of infarction characterized by hyperintensity on T1w, hypointensity on T2w, and nonenhancement on DCE (Fig. 6.6A and B).[55] Many other minimally invasive technologies are available for the treatment of BPH including laser-based procedures such as holmium laser enucleation of the prostate (HoLEP) and photoselective vaporization of the prostate (PVP), as well as thermal ablation procedures such as water vapor thermal therapy (Rezum).[53] These result in reduction in volume of periurethral prostatic tissue. UroLift is another option for the treatment of BPH. It is a permanent metallic implant used to pull open the prostatic urethra without an associated decrease in prostate size (Fig. 6.7). Imaging appearance of posttreatment prostate can be distinctive based on the treatment option utilized and imaging can also be utilized to evaluate posttreatment complications like bleeding, infection, erosion (Fig. 6.8), capsular perforation, osteomyelitis, and stricture formation.

6.3.2 Prostatitis

Prostatitis is a common condition affecting nearly 8% of adult men and can be a challenging clinically diagnosis.[56] Four categories have been described by National Institutes of Health consensus statement: acute bacterial prostatitis, chronic bacterial prostatitis, chronic pelvic pain syndrome, and asymptomatic inflammatory prostatitis.[57] Acute bacterial prostatitis is usually caused by an ascending uretheral infection by *Escherichia coli*, which if left untreated can lead to chronic bacterial prostatitis.[58,59] Imaging features of bacterial prostatitis can overlap with carcinoma with areas of hypointensity on T2w and DWI restriction corresponding to areas of inflammation however the degree of signal loss on ADC is less than in neoplastic processes.[60,61] DCE can also show early enhancement however the morphology is wedge-shaped or diffuse rather than the ovoid or irregular morphology commonly seen in carcinoma (Fig. 6.9A–D).[62] Prostate abscesses have a typical appearance with rim enhancement

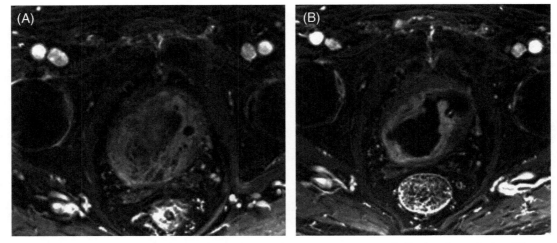

FIG. 6.6   Axial T1w postcontrast images which were obtained pre- and postprostate artery embolization shown in A and B, respectively. Image B demonstrates expected prostate infarction.

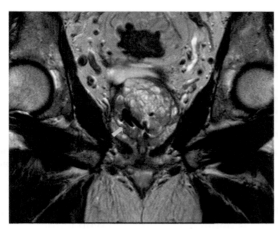

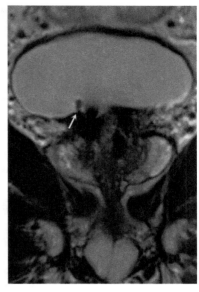

FIG. 6.7 Coronal T2w image demonstrates susceptibility artifact (yellow arrow) from an UroLift implant in a 64-year-old man. UroLift is a permanent metallic implant to mechanically constrict and retract the lateral lobes of prostate to open the urethral channel. The artifact is caused by a stainless steel tab placed along the urethral mucosa. It is connected by a monofilament to a nitinol tab placed on the outer surface of the prostate.

FIG. 6.8 Coronal T2w image demonstrating migration of a portion of the UroLift implant into the bladder lumen (yellow arrow) in this 65-year-old man.

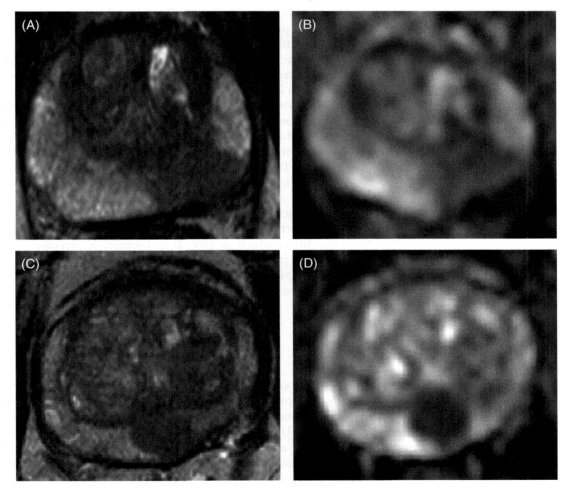

FIG. 6.9 (A) T2w and (B) ADC axial images demonstrating a wedge-shaped hypointense lesion with mild diffusion restriction in the left peripheral zone consistent with prostatitis. In contradistinction, (C) T2W and (D) ADC axial images demonstrating an oval marked hypointense lesion with marked diffusion restriction consistent with prostate cancer.

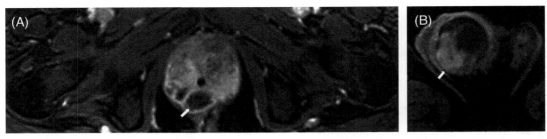

FIG. 6.10   (A) Contrast-enhanced axial T1w image demonstrating diffuse enhancement of the prostate and small abscess (white arrow) in this 57-year-old man suffering from acute prostatitis. (B) Contrast-enhanced axial T1w image in same patient demonstrates epididymo-orchitis manifesting as hyperenhancement on imaging (white arrow).

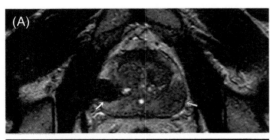

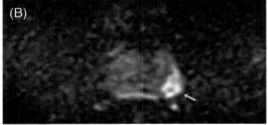

FIG. 6.11   A 62-year-old man with bladder cancer status post-BCG therapy, now with rising PSA. (A) Axial T2w image demonstrates a markedly T2 hypointense rounded lesion in the right peripheral zone (white arrow) and a more milder ill-defined confluent homogenous T2 hypointensity in the left peripheral zone (yellow arrow). (B) On high b-value axial DWI, the right lesion does not restrict diffusion whereas the left lesion demonstrates high signal signifying restricted diffusion. On biopsy, the right lesion demonstrated necrotizing granulomas whereas the left lesion demonstrated Gleason 4 + 3 prostate adenocarcinoma.

(Fig. 6.10A and B). Chronic pelvic pain syndrome or chronic nonbacterial prostatitis is defined as urogenital pain without identifiable infection lasting longer than 3 months.[56] While no MR imaging abnormality was observed in the prostate with chronic pelvic pain syndrome, two extraprostatic findings were found with periprostatic vein plexus dilatation in 70% and seminal vesicle enlargement in 30%.[63]

The last category asymptomatic inflammatory prostatitis encompasses a large variety of inflammatory processes such as granulomatous prostatitis. These conditions are found incidentally during prostatic biopsies. One notable cause for granulomatous prostatitis is intravesical injection of Bacillus–Calmete–Guerin for nonmuscle-invasive bladder cancer.[64] MRI imaging demonstrates hypointensity on T2w, hypointensity on ADC, and focal enhancement on DCE which can mimic prostatic carcinoma (Fig. 6.11A and B).[65] Florid granulomatous prostatitis may even demonstrate extraprostatic extension. Another inflammatory process, prostate amyloidosis, can appear as a T2 hypointense mass but usually does not demonstrate restricted diffusion or arterial enhancement.[66] Treatment of infectious prostatitis usually involves antibiotics (Fig. 6.12A and B). Other treatments for prostatitis may include anti-inflammatories, pain medications, stress management, pelvic floor therapy, and medications to improve urinary flow such as tamsulosin. Malakoplakia is another inflammatory condition which is rare. It is thought to develop from chronic urinary tract infection and affects the genitourinary tract. Isolated malakoplakia of the prostate is rare and has been clinically mistaken for prostatic malignancies.[67]

6.3.3 Miscellaneous

6.3.3.1 Calcifications

The pathogenesis of prostate calcification is thought to be possibly related to prostatic inflammation, urinary retention, or prostatic reflux. Prostate calcifications are usually asymptomatic and rarely mentioned in radiology reports. Recent studies have however shown that high-density material such as calcifications can have a significant impact on treatment delivery with high intensity focused ultrasound (HIFU), transurethral ultrasound ablation (TULSA), and brachytherapy (Fig. 6.13A–C).[68] Due to the diamagnetic effect of the calcium, calcification has low signal intensity on T2-weighted and ADC image and may create confusion. Lack of enhancement, persistent marked low signal intensity on DWI all b-values, and the occasional low T1w signal intensity may help. However, calcifications even sub-5 mm calcification can be problematic for therapeutic ultrasound of the prostate if they are in the vicinity of prostate cancer and calcifications this small may not be visible on MRI. CT remains gold standard for imaging of calcifications.

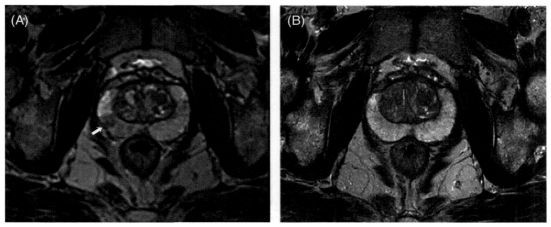

FIG. 6.12 (A) Axial T2w image demonstrating patchy T2 hypointensities in the prostate peripheral zone (white arrow). Symptoms of this 47-year-old man included pelvic pain, burning urination and fever. Urinalysis was positive. Antibiotic treatment was done and patient symptoms resolved. (B) Axial T2w image demonstrates resolution of patchy T2 hypointensities and clearing of the peripheral zone on follow-up.

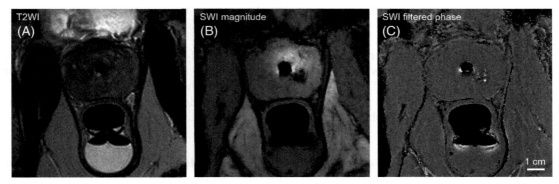

FIG. 6.13 **Example of the use of susceptibility-weighted imaging to identify prostate calcifications in a 71-year-old man with Gleason grade 2 prostate cancer considering undergoing transurethral prostate ablation.** (A) Axial T2w image for treatment planning does not demonstrate the calcification. (B) Magnitude reconstruction of the susceptibility-weighted image demonstrated a dark spot in left periurethral region. Both calcium and hemorrhage can have this appearance. (C) Filtered phase image of susceptibility-weighted image acquired during treatment planning demonstrates brightness in the region of the dark spot confirming calcifications as hemorrhage would remain dark.

6.3.3.2 Periprostatic vein

The periprostatic venous plexus is closely associated with the pseudocapsule of the prostate. It lies predominantly anterior and lateral to the prostate.[69] Prominent periprostatic veins are usually T2 hyperintense but can have low T2 signal and darkness on ADC depending velocity of blood flow. This may be difficult to differentiate from intraprostatic lesions, particularly at the apex where there is sparseness of the pseudocapsule leading to intermixing of the periprostatic and glandular tissue. Volume averaging on axial images and the oblique course of the veins at the apex contributes to the difficulty in delineating between intra- and extraprostatic structures. Brisk DCE signal, mirroring of blood pool signal and careful examination of coronal/sagittal planes can help demonstrate the continuity of apical veins with the remainder of the periprostatic venous plexus.

6.3.3.3 Periprostatic lymph nodes

Periprostatic lymph nodes are found in 4.4% of radical prostatectomy specimens.[69] They are most commonly located at the prostate base, laterally or posterolaterally. Malignant involvement of the periprostatic lymph nodes found in prostatectomy specimens is seen in 15% of cases. These can appear to lie within the prostate parenchyma on low spatial resolution images like DWI/ADC. T2w images can help confirm their location. MRI has limited sensitivity and specificity to differentiate benign from malignant lymph nodes. The detection of abnormal lymph nodes on MRI is usually done using size, shape, morphology, and enhancement pattern. In general, per PI-RADS, lymph nodes over 8 mm in short axis dimension are regarded as suspicious. PSMA PET and iron–oxide-enhanced MRI can detect smaller lymph nodes containing metastases but these too have limited sensitivity (Fig. 6.14A and B).

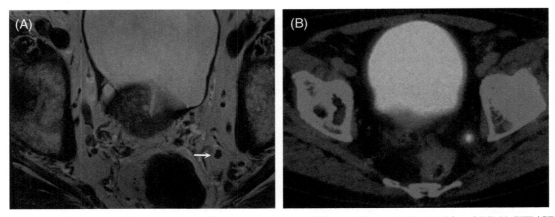

FIG. 6.14 **An 89-year-old man with biopsy-proven Gleason 4 + 4 cancer.** (A) Axial T2w and (B) Axial fused PSMA-PET/CT images demonstrate a left pelvic lymph node which is 5 mm in short axis on T2WI but intensely PSMA-avid and therefore much easier to see on the PET/CT images.

Lymphadenopathy may also be incidentally detected on prostate MRI. In the absence of a prostate lesion, bladder and rectum should be closely examined for a lesion. Systemic processes are also in the differential.

6.3.3.4 Atrophy

Prostatic atrophy can occur as a normal part of aging or inflammatory/infectious insults. It could be associated with wedge-shaped areas of low signal on T2w images as seen on prostatitis and mildly decreased signal on the ADC map from loss of glandular tissue.[4] The ADC is higher than cancer and there is often contour retraction and loss of volume. It might be asymmetric. There is positive association between degree of atrophy and PSA elevation. This counterintuitive elevation of PSA in atrophy is thought to be related to damaged epithelial cells in atrophic acini.[70]

6.3.3.5 Congenital cysts

There are two types of prostatic congenital cysts: utricular and Mullerian duct.[71] Utricular cysts are midline, intraprostatic, arise from the verumontanum and communicate with the posterior urethra.[72] These cysts are also diagnosed earlier in life due to associations with other urogenital conditions such as hypospadias and cryptorchidism. Mullerian duct cysts are found later in life due to focal failure of regression of the Mullerian duct and are also midline. Unlike utricular cysts, Mullerian duct cysts do not communicate with the urethra, usually extend above the prostate and are typically larger (Fig. 6.15A–C).[73] When asymptomatic, both cysts demonstrate hyperintensity on T2w and hypointensity on T1w.[72] However, utricular and Mullerian duct cysts can also display hemorrhage and become infected with corresponding increased signal on T1w. Carcinomas are a rare complication of prostatic cysts.[73] Also, ductal adenocarcinoma can present as a cystic mass and is usually higher grade than typical acinar adenocarcinoma.[66]

6.3.3.6 Hemorrhage

Normal prostate tissue has extraordinarily high amounts of citrate and zinc.[74] Citrate is secreted in prostatic fluid and is an energy substrate for the sperm. High zinc levels in prostatic epithelial cells inhibit oxidation of

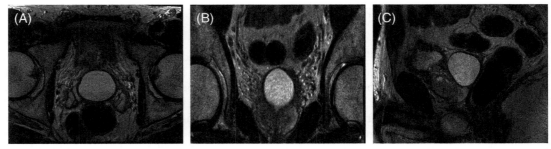

FIG. 6.15 (A) Axial, (B) Sagittal, and (C) Coronal T2w images demonstrating a classic Mullerian duct cyst in this asymptomatic 59-year-old man. Mullerian duct cysts do not communicate with the urethra, usually extend above the prostate and are typically larger.

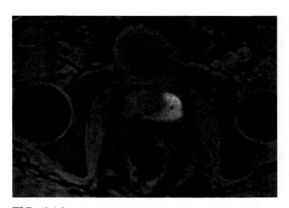

FIG. 6.16 **Axial T1w image without contrast demonstrating T1 hyperintense hemorrhage in the left hemiprostate whereas the right side is completely free of hemorrhage.** This 57-year-old patient had undergone transrectal ultrasound guided biopsy 3 weeks before this MRI and had Gleason 3 + 4 cancer only on the right side whereas all the left-sided cores were negative (hemorrhagic exclusion sign of cancer).

citrate to isocitrate by mitochondrial aconitase enzyme, thereby truncating the TCA cycle. Malignant prostate cells cannot accumulate zinc which results in increased citrate oxidation and coupled ATP production. This mismatch of citrate concentrations in benign and malignant prostate tissue has interesting connotations for prostate MRI, especially in MRI performed immediately after biopsy. As citrate is an anticoagulant, malignant prostate tissues do not bleed as much as normal prostate tissue and blood products do not persist. That is why MRI, if the purpose is detecting clinically significant prostate cancer, can be done after biopsy without any significant delay. Blood products can be T2 hypointense and can restrict diffusion. These can be easily differentiated from carcinoma using T1 hyperintensity and nonenhancement on DCE images (Fig. 6.16). If the purpose is staging, recommendation is to wait up to 6 weeks after biopsy to ensure resolution of blood products, as the most important sequence for staging is T2.

6.3.3.7 Uncommon tumors

Rarely, there can be benign solid lesions within the prostate including but not limited to leiomyoma (T2 homogenously hypointense), hemangioma (T2 hyperintensity with mirroring of blood pool on contrast-enhanced images), and cystadenoma (multilocular cystic lesion with or without soft tissue components) with typical imaging features (Fig. 6.17A–D).[66]

6.4 Conclusion

MRI is the modality of choice for noninvasive assessment of the prostate. Understanding prostate zonal anatomy and the MRI appearance is essential for the proper detection and characterization of prostatic lesions. The development of PI-RADS has standardized reporting and MRI techniques. With the knowledge of MRI sequences and MRI appearance of prostate anatomy, one can successfully discern clinically significant prostate cancer from benign prostatic lesions.

MRI protocol (details available including those pertaining to maximal in-plane pixel size for each sequence, TR/ TE in DWI/DCE, contrast dose, and injection rate in DCE: https://www.acr.org/-/media/ACR/Files/RADS/ Pi-RADS/PIRADS-V2-1.pdf).

Sequence	Specifications	Slice thickness	Planes	Utilization
T2W TSE 2D	FOV 20 cm	3 mm	Axial, coronal	Prostate zonal anatomy, primary sequence for transition zone lesions, staging
T2W TSE 3D (optional)	FOV 20 cm	1 mm	Axial	Detailed anatomy, contouring for fusion biopsy
T1W GRE with and/or without contrast	Large—to the level of aortic bifurcation	3 mm (minimum)	Axial	Hemorrhage, lymphadenopathy, metastases
DWI EPI with ADC (free breathing spin echo with spectral fat sat is recommended)	FOV 20 cm, B50/800/ 1600	3 mm	Axial	Primary sequence for peripheral zone lesions, secondary but still important for other zones
DCE 3DT1W GRE FS	FOV 20 cm, Temporal resolution 10 seconds, minimum observation time of 2 minutes	3 mm (minimum)— usually 1 mm	Axial	Troubleshooting sequence for determining clinically significant prostate lesions in the peripheral zone, posttreatment imaging

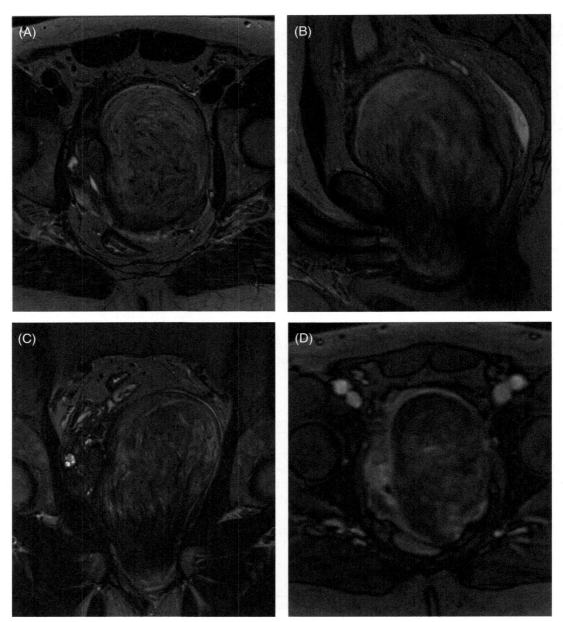

FIG. 6.17   (A) Axial, (B) Sagittal, (C) Coronal T2w images demonstrating a large T2 heterogenous mass arising from the left side of the prostate. (D) Postcontrast-enhanced T1w image demonstrates patchy enhancement of the tumor. This was resected and proven to be a leiomyoma. The lesion cells were positive for SMA, desmin, and caldesmon. They were negative for myogenin, MyoD1, HMB45, Melan-A, SOX10, S100, DOG1, CD117, and cytokeratin AE1/AE3.

Benign conditions mimics of prostate cancer (details will be discussed in the chapter dedicated to prostate neoplasia).

Prostatitis	Wedge-shaped or diffuse morphology, ADC usually not as dark
Benign prostatic hyperplasia	Well-defined margins and rounded contour
Calcification	Lack of enhancement, low intensity on all b-value images
Periprostatic veins	Look for continuity with remainder of periprostatic venous plexus

Teaching points

Central zone	Central zone T2w and ADC characteristics can mimic prostate carcinoma. Look for symmetrical appearance as a guide.
Anterior fibromuscular stroma	In younger patients, it can be bulky and mimic tumor morphology. Look for midline position and hypo-vascularity on DCE due to fibrous nature.
Surgical capsule	Surgical capsule T2w and ADC characteristics can mimic prostate carcinoma. Look for linear morphology.
Posttreatment prostate carcinoma	DCE is an essential tool for finding recurrent/residual disease.
3T vs. 1T	3T is almost always preferred except for patients with implanted hardware.
Endorectal coil	Advanced surface coils and 3T acquisitions offer excellent diagnostic images which can spare patients of endorectal coil placement.
DWI	Have patient evacuate as much as possible (which can be checked with scout images); however, enemas have not been shown to significantly benefit.

References

1. McNeal JE. The zonal anatomy of the prostate. *Prostate*. 1981;2(1):35–49.
2. Hricak H, Dooms G, McNeal J, et al. MR imaging of the prostate gland: normal anatomy. *Am J Roentgenol*. 1987;148(1):51–58.
3. Kayhan A. Multi-parametric MR imaging of transition zone prostate cancer: imaging features, detection and staging. *World J Radiol*. 2010;2(5):180.
4. Turkbey B, Rosenkrantz AB, Haider MA, et al. Prostate Imaging Reporting and Data System Version 2.1: 2019 update of Prostate Imaging Reporting and Data System Version 2. *Eur Urol*. 2019;76(3):340–351.
5. Vargas HA, Akin O, Franiel T, et al. Normal central zone of the prostate and central zone involvement by prostate cancer: clinical and MR imaging implications. *Radiology*. 2012;262(3):894–902.
6. Rosenkrantz AB, Taneja SS. Radiologist, be aware: ten pitfalls that confound the interpretation of multiparametric prostate MRI. *Am J Roentgenol*. 2014;202(1):109–120.
7. Bonekamp D, Jacobs MA, El-Khouli R, Stoianovici D, Macura KJ. Advancements in MR imaging of the prostate: from diagnosis to interventions. *Radiographics*. 2011;31(3):677–704.
8. Lakhoo J, Khatri G, Elsayed RF, et al. MRI of the male pelvic floor. *Radiographics*. 2019;39(7):2003–2022.
9. Sam P, Jiang J, LaGrange CA. *Anatomy, Abdomen and Pelvis, Sphincter Urethrae*. In StatPearls. StatPearls Publishing, Treasure Island, FL; 2021.
10. Sklinda K, Frączek M, Mruk B, Walecki J. Normal 3T MR anatomy of the prostate gland and surrounding structures. *Adv Med*. 2019;2019:1–9.
11. Kumar A, Patel VR, Panaiyadiyan S, Seetharam Bhat KR, Moschovas MC, Nayak B. Nerve-sparing robot-assisted radical prostatectomy: current perspectives. *Asian J Urol*. 2021;8(1):2–13.
12. Hinata N, Sejima T, Takenaka A. Progress in pelvic anatomy from the viewpoint of radical prostatectomy. *Int J Urol*. 2013;20(3):260–270.
13. Zhu XM, Yu GY, Zheng NX, et al. Review of Denonvilliers' fascia: the controversies and consensuses. *Gastroenterol Rep*. 2020;8(5):343–348.
14. Arroyo C, Martini A, Wang J, Tewari AK. Anatomical, surgical and technical factors influencing continence after radical prostatectomy. *Ther Adv Urol*. 2019;11:1–12.
15. Raychaudhuri B, Cahill D. Pelvic fasciae in urology. *Ann R Coll Surg Engl*. 2008;90(8):633–637.
16. Rocco B, Cozzi G. Denonvilliers' fascia: anatomy, surgical planes, use in reconstruction. In: John W. Davis (eds), *Robot-Assisted Radical Prostatectomy*: Springer International Publishing, Switzerland; 2016:113–118.
17. Steyn JH, Smith FW. Nuclear magnetic resonance imaging of the prostate. *Br J Urol*. 1982;54(6):726–728.
18. Barentsz JO, Richenberg J, Clements R, et al. ESUR prostate MR guidelines 2012. *Eur Radiol*. 2012;22(4):746–757.
19. Weinreb JC, Barentsz JO, Choyke PL, et al. PI-RADS Prostate Imaging - Reporting and Data System: 2015, Version 2. *Eur Urol*. 2016;69(1):16–40.
20. Barrett T, Vargas HA, Akin O, Goldman DA, Hricak H. Value of the hemorrhage exclusion sign on T1-weighted prostate MR images for the detection of prostate cancer. *Radiology*. 2012;263(3):751–757.
21. Tamada T, Sone T, Jo Y, et al. Prostate cancer: relationships between postbiopsy hemorrhage and tumor detectability at MR diagnosis. *Radiology*. 2008;248(2):531–539.
22. Pasoglou V, Michoux N, Peeters F, et al. Whole-body 3D T1-weighted MR imaging in patients with prostate cancer: feasibility and evaluation in screening for metastatic disease. *Radiology*. 2015;275(1):155–166.
23. Rosenkrantz AB, Neil J, Kong X, et al. Prostate cancer: comparison of 3D T2-weighted with conventional 2D T2-weighted imaging for image quality and tumor detection. *Am J Roentgenol*. 2010;194(2):446–452.
24. Westphalen AC, Noworolski SM, Harisinghani M, et al. High-resolution 3-T endorectal prostate MRI: a multireader study of radiologist preference and perceived interpretive quality of 2D and 3D T2-weighted fast spin-echo MR images. *Am J Roentgenol*. 2016;206(1):86–91.
25. Gibbs P, Tozer DJ, Liney GP, Turnbull LW. Comparison of quantitative T2 mapping and diffusion-weighted imaging in the normal and pathologic prostate. *Magn Reson Med*. 2001;46(6):1054–1058.
26. Kim CK, Park BK, Kim B. Diffusion-weighted MRI at 3 T for the evaluation of prostate cancer. *Am J Roentgenol*. 2010;194(6):1461–1469.
27. Hambrock T, Somford DM, Huisman HJ, et al. Relationship between apparent diffusion coefficients at 3.0-T MR imaging and Gleason grade in peripheral zone prostate cancer. *Radiology*. 2011;259(2):453–461.

28. Godley KC, Syer TJ, Toms AP, et al. Accuracy of high b-value diffusion-weighted MRI for prostate cancer detection: a meta-analysis. *Acta Radiol.* 2018;59(1):105–113.

29. Metens T, Miranda D, Absil J, Matos C. What is the optimal b value in diffusion-weighted MR imaging to depict prostate cancer at 3T? *Eur Radiol.* 2012;22(3):703–709.

30. Bittencourt LK. Feasibility study of computed vs measured high b-value (1400 s/mm^2) diffusion-weighted MR images of the prostate. *World J Radiol.* 2014;6(6):374.

31. Hansford BG, Peng Y, Jiang Y, et al. Dynamic contrast-enhanced MR imaging curve-type analysis: is it helpful in the differentiation of prostate cancer from healthy peripheral zone? *Radiology.* 2015;275(2):448–457.

32. Alonzi R, Padhani AR, Allen C. Dynamic contrast enhanced MRI in prostate cancer. *Eur J Radiol.* 2007;63(3):335–350.

33. Stanzione A, Imbriaco M, Cocozza S, et al. Biparametric 3T magentic resonance imaging for prostatic cancer detection in a biopsy-naïve patient population: a further improvement of PI-RADS v2? *Eur J Radiol.* 2016;85(12):2269–2274.

34. Beyersdorff D, Taymoorian K, Knösel T, et al. MRI of prostate cancer at 1.5 and 3.0 T: comparison of image quality in tumor detection and staging. *Am J Roentgenol.* 2005;185(5):1214–1220.

35. Rouvière O, Hartman RP, Lyonnet D. Prostate MR imaging at high-field strength: evolution or revolution? *Eur Radiol.* 2006;16(2):276–284.

36. Ullrich T, Quentin M, Oelers C, et al. Magnetic resonance imaging of the prostate at 1.5 versus 3.0 T: a prospective comparison study of image quality. *Eur J Radiol.* 2017;90:192–197.

37. Schnall MD, Lenkinski RE, Pollack HM, Imai Y, Kressel HY. Prostate: MR imaging with an endorectal surface coil. *Radiology.* 1989;172(2):570–574.

38. Gawlitza J, Reiss-Zimmermann M, Thörmer G, et al. Impact of the use of an endorectal coil for 3 T prostate MRI on image quality and cancer detection rate. *Sci Rep.* 2017;7:1–8.

39. de Rooij M, Hamoen EHJ, Witjes JA, Barentsz JO, Rovers MM. Accuracy of magnetic resonance imaging for local staging of prostate cancer: a diagnostic meta-analysis. *Eur Urol.* 2016;70(2):233–245.

40. Heijmink S, Scheenen TWJ, van Lin E, et al. Changes in prostate shape and volume and their implications for radiotherapy after introduction of endorectal balloon as determined by MRI at 3T. *Int J Radiat Oncol Biol Phys.* 2009;73(5):1446–1453.

41. Caglic I, Hansen NL, Slough RA, Patterson AJ, Barrett T. Evaluating the effect of rectal distension on prostate multiparametric MRI image quality. *Eur J Radiol.* 2017;90:174–180.

42. Lim C, Quon J, McInnes M, Shabana WM, El-Khodary M, Schieda N. Does a cleansing enema improve image quality of 3T surface coil multiparametric prostate MRI? *J Magn Reson Imaging.* 2015;42(3):689–697.

43. Wagner M, Rief M, Busch J, et al. Effect of butylscopolamine on the quality MRI images of the prostate. *Clin Radiol.* 2010;65(6):460–464.

44. Ullrich T, Quentin M, Schmaltz AK, et al. Hyoscine butylbromide significantly decreases motion artefacts and allows better delineation of anatomic structures in mp-MRI of the prostate. *Eur Radiol.* 2018;28(1):17–23.

45. Kabakus IM, Borofsky S, Mertan FV, et al. Does abstinence from ejaculation before prostate MRI improve evaluation of the seminal vesicles? *Am J Roentgenol.* 2016;207(6):1205–1209.

46. Grossfeld GD, Coakley FV. Benign prostatic hyperplasia: clinical overview and value of diagnostic imaging. *Radiol Clin North Am.* 2000;38(1):31–47.

47. Roehrborn CG. Benign prostatic hyperplasia: an overview. *Rev Urol.* 2005;7(Suppl 9(3 Suppl. A)):S3–S14.

48. Wasserman NF, Spilseth B, Golzarian J, Metzger GJ. Use of MRI for lobar classification of benign prostatic hyperplasia: potential phenotypic biomarkers for research on treatment strategies. *Am J Roentgenol.* 2015;205(3):564–571.

49. Oto A, Kayhan A, Jiang Y, et al. Prostate cancer: differentiation of central gland cancer from benign prostatic hyperplasia by using diffusion-weighted and dynamic contrast-enhanced MR imaging. *Radiology.* 2010;257(3):715–723.

50. Turkbey B, Huang R, Vourganti S, et al. Age-related changes in prostate zonal volumes as measured by high-resolution magnetic resonance imaging (MRI): a cross-sectional study in over 500 patients. *BJU Int.* 2012;110(11):1642–1647.

51. MacMahon PJ, Kennedy AM, Murphy DT, Maher M, McNicholas MM. Modified prostate volume algorithm improves transrectal US volume estimation in men presenting for prostate brachytherapy. *Radiology.* 2009;250(1):273–280.

52. Bezinque A, Moriarity A, Farrell C, Peabody H, Noyes SL, Lane BR. Determination of prostate volume. *Acad Radiol.* 2018;25(12):1582–1587.

53. Diaz T, Benson B, Clinkenbeard A, Long J, Kawashima A, Yano M. MRI evaluation of patients before and after interventions for benign prostatic hyperplasia: an update. *Am J Roentgenol.* 2021; 218(1), 88–99. Published online.

54. Sheu MH, Chiang H, Wang JH, Chang YH, Chang CY. Transurethral resection of the prostate-related changes in the prostate gland: correlation of MRI and histopathology. *J Comput Assist Tomogr.* 2000;24(4):596–599.

55. Frenk NE, Baroni RH, Carnevale FC, et al. MRI findings after prostatic artery embolization for treatment of benign hyperplasia. *Am J Roentgenol.* 2014;203(4):813–821.

56. Krieger JN, Lee SWH, Jeon J, Cheah PY, Liong ML, Riley DE. Epidemiology of prostatitis. *Int J Antimicrob Agents.* 2008;31(Suppl 1):85–90.

57. Krieger JN, Nyberg L, Nickel JC. NIH consensus definition and classification of prostatitis. *JAMA.* 1999;282(3):236–237.

58. Roberts RO, Lieber MM, Rhodes T, Girman CJ, Bostwick DG, Jacobsen SJ. Prevalence of a physician-assigned diagnosis of prostatitis: the Olmsted county study of urinary symptoms and health status among men. *Urology.* 1998;51(4):578–584.

59. Holt JD, Garrett WA, McCurry TK, Teichman JMH. Common questions about chronic prostatitis. *Am Fam Physician.* 2016;93(4):290–296.

60. Gürses B, Tasdelen N, Yencilek F, et al. Diagnostic utility of DTI in prostate cancer. *Eur J Radiol.* 2011;79(2):172–176.

61. Nagel KNA, Schouten MG, Hambrock T, et al. Differentiation of prostatitis and prostate cancer by using diffusion-weighted MR imaging and MR-guided biopsy at 3 T. *Radiology.* 2013;267(1):164–172.

62. Meier-Schroers M, Kukuk G, Wolter K, et al. Differentiation of prostatitis and prostate cancer using the Prostate Imaging - Reporting and Data System (PI-RADS). *Eur J Radiol.* 2016;85(7):1304–1311.

63. Clemente A, Renzulli M, Reginelli A, et al. Chronic prostatitis/pelvic pain syndrome: MRI findings and clinical correlations. *Andrologia.* 2019;51(9):1–6.

64. Shukla P, Gulwani HV, Kaur S. Granulomatous prostatitis: clinical and histomorphologic survey of the disease in a tertiary care hospital. *Prostate Int*. 2017;5(1):29–34.

65. Rais-Bahrami S, Nix JW, Turkbey B, et al. Clinical and multiparametric MRI signatures of granulomatous prostatitis. *Abdom Radiol*. 2017;42(7):1956–1962.

66. Li Y, Mongan J, Behr SC, et al. Beyond prostate adenocarcinoma: expanding the differential diagnosis in prostate pathologic conditions. *Radiographics*. 2016;36(4):1055–1075.

67. Heah NH, Tan TW, Tan YK. Malakoplakia of the prostate as a mimicker of prostate cancer on prostate health index and magnetic resonance imaging–fusion prostate biopsy: a case report. *J Endourol Case Rep*. 2017;3(1):74–77.

68. Singh S, Martin E, Tregidgo HFJ, Treeby B, Bandula S. Prostatic calcifications: quantifying occurrence, radiodensity, and spatial distribution in prostate cancer patients. *Urol Oncol Semin Orig Investig*. 2021;39(10) 728.e1-728.e6.

69. Kitzing YX, Prando A, Varol C, Karczmar GS, Maclean F, Oto A. Benign conditions that mimic prostate carcinoma: MR imaging features with histopathologic correlation. *Radiographics*. 2016;36(1):162–175.

70. Billis A, Meirelles LR, Magna LA, Baracat J, Prando A, Ferreira U. Extent of prostatic atrophy in needle biopsies and serum PSA levels: is there an association? *Urology*. 2007;69(5):927–930.

71. Curran S, Akin O, Agildere AM, Zhang J, Hricak H, Rademaker J. Endorectal MRI of prostatic and periprostatic cystic lesions and their mimics. *Am J Roentgenol*. 2007;188(5):1373–1379.

72. McDermott VG, Meakem TJ, Stolpen AH, Schnall MD. Prostatic and periprostatic cysts: findings on MR imaging. *Am J Roentgenol*. 1995;164(1):123–127.

73. Shebel HM, Farg HM, Kolokythas O, El-Diasty T. Cysts of the lower male genitourinary tract: embryologic and anatomic considerations and differential diagnosis. *Radiographics*. 2013;33(4):1125–1143.

74. Costello LC, Franklin RB. Novel role of zinc in the regulation of prostate citrate metabolism and its implications in prostate cancer. *Prostate*. 1998;35(4):285–296.

7

MRI of the prostate cancers

Sarah G. Winks, Jinxing Yu

Department of Radiology, Virginia Commonwealth University Health System, Richmond, VA, United States

7.1 Introduction

Prostate cancer (PCa) is the second most common cancer in men in the United States behind skin cancer and the second leading cause of cancer-related deaths in men in the United States, second only to lung cancer.[1] The American Cancer Society estimates that there will be 248,530 new cases of PCa and 34,130 deaths from PCa in the United States in 2021.[1] The prevalence of PCa in the United States is expected to increase as the population ages, as the majority of PCa occurs in older men.[1,2] Traditional screening methods for PCa have included monitoring of prostate-specific antigen (PSA) levels, digital rectal examination (DRE) and transrectal ultrasound-guided systematic (TRUS) prostate biopsy, which lacked sensitivity and specificity in detection of PCa. Recent advances in multiparametric magnetic resonance imaging (mp-MRI) of the prostate have allowed for increased use of prostate MRI for PCa screening and tumor detection, allowing for more targeted biopsies and more accurate diagnosis,[3] in addition to the traditional role of MRI in the staging of PCa. In this chapter, we discuss the role of mp-MRI in the detection and initial evaluation of PCa, the use of the Prostate Imaging Reporting & Data System (PI-RADS) v2.1 in the evaluation of PCa, potential mimics of PCa at mp-MRI, and imaging-guided prostate biopsy.

7.2 Prostate cancer at mp-MRI

7.2.1 Tumor detection

Detection of PCa at mp-MRI depends primarily on its appearance on T2-weighted imaging (T2WI) and diffusion-weighted imaging (DWI). PCa typically appears hypointense on T2WI with corresponding hyperintensity on DWI and hypointensity on apparent diffusion coefficient (ADC) map (i.e., restricted diffusion).[2] In the peripheral zone (PZ), tumors typically appear round or ill-defined (Fig. 7.1).[4] In the transition zone (TZ), in the setting of benign prostatic hyperplasia (BPH), there is often a background of benign nodules and stromal hyperplasia that demonstrates areas of T2 hypointensity and diffusion restriction, thus making detection of PCa in the TZ more challenging.[2,5] Tumors in the TZ often demonstrate an ill-defined or smudgy, T2 hypointense appearance, the so-called "erased charcoal sign," which may aid in tumor identification. Other features associated with TZ tumors include lenticular shape, spiculated margins, and lack of the capsule that is often seen with benign nodules (Fig. 7.2).[4] If the tumor is located in the anterior aspect of the TZ, high *b*-value (*b* > 1000) DWI may play an important role in demonstration of the diffusion restriction of the lesion. Invasion of adjacent structures by a lesion is concerning for malignancy regardless of the location of the lesion. Conversely, the presence of bilateral, relatively symmetric lesions is suggestive of benignity.

The use of dynamic contrast-enhanced (DCE) imaging of the prostate at mp-MRI is controversial, as PCa demonstrates variable enhancement patterns on DCE, and some benign lesions demonstrate similar enhancement patterns. However, DCE imaging may increase sensitivity for detection of PCa, particularly in the setting of image

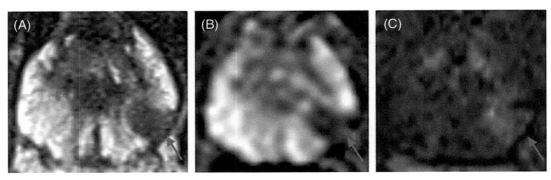

FIG. 7.1   PCa in the PZ. A 64-year-old male with elevated PSA of 5.2. Axial T2WI (A) from mp-MRI of the prostate demonstrates a hypointense lesion (blue arrow) in the left PZ. Axial ADC image (B) demonstrates associated diffusion restriction of the lesion (blue arrow). Axial DCE image (C) demonstrates postcontrast enhancement of the lesion (blue arrow). PI-RADS 4. Biopsy confirmed PCa, Gleason 3 + 4.

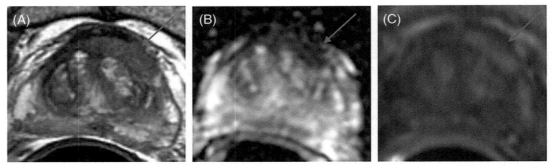

FIG. 7.2   PCa in the TZ. A 61-year-old male with elevated PSA of 4.8. Axial T2WI (A) from mp-MRI of the prostate demonstrates a homogeneous, lenticular hypointense lesion (blue arrow) in the left TZ anteriorly extending to the right. Axial ADC image (B) demonstrates associated diffusion restriction of the lesion (blue arrow). Axial DCE image (C) demonstrates postcontrast enhancement of the lesion (blue arrow). PI-RADS 5. Biopsy confirmed PCa, Gleason 3 + 4.

quality degradation on other sequences (e.g., artifact on DWI from hip prosthesis). In patients with a history of prior treatment for PCa, local recurrence may be best demonstrated on DCE imaging.[3,5] Its use is currently supported by PI-RADS v2.1, pending further research and particularly in the above settings.[4] DCE imaging may also help differentiate PCa from its mimics, as discussed in detail later in this chapter. At DCE imaging, PCa typically appears as focal, often vivid enhancement, appearing before or concurrently with enhancement of background prostate tissue, with corresponding abnormality on T2WI and/or DWI.[4]

It is important to note that some PCa is not well delineated on mp-MRI, with mp-MRI failing to identify up to 16% of clinically significant PCa lesions in one study.[6] Mp-MRI may also underestimate the size of some PCa lesions.[6] This may be of particular importance with the use of focal treatment for PCa such as cryotherapy or laser ablation.

7.2.2 Prostate cancer staging

In addition to detection of PCa, mp-MRI continues to play an important role in PCa staging. MRI typically depicts the location and size of the tumor within the prostate. Location of the tumor relative to the urethra, particularly in the apex at the level of the external urethral sphincter, may have implications for potential surgery or radiation therapy.[4] Prostate mp-MRI should also be assessed for evidence of extracapsular extension (ECE), including seminal vesicle involvement (SVI). ECE is often best demonstrated at T2WI due to the high resolution of the images. ECE may appear as direct visualization of tumor, typically T2 hypointensity, protruding beyond the capsule versus bulging or irregularity of the overlying capsule in less conspicuous cases (Fig. 7.3). Contact of the tumor with the capsule over a length of more than 1 cm should raise suspicion for ECE as well.[2,4] Potential involvement of the neurovascular bundles (NVBs) by ECE should also be described. SVI typically appears as abnormal T2 hypointensity, diffusion restriction, and/or postcontrast enhancement within the seminal vesicles (Fig. 7.4).[2] ECE and SVI may be subtle, sometimes only well-seen in one plane at T2WI.

At least one sequence through the entire pelvis should be included for each prostate MRI, allowing for assessment of pelvic nodal and metastatic disease. Evaluation of nodal involvement at mp-MRI is limited to assessment of pelvic nodal size and morphology, with nodes measuring larger than 0.8 cm in maximum short axis diameter, particularly those with rounded morphology, concerning for possible PCa involvement. Metastatic disease may be present in smaller nodes as well. Metastatic nodal disease, if present, may commonly be found in the proximal external iliac nodes on the same side as the PCa. Common iliac nodal involvement is also common. Osseous metastatic disease is the most common site of non-nodal metastatic disease in PCa, and pelvic bones should be assessed for potential lesions on the whole pelvis sequences as well, with bony metastases often demonstrating enhancement on T1WI. For patients at higher risk for metastatic disease, additional imaging, including nuclear medicine bone scan or PET/CT, may be necessary for complete staging.

7.2.3 Management of prostate cancer

Prostate mp-MRI also plays an important role in the management of PCa. In addition to PCa staging as above, mp-MRI can be used in the setting of active surveillance of PCa, both for initial patient selection for active surveillance and for continued monitoring of patients on active surveillance.[3] The role of mp-MRI in initial patient selection for active surveillance is to assess for more aggressive PCa that would warrant treatment rather than active surveillance. One study demonstrated upgrading of PCa in approximately 22% of patients on or considering active surveillance for PCa.[7] For patients already under active surveillance, mp-MRI can be used to monitor for disease progression that would warrant repeat biopsy and potentially treatment. Thus, periodic mp-MRI should be included in overall surveillance, particularly in the setting of other factors concerning for disease progression (e.g., rising PSA level). Prostate mp-MRI may also be used for guidance of local therapy for PCa, though such treatments are still evolving, and for detection of suspected recurrent PCa, which is discussed in more detail separately in this book.

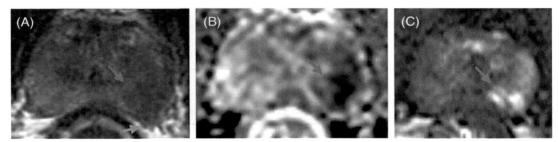

FIG. 7.3   **PCa in the PZ with evidence of extracapsular extension.** A 63-year-old male with elevated PSA of 18. Axial T2WI (A) from mp-MRI of the prostate demonstrates a hypointense lesion (blue arrow) in the left PZ with evidence of associated ECE (green arrow). Axial ADC image (B) demonstrates associated diffusion restriction of the lesion (blue arrow). Axial DCE image (C) demonstrates postcontrast enhancement of the lesion (blue arrow). Biopsy confirmed PCa, Gleason 3 + 4.

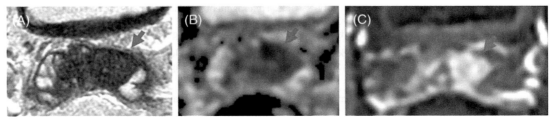

FIG. 7.4   **Seminal vesicle involvement.** A 61-year-old male with elevated PSA of 55 and lesion in the prostate consistent with PCa (not shown). Axial T2WI (A) from mp-MRI of the prostate demonstrates abnormal hypointensity in the seminal vesicles, left greater than right (blue arrow). Axial ADC image (B) demonstrates corresponding low ADC value (blue arrow), and axial DCE image (C) demonstrates associated enhancement (blue arrow). Findings are consistent with SVI.

7.3 PI-RADS v2.1

In 2012, the European Society of Urogenital Radiology (ESUR) published the PI-RADS v1 to aid in more accurate and standardized interpretations of prostate mp-MRI. Subsequently, a collaboration by the ESUR, American College of Radiology (ACR), and the AdMe Tech Foundation provided an updated version of PI-RADS (v2) to address prior limitations as well as evolving technology and data. The most recent version, PI-RADS v2.1, was published in 2019.[4,8] PI-RADS v2.1 provides background information on anatomy and pathology of the prostate, including PCa, clinical, and technical considerations for prostate MRI, suggestions for standardized reporting of prostate MRI as well as a scoring system for focal lesions as described below.

According to PI-RADS v2.1, focal abnormalities in the prostate should be scored on T2WI and DWI on a scale of 1–5 based on the presence of features concerning for PCa in each lesion. Evaluation of the scores from each sequence determines the overall PI-RADS score or assessment category, which reflects the likelihood of a lesion representing clinically significant PCa, with the overall PI-RADS scores ranging from 1, very low probability of clinically significant PCa, to 5, very high probability of clinically significant PCa (Table 7.1).[4] According to a recent review and meta-analysis, reported clinically significant PCa detection rates are 2% for PI-RADS 1 lesions, 4% for PI-RADS 2 lesions, 20% for PI-RADS 3 lesions, 52% for PI-RADS 4 lesions, and 89% for PI-RADS 5 lesions.[9] DWI is considered the "dominant" or "primary determining" sequence for the PZ, and T2WI is considered the dominant sequence for the TZ.[4] In other words, the appearance of a lesion on the dominant sequence contributes most to its overall PI-RADS score (Tables 7.2 and 7.3A and B). In the absence of limited DWI or T2WI, DCE imaging contributes little to the overall PI-RADS score: DCE imaging is scored as either present or absent abnormal enhancement. Positive enhancement in a PZ lesion that receives a score of 3 on DWI increases the overall PI-RADS score from 3 to 4; otherwise, the score at DCE imaging does not affect the overall PI-RADS score (Table 7.3A and B).

TABLE 7.1   PI-RADS v2.1 assessment categories.[4]

PI-RAD category	Interpretation	Clinically significant PCa detection rate[9]
PI-RADS 1	Clinically significant PCa highly unlikely	2%
PI-RADS 2	Clinically significant PCa unlikely	4%
PI-RADS 3	Intermediate probability (equivocal) for clinically significant PCa	20%
PI-RADS 4	Clinically significant PCa likely	52%
PI-RADS 5	Clinically significant PCa highly likely	89%

TABLE 7.2   Scoring of PZ and TZ lesions according to PI-RADS v2.1: imaging features.[4,39]

Score	DWI/ADC* DWI assessed on high *b*-value images	T2WI
1	Normal	PZ: Normal TZ: Normal or typical encapsulated nodule
2	Linear/wedge-shaped low signal intensity on ADC and/or linear/wedge-shaped high intensity on DWI	PZ: Linear/wedge-shaped or ill-defined, diffuse mild low signal intensity TZ: Partially encapsulated nodule or nonencapsulated but circumscribed nodule m area in between nodules that shows mildly low signal intensity
3	Focal low intensity on ADC and/or focal high intensity on DWI; can be markedly** low intensity on ADC OR markedly high signal intensity on DWI (not both)	PZ: Heterogeneous signal intensity or ill-defined or round moderately low signal intensity TZ: Nodule with heterogenous signal intensity and obscured margins
4	Focal markedly low intensity on ADC and markedly high signal intensity on DWI	PZ: Circumscribed, moderately low signal intensity TZ: Moderately low signal intensity; lenticular or noncircumscribed homogenous nodule
5	Features of 4 with maximum diameter >1.5 cm or extraprostatic extension/invasive behavior	PZ: Features of 4 with maximum diameter >1.5 cm or extraprostatic extension/invasive behavior TZ: Features of 4 with maximum diameter >1.5 cm or extraprostatic extension/invasive behavior

DWI/ADC: same criteria for PZ and TZ.
**Markedly: a more pronounced signal difference than any other focus, in the same zone.*

TABLE 7.3 Scoring of TZ and PZ lesions according to PI-RADS v2.1.

(A) Scoring of TZ lesions according to PI-RADS v2.1[4]

Score at T2WI	Score at DWI	Score at DCE	Overall PI-RADS Score
1	1–5	Absent or Present	1
2	1–3	Absent or Present	2
	4–5	Absent or Present	3
3	1–4	Absent or Present	3
	5	Absent or Present	4
4	1–5	Absent or Present	4
5	1–5	Absent or Present	5

(B) Scoring of PZ lesions according to PI-RADS v2.1[4]

Score at DWI	Score at T2WI	Score at DCE	Overall PI-RADS Score
1	1–5	Absent or Present	1
2	1–5	Absent or Present	2
3	1–5	Absent	3
		Present	4
4	1–5	Absent or Present	4
5	1–5	Absent or Present	5

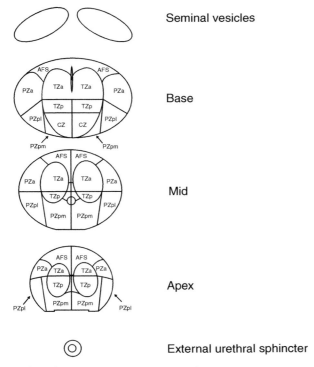

Seminal vesicles

Base

Mid

Apex

External urethral sphincter

FIG. 7.5   PI-RADS v2.1 sector map.[4] *a*, anterior; *AFS*, anterior fibromuscular stroma; *CZ*, central zone; *p*, posterior; *pl*, posterolateral; *pm*, posteromedial; *PZ*, peripheral zone; *TZ*, transition zone.

7.3.1 Reporting

PI-RADS v2.1 provides guidelines for reporting of mp-MRI of the prostate. The prostate should be measured in three dimensions, and its volume should be reported. PI-RADS 1 or 2 lesions do not need to be described but may be described if desired, particularly if they may be relevant to future imaging or procedures.[4] Up to four focal lesions with PI-RADS scores 3–5 may be reported, and an index or dominant lesion should be reported. If there are more than four lesions, the most suspicious and/or largest should be reported. Similarly, the index lesion is the largest or most aggressive-appearing lesion. For example, if one of multiple lesions demonstrates ECE, it should be classified as the index lesion even if it is not the largest.[4] At least the maximum dimension of each lesion on axial images should be reported. If the craniocaudal dimension of the lesion is greater than this value, this should also be reported. The location of each lesion within the prostate should be described. PI-RADS v2.1 recommends use of a sector map, which describes 41 regions: 38 within the prostate, one for each seminal vesicle, and one for the external urethral sphincter (Fig. 7.5).[4] Each lesion should be localized to a sector, and involvement of any adjacent sectors should be reported. Any ECE and involvement of adjacent structures should be described. Sample report templates are provided in PI-RADS v2.1.

TABLE 7.4 Pearls and pitfalls in diagnosis of PCa at mp-MRI.

PCa typically appears hypointense on T2WI with associated diffusion restriction and postcontrast enhancement
DWI-ADC is the dominant sequence for PZ lesions, and T2WI is the dominant sequence for TZ lesions
PZ lesions with mild or no diffusion restriction are likely benign
PCa in the TZ may demonstrate a smudgy appearance with ill-defined margins on T2WI, the so-called "erased charcoal sign," as well as lenticular shape and lack of a capsule
Symmetric bilateral lesions are typically benign
Use of DCE is controversial but may improve PCa detection and increase confidence in the diagnosis, particularly in setting of prior treatment or image degradation on other sequences
Some PCa, including clinically significant PCa, may be underestimated or not well seen at mp-MRI
PI-RADS 1 and 2 lesions do not need to be described
Up to 4 PI-RADS 3–5 lesions may be described
PI-RADS 4 and 5 lesions are typically biopsied; PI-RADS 3 lesions are often biopsied as well
MR/US fusion-guided biopsy has been becoming preferred technique for targeted biopsy
Systematic TRUS biopsy is controversial in setting of mp-MRI but may be of benefit, particularly for patients without prior systematic biopsy within several years
Nodal metastases may commonly be found in the common and external iliac nodes on the same side as the PCa
Lymph nodes >0.8 cm in maximum short axis diameter, particularly those with rounded morphology, are suspicious for metastatic disease

7.3.2 Limitations of PI-RADS v2.1 and potential future developments

While routine use of PI-RADS v2.1 allows for more accurate and standardized reporting of prostate mp-MRI, it does have limitations. For example, PI-RADS v2.1 provides recommendations for minimally acceptable scanning parameters and technical considerations, but specific guidelines for ideal MR technique are not provided. These are likely to be included in future versions.[4] It also does not address evolving MR techniques, but these may also be included in future versions as more data regarding such techniques becomes available.

PI-RADS v2.1 does not provide recommendations for management of focal lesions. PI-RADS 1 and 2 lesions are typically not biopsied, while biopsy should be considered for PI-RADS 4 and 5 lesions. Biopsy may also be considered for PI-RADS 3 lesions. At our institution, the majority of PI-RADS 3 lesions are biopsied with a tumor detection rate of approximately 38%. Management recommendations may be included in future versions of PI-RADS.[4]

PI-RADS v2.1 also does not address evaluation of recurrent PCa or management of disease progression in patients on active surveillance.[4]

Pearls and pitfalls in the diagnosis of PCa at mp-MRI and the use of PI-RADS are highlighted in Table 7.4.

7.4 Common and uncommon mimics of prostate cancer

Despite improved PCa detection on prostate MRI due to recent advances in mp-MRI, a wide variety of normal and abnormal entities can mimic PCa on mp-MRI and create diagnostic challenges.[10,11] As our department is one of the few large academic centers in the country performing MRI and US/MRI fusion-guided prostate biopsies, we have gained extensive experience in differentiating benign entities from malignant tumor in the prostate. Common entities mimicking PCa at MRI include but are not limited to chronic prostatitis, hypertrophic nodule, normal displaced central zone (CZ), postbiopsy hemorrhage, thickened surgical capsule, and ejaculatory ducts. Uncommon mimics of PCa at MRI include but are not limited to enlarged NVB, granulomatous prostatitis, insertion of capsule and fascia at the midline of the PZ, and prominent periprostatic fat. Although a number of these mimics have been the subject of formal scientific investigation and previously described in the peer-reviewed literature, others are reflection of our local experience. Recognition of the MR findings of these benign entities, along with the key MR features that may help to differentiate them from PCa, is important in avoiding unnecessary interventions and guiding appropriate clinical management.

7.4.1 Common mimics of PCa

7.4.1.1 *Chronic prostatitis*

Chronic prostatitis is very common, possibly resulting from undertreated acute prostatitis and recurrent infection but also occurring without prior history in older men with lower urinary tract obstruction. Routine cultures often

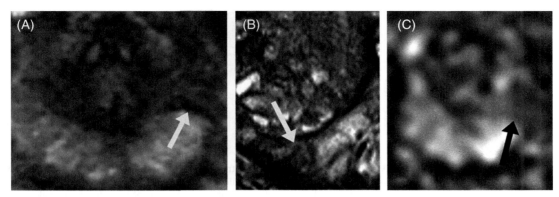

FIG. 7.6 **A 64-year-old male with elevated PSA to 4.8.** (A) Axial T2WI demonstrates a hypointensity in the left apex PZ (arrow). (B) Sagittal T2WI demonstrates the hypointensity in the left apex PZ (arrow). (C) ADC demonstrates mild diffusion restriction of the T2 hypointensity in the left apex PZ (arrow). There is mild increased enhancement of the focus (not shown). Biopsy confirmed prostatitis, not a tumor.

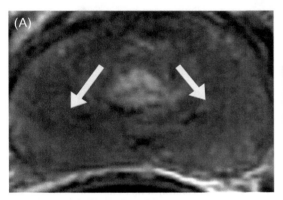

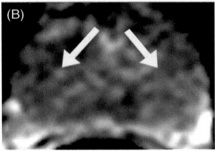

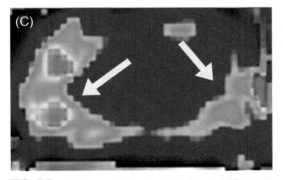

FIG. 7.7 **A 54-year-old male with elevated PSA to 15.** (A) Axial T2WI shows diffuse hypointensities in bilateral mid PZ without associated contour deformity (arrows). (B) ADC map demonstrates mild diffusion restriction in the PZ (arrows). (C) DCE shows bilateral symmetric vivid enhancement (arrows). Prostate biopsies confirmed prostatitis, not cancer.

do not allow identification of the causative organism. At histopathology, chronic prostatitis shows lymphocytes, usually accompanied by glandular atrophy.[12] Chronic prostatitis tends to be more indolent, often with no systemic symptoms. At MRI, the one of the most common benign entities that mimics PCa in the prostate is chronic prostatitis, particularly in the PZ. Chronic prostatitis may be diffuse or focal in the prostate with T2 hypointensity, diffusion restriction, and abnormal enhancement, mimicking PCa (Fig. 7.6).[13,14] There are clues to help differentiate chronic prostatitis from PCa. On T2WI, the hypointense areas in chronic prostatitis are usually geographic, ill-defined, and without associated contour deformity or mass effect on the adjacent normal prostate tissue or capsule.[14] On DCE, these areas may show bilateral symmetric enhancement (Fig. 7.7). Most importantly, chronic prostatitis has less degree of diffusion restriction than that seen in PCa, allowing for differentiation from PCa (Figs. 7.6B and 7.7B).[15,16]

7.4.1.2 Hypertrophic nodule

Hypertrophic nodules are present in the TZ in the majority of patients undergoing prostate MRI, with hyperplasia of the prostatic stromal and epithelial cells forming the nodules. Depending on the ratio of glandular to stromal tissue, these nodules may be hypo-, iso-, or hyperintense relative to the normal TZ on T2-weighted images. Due to the presence of prominent sclerotic, fibrous, or muscular elements, mixed and stromal nodules can demonstrate T2 hypointensity. These nodules may also demonstrate low ADC values and rapid contrast enhancement, mimicking PCa (Fig. 7.8).[17] Key clues for differentiation of a stromal nodule from PCa on T2WI include a well-defined contour (Fig. 7.8A), signal intensity potentially lower than that typically expected for PCa, and possible presence of small internal foci of T2 hyperintensity secondary to mixing with minimal glandular tissue.[18] Stromal nodules may show only mild diffusion restriction or may show abnormal signal intensity only on ADC map or DWI, but not on both. On DCE, enhancement of a stromal nodule may be similar to that of other benign nodules in the prostate (Fig. 7.8C).

Hypertrophic nodules can be seen in the PZ with T2 hypointensity, diffusion restriction, and rapid contrast enhancement, mimicking PCa (Fig. 7.9).[15,18] However, these nodules usually

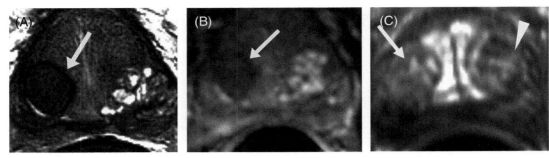

FIG. 7.8   A 65-year-old male with elevated PSA to 7.9. (A) Axial T2WI demonstrates a well-defined and markedly hypointense nodule in the right base TZ (arrow). (B) ADC map demonstrates diffusion restriction of the nodule in the right base TZ (arrow). (C) DCE shows mild enhancement of the nodule (arrow), similar to the left TZ (arrowhead). Biopsy confirmed not cancer (a stromal hypertrophy nodule).

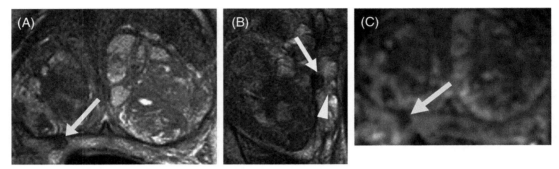

FIG. 7.9   A 79-year-old male with elevated PSA to 10. (A) Axial T2WI demonstrates a well-defined hypointense nodule in the right base PZ (arrow). (B) Sagittal T2WI shows the well-defined nodule in the right base PZ (arrow). The arrowhead indicates a layer of normal prostate tissue between the lesion and capsule. (C) ADC map shows diffusion restriction of the lesion (arrow). Biopsy confirmed no PCa.

demonstrate discrete, well-defined margins, measure less than 1 cm in diameter, and appear and rounded or spherical in shape. In addition, these nodules usually do not extend to the capsule on T2WI, so that normal prostate tissue is often present between the nodule and the capsule (Fig. 7.9A).[15,18] These nodules are often contiguous with the adjacent TZ in at least one plane on T2WI because most of these nodules arise from the TZ.

7.4.1.3 Normal displaced central zone

The CZ appears as a symmetric band of tissue between the peripheral and TZs, extending posterior to the TZ and urethra, proximal to the verumontanum, and surrounding the ejaculatory ducts.[19,20] The CZ exhibits homogenously decreased T2 signal intensity and low ADC value relative to the PZ. In patients with BPH, the TZ is hypertrophic and can compress and displace the CZ superiorly and laterally to the base, just inferior to the seminal vesicles.[12] If this process results in asymmetry of the right or left CZ, the displaced CZ in combination with its decreased T2 signal intensity and decreased ADC can mimic PCa (Fig. 7.10). However, on T2WI, the CZ is often visualized with sharp margins particularly in the posterior edge at the level of the ejaculatory ducts (Fig. 7.10A). Further, in contrast to the typical rapid enhancement of PCa, the CZ demonstrates no or minimal rapid enhancement on DCE.

7.4.1.4 Postbiopsy hemorrhage

Hemorrhage is commonly seen in the prostate after biopsy. It is more common in the PZ than in the TZ.[21] Hemorrhage can not only limit the ability of mp-MR imaging to delineate the extent or location of the tumor but also mimic PCa owing to the associated T2 hypointensity and diffusion restriction (Fig. 7.11). Key clues for differentiating postbiopsy hemorrhage from PCa include high T1 signal intensity of the area on T1WI and only mild associated diffusion restriction on ADC map.[21,22] If the hemorrhagic area has a very low ADC value, underlying tumor is not excluded. A follow-up prostate MRI in 3–6 months should be considered to reassess the area. In order to allow enough time for the resorption of blood products, most radiologists now recommend a postbiopsy delay of approximately 8 weeks before performing a prostate MRI.[15] PI-RADS v2.1 suggests a delay of at least 6 weeks after biopsy prior to prostate MRI.[4]

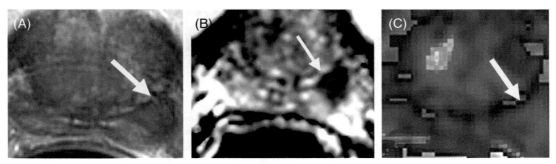

FIG. 7.10 **A 59-year-old male with elevated PSA to 8.5.** (A) Axial T2WI demonstrates a well-defined hypointensity in the left base (arrow). (B) ADC map shows diffusion restriction of the T2 hypointensity in the left base (arrow). (C) DCE shows no significant contrast enhancement of the focus in the left base (arrow). Biopsy confirmed normal prostate tissue (displaced left central zone).

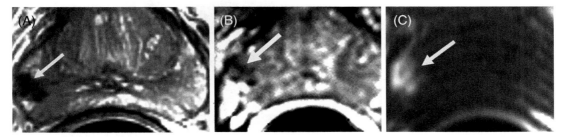

FIG. 7.11 **A 49-year-old male with elevated PSA to 11.2.** (A) Axial T2WI shows hypointensity in the right mid PZ (arrow). (B) ADC map shows diffusion restriction of the focus, mimicking PCa (arrow). (C) Axial T1WI shows high signal intensity of the region (arrow), consistent with hemorrhage. TRUS prostate biopsy prior to MRI demonstrated no tumor.

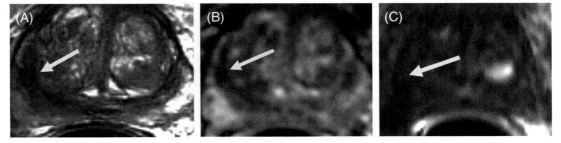

FIG. 7.12 **A 54-year-old male with elevated PSA to 6.2.** (A) Axial T2WI shows a band-like hypointensity between the right TZ and PZ (arrow). (B) ADC map shows diffusion restriction of the area (arrow), mimicking PCa. (C) DCE shows no significant contrast enhancement of the focus (arrow). Findings are consistent with right surgical capsule.

7.4.1.5 Thickened surgical capsule

In addition to the anatomic capsule of the prostate that surrounds the PZ, a "surgical" capsule surrounding the TZ has also been described, as it provides a landmark for surgery of BPH. This structure arises from the embryologic periurethral septum and is composed of fibrous and muscular tissue forming part of the network of supporting fibromuscular tissue in the prostate, including the anterior fibromuscular stroma.[15] The surgical capsule at MRI appears as an elongated T2 hypointensity with low ADC value, potentially mimicking PCa (Fig. 7.12). However, the classic location of the surgical capsule (between TZ and PZ) and its band-like or elongated, rather than mass-like, shape serve as clues to differentiate it from PCa.[23] Further, there is no associated postcontrast enhancement because the capsule is composed of dense fibromuscular tissue.

7.4.1.6 Ejaculatory ducts

The ejaculatory ducts are paired tubules that begin near the vas deferens behind the prostate and next to the seminal vesicles and are formed on each side by the union of the vas deferens and the duct of the seminal vesicle. They course through the prostate and empty into the prostatic urethra at the verumontanum. The ducts are visualized at

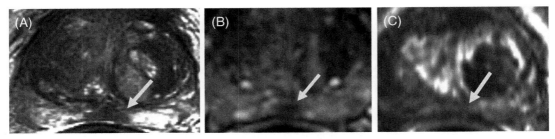

FIG. 7.13   **A 64-year-old male with elevated PSA to 5.4.** (A) Axial T2WI shows a hypointensity at the midline PZ at the level of the mid-gland (arrow). (B) ADC map shows diffusion restriction of the focus (arrow) at the midline of the PZ, mimicking PCa. (C) DCE shows no significant contrast enhancement of the focus (arrow). Findings are consistent with ejaculatory ducts.

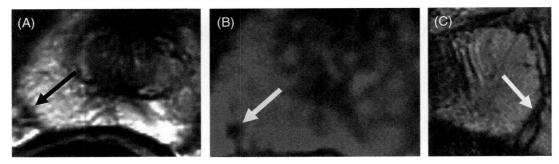

FIG. 7.14   **A 57-year-old male with elevated PSA to 7.0.** (A) Axial T2WI shows a small hypointensity along the right lateral aspect of the PZ (arrow). (B) ADC map shows diffusion restriction of the focus along the right lateral aspect of the PZ, mimicking PCa. (C) Sagittal T2WI shows that the hypointensity is elongated and located outside of prostate (arrow), consistent with prominent neurovascular bundle.

the level of the base to mid-gland in the medial aspect of the PZ near the midline. Since the ducts are encased by intermittent bundles of longitudinal fibers, at times with fibrotic tissue, they present low signal intensity on T2WI and ADC map, mimicking PCa (Fig. 7.13).[24] Their typical location, bilateral and elongated appearance, which may be better appreciated on the coronal and/or sagittal planes, and lack of rapid contrast enhancement on DCE help in differentiating the ejaculatory ducts from PCa.

7.4.2 Uncommon mimics

7.4.2.1 *Enlarged neurovascular bundle*

The NVBs include the nervous plexus, arteries, veins, and additional smaller nerve branches that supply the prostate gland. They have classically been viewed as discrete structures coursing along the posterolateral margins of the prostate near the prostate capsule at approximately the 5- and 7-o'clock positions.[25] The structures exhibit low signal intensity on T2WI and ADC map. The discrete rounded appearance of the NVB may be mistaken for PCa due to the proximity to the PZ (Fig. 7.14). Moreover, on the ADC map, NVB may appear to be located within the PZ relating to anatomic distortion of the prostate on this particular image set. Key clues in differentiating the NVB from PCa include tubular appearance when tracked across multiple consecutive slices, rounded contour if viewed en face on an individual axial slice, and typical location along the outer edge of the prostate capsule.[26,27]

7.4.2.2 *Granulomatous prostatitis*

Granulomatous prostatitis is an uncommon benign inflammatory condition often presenting as a firm nodule on digital rectal exam with elevated PSA that clinically mimics PCa.[28] Idiopathic granulomatous prostatitis is the most common type, making up 60–77.7% of granulomatous prostatitis cases in reported series.[29] It has no clear cause and no associated systemic disease and is often self-limiting. Infective granulomatous prostatitis can be caused by

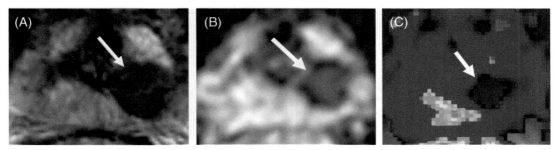

FIG. 7.15 A 69-year-old male with elevated PSA to 4.1. (A) Axial T2WI shows a hypointensity in the left apex PZ (arrow). (B) ADC map shows diffusion restriction of the lesion (arrow), concerning for PCa. (C) DCE demonstrates no enhancement of the lesion (arrow), not supportive of the suspicion of PCa. Biopsy of the lesion in the left apex confirmed granulomatous prostatitis.

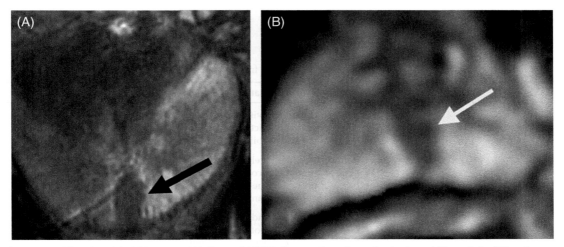

FIG. 7.16 A 73-year-old male with PSA to 5.7. (A) Coronal T2WI shows a hypointensity in the midline of the PZ at the apex (arrow). (B) ADC map shows diffusion restriction of the region (arrow) mimicking PCa. There is no rapid enhancement of the region (not shown). Biopsy confirmed no cancer. Findings are consistent with fusion of capsule and fascia in the midline of the PZ.

Mycobacterium tuberculosis (via hematogenous spread or direct extension from adjacent organs) or develop after intravesical bacillus Calmette–Guérin (BCG) therapy for bladder cancer. On MR imaging, this entity appears as a discrete mass with significant hypointensity on T2WI and ADC map mimicking PCa (Fig. 7.15). Additionally, there may be associated infiltration of the periprostatic fat as this is an inflammatory process, which can appear similar to extraprostatic tumor extension.[15] One clue in differentiation is that granulomatous prostatitis may have a large area without enhancement due to foci of necrosis within the lesion (Fig. 7.15C).[16]

7.4.2.3 *Insertion of capsule and fascia at the midline of the peripheral zone*

A T2 hypointensity at the midline of the PZ may be encountered at mp-MRI at the level of the mid-gland to apex. Fusion of the prostatic capsule and fascia at this region is believed to be responsible for this T2 hypointensity.[16] This focus at midline may also show diffusion restriction on ADC map, mimicking PCa (Fig. 7.16). MRI features including concave contour of the prostate at the focus, midline location of the focus, and lack of associated dynamic contrast enhancement are the key clues for differentiating this entity from PCa.[16]

7.4.2.4 *Prominent periprostatic fat*

Susceptibility effects from chemical shift artifacts caused by periprostatic fat can lead to significant diffusion restriction which mimics PCa (Fig. 7.17).[10] However, unlike PCa, periprostatic fat is located adjacent to but outside the prostate,[10,25] with high T1 and T2 signal intensity (Fig. 7.17B) and without contrast enhancement.

Key clues for differentiating PCa from its common and uncommon mimics are summarized in Tables 7.5 and 7.6.

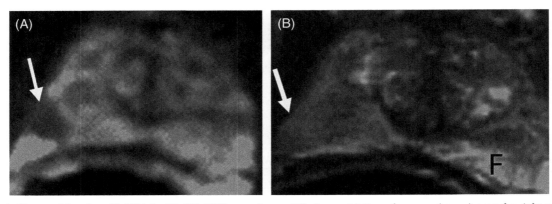

FIG. 7.17   A 69-year-old male with PSA to 4.9. (A) ADC map shows diffusion restriction of an area (arrow) near the right apex of the PZ, mimicking PCa. (B) Axial T2WI shows high T2 signal of the corresponding focus (arrow), identical to that of the adjacent fat (F), excluding PCa. Findings are consistent with periprostatic fat.

TABLE 7.5   Key MR clues that help in differentiating common mimics from prostate cancer.

Mimic	Key clues in differentiation
Chronic prostatitis	• Ill-defined margins with no associated contour deformity • Slight diffusion restriction • Possible symmetric, bilateral contrast enhancement
Hypertrophic nodule	• Round shape with well-defined margins • Lack of "erased charcoal" appearance if in TZ • Layer of normal tissue between nodule and prostate capsule if in PZ • Size typically less than 1 cm if in PZ
Normal displaced central zone	• Typical symmetric and well-defined appearance • Location at the level of ejaculatory ducts • Lack of rapid contrast enhancement
Postbiopsy hemorrhage	• Very abnormal T2 signal intensity with only mild diffusion restriction • High T1 signal intensity
Thickened surgical capsule	• Band-like or crescentic shape • Location at the junction of the PZ and TZ • Lack of rapid contrast enhancement
Ejaculatory ducts	• Location at the medial aspect of the PZ near the midline from the base to mid-gland • Bilateral and elongated appearance • Lack of rapid contrast enhancement

TABLE 7.6   Key MR clues that help in differentiating uncommon mimics from prostate cancer.

Mimic	Key clues in differentiation
Enlarged neurovascular bundle	• Tubular appearance on at least one plane • Location along outer edge of the prostate capsule
Granulomatous prostatitis	• Large areas of nonenhancement due to foci of necrosis within the lesion • Possible history of BCG treatment for bladder cancer
• Insertion of capsule and fascia at the midline of the PZ	• Midline location with concave contour of the prostate at the focus • Lack of rapid enhancement
Prominent periprostatic fat	• High T1 and T2 signal intensity • Location adjacent to but outside the prostate • Lack of rapid enhancement

7.5 Imaging-guided prostate biopsy

Screening for PCa is evolving given the improved PCa detection due to recent advances in mp-MRI of the prostate. Traditionally, PCa screening has included DRE of the prostate, monitoring of PSA levels, and systematic TRUS prostate biopsy. During a TRUS biopsy, the prostate is divided into segments, and a sample is obtained from each segment. When systematic TRUS biopsy was first introduced, the prostate was typically divided into sextants (i.e., bilateral base, mid-gland, and apex), and a sample was obtained from each sextant. In recent decades, the number of samples typically obtained has increased to improve detection of PCa, now with 10–18 samples typically obtained.[30,31] When performing systematic TRUS biopsies, we typically obtain 12 cores, as is common practice for many providers. In a typical 12-core biopsy, medial and lateral samples are obtained from each sextant. Additional, or fewer, samples may be taken based on individual factors such as prostate size, biopsy history, and clinician preference. Samples may be obtained from focal lesions if identified, but ultrasound is less sensitive and specific for identification of focal PCa when compared to mp-MRI.[3] Systematic TRUS biopsy may miss a significant number, potentially 50–80%, of clinically significant PCa,[32] particularly lesions located in the anterior aspect of the prostate and in the apex.[32] However, with recent advances in mp-MRI allowing for use of mp-MRI as a screening tool for PCa, potentially prior to TRUS biopsy, focal lesions concerning for PCa at mp-MRI can be targeted accurately using the methods described below.

7.5.1 In-gantry MRI-guided prostate biopsy

One method for biopsy of lesions concerning for PCa at mp-MRI is in-gantry MRI-guided prostate biopsy. The patient is typically positioned prone on the MR scanner table, and an endorectal needle guide is utilized. The biopsy needle is advanced to the area of concern under the guidance of serial MR scanning (Fig. 7.18).[30,33] This biopsy method allows for precise biopsy of target lesions but has disadvantages as well, including the length and cost of the procedure, use of MR scanner time, steep learning curve for the operator, and limited ability to perform a systematic prostate biopsy in the same setting.[31,33,34] The utility of systematic prostate biopsy for PCa screening in conjunction with mp-MRI and targeted biopsy is currently controversial, but it may be beneficial, as targeted biopsy based on mp-MRI alone may miss clinically significant PCa in up to 23% of cases.[30,34,35] Given its disadvantages, in-gantry MRI-guided prostate biopsy has been replaced in many institutions by MR/US fusion-guided prostate biopsy, which addresses some of the limitations of in-gantry MRI-guided prostate biopsy.

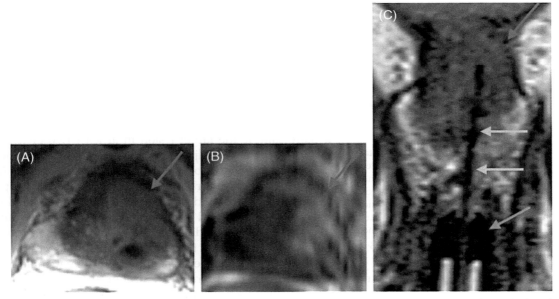

FIG. 7.18 Transrectal in-gantry MRI-guided targeted prostate biopsy. A 69-year-old male with history of elevated PSA of 26.5 and prior negative TRUS biopsy. Axial T2WI (A) from mp-MRI of the prostate demonstrates an ill-defined hypointense lesion (blue arrow) in the anterior left TZ. There is mild-associated diffusion restriction (not shown). Axial DCE image (B) demonstrates postcontrast enhancement of the lesion (blue arrow). Oblique axial T2WI (C) from in-gantry MRI-guided biopsy demonstrates the needle (yellow arrows) extending into the lesion (blue arrow) via a needle guide (green arrow) in the rectum. Pathology demonstrated PCa, Gleason score 4 + 3.

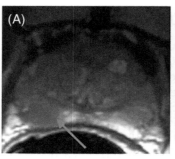
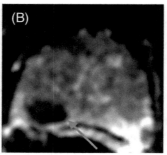
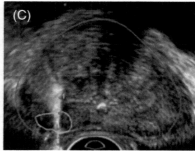

FIG. 7.19 **Transrectal MR/US fusion-guided targeted prostate biopsy.** An 82-year-old male with history of elevated PSA of 9.2. Axial T2WI (A) and axial ADC image (B) from mp-MRI of the prostate demonstrate a suspicious lesion (blue arrows) in the right peripheral zone. Grayscale ultrasound image with MR fusion overlay (C) demonstrates a biopsy needle (yellow line) extending into the target lesion (green outline) in the prostate (purple outline) via a needle guide on the transrectal ultrasound transducer. Pathology demonstrated PCa, Gleason score 4 + 3.

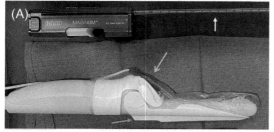

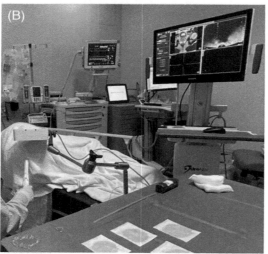

FIG. 7.20 **Transrectal MR/US fusion-guided targeted prostate biopsy.** (A) With the UroNav system (Philips), a navigation sensor (yellow arrow) is attached to a transrectal ultrasound transducer. The biopsy needle (white arrow, Bard) is inserted through the needle guide (green arrow) on the transducer. (B) The UroNav electromagnetic field generator (orange arrow) is positioned above the patient's pelvis to allow for probe tracking.

7.5.2 MR/US fusion-guided prostate biopsy

With the increased use of mp-MRI for evaluation of PCa, there has also been increased use of MR/US fusion technology for prostate biopsy. With the MR/US fusion technique, the operator defines the prostate boundary and target lesion(s) on the MR images in the software prior to the biopsy. During the procedure, real-time ultrasound is utilized instead of MRI, thus decreasing the typical length and cost of the procedure, freeing up MR scanner time, and more easily allowing for systematic prostate biopsy in the same setting if desired. Depending on the biopsy system utilized, the MR prostate boundary is either overlaid on the real-time ultrasound images using landmarks for registration or fused with a boundary of the prostate defined at ultrasound.[36] The target lesion(s) are then overlaid on the fused boundary, allowing for targeted biopsy of those areas (Fig. 7.19). The accuracy of the fusion of the MR and US images can significantly affect the accuracy of the biopsy itself. Care should be taken to account for differences in patient positioning and differences in the shape of the prostate due to factors such as pressure on the prostate from the ultrasound transducer or distention of the adjacent urinary bladder.[34,37] Attention should also be paid to the registration of the prostate boundary with the prostate on the real-time ultrasound images, which is facilitated by probe-tracking technologies, including electromagnetic systems, angle-sensing systems, and completely software-based systems (Fig. 7.20).[34,37] We usually sample the target lesion in at least two areas, potentially including the tissue adjacent to the target defined by the software, to avoid sampling error due to misregistration of the MRI target with the real-time ultrasound. Depending on the biopsy system utilized, the ultrasound and biopsy may be performed via a transrectal or transperineal approach. With a transrectal approach, the biopsy needle is introduced via a needle guide on the transrectal ultrasound transducer, through the wall of the rectum, and into the prostate. With a transperineal approach, the patient is placed in the dorsal lithotomy position, and the biopsy needle is introduced percutaneously through the perineum and into the prostate, typically still under the guidance of transrectal ultrasound with the ultrasound transducer held in place with a stepper device. Biopsy via a transperineal approach typically has a decreased risk of infection compared with a transrectal approach.[38] However, transperineal prostate biopsy may require additional equipment and increased anesthesia. In our practice, we have been able to significantly reduce our infection rate for transrectal biopsy by using 2000 mg intravenous ceftriaxone as antibiotic prophylaxis and prefer to use a transrectal approach.

7.5.3 "Cognitive fusion" targeted prostate biopsy

When resources necessary for in-gantry MRI-guided or MR/US fusion-guided targeted prostate biopsy are not available, targeted TRUS biopsy may be performed using a "cognitive fusion" technique. Using this method, a target lesion seen on mp-MRI is localized with transrectal ultrasound based on knowledge of its location and adjacent landmarks on MRI. This technique is more dependent on the experience of the operator and their familiarity with the MR images,[37] but it was shown to be superior to systematic TRUS biopsy in some studies and is thus preferred when other methods are not available.[3,8,30,34]

7.6 Conclusion

Recent advances in mp-MRI have allowed for an expanded role of prostate MRI in the detection, staging, and management of PCa. As prostate mp-MRI becomes more widely available and the population ages, the use of mp-MRI will likely continue to increase. A variety of common and uncommon benign entities of the prostate can mimic PCa at mp-MRI, creating diagnostic challenges. Radiologists should be familiar with evaluation of PCa at mp-MRI, including PI-RADS v2.1, as well as PCa mimics in order to optimize the use of mp-MRI in this setting, establish correct diagnoses, and avoid unnecessary interventions.[30]

References

1. American Cancer Society. Key Statistics for Prostate Cancer. Accessed Feb 08, 2021. https://www.cancer.org/cancer/prostate-cancer/about/key-statistics.html.
2. Johnson LM, Turkbey B, Figg WD, Choyke PL. Multiparametric MRI in prostate cancer management. *Nat Rev Clin Oncol.* 2014;11(6):346–353. doi:10.1038/nrclinonc.2014.69.
3. Mendhiratta N, Taneja SS, Rosenkrantz AB. The role of MRI in prostate cancer diagnosis and management. *Future Oncol.* 2016;12(21):2431–2443. doi:10.2217/fon-2016-0169.
4. Turkbey B, Rosenkrantz AB, Haider MA, et al. Prostate Imaging Reporting and Data System Version 2.1: 2019 update of Prostate Imaging Reporting and Data System Version 2. *Eur Urol.* 2019;76(3):340–351. doi:10.1016/j.eururo.2019.02.033.
5. Barrett T, Rajesh A, Rosenkrantz AB, Choyke PL, Turkbey B. PI-RADS version 2.1: one small step for prostate MRI. *Clin Radiol.* 2019;74(11):841–852. doi:10.1016/j.crad.2019.05.019.
6. Borofsky S, George AK, Gaur S, et al. What are we missing? False-negative cancers at multiparametric MR imaging of the prostate. *Radiology.* 2018;286(1):186–195. doi:10.1148/radiol.2017152877.
7. Yu J, Fulcher AS, Winks S, et al. Utilization of multiparametric MRI of prostate in patients under consideration for or already in active surveillance: correlation with imaging guided target biopsy. *Diagnostics (Basel).* 2020;10(7):441. doi:10.3390/diagnostics10070441, PMID: 32610595; PMCID: PMC7400343.
8. Dutruel SP, Jeph S, Margolis DJA, Wehrli N. PI-RADS: what is new and how to use it. *Abdom Radiol (NY).* 2020;45(12):3951–3960. doi:10.1007/s00261-020-02482-x.
9. Oerther B, Engel H, Bamberg F, et al. Cancer detection rates of the PI-RADSv2.1 assessment categories: systematic review and meta-analysis on lesion level and patient level. *Prostate Cancer Prostatic Dis.* 2022;25:256–263. doi:10.1038/s41391-021-00417-1.
10. Bonekamp D, Jacobs MA, El-Khouli R, Stoianovici D, Macura KJ. Advancements in MR imaging of the prostate: from diagnosis to interventions. *Radiographics.* 2011;31(3):677–703. doi:10.1148/rg.313105139.
11. Vargas HA, Akin O, Franiel T, et al. Diffusion-weighted endorectal MR imaging at 3 T for prostate cancer: tumor detection and assessment of aggressiveness. *Radiology.* 2011;259(3):775–784. doi:10.1148/radiol.11102066.
12. Kitzing YX, Prando A, Varol C, Karczmar GS, Maclean F, Oto A. Benign conditions that mimic prostate carcinoma: MR imaging features with histopathologic correlation. *Radiographics.* 2016;36(1):162–175. doi:10.1148/rg.2016150030.
13. Franiel T, Ludemann L, Rudolph B, et al. Evaluation of normal prostate tissue, chronic prostatitis, and prostate cancer by quantitative perfusion analysis using a dynamic contrast-enhanced inversion-prepared dual-contrast gradient echo sequence. *Invest Radiol.* 2008;43(7):481–487. doi:10.1097/RLI.0b013e31816b2f63.
14. Shukla-Dave A, Hricak H, Eberhardt SC, et al. Chronic prostatitis: MR imaging and 1H MR spectroscopic imaging findings—initial observations. *Radiology.* 2004;231(3):717–724. doi:10.1148/radiol.2313031391.
15. Rosenkrantz AB, Taneja SS. Radiologist, be aware: ten pitfalls that confound the interpretation of multiparametric prostate MRI. *AJR Am J Roentgenol.* 2014;202(1):109–120. doi:10.2214/AJR.13.10699.
16. Yu J, Fulcher AS, Turner MA, Cockrell CH, Cote EP, Wallace TJ. Prostate cancer and its mimics at multiparametric prostate MRI. *Br J Radiol.* 2014;87(1037):20130659. doi:10.1259/bjr.20130659.
17. Li H, Sugimura K, Kaji Y, et al. Conventional MRI capabilities in the diagnosis of prostate cancer in the transition zone. *AJR Am J Roentgenol.* 2006;186(3):729–742. doi:10.2214/AJR.04.0775.
18. Yu J, Fulcher AS, Winks SG, et al. Diagnosis of typical and atypical transition zone prostate cancer and its mimics at multiparametric prostate MRI. *Br J Radiol.* 2017;90(1073):20160693. doi:10.1259/bjr.20160693.
19. McNeal JE. The zonal anatomy of the prostate. *Prostate.* 1981;2(1):35–49. doi:10.1002/pros.2990020105.
20. Vargas HA, Akin O, Franiel T, et al. Normal central zone of the prostate and central zone involvement by prostate cancer: clinical and MR imaging implications. *Radiology.* 2012;262(3):894–902. doi:10.1148/radiol.11110663.

21. Tamada T, Sone T, Jo Y, et al. Prostate cancer: relationships between postbiopsy hemorrhage and tumor detectability at MR diagnosis. *Radiology*. 2008;248(2):531–539. doi:10.1148/radiol.2482070157.

22. Rosenkrantz AB, Kopec M, Kong X, et al. Prostate cancer vs. post-biopsy hemorrhage: diagnosis with T2- and diffusion-weighted imaging. *J Magn Reson Imaging*. 2010;31(6):1387–1394. doi:10.1002/jmri.22172.

23. Semple JE. Surgical capsule of the benign enlargement of the prostate. Its development and action. *Br Med J*. 1963;1(5346):1640–1643. doi:10.1136/bmj.1.5346.1640.

24. Gray H. *The Unabridged Gray's Anatomy*: Running Press Kids; 1999.

25. Nunes LW, Schiebler MS, Rauschning W, et al. The normal prostate and periprostatic structures: correlation between MR images made with an endorectal coil and cadaveric microtome sections. *AJR Am J Roentgenol*. 1995;164(4):923–927. doi:10.2214/ajr.164.4.7726049.

26. Poon PY, Bronskill MJ, Poon CS, McCallum RW, Bruce AW, Henkelman RM. Identification of the periprostatic venous plexus by MR imaging. *J Comput Assist Tomogr*. 1991;15(2):265–268. doi:10.1097/00004728-199103000-00014.

27. Tempany CM, Rahmouni AD, Epstein JI, Walsh PC, Zerhouni EA. Invasion of the neurovascular bundle by prostate cancer: evaluation with MR imaging. *Radiology*. 1991;181(1):107–112. doi:10.1148/radiology.181.1.1887017.

28. Bour L, Schull A, Delongchamps NB, et al. Multiparametric MRI features of granulomatous prostatitis and tubercular prostate abscess. *Diagn Interv Imaging*. 2013;94(1):84–90. doi:10.1016/j.diii.2012.09.001.

29. Mohan H, Bal A, Punia RP, Bawa AS. Granulomatous prostatitis—an infrequent diagnosis. *Int J Urol*. 2005;12(5):474–478. doi:10.1111/j.1442-2042.2005.01068.x.

30. Das CJ, Razik A, Sharma S, Verma S. Prostate biopsy: when and how to perform. *Clin Radiol*. 2019;74(11):853–864. doi:10.1016/j.crad.2019.03.016.

31. Hong CW, Amalou H, Xu S, et al. Prostate biopsy for the interventional radiologist. *J Vasc Interv Radiol*. 2014;25(5):675–684. doi:10.1016/j.jvir.2013.12.568.

32. Benelli A, Vaccaro C, Guzzo S, Nedbal C, Varca V, Gregori A. The role of MRI/TRUS fusion biopsy in the diagnosis of clinically significant prostate cancer. *Ther Adv Urol*. 2020;12:1756287220916613. doi:10.1177/1756287220916613.

33. Verma S, Bhavsar AS, Donovan J. MR imaging-guided prostate biopsy techniques. *Magn Reson Imaging Clin N Am*. 2014;22(2):135–144. doi:10.1016/j.mric.2014.01.002.

34. Das CJ, Razik A, Sharma S. Magnetic resonance imaging-transrectal ultrasound fusion biopsy of the prostate—an update. *Semin Roentgenol*. 2018;53(3):219–226. doi:10.1053/j.ro.2018.04.003.

35. Rosenkrantz AB, Verma S, Choyke P, et al. Prostate magnetic resonance imaging and magnetic resonance imaging targeted biopsy in patients with a prior negative biopsy: a consensus statement by AUA and SAR. *J Urol*. 2016;196(6):1613–1618. doi:10.1016/j.juro.2016.06.079.

36. Wegelin O, van Melick HHE, Hooft L, et al. Comparing three different techniques for magnetic resonance imaging-targeted prostate biopsies: a systematic review of in-bore versus magnetic resonance imaging-transrectal ultrasound fusion versus cognitive registration. Is there a preferred technique? *Eur Urol*. 2017;71(4):517–531. doi:10.1016/j.eururo.2016.07.041.

37. Sarkar S, Verma S. MR imaging-targeted prostate biopsies. *Radiol Clin North Am*. 2018;56(2):289–300. doi:10.1016/j.rcl.2017.10.010.

38. Thomson A, Li M, Grummet J, Sengupta S. Transperineal prostate biopsy: a review of technique. *Transl Androl Urol*. 2020;9(6):3009–3017. doi:10.21037/tau.2019.12.40.

39. Barentsz JO, Weinreb JC, Verma S, et al. Synopsis of the PI-RADS v2 guidelines for multiparametric prostate magnetic resonance imaging and recommendations for use. *Eur Urol*. 2016;69(1):41–49. doi:10.1016/j.eururo.2015.08.038.

8

MRI of the recurrent prostate cancers

Jinxing Yu, Sarah G. Winks

Department of Radiology, Virginia Commonwealth University
Health System, Richmond, VA, United States

8.1 Introduction

Prostate cancer (PCa) recurrence after treatment is a significant issue. Despite advances in diagnosis and management of PCa, the disease still recurs after definitive treatment in up to 40% of patients.[1] Early diagnosis of local recurrence is important for making prompt treatment decisions and is strongly associated with patient prognosis. Without salvage therapy, the average time from development of local recurrence to distant metastasis is approximately 3 years.[2] Biochemical recurrence (BCR) does not differentiate local recurrence from systemic disease, and there is no reliable way to diagnose local recurrence clinically. Fortunately, recent advances in multiparametric MRI (mp-MRI) techniques have markedly improved detection of local recurrence following therapy.[3] Most local recurrences exhibit specific features at mp-MRI that make them readily detectable.[4] However, a variety of pitfalls can mimic recurrent PCa at mp-MRI, creating a diagnostic challenge. Following radical prostatectomy (RP), entities mimicking a local recurrence may include, but are not limited to, residual prostatic tissue, fibrotic scar, prominent vascular structures, granulation tissue, retained seminal vesicles (SVs), and contrast enhancement of the proximal urethra. After radiation therapy, mimics including focal regions of severe posttreatment change, well-preserved hypertrophic nodules in the central gland, and marked and asymmetric hypertrophic fibromuscular stroma may be encountered. The purpose of this chapter is to provide an overview of the MRI features of locally recurrent PCa and its mimics, emphasizing the key MRI features that will lead to make a definitive diagnosis of local recurrence and that help to differentiate local recurrence from its mimics, allowing for prompt, appropriate clinical management.

8.2 Key features of recurrent PCa at mp-MRI

8.2.1 Following radical prostatectomy

RP is a very common active treatment for PCa patients with localized disease, with around 40% of patients undergoing definitive therapy choosing this option.[5] Prostate-specific antigen (PSA) should drop to undetectable levels within 2–3 weeks after successful surgery, and patients should be followed with serial serum PSA measurements for early detection of possible BCR. According to the American Urological Association (AUA) guidelines, BCR after RP is defined as a serum PSA measurement ≥ 0.2 ng/mL, followed by a second confirmatory serum PSA measurement ≥ 0.2 ng/mL.[6]

Prostate mp-MRI can play a unique and important role in the evaluation if a local recurrence seems likely.[3,4] After surgery, the vesicourethral anastomosis (VUA) is often visualized as a ring of postoperative fibrosis, exhibiting low signal intensity on all sequences of mp-MRI.[7] SVs may be left behind in up to 20% of cases and are seen in their presurgical location with their characteristic tubular structure on T2W imaging.[8]

Locally recurrent PCa in the post-RP patient may occur anywhere in or around the surgical bed but most commonly occurs at the VUA.[9-11] T2W imaging is always used in the evaluation of postsurgery to determine anatomy and evaluate for potential soft tissue mass with certain signal patterns suspicious for recurrence. Recurrence tends to appear nodular and relatively hyperintense in comparison to pelvic muscle signal intensity on T2W imaging.[12] On DCE, the focal recurrence readily enhances as a focal nodule at the surgical bed during the arterial phase (Fig. 8.1).[13] In one study evaluating 72 post-RP BCR patients, when DCE was combined with T2WI, compared to T2WI alone, Cirillo et al. found a sensitivity of 84.1% (compared to 61.4%) and specificity of 89.3% (compared to 82.1%).[10] In general, the utility of diffusion-weighted imaging (DWI) is highly compromised due to surgical clips at the surgical bed.[9] However, in some cases, a diffusion restricted focus corresponding to the abnormality detected on T2WI and DCE is observed at high b number images ($b \geq 1000$) (Fig. 8.2).[10] Overall, early postcontrast enhancement at DCE is the most important finding, as DWI is likely to be degraded, and small foci of recurrent PCa may not be well seen at T2WI.

8.2.2 Following radiation therapy

Up to 40% of patients over 65 years old and 25% of patients under 65 years old choose RT as the definitive treatment for PCa, making it the second most common treatment.[14] RT can be offered as external-beam RT (EBRT) or brachytherapy. EBRT involves the use of ionizing radiation directed at the prostate and surrounding tissues through multiple portals. Using advanced computer-based planning systems, most modern methods in EBRT allow for highly targeted radiation with reduced dose to normal tissue by delivering photons or protons. In brachytherapy, radioactive sources (seeds or needles) are implanted directly into the prostate gland to deliver a high dose of radiation to the tumor while sparing the bladder and the rectum. Following RT, up to 30% of patients with high-risk disease can have BCR.[15] Majority of post-RT recurrences have been shown to be local, with the most common site

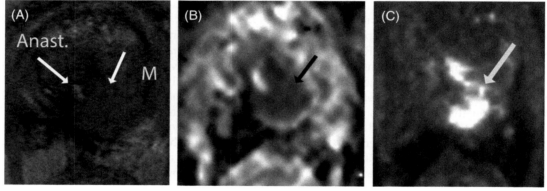

FIG. 8.1   A 68-year-old male status post prostatectomy with current PSA 5.5. (A) Axial T2WI shows a soft tissue mass (arrow) with slightly higher T2 signal intensity compared to the adjacent muscle (M), at the left of the vesicourethral anastomosis. (B) ADC demonstrates diffusion restriction of the mass (arrow). (C) DCE shows vivid enhancement of the mass (arrow). US/MRI fusion-guided biopsy confirmed recurrent PCa.

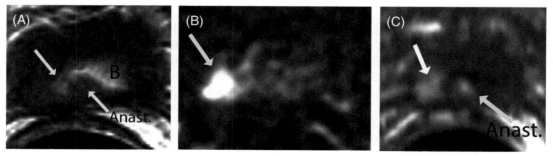

FIG. 8.2   A 65-year-old male status post prostatectomy with current PSA 0.7. (A) Axial T2WI shows a soft tissue mass (arrow) to the right of the vesicourethral anastomosis (Anast.) and the bladder neck (B). (B) DWI ($b = 1000$) demonstrates diffusion restriction of the mass (arrow). (C) DCE shows vivid enhancement of the mass (arrow) to the right of the anastomosis (Anast.). US/MRI fusion-guided biopsy confirmed recurrent PCa.

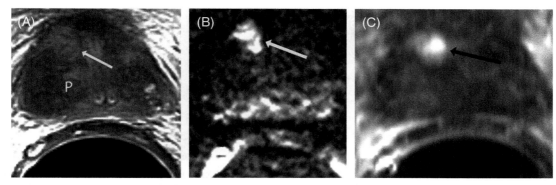

FIG. 8.3 **A 73-year-old male status post external radiation therapy for PCa GS 8 in the right base with current PSA 3.0.** (A) Axial T2WI shows a soft tissue mass with slightly higher T2 signal intensity (arrow) as compared to the background of the radiated prostate (P). (B) DWI (b = 1000) demonstrates diffusion restriction of the mass (arrow). (C) DCE shows vivid enhancement of the mass (arrow). US/MRI fusion-guided biopsy confirmed recurrent PCa GS 8.

of recurrence being the prostate. Therefore, evaluation with prostate mp-MRI is essential in the follow-up of BCR in these patients.[16]

8.2.2.1 Recurrent PCa in patients after external radiation therapy

The differentiation of the zones of the prostate is effaced in the irradiated prostate, which is smaller as a result of gland atrophy.[17] The entire prostate is hypointense on T2W imaging, further complicating differentiation between zones as well as distinction between benign versus tumor tissue.[18] Accurate localization of focal recurrence is essential for possible salvage radiation therapy. Recurrence most commonly appears at the original site of the primary tumor, with only 4–9% of local recurrent disease appearing elsewhere.[19,20] Unfortunately, T2W imaging has marked limitations even though malignant tumors are still most often recognized as lesions of relatively lower T2 signal intensity than that of surrounding noncancerous prostate. Because the postradiation gland fibrosis is less cellular and has diminished vascularity compared to pretreatment prostate tissue, the DWI and DCE appearance of the prostate is impacted after RT as well. However, the functional sequences of mp-MRI still play a more dominant role in the detection of post-RT recurrence because changes on DWI and DCE are not as drastic as on T2WI. On DWI, signal characteristics of post-RT recurrence are very similar to characteristics of primary PCa, with focal hypointensity on the ADC map and hyperintensity on high b-value DWI corresponding to a nodular area on T2W imaging. Although the vascularity of the overall irradiated prostate decreases with gland atrophy, recurrent tumors will retain their highly vascular network.[21] Recurrence will show early hyperenhancement relative to the treated prostate on DCE imaging. Focal, early enhancement is particularly suspicious for recurrent PCa if it correlates with abnormalities on T2WI and DWI (Fig. 8.3).[22]

8.2.2.2 Recurrent PCa in patients after brachytherapy

Posttreatment changes to the prostate following brachytherapy are very similar to those seen after EBRT, with the additional finding of visualization of the radioactive seeds used. Brachytherapy seeds can distort images by introducing MR susceptibility artifacts, particularly on DWI, making interpretation difficult. On T2W imaging, the brachytherapy seeds appear as small, hypointense, ellipsoid structures scattered throughout the prostate. The seeds gradually migrate peripherally within the gland as it shrinks in size. Following brachytherapy, the most common site of recurrence is at the location of the original tumor, which is similar to EBRT. Recurrence appears as a hypointense nodule on T2W imaging with paucity of radiation seeds nearby that shows rapid hyperenhancement on DCE imaging, with or without associated diffusion restriction (Fig. 8.4).[23]

In recent years, a new form of brachytherapy has been offered in temporary high-dose rate form (HDR). As the seeds in HDR brachytherapy are removed, image quality does not suffer from susceptibility artifacts related to the seeds. The data validating the use of mp-MRI post-HDR are limited because HDR is relatively new and BCR post-brachytherapy occurs less frequently. T2WI sensitivity in detecting the recurrence is limited due to the background changes in the gland. DWI shows high sensitivity for detection of recurrence in this setting. Early hyperenhancement of recurrent PCa at DCE imaging remains important as well.[24]

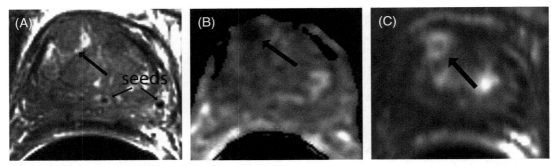

FIG. 8.4   A 76-year-old male status post internal radiation treatment for PCa, with current PSA 3.2. (A) Axial T2WI shows an ill-defined T2 hypointense lesion in the right anterior TZ (arrow). Radiation seeds are noted (seeds). (B) ADC demonstrates diffusion restriction of the lesion (arrow). (C) DCE shows vivid enhancement of the lesion (arrow). Targeted biopsy confirmed recurrent PCa.

8.2.3 Focal therapy

Focal therapy seems to demonstrate reasonable efficacy even though it is still in its investigative stages. Focal therapy relies on use of various energies for local destruction of the index tumor in the gland, such as microwave, focal laser ablation, cryotherapy, and high-intensity focused ultrasound. Depending on the extent of the treatment, loss of zonal differentiation, thickening of the prostatic capsule, and periprostatic fibrosis and scarring may be present. Local recurrence after focal therapy is typically located at the periphery of the previously treated area.[25] In general, enhancing soft tissue lesions with diffusion restriction after focal treatment should be considered suspicious for recurrence, just as they are after other forms of treatment (Fig. 8.5).[26]

8.3 Diagnosis of mimics of recurrent PCa

Recent advances in mp-MRI have markedly improved the detection of local PCa recurrence following all kinds of treatment, and there is increasing acceptance of emerging management options for local recurrence.[27-30] These advanced management options, such as imaging-guiding local targeted therapies, require reliable estimation of local recurrence.[31] Therefore, optimization of the interpretation of prostate MRI and distinguishing recurrent PCa versus its mimics is critical.[32]

8.3.1 Following radical prostatectomy

8.3.1.1 *Residual normal prostate tissue*

Following RP, a small amount of normal, nodular prostatic tissue may be present in the surgical bed and can be responsible for slight elevation of PSA, mimicking recurrent or residual PCa clinically.[33] In this clinical scenario, MR

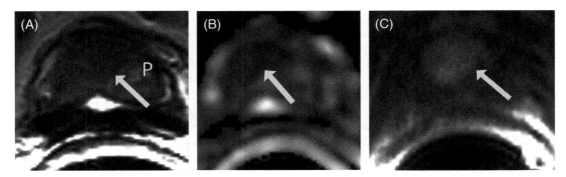

FIG. 8.5   A 64-year-old male status post-HIFU treatment for PCa with current PSA 4.1. (A) Axial T2WI shows an ill-defined T2 hypointense lesion in the right TZ (arrow) in a post-HIFU treated prostate (P). (B) ADC demonstrates diffusion restriction of the lesion (arrow). (C) DCE shows vivid enhancement of the lesion (arrow). US/MRI fusion-guided biopsy confirmed recurrent PCa GS 7.

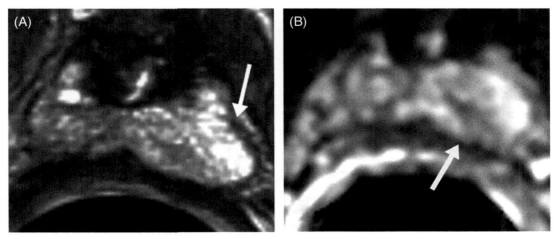

FIG. 8.6   A 68-year-old male status post prostatectomy with current PSA 0.2. (A) Axial T2WI shows a high T2 signal intensity mass (arrows) in the left aspect of the surgical bed. (B) ADC map demonstrates no diffusion restriction of the mass (arrow), excluding recurrence. Findings are consistent with residual prostate tissue.

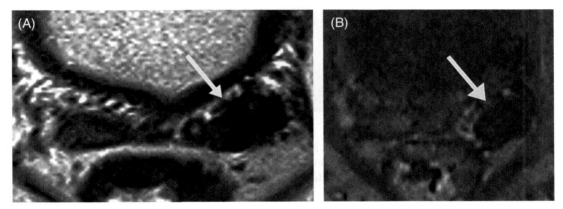

FIG. 8.7   A 64-year-old male status post prostatectomy with current PSA 3.4. (A) Axial T2WI shows a soft tissue mass (arrow) near the left seminal vesicle with marked T2 hypointensity. (B) DCE shows no enhancement of the mass (arrow). Findings are consistent with fibrotic scar.

imaging may be useful to help determine the amount and extent of residual prostate and to rule out residual or recurrent PCa. Benign residual prostate should have signal intensity similar to that of untreated prostate: that is, homogenous high signal intensity in the PZ and heterogeneous signal intensity in the TZ on T2-weighted images, without diffusion restriction (Fig. 8.6) or abnormal enhancement at DCE. The most important clinical information is the value of PSA and its stability over time. With residual prostatic tissue, patients typically have low PSA, usually less than 0.4 ng/mL, with little change over time.[33] The value of PSA in a patient of local recurrence usually gradually increases, with a doubling time of about 6–12 months.

8.3.1.2 *Fibrotic scar*

Fibrotic scar is commonly present in the surgical bed and appears as a soft tissue focus that can mimic a recurrence, particularly if the fibrosis has a nodular appearance. The key distinguishing feature of fibrotic scar from recurrent PCa is very low T2 signal intensity compared to muscle on T2-weighted images, with no or slightly delayed enhancement at DCE (Fig. 8.7). Typically, no significant diffusion restriction is noted in the scar, even though fibrotic tissue is highly cellular. The diffusion-weighted images may also be degraded due to surgical clips, limiting their utility.[34]

8.3.1.3 *Granulation tissue*

Granulation tissue in the surgical bed may occasionally be present as a result of surgery and resultant inflammation, most commonly in the perianastomotic region. The tissue shows higher signal intensity on T2WI relative to muscle

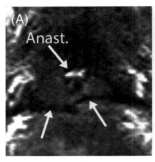
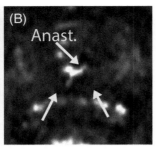

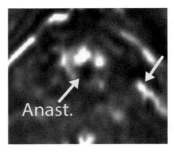

FIG. 8.8 **A 67-year-old male status post prostatectomy with current PSA 0.4.** (A) Axial T2WI shows soft tissue foci (arrows) posterior to the vesicourethral anastomosis (Anast.) bilaterally, with slightly higher T2 signal intensity than the adjacent muscle. (B) DCE shows no enhancement of the soft tissue foci (arrows) posterior to the vesicourethral anastomosis (Anast.). Findings are consistent with granulation tissue.

FIG. 8.9 **A 58-year-old male status post prostatectomy with current PSA 0.2.** DCE demonstrates an elongated and continuous structure at the left lateral aspect of the vesicourethral anastomosis (Anat.) with contrast enhancement (arrow). T2WI did not show corresponding abnormality (not shown). Findings are consistent with periprostatic vessel.

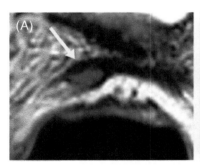
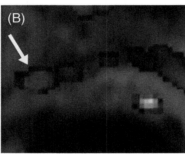

FIG. 8.10 **A 56-year-old male status post prostatectomy with current PSA 0.9.** (A) Axial T2WI shows homogeneous soft tissue in the expected location of the right seminal vesicle (arrow). (B) DCE demonstrates no associated contrast enhancement (arrow). US/MRI fusion-guided biopsy confirmed retained seminal vesicle, not recurrent tumor.

and some enhancement on DCE, potentially mimicking a local recurrence (Fig. 8.8).[35] However, granulation tissue usually demonstrates no rapid contrast enhancement as local recurrence typically does. If it is difficult to make a distinction, MRI/ultrasound fusion (MRI/US)-guided biopsy of the soft tissue mass at the surgical bed can be performed to confirm the diagnosis.

8.3.1.4 *Prominent vascular structures*

After removal of the prostate, prominent residual periprostatic vascular structures may be present in the surgical bed, demonstrating rapid contrast enhancement, mimicking recurrence. At T2WI, these vascular structures do not usually have the appearance of a soft tissue mass in the surgical bed and are frequently located in the anterior and lateral aspects of the surgical bed, with an elongated and continuous appearance noted on the consecutive images at DCE (Fig. 8.9).[28] In contrast, a local recurrence appears as rounded soft tissue with enhancement.

8.3.1.5 *Retained seminal vesicles*

After RP, retained SVs are observed in approximately 20% of patients.[36] Most retained SVs are very low in signal intensity on both T1- and T2-weighted images, presumably due to fibrosis, though they may demonstrate preservation of their convoluted tubular appearance.[37] If a retained SV shows focal abnormal T2 signal intensity, it may mimic a recurrence (Fig. 8.10). The clue to distinguish retained SV from recurrent PCa is lack of diffusion restriction or rapid contrast enhancement of the retained SV at DCE. Recognition of normal residual SVs is of paramount importance because such recognition prevents unnecessary biopsies for suspicion of recurrent tumor.

8.3.1.6 *Contrast enhancement of the proximal urethra*

Normal periurethral contrast enhancement at the proximal urethra at midline immediately below the VUA is commonly encountered, with similar periurethral enhancement in patients with no prior surgery. This enhancement usually has a circular and symmetrical shape that can be confidently recognized by experienced radiologists.[38] If the enhancement is lobulated and asymmetric, it may mimic a recurrence (Fig. 8.11). Continuation of the enhancement with the proximal or distal urethra and lack of corresponding soft tissue nodule at T2WI aid in making the distinction.

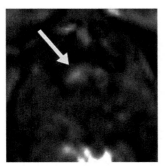

FIG. 8.11 **A 69-year-old male status post prostatectomy with current PSA 0.3.** DCE demonstrates asymmetric enhancement at the right lateral aspect of the vesicourethral anastomosis (arrow), continuous with the enhancement of the urethral mucosa (not shown). T2WI does not show corresponding abnormality (not shown). Findings are consistent with asymmetric enhancement of urethral mucosa at the anastomosis.

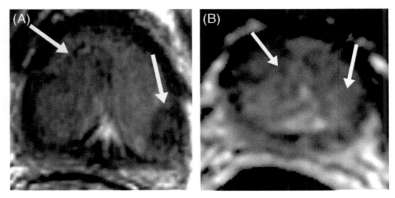

FIG. 8.12 **A 59-year-old male status post external-beam radiation therapy with a digital rectal exam demonstrating nodules at the right and left mid prostate.** (A) Axial T2WI demonstrates two focal areas of low T2 signal intensity in the transition zone (arrows). (B) ADC map demonstrates no diffusion restriction (arrows) in these two nodules, excluding recurrence.

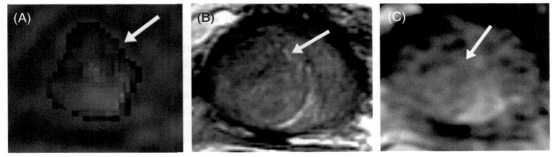

FIG. 8.13 **A 64-year-old male status post external-beam radiation therapy with nodular contour of the prostate.** The original PCa was in the left mid PZ. (A) DCE demonstrates a large area of focal, vivid enhancement in the right transition zone (arrow). (B) Axial T2WI demonstrates a corresponding well-defined nodule in the right transition zone (arrow). (C) ADC map demonstrates no diffusion restriction of the enhancing focus (arrow). Biopsy confirmed benign prostatic tissue.

8.3.2 Following radiation therapy

8.3.2.1 Focal region of severe posttreatment change

Following radiation therapy, focal areas of marked low T2 signal intensity, lower than the rest of the treated prostate, are common due to the uneven distribution of severe postradiation changes and treated tumor, potentially mimicking recurrence (Fig. 8.12A).[39] If pretreatment imaging is available, the focal hypointensity on T2WI related to the treated tumor can be easily identified. In addition, these areas of severe posttreatment change do not demonstrate diffusion restriction (Fig. 8.12B) or abnormal enhancement, distinguishing them from focal recurrence.[40]

8.3.2.2 Well-preserved hypertrophic nodule in the transition zone

Following radiation therapy, hypertrophic nodules in the TZ may be well preserved with little or no radiation-related changes, particularly in the median lobe. These nodules may demonstrate rapid contrast enhancement, mimicking recurrence (Fig. 8.13). Theses nodules can be differentiated from recurrence by well-defined margins, lack of internal smudgy appearance on T2WI (Fig. 8.13B), lack of significant diffusion restriction (Fig. 8.13C), and a location different than that of the original tumor.[39]

8.3.2.3 Marked hypertrophic fibromuscular stroma

Following radiation therapy, the prostate is typically small and atrophic. However, the anterior fibromuscular stroma may be hypertrophic with a mass-like appearance. The enlarged stroma may be asymmetric with a low T2 signal intensity and low ADC value due to fibrotic content, potentially mimicking a recurrence (Fig. 8.14). The key features

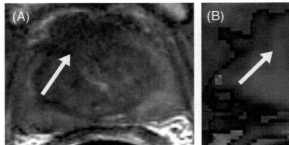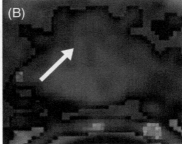

FIG. 8.14   A 71-year-old male status post external-beam radiation therapy with recent elevation of PSA to 3.0. (A) Axial T2WI demonstrates a low T2 signal intensity soft tissue mass in the anterior aspect of the right transition zone near the midline (arrow). (B) DCE shows no enhancement of the mass (arrow). US/MRI-guided biopsy confirmed benign fibromuscular stroma.

differentiating the stroma from recurrence are location anteriorly at or near the midline, significantly low signal intensity of the stroma on T2WI, lower than that of most recurrences, and lack of enhancement at DCE.[28]

8.4 Conclusion

MR imaging plays an important role not only in initial staging of PCa but also in evaluation for suspected residual or recurrent disease after treatment. All forms of treatment alter the MR imaging features of the prostatic region to some extent. Pathologic conditions of the prostate and prostatectomy bed following treatment have mp-MRI characteristics that overlap with local recurrence, creating a diagnostic challenge. The radiologist plays an important role in subsequent clinical management and potential treatment of PCa recurrence by recognizing the typical appearance of posttreatment changes and distinguishing them from the features of recurrent cancer (Table 8.1). Familiarity with the MR features of mimics and key clues in distinction after RP (Table 8.2) or radiation therapy (Table 8.3) is crucial in diagnosis and is important to avoid unnecessary intervention.

TABLE 8.1   Typical imaging features of recurrent PCa at mp-MRI.

PCa treatment	Typical MR features of recurrence
Prostatectomy	Soft tissue mass in the surgical bed with slightly higher T2 signal intensity than adjacent muscle, abnormal enhancement at DCE, and possible associated diffusion restriction at high b number images (such as $b \geq 1000$)
External radiation therapy	Mass-like T2 hypointense lesion, most commonly at the site of original tumor, with diffusion restriction and abnormal enhancement at DCE
Internal radiation therapy	T2 hypointense lesion, most commonly at the site of the original tumor, with paucity of radiation seeds nearby and abnormal enhancement at DCE
Focal therapy	T2 hypointense lesion, at the periphery of the previously treated area, with diffusion restriction and abnormal enhancement at DCE

TABLE 8.2   Key features that help differentiate recurrent PCa following radical prostatectomy from its mimics.

Mimic	Key features for differentiation
Residual normal prostate tissue	Low, stable PSA level, usually less than 0.4 ng/mL; no diffusion restriction or abnormal enhancement of the tissue
Fibrotic scar	Very low T2 signal intensity, even lower than that of adjacent muscle; lack of or only mild delayed enhancement
Granulation tissue	High signal relative to muscle on T2WI; lack of early rapid contrast enhancement at DCE
Prominent vascular structure	Lack of soft tissue mass in the surgical bed on T2WI; location in the anterior and lateral aspects of the surgical bed with an elongated and continuous appearance of enhancing focus at DCE
Retained seminal vesicles	Lack of diffusion restriction or rapid contrast enhancement at DCE; preservation of convoluted tubular appearance of SV
Contrast enhancement of the proximal urethra	Typical circular and symmetric shape; continuation of the enhancement with the urethra; lack of corresponding soft tissue nodule at T2WI

TABLE 8.3 Key MR features that help differentiate recurrent PCa following radiation therapy from its mimics.

Mimic	Key features for differentiation
Focal region of severe posttreatment change	Very low T2 signal intensity; lack of diffusion restriction or abnormal enhancement at DCE
Well-preserved hypertrophic nodule in the transition zone	Well-defined margins on T2WI; location different from that of the original tumor; lack of or only mild diffusion restriction
Markedly hypertrophic fibromuscular stroma	Typical location anteriorly at midline; symmetric or nearly symmetric appearance; very low signal intensity on T2WI, lower than that of typical recurrence; lack of enhancement at DCE

References

1. Babaian RJ, Troncoso P, Bhadkamkar VA, Johnston DA. Analysis of clinicopathologic factors predicting outcome after radical prostatectomy. *Cancer*. 2001;91(8):1414–1422 [PubMed: 11301387].
2. Bianco FJ, Scardino PT, Stephenson AJ, DiBlasio CJ, Fearn PA, Eastham JA. Long term oncologic results of salvage radical prostatectomy for locally recurrent prostate cancer after radiotherapy. *Int J Radiat Oncol Biol Phys*. 2005;62(2):448–453.
3. Mertan FV, Greer MD, Borofsky S, et al. Multiparametric magnetic resonance imaging of recurrent prostate cancer. *Top Magn Reson Imaging*. 2016;25(3):139–147 [PubMed: 27187164].
4. Vargas H, Wassberg C, Akin O, Hricak H. MR imaging of treated prostate cancer. *Radiology*. 2012;262(1):26–42.
5. Adamis S, Varkarakis IM. Defining prostate cancer risk after radical prostatectomy. *Eur J Surg Oncol*. 2014;40(5):496–504 [PubMed: 24613741].
6. Stephenson AJ, Kattan MW, Eastham JA, et al. Defining biochemical recurrence of prostate cancer after radical prostatectomy: a proposal for a standardized definition. *J Clin Oncol*. 2006;24(24):3973–3978 [PubMed: 16921049].
7. SD Allen, Thompson A, Sohaib SA. The normal post-surgical anatomy of the male pelvis following radical prostatectomy as assessed by magnetic resonance imaging. *Eur Radiol*. 2008;18(6):1281–1291 [PubMed: 18270715].
8. Sella T, Schwartz LH, Hricak H. Retained seminal vesicles after radical prostatectomy: frequency, MRI characteristics, and clinical relevance. *AJR Am J Roentgenol*. 2006;186(2):539–546 [PubMed: 16423965].
9. Cha D, Kim CK, Park SY, Park JJ, Park BK. Evaluation of suspected soft tissue lesion in the prostate bed after radical prostatectomy using 3T multiparametric magnetic resonance imaging. *Magn Reson Imaging*. 2015;33(4):407–412 [PubMed: 25527395].
10. Cirillo S, Petracchini M, Scotti L, et al. Endorectal magnetic resonance imaging at 1.5 Tesla to assess local recurrence following radical prostatectomy using T2-weighted and contrast-enhanced imaging. *Eur Radiol*. 2009;19(3):761–769 [PubMed: 18825386].
11. Lopes Dias J, Lucas R, Magalhaes Pina J, et al. Post-treated prostate cancer: normal findings and signs of local relapse on multiparametric magnetic resonance imaging. *Abdom Imaging*. 2015;40(7):2814–2838 [PubMed: 26105522].
12. Grant K, Lindenberg ML, Shebel H, et al. Functional and molecular imaging of localized and recurrent prostate cancer. *Eur J Nucl Med Mol Imaging*. 2013;40(Suppl 1):S48–S59 [PubMed: 23649462].
13. Sella T, Schwartz LH, Swindle PW, et al. Suspected local recurrence after radical prostatectomy: endorectal coil MR imaging. *Radiology*. 2004;231(2):379–385 [PubMed: 15064390].
14. Siegel R, DeSantis C, Virgo K, et al. Cancer treatment and survivorship statistics, 2012. *CA Cancer J Clin*. 2012;62(4):220–241 [PubMed] [Google Scholar].
15. Rosenbaum E, Partin A, Eisenberger MA. Biochemical relapse after primary treatment for prostate cancer: studies on natural history and therapeutic considerations. *J Natl Compr Canc Netw*. 2004;2(3):249–256 [PubMed] [Google Scholar].
16. Zumsteg ZS, Spratt DE, Romesser PB, et al. Anatomical patterns of recurrence following biochemical relapse in the dose escalation era of external beam radiotherapy for prostate cancer. *J Urol*. 2015;194(6):1624–1630 [PMC free article] [PubMed] [Google Scholar].
17. Sugimura K, Carrington BM, Quivey JM, Hricak H. Postirradiation changes in the pelvis: assessment with MR imaging. *Radiology*. 1990;175(3):805–813 [PubMed: 2343132].
18. Chan TW, Kressel HY. Prostate and seminal vesicles after irradiation: MR appearance. *J Magn Reson Imaging*. 1991;1(5):503–511 [PubMed: 1790374].
19. Arrayeh E, Westphalen AC, Kurhanewicz J, et al. Does local recurrence of prostate cancer after radiation therapy occur at the site of primary tumor? Results of a longitudinal MRI and MRSI study. *Int J Radiat Oncol Biol Phys*. 2012;82(5):e787–e793 [PMC free article] [PubMed] [Google Scholar].
20. Jalloh M, Leapman MS, Cowan JE, et al. Patterns of local failure following radiation therapy for prostate cancer. *J Urol*. 2015;194(4):977–982 [PubMed] [Google Scholar].
21. Franiel T, Ludemann L, Taupitz M, Bohmer D, Beyersdorff D. MRI before and after external beam intensity-modulated radiotherapy of patients with prostate cancer: the feasibility of monitoring of radiation-induced tissue changes using a dynamic contrast-enhanced inversion-prepared dual-contrast gradient echo sequence. *Radiother Oncol*. 2009;93(2):241–245 [PubMed] [Google Scholar].
22. Barchetti F, Panebianco V. Multiparametric MRI for recurrent prostate cancer post radical prostatectomy and postradiation therapy. *Biomed Res Int*. 2014;2014:316272 [PubMed: 24967355].
23. Rouviere O, Vitry T, Lyonnet D. Imaging of prostate cancer local recurrences: why and how? *Eur Radiol*. 2010;20(5):1254–1266 [PubMed: 19921202].
24. Tamada T, Sone T, Jo Y, et al. Locally recurrent prostate cancer after high-dose-rate brachytherapy: the value of diffusion-weighted imaging, dynamic contrast-enhanced MRI, and T2-weighted imaging in localizing tumors. *AJR Am J Roentgenol*. 2011;197(2):408–414 [PubMed: 21785087].

25. Marra G, Valerio M, Emberton M, et al. Salvage local treatments after focal therapy for prostate cancer. *Eur Urol Oncol.* 2019;2:526–538.

26. McCammack KC, Raman SS, Margolis DJ. Imaging of local recurrence in prostate cancer. *Future Oncol.* 2016;12(21):2401–2415 [PubMed: 27306275].

27. Mertan FV, Greer MD, Borofsky S, et al. Multiparametric magnetic resonance imaging of recurrent prostate cancer. *Top Magn Reson Imaging.* 2016;25(3):139–147 [PubMed: 27187164].

28. Notley M, Yu J, Fulcher AS, Turner MA, Cockrell CH, Nguyen D. Pictorial review. Diagnosis of recurrent prostate cancer and its mimics at multiparametric prostate MRI. *Br J Radiol.* 2015;88(1054):20150362 [PubMed: 26268143].

29. Abd-Alazeez M, Ramachandran N, Dikaios N, et al. Multiparametric MRI for detection of radiorecurrent prostate cancer: added value of apparent diffusion coefficient maps and dynamic contrast-enhanced images. *Prostate Cancer Prostatic Dis.* 2015;18(2):128–136 [PubMed: 25644248].

30. Weinreb JC, Barentsz JO, Choyke PL, et al. PI-RADS Prostate Imaging - Reporting and Data System: 2015, version 2. *Eur Urol.* 2016;69(1):16–40 [PubMed: 26427566].

31. Barret E, Harvey-Bryan KA, Sanchez-Salas R, Rozet F, Galiano M, Cathelineau X. How to diagnose and treat focal therapy failure and recurrence? *Curr Opin Urol.* 2014;24(3):241–246 [PubMed: 24625430].

32. Barentsz JO, Richenberg J, Clements R, et al. ESUR prostate MR guidelines 2012. *Eur Radiol.* 2012;22:746–757.

33. Vargas H, Wassberg C, Akin O, Hricak H. MR imaging of treated prostate cancer. *Radiology.* 2012;262(1):26–42.

34. Moman MR, van den Berg CAT, Bocken Kroger AE, et al. Focal salvage guided by T2-weighted and dynamic contrast-enhanced magnetic resonance imaging for prostate cancer recurrences. *Int J Radiat Oncol Biol Phys.* 2010;76(3):741–746.

35. Gaur S, Turkbey B. Prostate MR imaging for posttreatment evaluation and recurrence. *Radiol Clin N Am.* 2018;56(2):263–275.

36. Sella T, Schwartz LH, Hricak H. Retained seminal vesicles after radical prostatectomy frequency, MRI characteristics, and clinical relevance. *AJR Am J Roentgenol.* 2006;186(2):539–546.

37. Hricak H, Carrington BM. *MRI of the Pelvis: A Text Atlas.* London, England: Martin Dunitz; 1991.

38. Rischke HC, Schäfer AO, Nestle U, et al. Detection of local recurrent prostate cancer after radical prostatectomy in terms of salvage radiotherapy using dynamic contrast enhanced MRI without endorectal coil. *Radiat Oncol.* 2012;7:185. doi:10.1186/1748-717X-7-185.

39. Morgan VA, Riches SF, Giles S, Dearnaley D, deSouza NM. Diffusion-weighted MRI for locally recurrent prostate cancer after external beam radiotherapy. *AJR Am J Roentgenol.* 2012;198(3):596–602.

40. Panebianco V, Barchetti F, Barentsz J, et al. Pitfalls in interpreting mp-MRI of the prostate: a pictorial review with pathologic correlation. *Insights Imaging.* 2015;6:611–630. https://doi.org/10.1007/s13244-015-0426-9.

9

MRI of scrotum and testicles

Alex Chan[a], Pardeep Mittal[b], Courtney Moreno[c]

[a]Department of Radiology, Mayo Clinic Radiology, Rochester, MN, United States, [b]Department of Radiology and Imaging: Diagnostic, Medical College of Georgia, Augusta University Medical Center, Augusta, GA, United States, [c]Department of Radiology and Imaging Sciences, Emory University, Atlanta, GA, United States

9.1 Introduction

In this chapter, we will first review the basic MRI anatomy of the scrotum along with describing a standard MRI protocol that leverages its inherent superior soft tissue resolution and multiplanar capabilities. The remainder of the chapter will discuss a wide variety of example cases in the MRI evaluation of scrotal disorders organized by congenital abnormalities, scrotal pain, and scrotal masses. Although the intention of this chapter is not an encyclopedic account of all scrotal pathology, we hope to enhance the understanding of the evolving role scrotal MRI as a problem-solving tool at the diagnostic and pretreatment stages of patient management; all while serving as a practical daily reference. Throughout each section, many conditions will be briefly discussed along with their MRI features, and associated images. The ultrasound features and more detailed key clinical information about each disorder are summarized in Tables 9.1–9.3.

9.2 MRI anatomy of the scrotum and testicle

The basis for interpreting scrotal MRI begins with understanding the normal appearance of the scrotum and testicle on key MRI sequences. Standard T1- and T2-weighted images provide excellent contrast resolution between normal structures in the background of fat, which facilities the depiction of pathology. The testis should normally appear homogenous hypointense on T1-weighted images resembling surrounding musculature.[4] On T2-weighted images, the normal testis parenchyma should be hyperintense, although to a lesser degree than free fluid, and furthermore, the internal architecture of the testis should be clearly contrasted from this background. Thin fibrous septa surround lobules and portrayed as T2 hypointense lines that radiate toward the mediastinum. The tunica albuginea, a dense fibrous tissue surrounding the testis, is depicted as a T2 hypointense structure that homogenously enhances following the administration of gadolinium, which is likely related to the intact blood–testis barrier.[4] On DWI and ADC maps, the testicular parenchyma demonstrates high and low signal, respectively, likely on the basis of its densely packed seminiferous tubules surrounded by fibrous septa containing fibroblasts, lymphovasculature, and Leydig cells restricting the normal diffusion of water molecules.[4] In additional to the intratesticular structures, extratesticular structures are of paramount of importance. The spermatic cord displays as a long tubular T2 hypointense structure traversing the inguinal canal advantageously contrasted by the background of T2 hypertense fat in the coronal plane, which can also be used to compare to the other side for asymmetry. The epididymis exhibits T1 hypointensity and T2 hyperintensity that envelops the testis, conspicuously contrasted by the normal T2 hyperintense testicular parenchyma and favorably depicted on the sagittal orientation (Fig. 9.1).

TABLE 9.1 MRI and ultrasound appearance, clinical information, and management options for congenital and acute testicular pathologies

Lesion	MRI and ultrasound appearances	Clinical information	Management options
Polyorchidism	MRI: -Supranumerary testes follows signal intensities as adjacent testicle.[1] US: -Extratesticular mass that demonstrates close to near identical echogenicity and Doppler pattern as the normal testis.[1]	-Mean age of 15–20 years old.[1] -Most commonly, the supernumerary testis may be located in the scrotum (60–70%), either superior or inferior to the testes, inguinal canal (25%) or retroperitoneum.[30] -Low risk of malignancy of supernumerary testes, however, difficult to measure due to low incidence.[31,32] -Surgical management of polyorchidism in a patient with fertility problems.[33]	-No consensus on conservative or surgical management. -Some suggest conservative approach if there are no risk factors, lack of tumor markers, and no imaging evidence of malignancy.[34]
Cryptorchidism	Abnormal location of undescended testis along the expected descent pathway.[1]	-Occurs in 1–3% of full-term and up to 30% of premature male infants.[6,7] -Undescended testis is most commonly located in the inguinal canal. -Increased risk of malignancy of undescended AND normally descended testis.[6,7] -Risk of development of germ cell tumors, most commonly seminoma, accounting for approximately 10% of cases.[35]	-Increased risk of infertility of undescended testis which is proportional to the time the affected testis remains undescended (Tasian,[6,7]). -Age of surgical management, typically with orchiopexy, has been shown to decrease the development of both infertility and testicular cancer; by 2 years old and 12 years old, respectively.[36]
Testicular hematoma	Appearance of testicular hematoma varies with the age of the hematoma[1] MRI: -Acute hematoma: T1 and T2 hyperintense -Chronic hematoma: T2 hypointense rim surrounding the hematoma indicating hemosiderin US: -Acute hematomas are echogenic, whereas chronic hematomas become anechoic over time, may develop septa and lobulations, and may show fluid–fluid levels along with echoes indicative of clots.[37,38]	-Most common following blunt trauma.[1,37] -May occur as complication after orchiectomy, inguinal herniorrhaphy.[1,37] -Decreased Doppler signal of the hematoma can mimic testicular torsion.[1]	Extratesticular hematoma: -Evacuation of an extratesticular hematoma may result in restoration of normal testicular blood flow.[1] Intratesticular hematoma: -Mild to moderate pain with stable size of hematoma → observation. -Significant pain or enlarging hematoma → surgical exploration. -Serial ultrasound should be performed within 72 hours of blunt trauma.[16]
Testicular rupture	MRI: -Disruption of T1 and T2 hypointense tunica albuginea.[1] -T1 hyperintensity indicating blood products.[1] US: -High sensitivity for depicting testicular injuries and can be associated with abnormal focal parenchymal heterogenous echotexture related to injury, hypoechoic fracture line, testicular contour abnormality, and disruption of the tunica albuginea, and extratesticular hydrocele and/or hematocele.[39]	-Prompt diagnosis is crucial and often difficult due to many overlapping etiologies of acute scrotal pain.[39]	-Surgical exploration and repair should be performed within 72 hours and delay decreases salvage from 80–90% to 45–55%.[39]

Lesion	MRI and ultrasound appearances	Clinical information	Management options
Epididymitis/ orchitis	MRI: - Testicular enlargement with heterogenous T2 signal and intense postgadolinium enhancement.[1] - ± Extratesticular fluid collections[1,5] - Edematous and inflamed spermatic cord.[5] US: - Low parenchymal echogenicity (or high echogenicity if there is coexisting hemorrhage) along with enlargement and hypervascular epididymis and testicle.[18] - Pitfall: scrotal trauma can cause epididymal enlargement and hypervascularity,[18] - May be associated with reactive hydrocele or pyocele and scrotal wall edema.[14] Tuberculosis epididymo-orchitis: MRI: - Signs of chronic destructive inflammation such as fistulous or sinus tracts.[1] US: - Literature describes several appearances ranging from diffuse heterogenous hypoechoic epididymis and/or testis to a nodular heterogenous hypoechoic appearance.[1,20]	- Acute scrotal pain in young males. - About 10–20% of patients with epididymitis/orchitis form abscess.[12,40] - Tuberculosis epididymo-orchitis: - Painless or slightly painful scrotal mass.[20] - Overlapping clinical presentation and physical exam with testicular infarct.[21,24]	- Treated with antibiotics.
Testicular infarct	Segmental testicular infarction: MRI: - T2 hypointensity and intense peripheral enhancement with or without increased T1 signal to signify hemorrhage.[1] US: - Small ill-defined avascular wedge-shaped hypoechoic lesion.[4] - May resemble tumor if the appearance is more well-defined borders with equivocal vascularity.[4] Global testicular infarction: MRI: - Lack of enhancement of the involved testicle and edematous diffusely heterogenous T2 related to edema.[25] US: - Diffuse loss of Doppler signal and heterogenous echotexture.[1,4]	- Segmental infarct typically idiopathic and usually affects patients between the second and the fourth decades of life.[41] - Most commonly manifests as acute scrotal pain (shen,[41]), and may be indistinguishable from other etiologies of acute scrotal pain.[41,42] - Rare complication of epididymo-orchitis - Global infarct often seen in 12–18-year old[1]	Segmental infarct: - Controversial; testis-sparing surgery in younger patients is preferred. However, malignancy is a mimic and orchiectomy may be performed for pathologic exclusion.[41] - Some studies suggest conservative management with good results.[41] Segmental testicular infarction: conservative management is feasible and safe.[43]
Testicular abscess	- Usually, an ill-defined avascular hypoechoic lesion with shaggy walls containing mixed or low-level internal echoes related to contents such as fluid, gas, and purulent material.[1,44]	- Intratesticular abscess is rare. - Atypical etiologies of testicular abscess include following trauma and mumps.[1]	- Up to 50% of patients with testicular abscess undergo orchiectomy.[45,46]
Testicular torsion	MRI: - T2 hyperintense fluid collection with variable T1 signal intensity and peripheral enhancement.[1] - Restricted diffusion.[1] US: - Decreased or lack of Doppler flow, parenchymal heterogeneity, and with or without reactive hydrocele.[47]	- Bimodal peak; 1 year old and second peak; adolescence.[1] - Pain <24 hours, nausea/vomiting, abnormal cremasteric reflex, and high position of testis.[47] - Beware of intermittent or partial torsion, which can demonstrate flow.[44]	- Treatment with manual detorsion may be combined with elective orchiopexy.[48]

TABLE 9.2 MRI and ultrasound characteristics, clinical information, and management options for benign testicular and extratesticular pathologies

Lesion	MRI and ultrasound characteristics	Clinical information	Management options
Testicular fibrosis	MRI: -Hypointense T1 and very hypointense T2 signal.[54-56] -No internal enhancement.[54-56] US: -Focal hypoechoic or hyperechoic lesions and diffuse heterogeneity of testicular parenchyma.[88]	-Presents following testicular parenchymal insult.[4] -Can mimic testicular neoplasm.[54-56]	-Indeterminate findings may lead to surgical explorations such as orchiectomy.[88]
Ectasia of rete testis	MRI: -T2 hyperintense and T1 hypointense cystic–multicystic structure centered at the mediastinum testis region.[49,60] -No enhancement.[49,60] US: -Often characteristic appearance showing tiny dilated cystic rete testis at the hilum of the testis without Doppler flow.[57] -Often bilateral, encouraging the diagnosis.[57] -Can be associated with spermatocele.[57]	-Common over 55 years old.[18] -Usually asymptomatic.[18,57]	-Typically not treated. -Exception in pediatric population where cystic dysplasia of the rete testis can occur. Although, a benign tumor, surgical excision, or orchiectomy may be necessary to exclude malignant process.[89]
Testicular epidermoid cyst	MRI: "Target" and "onion-ring" appearance.[18,49,54] MRI: -Alternating hyperintense and hypointense bands, hyperintense mid zone, and peripheral hypointense rim.[54] -No enhancement.[54] US: -Hypoechoic concentric rings with echogenic center.[18,49] -Alternating hypoechoic and hyperechoic concentric rings.[18,49]	-Most common benign intratesticular neoplasm. -Typically presents in younger men and adolescents.[18,49] -Painless.[18,49]	-Treated with enucleation.[90]
Testicular adrenal rest	MRI: -Nonspecific.[1] -T1 isointense to testicular parenchyma.[1] -T2 hypo- to hyperintense.[1,54] -Diffuse contrast enhancement.[1,54] US: -Typically hypoechoic and can be homogenous or heterogenous or homogenously isoechoic.[92]	-Prevalence in 40% of patients with congenital adrenal hyperplasia.[91]	-No clear guidelines. -Glucocorticoid therapy to suppress ACTH and restore fertility.[91]
Testicular hemangioma	MRI: - Slight increased T1 hyperintensity relative to muscle.[54,64_69] -Marked T2 hyperintensity.[54,64-69] -Contrast enhancement.[54,64-69] -Areas of signal void reflecting the heterogeneity of internal fibrous, fatty, or smooth muscle components, organized thrombus, or fast-flowing blood.[54,64-69] US: -Hypoechoic nodule with increased Doppler flow.[64]	-Rare. -Mean age between 6 months and 80 years old; most in children or young adults with 59% in patients <19 years old.[93] -Most commonly occurs during childhood and adolescence.[66] -Unilateral testicular enlargement, with or without tenderness, is the main presenting symptom, which is similar to that of malignant testicular tumors on clinical presentation.[65,66] -Pain is an inconsistent feature.[65] -All cases of testicular hemangioma have been benign.[65]	-Can be treated by enucleation if confirmed benign.[65] -Surgical excision with other therapies such as laser fulguration, intralesional sclerotherapy, and cryotherapy.[65]

Lesion	MRI and ultrasound characteristics	Clinical information	Management options
Epididymal cyst	MRI: -T2 hyperintense and T1 hypointense. -No enhancement. US: -Characteristic extratesticular anechoic lesion. -Sometimes difficult to distinguish from hydrocele if large; a helpful characteristic is that hydrocele envelopes and extratesticular cysts causes mass effect on the testicle.[52]	-Painless.[52,94] -Spermatoceles can be seeing following postvasectomy.[52,94] -75% in some studies.[94]	-Treated only if symptomatic. -Success with percutaneous sclerotherapy.[95]
Tunica albuginea cyst	MRI: -T2 hyperintense and T1 hypointense. -No enhancement. US: -Tiny vascular anechoic structures along the tunica that are characteristically located at the upper anterior or lateral aspect of the testicle.[96]	-Very common. -Mean age of 40 years old and seen in the fifth and sixth decades.[96]	-Conservation treatment for asymptomatic cysts.[97] -Surgical intervention can be performed based on patient factors and size of cyst.[97]
Varicocele	MRI: -Signal intensity depends on the flow rate of dilated vessels.[52] -Typically intermediate on T1- and T2-weighted images.[52] -Signal void in vessels with higher velocities.[52] US: -Dilated and serpiginous vessels superior and posterior to the testis.[52]	-Most common mass of the spermatic cord.[52,98] -Seen in 15% of population and 40% in infertile men.[52]	Varicocelectomy, conventional or other variants.[98] -Angiographic embolization. -Rising interest in using antioxidant therapy.[98]
Inguinal hernia	Imaging appearance depends on herniated components. MRI: -Bowel gut signature. -T1 and T2 hyperintensity of herniated fat. US: -Bowel can show peristalsis; fat appears hyperechoic. -Most important component to evaluation is using Valsalva to detect transient hernias that can completely reduce at rest.[80]	-Can cause testicular torsion due to compression of testicular artery.[99]	-Treatment is surgical, especially if presenting with large inguinoscrotal hernia.[100] -Proposed separate or combined open abdominal and inguinal approach.[100]
Lipoma	MRI: - T1- and T2-hyperintense.[1] -India ink artifact at fat-water interface on out-of-phase T1 sequence.[1] -No enhancement.[1] US: -Avascular hyperechoic lesions.[1]	-Usually nontender. -Most common extratesticular neoplasm.[52]	-If large, surgical excision through scrotal or combined scrotal and inguinal incision.[101]
Fibrolipoma	MRI: -T1 hyperintense.[81] -T2 heterogenous hyperintense.[81] -Signal loss on fat-saturated sequences.[81] US: -Typically hyperechoic avascular mass.[81]	-Benign. -Slowly enlarging. -Asymptomatic or mildly symptomatic. -Palpable but not fixed mass.[81]	-Surgical excision.[81]

(Continued)

TABLE 9.2 (Cont'd)

Lesion	MRI and ultrasound characteristics	Clinical information	Management options
Fibrous pseudotumor	MRI: -T1 and T2 hypointense.[82,83] -Variable contrast enhancement.[82,83] US: -Isoechoic to hypoechoic relative to the testis with Doppler flow.[83]	-Most common in the third decade of life. -Rare before 18 years old. -Usually painless nodule; however, 30% patients can present with diffuse nodular thickening in the setting of trauma or infection.[49]	-Often surgical resection because of overlapping features with testicular malignancies. -Alternatively, scrotal exploration and frozen biopsy and upon diagnosis, resection or tumor and tunica vaginalis.[102]
Extratesticular epidermoid inclusion cyst	MRI: -T1 hypointense and T2 hyperintense.[85] -T2 hypointense capsule.[85] -No enhancement.[85] US: -Commonly hypoechoic containing scattered reflectors.[84]	-Very rare. -Typically remain asymptomatic until complications such as rupture, superinfection or lesion enlargement causing locoregional mass effect.[84]	-Limited literature due to rarity of lesion. -Surgical excision is the suggested treatment of choice.[84]
Adenomatoid tumor	MRI: -T2 hypointense.[49] -Variable contrast. Enhancement related to granulation tissue.[49] US: -Variable in appearance.[1]	-Second most common extratesticular tumor. -Adenomatoid tumors are often painless and found incidentally on imaging in men between the ages of 20 and 50 years old, with the majority found in patients between 20 and 25 years old.[1,49] -Not been shown to recur or undergo malignant degeneration.[103]	-Excisional biopsy.[103]
Sclerosing lipogranuloma	MRI: -Heterogenous T1- and T2 signal.[1] -Heterogenous. Enhancement.[1] -Intravoxel fat.[1] -Can contain necrotic components; T2 hyperintense.[1] US: -Typically hypoechoic.[1]	-Majority of cases are secondary to injection of foreign bodies such as liquid paraffin, mineral oil, or silicone -Some cases occurred without injection, primary, and though to be related to breakdown of endogenous lipids.[1,105,106,115]	-Conservative (first line)—close observation, symptomatic treatment, antibiotics to steroids. -Surgical—partial or total excision with or without skin flap reconstruction.[104]

TABLE 9.3 MRI and ultrasound appearance, clinical information, and management options for testicular tumors

Lesion	MRI and ultrasound appearance	Clinical information	Management options
Seminoma	MRI: -Nonencapsulated, nodular, fibrovascular septa.[49,104] Isointense on T1- and homogenously hypointense on T2-weighted images.[49,104] -Contrast enhancement.[49,104] -Typically does not demonstrate internal hemorrhagic or cystic components.[49,104] US: -Typically homogenously hypoechoic relative to background testis and may be lobulated or multinodular. -Can have internal echogenic foci reflecting calcifications or contain cystic spaces.[119]	-Painless. -Median age of 35-39 years old. -Tumor markers: HCG, LDH, PlAP; at least 1 marker elevated in 84%.[120]	-Depends on stage[118]: I: Active surveillance or alternatively, single agent carboplatin or radiotherapy. II: Radiotherapy for lower stage II, chemotherapy for higher stage II. III: Chemotherapy.
Nonseminomatous tumor	MRI: -Encapsulated and without fibrovascular septa.[49,104] -Heterogenous on T1- and T2-weighted images.[49,104] -Heterogenous enhancement.[49,104] -Hemorrhagic or cystic components.[49,104] US: -Appears similar to seminoma except nonseminomas are typically heterogenous.[121]	-Typically painless.[112] -Age of presentation depends on tumor, as below.	-Depends on stage:[118] I: Active surveillance or alternatively, retroperitoneal lymph node dissection. II: Retroperitoneal lymph node dissection or chemotherapy for lower stage II, chemotherapy ± retroperitoneal lymph node dissection for higher stage II. III: Chemotherapy (baird,[119]).
Embryonal carcinoma	MRI: -As described above. US: -Heterogenously hypoechoic and diffuse infiltration.[122]	-Median age of 25-35 years old.[1] -Tumor marker: AFP. -More common as a component of mixed germ cell tumors than pure form.[1]	
Yolk sac tumor	Focal—usually solid and ovoid, with a homogeneous echo texture or multiple random anechoic spaces, and hypervascular.[1+] Diffuse neoplasms had heterogeneous echo textures; most were hypervascular.[123]	-Before 2 years ago.[1] -Most common testicular tumor in children.[1] -Tumor marker: AFP.[1]	
Choriocarcinoma	Infiltrative, heterogeneous mass.[124]	-Pure form is extremely rare.[1] -Most commonly in second or third decade of life.[1] -Very aggressive. -Tumor marker: HCG.[1]	
Teratoma	-Typically complex cystic mass.[1] -Areas of T1 hyperintensity representing intralesional fat.	-Can occur in any age group.[1] -Second most common testicular tumor in children.[1] -Pure form of teratoma is rare in adults.[1]	
Mixed germ cell tumor	-Appearances depend tumor composition. -Heterogeneity of the tumor reflects internal hemorrhage, necrosis, and calcifications.[1]	-Average age of 30 years old.[1] -Tumor markers reflect on germ cell components.[1]	
Leydig cell tumor	MRI: -T1 isointense.[108] -T2 hypointense.[108] -Rapid wash-in and prolonged wash out following contrast.[108] US: -Typically small hyperechoic or hypoechoic nodules.[1]	-Occur in all age groups, but the peak incidences are at ages 5-10 years and 30-35 years.[125] -Most common sex cord stromal tumor.[125]	-Traditionally treated with radical orchiectomy. -Some evidence suggest testis-sparing surgery is safe for patients for tumor size <2.5 cm.[126]

(Continued)

TABLE 9.3 (Cont'd)

Lesion	MRI and ultrasound appearance	Clinical information	Management options
Sertoli cell tumor	MRI: -Homogeneous intermediate T1 signal intensity.[1] -High T2 signal intensity.[1] -Homogeneous enhancement.[1] US: -Variable and can include a multicystic spoke-wheel appearance or increased echogenicity.[1]	-Typically occur in the first four decades of life.[1] -Second most common sex cord stromal tumor.[1]	-Recent meta-analysis show low local recurrent following testis-sparing surgery and no adjuvant therapy.[127]
Granulosa cell tumor	MRI: -T2 hypointense.[1] -T1 hypo- to isointense.[1] -Intense contrast enhancement.[1] US: -Well-defined hypoechoic mass with few internal echoes and increased peripheral and low central vascularity.[1]	-Uncommon with less than 150 reported cases.[128] -Juvenile: 90% presented 6 months of age or younger.[128] -Adult: median age of 44 years old.[128] -Painless.[128] -Gynecomastia.[128]	-Treated with radical orchiectomy.[128] -Good response to induction[128] chemotherapy with regional lymph node metastasis.[128]
Testicular lymphoma	Can be focal or infiltration in appearance. MRI: -T1 and T2 hypointense.[1] -Mildly homogenous enhancement.[1] US: -Single or multiple focal regions with decreased echogenicity of variable size or as a diffuse enlargement and decreased echogenicity of the entire testis, maintaining the normal testicular shape. -Internal vascularity.[1,112,129]	-Rare. -Old than 60 years old. -Most common bilateral testicular tumor.[112] -Can be secondary or primary.[112]	-Evolving data suggest significant gains with addition of radiation therapy, anthracycline-based chemotherapy, rituximab, and CNS-directed prophylaxis.[129]
Liposarcom77a	MRI: -T1 and T2 hyperintense.[1] -Signal loss on fat-suppressed images.[1] -Heterogenous contrast enhancement.[1] US: -Predominantly hyperechoic owing to their predominate fat composition but have variable echogenicity because of variable amounts of internal soft-tissue septa and calcifications.[1] -Appearance also related to different histologic subtypes.[130]	-Mean age at presentation is 56 years (reported range of 16–90 years old).[1,52] -Immunoreactive for MDM2 and CDK4 markers, differentiating from lipoma.[1,52] -Most specific marker is S-100 protein (positive in 90%).[52]	-Surgical resection with wide excision including orchiectomy and high ligation of spermatic cord.[132] -Literature describes up to 25% of patients develop local recurrence following complete surgical resection.[131] -More than one-third of patients undergoing complete section developed distant metastasis.[131]
Rhabdomyosarcoma	MRI: -T2 hyperintense.[130] -T1 isointense.[130] -Contrast enhancement.[130] US: -Variable appearance.[1] -Increased vascularity.[1] -May have hydrocele.[1]	-Median of 7 years old.[1,135] -Painless.[135]	-Surgery (orchiectomy and lymph node dissection) chemotherapy, and radiation therapy.[133,134,135,137]
Metastasis	-Nonspecific and variable.[1,116,117]	-Rare. -Most commonly from prostate adenocarcinoma.[133]	-Treatment includes high inguinal orchiectomy directed to the primary neoplasm if extratesticular involvement.[133]

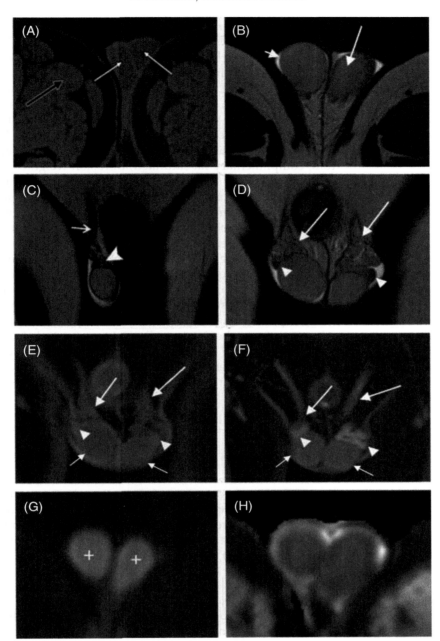

FIG. 9.1 Normal testes anatomy. (A) Axial T1-weighted MR image through the scrotum shows normal testes (white arrows) with signal intensity similar to that of the surrounding muscles (black arrow). (B) Axial T2-weighted MR image shows the hyperintense parenchyma of normal testes (white arrows) surrounded by a thin lining of hypointense tunica albuginea (black arrows). (C) Coronal T2-weighted MR image shows the normal right spermatic cord (arrow), and epididymal head (arrowhead), which are hypointense compared with the testis. (D) Additional coronal T2-weighted MR image shows symmetric normal bilateral spermatic cords (arrow), and epididymal heads (arrowhead). (E and F) Coronal fat-sat precontrast T1-weighted and postcontrast enhancement MR images show the normal symmetric enhancement of bilateral spermatic cords (arrow) epididymal heads (arrowhead), and testes (shorter arrows). Which are hypointense compared with the testis. (G) Axial diffusion-weighted MR image ($b = 800$ s/mm^2) depicts normal testicles with high signal intensity (plus signs). (H) Apparent diffusion coefficient (ADC) image shows normal appearance of bilateral testicles.

Images (A–D) were reproduced with the permission of the RSNA as the copyright holder. from Vol. 38, No. 3, 806–830.

9.3 MRI scrotal and testicle protocol

While a detailed MR protocol has been wonderfully described by other authors, the authors feel compelled to highlight the utility of specific MR sequences that leverage the capabilities of MRI to problem solve the main clinical settings described in this chapter.[1,3,4] Within all clinical settings, the depiction of testicular and extratesticular anatomy, using small and large field of view, respectively, is paramount for lesion localization and characterization. The key anatomic sequences typically include T1-and T2-weighted spin echo sequences, in at least the axial plane, with additional coronal and sagittal orientations as needed for the specific clinical situation. In the setting of characterizing congenital scrotal anomalies, small and large field of view T1- and T2-weighted sequences allow lesion detection within and outside the scrotum; complimentary fat-saturated, diffusion-weighted, and postcontrast 3D sequences may increase lesion conspicuity. In the setting of scrotal pain, especially in the acute trauma setting, the depiction of blood products along with parenchymal and tunica albuginea compromise is important for diagnosing critical pathologies such as testicular rupture. Complementing the detection of edema and fluid with fat-saturated T2-weighted images, the addition of T1-weighted dual echo in- and out of phase sequences can increase the sensitivity of blood products.[1] For evaluating nontraumatic etiologies of scrotal pain, characterizing the location and extent of edema along with associated secondary findings such as fluid collections using diffusion-weighted, fat-saturated T2-weighted, and postcontrast T1-weighted sequences can increase the confidence of either an infection or inflammatory process. Lastly, in the evaluation of a scrotal mass, the entire spectrum of T1- and T2-weighted sequences along with diffusion-weighted and postcontrast sequences should be employed, in multiple orientations with key sequences such as T2-weighted and postcontrast sequences. The multiparametric capability of MRI can detect specific features that can lead the diagnosis from a benign to malignant process, and vice versa, or direct testis-sparing surgery rather than orchiectomy. Throughout the chapter, we will describe lesion-specific features that are resolvable by MRI in hopes to increase diagnostic confidence of scrotal diseases.

9.4 Congenital abnormalities

9.4.1 Introduction

The spectrum of congenital abnormalities of the testes comprises of aberrations in the presence or absence, size, number, and location of testes. Common congenital abnormalities involve the number and location of testes, such as polyorchidism and cryptorchidism, respectively. The role of MR imaging in the investigation of testicular congenital abnormalities utilizes the large field of view and multiplanar capabilities along with the superior tissue contrast to determine the location and characterization of suspected abnormalities.

9.4.2 Polyorchidism

Polyorchidism is defined by the presence of more than two testes. Although the etiology of polyorchidism is unclear, it is postulated to be the consequence of abnormal division of the genital ridge by formation of peritoneal bands.[1] The supernumerary testes can harbor malignant potential; the most common of which are germ cell tumors, particularly, embryonal carcinoma and seminoma.[1] Polyorchidism may be associated with ipsilateral inguinal hernia with the highest association when the supernumerary testis is located in the retroperitoneum.[5] MR imaging can be used in equivocal cases, for which the display of reassuring signal intensities of the supernumerary testes similar to the normal testis on T1, T2, and postgadolinium sequences (Fig. 9.2). MR imaging also offers the detection of complications involving the supernumerary testis, including cryptorchidism and neoplasm.[1]

9.4.3 Cryptorchidism

Cryptorchidism is referred to an undescended testicle. There are known risks of developing malignancy in the undescended, therefore, the diagnosis and characterization of the undescended testis is important for management which furthers the need for detection and treatment. While ultrasound is the most common initial modality to evaluate cryptorchidism, there is less reliability in the setting of undescended and nonpalpable testis, especially in the setting of an abdominopelvic/inguinal location.[6,7] Ultrasound is especially limited in the case of undescended testes residing in the abdomen, which consists of 20% of cases.[8]

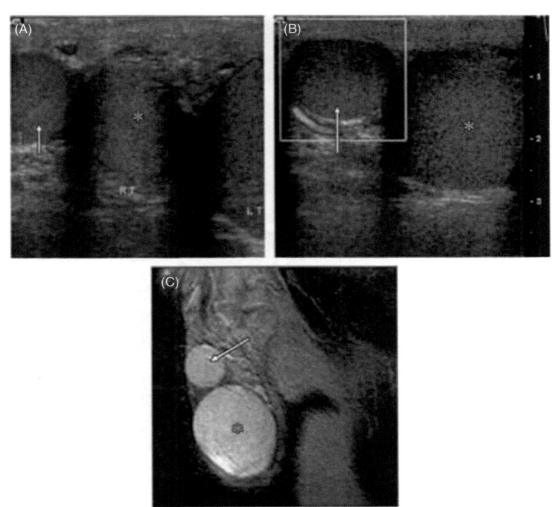

FIG. 9.2 Polyorchidism. (A and B) Grayscale (A), and color Doppler (B) US images of the scrotum show a well-defined rounded mass (arrow) superior and lateral to the right testis (RT; *) demonstrates isoechogenicity to the adjacent testis with internal Doppler flow.
Images were reproduced with the permission of the RSNA as the copyright holder. from Vol. 38, No. 3, 806–830.

On the other hand, MR imaging of cryptorchidism demonstrates a sensitivity and specificity of 96% and 100%, respectively.[9] On MRI, the undescended testes demonstrate low T1 signal intensity and intermediate to high T2 signal intensity; low T2 signal intensity can be seen depending on the amount of fibrosis or atrophic status (Figs. 9.3 and 9.4).[5] Despite the perceived benefits of MRI in the evaluation of undescended testes, a meta-analysis study showed a 62% sensitivity in detecting nonpalpable cryptorchid testes, although with 100% specificity.[10] Furthermore, the study reveals that MRI has a limited value in locating viable cryptorchid testes in the abdomen due to the inability to detect atrophied undescended testes.[10]

9.5 Acute scrotum

9.5.1 Introduction

Ultrasound is the preferred initial imaging modality in the evaluation of scrotal pain, particularly in the acute scrotum setting owing to its high-resolution evaluation of superficial structures, rapid imaging, and the ability to assess vascularity with color Doppler.[11] Not uncommonly, the acute scrotum presents with vague symptomology

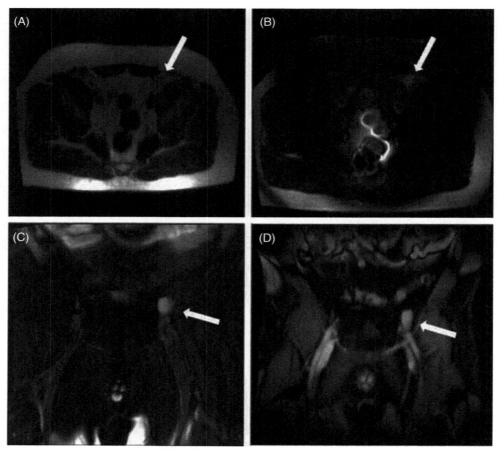

FIG. 9.3 Cryptorchidism. (A) Axial T2-weighted MR image through the pelvis shows a T2 hyperintense structure along the left distal external iliac region, corresponding to the undescended testis (white arrow). (B) Axial fat sat T2-weighted MR image shows the same undescended testis (white arrow), which is more conspicuous compared to saturated surrounding fat. (C) Coronal fat sat T2-weighted MR image shows the same undescended testis (white arrow). (D) Coronal contrast-enhanced MR image shows homogenous enhancement of the undescended testis (white arrow). *Images were reproduced with the permission of the RSNA as the copyright holder. from Vol. 38, No. 3, 806–830.*

and ambiguous clinical findings, for which ultrasound has been well validated to play a significant role in this setting.[12] The acute scrotum can be broadly categorized into nontraumatic and traumatic, with clinical management depends on the presence or absence of testicular rupture in the acute trauma setting and testicular torsion in the nontraumatic setting. Leveraging advantages of MRI in the evaluation of scrotal and testicular masses, MRI can offer additional management altering information when evaluating acute scrotal pathologies. Recent studies have studied the benefits of MRI in the traumatic setting with high accuracy in diagnosis following blunt scrotal trauma, identified extent of posttraumatic disease, as well as proving sequela of posttraumatic injury rather than suspected tumor based on initial ultrasound evaluation.[2,13,14] Furthermore, Makela et al. evaluated the ability of using dynamic contrast-enhanced MRI to detect testicular torsion from other causes of acute scrotum.[15] Their study demonstrate increasing region of interest in the setting of normal testicles, while a constantly low ROI was seen in altered testicular perfusion and other causes of acute scrotum such as epididymitis and torsion of testicular appendage demonstrated normal testicular perfusion.[15] The following section will discuss a variety of acute scrotal conditions and highlight specific use cases of MRI.

9.5.2 Traumatic conditions

9.5.2.1 *Testicular hematoma*

Testicular hematoma occurs most commonly presents following acute blunt scrotal trauma in younger men and reside within the tunica vaginalis and scrotal wall.[1,16,17] The imaging appearance of testicular hematomas vary

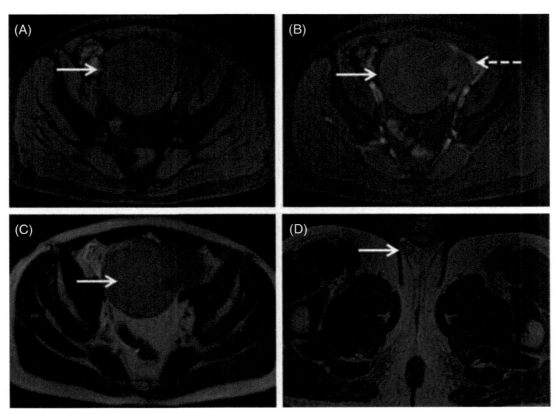

FIG. 9.4 **Seminoma in an undescended testis.** (A) Axial T1-weighted MR image shows a large hypointensity mass (arrow) in the pelvis. (B) Axial contrast-enhanced T1-weighted MR image shows enhancement of the mass (solid arrow) and prominent vessels along the left lateral aspect of the mass (dashed arrow). These vessels drain into the left renal vein (not shown). (C) Axial T2-weighted MR image shows low signal in the mass (arrow). (D) Axial T2-weighted MR image at a more inferior level shows the right spermatic cord (arrow) but without the left spermatic cord, signifying undescended testes.
Images were reproduced with the permission of the RSNA as the copyright holder. from Vol. 35, No. 2, 400–415.

depending on the chronicity; typically more acute hematomas display hyperintensity on T1- and T2-weighted images, while a dark hemosiderin T2 hypointense rim surrounding the hematoma indicates chronicity (Figs. 9.5A and 9.5B).[1] In the setting of extratesticular hematomas, mass effect on the adjacent testicular vessels by the hematoma may cause reduce blood flow to the testicle and potentially mimic testicular torsion on initial ultrasound evaluation.[1] MRI may play a role in the management of these patients by assessing the location and confirmation of the hematoma, therefore aiding in the planning for intervention and assessment of testicular parenchymal compromise using pulse sequence and postgadolinium enhancement characteristics. Furthermore, an indeterminate ultrasound can be further characterized with MRI. In the study by Muglia et al., the authors showed the benefit of using MRI to confirm a testicular hematoma rather than suspected neoplasm (Fig. 9.6).[14]

9.5.2.2 *Testicular rupture*

Consequences of testicular trauma include contusion, hematoma, and most seriously, testicular rupture. While ultrasound serves an important initial role in the detection of testicular rupture, MRI can serve as a useful alternative, primarily if disruption of the tunica albuginea remains sonographically equivocal. In a study performed by Kim et al., a prospective study demonstrated superior diagnosis of testicular rupture, especially in the setting of an inconclusive ultrasound.[1,13] On MRI, the tunica albuginea is T2 hypointense, tunica albuginea is the primary finding for testicular rupture, for which detection is readily apparent on MRI and can be difficult to characterize on ultrasound (Fig. 9.7).

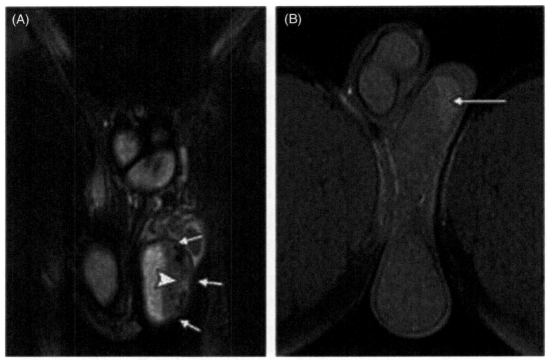

FIG. 9.5A   Testicular trauma with an intact tunica albuginea. (A) Coronal T2-weighted MR image of the scrotum shows abnormal areas of low signal intensity involving the left testis (arrowhead), with preserved low signal tunica albuginea (arrows). (B) Corresponding axial T1-weighted MR image shows areas of high signal intensity (arrow) related to blood products.
Images were reproduced with the permission of the RSNA as the copyright holder. from Vol. 38, No. 3, 806–830.

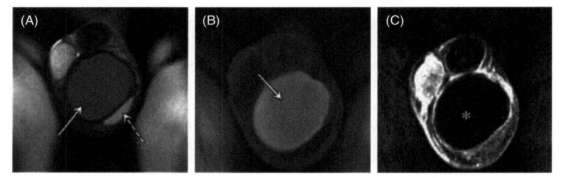

FIG. 9.5B   Chronic organized extratesticular hematoma presenting with chronic asymmetric left testicular swelling. Normal tumor markers. (A) Coronal T2-weighted MR image of the scrotum shows a well-encapsulated intermediate intensity lesion (solid arrow) with a hypointense periphery, which is due to hemosiderin causing mass effect and displacement of an otherwise normal left testis (dashed arrow). The structure causes mass effect and displacement of the adjacent testis, confirming extratesticular location. (B and C) Coronal T1-weighted (B) and contrast-enhanced subtraction (C) MR images show that hyperintense internal contents (arrow in B) and without contrast enhancement (* in C).
Images were reproduced with the permission of the RSNA as the copyright holder. from Vol. 38, No. 3, 806–830.

9.5.3 Nontraumatic conditions

9.5.3.1 *Epididymitis/orchitis*

Epididymitis/orchitis reflects the inflammation of testicular structures usually due to sexually transmitted disease or retrograde spread of bacterial infections stemming from the bladder.[18] The course of disease typically begins at the epididymal tail and traverses to the epididymal head, and in approximately 20–40% of cases, the infection spreads to the adjacent testicle.[18] While ultrasound remains the primary mode of diagnosis, with hypervascularity of the being a well-established finding, MR imaging can be used to detect secondary signs of testicular inflammation

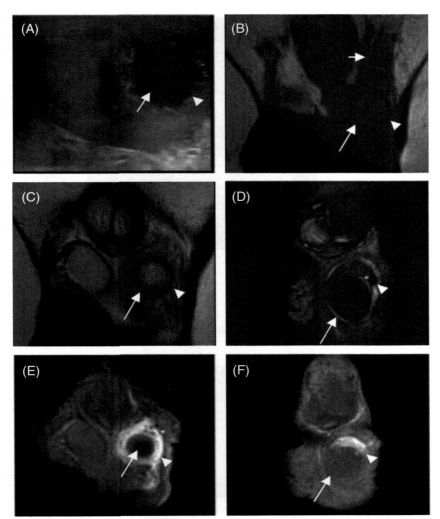

FIG. 9.6 Left testicular pain in a man following fall. (A) Initial evaluation with scrotal ultrasound shows a near anechoic rounded structure (arrow) in the left testis with heterogenous peripheral hyperechogenicity (arrowhead). Differential diagnosis was intratesticular hematoma or testicular infarct; further characterization with MRI was performed. (B) Coronal T1-weighted MR image shows a mildly T1 hyperintense structure (long arrow), corresponding to the ultrasound findings, with T1 hypointense rim (arrowhead). The left spermatic cord (short arrow) is thickened compared to the contralateral right side (short arrow). (C) Coronal T2-weighted MR image shows the peripheral T2 hypointensity (arrowhead) and central hyperintensity (arrow). (D) Corresponding fat sat sagittal T2-weighted MR image shows diffuse low T2 signal of the left testicle (arrow) and thickened epididymis (arrowhead). (E) Coronal contrast-enhanced T1-weighted MR image shows intense peripheral enhancement of the structure (arrowhead) with central nonenhancement of the structure (arrow). (F) Sagittal contrast-enhanced MR image shows heterogenous enhancement of the left testicle (arrow) and adjacent epididymis (arrowhead). Findings consistent with testicular infarct with hemorrhage.

to distinguish from clinically and imaging equivocal cases such as testicular torsion.[18] In addition to testicular enlargement, the inflamed testis can demonstrate heterogenous T2 signal and intense postgadolinium enhancement, which may be accompanied by pyoceles and heterogenous T2 signal infected extratesticular fluid collections (Figs. 9.8 and 9.9).[1,5] Furthermore, the spermatic cord is often edematous and enhancing, as well as the surrounding tissues; these features are typically not present in noninflammatory processes such as testicular torsion.[5]

A chronic form of epididymitis can be seen in the setting of atypical infections such as with *Mycobacterium tuberculosis*, which represents the most common form of extrapulmonary tuberculosis.[1] Tuberculosis infection of the scrotal may be from retrograde spread from the prostate and seminal vesicle or through hematogenous spread.[1] Typically, cases of tuberculosis epididymo-orchitis occurs in the setting of pulmonary tuberculosis, and rarely, as an isolated event.[19] The spread of infection usually begins at the epididymal tail, owing to its greater blood supply and/or initial point of exposure to urinary reflux, and eventually progressing to involve the testicle.[20] In the case report by Badmos, the presentation of tuberculous epididymo-orchitis can simulate a testicular tumor, especially in the setting of no

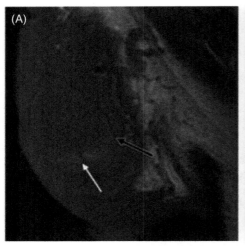

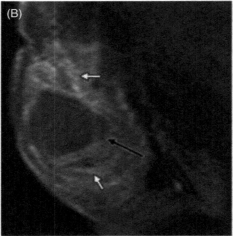

FIG. 9.7 Scrotal trauma with rupture of the tunica albuginea. (A) Sagittal nonenhanced T1-weighted MR image shows a linear area of hyperintense T1 signal at the junction of the middle and lower thirds of the left testis, suggestive of a fracture line, with a hematoma (white arrow), and associated comprise of the tunica albuginea (black arrow), indicating rupture. (B) Sagittal contrast-enhanced T1-weighted MR image shows enhancement of paratesticular tissues (white arrow) surrounding the area of the tunica albuginea rupture (black arrow).
Images were reproduced with the permission of the RSNA as the copyright holder. from Vol. 38, No. 3, 806–830.

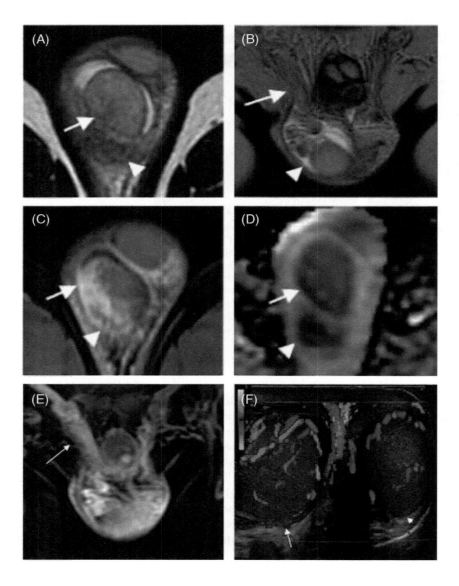

FIG. 9.8 Acute epididymo-orchitis in a man with right testicular pain. (A) Axial T2-weighted MR image through the scrotum shows focal heterogenous hypointense signal in the right testis (white arrow) and adjacent enlarged right epididymis (arrowhead). (B) Coronal T2-weighted MR image shows the enlarged and thickened right spermatic cord (white arrow), and reactive right hydrocele (arrowhead). (C) Axial contrast-enhanced T1-weighted MR image shows heterogenous enhancement of the enlarged right epididymis (arrowhead), and part of the right testis (white arrow). (D) Axial ADC MR image shows restricted diffusion in the areas of contrast enhancement in the right testis and epididymitis. Coronal T2-weighted MR image shows the normal right spermatic cord (arrow) and epididymal head (arrowhead), which are hypointense compared with the testis. (E) Coronal contrast-enhanced MR image shows asymmetric contrast enhancement of the right spermatic cord. (F) Transverse color Doppler image of bilateral testicles in cleavage view shows increased Doppler flow in the right testis (long arrow) compared to the normal Doppler flow in the left testis (arrowhead).

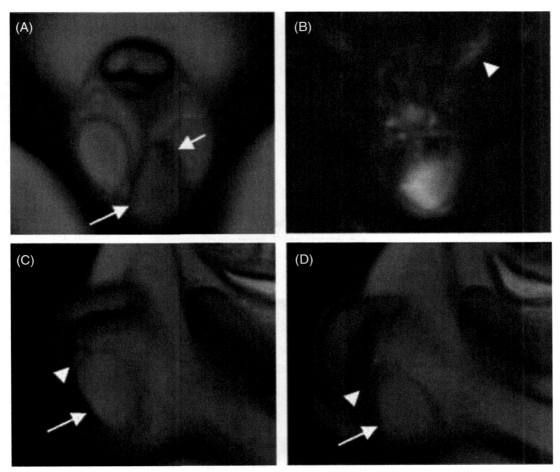

FIG. 9.9   Chronic left epididymo-orchitis in a man with ongoing left testicular pain. (A) Coronal T2-weighted MR image shows asymmetric diffuse heterogenous hypointense T2 signal in the left testis (white arrow) and adjacent mildly enlarged left epididymis (arrowhead). (B) Coronal fat-saturated T2-weighted MR image show asymmetric mildly edematous left spermatic cord (arrowhead). (C) Sagittal T2-weighted MR image shows the normal right-sided epididymis (arrowhead), and testis. (D) Sagittal T2-weighted MR image shows the asymmetrically thickened left epididymis and heterogenous T2 hypointense left testis (arrow).

systemic tuberculosis infection.[19] The ultrasound appearance of tuberculosis epididymo-orchitis may be variable and challenging. On MRI, the lesion portrays characteristics of chronic inflammation and may characterize the sequela of destructive inflammatory process as sinuses or fistulous tracts that signify tuberculosis infection (Fig. 9.10).[1] If imaging findings remain inconclusive, pathological confirmation may be needed to guide management.

Testicular infarct is another rare complication of epididymo-orchitis, which is a difficult diagnosis given overlapping clinical presentation and physical examination with uncomplicated epididymo-orchitis.[21,22,29] The proposed pathophysiology of testicular infarct related to epididymo-orchitis is multifactorial and likely involves bacterial exotoxins causing endothelial damage and vascular thrombosis along with inflammatory infiltration/edema causing compression on testicular vascular structures.[23] MR imaging offers a complimentary role to ultrasound in this clinically and radiologically challenge disease by providing more accurate assessment of testicular perfusion and resultant nonenhancement testis of parenchymal infarction in the background of inflammatory changes as described above (Fig. 9.11).[24] A potential path if undetected may eventually proceed to testicular rupture.[25]

9.5.3.2 *Testicular abscess*

Testicular abscesses occur most often as sequela of scrotal infections such as epididymo-orchitis, and less commonly following trauma, infarction, mumps, and tuberculosis.[1] The appearance of testicular abscess is similar in characteristics to abscesses in located in other parts of the body presenting as a T2 hyperintense fluid collection with variable T1 signal intensity and peripheral enhancement along with restricted diffusion.[1] The role of MR imaging

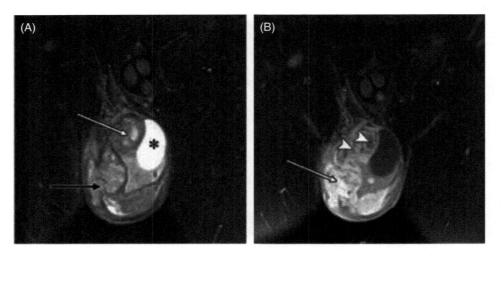

FIG. 9.10 Tuberculous epididymo-orchitis in a man with scrotal pain and swelling. (A) Coronal fat-suppressed T2-weighted MR image through the scrotum shows a diffusely thickened epididymis and a heterogeneous right testis, which is displaced (white arrow). There is a disruption of the tunica vaginalis (black arrow), adjacent hydrocele (*) and associated secondary findings of inflammation such as thickened overlying subcutaneous tissues. (B) Coronal contrast-enhanced T1-weighted MR image shows heterogeneous enhancement of the thickened epididymis and testis (arrow). Multiple tiny nonenhancing areas (arrowheads) within the epididymis and testis show T2 signal intensity in image a, which are consistent with microabscesses.

Images were reproduced with the permission of the RSNA as the copyright holder. from Vol. 38, No. 3, 806–830.

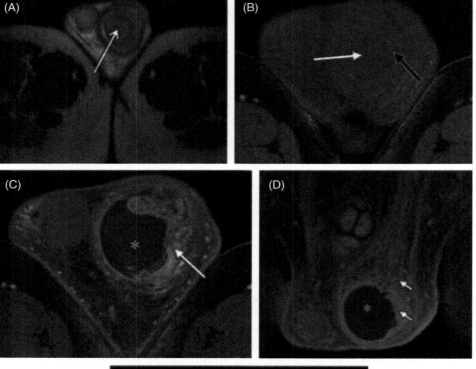

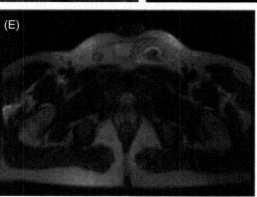

FIG. 9.11 Segmental testicular infarction following in episode of epididymo-orchitis in a patient with acute left testicular pain. (A) Axial T2-weighted MR image shows an area of heterogeneous low signal intensity in the left testis (arrow). (B) Axial non-enhanced T1-weighted MR image through the scrotum shows a corresponding area that is isointense to the testis (white arrow) with peripheral hyperintense signal, indicating hemorrhage (black arrow). (C and D) Axial (C) and coronal (D) contrast-enhanced T1-weighted MR images show rim enhancement (arrow in C) in the region of the infarcted testis (*), with enhancement of viable parts of testis, and epididymis (arrows in D). (E) Axial T2-weighted MR image at the level of the lesser trochanter shows fluid surrounding the left spermatic cord (arrows).

Images were reproduced with the permission of the RSNA as the copyright holder. from Vol. 38, No. 3, 806–830.

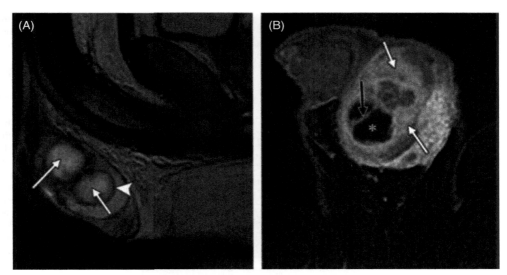

FIG. 9.12   **Testicular abscess in man presenting with fever and scrotal swelling.** (A) Sagittal T2-weighted MR image demonstrates areas of hyperintensity (arrows) and a hypointense rim (arrowhead) involving the left testis. (B) Corresponding axial contrast-enhanced T1-weighted MR image through the scrotum shows no internal enhancement (*) but shows enhancing septa (black arrow), indicating abscess, and enhancement of the surrounding parenchyma (white arrows), as additional signs of inflammation.
Images were reproduced with the permission of the RSNA as the copyright holder. from Vol. 38, No. 3, 806–830.

in the setting of testicular abscess can serve to better characterize the extent of disease such as extratesticular extension and detection of infectious tracts.[17] Additionally, MRI can be useful in the setting of an equivocal clinically history or physical examination for other acute scrotal pathologies such as testicular torsion, in which case, the affected testicle may be orientated in an abnormal position, decreased enhancement of the ipsilateral spermatic cord, and no epididymal hypervascularity (Fig. 9.12).[5,18] Clinical history of trauma may help differentiate testicular abscess from an avascular hematoma.[18]

9.5.3.3 *Testicular torsion*

Testicular torsion occurs when the testicle twists on the spermatic cord resulting in decreased testicular blood flow (Fig. 9.13). Testicular torsion can be broadly characterized as complete, partial, or incomplete/intermittent, depending on the degree of testicular twisting. The clinical presentation of testicular torsion in the acute setting often represents a diagnostic challenge since it can mimic other acute pathologies of the scrotum, such as epididymitis, however, a

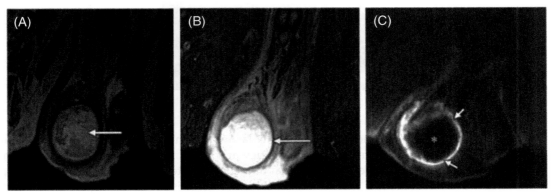

FIG. 9.13   **Missed torsion and testicular infarction in a man presenting with acute right testicular pain.** The patient had experienced similar pain a few months earlier for a short period of time, which was relieved without medical intervention. (A) Coronal T2-weighted MR image demonstrates an ill-defined and heterogeneous signal intensity in the right testis (arrow). (B) Corresponding coronal contrast-enhanced T1-weighted MR image shows diffuse hyperintensity thought the testis (arrow), indicating parenchymal hemorrhage. (C) Complimentary contrast-enhanced subtraction MR image shows no enhancement in the involved testicular parenchyma (*). The peripheral rim of enhancement is due to vascularity from capsular enhancement (arrows).
Images were reproduced with the permission of the RSNA as the copyright holder. from Vol. 38, No. 3, 806–830.

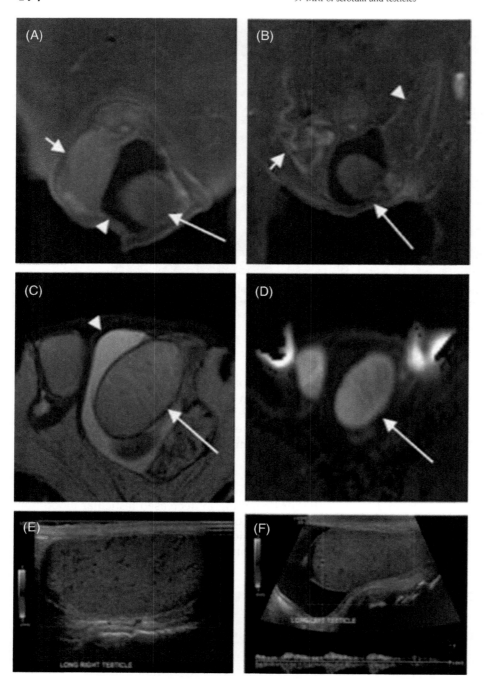

FIG. 9.14 Intermittent torsion in a man who relapsing left testicular pain. (A) Coronal fat-saturated T1-weighted MR image demonstrates abnormal position and diffuse low T1 signal of the left testis (long arrow), left hydrocele (arrowhead), and normal right testis (short arrow). (B) Corresponding coronal contrast-enhanced T1-weighted MR image shows lack of enhancement of the left testicular vessels (arrowhead) relative to the right side (short arrow), and abnormal position and signal of the left testis (long arrow). (C) Axial T2-weighted image shows mildly heterogeneous striated appearance of the left testicle (arrow), and adjacent hydrocele (arrowhead). (D) Axial ADC image shows the mild asymmetric restricted diffusion of the left testis (arrow). (E) Longitudinal color Doppler image of the right testicle shows normal echotexture and Doppler flow. (F) Contralateral longitudinal color Doppler image of the left testicle shows mildly heterogenous echotexture with decreased color Doppler, and blunted spectral waveform along with adjacent reaction hydrocele.

misdiagnosis can lead to grave consequences such as testicular infarction. Ultrasound remains the quintessential imaging modality for establishing the diagnosis of acute testicular torsion, however, a dilemma exists in the setting of incomplete testicular torsion.[26] The clinical presentation of incomplete testicular torsion can be nonspecific with a high false-negative rate of diagnosis by ultrasound.[26] Although there is limited data, MRI has been shown to demonstrate the sequela of reduced testicular blood flow in the clinical setting of incomplete torsion, along with other suggestive morphologic signs such as rotated cord structures and increased testicular size (Fig. 9.14).[26] Despite preliminary studies described the limited utility of MRI in the evaluation of intermittent torsion, a cost–benefit analysis by Serra et al. concluded that MRI can save cost in the management plan of patients with indeterminate scrotal pathology, however, the study was limited due to lack of patients presents with testicular torsion.[27]

9.5.3.4 *Testicular infarction*

Testicular infarction occurs following testicular vascular compromise and characterized as global or segmental testicular torsion depending on the severity of parenchymal involvement. Segmental testicular infarction can occur in patients with a predisposition to small vessel ischemic diseases such as sickle cell disease and vasculitis as well as infection and trauma.[4] On imaging, segmental testicular infarct can present like a testicular tumor, thus, requiring surgical intervention.[28] In this scenario, the utility of MRI can offer testis-sparing management by demonstrating typical imaging characteristics of T2 hypointensity and intense peripheral enhancement with or without increased T1 signal to signify hemorrhage, respectively (Fig. 9.15). On the other end of the spectrum, global testicular infarction involves a larger portion of the testicle and can be seen following torsion of the spermatic cord, incarcerated hernia, severe epididymitis and iatrogenic injury. In a study by Wantanbe et al., the MRI diagnosis of global testicular infarct reaches near 100% specificity by demonstrating lack of enhancement of the involved testicle and associated diffuse heterogenous T2 hyperintensity owing to edema.[23,29] Global testicular infarct can present as an exceedingly rare complication of epididymo-orchitis and a difficult diagnosis on ultrasound evaluation.[24]

The utility of MRI may be beneficial in patients who demonstrate persistence or worsening of symptoms despite antibiotic treatment to confirm nonglobal ischemic changes and initial appropriate surgical treatment prior to the development of global involvement.[24]

9.6 Scrotal masses

9.6.1 Introduction

One of the overarching goals of scrotal imaging is to determine the intra or extratesticular location of a lesion since an intratesticular solid mass is typically malignant, whereas an extratesticular mass is usually benign.[4] Recent evidence has proved the ability of MRI to adequately depict the location and morphologic characteristics of a scrotal mass.[49-52] Additionally, MRI has been shown to be a cost-effective modality in the evaluation of scrotal disease when presented with equivocal or inconsistent results on ultrasound.[53]

Reassuringly, the management of a benign intratesticular lesion includes less aggressive options such as follow-up, lesion biopsy, tumor enucleation, and more recently, testis-sparing surgery.[4] Therefore, it is paramount for the radiologist to combine knowledge of clinical information and imaging characteristics of benign masses to allow for confident diagnosis.

9.6.2 Benign intratesticular masses

9.6.2.1 *Testicular fibrosis*

Testicular fibrosis occurs as a result following parenchymal insult such as infection, inflammation, or traumatic process, and in the setting following radiation treatment and postbiopsy changes.[54] Although a benign finding, the sonographic appearance of testicular fibrosis can mimic a malignant testicular neoplasm, therefore, prompting evaluation with MRI which shows low T1 and very low T2 signal intensities without enhancement, which favors a non-neoplastic process (Fig. 9.16).[54-56]

9.6.2.2 *Ectasia of rete testis*

Ectasia of rete testis is the cystic dilation rete testis due to efferent ductal obstruction related to sequela of surgery, such as vasectomy, and other nonsurgical etiologies, for example, epididymitis.[49] Recent study described that ectasia of rete testis has been seen in patients with chronic kidney disease on long-term dialysis, which has been presumed to be related to retention of calcium oxalate crystals.[57] Ectasia of the rete testis is commonly seen in patients over 55 years old, involves both testicles in approximately one-third of cases and can be associated with spermatoceles.[49,58] MRI can be used as a confirmatory role when discerning from a cystic tumor remains a challenge by ultrasound or is the lesion demonstrates atypical features.[49,60] On MR imaging, ectasia of rete testis appears as a T2 hyperintense and T1 hypointense multicystic structure centered at the mediastinum testis region without enhancement following gadolinium administration (Fig. 9.17).[49,60] Additionally, if the diagnosis of ectasia of rete testis remains uncertain, the mediastinum location, presence of epididymal cysts, and bilaterality of the lesion can potentially encourage the diagnosis.[57]

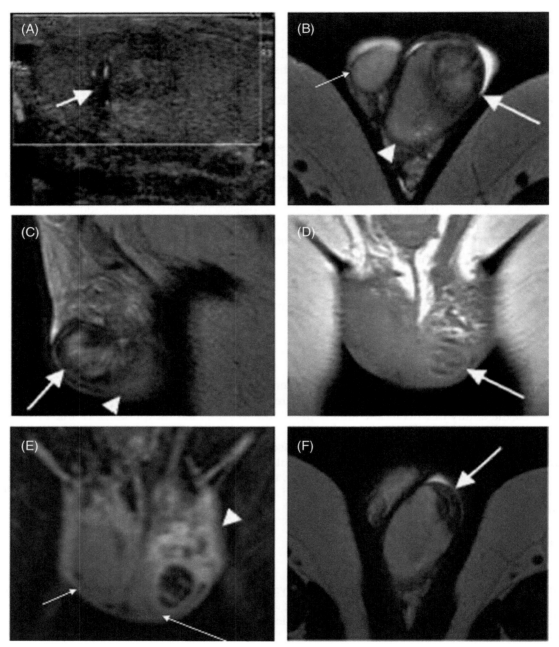

FIG. 9.15   Segmental testicular infarction man who presented with acute to subacute left testicular pain. (A) Initial evaluation with scrotal ultrasound shows a relatively ill-defined focal heterogeneously hypoechoic area in the left testicle with equivocal internal Doppler signal. (B) Axial T2-weighted MR image shows a T2 hyperintense structure in the right testis with a rim of low T1 signal (arrow). The surrounding left testis (arrowhead) shows relatively symmetric T2 intensity compared to the right testis (short arrow). (C) Corresponding sagittal T2-weighted MR image shows the T2 hyperintense structure (arrow) in the left testis (arrowhead), and confirming complete intratesticular location. (D) Coronal T1-weighted MR image shows the heterogenous, and striated appearance with mild increase T1 signal, suggesting hemorrhage. (E) Coronal contrast-enhanced MR image shows no enhancement of the left intratesticular structure, however, there is asymmetric enhancement of the paratesticular tissues, and spermatic cord (arrowhead). Note that both testes show symmetric contrast enhancement (arrows). (F) Three-month follow-up axial T2-weighed MRI image shows decrease in size of the left testicular structure.

9.6.2.3 *Testicular epidermoid cyst*

Testicular epidermoid cyst is the most common benign intratesticular neoplasm and accounts for 1–2% of all testicular lesions.[4,61] The appearance of a testicular epidermoid cyst follows the histopathologic morphology of a hard while lesion with concentric rings of white–yellow paste like material.[61] While the known characteristic appearance

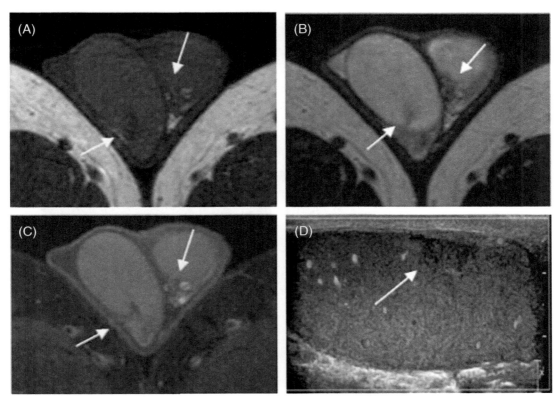

FIG. 9.16 Segmental testicular infarction man who presented with acute to subacute left testicular pain. (A) Initial evaluation with scrotal ultrasound shows a relatively ill-defined focal heterogeneously hypoechoic area in the left testicle with equivocal internal Doppler signal. (B) Axial T2-weighted MR image shows a T2 hyperintense structure in the right testis with a rim of low T1 signal (arrow). The surrounding left testis (arrowhead) shows relatively symmetric T2 intensity compared to the right testis (short arrow). (C) Corresponding sagittal T2-weighted MR image shows the T2 hyperintense structure (arrow) in the left testis (arrowhead) and confirming complete intratesticular location. (D) Coronal T1-weighted MR image shows the heterogenous and striated appearance of the with mild increase T1 signal, suggesting hemorrhage. (E) Coronal contrast-enhanced MR image shows no enhancement of the left intratesticular structure, however, there is asymmetric enhancement of the paratesticular tissues and spermatic cord (arrowhead). Note that both testes show symmetric contrast enhancement (arrows). (F) Three-month follow-up axial T2-weighed MRI image shows decrease in size of the left testicular structure.

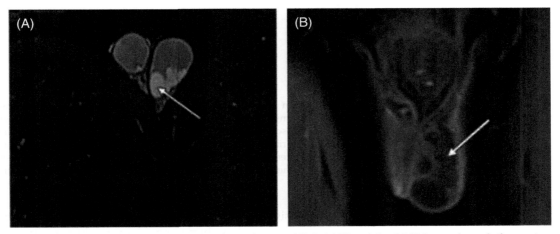

FIG. 9.17 Tubular ectasia of the rete testis in an asymptomatic man. (A) Axial T2-weighted MR image through the scrotum shows hyperintense cystic tubular structures in the region of the left mediastinum testis (arrow). (B) Coronal contrast-enhanced T1-weighted MR image demonstrates nonenhancement of the structure (arrow).

Images were reproduced with the permission of the RSNA as the copyright holder. from Vol. 38, No. 3, 806–830.

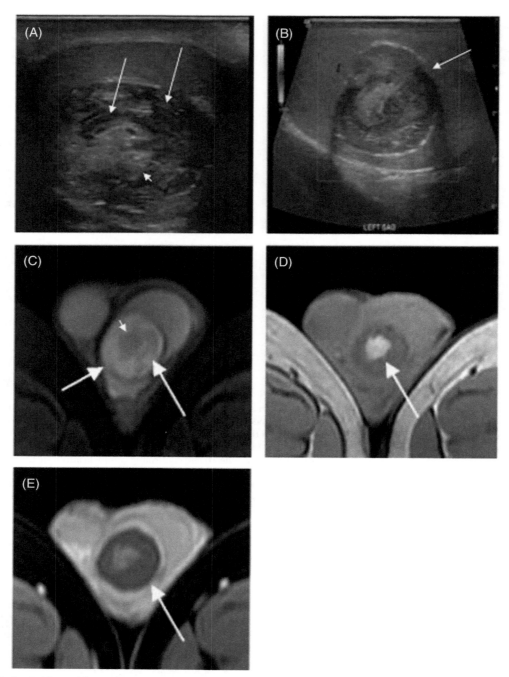

FIG. 9.18   Testicular epidermoid cyst found incidentally in a man with right testicular pain. (A) Transverse grayscale ultrasound image shows a left testicle lesion of "target" morphology depicted by alternating hypoechoic, and hyperechoic concentric rings (arrows) with echogenic center (arrowhead). (B) Corresponding color Doppler image shows avascularity of the lesion. (C) Axial fat-saturated T2-weighted image through the scrotum shows axial T2-weighted MR image shows hypointense rim and areas of alternating hyperintense and hypointense bands (long arrow), and central low intensity area of heterogeneous low signal intensity in the left testis (arrow). (D) Axial nonenhanced T1-weighted MR image through the scrotum shows a corresponding hypointense peripheral areas with hyperintense center (arrow). (E) Axial contrast-enhanced MR image confirms nonenhancement of the lesion.

of testicular epidermoid cyst leads to a confident diagnosis, an atypical appearance may mimic a worrisome mass.[54] As described by Maizlin et al., testicular epidermoid cysts can show homogenous hypoechogenicity, which can be seen in seminomas.[62] Additionally, Maizlin et al. described testicular teratomas that demonstrated characteristic of epidermoid cysts, confirmed by pathology.[62] In equivocal ultrasound cases, MRI may offer a degree of reassurance of benignity and potentially deter orchiectomy (Fig. 9.18). On MR, testicular epidermoid cyst can demonstrate a similar "target" and "onion-ring" appearance; alternating hyperintense and hypointense bands, hyperintense mid zone, and a peripheral hypointense rim, respectively; both patterns show no enhancement following gadolinium administration.[54]

9.6.2.4 Testicular adrenal rest

Testicular adrenal rest tumors are the result of overstimulation of aberrant adrenal cells within the testes most commonly in patients with congenital adrenal hyperplasia and less commonly in men with Cushing syndrome.[54] Testicular adrenal rest tumors are usually present at the mediastinum testis, multiple, bilateral, and benign, however, their appearance can overlap with malignant testicular tumors. Ultrasound is the modality of choice in the diagnosis, characterization, and follow-up of testicular adrenal rest tumors.[54] On MRI, the lesion(s) can be T1 isointense against adjacent testis and T2 hypointense to hyperintense with diffuse contrast enhancement (Fig. 9.19).[1,54] Upon diagnosis and appropriate initiation of treatment, these lesions typically decrease in size following therapy.[4,54] In the event the lesions are treatment resilient, the next step is often testis-sparing surgery.[4,54] If surgical intervention is desired, then further characterization of these lesions with MR imaging is required for planning to provide additional information on tumor size and margins as well as extent of disease.[54,63]

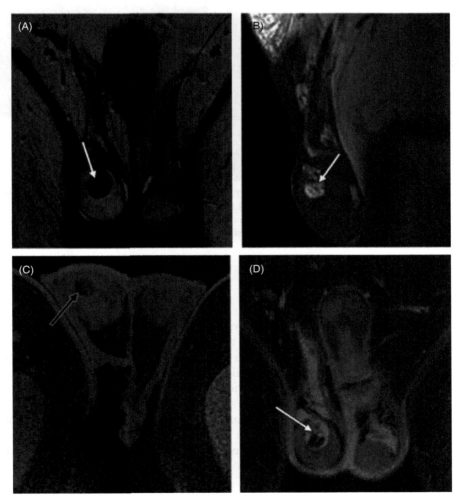

FIG. 9.19 **Adrenal rest tumor in a man with known congenital adrenal hyperplasia.** (A and B) Coronal T2-weighted (A) and sagittal T1-weighted (B) MR images show a mass (arrow) that is hypointense, and hyperintense to the normal testis, respectively. (C) Axial fat-suppressed T1-weighted MR image shows loss of signal within the lesion, consistent with internal macroscopic fat (arrow). (D) Coronal contrast-enhanced fat-suppressed T1-weighted MR image shows heterogeneously intense enhancement of the lesion (arrow). Considering the internal fat content, an imaging diagnosis of intratesticular lipoma or teratoma was suggested. Postorchiectomy pathology resulted in testicular adrenal rest tumor. *Images were reproduced with the permission of the RSNA as the copyright holder. from Vol. 38, No. 3, 806–830.*

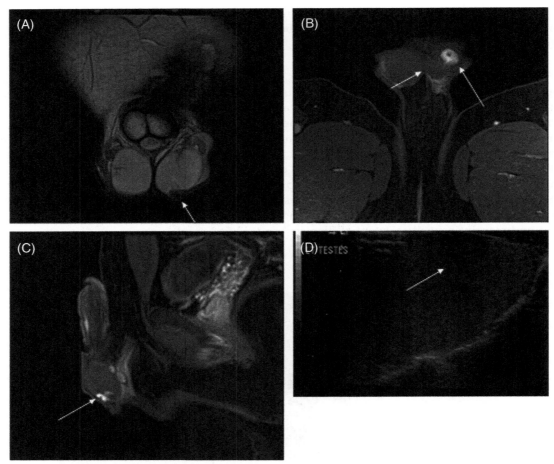

FIG. 9.20   (A) Coronal T2-weighted MR image shows a peripheral T2 hypointense lesion (arrow) in an otherwise unremarkable left testicle.
(B) Axial contrast-enhanced MR image shows intense enhancement of the lesion (long arrow) and surrounding testicular parenchyma (shorter
arrow). (C) Sagittal contrast-enhanced MR image shows the lesion in a different orientation, confirmed complete intratesticular location (arrow).
(D) Grayscale ultrasound image shows the lesion demonstrating ill-defined hypoechoic signal (arrow).

9.6.2.5 *Testicular hemangioma*

Testicular hemangioma is a rare benign vascular tumor with only approximately 50 reported cases in the literature.
Testicular hemangioma arise from the inner layer of the tunica albuginea and pathologically diagnosed by dilated
large vessels with thin walls.[64,65] The cavernous subtype is the most common subtype presenting during childhood.[66]
Given the confounding clinical presentation, such as testicular tenderness and rapid growth, and imaging appearance of testicular hemangiomas,[65–67] MRI may confirm the benign process and defer life changing orchiectomy.[65–67]
On MRI, testicular hemangiomas have been described to show slight increased T1 hyperintensity relative to muscle
and marked hyperintense T2 signal with contrast enhancement. Hemangiomas can show areas of signal void reflecting the heterogeneity of internal fibrous, fatty, or smooth muscle components, organized thrombus, or fast-flowing
blood (Fig. 9.20).[54,64–69] Furthermore, testicular hemangioma have been described to mimic testicular infarct, which
has been described above.[68,69]

9.6.3 Benign extratesticular masses

9.6.3.1 *Epididymal cystic lesions*

Epididymal cystic lesions are either epididymal cysts, which are lined by epithelium containing clear serous
fluid, or spermatoceles, that arise from obstructed and dilated seminiferous tubules as a result of insult.[70] These

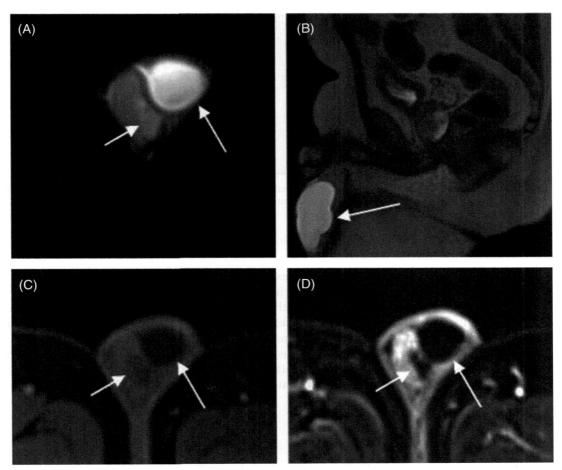

FIG. 9.21   Rete testis and spermatocele. (A) Axial T2-weighted MR image through the scrotum shows a left extratesticular T2 hyperintense lesion (long arrow) abutting an otherwise normal appearing left testis containing ectasia of rete testis (shorter arrow). (B) Sagittal MR image the extratesticular lesion demonstrating mild lobulation (arrow). (C) Axial fat-saturated T1-weighted MR image through the scrotum shows the hypointensity of extratesticular lesion (long arrow) and ectasia of the rete testis (short arrow). (D) Corresponding contrast-enhanced axial T1-weighted MR image shows no enhancement of the extratesticular lesion (long arrow) and ectasia of the rete testis (short arrow). The extratesticular cyst is presumed to represent a spermatocele given ectasia of rete testis.

lesions are typically indistinguishable by physical exam or ultrasound; however, spermatoceles contain spermatozoa and while both lesions can be seen at the epididymal head region, epididymal cysts can arise from anywhere along the epididymis.[71] A complex spermatoceles can demonstrate complex features such as internal septations and mobile debris, which are reliably detected and confirmed by ultrasound, however, nonmobile echoes may indicate a rare cystic epididymal neoplasm, rendering further characterization with MR imaging (Fig. 9.21).[70]

9.6.4 Tunica albuginea cysts

Tunica albuginea cyst is one the most common extratesticular benign lesions.[49,72] Tunica albuginea cysts arises from the fibrous tunica albuginea, under the tunica vaginalis and typically range from 2 to 5 mm in size tunica albuginea cysts may be associated with a history of trauma, hemorrhage, or infection and characteristically located at the upper anterior or lateral aspect of the testicle (Fig. 9.22).[73,74] Not uncommonly, tunica albuginea cysts are difficult to distinguish from tunica vaginalis cysts, however, both lesions demonstrate imaging characteristics of benign cysts. However, it is important to note that there are reports of complex tunica albuginea cysts that can mimic an intratesticular lesion for which MRI may be useful to confirm benignity prior to potential surgical intervention.[75]

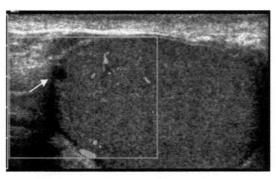

FIG. 9.22   **Incidentally found tunica albuginea cyst.** (A) Longitudinal color Doppler ultrasound through the scrotum demonstrates an avascular anechoic lesion abutting the overlying tunica albuginea, consistent with tunica albuginea cyst.

9.6.5 Varicocele

Varicocele is defined as dilation of the pampiniform plexus in the spermatic cord and represents the most commonly encounter "mass" in the spermatic cord.[76,77] The incidence of varicocele is estimated to be approximately 15% of the general population.[76] Ultrasound remains as the most frequently used modality to diagnose varicocele which shows characteristic dilated and serpiginous vessels superior and posterior to the testis.[76] MRI is seldomly used and required to diagnose varicocele, of which its imaging appearance is predicated upon the flow rate of the dilated vessels. Typically, varicoceles demonstrate contrast enhancement with intermediate signal intensity on T1- and T2-weighted images and signal void seen in vessels of higher velocities (Fig. 9.23).[76,77] Although there is a limited role of MRI in the diagnosis of varicocele, some studies show promise in detecting the sequela of varicoceles on the adjacent testicles.[78,79]

9.6.6 Inguinal hernia

Inguinal hernias are organized into direct or indirect hernia, depending on the structure through which herniated contents traverse, Hesselbach triangle or deep internal inguinal ring, respectively. Indirect hernias can extend to the scrotum and remains the most common cause of scrotal hernia.[80] Typically, the diagnosis of inguinal hernia is based on clinical presentation and physical examination, however, imaging offers a complimentary and problem-solving role in the evaluation of inguinal hernias.[80] While the detection of contents and movement within a hernia reassures the diagnosis on ultrasound, MR imaging may be used distinguish an omental fat containing hernia from a lipomatous lesion on ultrasound (Fig. 9.24).

9.6.7 Lipoma

Often arising from the spermatic cord, scrotal lipomas are the most common benign extratesticular mass, comprising of 45% of all extratesticular masses.[1,49] The role of MRI in the work up of scrotal lipoma can be confirmatory when ultrasonic features are atypical due to the heterogenous composition of the mass with other mesenchymal tissue such as fibrous connective or vascular tissue.[1,49] The MRI characteristics of a scrotal lipoma should follow macroscopic fat intensity, thus, hyperintensity on T1- and T2-weighted images without postgadolinium enhancement (Figs. 9.25 and 9.26).[1] On chemical shift imaging, India ink artifact is seen at water–fat interfaces with the lesion.[1]

9.6.8 Fibrolipoma

Scrotal fibrolipoma is a rare benign subtype of scrotal lipoma consisting of bundles of mature fibrous tissue traversing fatty lobules.[81] Due to the lipomatous tissue within the mass, the MR imaging appearance demonstrates a hyperechoic mass and high T1 and heterogenous T2 signal intensities with signal loss on fat-saturated sequences (Fig. 9.27). A case report in the literature presented a diagnostic conundrum in which a large fatty scrotal mass was difficult to differentiate a benign process such as lipoma or fibrolipoma versus a more malignant process such as a low-grade scrotal liposarcoma.[1,81] In such cases, the clinical presentation may further guide whether a conservative or surgical management is necessary.[81]

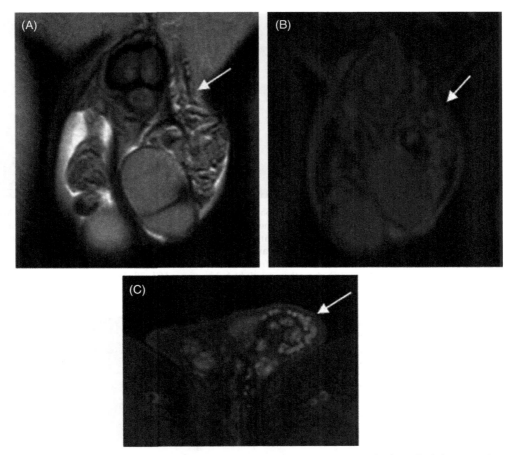

FIG. 9.23   Left varicocele. (A) Coronal T2-weighted MR image shows a dilated tubular vessels along the left spermatic cord extending to the left paratesticular tissues (arrow). (B) Corresponding coronal T1-weighted MR image shows similar findings (arrow). (C) Contrast-enhanced axial fat-saturated T1-weighted MR image through the scrotum shows intense enhancement of the tubular vessels, consistent with varicocele.

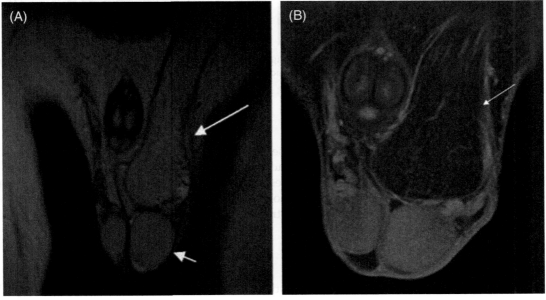

FIG. 9.24   Fat-containing left scrotal hernia. (A) Coronal T2-weighted MR image shows a fat signal extending along the inguinal canal into the left paratesticular tissues (arrow). Note the normal appearing and uninvolved left testicle (shorter arrow). (B) Corresponding contrast-enhanced axial T1-weighted MR image shows loss of signal of the herniated fat and without suspicious intralesional enhancement (arrow).

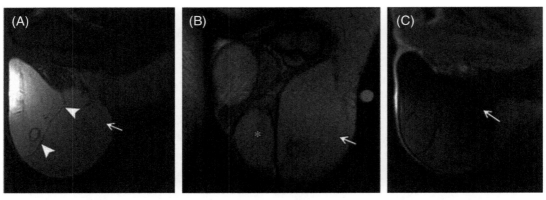

FIG. 9.25   Extratesticular lipoma in a 40-year-old man. (A and B) Sagittal T1-weighted (A) and coronal T2-weighted (B) MR images demonstrate a large well-encapsulated hyperintense mass (arrow) in the left hemiscrotum that displaces the left testis (* in B), indicating extratesticular location of the mass. There are scattered thin T2 hypointense septa within the mass (arrowheads in A). (C) Sagittal contrast-enhanced fat-suppressed T1-weighted MR image shows loss of internal signal intensity (arrow), signifying internal macroscopic fat without septa or solid enhancement. The lack of worrisome enhancement aids in the differentiation from a more aggressive liposarcoma.
Images were reproduced with the permission of the RSNA as the copyright holder. from Vol. 38, No. 3, 806–830.

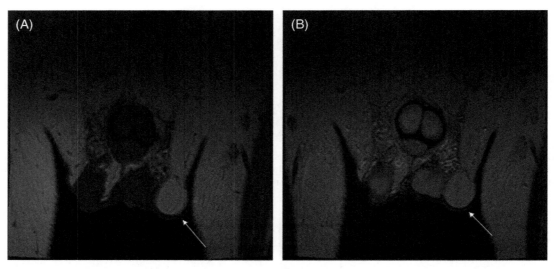

FIG. 9.26   Companion case of extratesticular lipoma. (A and B) Sagittal T1-weighted (A) and sagittal T2-weighted (B) MR images show a well-circumscribed lesion situation in the left lateral paratesticular space abutting the left testicle follows fat intensity (arrow), consistent with lipoma.

9.6.9 Adenomatoid tumor

Approximately 30% of extratesticular tumors are represented by adenomatoid tumors, which is the second most common extratesticular mass.[1,49] Approximately 40% of adenomatoid tumors arise from the epididymal tail.[1,49] MRI can be used to affirm the extratesticular location of the lesion rather than a mimicking peripherally location intratesticular mass.[59] On MRI, adenomatoid tumors can demonstrate T2 hypointensity relative to adjacent parenchyma (Fig. 9.28).[49] Following intravenous gadolinium administration, enhancement of adenomatoid tumors can be seen, possibly related to granulation tissue.[49]

9.6.10 Fibrous pseudotumor

Fibrous pseudotumor is the third most common extratesticular tumor is fibrous pseudotumor. Histopathologically, fibrous pseudotumor are formed from a proliferation of benign extratesticular fibrous tissue, and therefore, not necessarily a neoplasm.[49] Fibrous pseudotumors most commonly arise in the tunica vaginalis and likely consequence of a reactive proliferation of inflammatory and fibrous tissue.[82,83]

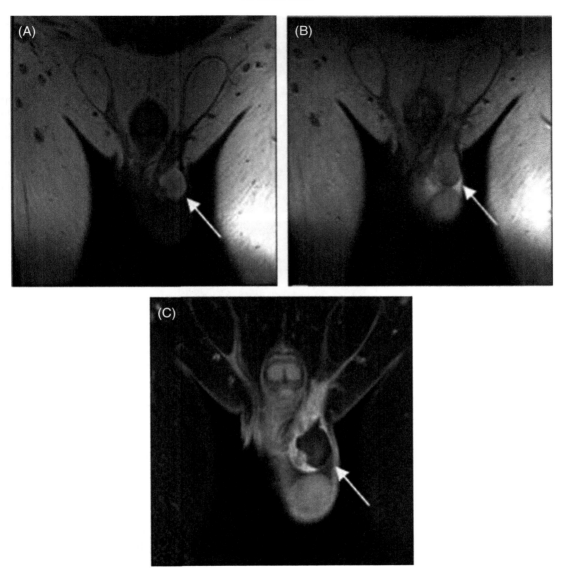

FIG. 9.27 **Extratesticular fibrolipoma.** (A and B) Sagittal T1-weighted (A) and sagittal T2-weighted (B) MR images show a heterogeneously hyperintense lesion on both sequences (arrows). (C) Corresponding fat-saturated contrast-enhanced coronal T1-weighted MR image shows no contrast enhancement and loss of signal of the lesion, indicative of macroscopic fat.

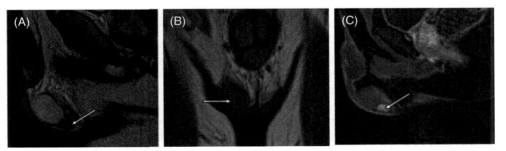

FIG. 9.28 **Adenomatoid tumor of the epididymis in a 32-year-old man with a right scrotal mass.** (A) Sagittal T2-weighted MR image shows a hypointense mass (arrow) in the tail of the epididymis. (B) Coronal T1-weighted MR image shows isointensity of the mass as adjacent testicular parenchyma (arrow). (C) Sagittal contrast-enhanced T1-weighted MR image shows enhancement of the mass (arrow).
Images were reproduced with the permission of the RSNA as the copyright holder. from Vol. 38, No. 3, 806–830.

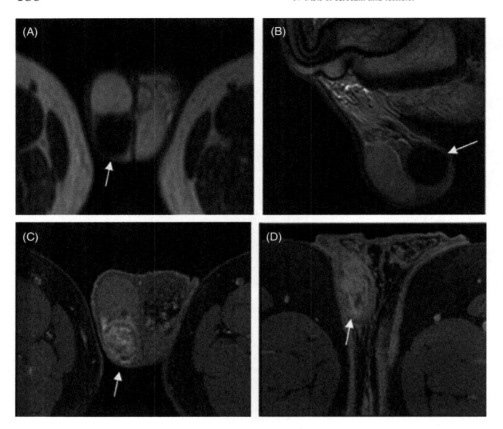

FIG. 9.29 Fibrous pseudotumor in man with right testicular lump. (A and B) Axial T2-weighted (A) and sagittal T2-weighted (B) MR images show a well circumscribed completely extratesticular T2 hypointense mass (arrows) posterior to the normal appearing right testicle. (C and D) Contrast-enhanced axial (C) and coronal (D) T1-weighted MR images show heterogenous enhancement of the mass (arrows).

Images (B–D) were reproduced with the permission of the RSNA as the copyright holder. from Vol. 38, No. 3, 806–830.

Similar to fibrous tumors in other parts of the body, fibrous pseudotumor exhibit T1 and T2 hypointensity with variable enhancement following gadolinium administration (Fig. 9.29).[82,83]

9.6.11 Extratesticular epidermoid inclusion cyst of the scrotum

Extratesticular epidermal inclusion cysts are thought to result from abnormal closure of the median raphe and urethral groove (Fig. 9.30).[84,85] Epidermoid inclusion cysts can be located along the midline of the median raphe, from the distal penis to the anus. These lesions can contain a variety of substances such as fluid, laminated keratin, cholesterol crystals, and debris, which guides their imaging appearances.[84] Clinically, patients typically remain asymptomatic until complications such as rupture, superinfection or lesion enlargement causing locoregional mass effect.[84] On MRI, these lesions demonstrate hypointensity on T1-weighted images and hyperintensity on T2-weighted images with a T2 hypointense capsule, and without contrast enhancement (Fig. 9.30).[85] In the setting of rupture, these lesions have been shown to demonstrate a lobulated morphology and internal Doppler flow.[85] Confident diagnosis of an epidermal inclusion cyst allows testis-sparing resection to prevent infection or rupture.[85]

9.6.12 Sclerosing lipogranuloma

Sclerosing lipogranuloma is a benign inflammatory process that can result from breakdown of endogenous lipids or caused by injection of an exogenous foreign body, such as liquid paraffin, vegetable oils, or silicon; the latter of which is more common.[1,86] As a result of chronic inflammation, the granuloma formed consists of epithelioid and a variety of immunologic cells which manifests as a hard scrotal nodule involving in the scrotum and penoscrotal junction.[1,87] On ultrasound, sclerosing lipogranuloma is typically hypoechoic. On MRI, these lesions demonstrate heterogenous T1- and T2 signal and heterogenous enhancement with intravoxel fat in the upper scrotum or penoscrotal junction.[1,87] Sclerosing lipogranuloma can also contain necrotic components which demonstrates areas of T2 hyperintensity (Fig. 9.31).[1,87] Caution is advised to include tuberculosis and fungal infections as important differential considerations for sclerosing lipogranuloma.[1] Sclerosing lipogranulomas has been shown to spontaneously resolve, and thus, may be managed conservatively or excised.[1]

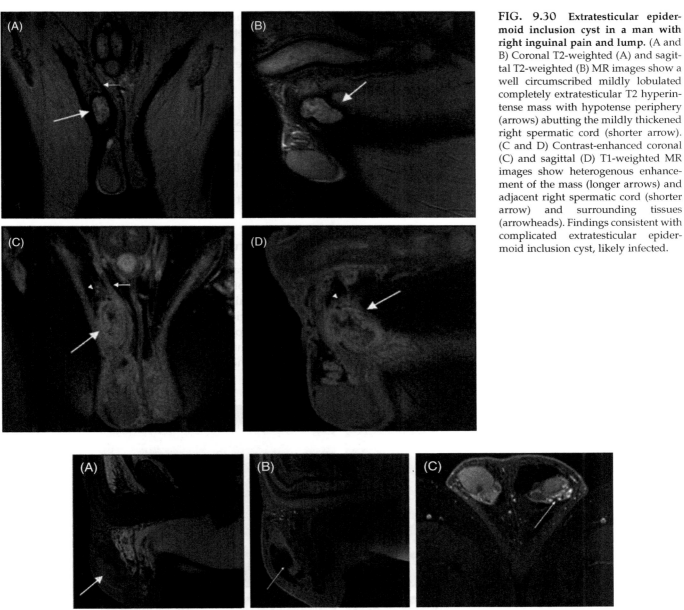

FIG. 9.30 Extratesticular epidermoid inclusion cyst in a man with right inguinal pain and lump. (A and B) Coronal T2-weighted (A) and sagittal T2-weighted (B) MR images show a well circumscribed mildly lobulated completely extratesticular T2 hyperintense mass with hypotense periphery (arrows) abutting the mildly thickened right spermatic cord (shorter arrow). (C and D) Contrast-enhanced coronal (C) and sagittal (D) T1-weighted MR images show heterogenous enhancement of the mass (longer arrows) and adjacent right spermatic cord (shorter arrow) and surrounding tissues (arrowheads). Findings consistent with complicated extratesticular epidermoid inclusion cyst, likely infected.

FIG. 9.31 Sclerosing lipogranuloma in a man after silicone injection into the penoscrotal region for penile enhancement. (A and B) Sagittal T1-weighted (A) and fat-suppressed T1-weighted (B) MR images demonstrate an ill-defined heterogenous mass-like lesion in the left hemiscrotum with focal areas of macroscopic fat suppression (arrow in B), indicated fat vacuole. (c) Axial contrast-enhanced fat-suppressed T1-weighted MR image shows focal areas of heterogeneous contrast enhancement (arrow) in the lesion.
Images were reproduced with the permission of the RSNA as the copyright holder. from Vol. 38, No. 3, 806–830.

9.7 Malignant scrotal masses

9.7.1 Introduction

In addition to recent literature that has proven MRI useful in characterizing scrotal lesion location and distinguishing between benign from malignant testicular masses, there is growing evidence for its use in specific diagnostic and preoperative settings. Studies that have shown that MRI reliably differentiates between seminomatous and nonseminomatous tumors, for which the distinction is important in guiding patient management. Furthermore, in the developing role of testis-sparing surgery for nongerm cell tumors, such as sex cord stromal tumors, there are some studies that demonstrate the utility of MRI to offer a confident preoperative diagnosis of certain sex cord stromal tumors that subsequently allow for treatment and surgical planning.[49] Moreover, in the setting of a known malignant testicular mass, MRI has been shown to accurately assess and detect the local extent and specific features of malignant testicular tumors, thereby enabling the potential for improved posttreatment results especially if testis-sparing surgery is considered.[49] The following sections will discuss the literature supporting these concepts in the setting of their respective pathologies.

9.8 Malignant intratesticular masses

As a minority in the overall percentage of solid tumors in men, testicular tumors are the most common solid malignancy occurring in men between the ages of 15–35 years old.[49] Germ cell tumors comprise of 95% of testicular malignancies and broadly divided into seminomatous and nonseminomatous subtypes, and the remaining, nongerm cell tumors (summarized in Table 9.3).[1] The following section will highlight the key and evolving findings from the growing evidence of MRI in the evaluation of testicular tumors.

9.8.1 Differentiation between seminoma and nonseminomatous tumors

In general, seminomas are sensitive to chemotherapy and radiation therapy while nonseminomatous germ cell tumors typically require lymph node dissection and chemotherapy, therefore, furthering the need confident preoperative diagnosis on imaging.[119] Many groups have shown consistently high accuracy of differentiation between seminomatous and nonseminomatous tumors by MR imaging characteristics.[49,107–109] Seminomas are typically non-encapsulated, exhibit a nodular morphology containing fibrovascular septa, and enhance following gadolinium administration with the septa enhancing to a greater degree than the tumor. Seminomas displays isointensity on T1-WI, homogenously hypointense on T2-WI and typically does not demonstrate internal hemorrhagic or cystic components (Figs. 9.32–9.34).[49,107]

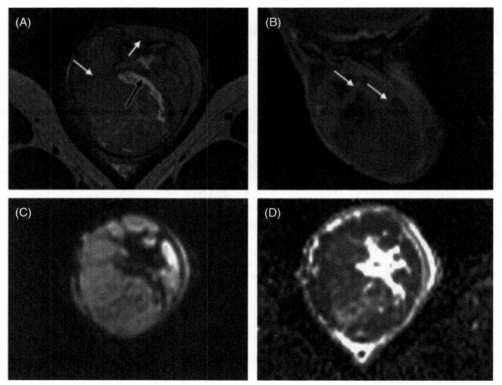

FIG. 9.32   **Seminoma in a mass who presented with a hard scrotal mass.** (A) Axial T2-weighted MR image shows a hypointense, lobulated, multinodular well-defined lesion in the right testis with band like areas of low signal intensity fibrovascular septa (white arrows), and central T2 hyperintensity secondary to necrosis (black arrow). (B) Sagittal contrast-enhanced T1-weighted MR image shows greater enhancement of the septa (arrows) in comparison with the mass. (C and D) Axial high *b*-value diffusion-weighted (C) and corresponding ADC map (D) shows restricted diffusion in the mass. Postorchiectomy histologic analysis revealed pure seminoma.
Images were reproduced with the permission of the RSNA as the copyright holder. from Vol. 38, No. 3, 806–830.

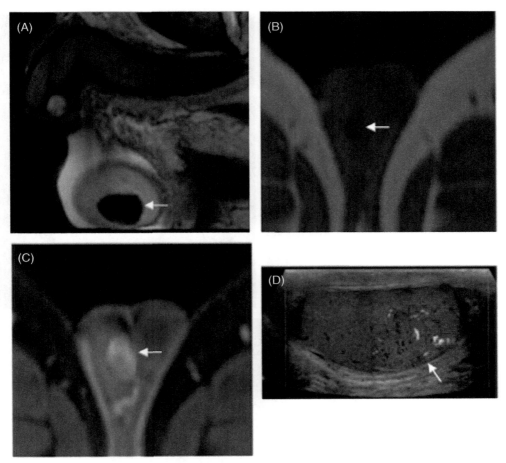

FIG. 9.33   **Companion case of seminoma incidentally found on CT (not shown).** (A) Sagittal T2-weighted MR image shows an intratesticular oval-shaped hypointense well-defined mass in the right testis (white arrows). (B) Axial T1-weighted image demonstrates T1 hypointensity of the mass (arrow). (C) Contrast-enhanced T1-weighted MR image shows relatively homogenous enhancement of the right testicular mass. (D) Longitudinal color Doppler ultrasound image shows the intensely vascular hypoechoic mass (arrow).

Nonseminomatous tumors can be encapsulated, heterogenous on T1- and T2-WI, and heterogenous enhancing with hemorrhagic or cystic components but without fibrovascular septa (Figs. 9.35–9.38).[49,107] There is also literature supporting the use of diffusion-weighted imaging to discriminate between seminomatous and nonseminomatous tumors such that a lower ADC values is observed in seminomas.[108] The differentiation between seminoma and nonseminomatous tumor may be warranted when chemotherapy is the recommended primary treatment in the setting of extensive metastasis.[59]

9.8.2   Differentiating between germ cell tumor versus nongerm cell tumor

Along the spectrum of tumor type differentiation, some MR imaging findings can differentiate between different germ cell tumors. While both Sertoli and Leydig cell tumors demonstrate marked contrast enhancement, Sertoli cell tumors can demonstrate T2 hyperintensity, and Leydig cell tumors can show T2 hypointensity (Figs. 9.39–9.41A and 9.41B).[1] Additionally, there are studies that showed the use of MRI to differentiate between germ cell and nongerm cell tumors. This distinction becomes important due to some evidence of utilizing testis-sparing surgery in patients with sex cord stromal tumors under certain circumstances, such as small size of tumors.[110] Continuing from above, Leydig cell tumors have been shown to demonstrate isointense T1 signal and hypointense T2 signal, which can mimic seminomas.[110] However, Manganaro et al. reported an accuracy of 93% in differentiating between Leydig cell tumors and seminomas most reliably using the markedly hypointense signal on T2-WI, rapid and marked wash-in followed by a prolonged washout as seen with Leydig cell tumors (Figs. 9.41A and 9.41B).[111]

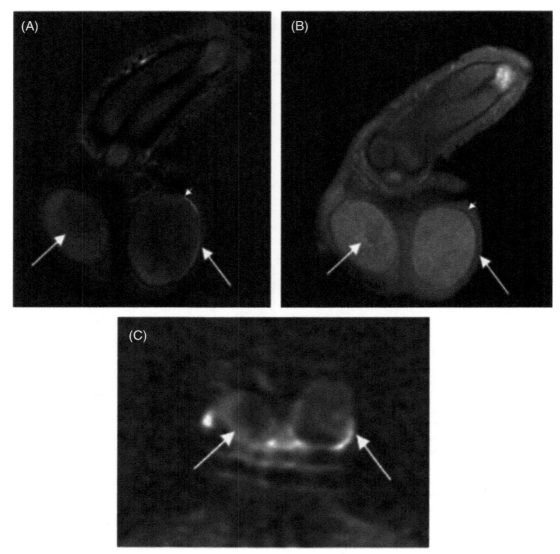

FIG. 9.34 Companion case of bilateral seminoma. (A) Sagittal T2-weighted MR image shows bilateral T2 hypointense masses (arrows) respecting the adjacent hypointense tunica albuginea (arrowheads). (B) Contrast-enhanced coronal T1-weighted MR images show enhancement of the masses (arrows). (C) Axial ADC images show restricted diffusion of these masses (arrows).

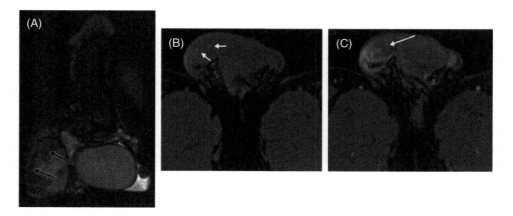

FIG. 9.35 Embryonal carcinoma in a man who presented with a painless right scrotal mass. (A) Coronal T2-weighted MR image shows a lobulated heterogeneous mass (arrows) with areas of low signal intensity that invades the adjacent tunica albuginea. (B) Corresponding axial nonenhanced T1-weighted MR image shows areas of high signal intensity due to hemorrhage (arrows). (C) Axial contrast-enhanced T1-weighted MR image shows heterogeneous enhancement of the mass (arrow).

Images were reproduced with the permission of the RSNA as the copyright holder. from Vol. 38, No. 3, 806–830.

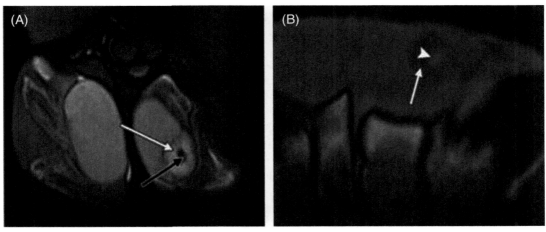

FIG. 9.36   Mature teratoma in a 40-year-old man with a left testicular mass. (A) Coronal T2-weighted MR image through the scrotum shows a well-defined lesion in the left testis with a hyperintense outer rim (white arrow), and central hypointensity (black arrow). (B) Corresponding axial fat-suppressed T1-weighted MR image reveals hypointense outer rim (arrow) due to fat along with internal hyperintensity (arrowhead) due to blood products. The heterogenous signal intensities of blood and fat are consistent with a mature teratoma.
Images were reproduced with the permission of the RSNA as the copyright holder. from Vol. 38, No. 3, 806–830.

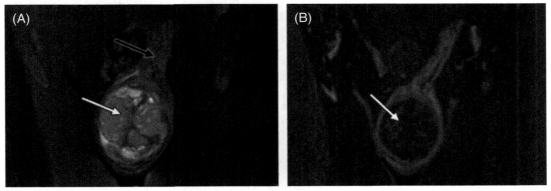

FIG. 9.37   Malignant teratoma in man with a painless left testicular mass. (A) Coronal fat-suppressed T2-weighted MR image through the scrotum shows a heterogeneous mixed cystic and solid lesion (white arrow) in the left testis associated with thickening of the spermatic cord (black arrow). (B) Coronal contrast-enhanced T1-weighted MR image shows heterogeneous enhancement of the lesion (arrow). Postorchiectomy histologic analysis revealed malignant teratoma.
Images were reproduced with the permission of the RSNA as the copyright holder. from Vol. 38, No. 3, 806–830.

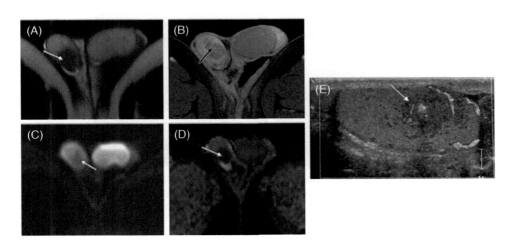

FIG. 9.38   Malignant mixed germ cell tumor with a right testicular mass. (A) Axial T2-weighted MR image shows an ill-defined hypointense mass (arrow) in the right testis. (B) Axial contrast-enhanced T1-weighted MR image shows heterogeneous enhancement (arrow). (C and D) Axial high *b*-value diffusion-weighted MR image (C), and corresponding ADC map (D) demonstrates internal restricted diffusion (arrow). (E) Color Doppler ultrasound of the same mass reveals calcification within the vascular hypoechoic mass (arrow). Postorchiectomy histopathologic analysis revealed malignant mixed germ cell tumor.
Images (A–D) were reproduced with the permission of the RSNA as the copyright holder. from Vol. 38, No. 3, 806–830.

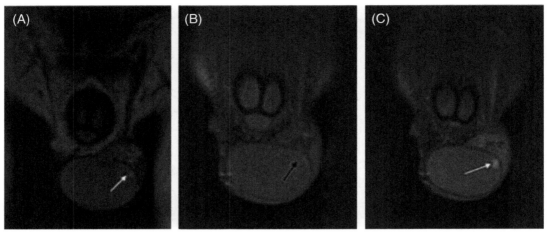

FIG. 9.39   Sertoli cell tumor in a young man with prior right orchiectomy for Sertoli cell tumor who presented with gynecomastia and testicular pain. (A) Coronal T2-weighted MR image shows a hyperintense nodule (arrow) in the left testis. (B) Coronal fat-saturated T1-weighted MR image shows the corresponding nodule (arrow) with isointense signal compared to adjacent testicle. (C) Corresponding coronal contrast-enhanced T1-weighted MR image shows marked contrast enhancement of the nodule (arrow).
Images were reproduced with the permission of the RSNA as the copyright holder. from Vol. 38, No. 3, 806–830.

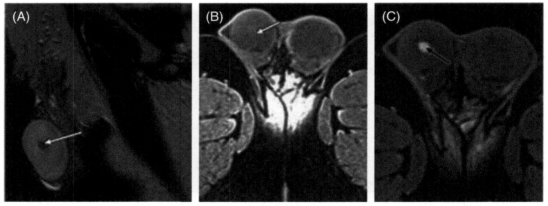

FIG. 9.40   Granulosa cell tumor in man with gynecomastia and a painless mass in the right testis. (A) Sagittal T2-weighted MR image demonstrates a hypointense nodule (arrow) in the right testis. (B) Axial T2-weighted MR image shows the nodule (arrow) nearly matching in signal relative to surrounding testicular parenchyma. (C) Axial contrast-enhanced T1-weighted MR image shows marked enhancement of the nodule (arrow).
Images were reproduced with the permission of the RSNA as the copyright holder. from Vol. 38, No. 3, 806–830.

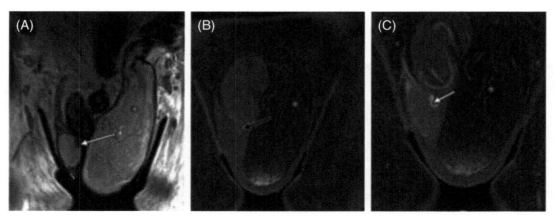

FIG. 9.41A   Leydig cell tumor in a 35-year-old man who presented with gynecomastia and decreased libido. *, incidental fat-containing left inguinal hernia. (A) Coronal T2-weighted MR image shows a hypointense nodule (arrow) in the right testis. (B) Corresponding nonenhanced T1-weighted MR image shows the mass (arrow) as nearly isointense to the testicular parenchyma. (C) Coronal contrast-enhanced T1-weighted MR image shows marked enhancement of the mass (arrow).
Images were reproduced with the permission of the RSNA as the copyright holder. from Vol. 38, No. 3, 806–830.

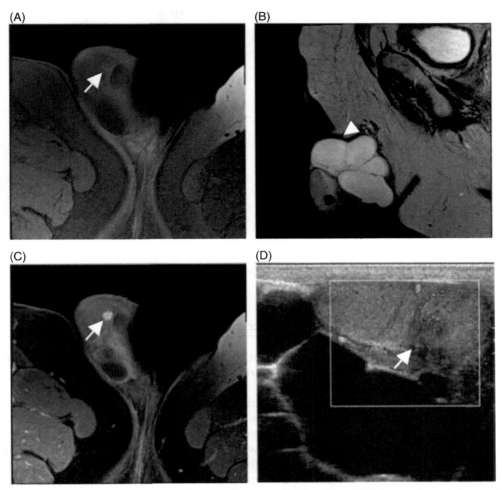

FIG. 9.41B Companion case of Leydig cell tumor. (A) Axial fat-saturated T1-weighted MR image through the scrotum shows a mildly hyperintense nodule in the right testes (arrow). (B) Sagittal T2-weighted MR image shows the nodule to have homogenously low T2 signal (arrow) and adjacent extratesticular lobulated extratesticular fluid collection (arrowhead) which represents with epididymal cyst or spermatocele. (C) Contrast-enhanced axial T1-weighted MR image shows intense contrast enhanced of the nodule (arrow) relative to the testicular parenchyma. (D) Color Doppler ultrasound image shows the hypoechoic nodule with increased internal Doppler flow (arrow).

An important nongerm cell tumor to consider is testicular lymphoma. Testicular lymphoma is most commonly the diffuse large B-cell non-Hodgkin's type, occurs in men greater than 60 years old and constitutes 1–9% of all testicular tumors.[1,112] Secondary involvement of the testis occurs more often than primary testicular lymphoma.[1,112] On imaging, primary testicular lymphoma has been described as a mildly enhancing homogenous mass with hypointense T1 and T2 signal while other studies describe an infiltrative appearance and bilaterality of the lesion with involvement of adjacent structures (Figs. 9.42 and 9.43).[1,112] The imaging appearance of testicular lymphoma can mimic seminoma, however, seminomas do not typically cause locoregional invasion or involve both testes.[49,112] Additional differential considerations of testicular lymphoma include epididymo-orchitis, sarcoidosis, and leukemia; clinical information and follow-up imaging after treatment may assist in the differentiation between these lesions from lymphoma.[1]

9.8.3 Local staging of tumor

The typical surgical treatment for malignant testicular masses is orchiectomy, however, the selection of testis-sparing surgery can be performed in certain settings.[113,114] The accuracy of utilizing MRI in the assessment of local extent of malignant testicular lesions was performed by Tsili et al.[54] By following the NCCN and the European germ cell cancer consensus group guidelines of local extent of malignant testicular lesions, the group reported an accuracy rate of 92.8% when using MRI for the detection of features that correspond to the T-stage (put in staging figure).[54] For example, the disruption of the tunica albuginea categorizes a lesion as T2 stage (Fig. 9.44). In addition, there is evidence to support facilitation of enucleation of tumor in the setting or testis-sparing surgery in the presence of a capsule identified by imaging.[49]

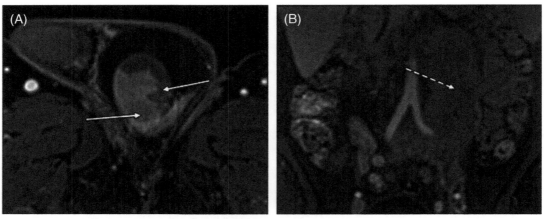

FIG. 9.42   Lymphoma in a man with left-sided scrotal swelling. (A) Axial contrast-enhanced fat-suppressed T1-weighted MR image shows a hypointense infiltrative lesion (arrows) in the left testis that enhances less than adjacent testicular parenchyma. (B) Coronal contrast-enhanced fat-suppressed T1-weighted MR image of the abdomen shows enlarged conglomerate of retroperitoneal lymph nodes (arrow).
Images were reproduced with the permission of the RSNA as the copyright holder. from Vol. 38, No. 3, 806–830.

9.9 Malignant extratesticular masses

Moving beyond separating between intratesticular from extratesticular location of masses, scrotal MRI has an advancing role in providing more confidence diagnoses and characterization of locoregional involvement of tumor, thereby facilitating effective pretreatment planning.[49]

Histopathologically, benign and malignant extratesticular masses can derive from nonepididymal tissues therefore representing mesenchymal origin.[114] Reassuringly, the majority of mesenchymal-derived extratesticular masses are benign with some of these tumors detailed in the previous section, including lipoma and fibrous pseudotumor, while other tumors are described by Wolfman et al.[114] On the malignant spectrum of extratesticular masses, spermatic cord sarcomas are the most common with the majority represented by rhabdomyosarcoma followed by liposarcoma and leiomyosarcoma, in decreasing order.[49]

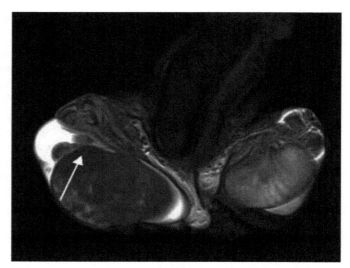

FIG. 9.43   Case of diffuse large B-cell lymphoma. Axial T2-weighted image shows a T2 hypointense mass infiltrating the testicle with extension into the epididymis (arrow).
-Reprinted under STM permissions guidelines graciously from Mathur M, Spektor M. MR imaging of the testicular and extratesticular tumors when do we need? 2018. Magn Resonance Imag Clin North Am. 27 (2019) 151–171.

FIG. 9.44   Case of seminoma with extratesticular extension. (A) Axial T2-weighted MR image of the scrotum demonstrates a hypointense mass replacing majority of the right testicle with extension of similar intensity tumor through the tunica albuginea and into the adjacent paratesticular tissues.

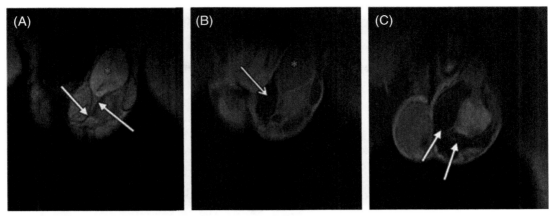

FIG. 9.45 **Scrotal liposarcoma in an older man.** (A and B) Coronal T2-weighted (A) and fat-suppressed T1-weighted (B) MR images demonstrate a nonwell circumscribed mass containing hypointense septa (arrows in A) and internal macroscopic fat (arrow in B) encasing the left testis (*). (C) Coronal contrast-enhanced fat-suppressed T1-weighted MR image shows enhancement of the internal septa (arrows), which is inconsistent with lipoma. *Images were reproduced with the permission of the RSNA as the copyright holder. from Vol. 38, No. 3, 806–830.*

9.9.1 Liposarcoma

Liposarcoma is an uncommon malignant neoplasm in the scrotum typically occurring in older men.[1,49] The ultrasound appearance of liposarcoma is variable and MRI can increase the confidence of diagnosis through the improved resolution in the detection of internal fat, as depicted by increased T1 and T2 intensity that loses signal on fat saturation sequences and chemical shift artifact at the junction of fat and soft tissue within the mass.[1,49] Additionally, MRI has the potential to detect thick soft tissue strands or nodules within fatty tissue, along with corroborating findings such as restricted diffusion, thus, differentiating from lipoma (Fig. 9.45).[1,49] However, it is important to recognize that a low-grade spermatic cord liposarcomas may be difficult to differentiate from a lipoma.[1,81] Furthermore, MRI has the potential to better define the involvement of surrounding tissue by the tumor with aims to achieve improved locoregional control of tumor if surgical resection is performed.[49]

9.9.2 Rhabdomyosarcoma

In contrast, rhabdomyosarcoma occurs much earlier in life relative to other sarcomas.[1] The predominant histologic subtype is embryonal rhabdomyosarcoma, accounting for 90% of all paratesticular rhabdomyosarcoma.[136] Rhabdomyosarcoma can locally invade testicular structures and possesses significant metastatic potential and favors lymphatic spread of disease.[1,134] Imaging findings are nonspecific with reports of MRI showing a homogenously or heterogeneously enhancing solid mass with slightly heterogenous hyperintense T2 signal intensity and T1 isointense to adjacent testicle (Fig. 9.46).[135,137,138] Shah et al. suggested the use of MRI in confirming diagnosis and potentially detect paratesticular spread of disease, thereby facilitating management.[135]

9.9.3 Testicular metastasis

Metastatic disease to the scrotum is rare, representing less than 8% of epididymal masses, and mostly occurring in the setting of prostate carcinoma, and subsequently in decreasing order, malignancies involving the kidney, stomach, colon, carcinoid tumor, ileum, and pancreas (Figs. 9.47 and 9.48).[49,116,117] Testicular metastasis can involve both testes in 8–15% of cases and may be suggested in the proper clinical setting.[116,117] The imaging features of scrotal metastasis are nonspecific, and suggestion of diagnosis is largely based on clinical suspicion (Figs. 9.47 and 9.48).[116,117]

9.9.4 Pearls and pitfalls

1. While ultrasound remains as the primary modality for the evaluation of scrotal pathology, there is emerging use of MRI to accurately assess the location of scrotal masses, which in and by itself is an indicator of malignant potential, and characterize sonographically indeterminate lesions.

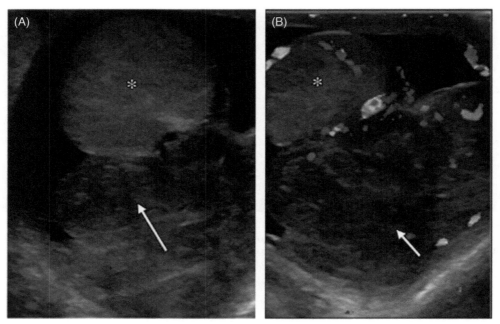

FIG. 9.46   Rhabdomyosarcoma in a 19-year-old man with left-sided scrotal swelling. Transverse grayscale (A) and color Doppler (B) US images of the left scrotum demonstrate a vascular large paratesticular heterogeneous mass (arrows) extending to the left testis (*). Biopsy results revealed rhabdomyosarcoma.
Images were reproduced with the permission of the RSNA as the copyright holder. from Vol. 38, No. 3, 806–830.

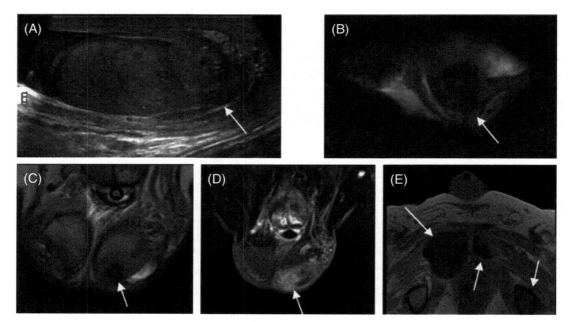

FIG. 9.47   Scrotal metastasis in a patient with metastatic prostate cancer. (A) Grayscale ultrasound in longitudinal view shows a heterogenous mass that straddles a part of the testicle and paratesticular tissues (arrow). (B and C) Axial T2-weighted (B) and sagittal T2-weighted (C) MR images show the hypointense mass corresponding to the mass on the ultrasound involving both the testicle and surrounding tissues. (D) Contrast-enhanced coronal T1-weighted MR image shows intense contrast enhancement of the mass (arrow). (E) Axial T2-weighted MR image shows heterogenous T2 hypointense masses elsewhere throughout the pelvis, consistent with metastatic disease.

Tips:

a. Determining the location of a scrotal mass is one of the main goals of scrotal imaging since an intratesticular solid mass is typically malignant, whereas an extratesticular mass is usually benign.[4] The authors suggest the use of multiplanar T2-weighted sequences to accurately localize lesions given the excellent contrast resolution between the testicle and extratesticular structures.

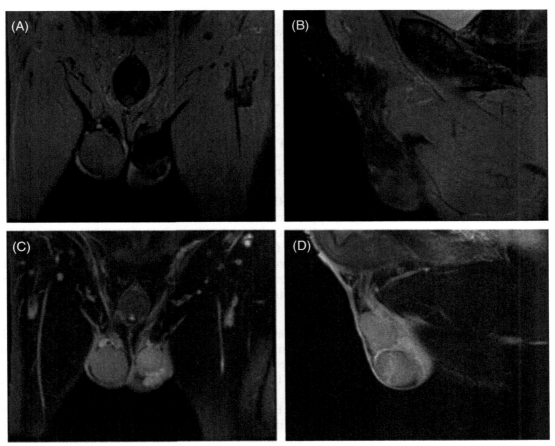

FIG. 9.48 Scrotal metastasis in a patient with metastatic sarcoma. (A and B) Coronal (A) and sagittal (B) T2-weighted MR images show an extratesticular T2 hypointense mass superior to and abutting the left epididymis (arrows). (C and D). Coronal (A) and sagittal (B) contrast-enhanced T1-weighted MR images show intense contrast enhancement of the mass with normal enhancement of the epididymis and testicle (short arrows).

 b. The secure diagnosis of a benign intratesticular lesion allows for less aggressive management options such as follow-up, lesion biopsy, tumor enucleation, and more recently, testis-sparing surgery versus orchiectomy.[4]

2. The inherent advantages of MRI allow multiplanar and multiparametric evaluation of scrotal pathologies providing additional value in the characterization of indeterminate lesions and may deter from originally planned surgical intervention. The ability to detect specific lesion characteristics (i.e., fat) could lead to a confident benign diagnosis, therefore, allowing conservative and nonsurgical management.

Tips:
- Scrotal MRI incorporates both large and small field of view in the acquisition of anatomic T1- and T2-weighted sequences as well as problem-solving sequences such as fat-saturated, dual echo, diffusion weighted, and postcontrast sequences.
- The variety of pulse sequences in different field of views facilitates in depicting key anatomical structures (i.e., tunica albuginea) and characterizing the extend of disease.
- In the authors' humble opinion, we believe that the small field of view T2-weighted sequence alone offers the most diagnostic value when compared to other individual pulse sequences. However, the advantageous acquisition of a palette of different pulse sequences grants the full potential of MRI.

3. Scrotal MRI can be used as a problem-solving tool in a variety of different settings, such as in the evaluation of congenital abnormalities, traumatic or nontraumatic scrotal pain, and scrotal masses. Within each setting, MRI has the potential to offer a complimentary and/or diagnostic role in the work up of scrotal pathologies thereby improving patient management.

Tips:

- MRI can be used in the localization of supernumerary or undescended testes when ultrasound remains equivocal or nondiagnostic. Studies have showed limited success with detecting nonpalpable crypto-orchid testes, however, MRI may prove useful prior to surgical evaluation.[10]
- In the case of indeterminate tunica albuginea involvement following scrotal trauma, Kim et al. have showed superior diagnosis of tunica disruption using MRI.[13] Key sequences include multiplanar small field of view T2-weighted images in different planes along with T1-weighted images, if equivocal.
- With the significant overlap of clinical presentations of many nontraumatic acute scrotal disorders, a confident clinical diagnosis may be challenging, especially in the setting of an indeterminate ultrasound result. For example, the diagnosis of intermittent testicular torsion remains a clinical and sonographic challenge, however, MRI can detect subtle testicular parenchymal signal and enhancement changes that can allude to the diagnosis (Fig. 9.14).
- Many benign scrotal masses have characteristic MRI appearances that may not be discernable on ultrasound evaluation. Familiarization of the imaging appearances of common scrotal lesions could, at least, offer the potential of benignity and initiating conservative/testis-sparing management, which may not have been a choice if solely based on indeterminate ultrasound findings.

4. Recent studies have shown the utility of MRI in the workup of scrotal masses; namely to differentiate between seminomas and nonseminomas, germ cell from nongerm cell tumor as well as characterization of known scrotal masses for accurate local staging, which collectively, facilitates optimal pretreatment planning.

Tips:

- Seminoma versus nonseminomatous tumors: Suggestive features for diagnosing seminoma include a nonencapsulated nodular enhancing mass with homogeneous low T2 signal and internal more enhancing T2 dark fibrovascular septa (Figs. 9.32–9.34). Features suggestive of nonseminomatous tumors include encapsulation with heterogeneous internal T1 and T2 signal intensities and enhancement along with hemorrhagic or cystic components (Figs. 9.35–9.38).
- Differentiating between types of germ cell tumors: Both Sertoli cell and Leydig cell tumors can enhance homogenously, however, Sertoli cell tumors can demonstrate T2 hyperintensity and Leydig cell tumors can show T2 hypointensity, therefore, allowing differentiation (Figs. 9.39, 9.41A, and 9.41B).
- MRI has been shown to provide accurate local staging by assessing tumor involvement of the testicle and extratesticular structures, thereby optimizing surgical management.[49,54,113,114] Key pulse sequences should contrast the tumor and its surrounding structures; the authors believe T2-weighted sequences allow excellent contrast resolution between tumor and its involvement to other structures (Fig. 9.44A).

9.10 Conclusion

While scrotal ultrasound remains the modality of choice in the evaluation of the scrotum under a variety of different clinical settings, we have discussed the role and highlighted recent evidence-based utilization of MRI in the evaluation of scrotal disorders. By first reviewing the normal MRI anatomy of the scrotum, followed by an extensive review of many case examples of scrotal lesions that leverage the benefits of MRI, we hope the reader has gained confidence to diagnose common scrotal lesions and potentially adapt some key concepts into practice.

Acknowledgments

We would like to thank Dr. Neeraj Lalwani for the opportunity to contribute to this wonderful book. We also want to thank all the researchers who have contributed to the wealth of knowledge, and without those efforts, this chapter could not be complete. None of the information here is the work of the authors and please excuse us if we have missed or inappropriately cited information presented in this chapter. Please contact the primary author Chan.Alex@ mayo.edu for any issues or comments. We thank you for your time and attention.

References

1. Mittal P, Abdalla A, Chatterjee A, et al. Spectrum of extratesticular and testicular pathologic conditions at Scrotal MR Imaging. *Radiographics.* 2018;38(3):806–830.
2. Parenti G, Feletti F, Brandini F, et al. Imaging of the scrotum: role of MRI. *Radiol Med (Torino).* 2009;114(3):414–424.
3. Tsili A, Argyropoulou M, Giannakis D, Sofikitis N, Tsampoulas K. MRI in the characterization and local staging of testicular neoplasms. *Am J Roentgenol.* 2010;194(3):682–689.
4. Tsili A, Giannakis D, Sylakos A, Ntorkou A, Sofikitis N, Argyropoulou M. MR imaging of scrotum. *Magn Reson Imaging Clin N Am.* 2014; 35(4):1033–1050.
5. Semelka R, Brown M, Altun E. *Abdominal-Pelvic MRI.* Chichester: Wiley Blackwell; 2016.
6. Tasian GE, Yiee JH, Copp HL. Imaging use and cryptorchidism: determinants of practice patterns. *J Urol.* 2011;185(5):1882–1887.
7. Tasian G, Copp H, Baskin L. Diagnostic imaging in cryptorchidism: utility, indications, and effectiveness. *J Pediatr Surg.* 2011;46(12):2406–2413.
8. Smolko MJ, Kaplan GW, Brock WA. Location and fate of the nonpalpable testis in children. *J Urol.* 1983;129(6):1204–1206.
9. Miyano T, Kobayashi H, Shimomura H, Yamataka A, Tomita TJ. Magnetic resonance imaging for localizing the nonpalpable undescended testis. *J Pediatr Surg.* 1991;26(5):607–609.
10. Krishnaswami S, Fonnesbeck C, Penson D, McPheeters M. Magnetic resonance imaging for locating nonpalpable undescended testicles: a meta-analysis. *Pediatrics.* 2013;131(6):e1908–e1916.
11. Yusuf G, Sidhu P. A review of ultrasound imaging in scrotal emergencies. *J Ultrasound.* 2013;16(4):171–178.
12. Chen P, John S. Ultrasound of the acute scrotum. *Appl Radiol.* 2006. https://appliedradiology.com/articles/ultrasound-of-the-acute-scrotum.
13. Kim SH, Park SC, Choi SH, Jeong WK, Choi JH. The efficacy of magnetic resonance imaging for the diagnosis of testicular rupture: a prospective preliminary study. *J Trauma: Injury Infect Crit Care.* 2009;66(1):239–242.
14. Muglia V, Tucci S, Elias J. Magnetic resonance imaging of scrotal diseases: when it makes the difference. *Urology.* 2002;59(3):419–423.
15. Mäkelä E, Lahdes-Vasama T, Ryymin P, et al. Magnetic resonance imaging of acute scrotum. *Scand J Surg.* 2011;100(3):196–201.
16. Bowen DK, Gonzalez CM. Intratesticular hematoma after blunt scrotal trauma: a case series and algorithm-based approach to management. *Central Eur J Urol.* 2014;67(4):427–429.
17. Parker R, Menias C, Quazi R, et al. MR imaging of the penis and scrotum. *Radiographics.* 2015;35(4):1033–1050.
18. Kim W, Rosen M, Langer J, Banner M, Siegelman E, Ramchandani P. US–MR imaging correlation in pathologic conditions of the scrotum. *Radiographics.* 2007;27(5):1239–1253.
19. Badmos KB. Tuberculous epididymo-orchitis mimicking a testicular tumour: a case report. *Afr Health Sci.* 2012;12(3):395–397.
20. Muttarak M, Peh WC, Lojanapiwat B, Chaiwun B. Tuberculous epididymitis and epididymo-orchitis: sonographic appearances: sonographic appearances. *Am J Roentgenol.* 2001;176(6):1459–1466.
21. Fehily SR, Trubiano JA, McLean C, et al. Testicular loss following bacterial epididymo-orchitis: case report and literature review. *J Can Urol Assoc.* 2015;9(3-4):E148–E151.
22. Fernández-Pérez GC, Tardáguila FM, Velasco M, et al. Radiologic findings of segmental testicular infarction. *Am J Roentgenol.* 2005;184(5):1587–1593.
23. Rhudd A, Moghul M, Reid G. Epididymo-orchitis causing testicular infarction: a serious complication of a common disorder. *J Surg Case Rep.* 2017;2017(10):rjx207.
24. Ramjit A, Shin C, Hayim M. Complete testicular infarction secondary to epididymoorchitis and pyocele. *Radiol Case Rep.* 2020;15(4):p420–p423.
25. Chia D, Penkoff P, Stanowski M, Beattie K, Wang AC. Testicular infarction and rupture: an uncommon complication of epididymo-orchitis. *J Surg Case Rep.* 2016;2016(5):rjw077.
26. Gotto GT, Chang SD, Nigro MK. MRI in the diagnosis of incomplete testicular torsion. *Br J Radiol.* 2010;83(989):e105–e107.
27. Serra A, Hricak H, Coakley F, et al. Inconclusive clinical and ultrasound evaluation of the scrotum: impact of magnetic resonance imaging on patient management and cost. *Urology.* 1998;51(6):1018–1021.
28. Shen YH, Lin YW, Zhu XW, Cai BS, Li J, Zheng XY. Segmental testicular infarction: a case report. *Exp Therap Med.* 2015;9(3):758–760.
29. Watanabe Y, Nagayama M, Okumura A, et al. MR imaging of testicular torsion: features of testicular hemorrhagic necrosis and clinical outcomes. *J Magn Reson Imaging.* 2007;26(1):100–108.
30. Kharrazi SM, Rahmani MR, Sakipour M, Khoob S. Polyorchidism: a case report and review of literature. *Urol J.* 2006;3(3):180–183.
31. Shabtai F, Schwartz A, Hart J, Halbrecht I, Kimche D. Chromosomal anomaly and malformation syndrome with abdominal polyorchidism. *J Urol.* 1991;146(3):833–834.
32. Mathur P, Prabhu K, Khamesra HL. Polyorchidism revisited. *Pediatr Surg Int.* 2002;18(5-6):449–450.
33. Pomara G, Cuttano MG, Romano G, Bertozzi MA, Catuogno C, Selli C. Surgical management of polyorchidism in a patient with fertility problems. *J Androl.* 2003;24(4):497–498.
34. Bayraktar A, Olcucuoglu E, Sahin I, Bayraktar Y, Tastemur S, Sirin E. Management of polyorchidism: surgery or conservative management? *J Hum Reprod Sci.* 2010;3(3):162–163.
35. Ferguson L, Agoulnik AI. Testicular cancer and cryptorchidism. *Front Endocrinol (Lausanne).* 2013;4:32.
36. Pettersson A, Richiardi L, Nordenskjold A, Kaijser M, Akre O. Age at surgery for undescended testis and risk of testicular cancer. *N Engl J Med.* 2007;356(18):1835–1841.
37. Garriga V, Serrano A, Marin A, Medrano S, Roson N, Pruna X. US of the tunica vaginalis testis: anatomic relationships and pathologic conditions. *Radiographics.* 2009;29(7):2017–2032.
38. Bhatt S, Dogra VS. Role of US in testicular and scrotal trauma. *Radiographics.* 2008;28(6):1617–1629.
39. Blok D, Flannigan M, Jones J. Testicular rupture following blunt scrotal trauma. *Case Rep Emerg Med.* 2019;2019:7058728.
40. Ludwig M. Diagnosis and therapy of acute prostatitis, epididymitis and orchitis. *Andrologia.* 2008;40(2):76–80.

41. Shen YH, Lin YW, Zhu XW, Cai BS, Li J, Zheng XY. Segmental testicular infarction: a case report. *Exp Therap Med*. 2015;9(3):758–760.

42. Shiraj S, Ramani N, Wojtowycz AR. Segmental testicular infarction, an underdiagnosed entity: case report with histopathologic correlation and review of the diagnostic features. *Case Rep Radiol*. 2016;2016:8741632.

43. Madaan S, Joniau S, Klockaerts K, et al. Segmental testicular infarction: conservative management is feasible and safe. *Eur Urol*. 2008;53(2):441–445.

44. Heller MT, Fargiano A, Rudzinski S, et al. Acute scrotal ultrasound: a practical guide. *Crit Ultrasound J*. 2010;2:65–73.

45. Desai KM, Gingell JC, Haworth JM. Localised intratesticular abscess complicating epididymo-orchitis: the use of scrotal ultrasonography in diagnosis and management. *Br Med J (Clin Res Ed)*. 1988;292(6532):1361–1362.

46. D Tena, F Leal, B Pozo, and J Bisquert, "Bilateral testicular abscess due to *Streptococcus pneumoniae*," Int J Infect Dis. 12(3):343-344.

47. Bandarkar AN, Blask AR. Testicular torsion with preserved flow: key sonographic features and value-added approach to diagnosis. *Pediatr Radiol*. 2018;48(5):735–744.

48. Demirbas A, Demir DO, Ersoy E, et al. Should manual detorsion be a routine part of treatment in testicular torsion? *BMC Urol*. 2017;17(1):84.

49. Mathur M, Spektor M. MR imaging of the testicular and extratesticular tumors. *Magn Reson Imaging Clin N Am*. 2019;27(1):151–171.

50. Thurnher S, Hricak H, Caroll PR, Pobiel RS, Filly RA. Imaging the testis: comparison between MR imaging and US. *Radiology*. 1998;167(3):631–636.

51. Akbar SA, Sayyed TA, Jafri SZ, Hasteh F, Neil S. Multimodality imaging of paratesticular neoplasms and their rare mimics. *Radiographics*. 2002;23(6):1461–1476.

52. Woodward PJ, Schwab CM, Sesterhenn IA. From the archives of the AFIP: extratesticular scrotal masses—radiologic-pathologic correlation. *Radiographics*. 2003;23(1):215–240.

53. Serra AD, Hricak H, Coakley FV, et al. Inconclusive clinical and ultrasound evaluation of the scrotum: impact of magnetic resonance imaging on patient management and cost. *Urology*. 1998;51(6):1018–1021.

54. Tsili AC, Bertolotto M, Rocher L, et al. Sonographically indeterminate scrotal masses: how MRI helps in characterization. *Diagn Intervent Radiol*. 2018;24(4):225–236.

55. Aguado A, Grant TH, Miller FH, Garnett J. Radiation-induced fibrosis of the spermatic cord: sonographic and MRI Findings. *Am J Roentgenol*. 2005;184(3 Suppl):S102–S103.

56. Yagan N. Testicular US findings after biopsy. *Radiology*. 2000;215(3):768–773.

57. Nair R, Abbaraju J, Rajbabu K, Anjum F, Sriprasad S. Tubular ectasia of the rete testis: a diagnostic dilemma. *Ann R Coll Surg Engl*. 2008;90(7):W1–W3.

58. Rouvière O, Bouvier R, Pangaud C, Jeune C, Dawahra M, Lyonnet D. Tubular ectasia of the rete testis: a potential pitfall in scrotal imaging. *Eur Radiol*. 1999;9(9):1862–1868.

59. Tsili AC, Argyropoulou MI, Dolciami M, Ercolani G, Catalano C, Manganaro L. When to ask for an MRI of the scrotum. *androl*. 2021;9(5):1395–1409.

60. Tartar V, Trambert M, Balsara Z, Mattrey R. Tubular ectasia of the testicle: sonographic and MR imaging appearance. *Am J Roentgenol*. 1993;160(3):539–542.

61. Loya A, Said J, Grant E. Epidermoid cyst of the testis: radiologic-pathologic correlation. *Radiographics*. 2004;24(Suppl 1):S243–S246.

62. Maizlin ZV, Belenky A, Baniel J, Gottlieb P, Sandbank J, Strauss S. Epidermoid cyst and teratoma of the testis: sonographic and histologic similarities. *J Ultrasound Med*. 2005;24(10):1403–1409.

63. Hamidi M, Nikolaidis P, Miller F, et al. Lesions without borders: scrotal lesions that involve both the intratesticular and extratesticular regions. *Am J Roentgenol*. 2018;210(2):W70–W79.

64. Ben Abda R, Bess D, Nieves-Robbins N. Testicular hemangioma mimicking a malignant neoplasm. *Radiol Case Rep*. 2016;11(2):121–123.

65. Tepeneu NF, Krafka K, Meglic S, Rogatsch H, Fasching G. Testicular cavernous hemangioma associated with testicular torsion – case report and review of literature. *Int J Surg Case Rep*. 2018;49:247–250.

66. Li F, Han S, Liu L, et al. Benign testicular cavernous hemangioma presenting with acute onset: a case report. *Mol Clin Oncol*. 2020;13(1):19–22.

67. Bonetti LR, Schirosi L, Sartori G, et al. Rapidly-growing hemangioma of the testicle clinically simulating an aggressive neoplasm. A case report. *Pathologica*. 2009;101(3):123–125.

68. Minagawa T, Murata Y. Testicular cavernous hemangioma associated with intrascrotal testicular torsion: a case report. *Hinyokika Kiyo*. 2009;55(3):161–163 Japanese.

69. Białek W, Rudzki S, Wronecki L. Capillary hemangioma of the testis. A case report of a rare benign tumor. *J Ultrasonogr*. 2016; 16(64):87–93.

70. Valentino M, Bertolotto M, Ruggirello M, Pavlica P, Barozzi L, Rossi C. Cystic lesions and scrotal fluid collections in adults: ultrasound findings. *J Ultrasound*. 2011;14(4):208–215.

71. Dogra V, Gottlieb R, Oka M, Rubens D. Sonography of the scrotum. *Radiology*. 2003;227(1):18–36.

72. Alvarez D, Bhatt S, Dogra V. Sonographic spectrum of tunica albuginea cyst. *J Clin Imag Sci*. 2011;1:5.

73. Dogra V, Gottlieb R, Rubens D, Liao L. Benign intratesticular cystic lesions: US features. *Radiographics*. 2001;21(Spec No:S273-81).

74. Bhatt S, Rubens D, Dogra V. Sonography of benign intrascrotal lesions. *Ultrasound Q*. 2006;22(2):121–136.

75. Poster RB, Spirt BA, Tamsen A, Surya BV. Complex tunica albuginea cyst simulating an intratesticular lesion. *Urol Radiol*. 1991; 13(2):129–132.

76. Woodward P, Schwab C, Sesterhenn I. From the archives of the AFIP. *Radiographics*. 2003;23(5):1245–1278.

77. Bhosale P, Patnana M, Viswanathan C, Szklaruk J. The inguinal canal: anatomy and imaging features of common and uncommon masses. *Radiographics*. 2008;28(3):819–835.

78. Karakas E, Karakas O, Cullu N, et al. Diffusion-weighted MRI of the testes in patients with varicocele: a preliminary study. *Am J Roentgenol*. 2014;202(2):324–328.

79. Tsili A, Xiropotamou O, Sylakos A, Maliakas V, Sofikitis N, Argyropoulou M. Potential role of imaging in assessing harmful effects on spermatogenesis in adult testes with varicocele. *World J Radiol*. 2017;9(2):34–45.

80. Jamadar DA, Jacobson JA, Morag Y, et al. Sonography of inguinal region hernias. *Am J Roentgenol*. 2006;187(1):185–190.

81. Mykoniatis I, Metaxa L, Nikolaou V, Filintatzi C, Kikidakis D, Sountoulides P. Giant scrotal fibrolipoma. *Rare Tumors*. 2015;7(4):6001.
82. Khallouk A, Ahallal Y, Tazi E, Tazi MF, Elfassi MJ, Farih MH. Benign paratesticular fibrous pseudotumor with malignant clinical features. *Rev Urol*. 2011;13(4):e203–e205.
83. Bulakci M, Tefik T, Kartal MG, et al. Imaging appearances of paratesticular fibrous pseudotumor. *Pol J Radiol*. 2016;81:10–14.
84. Yang WT, Whitman GJ, Tse GMK. Extratesticular epidermal cyst of the scrotum. *Am J Roentgenol*. 2004;183(4):1084.
85. Correa AF, Gayed BA, Tublin ME, Parwani AV, Gingrich JR. Epidermal inclusion cyst presenting as a palpable scrotal mass. *Case Rep Urol*. 2012;2012:498324.
86. Cassidy FH, Ishioka KM, McMahon CJ, et al. MR imaging of scrotal tumors and pseudotumors. *Radiographics*. 2010;30(3):665–683.
87. Mungan S, Karagüzel E, Turan C, Reıs A. A giant primary sclerosing lipogranuloma of the scrotum. *Türk patoloji dergis*. 2014;30(1):78–80.
88. Einstein DM, Paushter DM, Singer AA, Thomas AJ, Levin HS. Fibrotic lesions of the testicle: sonographic patterns mimicking malignancy. *Urol Radiol*. 1992;14(3):205–210.
89. Mac New HG, Terry NE, Fowler CL. Cystic dysplasia of the rete testis. *J Pediatr Surg*. 2008;43(4):768–770.
90. Ashouri KB, Heiman JM, Kelly EF, Manganiotis AN. Testicular epidermoid cyst: a rare case. *Urol Ann*. 2017;9(3):296–298.
91. Engels M, Span PN, van Herwaarden AE, Sweep FCGJ, Stikkelbroeck NMML, Claahsen-van der Grinten HL. Testicular adrenal rest tumors: current insights on prevalence, characteristics, origin, and treatment. *Endocr Rev*. 2019;40(4):973–987.
92. Ma L, Xia Y, Wang L, et al. Sonographic features of the testicular adrenal rests tumors in patients with congenital adrenal hyperplasia: a single-center experience and literature review. *Orphanet J Rare Dis*. 2019;14(1):242.
93. Wong NC, Dason S, Pozdnyakov S, Alexopoulou I, Greenspan M. Capillary hemangioma of the testis: a rare benign tumour. *Can Urol Assoc J*. 2015;9(3-4):133–135.
94. Holden A, List A. Extratesticular lesions: a radiological and pathological correlation. *Australas Radiol*. 1994;38(2):99–105.
95. Pieri S, Agresti P, Morucci M, Carnabuci A, De Medici L. A therapeutic alternative in the treatment of epididymal cysts: percutaneous sclerotherapy. *La Radiol Med*. 2003;105(5-6):462–470.
96. Alvarez DM, Bhatt S, Dogra VS. Sonographic spectrum of tunica albuginea cyst. *J Clin Imaging Sci*. 2011;1:5.
97. Fang Y, Zhao L, Yan F, Cui X, Zhou F. Strategy for treating simple testicular cyst in adults. *Am J Men's Health*. 2011;5(3):193–197.
98. Su JS, Farber NJ, Vij SC. Pathophysiology and treatment options of varicocele: an overview. *Andrologia*. 2021;53(1):e13576.
99. Chughtai K, Kallas J, Dogra VS. Inguinal hernia resulting in testicular ischemia. *Am J Sonogr*. 2018;1(3):3.
100. Staubitz JI, Gassmann P, Kauff DW, Lang H. Surgical treatment strategies for giant inguinoscrotal hernia -- a case report with review of the literature. *BMC Surg*. 2017;17(1):135.
101. Srivastava KN, Agarwal A, Siddharth Vikram SS, Gupta M. Huge scrotal lipoma posing a diagnostic dilemma: a case report and review of literature. *Urol Case Rep*. 2017;15:39–41.
102. Tobias-machado M, Corrêa Lopes Neto A, Heloisa Simardi L, Borrelli M, Wroclawski ER. Fibrous pseudotumor of tunica vaginalis and epididymis. *Urology*. 2000;56(4):670–672.
103. Schwartz EJ, Longacre TA Adenomatoid tumors of the female and male genital tracts express WT1. Int J Gynecol Pathol.23(2):123–128.
104. Singam P, Suriyani L, Ho C, Eng Hong G, Zainuddin Z. Primary sclerosing lipogranuloma: an unusual scrotal mass. *Libyan J Med*. 2010;5:10.
105. Tsili AC, Xiropotamou ON, Nomikos M, Argyropoulou MI. Silicone-induced penile sclerosing lipogranuloma: magnetic resonance imaging findings. *J Clin Imaging Sci*. 2016;6:3.
106. Ricchiuti VS, Richman MB, Haas CA, Desai D, Cai DX. Sclerosing lipogranuloma of the testis. *Urology*. 2002;60(3):515.
107. Liu R, Lei Z, Li A, Jiang Y, Ji J. Differentiation of testicular seminoma and nonseminomatous germ cell tumor on magnetic resonance imaging. *Medicine (Baltimore)*. 2019;98(45):e17937.
108. Tsili AC, Ntorkou A, Astrakas L, et al. Diffusion-weighted magnetic resonance imaging in the characterization of testicular germ cell neoplasms: effect of ROI methods on apparent diffusion coefficient values and interobserver variability. *Eur J Radiol*. 2017;89:1–6.
109. Tsili AC, Sylakos A, Ntorkou A, et al. Apparent diffusion coefficient values and dynamic contrast enhancement patterns in differentiating seminomas from nonseminomatous testicular neoplasms. *Eur J Radiol*. 2015;84(7):1219–1226.
110. Nicolai N, Necchi A, Raggi D, et al. Clinical outcome in testicular sex cord stromal tumors: testis sparing vs. radical orchiectomy and management of advanced disease. *Urology*. 2015;85(2):402–406.
111. Manganaro L, Vinci V, Pozza C, et al. A prospective study on contrast-enhanced magnetic resonance imaging of testicular lesions: distinctive features of Leydig cell tumours. *Eur Radiol*. 2015;25(12):3586–3595.
112. Coursey Moreno C, Small WC, Camacho JC, et al. Testicular tumors: what radiologists need to know—differential diagnosis, staging, and management. *Radiographics*. 2015;35(2):400–415.
113. International germ cell consensus classification: a prognostic factor-based staging system for metastatic germ cell cancers. International Germ Cell Cancer Collaborative Group. *J Clin Oncol*. 1997;15(2):594–603.
114. Wolfman DJ, Marko J, Gould CF, Sesterhenn IA, Lattin Jr GE. Mesenchymal extratesticular tumors and tumorlike conditions: from the radiologic pathology archives. *Radiographics*. 2015;35(7):1943–1954.
115. Akbar SA, Sayyed TA, Jafri SZH, Hasteh F, Neill JSA. Multimodality imaging of paratesticular neoplasms and their rare mimics. *Radiographics*. 2003;23(6):1461–1476.
116. Haupt HM, Mann RB, Trump DL, Abeloff MD. Metastatic carcinoma involving the testis: clinical and pathologic distinction from primary testicular neoplasms. *Cancer*. 1984;54(4):709–714.
117. Ulbright TM, Young RH. Metastatic carcinoma to the testis: a clinicopathologic analysis of 26 nonincidental cases with emphasis on deceptive features. *Am J Surg Pathol*. 2008;32(11):1683–1693.
118. Baird DC, Meyers GJ, Hu JS. Testicular cancer: diagnosis and treatment. *Am Fam Phys*. 2018;97(4):261–268.
119. Marko J, Wolfman DJ, Aubin AL, Sesterhenn IA. Testicular seminoma and its mimics: from the radiologic pathology archives. *Radiographics*. 2017;37(4):1085–1098.
120. Weissbach L, Bussar-Maatz R, Mann K. The value of tumor markers in testicular seminomas. Results of a prospective multicenter study. *Eur Urol*. 1997;32(1):16–22.
121. Dikici AS, Er ME, Alis D, et al. Is there any difference between seminomas and nonseminomatous germ cell tumors on shear wave elastography? A preliminary study. *J Ultrasound Med*. 2016;35(12):2575–2580.

122. Haque S, Tanvir R, Syed A, Haque S. Pure embryonal carcinoma of the testis presenting as an acute scrotal swelling. *Surg Case Rep*. 2020:1–2 Published online August 2020. DOI:10.31487/j.JSCR.2020.04.08.

123. Song QD. Ultrasound appearances of pediatric testicular yolk sac tumors: twenty-one cases in a single institution. *J Ultrasound Med*. 2018;37(10):2457–2463.

124. Aftan MK, Badrawi N, Abdulghaffar S, et al. Pure testicular choriocarcinoma Cannonball metastases as a presenting imaging feature: a case report and a review of literature. *Radiol Case Rep*. 2021;16(4):923–928.

125. Zhu J, Luan Y, Li H. Management of testicular Leydig cell tumor: a case report. *Medicine (Baltimore)*. 2018;97(25):e11158.

126. Loeser A, Vergho DC, Katzenberger T, et al. Testis-sparing surgery versus radical orchiectomy in patients with Leydig cell tumors. *Urology*. 2009;74(2):370–372.

127. Grogg J, Schneider K, Bode PK, et al. Sertoli cell tumors of the testes: systematic literature review and meta-analysis of outcomes in 435 patients. *Oncologist*. 2020;25(7):585–590.

128. Azizi M, Aydin AM, Cheriyan SK, et al. Therapeutic strategies for uncommon testis cancer histologies: teratoma with malignant transformation and malignant testicular sex cord stromal tumors. *Transl Androl Urol*. 2020;9(Suppl 1):S91–S103.

129. Cheah CY, Wirth A, Seymour JF. Primary testicular lymphoma. *Blood*. 2014;123(4):486–493.

130. Kryvenko ON, Rosenberg AE, Jorda M, Epstein JI. Dedifferentiated liposarcoma of the spermatic cord: a series of 42 cases. *Am J Surg Pathol*. 2015;39(9):1219–1225.

131. Ghadimi MP, Liu P, Peng T, et al. Pleomorphic liposarcoma: clinical observations and molecular variables. *Cancer*. 2011;117(23):5359–5369.

132. Chalouhy C, Ruck JM, Moukarzel M, Jourdi R, Dagher N, Philosophe B. Current management of liposarcoma of the spermatic cord: a case report and review of the literature. *Mol Clin Oncol*. 2017;6(3):438–440.

133. Debruyne FM, Bökkerink JP, de Vries JD. Current concepts in the management of paratesticular rhabdomyosarcoma. *Eur Urol*. 1985;11(5):289–293.

134. Stewart RJ, Martelli H, Oberlin O, et al. Treatment of children with nonmetastatic paratesticular rhabdomyosarcoma: results of the Malignant Mesenchymal Tumors studies (MMT 84 and MMT 89) of the International Society of Pediatric Oncology. *J Clin Oncol*. 2003;21(5):793–798.

135. Blyth B, Mandell J, Bauer SB, et al. Paratesticular rhabdomyosarcoma: results of therapy in 18 cases. *J Urol*. 1990;144(6):1450–1453.

136. Kim YJ, Huh JS, Hyun CL, Kim SD. A case of pediatric paratesticular rhabdomyosarcoma with epididymitis. *World J Men's Health*. 2012;30(2):146–149.

137. Yi J, Zhou DA, Huo JR, Wang YH, Ma JA. Primary intratesticular rhabdomyosarcoma: a case report and literature review. *Oncol Lett*. 2016;11(2):1016–1020.

138. Hanash KA. Metastatic tumors to the testicles. *Prog Clin Biol Res*. 1985;203:61–67.

CHAPTER

10

MRI of penis and penile prostheses

Ryan Clayton

Department of Radiology, VCU School of Medicine and
Health System, Richmond, VA, United States

10.1 Introduction

MRI is an important tool in evaluation of the penis, due to its exceptional contrast resolution and multiplanar abilities, and is commonly used in the evaluation of suspected penile fracture, Peyronie's disease (PD), priapism, the postoperative penis, and penile neoplasms. Often, other modalities such as ultrasound and CT are used as initial imaging modalities while MRI, with its exceptional contrast resolution, serves as a complimentary technique revealing unique details of multiple disease states and is an extremely useful problem-solving tool.

10.2 Penile anatomy

The penis is composed of three cylindrical endothelial lined cavernosal bodies, including the paired corpora cavernosa which are located dorsolaterally and the single corpus spongiosum located within the midline ventral portion of the penis. The corpora cavernosa are responsible for the mechanism of erection, and are composed of blood-filled sinusoidal spaces and surrounded by the durable fibrous/fascial layer of the tunica albuginea.[1] The tunica measures about 2–3 mm in flaccid state and 0.5 mm in the erect state.[2] Posteriorly, the corpora cavernosa splay laterally to form the crura which attach to the ischiopubic rami (Figs. 10.1–10.3).[3,4]

The corpus spongiosum is also surrounded by a fibrous layer of tunica albuginea, though less thick than the corpora cavernosa. The penile urethra runs within the corpus spongiosum. The distal portion of the corpus spongiosum forms the glans penis. Both the cavernosal and corporal bodies are surrounded by a contiguous layer of Buck fascia, which is less thick and on MRI is largely indistinguishable from the tunica albuginea, other than in the dorsal penis when it is sometimes visible as a distinct layer wrapping over the deep dorsal vein and dorsal arteries.[3]

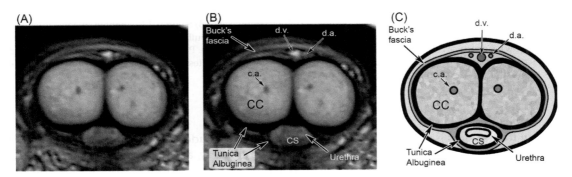

FIG. 10.1 **Penile anatomy.** (A) Axial T2-weighted image of a normal penis in the ventrally flexed position. (B and C) Annotated images showing the normal penis anatomy. *c.a.*, cavernosal artery; *CC*, corpus cavernosum; *CS*, corpus spongiosum; *d.a.*, dorsal artery; *d.v.*, deep dorsal vein.

Magnetic Resonance Imaging of The Pelvis.
DOI: https://doi.org/10.1016/B978-0-323-89854-6.00011-9

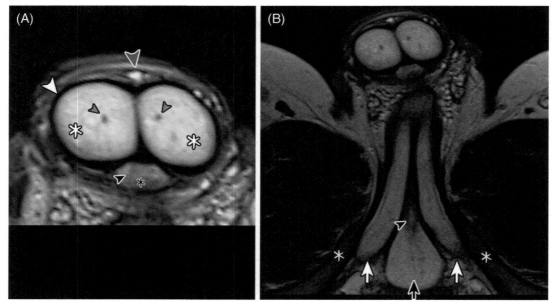

FIG. 10.2   **Normal penile MRI anatomy.** Axial T2-weighted MRI images of the penis. (A) Zoomed in axial image of the mid penile shaft flexed ventrally. The tunica albuginea and Buck's fascia appear as one continuous hypointense line (white arrowhead) surrounding the hyperintense corpora cavernosa (white asterisk) and corpus spongiosum (black asterisk). Dorsally, the tunica albuginea and Buck's fascia can sometimes be seen as separate structures as they divide around the deep dorsal vein (blue arrowhead). Cavernosal arteries run centrally within the corpora cavernosa (red arrowheads). The urethra (black arrowhead) is usually not well seen within the corpus spongiosum as it is collapsed. (B) Axial image through the root/base of the penis shows the crura of the corpora cavernosa (white arrows) splaying laterally to attach to the inferior pubic rami (yellow asterisk). The bulbous portion of the corpus spongiosum (black arrow) earns its name as it enlarges posteriorly.

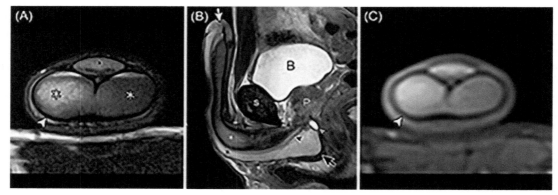

FIG. 10.3   **Normal MRI penile anatomy.** (A) Axial T2-weighted image of the mid penile shaft in the dorsiflexed position. The corpora cavernosa (white asterisk) demonstrate differential signal layering dependently, a normal finding. Corpus spongiosum (black asterisk) is seen anteriorly since the penis is dorsiflexed. T2-hypointense tunica albuginea (white arrowhead). (B) Sagittal T2-weighted image shows ideal dorsiflexed position of the penis. The corpus spongiosum (black asterisk) begins posteriorly as the bulbous portion (black arrow), and terminates distally as the glans (white arrow). Corpus cavernosum (white asterisk). Prostate (P). Bladder (B). Pubic symphysis (S). This patient happened to have a small Cowper duct cyst (yellow arrowhead). (C) Axial T1-weighted image demonstrates hypointense tunica albuginea (white arrowhead); small disruptions of the tunica can sometimes only be found on T1-weighted images.

Arterial supply to the penis is supplied by branches of the internal pudendal artery from the internal iliac artery. Branches include the dorsal artery of the penis, the bulbourethral artery, and perhaps most importantly, the cavernosal arteries which run within the center of the corpora cavernosa.[5] Venous drainage of the corpora is via the deep dorsal vein of the penis as well as the bulbar and cavernosal veins; the superficial dorsal vein is responsible for draining the tegumentary layers of the penis, and usually drains into the great saphenous vein.[6]

10.3 MRI technique

The most important sequences in evaluation of the penis are high resolution, small field-of-view T2-weighted images without fat saturation, obtained in three orthogonal planes, which afford detailed evaluation of small structures of the penile anatomy. We obtain high-resolution T2 turbo spin echo sequences with slice thickness ≤4 mm and small field-of-view (140–160 mm), using a surface receiver coil. Additional large field-of-view T2-weighted images are obtained of the pelvis to evaluate for lymphadenopathy and adjacent structures. Optimal imaging of the penis is achieved with the penis in a dorsiflexed position, gently secured against the abdomen (using tape). This position allows for improved image quality not only due to reduced motion, but it also reduces any air gap between the abdomen and penis which would otherwise cause additional artifacts.[3,4]

Whether or not to include contrast-enhanced sequences is up for debate. Although contrast is not necessary to make the diagnosis in many penile MRI indications, additional information can be obtained with contrast such as better delineation of hematomas in trauma, active inflammation in PD, staging of neoplasms, and further characterization of penile lesions. For these reasons, we include pre- and postcontrast fat-saturated T1-weighted sequences as part of our routine protocol (Table 10.1).

Another point of variability in building a penile MRI protocol is whether to perform imaging in the erect state via intracavernosal injection of prostaglandin-E_1. Many authors advocate imaging in the erect state as doing so can improve evaluation of the corpus cavernosum in the case of plaque detection in PD. However, intracavernosal injection of prostaglandin-E_1 is not entirely without risk, causing priapism in 1% of cases, with another 5% of men suffering discomfort.[7] The most commonly imaged disease states present a contraindication to its use (trauma, priapism). Therefore, it is not part of our standard protocol but may be added as deemed beneficial. Intracavernosal injection of prostaglandin-E1 is absolutely contraindicated in presence of penile prostheses. It is noteworthy that after PG-E1 induced erection the corpora may demonstrate dependent layering of the blood and it should not be taken as abnormal (Fig. 10.4).

TABLE 10.1 Recommended sequences for penile MRI.

Sequence	Comments
T2 axial	Large FOV to cover entire pelvis
T2 fat-sat axial	
T2 tse axial/sagittal/coronal	Small FOV (140–160 mm)
	High resolution (matrix size at least 256 × 192)
T1 fat-sat axial/sagittal	Thin section (≤4 mm)
	Surface coil
T1 fat-sat postcontrast sagittal	Small FOV
T1 fat-sat postcontrast axial	Large FOV
DWI	

DWI, diffusion-weighted images; *fat-sat*, fat-saturated; *FOV*, field-of-view; *tse*, turbo spin echo.

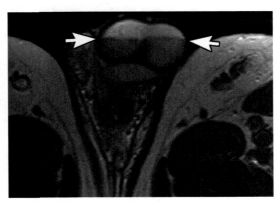

FIG. 10.4 Layering of blood in the corpora cavernosa (white arrows), a normal finding often seen when obtaining MRI after PG-E1 induced erection.

10.4 Penile trauma

10.4.1 Penile fracture

Penile fracture is defined as rupture of the corpus cavernosum with disruption of the tunica albuginea, caused by direct force to an erect penis. The tunica becomes thinner during erection and is predisposed to injury the corpora cavernosa are more susceptible to fracture than the corpora spongiosa. Classically attributed to forceful bending of the penis during sex (most commonly inadvertently thrusting the penis against the perineum or pubic symphysis) or vigorous masturbation, the epidemiology interestingly significantly differs based on geographic region. For example, in Middle Eastern and Mediterranean countries manual bending of the penis during erection (a practice sometimes known as "Taqnaadan") is a leading cause.[8-11]

In a typical presentation, patients will report hearing a snapping sound during sex followed by rapid loss of erection, penile pain, edema, bruising, and often a deformity with angulation of the penis. An associated urethral injury may occur 10–20% of the time, in which case the patient may have hematuria.[8,9] The clinical presentation can vary and may overlap with less severe injuries such as injury to a superficial fascia or vein with hematoma, sometimes referred to as "false penile fracture." It is important to confirm the diagnosis of penile fracture as surgical repair is the standard treatment, whereas less severe injuries may be managed conservatively.[12-14]

Often, the diagnosis can be made clinically however if there is uncertainty, radiologic studies can be used to confirm a tunica defect. Penile ultrasound is most commonly pursued as a first line imaging study due to high spatial resolution and widespread availability but has high false-negative rates. US can be limited in the presence of a large hematoma overlying a potential fracture. MRI, on the other hand, is less available but with its excellent contrast resolution provides superior sensitivity and specificity in detecting penile fracture.[15-17]

On MRI, a discontinuity of the tunica albuginea confirms the diagnosis of a penile fracture. A tunica defect is usually best visualized on high-resolution T2-weighted images due to the excellent resolution of the hypointense tunica compared with the typically T2-hyperintense cavernosal contents and adjacent fat.[4] The hypointense tunica is visible on both T1- and T2-weighted images, however, and it has been reported that T1-weighted images may better detect subtle defects possibly due to the presence of T2-hypointense hematoma which may obscure a small injury on T2-weighted images.[18] The site of a defect, if present, can be localized with MRI, helping the surgeon and potentially decreasing the size of an incision (small targeted incision versus exploration with penile degloving)[14,18] (Figs. 10.5 and 10.6). Conversely, in negative cases, MRI can identify the presence of a painful hematoma (either intra- or extracavernosal) without a tunica defect and obviate the need for surgery.[18]

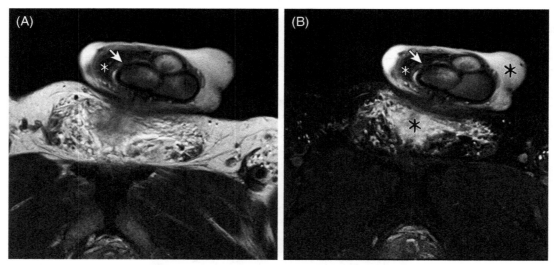

FIG. 10.5 Penile fracture. Patient with history pain during sex presenting with penile swelling. (A) Axial T2-weighted image reveals focal discontinuity of the tunica albuginea of the right corpus cavernosum (white arrow) with an adjacent acute hematoma (white asterisk). (B) An axial T2-weighted image of the same patient again shows focal discontinuity if the tunica (white arrow), adjacent hematoma (white asterisk), as well as generalized T2-hyperintense thickening of the penile soft tissues consistent with edema (black asterisk).

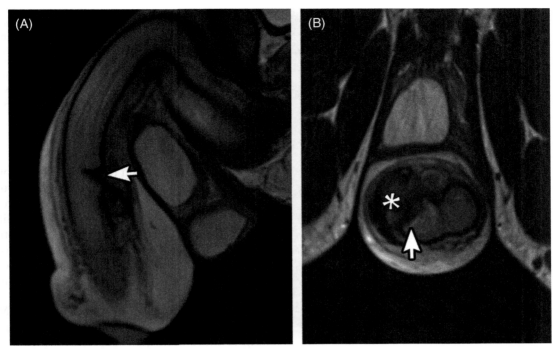

FIG. 10.6 **Penile fracture.** A different patient with penile fracture. (A and B) Sagittal and coronal T2-weighted images depict a defect of the tunica albuginea of the right corpus cavernosum (white arrow) and overlying hematoma (white asterisk).

Care should be taken to inspect the corpus spongiosum and, in turn, the urethra for injury as well, which as mentioned earlier can also be injured 10–20% of the time. Fortunately, only a small fraction of urethral injuries are clinically occult and they are usually minor.[8,18] Retrograde urethrogram is typically performed if a urethral injury is suspected as other modalities have not been shown to be superior in its detection.[18]

The use of contrast-enhanced sequences has been advocated by some, with reported improved visualization of a tunica defect, as well as improved visualization of an acute hematoma against the otherwise isointense corpus cavernosum.[19] However, the use of contrast will vary based on practice, as it lengthens the examination and the diagnosis can usually be made without it.[15,18]

10.4.2 Suspensory ligament injury

The suspensory ligament of the penis is a fibrous structure that supports the proximal penis in both the flaccid and erect states. It is actually composed of three different anatomic ligaments: the superficial/lateral fundiform ligament, the lateral bundle and the median bundle of the suspensory ligament proper which divide to encapsulate the dorsal vein before attaching to the tunica.[20] The fundiform ligament is thickened fascia extending from linea alba of the abdominal wall to the penis and scrotum. It does not fuse with the tunica but supports the scrotum as a hammock. The proper suspensory ligament fuses with tunica. These individual parts cannot be reliably distinguished at imaging, but the suspensory ligament as a whole unit is depicted on MRI as a hypointense structure connecting the pubic symphysis with the dorsal tunica.[4,20]

The usual mechanism of injury to the suspensory ligament is sexual trauma, similar to the scenario of penile fracture. The structure may also be congenitally absent, warranting reconstruction[21] or can be injured during a procedure. Knowledge of this structure has gained more relevance as the procedure of augmentation phalloplasty has become more common. In this procedure, the suspensory ligament is ligated to produce a visually longer penis in the treatment of penile dysmorphophobia.[22] In either case, absence or rupture of the suspensory ligament can be visualized on MRI as absence or disruption of the normally well-defined hypointense structure on T2-weighted sequences (Fig. 10.7).[4] In the case of injury and disruption to the suspensory ligament, surgical repair can resolve the deformity or instability and restore normal sexual function.[21]

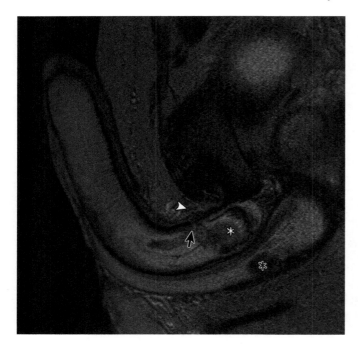

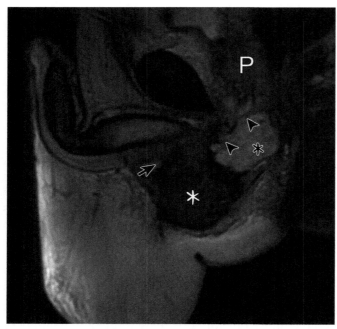

FIG. 10.8 Urethral injury. A sagittal T2-weighted image in a patient who suffered pelvic trauma. There is disruption of the posterior urethra involving the membranous and proximal bulbous portions (arrowheads). An associated T2-hyperintense collection (black asterisk) is consistent with an urinoma. More anteriorly, a large perineal hematoma is present (white asterisk). Prostate is mildly displaced upward (P).

FIG. 10.7 Suspensory ligament injury. Sagittal T2-weighted image in a patient who was kicked while playing soccer. There is focal discontinuity of the tunica albuginea dorsally at the base of the penis (black arrow). In addition, the normal T2-hypointense structures of the suspensory ligament are not visualized (white arrowhead), consistent with suspensory ligament injury. Hematomas are visualized in the corpus cavernosum (white asterisk) and spongiosum (black asterisk).

10.4.3 Urethral injury

MRI has not been shown to be superior to conventional retrograde urethrography and voiding cystourethrography (RUG, VCUG) or sonourethrography in the evaluation of the majority of urethral abnormalities (acute urethral injury, acquired stenosis, dilatation, diverticula/syringocele, fistula, etc.).[23,24] The exception to this is in the management of urethral injury in the setting of pelvic fracture (known as "pelvic fracture urethral injury").

Although not useful in the acute setting, MRI can be used to stage urethral injuries and in preoperative planning to more accurately depict the extent of injury. In particular, long segment posttraumatic obliterative strictures are more accurately depicted with MRI than conventional RUG/VCUG which can overestimate the length of stricture due to poor relaxation of the bladder and poor opacification of the prostatic urethra.[24,25] In addition, MRI provides information about prostate displacement and spongiosum fibrosis which are not depicted with RUG/VCUG.[24,25] MRI has been shown to more accurately estimate the length of urethral injury with better agreement with surgical findings than RUG/VCUG, changing management in 25–70% of cases (Fig. 10.8).[25-27] Optimal visualization of the urethra is achieved by infusion of sterile lubricating jelly through the external urethral meatus to dilate the distal urethra up to the stricture, gently tying gauze around the glans sulcus to prevent escape, and securing the penis against the midline anterior abdomen as per usual penile MRI positioning.[25]

10.5 Priapism

Priapism is an uncommon condition defined as an abnormal prolonged erection lasting more than 4 hours beyond or unrelated to sexual arousal.[28,29] The condition can be classified into two types, ischemic (veno-occlusive or "low-flow") and nonischemic (arterial or "high-flow") priapism. Distinguishing between these types is important in management because ischemic priapism is considered a medical emergency and if left untreated, low-flow priapism can lead to irreversible ischemia and erectile dysfunction. Furthermore, the two entities require different management.[30,31] The diagnosis of priapism usually starts with a thorough history and physical exam followed by aspiration of blood from the corpus cavernosum and blood gas analysis. Additional labwork may be helpful to determine if there is an underlying hematologic abnormality such as sickle cell disease.[31,32]

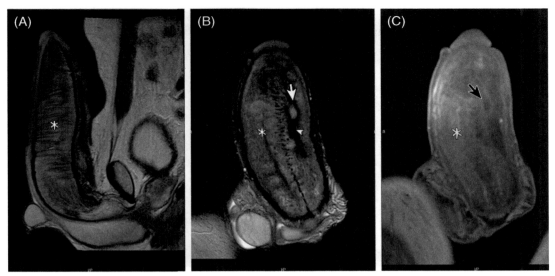

FIG. 10.9   **Ischemic priapism.** A man with history of sickle cell disease presented with priapism. Blood gases were consistent with ischemic priapism, as expected. (A and B) Sagittal and coronal T2-weighted images show an erect penis with markedly dilated cavernosal bodies with heterogeneous T2 signal (white asterisk). A particularly low signal area in the left corpus cavernosum likely represents fibrosis. The corpus spongiosum had normal signal (white asterisk). (C) Coronal T1-weighted image after contrast shows intact enhancement of the cavernosal bodies, with only a small T2-hyperintense focus demonstrating lack of enhancement consistent with a small area of necrosis (arrows). No permission required.

Ischemic priapism is by far the most common type, representing 95% of cases.[28] There are many recorded causes of ischemic priapism; the majority of cases are idiopathic with other common etiologies including sickle cell disease, alcohol, recreational drugs (cocaine), other pharmaceuticals including intracavernosal injections, underlying neoplasm and neurologic injury.[29,32-34] Ischemic priapism is characterized by marked rigidity and tenderness of the cavernosal bodies, while typically the corpus spongiosum and glans remain flaccid (Fig. 10.9). There is significant reduction or absence of cavernosal blood flow, with little to no cavernosal arterial inflow. Cavernosal blood gas is hypoxic, hypercarbic and acidotic.[32,33] Initial treatment strategy for ischemic priapism includes urgent evacuation of blood by corporal aspiration and intracavernosal injection of a sympathomimetic agent. Failing this, penile shunt surgery may be required.[31]

Nonischemic priapism by contrast is rare and is almost always due to trauma. It is the result of uncontrolled cavernosal arterial inflow, often associated with an arteriovenous fistula. The corporal bodies are soft and not painful, and cavernosal blood gasses are not hypercarbic or acidotic.[30,32,33] Treatment of nonischemic priapism is less urgent and begins with observation; as many as two thirds of cases spontaneously resolve. In nonresolving cases, selective angiography with penile artery embolization can be performed.[30,31]

Penile Doppler ultrasound is the first line imaging modality when evaluating priapism, in order to assess the arterial flow patterns.[32,35] Penile MRI is uncommonly used but can be helpful in determining the viability of penile smooth muscle in the case of ischemic priapism. MRI has been shown to be 100% sensitive in predicting nonviable smooth muscle and thus complete erectile impairment based on lack of gadolinium enhancement of the corpus cavernosum.[36] The presence or absence of enhancement may help guide treatment between routine management with follow-up versus penile prosthesis placement. In the case of nonischemic priapism, MRI/MRA can be used to detect a pseudoaneurysm or arteriovenous fistula, and in particular may be better than ultrasound in evaluation of the deeper posterior penis.[37]

10.6 Peyronie's disease

PD is a wound-healing disorder characterized by penile pain, curvature, and sexual dysfunction, described in the literature by Francois Gigot de la Peyronie as "induratio penis plastica" in 1743.[38] It is the result of abnormal healing in response to repeated microtrauma to the tunica albuginea with fibrotic plaque formation of the tunica, although only 20–30% of patients recall specific trauma.[39] Most commonly seen in men in their 50s and 60s, PD has a prevalence of up to 9% in the general population[40] and is often associated with penile curvature and erectile dysfunction (ED).[41] Plaques are usually seen along the dorsal surface of the penile shaft. It can be divided into two phases: an active inflammatory phase and a chronic "stable" phase. In the active phase, patients have periodic pain and progressive deformity. In the

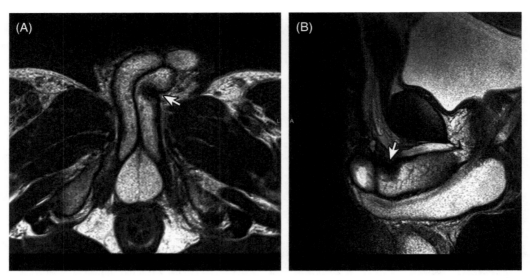

FIG. 10.10   **Peyronie's disease.** (A) Axial T2-weighted image of a patient with leftward penile curvature shows focal T2-hypointense thickening of the left corpus cavernosum at the point of curvature (white arrow). (B) Same finding is seen on sagittal image.

chronic phase, pain has resolved and the deformity is stable, and is usually assigned when symptoms have been present for at least 12 months and stable for 3–4 months.[41,42] Distinguishing between these two phases is important because their treatments differ; surgery is only offered in the chronic phase to avoid poor outcomes from active inflammation.[41,43]

The evaluation of PD begins with history and physical exam, followed by imaging. Objective measures on physical exam including degree of angulation and palpable plaques are recorded (Fig. 10.10). The goal of imaging is to identify and characterize tunica plaques, which can be done with both ultrasound and MRI, though each modality has its strengths and weaknesses in this task. Ultrasound is cheaper and more widely available, able to characterize complex plaque geometry, identify nonpalpable plaques, degree of plaque calcification, and using Doppler techniques can assess penile vasculature in the case of associated ED.[44,45] MRI, on the other hand, has difficulty identifying plaque calcifications (Fig. 10.11);[45] the addition of SWI sequences may improve detection of calcification.[46] The presence of calcification indicates a chronic plaque. MRI is better than US at visualizing plaques proximal to the penile base, can better depict complex deformities, and is superior in establishing the position of plaque, tunica thickness, and cavernosal diameter, all of which influence the surgical approach.[4,44,46,47]

A potential benefit of MRI is to evaluate for the presence of active inflammation based on the presence or absence of plaque enhancement (Fig. 10.12). Studies have shown that the presence of enhancement of a tunica plaque is associated with histological inflammation[48] however no studies to date have established a positive correlation between plaque enhancement and pain, the established clinical indicator of active PD.[4,49]

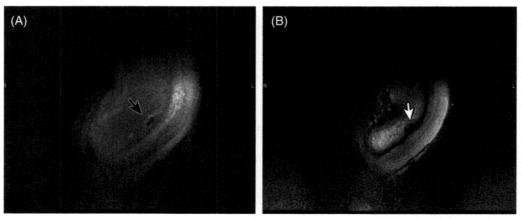

FIG. 10.11   **Calcification in Peyronie's disease.** (A) Coronal T1-weighted and (B) coronal T2-weighted images demonstrate a plaque in Peyronie's disease, with focal T1-hypointensity likely representing calcification. US is better than MRI for detecting calcification.

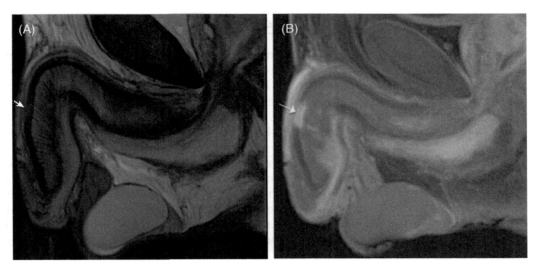

FIG. 10.12 **Peyronie's disease with active inflammation.** (A) Sagittal T2-weighted image shows focal abnormality of the tunica albuginea dorsally (white arrow), consistent with fibrous plaque. (B) Sagittal T1-weighted image with fat saturation after contrast shows enhancement of the plaque (yellow arrow), likely representing active inflammation.

On MRI, plaques are seen as hypointense localized areas of thickening on both T1- and T2-weighted images. Most investigators perform the MRI in both the flaccid and tumescence phases after the intracavernosal injection of prostaglandin-E_1, the concept being that during erection, the tunica is stretched and thinned and areas of abnormal thickening are more accurately identified.[4,49] A thickened area of tunica with increased T1 signal and enhancement likely represents active inflammation but as mentioned earlier, there is not agreement regarding whether this accurately indicates active phase PD.[49] Associated deformities including curvature and cavernosal narrowing (waisting) are also depicted.[4]

Medical treatment may include oral pentoxifylline or local collagenase injections.[50] Surgical treatments may include plication and grafting. Insertion of penile implants remains the treatment of choice for PD with erectile dysfunction. Plication includes a surgical procedure to correct the curvature deformity.[50] To straighten the curvature, plication involves tightening the surface of the opposite side of curvature with stitches. This stitching typically involves multiple pairs of calculated incisions along the side of the penis. Occasionally, sutures may fail during an aggressive sexual act and the patient may present with return of the curvature.[51] (Fig. 10.13).

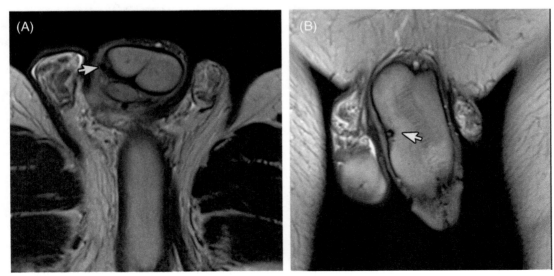

FIG. 10.13 **Plication for treatment of Peyronie's disease.** Patient experiencing recurrent penile curvature after treatment for Peyronie's disease. (A) Axial T2-weighted and (B) coronal T2-weighted MRI images demonstrate focal thickening with susceptibility artifact of the tunica albuginea, corresponding with the site of plication suture (yellow arrow). The suture had failed in the patient resulting in recurrent curvature.

10.7 Neoplasms

Primary penile squamous cell carcinoma (PSCC, commonly referred to as penile cancer) has exceedingly low incidence rates globally; age-standardized incidence of penile cancer worldwide is 0.84 cases per 100,000 person-years.[52] In the United States and Europe, penile cancer represents less than 1% of cancers in men.[53-55] Distinct differences are found when comparing industrialized countries with emerging and developing countries; incidence rates are highest in certain countries in South America and Africa, while lowest rates are found in Israel and Kuwait. Even in the United States, incidence differs more than threefold based on ethnicity and geographic region (Figs. 10.14 and 10.15).[56]

Phimosis is a crucial risk factor in the formation of penile cancer, and explains the decreased incidence of penile cancer in regions with higher circumcision rates. Additional risk factors for PSCC include HPV infection, smoking, and history of penile-specific medical conditions including genital warts, trauma, and urethral stricture.[56,57]

The most common location of PSCC is the glans followed by the foreskin, and physical exam almost always reveals a visible skin lesion. Inguinal lymph nodes are commonly involved and pathologic inguinal lymph nodes are found in 50% of cases at initial presentation. After a biopsy confirms the diagnosis of PSCC, imaging is used to further stage the disease.[57,58]

MRI in penile cancer is useful in staging the primary tumor (T-stage), helping in surgical planning by identifying penile shaft length, presence of satellite nodules, urethral involvement, etc., and evaluating for lymph node spread (N-stage). The TNM staging system the PSCC was recently updated in 2018 with the addition of lymphovascular invasion for T staging (Table 10.2).[59,60]

On MRI, penile cancer typically appears as an infiltrative mass, hypointense compared with the corpora on T1- and T2-weighted images, and hyperintense relative to the fascia and tunica on T2-weighted images. Superficial tumor dimensions can be easily obtained on physical exam, but tumor depth (vertical measurement from the top of the tumor to the deepest limit) is much better assessed with MRI and is directly related to survival rates.[58,61] T-staging is best determined on T2-weighted images, as invasion of the corpus cavernosum and corpus spongiosum is most clearly seen.[58] Invasion of the corpus cavernosum confers T3 disease.[58] Care should be taken to not overstage

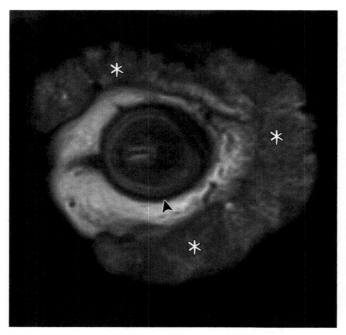

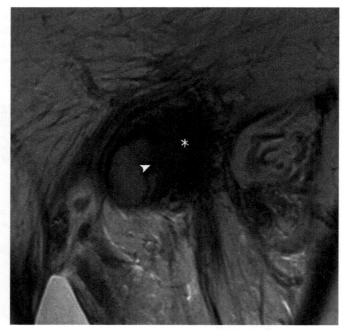

FIG. 10.14 **PSCC confined to skin.** A coronal T2-weighted image in a man with a large exophytic growth of the distal penis and biopsy showing squamous cell carcinoma. Coronal T2-weighted image shows a large cauliflower-like mass of the distal penis (asterisk) arising from the foreskin. The underlying glans and tunica (arrowhead) were not involved, consistent with T1 disease.

FIG. 10.15 **PSCC T3.** A patient with biopsy-proven PSCC presented for MRI staging. A coronal T2-weighted image shows a mass (asterisk) which is T2-hypointense compared to the corpus cavernosum, with clear invasion of the tunica albuginea (arrowhead), consistent with T3 tumor.

TABLE 10.2 TNM staging of PSCC, AJCC 8th edition.

T		
	Tis	Carcinoma in situ (PeIN)
	Ta	Noninvasive localized SCC
	T1	Glans: tumor invades lamina propria Foreskin: tumor invades dermis, lamina propria, or dartos fascia Shaft: tumor invades connective tissue between epidermis and corpora regardless of location T1a: without LVI or PNI and is not high grade (grade 3 or sarcomatoid) T1b: with LVI and/or PNI or is high grade (grade 3 or sarcomatoid)
	T2	Tumor invades corpus spongiosum with or without urethral invasion
	T3	Tumor invades corpora cavernosum with or without urethral invasion
	T4	Tumor invades other adjacent structures
PN		
	PN1	≤2 unilateral ILN metastases, no ENE
	PN2	≥3 unilateral or bilateral ILN metastases
	PN3	ENE of ILN metastases or pelvic lymph node(s), unilateral or bilateral

AJCC, American Joint Committee on Cancer; *ENE*, extranodal extensión; *ILN*, inguinal lymph node; *LVI*, lymphovascular invasion; *M*, distant metastases; *PeIN*, penile intraepithelial neoplasia; *pN*, pathologic stage of regional lymph nodes; *PNI*, perineural invasion; *SCC*, squamous cell carcinoma; *T*, primary tumor.

a tumor only involving Buck's fascia (T1 disease) as involving the tunica albuginea (T3 disease); as these layers appear as a single hypointense structure on MRI, T3 disease should only be assigned when there is definite involvement of the innermost layer of the T2-hypointense line, i.e., unequivocal involvement of the tunica albuginea. Urethral invasion, often difficult to determine on MRI, is less important than cavernosal invasion as it can be present in both T2 and T3 disease in the most updated TNM criteria.[58] MRI is highly accurate in identifying involvement of adjacent structures such as the prostate, T4 disease.[62] It should be noted that contrast-enhanced sequences are not necessary to accurately stage penile cancer, but may help identify small satellite nodules.[58] DWI/ADC and postcontrast images can be helpful when evaluating for penile neoplasms, especially recurrent or residual tumor at the site of primary or nodal resection (Fig. 10.16).

The primary route of lymph node spread in skin-based tumors is to superficial inguinal lymph nodes. Lymphatic drainage from the glans is into deep inguinal and external iliac nodes, while drainage of the erectile bodies and urethra is to internal iliac nodes. MRI lymph node staging is, unsurprisingly, superior to clinical staging.[62] The important factors to consider when evaluating lymph node involvement are number of lymph nodes involved, laterality (unilateral or bilateral), and whether "bulky" lymph nodes are present. "Bulky" lymph nodes are defined

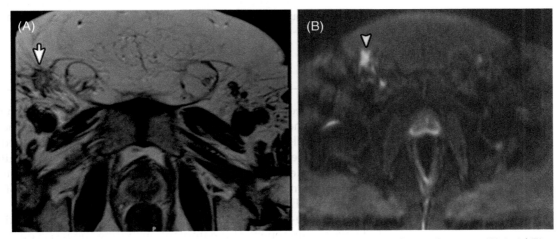

FIG. 10.16 Recurrence after penectomy. Patient underwent restaging MRI after penectomy for penile cancer. (A) Axial T2-weighted image reveals spiculated area of intermediate T2 signal in the right groin (white arrow), in the area of lymph node dissection. (B) DWI demonstrates associated restricted diffusion (yellow arrowhead) indicative of recurrence.

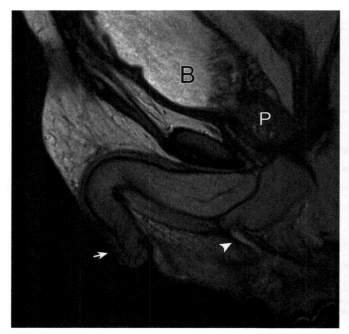

FIG. 10.17 **Partial penectomy.** Sagittal T2-weighted MRI image in a patient who underwent partial penectomy for PSCC. The distal penile resection margin (white arrow) showed no evidence of recurrence. The patient has a continent perineal urethral diversion (white arrowhead). Bladder (B) and prostate (P).

FIG. 10.18 **Penile metastasis.** A patient with history of prostate cancer and penile lesion presented for MRI evaluation. An axial T1-weighted image without contrast reveals a round T1-hypointense mass (asterisk) within the corpus cavernosum, consistent with metastasis.

as longest dimension of contiguous lymph nodes of >4 cm in the axial plane.[57] Accurate N staging is important because regional lymph node involvement is the strongest predictor of survival and bulky, fixed, and bilateral lymph node metastases are treated with neoadjuvant therapy.[57,58,63]

When possible, penile-sparing surgery is done. In larger and more invasive tumors, glans amputation, partial or radical penectomy with reconstruction may be needed.[64] In either case, MRI can be used in postoperative patients to evaluate for recurrent tumor (Fig. 10.17).

Unfortunately, PSCC is not the only cancer that can involve the penis. Other uncommon neoplasms that can involve the penis include metastases (usually from other pelvic neoplasms such as prostate or bladder cancer), which may appear as either multiple or solitary lesions with nonspecific imaging characteristics,[65] and may present with priapism.[66] Sarcomas make up less than 5% of primary penile cancers, with vascular sarcomas being the most common of these followed my rhabdomyosarcomas, leiyomyosarcomas, and fibrosarcomas.[67] Urothelial carcinomas which arise in the penis are usually found in the bulbous or membranous portions of the urethra.[68] Primary penile lymphoma is extremely rare and may appear as a well-defined hypoenhancing mass (Fig. 10.18).[69]

10.8 Implants

Penile prosthetic (PP) implants have emerged as an effective definitive treatment for erectile dysfunction unresponsive to medical management.[47] Devices have undergone substantial progressive improvements over the past four decades, evolving into the current widely preferred dual-chamber inflatable devices.[70-72] Despite continued improvements, device-related complications are not rare. Indeed, device explant rates remain high. In the United States, although the rate of device implantation has recently declined, the patients undergoing PP surgery have increased comorbidities with likely increase in complications seen.[71,72] MRI is an effective tool in the evaluation of complications which can involve different device components (Figs. 10.19 and 10.20).

MR protocol may be slightly modified to include pre- and postinflation orthogonal T2W images in axial, coronal and sagittal planes. It is important to include every component of the implant, including the reservoir in the space of Retzius and the pump in the scrotum.[2] If necessary, T2W images of the entire pelvis may be added before and after inflation. Cylinders must be evaluated on postinflation sequences to prevent overdiagnosis of pathologies.

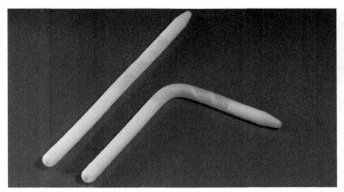

FIG. 10.19 **Malleable penile prosthesis.** A malleable penile prosthesis, the "Genesis" from Coloplast, made of silicone around a malleable core. From ColoplastMD. (n.d.). Retrieved August 29, 2021, from https://www.coloplastmd.com/.

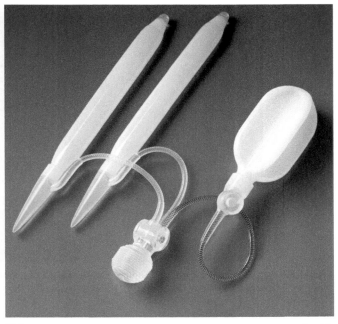

FIG. 10.20 **Inflatable penile prosthesis.** A three-part inflatable penile prosthesis, the "Titan" from Coloplast, consisting of the inflatable cylinders, valve, reservoir, and tubing. From ColoplastMD. (n.d.). Retrieved August 29, 2021, from https://www.coloplastmd.com/.

PP devices can be broadly divided into two types: semirigid or malleable and inflatable. The earliest implanted devices were actually completely rigid, beginning with the use of rib cartilage graft to create an os penis in 1936, followed by acrylic devices. Eventually, in 1973, the inflatable penile prosthesis (IPP) was developed and has been continuously refined.[73] IPPs are favored over malleable devices because they better replicate normal physiologic erection and are able to be fully deflated. Malleable devices are preferable in some circumstances as they require less manual dexterity by the patient, can be performed under local anesthesia, and are less prone to malfunction; however, they are permanently firm and have lower overall satisfaction compared with IPPs. Two-cylinder IPPs are also available without a separate reservoir and can be used when reservoir implantation would be unsuitable, however these devices cannot fully deflate.[70]

At surgery, the cylinders of the PP are placed in the corpora cavernosa. The pump and release valve are placed low hanging into the midline scrotum. The fluid reservoir is usually placed in the extraperitoneal space in the pelvis near the bladder (space of Retzius) and tubing is placed through the inguinal canal, although placement can vary based on the patient's anatomy. The reservoir can alternatively be placed into the abdominal wall, subcutaneous tissue, or rarely within the inguinal canal.[70,74] The surgical procedure can be performed via subpubic or trans scrotal approach. Placement of the reservoir within the space of Retzius is usually a blind procedure.

As mentioned, complications of PPs are not uncommon; infections occur 2–4% of the time and 5-year mechanical failure rates have improved to ~10%.[75,76] Nonspecific pain is often the only presenting symptom. MRI is the preferred imaging modality to evaluate IPP complications due to its exceptional contrast resolution and multiplanar capabilities. The exception to this is when infection is suspected, as CT is more available and can often better delineate the extent of an infection.[74] Currently, all IPPs being used in the United States are MRI compatible.[74] The cylinders and reservoir are filled with saline and therefore readily depicted as hyperintense on T2-weighted images. Malleable prostheses, on the other hand, are composed of silicone and are T2-hypointense.[4]

10.8.1 Infection

When infection is suspected, CT is usually performed. MRI can assist in determining the extent of infection and involvement of various prosthetic components. If MRI is used, findings such as increased soft tissue thickening, increased T2 signal and enhancement surrounding a component indicate the presence of infection. Abscess can be found by the presence of an associated loculated fluid collection.[74] Infection requires device explantation with antibiotics; reimplantation can be considered 6–12 months later.[75] Salvageable surgery requires earlier replacement of infected implant component. Delay can lead to fibrosis and replacement can be challenging over the long term. Chronic infections along the infected reservoir may form pelvic pseudocysts.

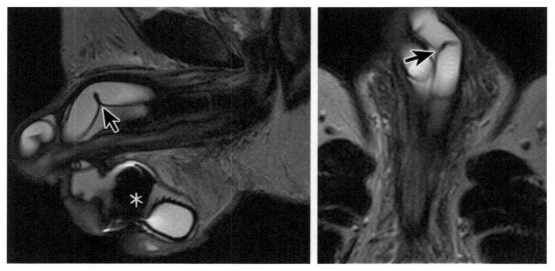

FIG. 10.21   Cylinder buckling. (A) Sagittal and (B) axial T2-weighted image of patient with IPP inflated shows buckling of the left cylinder (arrows). The patient was experiencing pain. IPP pump noted in the scrotum (asterisk).

10.8.2 Cylinder complications

When patients present with pain during inflation of the prosthesis, a common cause is buckling of the cylinder(s) (Fig. 10.21). In one study, buckling was found in all patients who were experiencing pain but was only clinically evident in one third.[77] Buckling is, however, rarely also found in asymptomatic patients. Buckling usually occurs due to oversizing of the cylinders.[4] Undersized cylinders can lead to "Concorde" deformation of the penis, where the tip is inclined downward as a supersonic transporter.[2] Although buckling requires an MRI assessment in the fully inflated state (to avoid overdiagnosis), Concorde deformity is often diagnosed clinically.

There are many other reported cylinder complications detectable with MRI including:[1,78]

- Cylinder displacement/migration (Fig. 10.22)
- Tunical erosion or extrusion

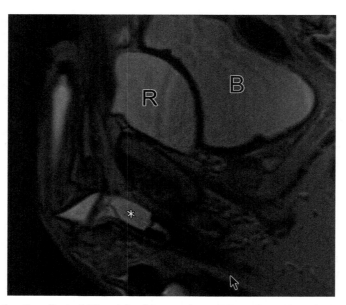

FIG. 10.22   Posterior cylinder migration. Sagittal T2-weighted image shows IPP in place. The cylinder (white asterisk) has migrated posteriorly, with T2-hypointense base extending posteriorly out of the corpus cavernosum (black arrow). Reservoir (R) and bladder (B) noted.

- Cylinder crossover (one cylinder erodes into the contralateral corpus cavernosum or spongiosum) (Fig. 10.23)
- Focal cylinder dilatation (aneurysm) (Fig. 10.24)
- Incomplete cylinder inflation
- Cylinder rupture (Figs. 10.25 and 10.26)

10.8.3 Reservoir and tubing complications

Reservoir complications are less common than cylinder complications. Rarely the reservoir may herniate into the scrotum in penoscrotally placed prostheses.[79] Even more rarely, the reservoir can erode into adjacent organs such as the urinary bladder. Alternate reservoir placements other than the prevesical space (space of Retzius) are gaining popularity to avoid such complications in patients who have had prior major abdominal or pelvic surgeries.[79,80] Abnormal folding of the reservoir is a problem affecting a specific low-profile reservoir called the "Conceal Low-Profile reservoir" where abnormal folding of the reservoir envelops and occludes the coupler, obstructing flow out of the reservoir.[1,81] Rupture of the reservoir has been reported Fig.10.27.[74,80] It should be noted that after rupture, the fluid may be reabsorbed and the only imaging discovery incudes a completely decompressed reservoir without fluid (Fig. 10.28). Finally, the reservoir can migrate into the inguinal canal in the early post-op phase due increased intraabdominal pressure due to coughing or vomiting (Fig. 10.29).

Erosion of tubing either through the skin or into adjacent structures such as the urethra is a rarely reported complication.[82,83] Kinking and obstruction of the prosthesis tubing was a problem found in older devices but based on reporting seems to have been largely resolved by the advent of kink-resistant tubing introduced in the 1980s.[84,85]

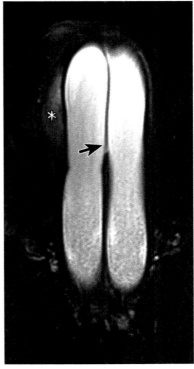

FIG. 10.23 **Cylinder crossover.** Coronal fat-saturated T2-weighted image with IPP inflated shows crossing of the right cylinder over the intercavernosal septum (arrow) and into the left corpus cavernosum.

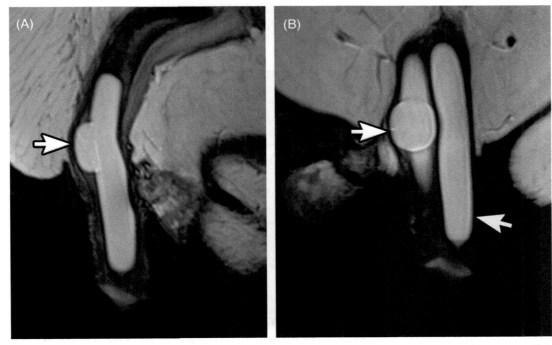

FIG. 10.24 **Focal aneurysmal cylinder dilatation.** (A and B) Sagittal and coronal T2-weighted MRI images of a patient with inflatable penile prosthesis demonstrate focal dilatation of the left cylinder dorsally (white arrow). Normal left cylinder (yellow arrow).

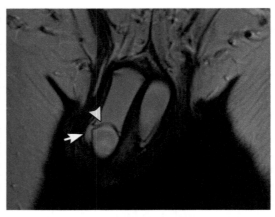

FIG. 10.25   **IPP cylinder rupture.** A patient with IPP dysfunction underwent MRI with device inflated. Coronal T2-weighted image reveals increased asymmetric fluid adjacent to the right cylinder (white arrow) and infolding of the cylinder (yellow arrowhead), consistent with cylinder rupture.

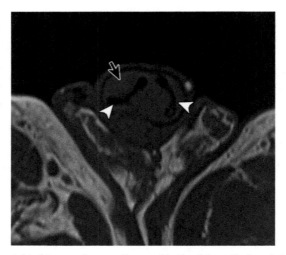

FIG. 10.26   **IPP cylinder collapse.** T1-weighted image shows collapse of both of the cylinders (white arrowheads), with adjacent otherwise normal-appearing contents of the corpus cavernosum (black arrow).

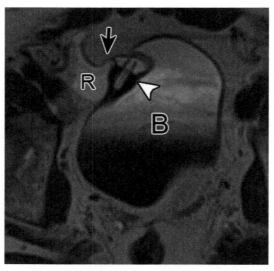

FIG. 10.27   **Abnormal folding of Conceal Low-Profile reservoir.** The reservoir (R) is positioned within the anterior perivesicular space (space of Retzius), the usual location adjacent to the bladder (B). There is abnormal folding of the reservoir (black arrow) which envelops and occludes the coupler (white arrowhead), obstructing flow to the cylinders (not pictured).

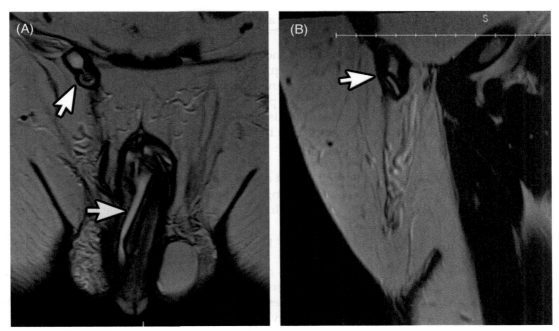

FIG. 10.28   Reservoir rupture. (A and B) Coronal and sagittal T2-weighted images reveal a completely deflated IPP reservoir (white arrow) located near the deep inguinal ring. Note deflated cylinder (yellow arrow).

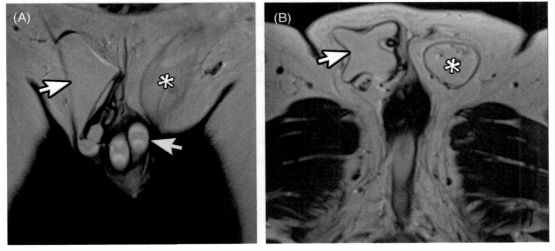

FIG. 10.29   Migration of reservoir. (A and B) Coronal and axial T2-weighted MRI images reveal abnormal location of the IPP reservoir in the right groin, below the inguinal ligament. Incidental fatty left inguinal hernia (white asterisk). IPP cylinders (yellow arrow).

Search pattern and reporting of penile prostheses

1. Identify the prosthesis: Malleable vs two or three piece IPP.
2. Intracavernosal position of the cylinders: Confirm on axial and coronal. Assess for proximal, distal or lateral migration. Ascertain if tunica is intact throughout.
3. Locations of pump and reservoir: Appropriate or ectopic?
4. Pre- and postinflation: (1) size of reservoir, (2) size of cylinders (most of the current IPP reservoir have 65–100 cc volume).
5. Assess for integrity of cylinders (*postinflation*): Any buckling, aneurysmal dilatation, or cross over?
6. Are tubing intact and continuous?
7. Is there any abnormal fluid collection?
8. Is there any sign of infection?

10.9 Pearls and pitfalls

1. MRI is the modality of choice for surgical planning and cancer staging of penile cancer.
2. MRI is the first modality for the evaluation of penile prostheses.
3. Tunica albuginea is a fibrous structure and does not enhance in the absence of pathology.
4. MRI can reduce the rates of unnecessary surgeries in patients with suspected fractures.
5. PD is commonly seen along the dorsal surface of penis.
6. Enhancement of plaque suggests active inflammation in the PD.
7. Cylinders in malleable implants are T2W hypointense (metallic). Inflatable implants have T2W hyperintense cylinders (saline).
8. Low-profile reservoirs are predisposed to fluid lock out due to improper folding and can lead to implant failure.
9. A thorough surgical history is mandatory before calling an ectopic location of reservoir.
10. Cylinders of inflatable implants should be evaluated in pre- and postinflation state to avoid overdiagnosis of pathologies.
11. While evaluating inflatable implants, images of entire pelvis can be acquired in pre- and postinflation state to include reservoir and pump.
12. MRI can be critical to evaluate postimplant infections as it can differentiate infections confined to the superficial structures versus infections related o periprosthetic space.
13. Reservoir dysfunction may occur due to fibrosis/adhesions caused by prior pelvic surgeries or radiation. No significant change in the caliber of reservoir and/or cylinders after inflation should prompt this diagnosis. However, similar findings can also be seen with pump failure.

10.10 Conclusion

MRI is a powerful tool in the evaluation of penile pathologies, and is a preferred method to assess penile trauma, neoplasms, and complications of penile prostheses. While it does not serve as the first-line imaging modality for all penile indications, it is often valuable as an adjunct to problem-solve in cases of priapism, PD. Penile anatomy is exceptionally depicted using the correct MRI protocol, and familiarity with both normal penile anatomy and findings of penile abnormalities at MRI will help lead to the correct diagnosis.

Acknowledgment

Dr. A.R. Abualruz, Assistant Professor of Radiology, Augusta University, GA for contributing cases and images.

References

1. Abualruz AR, O'Malley R, Ponnatapura J, et al. MRI of common penile pathologies and penile prostheses. *Abdom Radiol (NY)*. 2020;45(9):2825–2839. doi:10.1007/s00261-019-02080-6.
2. Uski A, Piccolo LM, Abud CP, et al. MRI of penile prostheses: the challenge of diagnosing postsurgical complications. *Radiographics*. 2022;42(1):159–175. doi:10.1148/rg.210075.
3. Lindquist CM, Nikolaidis P, Mittal PK, Miller FH. MRI of the penis. *Abdom Radiol*. 2020;45(7):2001–2017. doi:10.1007/s00261-019-02301-y.
4. Kirkham AP, Illing RO, Minhas S, Minhas S, Allen C. MR imaging of nonmalignant penile lesions. *Radiographics*. 2008;28(3):837–853. doi:10.1148/rg.283075100.
5. Wahl SI, Rubin MB, Bakal CW. Radiologic evaluation of penile arterial anatomy in arteriogenic impotence. *Int J Impotence Res*. 1997;9(2):93–97. doi:10.1038/sj.ijir.3900273.
6. Moscovici J, Galinier P, Hammoudi S, Lefebvre D, Juricic M, Vaysse P. Contribution to the study of the venous vasculature of the penis. *Surg Radiol Anat*. 1999;21(3):193–199. doi:10.1007/bf01630901.
7. Linet OI, Ogrinc FG. Efficacy and safety of intracavernosal alprostadil in men with erectile dysfunction. *New Engl J Med*. 1996;334(14):873–877. doi:10.1056/NEJM199604043341401.
8. Amer T, Wilson R, Chlosta P, et al. Penile fracture: a meta-analysis. *Urol Int*. 2016;96(3):315–329. doi:10.1159/000444884.
9. Koifman L, Barros R, Júnior RA, Cavalcanti AG, Favorito LA. Penile fracture: diagnosis, treatment and outcomes of 150 patients. *Urology*. 2010;76(6):1488–1492. doi:10.1016/j.urology.2010.05.043.
10. Majzoub AA, Canguven O, Raidh TA. Alteration in the etiology of penile fracture in the Middle East and Central Asia regions in the last decade; a literature review. *Urol Ann*. 2015;7(3):284–288. doi:10.4103/0974-7796.157973.
11. Rodriguez D, Li K, Apoj M, Munarriz R. Epidemiology of penile fractures in United States Emergency Departments: access to care disparities may lead to suboptimal outcomes. *J Sex Med*. 2019;16(2):248–256. doi:10.1016/j.jsxm.2018.12.009.
12. Ateyah A, Mostafa T, Nasser TA, Shaeer O, Hadi AA, Al-Gabbar MA. Penile fracture: surgical repair and late effects on erectile function. *J Sex Med*. 2008;5(6):1496–1502. doi:10.1111/j.1743-6109.2007.00769.x.
13. El-Assmy A, El-Tholoth HS, Abou-El-Ghar ME, Mohsen T. Ibrahiem el HI. False penile fracture: value of different diagnostic approaches and long-term outcome of conservative and surgical management. *Urology*. 2010;75(6):1353–1356. doi:10.1016/j.urology.2009.11.086.

14. Falcone M, Garaffa G, Castiglione F, Ralph DJ. Current management of penile fracture: an up-to-date systematic review. *Sex Med Rev.* 2018;6(2):253–260. doi:10.1016/j.sxmr.2017.07.009.

15. Esposito AA, Giannitto C, Muzzupappa C, et al. MRI of penile fracture: what should be a tailored protocol in emergency? *La radiol med.* 2016;121(9):711–718. doi:10.1007/s11547-016-0651-4.

16. Saglam E, Tarhan F, Hamarat MB, et al. Efficacy of magnetic resonance imaging for diagnosis of penile fracture: a controlled study. *Investig Clin Urol.* 2017;58(4):255–260. doi:10.4111/icu.2017.58.4.255.

17. Zare Mehrjardi M, Darabi M, Bagheri SM, Kamali K, Bijan B. The role of ultrasound (US) and magnetic resonance imaging (MRI) in penile fracture mapping for modified surgical repair. *Int Urol Nephrol.* 2017;49(6):937–945. doi:10.1007/s11255-017-1550-x.

18. Uder M, Gohl D, Takahashi M, et al. MRI of penile fracture: diagnosis and therapeutic follow-up. *Eur Radiol.* 2002;12(1):113–120. doi:10.1007/s003300101051.

19. Choi M-H, Kim B, Ryu J-A, Lee SW, Lee KS. MR imaging of acute penile fracture. *Radiographics.* 2000;20(5):1397–1405. doi:10.1148/radiographics.20.5.g00se051397.

20. Hoznek A, Rahmouni A, Abbou C, Delmas V, Colombel M. The suspensory ligament of the penis: an anatomic and radiologic description. *Surg Radiol Anat.* 1998;20(6):413–417. doi:10.1007/bf01653133.

21. Li CY, Agrawal V, Minhas S, Ralph DJ. The penile suspensory ligament: abnormalities and repair. *BJU Int.* 2007;99(1):117–120. doi:10.1111/j.1464-410X.2007.06551.x.

22. Spyropoulos E, Christoforidis C, Borousas D, Mavrikos S, Bourounis M, Athanasiadis S. Augmentation phalloplasty surgery for penile dysmorphophobia in young adults: considerations regarding patient selection, outcome evaluation and techniques applied. *Eur Urol.* 2005;48(1):121–127. doi:10.1016/j.eururo.2005.02.021 discussion 127-128.

23. Pavlica P, Barozzi L, Menchi I. Imaging of male urethra. *Eur Radiol.* 2003;13(7):1583–1596. doi:10.1007/s00330-002-1758-7.

24. Sung DJ, Kim YH, Cho SB, et al. Obliterative urethral stricture: MR urethrography versus conventional retrograde urethrography with voiding cystourethrography. *Radiology.* 2006;240(3):842–848. doi:10.1148/radiol.2403050590.

25. Oh MM, Jin MH, Sung DJ, Yoon DK, Kim JJ, du Moon G. Magnetic resonance urethrography to assess obliterative posterior urethral stricture: comparison to conventional retrograde urethrography with voiding cystourethrography. *J Urol.* 2010;183(2):603–607. doi:10.1016/j.juro.2009.10.016.

26. Pandian RM, John NT, Eapen A, Antonisamy B, Devasia A, Kekre N. Does MRI help in the pre-operative evaluation of pelvic fracture urethral distraction defect? -- A pilot study. *Int Braz J Urol.* 2017;43(1):127–133. doi:10.1590/s1677-5538.Ibju.2016.0252.

27. da Silva Gaspar SR, Ferreira ND, Oliveira T, Oliveira P, Dias JS, Lopes TM. Magnetic resonance imaging and pelvic fracture urethral injuries. *Urology.* 2017;110:9–15. doi:10.1016/j.urology.2017.06.041.

28. Broderick GA, Kadioglu A, Bivalacqua TJ, Ghanem H, Nehra A, Shamloul R. Priapism: pathogenesis, epidemiology, and management. *J Sex Med.* 2010;7(1 Pt 2):476–500. doi:10.1111/j.1743-6109.2009.01625.x.

29. Eland IA, van der Lei J, Stricker BH, Sturkenboom MJ. Incidence of priapism in the general population. *Urology.* 2001;57(5):970–972. doi:10.1016/s0090-4295(01)00941-4.

30. Acampora C, Borzelli A, Di Serafino M, et al. High-flow post-traumatic priapism: diagnostic and therapeutic workup. *J Ultrasound.* 2021;24(4):539–545. doi:10.1007/s40477-020-00449-8.

31. Burnett AL, Sharlip ID. Standard operating procedures for priapism. *J Sex Med.* 2013;10(1):180–194. doi:10.1111/j.1743-6109.2012.02707.x.

32. Montague DK, Jarow J, Broderick GA, et al. American Urological Association guideline on the management of priapism. *J Urol.* 2003;170(4 Pt 1):1318–1324. doi:10.1097/01.ju.0000087608.07371.ca.

33. James Johnson M, Hallerstrom M, Alnajjar HM, et al. Which patients with ischaemic priapism require further investigation for malignancy? *Int J Impotence Res.* 2020;32(2):195–200. doi:10.1038/s41443-019-0141-z.

34. Montgomery S, Sirju K, Bear J, Ganti L, Shivdat J. Recurrent priapism in the setting of cannabis use. *J Cannabis Res.* 2020;2(1):7. doi:10.1186/s42238-020-0015-8.

35. Sadeghi-Nejad H, Sharma A, Irwin RJ, Wilson SK, Delk JR. Reservoir herniation as a complication of three-piece penile prosthesis insertion. *Urology.* 2001;57(1):142–145. doi:10.1016/s0090-4295(00)00864-5.

36. Ralph DJ, Borley NC, Allen C, et al. The use of high-resolution magnetic resonance imaging in the management of patients presenting with priapism. *BJU Int.* 2010;106(11):1714–1718. doi:10.1111/j.1464-410X.2010.09368.x.

37. El-Assmy A, Hekal IA, Abou-El-Ghar ME. Use of magnetic resonance angiography in diagnosis and decision making of post-traumatic, high-flow priapism. *Sci World J.* 2008;8:176–181. doi:10.1100/tsw.2008.35.

38. Akkus E. Historical review of Peyronie's disease. In: Levine LA, ed. *Peyronie's Disease: A Guide to Clinical Management*: Humana Press; 2007:1–8.

39. Bjekic MD, Vlajinac HD, Sipetic SB, Marinkovic JM. Risk factors for Peyronie's disease: a case-control study. *BJU Int.* 2006;97(3):570–574. doi:10.1111/j.1464-410X.2006.05969.x.

40. Mulhall JP, Creech SD, Boorjian SA, et al. Subjective and objective analysis of the prevalence of Peyronie's disease in a population of men presenting for prostate cancer screening. *J Urol.* 2004;171(6 Pt 1):2350–2353. doi:10.1097/01.ju.0000127744.18878.f1.

41. Ziegelmann MJ, Bajic P, Levine LA. Peyronie's disease: contemporary evaluation and management. *Int J Urol.* 2020;27(6):504–516. doi:10.1111/iju.14230.

42. Nehra A, Alterowitz R, Culkin DJ, et al. Peyronie's disease: AUA guideline. *J Urol.* 2015;194(3):745–753. doi:10.1016/j.juro.2015.05.098.

43. Chung E, Wang R, Ralph D, Levine L, Brock G. A worldwide survey on Peyronie's disease surgical practice patterns among surgeons. *J Sex Med.* 2018;15(4):568–575. doi:10.1016/j.jsxm.2018.01.025.

44. Chen JY, Hockenberry MS, Lipshultz LI. Objective assessments of Peyronie's disease. *Sex Med Rev.* 2018;6(3):438–445. doi:10.1016/j.sxmr.2017.12.006.

45. Parmar M, Masterson JM, Masterson 3rd TA. The role of imaging in the diagnosis and management of Peyronie's disease. *Curr Opin Urol.* 2020;30(3):283–289. doi:10.1097/mou.0000000000000754.

46. Wang HJ, Guan J, Lin JH, Pan BT, Deng CH, Guo Y. Diagnostic value of high-field MRI for Peyronie's disease. *Zhonghua Nan Ke Xue.* 2016;22(9):787–791.

47. Levine LA, Lenting EL. A surgical algorithm for the treatment of Peyronie's disease. *J Urol.* 1997;158(6):2149–2152. doi:10.1016/s0022-5347(01)68184-9.

48. Helweg G, Judmaier W, Buchberger W, et al. Peyronie's disease: MR findings in 28 patients. *Am J Roentgenol.* 1992;158(6):1261–1264. doi:10.2214/ajr.158.6.1590119.

49. Hauck EW, Hackstein N, Vosshenrich R, et al. Diagnostic value of magnetic resonance imaging in Peyronie's disease–a comparison both with palpation and ultrasound in the evaluation of plaque formation. *Eur Urol*. 2003;43(3):293–299. doi:10.1016/s0302-2838(03)00003-4 discussion 299-300.

50. Babu A, Kayes O. Recent advances in managing Peyronie's disease. *F1000Research*. 2020;9:F1000. doi:10.12688/f1000research.20557.1. Faculty Rev-381.

51. Mobley EM, Fuchs ME, Myers JB, Brant WO. Update on plication procedures for Peyronie's disease and other penile deformities. *Ther Adv Urol*. 2012;4(6):335–346. doi:10.1177/1756287212448224.

52. Montes Cardona CE, García-Perdomo HA. Incidence of penile cancer worldwide: systematic review and meta-analysis. *Rev Panam Salud Publica*. 2017;41:e117. doi:10.26633/RPSP.2017.117 -e117.

53. Arya M, Li R, Pegler K, et al. Long-term trends in incidence, survival and mortality of primary penile cancer in England. *Cancer Causes Control*. 2013;24(12):2169–2176. doi:10.1007/s10552-013-0293-y.

54. Hansen BT, Orumaa M, Lie AK, Brennhovd B, Nygård M. Trends in incidence, mortality and survival of penile squamous cell carcinoma in Norway 1956-2015. *Int J Cancer*. 2018;142(8):1586–1593. doi:10.1002/ijc.31194.

55. Siegel RL, Miller KD, Jemal A. Cancer statistics, 2018. *CA: Cancer J Clin*. 2018;68(1):7–30 doi:https://doi.org/10.3322/caac.21442.

56. Colberg C, van der Horst C, Jünemann KP, Naumann CM. Epidemiologie des Peniskarzinoms. *Der Urol*. 2018;57:408–412.

57. Chahoud J, Kohli M, Spiess PE. Management of advanced penile cancer. *Mayo Clin Proc*. 2021;96(3):720–732. doi:10.1016/j.mayocp.2020.06.031.

58. Krishna S, Shanbhogue K, Schieda N, et al. Role of MRI in staging of penile cancer. *J Magn Reson Imaging*. 2020;51(6):1612–1629. https://doi.org/10.1002/jmri.27060.

59. Amin MB, Greene FL, Edge SB, et al. The Eighth Edition AJCC Cancer Staging Manual: continuing to build a bridge from a population-based to a more "personalized" approach to cancer staging. *CA Cancer J Clin*. 2017;67(2):93–99. doi:10.3322/caac.21388.

60. Khalil MI, Kamel MH, Dhillon J, et al. What you need to know: updates in penile cancer staging. *World J Urol*. 2021;39(5):1413–1419. doi:10.1007/s00345-020-03302-z.

61. Lopes A, Hidalgo Geraldo S, Kowalski Luiz P, Torloni H, Rossi Benedito M, Fonseca Francisco P. Prognostic factors in carcinoma of the penis: multivariate analysis of 145 patients treated with amputation and lymphadenectomy. *J Urol*. 1996;156(5):1637–1642. doi:10.1016/S0022-5347(01)65471-5.

62. Lucchesi FR, Reis RB, Faria EF, et al. Incremental value of MRI for preoperative penile cancer staging. *J Magn Reson Imaging*. 2017;45(1):118–124. doi:10.1002/jmri.25339.

63. Azizi M, Chipollini J, Peyton CC, Cheriyan SK, Spiess PE. Current controversies and developments on the role of lymphadenectomy for penile cancer. *Urol Oncol*. 2019;37(3):201–208. doi:10.1016/j.urolonc.2018.08.017.

64. Hakenberg OW, Dräger DL, Erbersdobler A, Naumann CM, Jünemann K-P, Protzel C. Diagnostik und Therapie des Peniskarzinoms. *Dtsch Arztebl Int*. 2018;115(39):646–652.

65. Mearini L, Colella R, Zucchi A, Nunzi E, Porrozzi C, Porena M. A review of penile metastasis. *Oncol Rev*. 2012;6(1):e10. doi:10.4081/oncol.2012.e10 -e10.

66. Schroeder-Printzen I, Vosshenrich R, Weidner W, Ringert RH. Malignant priapism in a patient with metastatic prostate adenocarcinoma. *Urol Int*. 1994;52(1):52–54. doi:10.1159/000282571.

67. Lucia MS, Miller GJ. Histopathology of malignant lesions of the penis. *Urol Clin North Am*. 1992;19(2):227–246.

68. Zhang M, Adeniran AJ, Vikram R, et al. Carcinoma of the urethra. *Hum Pathol*. 2018;72:35–44. doi:10.1016/j.humpath.2017.08.006.

69. Chiang KH, Chang PY, Lee SK, et al. MR findings of penile lymphoma. *Br J Radiol*. 2006;79(942):526–528. doi:10.1259/bjr/55555394.

70. Levine LA, Becher EF, Bella AJ, et al. Penile prosthesis surgery: current recommendations from the international consultation on sexual medicine. *J Sex Med*. 2016;13(4):489–518. doi:10.1016/j.jsxm.2016.01.017.

71. Lee DJ, Najari BB, Davison WL, et al. Trends in the utilization of penile prostheses in the treatment of erectile dysfunction in the United States. *J Sex Med*. 2015;12(7):1638–1645. doi:10.1111/jsm.12921.

72. Li K, Brandes ER, Chang SL, et al. Trends in penile prosthesis implantation and analysis of predictive factors for removal. *World J Urol*. 2019;37(4):639–646. doi:10.1007/s00345-018-2491-4.

73. Carrion H, Martinez D, Parker J, et al. A history of the penile implant to 1974. *Sex Med Rev*. 2016;4(3):285–293. doi:10.1016/j.sxmr.2016.05.003.

74. Hartman RP, Kawashima A, Takahashi N, LeRoy AJ, King BF. Inflatable penile prosthesis (IPP): diagnosis of complications. *Abdom Radiol*. 2016;41(6):1187–1196. doi:10.1007/s00261-016-0686-y.

75. Carson CC. Diagnosis, treatment and prevention of penile prosthesis infection. *Int J Impotence Res*. 2003;15(5):S139–S146. doi:10.1038/sj.ijir.3901091.

76. Mulcahy JJ, Austoni E, Barada JH, et al. The penile implant for erectile dysfunction. *J Sex Med*. 2004;1(1):98–109. doi:10.1111/j.1743-6109.2004.10115.x.

77. Moncada I, Hernandez C, Jara J, et al. Buckling Of Cylinders May Cause Prolonged Penile Pain After Prosthesis Implantation: A Case Control Study Using Magnetic Resonance Imaging Of The Penis. *J Urol*. 1998;160(1):67–71. doi:10.1016/S0022-5347(01)63033-7.

78. McPhail EF, Nehra A, Bruner BC, Kawashima A, King BF, Kim B. MRI and its role in the evaluation and surgical decision making in patients with challenging IPP presentations: descriptions of MRI findings and algorithm for patient management. *BJU Int*. 2012;109(12):1848–1852. doi:10.1111/j.1464-410X.2011.10683.x.

79. Sadeghi-Nejad H, Dogra V, Seftel AD, Mohamed MA. Priapism. *Radiol Clin North Am*. 2004;42(2):427–443. doi:10.1016/j.rcl.2004.01.008.

80. Clavell-Hernández J, Shah A, Wang R. Non-infectious reservoir-related complications during and after penile prosthesis placement. *Sex Med Rev*. 2019;7(3):521–529. doi:10.1016/j.sxmr.2018.12.005.

81. Navarrete RA, Cui T, Carson C, Terlecki R. Failure of the inflatable penile prosthesis due to abnormal folding of a low-profile reservoir – a selected case from an overall series and systematic review. *Urol Case Rep*. 2017;14:56–58. https://doi.org/10.1016/j.eucr.2017.06.009.

82. Brown ET, Saunders SE, Zaslau S. Penile prosthesis pump tubing erosion into urethra appearing as inability to catheterize: a case report. *J Sex Med*. 2008;5(12):2960–2962. doi:10.1111/j.1743-6109.2008.00868.x.

83. Morales A. Tubing erosion of an inflatable penile prosthesis long after implantation. *Sex Med*. 2014;2(2):103–106. doi:10.1002/sm2.30.

84. Fein Richard L, Needell Mervin H. Early problems encountered with the mentor inflatable penile prosthesis. *J Urol*. 1985;134(1):62–64. doi:10.1016/S0022-5347(17)46979-5.

85. Rodriguez KM, Pastuszak AW. A history of penile implants. *Transl Androl Urol*. 2017;6(Suppl 5):S851–S857. doi:10.21037/tau.2017.04.02.

11

MRI of female infertility*

Mark D. Sugi[a], Liina Põder[a], Margaret Houser[b],
Joanna Riess[b], Nadia J. Khati[b]

[a]Department of Radiology & Biomedical Imaging, Division of Abdominal Imaging and Ultrasound, University of California, San Francisco, CA, United States [b]Department of Radiology, The George Washington University Hospital, Washington, DC, United States

11.1 Introduction

Infertility is defined as a couple's inability to achieve a clinical pregnancy after a year of unprotected, regular sexual intercourse in women less than 35 years of age.[1] According to the American College of Obstetricians and Gynecologists (ACOG) and the American Society for Reproductive Medicine (ASRM), women older than 35 years should undergo evaluation earlier, after only 6 months of failed attempts at successful conception, while women 40 years of age and older should get evaluated immediately.[1] The World Health Organization (WHO) classifies infertility as a disease affecting 12–15% of couples in the world.[1,2] Causes for infertility are multifactorial with 40% of etiologies identified as male and 40% female.[3] Affected couples should have a comprehensive diagnostic evaluation including a complete review of medical history, detailed physical examination, laboratory assessment consisting of semen and hormonal analysis, and imaging examinations. The latter plays a crucial role in the assessment of female infertility and consists of a multimodality imaging approach of the reproductive organs. Depending on the suspected etiologies, these may range from ultrasound (US) to hysterosalpingography (HSG) and magnetic resonance imaging (MRI). This chapter will focus on the current role of MR imaging in the evaluation of female infertility, including its limitations. We will discuss the imaging findings of disorders associated with female infertility which include a variety of ovarian, tubal and peritubal, and uterine (acquired and congenital) abnormalities as well as briefly discuss pelvic deep infiltrating endometriosis.

11.2 Embryology/anatomy

The reproductive organs of the female pelvis consist of the vagina, cervix, uterus, fallopian tubes, and ovaries. During embryology, the absence of Mullerian-inhibiting factor in female fetuses allows development of the paired Mullerian or paramesonephric ducts. These ducts fuse caudally to form the uterus, cervix, and upper two-thirds of the vagina, while the unfused cranial portions form the fallopian tubes. The fused Mullerian ducts are initially separated by a midline septum which progressively regresses to form a single uterine cavity (Fig. 11.1). Failure of development of one or both Mullerian ducts, absence of fusion or abnormal/incomplete resorption of the midline septum will result in a group of congenital abnormalities referred to as Mullerian duct anomalies (MDAs). This sometimes-complex spectrum of abnormalities is often associated with a high risk of infertility, endometriosis, amenorrhea, and obstetric complications such as recurrent miscarriages or preterm delivery. In women of reproductive age, the uterus usually measures roughly 8 cm long, 4 cm in anterior-posterior dimension and 5 cm wide. The fallopian tubes run within the superior aspect of the broad ligament and typically measure between 7 cm and 12 cm long. They are divided into 4 segments: a short interstitial portion, isthmic, ampullary, and distal funnel-shaped infundibular

---

* The authors declare that they had full access to this manuscript and take complete responsibility for the integrity and the accuracy of the submitted manuscript.

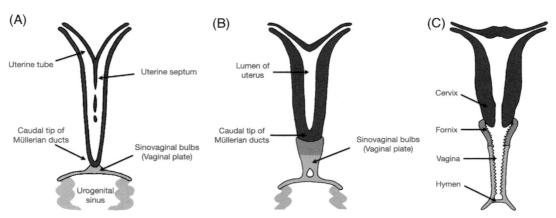

FIG. 11.1   **Development of the uterus and vagina.** (A) The caudal portions of paired Mullerian ducts migrate medially and fuse to form the uterovaginal primordium. A uterine septum initially persists. (B) Resorption of the uterine septum occurs between the 9th and 12th week of gestation, creating the uterine cavity. Simultaneously, the distal aspect of the Mullerian duct contacts the urogenital sinus inducing formation of the vagina. (C) The uterine cavity continues to grow with development of the cervix and by the 5th month of gestation, the vagina is entirely canalized. *Adapted from Fig. 11.2, Congenital anomalies causing hemato/hydrocolpos: imaging findings, treatment, and outcomes published in Japanese Journal of Radiology (2021) 30:733–740. (Licensed under a Creative Commons Attribution 4.0 International License, http://creativecommons.org/licenses/by/4.0/).*

portions. This latter part opens freely into the peritoneal cavity. The ovaries have a different embryologic origin than the uterus and derive from mesenchymal and epithelial cells of the gonadal ridge. These paired organs are located within the ovarian fossa along the pelvic side wall and are attached by the mesovarium to the posterior surface of the broad ligament. Ovarian size is best assessed using a volume measurement which can be up to 22 cc in women of reproductive age.

11.2.1 MR imaging: indications, limitations, technique, protocols

The imaging investigation of female infertility is most often performed using a multimodality approach. Depending on the suspected etiology early in the work-up, imaging may start with a pelvic US as a first screening examination, and this may be followed by an HSG or more recently hysterosalpingo-contrast sonography (HyCoSy) to assess tubal patency and evaluate the uterine cavity.[4] MR imaging is an excellent problem-solving tool due its multiplanar capabilities, superior soft tissue resolution, noninvasive nature and lack of ionizing radiation. Unlike US, it is not as operator dependent, is more reproducible given a specific imaging protocol and technique and is not as affected by body size or overlying structures. In addition, there is very little inter-reader variability when studies are interpreted by experienced radiologists. MRI is extremely helpful in the diagnosis and pretreatment planning of uterine fibroids, adenomyosis, deep infiltrating endometriosis (DIE), tubal and peritubal adhesions as well as MDAs.[4,5] It serves as an optimal adjunct imaging modality to better characterize atypical endometriomas seen on US, or to differentiate hydro/hematosalpinx from atypical cystic adnexal masses. More recently, MR-HSG has been found to have similar diagnostic accuracy to conventional HSG in the detection of uterine cavity abnormalities and tubal patency.[6] Although innovative with promising results, this imaging technique is not widely available and further research is required.

Imaging protocols vary by institution and consist of a combination of T1 and T2 weighted sequences, performed on a 1.5 or 3 Tesla magnet using a body phase array coil. T2 weighted sequences are essential in imaging the female pelvis given their ability to depict the zonal anatomy of the uterus and provide detailed visualization of the ovaries and adnexal regions. T1 weighted sequences with fat suppression are also important due to their ability to demonstrate blood products related to hematosalpinges, endometriomas, hemorrhagic cysts, and endometriosis. Adding in- and out-of-phase T1 weighted sequences is necessary to distinguish dermoid cysts from other T1 bright lesions. Administering a spasmolytic agent at the time of the scan is recommended to reduce artifact from peristalsing bowel and uterine contractions, while fasting and/or the routine use of a bowel preparation are not necessary. Depending on the suspected etiology, imaging protocols should be tailored to specific disease processes (Table 11.1). For example, when DIE is of concern, using vaginal and/or rectal gel (Fig. 11.2) or water may be warranted to increase the conspicuity of implants in the vaginal fornices and along the rectal wall as well as cul-de-sac structures.[7] Aqueous

TABLE 11.1 Imaging protocols: Society of Abdominal Radiology Endometriosis DFP MRI protocol.

Body phased array sequence	Plane	Comment
Scout	3 planes	
T2 turbo spin echo (TSE)/fast spin echo (FSE)	Sag	• Nonbreath hold • Small field of view • Cover femoral head to femoral head right to left and all female pelvis anatomy • Add anterior saturation band • Use 4–6 mm slices
T2 TSE/FSE	Straight Ax or oblique Ax	• Axial straight • Cover female pelvis
Diffusion weighted imaging (DWI)	Ax	• Diffusion B = 0, 50, 800 • Cover female anatomy or suspicious pathology
T2 TSE	Coronal or oblique coronal	• Coronal oriented parallel to uterus • Nonbreath hold 2–3 acquisitions • Small FOV
T1 in/out dixon	Ax	• Small FOV • Cover female organs only
T1 WI with fat suppression precontrast	Sag	• Small slab/FOV • 2 mm slice thickness
T1 WI with fat suppression precontrast large field of view	Ax	• Aortic bifurcation to symphysis pubis
T1 WI with fat suppression postcontrast	Sag	• Small slab/FOV • 2 mm slice thickness
T1 WI with fat suppression postcontrast large field of view	Ax	• Aortic bifurcation to symphysis pubis

Reference: Society of Abdominal Radiology (SAR) Endometriosis Disease-Focused Panel (DFP) MRI protocol.
MRI: 1.5T or 3T with phased array coil.
Patient Preparation:
Moderate urinary bladder filling: conditionally recommended.
Vaginal contrast: conditionally recommended (30–60 cc aqueous gel).
Rectal contrast: conditionally recommended (60–180 cc aqueous gel).
Antiperistaltic agent: Highly recommended (1 mg IV Glucagon).

gel is most commonly used as it is widely available, easy to use and less prone to leak. A volume of 60–180 mL is placed in one or more syringes and administered by physician or other trained medical personnel with the patient lying in a lateral decubitus position on the MRI table. More contrast may be administered as needed based on subsequent imaging. If an MDA is suspected, images are obtained parallel to the long and short axis of the uterine corpus (Fig. 11.3) in order to characterize the outside fundal contour. In addition, a coronal T2 weighted single-shot fast spin echo (SSFSE) with wide field of view to include the upper abdomen is performed to evaluate for the presence of concurrent renal agenesis/anomalies. Although contrast is not routinely required in the evaluation of female infertility[5,8,9] its use helps assess the presence and degree of fibroid enhancement for pretreatment planning and allows further characterization of any suspicious findings seen on the noncontrast sequences. Intravenous contrast also improves conspicuity of inflammatory endometrial deposits along the peritoneal surfaces as well as areas of inflammatory adhesions.[7] Subtraction imaging is necessary when postcontrast sequences are obtained as it allows better assessment of enhancement of intrinsically T1 bright lesions, malignant transformation of endometriomas or small endometrial implants.[9] The Society of Abdominal Radiology endometriosis disease-focused panel has recently published a consensus statement detailing their recommendations to optimize MR imaging techniques and protocols in the evaluation of endometriosis.[9]

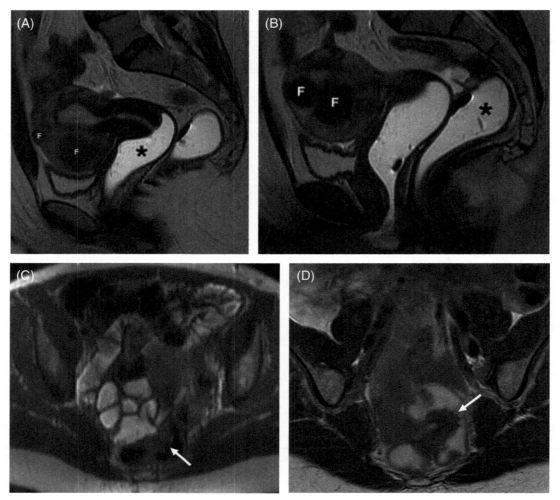

FIG. 11.2   **Utility of vaginal and rectal gel for evaluation of deep infiltrating endometriosis.** (A and B) Sagittal T2-weighted MR images of the pelvis with gel (*) in the vagina (A) and rectum (B). The presence of gel nicely distends the vagina allowing better visualization of the vaginal fornices. F: fibroids. (C and D) Axial T2-weighted MR images in a different patient acquired 3 months apart without (C) and with (D) rectal gel showing the "mushroom cap" lesion (arrow), indicative of bowel-invasive DIE. The lesion is significantly better visualized on the follow-up examination outlined by intraluminal gel.

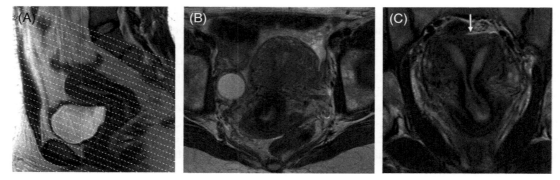

FIG. 11.3   **Multiplanar imaging of the uterus for assessment of suspected Mullerian duct anomaly.** Sagittal T2-weighted MR localizing image through the uterus showing the acquisition plane of images obtained parallel to the long axis of the uterus (A) with corresponding single shot fast spin echo (SSFSE) images of the uterus (B) showing the external uterine fundal contour (arrow). SSFSE coronal oblique MR image of the uterus in a different patient (C) acquired to optimize visualization of the uterine fundus and uterine cavity, demonstrating a septate uterus with flat uterine fundus (arrow).

TABLE 11.2 Endometriosis: compartments of the female pelvis.

Anterior compartment	• Prevesical space • Vesicouterine space • Vesicocervical/vesicovaginal spaces • Round ligament • Bladder and ureters
Middle compartment	• Uterus • Vagina • Ovaries
Posterior compartment	• Rectouterine • Retrocervical/rectocervical space • Rectovaginal space • Uterosacral ligaments

11.3 Structured reporting

When reviewing pelvic MRIs in the workup of female infertility, radiologists should use a systematic approach for accuracy and completeness. Given the complexity of some cases, radiology reports must include a comprehensive description of findings using a universal lexicon and a structured report. This allows for a more efficient way to convey valuable information to clinicians in a clear and concise manner.[10] The benefits of using structured reports have been previously reported in the literature with some advantages including a decrease in diagnostic errors, an increased likelihood of adhering to consensus guidelines, and higher reimbursements as reports are more complete and comprehensive.[10]

Structured MRI reports in patients with infertility should include evaluation of the ovaries, fallopian tubes, and uterus.[11] In addition, the anterior and posterior anatomic compartments of the female pelvis (Table 11.2) must be carefully evaluated in cases of deep infiltrating endometriosis.[12] A more detailed description of these compartments is beyond the scope of this chapter as they will be the subject of a separate chapter in this book entitled "MRI of endometriosis."

11.4 Ovarian causes

Ovarian causes of infertility include primary conditions such as congenital absence of the ovaries or gonadal dysgenesis, ovulatory dysfunction, nonfunctional ovaries, or premature ovarian failure. Imaging plays an insignificant role in the diagnosis of such entities as these are mainly evaluated using clinical and hormonal level assessment.[13,14] Imaging plays a crucial role in the diagnosis of secondary conditions of infertility such as polycystic ovarian morphology (PCOM) and polycystic ovarian syndrome (PCOS) as well as endometriomas. Polycystic ovarian syndrome is a complex disease process affecting up to 10% of women of childbearing age[15] and is characterized by chronic hyperandrogenism resulting in anovulation. This is in distinction to PCOM which is an imaging diagnosis consisting of multiple ovarian follicles in women with no or only mild PCOS symptoms and has been reported in 30% of the general female population.[16] Based on the 2003 Rotterdam criteria, PCOS is diagnosed when 2 out of 3 of the following findings are present: (1) clinical and/or biochemical evidence of hyperandrogenism, (2) oligo/amenorrhea, and (3) one or both ovaries having a PCO morphology.[17] The most widely accepted definition of PCOM is that of an ovary containing 12 or more follicles measuring 2–9 mm each and/or having a volume greater than 10 cc.[15] These criteria were mainly based on studies using older US equipment or a transabdominal scanning approach. More recently, the Androgen Excess and Polycystic Ovary Syndrome Society Task Force has recommended increasing the threshold of follicle number to 25 or greater given the advent of higher resolution transvaginal transducers (frequency >8 MHz) which provide better visualization of follicles.[16] While US is undoubtedly the gold standard imaging modality for the diagnosis of PCOM, MR imaging without intravenous contrast is the best alternative in obese adolescent girls or in those who cannot tolerate a transvaginal US.[15,18] At MR imaging, findings suggesting PCO morphology include a classic hypointense T2 central stroma, multiple peripherally arranged follicles (Fig. 11.4) and increased ovarian volume greater than 10 cc (Fig. 11.5). More recently, Badeeb et al. have found that a continuous dark T2 cortical rim (Fig. 11.6) was present in ovaries of women with PCOS in 71% of cases compared with only 25% of controls.[19] They speculated this finding corresponded to superficial cortical fibrosis.

Endometriosis is defined as the presence of endometrial glands and stroma outside the uterus and affects 10% of women of childbearing age.[20,21] Affected women often present with chronic cyclic pelvic pain and up to 50% have

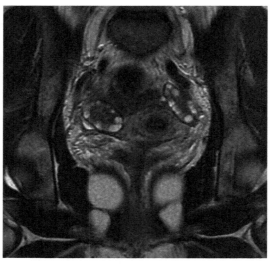

FIG. 11.4   Polycystic ovarian morphology, normal ovarian volume. Coronal T2-weighted MR image of normal-sized ovaries with multiple, peripherally arranged small follicles.

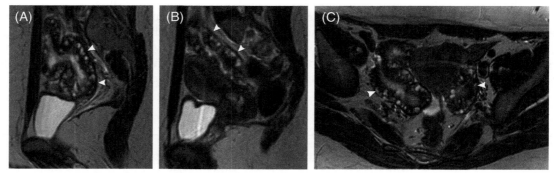

FIG. 11.5   Polycystic ovarian morphology, enlarged ovaries. Sagittal T2-weighted (A and B) and axial (C) MR images in a patient with PCOS, shows peripherally arranged follicles (arrowheads), most of which measures between 2 mm and 9 mm, and bilateral ovarian enlargement (each >10 cc in volume).

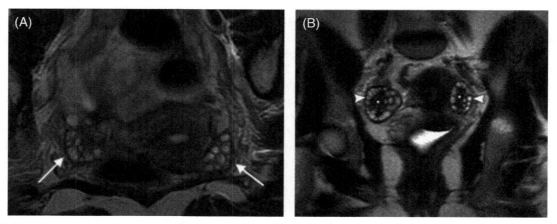

FIG. 11.6   Polycystic ovarian morphology, T2 hypointense cortical rim and hypointense central stroma. Axial T2-weighted MR image (A) shows a continuous dark T2 cortical rim around both ovaries (arrows). Coronal T2-weighted MR image (B) shows a classic hypointense appearance of the central stroma (*) with multiple peripherally arranged follicles (arrowheads) in a different patient with PCOS.

infertility.[22] Endometriomas represent a form of endometriosis whereby implants within the ovary bleed cyclically resulting in endometriotic cysts. They are present in up to 44% of patients with endometriosis.[23] MR signal characteristics of endometriomas are the result of their high viscosity and highly concentrated blood and protein contents. For that reason, these cysts are classically hyperintense on T1 weighted fat-suppressed sequences and demonstrate hypointensity (Fig. 11.7) or the classic "shading sign" on T2 weighted sequences (Fig. 11.8). These MR imaging characteristics were first described by Togashi et al. in 1991 whose study results showed a sensitivity and specificity of 90% and 98% respectively and an accuracy of 96% in making the diagnosis and differentiating endometriomas from other hemorrhagic adnexal lesions.[24] Although the T2 "shading sign" is a distinguishing imaging finding which is helpful in differentiating endometriomas from other T1 hyperintense lesions such as hemorrhagic or dermoid cysts, it has recently been found not to be an exclusive and reliable sign (Fig. 11.9). According to Dias et al. it can also be seen in other adnexal lesions such as other benign and malignant nonendometrioid tumors (Fig. 11.10).[25] Rather than using the presence or absence of the T2 shading sign to characterize an adnexal lesion as an endometrioma, they evaluated the pattern of shading within the cyst. Their study concluded that a homogeneous shading pattern was more frequently seen in endometriomas (Fig. 11.11).[25] Two additional MR findings are helpful in making the diagnosis of endometriomas and differentiating them from hemorrhagic cysts: the T2 dark spot sign and T2 dark rim sign. The T2 dark spot sign was first described by Corwin et al. as small markedly hypointense foci within T2 hypointense cystic adnexal lesions.[26] They speculated that these small T2 hypointense foci corresponded to areas of chronically retracted blood clot within a cyst and concluded that the sign was 93% specific in differentiating endometriomas from hemorrhagic cysts (Fig. 11.12). These results were confirmed by Cansu et al.[27] whose study included 50 endometriomas and 22 hemorrhagic cysts and found the T2 dark spot sign to be present in 52% of the endometriomas and none of the hemorrhagic cysts yielding a specificity and positive predictive value 100% for this sign. The T2 dark rim sign, which corresponds pathologically to the thick hemosiderin fibrous capsule of endometriomas, was observed in 98% of endometriomas compared to 86.3% of hemorrhagic cysts[27] with an incomplete rim

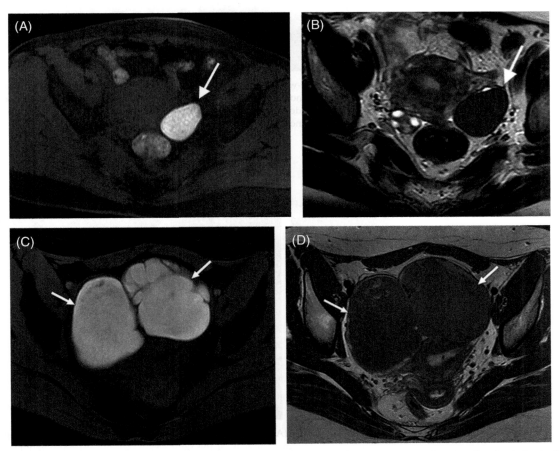

FIG. 11.7 **Endometrioma.** Axial T1-weighted fat-suppressed (A) and T2-weighted (B) MR images showing the classic intrinsic T1 hyperintensity and T2 hypointensity of a left endometrioma (arrows). Axial T1-weighted fat-suppressed (C) and T2-weighted (D) MR images in another patient showing bilateral T1 hyperintense and T2 hypointense endometriomas (arrows).

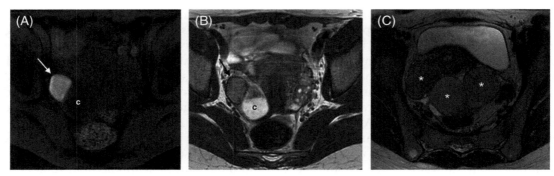

FIG. 11.8   **Endometrioma with T2 shading sign.** Axial T1-weighted fat-suppressed (A) and T2-weighted (B) MR images show a right endometrioma with intrinsic T1 hyperintensity and "T2 shading" with intermediate signal (arrows). C: cyst. (C) Axial T2-weighted MR image in a different patient shows different levels of intermediate signal within the endometriomas (*). The degree of "shading" may be nonuniform across different endometriomas owing to variability in the age of blood products.

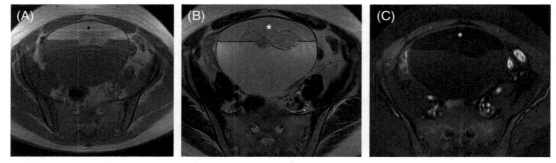

FIG. 11.9   **Dermoid cyst with T2 shading.** Axial T1- (A) and T2-weighted (B) MR images showing a large cystic ovarian mass with a fluid-fluid level. The antidependent layer (*) is T1 hyperintense and demonstrates T2 shading. On the axial T1 weighted fat-suppressed MR image, the antidependent layer (*) is hypointense representing fat within a dermoid cyst. This example emphasizes the nonspecific nature of T2 shading within an ovarian lesion as well as the use of fat-suppressed sequences.

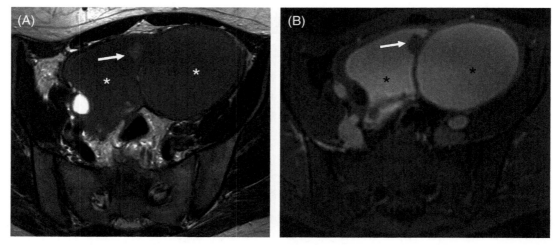

FIG. 11.10   **Endometrioid adenocarcinoma with T2 shading sign.** (A) Axial T2-weighted MR image shows the T2 shading sign in bilateral adnexal cystic lesions (*) with a hyperintense papillary projection along the wall of the right lesion (arrow). (B) Axial gadolinium-enhanced T1-weighted fat-suppressed MR image at the same level shows intrinsic T1 hyperintensity of the hemorrhagic lesions (*) and the papillary projection along the wall (arrow). Surgical pathology showed endometrioid adenocarcinoma, FIGO grade 3, arising within endometriosis and confined to the ovary.

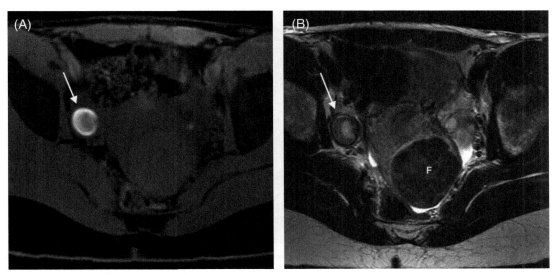

FIG. 11.11   Heterogeneous T2 shading, hemorrhagic cyst. Axial T1-weighted fat suppressed (A) and T2-weighted (B) MR images show a right adnexal cystic lesion with heterogeneous T1 hyperintensity and heterogeneous T2 shading. This was compatible with a hemorrhagic cyst. F: fibroid.

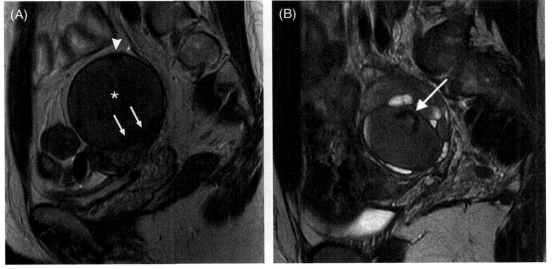

FIG. 11.12   Endometrioma with T2 dark spot sign. (A) Sagittal T2-weighted MR image in a patient with deep infiltrating endometriosis shows multiple T2 dark spots (arrows) along the inferior wall of a large endometrioma. Note also the T2 dark rim sign (arrowhead) and T2 shading sign (*). (B) Sagittal T2-weighted MR image in a different patient showing an endometrioma with T2 dark spot (arrow).

seen more commonly in endometriomas, rendering the morphology of the rim rather than its presence a more reliable feature (Fig. 11.13). Diffusion weighted imaging, which is widely used in abdominal and pelvic MR imaging protocols, provides added value in distinguishing endometriomas from hemorrhagic cysts. Balaban et al. found that endometriomas had significantly lower apparent diffusion coefficient values than hemorrhagic cysts at all b values, with b values of 1000 having a higher sensitivity and specificity.[28] The anatomic location of the ovaries within the female pelvis may also be a valuable indicator of endometriosis and hence of possible associated infertility. Due to the significant amount of peri- and paraovarian adhesions seen in some cases of deep infiltrating endometriosis, the ovaries may be displaced medially out of the ovarian fossae, a sign referred to as the "ovarian kissing sign." They may also become retropositioned in the pouch of Douglas.[12] This sign can be seen in the setting of otherwise morphologically normal ovaries (Fig. 11.14) or in cases of bilateral endometriomas (Fig. 11.15), a finding seen in over 50% of cases.[29] Recognizing this imaging appearance on MRI is important given its strong association with stages 3/4 endometriosis.[30] Williams et al. found kissing ovaries to have a sensitivity and specificity of 41% and 95% respectively for stage 4 endometriosis. Furthermore, identifying either kissing ovaries regardless of the presence of

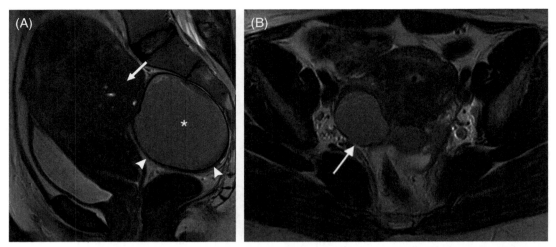

FIG. 11.13   Endometrioma with T2 dark rim sign. (A) Sagittal T2-weighted MR image in a patient with adenomyosis (arrow) and a large endometrioma in the cul-de-sac demonstrates the T2 dark rim sign (arrowhead) and T2 shading sign (*). (B) Axial T2-weighted MR image showing a discontinuous T2 dark rim sigh (arrow) within a right endometrioma.

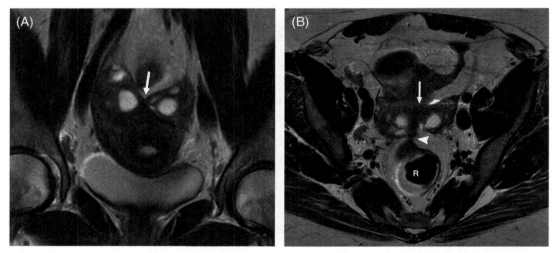

FIG. 11.14   Kissing ovaries in deep infiltrating endometriosis. Coronal (A) and axial (B) T2-weighted MR images show medialization of normal appearing ovaries in a "kissing" configuration (arrows) caused by adhesions, which also extend to the anterior serosa of the rectum (R) in B (arrowhead).

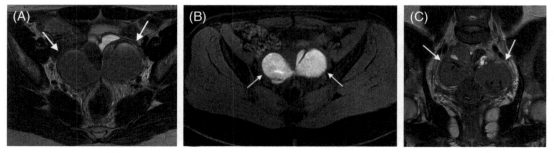

FIG. 11.15   Kissing bilateral endometriomas. Axial T2 (A) and T1-weighted (B) MR images and coronal T2-weighted (C) MR images show bilateral "kissing" T1 hyperintense endometriomas with T2 shading (white arrows). Note the T2 dark spots within both lesions (small black arrows).

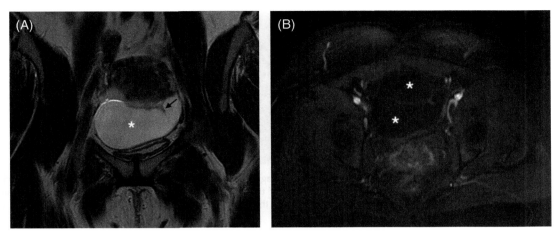

FIG. 11.16 Hydrosalpinx. (A) Coronal T2-weighted MR image shows a hyperintense tubular structure (*) in the left adnexa with a small incomplete endosalpingeal fold (arrow) consistent with a hydrosalpinx. The simple fluid within the dilated fallopian tube in this case (*) is hypointense on the corresponding axial T1-weighted fat-suppressed image (B).

endometriomas or retropositioned ovaries allows for improved preoperative planning and hence better patient outcome. Endometriosis may distort pelvic anatomy and lead to functional changes in the tube or uterus that decrease fertility. Surgical intervention for chronic pelvic pain due to DIE may affect ovarian reserve and postsurgical inflammatory changes may have an impact on the ability of the ovum to reach the uterine cavity. Current controversies exist regarding treatment of infertility in the setting of endometriosis however individualized treatment is aided by identifying the extent and spectrum of disease identified on imaging.[31,32]

11.4.1 Tubal causes: tubal occlusion, peritubal adhesions, PID, pyo/hematosalpinx

Tubal pathology is a common cause of infertility in women of childbearing age, representing 30–40% of causes.[8] Abnormalities of the tubes can manifest as irregularities, occlusions or peritubal adhesions with resultant dilated tubes. The latter is an important diagnosis specifically for IVF patients as this may result in a 50% decreased pregnancy rate. Hysterosalpingography is the first-line imaging modality when assessing for tubal patency. Pelvic US is an excellent modality for assessing dilated tubes, although there could be overlapping imaging features between hydrosalpinx and some atypical ovarian cystic lesions. Newer emerging imaging techniques such as HyCoSy, CT virtual HSG, and three-dimensional dynamic MR HSG are all very promising tools in the evaluation of tubal patency.[33–35] HyCoSy is reported to have similar diagnostic accuracy and cost to HSG for tubal patency evaluation without any radiation. In addition, it provides morphologic information about the uterus, endometrium, and adnexae.[36] MR has the added advantage of offering comprehensive imaging of peritubal adhesions which result from pelvic inflammatory disease (PID) and endometriosis, both common causes of female infertility. Unfortunately, infertility complicates PID in up to 50% of cases with up to 80% of women having subclinical PID, resulting in late diagnosis.[37,38] Tubal occlusion at the ampullary portion is commonly due to scarring or peritoneal adhesions, resulting in dilation of the tube proximally. The MR imaging characteristics will depend on the tubal fluid content with simple fluid, pus or blood seen in hydrosalpinx, pyosalpinx, and hematosalpinx respectively. A hydrosalpinx appears as a thin-walled C or S-shaped tubular structure folded on itself, within the adnexa and is hypointense on T1 and hyperintense on T2 weighted sequences (Fig. 11.16). Fallopian tubes contain incomplete internal folds resulting in the classic "cogwheel" appearance of a hydrosalpinx. MR is particularly helpful at distinguishing markedly dilated tubes from cystic ovarian neoplasms which they can sometimes mimic. A pyosalpinx has a thick, enhancing wall with contents of variable signal intensities on T1 and T2 weighted sequences depending on the protein contents and the amount of debris within the tube (Fig. 11.17).[39,40] DW imaging can help differentiate a hydrosalpinx from a pyosalpinx in debatable cases by showing restricted diffusion of the tube contents and its walls in the latter.[38] Hematosalpinx is usually seen in the context of endometriosis and is the result of tubal damage in the form of serosal/subserosal or less commonly intraluminal mucosal isthmic endometrial implants. Repeated hemorrhages of these implants lead to fibrosis/peritubal adhesions and hematosalpinx respectively.[40] These findings are discovered at laparoscopy in 30% of women with endometriosis. On MR, hematosalpinx has a characteristic high signal on T1 fat-suppressed sequences (Fig. 11.18). Its signal on T2 weighted sequences may vary from hyperintense to hypointense and less often with T2 shading considering that the intraluminal type of endometriosis is less common (Fig. 11.19).[41–43]

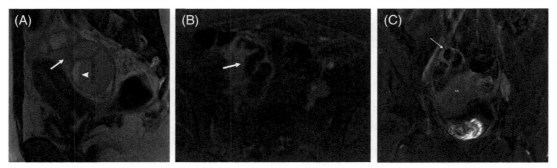

FIG. 11.17   Pyosalpinx in a patient with abdominal pain and fever. (A) Sagittal T2-weighted MR image shows a dilated, mildly thick-walled right fallopian tube containing a fluid-fluid level (arrowhead) with stranding of the adjacent fat (arrow). (B) Axial and coronal gadolinium-enhanced T1-weighted fat-suppressed MR images show diffuse mural enhancement of the thickened tube (arrow), consistent with a pyosalpinx. Ut: uterus.

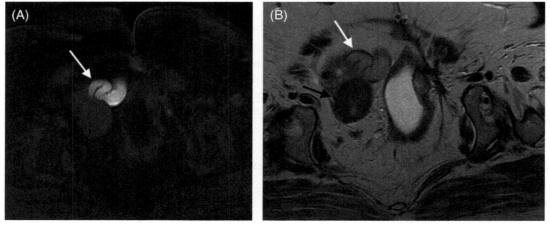

FIG. 11.18   Hematosalpinx. (A) Axial T1-weighted fat-suppressed MR image shows a T1 hyperintense tubular structure within the right adnexa (arrow). This structure is T2 hypointense (white arrow) on the corresponding axial T2-weighted image (B). This patient had a didelphys uterus with the right uterine horn seen in the right adnexa (black arrow).

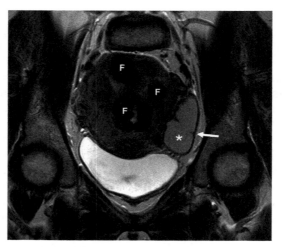

FIG. 11.19   Tubal endometriosis with T2 shading. Coronal T2-weighted MR image in a patient with deep infiltrating endometriosis shows a dilated tubular structure in the left adnexa with incomplete folds (arrow) and T2 shading of the internal contents (*), compatible with tubal endometriosis in this clinical setting. F: fibroids.

11.4.2 Uterine, cervical, and vaginal causes: congenital and acquired

The basis for uterine causes of infertility is impaired implantation of the blastocyst, either due to structural abnormalities or diminished receptivity of the endometrium. Uterine causes of infertility may be congenital or acquired and include MDAs, adenomyosis, endometriosis, fibroids, adhesions, and malignancy. Ovarian and hormonal abnormalities may also contribute to inadequate levels of progesterone needed to stimulate endometrial proliferation and maintenance of an intrauterine pregnancy until the placenta becomes the primary source of progesterone, after 6–8 weeks of gestation.[44]

MDAs are classically divided according to the embryologic stage at which the anomaly is thought to occur: early developmental anomalies causing hypoplasia; fusion anomalies; and resorption anomalies (Table 11.3).[45] The original classification by Buttram and Gibbons in 1979 included six classes of Mullerian duct anomalies and associated five classes of urinary tract anomalies.[46] Congenital uterine anomalies are often one component of a spectrum of anomalies affecting the uterus, cervix, and vagina due to developmental anomalies related to the Mullerian ducts. The incidence of primary infertility may be increased in women with congenital uterine anomalies (9%), however these may be due to nonuterine factors including hormonal or metabolic abnormalities, endometriosis, or tubal factors.[47]

Among the extrauterine anomalies, vaginal hypoplasia often presents first clinically as amenorrhea in an adolescent female and is often associated with other anomalies as part of Mayer-Rokitansky-Küster-Hauser syndrome (MRKHS),

TABLE 11.3 Imaging features and classification of Mullerian duct anomalies (ASRM and CUME).

Embryology	Diagnosis	Imaging Features and Criteria (US and MRI)
Normal	**Normal/arcuate**	ASRM makes no distinction between normal and arcuate
	Fundus	Convex
	Internal indentation	Indentation depth* <1 cm, angle of divergence** >90°
	Cervix	Single
	Vagina	Single
Resorption anomaly class V	**Septate**	
	Fundus	Convex or flat; minimal external indentation <1 cm†
	Internal indentation	Muscular or fibromuscular septum Complete: division to the internal cervical os; partial: above
	ASRM	>1.5 cm, <90°
	CUME	≥1.0 cm, <140°
	Cervix	Single, septate, or double (MICD 5.4 mm)
	Vagina	Single, longitudinal or transverse septum
Fusion anomaly class III–IV	**Bicornuate**	
	Fundus	External indentation >1 cm
	Internal indentation	Muscular or fibromuscular septum Complete: division to the internal cervical os; partial: above
	Cervix	Single (unicollis) Septate (bicollis): septum of variable length (MICD 5.4 mm)
	Vagina	Single, longitudinal or transverse septum
	Didelphys	Two separate uterine cavities with double cervix
	Uterine bodies	May be separated or partially fused with deep external indentation
	Endometrium	No communication between the endometrial cavities
	Cervix	Double (MICD 12.1 mm)
	Vagina	Longitudinal or oblique septum (e.g., OHVIRA)

(Continued)

TABLE 11.3   *(Cont'd)*

Developmental anomaly class I–II	**Unicornuate**	
	Uterine body	Elongated (banana-shaped) and deviated to the right or left pelvis
		Isolated (35%), or with rudimentary horn (noncavitary 33%, cavitary noncommunicating 22%, cavitary communicating 10%)
	Cervix	Single
	Vagina	Single
	Associations	Renal agenesis on the same side as absent or rudimentary horn
	Hypoplasia or agenesis	MRKH syndrome or vaginal agenesis
	Uterine body	Unilateral or bilateral rudimentary horns (92%), or absent
		Rudimentary horns often connected by low signal fibrous bands (48%)
	Endometrium	Variable 3-layer differentiation (1 > 2 > 3 layers)
	Cervix	Absent, or replaced by triangular soft tissue
	Vagina	Hypoplastic or absent; rectovaginal septum may be visible
	Ovaries	Abnormal location (40%); cephalad relationship to rudimentary uteri

US and MRI criteria from the ASRM and CUME guidelines.

External indentation is the depth from a line connecting the apex of the right and left uterine horns to the lowest point of the indentation of the uterine fundus in the midline.

*Internal indentation is the depth from the interstitial line to the lowest point of the indentation of the uterine cavities.

**Angle of indentation or divergence is the angle formed by the apex of the endometrial cavity and the interstitial line.

†Inclusion of uteri with minimal external fundal indentation < 1 cm as septate is controversial; this morphology has been referred to as a combined fusion/resorption anomaly.

ASRM, American Society for Reproductive Medicine Classification System; *CUME*, Congenital Uterine Malformation by Experts Classification; *ESHRE/ESGE*, European Society of Human Reproduction and Embryology-European Society for Gynaecological Endoscopy Classification; *MICD*, mean intercervical distance.

References:

– Practice Committee of the American Society for Reproductive Medicine. Uterine septum: a guideline. Fertil Steril. 2016.

– Ludwin *et al*. Congenital Uterine Malformation by Experts (CUME): better criteria for distinguishing between normal/arcuate and septate uterus? Ultrasound Obstet Gynecol. 2018. Jan;51(1):101-109

– Sugi *et al*. Müllerian duct anomalies: role in fertility and pregnancy. Radiographics. 2021 Oct; 41(6):1857-1875.

also known as Mullerian agenesis (Fig. 11.20). This term is somewhat of a misnomer as the anomalies that characterize this syndrome are often related to hypoplasia rather than true agenesis. Axial nonfat-saturated, T2-weighted sequences are useful for evaluating the degree of hypoplasia or aplasia of the vagina, which is often replaced by fibrofatty tissue across a variable length of the lower vagina and may involve the entire vagina. The normal, collapsed vagina on axial T2-weighted images assumes a "W" or "H" morphology owing to the increased tensile strength of the lateral walls of the vagina relative to the anteroposterior walls. This results in a characteristic appearance on axial T2-weighted images in which the hyperintense vaginal mucosa is outlined by a T2 hypointense rim (Fig. 11.21). On sagittal T2-weighted images, a low signal fibrous rectovaginal septum may be evident between the bladder and expected location of the vagina in patients with vaginal hypoplasia.[48] Vaginal dilation is a therapeutic option for patients with MRKHS that aims to restore the vaginal cavity to allow for normal sexual activity. This syndrome is associated with hypoplasia of the uterus, most often rudimentary uteri (92% of cases), which are usually bilateral and can have varying degrees of differentiation into more than one layer.[49] The rudimentary uteri classically assume a caudal relationship to the ovaries in this condition, which is particularly helpful for localization as the ovaries are often positioned outside of their normal location in the pelvis (Fig. 11.22).[49] When functional endometrial tissue is present, the rudimentary uterus can be a cause of pain and is associated with increased risk for adenomyosis, endometriosis, and hematometra. Rudimentary horns (RH) may also be present in the setting of a unicornuate uterus (class II anomaly), and may be cavitary (containing functional endometrial tissue) or noncavitary, and communicating (uterine cavity communicates with that of the unicornuate uterus) or

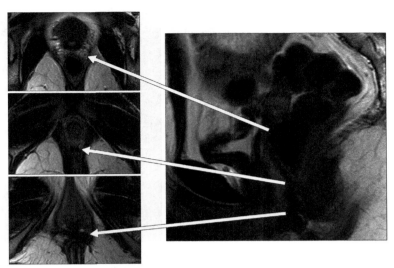

FIG. 11.20 **Hypoplasia of the upper two-thirds of the vagina in a patient with Müllerian agenesis/hypogenesis, or Mayer-Rokitansky-Küster-Hauser syndrome (MRKHS).** Axial T2-weighted MR images (left) of the upper, mid, and lower vagina corresponding to different levels of the vagina on the sagittal T2-weighted MR image (right). Patients with MRKH have variable degrees of vaginal hypoplasia. In patients with true vaginal agenesis, two-thirds will have a rectovaginal septum that appears as a distinct layer between the bladder and rectum.

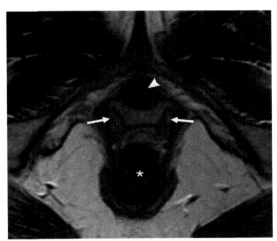

FIG. 11.21 **Normal appearance of the lower vagina.** Axial T2-weighted MR image shows the normal low signal appearance of the collapsed vagina, which forms a characteristic "H" (or "W") shape due to increased tensile strength of the lateral walls (arrows) compared to the anterior/posterior walls. Note the rectum posteriorly (*) and urethra (arrowhead) anteriorly.

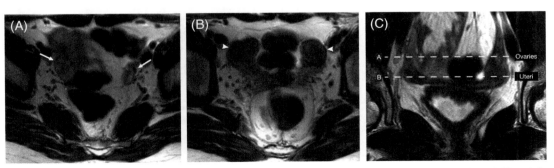

FIG. 11.22 **Rudimentary uteri and their caudal relationship to the ovaries in MRKHS.** (A and B) Sequential axial T2-weighted MR images from cranial to caudal show the bilateral ovaries (arrows) positioned cephalad to the rudimentary uteri (arrowheads). (C) Coronal T2-weighted MR image shows this relationship to better advantage, which is constant for patients with MRKHS and can be useful for locating the ovaries or rudimentary uteri, particularly when positioned outside of their expected locations in the pelvis.

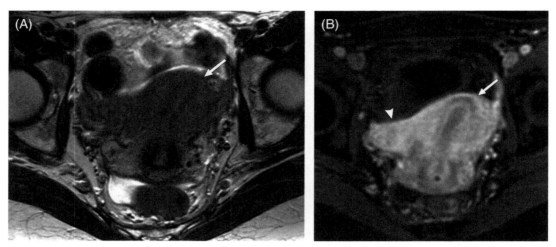

FIG. 11.23   **Unicornuate uterus with noncavitary right rudimentary horn.** (A and B) Axial T2-weighted (A) and gadolinium-enhanced T1-weighted fat-suppressed (B) MR images show the "banana-shaped" unicornuate uterus (arrows) deviated to the left pelvis. A noncavitary right rudimentary horn is better seen on the gadolinium-enhanced image (arrowhead).

noncommunicating (Fig. 11.23).[50,51] The most common type of unicornuate uterus is the isolated variant in which no RH is present, accounting for 35% of cases.[50] The diagnosis of unicornuate uterus can be suggested at HSG by fusiform opacification of the uterine cavity deviated to one side of the pelvis in a "banana shape" and opacification of a single fallopian tube. MRI should be performed for further characterization to determine whether a RH is present, as both noncavitary and noncommunicating horns will not opacify at HSG (Fig. 11.24). Since the RH results from a partial fusion anomaly, the uterine cavity of the dominant horn may be more medial than that seen in a simple unicornuate uterus without RH.[51] The presence of cavitation on MRI is suggested by linear increased T2 signal within the RH, however variable signal intensity may be present if there is sufficient functional endometrial tissue to cause hematometra, in which case the rudimentary uterine cavity may be expanded by low T2 signal blood products. A centrally necrotic fibroid with central T2 hyperintensity may mimic a cavitary RH.[52] Urinary tract anomalies such as renal agenesis are common and almost always occur ipsilateral to the absent or RH.[51] From a fertility standpoint, recognition of a unicornuate uterus has implications for management of tubal ectopic pregnancy as salvage of the solitary fallopian tube may be especially important.

Uterus didelphys and bicornuate uterus (class III and IV anomalies, respectively) are fusion anomalies associated with increased risk for preterm delivery and fetal malpresentation, but not directly associated with infertility.[53] These anomalies are grouped together under the European Society of Human Reproduction and Embryology (ESHRE) and the European Society for Gynecological Endoscopy (ESGE) classification as class U3 "bicorporeal uterus," which includes a bicorporeal septate anomaly that incorporates features of both fusion and resorption anomalies.[54] By ASRM criteria, uterus didelphys

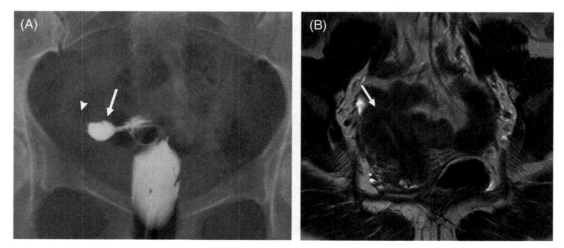

FIG. 11.24   **Isolated unicornuate uterus at HSG and MRI in a 38-year-old woman with successful pregnancy following HSG.** (A) AP radiograph of the pelvis acquired during HSG shows opacification of the uterine cavity (arrow), deviated to the right pelvis, and opacification of a single fallopian tube (arrowhead). (B) Axial oblique T2-weighted MR image shows the right unicornuate uterus (arrow). Although dedicated abdominal images were not acquired, left-sided renal agenesis (ipsilateral to the side of the absent left horn) was evident on the scout sequence.

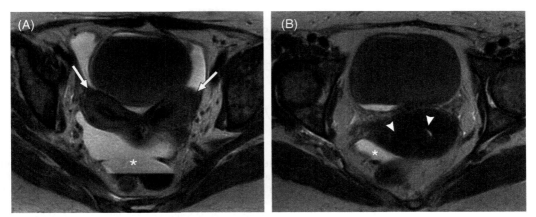

FIG. 11.25   Uterus didelphys and left renal agenesis in a 38-year-old woman. (A and B) Axial T2-weighted MR images show two separate uterine bodies (arrows) converging in the midline at the level of the cervix, which is duplicated with two distinct cervical canals (arrowheads). Incidental note of free fluid (*) and small layering hemoperitoneum due to a ruptured hemorrhagic cyst. Low signal in the bladder is due to gadolinium contrast excretion. (C) Coronal T2-weighted MR image shows an empty left renal fossa (*) with lying down adrenal gland (arrowhead) consistent with left renal agenesis and compensatory hypertrophy of the right kidney (arrow).

is defined as two separate uterine cavities with duplication of the cervix, often associated with a longitudinal vaginal septum (Fig. 11.25). On MRI, both uterus didelphys and bicornuate uterus are defined by an external fundal indentation >10 mm, which is best seen on T2-weighted coronal oblique views of the uterus. The uterine corpi are widely divergent in uterus didelphys, to a lesser degree in bicornuate uterus, with normal zonal anatomy.[55] Unlike uterus didelphys, bicornuate uterus may be partial or complete depending on whether or not the muscular or fibromuscular septum divides the uterine cavities above or to the level of the internal cervical os, respectively. In cases in which a septum divides the cervix and/or vagina, bicornuate uterus may be indistinguishable from uterus didelphys by imaging.

The most common congenital uterine anomaly is septate uterus (class V anomaly), accounting for more than half of MDAs.[56] Women with infertility have a higher incidence of septate uterus, however the role of the septum as a cause for infertility has not been proven and the role for intervention, if any, is controversial.[57] The proposed pathophysiology of infertility in the setting of a uterine septum is based on the idea that implantation of the blastocyst at this site incurs variable risks for reproductive waste.[58,59] This is thought to be related in part to the composition and vascularity of the septum, which can be muscular and highly vascularized, appearing as V-shaped internal myometrial indentation on the uterine cavity, or fibrous and relatively avascular, appearing as a linear band of low signal tissue on MRI extending caudally from the top of the uterine cavity (Fig. 11.26). In practice, a combination of muscular and fibrous components (i.e., fibromuscular septum) is often seen. Abnormalities of the endometrium overlying the septum including decreased number of glandular cells may also impair implantation.[59,60] Based on

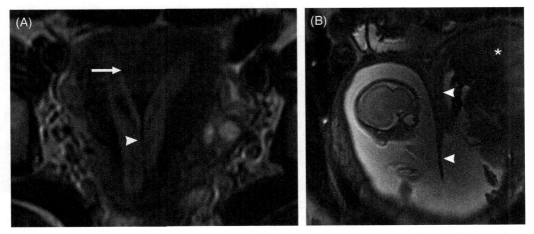

FIG. 11.26   Imaging appearance of various compositions of the uterine septum. (A) Axial T2-weighted MR image shows a septate uterus with a prominent muscular septum (arrow) causing internal indentation of the uterine cavity with a fibrous septum extending through the mid uterus to the level of the cervix (arrowhead). (B) Coronal T2-weighted MR image in a different patient with an incomplete fibromuscular septum (arrowheads), which is readily apparent due to the surrounding amniotic fluid in this pregnant patient. Note the placenta (*).

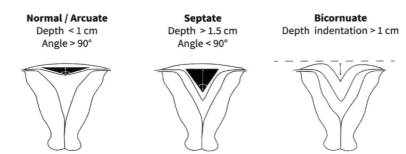

Normal / Arcuate
Depth < 1 cm
Angle > 90°

Septate
Depth > 1.5 cm
Angle < 90°

Bicornuate
Depth indentation > 1 cm

FIG. 11.27   American Society of Reproductive Medicine (ASRM) 2016 guideline definitions of normal/arcuate, septate, and bicornuate uterus. In this guideline, no differentiation is made between normal and arcuate uterus, which is defined by a depth of internal indentation <1 cm and angle >90°. Septate is defined by depth of internal indentation >1.5 cm and angle <90°. Bicornuate is defined by depth of external or fundal indentation >1 cm.
Adapted from Fig. 11.1, Mullerian Anomalies published in ASRM's Practice Guideline: Uterine Septum a Guideline, copyrighted by ASRM 2016.

updated 2016 guidelines, however, the ASRM suggests that there is insufficient evidence to conclude that a uterine septum is associated with infertility.[57] Septate uterus is the result of partial or complete failure of resorption of the septum around the 20th week of gestation. In order to define the length of the septum and make this diagnosis using either coronal T2-weighted MRI or 3D sonography, certain landmarks are first defined. The interstitial line is a horizontal line drawn between the interstitial segments of the fallopian tubes. The length of the septum is defined by a vertical line drawn from the interstitial line to the apex of the internal indentation of the uterine cavity (i.e., the top of the uterine cavity in the midline). By ASRM criteria, septate uterus is defined by a septum measuring >1.5 cm and angle of internal indentation measuring <90° (Fig. 11.27). Complete septate uterus refers to a septum that extends from the top of the interstitial line to the level of the internal cervical os, whereas partial septate (or subseptate) uterus refers to a septum that terminates above the level of the internal cervical os (Fig. 11.28). The septum may extend into the cervix and/or vagina. When the septum extends through the full length of the cervix, the cervix assumes the appearance of a "double cervix" on axial or coronal MRI, i.e. two separate cervical canals are present. Septate uterus is at least as common as uterus didelphys in patients with a double cervix due to the higher prevalence of septate uterus among MDAs, although the cervical canals tend to be spaced farther apart in the axial plane in association

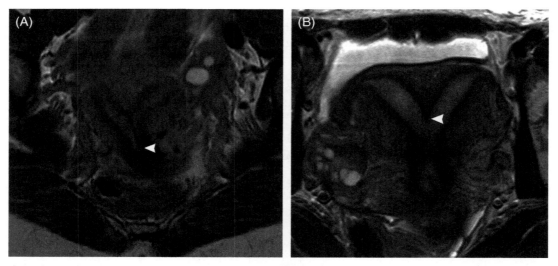

FIG. 11.28   **Complete and partial septate uteri.** (A) Axial T2-weighted MR image shows a complete septate uterus with a fibromuscular septum extending to the level of the internal cervical os (arrowhead). The septum may extend through the cervix and/or vagina. (B) Axial T2-weighted MR image shows a partial septate (subseptate) uterus with a predominantly muscular septum terminating in the mid uterine body (arrowhead) with fusion of the uterine cavities in the lower uterus.

with uterus didelphys (12 mm) compared to those associated with septate uterus (5 mm) (Fig. 11.29).[61] Recognition of a double cervix is important in patients seeking assisted reproduction with techniques such as intrauterine insemination (IUI). In this procedure, sperm is injected via a catheter placed into the uterus typically one day following the luteinizing hormone surge, indicative of ovulation.[62] In patients with unrecognized MDAs including a double cervix, supplementing this procedure with transabdominal sonography allows for identification of the side of ovulation and placement of the catheter in the ipsilateral uterine cavity. This is particularly relevant for patients with an incomplete cervical septum that is not evident on speculum exam, but that could result in inadvertent sperm insemination in the uterine cavity contralateral to the side of ovulation.[63]

Outside of assisted reproductive technologies, the importance of a longitudinal septum extending to the cervix and vagina may have less relevance for infertility.[64] In a study of 67 women with complete septate uterus including the cervix and longitudinal vaginal septum, Heinonen found no association with primary infertility and a live birth rate of 72% in the cohort of women not undergoing metroplasty.[65] Vaginal septa may be longitudinal or transverse and are best visualized on coronal or sagittal T2-weighted MRI sequences oriented to the vaginal canal as linear, low signal bands of tissue. An important variation of vaginal septum orientation is seen in cases of obstructive hemivagina ipsilateral renal anomaly (OHVIRA, also known as Herlyn-Werner-Wunderlich syndrome), a potential

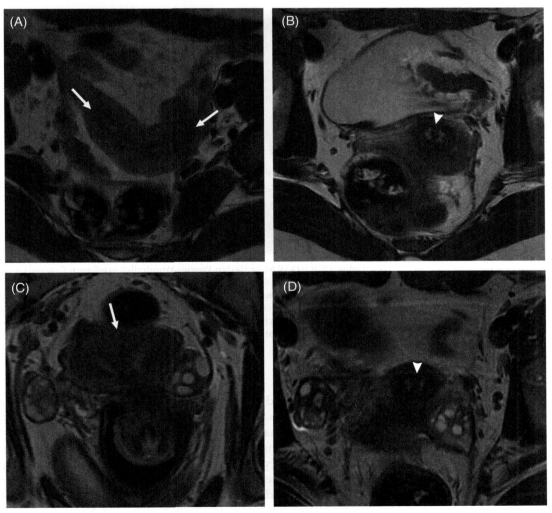

FIG. 11.29 **Septate cervix associated with fusion and resorption congenital uterine anomalies.** (A and B) Axial T2-weighted MR images show a Müllerian duct anomaly along the spectrum of fusion anomalies (i.e., bicornuate to didelphys) with incompletely fused uterine bodies (arrows) and a septate cervix (arrowhead). (C and D) Coronal oblique T2-weighted MR images in a different patient with septate uterus show a flattened fundal contour (arrow) and septate cervix divided centrally by a fibrous septum (arrowhead). Compare these to the duplicated cervix associated with uterus didelphys in Fig. 11.24B.

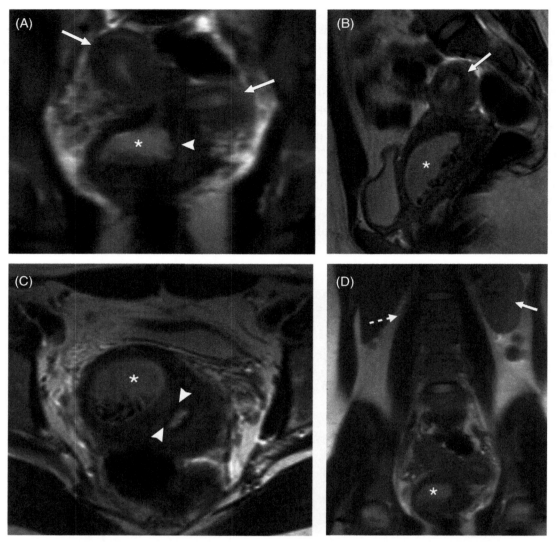

FIG. 11.30   Obstructed hemivagina ipsilateral renal anomaly (OHVIRA), or Herlyn-Werner-Wunderlich syndrome. Coronal (A), sagittal (B), and axial (C) T2-weighted MR images show uterus didelphys with separated uterine bodies (arrows), two cervices, and a longitudinal vaginal septum (arrowheads) dividing the vagina. The fluid-filled, distended right hemivagina (*) shows evidence of chronic obstruction with layering debris. At surgery, a bulge against the medial wall of the left vagina was seen and a 4 cm septum was excised to the level of the cervix, yielding yellowish fluid from the obstructed side. (D) Wide-field coronal T2-weighted MR image including the upper abdomen shows a left kidney (arrow) and empty right renal fossa (dashed arrow) in keeping with hypoplasia or agenesis ipsilateral to the side of the obstructed hemivagina (*).

cause of lower abdominal or pelvic pain in females around the time of menarche. In patients with this association, a longitudinal oblique vaginal septum divides the vagina and obstructs one side in association with a uterine anomaly such as uterus didelphys.[66] Since one vaginal canal communicating with the uterine cavity remains open, the hematocolpos or hematometrocolpos that occurs during menses on the completely or partially obstructed side may be clinically occult. Detection of this condition often begins clinically with identification of a bulge in the medial wall of the patent vaginal canal. On MRI, this physical exam finding corresponds to an ovoid, intrinsically T1 hyperintense hemorrhagic fluid collection in the obstructed hemivagina (Fig. 11.30).[67] These patients typically have renal dysplasia, atrophy, or agenesis ipsilateral to the side of obstruction, which may also be associated with an ectopic ureter draining to the obstructed hemivagina.[66] For this reason, limited T2-weighted or delayed post gadolinium-enhanced T1-weighted imaging of the abdomen may be of use to assess for upper urinary tract anomalies. Renal scintigraphy using technetium-99m dimercaptosuccinic acid (DMSA) may also be used to localize the atrophic kidney.

MRI provides additional value for the evaluation of patients with conditions such as OHVIRA or other congenital anomalies of the female genital tract that have undergone intervention, given the complexity of the postsurgical anatomy. There is a reported 15–20% risk of recurrence following vaginoscopic resection of a vaginal septum due to fibrosis and adhesions.[68]

11.4.3 Abnormalities of the myometrium and endometrium

Abnormalities of the uterine parenchyma and endometrium impact fertility predominantly via their effects on implantation or embryo transfer, including extrinsic mass effect on the fallopian tubes or cervix. Myometrial abnormalities include adenomyosis and fibroids, which may contain submucosal or intracavitary components that can be readily assessed on MRI. Endometrial abnormalities include atrophy/hyperplasia, polyps, and synechia.

Adenomyosis is characterized by the presence of ectopic endometrial tissue within the myometrium, causing reactive changes in the myometrium including hypertrophy and hyperplasia. MRI has a reported diagnostic accuracy for adenomyosis of 85% using a thickness >12 mm for the junctional zone, which represents a distinct low signal layer of inner myometrium on T2-weighted sequences (Fig. 11.31).[69] The junctional zone is best visualized and measured in the sagittal plane. It is contiguous with the low signal inner fibromuscular stromal layer of the cervix and is distinct from the intermediate signal outer myometrium and high signal endometrium.[70] Other signs on MRI include subendometrial/myometrial microcystic changes, globular enlargement of the uterus and T2 hyperintense linear striations radiating from the endometrium into the myometrium, known as "pseudowidening of the endometrium" (Fig. 11.32).[69] Adenomyosis may be diffuse or focal, or may manifest as a distinct adenomyoma (Fig. 11.33). An adenomyoma appears as a mass in the myometrium with overall low T2 signal intensity and scattered internal foci of high signal intensity. It may mimic a fibroid but is typically not associated with the peripheral hypervascularity seen with fibroids and is often relatively less circumscribed. Unlike more aggressive neoplasms such as sarcomas, adenomyomas are associated with low signal intensity on diffusion-weighted imaging.[71] Atypical polypoid adenomyoma is a rare tumor containing atypical endometrial glands that is rarely associated with endometrial adenocarcinoma. The tumor is usually rounded and circumscribed with heterogeneous but overall slightly increased T2 signal intensity, irregular enhancement, and demonstrates increased radiotracer uptake on ^{18}F-FDG PET/CT (Fig. 11.34).[72,73] Mimics of adenomyosis include myometrial contractions, which can be identified based on changes in the morphology of the uterus on different sequences of the exam over time. Surgical excision of focal adenomyosis may result in morphologic distortion of the uterus that can persist and may even be exacerbated in

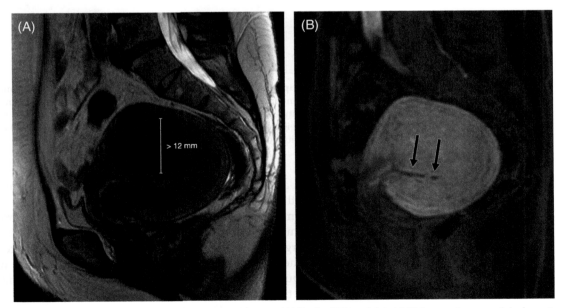

FIG. 11.31 **Adenomyosis with thickening of the junctional zone.** (A) Sagittal T2-weighted MR image shows a globular, retroflexed uterus with marked and diffuse thickening of the junctional zone (>12 mm), which has a diagnostic accuracy of 85% for adenomyosis. (B) Corresponding sagittal gadolinium-enhanced T1-weighted MR image shows the hypoenhancing endometrium (arrows) to better advantage.

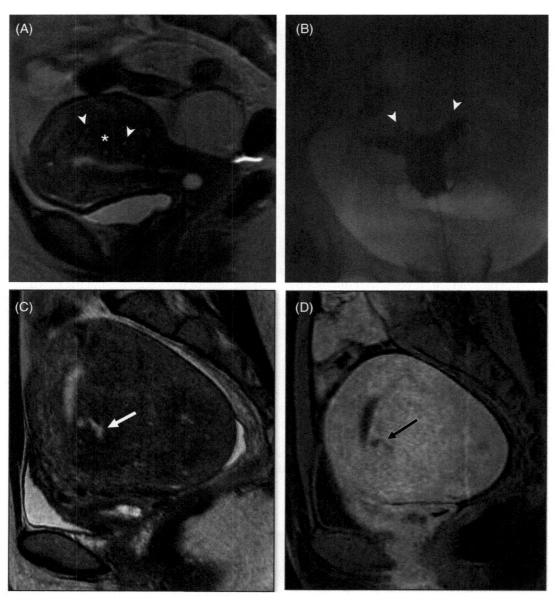

FIG. 11.32   Signs of adenomyosis on MRI and hysterosalpingography (HSG). (A) Sagittal T2-weighted MR image shows asymmetric thickening of the posterior junctional zone (*) with subendometrial and myometrial cystic change (arrowheads). (B) Fluoroscopic image acquired during HSG in the same patient shows irregularity of the uterine cavity with outpouchings of contrast extending into the myometrium (arrowheads) compatible with diffuse adenomyosis. (C and D) Sagittal T2-weighted (C) and sagittal gadolinium-enhanced T1-weighted fat-suppressed (D) MR images show glandular tracts invaginating into the myometrium (arrows) in another patient with adenomyosis.

pregnancy (Fig. 11.35). Uterine artery embolization has also been used to treat adenomyosis with close to 90% of patients reporting improvement in symptoms at 3 months in one case series by Kitamura et al.[74]

Uterine fibroids, also known as leiomyomas or myomas, are benign tumors comprised of smooth muscle cells and fibroblasts of the myometrium and are the most common tumors in the female pelvis. Fibroids are hormonally dependent on estrogen and progesterone and may undergo gradual growth in the reproductive years, often plateauing or decreasing in size at menopause. In addition to the previously discussed causes of infertility due to obstruction of the tubal ostia, other theories for fibroid contribution to subfertility include abnormal vascularization and effects on the endometrium, increased uterine contractility, and chronic inflammation.[75] A proposed consensus system for the nomenclature of fibroids was proposed by the International Federation of Gynecology and Obstetrics (FIGO) in 2011.[76] This system was devised with abnormal causes of uterine bleeding in reproductive females in mind, thus the classification gives special attention to submucosal involvement, including pedunculated intracavitary

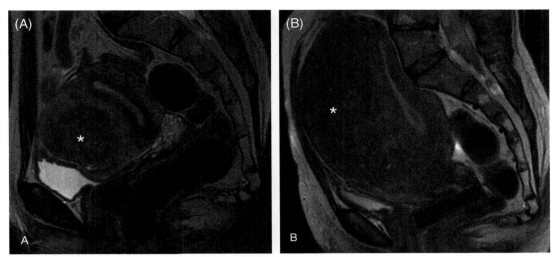

FIG. 11.33 **Progression of focal adenomyosis over time.** (A and B) Sagittal T2-weighted MR images in the same patient show focal adenomyosis involving the anterior myometrium (*) characterized by low T2 signal and scattered cystic change on initial MRI exam (A) and follow-up exam 6 years later (B). Both the uterine size and degree of myometrial involvement increased significantly between the two studies.

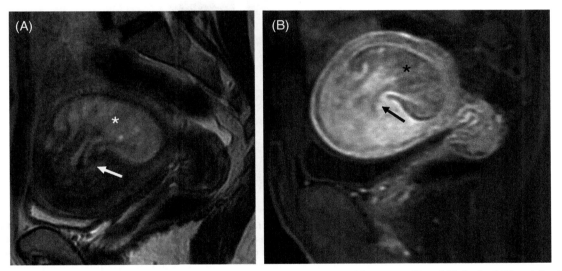

FIG. 11.34 **Polypoid adenomyoma mimicking uterine malignancy in a 34-year-old woman.** (A and B) Sagittal T2-weighted and sagittal gadolinium-enhanced T1-weighted fat-suppressed (B) MR images show an irregularly enhancing polypoid mass in the uterine cavity (*) with a stalk arising from the anterior myometrium (arrow), where there is low T2 signal with cystic change compatible with adenomyosis. (B) Surgical pathology showed features of polypoid adenoma without evidence of atypia or malignancy.

fibroids and submucosal fibroids with less than or greater than 50% intramural components (Fig. 11.36). The degree of submucosal and intramural extension can be delineated on T2-weighted imaging by assessing the relationship between the hyperintense endometrium and hypointense fibroid using methods adapted from the sonohysterography literature or by calculating the so-called interface-dimension ratio.[77-79] The first method involves measuring the diameter of the fibroid that protrudes into the uterine cavity and dividing it by the total diameter of the fibroid in the same plane (Fig. 11.37).[78] The second method is derived from the interventional radiology literature and involves measuring the length of the interface between the fibroid and endometrium, and dividing this number by the maximum diameter of the fibroid (Fig. 11.37).[79] Identification of a vascular stalk on MRI can assist with surgical planning for hysteroscopic resection.[80] Other FIGO descriptors include intramural, subserosal, pedunculated, and other (cervical, parasitic).[76] On MRI, fibroids typically demonstrate homogeneous low T2 signal with a cobblestone appearance (Fig. 11.38). Signal intensity on T1- and T2-weighted images can vary in the setting of degeneration,

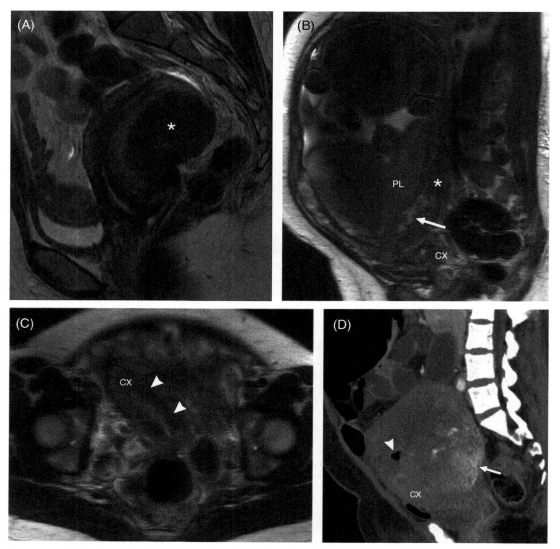

FIG. 11.35 **Postsurgical distortion of the uterus in a pregnant patient following excision of adenomyoma in a 35-year-old woman with recurrent pregnancy loss.** (A) Sagittal T2-weighted MR image shows acute retroflexion of the uterus due to a relatively circumscribed adenomyoma in the posterior uterus (*). The patient underwent surgical excision of this area and subsequently became pregnant. (B and C) Sagittal (B) and axial (C) T2-weighted MR images at 30 weeks' gestation shows myometrial vascular engorgement (arrow) underlying the placenta (PL) with persistent low signal changes in the posterior myometrium (*). The cervix (CX) is abnormally angulated to the right (arrowheads) due to architectural distortion from the adenomyoma and prior surgery. (D) Sagittal contrast-enhanced CT image performed for postpartum abdominal distention shows postsurgical changes of cesarean section with persistent retroflexion of the uterus relative to the cervix (CX) and hypervascularity of the myometrium at the site of the prior adenomyoma (arrow). Note small postsurgical gas in the uterine cavity (arrowhead). Malposition of the cervix led to the diagnosis of residual focal adenomyosis and the retroflexed orientation of the gravid uterus. It is important to recognize this configuration prior to cesarean section to prevent inadvertent incision into the cervix, which would be an obstetrical emergency.

necrosis, and calcification (Fig. 11.39). Enhancement is variable and characterized on dynamic, gadolinium-enhanced T1-weighted imaging, which provides valuable information for patients that may be candidates for therapeutic uterine artery embolization (UAE). Submucosal fibroids with an interface-dimension ratio >0.55 are at risk for intra-cavitary extension and spontaneous expulsion following UAE.[79] Submucosal fibroids may also prolapse into the endocervical canal and/or vagina in the absence of therapeutic interventions and are typically associated with a vascular stalk extending from the myometrium, distinguishing them from intrinsic cervical fibroids (Fig. 11.40). Imaging features that suggest malignancy include high b-1000 signal intensity, lower mean apparent diffusion coefficient (ADC of 0.978×10^{-3} mm^2/s), and intermediate T2 signal intensity.[80,81] These criteria along with higher patient

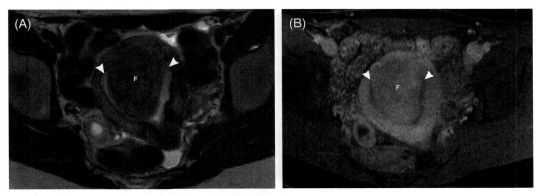

FIG. 11.36 Pedunculated intracavitary fibroid (FIGO 0). (A and B) Axial T2-weighted (A) and axial gadolinium-enhanced T1-weighted fat-suppressed (B) MR images show an intracavitary fibroid (F), which is well-delineated by the surrounding T2 hyperintense, hypoenhancing endometrium (arrowheads).

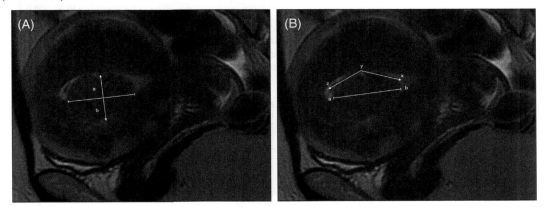

FIG. 11.37 Methods to measure the submucosal component of a fibroid. (A) Sagittal T2-weighted MR image shows an intramural fibroid with submucosal component. Using the method by Mavrelos et al. (Ultrasound Obstet Gynecol 2011), the submucosal fibroid protrusion ratio is calculated by $(a/(a+b)) \times 100$, in this case approximately 50%. Fibroids with less than 50% submucosal component have a higher risk of incomplete hysteroscopic resection. (B) Sagittal T2-weighted MR image in the same patient using the interface method by Verma et al. (AJR 2008). The interface of the fibroid with the endometrium $(xy + yz = xz)$ and maximum submucosal fibroid dimension (ab) are measured to calculate an interface-dimension ratio: (xz/ab).

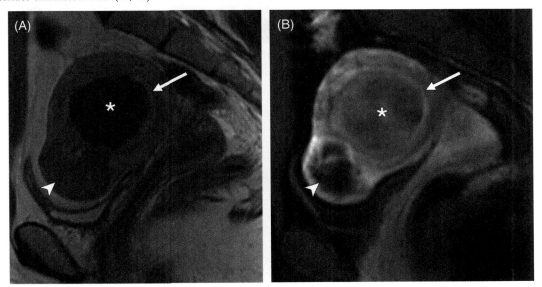

FIG. 11.38 Fibroid appearance on T2- and T1-weighted imaging in a 39-year-old woman with abnormal uterine bleeding. (A and B) Sagittal T2-weighted (A) and gadolinium-enhanced T1-weighted fat-suppressed (B) MR images shows a homogeneously T2 hypointense, heterogeneously enhancing intracavitary fibroid (*) with a thin rim of T2 hyperintense, enhancing endometrium (arrows). A centrally hypovascular subserosal fibroid is also present at the anterior fundus (arrowheads).

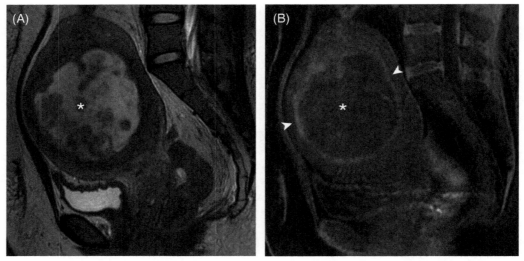

FIG. 11.39 **Carneous degeneration of a fibroid in a 31-year-old postpartum woman.** (A and B) Sagittal T2-weighted (A) and T1-weighted fat-suppressed (B) MR images shows an intramural fibroid (*) with variable T2 signal intensity and a rim of T1 hyperintensity (arrowheads), which is thought to represent hemorrhagic blood products confined to vessels surrounding the fibroid. Carneous degeneration is the most common form of fibroid degeneration during pregnancy.

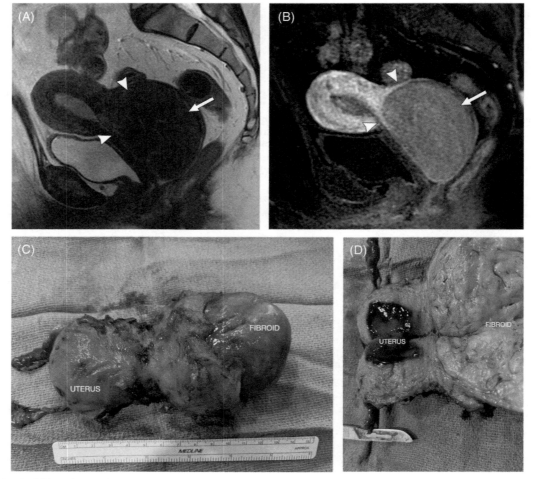

FIG. 11.40 **Cervical fibroid.** (A and B) Sagittal T2-weighted (A) and gadolinium-enhanced T1-weighted fat-suppressed (B) MR images show a homogeneously T2 hypointense, relatively hypoenhancing mass centered in the posterior lip of the cervix (arrows). A claw sign (arrowheads) is better seen on the postcontrast image and helps to differentiate this cervical fibroid from a prolapsed uterine fibroid in the endocervix. (C and D) Gross pathology specimens following elective hysterectomy show the large size of the fibroid relative to the uterus.

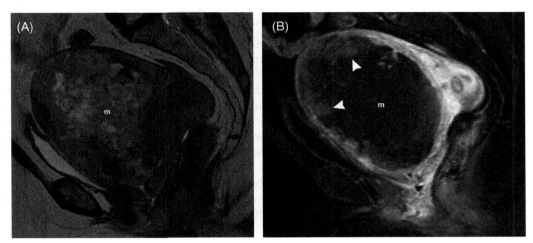

FIG. 11.41   Leiomyosarcoma. (A and B) Sagittal T2-weighted (A) and gadolinium-enhanced T1-weighted fat-suppressed (B) MR images show a heterogeneous mass (m) in the anterior uterus with solid areas of internal enhancement (arrowheads). Surgical pathology following hysterectomy showed an 18 cm leiomyosarcoma with lymphovascular invasion. Degenerating fibroids can mimic leiomyosarcoma, however growth in the postmenopausal state or invasion of adjacent structures should raise suspicion for malignancy.

age (mean 57 years) correctly classified benign and malignant lesions 92% of the time in one case series by Thomassin-Naggara et al. (Fig. 11.41).[81]

Assessing the endometrium on MRI, as with ultrasound, relies on recognizing the patient's phase of menstrual cycle. The normal endometrium is uniform in thickness and demonstrates homogeneous high signal intensity on T2-weighted imaging, with greater signal in the proliferative phase than in the luteal phase of the cycle. This distinction is important as endometrial lesions often appear as intermediate or low signal intensity masses within the uterine cavity and may be more readily differentiated during the proliferative phase.[82] Diffusion-weighted imaging and associated ADC values have some role in endometrial malignancy for predicting tumor grade, however physiologic variation in ADC values both spatially (lower uterus versus fundus) and temporally across phases of the menstrual cycle has been shown.[83,84] Endometrial polyps are caused by hyperplasia of endometrial glands and stroma around a central fibrovascular core and may be sessile or pedunculated. Patients with prior tamoxifen use, obesity, and hormone replacement therapy are at increased risk for developing polyps. A central fibrous core characterized by low signal intensity on T2-weighted imaging and high signal intralesional cysts may help to identify a polyp and distinguish it from endometrial carcinoma (Fig. 11.42).[85] Features more suggestive of polypoid adenomyoma or endometrial carcinoma include myometrial invasion, intratumoral hemorrhage, and necrosis.[86]

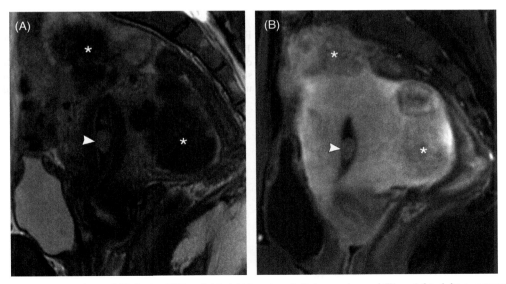

FIG. 11.42   Endometrial polyp. (A and B) Sagittal T2-weighted (A) and gadolinium-enhanced T1-weighted fat-suppressed (B) MR images show an enhancing polypoid lesion in the endometrium with heterogeneous low T2 signal centrally (arrowheads), consistent with an endometrial polyp. The uterus is myomatous with multiple intramural and subserosal fibroids, which show mildly heterogeneous enhancement (*).

11.4.4 Uterine pathology due to infection, inflammation, or intervention

Prior infection, inflammation, or surgery can lead to synechiae or adhesions within the uterine cavity that may have implications for fertility. When these adhesions are symptomatic, the condition is referred to as Asherman syndrome. Most adhesions occur following dilatation and curettage (90%), while others develop following myomectomy, cesarean section, or episodes of pelvic inflammatory disease.[87] Saline-infused sonohysterography (SIS) is the most sensitive modality for detecting intrauterine adhesions since distention of the uterine cavity allows for optimal visualization of synechiae, which are characterized by thin, sometimes irregular echogenic bands crossing the uterine cavity between the basal layers of the endometrium. In the absence of distention, MRI is less sensitive for diagnosis, however the synechiae may become evident following successful pregnancy as linear T2 hypointense bands extending across the amniotic sac (Fig. 11.43). These synechiae are usually not clinically significant for the fetus and are an entirely different entity from the intra-amniotic bands that cause fetal limb deformities in amniotic band syndrome.

Isthmocele is a fluid collection located at the site of a cesarean section scar and may contain blood products of varying ages due to retention of blood during menses (Fig. 11.44). This may interfere with sperm transport into the uterus by

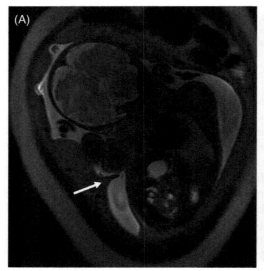
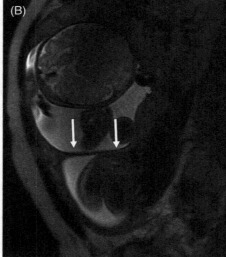

FIG. 11.43 Uterine synechiae during pregnancy. (A and B) Coronal (A) and sagittal (B) T2-weighted MR images of a gravid uterus show a thin fibrous band (arrows) that extends across the uterus outside of the amniotic sac, consistent with a uterine synechia.

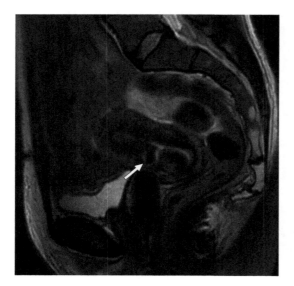

FIG. 11.44 Isthmocele status post cesarean section. Sagittal T2-weighted MR image in a patient post cesarean section shows a focal defect in the anterior lower uterus (arrow), which is filled with low signal blood products. Isthmoceles may act as reservoirs for blood products that contribute to abnormal intermenstrual bleeding.

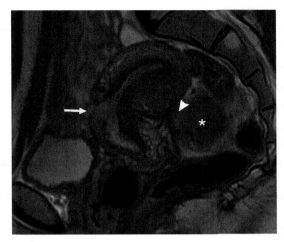

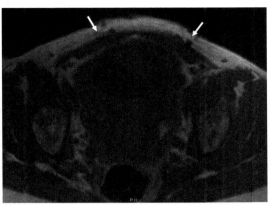

FIG. 11.45   Anteverted, retroflexed uterus in a patient post cesarean section with isthmocele and deep infiltrating endometriosis. Sagittal T2-weighted MR image shows the anteverted (cervix relative to vagina), retroflexed (uterus relative to cervix) orientation with a focal defect in the anterior lower uterus consistent with an isthmocele (arrow). While more than a quarter of patients following cesarean section have this uterine orientation, the uterus in this patient is also retroflexed due to focal tethering at the torus uterinus by an endometriotic implant (arrowhead), which also causes medialization of an endometrioma in the cul-de-sac (*).

FIG. 11.46   Postsurgical changes evidenced by blooming artifact on in-phase chemical shift MRI. Axial T1-weighted in-phase image shows blooming artifact at the site of a prior cesarean section. Identification of the prior incision site can be useful for evaluating areas at increased risk for placenta accreta spectrum disorder.

altering the constitution of the cervical mucous.[88] Sagittal T2-weighted images of the uterus show focal myometrial thinning at the site of the cesarean section scar with low or heterogeneous signal intensity fluid within the scar niche. The fluid may show increased signal intensity on T1-weighted images due to blood products. A characteristic orientation of the uterus following cesarean section is the anteverted, retroflexed uterus, which occurs in about 27% of patients after cesarean delivery but can also be seen with endometriosis involving the torus uterinus (Fig. 11.45).[89]

Radical vaginal trachelectomy, or surgical resection of the cervix, is usually performed in the setting of early-stage cervical cancer. Preservation of fertility and childbearing can be achieved following trachelectomy, although these pregnancies carry an increased risk of premature delivery.[90] MRI may also show secondary evidence of cervical stenosis related to prior surgery or instrumentation such as hydro- or hematometra. Postsurgical changes are most apparent on the in-phase images of chemical shift MRI sequences as blooming artifact related to suture or surgical clips (Fig. 11.46).

Pearls and pitfalls for MR imaging of the female pelvis in infertility are summarized in Table 11.4.

TABLE 11.4   MR imaging of the pelvis in female infertility: pearls and pitfalls.

- A spasmolytic agent helps to reduce motion artifact related to bowel peristalsis and uterine contractions

- Vaginal and/or rectal gel may be administered for patients with suspected DIE

- When an MDA is suspected, MR images are obtained parallel to the long and short axis of the uterine corpus to better assess the outside fundal contour

- Structured reporting using a universal lexicon allows for improved adherence to consensus guidelines

- Dark T2 ovarian cortical rim is present in 71% of patients with PCOS

- Endometriomas classically show T1 hyperintensity, T2 shading and may also show T2 dark spot and T2 dark rim signs. T2 dark rim is more specific than T2 shading

- Endometriomas usually show lower ADC values than hemorrhagic cysts (ideal b-value 1000)

- Kissing ovaries highly sensitive and specific for stages 3/4 DIE

- MRKHS: vaginal hypoplasia of varying degrees, useful to assess on both axial and sagittal T2-weighted images without fat saturation

- Rudimentary uteri are usually bilateral and classically assume a caudal relationship to the ovaries in MRKHS

- Unicornuate uterus deviates to one side of the pelvis with "banana shape"

(Continued)

TABLE 11.4 *(Cont'd)*

- Urinary tract anomalies including renal agenesis typically occur ipsilateral to the absent or rudimentary horn

- Didelphys uterus is defined by two separate uterine cavities and a double cervix

- Bicornuate uterus by ASRM criteria is defined by external fundal indentation >10 mm

- Septate uterus by ASRM criteria is defined by a septum >1.5 cm and angle of internal indentation <90° and may be complete or partial

- OHVIRA (Herlyn-Werner-Wunderlich syndrome): obstructive hemivagina ipsilateral renal anomaly is characterized by a longitudinal oblique vaginal septum obstructing one side of the vagina in the setting of an MDA (e.g. uterus didelphys)

- Adenomyosis is characterized by thickening of the junctional zone >12 mm, myometrial microcystic change, T2 hyperintense linear striations radiating to the myometrium, and globular uterine enlargement

- Imaging features of endometrial lesions that suggest malignancy include intermediate T2 signal, high b-1000 signal intensity, and low ADC values

- Endometrial polyps sometimes show a central low T2 signal fibrous core and high signal cystic change

- Isthmocele is a fluid collection often containing old blood products in the cesarean scar niche in the anterior lower uterus that can contribute to intermenstrual bleeding

11.5 Conclusion

MRI is highly sensitive for the diagnosis and characterization of multiple causes of infertility, including ovarian, tubal, uterine, cervical, and vaginal etiologies. T2-weighted, nonfat saturated MRI sequences are the principal sequences used for anatomic evaluation of the female pelvis. Structured reporting with a comprehensive description of findings using a consensus lexicon ensures that clinically important findings are systemically reviewed and allows for succinct, relevant communication with clinicians.

Funding sources

None.

Conflicts of interest

None.

References

1. Infertility workup for the women's health specialist: ACOG committee opinion, number 781. *Obstet Gynecol.* 2019;133(6):e377–e384.
2. Vander Borght M, Wyns C. Fertility and infertility: definition and epidemiology. *Clin Biochem.* 2018;62:2–10.
3. Jeelani R, Puscheck EE. Imaging and the infertility evaluation. *Clin Obstet Gynecol.* 2017;60(1):93–107.
4. Merritt BA, Behr SC, Khati NJ. Imaging of infertility, part 1: hysterosalpingograms to magnetic resonance imaging. *Radiol Clin North Am.* 2020;58(2):215–225.
5. Wu V, Mar W, Milad MP, Horowitz JM. Magnetic resonance imaging in the evaluation of female infertility. *Curr Probl Diagn Radiol.* 2022;51(2):181–188.
6. Volondat M, Fontas E, Delotte J, Fatfouta I, Chevallier P, Chassang M. Magnetic resonance hysterosalpingography in diagnostic work-up of female infertility – comparison with conventional hysterosalpingography: a randomised study. *Eur Radiol.* 2019;29(2):501–508.
7. Schneider C, Oehmke F, Tinneberg H-R, Krombach GA. MRI technique for the preoperative evaluation of deep infiltrating endometriosis: current status and protocol recommendation. *Clin Radiol.* 2016;71(3):179–194.
8. Imaoka I, Wada A, Matsuo M, Yoshida M, Kitagaki H, Sugimura K. MR imaging of disorders associated with female infertility: use in diagnosis, treatment, and management. *Radiographics.* 2003;23(6):1401–1421.
9. Tong A, VanBuren WM, Chamié L, et al. Recommendations for MRI technique in the evaluation of pelvic endometriosis: consensus statement from the Society of Abdominal Radiology Endometriosis Disease-Focused Panel. *Abdom Radiol N Y.* 2020;45(6):1569–1586.
10. Goldberg-Stein S, Chernyak V. Adding value in radiology reporting. *J Am Coll Radiol JACR.* 2019;16(9):1292–1298 Pt B.

11. Wallace WHB, Kelsey TW, Anderson RA. Fertility preservation in pre-pubertal girls with cancer: the role of ovarian tissue cryopreservation. *Fertil Steril.* 2016;105(1):6–12.
12. Jha P, Sakala M, Chamie LP, et al. Endometriosis MRI lexicon: consensus statement from the society of abdominal radiology endometriosis disease-focused panel. *Abdom Radiol.* 2020;45(6):1552–1568.
13. DeBenedectis C, Ghosh E, Lazarus E. Pitfalls in imaging of female infertility. *Semin Roentgenol.* 2015;50(4):273–283.
14. Sadow CA, Sahni VA. Imaging female infertility. *Abdom Imaging.* 2014;39(1):92–107.
15. Barber TM, Alvey C, Greenslade T, et al. Patterns of ovarian morphology in polycystic ovary syndrome: a study utilising magnetic resonance imaging. *Eur Radiol.* 2010;20(5):1207–1213.
16. Dewailly D, Lujan ME, Carmina E, et al. Definition and significance of polycystic ovarian morphology: a task force report from the Androgen Excess and Polycystic Ovary Syndrome Society. *Hum Reprod Update.* 2014;20(3):334–352.
17. Lee TT, Rausch ME. Polycystic ovarian syndrome: role of imaging in diagnosis. *Radiogr Rev Publ Radiol Soc N Am Inc.* 2012;32(6):1643–1657.
18. Kayemba-Kay's S, Pambou A, Heron A, Benosman SM. Polycystic ovary syndrome: pelvic MRI as alternative to pelvic ultrasound for the diagnosis in overweight and obese adolescent girls. *Int J Pediatr Adolesc Med.* 2017;4(4):147–152.
19. Badeeb A, Brook A, Lee KS. Dark cortical rim: an MRI feature of polycystic ovarian syndrome. *Abdom Radiol N Y.* 2021;46(3):1148–1156.
20. de Venecia C, Ascher SM. Pelvic endometriosis: spectrum of magnetic resonance imaging findings. *Semin Ultrasound CT MR.* 2015;36(4):385–393.
21. Kaproth-Joslin K, Dogra V. Imaging of female infertility: a pictorial guide to the hysterosalpingography, ultrasonography, and magnetic resonance imaging findings of the congenital and acquired causes of female infertility. *Radiol Clin North Am.* 2013;51(6):967–981.
22. Steinkeler JA, Woodfield CA, Lazarus E, Hillstrom MM. Female infertility: a systematic approach to radiologic imaging and diagnosis. *Radiogr Rev Publ Radiol Soc N Am Inc.* 2009;29(5):1353–1370.
23. Cranney R, Condous G, Reid S. An update on the diagnosis, surgical management, and fertility outcomes for women with endometrioma. *Acta Obstet Gynecol Scand.* 2017;96(6):633–643.
24. Togashi K, Nishimura K, Kimura I, et al. Endometrial cysts: diagnosis with MR imaging. *Radiology.* 1991;180(1):73–78.
25. Dias JL, Veloso Gomes F, Lucas R, Cunha TM. The shading sign: is it exclusive of endometriomas? *Abdom Imaging.* 2015;40(7):2566–2572.
26. Corwin MT, Gerscovich EO, Lamba R, Wilson M, McGahan JP. Differentiation of ovarian endometriomas from hemorrhagic cysts at MR imaging: utility of the T2 dark spot sign. *Radiology.* 2014;271(1):126–132.
27. Cansu A, Bulut E, Dinc G, et al. Diagnostic efficacy of T2 dark spot, T2 dark rim signs, and T2 shading on magnetic resonance imaging in differentiating endometriomas from hemorrhagic cysts. *J Comput Assist Tomogr.* 2019;43(4):619–622.
28. Balaban M, Idilman IS, Toprak H, Unal O, Ipek A, Kocakoc E. The utility of diffusion-weighted magnetic resonance imaging in differentiation of endometriomas from hemorrhagic ovarian cysts. *Clin Imaging.* 2015;39(5):830–833.
29. Kokilavani J, Indiran V. Kissing ovaries sign on MRI. *Abdom Radiol N Y.* 2018;43(10):2880–2881.
30. Williams JC, Burnett TL, Jones T, Venkatesh SK, VanBuren WM. Association between kissing and retropositioned ovaries and severity of endometriosis: MR imaging evaluation. *Abdom Radiol N Y.* 2020;45(6):1637–1644.
31. Giudice LC. Clinical practice. endometriosis. *N Engl J Med.* 2010;362(25):2389–2398.
32. Jayaprakasan K, Becker C, Mittal M on behalf of the Royal College of Obstetricians and Gynecologists. The effect of surgery for endometriomas on fertility. *BJOG Int J Obstet Gynaecol.* 2018;125(6):e19–e28.
33. Alcázar JL, Martinez-Astorquiza Corral T, Orozco R, Dominguez-Piriz J, Juez L, Errasti T. Three-dimensional hysterosalpingo-contrast-sonography for the assessment of tubal patency in women with infertility: a systematic review with meta-analysis. *Gynecol Obstet Invest.* 2016;81(4):289–295.
34. Carrascosa PM, Capuñay C, Vallejos J, Martín López EB, Baronio M, Carrascosa JM. Virtual hysterosalpingography: a new multidetector CT technique for evaluating the female reproductive system. *Radiographics.* 2010;30(3):643–663.
35. Wiesner W, Ruehm S, Bongartz G, Kaim A, Reese E, De Geyter C. Three-dimensional dynamic MR hysterosalpingography: a preliminary report. *Eur Radiol.* 2001;11(8):1439–1444.
36. Lim CP, Hasafa Z, Bhattacharya S, Maheshwari A. Should a hysterosalpingogram be a first-line investigation to diagnose female tubal subfertility in the modern subfertility workup? *Hum Reprod.* 2011;26(5):967–971.
37. Revzin MV, Mathur M, Dave HB, Macer ML, Spektor M. Pelvic inflammatory disease: multimodality imaging approach with clinical-pathologic correlation. *Radiogr Rev Publ Radiol Soc N Am Inc.* 2016;36(5):1579–1596.
38. Czeyda-Pommersheim F, Kalb B, Costello J, et al. MRI in pelvic inflammatory disease: a pictorial review. *Abdom Radiol N Y.* 2017;42(3):935–950.
39. Tukeva TA, Aronen HJ, Karjalainen PT, Molander P, Paavonen T, Paavonen J. MR imaging in pelvic inflammatory disease: comparison with laparoscopy and US. *Radiology.* 1999;210(1):209–216.
40. Foti PV, Ognibene N, Spadola S, et al. Non-neoplastic diseases of the fallopian tube: MR imaging with emphasis on diffusion-weighted imaging. *Insights Imaging.* 2016;7(3):311–327.
41. Rezvani M, Shaaban AM. Fallopian tube disease in the nonpregnant patient. *Radiogr Rev Publ Radiol Soc N Am Inc.* 2011;31(2):527–548.
42. Mason BR, Chatterjee D, Menias CO, Thaker PH, Siegel CL, Yano M. Encyclopedia of endometriosis: a pictorial rad-path review. *Abdom Radiol N Y.* 2020;45(6):1587–1607.
43. Hindman N, VanBuren W. Imaging spectrum of endometriosis (endometriomas to deep infiltrative endometriosis). *Radiol Clin North Am.* 2020;58(2):275–289.
44. Tuckey RC. Progesterone synthesis by the human placenta. *Placenta.* 2005;26(4):273–281.
45. Behr SC, Courtier JL, Qayyum A. Imaging of Müllerian duct anomalies. *Radiographics.* 2012;32(6):E233–E250.
46. Buttram VC, Gibbons WE. Müllerian anomalies: a proposed classification (an analysis of 144 cases). *Fertil Steril.* 1979;32(1):40–46.
47. Heinonen PK, Pystynen PP. Primary infertility and uterine anomalies: A preliminary report was presented at the Twenty-Second Congress of the Scandinavian Association of Obstetricians and Gynecologists, June 7 to 10, 1982, Helsinki, Finland. *Fertil Steril.* 1983;40(3):311–316.
48. Huebner M, Rall K, Brucker SY, Reisenauer C, Siegmann-Luz KC, DeLancey JOL. The rectovaginal septum: visible on magnetic resonance images of women with Mayer-Rokitansky-Küster-Hauser syndrome (Müllerian agenesis). *Int Urogynecology J.* 2014;25(3):323–327.
49. Hall-Craggs MA, Williams CE, Pattison SH, Kirkham AP, Creighton SM. Mayer-Rokitansky-Kuster-Hauser syndrome: diagnosis with MR imaging. *Radiology.* 2013 1;269(3):787–792.

50. Khati NJ, Frazier AA, Brindle KA. The unicornuate uterus and its variants. *J Ultrasound Med*. 2012;31(2):319–331.

51. Brody JM, Koelliker SL, Frishman GN. Unicornuate uterus: imaging appearance, associated anomalies, and clinical implications. *Am J Roentgenol*. 1998;171(5):1341–1347.

52. Devine K, McCluskey T, Henne M, Armstrong A, Venkatesan AM, DeCherney A. Is MRI sufficient to diagnose rudimentary uterine horn? A case report and review of the literature. *J Minim Invasive Gynecol*. 2013;20(4):533–536.

53. Chan YY, Jayaprakasan K, Tan A, Thornton JG, Coomarasamy A, Raine-Fenning NJ. Reproductive outcomes in women with congenital uterine anomalies: a systematic review. *Ultrasound Obstet Gynecol*. 2011;38(4):371–382.

54. Grimbizis GF, Gordts S, Di Spiezio Sardo A, et al. The ESHRE/ESGE consensus on the classification of female genital tract congenital anomalies. *Hum Reprod*. 2013 1;28(8):2032–2044.

55. Li Y, Phelps A, Zapala MA, MacKenzie JD, MacKenzie TC, Courtier J. Magnetic resonance imaging of Müllerian duct anomalies in children. *Pediatr Radiol*. 2016 1;46(6):796–805.

56. Troiano RN, McCarthy SM. Müllerian duct anomalies: imaging and clinical issues. *Radiology*. 2004;233(1):19–34.

57. Uterine septum: a guideline. *Fertil Steril*. 2016 1;106(3):530–540.

58. Rikken JFW, Leeuwis-Fedorovich NE, Letteboer S, et al. The pathophysiology of the septate uterus: a systematic review. *BJOG Int J Obstet Gynaecol*. 2019;126(10):1192–1199.

59. Grimbizis GF. The pathophysiology of septate uterus. *BJOG Int J Obstet Gynaecol*. 2019;126(10):1200.

60. Cox JM, Heitmann RJ, Hailstorks T, Armstrong AY. MRI evidence of embryo implantation onto the fibromuscular uterine septum. *J Minim Invasive Gynecol*. 2014;21(4):535–536.

61. Smith BC, Brown DL, Carter RE, Famuyide AO. Double cervix: clarifying a diagnostic dilemma. *Am J Obstet Gynecol*. 2014;211(1) 26. e1–26.e5.

62. Khattab AF, Mustafa FA, Taylor PJ. The use of urine LH detection kits to time intrauterine insemination with donor sperm. *Hum Reprod*. 2005;20(9):2542–2545.

63. Ziel HK, Paulson RJ. Contralateral corpus luteum in ectopic pregnancy: what does it tell us about ovum pickup? *Fertil Steril*. 2002;77(4):850–851.

64. Haddad B, Louis-Sylvestre C, Poitout P, Paniel B-J. Longitudinal vaginal septum: a retrospective study of 202 cases. *Eur J Obstet Gynecol Reprod Biol*. 1997;74(2):197–199.

65. Heinonen PK. Complete septate uterus with longitudinal vaginal septum. *Fertil Steril*. 2006;85(3):700–705.

66. Schlomer B, Rodriguez E, Baskin L. Obstructed hemivagina and ipsilateral renal agenesis (OHVIRA) syndrome should be redefined as ipsilateral renal anomalies: cases of symptomatic atrophic and dysplastic kidney with ectopic ureter to obstructed hemivagina. *J Pediatr Urol*. 2015;11(2) 77.e1–77.e6.

67. Bajaj SK, Misra R, Thukral BB, Gupta R. OHVIRA: uterus didelphys, blind hemivagina and ipsilateral renal agenesis: advantage MRI. *J Hum Reprod Sci*. 2012;5(1):67–70.

68. Han JH, Lee YS, Im YJ, Kim SW, Lee M-J, Han SW. Clinical implications of obstructed hemivagina and ipsilateral renal anomaly (OHVIRA) syndrome in the prepubertal age group. *PLoS One*. 2016;11(11):e0166776.

69. Novellas S, Chassang M, Delotte J, et al. MRI characteristics of the uterine junctional zone: from normal to the diagnosis of adenomyosis. *Am J Roentgenol*. 2011;196(5):1206–1213.

70. Yitta S, Hecht EM, Mausner EV, Bennett GL. Normal or abnormal? Demystifying uterine and cervical contrast enhancement at multidetector CT. *Radiographics*. 2011;31(3):647–661.

71. Takeuchi M, Matsuzaki K. Adenomyosis: usual and unusual imaging manifestations, pitfalls, and problem-solving MR imaging techniques. *Radiographics*. 2011;31(1):99–115.

72. Maeda T, Tateishi U, Sasajima Y, et al. Atypical polypoid adenomyoma of the uterus: appearance on [18] F-FDG PET/MRI fused images. *Am J Roentgenol*. 2006;186(2):320–323.

73. Nakai G, Kitano R, Yamamoto K, et al. Magnetic resonance imaging findings in atypical polypoid adenomyoma. *J Comput Assist Tomogr*. 2015;39(1):32–36.

74. Kitamura Y, Allison SJ, Jha RC, Spies JB, Flick PA, Ascher SM. MRI of adenomyosis: changes with uterine artery embolization. *Am J Roentgenol*. 2006;186(3):855–864.

75. Walker WJ, Bratby MJ. Magnetic resonance imaging (MRI) analysis of fibroid location in women achieving pregnancy after uterine artery embolization. *Cardiovasc Intervent Radiol*. 2007;30(5):876–881.

76. Munro MG, Critchley HOD, Fraser IS. The FIGO classification of causes of abnormal uterine bleeding in the reproductive years. *Fertil Steril*. 2011;95(7):2204–2208 e3.

77. Dudiak CM, Turner DA, Patel SK, Archie JT, Silver B, Norusis M. Uterine leiomyomas in the infertile patient: preoperative localization with MR imaging versus US and hysterosalpingography. *Radiology*. 1988;167(3):627–630.

78. Mavrelos D, Naftalin J, Hoo W, Ben-Nagi J, Holland T, Jurkovic D. Preoperative assessment of submucous fibroids by three-dimensional saline contrast sonohysterography. *Ultrasound Obstet Gynecol*. 2011;38(3):350–354.

79. Verma SK, Bergin D, Gonsalves CF, Mitchell DG, Lev-Toaff AS, Parker L. Submucosal fibroids becoming endocavitary following uterine artery embolization: risk assessment by MRI. *Am J Roentgenol*. 2008;190(5):1220–1226.

80. Gomez E, Nguyen M-LT, Fursevich D, Macura K, Gupta A. MRI-based pictorial review of the FIGO classification system for uterine fibroids. *Abdom Radiol*. 2021;46(5):2146–2155.

81. Thomassin-Naggara I, Dechoux S, Bonneau C, et al. How to differentiate benign from malignant myometrial tumours using MR imaging. *Eur Radiol*. 2013;23(8):2306–2314.

82. Shitano F, Kido A, Kataoka M, et al. MR appearance of normal uterine endometrium considering menstrual cycle: differentiation with benign and malignant endometrial lesions. *Acta Radiol*. 2016;57(12):1540–1548.

83. Nougaret S, Reinhold C, Alsharif SS, et al. Endometrial cancer: combined MR volumetry and diffusion-weighted imaging for assessment of myometrial and lymphovascular invasion and tumor grade. *Radiology*. 2015;276(3):797–808.

84. Fornasa F, Montemezzi S. Diffusion-weighted magnetic resonance imaging of the normal endometrium: temporal and spatial variations of the apparent diffusion coefficient. *Acta Radiol Stockh Swed*. 1987;53(5):586–590 2012 Jun 1.

85. Grasel RP, Outwater EK, Siegelman ES, Capuzzi D, Parker L, Hussain SM. Endometrial polyps: MR imaging features and distinction from endometrial carcinoma. *Radiology.* 2000;214(1):47–52.

86. Kawaguchi M, Kato H, Suzui N, et al. MR imaging findings differentiating uterine submucosal polypoid adenomyomas from endometrial polyps. *Br J Radiol.* 2019;92(1095):20180430.

87. Alamo L, Vial Y, Denys A, Andreisek G, Meuwly J-Y, Schmidt S. MRI findings of complications related to previous uterine scars. *Eur J Radiol Open.* 2018;5:6–15.

88. Montoliu-Fornas G, Martí-Bonmatí L. Magnetic resonance imaging structured reporting in infertility. *Fertil Steril.* 2016;105(6):1421–1431.

89. Sanders RC, Parsons AK. Anteverted retroflexed uterus: a common consequence of cesarean delivery. *Am J Roentgenol.* 2014;203(1):W117–W124.

90. Speiser D, Mangler M, Köhler C, et al. Fertility outcome after radical vaginal trachelectomy: a prospective study of 212 patients. *Int J Gynecol Cancer Off J Int Gynecol Cancer Soc.* 2011;21(9):1635–1639.

12

MRI of benign uterine pathologies

Jill Bruno[a], Christina Miller[b]

[a]Department of Radiology, Virginia Commonwealth University/VCU Health, Richmond, VA, United States [b]Department of Radiology, Women's Imaging, Augusta Health, Fishersville, VA, United States

12.1 Introduction

Commonly encountered benign uterine pathologies may originate from the myometrium or endometrium and may include leiomyomas, adenomyosis, endometrial hyperplasia and atrophy, and endometrial polyps. In addition, numerous extrauterine pathologies can sometimes mimic uterine pathologies on imaging and must be differentiated to help determine appropriate management. MRI plays a crucial role in characterizing uterine pathologies and distinguishing between mimics while providing a global view of the pelvis.

In this chapter, we deal with the broad spectrum of benign uterine pathologies and malignant conditions that may mimic benign uterine pathologies. The full range of malignant conditions of the uterus is beyond the scope of this chapter; however, given that degenerating leiomyomas and leiomyosarcomas may have overlapping MRI imaging features, attention will be given to this topic given the importance of distinguishing these two disease processes. Finally, the last section, "How I do it," will provide a practical framework for assessing benign conditions of the uterus.

12.2 Imaging of female pelvis

In clinical practice, pelvic ultrasound is often the initial imaging modality for characterizing pathologic processes of the female pelvis, given several advantages. Ultrasound is well suited as a first line modality for evaluating female pelvic pathology as it is widely accessible, does not emit ionizing radiation, and is generally well-tolerated by patients. However, ultrasound may be limited due to operator dependence and/or skill level and experience of the sonographer. Ultrasound may be limited in its ability to characterize some uterine pathologies due to decreased contrast resolution as compared to MRI. While transvaginal ultrasound may provide high-resolution images, some patients may be reluctant to undergo transvaginal imaging for a variety of reasons, or may have underlying pathologic processes such as vaginal atrophy or stenosis that prevent transvaginal acquisition of images. Other patient-related factors that may limit ultrasound assessment of the pelvis include body habitus, inability to position patient for optimal ultrasound assessment, and bowel gas, which may obscure intrapelvic structures. Pelvic pain and position of the uterus may limit the sonographer's ability to optimally evaluate the uterus via transvaginal ultrasound. It has been stated that ultrasound imaging is similar to shining a flashlight in a dark room to look for an object; you will only see what the flashlight shines upon, in much the same way that sonographically acquired images will only depict what is directly scanned by the transducer. In contrast to ultrasound, MRI imaging allows for global cross-sectional images to be obtained of the entire pelvis, and abdomen if needed, and thus MRI obviates concern that any portion of the pelvis could be excluded from view.

While CT is a valuable imaging modality for evaluating many pathologic processes, CT is limited in its ability to assess the uterine architecture due to decreased contrast resolution and due to the fact that it exposes patients to ionizing radiation. In applying the ALARA principle (as low as reasonably achievable), MRI is advantageous in that no ionizing radiation is imparted to the patient during MR imaging. In addition, the anatomic zones of the uterus

Magnetic Resonance Imaging of The Pelvis.
DOI: https://doi.org/10.1016/B978-0-323-89854-6.00022-3

are generally not well distinguished with CT, nor are pathologic processes that disrupt these anatomic zones. MRI more clearly distinguishes uterine anatomy and pathology, as we will see in the next sections.

PET-CT has a role in assessing metastatic disease and malignant recurrence, but false positives, particularly in the pelvis, may occur. Frequent sources of false positives on PET-CT include the physiologic excretion of radiotracer in the ureters and urinary bladder, which may obscure or mimic malignancy. Physiologic uptake of radiotracer throughout the gastrointestinal tract is also a potential source of a false positive result. Physiologic uptake of radiotracer may also be seen in the endometrium and within the ovaries. In the postsurgical or postradiation setting, false positives on PET-CT may also occur. PET-CT is also limited by reduced spatial resolution and reduced contrast resolution. MR imaging of the pelvis allows for greater spatial resolution and excellent definition of the fine anatomic structures of the uterus, adnexa, and other structures within the pelvis. Additional advantages of MR include lack of ionizing radiation and ability to depict fine structural detail of adjacent pelvic organs that may be involved in pathologic processes affecting the uterus. MRI is generally well tolerated by patients as the patient can lie supine in the MRI scanner. Aside from placement of an intravenous line for contrast administration, there is no invasive component when evaluating benign uterine pathologies. A wider range of body habitus types are amenable to MRI imaging with newer MRI scanners that can accommodate nearly all patients (Fig. 12.1). Bowel gas typically does not pose a problem or cause significant image artifact with MRI imaging. Antiperistaltic agents may be administered to the patient prior to MRI scanning to decrease artifact related to bowel peristalsis on a case-by-case basis. Table 12.1 summarizes advantages and disadvantages of imaging modalities for evaluation of the female pelvis.

12.3 MR technique

MR imaging of the pelvis is the diagnostic investigation of choice for many pelvic conditions, including both benign and malignant uterine processes.

As with any MRI exam, patient preparation is important in order to optimize image quality.

In general, it is critical for the patient to know what to expect, particularly for the patient's first MRI exam. Most institutions provide patients with specific instructions regarding what to expect during an MRI exam. While specifics regarding patient preparation may vary across institutions, in general, fasting prior to the MRI exam is recommended; patients are generally informed that it is acceptable to have small sips of water in order to take prescribed medications. For MRI of the female pelvis, patients are advised to avoid eating 4–6 hours prior to the exam, which is helpful to reduce bowel peristalsis and to improve image quality.

Patients are typically asked to void 30 minutes to 1 hour prior to MRI, allowing for increased patient comfort and decreased patient motion during the exam. As a distended urinary bladder can produce phase ghost artifacts and can cause partial compression of the uterus, taking care to ensure that the patient has emptied the bladder prior to the MRI is recommended.

Patients are typically advised to avoid moving during the MRI, as patient motion may greatly limit image quality. Care is taken to ensure the patient is in a comfortable position in the MRI scanner to improve the patient experience as well as to minimize patient motion, thereby reducing motion artifact.

Pelvic MRI may be performed at both 1.5 Tesla and 3 Tesla magnet strength. Both 1.5T and 3T MRI scanners have the ability to produce images of the pelvis with exquisite anatomic detail. High-field 3 Tesla MRI provides improved signal-to-noise ratio (SNR), spatial resolution and anatomic detail with faster table times; in turn, faster table times allow for increased comfort for the patient and increased workflow efficiency. When possible, a multicoil array should be used for smaller field of view (FOV) and higher spatial resolution.[1] MR technique decidedly demonstrates the best soft tissue contrast with the added advantage of 3-D depiction of anatomy and pathology and lack of ionizing radiation. MR is most valuable for determining local extent of disease in patients with pelvic malignancy and is of great importance in surgical and treatment planning, as well as problem solving following pelvic ultrasound.[1]

Although there are many sequences that can be obtained for focused clinical questions, suggested sequences per the current ACR practice guidelines are as follows: Axial T1-weighted imaging, orthogonal high-resolution T2-weighted fast spin-echo sequences (relative to the uterus and/or cervix), long- or short-axis precontrast and dynamic postcontrast 2-D T1-weighted or 3-D weighted acquisition (with fat suppression), axial T2-weighted imaging of the pelvis to include the perineum, and diffusion-weighted imaging (DWI) with ADC map.[1] High-resolution long- and short-axis T2-weighted imaging with small field of view of the uterine body is optimal for visualizing the myometrium and zonal anatomy.

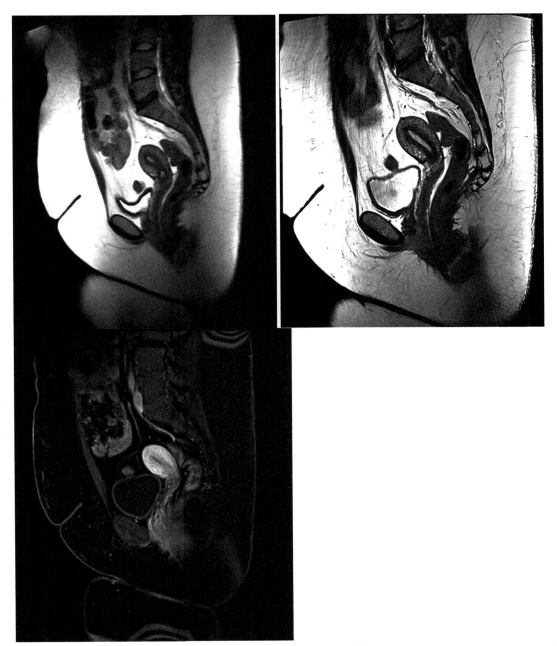

FIG. 12.1 **Normal uterus, increased BMI.** 30-year-old female with BMI of 46 kg/m². Standard sagittal T2-weighted image (A), sagittal high resolution T2-weighted image (B), sagittal T1-fat saturated image following contrast administration (C). These images demonstrate the ability of MRI to depict the normal zonal anatomy of the uterus with exquisite detail even in the setting of an increased BMI.

Imaging of the uterus should be performed with a small field of view (20–24 cm) and thin section imaging should be acquired. Targeted thinner slice sequences can be used to better depict the origin of a suspected fibroid if there is a question, for instance in the setting of an ovarian mass abutting the uterus versus pedunculated uterine fibroid interposed between the uterus and ovary. Matrix size should be as large as possible.

The T2-weighted sequence is one of the most important sequences for depicting fine anatomic detail of the uterus and pelvic structures. Imaging in the sagittal plane is well suited for evaluation of uterine anatomy, with oblique coronal and axial imaging performed along the long and short axis of the endometrial canal. Including reference online or hardcopy diagrams to the MRI technologist protocols to assist technologists acquiring desired planes can be extremely helpful.

A comprehensive MRI protocol is elaborated in Table 12.2.

TABLE 12.1 Advantages and disadvantages of imaging modalities for the female pelvis.

Modality	Advantages	Disadvantages
Ultrasound	• Widely accessible • Well-tolerated • No ionizing radiation • Least costly modality	• Contrast resolution varies • Operator dependent • Transvaginal imaging not always possible • Bowel gas may obscure pelvic structures particularly with transabdominal approach
CT	• Allows a global view of surrounding organs/pathology • Well tolerated	• Limited contrast resolution • Ionizing radiation
PET/CT	• Assesses metastatic disease and malignant recurrence	• Reduced spatial resolution • Reduced contrast resolution • False positives from excretion of radiotracer in the ureters/bladder • False positives from physiologic uptake in the GI tract, endometrium, and ovaries • Ionizing radiation
MRI	• Excellent contrast resolution • Excellent spatial resolution • No ionizing radiation • Usually well tolerated • Bowel gas typically not problematic	• IV placement for contrast administration • Sensitive to motion artifact • Implantable devices must be MRI compatible • Less cost effective than other modalities

TABLE 12.2 MRI pelvis evaluation of benign uterus.
Suggested protocol, vendor specifications may vary.

Plane	Sequence	Type	FOV	Coverage
Axial/Sag/Cor	T2 single shot TSE/FSE	2D	300 mm	Coronal to cover whole abdomen and pelvis
Axial	T2 TSE fat sat	2D	380 mm	Whole pelvis
Axial	T1	2D	380 mm	Whole pelvis
Axial	T1 fat sat	2D	220 mm	Uterus/adnexa
Axial	T2 TSE Hi-Res	2D	220 mm	Uterus/adnexa
Long-axis uterus	T2 TSE Hi-Res	2D	200 mm	Uterus/adnexa
Sagittal	T2 TSE Hi-Res	2D	220 mm	Uterus/adnexa
Sagittal	T1 VIBE fat sat precontrast	3D	220 mm	Uterus/adnexa
Axial	TI VIBE fat sat precontrast	3D	330 mm	Whole pelvis
Contrast injection				
Sagittal	Dynamic postcontrast T1 VIBE fat sat × 3*	3D	220 mm	Uterus/adnexa
Axial	T1 VIBE fat sat postcontrast	3D	330 mm	Whole pelvis
Axial	DWI b50, b400, b800**	2D	380 mm	Whole pelvis

*Subtracted postcontrast images should be created by the MRI technologist to accompany these sequences.
**DWI sequence use varies by institution.

12.4 Normal anatomy

The uterus is classically divided into three anatomic parts, the uterine fundus, the uterine body, and the cervix. The fundus describes the portion of the uterus from which the fallopian tubes arise. The isthmus is the portion of the lower uterine body that becomes narrowed, separating the uterine body from the cervix (Fig. 12.2).

The position of the uterus may be described as being anteverted or retroverted, regarding the orientation of the long axis of the uterine fundus with respect to the vagina. Anteverted or retroverted position of the uterus may be a fixed position in some patients, while in other patients the position of the uterus may change depending on degree of fullness of the urinary bladder. Thus on one exam the uterus may be anteverted, and on a subsequent exam for the same patient, the uterus may be retroverted. Further, the uterus may be described as anteflexed or retroflexed, regarding the position of the fundus with respect to the cervix. If the uterine fundus is flexed toward the anterior aspect of the patient, this is termed anteflexed; likewise, if the uterine fundus is flexed posteriorly toward the sacrum, this is termed retroflexed.

12.4.1 Zonal anatomy

Zonal anatomy is well depicted with MRI and includes the myometrium, endometrium, and the junctional zone. These anatomic distinctions are best delineated on mid sagittal high-resolution T2-weighted sequences; the mid sagittal T2-weighted images are used to measure the thickness of the junctional zone and endometrium (Figs. 12.2 and 12.3).

The junctional zone was first described as an MRI finding in 1986 by Hricak et al., calling it "the low intensity line" between the endometrium and myometrium.[2,3] This zone has since been histologically correlated to the innermost layer of the myometrium and demonstrates myocytes with slightly different morphology compared to the outer layers of the myometrium.[4]

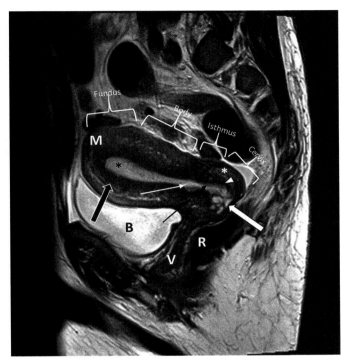

FIG. 12.2 **Uterine anatomy on sagittal T2-weighted imaging.** M-myometrium, black thick arrow-junctional zone, Black asterisk-endometrium, Thin white arrow-high T2 signal mucus, Black thin arrow-High T2 endocervix (slightly lower T2 signal than mucus), White arrowhead-Low T2 signal fibromuscular stromal layer of cervix (continuous with the junctional zone), White asterisk-Outer fibromuscular stromal layer of cervix (continuous with the outer myometrium), White thick arrow-cervical os, B-bladder, V-vagina, R-rectum. Note the incidental high T2 signal cervical Nabothian cysts.

Junctional zone myocytes demonstrate a greater relative nuclear area and looser extracellular matrix, as well as different architectural organization in a concentric rather than longitudinal orientation, all contributing to the characteristic low signal on T2-weighted imaging[4] (Fig. 12.3). The zonal anatomy of the uterus may appear different during premenarche, pregnancy, and postmenopause, due to progressive dehydration of the smooth-muscle tissue associated with fibrous involution of the extracellular matrix.[4] Of note, the junctional zone may not be well seen in 30% of postmenopausal women.[5] Also, in reproductive-aged women taking oral contraceptive pills, the separation of the myometrium and endometrium on MRI is often less distinct; endometrial atrophy is common in this scenario, and the junctional zone may not be visible. There have been multiple studies to determine normal junctional zone thickness. Currently, literature review demonstrates an acceptable thickness of up to 8 mm in both premenopausal and postmenopausal patients.[4] This will be further discussed in the section to follow regarding adenomyosis.

12.4.2 Endometrium

The normal MR appearance of the endometrium is best seen in the central aspect of the uterus, typically parallel to the long axis of the uterus on sagittal T2-weighted imaging. The normal endometrium demonstrates uniform high signal intensity on T2-weighted images, in contrast to the uniform low T2 signal intensity of the junctional zone.[6] In the absence of endometrial fluid or mass, the endometrium will appear uniformly hyperintense on T2-weighted images and should be measured at the point of greatest thickness on sagittal images (Fig. 12.3). While the normal endometrium is hyperintense on T2-weighted images, if fluid is present in the endometrial canal, it is typically of even greater T2 hyperintensity, similar to the T2 hyperintense signal of cerebrospinal fluid. When fluid is present within the endometrial canal, to evaluate endometrial thickness, the two sides of the endometrium should be measured separately on the sagittal images (excluding the central T2 hyperintense fluid) and these two measurements added together, in a similar technique as is performed with ultrasound. There is variability in the endometrial thickness in both premenopausal and postmenopausal women related to hormonal changes during the menstrual cycle and patients on hormone therapy.[7,8] The endometrium reaches maximum thickness during the mid-secretory phase and may measure up to 16 mm in thickness in the premenopausal patient.[6] In contrast, the postmenopausal endometrium should appear thin, with a double layer thickness of less than 5 mm consistent with atrophy.[6] Postmenopausal patients may be considered for biopsy when endometrial thickness exceeds 8 mm even in the presence of hormone therapy, and in the clinical scenario of postmenopausal bleeding, biopsy may be considered at any thickness greater than 5 mm.[6]

12.4.3 Cervix

The uterine cervix can be subdivided into the supravaginal cervix (endocervix) and the portio (or ectocervix), which protrudes into the vagina.[9] The epithelial lining of the portio is composed of squamous cells, while the glandular epithelium of the endocervical canal is covered by columnar cells.[10] With age, squamous cells grow to cover the columnar cells, and this transformation zone is called the squamocolumnar junction.[10] This squamocolumnar junction is almost exclusively where cervical cancer develops.[10] Normal MR appearance of the cervix demonstrates a trilaminar pattern of signal intensity, with a central high signal intensity zone secondary to endocervical mucosal glands, surrounded by a low signal intensity stroma, and then surrounded by a rim of intermediate signal smooth muscle.[9] The plicae palmatae are normal low T2 signal folds along the anterior and posterior walls of the cervical canal, seen in up to 50% of reproductive aged women, and should not be mistaken for a septum (Fig. 12.4).

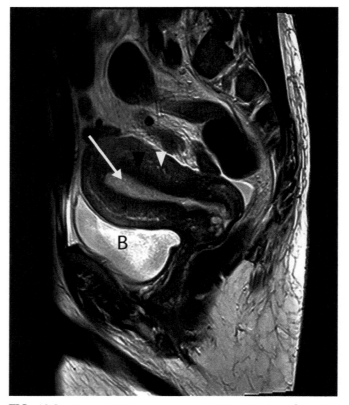

FIG. 12.3 Normal MRI uterus, normal BMI of 21.5 kg/m². Sagittal T2-weighted image of the pelvis demonstrates a normal uterus. Note that a low T2 signal saturation band has been placed by the MRI technologist over the superficial soft tissues of the anterior pelvis, which reduces scan artifact. The endometrium (white arrow) is uniformly T2 hyperintense, though slightly lower in T2 signal intensity as compared to fluid in the urinary bladder (B). The middle layer, a low T2 signal band surrounding the endometrium is the junctional zone (black arrowhead). Note the normal thickness and uniform appearance of the junctional zone, and absence of subendometrial cysts. The outermost layer is the myometrium (white arrowhead), intermediate in signal, normal in appearance and without focal mass or disruption. Incidental note is made of small, T2 hyperintense cervical Nabothian cysts.

12.5 Benign cervical lesions and mimics

Perhaps the most common benign entity involving the cervix is the Nabothian cyst, which may occur as a single cyst or as multiple cysts (Fig. 12.2). These are common retention cysts of the cervix that result following chronic cervicitis.[10] During chronic inflammation, squamous cells grow to cover the columnar cells. When these columnar cells produce mucin, the mucin becomes entrapped and forms a retention cyst.[10] Nabothian cysts are usually several millimeters in size but can reach up to 4 cm in size.[10] A specific subtype of Nabothian cysts is called a tunnel cluster, characterized by multicystic dilatation of the endocervical glands.[10] Nabothian cells follow expected signal intensity of cysts, but may demonstrate intermediate or high signal intensity on T1-weighted imaging and high signal intensity on T2-weighted imaging. No solid or enhancing components should be visualized.

Adenoma malignum, although a malignant process, will briefly be discussed here because it is an important yet rare mimic of Nabothian cysts. Adenoma malignum, also known as minimal deviation adenocarcinoma, is a well-differentiated adenocarcinoma of the cervix with an unfavorable prognosis. Histologically, small cystic spaces filled with mucin are identified, and lined by mucin-containing columnar epithelial cells, with these glands demonstrating

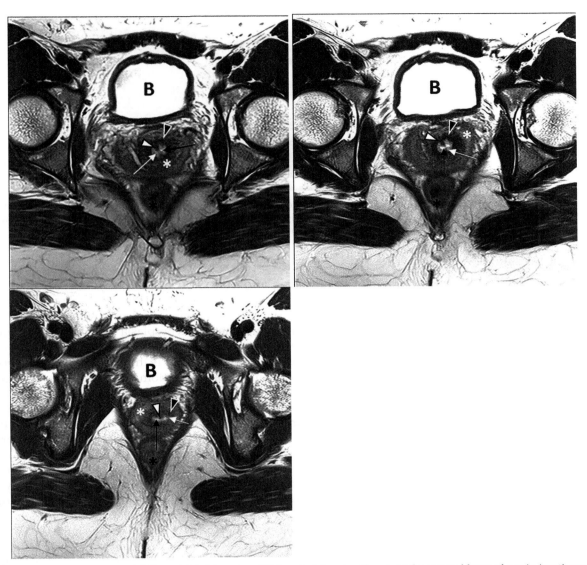

FIG. 12.4   Cervical anatomy on axial T2-weighted imaging. White asterisk-outer fibromuscular stromal layer of cervix (continuous with the myometrium), Black arrowhead-low T2 signal fibromuscular stromal layer of cervix (continuous with the junctional zone), White arrowhead-plicae palmatae (normal low T2 signal folds along the anterior and posterior walls of the cervical canal, seen in up to 50% of reproductive aged women and should not be mistaken for a septum), White thin arrow-high T2 endocervix (slightly lower T2 signal than mucus), Black thin arrow-high T2 signal mucus, B-bladder; black asterisk-rectum.

cellular atypia and dysplasia.[11] This entity makes up less than 3% of all cervical adenocarcinomas and the most classical presentation is watery vaginal discharge associated with Peutz–Jeghers syndrome, which also is associated with mucinous tumors of the ovary. To briefly review, Peutz–Jeghers syndrome is an autosomal dominant polyposis syndrome characterized by multiple hamartomas and mucocutaneous melanin pigmentation, but with increased risk of multiple cancers, including adenoma malignum. Adenoma malignum is characterized on MR imaging as a multiloculated cystic lesion with high T2 signal, but with the added observation of enhancing solid components within the deep cervical stroma, which helps differentiate this tumor from Nabothian cysts.[11,12] In contradistinction, Nabothian cysts are centered superficially in the cervix and should not have solid enhancing components.[13] Cervical polyps are not uncommon and most commonly occur in the endocervical canal.[10]

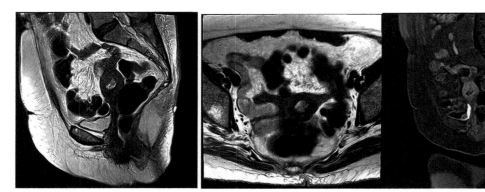

FIG. 12.5 **Endometrial polyp.** Sagittal and axial T2-weighted images, followed by sagittal T1-weighted, fat-saturated, contrast enhanced image. These images demonstrate a small, ill-defined intermediate T2 signal structure projecting into the endometrial canal, showing enhancement on the sagittal contrast enhanced image. Upon hysterectomy, pathology confirmed the diagnosis of endometrial polyp.

12.6 Endometrial hyperplasia and endometrial polyps

Endometrial hyperplasia is defined as irregular proliferation of the endometrial glands with increased gland to stroma ratio when compared to proliferative endometrium.[14] Endometrial hyperplasia includes noncancerous and precancerous intraepithelial neoplasms (complex endometrial hyperplasia with atypia).[14] There is strong evidence that endometrial hyperplasia may be a precursor of endometrial cancer, which is the most common gynecological malignancy in the Western world.[14] Although many studies demonstrate an endometrial thickness of 5 mm or less as normal, changes in morphology of the endometrial stripe may be a better predictor of hyperplasia.[14]

Endometrial polyps are localized overgrowths of endometrial glands and stroma with a vascular core, most of which are asymptomatic.[15] Endometrial polyps may occur with or without endometrial hyperplasia, with endometrial polyps being a more common cause of pathologic endometrial thickening than endometrial hyperplasia.[16] Endometrial polyps may appear sessile or pedunculated, and more commonly demonstrate more mass like shape and appear well circumscribed.[17] Histologically, these polyps demonstrate a stroma of dense fibrous or smooth muscle tissue and glandular cystic dilatation.[17] Polyps tend to have a low or intermediate signal intensity core on T2-weighted imaging, along with intra-tumoral cysts demonstrating high T2 signal intensity, with or without hemorrhage, with variable enhancement characteristics, most commonly following the enhancement of the myometrium[17] (Fig. 12.5). Grasel et al. showed that endometrial polyps are typically intermediate in signal on T1-weighted images, demonstrating heterogeneous, intermediate to high signal on T2-weighted images.[16] In contradistinction to endometrial carcinoma, endometrial polyps tend to show a central low T2 signal fibrous core and high T2 signal intratumoral cysts. Myometrial invasion and necrosis were more predictive of carcinomas.[16] Despite MR features that help to distinguish endometrial polyps from endometrial carcinoma, biopsy and histopathologic correlation remain necessary for diagnosis, in part because endometrial polyps and carcinoma frequently occur together, and as endometrial hyperplasia and carcinoma may appear similar (Fig. 12.6).

12.7 Uterine fibroids

Uterine leiomyomas, or fibroids, are the most common benign uterine tumor, estimated to occur in 70% of white women and more than 80% of black women by the age of 50.[18,19] Uterine fibroids are tumors arising from uterine smooth muscle, with the tumors histologically demonstrating disordered smooth-muscle cells within ample extracellular matrix.[18] Tumor growth is heavily dependent on estrogen and progesterone, with ovarian activity essential for fibroid growth, and with fibroids diminishing in size following menopause.[18] The location and size of the fibroid is a primary factor in clinical presentation, with symptoms including excessive uterine bleeding, anemia, preterm labor and obstruction of labor, pregnancy loss, pelvic pain, and urinary incontinence.[20]

Uterine fibroids are generally classified by location as subserosal, intramural, and submucosal[21] (Fig. 12.7). Leiomyomas arise from the myometrium of the uterine corpus but may also occur in the cervix; however, cervical leiomyomas are rare and reported to be less than 10% of all leiomyomas.[10,22] Submucosal fibroids represent about 5% of leiomyomas, but are more likely to cause symptoms given their projection into the endometrial canal (Fig. 12.8).

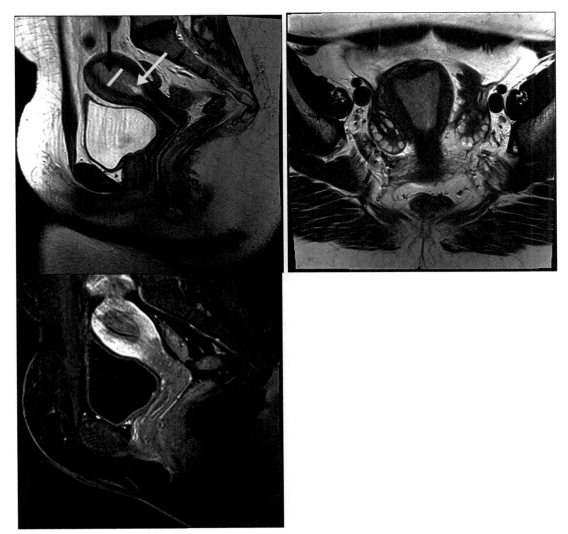

FIG. 12.6 **Endometrial carcinoma.** 27-year-old female experienced abnormal daily bleeding for three months which prompted pelvic ultrasound demonstrating abnormal thickening of the endometrium of 2.1 cm. A subsequent endometrial biopsy showed complex atypical hyperplasia and could not exclude endometrial adenocarcinoma. Sagittal T2-weighted image shows abnormally thickened endometrium measuring 2.1 cm in thickness (A) (black arrow). White line perpendicular to the endometrium shows how the endometrium should be measured, at the thickest point perpendicular to the long axis of the endometrial canal on sagittal T2-weighted image. Trace T2 hyperintense fluid in the endometrial canal is demarcated by the white arrow (A). Note the low T2 signal junctional zone is not widened and is intact (A, B). Pathology showed a 3 × 2 × 0.5 cm endometrial carcinoma, endometrioid type, FIGO grade 1. These imaging findings can be seen with both endometrial hyperplasia and endometrial carcinoma, and this case highlights the fact that features of endometrial hyperplasia and carcinoma overlap, necessitating biopsy. Given the unusually young age for developing malignancy, genetic testing for potential hereditary cancer was pursued.

Submucosal fibroids may become pedunculated with prolapse into the cervical or vaginal canal[23] (Fig. 12.9). Unusual locations of fibroids include the vulva, ovaries, urinary bladder, urethra and vagina.[24,25] A vaginal fibroid is shown in Fig. 12.7.

Subserosal fibroids are typically exophytic fibroids, projecting into the pelvic and/or abdominal cavity. These may be broad-based or may demonstrate a pedunculated appearance, attached to the uterus by a stalk. Pedunculated subserosal fibroids can cause significant pain if undergoing torsion or infarction.[21] They may become very large, in which case the imaging protocol can be expanded to include the abdomen and pelvis (Fig. 12.10).

Fibroids may demonstrate various types of degeneration including hyaline, cystic, myxoid, and red or carneous degeneration.[22,26,27] Fibroid degeneration has been attributed to conditions that alter blood supply to the fibroids including pregnancy, menopause associated atrophy, and posttraumatic or postprocedural changes.[26] MRI can suggest various types of degeneration, but there may be overlap of imaging features and more than one type can occur concurrently (Table 12.3).[26]

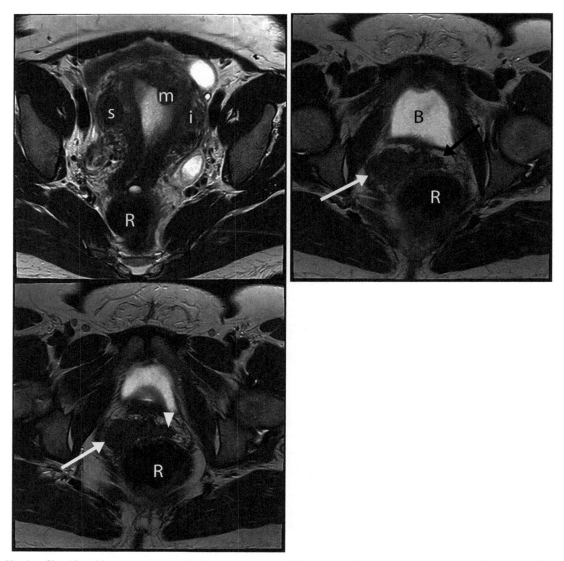

FIG. 12.7   Uterine fibroids with concurrent vaginal leiomyoma. Axial T2-weighted images depict subserosal (s) intramural (i), and submucosal (m) fibroids (A) as well as an ovoid, circumscribed vaginal fibroid arising from the right, superolateral aspect of the vaginal wall (B, C). The vaginal fibroid (white arrow) demonstrates similar signal characteristics when compared to other uterine fibroids on all sequences. Clinical exam and sonographic assessment were also consistent with vaginal fibroid. The left side of the vagina appears normal, with a low T2 signal thin band representing the outer muscular layer (black arrow) surrounding increased T2 signal vaginal mucosa and secretions centrally (white arrowhead). B demarcates urinary bladder. R demarcates rectum.

The classic MR imaging appearance of nondegenerated fibroids demonstrates well-circumscribed masses with low signal intensity on T2-weighted imaging and low to isointensity on T1-weighted imaging. Classic or usual fibroids enhance following contrast administration, though enhancement pattern is variable.[26,27]

Hyaline degeneration can appear similar with low signal intensity on T1-weighted imaging, but with minimal heterogeneous enhancement and a heterogeneous whorled appearance on T2-weighted imaging due to extensive hyalinization, which begins in the stromal components separating smooth muscle cells and with eventual replacement of the smooth muscle cells.[22,27]

Edema is commonly seen in up to 50% of leiomyomas and may not be secondary to degeneration.[27] Edema is usually seen throughout the fibroid, greatest at the periphery, and which if present lends to high signal intensity on T2-weighted imaging.

Cystic degeneration involves varying levels of edema and collagen with both large and small cystic spaces developing throughout the fibroid, which demonstrate round well-defined fluid signal intensity without enhancement (Figs. 12.11–12.13).

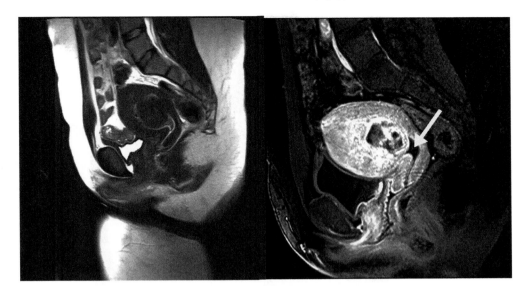

FIG. 12.8 24-year-old female with submucosal and intramural uterine fibroids. Sagittal T2-weighted image (A) shows the dominant, low T2 signal submucosal fibroid splaying the endometrial canal. Sagittal T1 fat saturated image subtracted post contrast image (B) demonstrates heterogeneous enhancement of the dominant submucosal fibroid. Note the non-enhancing low T1 signal fluid just inferior to the submucosal fibroid, just above the endocervical canal (white arrow).

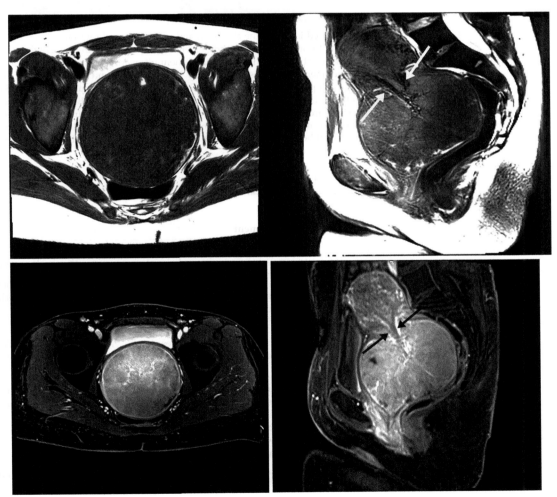

FIG. 12.9 39-year-old female with prolapsing uterine fibroid. (A) Axial and (B) sagittal T2-weighted images demonstrate low T2 signal circumscribed mass extending from the central uterus into the cervix, splaying and thinning the surrounding cervix. The mass is attached to the central uterus by a stalk; note the beak-like appearance of the central uterus extending toward the prolapsing fibroid on sagittal images (white arrows). The internal architecture and well-defined low T2 signal appearance are typical for a uterine fibroid. Note the intact, thin, low T2 signal fibrous cervix surrounding the fibroid. (C) Axial and (D) sagittal T1 fat-saturated subtracted post contrast images demonstrate homogeneous enhancement of the prolapsing fibroid. Beak-like appearance demarcated with black arrows on (D).

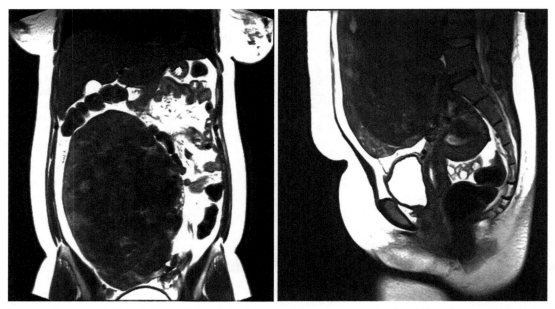

FIG. 12.10 Large, pedunculated fibroid. Coronal T2-weighted image of the abdomen and pelvis (A), and sagittal T2-weighted image of the pelvis (B) demonstrate a large pedunculated fibroid occupying the abdomen and pelvis, extending superiorly to the level of the transverse colon. This 31-year-old female presented for evaluation of irregular menstrual bleeding with subsequent ultrasound demonstrating an incidental 20 cm abdominopelvic mass. The patient then underwent CT abdomen and pelvis followed by MRI abdomen and pelvis. The patient underwent abdominal myomectomy several days following the MRI, with pathology confirming 25 × 20 × 11 cm leiomyoma weighing 3245 grams. Intra-operatively, the fibroid was shown to be pedunculated, attached to the anterior uterine fundus by a 4 cm stalk. The sagittal T2-weighted image shows a low T2 signal beak-like appearance of the stalk arising from the anterior uterine fundus; the stalk is noted immediately anterior to L5-S1 on the sagittal image. This case underscores the importance of reviewing prior imaging studies as well as the MRI localizer images prior to obtaining the remaining sequences, as this fibroid extends well beyond the confines of the pelvis and thus a combined abdomen/pelvis MRI was needed to include the entire fibroid.

TABLE 12.3 MRI imaging characteristics for various fibroid degenerations and variants.

MRI characteristics of uterine fibroids and variants	T1	T2	Enhancement	DWI/ADC	Comment
Classic/usual type (no degeneration)	Hypo- or Isointense	Hypointense	Enhance, variable appearance	Hypointense/ hypointense	Low T1 and T2 signal due to smooth muscle content
Cystic degeneration	Hypo- or Isointense	Hyperintense foci in hypointense fibroid	Cystic portions do not enhance; nondegenerated portions enhance	No restricted diffusion	Degree of cystic degeneration determines T2 hyperintensity
Hyaline degeneration	Hypo- or Isointense	Hypointense	Little or no Enhancement	No restricted diffusion	Most common type of degeneration. Calcific degeneration may be seen
Myxoid degeneration	Hypointense	Extremely Hyperintense	Internal mucinous areas do not enhance; myxoid stroma with delayed enhancement	No restricted diffusion	Myxoid degeneration may be seen in benign fibroids and in LMS
Red/carneous degeneration post-UAE	T1 hyperintense rim or diffuse T1 hyperintensity	T2 hypointense rim or diffuse T2 hypointensity	No early enhancement	No restricted diffusion	Red/carneous degeneration and post-UAE change appear similar
Calcific degeneration	Hypointense	Hypointense	None	No restricted diffusion	Dense, central or peripheral calcification indicate benign fibroid. Occurs with hyaline degeneration, post-UAE, autoinfarction

MRI characteristics of uterine fibroids and variants	T1	T2	Enhancement	DWI/ADC	Comment
Cellular	T1 signal varies	Homogeneous T2 hyperintensity	Pronounced early enhancement	Restriction of diffusion	Both cellular and LMS cause restricted diffusion, but cellular fibroids are more homogeneous
Lipoleiomyoma	Heterogeneous with areas following fat signal on all sequences	Heterogeneous with areas following fat signal on all sequences	Enhancement of bands of tissue traversing the fatty portions	Needs further investigation	Internal fatty content is also well visualized on CT
STUMP	Heterogeneous T1 hyperintense areas	Heterogeneous T2 hyperintense areas	Variable	Needs further investigation	Can mimic classic or usual fibroids. Greater risk of recurrence after removal, may recur as LMS

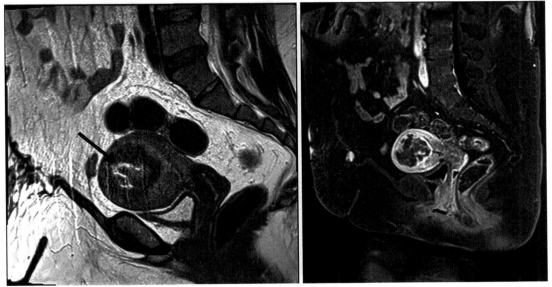

FIG. 12.11   **Cystic degeneration.** Sagittal T2-weighted image (A) and sagittal T1-fat saturated contrast enhanced image (B) show an intracavitary fibroid, the background of which is low in T2 signal, with increased T2 signal within reflecting cystic degeneration.

Myxoid degeneration appears similar with areas of cystic fluid signal, as well as markedly T2 hyperintense gelatinous mucoid areas which may demonstrate some progressive enhancement[26] (Fig. 12.14).

Red or carneous degeneration is unique, in that it usually causes more acute clinical symptoms compared to the other types of degeneration.[27] Red degeneration is secondary to massive infarction of the leiomyoma secondary to obstruction of peripheral venous drainage, and most often occurs during pregnancy.[22,26] MR imaging demonstrates low signal intensity on T1- and T2-weighted imaging without enhancement, and with a peripheral rim of high signal intensity on T1-weighted images, corresponding to peripheral vessels. Red or carneous degeneration appears similar to post-UAE changes. The presence of calcification within fibroids can further alter MR imaging characteristics, with signal voids identified in dense area of calcifications which are typically present along the periphery of the fibroid, and which can occur following hemorrhage and necrosis[27] (Fig. 12.15).

Lipoleiomyoma is a rare benign tumor of the uterus of undetermined exact origin, but which may represent a leiomyoma with fatty degeneration. These occur most frequently in postmenopausal women and may range in size from 3 mm to 32 cm, with an average of 5–10 cm.[28] Lipoleiomyomas present as a well-demarcated mass with moderate T1 signal intensity which suppresses on fat-saturated sequences and may appear of moderate T2 signal intensity with variable enhancement[29] (Fig. 12.16). Lipoleiomyomas histologically are comprised of smooth muscle cells, mature adipose tissue, and fibrous tissue.[28] Pathologically, lipomatous uterine tumors may be classified into three

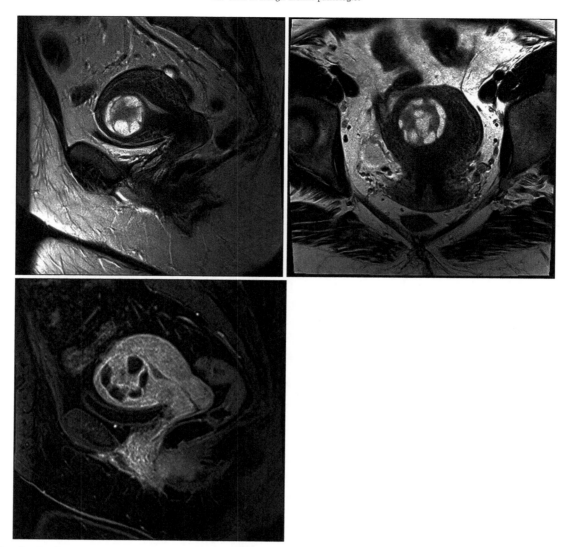

FIG. 12.12 Cystic degeneration within an intramural fibroid in different patient is shown in (A–C) causing mass effect upon the endometrium.

general categories: (1) pure lipoma, (2) lipoleiomyoma and other variants such as angiomyolipoma or fibromyolipoma, and (3) malignant neoplasms, predominantly liposarcoma.[28]

12.8 Additional leiomyoma variants

Leiomyoma variants also include mitotically active, cellular, and atypical leiomyomas in addition to smooth muscle tumors of uncertain malignant potential or STUMP tumors.[29] These variants require thorough evaluation by a pathologist for diagnosis as imaging features are nonspecific.[29] Most leiomyoma variants behave in a benign manner, however atypical leiomyomas and STUMP tumors, if discovered, need clinical and imaging surveillance, though universally agreed upon guidelines have not been established. STUMP tumors have a greater risk of recurrence after removal and may recur as leiomyosarcoma. Given the rarity of atypical leiomyomas and STUMP tumors, management in a multidisciplinary fashion including consultation with a gynecologic oncologist is considered prudent. It is generally accepted that unusual uterine masses are best managed with myomectomy or hysterectomy as opposed to medical management, embolization, or morcellation.

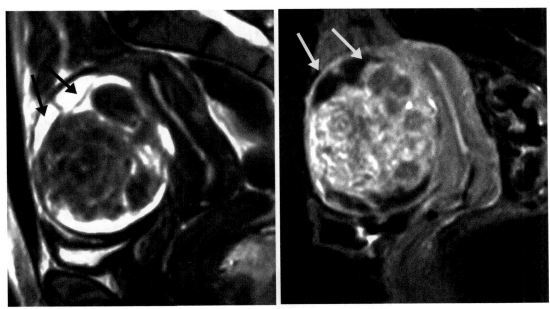

FIG. 12.13   Cystic degeneration. Sagittal T2-weighted image (A) and sagittal T1-weighted, fat saturated, contrast enhanced image (B) depict a large anterior uterine fibroid with focal areas of cystic degeneration. The black arrows depict areas of T2 hyperintensity reflecting cystic degeneration within the fibroid. The white arrows show absence of enhancement within the areas of cystic degeneration. A crescent of T2 hyperintense fluid is also noted along the inferior aspect of the fibroid, also reflecting cystic degeneration. The bulk of the fibroid demonstrates the T2 hypointense signal (A) and heterogeneous enhancement (B) expected for a fibroid.

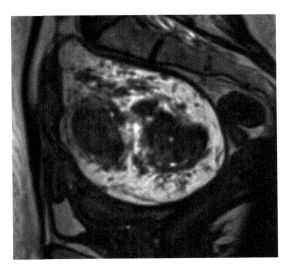

FIG. 12.14   Myxoid degeneration. Sagittal T2-weighted image shows a large fibroid with areas of marked T2 hyperintensity throughout the fibroid, as can be seen with myxoid degeneration, though leiomyosarcoma may have similar imaging features. Pathology showed myxoid degeneration and focal hyalinization.

12.9 Fibroid mimics

12.9.1 Mimics of intramural uterine fibroids

Transient myometrial contractions commonly mimic intramural uterine fibroids on both ultrasound and on MR imaging, and are often seen in pregnant patients. It is important to distinguish myometrial contractions from fibroids, particularly in pregnant patients, as management may be altered in the presence of uterine fibroids, whereas transient myometrial contractions resolve spontaneously and are not of clinical concern. When discovered during

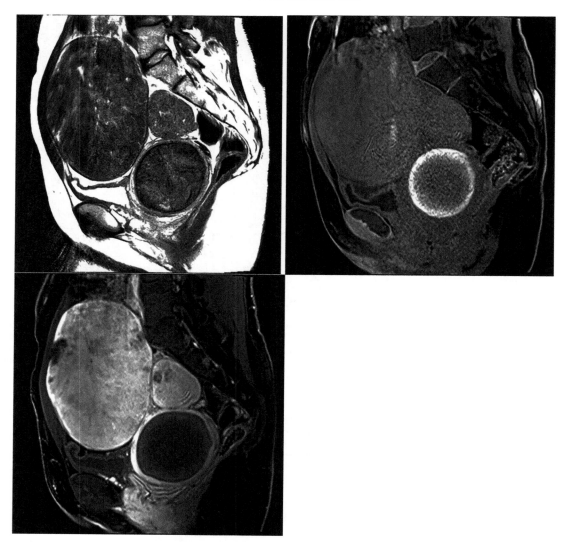

FIG. 12.15 **Red/carneous degeneration.** Sagittal T2-weighted image (A) shows 3 dominant fibroids, all of which are low in T2 signal. The inferior-most fibroid has a very low T2 signal rim (A) with a corresponding high T1 signal rim on the sagittal T1-weighted, fat saturated image (B) which has the appearance of a white, circular rim on (B). The low T2 / high T1 signal rim reflects the thrombosed vessels with intracellular methemoglobin that occur with red or carneous degeneration. On the sagittal T1-weighted, fat saturated, contrast enhanced image (C) the inferior-most fibroid is completely devoid of enhancement, also characteristic of red degeneration. These findings may look identical to those following uterine fibroid embolization, which will be addressed in a separate chapter.

an ultrasound exam, reimaging after several minutes have passed can demonstrate resolution of the myometrial contraction. On MRI, transient myometrial contractions demonstrate a low signal, ovoid, mass-like appearance of the myometrium on T2-weighted imaging, similar in appearance to that of the low T2 signal uterine fibroid. Transient myometrial contractions are often somewhat less distinct than fibroids, and often lack the lobulated internal architecture of fibroids. However, given that contractions are transient, these masses are not consistently seen on all sequences and if there is any question, repeat T2-weighted imaging can be obtained to ensure a transient nature (Fig. 12.17).

Adenomyosis is discussed in more detail later in this chapter, however we will briefly touch upon adenomyomas, which appear as a mass-like conglomerate of adenomyotic glands and may mimic fibroids both clinically and on imaging.[4] Clinical findings include menorrhagia (most commonly) as well as pelvic pain, metrorrhagia, dysmenorrhea, and dyspareunia. Up to one-third of women with adenomyosis are asymptomatic.[30] While ultrasound is typically the first line imaging modality for investigation of adenomyosis and can be as accurate as MRI in diagnosing

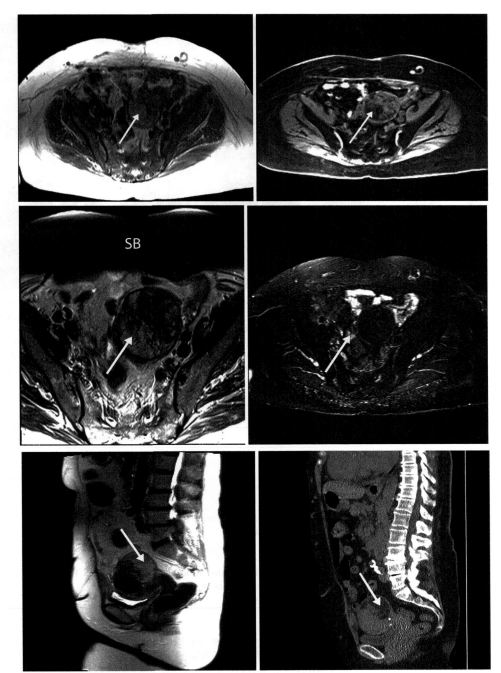

FIG. 12.16. **65-year-old female with uterine mass demonstrating signal characteristics consistent with lipoleiomyoma.** Axial T1-weighted image without fat saturation (A) and with fat saturation (B). Crescent-shaped area of macroscopic fat (white arrow) is noted in the posterior right aspect of the lipoleiomyoma. Axial T2-weighted image without (C) with fat saturation (D). Crescent- shaped area of macroscopic fat is noted in the posterior right aspect of the lipoleiomyoma. Note the saturation band (SB) placed on the anterior tissues of the pelvis to reduce scan artifact. Sagittal T2-weighted MRI image of the pelvis (E) and corresponding sagittal CT image (F) of the abdomen and pelvis, both demonstrating crescent shaped area of macroscopic fat (white arrow) in the posterior aspect of the lipoleiomyoma.

adenomyosis,[30,31] MRI can be an exceptional tool to help distinguish adenomyomas from fibroids.[30,32] MRI can also help to define other uterine pathologies that may coexist with adenomyosis, including endometriosis and endometrial and cervical polyps.[33-35] Mark et al. and Togashi et al. performed early investigations demonstrating the value of MRI in diagnosing adenomyosis.[36,37] Briefly, fibroids tend to have a well-defined border, whereas adenomyomas are less well defined. Fibroids, particularly if large, tend to cause significant mass effect, whereas focal adenomyosis

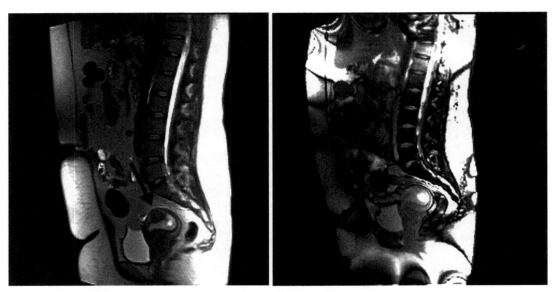

FIG. 12.17 Fibroid mimics—transient myometrial contractions. 23-year-old female, 6 weeks pregnant, presented with abdominal pain including rebound and guarding on exam. A non-contrast MRI abdomen and pelvis was performed to evaluate for appendicitis or other source of abdominal pain. The MRI demonstrated a normal appendix and no etiology to account for the patient's pain. Images below demonstrate a low T2 signal structure in the anterior uterus on the sagittal T2-weighted image (A). This was not present on the initial localizer image (B), or any other sequences. An ultrasound performed on the same day demonstrated no uterine fibroid, nor did any prior or subsequent ultrasound exams. This is consistent with a transient myometrial contraction, which due to its low T2 signal and ovoid appearance, can mimic a fibroid. Note the high T2 signal gestational sac within the endometrial canal.

TABLE 12.4 Distinguishing fibroids from adenomyomas.

Feature	Fibroid	Adenomyoma
Border	Well-defined	Ill-defined
Shape	Round/spherical	Oval, long axis parallel to endometrium
Mass effect	Fibroids cause mass effect	Adenomyomas cause little to no mass effect
Pseudocapsule	Fibroids compress adjacent myometrium, resulting in pseudocapsule	No pseudocapsule
Prominent vessels at myometrial interface	Present	Absent
Internal architecture	Classically low T2 signal throughout, unless cystic degeneration which produces larger T2 hyperintense cystic spaces	Often see small T2 hyperintense foci throughout

causes little to no mass effect. The appearance of a pseudocapsule surrounding the fibroid is a manifestation of mass effect caused by the fibroid compressing adjacent myometrium. This pseudocapsule is well depicted with MRI and can be used to distinguish fibroids from adenomyomas, which do not compress adjacent myometrium and therefore are not surrounded by a pseudocapsule. Fibroids are more often round/spherical in shape, whereas adenomyomas tend to be more ovoid in configuration with the long axis parallel to the long axis of the uterus. Fibroids may be associated with dilated vessels along the border of the fibroid and myometrium, which are well depicted as low T2 signal flow voids on T2-weighted images or as enhancing vessels on contrast-enhanced images. Focal adenomyosis does not typically have dilated vessels along the myometrial interface.[38] Adenomyomas often contain small T2 hyperintense foci within.[4] Table 12.4 summarizes features of fibroids versus adenomyomas.

12.9.2 Mimics of subserosal uterine fibroids

A variety of pelvic masses may mimic subserosal uterine fibroids, including masses of adnexal and ovarian origin, such as ovarian neoplasms, endometriomas, tuboovarian abscesses, among others. In particular, ovarian fibromas or fibrothecomas are benign solid ovarian neoplasms that may resemble broad ligament fibroids on MRI imaging given their ovoid, circumscribed appearance, and uniformly low signal on T2-weighted images.[39] Bowel masses and other pelvic masses in juxtauterine location may mimic fibroids as well. The bridging vascular sign has been shown to be a useful sign in determining uterine versus adnexal/ovarian masses.[40] One study evaluated the use of the bridging vascular sign in distinguishing exophytic uterine leiomyomas from adnexal masses; the sign was found in 20 of 26 cases of leiomyomas and in no cases of other adnexal masses.[41] Another study found that these bridging vessels were present in 39 of 41 subserosal fibroids when evaluating with MR ultrasound, or both; only 3 of 27 extrauterine tumors were shown to have the bridging vessel sign, all three being malignant ovarian neoplasms that directly invaded the uterus.[42] In the case of malignant ovarian neoplasm directly invading the uterus, there is usually not a diagnostic dilemma, as features such as irregular border and direct invasion of the uterus are typically readily distinguished from uterine fibroids.

12.9.3 Mimics of submucosal uterine fibroids

Endometrial polyps may mimic submucosal uterine fibroids, however, the signal characteristics favoring polyps include low T2 signal core, and T2 hyperintense foci often found within polyps. Submucosal fibroids are also round or ovoid structures within the endometrial canal, however, fibroids more commonly demonstrate uniformly low T2 signal, whereas polyps tend to have internal foci of high T2 signal. Polyps tend to have a single vascular stalk, whereas fibroids may have more than one feeding vessel.[43] Another potential mimic of a submucosal uterine fibroid is retained products of conception.[44] Usually the clinical scenario and sonographic correlation would allow these two entities to be distinguished. An example of retained products of conception on MRI is included (Fig. 12.18).

12.9.4 Disseminated peritoneal leiomyomatosis, benign metastasizing leiomyoma and intravenous leiomyomatosis

Disseminated peritoneal leiomyomatosis. This extremely rare condition of benign vascular leiomyomas developing in the submesothelial peritoneum of the abdomen and pelvis is usually found in women of reproductive age. This is thought to be governed by hormonal factors given association with pregnancy, long-term oral contraceptive use, and granulosa cell tumors of the ovary. Cases have also been documented in men and postmenopausal women without known excess of hormones, which may be due to increased responsiveness of tumor cell estrogen and progesterone receptors to a normal hormonal milieu. These tumors often regress in the postpartum state or after cessation of excess hormone exposure.[25] Disseminated peritoneal leiomyomatosis (DPL) has been reported as a rare complication of laparoscopic myomectomy for treatment of uterine fibroids, as these tumors have been found along the laparoscopic tract.[45,46] It has been hypothesized that DPL may be a result of smooth muscle metaplasia in the subcoelomic mesenchyme, which is the embryologic tissue from which peritoneal lining and female internal genitalia derive. The condition appears to be associated with endometriosis.[25] MRI imaging features include multiple circumscribed masses with signal intensity similar to skeletal muscle and smooth muscle on T1- and T2-weighted images; these masses enhance after contrast administration. Given nonspecific imaging findings, the differential diagnosis of DPL is broad and includes peritoneal carcinomatosis, primary peritoneal mesothelioma, lymphoma, tuberculosis, desmoid tumors. Splenosis can also present as multiple enhancing masses throughout the abdomen and pelvis with a clinical history of splenectomy. F-18 FDG PET/CT may be helpful in narrowing the differential, as DPL generally does not show uptake, whereas increased FDG avidity may indicate a malignant condition. Image-guided percutaneous biopsy can suggest the diagnosis, but ultimately, exploratory laparotomy and surgical biopsy are generally required for diagnosis of diffuse peritoneal leiomyomatosis.[25] CT and MRI images of disseminated peritoneal leiomyomatosis are shown in Figs. 12.19 and 12.20.

Benign metastasizing leiomyoma. Another extremely rare condition is benign metastasizing leiomyoma, and as the name suggests, is defined by well-differentiated leiomyomas located far from the uterus (Fig. 12.21). Histologically they are identical to uterine leiomyomas.[25] This is usually seen in middle-aged women with multiple incidental lung nodules, and there is often a prior history of hysterectomy for fibroids. The heart, brain, lymph nodes, bone, and skin are reported to be rarely involved.[25] While most patients are asymptomatic middle-aged women, reports in men exist. Some patients have presented with chest pain, shortness of breath or cough. While the disease usually progresses slowly, cases with rapid progression in the lungs have been described. The predominant theory is that these represent hematogenous metastases of benign tumors, though another theory suggests these may be sequelae of multiple independent foci of proliferating smooth muscle.[25] Imaging features

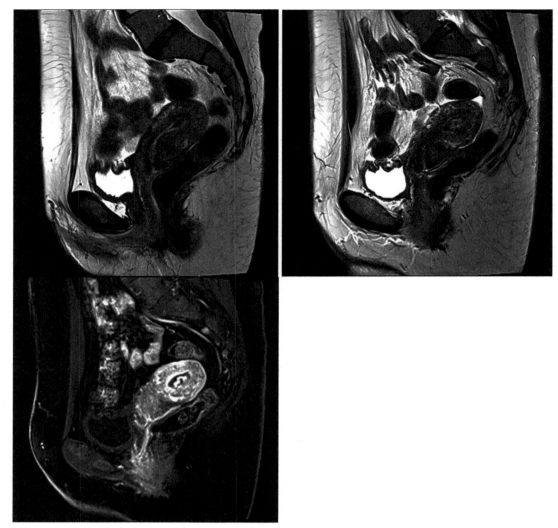

FIG. 12.18 **Fibroid mimics—retained products of conception mimicking submucosal fibroid.** Sagittal T2-weighted image obtained at the midline of the uterus shows a low T2 signal mass within the endometrial canal (A). Sagittal T2-weighted image slightly off midline shows ill-defined, heterogeneous T2 signal within this mass (B). Sagittal T1 fat saturated subtracted post-contrast image demonstrates heterogeneous enhancement of this structure (C). Prior to MRI, retained products of conception were suspected in this patient without history of fibroids. Upon tissue sampling, 3.0 × 2.2 × 0.7 cm specimen was determined by pathology to be retained products of conception, with chorionic villi and degenerated decidua noted in the specimen.

on both CT and MRI are nonspecific; lung nodules typically enhance and may cavitate and pneumothorax may be associated. Given the similar appearance to malignant pulmonary metastases, image-guided core biopsy is often needed for diagnosis, though spontaneous resolution has been reported.[25] Benign metastasizing leiomyoma may be associated with diffuse peritoneal leiomyomatosis, intravenous leiomyomatosis, and diffuse uterine leiomyomatosis and may indicate a common pathologic origin.[25]

Intravenous leiomyomatosis is a rare, histologically benign condition but can behave in a clinically aggressive manner, with growth of leiomyomata in intrauterine, parametrial, and systemic veins. These represent implants from concurrent or previously resected uterine fibroids. Clinical course varies and depends on disease burden. MRI images show enhancing pelvic venous tumor nodules, low to intermediate in T1 and T2 signal.[25] CT images show similar findings, with enhancing, circumscribed tumor nodules within the lumen of venous structures.

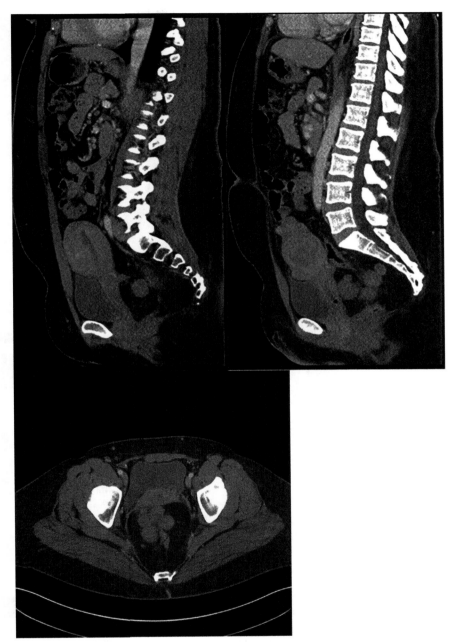

FIG. 12.19 Disseminated peritoneal leiomyomatosis. A 37-year-old female presented to the emergency department for pelvic pain, ongoing heavy menstrual bleeding, and constipation. Pertinent past medical history included two prior spontaneous vaginal deliveries with post-partum bilateral tubal ligation. Sagittal contrast enhanced CT images (A, B) and axial contrast enhanced CT image (C) demonstrate an enlarged, leiomyomatous uterus as well as multiple circumscribed, round and ovoid pelvic masses demonstrating homogeneous enhancement, many located in the perirectal region. Thickening and tethering of the right side of the rectal wall prompted a colonoscopy, which was negative.

12.9.5 Parasitic (broad ligament) leiomyoma

Leiomyomas may become attached to adjacent pelvic structures including the broad ligament, omentum, or connective tissue in the vicinity. These parasitic leiomyomas may cause mass effect upon the urethra, bladder, or ureter, which may in turn cause urinary symptoms including outflow obstruction or hydronephrosis. Ultrasound is helpful

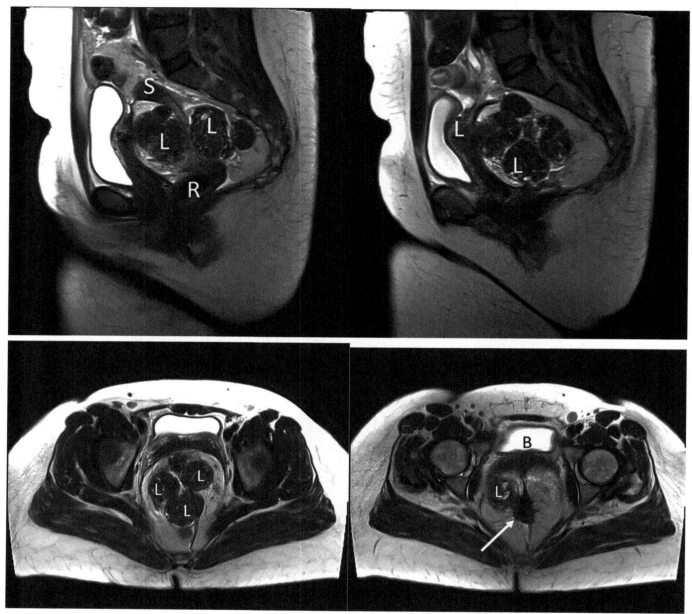

FIG. 12.20   Disseminated peritoneal leiomyomatosis. Approximately twenty-seven months later, due to ongoing symptoms, the same patient as presented above in Fig 12.19 underwent robotic total laparoscopic hysterectomy utilizing morcellation technique, and bilateral salpingectomy. Pathology indicated aggregate of morcellated uterine tissue fragments including fragments of leiomyomas. An MRI of the abdomen and pelvis was performed less than two weeks after hysterectomy. Sagittal (A and B) and axial (C and D) T2-weighted images of the pelvis, as well as sagittal T1 fat saturated contrast enhanced subtracted images of the pelvis (E and F) and axial T1 fat saturated contrast enhanced image of the pelvis (G) depict absence of uterus and presence of multiple, circumscribed low T2-signal masses throughout the pelvis, many in a perirectal location, all enhancing avidly. MRI appearance is consistent with disseminated peritoneal leiomyomatosis. Subsequent to the MRI, the patient was re-operated upon and all masses were removed; pathology indicated thirteen leiomyomata. S-Sigmoid colon. L-Leiomyoma. R-Rectum. B-Bladder. Small white arrow on axial T2-weighted image (d)-Rectum. Multiple white arrows on T1-weighted, fat saturated contrast enhanced images (E–G), leiomyomata.

in its ability to establish presence or absence of communication with the mass and the uterus or ovaries. MRI can also be extremely helpful in distinguishing broad ligament fibroids from ovarian or tubal masses. MRI can also demonstrate the typical imaging features of fibroids, as discussed in prior sections, which may also suggest this diagnosis.[25] A broad ligament leiomyoma is shown in Fig. 12.22.

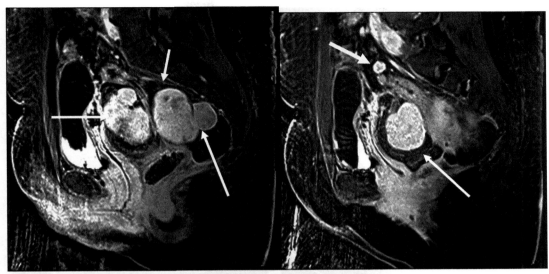

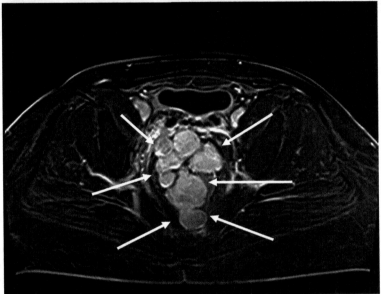

FIG. 12.20 *(Continued)*

12.10 Leiomyosarcoma

Leiomyosarcoma, although a malignant tumor, will briefly be discussed as it can mimic a degenerating fibroid and benign leiomyomas may rarely undergo malignant transformation. Leiomyosarcomas are rare, representing less than 1.5% of uterine malignancies, and are the most common histological variant of uterine sarcomas with a poor prognosis, with 5-year survival ranging from 18.8% to 68%.[26,47] Unfortunately, both the clinical presentation and imaging features of leiomyosarcoma are nonspecific.[46] Classic clinical presentation involves a rapidly growing pelvic mass, with abdominopelvic pain and/or vaginal bleeding. However, it has been shown that rapid growth of a uterine mass is not a reliable indicator of leiomyosarcoma.[29,48,55] The great majority of these are thought to arise de novo but may rarely arise from sarcomatous transformation of a benign leiomyoma in 0.2% of cases.[47]

At MR imaging, leiomyosarcomas commonly present as a large solitary infiltrating mass with ill-defined margins and heterogenous hypointense signal on T1-weighted imaging. On T2-weighted imaging, leiomyosarcomas generally demonstrate intermediate-to-high signal intensity with central hyperintensity signifying areas of necrosis, and

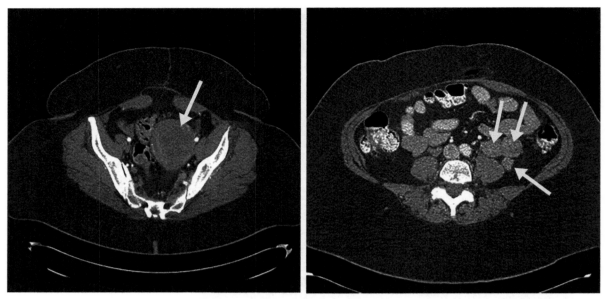

FIG. 12.21   Benign metastasizing leiomyoma with suspected associated intravascular leiomyomatosis. Axial contrast enhanced CT image of the pelvis demonstrates a dominant, circumscribed left pelvic mass demarcated by the white arrow (A). Additional similar, circumscribed enhancing masses along the course of the left gonadal vasculature are demarcated by the white arrows (B). This patient was a 63-year-old female who had undergone hysterectomy for uterine leiomyoma 20 years prior, and was re-operated upon for pelvic and periaortic masses. Pathology of the dominant pelvic mass indicated a 15 cm mass consistent with leiomyoma. The left periaortic masses were shown by pathology to represent three distinct masses consistent with leiomyomatosis, with no lymph tissue in the specimen. Based on pathologic findings as well as intraoperative and radiographic findings, a component of intravascular leiomyomatosis was suspected. This patient also had three circumscribed lung nodules (not shown), the largest measuring 7 mm, with CT thorax exams documenting stability over many years. These lung nodules were suspected to represent leiomyomatosis, the most common site of metastasis in the setting of benign metastasizing leiomyoma. No biopsy had been performed given stability and benign appearance.

with early heterogenous enhancement (Fig. 12.23).[47] Hemorrhage is common and calcifications may also be present secondary to both hemorrhage and necrosis.

Of note, four features most associated with leiomyosarcoma were shown by Lakhman et al. to be nodular borders, hemorrhage, areas of decreased signal intensity on T2-weighted images, and central areas with absent enhancement.[45,46,49] Ill-defined margins of a uterine mass should also raise suspicion for leiomyosarcoma.[29] DWI appears to be emerging as a powerful tool in problem solving of atypical uterine tumors. Tumors that demonstrate increased signal intensity on T2-weighted imaging and increased signal intensity on high-*b*-value DWI, with corresponding low ADC value are predictors of malignancy.[50] A study by Sato et al. in 2014 categorized tumors with an ADC value of 1.1 or greater at low risk while an ADC value of 1.1 or less was considered high risk, with data demonstrating at this algorithm yielded 100% sensitivity and 94% specificity, with accuracy of 94.6%.[26,50] In contrast, classic leiomyomas demonstrate homogeneously hypointense signal intensity on T2-weighted imaging, and appears hypointense on DWI and ADC compared to normal smooth muscle, also known as the "blackout phenomenon."[26,47] In summary, MRI is an important and powerful modality in the preoperative management of fibroids, but it should be noted that currently, there remains some overlap in appearance between leiomyomas and leiomyosarcomas. Leiomyosarcomas will be addressed in more detail in a separate chapter.

12.10.1   Uterine artery embolization: role of MRI

Not only is pelvic MRI an optimal imaging tool for characterization and classification of fibroids pre- and posttherapeutic intervention, but MRI can demonstrate mass effect of fibroids on nearby organs, and can help to guide clinical decisions in selecting fibroid therapies. MRI of the pelvis is advantageous in its ability to depict even the largest of uterine fibroids, and if needed in the case of a markedly enlarged uterus, additional imaging of the abdomen during the same imaging session can be performed to characterize the entirety of the enlarged uterus. If an enlarged, fibroid uterus causes mass effect upon the ureters resulting in hydronephrosis, this can be imaged with abdominal and pelvic MRI and is an important finding to be aware of in the pre- or posttreatment setting. Fibroids often cause mass effect upon the urinary bladder, and MRI can provide a pictorial demonstration of how fibroids cause symptoms of urinary frequency and urgency. Clinicians discussing possible therapies for uterine fibroids can review pelvic MRI images with their patients, which clearly depict how an enlarged, leiomyomatous uterus can contribute to urinary symptoms and other bulk symptoms such as back and leg pain, pelvic pressure and pain, or heaviness, bloating, constipation, and possibly lower extremity swelling if there is compression of the pelvic vasculature. In addition, contrast-enhanced MRI can provide valuable information regarding the arterial supply of fibroids or any parasitic branches from the ovarian artery. Information about preexisting degeneration or necrosis or lack of improvement can predict a possible lack of response to the treatment. Subtraction sequences can be particularly helpful when assessing the enhancement characteristics of fibroids, especially following uterine fibroid embolization.

Hysterectomy and myomectomy have traditionally been the standard procedures performed for treatment of fibroids, with more recent treatment options including uterine fibroid embolization and morcellation techniques. Uterine fibroid embolization is discussed further in a separate chapter. Morcellation technique involves the use of a device that mechanically reduces solid tissue specimen into smaller pieces that can then be removed through smaller incisions, but initially was an open, uncontained procedure within the peritoneal cavity that dispersed tissue fragments within the peritoneum and surgical ports.[51] Disseminated leiomyomatosis can therefore occur following morcellation procedures. Preoperative MRI is therefore extremely important to help identify potential cases of sarcoma for which dissemination would be disastrous. Given case reports of patients with disseminated leiomyosarcoma following morcellation, the FDA released an updated safety communication in December 2020 that laparoscopic power morcellation for myomectomy or hysterectomy only be performed with a tissue containment system and only in appropriately selected patients.[51] However, the use of a tissue containment system is yet unknown to stop the spread of disseminated benign or malignant tissue.[51] Because of the higher prevalence of leiomyosarcoma in older women, the FDA guidance also recommended against the use of morcellation in postmenopausal women or women older than age 50.[51] The management of uterine fibroids is therefore not without risks and preprocedural MRI remains an important tool in clinical decision making.

12.11 Adenomyosis

Adenomyosis is characterized by ectopic endometrial glands and stroma within the myometrium, with reactive hypertrophy of the surrounding myometrial smooth muscle.[21] Adenomyosis may present as a diffuse or focal process, and as a more mass-like process as an adenomyoma.[4,21]

The clinical presentation of adenomyosis may be identical to that of uterine fibroids; however, many patients with adenomyosis are asymptomatic, with actual prevalence unknown.[4] Now that sonography is widely used for the assessment of pelvic pain, it has been reported more recently that up to one-third of patients with adenomyosis are asymptomatic.[52]

Critical to the imaging diagnosis of adenomyosis is understanding of the junctional zone, or the innermost layer of the myometrium. The junctional zone (inner myometrium) is composed of myocytes but unlike the outer myometrium, the junctional zone myocytes are greater in nuclear area, are part of a looser extracellular matrix, and have a lower water content; this lower water content causes the junctional zone to appear as a low T2 signal band interposed between the outer myometrium and the endometrium.[4]

The classic appearance of diffuse adenomyosis is diffuse thickening of the junctional zone, with a thickness of 12 mm or greater highly predictive of adenomyosis (Fig. 12.24).[4,21] The diffuse low signal on T2-weighted imaging is secondary to the dense smooth muscle hypertrophy surrounding the ectopic endometrial tissue, with a few scattered small foci of increased signal on T2-weighted imaging secondary to the endometrial glands.[21] If this process does not affect the entire junctional zone but is limited to a smaller portion, it is called focal adenomyosis.

Adenomyoma represents a less common form of adenomyosis as compared to diffuse and focal adenomyosis. Adenomyomas are comparable to leiomyomas given their low signal on T2-weighted imaging; however, adenomyomas will often also demonstrate high signal intensity foci on T2-weighted imaging.[4] Fibroids generally have a well-defined outline and have a mass effect, while adenomyosis is ill-defined and has no mass effect. Adenomyomas are not associated with a pseudocapsule or peripheral vessels, unlike fibroids. Please see above section regarding fibroid mimics for additional discussion of adenomyomas and distinguishing features.

Adenomyosis and fibroids may occur in the same patient, and MRI is beneficial in defining these two pathologies when they occur concurrently (Fig. 12.24).

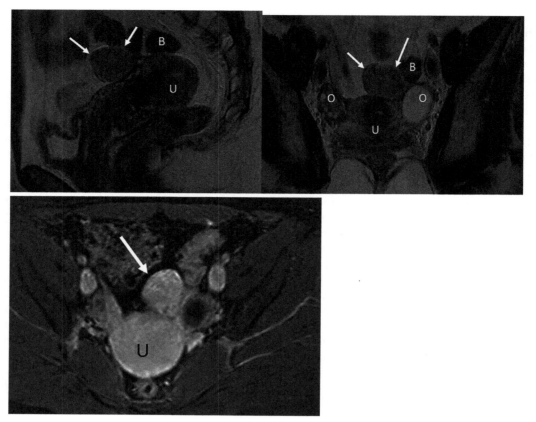

FIG. 12.22   Broad ligament leiomyoma. Sagittal and coronal T2-weighted images (A and B) and axial T1 fat-saturated, contrast-enhanced image (C) of the pelvis demonstrate a circumscribed, low T2 signal broad ligament fibroid in juxtauterine location, abutting the anterior left side of the uterine body, demarcated by white arrows (A–C). B indicates adjacent bowel loop. O indicates the ovaries (B); note normal follicles in the right ovary, as well as T2 hyperintense, non-enhancing benign cyst in the left ovary. U indicates the uterus.

12.11.1 Intrauterine devices

Ultrasound is the modality of choice for evaluation of intrauterine devices. As females of reproductive age will represent many of the patients undergoing MRI for uterine pathologies, it is important to recognize intrauterine devices on MRI exams. Depending on the protocol and technique utilized, these can be subtle and it is important to review all sequences and to note the presence and position of an IUD, and to comment on appropriate positioning or lack thereof.[53] The images in Fig. 12.25 demonstrate a well-positioned intrauterine device in the endometrial canal.

12.12 How I do it—protocol creation and selection, patient preparation, history review, and reporting

12.12.1 Protocol creation and selection

Ongoing review of department protocols and image quality is advised to ensure that the most current techniques are being employed to obtain the best quality imaging. Addressing image artifacts and other scan limitations in a systematic way, including frequent communication with a lead MRI technologist to address such issues, can result in improved image quality. Selecting the appropriate protocol is critical to reaching the correct diagnosis. Review of patient history and prior imaging exams can help to tailor the protocol based on suspected or known underlying uterine pathology. There are various ways to tailor an MRI protocol, with the basics of uterine imaging to include the following: Axial T1-weighted imaging, orthogonal high-resolution T2-weighted fast spin-echo sequences (relative to the uterus and/or cervix), long- or short-axis precontrast and dynamic postcontrast 2-D T1-weighted or 3-D

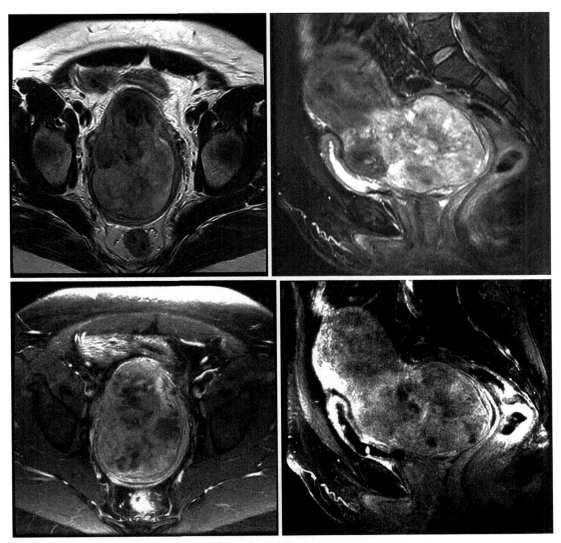

FIG. 12.23 Fibroid mimics – Leiomyosarcoma. 49-year-old female presented with vaginal bleeding, pelvic mass. The patient underwent modified radical hysterectomy (TAH/BSO) and on pathology was found to have an 11.2 cm high grade leiomyosarcoma extensively involving uterine cervix and myometrium. The T2-weighted images without fat saturation (A) and with fat saturation (B) from the pre-operative MRI demonstrate a large, heterogeneous mass with heterogeneous increased T2 signal throughout, along with scattered, ill-defined areas of lower T2 signal throughout the mass involving the lower uterine segment and cervix, protruding into and distending the cervix. The T1 fat saturated axial (C) and sagittal (D) post contrast images demonstrate diffuse, heterogeneous enhancement of the mass, will ill-defined borders, findings in keeping with uterine leiomyosarcoma.

weighted acquisition (with fat suppression), axial T2-weighted imaging of the pelvis to include the perineum, and DWI with ADC map.[1] High-resolution long- and short-axis T2-weighted imaging with small field of view of the uterine body is optimal for visualizing the myometrium and zonal anatomy.

Several actions can be performed to improve image quality, as discussed in the next section, including placement of saturation bands, patient preparation, and review of history and prior scans to assist in selecting the appropriate MRI protocol.

12.12.2 Saturation band placement

The MRI technologist can be advised to place a saturation band over the anterior lower abdominal/pelvic subcutaneous fat to help reduce image artifact. Placing a saturation band over the subcutaneous fat of the anterior pelvis takes only a few seconds and greatly reduces ghosting artifact related to respiratory motion artifact.

12.12.3 Patient preparation

Ensuring that the patient has not eaten prior to the exam helps to reduce bowel peristalsis that could result in artifact related to bowel motion. Antiperistalsis agents can also be administered to the patient to reduce bowel peristalsis. Asking the patient to empty the urinary bladder 30 minutes to 1 hour prior to undergoing MRI can help to keep the patient comfortable during the exam and can help the patient to remain as motionless as possible during the exam. MRI technologist and/or radiologist discussion with the patient prior to MRI will allow the patient to understand that image quality depends upon the patient's ability to remain still during the exam; this, in turn, can result in highest quality images. Once the patient is on the exam table, care should be taken to ensure that the patient is well-positioned and is comfortable, as this will reduce the chance for patient motion and/or early exam termination.

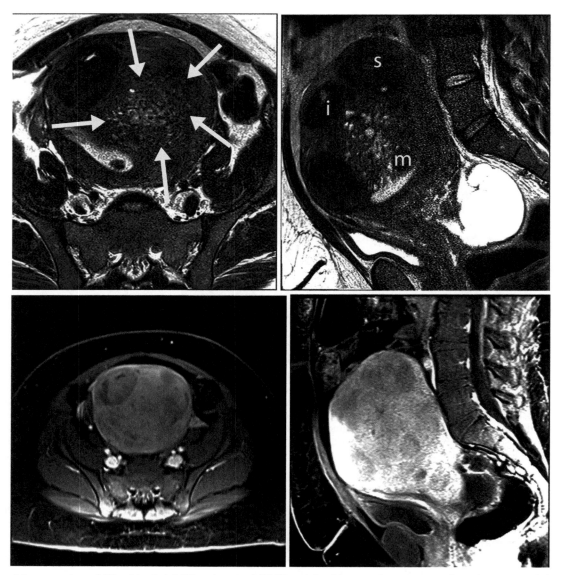

FIG. 12.24   Adenomyosis and Fibroids. Axial (A) and sagittal (B) T2-weighted images demonstrate enlarged, retroverted, leiomyomatous uterus as well as a large, mass-like area of adenomyosis (white arrows) occupying the anterior uterine body and fundus. The dominant area of adenomyosis is diffusely heterogeneous with innumerable small T2 hyperintense foci throughout a thickened junctional zone. The mass-like area of adenomyosis measures up to 6 x 7 x 7 cm. The uniformly T2 hyperintense endometrium is mildly thickened and displaced posteriorly and to the right by the large area of adenomyosis. Numerous low T2 signal, ovoid, circumscribed leiomyomata are noted in subserosal (s), intramural (i), and submucosal (m) locations. Incidentally noted in this patient is a hydrosalpinx, best seen as a T2 hyperintense structure posterior to the uterus on the sagittal T2-weighted image. Corresponding axial (C) and sagittal (D) T1-fat saturated post contrast images, from the same patient's MRI as (A) and (B) above, demonstrate heterogeneous enhancement of the fibroids and adenomyosis. The low T2 signal of the small fibroid protruding into the endometrial canal (A) as well as the enhancement pattern demonstrate features consistent with submucosal fibroid, as opposed to an endometrial polyp, which would typically be more intermediate in signal on T2 weighted images.

12.12.4 History review

Before protocol selection and prior to analyzing and interpreting the MRI images, as much information as possible is gathered. The clinical indication and history provided by the ordering clinician are reviewed, as well as any history provided by the patient. Sources of history include review of pertinent medical records, technologist communication sheets, and if necessary, discussion with the ordering provider and/or patient to clarify any historical information that may be unclear. It is also important to review any prior outside imaging available, including prior CT, PET/CT, MRI, ultrasound, and/or radiographic images that may contribute to the interpretation.

12.12.5 Reporting

After history and outside studies have been reviewed and the indication for imaging is known, a detailed assessment of the uterus and adjacent structures is performed. When describing the uterus in the radiology report, the uterine measurements in three dimensions should be provided. As some physicians and patients may be considering transvaginal hysterectomy, it is important to report the size of the uterus so that the surgeon can assess candidacy for this procedure. Another reason to report the size of the uterus is that, particularly in the setting of an enlarged, leiomyomatous uterus, the initial MRI of the uterus can provide a baseline prior to medical therapy or uterine fibroid embolization, so that efficacy of these interventions can be assessed with subsequent imaging, and degree of uterine size reduction can be compared on pre- and posttherapy imaging. Typically, the uterine length is measured on the sagittal T2-weighted image of the uterus as the long axis from the superior aspect of fundus to inferior aspect of the cervix. The AP dimension of the uterus is obtained as a line perpendicular to the uterine long axis on sagittal image. The transverse dimension of the uterus is often obtained from the axial T2-weighted images, as they best depict the uterine margins in relationship to adjacent structures.

As previously stated, the endometrium is a T2 hyperintense band within the central uterus, slightly lower in signal than markedly T2 hyperintense fluid in the bladder or cerebrospinal fluid. The endometrial thickness is measured on sagittal T2-weighted images as the AP dimension of the endometrium perpendicular to the long axis of the uterus. Simple fluid in the endometrial canal manifests as markedly T2 hyperintense fluid within the central portion of the slightly less T2 hyperintense signal of the endometrium. If there is fluid in the endometrial canal, as with ultrasound, the endometrial measurement should exclude the central, more T2 hyperintense fluid compo-

TABLE 12.5 Pearls and pitfalls to be aware of when interpreting pelvic MRI.

Pearls and pitfalls
While ultrasound remains the first-line modality for evaluating benign uterine pathologies, MRI is an excellent tool for evaluating complex or indeterminate pathologies due to its noninvasive nature, excellent contrast resolution, multiplanar imaging capabilities and lack of ionizing radiation.
Ordinary or usual leiomyomas have characteristic imaging features including round or oval shape, well-defined border, low T2 signal, pseudocapsule, and variable enhancement.
Fibroids can undergo various types of degeneration: cystic, hyaline, myxoid, red/carneous, and calcific. Imaging features can suggest the type of degeneration, though features may overlap. Multiple types of degeneration can occur concurrently.
Red or carneous degeneration more commonly causes acute symptoms as compared to other types of degeneration. Torsion of a pedunculated fibroid also causes acute symptoms.
Fibroids and adenomyomas may look similar. Fibroids tend to be round, well-defined, cause mass effect, have a pseudocapsule, and demonstrate low T2 signal. Adenomyomas are more often oval, ill-defined, cause no mass effect, and are low in T2 signal with numerous internal high T2 signal foci.
Fibroids and other juxtauterine masses may look similar. The bridging vascular sign has been shown to be a useful sign in distinguishing fibroids from other types of juxtauterine masses.
Fibroids and leiomyosarcomas may have overlapping imaging features. When a fibroid has three or more of the following features, malignancy must be considered: nodular borders, hemorrhage, areas of low T2 signal, central nonenhancing areas. Irregular border of a uterine tumor is also a red-flag for possible malignancy. Suspicious features should prompt further investigation with multidisciplinary evaluation.
The most common symptoms of uterine sarcomas are abnormal vaginal bleeding, pain, or rapid growth of a uterine mass.
A new or rapidly enlarging uterine mass in a postmenopausal woman should always raise suspicion for possible leiomyosarcoma and should be evaluated promptly, however, most patients operated on for rapidly growing fibroids do not have sarcoma.
Despite MRI features that help to distinguish endometrial polyps and hyperplasia from carcinoma, biopsy must be performed, as imaging features overlap and these may occur concurrently.

nent. The endometrium should be carefully assessed for uniformity (or lack thereof), fluid, including simple fluid, blood or other complex T1 hyperintense fluid, polyps or masses as evidenced by enhancement, or any foreign objects or medical devices such as an intrauterine device. An intrauterine device typically appears as a low T2 signal linear or T-shaped structure in the endometrial canal. The IUD should be inspected for appropriate positioning; if the IUD is malpositioned, this is described in the radiology report. If the patient has had prior placement of coil type permanent birth control device into the fallopian tubes, careful inspection of the cornual regions and uterine fundus should be performed. These coils are easily visualized on plain radiography, standard and sonographic hysterosonography, and can also be seen on MRI as areas of signal void within the proximal portions of the fallopian tubes at the level of the uterine cornua.[54]

Next, the junctional zone should be assessed. The thickness of the junctional zone is measured on the sagittal T2-weighted image in a similar fashion as was used for measuring the endometrium. The normal junctional zone should be a low T2 signal band surrounding the endometrium. The junctional zone should be analyzed for uniformity (or lack thereof), with focal or diffuse areas of thickening, and/or the presence of T2 hyperintense subendometrial cysts, which would suggest adenomyosis. If a discrete adenomyoma is observed, the location and measurements in at least two planes but preferably three planes should be described.

The myometrium is then assessed and described as homogeneous or heterogeneous, and the presence of any pathologic condition should be discussed. If there are uterine fibroids, the locations of fibroids (subserosal, intramural, submucosal) should be discussed. The imaging features, signal characteristics, presence of usual or

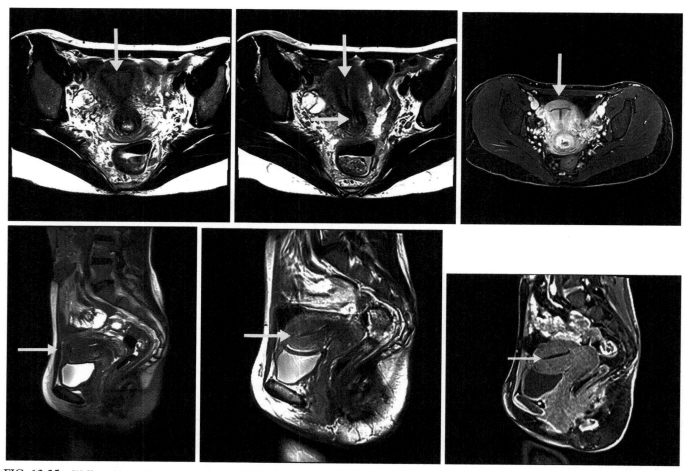

FIG. 12.25 **Well-positioned intrauterine device (IUD).** The IUD is well-visualized on the axial T2-weighted images as a T2 hypointense, T-shaped structure centered in the endometrial canal (A and B) and on the axial T1 fat-saturated contrast enhance image (C). Note that the standard T2-weighted image in the same patient (D) does not show the IUD as well as the axial sequences (A–C) or the sagittal T2 high resolution image (E) or sagittal T1 weighted image (F), underscoring the importance of evaluating all sequences to locate the intrauterine device. The strings of the IUD can be seen traversing the cervix on the second axial T2-weighted image, demarcated by the horizontal white arrow (B).

classic type of fibroid versus atypical imaging features should be discussed. Careful attention should be paid to any feature that may indicate the potential for an underlying leiomyosarcoma.

Whether addressing benign or malignant conditions of the uterus, structured reporting lends itself well to communicating exam findings to the ordering clinician, and helps to ensure that all important elements of the radiology report are included. A sample report template is illustrated in Fig. 12.26.

Sample report template MRI Pelvis with and without contrast

CLINICAL HISTORY: Fibroids.
EXAMINATION: MRI Pelvis with and without contrast +/- MRA Pelvis with and without contrast
DATE:
COMPARISON:
TECHNIQUE: MRI technique as per institution protocol should be included
CONTRAST DOSE: include dose (ml) and type of intravenous contrast agent utilized

FINDINGS:
UTERUS: Measures (Length x AP x TV)
Fibroid burden:
Index fibroids:
Fibroid 1: (Type, location, current and prior dimensions (CC x AP x TV cm)
Signal intensity compared to myometrium:
T1-weighted sequences:
T2-weighted sequences:
Enhancement: Yes or no; describe
DWI/ADC: (If performed)

ENDOMETRIUM:
JUNCTIONAL ZONE:
CERVIX:
OVARIES/ADNEXA:
    Right:
    Left:
MR ARTERIOGRAPHY: (if applicable)
PERITONEUM / RETROPERITONEUM:
GASTROINTESTINAL TRACT:
LYMPH NODES:
BLADDER:
MUSCULOSKELETAL / SOFT TISSUES:
OTHER / PELVIC FREE FLUID:

IMPRESSION:

FIG. 12.26 Sample report template MRI Pelvis with and without contrast. This can be tailored as per institution.

12.13 Pearls and pitfalls

Given the overlapping imaging appearances of many uterine pathologies, Table 12.5 provides a summary of pearls and pitfalls to be aware of when interpreting pelvic MRI (Table 12.5).

12.14 Conclusion

MRI is an extremely important tool in the evaluation of benign uterine pathologies, particularly when ultrasound is limited or inconclusive, or when complex or overlapping pathologies are present. MRI is well-established in its ability to evaluate overall fibroid burden and can provide a comprehensive map of size, number, and location of fibroids. MRI can depict degenerating and nondegenerating fibroids for treatment planning purposes. Prior to fibroid treatment, MRI can also identify any concurrent pathologies that may affect the treatment strategy, such as adenomyosis, endometriosis, endometrial pathologies, or underlying pelvic malignancies. As the role of MRI continues to expand, it is imperative for the radiologist interpreting pelvic MRI to be aware of the MRI appearances of uterine pathologies and to understand the overlapping imaging features of some of these processes. Forging relationships with clinicians to discuss MRI results in order to address complex scenarios in a multidisciplinary fashion can help to achieve the best outcomes for the patient.

Acknowledgment

We want to extend our gratitude to Dr. Susan Ascher MD, Georgetown University Hospital, Washington, DC for the images (Figs. 12.13 and 12.14) contributed to this chapter.

References

1. ACR-SAR-SPR Practice Parameter for the Performance of Magnetic Resonance Imaging (MRI) of the Soft-Tissue Components of the Pelvis. ACR. Resolution 28. Revised 2020.
2. Hricak H. MRI of the female pelvis: a review. *AJR*. 1986;146:1115–1122.
3. Hricak H, Alpers C, Crooks LE, Sheldon PE. Magnetic resonance imaging of the female pelvis: initial experience. *AJR*. 1983;141:1119–1128.
4. Novellas S, Chassang M, Delotte J, et al. MRI characteristics of the uterine junctional zone: from normal to the diagnosis of adenomyosis. *AJR*. 2011;196:1206–1213.
5. Bazot M, Cortez A, Darai E, et al. Ultrasonography compared with magnetic resonance imaging for the diagnosis of adenomyosis: correlation with histopathology. *Hum Reprod*. 2001;16(11):2427–2433.
6. Nalaboff KM, Pellerito JS, Ben-Levi E. Imaging the endometrium: disease and normal variants. *Radiographics*. 2001;21:1409–1424.
7. Langer JE, Oliver ER, Lev-Toaff AS, Coleman BG. Imaging of the female pelvis through the life cycle. *Radiographics*. 2012;32:1575–1597.
8. Demas B, Hricak H, Jaffe RB. Uterine MR imaging: effects of hormonal stimulation. *Radiology*. 1986;159:123–126.
9. Freeman SJ, Aly AM, Kataoka MY, Addley HC, Reinhold C, Sala E. The revised FIGO staging system for uterine malignancies: implications for MR imaging. *Radiographics*. 2012;32(6):1805–1827.
10. Okamoto Y, Tanaka YO, Masato N, Tsunoda H, Yoshikawa H, Itai Y. MR imaging of the uterine cervix: imaging-pathologic correlation. *Radiographics*. 2003;23(2):425–445.
11. Park SB, Lee JH, Lee YH, Song MJ, Choi HJ. Multilocular cystic lesions in the uterine cervix: broad spectrum of imaging features and pathologic correlation. *AJR*. 2010;195:517–523.
12. Doi T, Yamashita Y, Yasunaga T, et al. Adenoma malignum: MR imaging and pathologic study. *Radiology*. 1997;204(1):39–42.
13. Yamashita Y, Takahashi M, Katabuchi H, Fukumatsu Y, Miyazaki K, Okamura H. Adenoma malignum: MR appearances mimicking Nabothian cysts. *AJR*. 1994;162:649–650.
14. Natarajan P, Vinturache A, Hutson R, Nugent D, Broadhead T. The value of MRI in management of endometrial hyperplasia with atypia. *World J Surg Oncol*. 2020;18:34.
15. Sadro CT. Imaging the endometrium: a pictorial essay. *Can Assoc Radiol J*. 2016;67:254–262.
16. Grasel R, Outwater E, Sigelman E, Capuzzi D, Parker L, Hussain S. Endometrial polyps: MR imaging features and distinction from endometrial carcinoma. *Radiology*. 2000;214:47–52.
17. Soichiro H, Mitsumori A, Inai R, et al. Endometrial polyps: MR imaging features. *Acta Med Okayama*. 2012;66(6):475–485.
18. Bulun SE. Uterine fibroids. *NEJM*. 2013;369:1344–1355.
19. Baird DB, Dunson DB, Hill MC, Cousins D, Schectman JM. High cumulative incidence of uterine leiomyoma in black and white women: ultrasound evidence. *Am J Obstet Gynecol*. 2003;188(1):100–107.
20. De La Cruz M, Buchanan E. Uterine fibroids: diagnosis and treatment. *Am Fam Physician*. 2017;95(2):100–107.
21. Murase E, Siegelman ES, Outwater EK, Perez-Jaffe LA, Tureck RW. Uterine leiomyomas: histopathologic features, MR imaging findings, differential diagnosis, and treatment. *Radiographics*. 1999;19:1179–1197.
22. Fennessey, F. MRI of benign female pelvis. ARRS Categorical Course Body MRI. 2013;223-230.

23. Panageas E, Kier R, McCauley TR, McCarthy S. Submucosal uterine leiomyomas: diagnosis of prolapse into the cervix and vagina based on mri imaging. *Am J Radiol*. 1992;159:555–558.

24. Sherer D, Cheung W, Gorelick C, et al. Sonographic and magnetic resonance imaging findings of an isolated vaginal leiomyoma. *J Ultrasound Med*. 2007;26:1453–1456.

25. Fasih N, Shanbhogue AKP, Macdonald DB, et al. Leiomyomas beyond the uterus: unusual locations, rare manifestations. *Radiographics*. 2008;28:1931–1948.

26. DeMulder D, Ascher SM. Uterine leiomyosarcoma: can MRI differentiate leiomyosarcoma from benign leiomyoma before treatment? *AJR*. 2018;211:1405–1415.

27. Ueda H, Togashi K, Konishi I, et al. Unusual appearances of uterine leiomyomas: MR imaging findings and their histopathologic backgrounds. *Radiographics*. 1999;19:S131–S145.

28. Kitajima K, Kaji Y, Imanaka K, Sugihara R, Sugimura K. MRI findings of uterine lipoleiomyoma correlated with pathologic findings. *AJR*. 2007;189:W100–W104.

29. Arleo EK, Schwartz PE, Hui P, McCarthy S. Review of leiomyoma variants. *AJR*. 2015;205:912–921.

30. Cunningham R, Horrow M, Smith R, Springer J. Adenomyosis: a sonographic diagnosis. *Radiographics*. 2018;38:1576–1589.

31. Reinhold C, McCarthy S, Bret PM, et al. Diffuse adenomyosis: comparison of endovaginal us and MR imaging with histopathologic correlation. *Radiology*. 1996;199(1):151–158.

32. Ascher SM, Arnold LL, Patt RH, et al. Adenomyosis: prospective comparison of MR imaging and transvaginal sonography. *Radiology*. 1994;190(3):803–806.

33. Larsen S, Lundorf E, Forman A, Dueholm M. Adenomyosis and junctional zone changes in patients with endometriosis. *Eur J Obstet Gynecol Reprod Biol*. 2011;157:206–211.

34. Kunz G, Beil D, Huppert P, Noe M, Kissler S, Leyendecker G. Adenomyosis in endometriosis-prevalence and impact on fertility. Evidence from magnetic resonance imaging. *Hum Reprod*. 2005;20:2309–2316.

35. Bazot M, Fiori O, Darai E. Letter to the editor - Adenomyosis in endometriosis-prevalence and impact on fertility. evidence from magnetic resonance imaging. *Hum Reprod*. 2006;21:1101–1102.

36. Mark AS, Hricak H, Heinrichs LW, et al. Adenomyosis and leiomyoma: differential diagnosis with mr imaging. *Radiology*. 1987;163:527–529.

37. Togashi K, Ozasa H, Konishi I, et al. Enlarged uterus: differentiation between adenomyosis and leiomyoma with mr imaging. *Radiology*. 1989;171:531–534.

38. Tamai K, Togashi K, Ito T, Morisawa N, Fujiwara T, Koyama T. MR imaging findings of adenomyosis: correlation with histopathologic features and diagnostic pitfalls. *Radiographics*. 2005;25:21–40.

39. Shinagare AB, Meylaerts LJ, Laury AR, Mortele KJ. MRI features of ovarian fibroma and fibrothecoma with histopathologic correlation. *AJR*. 2012;198:W296–W303.

40. Madan R. The bridging vascular sign. *Radiology*. 2006;238:371–372.

41. Kim JC, Kim SS, Park JY. Bridging vascular sign in the mr diagnosis of exophytic uterine leiomyoma. *J Comput Assist Tomogr*. 2000;24(1):57–60.

42. Kim SH, Sim JS, Seong CK. Interface vessels on color/power doppler us and MRI: a clue to differentiate subserosal uterine myomas from extrauterine tumors. *J Comput Assist Tomogr*. 2001;25:36–42.

43. Gupta A, Desai A, Bhatt S. Imaging of the endometrium: physiologic changes and diseases: womens imaging. *Radiographics*. 2017;37(7):2206–2207.

44. Sellmyer M, Desser T, Maturen K, Jeffrey Jr RB, A Kamaya. Physiologic, histologic, and imaging features of retained products of conception. *Radiographics*. 2013;33:781–796.

45. Thian YL, Tan KH, Kwek JW, Wang J, Chern B, Yam KL. Leiomyomatosis peritonealis disseminata and subcutaneous myoma – a rare complication of laparoscopic myomectomy. *Abdom Imaging*. 2009;34:235–238.

46. Kumar S, Sharma JB, Verma D, Gupta P, Roy KK, Malhotra N. Disseminated peritoneal leiomyomatosis: an unusual complication of laparoscopic myomectomy. *Arch Gynecol Obstet*. 2008;278(1):93–95.

47. Santos P, Cunha TM. Uterine sarcomas: clinical presentation and MRI features. *Diag Interv Radiol*. 2015;21:4–9.

48. Parker WH, Fu YS, Berek JS. Uterine sarcoma in patients operated on for presumed leiomyoma and rapidly growing leiomyoma. *Obstet Gynecol*. 1994;83:414–418.

49. Lakhman Y, Veeraraghavan H, Chaim J, et al. Differentiation of uterine leiomyosarcoma from atypical leiomyoma: diagnostic accuracy of qualitative MR imaging features and feasibility of texture analysis. *Eur Radiol*. 2017;27(7):2903–2915.

50. Sato K, Yuasa N, Fujita M, Fukushima Y. Clinical application of diffusion-weighted imaging for preoperative differentiation between uterine leiomyoma and leiomyosarcoma. *Am J Obstet Gynecol*. 2014;210(4):368.e1-368.e8.

51. ACOG Committee Opinion. Uterine morcellation for presumed leiomyomas. number 822. *Obstet Gynecolo*. 2021;137(3):e63–e74.

52. Struble J, Reid S, Bedaiwy MA. Adenomyosis: a clinical review of a challenging gynecologic condition. *J Minim Invasive Gynecol*. 2016;23(2):164–185.

53. Boortz H, Martolis J, Ragavendra N, Patel M, Kadell B. Migration of intrauterine devices: radiologic findings and implications for patient care. *Radiographics*. 2012;32:335–352.

54. Khati N, Parghi C, Brindle K. Multimodality imaging of the essure permanent birth control device: emphasis on commonly overlooked abnormalities. *AJR*. 2011;196:W648–W658.

55. Wu TI, Yen TC, Lai CH. Clinical presentation and diagnosis of uterine sarcoma, including imaging. *Best Pract Res Clin Obstet Gynaecol*. 2011;25:681–689.

13

MRI of malignant uterine tumors

Raj Mohan Paspulati

Department of Radiology, Moffitt Cancer Center, Tampa, FL, United States

13.1 Introduction

Endometrial malignancies can be of epithelial or nonepithelial origin. Epithelial malignancies are more common and endometrial adenocarcinoma cancer is the most common gynecologic malignancy in the developed world. The overall survival, prognosis and the type of management depends on initial stage at the time of diagnosis and the histologic type of malignancy. The final surgical stage, histologic type, grade, size of the tumor, and age of the patient are important prognostic factors of endometrial cancer. Knowledge of genetic mutations and molecular biology of the endometrial cancer has provided a new insight in management and prognosis. Magnetic resonance imaging (MRI) of the pelvis provides important information about the size of the tumor, its location, depth of myometrial invasion and regional extrauterine invasion for proper treatment planning. Contrast enhanced computed tomography (CT) and FDG PET/CT are used to asses lymph nodal and distant metastases for complete staging. This manuscript provides information about MRI technique, role of MRI in local staging of endometrial carcinoma, case-based illustration of different stages of endometrial cancer, key MR imaging features in treatment planning and pitfalls in staging. It also provides case-based illustration of different types of nonepithelial endometrial malignancies. Role of FDG PET/CT, PET/MRI and other novel imaging techniques in assessment of lymph nodal and distant metastases are also reviewed.

13.2 Endometrial carcinoma

Endometrial (Adenocarcinoma) carcinoma is the most common type of uterine malignancy. It is the fourth most common female malignancy and most common gynecologic malignancy in the United States. It is the sixth most common cause of cancer related death among women in the United States. 70% of endometrial carcinomas are seen in women over 50 years of age. According to American Cancer Society, about 66,570 new cases of endometrial cancer will be diagnosed with 12,940 deaths in 2021.[1] Though it is still predominantly a cancer of postmenopausal women, there is increasing incidence in young adult women before the age of 40 years due to increasing prevalence of obesity in young women. This new data suggests that surveillance for endometrial cancer should start at much earlier age before menopause. Age is also considered to be an important prognostic factor as women over the age of 65 years have poor prognosis due to high tumor grade with deeper myometrial invasion presenting at more advanced stage.[1,2] Though the incidence of endometrial cancer is slightly higher among white women than Black women, the five-year survival rate is 84% in White women and 63% in Black women. This survival difference is due to more aggressive histologic types, grade and more advanced stage of the disease at initial diagnosis in Black women.[3] Apart from age, obesity, nulliparity, and early menopause are important risk factors for endometrial carcinoma. As compared to women of healthy weight, endometrial cancer is three times more common in women with body mass index (BMI) more than 30.[4] Using estrogen alone without progesterone for menopausal symptoms, diabetes mellitus are other risk factors.[5] Breast cancer patients treated with Tamoxifen have slight increased risk of developing endometrial cancer due to mild estrogenic effect on endometrium. The risk of developing endometrial cancer with Tamoxifen use is <1% per year and the benefits outweigh the risk.[5] Hereditary nonpolyposis colon cancer (HNPCC) or Lynch 2 has also increased risk of endometrial cancer in addition to colon and ovarian cancer. This is most commonly due to defect in the mismatch repair genes MLH1 or MSH2. Five other genes associated with HNPCC include MLH3, MSH6, TGBR2, PMS1, and PMS2.[6,7] Due to its clinical presentation with postmenopausal bleeding, endometrial carcinoma is most often detected at an early stage. Two basic types of endometrial carcinoma have been described by Bokhman based on pathogenesis.[8] One is associated with atypical hyperplasia due to hyperestrogenism and the second one developing in an atrophic endometrium. Those developing from atypical hyperplasia have relatively better prognosis compared to those developing from atrophic endometrium. This simple classification is being replaced by new classification based on molecular pathogenesis of endometrial carcinoma. These molecular subtypes based on tumor genomic architecture provide better insight into the pathogenesis and prognostic value.[9,10] The prognosis and the type of management depends on several factors including the histologic type, grade, lymphovascular invasion, nodal status, and depth of myometrial invasion at initial presentation.[11,12] Preoperative knowledge of these factors is helpful in proper management. Though the histologic type is determined by the initial endometrial biopsy, the final histologic diagnosis with molecular subtype and grade is only provide by the histopathology of the hysterectomy specimen. Incidence of lymph nodal metastases increases with the degree of myometrial invasion.[12] The size of the tumor and its location are also important in determining the management and prognosis.[13] Tumors in the lower uterine segment compared to the fundus are more likely invade the cervix and studies have shown that low lying endometrial carcinoma has higher incidence of pelvic nodal metastases compared to fundal tumors.[12] The exact size, location of the tumor in the endometrial cavity, depth of myometrial invasion, invasion of cervical stroma, and regional lymph nodal metastases are important prognostic factors that can be provided preoperatively by MR imaging.

13.2.1 Histologic types

Endometrioid endometrial carcinoma is the most common type and constitutes 80% of endometrial carcinomas

Less common types include endometrioid carcinoma with squamous differentiation, serous carcinoma, clear cell carcinoma, and undifferentiated carcinoma. Papillary serous carcinoma is the most aggressive type with poor survival.

13.2.2 Risk factors (Table 13.1)

Clinical features:
  Abnormal uterine bleeding: It is the most common presenting symptom (>75%) of endometrial carcinoma.
  Abnormal cytology on screening Pap smear.
  Incidental finding on imaging.
  Incidental finding at hysterectomy for benign disease.
  Staging of endometrial carcinoma (Table 13.2).

TABLE 13.1   Risk Factors.

Risk factors for Endometrial carcinoma	Genetic factors
Age: Postmenopausal and elderly	Genetic predisposition
Hormonal factors	Family History of endometrial, ovarian, breast, or colon cancer
Unopposed estrogen therapy	Lynch syndrome
Tamoxifen therapy	Cowden syndrome
Early menarche	
Late menopause	
Nulliparity	
Polycystic ovary syndrome/chronic anovulation	
Estrogen secreting ovarian tumor (Granulosa cell Tumor)	
Obesity	
Diabetes mellitus	

TABLE 13.2 Staging of endometrial carcinoma (AJCC).

Stage	Stage grouping	FIGO stage	Stage description
I	T1 N0 M0	I	The cancer is growing inside the uterus. It may also be growing into the glands of the cervix, but not into the supporting connective tissue of the cervix (T1). It has not spread to nearby lymph nodes (N0) or to distant sites (M0).
IA	T1a N0 M0	IA	The cancer is in the endometrium (inner lining of the uterus) and may have grown less than halfway through the underlying muscle layer of the uterus (the myometrium) (T1a). It has not spread to nearby lymph nodes (N0) or to distant sites (M0).
IB	T1b N0 M0	IB	The cancer has grown from the endometrium into the myometrium. It has grown more than halfway through the myometrium, but has not spread beyond the body of the uterus (T1b). It has not spread to nearby lymph nodes (N0) or to distant sites (M0).
II	T2 N0 M0	II	The cancer has spread from the body of the uterus and is growing into the supporting connective tissue of the cervix (called the cervical stroma). But it has not spread outside the uterus (T2). It has not spread to nearby lymph nodes (N0) or to distant sites (M0).
III	T3 N0 M0	III	The cancer has spread outside the uterus, but has not spread to the inner lining of the rectum or urinary bladder (T3). It has not spread to nearby lymph nodes (N0) or to distant sites (M0).
IIIA	T3a N0 M0	IIIA	The cancer has spread to the outer surface of the uterus (called the serosa) and/or to the fallopian tubes or ovaries (the adnexa) (T3a). It has not spread to nearby lymph nodes (N0) or to distant sites (M0).
IIIB	T3b N0 M0	IIIB	The cancer has spread to the vagina or to the tissues around the uterus (the parametrium) (T3b). It has not spread to nearby lymph nodes (N0) or to distant sites (M0).
IIIC1	T1–T3 N1, N1mi or N1a M0	IIIC1	The cancer is growing in the body of the uterus. It may have spread to some nearby tissues, but is not growing into the inside of the bladder or rectum (T1 to T3). It has also spread to pelvic lymph nodes (N1, N1mi, or N1a), but not to lymph nodes around the aorta or distant sites (M0).
IIIC2	T1–T3 N2, N2mi or N2a M0	IIIC2	The cancer is growing in the body of the uterus. It may have spread to some nearby tissues, but is not growing into the inside of the bladder or rectum (T1 to T3). It has also spread to lymph nodes around the aorta (para-aortic lymph nodes) (N2, N2mi, or N2a), but not to distant sites (M0).
IVA	T4 Any N M0		The cancer has spread to the inner lining of the rectum or urinary bladder (called the mucosa) (T4). It may or may not have spread to nearby lymph nodes (Any N), but has not spread to distant sites (M0).
IVB	Any T Any N M1	IVB	The cancer has spread to inguinal (groin) lymph nodes, the upper abdomen, the omentum, or to organs away from the uterus, such as the lungs, liver, or bones (M1). The cancer can be any size (Any T) and it might or might not have spread to other lymph nodes (Any N).

13.3 Imaging technique

13.3.1 Ultrasonography

Transvaginal ultrasonography (TVUS) is useful in identifying abnormal endometrial thickness and endometrial mass in women with postmenopausal bleeding. Color Doppler is useful in differentiating abnormally thickened endometrium from hemorrhagic blood products. Ultrasonography (US) has low sensitivity and accuracy in detection of depth of myometrial invasion and is not used for staging (Fig. 13.1).

13.3.2 Computed tomography and FDG PET imaging

CT and PET imaging are useful for detection of nodal and distant metastases and not useful for depth of myometrial invasion due to poor soft tissue contrast resolution of CT imaging (Fig. 13.2).

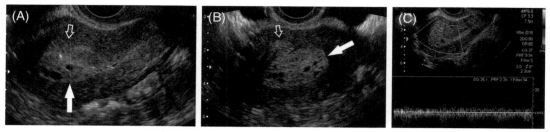

FIG. 13.1 Sagittal (A) and axial (B) TVUS images show thick polypoidal endometrium with cystic foci (arrow). Lobulated focus (open arrow) near enodomyometrial junction suspicious for inner myometrial invasion. Sagittal TVUS image with Doppler (C) demonstrates low resistance arterial flow in the endometrial mass.

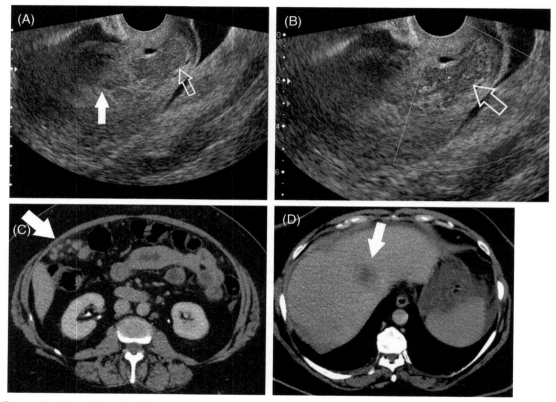

FIG. 13.2 Gray scale (A) and Doppler (B) sagittal TVUS images demonstrate large endometrial mass (arrow) invading into cervix stroma (open arrow). Contrast enhanced CT images of the abdomen show peritoneal implants (C) and liver metastasis (D).

13.3.3 MR imaging

MR imaging technique: High resolution, small field of view, T2 weighted fast spin echo (FSE) and dynamic contrast enhanced T1 weighted fat saturated images in sagittal and axial (perpendicular to the endometrial cavity) are mandatory for detection of primary tumor and accurate staging of myometrial invasion. Diffusion weighted images are complementary to T2 weighted and delayed contrast T1 weighted images in assessment of myometrial invasion and also useful to assess treatment response after chemoradiation treatment.[14–16] Large FOV T2weighted and contrast enhanced T1 weighted images of the entire pelvis are useful to evaluate lymph nodes and extra nodal metastatic disease.

13.4 MR protocol (Table 13.3)

T2 weighted MR images provide good zonal anatomy of the uterus with clear delineation of endometrium, junctional zone and myometrium (Fig. 13.3). Depth of myometrial and cervical stromal invasion can be well delineated

TABLE 13.3 MRI protocol.

- IM Glucagon prior to imaging
- SS T2 COR (HASTE, SINGLE SHOT TSE OR FSE) (large FOV, 5 mm no gaps)
- SS T2 AX (HASTE, SINGLE SHOT TSE OR FSE) (large FOV, 5 mm no gaps)
- SS T2 SAG (HASTE, SINGLE SHOT TSE OR FSE) (large FOV, 5 mm no gaps)
- High resolution T2 FSE with small FOV (200–240)
- T2 TSE SAG without fat saturation
- T2 TSE without fat saturation coronal to Long Axis of uterus (3–4 mm thickness, no gap)
- T2 TSE without fat saturation Short Axis of uterus perpendicular to endometrial cavity (3–4 mm thickness, no gap)
- T2 TSE with fat saturation short axis of uterus perpendicular to endometrial cavity (3–4 mm thickness, no gap)—optional
- Axial DWI with ADC- 4–5 mm (b values 50, 600 and 1000)
- Precontrast T1 3D with fat saturation Axial (VIBE, THRIVE, LAVA, TIGRE)
- Postcontrast T1 3D Axial with fat saturation (VIBE, THRIVE, LAVA-XV, TIGRE) 25 seconds and 90 seconds delayed
- Postcontrast T1 3D Sagittal and Coronal (VIBE, THRIVE, LAVA, TIGRE)
- Delayed Postcontrast T1 3D Axial with fat saturation (VIBE, THRIVE, LAVA-XV, TIGRE)

due to difference in contrast signal intensity of the tumor from junctional zone and cervical stroma.[17] Delayed phase T1 contrast enhanced MR images and diffusion weighted images (DWI) also provide additional confirmation of the depth of myometrial invasion due to differential contrast enhancement and diffusion restriction of the tumor from myometrium and cervical stroma[14] (Fig. 13.3). DWI with ADC and dynamic contrast enhanced (DCE) images with quantification of apparent diffusion and contrast enhancement are useful biomarkers in further assessment of tumor response after neoadjuvant treatment.[18,19]

13.4.1 Imaging findings

Role of imaging is for staging of endometrial carcinoma after it is diagnosed by endometrial biopsy.

13.4.2 Ultrasonography

Stage 1A: Focal or diffuse thick and echogenic endometrium with a clear demarcation of endometrial-myometrial junction (subendometrial halo).

Ultrasonography: Endometrial mass and Color Doppler demonstrates multiple feeding vessels with low resistance arterial flow (Fig. 13.4A and B).

Stage 1B: Endometrial thickening or mass with disruption of the endometrial-myometrial junction (Fig. 13.1B).

13.4.3 Computed tomography

Not useful for detecting depth of myometrial invasion due to poor soft tissue contrast resolution. CT is used for lymph nodal and extra nodal distant metastases.

13.4.4 MR imaging

MR imaging is more accurate for T staging of endometrial carcinoma due to excellent demonstration of the zonal anatomy of the uterus. MRI is more accurate in depth of myometrial invasion, extension to cervix, vagina, and adnexa. Detection of lymph nodal metastases has similar accuracy to CT and is based on size criteria.[20,21]

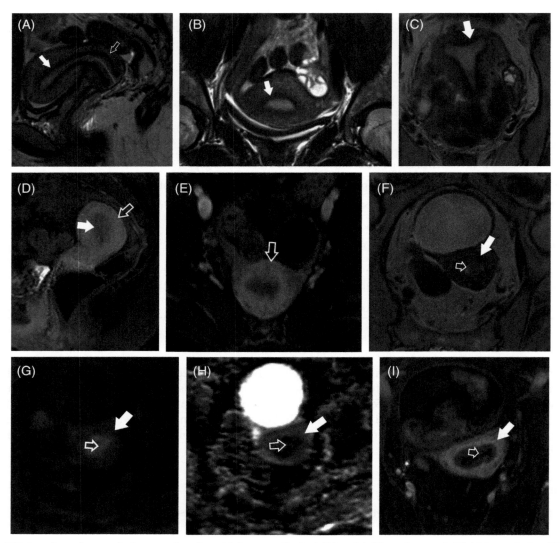

FIG. 13.3   MR imaging of normal uterus and endometrial cancer. Sagittal (A), axial (B), and coronal (C) high resolution T2 FSE images demonstrate good zonal anatomy with T2 hypointense junctional zone (arrow) surrounding the hyperintense endometrial lining. Delayed contrast enhanced T1 GRE images in sagittal (D) and axial (E) plane show normal homogeneous enhancement of the myometrium (open arrow) and hypointense endometrial lining (arrow). Axial T2 (F), DWI (G), ADC (H) and delayed postcontrast T1 GRE (I) images of uterus with endometrial cancer demonstrate good contrast resolution between the endometrial cancer (open arrow) and myometrium (arrow).

13.4.5 Imaging features

T1 weighted images: Tumor is isointense to normal endometrium and demarcation from adjacent myometrium is less distinct. Hematoma is hyperintense to the tumor.

T2 weighted images: Tumor is isointense or hypointense to the normal endometrium. Hyperintense relative to the myometrium (Fig. 13.4C and D).

Contrast enhanced T1 weighted images: 3 different phase of contrast enhancement of the uterus.

Early (<1 minute) phase: The inner myometrium or the junctional zone enhances first and provides clear demarcation between the endometrial tumor and outer myometrium. Disruption of this enhancing rim by the hypointense tumor is the earliest sign of myometrial invasion.

Equilibrium (2–3 minutes) phase: Enhancement of the outer myometrium.

Delayed (4–5 minutes) phase: Enhancement of the cervical stroma.

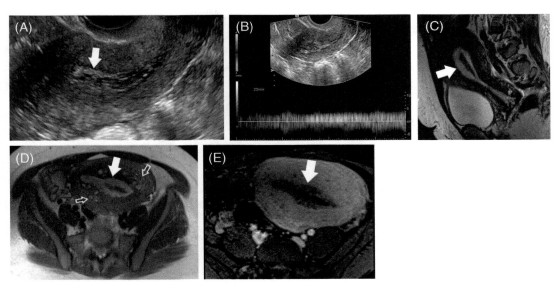

FIG. 13.4   **Stage 1A endometrial cancer.** Sagittal TVUS images color Doppler (A and B) show endometrial thickening (arrow) with low resistance arterial flow. Sagittal (C) and axial (D) T2 weighted images show hyperimtense endometrial thickening with multiple T2 hyperintense foci (open arrow) in the myometrium due to incidental adenomyosis. Axial delayed postcontrast T1 GRE image (E) shows hyointense thick endometrium (arrow) compared to enhancing myometrium without invasion.

Endometrial carcinoma enhances earlier than normal endometrium and later than the inner myometrium. Maximum tumor-myometrium contrast is in the equilibrium phase (Fig. 13.4E).

Stage 1A: Focal or diffuse endometrial thickening with smooth interface between the endometrium and the junctional zone or Invasion into the inner half of the myometrium. The junctional zone is hypointense on T2w images and seen as an intense enhancing layer in the early contrast enhanced T1w images (Figs. 13.4 and 13.5).

T2 weighted images: Disruption of the smooth interface between the hyperintense tumor and the hypointense junctional zone.

Contrast enhanced T1 weighted images: Disruption of the interface between the hypointense tumor and enhancing junctional zone in the early contrast enhanced phase (<1 minute). Deeper myometrial invasion beyond the junctional zone is seen in equilibrium phase as hypointense tumor within the enhancing myometrium. Maximum depth of myometrial invasion is less than 50% of myometrial thickness.

Stage 1B: Full thickness disruption of the junctional zone with >50% invasion into the myometrium and an intact peripheral rim of myometrium.

Stage 2: Tumor extension to cervix.

Stage 2A: Tumor extension through the internal os into the endocervix without invasion of the cervical stroma. Clear demarcation of hyperintense tumor mass from the hypointense cervical stroma on T2 weighted images. On delayed contrast enhanced T1 weighted images (3–5 minutes), no invasion of the enhancing stroma by the hypointense tumor in the endocervix (Fig. 13.6).

Stage 2B: Tumor invasion into the cervical stroma (Figs. 13.7, 13.8, and 13.9).

T2 weighted images show hyperintense tumor extending into hypointense cervical stroma and delayed contrast enhanced T1GRE images show hypointense tumor extending into enhancing cervical stroma.

Stage 3: Tumor extension beyond the uterus.

Stage 3A: Full thickness myometrial invasion with Irregular uterine contour and with or without parametrial mass.

Stage 3B: Tumor extension inferior to the cervix with invasion of the upper vagina. Disruption of the hypointense vaginal wall on T2 weighted images.

Stage 3C: Enlarged pelvic lymph nodes.

Stage 4: Tumor extension beyond pelvis or invasion of bladder or rectum.

Stage 4A: Disruption of the hypointense rectal or bladder wall with intraluminal tumor extension.

Stage 4B: Ascites, peritoneal implants and distant metastases (Figs. 13.10 and 13.11).

Contrast enhanced CT, PET-CT or PET-MR are useful in demonstrating the extent of distant metastases in stage 4 disease (Figs. 13.10 and 13.11).

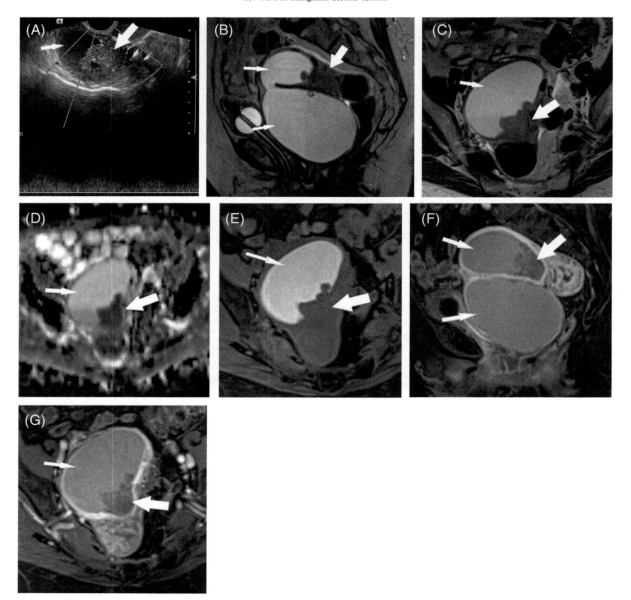

FIG. 13.5   Stage 1A endometrial carcinoma in the lower uterine segment with hematometra. Sagittal TVUS with spectral Doppler (A) shows large polypoid mass with arterial flow (large arrow) obstructing the endometrial cavity with echogenic fluid in the endometrial cavity (small arrow). Sagittal (B) and axial (C) T2 weighted images show an obstructing T2 hypointense mass (large arrow) in the lower uterine segment with fluid distended endometrial cavity (small arrows). Axial ADC image (D) show lower uterine segment mass (arrow) with diffusion restriction. Axial unenhanced T1 GRE image (E) shows hypointense lower uterine endometrial mass (large arrow) and T1 hyperintense endometrial fluid (small arrow) due to hematometra. Sagittal (F) and axial (G) postcontrast T1 GRE images show polypoidal low intensity lower uterine segment mass (large arrow) without invasion into the enhancing myometrium and hematometra (small arrows).

13.4.6 Pitfalls

Pitfalls in staging of endometrial carcinoma due to erroneous assessment of the depth of myometrial invasion can occur if the junctional zone is not well visualized. This can occur with adenomyosis, leiomyomas and bulky endometrial tumor resulting in a thin surrounding myometrium. Tumor extension to uterine cornua can be mistaken for full thickness myometrial invasion. Poor tumor-myometrium contrast in postcontrast T1 weighted images can over or under stage the depth of myometrial invasion[22,23] (Fig. 13.12).

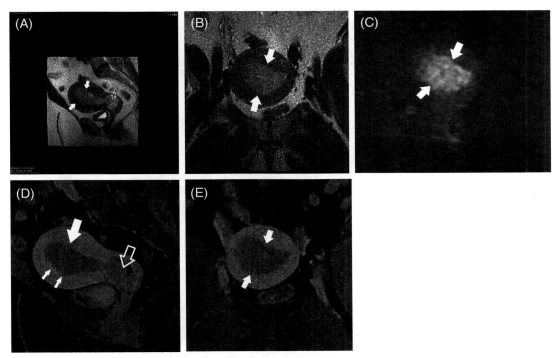

FIG. 13.6   Bulky stage 2A endometrial cancer extending to endocervix without cervical stromal invasion. Sagittal and axial T2 weighted images bulky T2 hyperintense endometrial mass (arrows) extending into endocervical canal (open arrow). Axial DWI (C) shows diffusion restriction of the endometrial mass. Sagittal (D) and axial (E) delayed postcontrast T1 GRE images show endometrial mass (arrows) with inner myometrial invasion (small arrows) and extending into endocervix (open arrow) without cervical stromal invasion.

13.4.7   Undifferentiated endometrial carcinoma (UEC)

UEC is a rare form of endometrial carcinoma accounting for <10% endometrial carcinomas. Compared to other Grade 3 endometrial carcinomas, they are more aggressive with initial presentation at more advanced stage and poor prognosis. Though the median age of incidence is between 50 and 60 years, can affect at younger age before 40 years. Morphologically can present as endometrial thickening or polypoid mass with myometrial and adnexal invasion. There is also more frequent involvement of the lower uterine segment and cervix. Large areas of tumor necrosis and early vascular invasion are other features of this UEC (Figs. 13.13 and 13.14). They can be associated with hereditary nonpolyposis colorectal carcinoma or Lynch syndrome. They can be mistaken histopathologically for Grade 3 endometrioid carcinoma. Local staging of the extent of tumor invasion is better assessed with MR imaging. Nodal and distant metastases are also more common and better assessed with CT or FDG PET imaging[24,25] (Figs. 13.13 and 13.14).

13.5   Nonepithelial malignancies

These include mixed epithelial and mesenchymal tumors and pure stromal sarcomas. These tumors are thought to arise from either endometrial stroma or uterine muscle.[26–28] Malignant tumors arising from uterine stroma may be associated with epithelial component which can be benign or malignant. These heterogeneous uterine tumors are grouped as uterine sarcomas with different classifications and the GOG classification placing them in two broad categories as nonepithelial neoplasms and mixed epithelial nonepithelial neoplasms. Uterine sarcomas in general represent, 10% of malignant uterine tumors with varying incidence of the subtypes. The most common, in order of decreasing incidence, are carcinosarcoma, leiomyosarcoma, endometrial stromal sarcoma, and adenosarcoma. In general, the incidence of uterine sarcomas is slightly higher in Black females and relatively earlier age incidence of leiomyosarcomas compared to carcinosarcomas. The risk factors for carcinosarcoma are similar to endometrial carcinoma and prior pelvic radiation

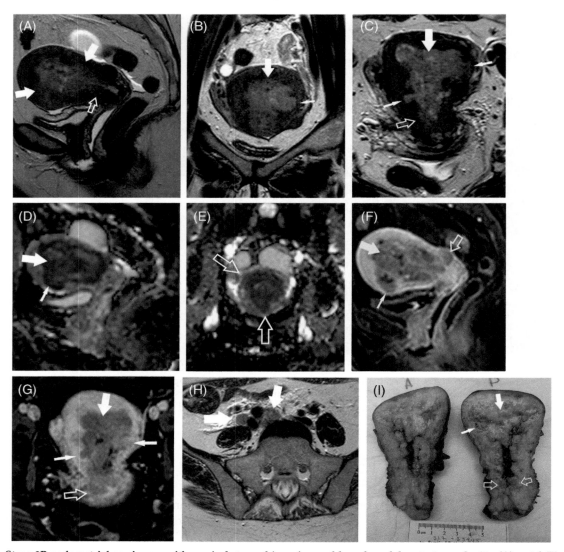

FIG. 13.7 Stage 2B endometrial carcinoma with cervical stromal invasion and lymph nodal metastases. Sagitta (A), axial (B), and coronal (C) T2 weighted images show large endometrial mass (large arrow) extending into cervix (open arrows) with myometrial invasion (small arrows). Sagittal (D) and axial (E) ADC images show diffusion restricting endometrial and cervical mass (large arrow) with myometrial (small arrows) and cervical stromal invasion (open arrows). Sagittal (F) and coronal (G) delayed postcontrast T1 GRE images confirm >50% myometrial invasion (small arrows) and cervical stromal invasion (open arrows). Axial T2 weighted image (H) shows enlarged right common iliac lymph nodes (arrows). Coronal Gross pathology specimen image (I) shows large infiltrating endometrial mass (large arrow) involving the entire endometrial cavity and cervix with invasion into myometrium (small arrow) and cervical stroma (open arrows).

is also considered to be a risk factor, especially for carcinosarcoma. Though leiomyosarcoma may be associated with uterine benign leiomyoma, they are considered to arise independent of leiomyoma.[29]

13.6 Imaging of uterine sarcomas

13.6.1 Carcinosarcoma

They account for less than 5% of uterine malignancies and typically seen in elderly women. Though it may be classified in the uterine sarcoma, it is now considered to be primarily an epithelial neoplasm with sarcomatous transformation.[30,31] Similar to endometrial carcinoma, may present in earlier stages as endometrial thickening or a

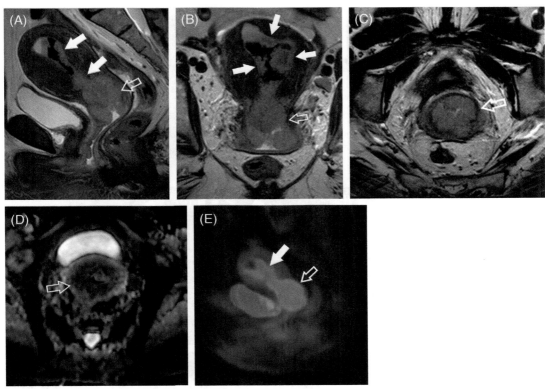

FIG. 13.8   Stage 2B endometrial carcinoma with myometrial and cervical stromal invasion. Sagittal (A), coronal (B), and axial (C) T2 FSE images show lobulated endometrial mass invading into >50% myometrium (large arrows) and into cervical stroma (open arrows). Axial ADC image (D) of the cervix confirms cervical stroma invasion (open arrow). Sagittal FDG PET CT image shows hypermetabolic endometrial (arrow) and cervical (open arrow) mass.

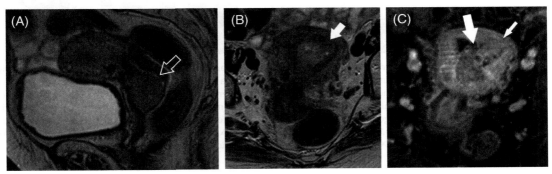

FIG. 13.9   Stage 1B endometrial carcinoma with second separate endometrial carcinoma in the endocervix invading into cervical stroma. Sagittal T2 weighted image (A) shows T2 hyperintense cervical mass invading into cervical stroma (open arrow). Axial T2 weighted image of the uterine fundus (B) shows fundal endometrial mass invading into the myometrium (arrow). Axial delayed postcontrast T1 GRE image show heterogeneously enhancing endometrial mass (large arrow) invading into inner half of the myometrium (small arrow).

polypoid mass. At more advanced stage they present as bulky mass in the endometrial cavity, with hemorrhage and necrosis, extension into the endocervix and vagina with varying degrees of myometrial invasion, extension to adnexa and surrounding viscera. The true extent of the mass is better delineated on MR imaging.[32] High T2 signal intensity with prolonged intense enhancement on contrast enhanced images are commonly observed[33] (CT and PET imaging are useful for nodal and distant metastases). Spread to pelvic and para aortic lymph nodes is common and distant metastases may occur to lung, liver, and bones. There are no definite imaging features to differentiate endometrial carcinoma from carcinosarcoma. Histologic diagnosis depends on identifying high grade epithelial and mesenchymal components. The epithelial component may include high grade endometrioid, clear cell, serous, undifferentiated type or even squamous type and the mesenchymal element can be homologous or heterologous.

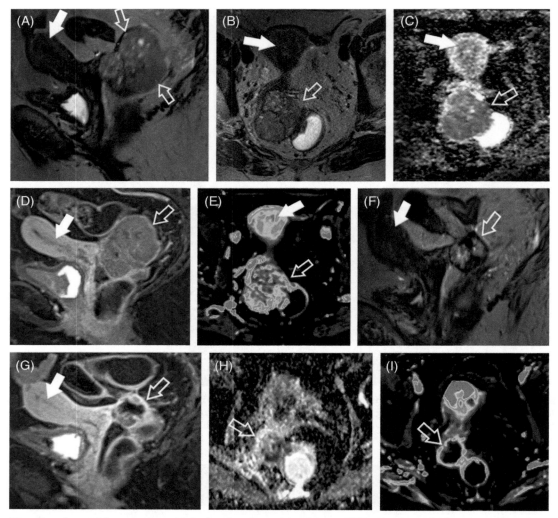

FIG. 13.10 **Stage 4 endometrial carcinoma with isolated peritoneal implant on PET-MRI.** Sagittal (A) and axial (B) T2 weighted images show Hyperintense thick endometrium without myometrial invasion (arrow) and a large heterogeneous signal intensity peritoneal mass (open arrow) in the cul-de-sac. Axial ADC image (C) shows diffusion restriction of the peritoneal implant (open arrow). Sagittal delayed postcontrast T1GRE image (D) show hypointense endometrial thickening (arrow) without myometrial invasion with large minimally enhancing peritoneal implant (open arrow). Axial FDG PET MR image (E) shows uptake in the endometrial ling (arrow) and within the peritoneal implant (open arrow). Post chemotherapy F/U sagittal T2 (F), sagittal postcontrast T1 GRE (G), axial ADC (H), and axial PET-MR image (I) show decrease in size of the peritoneal implant with improved ADC and decreased FDG uptake indicating good response to chemotherapy.

The heterologous type may include, rhabdomyoblasts, malignant cartilage and rarely liposarcomatous or osteosarcomatous types[34] (Figs. 13.14 and 13.15).

13.6.2 Endometrial stromal sarcoma

Endometrial stroma nodule is the benign counterpart of the endometrial stromal sarcoma. The endometrial stromal nodules are well defined displacing the myometrium without invasive margins. Endometrial stromal sarcoma is a low grade well differentiated tumor with favorable prognosis compared to other sarcomas.[35] However the prognosis and final outcome depends on the histopathologic grade and initial extent of the tumor at presentation.[36] They are characterized by late recurrence several years after surgery even with stage I disease and hence long term follow up is mandatory.[37] They occur in pre and postmenopausal age group between 40 and 55 years.

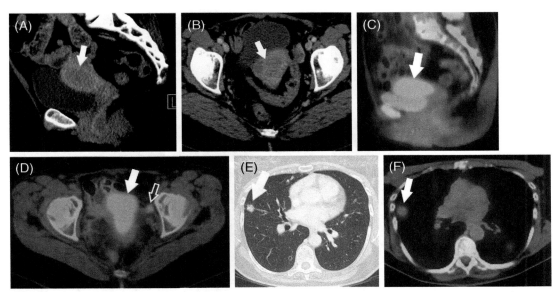

FIG. 13.11 **Stage 4 endometrial carcinoma with lung metastases.** Sagittal (A) and axial (B) contrast enhanced CT images of the pelvis show endometrial mass (arrow) invading into the myometrium. Sagittal (C) and axial (D) FDG PET-CT images show hypermetabolic endometrial mass (arrow). Axial CT of the chest (E) and corresponding axial FDG PET-CT (F) images show hypermetabolic lung metastasis (arrow).

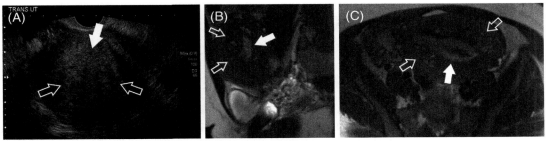

FIG. 13.12 **Endometrial carcinoma with adenomyosis with difficulty in in assessing the depth of myometrial invasion.** Sagittal TVUS image of the uterus echogenic endometrial mass (arrow) with ill defined, echogenic surrounding myometrium (open arrows). Sagittal (B) and axial (C) T2 FSE images demonstrate thick T2 hyperintense endometrium (arrow) and multiple cystic foci (open arrows) in the surrounding myometrium due to adenomyosis.

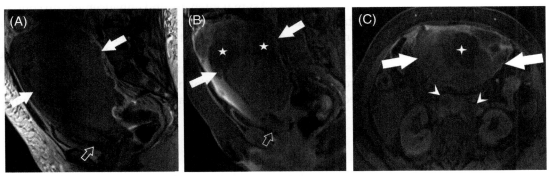

FIG. 13.13 **Undifferentiated carcinoma.** Sagittal T2 FSE (A) and sagittal delayed contrast enhanced T1 GRE (B) images demonstrate a large heterogeneously enhancing mass involving the entire uterine corpus and cervix with areas of necrosis (stars), full thickness myometrial invasion (arrows) and cervical stromal invasion (open arrow). Axial contrast enhanced T1 GRE image of the pelvis shows locally invasive endometrial mass (arrows) with necrosis (star) and metastatic iliac lymph nodes (arrow heads).

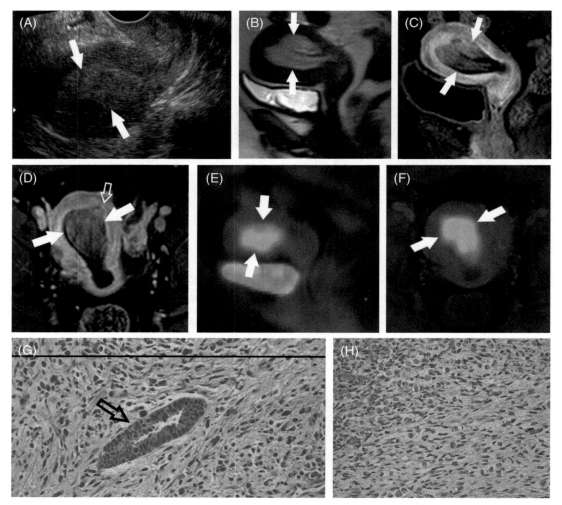

FIG. 13.14 Carcinosarcoma PET-MR imaging. Sagittal TVUS image (A) of the uterus shows diffuse heterogeneous echogenic endometrial mass (arrows). Sagittal T2 FSE MR image shows a bulky T2 hyperintense mass involving the entire endometrial cavity (arrows). Sagittal (C) and coronal (D) contrast enhanced T1 GRE MR images show heterogeneous enhancement of the endometrial mass (arrows) with focal <50% myometrial invasion (open arrow). Sagittal (E) and coronal (F) fused PET-MR image shows intense FDG uptake of the endometrial mass. Histopathology images (G and H) show hybrid serous glandular (arrow) and spindle cell stroma.

13.6.3 MR imaging

MRI is extremely useful in initial assessment of the extent of the tumor which determines the final outcome in these patients. Large polypoid mass lesions with heterogeneous T2 signal intensity and enhancement on contrast enhanced T1 weighted images. The mass may distend the endometrial cavity with myometrial, cervical, and adnexal invasion. The tumor has tendency for lymphovascular invasion and serpiginous tumor extension within the myometrium and adnexa can be seen on T2 weighted images and contrast enhanced T1 weighted images. Large bulky tumor mass, increased enhancement, nodular extension into the myometrium and perivascular extension are some of the imaging features of endometrial stromal sarcoma useful in differentiating from endometrial carcinoma.[38,39] Local recurrence after surgery can be best evaluated with MRI for better evaluation of the extent of the tumor and treatment planning[40,41] (Fig. 13.16).

13.6.4 Leiomyosarcoma

Leiomyosarcoma of the uterus are most often a pathological diagnosis after surgery and preoperative diagnosis remains a clinical challenge.[42,43] Differentiation of a leiomyoma from leiomyosarcoma is difficult with imaging and any rapid increase in size of a known myometrial mass especially in postmenopausal women should raise concern for leiomyosarcoma.[44,45] Any myometrial mass with invasive margins on CT imaging should be further evaluated

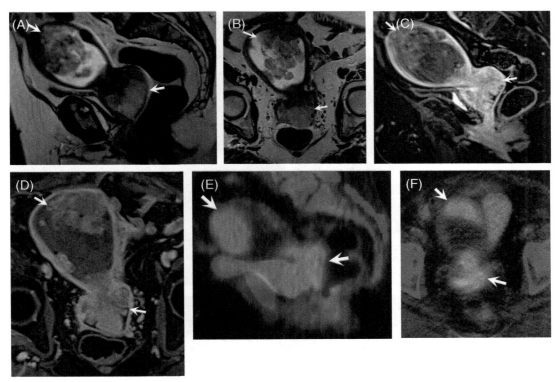

FIG. 13.15   Carcinosarcoma MRI and PET-CT imaging. Sagittal (A) and coronal (B) T2 FSE MR images show T2 hyperintense mass in the cervix (arrow) invading the stroma and large lobulated endometrial mass (arrow) with endometrial fluid due to cervical obstruction. Contrast enhanced T1 GRE images in sagittal (C) and coronal (D) planes show enhancement of both the endometrial and cervical masses (arrow). Corresponding sagittal (E) and coronal (F) FDG PET-CT images show intense FDG uptake of both masses (arrows).

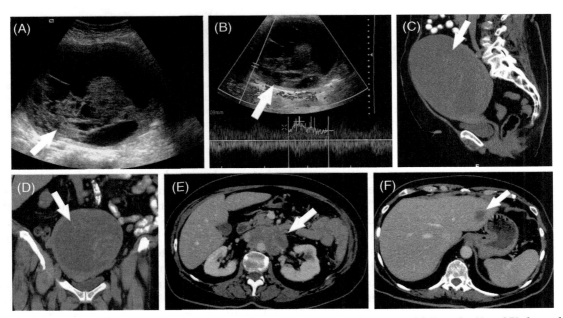

FIG. 13.16   Endometrial stromal sarcoma with distant metastases transabdominal US images with Doppler (A and B) show a large necrotic endometrial mass. Contrast enhanced sagittal (C) and coronal (D) CT images of the pelvis show a large endometrial mass with areas of necrosis distending the endometrial cavity (arrow). Contrast enhanced CT images of the upper abdomen demonstrate retroperitoneal metastatic lymph nodes (E) and liver metastasis (F).

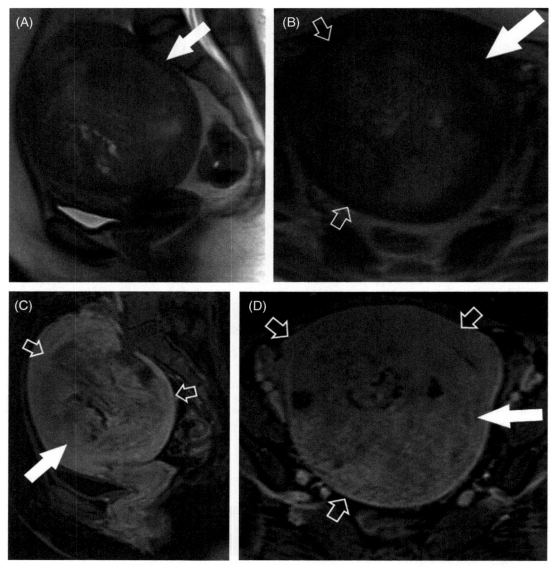

FIG. 13.17   Large degenerating leiomyoma. Sagittal (A) and axial (B) T2 FSE MR images of the pelvis show enlarged uterus with a large posterior myometrial mass (arrow) of heterogeneous signal intensity containing mixed hyperintense and hypointense signal intensity. Corresponding sagittal (C) and axial (D) postcontrast T1GRE images show heterogeneous enhancement of the mass (arrow) with peripheral normal enhancing compressed myometrium (open arrows). Histopathology diagnosis was a leiomyoma with myxoid degeneration.

with MRI and tissue diagnosis. There is significant overlap between benign degenerating leiomyoma and leiomyosarcoma. Cystic degeneration, hemorrhage, and pattern of enhancement are not reliable features of differentiation between leiomyoma and leiomyosarcoma[46] (Fig. 13.17). Vascular extension into myometrial and adnexal veins can be seen in both.[47,48] Tissue diagnosis should always be obtained before uterine artery embolization or Laparoscopic morcellation when a suspected leiomyoma has atypical imaging features. MR imaging demonstrates large infiltrating mass with variable signal intensity on T1 and T2 weighted images due to areas of necrosis and hemorrhage. Contrast enhanced T1 weighted images differentiates enhancing tumor from areas of necrosis. Invasion into the parametrium and surrounding viscera is common at initial presentation. Irregular and invasive margins of the mass even when confined to the uterus are differentiating features from a benign leiomyoma.[49–51] DWI with ADC map is found to be useful in differentiating benign leiomyoma from leiomyosarcoma. Though there is some overlap of DWI and ADC between a benign leiomyoma and leiomyosarcoma, it has a potential role in differentiating the two and tissue confirmation of those with suspicious DWI features should be considered before surgical management[52–54] (Figs. 13.17, 13.18, 13.19, and 13.20).

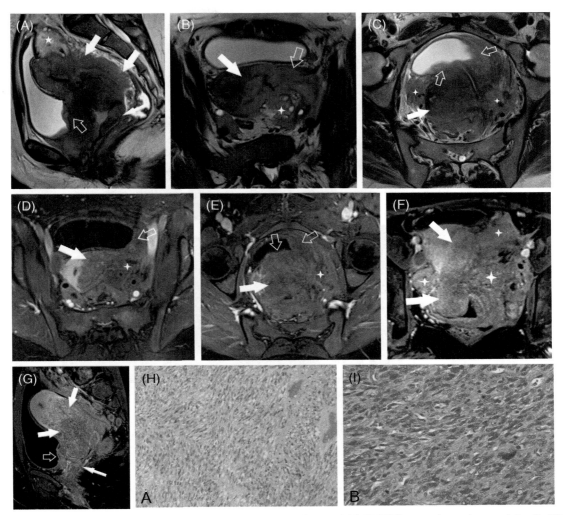

FIG. 13.18   Leiomyosarcoma (epithelioid type). Sagittal (A), axial (B), and coronal (C) T2 FSE images show a large, minimally T2 hyperintense infiltrating mass of the uterine myometrium extending to cervical stroma (small arrow), parametrium (large arrows), ovaries (star) and posterior bladder wall (open arrow). Corresponding delayed postcontrast T1 GRE images in axial (D and E), coronal (F), and sagittal (G) plane show hypoenhancing mass myometrial mass (large arrows), infiltrating the cervical stroma (small arrow), adnexa and ovaries (stars) and posterior bladder wall (open arrow). Histopathology images at low (H) and high (I) power show hypercellular tumor composed of pleomorphic cells with hyperchromatic nuclei and prominent nucleoli consistent with a high-grade epithelioid type leiomyosarcoma.

13.6.5 Mullerian adenosarcoma

Adenosarcoma is a mixed tumor with epithelial and stromal components in which the epithelial component is benign or atypical and the stromal component is low grade malignant. It is less common type of sarcoma with low malignant potential and good prognosis. The uterine corpus is the most common site of location of female genital tract, but can arise primarily in cervix, vagina, and ovary. Histologically, the epithelial component is glandular of endometrioid type and resembles proliferative endometrium. Uncommonly, the epithelial component may present as atypical hyperplasia, intraepithelial neoplasia or carcinoma. The stromal component which is usually of low grade composed of spindle or round cells. If the sarcomatous component is more than 25% of the tumor volume, it is referred to as sarcomatous overgrowth.[55–57]

They can arise within the endometrial lining or within the myometrium from adenomyosis. They present as large polypoid mass distending the endometrial cavity and extending into the endocervical canal and may prolapse into the vagina. The mass is heterogeneous due to cystic and solid enhancing components. MR imaging differentiates true invasion of myometrium and cervix from mass effect and prolapse into the cervix. Local invasion into the adnexa and ovaries is also well evaluated with MR imaging. Postcontrast T1 weighted images differentiate enhancing tumor from necrosis and hemorrhage. Majority are confined to endometrial lining and about 15% invade into

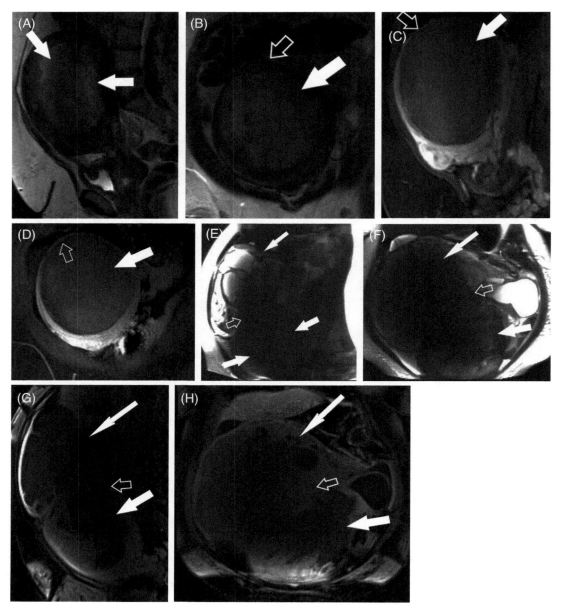

FIG. 13.19 Leiomyoma with sarcomatous transformation. Sagittal (A) and axial (B) T2 FSE MR images show a large myometrial mass (arrows) in the body and fundus of the uterus with predominantly hyperintense T2 signal intensity and foci low T2 signal intensity with peripheral intact T2 hypointense rim of myometrium (open arrow). Corresponding delayed postcontrast T1 GRE images in sagittal (C) and axial (D) plane show mild homogeneous enhancement of the mass (arrows) without necrosis and peripheral thin intact enhancing myometrium (open arrow). Follow up MRI after 2 years. Sagittal (E) and axial (F) T2 FSE MR images show previous myometrial mass (arrows) extending through the myometrium (open arrow) into peritoneal cavity with large extrauterine mass (Small arrow) with cystic areas of necrosis and layering hemorrhage. Corresponding delayed postcontrast T1 GRE images in sagittal (G) and axial (H) planes show heterogeneous enhancement with necrosis of the original myometrial mass (arrow) extending through the myometrium (open arrow) with large extrauterine mass (small arrow) demonstrating large areas of necrosis.

the inner half of myometrium or cervical stroma. Adenosarcoma with sarcomatous overgrowth is a more aggressive variant with early and more extensive myometrial and adnexal invasion. The sarcoma in this type is high grade and may be rhabdomyosarcoma or undifferentiated sarcoma[49,58–60] (Figs. 13.21 and 13.22).

13.6.6 Rhabdomyosarcoma

Rhabdomyosarcoma is predominantly a childhood extrauterine malignancy. Adult primary rhabdomyosarcoma of uterus is extremely uncommon with less than 35 cases reported. They are very aggressive with early invasion into

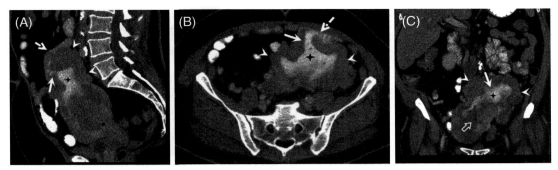

FIG. 13.20 Leiomyosarcoma invading into bowel. Sagittal (A), axial (B), and coronal (C) contrast enhanced CT images demonstrate a diffuse infiltrating uterine mass (arrow heads) invading the adjacent small bowel (stem arrow) with fistula (arrow) and oral contrast within the endometrial cavity (star).

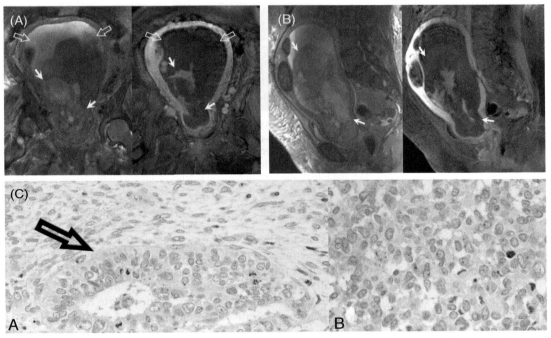

FIG. 13.21 Adenosarcoma. coronal T2 FSE and contrast enhanced T1 GRE (A) images; sagittal T2 FSE and contrast enhanced T1 GRE sagittal MR images (B) demonstrate a large mass within the endometrial cavity extending into the cervix with large areas of necrosis (open arrows) and small enhancing solid components (arrows) and with peripheral intact enhancing myometrium without full thickness invasion. Histopathology images (C) demonstrate low grade mixed glandular epithelial component (arrow in A) and malignant stromal cells in image B.

myometrium and adnexa. Rhabdomyosarcomas of the female genital tract in infancy and childhood are embryonal type and adult rhabdomyosarcoma in postmenopausal uterus are usually of pleomorphic type.[61,62] MR imaging features are similar to other stromal sarcomas with large mass in the endometrial cavity with varying degrees of cystic degeneration and enhancement.[49,63,64] There are different histologic subtypes with the most frequent pleomorphic type has poor prognosis and embryonal type having better prognosis. Alveolar is the least common type with also poor prognosis (Fig. 13.23).

13.7 Recurrence of endometrial malignancies

Although the prognosis for endometrial cancer is better than other gynecologic malignancies, prognosis for recurrent disease is poor. Most common time frame for recurrence is within 3 years of the initial diagnosis. The factors associated with recurrence include age, histologic type, ER& PR status, lower uterine segment and cervical involvement, depth of myometrial invasion, lymphovascular space invasion, ovarian involvement, and peritoneal cytology

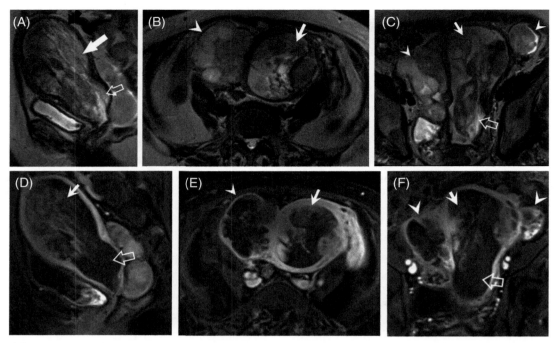

FIG. 13.22 **Adenosarcoma with sarcomatous overgrowth.** Sagittal (A), axial (B), and coronal (C) T2 FSE MR images of the pelvis show a large polypoid mass (arrow) distending the endometrial cavity and extending into the endocervix (open arrow) with invasion into bilateral adnexa (arrow heads). The mass has mixed T2 hyperintense and hypointense components. Corresponding sagittal (D), axial (E), and coronal (F) T1 contrast enhanced GRE images show mixed enhancing and nonenhancing components of the endometrial (arrow), endocervical (open arrow) mass invading into bilateral adnexa (arrow heads). Histopathology showed high grade Adenosarcoma with predominant (>70%) smooth muscle sarcomatous component.

at the initial surgical staging.[65–68] Recurrence can be localized to vagina, regional to pelvis or more wide spread involving general abdominal cavity or distant metastases.[37,69–71] Vaginal recurrence is most commonly located at vaginal apex/cuff. Distal vaginal recurrence is seen in patients with positive lymphovascular invasion of the final hysterectomy histopathology.[71] Local vaginal cuff recurrence presents with vaginal bleeding and diagnosed by gynecological examination and biopsy. Transvaginal ultrasonography may demonstrate recurrent vaginal mass but MR imaging of the pelvis better demonstrates the actual extent of the recurrence and invasion of adjacent organs for proper treatment planning. Contrast enhanced CT and FDG-PET imaging are more appropriate for assessment of distant nodal and hematogenous metastases. Combined PET-MR can be used as a single imaging modality for assessment of both local recurrence and distant metastases[69,70,72] (Figs. 13.24 and 13.25).

13.8 Primary endometrial malignancy with associated ovarian mass

Simultaneous primary endometrial and ovarian carcinoma can occur in about 10% of women. Surgical histopathology will differentiate synchronous primary ovarian carcinoma from metastases to the ovary from primary endometrial carcinoma. Synchronous primary endometrial and ovarian carcinoma has surprisingly better prognosis and survival after surgery compared to endometrial carcinoma with metastases to ovary. This is due to the predominant endometrioid histologic type and low grade of both primary malignancies[73–75] (Fig. 13.26).

13.9 Cervical versus endometrial carcinoma

Differentiation of cervical from endometrial adenocarcinoma is important due to differences in staging, prognosis, and treatment. Presurgical biopsy is not accurate and MR imaging is also not completely fool proof in differentiation between the two types. Several MR imaging features are described such as tumor epicenter (uterine corpus or cervix), tumor hypervascularity in the early arterial DCE images, mass in the endometrial cavity, depth of myometrial,

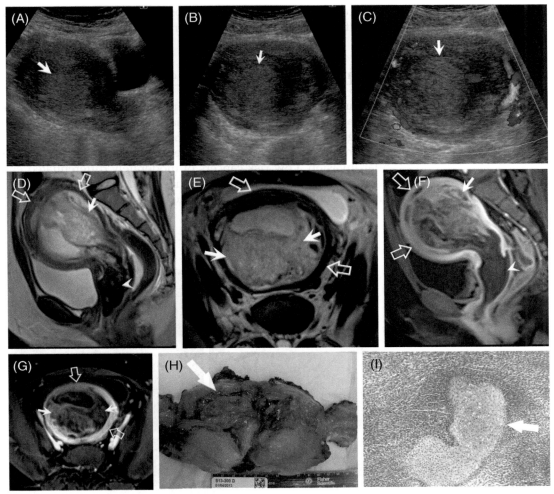

FIG. 13.23 **Rhabdomyosarcoma.** Sagittal and axial gray scale and color Doppler US images (A–C) demonstrate an echogenic endometrial mass (arrow). Sagittal (D) and axial (E) T2 FSE MR images show a large mixed solid and cystic endometrial mass extending into the lower uterine segment (arrow) with peripheral hypointense myometrium (open arrow) and T2 hypointense endocervical contents due to hemorrhage (arrow head). Corresponding sagittal (F) and axial (G) contrast enhanced T1 GRE images show heterogeneous enhancement of the mass (arrow) with nonenhancing necrotic foci, peripheral compressed enhancing intact myometrium (open arrows) and nonenhancing hemorrhagic blood products in the endocervix (arrow head). Gross pathology specimen image of the uterus (H) shows a large polypoid mass with areas of hemorrhage within the endometrial cavity (arrow). Histopathology image (I) demonstrates sheets of spindle and round cells with focus of cartilage (arrow). Immunohistochemical stains positive for desmin and myogenin confirming rhabdomyosarcoma.

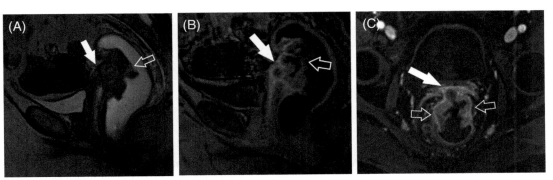

FIG. 13.24 **Recurrent endometrial carcinoma at the vagina.** Sagittal T2 FSE MR image (A) demonstrates a lobulated T2 hypointense mass at the vaginal cuff (arrow) invading the anterior rectal wall (open arrow) Rectum is well distended with T2 hyperintense gel to demonstrate the size and extent of the rectal invasion. Contrast enhanced T1 GRE images in sagittal (B) and axial (C) planes show lobulated heterogeneously enhancing vaginal cuff mass (arrow) invading the anterior rectal wall (open arrow).

and cervical stromal invasion. Of these features, tumor epicenter is the most reliable, but with large bulky tumors involving the entire uterus and cervix, it is difficult to determine the epicenter of the tumor.[76–79]

13.10 Nodal metastases in endometrial carcinoma

Lymph nodal involvement important in staging, treatment planning, and prognosis. Management of endometrial cancer is heterogeneous regarding lymph nodal staging and resection at initial hysterectomy. Endometrial carcinoma is staged on lymph nodal involvement as stage 3C1 with positive pelvic lymph nodes and stage 3C2 with positive para aortic lymph nodes. Risk factors for lymph nodal metastases include, nonendometrioid type, grade 3, deep myometrial invasion, and lympho vascular invasion. Low risk cancers of moderately differentiated endometrioid type cancers of less than 2 cm and less than 50% myometrial invasion are reported to have <1% nodal metastases. Lymph nodal distribution depends upon the location of the primary tumor. The mid and lower uterine segment

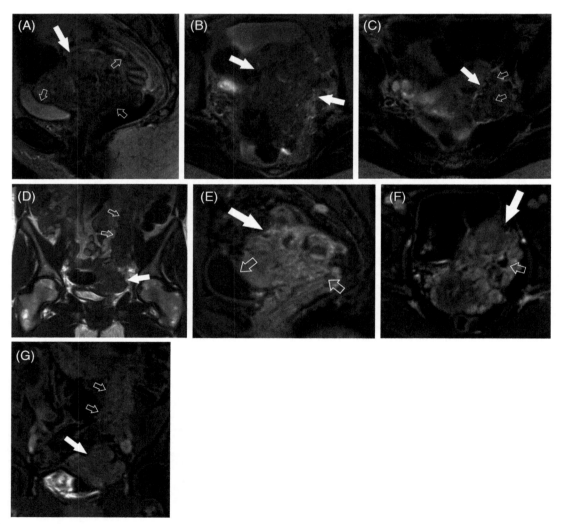

FIG. 13.25   Recurrent stromal sarcoma. Sagittal (A) and axial (B and C) T2 FSE MR images of the pelvis demonstrate a large, lobulated, serpiginous minimally T2 hyperintense mass (arrows) from the vaginal cuff invading into the left adnexa encasing and involving the let adnexal vessels. Involves the posterior bladder wall and anterior rectal wall (open arrows). Coronal T2 FSE (D) of the pelvis and lower abdomen shows serpiginous tumor extension along the left ovarian vein (open arrow). Corresponding sagittal (E) and axial (F and G) contrast enhanced T1 GRE images show intense enhancement of recurrent mass (arrows) invading into the left adnexa and encasing and intravenous extension of the adnexal and left ovarian veins. Tumor extension to adjacent bladder and rectum (open arrows).

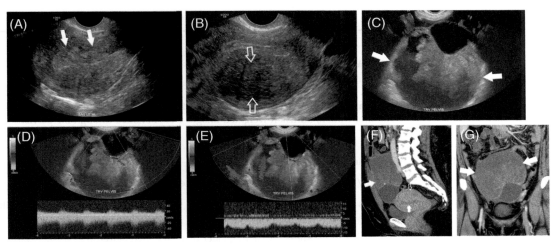

FIG. 13.26 Endometrial carcinoma with synchronous left ovarian carcinoma. Sagittal TVUS images of the pelvis (A and B) show echogenic endometrial thickening with invasion into the inner myometrium (solid arrows) and diffuse hypoechoic thickening of posterior myometrium due to adenomyosis (open arrows). TVUS of the left adnexa (C–E) demonstrates a large mixed cystic and solid mass (solid arrows) with arterial and venous Doppler flow within the solid component. Sagittal contrast enhanced CT image of the pelvis (F) shows thick endometrial lining (solid arrow) and diffuse posterior myometrial thickening (open arrow) due to adenomyosis. Coronal contrast enhanced CT image of the pelvis and lower abdomen (G) shows a large left mixed cystic and enhancing solid adnexal mass (solid arrows). CT of the chest, abdomen and pelvis did not demonstrate distant metastases. Hysterectomy and bilateral salpingo-oophorectomy with histopathology demonstrated endometrial carcinoma with serous differentiation and endometroid carcinoma of the left ovary distinct from endometrial carcinoma. Histopathogy also showed adenomyosis of the uterus.

tumors drain into the parametrium and involve paracervical and obturator lymph nodes and tumors of upper uterine segment and fundus involve common iliac and paraaotic lymph nodes. Inguinal lymph nodes are not regional lymph nodes and their involvement represent stage 4 disease. Studies have shown that five-year disease free survival is up to 90% without lymph nodal metastases, 75% with pelvic lymph nodal metastases and 38% with para aortic lymph nodal metastases.[80] The overall recurrence rate is also reported to be about 48% with positive lymph nodes and 8% with negative lymph nodes.[81] The recurrence rate is also reported to be higher in positive para aortic lymph node group compared to only positive pelvic lymph nodes.[82,83] The nodal staging prior to surgery is crucial for proper treatment planning and adjuvant chemotherapy is necessary for those with positive lymph nodes on surgical pathology. Role of routine lymphadenectomy in early stage endometrial carcinoma is controversial and its therapeutic benefits over potential complications is not well established. Preoperative detection of lymph nodal metastases by imaging is desirable with contrast enhanced CT, PET-CT, and MRI. Conventional nodal assessment on CT and MRI using short axis diameter of 10 m and larger to identify positive lymph nodes has sensitivity of only 48%[84] (Figs. 13.7, 13.11, and 13.13). DWI with ADC quantification may aid in improving the sensitivity and specificity but obtaining reliable ADC quantification is challenging due to small size of the lymph nodes.[85–89] Computer aided segmentation and DW radiomics have a potential role in improving diagnostic performance over standard size criteria and ADC measurements.[90] 18 F- FDG PET/CT is reported to have higher sensitivity, specificity, and accuracy over cross sectional imaging in assessment of lymph nodal metastases, especially for paraaortic nodal metastases[91,92] (Fig. 13.11). Prediction of nodal metastases can be improved by analyzing radiomic PET features of the primary endometrial cancer.[93]

13.11 MRI report

MRI dictation report for staging endometrial carcinoma should have a standardized template including technique of the examination, body and a conclusion easy for the requesting physician to understand and for follow up after management (Table 13.4). Standardized reporting will provide clarity and consistency for both the treating clinician and for the radiologists in follow up surveillance imaging.

TABLE 13.4 Standardized MRI Report.

Study: MRI pelvis without and with contrast

Clinical information/history: [free text]

Comparison: [free text]

Technique: Prior to and following the uneventful intravenous administration of contrast, T1 and T2 weighted images in multiple planes were obtained through the pelvis. Prior to contrast administration, diffusion-weighted images were obtained through the pelvis.

Findings:

UTERUS: Measures [] x [] x [] cm [Describe other uterine findings, excluding the tumor.]

TUMOR SITE: [Describe the tumor location: posterior/anterior/fundal/body/lower uterine segment]

TUMOR SIZE: [Give 3 dimensions unless the tumor is too small or ill-defined to measure, then dictate: tumor too small or too ill-defined to measure.]

MYOMETRIAL INVASION: [less than 50% myometrial wall thickness invasion/greater than 50% myometrial wall thickness invasion]

INVASION of the tumor into the cervix stroma: [yes/no/indeterminate]

EXTENSION of tumor into adjacent structures: [None/vagina/parametrium/bowel/bladder]; [presence/absence of ureteral dilatation]

ADDITIONAL COMMENTS: [None or add any specific comments related to the tumor here if appropriate]

OVARIES: The ovaries are [not visualized/visualized] and are [normal/abnormal] in appearance. [Right Ovary measures # x # x #cm and left ovary measures # x # x #cm.] [If abnormal describe.]

LYMPH NODES:

There are [no/few/many] lymph nodes; [The largest pelvic lymph node is located (give location) and measures (give size).] [The largest para-aortic lymph node measures (give size)]. These lymph nodes are [likely/possibly/less likely to be/unlikely to be] malignant.

ADDITIONAL PELVIC FINDINGS: [None; presence/absence pelvic fluid; presence/absence pelvic peritoneal implants; other findings]

BONES: [No aggressive bone lesions]

Impression:

Endometrial cancer [summarize the endometrial tumor, including extent of invasion and provide your impression of whether there are suspicious lymph nodes].

13.12 Pearls and pitfalls

MRI cannot differentiate endometrial hyperplasia from malignancy when there is no myometrial invasion.

T2 weighted and delayed postcontrast T1 weighted images perpendicular to the endometrial lining are useful for depth of myometrial invasion.

Erroneous assessment of myometrial invasion due to poor delineation of endo-myometrial interface in the presence of adenomyosis or leiomyoma and in the cornual regions due to thin and difficult delineation of myometrium. DWI and DCE images can help to assess myometrial invasion at these locations.

Lower uterine segment involvement has poor prognosis with higher incidence of pelvic lymph nodes compared to same stage fundal tumors.

Differentiation of a leiomyoma from leiomyosarcoma is difficult with imaging and any rapid increase in size of a known myometrial mass especially in postmenopausal women should raise concern for leiomyosarcoma.

Cystic degeneration, hemorrhage, and pattern of enhancement are not reliable features of differentiation between leiomyoma and leiomyosarcoma.

Vascular extension into myometrial and adnexal veins can be seen in benign leiomyoma and leiomyosarcoma and is not a differentiating feature.

Tissue diagnosis should always be obtained before uterine artery embolization or Laparoscopic morcellation when a suspected leiomyoma has atypical imaging features.

Synchronous primary endometrial and ovarian carcinoma has better prognosis and survival after surgery compared to endometrial carcinoma with metastases to ovary due to predominantly low grade endometrioid type carcinoma in both.

13.13 Conclusion

Endometrial carcinoma is the most common uterine malignancy and nonepithelial malignancies constituting <10% of uterine malignancies. Surgery is the most definitive treatment of uterine malignancies and exact disease extent especially the presence of extrauterine direct extension, nodal and distant metastases is crucial for surgical management. The depth of myometrial invasion has direct correlation with the presence of nodal disease and likely hood of local recurrence after surgical management. MR imaging of the pelvis has high accuracy in assessing the local T staging and is important to optimize treatment decision making. CT and PET-CT are useful to assess the nodal and distant metastases. Newer imaging techniques such as PET-MR are useful in providing a complete TNM staging with single imaging modality. MRI and PET-MRI are also useful in surveillance for recurrent disease after initial surgical management for local recurrence and distant metastases.

References

1. Jolly S, Vargas CE, Kumar T, et al. The impact of age on long-term outcome in patients with endometrial cancer treated with postoperative radiation. *Gynecol Oncol.* 2006;103:87.
2. Lee NK, Cheung MK, Shin JY, et al. Prognostic factors for uterine cancer in reproductive-aged women. *Obstet Gynecol.* 2007;109:655.
3. Maxwell GL, Tian C, Risinger J, et al. Racial disparity in survival among patients with advanced/recurrent endometrial adenocarcinoma: a Gynecologic Oncology Group study. *Cancer.* 2006;107:2197.
4. Zhang Y, Liu H, Yang S, Zhang J, Qian L, Chen X. Overweight, obesity and endometrial cancer risk: results from a systematic review and meta-analysis. *Int J Biol Markers.* 2014;29(1):e21–e29.
5. American Cancer Society. *Cancer Facts and Figures.* 2021.
6. Barrow E, Robinson L, Alduai W. Cumulative lifetime incidence of extracolonic cancers in Lynch syndrome: a report of 121 families with proven mutations. *Clin Genet.* 2009;75:141–149.
7. Bonadona V, Bonaïti B, Olschwang S, et al. Cancer risks associated with germline mutations in MLH1, MSH2, and MSH6 genes in Lynch syndrome. *JAMA.* 2011;305(22):2304–2310.
8. Bokhman JV. Two pathogenetic types of endometrial carcinoma. *Gynecol Oncol.* 1983;15:10–17.
9. McConechy MK, Ding J, Cheang MC, et al. Use of mutation profiles to refine the classification of endometrial carcinomas. *J Pathol.* 2012;228:20–30.
10. Kuhn E, Wu RC, Guan B, et al. Identification of molecular pathway aberrations in uterine serous carcinoma by genome-wide analyses. *J Natl Cancer Inst.* 2012;104:1503–1513.
11. Fujimoto T, Nanjyo H, Fukuda J, et al. Endometrioid uterine cancer: histopathological risk factors of local and distant recurrence. *Gynecol Oncol.* 2009;112(2):342–347.
12. Singh N, Hirschowitz L, Zaino R, et al. Pathologic prognostic factors in endometrial carcinoma (Other than tumor type and grade). *Int J Gynecol Pathol.* 2019;38:93–113.
13. Doll KM, Denslow S, Tseng J, Gehrig PA, Fader AN. High-grade endometrial cancer: revisiting tumor size and the lower uterine segment. *J Clin Oncol.* 2013;31:15.
14. Beddy P, Moyle P, Kataoka M. Evaluation of depth of myometrial invasion and overall staging in endometrial cancer comparison of diffusion-weighted and dynamic contrast-enhanced MR imaging. *Radiology.* 2012;262:530–537.
15. Rechichi G, Galimberti S, Signorelli M. Endometrial cancer correlation of apparent diffusion coefficient with tumor grade, depth of myometrial invasion, and presence of lymph node metastases. *AJR Am J Roentgenol.* 2011;197:256–262.
16. Sala E, Crawford R, Senior E. Added value of dynamic contrast-enhanced magnetic resonance imaging in predicting advanced stage disease in patients with endometrial carcinoma. *Int J Gynecol Cancer.* 2009;19:141–146.
17. Bi Q, Chen Y, Chen J, et al. Predictive value of T2-weighted imaging and dynamic contrast-enhanced MRI for assessing cervical invasion in patients with endometrial cancer: a meta-analysis. *Clin Imaging.* 2021;78:206–213.
18. Fasmer KE, Bjørnerud A, Ytre-Hauge S, et al. Preoperative quantitative dynamic contrast-enhanced MRI and diffusion-weighted imaging predict aggressive disease in endometrial cancer. *Acta Radiol.* 2018;59(8):1010–1017.
19. Hameeduddin A, Sahdev A. Diffusion-weighted imaging and dynamic contrast-enhanced MRI in assessing response and recurrent disease in gynaecological malignancies. *Cancer Imaging.* 2015;15(1):3.
20. Bi Q, Chen Y, Wu K, et al. The diagnostic value of MRI for preoperative staging in patients with endometrial cancer: a meta-analysis. *Acad Radiol.* 2020;27(7):960–968.
21. Nougaret S, Horta M, Sala E, et al. Endometrial cancer Mri staging: updated guidelines of the European Society of Urogenital Radiology. *Eur Radiol.* 2019;29(2):792–805.
22. Sanjuán A, Escaramís G, Ayuso JR, et al. Role of magnetic resonance imaging and cause of pitfalls in detecting myometrial invasion and cervical involvement in endometrial cancer. *Arch Gynecol Obstet.* 2008;278(6):535–539.
23. Kinkel K. Pitfalls in staging uterine neoplasm with imaging: a review. *Abdom Imaging.* 2006;31(2):164–173.
24. Al-Loh S, Al-Hussaini M. Undifferentiated endometrial carcinoma: a diagnosis frequently overlooked. *Arch Pathol Lab Med.* 2013;137(3):438–442.
25. AlHilli M, Elson P, Rybicki L, et al. Undifferentiated endometrial carcinoma: a National Cancer Database analysis of prognostic factors and treatment outcomes. *Int J Gynecol Cancer.* 2019;29(7):1126–1133.
26. Chuang JT, Van Velden DJ, Graham JB. Carcinosarcoma and mixed mesodermal tumor of the uterine corpus. Review of 49 cases. *Obstet Gynecol.* 1970;35(5):769–780.

27. Clement PB, Young RH, Keh P, Ostör AG, Scully RE. Malignant mesonephric neoplasms of the uterine cervix. A report of eight cases, including four with a malignant spindle cell component. *Am J Surg Pathol.* 1995;19(10):1158–1171.

28. Bagué S, Rodríguez IM, Prat J. Malignant mesonephric tumors of the female genital tract: a clinicopathologic study of 9 cases. *Am J Surg Pathol.* 2004;28(5):601–607.

29. Barral M, Placé V, Dautry R, et al. Magnetic resonance imaging features of uterine sarcoma and mimickers. *Abdom Radiol (NY).* 2017;42(6):1762–1772.

30. Denschlag D, Ulrich UA. Uterine carcinosarcomas: diagnosis and management. *Oncol Res Treat.* 2018;41(11):675–679.

31. Sagebiel TL, Bhosale PR, Patnana M, Faria SC, Devine CE. Uterine carcinosarcomas. *Semin Ultrasound CT MR.* 2019;40(4):295–301.

32. Takeuchi M, Matsuzaki K, Harada M. Carcinosarcoma of the uterus: MRI findings including diffusion-weighted imaging and MR spectroscopy. *Acta Radiol.* 2016;57(10):1277–1284.

33. Tanaka YO, Tsunoda H, Minami R, Yoshikawa H, Minami M. Carcinosarcoma of the uterus: MR findings. *J Magn Reson Imaging.* 2008;28(2):434–439.

34. Lopez-Garcia MA, Palacios J. Pathologic and molecular features of uterine carcinosarcomas. *Semin Diagn Pathol.* 2010;27(4):274–286.

35. Conklin CM, Longacre TA. Endometrial stromal tumors: the new WHO classification. *Adv Anat Pathol.* 2014;21(6):383–393.

36. Sciallis AP, Bedroske PP, Schoolmeester JK, et al. High-grade endometrial stromal sarcomas: a clinicopathologic study of a group of tumors with heterogenous morphologic and genetic features. *Am J Surg Pathol.* 2014;38(9):1161–1172.

37. Gangireddy M, Chan Gomez J, Kanderi T, Joseph M, Kundoor V. Recurrence of endometrial stromal sarcoma, two decades post-treatment. *Cureus.* 2020;12(7):e9249.

38. Koyama T, Togashi K, Konishi I, et al. MR imaging of endometrial stromal sarcoma: correlation with pathologic findings. *AJR Am J Roentgenol.* 1999;173(3):767–772.

39. Ueda M, Otsuka M, Hatakenaka M, et al. MR imaging findings of uterine endometrial stromal sarcoma: differentiation from endometrial carcinoma. *Eur Radiol.* 2001;11(1):28–33.

40. Chin TH, Lin G, Wu RC, Lai CH. Recurrence after fertility-preserving surgery for low-grade endometrial stromal sarcoma. *J Obstet Gynaecol Res.* 2018;44(9):1836–1842.

41. Lee SI, Catalano OA, Dehdashti F. Evaluation of gynecologic cancer with MR imaging, 18F-FDG PET/CT, and PET/MR imaging. *J Nucl Med.* 2015;56(3):436–443.

42. Cui RR, Wright JD, Hou JY. Uterine leiomyosarcoma: a review of recent advances in molecular biology, clinical management and outcome. *BJOG.* 2017;124(7):1028–1037.

43. Juhasz-Böss I, Gabriel L, Bohle RM, Horn LC, Solomayer EF, Breitbach GP. Uterine leiomyosarcoma. *Oncol Res Treat.* 2018;41(11):680–686.

44. Sun S, Bonaffini PA, Nougaret S, et al. How to differentiate uterine leiomyosarcoma from leiomyoma with imaging. *Diagn Interv Imaging.* 2019;100(10):619–634.

45. Bura V, Pintican RM, David RE, et al. MRI findings in-between leiomyoma and leiomyosarcoma: a RAD-path correlation of degenerated leiomyomas and variants. *Br J Radiol.* 2021;94(1125):20210283.

46. DeMulder D, Ascher SM. Uterine leiomyosarcoma: can MRI differentiate leiomyosarcoma from benign leiomyoma before treatment? *AJR Am J Roentgenol.* 2018;211(6):1405–1415.

47. Declas E, Lucot JP. La léiomyomatose extra-utérine : revue de la littérature [extra uterine leiomyomatosis: review of the literature]. *Gynecol Obstet Fertil Senol.* 2019;47(7-8):582–590.

48. Pacheco-Rodriguez G, Taveira-DaSilva AM, Moss J. Benign metastasizing leiomyoma. *Clin Chest Med.* 2016;37(3):589–595.

49. Santos P, Cunha TM. Uterine sarcomas: clinical presentation and MRI features. *Diagn Interv Radiol.* 2015;21(1):4–9.

50. Pattani SJ, Kier R, Deal R, Luchansky E. MRI of uterine leiomyosarcoma. *Magn Reson Imaging.* 1995;13(2):331–333.

51. Takemori M, Nishimura R, Sugimura K. Magnetic resonance imaging of uterine leiomyosarcoma. *Arch Gynecol Obstet.* 1992;251(4):215–218.

52. Li HM, Liu J, Qiang JW, Zhang H, Zhang GF, Ma F. Diffusion-weighted imaging for differentiating uterine leiomyosarcoma from degenerated leiomyoma. *J Comput Assist Tomogr.* 2017;41(4):599–606.

53. Tamai K, Koyama T, Saga T, et al. The utility of diffusion-weighted MR imaging for differentiating uterine sarcomas from benign leiomyomas. *Eur Radiol.* 2008;18(4):723–730.

54. Sato K, Yuasa N, Fujita M, Fukushima Y. Clinical application of diffusion-weighted imaging for preoperative differentiation between uterine leiomyoma and leiomyosarcoma. *Am J Obstet Gynecol.* 2014;210(4) 368.e1–368.e8.

55. Ulrich UA, Denschlag D. Uterine adenosarcoma. *Oncol Res Treat.* 2018;41(11):693–696.

56. Wang Y, Liu AJ, Chen X, Song X. Prognosis-related clinicopathologic characteristics of FIGO stage I Müllerian adenosarcoma of uterus. *Zhonghua Bing Li Xue Za Zhi.* 2018;47(5):334–338.

57. Gallardo A, Prat J. Mullerian adenosarcoma: a clinicopathologic and immunohistochemical study of 55 cases challenging the existence of adenofibroma. *Am J Surg Pathol.* 2009;33(2):278–288.

58. Fujii S, Nosaka K, Mukuda N, Fukunaga T, Sato S, Ogawa T. MR imaging of an intramural adenosarcoma with pathologic correlation. *Magn Reson Med Sci.* 2018;17(1):1–2.

59. Takeuchi M, Matsuzaki K, Yoshida S, et al. Adenosarcoma of the uterus: magnetic resonance imaging characteristics. *Clin Imaging.* 2009;33(3):244–247.

60. Krivak TC, Seidman JD, McBroom JW, MacKoul PJ, Aye LM, Rose GS. Uterine adenosarcoma with sarcomatous overgrowth versus uterine carcinosarcoma: comparison of treatment and survival. *Gynecol Oncol.* 2001;83(1):89–94.

61. Alavi S, Eckes L, Kratschell R, et al. Pleomorphic rhabdomyosarcoma of the uterus: case report and a systematic review of the literature. *Anticancer Res.* 2017;37(5):2509–2514.

62. Chang WC, Lin WC, Lee HC, et al. Pure rhabdomyosarcoma of the corpus uteri in a postpartum patient: report of a case and review of the literature. *Zhonghua Yi Xue Za Zhi (Taipei).* 1992;50(1):73–76.

63. Li ZJ, Li CL, Wang W, Fu XY, Zhen YQ. Diagnosis and treatment of pleomorphic rhabdomyosarcoma of the uterus: a rare case report and review of the literature. *J Int Med Res.* 2021;49(5):3000605211014360.

64. Yamada S, Harada Y, Noguchi H, et al. Embryonal rhabdomyosarcoma arising from the uterine corpus in a postmenopausal female: a surgical case challenging the genuine diagnosis on a cytology specimen. *Diagn Pathol*. 2016;11:3.

65. Francis SR, Ager BJ, Do OA, et al. Recurrent early stage endometrial cancer: patterns of recurrence and results of salvage therapy. *Gynecol Oncol*. 2019;154(1):38–44.

66. Laban M, El-Swaify ST, Ali SH, et al. The prediction of recurrence in low-risk endometrial cancer: is it time for a paradigm shift in adjuvant therapy? *Reprod Sci*. 2022;29(4):1068–1085.

67. Mundt AJ, McBride R, Rotmensch J, Waggoner SE, Yamada SD, Connell PP. Significant pelvic recurrence in high-risk pathologic stage I–IV endometrial carcinoma patients after adjuvant chemotherapy alone: implications for adjuvant radiation therapy. *Int J Radiat Oncol Biol Phys*. 2001;50(5):1145–1153.

68. Takahashi A, Matsuura M, Matoda M, et al. Clinicopathological features of early and late recurrence of endometrial carcinoma after surgical resection. *Int J Gynecol Cancer*. 2017;27(5):967–972.

69. Kurra V, Krajewski KM, Jagannathan J, Giardino A, Berlin S, Ramaiya N. Typical and atypical metastatic sites of recurrent endometrial carcinoma. *Cancer Imaging*. 2013;13(1):113–122.

70. Albano D, Zizioli V, Odicino F, Giubbini R, Bertagna F. Clinical and prognostic value of ^{18}F-FDG PET/CT in recurrent endometrial carcinoma. *Rev Esp Med Nucl Imagen Mol (Engl Ed)*. 2019;38(2):87–93.

71. Steiner A, Alban G, Cheng T, et al. Vaginal recurrence of endometrial cancer: MRI characteristics and correlation with patient outcome after salvage radiation therapy. *Abdom Radiol (NY)*. 2020;45(4):1122–1131.

72. Lee SI, Catalano OA, Dehdashti F. Evaluation of gynecologic cancer with MR imaging, 18F-FDG PET/CT, and PET/MR imaging. *J Nucl Med*. 2015;56(3):436–443.

73. Castro IM, Connell PP, Waggoner S, et al. Synchronous ovarian and endometrial malignancies. *Am J Clin Oncol*. 2000;23:521–525.

74. Zaino R, Whitney C, Brady MF, et al. Simultaneously detected endometrial and ovarian carcinomas: a prospective clinicopathologic study of 74 cases: a gynecologic oncology group study. *Gynecol Oncol*. 2001;83:355–362.

75. Heitz F, Amant F, Fotopoulou C, et al. Synchronous ovarian and endometrial cancer: an international multicenter case-control study. *Int J Gynecol Cancer*. 2014;24:54–60.

76. Haider MA, Patlas M, Jhaveri K, Chapman W, Fyles A, Rosen B. Adenocarcinoma involving the uterine cervix: magnetic resonance imaging findings in tumours of endometrial, compared with cervical, origin. *Can Assoc Radiol J*. 2006;57:43–48.

77. Vargas HA, Akin O, Zheng J, Moskowitz C, et al. The value of MR imaging when the site of uterine cancer origin is uncertain. *Radiology*. 2011;258:785–792. doi:10.1148/radiol.10101147.

78. He H, Bhosale P, Wei W, Ramalingam P, Iyer R. MRI is highly specific in determining primary cervical versus endometrial cancer when biopsy results are inconclusive. *Clin Radiol*. 2013;68:1107–1113.

79. Bourgioti C, Chatoupis K, Panourgias E, et al. Endometrial vs. cervical cancer: development and pilot testing of a magnetic resonance imaging (MRI) scoring system for predicting tumor origin of uterine carcinomas of indeterminate histology. *Abdom Imaging*. 2015; 40:2529–2540.

80. Morrow CP, Bundy BN, Kurman RJ, et al. Relationship between surgical-pathological risk factors and outcome in clinical stage I and II carcinoma of the endometrium: a Gynecologic Oncology Group study. *Gynecol Oncol*. 1991;40(1):55–65.

81. Lurain JR, Rice BL, Rademaker AW, Poggensee LE, Schink JC, Miller DS. Prognostic factors associated with recurrence in clinical stage I adenocarcinoma. *Obstet Gynecol*. 1991;78(1):63–69.

82. Aalders JG, Thomas G. Endometrial cancer-Revisiting the importance of pelvic and para aortic lymph nodes. *Gynecol Oncol*. 2007;104(1):222–231.

83. Hirahatake K, Hareyama H, Sakuragi N, Nishiya M, Makinoda S, Fujimoto S. A clinical and pathologic study on para-aortic lymph node metastasis in endometrial carcinoma. *J Surg Oncol*. 1997;65(2):82–87.

84. Reijnen C, IntHout J, Massuger L, et al. A diagnostic accuracy of clinical biomarkers for preoperative prediction of lymph node metastasis in endometrial carcinoma: a systematic review and meta-analysis. *Oncologist*. 2019;24:e880–e890.

85. Roy C, Bierry G, Matau A, Bazille G, Pasquali R. Value of diffusion-weighted imaging to detect small malignant pelvic lymph nodes at 3T. *Eur Radiol*. 2010;20:1803–1811.

86. Nakai G, Matsuki M, Inada Y, et al. Detection and evaluation of pelvic lymph nodes in patients with gynecologic malignancies using body diffusion-weighted magnetic resonance imaging. *J Comput Assist Tomogr*. 2008;32:764–768.

87. Rechichi G, Galimberti S, Oriani M, Perego P, Valsecchi MG, Sironi S. ADC maps in the prediction of pelvic lymph nodal metastatic regions in endometrial cancer. *Eur Radiol*. 2013;23:65–74.

88. Lin G, Ho KC, Wang JJ, et al. Detection of lymph node metastasis in cervical and uterine cancers by diffusion-weighted magnetic resonance imaging at 3T. *J Magn Reson Imaging*. 2008;28:128–135.

89. Kwee TC, Takahara T, Luijten PR, Nievelstein RA. ADC measurements of lymph nodes: inter- and intra-observer reproducibility study and an overview of the literature. *Eur J Radiol*. 2010;75:215–220.

90. Yang LY, Siow TY, Lin YC, et al. Computer-Aided segmentation and machine learning of integrated clinical and diffusion-weighted imaging parameters for predicting lymph node metastasis in endometrial cancer. *Cancers (Basel)*. 2021;13(6):1406.

91. Bollineni VR, Ytre-Hauge S, Bollineni-Balabay O, Salvesen HB, Haldorsen IS. High diagnostic value of 18F-FDG PET/CT in endometrial cancer: systematic review and meta-analysis of the literature. *J Nucl Med*. 2016;57(6):879–885.

92. Crivellaro C, Landoni C, Elisei F, et al. Combining positron emission tomography/computed tomography, radiomics, and sentinel lymph node mapping for nodal staging of endometrial cancer patients. *Int J Gynecol Cancer*. 2020;30:378–382.

93. Taşkin S, Varli B, Ersöz CC, Altin D, Soydal Ç, Ortaç F. Complementary role of 18F-FDG PET/CT for sentinel lymph node algorithm in endometrial cancer with high-risk factors for lymphatic metastasis. *Nucl Med Commun*. 2020;41(4):389–394.

14

MRI of cervical cancer

Janardhana Ponnatapura[a], Neeraj Lalwani[b]

[a]Department of Radiology, Wake Forest University School of Medicine, Winston Salem,
NC, United States [b]Professor of Radiology, Virginia Commonwealth University School of Medicine
and Health System, Richmond, VA, United States

14.1 Introduction

Cervical cancer is the fourth most frequent cancer in women globally, after breast, colorectal, and lung cancers; over half a million new cases of cervical cancer are diagnosed each year.[1] Adequate diagnosis, proper staging, and correct management using modern imaging techniques and novel, minimally invasive surgery helps to reduce the mortality rate. The International Federation of Gynecology and Obstetrics (FIGO) staging system continues to be the most frequently used globally in clinical practice and for gynecologic cancer database reporting, although a parallel TNM system has been described by the American Joint Committee on Cancer.

Traditionally, the FIGO staging of cervical cancer has prescribed assessments of the extent of the disease to be mainly based on clinical examination, including bimanual pelvic examination, cystoscopy, and colonoscopy. The third edition of the FIGO Cancer Report, published in 2018, presents a current update on the state-of-the-art management of gynecological cancers that accommodates novel imaging and surgical techniques.[2] The imaging plays a central role in this updated staging system for uterine cervical cancer. A thorough knowledge of the updated FIGO system and revisions is essential for appropriate radiological reporting.

14.2 Anatomy of the cervix

The cervix is a fibromuscular organ which connects the uterine cavity to the vaginal cavity. It is approximately 4 cm in length and 3 cm in diameter and is composed of the portio (or portio vaginalis or ectocervix), which protrudes into the vagina, and the supravaginal portion (or endocervix). The opening of the ectocervix into the vagina is called the external os, whereas the opening of the endocervix into the uterus is called the internal os. The nonkeratinized squamous epithelium covers the ectocervix and the endocervix is lined with a mucus secreting columnar epithelium. The transitional area between the two epithelial linings is called as squamocolumnar junction (SCJ) (Fig. 14.1).

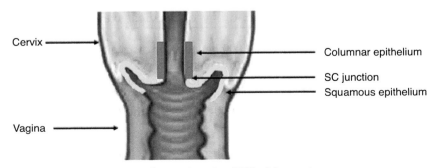

FIG. 14.1 Graphical image representing squamous-columnar junction (SCJ) of the cervix.

SCJ is the result of a continuous remodeling process resulting from age and physiological hormonal status. Carcinoma of the cervix develops almost exclusively within the transitional zone of SCJ.

14.3 Development of the cervix

The cervix is developed around the sixth week of embryogenesis. In the course of development, outer and vertical portion of the two paramesonephric ducts (also called Müllerian ducts) merge to form a single canal that becomes the upper vagina, cervix and uterus.[3] The cervix is significantly larger than the uterine body in fetal life. However, the cervix measures twice the size of the uterus during childhood but ends up getting its adult size after puberty.

14.4 Neurovasculature of the cervix

The descending branches of the uterine artery (a branch of the internal iliac artery) supply the cervix. The uterine venous plexus drains into the internal iliac vein via uterine vein.[4]

Nerve supply of the cervix originates in the inferior hypogastric plexus. Sympathetic component emerges from the T12/L1 segments, while the parasympathetic component originates from the S2–S4 spinal segments. The neurovascular bundle runs through the lateral uterine ligaments formed by the peritoneal reflections connecting the lateral wall of the uterus to the pelvic wall.[4]

14.5 Lymphatic drainage of the cervix

The cervical lymphatics converge in smaller anterior and posterior trunks and larger lateral trunks. The bilateral lateral trunks pass through the parametrium and drain into the ipsilateral hypogastric, external iliac, obturator, and common iliac territories.[5]

The smaller anterior trunks pass behind the bladder and end in the external iliac glands. Similarly, the posterior channels directly drain into the common iliac and paraaortic nodes and the superior rectal nodes.

14.6 The spread of cervical cancer

Cervical cancer can be spread locally by direct spread or at a distance by lymphatic or blood-borne spread. Direct spread may involve the uterine body, vagina, parametria, bladder or rectum, and peritoneal cavity. The most common sites of haematogenic spread can include the liver, lungs, and bones.

The distribution of sites of nodal metastasis are external iliac (43%), obturator (26%), parametrial (21%), common iliac (7%), presacral (1%), and para-aortic (1%).[6]

Typically, paraaortic nodal spread occurs with an orderly and gradual involvement of pelvic and common iliac glands. However, cervical cancer may sometimes metastasize directly into the para-aortic glands via the posterior trunks. In addition, left supraclavicular nodes can also be involved via thoracic duct in 0.1–1.5% cases.[7] The thoracic duct communicates with the systemic venous system at the confluence of the left internal jugular and subclavian veins. As a result, the left supraclavicular lymph nodes may represent the ultimate pathway of infra-diaphragmatic lymphatic drainage or malignancies.[8] Involvement of supraclavicular nodes in cervical cancers can be a manifestation of high tumor burden and poor prognosis.[9] Therefore, careful examination of the supraclavicular areas is critical when evaluating patients with cervical cancer (Fig. 14.2).

14.7 The epidemiology of cervical cancer

In 2020, cervical cancer accounted for an estimated 604,000 new cancer cases and 342,000 deaths worldwide[10] and was the fourth most common cancer in females. Eighty-four percent of cervical cancer cases were from resource-limited regions.[11] In the United States, about 4000 women die from cervical cancer annually with African Americans, Hispanics, and women in low-resource areas having higher disparities in evidenced-based care and a much higher mortality rate.[12]

The racial variation in cervical cancer rates per 100,000 women in the United States is as follows (Surveillance Epidemiology and End Results; SEER 21 2014–2018):

Hispanic: 9.3
African American: 8.6
American Indian/Alaska Native: 7.6

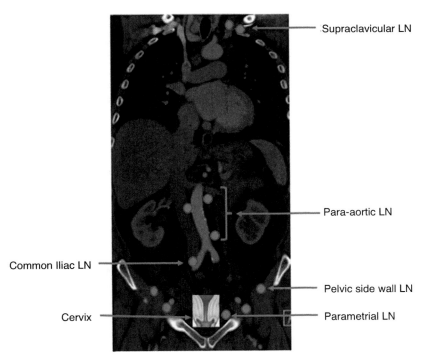

Supraclavicular LN

Para-aortic LN

Common Iliac LN

Pelvic side wall LN

Cervix

Parametrial LN

FIG. 14.2   Sites of lymph nodal (LN) metastasis from cervical carcinoma.

White: 7.3
Asian/Pacific Islander: 6.4

14.8 Risk factors for cervical cancer

The cervical cancer is broadly classified into HPV-related and non-HPV-related. HPV consists of a heterogenous group of DNA viruses. Over 90% of all cervical cancers globally are caused by 8 types of HPV: 16, 18, 31, 33, 35, 45, 52, and 58. It is worth noting that three types, 16, 18, and 45, account for 94% of cervical adenocarcinomas.[13] Of these three variants, type 16 HPV may pose a higher cancer risk than others.[14]

Non-HPV related risk factors include low socioeconomic status, oral contraceptive use, cigarette smoking, and genetics.

14.9 The clinical presentation of cervical cancer

Early cervical cancer is often asymptomatic, making screening important. In people with symptoms, the most common symptoms of presentation are irregular or profuse vaginal bleeding, and postcoital bleeding. Some patients have vaginal discharge that may be watery, mucoid, or purulent and malodorous imitating vaginitis or cervicitis. Advanced disease can exhibit pelvic or lumbar pain, which can radiate along the posterior side of the lower limbs. Intestinal or urinary symptoms, such as complaints related to pressure, hematuria, hematochezia, or vaginal passage of urine or stool, are rare and suggest advanced disease or local spread to the pelvic organs.[15]

14.10 FIGO staging

The 2009 version of the FIGO staging system has been shown to be inaccurate. It underestimated Stage IB–IIIB cancers by 20–40% and overestimated Stage IIIB cancers by 64%.[16] Lymph node metastases are a key factor in cervical cancer prognosis and treatment planning. Moreover, radical trachelectomy, an emerging fertility preservation technique, is currently considered in management techniques. Modern cross-sectional and functional imaging techniques, such as computed tomography (CT), magnetic resonance imaging (MRI), and fluorine 18 fluorodeoxyglucose positron emission tomography (FDG PET), have been included in treatment planning for invasive cervical cancer in most of the developed world. To incorporate all this crucial information, the FIGO classification was revised in 2018 (Fig. 14.3).

Stage	Description
I	The carcinoma is strictly confined to the cervix (extension to the uterine corpus should be disregarded)
IA	Invasive carcinoma that can be diagnosed only by microscopy, with maximum depth of invasion <5 mm[a]
IA1	Measured stromal invasion <3 mm in depth
IA2	Measured stromal invasion ≥3 mm and <5 mm in depth
IB	Invasive carcinoma with measured deepest invasion ≥5 mm (greater than Stage IA), lesion limited to the cervix uteri[b]
IB1	Invasive carcinoma ≥5 mm depth of stromal invasion, and <2 cm in greatest dimension
IB2	Invasive carcinoma ≥2 cm and <4 cm in greatest dimension
IB3	Invasive carcinoma ≥4 cm in greatest dimension
II	The carcinoma invades beyond the uterus, but has not extended onto the lower third of the vagina or to the pelvic wall
IIA	Involvement limited to the upper two-thirds of the vagina without parametrial involvement
IIA1	Invasive carcinoma <4 cm in greatest dimension
IIA2	Invasive carcinoma ≥4 cm in greatest dimension
IIB	With parametrial involvement but not up to the pelvic wall
III	The carcinoma involves the lower third of the vagina and/or extends to the pelvic wall and/or causes hydronephrosis or nonfunctioning kidney and/or involves pelvic and/or para-aortic lymph nodes[c]
IIIA	The carcinoma involves the lower third of the vagina, with no extension to the pelvic wall
IIIB	Extension to the pelvic wall and/or hydronephrosis or nonfunctioning kidney (unless known to be due to another cause)
IIIC	Involvement of pelvic and/or para-aortic lymph nodes, irrespective of tumor size and extent (with r and p notations)[c]
IIIC1	Pelvic lymph node metastasis only
IIIC2	Para-aortic lymph node metastasis
IV	The carcinoma has extended beyond the true pelvis or has involved (biopsy proven) the mucosa of the bladder or rectum. (A bullous edema, as such, does not permit a case to be allotted to Stage IV)
IVA	Spread to adjacent pelvic organs
IVB	Spread to distant organs

When in doubt, the lower staging should be assigned.

[a] Imaging and pathology can be used, where available, to supplement clinical findings with respect to tumor size and extent, in all stages.

[b] The involvement of vascular/lymphatic spaces does not change the staging. The lateral extent of the lesion is no longer considered.

[c] Adding notation of r (imaging) and p (pathology) to indicate the findings that are used to allocate the case to Stage IIIC. Example: If imaging indicates pelvic lymph node metastasis, the stage allocation would be Stage IIIC1r, and if confirmed by pathologic findings, it would be Stage IIIC1p. The type of imaging modality or pathology technique used should always be documented.

FIG. 14.3 FIGO staging of cancer of the cervix uteri 2018 (adapted, under a CC BY license, from reference 2).

The major changes in FIGO 2018 cervical cancer staging are described in Table 14.1.

Stage 1B:

One of the major changes in the updated staging system is that stage IB disease (i.e., invasive carcinoma limited to the cervix) now includes three, rather than two, subgroups based on tumor size measured at its maximal dimension. Previously, stage IB1 disease was subdivided into two groups (Table 14.2).

This revision is based on observational data[17] that define two clinically distinct patient populations, as described below.

Survival outcome: Survival is significantly different between 2018 FIGO stage IB1 and IB2 diseases, with a nearly two-fold increased risk in cervical cancer mortality in stage IB2 disease compared to IB1 disease.

Risk-stratification: In stage IB cervical cancer, the current guidelines recommend radical trachelectomy, a fertility-sparing treatment for cervical cancer in which the uterine cervix, parametria, and vaginal cuff are resected, for 2018 FIGO stage IB1 disease but not for stage IB2.[17]

TABLE 14.1 Changes in 2018 FIGO cervical cancer staging.

Characteristics	2014 FIGO staging	2018 FIGO staging
Stage IB1	Tumor size ≤4 cm	Tumor size <2 cm
Stage IB2	Tumor size ≥4 cm	Tumor size 2–3.9 cm
Stage IB3	-	Tumor size ≥4 cm
Stage IIIC1	-	Pelvic lymph node metastasis only
Stage IIIC2	-	Para-aortic lymph node metastasis

TABLE 14.2 Stage IB classification under 2018 FIGO cervical cancer staging.

Stage	FIGO 2018
IB1	Tumor size <2 cm
IB2	Tumor size 2–3.9 cm
IB3	Tumor size ≥4 cm

TABLE 14.3 Stage IIIC classification under 2018 FIGO cervical cancer staging.

New inclusion of stage	FIGO 2018
IIIC1	Pelvic lymph node metastasis only
IIIC2	Para-aortic lymph node metastasis

Criteria for radical trachelectomies are as follows:

- The patient is of childbearing age and wishes to preserve fertility, without any clinical proof of impaired fertility.
- The cancer is contained in the cervix and is IB1 (or less).
- The tumor is located ≥1 cm from the cervical internal os.
- Absent stromal and deep lymphovascular invasion (LVSI) and pelvic or distant metastases.
- Certain histological subtypes such as neuroendocrine, squamous cell or serous/clear cell adenocarcinomas are excluded as they are considered to be more aggressive.

Surgical management: Minimally invasive surgical approaches are associated with decreased survival in stage IB2 disease but not in stage IB1 disease.

Characteristics: Stage IB1 disease was more likely to have an adenocarcinoma histology and to be low grade, whereas stage IB2 disease was more likely to have a squamous histology and to be high grade.

Stage III:

The assessment of abdominopelvic retroperitoneal lymph nodes in cervical cancer staging, which was not in any previous versions of the FIGO system, was introduced in the 2018 update (Table 14.3).

Patients with pelvic and/or para-aortic lymph node metastases are designated as having a stage IIIC disease, irrespective of the primary tumor size or local pelvic spread. Stage IIIC1 corresponds to nodal metastases confined to the pelvis and stage IIIC2 to para-aortic nodal metastases. Lymph node status is to be assigned based on imaging and/or pathologic analysis, and the methodology is to be recorded.[18] Lymphadenopathy is an important determinant in treatment planning and a major prognostic factor for survival outcomes.[19]

Treatment planning: The two conventional curative treatment options for invasive cervical cancer are:

- A radical hysterectomy with lymphadenectomy in early stage diseases (IA, IB1, and IIA1)
- Radiation therapy with concurrent platinum-based chemotherapy for patients with locoregionally advanced diseases (tumor >4 cm, stage IIB or greater).

However, 10–30% of patients with early stage disease harbor lymph node metastases; hence, surgery is not curative.[20] The identification and upstaging of these patients according to FIGO 2018 spare them from unnecessary surgery and potential long-term morbidity.[21]

Survival outcomes: Stage IIIC1 have superior cervical cancer-specific survival outcomes compared to those with stage IIIA-B disease. Important determinants of survival are local tumor factors, nodal status, and the degree of lymph node metastasis (isolated tumor cells vs. microscopic vs. macroscopic). Physicians should be aware that stage IIIC1 cervical cancer is not a single disease entity but instead reflects a heterogeneous group of tumors with a wide range of survival statistics ranging from 39.3% to 74.8%.[17,22] The literature notes that up to 30% of patients with early stage disease and lymph nodal disease can develop recurrent disease, so lymphadenectomy is regularly performed during the early stages.[20]

TABLE 14.4 Choice of imaging modality to asses cervical cancer, based on staging system and available resources.

FIGO 2018 staging	Limited resources available	Enhanced resources
IB Tumor size	TR/TV pelvic US	Pelvic MRI
IIA Upper vaginal spread	TR/TV pelvic US	Pelvic MRI
IIB Parametrial involvement	TR/TV pelvic US/pelvic CT	Pelvic MRI
IIIA Lower vaginal spread	TR/TV pelvic US	Pelvic MRI
IIIB Pelvic wall Hydronephrosis	TR/TV pelvic US/pelvic CT Abdominal US/IVU/CT	Pelvic MRI Abdominopelvic MRI/PET-CT
IIIC Pelvic lymphadenopathy Para-aortic lymphadenopathy	TR/TV pelvic US Abdominal US/CT	Torso PET/CT
IVA Adjacent pelvic organs	TR/TV pelvic US/pelvic CT	Pelvic MRI/PET-CT
IVB Lung metastasis	Chest radiograph	Chest radiograph/PET-CT

14.11 Choice of imaging based on staging and available resources

The choices of imaging modality to assess cervical cancer, based on the 2018 FIGO staging system and on available resources, are described in Table 14.4.

Imaging is appropriate in women with tumor invasive to a depth greater than or equal to 5 mm.

TR—Transrectal, TV—Transvaginal, US—Ultrasound, MRI—Magnetic resonance imaging, CT—Computed tomography, PET—Positron emission tomography, IVU—Intravenous urogram.

14.12 The role of MRI

MRI imaging can provide highly accurate information on the exact extent of tumors because of its fine contrast resolution and is thus invaluable for identifying important prognostic factors and optimizing treatment strategies. MRI can prevent unnecessary use of invasive procedures such as cystoscopy and proctoscopy, especially if there is no evidence of local spread. It is preferred for evaluation of the lymph nodes and to detect fistulous tracts and is also an important tool to optimize brachytherapy and external beam therapy by evaluating the shape and direction of lesion growth.

14.12.1 MRI anatomy of the cervix

On MRI imaging, the cervix demonstrates a trilaminar pattern. The high signal intensity of the endocervical mucous glands is surrounded by a low signal intensity stroma, followed by outer smooth muscles of intermediate signal intensity (Fig. 14.4).

Cervical cancer appears as an intermediate or hyperintense lesion on T2-weighted images, regardless of their histopathological type.[23]

14.12.2 MRI protocol

Pelvic MRI is the imaging modality of choice for evaluating primary tumor size and its extension into the soft tissues of the central pelvis, especially invasions into the parametria (stage IIB) and pelvic sidewall (stage IIIB). An

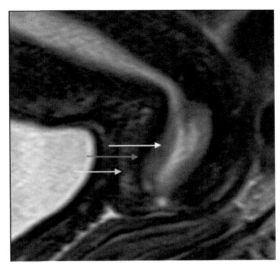

FIG. 14.4 Sagittal T2 weighted MR image demonstrates normal trilaminar pattern of signal intensity, with high-signal-intensity endocervical mucosal glands (white arrow) surrounded by low signal-intensity stroma (red arrow) and a rim of intermediate signal-intensity smooth muscle (yellow arrow).

TABLE 14.5   MRI protocol to image uterine cervical cancer.

Sequence	Plane	Field of view	Reason	Tumor characteristics
T1 weighted	Axial	Large (renal hila to symphysis pubis)	Identify pelvic lymph nodes; assess bone marrow	Isointense compared with pelvic muscles
T2 weighted	Axial	Large (renal hila to symphysis pubis)	Overview of pelvic sidewalls; assess for hydronephrosis	High signal intensity relative to low-signal-intensity cervical stroma
T2 weighted	Sagittal	Large	Assess tumor position and invasion of vagina and/or adjacent tissues	
T2 weighted	Oblique axial (perpendicular to long axis of cervix)	Small	Assess for parametrial invasion	
Diffusion-weighted imaging (DWI)	Axial or oblique axial	Large	Tumor assessment and an aid in detection of lymph nodes metastasis and peritoneal carcinomatosis	Tumor, nodes and peritoneal deposits demonstrate restricted diffusion

abdominopelvic MRI helps to evaluate hydronephrosis (stage IIIB) and lymphadenopathy (stage IIIC). The MRI protocol for imaging uterine cervical cancer is shown in Table 14.5.

The usefulness of dynamic contrast material-enhanced (DCE) studies in diagnosing peritoneal, nodal, and bone metastases has been documented.[24] DCE studies can also assist in predicting radio-sensitivity.[25] Oblique MRI sequences in staging cervical cancer should be planned along the long axis of the cervix and perpendicular to the long axis, which increases the sensitivity for detecting parametrial invasions (stage IIB) (Fig. 14.5).

14.12.3 The role of MRI in stage I

Stage IA is defined as a microinvasive tumor that cannot be demonstrated via MR imaging. Stage IB is defined as a clinically invasive tumor, although it is confined to the cervix and does not invade the vagina or parametrium (Fig. 14.6).

Tumors appear hyperintense on a T2-weighted sequence with surrounding hypointense normal cervical stroma (Fig. 14.7).

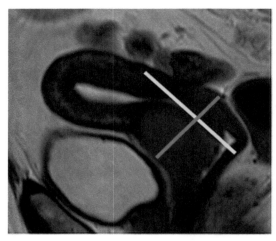

FIG. 14.5   Planning of MRI sequence in cervical cancer along the long axis of the cervix (oblique axial and coronal). Yellow line indicates the coronal plane, red line indicates the axial oblique plane.

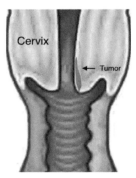

FIG. 14.6   Graphical representation of 2018 FIGO Stage I cervical cancer.

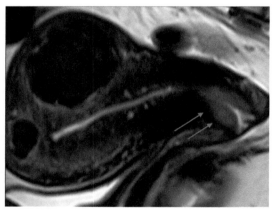

FIG. 14.7   **FIGO 2018 Stage IB cervical cancer.** Sagittal T2-weighted MR sequence demonstrates abnormal hyperintensity signal confined to the cervix (red arrows) suggesting cervical cancer.

MRI aids in categorizing stage IB tumors into IB1, IB2, and IB3 and further helps in planning appropriate management. MRI has a sensitivity of 90% and a specificity of 98% for the staging of early IB1 tumors. Adding diffusion weighted images (DWI) and DCE imaging allows the detection of tumors less than 1 cm.[26,27]

14.12.4 The role of MRI in stage II

Stage IIA is defined as a tumor that invades the upper two-thirds of the vagina without parametrial invasion (Fig. 14.8).

On MRI, T2-weighted images demonstrate the extension of a cervical tumor with segmental disruption of the hypointense vaginal wall (Fig. 14.9).[28]

MRI shows high accuracy (86–93%) for the assessment of vaginal invasions.[29,30] When a tumor extends beyond the uterus by a parametrial invasion without reaching the pelvic wall, it is defined as stage IIB (Fig. 14.10).

During MR imaging, a triangular protrusion of the tumor across the interrupted hypointense ring of the cervical stroma is observed.

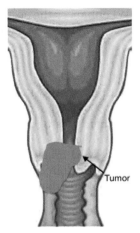

FIG. 14.8 Graphical representation of 2018 FIGO stage IIA cervical cancer extending up to upper vagina.

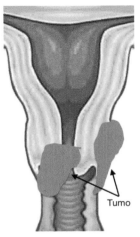

FIG. 14.10 Graphical representation of 2018 FIGO stage IIB cervical cancer extending laterally to involve parametrium.

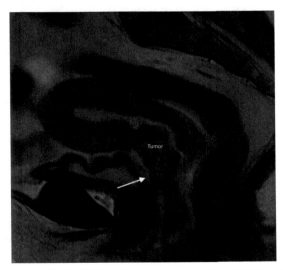

FIG. 14.9 FIGO 2018 Stage IIA cervical cancer. Sagittal T2-weighted MR sequence demonstrates cervical cancer extending into upper one-third of the vagina (white arrow).

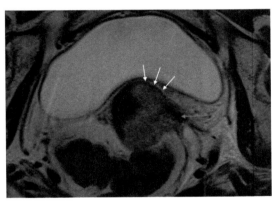

FIG. 14.11 FIGO 2018 stage IIB cervical cancer. Oblique axial T2-weighted MR sequence demonstrates cervical cancer extending into parametrium along the left lateral wall of cervix (red arrow). Normal cervical stromal ring appearing as hypointense rim on T2-weighted sequence (white arrows).

14.12.5 The concept of parametrial invasion

The radial spread of a tumor out of the uterine cervix into the parametria correlates with stage IIB disease. Stage IIB is often associated with metastasis, disease recurrence and compromised survival, virtually limiting available management options. With MRI, this is best seen on fast spin-echo T2 long-axis oblique views of the cervix where the isointense tumor extends beyond the dark stromal ring of the cervix (Fig. 14.11).[31]

Preservation of a stromal ring thickness of >3mm excludes parametrial involvement (specificity, 96–99%; NPV, 94–100%).[26,29]

For detecting parametrial involvement, MRI is more sensitive than a physical examination. Hricak et al. demonstrated that, in patients with early-stage tumors intended for curative surgery, the sensitivity of MRI versus clinical examination to help detect parametrial extension was 53% versus 29%.[32] Furthermore, the false-negative rate with MRI for parametrial extension is very low (<3%).[33] However, large tumors with peritumoral edema manifest as a T2 hyperintense signal and mimic cervical stromal disruption, which decreases the specificity of MRI in detecting parametrial invasion.[34] The combined analysis of T2-weighted imaging and DWI enhances the accuracy of detecting parametrial invasion in patients with cervical cancer when compared with T2-weighted imaging alone.[35]

14.12.6 The role of MRI in stage III

At stage IIIA, vaginal involvement reaches the lower third of the vaginal canal but does not extend to the pelvic wall (Figs. 14.12 and 14.13).

When the tumor extends to the pelvic wall or causes hydronephrosis, it is defined as stage IIIB (Fig. 14.14).

On MRI, the tumor obliterates the entire cardinal ligament and extends to the pelvic muscles. MR urography can be used to detect hydronephrosis caused by tumor extension. Large field-of-view MRI images (e.g., gradient-echo T1-weighted or echo planar T2-weighted images) from the level of the renal hilum through the pelvic floor are also obtained in the axial plane to evaluate for hydronephrosis (stage IIIB) (Fig. 14.15) and lymphadenopathy (stage IIIC).

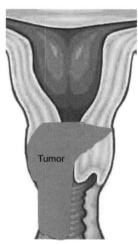

FIG. 14.12   Graphical representation of 2018 FIGO stage IIIA cervical cancer with involvement of lower third of the vagina.

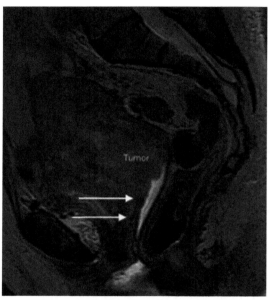

FIG. 14.13   FIGO 2018 stage IIIA cervical cancer. Sagittal T2-weighted MR sequence with vaginal gel demonstrates cervical cancer extending into lower third of the vagina (white arrows).

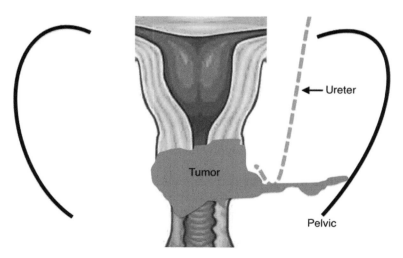

FIG. 14.14   Graphical representation of 2018 FIGO stage IIIB cervical cancer extending and involving the ureter and the pelvic wall.

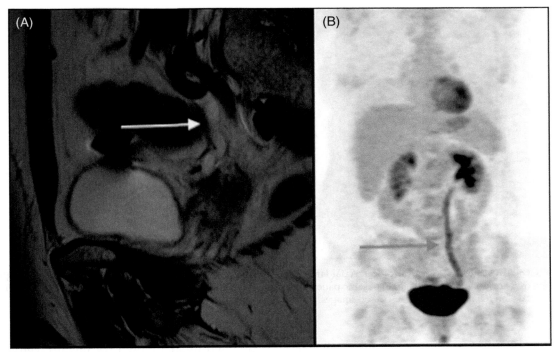

FIG. 14.15 FIGO 2018 stage IIIB cervical cancer. Sagittal T2-weighted MR sequence (A) demonstrates hydroureter secondary to cervical cancer (white arrow). Coronal PET image of same patient demonstrates left hydroureteronephrosis (red arrow).

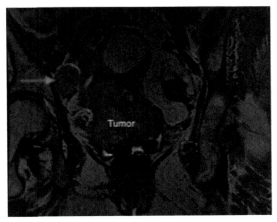

FIG. 14.16 FIGO 2018 stage IIIC1 cervical cancer. Coronal oblique T2-weighted MR sequence demonstrates cervical cancer with enlarged right pelvic sidewall lymphadenopathy (red arrow).

14.12.7 *Detection of lymphadenopathy* (stage IIIC1 and IIIC2)

A T2-weighted MRI sequence is best for detecting lymph nodes that display an intermediate signal intensity and can be distinguished from hypointense muscles and blood vessels (Fig. 14.16).

Adding a DWI sequence would provide greater sensitivity and specificity for detecting lymph node metastases.[36] An addition of DWI and apparent diffusion coefficient (ADC) maps has also been shown to increase reader confidence and enhance tumor detection.

Lymph node disease detection is based on size and morphology criteria. The most widely accepted size criterion is a transverse diameter exceeding 8 mm.[37] A size of 8–10 mm is reported as "likely" involved and a size of >15 mm is reported as "almost certainly" involved on CT examination. Based on morphology criteria, the malignant infiltration of lymph nodes may be indicated by certain imaging features. Some of these suspicious features

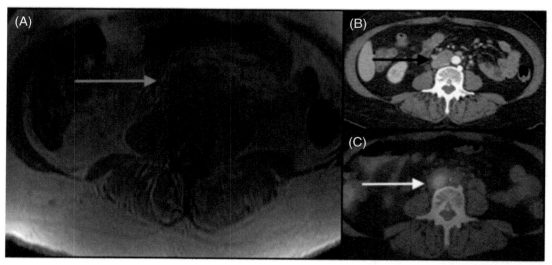

FIG. 14.17   **FIGO 2018 stage IIIC2 cervical cancer.** Axial large field of view T2-weighted MR sequence (A) demonstrates right para-aortic lymphadenopathy (red arrow). Axial CT image (B) of same patient demonstrates right para-aortic lymphadenopathy (black arrow) which shows hypermetabolic uptake on (C) axial FDG PET-CT fused images (white arrow).

may include a spherical shape and irregular contour, altered signal intensity on T2W images, central necrosis, and the formation of nodal conglomerates. Central node necrosis has 100% PPV for the diagnosis of nodal metastasis.[38]

MR has a wide range of sensitivity and specificity for the detection of lymph node metastases ranging from 38% to 89% and 78% to 99%, respectively.[39] The lack of discrimination between enlarged inflammatory or metastatic lymph nodes on MRI may explains the variability. The MRI also shows unsatisfactory diagnostic precision in micro-metastases.[40] Additionally, occasionally ovarian follicles, neural or radicular tumors, and other nonspecific pelvic masses can be misinterpreted as pelvic metastatic adenopathy.

In spite of these disadvantages, studies have shown that pretreatment imaging of lymph nodes using MRI has decreased patient morbidity by avoiding the short and long-term complications of lymphadenectomy.[41] Para-aortic lymphadenopathy (stage IIIC2) is clinically significant as it not only upstages the patient, but also expands the fields for radiation therapy. MRI or CT is a second-line alternative, with both modalities demonstrating similar diagnostic performance when PET/CT, which is more sensitive than MRI for detecting metastatic lymph nodes from cervical carcinoma, is unavailable (Fig. 14.17).[42]

The main disadvantage of PET in assessing lymph nodes is that necrotic lymph shows poor or no FDG uptake; this drawback can be alleviated by correlation with corresponding CT images.

14.12.8 The role of MRI in stage IV

If the tumor invades the vesical or rectal mucosa, it is classified as stage IVA. Segmental disruption of the hypointense vesical or rectal wall or a segmental thickened rectal wall is seen on MRI (Figs. 14.18 and 14.19).

Once any distant metastases occur, the stage is defined as IVB. Cervical cancer occasionally causes carcinomatous lymphangitis of the lung or hematogenous hepatic metastases. CT plays a major role in diagnosing such advanced disease.

14.13 Bladder and rectum involvement

MRI has a 100% negative predictive value for the exclusion of bladder and rectal invasions; therefore, cystoscopy and endoscopic staging procedures are not mandated by FIGO if the staging MRI is negative. MRI also shows an accuracy of 71–100% for bladder invasion, and 88–91% for rectal invasion.[43,44] However, when MRI findings are equivocal or assessment is difficult due to the presence of bullous edema, endoscopy may be used to depict or exclude mucosal invasion.[45]

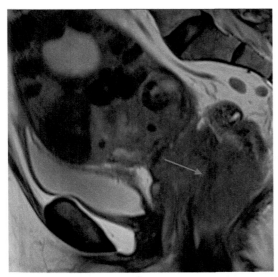

FIG. 14.18 FIGO 2018 stage IV cervical cancer. Sagittal T2-weighted MR sequence demonstrates extension of cervical cancer posteriorly into the rectum (red arrow).

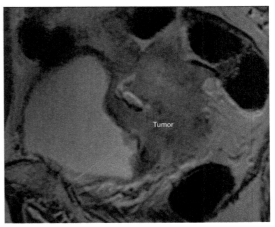

FIG. 14.19 FIGO 2018 STAGE IV cervical cancer. Sagittal T2-weighted MR sequence demonstrates extension of cervical cancer anteriorly into the urinary bladder (red arrow).

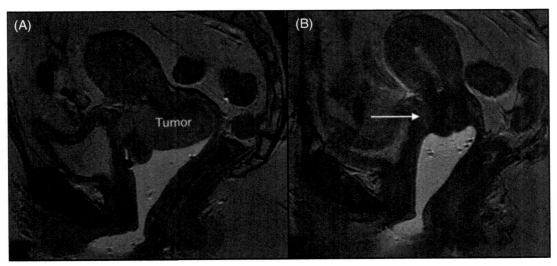

FIG. 14.20 Role of MRI in assessing post-treatment changes in cervical cancer. Sagittal T2-weighted sequence MRI (A) pretreatment staging demonstrated cervical cancer abutting the posterior wall of urinary bladder. Post-treatment MR after radiation therapy shows significant interval resolution of the tumor with residual tumor along the posterior wall of the urinary bladder (white arrow).

Adding DWI can help identify subtle serosal or peritoneal deposits that can easily be missed on T2WI. The DWI protocol should include at least one plane with a minimum of two b values (e.g., b = 0, b = 1000). Scanning T2WI and DWI at the same plane enables image fusion and optimizes anatomical correlation. The addition of DWI also helps to improve evaluations, particularly where gadolinium cannot be administered. To avoid any pitfalls, DWI images should always be assessed with ADC maps and anatomical images.[29]

14.13.1 The role of MRI in post-treatment

MRI can be helpful in detecting local recurrence after surgery or radiation therapy.[46] Disease recurrence would appear as intermediate-to-high signal intensity on T2-weighted images (Fig. 14.20).

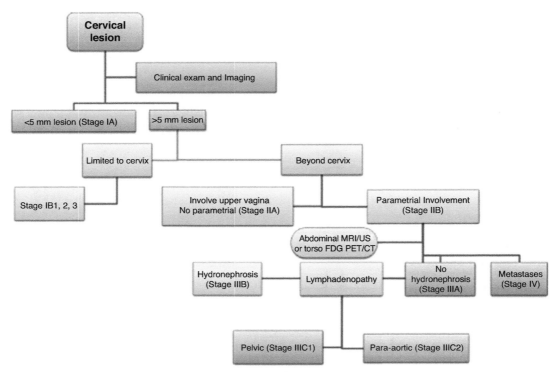

FIG. 14.21   2018 FIGO cervical cancer staging and patient triage algorithm.

It is important to distinguish between postradiation changes and local recurrence in patients receiving radiation therapy. The contrast enhanced images may aid in this process; recurrent tumor usually shows early enhancement (45–90 s) and corresponding restriction on DWI sequences. Whereas fibrosis does not show any significant enhancement or enhances only in delayed phases. Tumor recurrence and inflammatory changes both may show hyperintensity at a high b-value, but only recurring tumors will have a corresponding lower signal intensity on the ADC map.[47]

2018 FIGO cervical cancer staging, and patient triage algorithm is summarized in Fig. 14.21. Refer to Fig. 14.22 for treatment algorithm.

Table 14.6 provides a list of key teaching points that may play a critical role in the interpretation of radiological images.

14.14 Other imaging modalities

14.14.1 Chest radiography

Consensus guidelines suggest that the initial choice for chest imaging is radiography instead of CT (especially if PET/CT is not performed).[24] However, CT is taken as a superior modality to detect pleural effusion or pulmonary metastases compared to chest radiography (Fig. 14.23).[24]

14.14.2 Ultrasound

Cervical cancer appears as homogeneously solid and hypoechoic relative to the uterine cervical stroma (Fig. 14.24).[48]

Transrectal ultrasound (TRUS) or transvaginal ultrasound with a high frequency transducer (7–9 MHz) is a useful tool to detect early local spread into the cervical stroma (stage IB) or parametrial invasion (stage IIB). The accuracies of TRUS and MRI are similar for tumor detection and parametrial infiltration.[24] In low resource countries, ultrasound can be used in patients suspected of having advanced disease to evaluate for hydronephrosis (stage IIIB) and retroperitoneal lymph nodes if cross-sectional imaging with CT, MRI, or PET-CT cannot be not performed.[16]

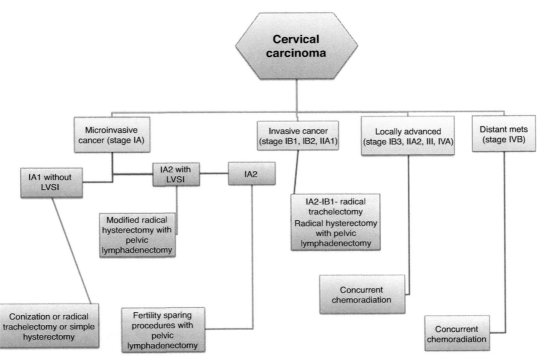

FIG. 14.22 2018 FIGO cervical cancer treatment algorithm.

TABLE 14.6 Pearls and pitfalls of MR imaging in staging cervical cancer.

2018 FIGO staging	Pitfall	Pearl
Stage I	Difficult to detect tumors stage IA and IB1 (especially <1 cm tumors)	Addition of DWI and DCE sequences helps to detect
	Overstaging of IB3 as stage IIA in large tumors	Vaginal walls can be distended with vaginal gel
	Overstaging of IB2 as stage IIB due to cervical edema in large tumors	DWI and DCE sequences improve the accuracy of T2 images
Stage II	Understaging IIB as stage IB2-IB3 tumors in tumors with diffuse T2 signal inhomogeneity of the cervical rim due to invasion	The cervical rim must be thick (>3 mm) and homogeneous on T2 to exclude parametrial invasion
Stage III	Misinterpretation of benign lymphadenopathy and hydronephrosis as stage IIIC and IIIB tumors	Use large field of view MRI or other cross section imaging like CT and PET-CT or perform tissue biopsy
Stage IV	Misinterpretation of bladder wall edema (bullous edema) as stage IVA	DWI and DCE sequence aid to differentiate invasion of bladder. Preserved fat plane between tumor and bladder excludes invasion. Perform cystoscopy
Post-treatment	Post biopsy changes can overestimate the size and parametrial invasion	Perform imaging after 10 days of biopsy. Addition of DWI sequence may help. Repeat MRI in 6 weeks if required

14.14.3 Computed tomography

If a pelvis CT is conducted for an evaluation of a tumor as an alternative to pelvic MRI, contrast administration is strongly advised, even though it is highly discouraged as the tumor enhances similar to normal cervical tissue and thus makes CT evaluation suboptimal for assessing the spread and measurement of the tumor. Abdominopelvic CTs are relevant for evaluating retroperitoneal lymphadenopathy (Stage IIIC) as a part of PET/CT or as an alternative to an abdominopelvic MRI. According to consensus guidelines for solid tumor measurement, tumor involvement

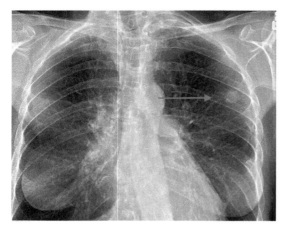

FIG. 14.23 Role of chest radiography in cervical cancer staging. Frontal chest radiography in a patient with cervical cancer shows pulmonary nodule in the left upper lung (red arrow) favoring metastasis (stage IVB).

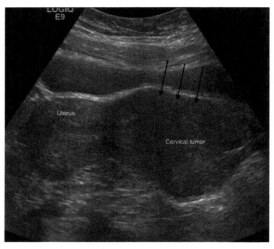

FIG. 14.24 Role of ultrasound in cervical cancer staging. Sagittal grey scale image of uterus shows hypoechoic mass in the cervix (black arrows), concerning for cervical cancer.

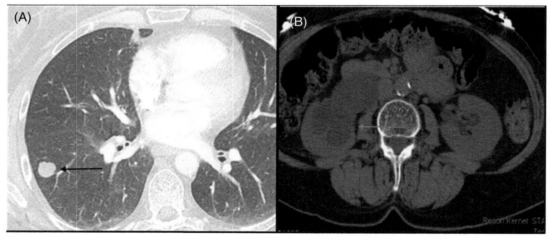

FIG. 14.25 Role of CT in cervical cancer staging. Axial CT image lung window (A) shows right lower lobe pulmonary metastasis (black arrow). Axial CT image soft tissue window (B) demonstrates right hydronephrosis (red arrow).

is reported as "likely" if the lymph node measures greater than or equal to 8 mm and as "almost certainly" if it measures greater than or equal to 15 mm on a short axis.[49] A CT urogram study can be performed to evaluate hydronephrosis (stage IIIB), again as an alternative to an abdominopelvic MRI.

A chest CT, with or without contrast, is performed to follow up an abnormal chest radiograph to evaluate spread distance (stage IVB), including pulmonary nodules and the involvement of supraclavicular lymph nodes (Fig. 14.25).

14.14.4 Positron emission tomography

PET/CT is best used to evaluate for hydronephrosis (stage IIIB), retroperitoneal lymphadenopathy (stage IIIC), and distant metastases (stage IVB) (Fig. 14.26).

PET demonstrates a higher sensitivity (75%) and comparable specificity (98%) to MRI and CT in detecting lymph node metastases greater than 10 mm. PET and PET/CT are strong predictors of disease-specific survival due to their sensitivity in depicting lymph node metastases.[50] PET/CT is indicated and is the preferred examination for whole-body staging in patients with local-regionally advanced cancer at pelvic examination (i.e., clinical stage IB3, IIA2, >IIB) and in patients in whom radiography, CT, or MRI indicates the extrauterine spread of the primary tumor.

Commonly involved distant sites of metastasis include the lungs, peritoneum, supraclavicular and thoracic lymph nodes, and bones, in order of prevalence. The majority of these distant metastases, including thoracic lymphadenopathy,

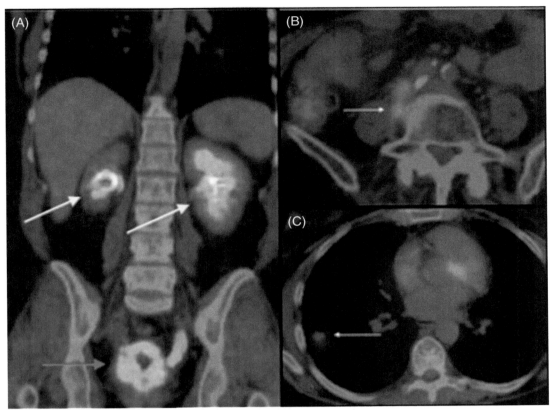

FIG. 14.26 **Role of FDG PET-CT in cervical cancer staging.** Coronal fused PET-CT image (A) shows FDG avid cervical tumor (red arrow) with bilateral hydronephrosis (white arrows) (stage IIIB). Axial fused PET-CT image (B) shows FDG avid para-aortic lymphadenopathy (white arrow) (stage IIIC2) and axial fused PET-CT image (C) shows FDG hypermetabolic right pulmonary metastasis (red arrow) (stage IVB).

pulmonary nodules <1 cm, and bone metastases, are challenging to assess with pelvic MRI and chest radiography, which are only recommended as alternative modalities if PET/CT is unavailable.[51] Although PET/CT shows high specificity and positive predictive value in detecting distant metastases, it should be confirmed with a biopsy because a designation of stage IVB is associated with a significant change in treatment strategy.[16]

14.15 Case-based learning

Case 1: A 60-year-old female with abnormal vaginal bleeding (Fig. 14.27).

A sagittal T2-weighted MRI image (A) shows an abnormal hyperintense signal in the cervix (red arrows) measuring up to 2.2 cm. The sagittal postcontrast T1-weighted MRI images (B) show an enhancing lesion, suggesting cervical cancer.

Question: Which stage should be assigned?

Answer: Earlier FIGO staging would classify this lesion as stage IB1. However, according to 2018 FIGO staging, it is assigned to stage IB2.

Teaching points: One of the major changes in the updated staging system is that stage IB disease now includes three, rather than two, categories. Survival outcome, risk stratification, and surgical management are different in these subgroups.

Case 2: A 50-year-old female with pelvic pain and vaginal bleeding (Fig. 14.28).

A coronal T2-weighted MRI image (A) demonstrates a hyperintense cervical lesion involving the lower third of the vagina with a large right iliac chain lymph node (red arrows). An axial PET-CT fused image (B) shows an uptake in the cervical mass and in the right iliac chain lymph node (red arrow).

Question: Which stage should be assigned?

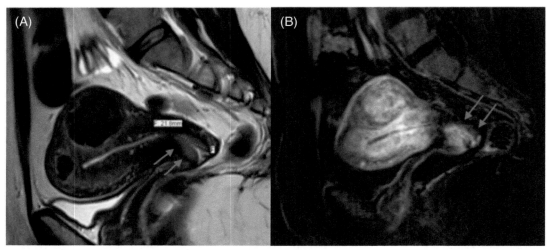

FIG. 14.27   **Case based learning.** Case 1.

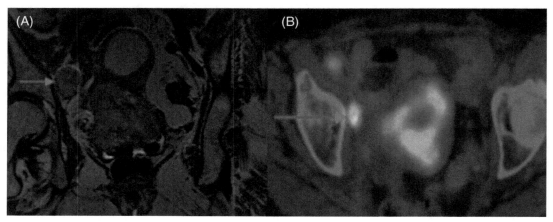

FIG. 14.28   **Case based learning.** Case 2.

Answer: Earlier FIGO staging would classify this lesion as stage IIIA. However, according to 2018 FIGO staging, it is assigned to stage IIIC1r.

Teaching points: The 2018 FIGO enables the identification and upstaging of patients based on pretreatment lymph nodes. Lymphadenopathy is a major prognostic factor for survival and an important determinant in treatment planning.

Case 3: A 52-year-old female with abnormal vaginal bleeding (Fig. 14.29).

A sagittal T2-weighted MRI image (A) demonstrates a hyperintense cervical lesion measuring 3.2 cm in the craniocaudal dimension. An axial postcontrast T1-weighted MRI image (B) demonstrates a hyperintense lesion limited to the cervix measuring 4.4 cm in the horizontal dimension.

Question: Which stage should be assigned?

Answer: Earlier FIGO staging would classify this lesion into stage IB2 (>4 cm). However, according to 2018 FIGO staging, it is assigned to stage IB2 (2–3.9 cm).

Teaching points: The horizontal dimension is no longer considered in the 2018 FIGO revision since it is subject to many artifactual errors.

Case 4: A 64-year-old female with pelvic pain and abnormal vaginal discharge (Fig. 14.30).

A transvaginal grey scale ultrasound image of the uterus in the sagittal plane (A) demonstrates an enlarged cervix with a hypoechoic lesion (white arrows). A sagittal T2-weighted MRI image (B) demonstrates a hyperintense cervical lesion extending into the upper third of the vagina (red arrow). A postradiation sagittal T2-weighted MRI image (C) demonstrates an interval resolution of the cervical lesion with a diffuse T2 hypointense signal in the cervix (yellow arrow). An FDG PET/CT was negative (not shown).

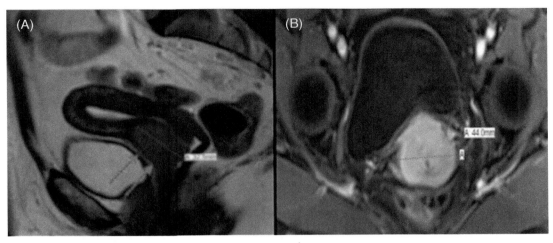

FIG. 14.29   **Case based learning.** Case 3.

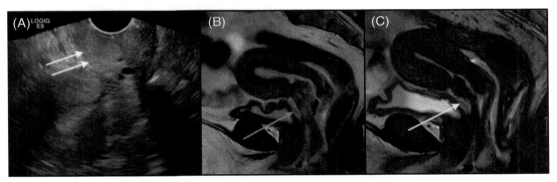

FIG. 14.30   **Case based learning.** Case 4.

Question 1: Which stage should be assigned?

Answer: According to 2018 FIGO staging, it is assigned to stage IIA because the tumor involves the upper third of the vagina and spares the lower part.

Question 2: How should it be evaluated for post-treatment MRI?

Answer: It is important to differentiate between postradiation changes and local recurrence in patients treated with radiation. Disease recurrence would appear as an intermediate-to-high signal intensity on T2-weighted images. In this case, post-treatment MRI image shows diffuse T2 hypointensity, suggesting no residual tumor.

Teaching points: It is important to distinguish between postradiation changes and local recurrence in patients receiving radiation therapy. Postcontrast images facilitate this process, as recurrence shows early improvement (45–90 s) and restriction on DWI sequences. The fibrosis shows delayed enhancement. Tumor recurrence and inflammatory changes may demonstrate overlapping features on high b-value DWI, but only recurrent tumors will have a lower signal intensity on the ADC map.

Case 5: A 48-year-old female with postcoital pain and bleeding (Fig. 14.31).

A sagittal T2-weighted MRI image (A) demonstrates a hyperintense cervical tumor. An axial unenhanced CT image (B) and axial fused PET/CT image (C) demonstrate an FDG avid cervical tumor (yellow arrow) with an FDG-avid enlarged right external iliac chain lymph node (white arrow). A postradiation sagittal T2-weighted MRI image (C) demonstrates the interval resolution of a cervical lesion with a diffuse T2 hypointense signal in the cervix (red arrow). An axial fused PET/CT image (E) shows a complete resolution of an FDG-avid cervical tumor and right external iliac lymph node.

Question 1: Which stage should be assigned?

Answer: According to 2018 FIGO staging, it is assigned to stage IIIC1r due to the presence of FDG-avid right pelvic side wall lymphadenopathy.

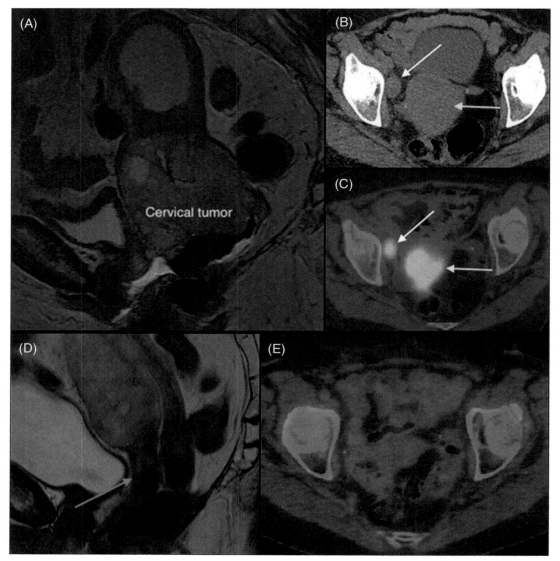

FIG. 14.31   **Case based learning.** Case 5.

Teaching points: Lymph node disease detection is based on size and morphology criteria. A size of 8–10 mm is reported as "likely" involved and a size of >15 mm is reported as "almost certainly" involved upon CT examination. PET/CT is the recommended imaging modality for the assessment of lymph nodal disease in cervical cancer.

Case 6: A 58-year-old female with excessive vaginal bleeding and right flank pain (Fig. 14.32).

A transvaginal grey scale ultrasound image of a uterus in the sagittal plane (A) demonstrates an enlarged cervix with a hypoechoic lesion (white arrow). A coronal whole-body fused FDG PET/CT and PET images (B and C) demonstrate an FDG-avid cervical cancer with right hydronephrosis. A sagittal T2-weighted MRI image (D) demonstrates a cervical tumor (red arrow), and a postradiation sagittal T2-weighted MRI image (E) demonstrates the interval resolution of a cervical lesion with a diffuse T2 hypointense signal in the cervix (red arrow).

Question 1: Which stage should be assigned?

Answer: According to 2018 FIGO staging, it is assigned to stage IIIB due to the involvement of the right ureter, causing hydroureteronephrosis.

Teaching points: Large field-of-view MRI images from the level of the renal hilum through the pelvic floor are obtained in the axial plane to evaluate for hydronephrosis (stage IIIB) and lymphadenopathy (stage IIIC). Alternatively, MR urography can be used to detect hydronephrosis caused by tumor extension. In low resource locations, hydronephrosis can be detected using ultrasound or CT imaging.

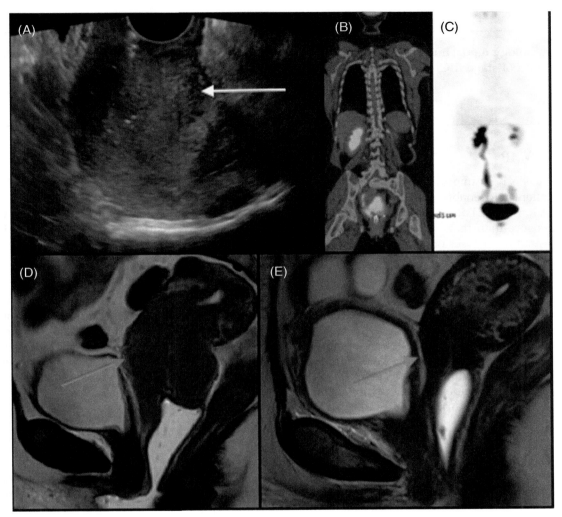

FIG. 14.32 **Case based learning.** Case 6.

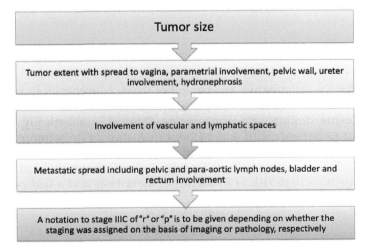

FIG. 14.33 Radiology reporting format.

Magnetic resonance imaging of the pelvis

14.16 Standardized reporting

A standard radiology report must include detailed descriptions of tumor size, tumor extent, and metastatic spread with the notation of stage IIIC, as shown in Fig. 14.33.

14.17 Future directions

14.17.1 PET-MR

FDG PET-MR is a new hybrid imaging technique that allows concurrent acquisition of MR and PET images. It provides excellent MRI-enabled soft tissue contrast and high-resolution morphological details combined with metabolic information on PET imaging. It has the advantage of providing multiparametric tumor imaging with lower radiation exposure than that of PET-CT. Sarabhai et al. reported higher sensitivity and specificity in identifying nodal and distant metastases on PET-MRI compared to MRI alone.[52]

14.17.2 ADC imaging

DWI with ADC maps can provide additional information about internal tumor microstructure that can correlate with treatment response and aggressive behavior. Higher ADC levels are associated with favorable histology and differentiation. Adenocarcinomas demonstrates highest ADC values (mean 0.894) followed by adenosquamous histology (mean 0.894). Squamous cell carcinoma has the lowest ADC values (mean 0.694). Similarly, well differentiated tumors show higher ADC values (mean 0.841) and poorly differentiated tumors show lower values (mean 0.648). Typically, tumors with low ADC (mean 0.648–0.694) are associated with unfavorable histologies (like squamous cell), high-grade tumors, parametric invasion, and low survival rates.[53,54]

Measuring tumor ADC during chemo-radiotherapy can be a potentially useful biomarker of the response to early treatment.[55]

14.17.3 DCE MRI

Certain solid tumors, including cervical cancers, demonstrate tumor hypoxia, which may explain resistance of the tumor to neoadjuvant or adjuvant therapy. Consequently, tumor hypoxia may play a central role in mechanisms leading to uncontrolled tumor growth and potential metastatic dissemination.[56,57]

Tumor microvasculature and the angiogenic profile of tumor tissue in vivo can be quantitatively assessed by DCE MRI. Pretreatment DCE-MRI may help predict the potential tumors with low radio responsiveness, treatment response and survival in cervical cancer patients.

14.17.3.1 MR spectroscopy (MRS)

In vivo MRS registers signals from chemical nuclei (typically hydrogen) and obtains noninvasive biochemical information from a selected volume tumor tissue. High lipid resonance rates on MRS are reported to predict poor prognostic HPV genotypes and persistent illnesses following chemotherapy in cervical cancer.[58]

14.17.3.2 Bioluminescence imaging (BLI)

The technique of BLI allows for the quantitative assessment of tissue concentrations of ATP, glucose, and lactate at quasi-identical locations and thus can help establish spatial correlations between the respective distribution images. A study on cervical cancer using bioluminescence imaging showed a statistically highly significant difference between tumor lactate content in patients with and without metastasis. Furthermore, the overall and disease-free survival probabilities for patients with low tumor lactate values were significantly higher than those for patients with high lactate values in viable tumor tissue. These findings indicate that high local levels of lactate within cervical cancers may be associated with a high risk of incidence of metastasis and a bad prognosis for survival.[59]

14.17.3.3 Ultrasmall super paramagnetic iron oxide (USPIO)

The assessment of lymph node metastases can be further improved with the use of USPIO particles. USPIO may be absorbed by normal macrophage in the lymph nodes. Metastatic lymph nodes lack macrophage, preventing the uptake of USPIO. USPIO increases MRI sensitivity by as much as 93% to detect nodal metastases.[60–62]

14.18 Conclusion

It is pertinent for radiologists to have a thorough knowledge of the updated 2018 FIGO staging system for uterine cervical cancer in which imaging plays an essential role in patient management. The revision demands a more comprehensive depiction of primary tumor size, which should be measured with MRI, especially for trachelectomy planning in early-stage tumors. MRI plays an important role in locoregional staging, the detection of metastases, evaluating responses to treatment, and detecting tumor recurrence and potential complications. Radiologists should arrive at consensus standards and criteria for image acquisition, interpretation, and reporting to achieve optimum quality in the care of uterine cervical cancer.

Acknowledgments

None.

References

1. Arbyn M, Weiderpass E, Bruni L, et al. Estimates of incidence and mortality of cervical cancer in 2018: a worldwide analysis. *Lancet Glob Health*. 2020;8(2):e191–e203. doi:10.1016/s2214-109x(19)30482-6.
2. Bhatla N, Aoki D, Sharma DN, Sankaranarayanan R. Cancer of the cervix uteri. *Int J Gynaecol Obstet*. 2018;143(Suppl 2):22–36. doi:10.1002/ijgo.12611.
3. Moncada-Madrazo M, Rodríguez Valero C. Embryology, uterus. [Updated 2021 Jul 31]. *StatPearls*. Treasure Island (FL): StatPearls Publishing; 2022 Jan-. Available from: https://www.ncbi.nlm.nih.gov/books/NBK547748/.
4. Ferenczy A. Anatomy and histology of the cervix. In: Blaustein A, ed. *Pathology of the Female Genital Tract*. New York: Springer; 1977:102–123.
5. Buchsbaum HJ. Extrapelvic lymph node metastases in cervical carcinoma. *Am J Obstet Gynecol*. 1979;133(7):814–824. doi:10.1016/0002-9378(79)90118-2.
6. Bader AA, Winter R, Haas J, Tamussino KF. Where to look for the sentinel lymph node in cervical cancer. *Am J Obstet Gynecol*. 2007;197(6):678. e1-7. doi:10.1016/j.ajog.2007.09.053.
7. Henriksen E. The lymphatic spread of carcinoma of the cervix and of the body of the uterus; a study of 420 necropsies. *Am J Obstet Gynecol*. 1949;58(5):924–942. doi:10.1016/0002-9378(49)90200-8.
8. Ellison E, LaPuerta P, Martin SE. Supraclavicular masses: results of a series of 309 cases biopsied by fine needle aspiration. *Head Neck*. 1999;21(3):239–246. doi:10.1002/(sici)1097-0347(199905)21:3<239::aid-hed9>3.0.co;2-b.
9. López F, Rodrigo JP, Silver CE, et al. Cervical lymph node metastases from remote primary tumor sites. *Head Neck*. 2016;38(Suppl 1):E2374–E2385. doi:10.1002/hed.24344.
10. Sung H, Ferlay J, Siegel RL, et al. Global cancer statistics 2020: GLOBOCAN estimates of incidence and mortality worldwide for 36 cancers in 185 countries. *CA Cancer J Clin*. 2021;71(3):209–249. doi:10.3322/caac.21660.
11. Bray F, Ferlay J, Soerjomataram I, Siegel RL, Torre LA, Jemal A. Global cancer statistics 2018: GLOBOCAN estimates of incidence and mortality worldwide for 36 cancers in 185 countries. *CA Cancer J Clin*. 2018;68(6):394–424. doi:10.3322/caac.21492.
12. Rauh-Hain JA, Melamed A, Schaps D, et al. Racial and ethnic disparities over time in the treatment and mortality of women with gynecological malignancies. *Gynecol Oncol*. 2018;149(1):4–11. doi:10.1016/j.ygyno.2017.12.006.
13. de Sanjose S, Quint WG, Alemany L, et al. Human papillomavirus genotype attribution in invasive cervical cancer: a retrospective cross-sectional worldwide study. *Lancet Oncol*. 2010;11(11):1048–1056. doi:10.1016/s1470-2045(10)70230-8.
14. Bouvard V, Baan R, Straif K, et al. A review of human carcinogens–Part B: biological agents. *Lancet Oncol*. 2009;10(4):321–322. doi:10.1016/s1470-2045(09)70096-8.
15. Eze JN, Emeka-Irem EN, Edegbe FO. A six-year study of the clinical presentation of cervical cancer and the management challenges encountered at a state teaching hospital in southeast Nigeria. *Clin Med Insights Oncol*. 2013;7:151–158. doi:10.4137/CMO.S12017.
16. Lee SI, Atri M. 2018 FIGO staging system for uterine cervical cancer: enter cross-sectional imaging. *Radiology*. 2019;292(1):15–24. doi:10.1148/radiol.2019190088.
17. Matsuo K, Machida H, Mandelbaum RS, Konishi I, Mikami M. Validation of the 2018 FIGO cervical cancer staging system. *Gynecol Oncol*. 2019;152(1):87–93. doi:10.1016/j.ygyno.2018.10.026.
18. Bhatla N, Berek JS, Cuello Fredes M, et al. Revised FIGO staging for carcinoma of the cervix uteri. *Int J Gynaecol Obstet*. 2019;145(1):129–135. doi:10.1002/ijgo.12749.
19. Kidd EA, El Naqa I, Siegel BA, Dehdashti F, Grigsby PW. FDG-PET-based prognostic nomograms for locally advanced cervical cancer. *Gynecol Oncol*. 2012;127(1):136–140. doi:10.1016/j.ygyno.2012.06.027.
20. Signorelli M, Guerra L, Montanelli L, et al. Preoperative staging of cervical cancer: is 18-FDG-PET/CT really effective in patients with early stage disease? *Gynecol Oncol*. 2011;123(2):236–240. doi:10.1016/j.ygyno.2011.07.096.
21. Landoni F, Maneo A, Colombo A, et al. Randomised study of radical surgery versus radiotherapy for stage IB-IIA cervical cancer. *Lancet*. 1997;350(9077):535–540. doi:10.1016/s0140-6736(97)02250-2.
22. Quinn MA, Benedet JL, Odicino F, et al. Carcinoma of the cervix uteri. FIGO 26th annual report on the results of treatment in gynecological cancer. *Int J Gynaecol Obstet*. 2006;95(Suppl 1):S43–103. doi:10.1016/s0020-7292(06)60030-1.
23. Abe Y, Yamashita Y, Namimoto T, et al. Carcinoma of the uterine cervix. High-resolution turbo spin-echo MR imaging with contrast-enhanced dynamic scanning and T2-weighting. *Acta Radiol*. 1998;39(3):322–326. doi:10.1080/02841859809172203.

24. Siegel CL, Andreotti RF, Cardenes HR, et al. ACR appropriateness criteria® pretreatment planning of invasive cancer of the cervix. *J Am Coll Radiol.* 2012;9(6):395–402. doi:10.1016/j.jacr.2012.02.021.

25. Yamashita Y, Takahashi M, Sawada T, Miyazaki K, Okamura H. Carcinoma of the cervix: dynamic MR imaging. *Radiology.* 1992;182(3):643–648. doi:10.1148/radiology.182.3.1535875.

26. Sala E, Rockall AG, Freeman SJ, Mitchell DG, Reinhold C. The added role of MR imaging in treatment stratification of patients with gynecologic malignancies: what the radiologist needs to know. *Radiology.* 2013;266(3):717–740. doi:10.1148/radiol.12120315.

27. Wakefield JC, Downey K, Kyriazi S, deSouza NM. New MR techniques in gynecologic cancer. *AJR Am J Roentgenol.* 2013;200(2):249–260. doi:10.2214/ajr.12.8932.

28. Sironi S, Belloni C, Taccagni GL, DelMaschio A. Carcinoma of the cervix: value of MR imaging in detecting parametrial involvement. *AJR Am J Roentgenol.* 1991;156(4):753–756. doi:10.2214/ajr.156.4.2003441.

29. Patel-Lippmann K, Robbins JB, Barroilhet L, Anderson B, Sadowski EA, Boyum J. MR imaging of cervical cancer. *Magn Reson Imaging Clin N Am.* 2017;25(3):635–649. doi:10.1016/j.mric.2017.03.007.

30. Otero-Garcia MM, Mesa-Alvarez A, Nikolic O, et al. Role of MRI in staging and follow-up of endometrial and cervical cancer: pitfalls and mimickers. *Insights Imaging.* 2019;10(1):19. doi:10.1186/s13244-019-0696-8.

31. Okamoto Y, Tanaka YO, Nishida M, Tsunoda H, Yoshikawa H, Itai Y. MR imaging of the uterine cervix: imaging-pathologic correlation. *Radiographics.* 2003;23(2):425–445. doi:10.1148/rg.232025065.

32. Hricak H, Gatsonis C, Chi DS, et al. Role of imaging in pretreatment evaluation of early invasive cervical cancer: results of the intergroup study American College of Radiology Imaging Network 6651-Gynecologic Oncology Group 183. *J Clin Oncol.* 2005;23(36):9329–9337. doi:10.1200/jco.2005.02.0354.

33. Epstein E, Testa A, Gaurilcikas A, et al. Early-stage cervical cancer: tumor delineation by magnetic resonance imaging and ultrasound: a European multicenter trial. *Gynecol Oncol.* 2013;128(3):449–453. doi:10.1016/j.ygyno.2012.09.025.

34. Nicolet V, Carignan L, Bourdon F, Prosmanne O. MR imaging of cervical carcinoma: a practical staging approach. *Radiographics.* 2000;20(6):1539–1549. doi:10.1148/radiographics.20.6.g00nv111539.

35. Qu JR, Qin L, Li X, et al. Predicting parametrial invasion in cervical carcinoma (Stages IB1, IB2, and IIA): diagnostic accuracy of T2-weighted imaging combined with DWI at 3T. *AJR Am J Roentgenol.* 2018;210(3):677–684. doi:10.2214/ajr.17.18104.

36. Shen G, Zhou H, Jia Z, Deng H. Diagnostic performance of diffusion-weighted MRI for detection of pelvic metastatic lymph nodes in patients with cervical cancer: a systematic review and meta-analysis. *Br J Radiol.* 2015;88(1052):20150063. doi:10.1259/bjr.20150063.

37. Scheidler J, Hricak H, Yu KK, Subak L, Segal MR. Radiological evaluation of lymph node metastases in patients with cervical cancer: a meta-analysis. *JAMA.* 1997;278(13):1096–1101.

38. Bourgioti C, Chatoupis K, Moulopoulos LA. Current imaging strategies for the evaluation of uterine cervical cancer. *World J Radiol.* 2016;8(4):342–354. doi:10.4329/wjr.v8.i4.342.

39. Choi HJ, Ju W, Myung SK, Kim Y. Diagnostic performance of computer tomography, magnetic resonance imaging, and positron emission tomography or positron emission tomography/computer tomography for detection of metastatic lymph nodes in patients with cervical cancer: meta-analysis. *Cancer Sci.* 2010;101(6):1471–1479. doi:10.1111/j.1349-7006.2010.01532.x.

40. Choi HJ, Roh JW, Seo SS, et al. Comparison of the accuracy of magnetic resonance imaging and positron emission tomography/computed tomography in the presurgical detection of lymph node metastases in patients with uterine cervical carcinoma: a prospective study. *Cancer.* 2006;106(4):914–922. doi:10.1002/cncr.21641.

41. Achouri A, Huchon C, Bats AS, Bensaid C, Nos C, Lécuru F. Complications of lymphadenectomy for gynecologic cancer. *Eur J Surg Oncol.* 2013;39(1):81–86. doi:10.1016/j.ejso.2012.10.011.

42. Mitchell DG, Snyder B, Coakley F, et al. Early invasive cervical cancer: tumor delineation by magnetic resonance imaging, computed tomography, and clinical examination, verified by pathologic results, in the ACRIN 6651/GOG 183 intergroup study. *J Clin Oncol.* 2006;24(36):5687–5694. doi:10.1200/jco.2006.07.4799.

43. Rockall AG, Ghosh S, Alexander-Sefre F, et al. Can MRI rule out bladder and rectal invasion in cervical cancer to help select patients for limited EUA? *Gynecol Oncol.* 2006;101(2):244–249. doi:10.1016/j.ygyno.2005.10.012.

44. Sahdev A, Jones J, Shepherd JH, Reznek RH. MR imaging appearances of the female pelvis after trachelectomy. *Radiographics.* 2005;25(1):41–52. doi:10.1148/rg.251045047.

45. Freeman SJ, Aly AM, Kataoka MY, Addley HC, Reinhold C, Sala E. The revised FIGO staging system for uterine malignancies: implications for MR imaging. *Radiographics.* 2012;32(6):1805–1827. doi:10.1148/rg.326125519.

46. Balleyguier C, Sala E, Da Cunha T, et al. Staging of uterine cervical cancer with MRI: guidelines of the European Society of Urogenital Radiology. *Eur Radiol.* 2011;21(5):1102–1110. doi:10.1007/s00330-010-1998-x.

47. Park KJ, Braschi-Amirfarzan M, DiPiro PJ, et al. Multimodality imaging of locally recurrent and metastatic cervical cancer: emphasis on histology, prognosis, and management. *Abdom Radiol (NY).* 2016;41(12):2496–2508. doi:10.1007/s00261-016-0825-5.

48. Alcázar JL, Arribas S, Mínguez JA, Jurado M. The role of ultrasound in the assessment of uterine cervical cancer. *J Obstet Gynaecol India.* 2014;64(5):311–316. doi:10.1007/s13224-014-0622-4.

49. Eisenhauer EA, Therasse P, Bogaerts J, et al. New response evaluation criteria in solid tumours: revised RECIST guideline (version 1.1). *Eur J Cancer.* 2009;45(2):228–247. doi:10.1016/j.ejca.2008.10.026.

50. Berek JS, Matsuo K, Grubbs BH, et al. Multidisciplinary perspectives on newly revised 2018 FIGO staging of cancer of the cervix uteri. *J Gynecol Oncol.* 2019;30(2):e40. doi:10.3802/jgo.2019.30.e40.

51. Chao A, Ho KC, Wang CC, et al. Positron emission tomography in evaluating the feasibility of curative intent in cervical cancer patients with limited distant lymph node metastases. *Gynecol Oncol.* 2008;110(2):172–178. doi:10.1016/j.ygyno.2008.03.018.

52. Sarabhai T, Schaarschmidt BM, Wetter A, et al. Comparison of (18)F-FDG PET/MRI and MRI for pre-therapeutic tumor staging of patients with primary cancer of the uterine cervix. *Eur J Nucl Med Mol Imaging.* 2018;45(1):67–76. doi:10.1007/s00259-017-3809-y.

53. Nakamura K, Joja I, Kodama J, Hongo A, Hiramatsu Y. Measurement of SUVmax plus ADCmin of the primary tumour is a predictor of prognosis in patients with cervical cancer. *Eur J Nucl Med Mol Imaging.* 2012;39(2):283–290. doi:10.1007/s00259-011-1978-7.

54. Karunya RJ, Tharani P, John S, Kumar RM, Das S. Role of functional magnetic resonance imaging derived parameters as imaging biomarkers and correlation with clinicopathological features in carcinoma of uterine cervix. *J Clin Diagn Res.* 2017;11(8):xc06–xc11. doi:10.7860/jcdr/2017/29165.10426.

55. Onal C, Erbay G, Guler OC. Treatment response evaluation using the mean apparent diffusion coefficient in cervical cancer patients treated with definitive chemoradiotherapy. *J Magn Reson Imaging.* 2016;44(4):1010–1019. doi:10.1002/jmri.25215.

56. Carmeliet P, Jain RK. Molecular mechanisms and clinical applications of angiogenesis. *Nature.* 2011;473(7347):298–307. doi:10.1038/nature10144.

57. Leach MO, Morgan B, Tofts PS, et al. Imaging vascular function for early stage clinical trials using dynamic contrast-enhanced magnetic resonance imaging. *Eur Radiol.* 2012;22(7):1451–1464. doi:10.1007/s00330-012-2446-x.

58. Lin G, Lai CH, Tsai SY, et al. (1) H MR spectroscopy in cervical carcinoma using external phase array body coil at 3.0 Tesla: prediction of poor prognostic human papillomavirus genotypes. *J Magn Reson Imaging.* 2017;45(3):899–907. doi:10.1002/jmri.25386.

59. Walenta S, Wetterling M, Lehrke M, et al. High lactate levels predict likelihood of metastases, tumor recurrence, and restricted patient survival in human cervical cancers. *Cancer Res.* 2000;60(4):916–921.

60. Dappa E, Elger T, Hasenburg A, Düber C, Battista MJ, Hötker AM. The value of advanced MRI techniques in the assessment of cervical cancer: a review. *Insights Imaging.* 2017;8(5):471–481. doi:10.1007/s13244-017-0567-0.

61. Rockall AG, Sohaib SA, Harisinghani MG, et al. Diagnostic performance of nanoparticle-enhanced magnetic resonance imaging in the diagnosis of lymph node metastases in patients with endometrial and cervical cancer. *J Clin Oncol.* 2005;23(12):2813–2821. doi:10.1200/jco.2005.07.166.

62. Keller TM, Michel SC, Fröhlich J, et al. USPIO-enhanced MRI for preoperative staging of gynecological pelvic tumors: preliminary results. *Eur Radiol.* 2004;14(6):937–944. doi:10.1007/s00330-004-2258-8.

15

MRI evaluation of abdominal pain during pregnancy and abnormal placentation

Pamela Argiriadi, Bachir Taouli

Department of Diagnostic, Molecular, & Interventional Radiology, Icahn School of Medicine at Mount Sinai, New York, NY, United States

15.1 Introduction

Abdominal pain is a common complaint in pregnancy that requires early and accurate diagnosis and treatment. The term "abdominal pain" encompasses pain in all four abdominal quadrants, including pelvic pain. It can arise from a variety of different causes, including gastrointestinal, genitourinary, and gynecologic pathologic processes. Accurate diagnosis is confounded by multiple factors, including nonspecific clinical symptoms and distorted anatomy in the gravid patient.[1] It has been reported that approximately 0.2–1.0% of pregnant patients require surgery for a nonobstetrical problem.[2] Early and accurate diagnosis is essential and delay in diagnosis is the single greatest factor in morbidity and morbidity in pregnant patients.[2] Magnetic resonance imaging (MRI) of the abdomen and pelvis, with its increasing availability at many institutions, is an essential diagnostic tool to diagnose the cause of pain with its superior anatomical depiction and its high contrast resolution. MRI is also increasingly used to evaluate abnormal placentation, which is critical to maternal and fetal outcomes.[3]

15.1.1 Imaging in the pregnant patient

Typically, transabdominal ultrasound (US) is the first line modality in the evaluation of abdominal pain in the pregnant patient and to evaluate pregnant patients for potential abnormal placentation. Ultrasound is accessible, inexpensive, portable, and does not expose the patient to ionizing radiation. However, US has limitations, including inter-operator variability, image obscuration from the patient's gravid uterus and bowel gas.[4]

Computed tomography (CT) has also been used in the diagnosis of abdominal pain in pregnancy.[5] CT provides excellent anatomic detail, but at the expense of harmful ionization radiation to the fetus.[6]

MRI is at the forefront for evaluation of the pregnant patient with abdominal pain and can accurately make an early diagnosis at many institutions 24 hours a day. MRI also plays a critical role in diagnosing placental location, placental variants, and extent of placental invasion.[3] MRI provides superior soft tissue contrast resolution and multiparametric capability. Multiple organ systems can be depicted simultaneously and quickly. No study to date has demonstrated adverse effects on the developing fetus.[7] Theoretical risks of MRI during pregnancy still exist and include exposure to the static magnetic field with potential abnormal cell migration and risk for miscarriage.[6–8] Energy deposition in the pregnant patient with specific absorption rate has a potential to heat tissues in organogenesis.[6–8] Acoustic noise secondary to varying field gradients could theoretically damage the fetal ear.[6–8] According to the American College of Radiology (ACR) Guidance Document on MR Safe practices: 2013, "present data *have not* conclusively documented any deleterious effects of MR imaging exposure on the developing fetus. Therefore, no special consideration is recommended for the first, versus any other, trimester in pregnancy."[9]

TABLE 15.1 Suggested MRI protocol for abdominal pain in pregnancy.

Sequence	Plane	TR	TE	FA	ST (mm)	Matrix
T2 HASTE/SSFSE*	Axial Coronal Sagittal	Min	90	180	5–9	256 × 192
Fat-suppressed T2 FSE	Axial	5000	117	160	4	256 × 192
T1 GRE in/out	Axial	225	2.2 4.4	80	4	256 × 128
Fat-suppressed 3D GRE T1	Axial	Min	Min	10–15	4.4	224 × 160
DWI SS EPI**	Axial	1,5000	Min		7	129 × 192
2D TruFISP/FIESTA	Axial Coronal	6.71	3.36	65	7	224 × 320

DWI SS EPI, diffusion weighted imaging single shot echo planar imaging; *FA*, flip angle (degrees); *GRE*, gradient-echo; *HASTE*, half-Fourier acquisition single-shot turbo spin echo imaging; *SSFSE*, single-shot fast spin echo; *ST*, slice thickness (mm); *TE*, echotime (ms); *TR*, repetition time (ms).
Field of view (FOV) adapted to maternal size with additional sequences obtained to survey an area of interest.
***Respiratory triggered, multiple B values obtained (50–800 s/mm²). Sagittal DWI images obtained for abnormal placentation.*

15.1.2 MRI protocol

At our institution, there is a dedicated MRI protocol for pregnant patients with abdominal pain (Table 15.1). Goals include rapid acquisition of sequences with minimal table time to minimize patient discomfort. No intravenous contrast is administered as per ACR guidelines[9] with theoretical concern of MR contrast agent crossing the placenta and being absorbed by the fetus and excreted in the amniotic fluid, where it may remain for an indeterminate amount of time.[9]

State of the art protocol is performed on a 1.5T system using high performance gradients and a phase array coil. No harmful fetal effects have been documented on either 1.5 T or 3T systems.[9] A combination of multiplanar T2-weighted imaging (T2WI) single-shot fast spin echo (SSFSE/HASTE), fat-saturated FSE T2WI, T1WI in- and opposed-phase, echoplanar diffusion weighted imaging (DWI) with two different b values (50 and 800 s/mm²), and noncontrast fat-saturated 3D T1 gradient echo sequences (VIBE/LAVA) are obtained with tailoring field of view to the maternal abdomen and pelvis. Additional sequences, including true fast imaging with steady-state free procession (TrueFISP), fast imaging employing steady state precession (FIESTA), or MR cholangiopancreatography (MRCP) can be added.

T2 SSFSE/HASTE images are the most valuable sequences and often immediately yield an accurate diagnosis, allowing imaging of the bowel and uterus with little motion artifact. Three planes of acquisition allow for triangulation of pertinent structures, such as the appendix or the ovaries. Fat-saturated T2 FSE (FSFSE) images are added to increase the conspicuity of inflammation, particularly in the mesenteric fat or along the retroperitoneum. T1 GRE in/out imaging characterizes masses for potential fat and detects susceptibility artifact from either air or calcification. DWI adds confidence for inflammation assessment and helps characterize solid versus cystic masses. Noncontrast T1 sequences allow for hemorrhage detection, while TrueFISP/FIESTA increases conspicuity of peri-uterine vessels.

At our institution, there is an analogous dedicated MRI protocol for pregnant patients with suspected abnormal placentation beyond 24 weeks gestational age. Similar multiplanar sequences are performed. The T2W HASTE/SSFSE sequences are again the most valuable sequences for evaluation of placental architecture and uterine layers. Fat-saturated T2WI sequences and TrueFISP/FIESTA accentuate intraplacental vessels and help differentiate from intraplacental bands.[10] T1W1 sequences allow for the assessment of subchorionic and retroplacental hemorrhage.[10] DWI demonstrates a strong contrast border between the placental high signal intensity as compared to the adjacent myometrium.[11]

15.2 Discussion

15.2.1 Normal anatomy

Knowledge of expected maternal anatomy is crucial before evaluating a pregnant patient with abdominal pain. In the first trimester of pregnancy, the uterus maintains its normal shape and version and is best seen on sagittal images (Fig. 15.1). Uterine enlargement is contained with the bony pelvis. Location of abdominal pelvic organs is preserved.

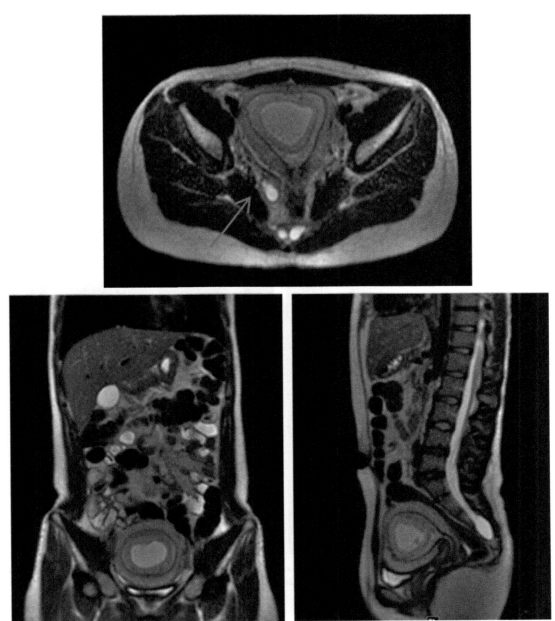

FIG. 15.1   **Normal maternal anatomy in a first trimester patient.** Axial, coronal, and sagittal T2 HASTE images demonstrate a gravid uterus with a small fetal pole. Uterine enlargement is contained within the bony pelvis and abdominal and pelvic viscera, including the ovaries, are preserved. Right ovary (red arrow) located in the posterior cul-de-sac.

The ovaries maintain normal position lateral or posterior to the uterus, suspended by the broad and suspensory ligaments.[12]

In the second and third trimesters of pregnancy, the gravid uterus continues to enlarge (Fig. 15.2). The uterus displaces the ovaries laterally and the bowel laterally and superiorly. All retroperitoneal structures, including the pancreas and kidneys, maintain their respected locations.

After a general overview of maternal anatomy, localization of the appendix is critical to assess for appendicitis in a pregnant patient. In the first trimester, the appendix is often located in the right lower quadrant since bowel is not distorted by the gravid uterus. In the second and third trimesters, localization is more difficult, and the appendix can be subhepatic or retrocecal in location (Fig. 15.3). A normal appendix measures 6 mm in caliber and does not

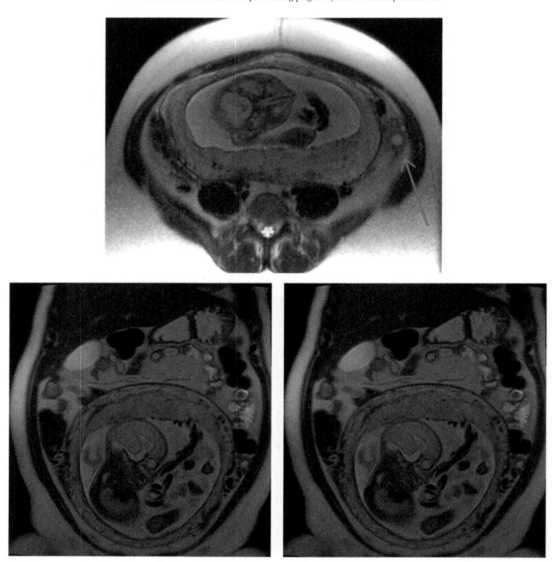

FIG. 15.2 **Normal maternal anatomy in a second trimester pregnant patient.** Axial, coronal, and sagittal T2 HASTE demonstrates a gravid uterus with superior and lateral displacement of intraperitoneal organs. Left ovary (red arrow) is displaced laterally in the peritoneal cavity. Bowel is displaced superiorly and laterally.

demonstrate any significant wall thickening (2 mm) or inflammation with preservation of the surrounding fat on T2 HASTE and T2 FSFSE images. Susceptibility artifact from air on T1W images is reassuring when it is seen throughout the entire lumen of the appendix.[13] A common pitfall is to mistake a normal terminal ileum for an inflamed appendix. Fig. 15.3 demonstrates a both a normal terminal ileum and a normal appendix on T2 coronal HASTE, differentiating the terminal ileum from the appendix by its normal folds.

15.2.2 Gastrointestinal causes of pain

15.2.2.1 *Acute appendicitis*

Appendicitis is the most common operative condition in the pregnant patient.[14] MRI has excellent performance for diagnosing appendicitis in pregnancy, with reported sensitivity of 90–100% and specificity of 94–98%.[15] An inflamed appendix is thick in diameter (greater than 7mm) and contains T2 hyperintense fluid on T2 HASTE and FSFSE sequences.[13] Periappendiceal inflammation manifests as T2 hyperintensity in the surrounding fat, accentuated on

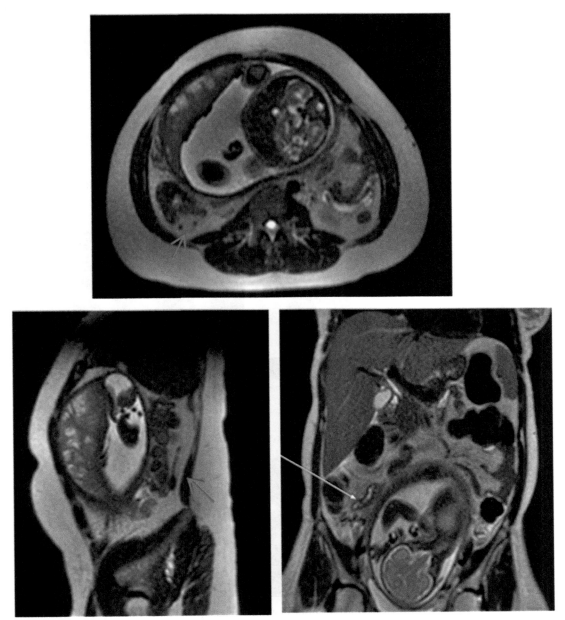

FIG. 15.3 **Normal appendix.** Axial and sagittal T2 HASTE images demonstrate a normal retrocecal appendix (red arrows), normal in caliber without inflammation. Appendix is above the right pelvic brim, subhepatic in location, anterior to the right retroperitoneum. Coronal T2 HASTE imaging demonstrates a normal terminal ileum (white arrow), which is often mistaken for an inflamed appendix.

fat suppressed T2 FSFSE sequences (Fig. 15.4). An appendix that measures 6–7 mm in diameter is considered equivocal[13] and the presence or absence of periappendiceal stranding, with or without added clinical data, can help escalate the diagnosis to definitive appendicitis. A fluid-filled and straightened retrocecal appendix demonstrates T2 hypointense appendicoliths within the lumen of the appendiceal base (Fig. 15.4). Axial DWI (B value 800) demonstrates appendiceal restricted diffusion within the appendiceal wall and accentuates the inflamed appendix (Fig. 15.4). According to Inci et al. appendiceal hyperintensity on high B value DWI imaging demonstrated a positive predictive value of 98.7% and negative predictive value of 100% in diagnosing acute appendicitis in the general population and demonstrated similar sensitivity and specificity of 100% and 98% respectively.[16]

Gangrenous appendicitis can develop when transmural inflammation progresses to transmural necrosis in the appendiceal wall. Susceptibility artifact from air on T1WI can be reassuring in a normal appendix if the air appears

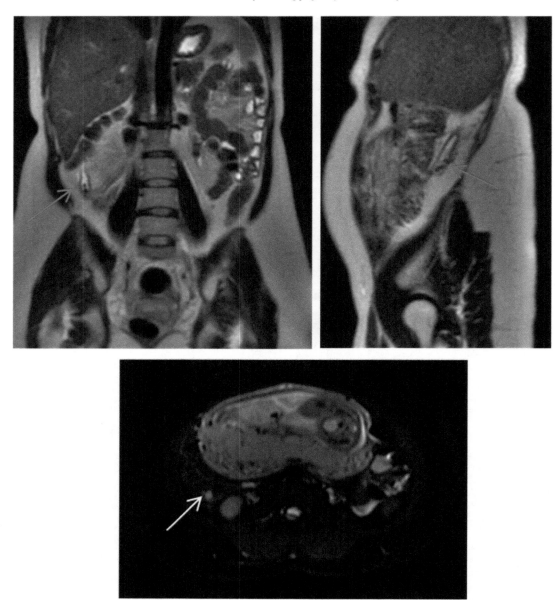

FIG. 15.4   Acute uncomplicated appendicitis with appendicoliths in an 18-week pregnant patient. Coronal and sagittal T2 HASTE images demonstrate distended fluid-filled appendix with multiple appendicoliths within the luminal base (red arrow). Axial DWI (B value = 800) demonstrates appendiceal restricted diffusion (white arrow).

throughout the appendiceal lumen.[12] However, if susceptibility artifact from air is only present at the appendiceal tip, gangrenous appendicitis should be considered (Fig. 15.5).

Often the diagnosis of appendicitis can be difficult if the patient has a paucity of intraperitoneal fat or if the appendix is located adjacent to periuterine vessels. DWI can help accentuate the appendix as previously described. FIESTA sequences can help differentiate periuterine vessels[13] (Fig. 15.6). Increasing the field of view with particular attention to the right lower quadrant can help identify the inflamed appendix (Fig. 15.7).

Complications of appendicitis include perforation and peritonitis. Fetal loss rate can increase to over 30% with perforation.[17] Fig. 15.8 demonstrates a 29 week pregnant patient with appendicitis and appendiceal abscess, which demonstrated avid hyperintensity on DWI with corresponding low ADC.

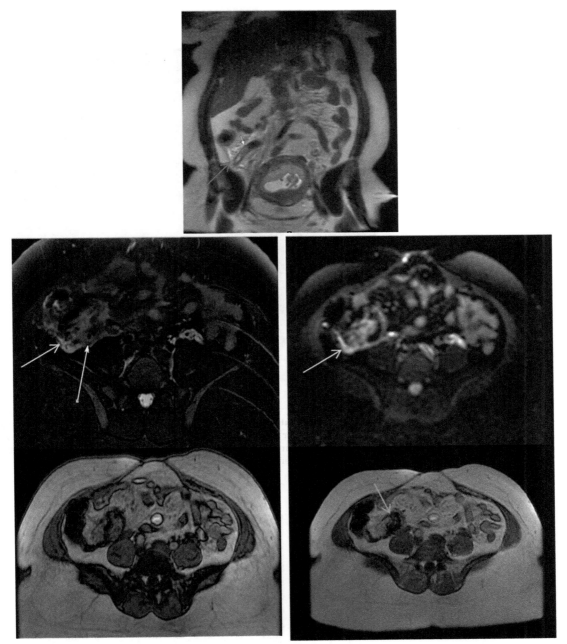

FIG. 15.5   Acute gangrenous appendicitis with appendicolith in a 14-week pregnant patient. Coronal T2 HASTE imaging demonstrates an inflamed and thickened appendix (red arrow). DWI (B value = 800) and T2 FSFSE demonstrates significant peritoneal inflammation (yellow arrows) with a central appendicolith (white arrow). T1-weighted in and out-of-phase imaging demonstrates blooming artifact (blue arrow), compatible with air in the wall of the appendiceal body and tip.

15.2.2.2 Bowel obstruction

Small bowel obstruction is rare in pregnancy, but poses risk of fetal loss and maternal morbidity.[18] Urgent MRI is recommended since laparotomy remains the treatment of choice for volvulus or internal hernia.[18] MRI findings in small bowel obstruction include dilated proximal bowel loops, distended with T2 hyperintensity, with collapsed distal loops or point of transition. Often partial obstructions are managed conservatively in patients, but identifying potential signs of bowel ischemia and identifying sub-sets of bowel obstruction, including closed loop obstruction and internal hernia is critical. CT signs for bowel ischemia in the setting of bowel obstruction are well documented[19] and include mesenteric vascular engorgement, surrounding ascites, and submucosal edema.

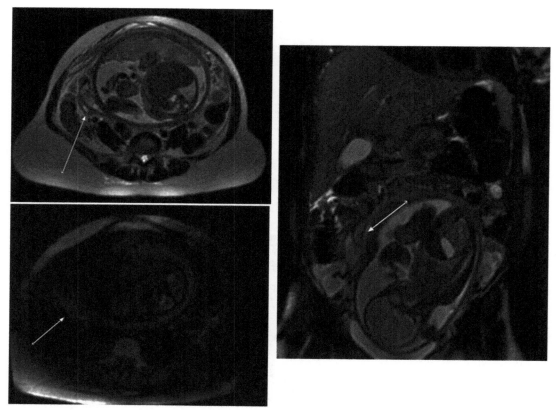

FIG. 15.6 **Acute appendicitis adherent to the lateral aspect of the uterus in a 23-week pregnant patient.** Axial T2 HASTE imaging demonstrated an inflamed appendix adherent to the right lateral uterine border (white arrow). Repeat coronal T2 HASTE with fat suppression accentuated inflamed appendix (white arrow) and differentiated appendix from peri-uterine vessels which can obscure diagnosis. DWI (B value = 800) demonstrates asymmetric restricted diffusion along the right lateral uterus border which supports diagnosis (white arrow).

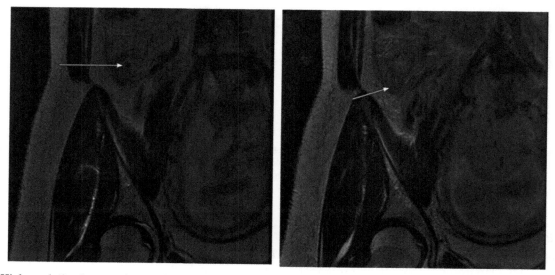

FIG. 15.7 **High resolution images of appendicitis in an 18-week pregnant patient with a paucity of intraperitoneal fat.** Small FOV coronal T2 HASTE images were obtained in this patient with a paucity of intraperitoneal fat and demonstrated an appendicolith at the base of the appendix with a thickened appendiceal base and right retroperitoneal thickening (white arrows).

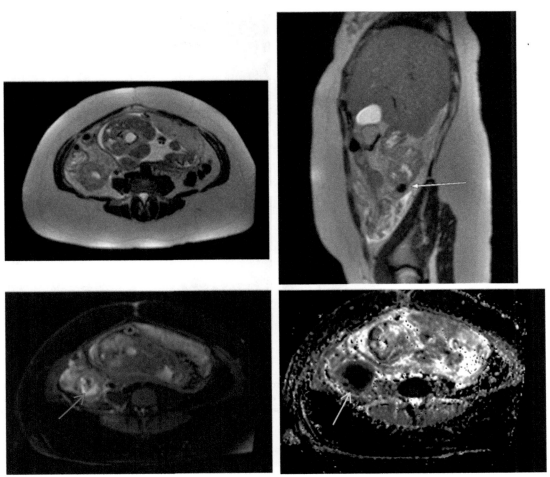

FIG. 15.8 **Perforated appendicitis in a 29-week pregnant patient.** Axial and sagittal T2 HASTE images demonstrate a thick-walled peri-appendiceal abscess with fluid in the right retroperitoneum. An appendicolith **is** present at the base of the collection (white arrow). Axial T2 FSFSE images demonstrate purulent, complex material within the abscess and surrounding T2-hyperintense inflammation (red arrow). ADC map calculated from DWI imaging demonstrates low ADC value within the abscess (yellow arrow).

MRI can demonstrate similar distended small bowel with a whorled appearance and with surrounding ascites and mesenteric engorgement (Fig. 15.9). Ischemic small bowel is edematous with T2 hyperintensity in the submucosal layer and a targetoid appearance. Bowel obstruction can occur in any abdominal quadrant. Paraduodenal or mesocolic hernias account for over 50% of all internal hernias[20] and occur when small bowel herniates behind the fourth portion of the duodenum causing obstruction (Fig. 15.10).

15.2.2.3 *Inflammatory bowel disease*

Inflammatory bowel disease often affects women of reproductive age with disease activity at conception predicting disease activity during the course of the pregnancy.[21] MRI has an overall sensitivity of 91% and specificity of 71% for the detection of active disease.[22] MRI findings in Crohn's disease include bowel wall thickening and strictures with mucosal DWI hyperintensity and mesenteric engorgement. The terminal ileum being the most commonly involved segment. MRI defines extent of disease, which helps clinicians either to optimize medical therapy or to refer to surgery. Fistulization and abscess are common Crohn's complications that can be detected on MRI.

Fig. 15.11 details a woman with prepregnancy terminal ileitis (Fig. 15.11a) who 4 years later, presented at 27 weeks gestational age with upper abdominal pain and early satiety. The patient's terminal ileum is displaced superiorly by the gravid uterus and fistulizes to the adjacent duodenum with duodenitis and gastric outlet obstruction (Fig. 15.11b).

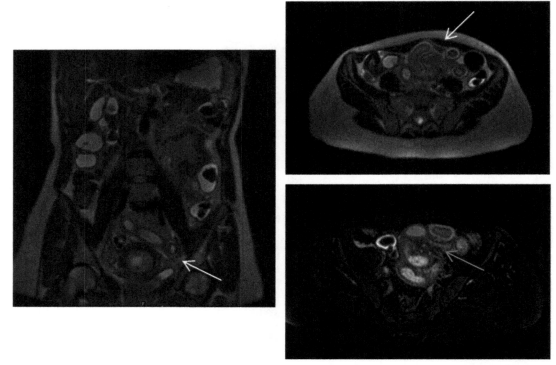

FIG. 15.9 Closed loop obstruction in a 7-week pregnant patient. Coronal, axial T2 HASTE, and axial T2 FSFSE images demonstrate excluded, thickened, and edematous small bowel in the left lower quadrant with a swirled configuration (white arrows). Engorgement of the mesenteric vessels and bowel wall stratification, with edematous bowel submucosa, is a poor prognostic sign (red arrow). Emergent surgical exploration confirmed 50 cm of ischemic small bowel.

Terminal ileal displacement is seen again in the next case in patient with intestinal malrotation and Crohn's disease (Fig. 15.12). The terminal ileum is thickened in the left lower quadrant with proximal obstruction.

MRI findings in ulcerative colitis include contiguous wall thickening, narrowing, and a haustration of the colon in a retrograde fashion. Fig. 15.13 demonstrates a pregnant patient with known ulcerative colitis and abdominal pain at 19 weeks gestational age. Findings are subtle, but demonstrate wall thickening with transmural restricted diffusion.

15.2.2.4 *Additional gastrointestinal causes of pain*

Nonoperative causes of abdominal pain in a pregnant pain include epiploic appendagitis, omental infarct, and transient intussusception, all of which can be managed conservatively. Fig. 15.14 demonstrates well-encapsulated fat in the right lower quadrant adjacent to a normal appendix in a pregnant patient at 17 weeks gestational age. A transient intussusception is seen in the next case in a pregnant patient at 15 weeks gestation with resolution on subsequent MRI (Fig. 15.15).

15.2.3 Hepatobiliary/pancreatic causes of pain

15.2.3.1 *Acute cholecystitis*

Bile stasis during pregnancy increases risk for cholelithiasis. It is estimated that 2–4% of pregnant patients have gallstones[23] and acute cholecystitis is the second most common disease requiring surgery in pregnant patients.[15] Transabdominal US is often the modality of choice to diagnose acute cholecystitis, but body habitus and nonlocalization of a sonographic Murphy's sign can hinder the diagnosis on US. MRI can be a helpful adjunct tool with findings including gallstones, gallbladder wall thickening, and wall irregularity with surrounding T2 hyperintense pericholecystic fluid (Fig. 15.16). Additional MRCP images can be obtained to assess for choledocholithiasis as well (Fig. 15.17). Laparoscopic cholecystectomy during pregnancy is not associated with increased morbidity or mortality

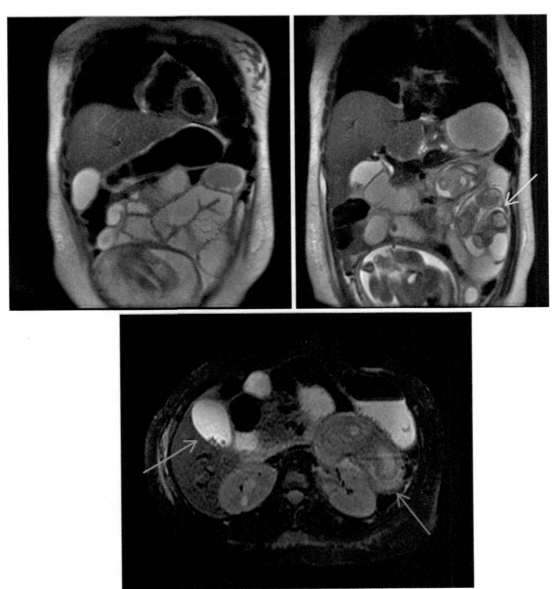

FIG. 15.10 Left paraduodenal hernia in a second trimester pregnant patient. Coronal T2 HASTE and axial T2 FSFSE demonstrates proximal small bowel obstruction (red asterisk) and encapsulated small bowel loop in the left upper quadrant (yellow arrow). Surrounding ascites and bowel wall stratification is a poor prognostic sign (red arrow). Cholelithiasis is incidentally noted (blue arrow).

to mother or fetus[24] and endoscopic retrograde cholangiopancreatography (ERCP) retrieval of common bile ducts is considered safe if fluoroscopy is performed conservatively.[25]

15.2.3.2 Intraductal stones

Bile stasis in pregnancy is not limited to cholelithiasis or choledocholithiasis, but also can be seen with intrahepatic cholestasis. Intrahepatic cholestasis is the most common liver disease in pregnancy[26] and is suspected in pregnancy when patients develop pruritus without rash. Often patients are treated conservatively with ursodeoxycholic acid and are not imaged if pruritus is the only symptom. In the setting of abdominal pain, MRI and MRCP can assess for potential biliary obstruction. Fig. 15.18 demonstrates a pregnant patient (15 weeks gestational age) with T1 hyperintense intraductal stones and corresponding filling defects within the biliary tree on MRCP, but without significant biliary obstruction.

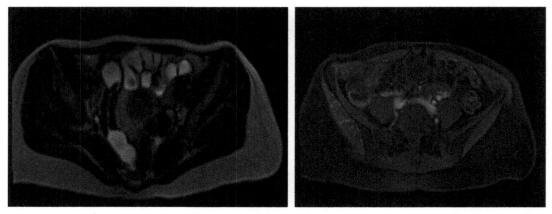

FIG. 15.11a   Terminal ileitis. 32-year-old nonpregnant woman with Crohn's terminal ileitis and with skip lesions in the right lower quadrant. Axial T2 HASTE and axial postcontrast T1 VIBE images demonstrate wall thickening with enhancement of the terminal ileum and 4 cm distal ileum with intervening skip lesion.

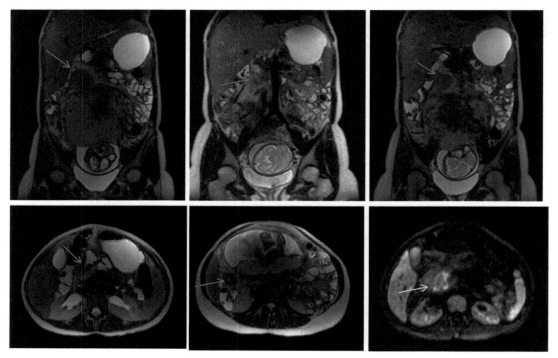

FIG. 15.11b   Crohn's terminal ileitis and duodenitis with fistulization. Same patient (4 years later) is 27 weeks pregnant with upper abdominal pain and early satiety. Coronal and axial T2 HASTE images demonstrate displacement of the terminal ileum into the right upper quadrant with fistulization to the adjacent duodenum (red arrows). Axial DWI (B value = 800) demonstrates restricted diffusion with duodenitis in the second portion of the duodenum with distended stomach and gastric outlet obstruction (yellow arrow).

15.2.3.3 *Acute pancreatitis*

Acute pancreatitis is rare in pregnancy with over 50% of pregnant patients often diagnosed in the third trimester.[27] Over 50% of acute pancreatitis cases are secondary to gallstones, while other causes include hyperlipemia and alcohol abuse.[27] Abdominal pain, vomiting, and elevated lipase are common symptoms, and treatment recommendations depend on the trimester with conservative management in the first trimester and laparoscopic cholecystectomy in the second trimester. Typical MRI findings include pancreatic enlargement with diminished or heterogeneous signal intensity on T1WI imaging and with corresponding T2-hyperintense peripancreatic inflammation and with restricted diffusion. Fig. 15.19 demonstrates a pregnant patient (11-week twin gestation) with diffuse pancreatitis

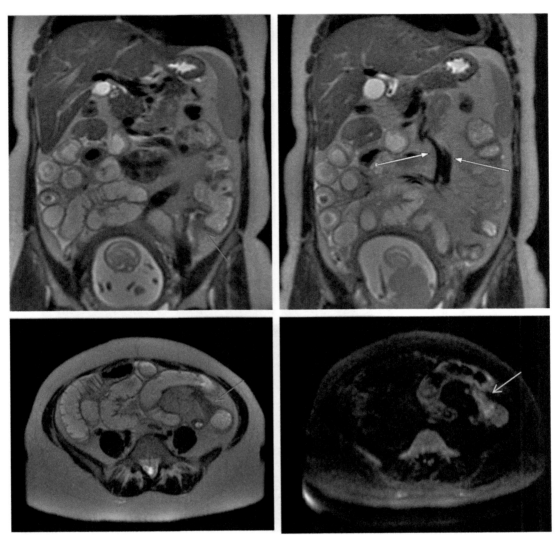

FIG. 15.12   **Left lower quadrant Crohn's disease in a patient with intestinal malrotation.** Acute terminal ileitis in the left lower quadrant with proximal small bowel obstruction. Coronal and axial T2 HASTE demonstrates long segment wall thickening of terminal ileum with proximal obstruction (red arrows). DWI (B value = 800) demonstrates mucosal restricted diffusion suggesting acute disease (yellow arrow). Cecum is located in the left lower quadrant. SMA is located to the right of the SMV (white arrows).

and diffuse peripancreatic inflammation. Patient was managed conservatively until lipase normalized with patient subsequently electing for second trimester cholecystectomy.

Focal acute pancreatitis can occur in 20% of all pancreatitis patients[28] and has similar MRI findings to diffuse pancreatitis, but in a more localized area of the pancreas. Focal enlargement of a portion of the pancreas occurs (Fig. 15.20) with surrounding T2 hyperintensity and inflammation, which helps distinguish between focal pancreatitis and a focal pancreatic mass, such as solid pseudopapillary endothelial neoplasm (SPEN) (Fig. 15.21).

15.2.4 Genitourinary causes of pain

15.2.4.1 Obstructive hydronephrosis

Obstructive uropathy in pregnancy occurs in approximately 1:200 to 1:1:1500 patients with increased frequency in the second and third trimesters.[29] The majority pregnant patients are treated conservatively with hydration and analgesia, since over 70% of patients pass their stones with conservative management.[30] Clinical signs including persistent pain, fever, and progressive renal obstruction may warrant intervention such as utereroscopy or percutaneous nephrostomy.[29]

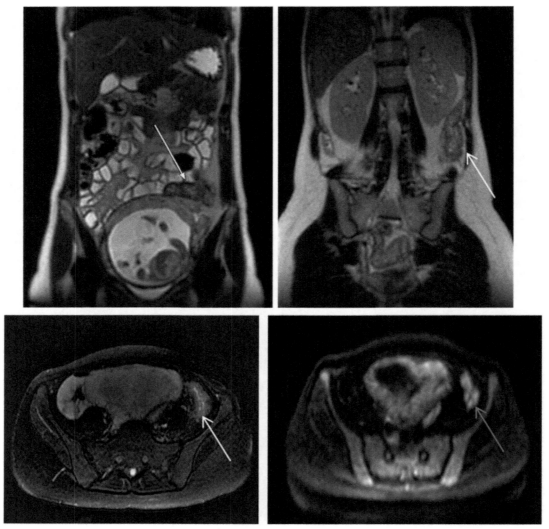

FIG. 15.13   Ulcerative colitis in a 19-week pregnant patient. Coronal T2 HASTE and axial T2 FSFSE demonstrates contiguous wall thickening and pericolonic stranding extending from the anus to the splenic flexure in this patient with ulcerative colitis (white arrows). Axial DWI (B value = 800) demonstrates restricted diffusion in the colonic mucosa (red arrow).

Physiologic hydronephrosis can be seen in up to 90% of pregnant patients from the second trimester to 6 weeks postpartum.[30] Often the right renal collecting system is affected more than the left renal collecting system as the sigmoid colon protects from compression on the left side (Fig. 15.22). Urinary stasis in physiologic hydronephrosis can promote stone formation[30] and result in obstructing uropathy with subsequent hydronephrosis, renal parenchymal thinning, and calyceal/forniceal rupture (Fig. 15.23). Initial imaging for renal calculi is US, but when ultrasound fails to differentiate between physiologic hydronephrosis and obstructive uropathy, MRI can help detect perinephric fluid and inflammation on fluid sensitive sequences.[31] Although MRI is limited at calcification detection, well-circumscribed filling defects in the T2 hyperintense collecting system and T1-weighted susceptibility artifact can help detect stones.

15.2.4.2 *Pyelonephritis*

Urinary stasis in pregnancy can also progress to pyelonephritis, which presents with fever, costovertebral angle tenderness, and bacteriuria. MR findings are similar to CT findings and include renal enlargement, perinephric fluid or collections, and renal parenchymal striation.[32] DWI has higher sensitivity in the diagnosis of pyelonephritis[33] by demonstrating obstructive right hydroureteronephrosis with focal pyelonephritis in the superior right kidney (Fig. 15.24).

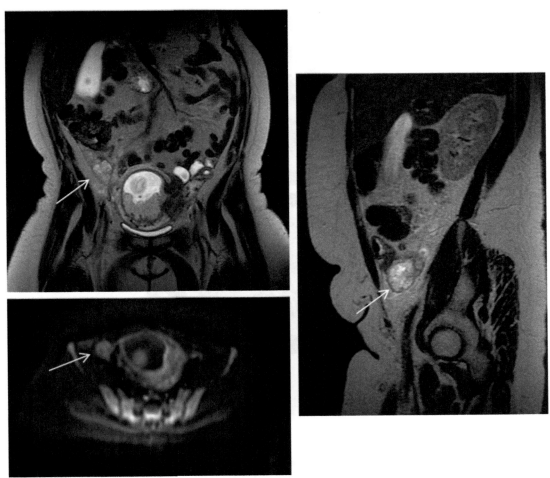

FIG. 15.14 **Suspected omental infarct in a 19-week pregnant patient.** Coronal and sagittal HASTE in this first trimester patient demonstrates fat necrosis in the right lower quadrant with encapsulated and inflamed fat (white arrows). A normal appendix is seen superiorly on sagittal images (red arrow). Axial DWI (B value = 800) demonstrates restricted diffusion in the fat-containing mass (yellow arrow), suspicious for omental infarct. Patient recovered with supportive care.

Chronic pyelonephritis, including xanthogranulomatous pyelonephritis, is exceeding rare in pregnancy, but presents with clinical and MRI findings similar to nongravid patients. Marked renal enlargement with a central calculus and surrounding inflammation of the perinephric fat.[32] T2wi is striking with patulous T2-hyperintense medullary pyramids distended with inflammation, fluid, and debris (Fig. 15.25).

15.2.4.3 *Adrenal hemorrhage*

Nontraumatic adrenal hemorrhage can occur in any patient enduring stress, including patients with recent surgery, sepsis, and pregnancy.[34] Acute hemorrhage presents as a nonenhancing mass in the adrenal gland with either high or evolving signal intensity on T1wi[34] and with corresponding heterogeneous T2 signal intensity (Fig. 15.26). Observation and serial imaging is important as bilateral adrenal hemorrhage increases risk for adrenal insufficiency.[35] Imaging features of chronic adrenal hemorrhage include evolution into a nonenhancing cystic mass (Fig. 15.27).

15.2.5 Gynecologic causes of pain

15.2.5.1 *Spontaneous hemoperitoneum*

Spontaneous hemoperitoneum in pregnancy (SHiP) presents with acute or subacute abdominal or flank pain and can be secondary to multiple causes, from pelvic endometriosis to ruptured peri-uterine vessels.[36] In early pregnancy,

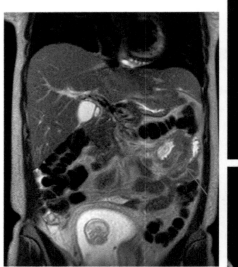

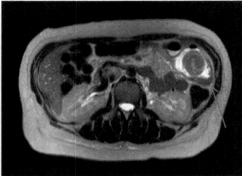

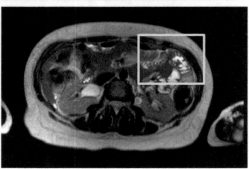

FIG. 15.15 Transient intussusception in a 15-week pregnant patient. Coronal and axial T2 HASTE images demonstrate a telescoping jejunal segment (red arrows), compatible with intussusception in this pregnant woman pregnant. Repeat MR images two days later demonstrate resolution of the intussusception (yellow box).

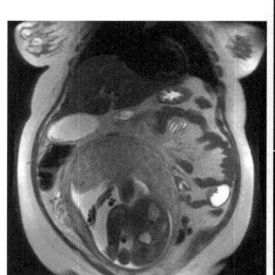

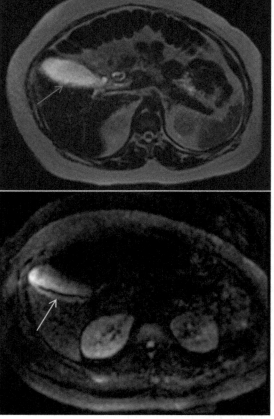

FIG. 15.16 Cholecystitis in a 24-week pregnant patient. Coronal and axial T2 HASTE images in this pregnant patient demonstrate gallbladder distention, gallbladder wall thickening and irregularity (red arrows). Axial DWI (B value = 800) demonstrates restricted diffusion in the gallbladder wall (yellow arrow).

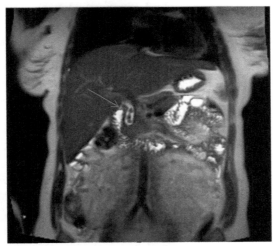

FIG. 15.17   Choledocholithiasis in a 34-week pregnant patient. Coronal and axial T2 HASTE images demonstrate multiple filling defects within the common bile duct, compatible with choledocholithiasis (red arrow), in this second trimester pregnant patient.

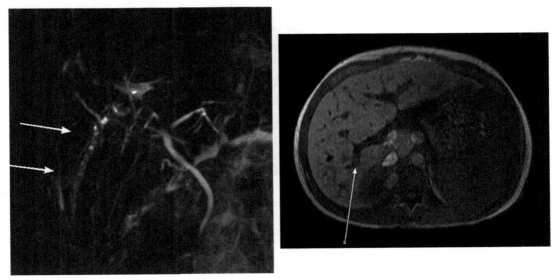

FIG. 15.18   Intraductal stones in a 15-week pregnant patient. Second trimester pregnant patient presented with abdominal pain along with elevated LFTs and pruritus. MRCP images were added to further evaluate for abdominal pain. Thick MRCP image demonstrates multiple filling defects within the right intrahepatic biliary tree with corresponding T1 hyperintensity, compatible with multiple intraductal stones (white arrows).

beta HCG levels and sonographic evaluation of the intrauterine gestational sac should be performed to exclude ruptured ectopic or cornual pregnancy. MRI can help see the extent and volume of hemoperitoneum and find secondary causes such as T1 hyperintense endometriotic implants or involuted hemorrhagic cyst. Fig. 15.28 demonstrates a first trimester pregnant patient with viable intrauterine pregnancy and hyperacute hemorrhage in the pelvis with mild T1 hyperintensity and T2 heterogenous fluid. Presumed diagnosis was a ruptured right corpus luteum and the patient recovered.

15.2.5.2 Ovarian masses and torsion

Ovarian cysts and masses in pregnancy are often asymptomatic, but can cause abdominal-pelvic main if they rupture, enlarge, or serve as a lead point for ovarian torsion.[12,37] MRI can provide excellent differentiation of ovarian

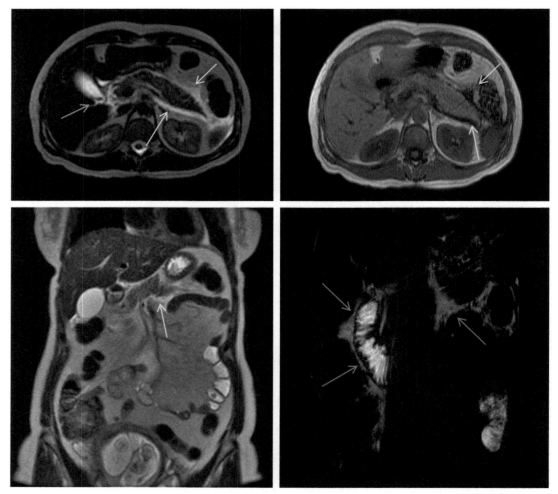

FIG. 15.19   Gallstone pancreatitis in an 11-week pregnant patient. Axial T2 HASTE, axial T1 in-phase imaging, and coronal T2 HASTE demonstrates diffuse peripancreatic fluid (yellow arrows), compatible with diffuse interstitial pancreatitis in this first trimester pregnant patient with dichorionic/diamniotic twins. Cholelithiasis (blue arrow) is present on axial images. MRCP demonstrates diffuse peripancreatic fluid (red arrows), but no bile duct or pancreatic ductal dilatation.

cysts and masses with its depiction of intralesional fat and hemorrhage as seen in as case of bilateral dermoid cysts (Fig. 15.29). Risk for ovarian torsion increases with the presence of an ovarian cyst or mass and affects 7% of ovarian masses in pregnancy.[12] The most common finding of ovarian torsion is enlargement (>4 cm), but is nonspecific; the most specific sign of ovarian torsion is a twisted vascular pedicle.[38] Additional signs include surrounding ascites, peripheralization of follicles, and asymmetric restricted diffusion of the affected ovary. Late torsion and ovarian ischemia demonstrate T2 hyperintensity with hemorrhagic follicles. Fig. 15.30 demonstrates a case of a 32-week pregnant patient with ovarian torsion. No ovarian mass or cyst is seen on MR, which can occur in approximately 10% of ovarian torsion cases,[1,39] but peripheralization of follicles on T2 FSFSE with restricted diffusion raises suspicion for diagnosis. This patient underwent timely ovarian sparing surgery with preservation of the ovary. Fig. 15.31 demonstrates a massive simple right ovarian cyst acting as a lead point for ovarian torsion with a twisted and engorged vascular pedicle and with deviation of the gravid uterus towards the left.

15.2.5.3 *Ovarian hyperstimulation syndrome*

A common diagnostic pitfall for ovarian torsion is massively enlarged ovaries in the setting of ovarian hyperstimulation.[38] Both ovaries are symmetrically enlarged and edematous as demonstrated on T2-weighted imaging (Fig. 15.32). Doppler sonography with documented color flow centrally and peripherally can be reassuring in these cases. Asymmetric ovarian size or ipsilateral hemorrhage can raise suspicion for torsion on one side.[38]

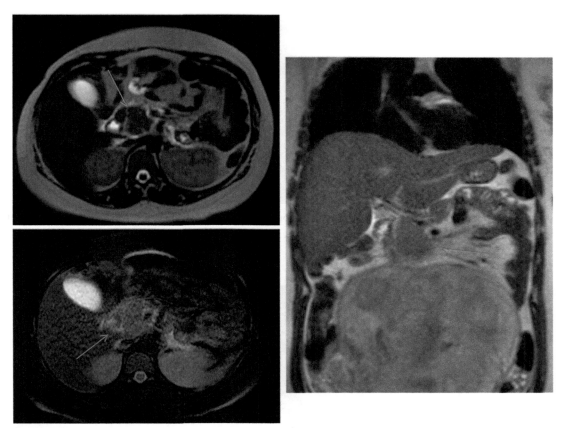

FIG. 15.20 **Focal pancreatitis in a 27-week pregnant patient.** Axial T2 HASTE, coronal T2 HASTE, and T2 FSFSE demonstrates focal enlargement of the pancreatic head with pancreatic fluid surrounding (red arrows). Symptoms resolved and lipase returned to normal with conservative management.

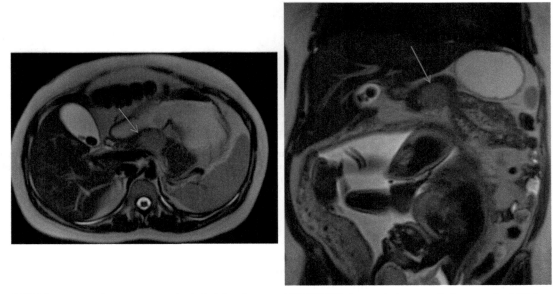

FIG. 15.21 **SPEN in a 30-week pregnant patient.** Axial and coronal T2 HASTE demonstrates a well-circumscribed T2 hyperintense solid mass (red arrow), but without peripancreatic inflammation. In a young woman, most likely diagnosis is a solid papillary endothelial neoplasm (SPEN), which can be a mimic of focal pancreatitis.

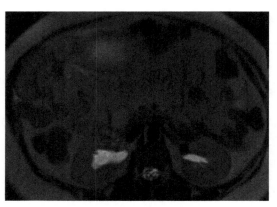

FIG. 15.22 **Physiologic hydronephrosis.** Axial T2 HASTE demonstrates fullness of the renal pelvises with mild right physiologic hydronephrosis.

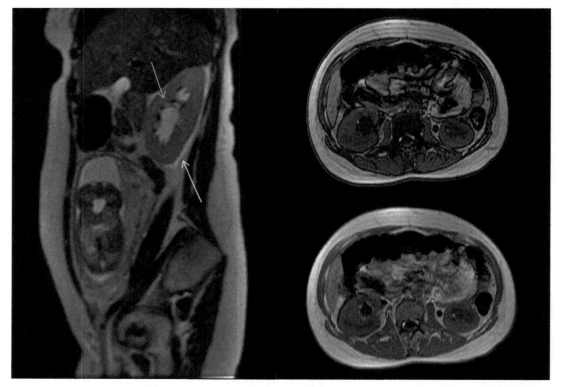

FIG. 15.23 **Forniceal rupture with urolithiasis in a 23-week pregnant patient.** Sagittal T2 HASTE demonstrates mild right hydronephrosis (blue arrow) and right perinephric fluid (yellow arrow), suggesting forniceal rupture. T1 in-phase imaging demonstrated susceptibility artifact in the right proximal ureter suggesting an obstructing stone (red arrow).

15.2.5.4 *Degenerating uterine fibroids*

As the uterus enlarges, the blood supply to the uterus changes, symptomatically affecting pregnant patients.[6] Depending on location and size, fibroids can degenerate and twist with pedunculated fibroids being the most affected. Most fibroids are asymptomatic, but pregnant patients can experience severe localized abdominal pain with either torsion, impaction, or hemorrhagic ("red") degeneration.[40] Conservative management is preferred, but myomectomy can be performed in cases of unresolved severe pain.[40] Ultrasound can identify the presence of fibroids, but MR is superior at detecting cystic or hemorrhagic degeneration and helps differentiate between pedunculated

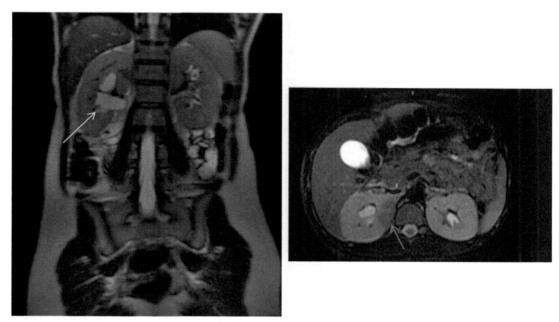

FIG. 15.24   Focal pyelonephritis in a 33-week pregnant patient. Coronal HASTE and axial T2 FSFSE demonstrates wedge-shaped T2 hypointensity (red arrow) in the superior right kidney with right hydroureteronephrosis (yellow arrow), compatible with focal pyelonephritis.

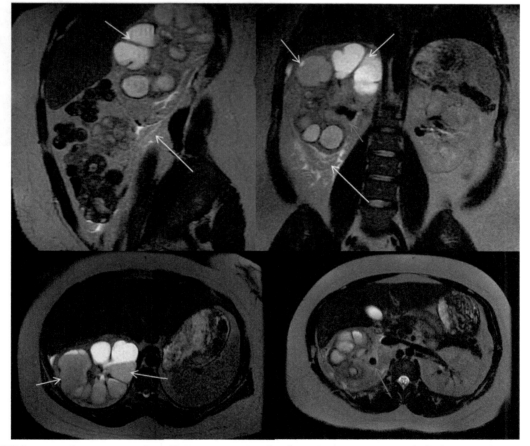

FIG. 15.25   XGP in a 5-week pregnant patient. Pregnant woman in her first trimester presents with flank pain and history of chronic UTI. Sagittal, coronal, and axial T2 HASTE demonstrates enlargement of the right kidney with amorphous expansion and T2 hyperintensity of the right medullary pyramids with layering debris (yellow arrows), compatible with xanthogranulomatous pyelonephritis (XGP). Perinephric inflammation (white arrows) and staghorn calculus (red arrow) present as well.

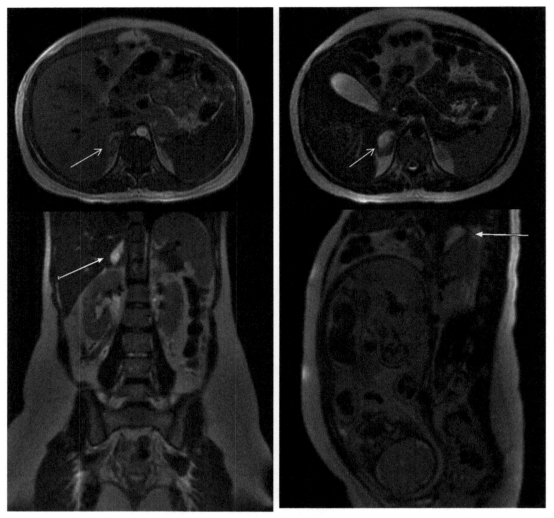

FIG. 15.26 **Adrenal hemorrhage.** Axial T1 in-phase and T2 HASTE images demonstrate T1 hyperintense/T2 hypointense hemorrhage in the right adrenal gland (white arrows), confirmed on coronal imaging in this 34-week pregnant patient.

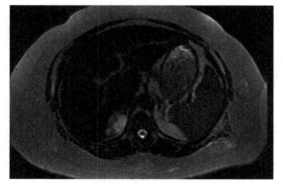

FIG. 15.27 **Chronic adrenal hemorrhage.** Axial T2 HASTE images demonstrate cystic T2 hyperintense chronic hemorrhage in the right adrenal gland in a patient with previous HELLP and adrenal hemorrhage during pregnancy.

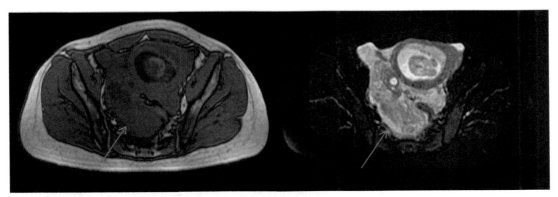

FIG. 15.28   **Spontaneous hemoperitoneum in pregnancy.** Axial T2 T1opposed phase and T2 FSFSE demonstrates T2 mildly hyperintense/ T1 isointense fluid in the pelvis (red arrows), compatible with hyperacute hemorrhage in this 14-week pregnant patient with acute onset abdominal pain. No causality was found on this MRI and the patient was managed conservatively.

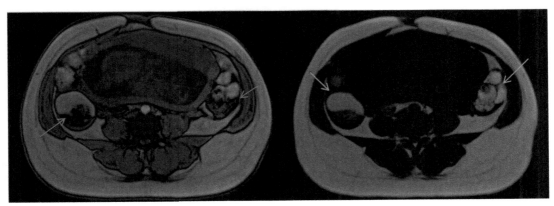

FIG. 15.29   **Bilateral ovarian dermoids in a 16-week pregnant patient.** Axial T2 HASTE images demonstrate bilateral ovarian cystic masses which demonstrate chemical shift artifact on T1 opposed phased imaging (red arrow) and fat signal on multi-point Dixon (blue arrow).

fibroids and adnexal masses. Fig. 15.33 demonstrates a subserosal fibroid in a 20-week pregnant patient. Fibroid demonstrates internal T2-hyperintensity and mild T1-hyperintensity suspicious for hemorrhagic degeneration.

15.2.6 Additional causes of pain

Lastly, it is important to recognize causes of abdominal pain that are either vascular or extraperitoneal in etiology. Although assessment of vascularity is limited on noncontrast MRI, T2 weighted sequences, including FSFSE and FIESTA can help assess the vasculature as in this pregnant patient with segmental right portal thrombus and nonocclusive SMV thrombus (Fig. 15.34). MRI can also evaluate extraperitoneal pathology that can manifest as referred abdominal pain as in a one patient with a supraumbilical hernia (Fig. 15.35) or in this sickle cell patient with right hip avascular necrosis (Fig. 15.36).

15.2.7 Abnormal placentation

Placenta previa and placenta accreta spectrum (previously known as morbidly adherent placenta) are part of a broad spectrum under the term abnormal placentation.[3] Risk factors include prior uterine surgery (including Cesarean section, myomectomy, or dilation and curettage), advanced maternal age, and previous pregnancy with abnormal placentation.[41] Abnormal placental adherence or location can cause life-threatening maternal hemorrhage during delivery.[42,43] Prenatal recognition directs management in patients with suspected placenta accreta spectrum as a multidisciplinary care team with a planned delivery and/or surgical approach before 36 weeks is recommended.[43,44]

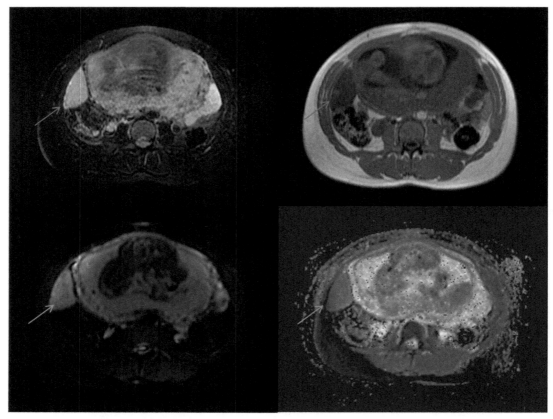

FIG. 15.30   **Ovarian torsion.** 32-week pregnant patient with pelvic pain. Axial T2 FSFSE and T1 inphase imaging demonstrates an edematous right ovary with peripheral follicles (red arrows). Axial DWI (B value = 800) with corresponding low ADC confirms ovarian torsion diagnosis (blue arrows).

15.2.7.1 *Normal placental anatomy and variants*

Before evaluating for abnormal placental adherence, basic anatomical placental location should be described and the umbilical cord should be located to assess for placenta previa and/or vasa previa. The placenta can be anterior, posterior, fundal, or lateral in location. The relationship between the inferior placental edge and the internal cervical os should be described (Fig. 15.37). A normal placental edge should be at least 2 cm away from the internal cervical os (after 24 weeks gestational age).[45] A low-lying placenta has its inferior placental edge within 2 cm from the internal os, while a marginal placental edge abuts the edge of the cervical os. Placenta previa occurs when the placenta covers the cervical os, and it can be partial or complete.[45] Placenta previa is present in more than 80% of cases of placenta accreta spectrum.

Umbilical cord insertion and accessory lobes should also be identified. The umbilical cord usually inserts centrally, but can insert in various locations (Fig. 15.38). A velamentous cord attaches to the placental edge through placental membranes and increases the risk of vasa previa.[45] The risk for vasa previa also increases with accessory lobes, such as succenturiate placenta.

15.2.7.2 *Grades of abnormal placental adherence*

Placenta accreta spectrum is abnormal extension of chorionic villi into the uterus. In a normal placenta, normal decidua with a fibrinous layer separates the chorionic villi from the uterine myometrium (Fig. 15.39). In placenta accreta (which accounts for the majority of placenta accreta cases), the normal decidua is absent and the chorionic villi of the placenta are in direct contact with the uterine myometrium. Chorionic villi invade the myometrial wall in placenta increta and invade past the uterine serosa in placenta percreta (Fig. 15.39).

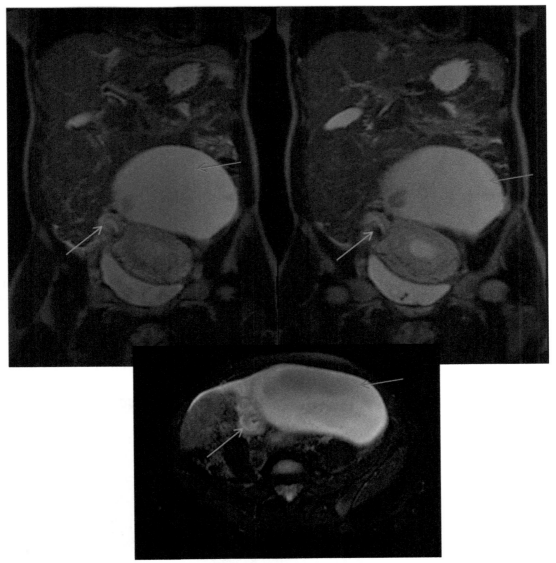

FIG. 15.31 **Ovarian torsion in a 12-week pregnant patient.** Axial T2 HASTE and coronal T2 FSFSE demonstrates an enlarged ovary with a 14 cm simple cyst (red ovary) and a twisted edematous right ovarian pedicle (blue arrows).

15.2.7.3 *Ultrasound vs. MRI*

Ultrasound is in the initial diagnostic tool to describe the placental location and to assess for possible abnormal placental adherence with imaging features such as absent retroplacental hypoechoic zone and bizarre placental lacunae.[43] A meta-analysis by Meng et al. demonstrates a sensitivity of 83% and a specificity of 95%[46] in the diagnosis of placenta accreta spectrum. Ultrasound is low cost and readily available, but is limited by patient body habitus, posterior placental location, and sonographic skill.[3]

MRI with placenta protocol is performed when ultrasound screening for abnormal placental adherence is positive, equivocal, or limited. MRI can also be performed in patients with negative screening US but with prior history of placenta accreta spectrum. A large meta-analysis by D'Antonio et al. demonstrated a sensitivity of 90.2% and a specificity of 88.2% in the detection of abnormal placental adherence for MRI.[47]

15.2.7.4 *MRI of normal placenta*

In the early second trimester, MRI appearance of the placenta is very homogeneous with diffuse T2 hyperintensity and with a discrete T2 hypointense decidual layer, which separates the placenta from the myometrium (Fig. 15.40).

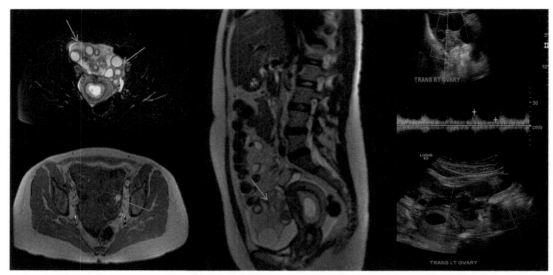

FIG. 15.32   Ovarian hyperstimulation in an 8-week pregnant patient. Axial T2FSFSE and sagittal T2 HASTE demonstrate bilateral enlarged and edematous ovaries with multiple follicles in the setting of IVF (blue arrows). Pelvic ascites is present. Axial T1 in-phase imaging demonstrates symmetric punctuate bilateral hemorrhagic cysts (red arrow). Doppler US confirms vascularity to both ovaries.

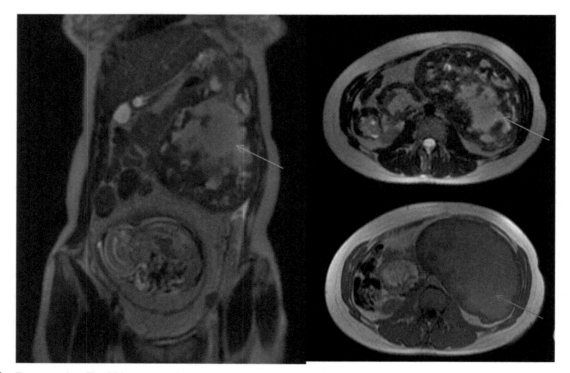

FIG. 15.33   Degenerating fibroid in a 17-week pregnant patient. Coronal and axial T2 HASTE demonstrate a subserosal fibroid with central T2 hyperintense degeneration (blue arrows). T1 in-phase axial images demonstrate mild T1 hyperintensity suggesting carneous or hemorrhagic degeneration (red arrow).

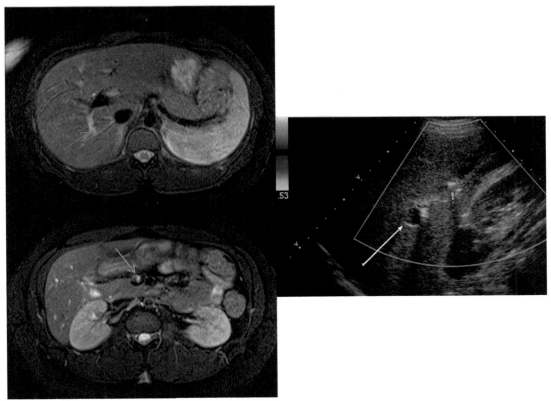

FIG. 15.34   Portal vein thrombus in 34-week pregnant patient. Axial T2 FSFSE demonstrates loss of normal flow void in the right posterior portal vein (red arrow), confirmed on Doppler US (white arrow), compatible with thrombus. Nonocclusive thrombus is also suspected in the SMV with disruption of the flow void on T2FSFSE (blue arrow).

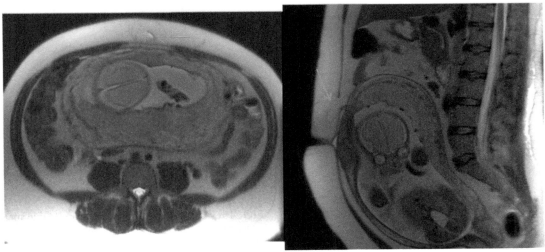

FIG. 15.35   Umbilical hernia in a 25-week pregnant patient. Axial and sagittal T2 HASTE demonstrates a focal fat-containing supraumbilical hernia without strangulation (blue arrows).

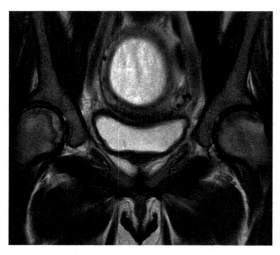

FIG. 15.36 Avascular necrosis in a 35-week pregnant patient. Coronal T2 HASTE demonstrates serpiginous T2 curvilinear signal with flattening if the right femoral head, compatible with avascular necrosis.

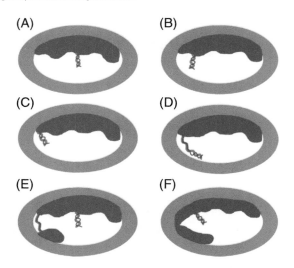

FIG. 15.38 Umbilical cord insertion and placental lobe variants. (A) central cord insertion, (B) eccentric cord insertion, (C) marginal cord insertion, (D) velamentous cord insertion, (E) placenta with succenturiate lobe, and (F) bilobed placenta.

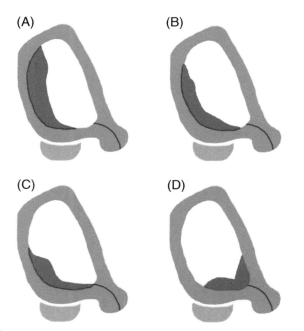

FIG. 15.37 Types of placenta previa. (A) low-lying placenta, (B) marginal placenta, (C) partial or incomplete placenta previa, and (D) complete placenta previa.

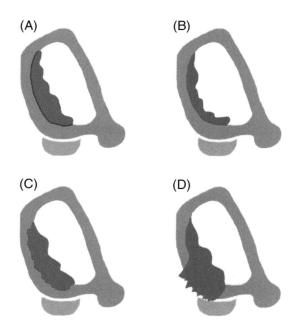

FIG. 15.39 Placenta accreta spectrum. (A) normal placenta with intact basement membrane, (B) placenta accrete, (C) Placenta increta, and (D) placenta percreta.

In early pregnancy, the placental edge can be in close proximity to the cervical os since the uterus is not fully enlarged and the placenta is not fully mature.

Beyond 24 weeks, the placenta increases in heterogeneity with intermittent flow voids particularly at the placental myometrial junction, but with preservation of the T2 hypointense decidual layer (Fig. 15.41). The placenta should be relatively uniform in thickness (from 2 cm to 4 cm) with tapered edges.[43] The uterine myometrium also has distinct appearance on MRI. Between 24 and 30 weeks, the myometrium demonstrates three layers, with a thin T2 hypointense inner and outer layer and a middle T2 hyperintense layer, which has increased hyperintensity as compared

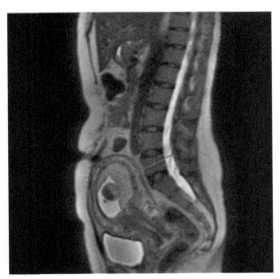

FIG. 15.40 Normal placental anatomy before 24 weeks. 17-week pregnant patient demonstrates a posterior homogeneous placenta with normal T2 hypointense decidual layer (red arrow). Inferior aspect of the placenta covers the internal cervical os, which can be a normal finding as the placenta is not fully mature.

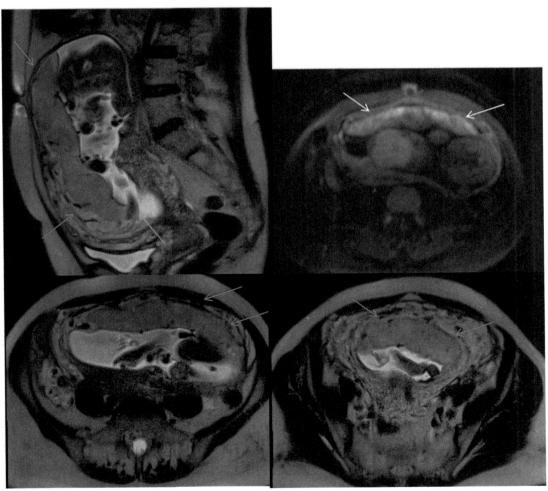

FIG. 15.41 Normal placenta after 24 weeks. Sagittal and axial T2 HASTE demonstrates an anterior placenta with intact T2 hypointense decidual layer (red arrows) and with normal three-layered myometrial architecture. Placenta is low-lying with a marginal cord insertion (blue arrow). Axial DWI images accentuate the well-defined myometrial/placental interface (white arrow).

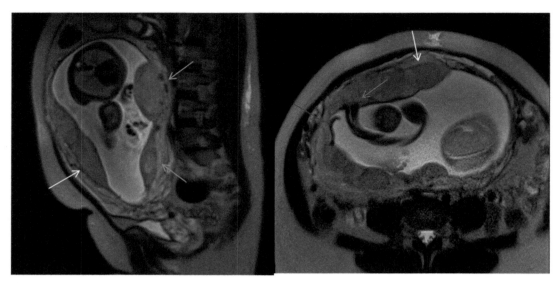

FIG. 15.42 Placental variants (30 weeks). Sagittal and axial T2 HASTE images demonstrate a succenturiate placenta (blue arrow) with continuation of the umbilical cord from the accessory succenturiate lobe to the anterior lobe (purple arrow). Eccentric insertion of the cord is present in the anterior lobe (red arrow). Three layered myometrial architecture and T2 hypointense decidual layer is preserved deep to both lobes (white arrows).

to the adjacent placenta.[43] As the gestation progresses into the third trimester, uterine myometrium stretches and thins with the layers becoming less distinct.[43] In cases of multiple placenta lobes or a bilobed placenta, uterine and placental architecture is preserved for all lobes (Fig. 15.42). DWI is a helpful adjunct sequence as it accentuates the normal placental-myometrial border.[48]

15.2.7.5 *Placenta accreta spectrum*

With abnormal placentation, the placenta becomes adherent and tethered. Placenta thickness becomes nonuniform in thickness and can lose its normal tapering edge.[43] Therefore, MRI findings of placenta accreta spectrum include abnormal uterine bulging along its exterior border and irregular interior contour as well (Fig. 15.43). Placental abruption can occur with abnormal placental adherence. T1wi can identify placental hematoma in the setting of either retroplacental or marginal abruption (Fig. 15.43).

Additional MR features of placenta accreta spectrum include increase in placental heterogeneity and T2-hypointense intraplacental bands[43] which can be focal or diffuse in distribution (Fig. 15.44) and defects along utero-placental interface.[3]

Placenta accreta and placenta increta appear identical on MRI, but MRI can identify extraplacental extension in placenta percreta.[43] Placenta tethering to the anterior abdominal wall, full thickness T2 hypointensity through the uterine myometrium with loss and contraction of uterine architecture, and urinary bladder wall invasion all suggest the presence of placenta percreta.[43] Partial urinary bladder distension helps assess for maternal bladder invasion, which changes surgical and delivery management. Coronal imaging and dedicated high resolution images through the uterine bladder interface can help assess for placenta percreta into the urinary bladder or into the cervical os (Fig. 15.45).

15.3 Pearls and pitfalls

- MRI is a safe effective way to evaluate for pain in the pregnant patient and to evaluate for abnormal placentation.
- In first trimester pregnant patients, visceral organ position is predominantly maintained.
- In second and third trimester patients, ovaries are often displaced superiorly and laterally. Appendix and terminal ileum can be displaced to the right upper quadrant.

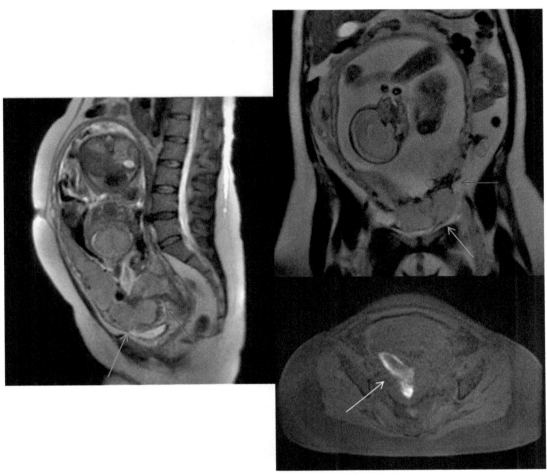

FIG. 15.43   Placenta accreta spectrum with subchorionic hemorrhage (32 weeks). Coronal and sagittal T2 HASTE demonstrates complete placenta previa (red arrow) with varying placental thickness, interior placental contour irregularity, and abnormal uterine exterior bulge (blue arrows). Coronal image demonstrates complete loss of normal myometrial architecture with T2 hypointense band on the left inferior uterine border (purple arrow). T1 imaging demonstrates placenta abruption with marginal placenta hematoma funneling into the internal os (white arrow).

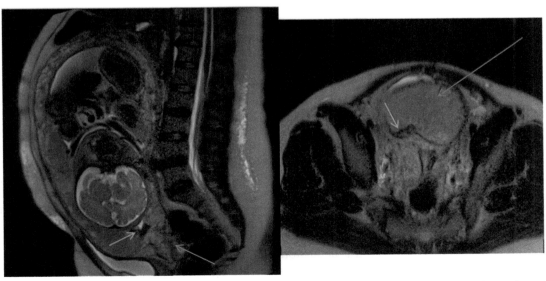

FIG. 15.44   Focal placenta accreta spectrum (35 weeks). Sagittal and axial T2 HASTE demonstrates complete placental previa (red arrows) with interruption of the decidual layer and focal T2 hypointense band to the right of the internal os (blue arrows). Caesarian section with hysterotomy confirmed focal placenta accreta.

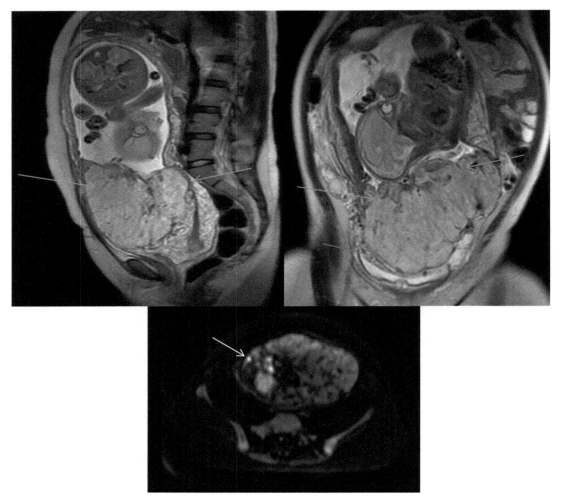

FIG. 15.45 **Placental percreta at 25 weeks.** Coronal T2 HASTE and sagittal T2 FIESTA demonstrates complete placenta previa and abnormal uterine bulge and contour in the anterior lower uterine contour (blue arrows). Irregularity of the superior bladder wall is suspicious for placenta percreta (red arrows). DWI accentuates placental irregularity at the right inferior aspect of the placenta (white arrow).

- An inflamed appendix measures greater than 7 mm in diameter and is distended with fluid on T2W sequences with surrounding T2-hyperintense periappendiceal inflammation.
- An appendix that measures 6–7 mm in diameter is considered equivocal. Periappendiceal stranding and restricted diffusion can help establish a diagnosis of appendicitis.
- Susceptibility or "blooming" artifact on T1W in-phase images only in the appendiceal tip raises concern for gangrenous appendicitis.
- High resolution T2W images with large FOV can help identify the appendix in patients with a paucity of intraperitoneal fat and can help differentiate a normal terminal ileum from an inflamed appendix with the presence of mucosal folds. T2 FIESTA images can differentiate normal periuterine vessels from the appendix.
- Signs of bowel ischemia, in the setting bowel obstruction, include mesenteric vascular engorgement, bowel wall stratification with submucosal edema, and localized ascites adjacent to distended small bowel loops.
- The terminal ileum can be displaced to the right upper quadrant or the left lower quadrant in pregnant patients with Crohn's disease. Assessment for fistula and abscess in these locations is critical.
- Bile stasis during pregnancy increases risk for cholelithiasis, and its associated diagnoses, including pancreatitis, choledocholithiasis, and intraductal stones. MRCP sequence should be added when choledocholithiasis is suspected. Intraductal stones are often hyperintense on T1W images.
- Solid pseudopapillary endothelial neoplasm (SPEN) can mimic focal pancreatitis in a young woman. Peripancreatic stranding is present only with pancreatitis and can help distinguish the two diagnoses.

- Physiologic hydronephrosis is common in pregnancy. MRI features in pyelonephritis include geographic area of restricted diffusion with corresponding T2 hypointensity. MRI features of forniceal rupture and pyelonephritis include asymmetric T2 hyperintense perinephric stranding.
- MRI features of ovarian torsion include ovarian enlargement with asymmetric restricted diffusion, peripheralization of follicles, and a twisted vascular pedicle.
- Due to the varying blood supply to the uterus, fibroids can degenerate in pregnancy with either T2-hyperintense cystic degeneration, T1-hyperintense "carneous" degeneration. Restricted diffusion on high B value images can help diagnosis torsion of pedunculated fibroids.
- Placental evaluation on MRI should include the presence of accessory placental lobes, location of umbilical cord insertion, and relationship of the placental edge to the internal os.
- Placental heterogeneity increases on MRI with increasing gestational age, but the T2-hypointense placental myometrial junction should be preserved throughout the pregnancy. DWI is a helpful adjunct, accentuating the placental interface.
- MRI features of abnormal placentation include abnormal uterine bulge and T2-hypointense intraplacental bands. Tethering to the abdominal wall and interruption of the urinary bladder wall suggest the presence of placenta percreta.

15.4 Conclusion

In conclusion, abdominal MRI is an invaluable imaging tool in pregnancy from assessing pregnant patients with abdominal pain to assessing abnormal placental implantation. MRI improves pregnant patient outcomes with early and accurate diagnosis and treatment of abdominal pain and with detailed placental anatomy that can prepare both the patient for and the obstetrician for delivery.

Acknowledgement

I would like to acknowledge the abdominal imaging and body MRI section in the Department of Diagnostic, Molecular, & Interventional Radiology at the Icahn School of Medicine at Mount Sinai.

Financial disclosures

None.

References

1. Spalluto LB, et al. MR imaging evaluation of abdominal pain during pregnancy: appendicitis and other nonobstetric causes. *Radiographics*. 2012;**32**(2):317–334.
2. Diegelmann L. Nonobstetric abdominal pain and surgical emergencies in pregnancy. *Emerg Med Clin North Am*. 2012;**30**(4):885–901.
3. Azour L, et al. The gravid uterus: MR imaging and reporting of abnormal placentation. *Abdom Radiol (NY)*. 2016;**41**(12):2411–2423.
4. Kennedy A. Assessment of acute abdominal pain in the pregnant patient. *Semin Ultrasound CT MR*. 2000;**21**(1):64–77.
5. Rosen MP, et al. Impact of abdominal CT on the management of patients presenting to the emergency department with acute abdominal pain. *AJR Am J Roentgenol*. 2000;**174**(5):1391–1396.
6. Birchard KR, et al. MRI of acute abdominal and pelvic pain in pregnant patients. *AJR Am J Roentgenol*. 2005;**184**(2):452–458.
7. Tremblay E, et al. Quality initiatives: guidelines for use of medical imaging during pregnancy and lactation. *Radiographics*. 2012;**32**(3):897–911.
8. De Wilde JP, Rivers AW, Price DL. A review of the current use of magnetic resonance imaging in pregnancy and safety implications for the fetus. *Prog Biophys Mol Biol*. 2005;**87**(2-3):335–353.
9. Expert Panel on, M.R.S. ACR guidance document on MR safe practices: 2013. *J Magn Reson Imaging*. 2013;**37**(3):501–530.
10. Derman AY, et al. MRI of placenta accreta: a new imaging perspective. *AJR Am J Roentgenol*. 2011;**197**(6):1514–1521.
11. Morita S, et al. Feasibility of diffusion-weighted MRI for defining placental invasion. *J Magn Reson Imaging*. 2009;**30**(3):666–671.
12. Spalluto LB, Grand DJ. MRI of acute appendicitis in the pregnant patient. *Med Health R I*. 2012;**95**(2):39–40.
13. Dewhurst C, Beddy P, Pedrosa I. MRI evaluation of acute appendicitis in pregnancy. *J Magn Reson Imaging*. 2013;**37**(3):566–575.
14. Pedrosa I, et al. MR imaging evaluation of acute appendicitis in pregnancy. *Radiology*. 2006;**238**(3):891–899.
15. Sharp HT. The acute abdomen during pregnancy. *Clin Obstet Gynecol*. 2002;**45**(2):405–413.
16. Inci E, et al. Utility of diffusion-weighted imaging in the diagnosis of acute appendicitis. *Eur Radiol*. 2011;**21**(4):768–775.
17. Mazze RI, Kallen B. Appendectomy during pregnancy: a Swedish registry study of 778 cases. *Obstet Gynecol*. 1991;**77**(6):835–840.

18. Webster PJ, et al. Small bowel obstruction in pregnancy is a complex surgical problem with a high risk of fetal loss. *Ann R Coll Surg Engl.* 2015;**97**(5):339–344.

19. Cox VL, et al. Bowel obstruction complicated by ischemia: analysis of CT findings. *Abdom Radiol (NY).* 2018;**43**(12):3227–3232.

20. Schizas D, et al. Paraduodenal hernias: a systematic review of the literature. *Hernia.* 2019;**23**(6):1187–1197.

21. Laube R, Paramsothy S, Leong RW. Review of pregnancy in Crohn's disease and ulcerative colitis. *Therap Adv Gastroenterol.* 2021;**14**:17562848211016242.

22. Koh DM, et al. MR imaging evaluation of the activity of Crohn's disease. *AJR Am J Roentgenol.* 2001;**177**(6):1325–1332.

23. Melnick DM, Wahl WL, Dalton VK. Management of general surgical problems in the pregnant patient. *Am J Surg.* 2004;**187**(2):170–180.

24. Nasioudis D, Tsilimigras D, Economopoulos KP. Laparoscopic cholecystectomy during pregnancy: a systematic review of 590 patients. *Int J Surg.* 2016;**27**:165–175.

25. Daas AY, et al. ERCP in pregnancy: is it safe? *Gastroenterol Hepatol (NY).* 2009;**5**(12):851–855.

26. Sasamori Y, Tanaka A, Ayabe T. Liver disease in pregnancy. *Hepatol Res.* 2020;**50**(9):1015–1023.

27. Mali P. Pancreatitis in pregnancy: etiology, diagnosis, treatment, and outcomes. *Hepatobiliary Pancreat Dis Int.* 2016;**15**(4):434–438.

28. Miller FH, et al. MRI of pancreatitis and its complications: part 1, acute pancreatitis. *AJR Am J Roentgenol.* 2004;**183**(6):1637–1644.

29. Semins MJ, Matlaga BR. Management of stone disease in pregnancy. *Curr Opin Urol.* 2010;**20**(2):174–177.

30. McAleer SJ, Loughlin KR. Nephrolithiasis and pregnancy. *Curr Opin Urol.* 2004;**14**(2):123–127.

31. Masselli G, et al. Imaging of stone disease in pregnancy. *Abdom Imaging.* 2013;**38**(6):1409–1414.

32. Craig WD, Wagner BJ, Travis MD. Pyelonephritis: radiologic-pathologic review. *Radiographics.* 2008;**28**(1):255–277; quiz 327-8.

33. Rathod SB, et al. Role of diffusion-weighted MRI in acute pyelonephritis: a prospective study. *Acta Radiol.* 2015;**56**(2):244–249.

34. Jordan E, et al. Imaging of nontraumatic adrenal hemorrhage. *AJR Am J Roentgenol.* 2012;**199**(1):W91–W98.

35. Mehrazin R, et al. Adrenal trauma: Elvis Presley Memorial Trauma Center experience. *Urology.* 2007;**70**(5):851–855.

36. Lier MCI, et al. Spontaneous hemoperitoneum in pregnancy (SHiP) and endometriosis: a systematic review of the recent literature. *Eur J Obstet Gynecol Reprod Biol.* 2017;**219**:57–65.

37. Cappell MS, Friedel D. Abdominal pain during pregnancy. *Gastroenterol Clin North Am.* 2003;**32**(1):1–58.

38. Duigenan S, Oliva E, Lee SI. Ovarian torsion: diagnostic features on CT and MRI with pathologic correlation. *AJR Am J Roentgenol.* 2012;**198**(2):W122–W131.

39. Pedrosa I, et al. MR imaging of acute right lower quadrant pain in pregnant and nonpregnant patients. *Radiographics.* 2007;**27**(3):721–743; discussion 743-753.

40. Lee HJ, Norwitz ER, Shaw J. Contemporary management of fibroids in pregnancy. *Rev Obstet Gynecol.* 2010;**3**(1):20–27.

41. Usta IM, et al. Placenta previa-accreta: risk factors and complications. *Am J Obstet Gynecol.* 2005;**193**(3 Pt 2):1045–1049.

42. Eller AG, et al. Optimal management strategies for placenta accreta. *BJOG.* 2009;**116**(5):648–654.

43. Kilcoyne A, et al. MRI of placenta accreta, placenta increta, and placenta percreta: pearls and pitfalls. *AJR Am J Roentgenol.* 2017;**208**(1):214–221.

44. Eller AG, et al. Maternal morbidity in cases of placenta accreta managed by a multidisciplinary care team compared with standard obstetric care. *Obstet Gynecol.* 2011;**117**(2 Pt 1):331–337

45. Fadl S, et al. Placental imaging: normal appearance with review of pathologic findings. *Radiographics.* 2017;**37**(3):979–998.

46. Meng X, Xie L, Song W. Comparing the diagnostic value of ultrasound and magnetic resonance imaging for placenta accreta: a systematic review and meta-analysis. *Ultrasound Med Biol.* 2013;**39**(11):1958–1965.

47. D'Antonio F, et al. Prenatal identification of invasive placentation using magnetic resonance imaging: systematic review and meta-analysis. *Ultrasound Obstet Gynecol.* 2014;**44**(1):8–16.

48. Sannananja B, et al. Utility of diffusion-weighted mr imaging in the diagnosis of placenta accreta spectrum abnormality. *Abdom Radiol (NY).* 2018;**43**(11):3147–3156.

16

MRI of endometriosis

Hannah Barnard, Myra K Feldman

Cleveland Clinic Imaging Institute, Cleveland, OH, United States

16.1 Introduction

Endometriosis is a common disorder, estimated to impact 11% of women of child-bearing age.[1] While traditionally thought of as a benign gynecologic condition, recent shifts in our understanding of the disease suggest endometriosis should be thought of as a chronic, systemic process.[2] Pelvic pain and infertility are the most common clinical manifestations of endometriosis, but women with endometriosis can present with variable symptoms, many of which are nonspecific and overlap with other disorders. In addition to clinical symptoms, women with endometriosis report a negative impact on their productivity, career trajectory, relationships and mental well-being.[3] This translates into a considerable economic burden to society with increased direct and indirect healthcare expenditures, similar to what is seen with patients with other chronic medical conditions.[4]

The cause and pathogenesis of endometriosis remains poorly understood. Histologically the disorder is characterized by ectopic endometrial glands and stroma, and hemosiderin laden macrophages. Fibrosis and smooth muscle hypertrophy are often seen in association with endometriosis. Estrogen dependence, progesterone resistance, inflammation and genetic predisposition all factor into the pathogenesis of endometriosis.[5] Endometriosis is commonly multifocal with most lesions located in the pelvis. Lesions can also be found outside of the pelvis, located in the abdomen, along the diaphragm, within the thorax and abdominal wall. The three phenotypes of endometriosis are superficial peritoneal disease, ovarian endometriomas and deep infiltrating endometriosis (DIE).

Treatment for endometriosis is variable and dependent upon the individual patient's goals. For some women, achieving fertility is a primary end-point for treatment while for others, therapies focus on controlling pain or other symptoms. Medical therapeutic approaches can be grouped into hormonal treatments that aim to block the hormonal effects of estrogen on disease progression, and analgesic or neuroleptic medications that aim to treat pain symptoms. Surgical resection is considered definitive therapy for medically refractory cases and for endometriosis related infertility.[6-9]

The role of imaging in the care of patients with endometriosis continues to evolve. Diagnostic laparoscopy with visual identification of lesions and histopathologic confirmation was traditionally considered the standard for establishing a diagnosis of endometriosis. Magnetic resonance (MR) imaging is known to be sensitive and specific for the diagnosis of ovarian endometriomas and pelvic DIE, the two most severe forms of the disease.[10-14] Given that clinical manifestations of endometriosis are variable and nonspecific, pelvic MR is useful as a noninvasive tool to establish a diagnosis of endometriosis or to suggest an alternative diagnosis. When surgical resection is considered, a growing body of literature advocates for preoperative imaging to map endometriotic lesions, either by dedicated endometriosis ultrasound or pelvic MR.[15-17] Preoperative imaging studies are critical as endometriosis is commonly multifocal and successful outcomes are predicated on complete excision of all lesions. Definitive surgical excision of endometriosis often requires multidisciplinary surgical teams with urology and colorectal surgeons in addition to gynecologic surgeons.[18] For women with endometriosis, the information gained by MR imaging mapping studies allows for improved patient preoperative counselling and comprehensive surgical planning.

16.2 Discussion

16.2.1 Anatomy and location of endometriosis

16.2.1.1 *Pelvis*

Endometriosis is often multifocal but most commonly occurs in the pelvis and tends to involve pelvic anatomic structures in a predictable pattern. When discussing endometriosis, is helpful to divide the pelvis into anterior, middle, and posterior compartments. These are not true anatomic spaces as they include both intra and extra peritoneal structures and spaces (Fig. 16.1).

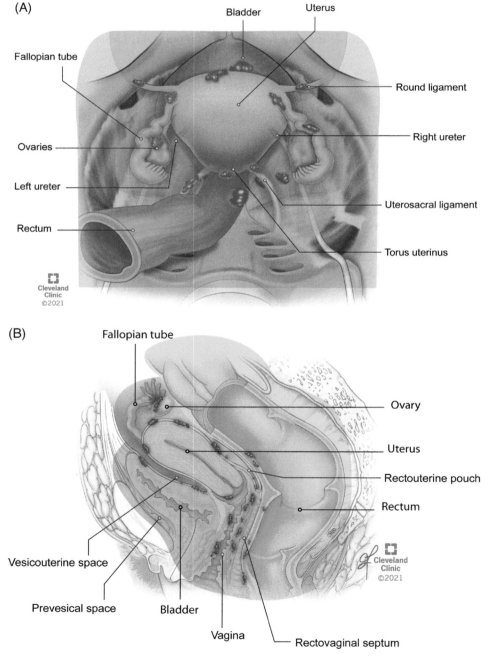

FIG. 16.1   Axial (A) and sagittal (B) illustrations of the female pelvis show anterior (red), middle (blue), and posterior (yellow) compartments. Anatomic structures in each compartment are indicated by labels and common sites for infiltrative endometriosis are indicated by pink nodules.

The borders of the anterior compartment are delineated by the pubic symphysis anteriorly and the anterior uterus and vagina posteriorly. Anatomic structures involved by endometriosis in the anterior compartment include the bladder, distal ureters, and round ligaments. Anatomic spaces involved by endometriosis in this compartment include the prevesical, vesicovaginal/vesicocervical and vesicouterine spaces. Of the three compartments, the anterior is the least common site of disease.[19–22]

The uterus, vagina, fallopian tubes, and ovaries are middle compartment structures commonly involved by DIE. Disease in the middle compartment often extends laterally to involve the pelvic side wall. Middle compartment endometriosis may also extend anteriorly to involve elements of the anterior compartment, or posteriorly to involve structures in the posterior compartment.

The posterior compartment is the most common site of DIE. The uterosacral ligaments are paired ligaments that insert posterior to the cervix forming the "torus uterinus," the most common site of deep infiltrating endometriosis, involved in as many as 69% of patients.[23] The uterosacral ligaments can be difficult to identify when normal, appearing as thin T2-hypointense bands, but are easier to identify when involved by DIE as they become thickened, foreshortened, or nodular (Fig. 16.2). Additional posterior com-

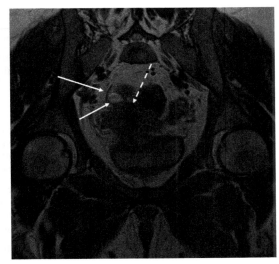

FIG. 16.2 Axial oblique T2 weighted (T2W) MR image through the pelvis shows the right uterosacral ligament (white arrows). A band-like area of thickening along the posterior cervix (dashed white arrow) is the torus uterinus.

partment structures and spaces that may be involved by endometriosis include the anterior wall of the rectosigmoid colon, the rectovaginal septum, retrocervical area, and rectouterine pouch.

16.2.1.2 Other locations

Common sites of extrarectal bowel endometriosis include the small bowel, appendix, and cecum.[24,25] The most common extraperitoneal locations of endometriosis include the inguinal canal, abdominal wall, and perineum. The most common abdominal visceral locations include the liver, kidney, pancreas, and biliary tract. The most common thoracic locations are the diaphragm, pleura, and lung.[26]

16.2.2 Imaging techniques and protocol

MR protocol optimization is critical for lesion detection and image interpretation. Several different patient preparation and image acquisition strategies have been explored. Evidence-based consensus guidelines for MR imaging of pelvic endometriosis have been issued by the European Society of Urogenital Radiology (ESUR) and the Society of Abdominal Radiology Endometriosis Disease Focused panel (SAR-EDFP).[27,28] Protocol recommendations from these two societies are summarized in this chapter and in Tables 16.1 and 16.2.

TABLE 16.1 Summary of patient preparation techniques with ESUR and SAR-EDFP recommendations.

Preparation	ESUR	SAR-EDFP	Method
Bowel preparation	Best practice	No recommendation	I.E. diet, laxatives, enemas
Rectal contrast	Option	Conditionally recommended	Water or ultrasound gel
Antiperistaltic	Recommended	Highly recommended	1 mg glucagon administered slowly over 1 minute
Fasting	Recommended	No recommendation	–
Vaginal contrast	Option	Conditionally recommended	60 cc self-administered sterile ultrasound gel
Bladder distention	Recommended	Conditionally recommended	No voiding within 1 hour of study initiation
Phased array coil	Recommended	Highly recommended	MR technologist placement
Endorectal coil	–	Highly not recommended	–

ESUR, European Society of Urogenital Radiology; SAR-EDFP, Society of Abdominal Radiology Endometriosis Disease Focused Panel.

TABLE 16.2   ESUR and SAR-EDFP MR sequence recommendations.

Sequence	Plane	Purpose	ESUR	SAR-EDFP
T2W without fat suppression	2–3 planes: sagittal, axial, and oblique through the uterus	Identification of deep infiltrating disease	T2W- recommended 3 planes—grade B	T2W- recommended 2 planes—highly recommended 3 planes-conditionally recommended
T1 without contrast with and without fat suppression	Axial	Increased conspicuity of hemorrhagic products. Differentiation of fat from blood products	T1W with AND without fat suppression recommended—grade B	T1W with AND without highly recommended—LE3
T1 postcontrast with fat suppression and with subtraction	Axial and sagittal	Characterization of benign versus malignant adnexal lesions, evaluation for infection	Option*	Highly recommended—LE4
Diffusion weighted imaging	Axial	Identifying malignant and infections processes	No recommendation	Highly recommended

*ESUR recommendations are specific to DIE, and did not take characterization of ovarian endometriomas into account.

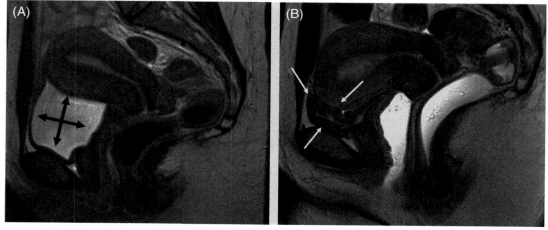

FIG. 16.3   Sagittal T2W MR image with a well distended bladder (A) shows the bladder wall is uniform in thickness (black arrows). This was achieved by asking the patient to void at check in, approximately 1 hour prior to scanning. Sagittal T2W MR image from the same patient 2 months earlier with a collapsed bladder (white arrows). The bladder wall is thickened making it more difficult to evaluate for focal thickening or involvement by endometriosis.

16.2.2.1 Patient preparation

Patient preparation strategies generally focus on improving lesion conspicuity (via techniques such as bladder distention, luminal contrast, and bowel preparation) or reducing bowel motion artifacts (via fasting or using anti-peristalsis agents).

The degree of bladder distention is important, as wall thickening, commonly seen with under-distention, may obscure small lesions involving the bladder wall (Fig. 16.3). Over-distention of the bladder can lead to detrusor contractions which can cause motion artifacts, potentially obscuring lesions of the bladder wall or perivesicular space. Moderate bladder distention can be achieved by asking patients not to void within 1 hour of imaging.[27,28]

Vaginal contrast has been studied as a method to improve conspicuity of lesions involving the vaginal wall and posterior compartment structures (Fig. 16.4). Sterile ultrasound gel is typically given to the patient in a prefilled syringe for self-administration.[28]

Bowel preparation and rectal contrast have both been studied as strategies to improve detection and characterization of rectosigmoid lesions and posterior compartment structures. Bowel preparations that have been described are variable but include special diets, laxative regimens and enemas.[27,28] Rectal contrast agents, either water or ultrasound gel, have been studied with conflicting data. Some studies found rectal contrast agents improved

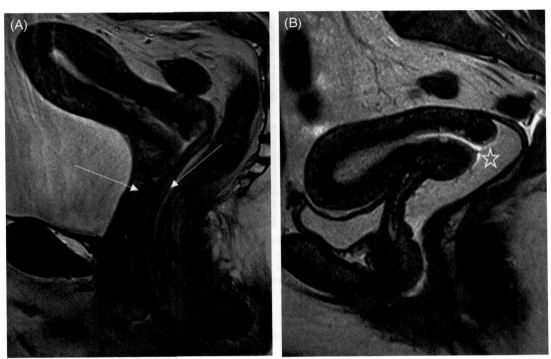

FIG. 16.4 Sagittal T2W MR image without vaginal contrast (A) shows the vagina is collapsed with poor soft tissue contrast between the closely opposed anterior and posterior vaginal walls (thin white arrow). Sagittal T2W MR image with vaginal contrast (B) (star) shows improved soft tissue contrast between the anterior and posterior vaginal walls. Although no lesion is present in this case, the improved soft tissue contrast has the potential to make vaginal lesion detection easier and more accurate.

evaluation of rectal and cul-de-sac lesions while others reported the practice degrades image quality, as it is associated with increased motion artifact, presumably from bowel spasm. Additional barriers to this practice include the potential for patient discomfort and workflow challenges.

Motion from small bowel peristalsis is a major source of artifact on endometriosis pelvic MR studies that utilize several time-intensive T2-weighted sequences. Fasting and administration of antiperistalsis agents are methods that have been advocated to reduce motion artifacts. The antiperistalsis agent available in the US is Glucagon, which is generally administered as 1 mg IV slowly over 1 minute. Barriers to using Glucagon include access to the medication (may not be available at outpatient centers without a pharmacy), personnel availability to administer the agent and increased scanner time.[29]

16.2.2.2 Technical considerations

Both 1.5 Tesla (T) and 3T systems are adequate for evaluation of endometriosis. Patients should be scanned in the supine position utilizing a phased array coil. Recommended MR sequences are described below and summarized in Table 16.2.

T2-weighted (T2W) sequences without fat suppression are the work-horse for lesion detection in endometriosis imaging. The most common planes used are sagittal (with a saturation band) (Fig. 16.5), axial and oblique axial through the uterus. Oblique axial T2W imaging through the uterus has been shown to improve visualization of the uterosacral ligaments (Fig. 16.2).[16,30,31] Three dimensional (3D) T2W sequences have been suggested as a way to help facilitate multiplanar imaging with less image acquisition, however these sequences are commonly regarded as visually less appealing due to reduced spatial resolution and motion artifacts.

T1-weighted (T1W) sequences with fat suppression without contrast are helpful to identify the hemorrhagic products that can be seen in association with endometriosis. These sequences are also important to include when postcontrast imaging is performed. T1W sequences without and with fat-suppression are important to differentiate fat from hemorrhagic material. Susceptibility-weighted imaging is sensitive in the detection of residual blood products from chronic hemorrhage but was not routinely recommended as it lacks sufficient specificity to accurately identify endometriosis.

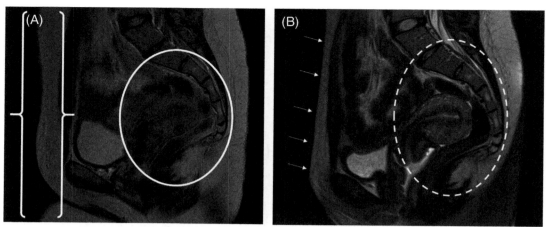

FIG. 16.5 Sagittal T2W MR image of the pelvis (A) was obtained without an anterior saturation band. The contour of the anterior abdominal wall is seen (brackets). Motion artifacts are present on the image causing the rectal wall, endometrium and junctional zone to look blurry (white oval). Sagittal T2W MR image through the pelvis on the same patient 18 months earlier (B) obtained with an angulated saturation band as evidenced by a dark angulated line obscuring the anterior abdominal wall (white arrows). In this image the rectal wall and posterior structures are clear and distinct (dashed white oval).

The primary value of postcontrast imaging in patients with suspected endometriosis is in its power to help characterize adnexal lesions. Patients with endometriosis are at a slight increased risk for developing ovarian cancers and postcontrast imaging is helpful in the differentiation of benign from potentially malignant ovarian lesions. The ESUR study, which only considered protocol recommendations specific to DIE, listed postcontrast imaging as "an option," whereas the SAR-EDFP, which considered protocol recommendations for all forms of endometriosis, "highly recommended" postcontrast imaging. Similarly, diffusion-weighted imaging, which is useful in helping to distinguish malignant and infectious process from benign disease, was highly recommended by the SAR-EDFP.[27,28]

As endometriosis can be found in many extra-pelvic sites, consideration should be given to tailoring the MR protocol when evaluation for suspected extra-pelvic sites is specifically requested by the ordering clinician. Some protocol modifications may include removing the saturation band on sagittal sequences and extending the field-of-view when evaluating for abdominal wall endometriosis, and adding T1/T2W sequences through the upper abdomen if diaphragmatic endometriosis is suspected.

16.2.3 Diagnostic criteria

While most radiologists have traditionally used the terms "endometrioma" and "endometriosis" interchangeably, there are three distinct forms of endometriosis, including superficial endometriotic implants, ovarian endometriomas, and DIE.[32] These subtypes can occur alone or in combination.

16.2.3.1 Ovarian endometriomas

Ovarian endometriomas are cystic ovarian or paraovarian structures that contain endometrial tissue and blood products of variable age due to episodes of cyclical bleeding. Endometriomas are typically uniformly hyperintense on T1W images due to the presence of chronic blood products (Fig. 16.6).

Endometriomas show low signal intensity on T2W images, sometimes referred to as "T2 shading." The T2 shading sign, originally described by Togashi et al.[33] refers to blunting of the T2 hyperintense signal due to blood products within the cyst, and may be homogenous or heterogeneous with layering. While Togashi's original paper showed high sensitivity, specificity and accuracy of the T2 shading sign in distinguishing endometriomas from other gynecologic lesions, subsequent studies have not reproduced this finding, and have shown T2 shading can be present in hemorrhagic cysts and neoplasms.[34-36] The T2 dark spot sign, originally described by Corwin as a T2 hypointense focus within an ovarian cystic structure that does not enhance on postcontrast imaging, is postulated to occur as a result of a blood clot within the endometrioma. A T2W dark spot was found to be 93% specific and 36% sensitive for the diagnosis of an endometrioma,[35] and can thus be a helpful finding in distinguishing hemorrhagic cysts from endometriomas when present (Fig. 16.6). Endometriomas may also have a hypointense rim on T2W images which is thought to be due to hemosiderin deposition or fibrous tissue.[37]

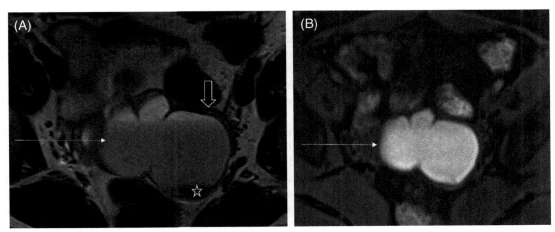

FIG. 16.6 Axial T2W MR image (A) shows a cystic ovarian lesion with T2 shading (thin white arrow) and a T2 dark-spot (star). Normal ovarian parenchyma is noted around the cystic lesion (open arrow). T1W MR image with fat saturation and no contrast (B) of the same lesion (thin white arrow) shows intrinsic T1 hyperintense signal. Imaging features of this lesion are characteristic of an ovarian endometrioma.

Endometriomas may have internal solid elements and septations due to hemorrhagic contents and blood clots. Contrast enhanced imaging is important to distinguish benign from neoplastic solid elements which typically show postcontrast enhancement. Subtraction images are helpful as it can be difficult to judge enhancement in the setting of intrinsic T1 hyperintense signal.

16.2.3.2 *Superficial endometriotic implants*

Superficial endometriotic implants, also known as peritoneal or superficial peritoneal endometriosis, are defined as implants with peritoneal invasion of less than 5 mm. These lesions may be associated with hemorrhagic material and fibrosis. Superficial lesions are commonly identified during laparoscopy where they have variable appearances based on the amount of associated blood products or fibrosis. These lesions are difficult to identify on MR due to small size and limitations of MR resolution. When superficial endometriotic implants are identified on MR studies, they can appear as a T1 isointense plaque, with or without punctate T1 hyperintense foci if accompanied by hemorrhage. Implants may appear T2 hypointense with or without T2 hyperintense foci due to functioning endometrial glands (Fig. 16.7).[38]

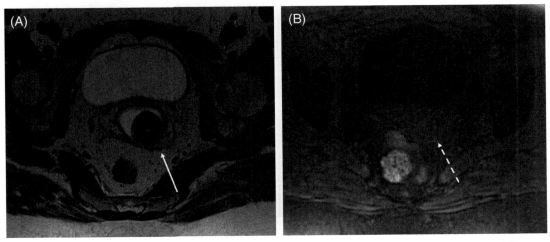

FIG. 16.7 Axial oblique T2W MR image through the lower pelvis (A) shows subtle asymmetric thickening of the left uterosacral ligament (white arrow). Axial T1W MR image obtained at the same level shows mild hyperintense signal at the same location. Surgery performed 1 year later showed superficial endometriosis involving both the left and right uterosacral ligaments.

16.2.3.3 *Deep infiltrating endometriosis*

DIE refers to implants that invade to a depth of at least 5 mm below the peritoneal surface.[39] Like superficial implants, these solid lesions are formed by endometrial glandular elements and fibrosis. On MR imaging studies, DIE can be conceptualized as having primary and secondary findings. Primary findings relate to the appearance of the DIE implant itself. Secondary findings are a result of the chronic inflammatory state incited by the primary process, including changes associated with fibrosis such as architectural distortion and muscular hyperplasia.

DIE lesions are primarily made up of fibrotic tissue with a solid, mass-like nodular or stellate shape (Fig. 16.8). Fibrotic elements can also appear as ligamentous thickening, nodules, or plaque-like lesions. Signal characteristics are similar to fibrous tissue in general with hypointense signal on T2W images, isointense signal on T1W images and progressive delayed enhancement. In some instances, T1W hyperintense foci or T2W hyperintense cystic foci are noted in association with DIE lesions. These findings are thought to relate to the functional endometrial glandular elements.[38,40]

Fibrosis associated with DIE may result in tethering of structures with resultant obliteration of potential spaces or architectural distortion. Given that endometriosis occurs in predictable locations, certain patterns of architectural distortion can be reliable indicators to the presence of DIE. These signs include kissing ovaries, uterine retroversion and elevation of the posterior vaginal fornix (Figs. 16.9 and 16.10). Kissing ovaries, or ovaries that are tethered together by fibrosis and located posterior to the uterus, have been found to be associated with more advanced (stage III or IV) endometriosis.[41]

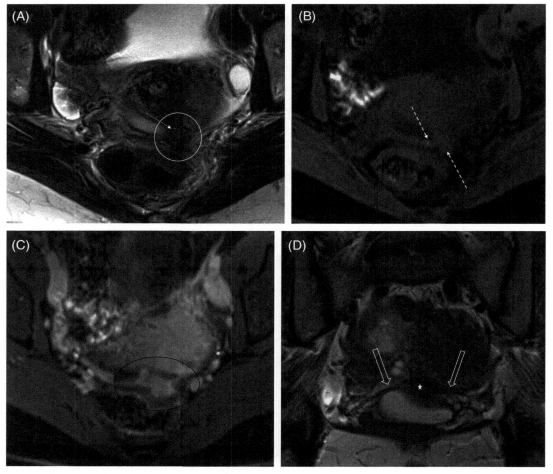

FIG. 16.8   Axial T2W MR image through the pelvis (A) shows a hypointense stellate shaped nodule in the rectouterine pouch (circle) with hyperintense, cystic foci (arrow). Axial T1W MR image at the same level (B) shows hyperintense foci in the nodule (dashed arrows). Axial T1W MR image with contrast at the same level (C) shows enhancement of the stellate nodule (black oval). Coronal T2W MR image (D) through the same nodule (star) shows thickening of the uterosacral ligaments adjacent to the nodule (open arrows). Imaging features are compatible with primary imaging findings of DIE.

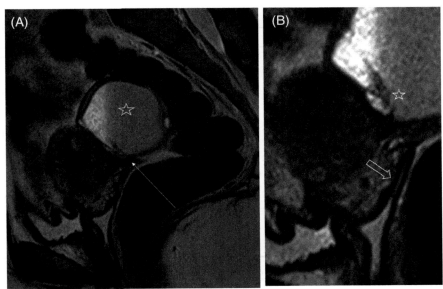

FIG. 16.9 Sagittal T2W MR image (A) shows retroflexion of the uterus and obliteration of the retrocervical area (thin arrow). Zoomed up sagittal T2W image from the same series show the posterior vaginal fornix (open arrow) is elevated. These secondary findings indicate the presence of posterior compartment DIE which was confirmed at surgery. An ovarian endometrioma (star) is tethered to this DIE lesion and the uterine body.

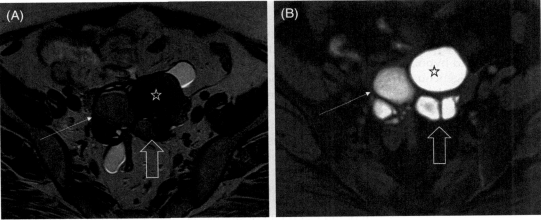

FIG. 16.10 Axial T2W (A) and T1W fat suppressed (B) MR images through the pelvis show the right (thin arrow) and left (open arrow) ovaries tethered together. Both ovaries contain multiple endometriomas with T2 shading and T1 hyperintense signal (example of one indicated by star). The ovaries were tethered together and located posterior to the uterus (not shown) in a "kissing ovary" configuration, indicative of DIE.

16.2.4 Endometriosis variants

16.2.4.1 *Polypoid*

Polypoid endometriosis is a rare subtype of endometriosis that is histologically similar to endometrial polyps, and is distinct from DIE, endometriomas, or superficial endometriotic implants. Polypoid endometriosis, unlike the three dominant phenotypes, presents similarly to endometrial polyps, as a T2 hyperintense mass with hypointense rim, and with enhancement characteristics identical to the endometrium. Patients are typically peri or postmenopausal and may be on an estrogen containing hormone therapy or Tamoxifen. Lesions tend to occur in the middle and posterior compartments.[42]

TABLE 16.3 Types of endometriosis with differential.

Type of endometriosis	Differential	Differentiating characteristics
Ovarian Endometrioma	Hemorrhagic cyst	T1 signal is typically less hyperintense than endometriomas or peripheral. No T2 dark spot. Resolves over time.
	Dermoid	Fat signal with loss of T1 hyperintensity on fat-saturated T1 sequences.
	Fibrous ovarian neoplasm	No T1 hyperintense signal, low-level enhancement.
	Abscess	Typically, less T1 hyperintense. Clinical symptoms of infection.
	Malignant neoplasm	Enhancement of nodular components, irregular walls or thick internal septae.
DIE	Infection	Clinical symptoms, restricted diffusion on DWI.
	Neoplasm	History of malignancy. Neoplasm may show increased signal on T2W sequences and restricted diffusion on DWI.
	Primary tumors, i.e. desmoids	Clinical history
	Postoperative change	History of surgery

16.2.5 Differential diagnosis

While some imaging features of endometriomas, superficial peritoneal disease and DIE are nonspecific, it is often possible to arrive at a confident diagnosis by synthesizing imaging characteristics with clinical information and temporal imaging findings (Table 16.3).

16.2.5.1 Endometrioma differential

The differential for ovarian endometrioma includes hemorrhagic cyst, abscess, and neoplasm.

Hemorrhagic cysts are common and pose the greatest diagnostic challenge as both lesions can have hyperintense signal on T1W images and hypointense signal on T2W images. For endometriomas, the T1W signal intensity tends to be greater, more homogeneous and occupy a greater portion of the lesion than hemorrhagic cysts due to higher concentrations of methemoglobin related to cyclic bleeding (Fig. 16.11). Increased T1W signal intensity is seen less frequently within hemorrhagic cysts (27%) and when present is more variable, with some lesions showing heterogeneous areas of increased signal, foci of increased signal or a peripheral rim of increased signal intensity.[43] As described in the diagnostic criteria section, T2 shading is not a reliable way to distinguish between hemorrhagic cysts and endometriomas. Identification of a T2 dark spot can be helpful in distinguishing an endometrioma from a hemorrhagic cyst, but unfortunately this finding is not sensitive. When in doubt, a follow-up imaging study at least 6 weeks apart can help distinguish these two lesions as hemorrhagic cysts should resolve over time while endometriomas persist.

Tubo-ovarian abscesses are typically hypointense on T1W sequences but can have increased signal intensity if complicated by hemorrhage or due to protein content. Clinical information can help narrow the differential as tubo-ovarian abscess is typically accompanied by infectious symptoms.[44]

Benign and malignant neoplasms can mimic endometriomas. Ovarian dermoids or benign mature teratomas have high signal intensity on T1W images without fat saturation due to fat content (Fig. 16.11). Evaluation of all ovarian lesions on T1W images with fat saturation is critical to differentiate endometriomas from a dermoids. Fibrous ovarian neoplasms can be confused for endometriomas as both lesions can have low signal intensity on T2W images. Fibromas lack hyperintense signal on T1W images and show low level enhancement. The appearance of malignant ovarian neoplasms is variable. Intrinsic T2W hypointense and T1W hyperintense signal is not common in malignant neoplasms, but can be present. Both neoplasms and endometriomas may have thick walls and internal septations, however walls and septae tend to be smooth in endometriomas and nodular in malignancy. Postcontrast sequences with subtraction are crucial to help identify enhancement of nodules or septations especially when the background T1W signal intensity is hyperintense (Fig. 16.12).[45–48] While diffusion restriction is a characteristic of many neoplastic processes, it is not specific for malignancy in the setting of endometriosis as hemorrhagic and proteinaceous contents in benign endometriomas are known to cause diffusion restriction. When focal areas of restricted diffusion are identified within a lesion and these foci correspond with enhancing nodules, the finding in suspicious for malignancy.[45]

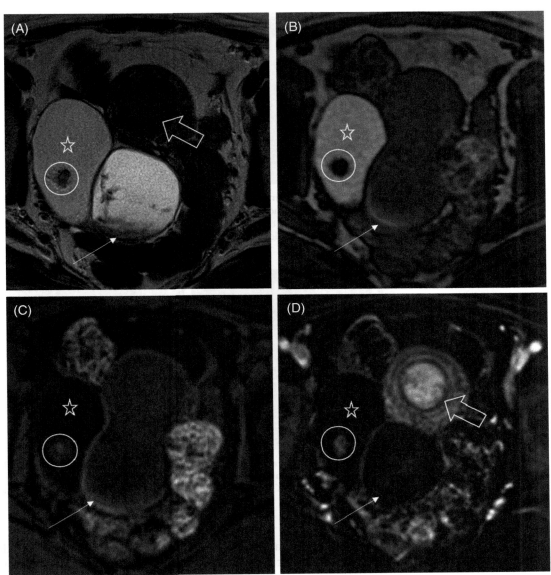

FIG. 16.11 Axial T2W MR image (A) shows 2 right ovarian lesions. The more lateral right ovarian cyst shows mild T2 shading (star) and a T2-hypointence focus (circle). The more medial lesion is hyperintense with layering hypointense material inferiorly (white arrow). Uterine fibroid is also present (open arrow). Axial T1W MR image without fat saturation (B) shows hyperintense signal in the lateral lesion. The medial lesion is mostly hypointense with layering hyperintense material (white arrow). Axial T1W MR image with fat saturation (C) shows signal loss in the lateral lesion indicating fat content compatible with ovarian dermoid. The more medial lesion remains predominately low signal with layering high signal intensity (white arrow). Axial T1W image with fat saturation, postcontrast enhancement and subtraction (D) shows no enhancement within either lesion. The medial lesion with very little, peripheral hyperintense T1W signal was felt to be compatible with a hemorrhagic cyst. At surgery the dermoid with central hair was confirmed. The lateral lesion had resolved, indicating it was a hemorrhagic cyst.

16.2.5.2 *Deep infiltrating and superficial peritoneal endometriosis differential*

The differential for DIE and superficial peritoneal endometriosis includes postoperative change, neoplastic and congenital anomalies. Postoperative change can be the most challenging differential, and is addressed in greater detail in Table 16.6 and in the section on imaging in the postsurgical setting.

Within the anterior compartment, DIE of the bladder wall may mimic bladder cancer. Endometriosis is an outward in process, beginning at the serosa before involving the muscular bladder wall and rarely involves the bladder mucosa. In contrast, bladder cancer arises from the mucosa and may grow to involve the muscle or extravesicular tissues.[49] Bladder neoplasms typically show mildly hyperintense signal on T2W images and are more common in older age groups.[49,50] Diverticula of the urinary tract and cystic lesions such as Gartner's ducts

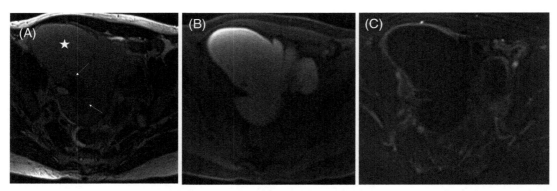

FIG. 16.12   Axial T2W MR image of the right ovary (A) shows a large cystic lesion with T2 shading (star) and hypointense papillary-like projections (white arrows). Axial T1W MR image with fat saturation and no contrast (B) shows intrinsic hyperintense signal within the lesion. The papillary projections are not well seen. Axial T1W MR image with fat saturation, contrast enhancement and subtraction (C) shows no enhancement of the papillary projection to suggest neoplasm. The lesion was removed with cystectomy and found to be compatible with a benign endometrioma.

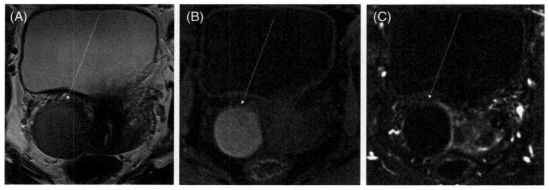

FIG. 16.13   Axial T2W MR image at the level of the cervix and vagina, above the pubic symphysis (A) shows a cystic vaginal lesion with T2 shading (white arrow). Axial T1W MR image with fat saturation at the same level (B) shows intrinsic hyperintense signal within the lesion. Axial T1W image with fat saturation, contrast enhancement and subtraction (C) shows no internal enhancement. Given characteristic location and no other findings of endometriosis, a Gartner's duct cyst was suspected.

cysts may have T1W hyperintense signal due to proteinaceous or hemorrhagic debris, mimicking endometriosis (Fig. 16.13). Gartner's duct cysts occur in a characteristic location, along the anterolateral wall of the vagina and can be seen in association with other congenital anomalies of the genitourinary tract.[51]

Middle compartment DIE involving the uterus can be confused for adenomyosis and leiomyomas. Adenomyosis occurs when endometrial tissue disrupts the endometrial basal layer and extends into the myometrium.[52] Adenomyosis can appear as T2W hypointense junctional zone thickening from smooth muscle hyperplasia, with or without T2W and T1W hyperintense foci representing endometrial glands (Fig. 16.14).[53] Endometriosis extends from the serosa inward. Full-thickness lesions that span the entire myometrium from serosa to endometrium may be impossible to differentiate from adenomyosis unless prior imaging is available for comparison. Leiomyomas are classically smoothly marginated T2W hypointense lesions, although they may mimic endometriosis when cystic or hemorrhagic degeneration are present.[54] Vaginal and cervical DIE can cause wall thickening which can be confused with other mass-like lesions such as neoplasm. Vaginal and cervical cancers have higher T2W signal intensity than endometriosis, and restrict diffusion.[55,56]

Endometriosis involving the rectosigmoid is often associated with focal wall thickening that can mimic other colorectal neoplasms or bowel wall metastasis. Adenocarcinoma of the colon and rectum develops from the inside-out, starting in the mucosa and extending outward towards and possibly through the muscular wall. Endometriosis develops from the outside-in, starting from the retrocervical area and working its way inward, often involving the muscular wall. Colon cancer tends to be T2-intermedate, while DIE lesions are T2W hypointense (Fig. 16.15).[57]

The differential for extrapelvic endometriosis includes desmoid tumors, hematomas, suture granulomas, and neoplasm. Desmoids may appear identical to the fibrotic components of endometrial implants, but are typically T1W hypointense and will not contain T1W hyperintense foci or T2W hyperintense cystic foci due to the lack of

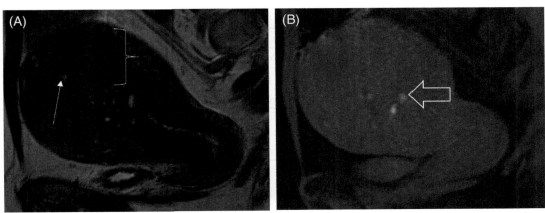

FIG. 16.14 Sagittal T2W MR image (A) shows diffuse junctional zone thickening (brackets) with predominately T2W hypointense signal and many cystic foci (thin white arrow) replacing the normal myometrial signal. Sagittal T1W MR image with fat saturation (B) shows several hyperintense foci in the myometrium (open arrow) consistent with blood products. Imaging findings are centered within the myometrium with no external component compatible with adenomyosis rather than endometriosis.

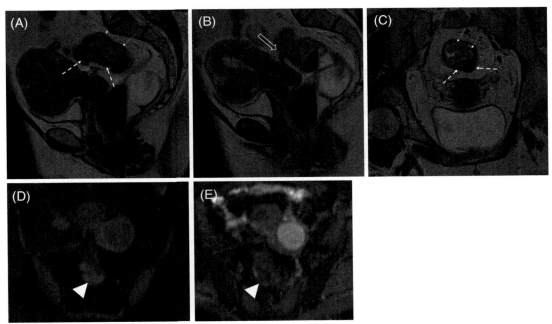

FIG. 16.15 Sagittal T2W MR image through the rectum (A) shows two rectal lesions. The more anterior lesion (dashed arrows) is markedly hypointense and shows a mushroom cap configuration typical of rectal endometriosis. The more posterior lesion (white arrows) is mildly hyperintense and shows a more irregular shape. A second sagittal T2W MR image (B) shows a thick fibrous stalk extending from the region of the posterior cervix (torus uterinus) to the more anterior rectal lesion (open arrow). Axial oblique T2W MR image (C) shows the anterior lesion extends from mesorectal fat to involve the rectal wall (dashed arrows). The posterior lesion extends from the inner, mucosal layer of the posterior wall and extends into the rectal lumen (white arrows). Axial MR high B value diffusion weighted image (D) with corresponding apparent diffusion coefficient map (E) show restricted diffusion within the posterior lesion (white arrowheads). At surgery the anterior lesion was confirmed to be muscle invasive rectal endometriosis and the posterior lesion was a rectal adenocarcinoma.

functioning endometrial tissue.[58] Hematomas often occur after an inciting incident, resolve over time, and are not associated with cyclic symptoms. Carcinomatosis and metastasis can be differentiated from multifocal endometriotic implants by evaluating the patient's history of malignancies, examining change over time, and by searching for a primary malignancy. Neoplastic lesions tend to have higher signal intensity on T2W images.

TABLE 16.4   Tri-compartmental division of the pelvis.

Location/compartment	Anatomic structures
Anterior compartment	Bladder, distal ureters; prevesical, vesicovaginal, vesicocervical and vesicouterine spaces, broad ligaments
Middle compartment	Uterus, vagina, fallopian tubes, ovaries, pelvic side wall
Posterior compartment	Uterosacral ligaments, torus uterinus, rectosigmoid colon; rectovaginal, retrocervical and rectouterine spaces

TABLE 16.5   Reporting template.

Compartment	Description, if endometriosis is present
Anterior compartment	
Bladder	Lesion size, proximity in relation to the ureters and trigone, depth of the implant
Ureters	Lesion size/length along ureter, proximity to the UVJ, presence/absence of hydroureteronephrosis
Round ligaments	Lesion size, segment involved, morphology (nodular, smooth, foreshortened)
Vesicouterine space	Lesion size, involvement of other structures (uterus or bladder)
Vesicovaginal space	Lesion size, obliteration of space, involvement of vagina or bladder
Prevesical space	Tethering, obliteration of space, associated invasion into the bladder
Middle compartment	
Ovaries	Size, location and number of endometriomas, DIE or superficial disease, tethering of adjacent structures
Fallopian tubes	Hematosalpinx or hydrosalpinx
Uterus	Location, lesion depth (with percent thickness of the uterine wall) and size
Cervix/vagina	Lesion size, depth (proximity to the endocervical canal) and circumferential extent
Posterior compartment	
Retrocervical space	Tethering, obliteration of space, associated invasion into cervix, vagina or rectum
Uterosacral ligament, Torus uterinus	Morphology-smooth and/or nodular thickening, associated tethering
Anterior rectal wall	Lesion length, lesion thickness/depth of invasion into muscle, circumferential extent, distance from anal verge, morphology (mushroom cap)
Rectovaginal space	Tethering, obliteration of space, associated invasion into vagina or rectum
Additional locations	
Sigmoid/other bowel	Location, size, depth of invasion
Appendix	Size of implant, associated tethering if present
Abdominal wall	Location, size, muscle involvement, landmarks for surgical localization
Nerves	Nerves involved, size of lesion, associated muscular atrophy

16.2.6 Search pattern and reporting

When interpreting and reporting pelvic MR studies for endometriosis, it is helpful to follow a systematic search pattern and report template utilizing the tri-compartmental approach previously introduced in the anatomy and location of endometriosis section (Fig. 16.1 and Table 16.4). This mirrors the approach used by the surgeon for surgical planning and helps ensure actionable items important for treatment planning are included in the report. (Table 16.5)[59,60] Subsequent scrutiny of additional abdominopelvic sites known to harbor endometriosis completes the MR evaluation.

16.2.6.1 *Anterior compartment*

The most common location of endometriosis in the anterior compartment is the vesicouterine space, which is an intraperitoneal pouch created by the peritoneal reflection over the bladder dome and uterine fundus. DIE in this location my lead to obliteration of the pouch and may be associated with bladder and uterine disease. Bladder DIE is more common in patients with a history of prior surgery for endometriosis (6–11% versus <1% in individuals with no prior surgery).[22,50,61] Muscle invasive bladder endometriosis is often identified as a focal area of mass-like wall thickening that shows signal intensity characteristic of DIE (Fig. 16.16).[62] These lesions can be definitively treated with partial cystectomy. Urology consultation may be required for lesions close to the trigone or ureter orifices as ureter reimplantation may be required. For bladder endometriosis, the size of the lesion, proximity of the implant in relation to the ureters and trigone, and the depth of the implant affect surgical planning, and must be reported.[50,61–63]

The distal ureters are more commonly involved than the proximal ureters, and implants are usually unilateral and associated with endometriosis elsewhere. Extrinsic ureter disease is more common and can be identified as T2-hypointese fibrosis encasing or tethering the ureter (Fig. 16.19). This type of disease can typically be resected off of the ureter by the gynecologist. Intrinsic DIE involves the muscular wall of the ureter and can appear as a T2-hypointense nodule with or without associated hydronephrosis (Fig. 16.17).[62] Intrinsic ureter disease often

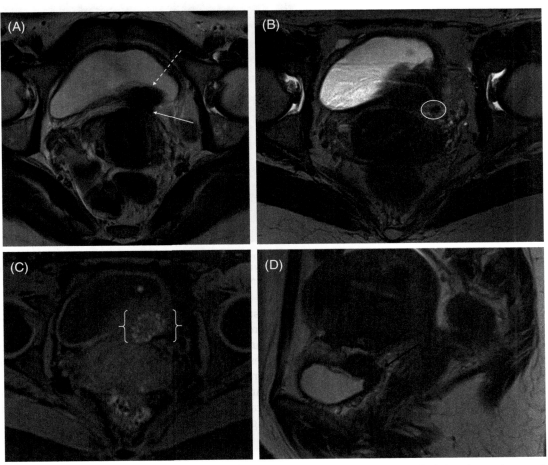

FIG. 16.16 Axial T2W MR image through the pelvis (A) shows a nodular lesion that extends from the left vesicouterine pouch (arrow) to the involve the left posterior lateral bladder wall in the region of the left uretorvesicular junction (dashed arrow). The lesion is predominately hypointense but also contains tiny cystic foci, primary imaging features of DIE. Axial T2W MR image a few slices cephalad to the first image (B) shows the distal left ureter (open circle) is thickened and hypointense, also involved by DIE. Axial T1W MR image with fat suppression and no contrast (C) shows multiple hyperintense foci within the left uterovesicular DIE lesion (brackets). Sagittal T2W MR image (D) shows the hypointense, nodular DIE lesion also extends to the vesicocervical/vesicovaginal space (black arrows). Distance from the inferior edge of the lesion to the trigone could be estimated on this view.

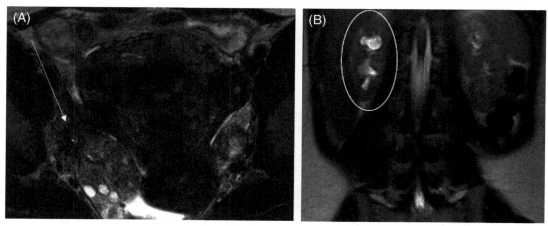

FIG. 16.17   Axial T2W MR image through the pelvis (A) shows a stellate shaped hypointense nodule surrounding the distal right ureter (white arrow). Coronal HASTE image (B) of the upper abdomen shows upstream hydronephrosis (oval). Intrinsic ureter disease was suspected and confirmed at surgery. Urology was consulted for segmental ureter resection with reconstruction.

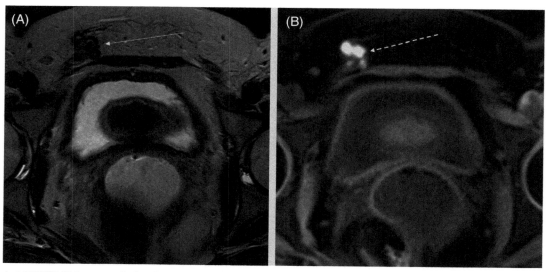

FIG. 16.18   Axial T2W MR image at the level of the inguinal canal (A) shows a cluster of cystic structures with T2W hypointense signal (white arrow). Axial T1W MR image with fat saturation and no contrast at the same level (B) shows hyperintense signal within the cysts (dashed arrow). Endometriosis involving the round ligaments within the inguinal canal, or "Canal of Nuck" was found at surgery.

requires Urology consultation for ureter resection and reconstruction. The proximity of the ureteral involvement to the UVJ, length of affected ureter, and degree of hydroureteronephrosis, if present, must be reported.

The prevesical and vesicovaginal/vesicocervical spaces are extraperitoneal and are rarely affected by endometriosis. Close scrutiny and reporting of lesions in these spaces is critical for surgical planning, as the peritoneum is not routinely traversed during surgical evaluation for endometriosis.

The round ligaments may become nodular, thickened, and foreshortened when involved by endometriosis.[19] Round ligament endometriosis can extend into the inguinal canal. When present, this should be reported as surgical resection may require collaboration with general surgery (Fig. 16.18).[63]

16.2.6.2 Middle compartment

The ovaries are the most common site of endometriosis in the middle compartment and can be involved by all three forms of endometriosis. The presence of multiple endometriomas and the "kissing ovary" morphology described earlier are predictive indicators for associated DIE and multifocal disease (Fig. 16.10).[40] DIE involving the ovaries is often associated with pelvic side wall disease. The surgical approach to ovarian endometriosis varies based on the individual patient's age, fertility goals, ovarian reserve, size, number and location of endometriomas (unilateral versus bilateral), and imaging features of each lesion. Different surgical approaches include oophorectomy,

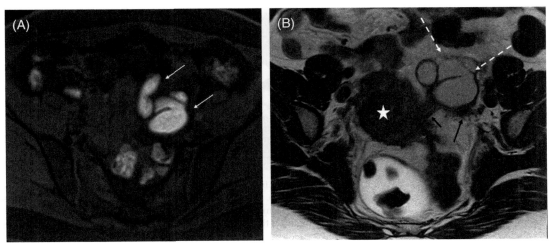

FIG. 16.19 Axial T1W MR image of the pelvis with fat saturation and no contrast (A) shows a dilated tubular structure with hyperintense signal (arrows). Axial T2W MR image (B) shows mild T2 shading within the same tubular structure compatible with hematosalpinx (dashed arrows). Bands of fibrotic tethering are present extending from the dilated fallopian tube to the uterus and left pelvic side wall (black arrows). The uterus with a fibroid is also noted (white star). DIE involving the left tube, ovary and pelvic sidewall was found at surgery.

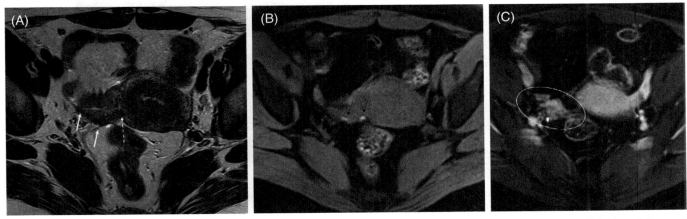

FIG. 16.20 Axial T2W MR image through the pelvis (A) shows hypointense thickening along the posterior aspect of the broad ligament (white arrows). The abnormal low signal intensity extended to the junction of the broad ligament and myometrium (dashed arrow). Axial unenhanced T1W MR image with fat saturation at the same level (B) shows hyperintense foci in the region of thickening shown on the T2W image. The combination of findings was suspicious for DIE. Axial contrast enhanced T1W MR image with fat suppression slightly cephalad to the first two images (C) shows enhancing tissue extends to surround the right ovary with a tethered appearance to the right pelvic side wall (oval). At surgery DIE was found involving the right broad ligament, fallopian tube (obliterated), right ovary and right pelvic side wall. Superficial disease along the myometrial surface was removed.

cystectomy, and cyst wall ablation. The number, size, and location of each endometrioma, and any evidence of ovarian involvement by DIE should be reported.[41] Imaging features suspicious for malignancy should be noted.

The fallopian tubes and broad ligament structures can be involved by superficial peritoneal or DIE implants.[64] Endometriosis may lead to tubal occlusion secondary to fibrosis and smooth muscle hypertrophy with or without associated hematosalpinx or hydrosalpinx (Figs. 16.19 and 16.20).[38,65] Tubal disease including presence of hematosalpinx or hydrosalpinx should be reported as these findings are important for patient counseling, especially for those who desire future fertility.

The uterus and vagina can be affected by DIE in association with anterior, middle or posterior compartment disease. Surgical treatment options for uterine endometriosis largely depend on the patient's desire to preserve fertility and include superficial excision, myomectomy and hysterectomy.[9] When myomectomy is considered for fertility preservation, the precise location, size, and lesion depth (with percent thickness of the uterine wall) should be reported. When the cervix is involved, the proximity to the endocervical canal and circumferential extent should be reported for surgical planning.[63]

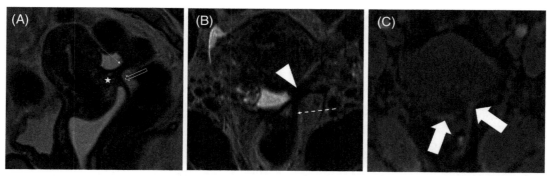

FIG. 16.21   Sagittal T2W MR image (A) shows hypointense bands of fibrotic tissue extending from the torus uterinus and posterior cervix (star) to the rectum (thin arrow) and posterior vaginal fornix (open arrow). Coronal oblique T2W MR image (B) shows the fibrotic signal replaces the left lateral vaginal wall (arrowhead) and is also contiguous with the anterior rectal wall (dashed arrow). Axial T1W MR image with fat suppression and no contrast (C) shows hyperintense foci in association with this lesion. Infiltrative endometriosis involving the torus uterinus, left uterosacral ligament, left vaginal wall and anterior rectal wall was found at surgery.

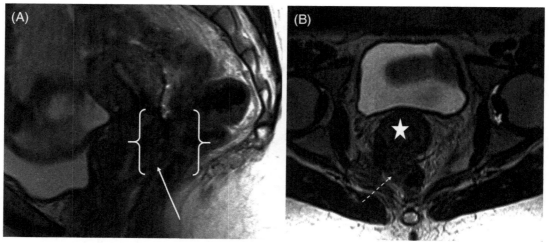

FIG. 16.22   Sagittal T2W MR image through the pelvis (A) shows obliteration of the normal fat plane of the rectovaginal space by hypointense tissue with cystic foci (brackets). The posterior vaginal fornix (white arrow) is encased by this tissue. Axial T2W image from the same level (B) shows the tissue involves the cervix (star) and anterior rectal wall (dashed white arrow). The extraperitoneal rectovaginal space was explored at surgery and DIE was found involving the rectal wall, cervix and vagina. Partial vaginectomy and segmental rectal resection was performed.

For vaginal endometriosis, the superior vaginal fornices are the most commonly affected site.[15,23] Involvement of the posterior vaginal fornix is often present in association with posterior compartment and rectal disease. When present, the location and depth of invasion should be reported to allow for planning of either superficial shaving or a partial vaginectomy.

16.2.6.3 *Posterior compartment*

The uterosacral ligaments are a common location for DIE and are typically involved close to the torus uterinus. When uterosacral ligament disease is identified, the torus uterinus, cervix, vagina, rectum, and adjacent nerves should be scrutinized for associated involvement by DIE. Lesion location, size, and adjacent structures involved should be reported.

DIE of the intraperitoneal rectouterine or retrocervical spaces is often part of a larger endometriotic complex involving multiple posterior compartment structures and spaces. When DIE is identified in these spaces, anatomic structures including the uterosacral ligaments, anterior rectal wall, and vaginal fornix should be evaluated for disease (Fig. 16.21). Lesion location, size, and all structures involved should be reported.[63]

The rectovaginal space and septum are extraperitoneal and not routinely evaluated during laparoscopy. Disease in these locations is rare and should be reported to alert the surgeon to the need for additional dissection (Fig. 16.22).

Rectosigmoid endometriosis is typically located along the anterior rectal wall, and can infiltrate into the muscularis propria. When DIE invades the muscular layer of the rectal wall, muscular hypertrophy with concomitant

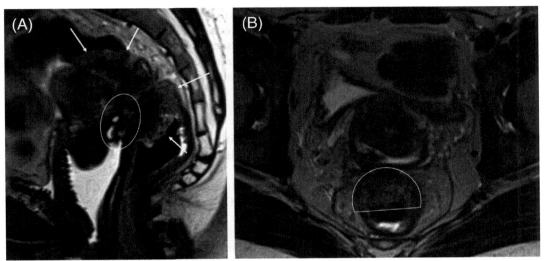

FIG. 16.23 Sagittal T2W MR image through the pelvis (A) shows a classic mushroom cap lesion DIE of the anterior rectal wall with hypointense fan shaped base and mildly hyperintense cap which corresponds with the rectal mucosa (white arrows). This lesion measured 6 cm in length. The vaginal fornix is also replaced by a DIE lesion (white oval). Axial obliqueT2W image through the lesion (B) shows the lesion involves about 50% of the rectal circumference (outline). This lesion was treated with surgical resection due to lesion size (length, circumference).

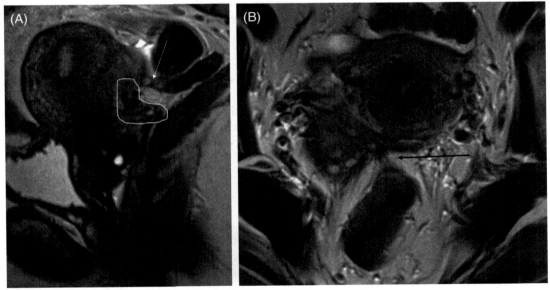

FIG. 16.24 Sagittal T2W MR image through the pelvis (A) shows posterior compartment DIE lesion involving the torus uterinus and rectrocervical area (outline). Thin fibrotic bands extend from this lesion to the anterior rectal wall (white arrow). Axial oblique T2W MR image at the same position (B) shows the fibrotic band only focally involves the anterior rectal wall (black arrow). This lesion did not involve the muscular rectal wall and was removed by the gynecologic surgeon.

shortening of the serosa often occurs resulting in nodular lesion. The mucosa is typically not involved by these lesions and appears as a T2-hyperintense crescentic cap overlying the nodule. Together these findings form the "mushroom cap sign" which indicates muscle-invasive rectal wall DIE (Fig. 16.23).[66,67] Surgical resection is offered to patients who are symptomatic from bowel disease. The three most common surgical approaches to rectosigmoid disease are rectal shaving, discoid resection and segmental resection with or without an ileostomy. Small lesions that do not involve the deep muscle layer can be removed by rectal shaving (partial thickness excision), a procedure usually performed by the gynecologist (Fig. 16.24). Lesions that involve the deep layer of muscle can be removed by discoid resection or segmental resection, often with the help of colorectal surgery. Lesions than are single, less than 3cm in length and involve less than 1/3 of the circumferential extent of the rectal wall can be removed with discoid resection, a full-thickness excision with reapproximation of the bowel. Due to risk of bowel angulation and dysfunction, lesions larger than 3 cm in length, those that occupy more than 1/3 of the circumferential rectal wall, and multifocal lesions are treated with segmental resection (Fig. 16.23). When lesions are in close proximity to the anal canal, many colon rectal surgeons will form a temporary diverting loop ileostomy to allow for optimal healing. For rectosigmoid DIE, it is critical report the number of lesions, distance between the lesions, and for each lesion the length and circumferential extent. Location of the implants in relation to both the anal verge and peritoneal reflection is also important. When possible, it is important to report the thickness or depth of mural invasion.[63,68]

16.2.6.4 Other locations

Abdominal wall endometriosis is one of the most common sites of extra pelvic endometriosis. It may occur spontaneously, but more often arises within surgical scars due to iatrogenic seeding of endometrial tissue (Fig. 16.25). Imaging features are similar to intra pelvic DIE. Postcontrast enhanced images are particularly helpful to determine the full extent of fibrosis.[38] Symptomatic lesions can be removed by surgical excision, and more recently treatment by high intensity focused ultrasound (HIFU), and cryoablation have been described.[69] Successful surgical treatment is predicated on a wide resection margin, so the depth, size, and specific location must be reported.

Small bowel endometriosis most commonly involves the terminal ileum, but any segment of bowel can be involved. Direct findings of small bowel DIE include discrete plaques or nodules. Secondary findings of tethering or angulated bowel loops can be helpful clues to the presence of disease. An MR enterography can be considered to further evaluate for small bowel endometriosis.[70] Terminal ileal, appendiceal, and cecal endometriosis can be coexistent, and all three sites should be evaluated if any single location is affected (Fig. 16.26). Appendiceal endometriosis may appear as T2W hypointense plaques. Luminal obstruction may occur, resulting in a dilated appendix with varying levels of T1W and T2W hyperintensity depending on the presence of hemorrhage. The resultant appearance may mimic that of an appendicular mucocele.[66] An effort should be made to identify and characterized the appendix on all studies, especially when intrapelvic DIE is identified.[71]

Diaphragmatic implants tend to occur along the right hepatic dome, and may present with pneumothorax (Fig. 16.27). Pulmonary endometriosis is less common.[26,38] T1W MR sequences with fat suppression through the diaphragm are helpful to localize diaphragmatic DIE. Some centers routinely include these sequences on pelvic MR studies done for endometriosis.

Neural involvement by endometriosis is rare, but can have significant morbidity. The nerves typically affected by endometriosis include the sciatic, obturator, pudendal, femoral, and greater lumbosacral plexus. Implants extend along and may encase nerves. Associated muscles may appear atrophic. Treatment options are typically medical however surgical excision has been described.[38,72,73]

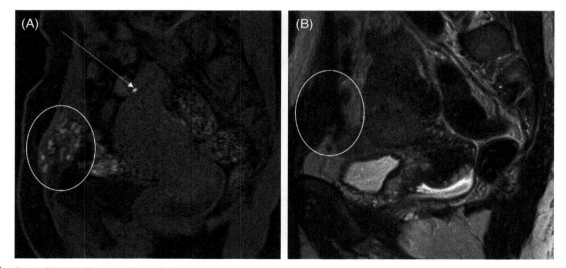

FIG. 16.25 Sagittal T1W MR image through the pelvis (A) shows multiple hyperintense foci in the region of the Cesarian section scar) (circle). Additional hyperintense focus noted on the uterine fundus (thin arrow). Sagittal T2W MR image from the same location (B) shows hypointense thickening of the left rectus abdominus (circle). DIE involving the Cesarian section scar was confirmed at surgery.

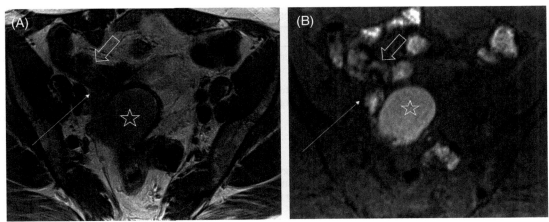

FIG. 16.26 Axial T2W MR image through the upper pelvis (A) shows an ovarian endometrioma with T2 shading (star). Spiculated hypointense tissue extends from the right ovary laterally to involve the right pelvic sidewall (white arrow) and anteriorly to involve the ileocecal valve (open arrow). Axial T1W MR image with fat saturation and no contrast (B) at the same level shows hyperintense signal within the right ovarian endometrioma (star) and foci of hyperintense signal in the region of the soft tissue (white arrow). DIE was confirmed at surgery involving the right ovary, right pelvic side wall and ileocecal valve.

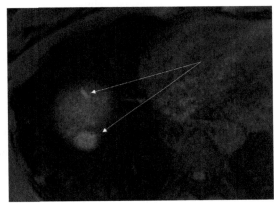

FIG. 16.27 T1W axial MR image of the right diaphragm showing T1-hyperintense endometriotic implants on the right hemidiaphragm (white arrows).

16.2.7 Imaging in special circumstances

16.2.7.1 Posttreatment

Medical therapy may be attempted as a first line of treatment for endometriosis.[74] Medical management is largely focused on decreasing estrogen production by the ovaries, thus decreasing the cyclic stimulation of ectopic endometrial tissue. Possible treatment effects are summarized in Table 16.6. Estrogen-progestin hormonal therapy is widely accessible, and is generally well tolerated, thus forming the backbone of medical therapy. Imaging findings after hormonal therapy may include a decrease in the size and number of endometriomas. GnRH agonists are considered second-line therapy. They have been shown to induce remission of disease in over 50% of patients, with resolution of implants noted via laparoscopy 5 months after initiating therapy, although the side-effect profile that results from the induction of pseudomenopause makes these medications poorly tolerated. Aromatase inhibitors have been shown to decrease the size of an endometriotic implant in at least one case.[8,75,76]

16.2.7.2 Imaging after surgical therapy

Surgery is pursued when medical therapy is poorly tolerated, in medically refractory cases with persistent debilitating symptoms, and when fertility is desired.[6,7,75,77] Accurate evaluation of postoperative findings requires understanding the patient's past surgeries. Postoperative changes can include alteration of the normal pelvic architecture and unwanted complications such as adhesions and fistulae. Operative techniques with possible postoperative imaging findings are summarized in Table 16.7.

TABLE 16.6 Current medical therapy and related imaging findings.

Therapy	Possible imaging findings	Examples of medication
Estrogen-progestin contraceptives	Decrease in size and number of endometriomas	Transdermal patch, vaginal ring, oral pill
Progestins	Decrease in size of endometriomas, possible decidualization, atrophy of plaques	IUD (off-label), dienogest, northindrone acetate, medroxyprogesterone acetate
Gonadotropin-releasing hormone agonists (GnRH)	Resolution of implants after 5 months of therapy in >50% of patients	Leuprolide, buserelin, nafarelin, goserelin, triptorelin
GnRH antagonists	Similar findings to GnRH agonists on laparoscopy, resolution of hematosalpinx with persistence of fibrotic implants has been noted on imaging after 2 years of therapy	Elagolix
Aromatase inhibitors	Documented case of the decrease in size of a vaginal lesion	Letrozole, anastrozole

TABLE 16.7 Surgical techniques with associated postoperative imaging findings.

Surgical technique	Postoperative finding
Posterior compartment DIE excision	Scar tissue/fibrosis Posterior compartment obliteration adhesions
Uterine wall lesion excision with or without ablation	Thinning of the uterine wall
Uterine lesion excision with cerclage	Annular foreign body
Full-thickness vaginal lesion excision	Partial colpectomy with absent fornix and scar fibrosis
Superficial vaginal lesion shaving	Preserved fornix, focal wall thinning, thickening at the site of shaving
Bowel wall shaving/resection with scissors with stitches—for small superficial lesions	Often occult on MR. Possible identification of sutures
Discoid resection of bowel lesions—for ventral lesions <3 cm long and ≤15 cm from anal verge. Shaving with subsequent transanal resection with stapler	Artifact from suture
Segmental bowel resection—for multifocal disease, lesions >3 cm long, or stenotic lesions	T2-hypointense anastomosis, scar fibrosis, fluid at the site of anastomosis—either free or loculated
Partial cystectomy	Focal bladder wall asymmetry, possible reduction in bladder volume
Ureterolysis with or without ureteral resection	T2-hypointense fibrotic ureteral wall thickening, higher neo-ureterovesical junction
Endometrioma cystectomy	Reduced ovarian size, possible persistent endometrioma if the wall was not removed. Ovarian fossa adhesions

The most common postoperative finding after excision of DIE is T2-hypointense scar.[78,79] Extensive pelvic adhesions are common, and my lead to anatomic distortion, fluid collections and peritoneal inclusion cysts (Fig. 16.28). Hematomas within the pouch of Douglas are common after colpectomy and are often due to vaginal wall trauma. Complications at the site of bowel resection and anastomosis may include leak, fistula, and stenosis. Bladder dysfunction secondary to neural injury can lead to imaging findings related to neurogenic bladder atony. Ureteral stenosis can occur after ureteral manipulation with varying degrees of upstream hydroureteronephrosis.

Recurrent and residual disease is a common finding on postoperative MR. Some sites of endometriosis may be intentionally left at the time of surgery, due to the complexity of the case, desire to preserve ovarian reserve, or other reasons.[77] Chronic findings secondary to endometriosis-related tissue damage can be difficult to differentiate

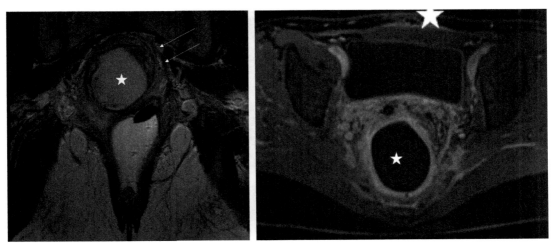

FIG. 16.28   Coronal T2W MR image through the pelvis with rectal contrast in a patient with prior segmental bowel resection for endometriosis (A) shows a thick-walled cystic structure (white star) adjacent to the rectum, displacing it to the left (white arrows). Axial T1W MR image with fat saturation and contrast enhancement (B) shows peripheral enhancement. Abscess was confirmed by percutaneous aspiration with drain placement.

from postoperative scarring, and findings may coexist, as recurrence has been noted in up to 21.5% of patients within 2 years, and 50% within 5 years.[79,80]

16.2.7.3 Endometriosis and malignancy

Although endometriosis is a benign disease, there is a well-established connection between endometriosis and ovarian malignancies. Women with endometriosis have a higher risk of developing ovarian carcinomas, especially endometrioid epithelial carcinomas and clear cell carcinomas.[81] Ovarian cancers that arise in the setting of endometriosis have been termed, "Endometriosis-associated ovarian carcinoma" (EAOC). These tumors make up a unique subtype of ovarian malignancies that tend to present at an earlier age and are associated with better prognosis.[45] It is imperative that MR imaging studies are scrutinized for imaging evidence of malignant transformation as these cases should be referred to gynecology oncology for definitive diagnosis and treatment. Imaging findings that can be used to distinguish ovarian malignancies from endometriomas were described in the Differential Diagnosis endometrioma section. One interesting imaging finding that can be a sign of malignant transformation is loss of shading on T2W images. It is thought that dilution of endometrioma contents by serous material produced by the neoplasm accounts for the change in signal on T2W images.[82] Lesion size has also been investigated as a potential risk factor for predicting malignancy in an endometrioma. The American College of Radiology took this into account when devising ORADS, upgrading the ORADS category for an endometrioma from 2 to 3 for lesions greater than 10 cm.[83]

Malignant transformation can also occur in association with extraovarian deep infiltrative endometriosis. On MR imaging, these lesions are typically solid and show intermediate signal on T1W and T2W images and show post-contrast enhancement (Fig. 16.29). Identification of a lesion such as this, in a background of endometriosis should raise suspicion for malignant transformation.[84]

16.2.7.4 Endometriosis in pregnancy

The ectopic endometrial elements of endometriosis are responsive to hormonal influences and are thus impacted by the hormonal changes of pregnancy. Given that pregnancy is dominated by higher progesterone levels and endometriosis is estrogen-dependent, most endometriosis lesions improve or completely resolve during pregnancy. A small percentage of endometriotic lesions enlarge during pregnancy.[85] This seemingly paradoxical response can be explained by the fact that progesterone supports the process of decidualization whereby the stromal layer of the endometrium hypertrophies and becomes more vascular. The ectopic endometrial elements in endometriomas and DIE may undergo decidualization during pregnancy giving rise to lesions with unusual imaging features.[86]

MR is well suited for the evaluation of endometriosis in the setting of pregnancy due to large field-of-view and excellent contrast resolution however gadolinium is not recommended in pregnancy due to an increased risk of rheumatologic, inflammatory and infiltrative skin conditions in the neonate as well as stillbirth and neonatal demise.[87]

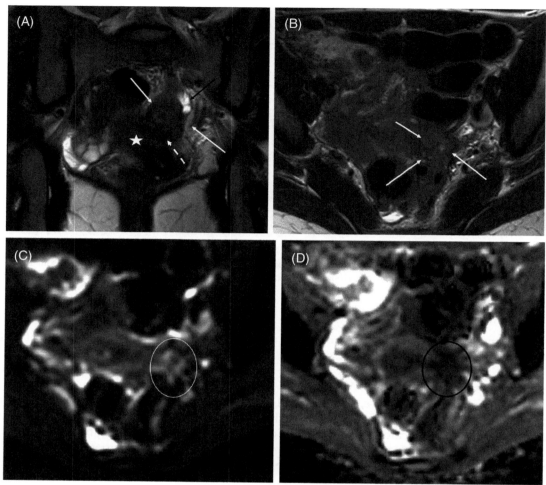

FIG. 16.29 Coronal (A) and axial (B) T2W MR images of the pelvis in a woman with endometriosis shows a left adnexal mass with mild hyperintense signal (white arrows) located between the uterus (white star) and left ovary (black arrow). Area of hypointense signal is present within the lesion posteriorly (dashed arrow). Axial high B value diffusion (C) and ADC map (D) show restricted diffusion within the lesion (white and black circle respectively). Due to these findings malignant transformation of endometriosis was suspected and the case was referred to gynecology oncology. Endometriosis with atypia was found on histopathology.

Decidualization of endometrial elements within ovarian endometriomas can result in intralesional vascular nodules and growth. On MR, the decidualized nodules are round and show similar signal characteristics as decidualized endometrium including hypointense signal on T2W sequences.[86] Decidualized DIE lesions show increased signal on T2W images compared to the pregravid state. The main differential lesions with these changes is malignancy. For ovarian lesions, smooth surface of the nodule suggests decidualization over malignancy which tends to be associated with irregular nodules. Decidualized nodules also have higher intrinsic T2W signal and higher ADC values than nodules seen in ovarian neoplasms. The presence of free fluid in the pelvis and elevated CA-125 are associated with malignancy but not pregnancy.[86]

16.3 Conclusion

MR is a powerful tool to help improve care and clinical management of endometriosis. Proper patient preparation and imaging protocol optimization can help improve lesion conspicuity. An organized search pattern and report template can help ensure that commonly involved pelvic structures are scrutinized and that actionable findings are relayed to clinicians in a reliable and useful manner (Table 16.8).

TABLE 16.8 Pearls and pitfalls.

Pearls	Pitfalls
Using a compartmental approach can reduce the risk of overlooking subtle sites of disease	Extra-pelvic sites of disease, including bowel, abdominal wall, and diaphragmatic endometriosis, are often overlooked
A specialized mr protocol aids in lesion detection	Failing to tailor the protocol to the clinical question (i.e., including sequences to evaluate the diaphragm in suspected diaphragmatic endometriosis) can result in a nondiagnostic study and suboptimal presurgical planning
Utilizing a reporting template facilitates multidisciplinary communication	Free-form dictation can undermine effective multidisciplinary communication
The T2 dark spot sign is more specific than T2 shading in distinguishing hemorrhagic cysts from endometriomas	Failing to closely scrutinize postcontrast imaging can result in missed diagnosis of malignant transformation
The posterior compartment is the most common site of die	Wall-adherent stool can be confused for colonic endometriosis
Anatomic distortion can be an indicator of die	Postoperative scar tissue is a classic DIE mimic
Middle and posterior compartment disease are often concomitant	Identification of disease in the middle compartment must prompt evaluation of the adjacent posterior compartment

References

1. Buck Louis GM, Hediger ML, Peterson CM, et al. Incidence of endometriosis by study population and diagnostic method: the ENDO study. *Fertil Steril.* 2011;96(2):360–365. doi:10.1016/j.fertnstert.2011.05.087.
2. Taylor HS, Kotlyar AM, Flores VA. Endometriosis is a chronic systemic disease: clinical challenges and novel innovations. *Lancet.* 2021;397(10276):839–852. doi:10.1016/S0140-6736(21)00389-5.
3. De Graaff AA, D'Hooghe TM, Dunselman GA, et al. The significant effect of endometriosis on physical, mental and social wellbeing: results from an international cross-sectional survey. *Hum Reprod.* 2013;28(10):2677–2685. doi:10.1093/humrep/det284.
4. Soliman AM, Yang H, Du EX, Kelley C, Winkel C. The direct and indirect costs associated with endometriosis: a systematic literature review. *Hum Reprod.* 2016;31(4):712–722. doi:10.1093/humrep/dev335.
5. Burney RO, Giudice LC. Pathogenesis and pathophysiology of endometriosis. *Fertil Steril.* 2012;98(3):511–519. doi:10.1016/j.fertnstert.2012.06.029.
6. Working group of ESGE, ESHRE, and WES, Saridogan E, Becker CM, et al. Recommendations for the surgical treatment of endometriosis-part 1: ovarian endometrioma. *Gynecol Surg.* 2017;14(1):27. doi:10.1186/s10397-017-1029-x.
7. Working group of ESGE, ESHRE, and WES, Keckstein J, Becker CM, et al. Recommendations for the surgical treatment of endometriosis. Part 2: deep endometriosis. *Hum Reprod Open.* 2020;2020(1):hoaa002. Published 2020 Feb 12. doi:10.1093/hropen/hoaa002.
8. Hindman N, Eswar C, Huang K, Tong A. Medical management of endometriosis: what the radiologist needs to know. *Abdom Radiol (NY).* 2020;45(6):1866–1871. doi:10.1007/s00261-020-02507-5.
9. Kho RM, Andres MP, Borrelli GM, Neto JS, Zanluchi A, Abrão MS. Surgical treatment of different types of endometriosis: Comparison of major society guidelines and preferred clinical algorithms. *Best Pract Res Clin Obstet Gynaecol.* 2018;51:102–110. doi:10.1016/j.bpobgyn.2018.01.020.
10. Medeiros LR, Rosa MI, Silva BR, et al. Accuracy of magnetic resonance in deeply infiltrating endometriosis: a systematic review and meta-analysis. *Arch Gynecol Obstet.* 2015;291(3):611–621. doi:10.1007/s00404-014-3470-7.
11. Chamié LP, Blasbalg R, Gonçalves MO, Carvalho FM, Abrão MS, de Oliveira IS. Accuracy of magnetic resonance imaging for diagnosis and preoperative assessment of deeply infiltrating endometriosis. *Int J Gynaecol Obstet.* 2009;106(3):198–201. doi:10.1016/j.ijgo.2009.04.013.
12. Grasso RF, Di Giacomo V, Sedati P, et al. Diagnosis of deep infiltrating endometriosis: accuracy of magnetic resonance imaging and trans-vaginal 3D ultrasonography. *Abdom Imaging.* 2010;35(6):716–725. doi:10.1007/s00261-009-9587-7.
13. Manganaro L, Fierro F, Tomei A, et al. Feasibility of 3.0T pelvic MR imaging in the evaluation of endometriosis. *Eur J Radiol.* 2012;81(6):1381–1387. doi:10.1016/j.ejrad.2011.03.049.
14. Bartlett DJ, Burkett BJ, Burnett TL, Sheedy SP, Fletcher JG, VanBuren WM. Comparison of routine pelvic US and MR imaging in patients with pathologically confirmed endometriosis. *Abdom Radiol (NY).* 2020;45(6):1670–1679. doi:10.1007/s00261-019-02124-x.

15. Krüger K, Behrendt K, Niedobitek-Kreuter G, Koltermann K, Ebert AD. Location-dependent value of pelvic MRI in the preoperative diagnosis of endometriosis. *Eur J Obstet Gynecol Reprod Biol*. 2013;169(1):93–98. doi:10.1016/j.ejogrb.2013.02.007.

16. Schneider C, Oehmke F, Tinneberg HR, Krombach GA. MRI technique for the preoperative evaluation of deep infiltrating endometriosis: current status and protocol recommendation. *Clin Radiol*. 2016;71(3):179–194. doi:10.1016/j.crad.2015.09.014.

17. Menakaya UA, Rombauts L, Johnson NP. Diagnostic laparoscopy in pre-surgical planning for higher stage endometriosis: Is it still relevant? *Aust N Z J Obstet Gynaecol*. 2016;56(5):518–522. doi:10.1111/ajo.12505.

18. Burkett BJ, Cope A, Bartlett DJ, et al. MRI impacts endometriosis management in the setting of image-based multidisciplinary conference: a retrospective analysis. *Abdom Radiol (NY)*. 2020;45(6):1829–1839. doi:10.1007/s00261-020-02417-6.

19. Gui B, Valentini AL, Ninivaggi V, Marino M, Iacobucci M, Bonomo L. Deep pelvic endometriosis: don't forget round ligaments. Review of anatomy, clinical characteristics, and MR imaging features. *Abdom Imaging*. 2014;39(3):622–632. doi:10.1007/s00261-014-0091-3.

20. Chapron C, Fauconnier A, Dubuisson JB, Barakat H, Vieira M, Bréart G. Deep infiltrating endometriosis: relation between severity of dysmenorrhoea and extent of disease. *Hum Reprod*. 2003;18(4):760–766. doi:10.1093/humrep/deg152.

21. Novellas S, Chassang M, Bouaziz J, Delotte J, Toullalan O, Chevallier EP. Anterior pelvic endometriosis: MRI features. *Abdom Imaging*. 2010;35(6):742–749. doi:10.1007/s00261-010-9600-1.

22. Chapron C, Chopin N, Borghese B, et al. Deeply infiltrating endometriosis: pathogenetic implications of the anatomical distribution. *Hum Reprod*. 2006;21(7):1839–1845. doi:10.1093/humrep/del079.

23. Kinkel K, Frei KA, Balleyguier C, Chapron C. Diagnosis of endometriosis with imaging: a review. *Eur Radiol*. 2006;16(2):285–298. doi:10.1007/s00330-005-2882-y.

24. Dallaudière B, Salut C, Hummel V, et al. MRI atlas of ectopic endometriosis. *Diagn Interv Imaging*. 2013;94(3):263–280. doi:10.1016/j.diii.2012.10.020.

25. Jaramillo-Cardoso A, Balcacer P, Garces-Descovich A, et al. Multimodality imaging and clinicopathologic assessment of abdominal wall endometriosis: knocking down the enigma. *Abdom Radiol (NY)*. 2020;45(6):1800–1812. doi:10.1007/s00261-018-1666-1.

26. Andres MP, Arcoverde FVL, Souza CCC, Fernandes LFC, Abrão MS, Kho RM. Extrapelvic endometriosis: a systematic review. *J Minim Invasive Gynecol*. 2020;27(2):373–389. doi:10.1016/j.jmig.2019.10.004.

27. Bazot M, Bharwani N, Huchon C, et al. European society of urogenital radiology (ESUR) guidelines: MR imaging of pelvic endometriosis. *Eur Radiol*. 2017;27(7):2765–2775. doi:10.1007/s00330-016-4673-z.

28. Tong A, VanBuren WM, Chamié L, et al. Recommendations for MRI technique in the evaluation of pelvic endometriosis: consensus statement from the Society of Abdominal Radiology endometriosis disease-focused panel. *Abdom Radiol (NY)*. 2020;45(6):1569–1586. doi:10.1007/s00261-020-02483-w.

29. Dillman JR, Smith EA, Khalatbari S, Strouse PJIv. glucagon use in pediatric MR enterography: effect on image quality, length of examination, and patient tolerance. *AJR Am J Roentgenol*. 2013;201(1):185–189. doi:10.2214/AJR.12.9787.

30. Bazot M, Gasner A, Ballester M, Daraï E. Value of thin-section oblique axial T2-weighted magnetic resonance images to assess uterosacral ligament endometriosis. *Hum Reprod*. 2011;26(2):346–353. doi:10.1093/humrep/deq336.

31. Bazot M, Jarboui L, Ballester M, Touboul C, Thomassin-Naggara I, Daraï E. The value of MRI in assessing parametrial involvement in endometriosis. *Hum Reprod*. 2012;27(8):2352–2358. doi:10.1093/humrep/des211.

32. Jha P, Sakala M, Chamie LP, et al. Endometriosis MRI lexicon: consensus statement from the society of abdominal radiology endometriosis disease-focused panel. *Abdom Radiol (NY)*. 2020;45(6):1552–1568. doi:10.1007/s00261-019-02291-x.

33. Togashi K, Nishimura K, Kimura I, et al. Endometrial cysts: diagnosis with MR imaging. *Radiology*. 1991;180(1):73–78. doi:10.1148/radiology.180.1.2052726.

34. Thotakura P, Dyer RB. The T2 shading sign. *Abdom Radiol (NY)*. 2016;41(12):2401–2403. doi:10.1007/s00261-016-0898-1.

35. Corwin MT, Gerscovich EO, Lamba R, Wilson M, McGahan JP. Differentiation of ovarian endometriomas from hemorrhagic cysts at MR imaging: utility of the T2 dark spot sign. *Radiology*. 2014;271(1):126–132. doi:10.1148/radiol.13131394.

36. Dias JL, Veloso Gomes F, Lucas R, Cunha TM. The shading sign: is it exclusive of endometriomas? *Abdom Imaging*. 2015;40(7):2566–2572. doi:10.1007/s00261-015-0465-1.

37. Cansu A, Bulut E, Dinc G, et al. Diagnostic efficacy of T2 dark spot, T2 dark rim signs, and T2 shading on magnetic resonance imaging in differentiating endometriomas from hemorrhagic cysts. *J Comput Assist Tomogr*. 2019;43(4):619–622. doi:10.1097/RCT.0000000000000892.

38. Mason BR, Chatterjee D, Menias CO, Thaker PH, Siegel CL, Yano M. Encyclopedia of endometriosis: a pictorial rad-path review. *Abdom Radiol (NY)*. 2020;45(6):1587–1607. doi:10.1007/s00261-019-02381-w.

39. Cornillie FJ, Oosterlynck D, Lauweryns JM, Koninckx PR. Deeply infiltrating pelvic endometriosis: histology and clinical significance. *Fertil Steril*. 1990;53(6):978–983. doi:10.1016/s0015-0282(16)53570-5.

40. Siegelman ES, Oliver ER. MR imaging of endometriosis: ten imaging pearls. *Radiographics*. 2012;32(6):1675–1691. doi:10.1148/rg.326125518.

41. Williams JC, Burnett TL, Jones T, Venkatesh SK, VanBuren WM. Association between kissing and retropositioned ovaries and severity of endometriosis: MR imaging evaluation. *Abdom Radiol (NY)*. 2020;45(6):1637–1644. doi:10.1007/s00261-019-02153-6.

42. Ghafoor S, Lakhman Y, Park KJ, Petkovska I. Polypoid endometriosis: a mimic of malignancy. *Abdom Radiol (NY)*. 2020;45(6):1776–1782. doi:10.1007/s00261-019-02143-8.

43. Kanso HN, Hachem K, Aoun NJ, et al. Variable MR findings in ovarian functional hemorrhagic cysts. *J Magn Reson Imaging*. 2006;24(2):356–361. doi:10.1002/jmri.20640.

44. Ha HK, Lim GY, Cha ES, et al. MR imaging of tubo-ovarian abscess. *Acta Radiol*. 1995;36(5):510–514.

45. Robinson KA, Menias CO, Chen L, et al. Understanding malignant transformation of endometriosis: imaging features with pathologic correlation. *Abdom Radiol (NY)*. 2020;45(6):1762–1775. doi:10.1007/s00261-019-01914-7.

46. Forstner R, Thomassin-Naggara I, Cunha TM, et al. ESUR recommendations for MR imaging of the sonographically indeterminate adnexal mass: an update [published correction appears in Eur Radiol. 2017 Jun;27(6):2258]. *Eur Radiol*. 2017;27(6):2248–2257. doi:10.1007/s00330-016-4600-3.

47. Takeuchi M, Matsuzaki K, Uehara H, Nishitani H. Malignant transformation of pelvic endometriosis: MR imaging findings and pathologic correlation. *Radiographics*. 2006;26(2):407–417. doi:10.1148/rg.262055041.

48. Mandai M, Yamaguchi K, Matsumura N, Baba T, Konishi I. Ovarian cancer in endometriosis: molecular biology, pathology, and clinical management. *Int J Clin Oncol*. 2009;14(5):383–391. doi:10.1007/s10147-009-0935-y.

49. Busard MP, Mijatovic V, Lüchinger AB, et al. MR imaging of bladder endometriosis and its relationship with the anterior uterine wall: experience in a tertiary referral centre. *Eur J Radiol*. 2012;81(9):2106–2111. doi:10.1016/j.ejrad.2011.08.007.

50. Juri H, Narumi Y, Panebianco V, Osuga K. Staging of bladder cancer with multiparametric MRI. *Br J Radiol*. 2020;93(1112):20200116. doi:10.1259/bjr.20200116.

51. Dwyer PL, Rosamilia A. Congenital urogenital anomalies that are associated with the persistence of Gartner's duct: a review. *Am J Obstet Gynecol*. 2006;195(2):354–359. doi:10.1016/j.ajog.2005.10.815.

52. Vercellini P, Viganò P, Somigliana E, Daguati R, Abbiati A, Fedele L. Adenomyosis: epidemiological factors. *Best Pract Res Clin Obstet Gynaecol*. 2006;20(4):465–477. doi:10.1016/j.bpobgyn.2006.01.017.

53. Agostinho L, Cruz R, Osório F, Alves J, Setúbal A, Guerra A. MRI for adenomyosis: a pictorial review. *Insights Imaging*. 2017;8(6):549–556. doi:10.1007/s13244-017-0576-z.

54. Bolan C, Caserta MP. MR imaging of atypical fibroids. *Abdom Radiol (NY)*. 2016;41(12):2332–2349. doi:10.1007/s00261-016-0935-0.

55. Balcacer P, Shergill A, Litkouhi B. MRI of cervical cancer with a surgical perspective: staging, prognostic implications and pitfalls. *Abdom Radiol (NY)*. 2019;44(7):2557–2571. doi:10.1007/s00261-019-01984-7.

56. Gardner CS, Sunil J, Klopp AH, et al. Primary vaginal cancer: role of MRI in diagnosis, staging and treatment. *Br J Radiol*. 2015;88(1052):20150033. doi:10.1259/bjr.20150033.

57. Horvat N, Carlos Tavares Rocha C, Clemente Oliveira B, Petkovska I, Gollub MJ. MRI of rectal cancer: tumor staging, imaging techniques, and management. *Radiographics*. 2019;39(2):367–387. doi:10.1148/rg.2019180114.

58. Braschi-Amirfarzan M, Keraliya AR, Krajewski KM, et al. Role of imaging in management of desmoid-type fibromatosis: a primer for radiologists. *Radiographics*. 2016;36(3):767–782. doi:10.1148/rg.2016150153.

59. Feldman MK, VanBuren WM, Barnard H, Taffel MT and Kho RM. Systematic interpretation and structured reporting for pelvis magnetic resonance imaging studies in patients with endometriosis: value added for improved patient care. Abdominal Radiology 2020;45(6); 1608–1622. doi:10.1007/s00261-019-02182-1.

60. Jaramillo-Cardoso A, Shenoy-Bhangle A, Garces-Descovich A, Glickman J, King L, Mortele KJ. Pelvic MRI in the diagnosis and staging of pelvic endometriosis: added value of structured reporting and expertise. *Abdom Radiol (NY)*. 2020;45(6):1623–1636. doi:10.1007/s00261-019-02199-6.

61. Chapron C, Bourret A, Chopin N, et al. Surgery for bladder endometriosis: long-term results and concomitant management of associated posterior deep lesions. *Hum Reprod*. 2010;25(4):884–889. doi:10.1093/humrep/deq017.

62. Agely A, Bolan C, Metcalfe A, VanBuren W, Menias C. Genitourinary manifestations of endometriosis with emphasis on the urinary tract. *Abdom Radiol (NY)*. 2020;45(6):1711–1722. doi:10.1007/s00261-019-02383-8.

63. Burnett TL, Feldman MK, Huang JQ. The role of imaging as a guide to the surgical treatment of endometriosis. Abdom Radiol. 2020; 45:1840–1846.

64. Bennett GL, Slywotzky CM, Cantera M, Hecht EM. Unusual manifestations and complications of endometriosis–spectrum of imaging findings: pictorial review. *AJR Am J Roentgenol*. 2010;194(6 Suppl):WS34–WS46. doi:10.2214/AJR.07.7142.

65. Kilcoyne A, O'Shea A, Gervais DA, Lee SI. Hysterosalpingography in endometriosis: performance and interpretation. *Abdom Radiol (NY)*. 2020;45(6):1680–1693. doi:10.1007/s00261-019-02373-w.

66. Jaramillo-Cardoso A, Shenoy-Bhangle AS, VanBuren WM, Schiappacasse G, Menias CO, Mortele KJ. Imaging of gastrointestinal endometriosis: what the radiologist should know. *Abdom Radiol (NY)*. 2020;45(6):1694–1710. doi:10.1007/s00261-020-02459-w.

67. Jung Hwan Y, Choi D, Jang K-T, Kim CK, Kim H, Lee SJ, Chun Ho-K, Lee WY, Yun SH. Deep rectosigmoid endometriosis: mushroom cap sign on T2-weighted MR imaging. *Abdom Imaging*. 2010 Dec;35(6):726–731. doi:10.1007/s00261-010-9643-3.

68. Rousset P, Buisson G, Lega JC, et al. Rectal endometriosis: predictive MRI signs for segmental bowel resection. *Eur Radiol*. 2021;31(2):884–894. doi:10.1007/s00330-020-07170-4.

69. Welch BT, Ehman EC, VanBuren WM, et al. Percutaneous cryoablation of abdominal wall endometriosis: the Mayo Clinic approach. *Abdom Radiol (NY)*. 2020;45(6):1813–1817. doi:10.1007/s00261-019-02379-4.

70. Bazot M, Kermarrec E, Bendifallah S, Daraï E. MRI of intestinal endometriosis. *Best Pract Res Clin Obstet Gynaecol*. 2021;71:51–63. doi:10.1016/j.bpobgyn.2020.05.013.

71. Mabrouk M, Raimondo D, Mastronardi M, et al. Endometriosis of the appendix: when to predict and how to manage—a multivariate analysis of 1935 endometriosis cases. *J Minim Invasive Gynecol*. 2020;27(1):100–106. doi:10.1016/j.jmig.2019.02.015.

72. Siquara De Sousa AC, Capek S, Amrami KK, Spinner RJ. Neural involvement in endometriosis: review of anatomic distribution and mechanisms. *Clin Anat*. 2015;28(8):1029–1038. doi:10.1002/ca.22617.

73. Moura Filho JP, Leão RV, Horvat N, et al. What abdominal radiologists should know about extragenital endometriosis-associated neuropathy. *Abdom Radiol (NY)*. 2020;45(6):1818–1828. doi:10.1007/s00261-018-1864-x.

74. Practice Committee of the American Society for Reproductive Medicine. Treatment of pelvic pain associated with endometriosis: a committee opinion [published correction appears in Fertil Steril. 2015 Aug;104(2):498]. *Fertil Steril*. 2014;101(4):927–935. doi:10.1016/j.fertnstert.2014.02.012.

75. Falcone T, Flyckt R. Clinical management of endometriosis. *Obstet Gynecol*. 2018 Mar;131(3):557–571. doi:10.1097/AOG.0000000000002469.

76. Harada T, Kosaka S, Elliesen J, Yasuda M, Ito M, Momoeda M. Ethinylestradiol 20 μg/drospirenone 3 mg in a flexible extended regimen for the management of endometriosis-associated pelvic pain: a randomized controlled trial. *Fertil Steril*. 2017;108(5):798–805. doi:10.1016/j.fertnstert.2017.07.1165.

77. Khan Z. Fertility-related considerations in endometriosis. *Abdom Radiol (NY)*. 2020;45(6):1754–1761. doi:10.1007/s00261-019-02307-6.

78. Guerra A, Daraï E, Osório F, et al. Imaging of postoperative endometriosis. *Diagn Interv Imaging*. 2019;100(10):607–618. doi:10.1016/j.diii.2018.11.003.

79. Chamié LP, Ribeiro D, Ribeiro G, Serafini PC. Postoperative imaging findings after laparoscopic surgery for deeply infiltrating endometriosis. *Abdom Radiol (NY)*. 2020;45(6):1847–1865. doi:10.1007/s00261-020-02434-5.

80. Guo SW. Recurrence of endometriosis and its control. *Hum Reprod Update*. 2009;15(4):441–461. doi:10.1093/humupd/dmp007.

81. Heidemann LN, Hartwell D, Heidemann CH, Jochumsen KM. The relation between endometriosis and ovarian cancer: a review. *Acta Obstet Gynecol Scand*. 2014;93(1):20–31. doi:10.1111/aogs.12255.

82. Tanaka YO, Yoshizako T, Nishida M, Yamaguchi M, Sugimura K, Itai Y. Ovarian carcinoma in patients with endometriosis: MR imaging findings. *AJR Am J Roentgenol.* 2000;175(5):1423–1430. doi:10.2214/ajr.175.5.1751423.

83. Strachowski LM, Jha P, Chawla TP, et al. O-RADS for ultrasound: a user's guide, from the *AJR* special series on radiology reporting and data systems. *AJR Am J Roentgenol.* 2021;216(5):1150–1165. doi:10.2214/AJR.20.25064.

84. McDermott S, Oei TN, Iyer VR, Lee SI. MR imaging of malignancies arising in endometriomas and extraovarian endometriosis. *Radiographics.* 2012;32(3):845–863. doi:10.1148/rg.323115736.

85. Leeners B, Damaso F, Ochsenbein-Kölble N, Farquhar C. The effect of pregnancy on endometriosis-facts or fiction? *Hum Reprod Update.* 2018;24(3):290–299. doi:10.1093/humupd/dmy004.

86. Navarro R, Poder L, Sun D, Jha P. Endometriosis in pregnancy. *Abdom Radiol (NY).* 2020;45(6):1741–1753. doi:10.1007/s00261-020-02486-7.

87. Ray JG, Vermeulen MJ, Bharatha A, Montanera WJ, Park AL. Association between MRI exposure during pregnancy and fetal and childhood outcomes. *JAMA.* 2016;316(9):952–961. doi:10.1001/jama.2016.12126.

17

MRI of benign nonneoplastic female pelvic pathologies

Martina Sbarra[a], Teresa M. Cunha[b], Stephanie Nougaret[c,d]

[a]Departmental Faculty of Medicine and Surgery, Unit of Diagnostic Imaging and Interventional Radiology, Università Campus Bio-Medico di Roma, Rome, Italy [b]Department of Radiology, Instituto Português de Oncologia de Lisboa Francisco Gentil, Lisboa Codex, Portugal [c]IRCM, Montpellier Cancer Research institute, Montpellier, France [d]Department of Radiology, Montpellier Cancer institute, INSERM, University of Montpellier, Montpellier, France

17.1 Introduction

Magnetic resonance imaging (MRI) is routinely performed in female pelvic imaging. MRI offers a multiplanar capability and a high soft tissue contrast that allows an accurate anatomic characterization of the pelvis and an excellent depiction of the zonal anatomy. Therefore, it is very useful for loco-regional characterization of female pelvic diseases. In addition, MRI is crucial not only to establish a definitive diagnosis but also to guide the appropriate patient management. Thus, although ultrasound (US) is the first-line imaging modality in the evaluation of female pelvic pathologies, MRI has become more and more important for the assessment and management of gynecologic diseases into the clinical workflow.[1]

Benign female pelvic pathologies are very frequent conditions affecting women of all ages. They represent a common cause of gynecologic symptoms such as pelvic pain, menorrhagia, and infertility, but can also be an incidental finding in asymptomatic patients. The spectrum of common benign non-neoplastic pathologies of the female pelvis (ovarian and nonovarian) will be highlighted in this chapter with a special focus on MRI features and key imaging characteristics. A practical approach to define the origin of an unknown pelvic lesion at MRI will also be provided.

17.2 Magnetic resonance imaging

MRI continues to be an important problem-solving tool in the evaluation of congenital anomalies and acquired diseases of the female genital tract organs when ultrasound is technically suboptimal or the results are equivocal.[2] The increasing use of pelvic MRI in the recent years has been due to technological innovations and significant improvement in image quality. However, imaging quality is not only influenced by improved techniques but also by patient-related factors.[3]

17.2.1 Patient preparation

The female pelvis is an anatomic region more prone to MRI artifacts related to multiple factors, such as motion from respiration and bowel peristalsis, and susceptibility secondary to bowel gas.[4] Although technical developments, such as dedicated pelvic phase-array coils, saturation band, and accelerated acquisition are essential to improve the

Magnetic Resonance Imaging of The Pelvis.
DOI: https://doi.org/10.1016/B978-0-323-89854-6.00009-0

image quality, a proper patient preparation is crucial to reduce the image artifacts. Thereby, European Society of Urogenital Radiology (ESUR) guidelines have tried to standardize the patient preparation protocols.[5–7]

- Fasting is recommended (3–6 hours), especially when intravenous (iv) gadolinium injection is considered. Fasting should reduce the bowel motion artifacts and the risk of vomiting as a reaction of contrast medium injection.
- Use of antispasmodic drugs (intramuscular/intravenous butylscopolamine or intravenous glucagon) is recommended to reduce bowel motion artifacts unless it is contraindicated.
- A moderately full urinary bladder is suggested in clinical practice to correct the angle of uterine anteversion and to provide a better delineation of fat between the bladder and uterus; patients should empty their bladder 1 hour prior to examination to achieve a moderately filled urinary bladder.
- Rectal enema to clean the bowel is optional but it should be advocated as "best practice" in the study of pelvic bowel endometriosis.[8]
- Vaginal and/or rectal opacification with ultrasound gel is optional in the evaluation of deep pelvic posterior or bowel endometriosis.
- Scheduling exam according to menstrual cycle is not necessary.
- Avoid vaginal tampons.

17.2.2 Imaging protocols

High-resolution thin-section images acquired at 1.5 T or 3 T are recommended.
The imaging protocols should be tailored to the main indication for pelvic MRI.

- High resolution T2-weighted (T2-W) sequences without fat suppression are the best sequences to study the female pelvis; in this sense, at least two orthogonal T2-W planes should be performed in each examination. However, three-dimensional (3D)-T2-W sequence has recently become available and can potentially replace the standard two-dimensional (2D)-T2-W sequences acquired in multiple different planes (sagittal, axial, coronal, oblique). The 3D-T2-W sequence may allow multiplanar reformatting after the acquisition, especially useful in the assessment of the female genital tract congenital anomalies and may also serve to shorten abbreviated protocols.[6,7,9,10]
- Axial 2D-T2-W oblique planes should be oriented (1) perpendicular to the uterine body longitudinal axis to study uterine pathologies, (2) perpendicular to the endocervical canal to evaluate cervix pathologies, and (3) parallel to the uterine body longitudinal axis when a doubt remain if a pelvic mass originates from the ovaries or the uterus (Fig. 17.1).[5,11]
- Axial T1-W sequence with and without fat suppression is useful to detect high signal intensity lesions. T1-W sequence with fat saturation allows the characterization and distinction of hemorrhagic and fatty lesions (lipoleiomyoma vs. leiomyoma with hemorrhagic degeneration; hematometra, hematocolpos, endometriosis, teratomas).[5,7]

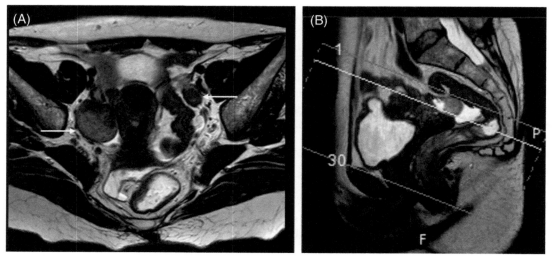

FIG. 17.1   **Axial 2D-T2-W oblique plane.** Axial oblique T2-W image (A) shows bilateral ovarian fibroma (arrows). The oblique plane is oriented parallel to the uterine body longitudinal axis (B).

- Large field of view T1-W or T2-W sequences of upper abdomen—acquired on axial or coronal plane from renal hila to pubic bone—allow visualization of the kidneys and ureters in the setting of the female genital tract congenital anomalies and help the evaluation of the secondary signs of pelvic mass effect such as hydronephrosis.[7,8]
- Diffusion-weighted imaging (DWI) has shown added value for lesion characterization.[12]
- Contrast-enhanced T1-W images with fat saturation allow lesion characterization and vascularization.
- MR-angiography is an additional study useful to determine details about pelvic vasculature before embolization treatment.[5]
- MR-urography can be added in cases of hydronephrosis secondary to ureteral obstruction (Fig. 17.2).

Learning point: *poor MRI protocols lead to poor MRI reports.*

17.2.3 Fast MRI protocols

Abbreviated MRI protocols are faster examinations and a potential lower-cost alternative to the standard MRI protocols. The rationale behind these new abbreviated MRI protocols is to reduce the number of sequences and to accelerate the acquisition time, without compromising diagnostic information.[9] Proposed abbreviated MRI protocols in the female pelvis are for postmenopausal ovarian cyst surveillance, cervical or uterine cancer staging and Mullerian duct anomalies evaluation (Table 17.1). Limited data are available about these new applications and some of these are not yet supported by professional society guidelines, therefore the abbreviated protocols should be used with caution in clinical practice.[9]

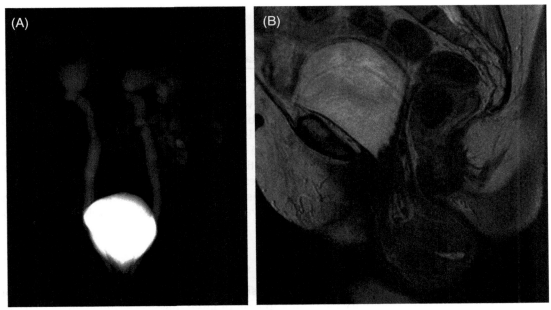

FIG. 17.2   **Uterine prolapse associated with bilateral hydronephrosis in a 75-year-old woman with a bulging perineal mass.** MR-urography (A) shows bilateral hydronephrosis secondary to uterine prolapse. Sagittal T2-WI (B) shows severe uterine prolapse (grade 3) in the middle pelvic compartment.

TABLE 17.1   Proposed abbreviated MRI protocols for the female pelvis.

Clinical indications	Abbreviated protocols
Postmenopausal ovarian cyst surveillance	- Axial T1-W sequence - 3D-T2-W sequence - Axial DWI
Cervical or uterine cancer staging	- High resolution axial oblique 2D-T2-W sequence - 3D-T2-W sequence - Axial DWI - Axial of the cervix or uterus DWI
Mullerian duct anomalies	- Axial T1-W sequence - 3D-T2-W sequence - Coronal T2-W sequence for upper abdomen

17.2.4 MRI and pregnancy

MRI is an imaging modality suitable for pregnant women because it does not use ionizing radiations; no harmful effects are known to the pregnant woman or to the fetus due to exposure to magnetic field and radiofrequency pulses used in the diagnostic setting.[13,14] In 2013, the American College of Radiology (ACR) asserted that pregnant women can undergo MRI when the potential benefits outweigh the theoretical risks, in particular (1) if the information requested cannot be obtained through alternative imaging modalities (e.g., ultrasound), (2) if the MRI provides information that can influence the patient care during pregnancy, and (3) when it is imprudent to postpone the imaging study after delivery.[15] The ACR also stated that there are no considerations for the first trimester of pregnancy. No scientific evidence suggests a significant increased risk for the fetus during the first trimester, which is the period of active organogenesis, but its long-term security has not been yet studied.[16,17] The examination should last as short as possible to reduce maternal fatigue and fetus' risks: fast sequences should be preferred (fast spin echo—FSE, SSFSE). Moreover, the radiofrequency pulses deposit energy in the body in form of heat that is quantified as specific absorption rate (SAR): to limit significant modification of fetal thermoregulation, low SAR sequences (steady state free precession—SSFP or gradient echo—GRE) should be favored.[14] The use of gadolinium-based contrast media should be avoided because it crosses the placenta. MR-angiography, MR-cholangiopancreatography, MR-urography could be used, alternative to contrast-enhanced imaging, to obtain high quality imaging of vascular system, biliary tree, and urinary tract.[17] The main applications of MRI during pregnancy are maternal acute abdomen (acute appendicitis), maternal neoplasms (benign and malignant), uterine anomalies (acquired or congenital) and placenta disorders.[18]

17.3 Benign non-neoplastic ovarian and adnexal pathologies

The vast majority of encountered ovarian lesions are benign and can be detected incidentally or associated with pelvic pain. US is the first line imaging modality in women with suspected ovarian pathology and in most cases other imaging examinations are not warranted.[19] However, about 20–25% of ovarian lesions remain indeterminate after initial ultrasound evaluation: in these cases, MRI should be considered as a problem-solver exam because of its higher ability to characterize adnexal pathologies.[20,21] Some studies suggest the use of MRI as a second examination to (1) decrease the number of sonographically false-positive diagnoses of tumor and (2) to potentially reduce the number of unnecessary surgical intervention for benign lesions.[22]

In the assessment of ovarian and adnexal lesions a stepwise approach should be followed: (1) define the exact origin of a pelvic lesion and (2) if the pelvic lesion is ovarian, differentiate physiological from pathological findings.[23]

17.3.1 How to define ovarian or extra-ovarian origin of a pelvic lesion

- Identification of a lesion completely separated from the ipsilateral ovary suggests its extra-ovarian origin. Instead, absence of normal ipsilateral ovary especially in case of large masses (*phantom organ sign*), or presence of ovarian follicles around a lesion suggest ovarian origin (Fig. 17.3).[24,25]
- If a normal ipsilateral ovary is not recognized, the ovarian vascular pedicle can be tracked from the retroperitoneum to the pelvis as an excellent anatomical landmark: if a gonadal vessel joins a pelvic lesion, the lesion has an ovarian origin (Fig. 17.4) (*ovarian vascular pedicle sign*).[26,27] The gonadal (ovarian) veins are located anterior to the psoas muscle. The right ovarian vein drains into the inferior vena cava and the left ovarian vein drains into the left renal vein.
- If the lesion abuts the ovary, the interface between the ovary and the lesion should be analyzed. When a mass deforms the edge of adjacent ovary into a "beak" shape, it is likely that the lesion arises from the ovary (Fig. 17.3) (*beak sign*). On the other hand, ovarian dull edges suggest that the mass compresses the ovary but does not arise from it.[28,29] In contrast, *claw sign* (Fig. 17.5) and *bridging vessels sign* (Fig. 17.6) are used to indicate that the mass originates from the uterus.[24,30,31]

Learning point: phantom organ sign, ovarian vascular pedicle sign, and beak sign are used to indicate that a lesion originates from the ovary.

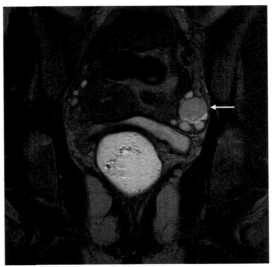

FIG. 17.3 Beak sign. Coronal T2-WI shows a cystic lesion (teratoma—arrow) with the beak sign in its contact surface with the left ovary. The presence of beak sign and follicles around the lesion are suggestive of its ovarian origin.

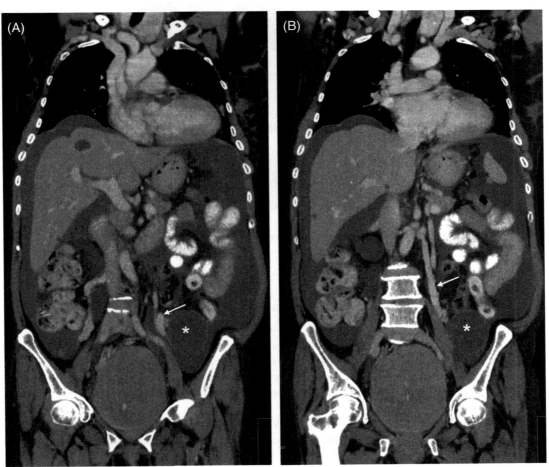

FIG. 17.4 Vascular pedicle sign. In these postcontrast coronal CT images (A and B) the left gonadal vein is distended (arrows), indicating increased blood flow from the tumor (asterisks) on the ipsilateral side, pointing out the origin of the tumor to the left ovary. The left gonadal vein joins the left ovarian tumor (A).

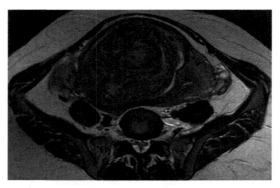

FIG. 17.5   Claw sign. A claw like extension of the myometrium surrounding the lesion is typically produced by subserosal uterine leiomyomas, as seen on this axial T2-WI.

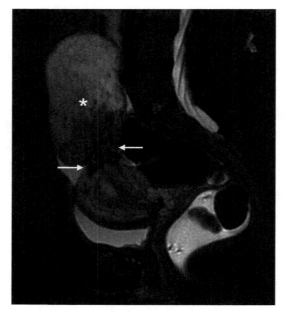

FIG. 17.6   Bridging vessels sign. Sagittal T2-WI with fat suppression shows the presence of bridging vessels (arrows) in the interface between a subserosal leiomyoma (asterisk) and the uterus; the subserosal leiomyoma has hydropic degeneration.

17.3.2 Normal ovaries in pre- and postmenopausal age and functional cysts

The typical ovarian position is laterally to the pelvic sidewall into a peritoneal depression known as ovarian fossa. The ovarian fossa is bounded posteriorly by the ureter and internal iliac artery, superiorly by the external iliac vein and anteriorly by the obliterated umbilical artery.[27] However, the position of the ovaries is variable (superior and posterior to the uterine fundus, in posterior pelvic cul-de-sac, above the pelvic rim in the paracolic gutter) due to ovarian mobility associated with ligamentous laxity especially in parous women, adhesions, inflammations, and surgery.[32]

The common appearance of normal ovaries changes over the female life's span, mainly because of the influence of the hormones on the reproductive organs.[33] Therefore, knowledge of MRI-related normal findings can be expected to aid the early identification of ovarian pathologies.[34]

In the premenopausal age, ovaries are easily recognized on MRI as ovoid structures with high T2 signal intensity (SI) follicles. The presence of follicles facilitates the identification of the ovaries in women in reproductive age. At MR imaging, most premenopausal ovaries on T2-weighted images (WI) exhibit a zonal anatomy with the medulla showing higher SI than the cortex (Fig. 17.7A).[35] On DWI sequences at any b value normal premenopausal ovaries show high SI, especially in the luteal phase (Fig. 17.7).[36,37]

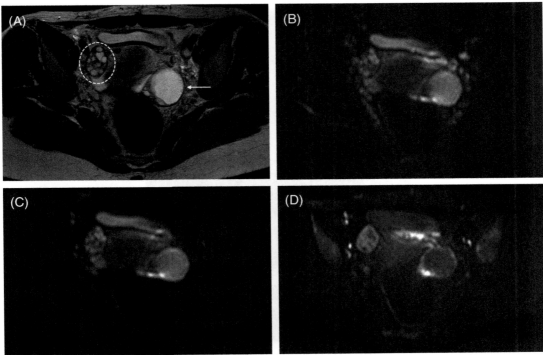

FIG. 17.7 **Normal ovaries in premenopausal age.** Axial T2-WI (A) shows normal ovaries with bilateral multiple follicles and a functional cyst in the left ovary (arrow). The normal zonal anatomy of the right ovary is shown as increased T2 signal intensity within the medulla relative to the cortex (A, white circle). On DWI images (B, b value: 0 s/mm^2; C, b value: 200 s/mm^2; D, b value: 1000 s/mm^2) the normal ovaries show high signal intensity at any b value.

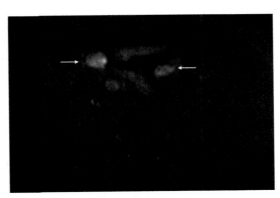

FIG. 17.8 **Bilateral ovarian metastases of a clear cell cervical carcinoma in postmenopausal age.** DWI image at high b value (b value: 1000 s/mm^2) shows ovaries with high SI (arrows), a finding that should suggest malignancy in postmenopausal age.

In the postmenopausal age, ovaries are smaller in size and generally lack of follicles. At MR imaging, postmenopausal ovaries usually show a more homogeneous low T2 SI, without exhibiting a zonal anatomy.[35,38] Diffusion restriction is not generally found on DWI sequences; therefore, high SI on DWI sequences in postmenopausal ovaries should suggest a pathologic finding (Fig. 17.8).

17.3.2.1 *Physiological cyst*

In women of reproductive age ovarian cysts ≤3 cm are called physiological cysts and include follicles at various stage of development and corpus luteum.[35,39] Follicles are unilocular simple cysts with high T2 SI, low T1 SI, and no enhancement on postcontrast T1-WI.[22] A dominant follicle can enlarge by 20–25 mm.[38]

Corpus luteum is a transient hormone-producing structure at the site of a follicle that has release an oocyte, generally visible in the secretory phase of the menstrual cycle and persist into the first trimester of pregnancy.[33] In nonpregnant women corpus luteum cyst derives from a failure of regression or hemorrhage into the corpus luteum.

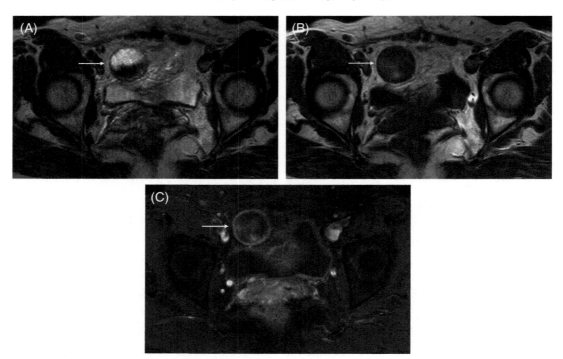

FIG. 17.9 **Corpus luteum cyst.** (A) Axial T2-WI shows a right ovarian cystic structure with variable SI due to blood products (arrow). (B) Axial T1-WI shows high SI along the inner and caudal portion of the right ovarian cyst (arrow), a finding that confirms the presence of blood products. (C) Axial postcontrast T1-WI with fat suppression shows a diffusely thick wall of the cystic structure that enhances (arrow).

The corpus luteum cyst has usually a diffusely thick wall that enhances on postcontrast T1-WI (Fig. 17.9).[22] A hemosiderin deposit with high T1 SI may be observed along the inner portion of the cyst (Fig. 17.9B).[38]

Learning point: follicles and corpus luteum cyst are normal findings; description in the MRI report is not required; follow up is not recommended.

17.3.2.2 *Unilocular functional cyst*

In the premenopausal age simple unilocular ovarian cysts >3 cm (but less than 10 cm) are considered functional cysts.[40] Functional cysts derive from a failure of follicular involution or ovulation.[38] They are generally asymptomatic and resolve spontaneously or become smaller within 3 months.[41] When simple cysts are greater than 3 cm, they should be described but do not need follow-up imaging unless they are greater than 5–7 cm.[41] The timing of follow-up is 2–6 months to evaluate resolution or characterization, and 6–12 months to assess the rate of growth.[41]

In the postmenopausal age simple ovarian cyst ≤1 cm is likely benign and can be safely ignored (cortical inclusion cyst, residual follicles, paraovarian cyst). In contrast, simple cysts greater than 1 cm should be described but do not need follow-up imaging unless they are greater than 3–5 cm.[41,42] The timing of follow-up is 3–6 months for characterization, and 6–12 months to assess rate of growth.[41]

At MR imaging the SI of simple fluid cyst is high on T2-WI, low on T1-WI, no enhancement on postcontrast T1-WI and no diffusion restriction on DWI (Fig. 17.10).

Learning point: size threshold for follow-up of simple ovarian cyst is greater than 5–7 cm in premenopausal age and greater than 3–5 cm in postmenopausal age.

17.3.2.3 *Hemorrhagic cyst*

The most common complication of functional cyst is bleeding, including follicular cyst, or corpus luteal cyst. The hemorrhage may be limited within the cyst or may cause external bleeding presenting with acute pelvic pain. The SI of hemorrhagic cyst is variable on T2-WI, T1-WI and DWI, depending on the different age of bleeding.[22,43] Subacute hemorrhage shows high T2 SI and high T1 SI (Fig. 17.11). The blood of hemorrhagic cyst can show high SI on DWI at high b value and low SI on ADC map; thereby they may mimic a malignant lesion. Correlating DWI with

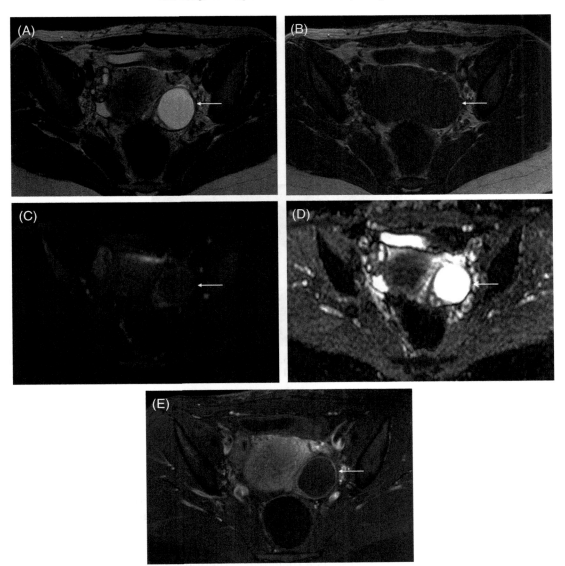

FIG. 17.10 **Unilocular left ovarian functional cyst in premenopausal age.** At MR imaging the signal intensity of simple fluid cyst is high on T2-WI (A, arrow), low on T1-WI (B, arrow), low on DWI (C, arrow) and high on ADC map (D, arrow), and no enhancement on postcontrast T1-WI with fat suppression (E, arrow).

the morphologic sequences (T2-WI and T1-WI) is mandatory to avoid potential pitfalls.[36] The main differential diagnosis of hemorrhagic cyst is endometrioma (Fig. 17.12).

17.3.2.4 *Paraovarian cyst*

Paraovarian (paratubal) cysts arise from the mesosalpinx between the ovary and fallopian tube. The ipsilateral ovary is not generally affected and maintains its normal morphology.[44,45] Paraovarian cysts are variable in size and most commonly occur in middle-aged women. Despite they are usually single cysts, multiple unilateral and bilateral paraovarian cysts have been reported.[46] At MR imaging, the identification of an adnexal cyst completely separated from the ipsilateral ovary is suggestive of paraovarian cyst (Fig. 17.13), which appears as a well-defined structure with high T2 SI and low T1 SI.[44,45] If the cyst is complicated by torsion or hemorrhage, may show high T1 SI and/ or thick wall.[45] The main differential diagnosis of paraovarian cyst include simple functional cyst, peritoneal inclusion cyst, or dilated tube.

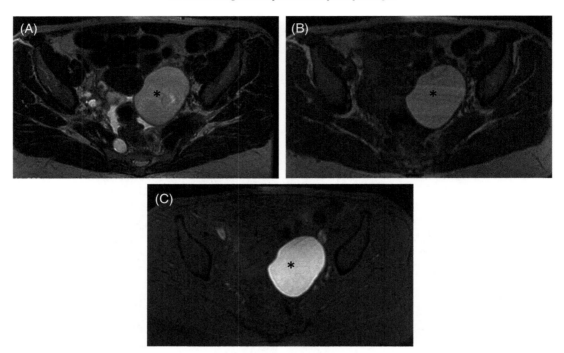

FIG. 17.11   Hemorrhagic left ovarian cyst in a 45-year-old woman. On MR imaging the signal intensity of hemorrhagic fluid is variable depending on age; late subacute hemorrhage is hyperintense on T2-WI (A, asterisk), hyperintense on T1-WI (B, asterisk) and hyperintense on T1-WI with fat suppression (C, asterisk).

17.3.3   Multicystic ovaries

17.3.3.1   *Multifollicular ovary*

Multifollicular ovary is a normal variant more frequent in young age and puberty. It is characterized by multiple small follicles (4–10 mm) with random distribution, located within a normal amount of ovarian stroma (Fig. 17.14).[47]

17.3.3.2   *Polycystic ovary*

Polycystic ovarian morphology (PCOM) represents a diagnostic criterion for polycystic ovary syndrome (PCOS) along with clinical/biochemical hyperandrogenism and chronic ovulatory disfunction.[48] Therefore, PCOM alone is not specific for the diagnosis of PCOS, especially in adolescent patients.[48] The imaging modality of choice to diagnose PCOS is transvaginal US, but MRI should be considered when ultrasound is limited (obese or virginal patients). The typical MRI features of PCOM are bilaterally enlarged ovaries with multiple (>20–25) peripherally located follicles (2–9 mm), associated with enlarged central stroma with low T2 and T1 SI (Fig. 17.15).[19,49] A dark cortical rim around the ovary on T2-WI, corresponding to superficial cortical fibrosis, is an MRI ancillary feature that can be used for the diagnosis of PCOS.[49]

   Learning point: imaging findings alone are not specific, but identification of multiple peripheral cysts beneath the ovarian capsule may help in the consideration of PCOS.

17.3.3.3   *Theca lutein cyst (hyperreactio luteinalis)*

Theca lutein cysts are rare functional ovarian masses secondary to overstimulation of the ovaries by endogenous or exogenous gonadotropins, usually in the setting of assisted fertility, gestational trophoblastic disease, or multiple gestations.[50] The imaging features are typical: bilateral marked ovarian enlargement (up to 10–20 cm in size) with multiple uniform-sized cysts (2–3 cm) that are composed of simple fluid. Residual ovarian parenchyma within the enlarged ovaries (high T2 SI, high SI on DWI, and intense enhancement on postcontrast imaging) may mimic solid tissue of multilocular cystic ovarian neoplastic mass; therefore, recognition of the morphologic features of theca lutein cysts, into the appropriate clinical context, is important in making the correct diagnosis (Fig. 17.16).[51]

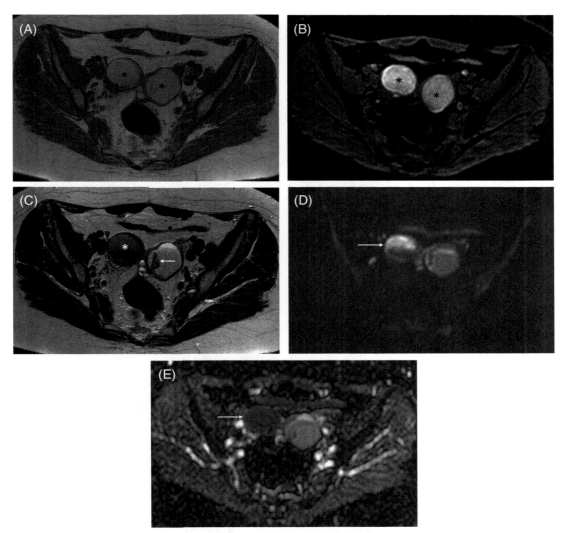

FIG. 17.12 Bilateral ovarian endometriomas in a 45-year-old woman. Axial T1-WI (A) and axial T1-WI with fat suppression (B) show bilateral adnexal lesions with spontaneous high signal intensity (asterisks). On axial T2-WI (C) the right adnexal lesion shows heterogeneous loss of signal (asterisk), whereas the left adnexal lesion shows high signal intensity with focus of hypointensity (T2 dark spot sign, arrow). DWI (D) and the corresponding ADC map (E) show a restricted diffusion of the adnexal lesions, more evident in the right side (arrow).

17.3.3.4 *Ovarian hyperstimulation syndrome (OHSS)*

OHSS is a rare and potentially fatal iatrogenic complication of ovulation induction or ovarian stimulation. It usually occurs during the luteal phase of the menstrual cycle or in early pregnancy, following endogenous or exogenous administration of luteinizing hormone or its surrogate, hCG.[52] OHSS is characterized by ovarian enlargement with multiple follicular cysts, acute fluid shift out of the intravascular space resulting in ascites, pleural effusion and hemoconcentration, and elevated serum estradiol.[52] On MR imaging, OHSS presents bilateral and symmetrical ovarian enlargement (>12 cm) with multiple variable-sized cysts representing enlarged follicles or corpus luteum cysts, usually associated with ascites.[52] The typical peripheral location of the follicles surrounding a central core of ovarian stroma has been described as a "spoke wheel" appearance.[53]

17.3.4 Tubal benign non-neoplastic disease

The normal fallopian tube is a thin serpentine structure between uterine fundus and ipsilateral ovary difficult to distinguish from adjacent vessels and ligaments at imaging, unless outlined with ascites.[33]

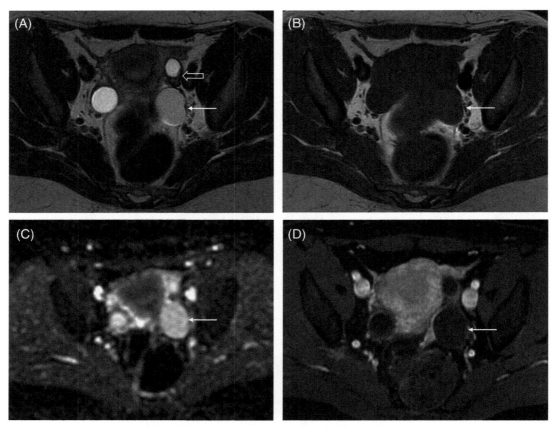

FIG. 17.13   **Left paraovarian cyst.** Axial T2-WI (A) shows a well-defined unilocular cystic lesion in the left adnexa (arrow) separated from the ipsilateral ovary (open arrow). It has simple fluid content: hyperintense on T2-WI (A, arrow), hypointense on T1-WI (B, arrow), no restricted diffusion with high signal intensity on ADC map (C, arrow), and no enhancement on postcontrast T1-WI with fat suppression (D, arrow). The MR findings are in support of a paraovarian cyst.

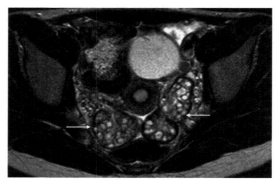

FIG. 17.14   **Multifollicular ovaries in a female adolescent patient.** Axial T2-WI shows multiple small follicles with random distribution in both ovaries (arrows). The amount of ovarian stroma is normal, and the typical ovarian zonal anatomy is seen as increased T2 signal intensity within the medulla relative to the cortex.

17.3.4.1 *Tubal dilation*

The terms hydrosalpinx, pyosalpinx, and hematosalpinx are used to indicate a dilated fallopian tube filled with fluid, pus, or blood, respectively. The most common cause of tubal dilation is pelvic inflammatory disease (PID). Other less frequent causes are endometriosis, adhesions from previous pelvic surgery or radiotherapy, tubal cancer, and tubal pregnancy.[54] At imaging, dilated fallopian tube appears as a tubular structure (sausage-like C- or S-shape cystic mass) with interdigitating incomplete mural septa.[54] It is usually separated from the ipsilateral ovary, although it may be attached by adhesions.[45] Multiplanar MR imaging is helpful (1) to confirm the tubular nature of the adnexal

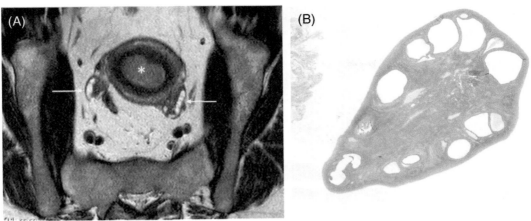

FIG. 17.15   Polycystic ovaries in a 52-year-old woman with endometrial tumor. Axial oblique T2-WI (A) shows ovaries with multiple peripherally located follicles associated with enlarged central stroma (arrows); it is also seen the coexistence of a pathologic endometrial tissue (asterisk). The corresponding pathological image (B) shows dilated follicle cysts with a peripherally distribution.

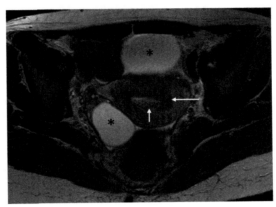

FIG. 17.16   Theca lutein cysts associated with hydatidiform invasive mole. Axial T2-WI show a focal distortion of the normal zonal anatomy (long arrow) and the presence of heterogeneous contents in the endometrial cavity (short arrow), associated with a marked enlargement of the ovaries, containing multiple cysts (asterisks).

lesion, depicting the ovary separated from the mass and differentiating the mass from the adjacent dilated bowel loops, and (2) to determine the cause of salpinx dilation, evaluating the nature of tubal fluid.[54-56]

- Hydrosalpinx contains simple fluid (low T1 SI, high T2 SI, and no restricted diffusion) (Fig. 17.17). The tubal wall is usually thin, and the presence of an enhancing solid component may be suggestive of tubal neoplasm or, in a specific clinical setting, of ectopic pregnancy.[54]
- Pyosalpinx contains pus (variable T1 and T2 SI, and restricted diffusion with high SI on DWI and low SI on ADC map) (Fig. 17.18). It is more likely to be bilateral with thickened and edematous enhancing wall, thickened utero-sacral ligaments, edema of the presacral fat and small bowel ileus.[45] The most common cause is pelvic inflammatory disease presenting with acute abdominal pain.
- Hematosalpinx contains blood products (high T1 and T1 fat sat SI, low T2 SI, and restricted diffusion) (Fig. 17.19). The most common cause is endometriosis, but other conditions may cause tubal bleeding such as tubal ectopic pregnancy, pelvic inflammatory disease, ovarian torsion, malignancy, and trauma.[45]

17.3.4.2 *Tubo-ovarian abscess (TOA)*

Tubo-ovarian abscess is a condition within the wide spectrum of pelvic inflammatory disease.[36] Identification of TOA is most common in women of reproductive age. In contrast, in postmenopausal women presenting with TOA, a concomitant pelvic malignancy should be excluded as there is a significant association with malignant disease.[57] On MR imaging, TOA appears as a complex mass with ill-defined borders, thickened walls and thickened septa

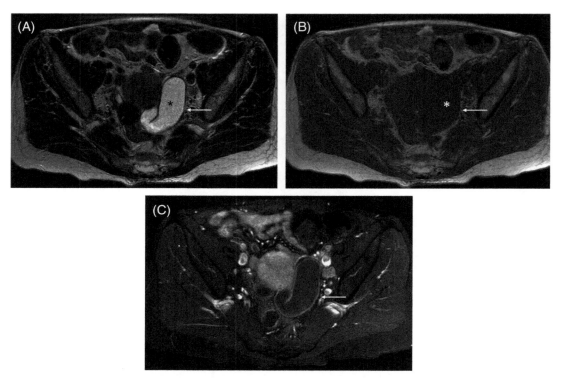

FIG. 17.17 Hydrosalpinx in a 52-year-old woman. Axial T2-WI (A) shows a tortuous tubular structure in the left adnexa (arrow), a finding suggestive of a dilated fallopian tube. The dilated tube contains simple fluid that is hyperintense on T2-WI (A, asterisk) and hypointense on T1-WI (B, asterisk). The tubal wall is thin with regular enhancement on postcontrast T1-WI with fat suppression (C, arrow).

with variable T1 SI, heterogeneous high T2 SI, and enhancement on postcontrast imaging.[54] In the evaluation of pelvic inflammatory disease, DWI sequence may improve the diagnostic accuracy, especially when contrast media is contraindicated.[36] TOA contains pus (viscous fluid) and proteinaceous plasma with high cellularity. Therefore, the higher the viscosity is, the higher will be the restricted diffusion (high SI on DWI and low SI on ADC map) (Fig. 17.20). However, false negatives on DWI can occur in cases of chronic abscesses, small abscesses (diameter <1 cm) and abscesses under antibiotic therapy.[58] When a complex TOA is associated with ascites and lymphadenopathy, it may be difficult to differentiate the abscess from a malignancy. Nevertheless, ovarian cancer is not frequently associated with tubal dilation.[59]

17.3.5 Ovarian endometriosis

Endometriosis is the presence of endometrial glands outside the uterus. Ovarian involvement may manifest as endometrioma (or endometriotic cyst) which is a chronic retention cyst with cyclic bleeding.[60] On MR imaging, endometriotic fluid has a very high T1 SI ("light bulb" appearance) and markedly low T2 SI (Fig. 17.21).[61] Homogeneous T2 shading is a characteristic finding of endometrioma. The shading sign refers to T2 shortening (low T2 SI) in an adnexal cyst that is hyperintense on T1-WI.[62] However, not all endometriomas show homogeneous T2 shading, depending on their age, the concentration of proteins and the amount of hemosiderin. On T2-WI dependent layering and hypointense fluid-fluid level may be seen within an endometrioma.[61,62] Another finding typical for chronic hemorrhagic lesion is the T2 dark spot sign, which is defined as discrete, markedly hypointense foci on T2-WI adjacent to the wall of the cyst (Fig. 17.21D). This sign has high specificity for chronic hemorrhage and may help to differentiate between endometrioma and hemorrhagic cyst (Table 17.2).[63] This topic will be discussed at length in the "MRI of Endometriosis" chapter.

17.3.6 Ovarian torsion and massive ovarian edema

Ovarian torsion is the twisting of the ovary along its axis, resulting in vascular compromise and ovarian infarction. The main risk factor for ovarian torsion is the presence of a benign ovarian mass greater than 5 cm.[64] On MR imaging,

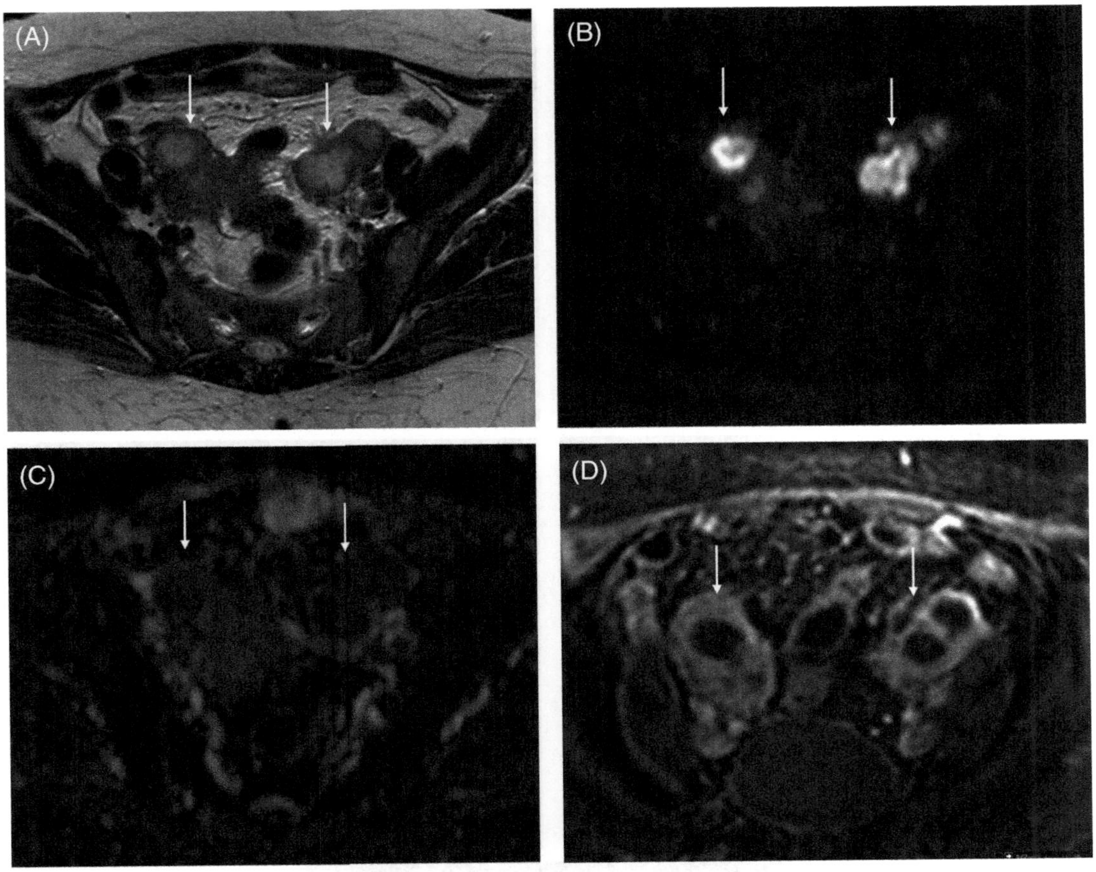

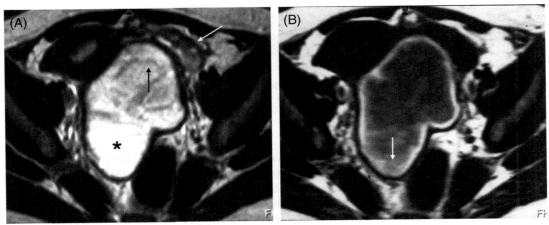

FIG. 17.18 Bilateral tuberculous pyosalpinx. MR images (A–D) show bilateral thick-walled, fluid-filled adnexal structures in keeping with dilated tubes (arrows). The tubes contain pus that is hyperintense on T2-WI (A) and has restricted diffusion with high signal intensity on DWI (B) and low signal intensity on ADC map (C). There is also avid enhancement of the thickened tubular walls and adjacent inflamed tissue after contrast media administration (D).

FIG. 17.19 Hematosalpinx. MR images (A and B) show a dilated left fallopian tube that is adjacent to the ipsilateral ovary (A, white arrow). On T2-WI (A) endoluminal content is hyperintense (asterisk) with fibrous bands (black arrow). High signal intensity along the inner portion due to hemosiderin deposit is seen on T1-WI (B, arrow).

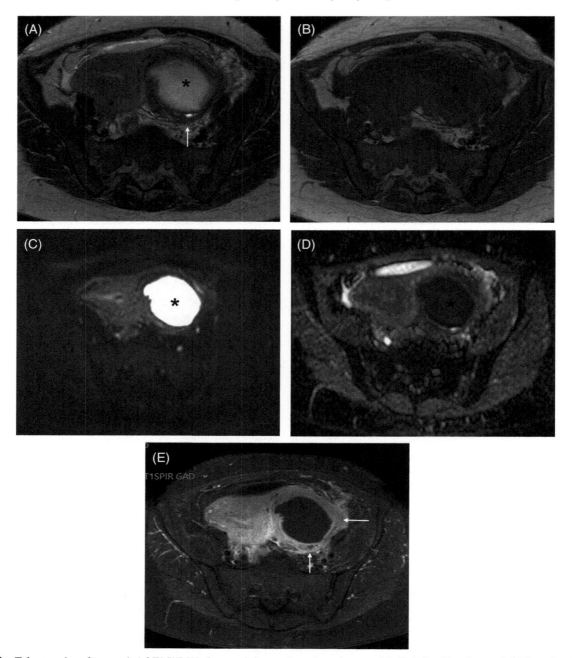

FIG. 17.20   **Tubo-ovarian abscess.** Axial T2-WI (A) shows a left complex adnexal mass with ill-defined borders and thickened walls (arrow). The adnexal mass contains pus (viscous fluid)—hyperintense on T2-WI (A, asterisk), hypointense on T1-WI (B, asterisk), hyperintense on DWI (C, asterisk) and hypointense on ADC map (D, asterisk). Postcontrast T1-WI with fat suppression (E) show a diffusely avid enhancement of the thickened walls and adjacent inflamed tissue (arrows).

the key features of ovarian torsion are: (1) massive ovarian enlargement, (2) high T2 SI of the ovarian central medulla, (3) peripherally dislocation of follicles as string of pearls, (4) vascular pedicle twist, (5) uterine displacement toward the side of the affected ovary, and (6) surrounding fat stranding and/or small volume of pelvic free fluid.[64] The stromal hemorrhage with high SI on T1-W imaging and the absence of enhancement, which are related to impaired arterial supply, are considered strongly predictive of ovarian nonviability, ischemia and necrosis.[64]

Massive ovarian edema is a rare benign entity affecting women between the second and third decades, although it may occur in any age including infancy.[65] The etiology is unclear, but the edema is most likely related to intermittent or partial ovarian torsion, causing venous and lymphatic drainage impairment. The pain of massive ovarian edema is usually mild, chronic, and intermittent compared to the severe and acute pain of ovarian torsion. Massive ovarian edema can be primary (85%) or secondary (15%) and is usually unilateral. Secondary massive edema may

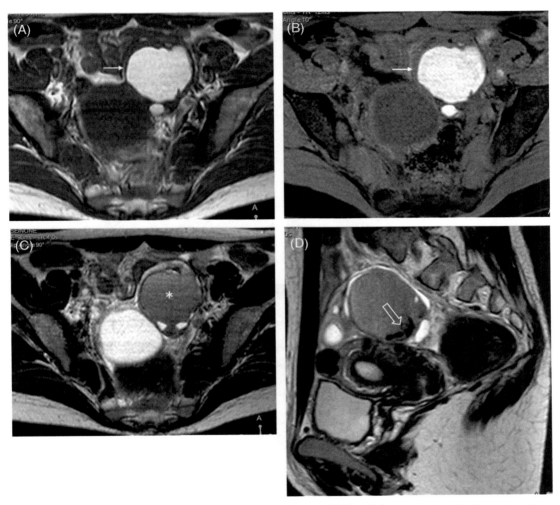

FIG. 17.21 Endometrioma in a 31-year-old woman. Axial T1-WI (A) and axial T1-WI with fat suppression (B) show a hyperintense cystic lesion in the left ovary (arrows). Axial T2-WI (C) demonstrates loss of signal within the lesion (asterisk), a finding that represents the "shading" sign. Sagittal T2-WI (D) shows markedly hypointense foci adjacent to the wall of the cyst (open arrow), a finding that is suggestive of the dark spot sign.

TABLE 17.2 MRI differentiation of ovarian endometrioma from hemorrhagic cyst.

	High T1 SI	Low T2 SI	T2 dark spot sign	DWI/ADC
Endometrioma	++	++	++	high/low
Hemorrhagic cyst	+	variable	−	high/low

be associated with ovarian fibromatosis, Meig syndrome, ovarian cystadenoma, polycystic ovaries, malignancy, ovarian lymphatic disfunction and drugs used for ovarian induction.[65] The affected ovary remains in general viable, unlike ovarian torsion where the arterial supply is usually compromised. The MR features of massive ovarian edema may mimic those of the ovarian torsion, but the presence of arterial supply and stromal enhancement, and the absence of a detectable vascular pedicle twist favor the diagnosis of massive ovarian edema (Fig. 17.22).[65]

17.3.7 Ovarian pregnancy

Ovarian pregnancy is a rare form of ectopic pregnancy, accounting for only 3% of all ectopic pregnancies. It occurs when the ovum is fertilized and implanted within the ovary.[66] The lack of an intrauterine pregnancy in a patient with positive results of a pregnancy test should be suggest an ectopic pregnancy.

On MR imaging the features of ovarian pregnancy include: (1) a gestational sac-like structure within the ovary characterized by thick wall with heterogenous high T2 SI, and high T1 SI foci adjacent to the wall suggesting

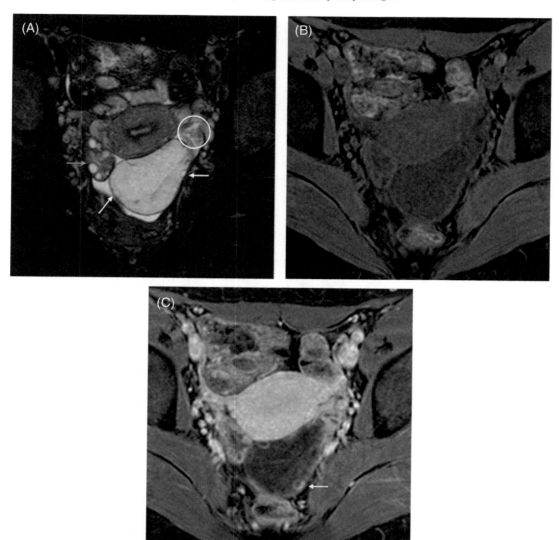

FIG. 17.22   Massive ovarian edema in a 26-year-old woman with mild, chronic, and intermittent pelvic pain. Axial fat saturated T2-WI (A) shows a massive enlargement of the left ovary with a markedly high signal intensity and peripherally located follicles (white arrows), edematous ispilateral fallopian tube (circle), and minimal free fluid; note the normal right ovary (orange arrow). Axial fat saturated T1-WI (B) shows a homogeneous low signal intensity of the left enlarged ovary, with no hemorrhagic foci. After contrast media injection (C) the left ovary shows mild stromal enhancement and follicular wall enhancement (arrow). *Case courtesy of Dr. Michele Dezio and Dr. Anna Maria Telesca, Madonna delle Grazie Hospital, Matera, Italy.*

hemorrhage; (2) normal fallopian tubes.[67] Hemoperitoneum is a finding with high positive predictive value for the diagnosis of ectopic pregnancy but is not necessarily associated with a ruptured ectopic pregnancy.[66] An important differential diagnosis of this condition is corpus luteum that is frequently associated with pregnancy.

17.3.8 Acute oophoritis

Oophoritis is an inflammation of the ovaries, commonly associated with salpingitis and pyosalpinx. The imaging findings of oophoritis include mild enlargement of the ovaries, measuring more than 3 cm, with hyperemia of the ovarian stroma, and a polycystic-like appearance of the ovaries with multiple small (2–10 mm) follicles within the increased ovarian stroma (Fig. 17.23). The main differential diagnosis to consider for oophoritis is ovarian torsion.[68]

17.3.9 Differential diagnosis of cystic adnexal lesion

The table 17.3 briefly describes the differential diagnosis of a benign cystic adnexal lesion.

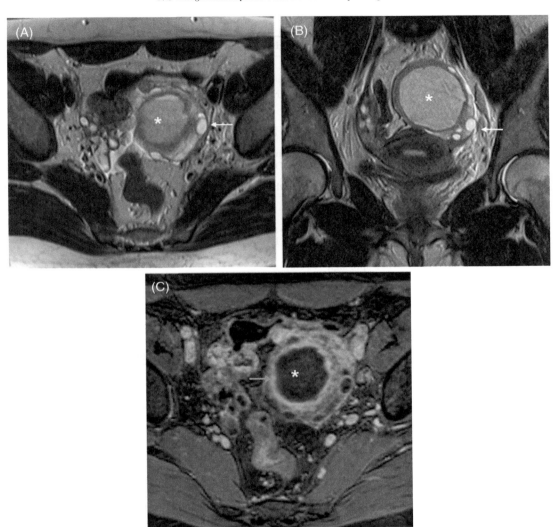

FIG. 17.23 Oophoritis and ovarian abscess. Axial T2-WI (A) and coronal T2-WI (B) show an edematous left ovary (white arrows) and an intra-ovarian fluid collection (asterisks) consistent with oophoritis and ovarian abscess. On fat saturated postcontrast T1-WI (C) the ovarian abscess (asterisk) shows rim enhancement (orange arrow).

TABLE 17.3 Diagnostic workup of cystic adnexal lesion.

Type of cystic adnexal mass	Clinical features and imaging findings
Unilocular cyst	
Functional cyst	Well-defined fluid ovarian cyst High T2 SI, Low T1 SI May resolve spontaneously Follow-up >5 cm in premenopausal age Follow-up >3 cm in postmenopausal age
Paraovarian cyst	Simple fluid cyst adjacent to the ovary High T2 SI, Low T1 SI More common in postmenopausal age
Cystadenoma	Simple fluid cyst increasing in size during follow-up High T2 SI, Low T1 SI No enhancing solid tissue

(Continued)

TABLE 17.3 (Cont'd)

Type of cystic adnexal mass	Clinical features and imaging findings
Multilocular Cyst	
Peritoneal inclusion cyst	Cystic lesion surrounding the ovary "Spider in a web" sign High T2 SI, Low T1 SI Previous history of surgery or PID
Cystadenofibroma	Cystic lesion with low T2 thick wall or septa No restricted diffusion on DWI
Tubal dilatation	Tubular cystic structure with incomplete septa and variable SI according to its content
Hemorrhagic Cyst	
Endometrioma	Chronic retention cyst with cyclic bleeding High SI on T1-WI and on T1-WI with fat suppression Low T2 SI (T2 shading) T2 dark spot sign
Hemorrhagic cyst	Cystic lesion with blood products Variable SI on T1-WI and T2-WI May resolve spontaneously
Cyst with fat	
Mature teratoma	Well-defined cystic lesion with high SI on T1-WI and signal drop on T1-WI with fat suppression

17.4 Benign nonovarian pathologies

Benign nonovarian pathologies include the common uterine diseases and the pathologic conditions involving the peritoneal cavity and the pelvic extraperitoneum.

17.4.1 Benign uterine pathologies

Benign uterine disease is mainly composed of leiomyomas, adenomyosis, and endometrial polyps. These pathologies are very frequent conditions that affect women of all ages, mostly during the premenopausal age.[1] Other less common benign uterine diseases include congenital malformations (also termed Mullerian duct anomalies), which should be taken in consideration due to the associated high risk of infertility.[69] For these pathologies MRI has becoming more and more important not only to make a diagnosis, but also to guide patient treatment.[1] In this chapter we are going to cover the most common benign uterine diseases, which will be discussed at length in the "MRI of Benign Uterine Pathologies" chapter.

17.4.1.1 *Leiomyoma*

Leiomyomas (also called myomas or fibroids) are the most common benign uterine disease affecting up to 20–30% of women during the reproductive age and may be solitary or, most frequently, multiple.[70] Leiomyomas commonly involve the myometrium and are classified according to their location as submucosal, intramural, and subserosal (PALM-COEIN).[71] On MR imaging, leiomyomas without degeneration are round lesion with low T2 SI, isointense T1 SI, and variable enhancement after contrast media injection. A high T2 signal rim, corresponding to a pseudocapsule of edema, may be detected in up to 23% of uterine leiomyomas.[72] Typical leiomyomas do not have restricted diffusion, showing low SI both on DWI and on corresponding ADC map ("blackout phenomenon"). It is important to remember that a low or intermediate DWI signal (lower than endometrium and lymph nodes) is highly suggestive of benign myometrial lesion, in contrast with leiomyosarcoma.[73]

Larger leiomyomas (≥5 cm), which exceed their blood supply, may degenerate. The types of degeneration are hyaline, cystic, myxoid, calcific and hydropic.[1] Besides degeneration, two subtypes of atypical leiomyoma should be considered: cellular leiomyoma and lipoleiomyoma. Cellular leiomyoma has an intermediate/high T2 SI, avid enhancement, and restricted diffusion, features that make it difficult to differentiate it from leiomyosarcoma. Lipoleiomyoma, which is more frequent in postmenopausal age, has fat components with high T1 SI, high T2 SI, and loss of SI on fat suppressed images (Fig. 17.24).[1]

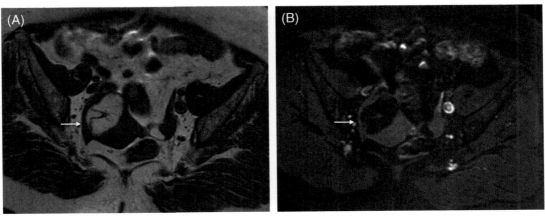

FIG. 17.24 Lipoleiomyoma in a 67-year-old woman. Axial T1-WI (A) shows a hyperintense uterine mass with lobulated margins (arrow). Axial T1-WI with fat suppression (B) demonstrates loss of signal within the mass (arrow), a finding that is suggestive of uterine lipoleiomyoma.

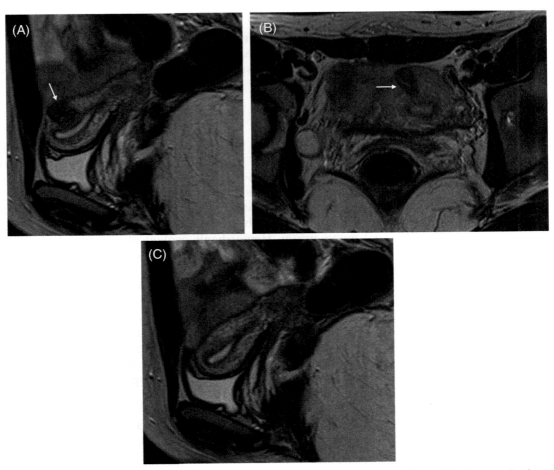

FIG. 17.25 Focal myometrial contraction. Sagittal T2-WI (A) and axial T2-WI (B) show a hypointense band perpendicular to the junctional zone (arrows). This finding is absent on subsequent sagittal T2-WI (C) that shows normal uterus, confirming the diagnosis of transient myometrial contraction.

Pitfall to avoid on MRI:

- Focal myometrial contractions: contractions may appear as low T2 SI focal myometrial lesions that may mimic a uterine leiomyoma (Fig. 17.25). Because they are transient and do not persist on all sequences, they may easily be differentiated from leiomyoma (Fig. 17.25C).
- Differentiate ovarian from uterine masses: it may be difficult to differentiate a uterine leiomyoma from an ovarian fibroma. Claw sign (uterine tissue draped around the mass) (Fig. 17.5) and bridging vessel sign (enlarged and tortuous vessels extending from the uterus to the mass) (Fig. 17.6) are useful to suggest the diagnosis of a uterine mass.
- Endometrial polyp: a submucosal leiomyoma may mimic an endometrial polyp. However, pedunculated submucosal leiomyomas show lower T2 SI (Fig. 17.26) than polyps (high T2 SI) and have a stalk that arises from the myometrium (Fig. 17.27).
- Leiomyosarcoma: the distinction of an atypical leiomyoma from a leiomyosarcoma is challenging and only a combination of MRI features may suggest the right diagnosis. In a study from Lakhman and colleagues,[74] the combination of 3 or more of 4 discriminated features, including nodular borders, hemorrhage (high T1 SI), T2-weighted dark areas, and central unenhanced areas, improve the sensitivity and the specificity for the diagnosis of leiomyosarcoma (Fig. 17.28).
- Adenomyoma: discussed later.

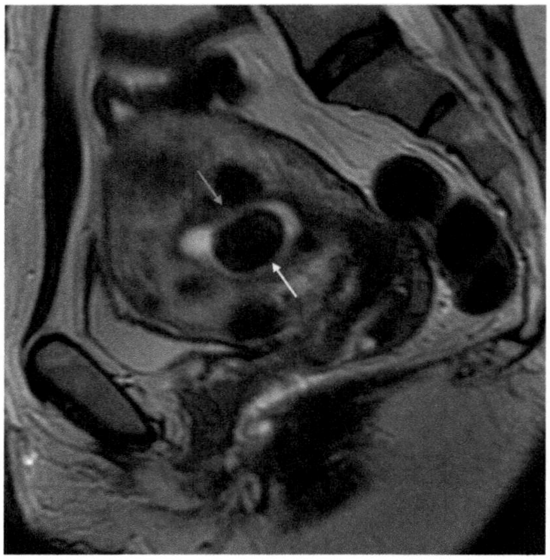

FIG. 17.26   **Submucosal leiomyoma.** Sagittal T2-WI shows peduncolate submucosal leiomyoma (white arrow), which is markedly hypointense and has a stalk that arise from the myometrium (orange arrow).

17.4.1.2 *Adenomyosis*

Adenomyosis is a common benign disease in women during reproductive age. It is a myometrial heterogeneous disease characterized by two specific features: (1) endometrial glands and stroma within the myometrium, and (2) smooth muscle cells hypertrophy and hyperplasia.[75] An MRI-based classification has been recently proposed by Bazot et al. and Kobayashi et al., describing different subtypes of adenomyosis.[75,76]

Internal adenomyosis: The main direct finding for adenomyosis on MR imaging is the presence of small myometrial cysts related to dilated ectopic endometrial glands. Typically, these cysts have water signal intensity (high T2 SI and low T1 SI) and are located in the internal myometrium. Hemorrhagic content may accumulate within the cysts showing high T1 SI.[76] Other indirect MRI findings for the diagnosis of internal adenomyosis is the thickening of the junctional zone (JZ) related to the myometrial hypertrophy. A maximum thickness of the JZ equal or greater than 12 mm (JZ_{max} ≥12 mm) and/or the ratio of JZ_{max} over the full myometrium thickness measured at the same place ($ratio_{max}$) >40% and/or big regular uterus, are indirect criteria that would be suggestive of adenomyosis when used in combination, according to Bazot et al (Fig. 17.29).[76]

Adenomyoma: Adenomyoma is a mass-like confluence of ectopic endometrial glands. In the presence of an isolated adenomyoma neither the JZ nor the uterine serosa are involved.[76] On MR imaging, adenomyoma is a low T2 SI myometrial mass with ill-defined borders and bright central cysts. Cystic adenomyoma is a rare subtype and is characterized by its predominant hemorrhage content, resulting in a cyst-like appearance with a high T1 SI and a low T2 SI rim. The cysts can be submucosal, intramural or subserosal (Fig. 17.30).[76,77]

External adenomyosis: External adenomyosis involves the outer part of the uterus, disrupting the serosa but not affecting the JZ. It is more frequently located in the posterior myometrium and is usually associated with deep endometriosis. On MR imaging, it appears as an ill-defined subserosal mass/pseudo-mass with a low T2 SI with or without internal bright foci (Fig. 17.31).[75] No data are available about the performance of MRI for the diagnosis of external adenomyosis, probably because it is rarely distinguishable from posterior deep endometriosis.[76]

Pitfall to avoid on MRI:

- Physiological changes of the JZ: the visualization of the JZ is dependent on patient's age and hormonal status. A pseudo-thickening of the JZ is frequently observed during menstrual cycle.[78] Therefore, MR examination

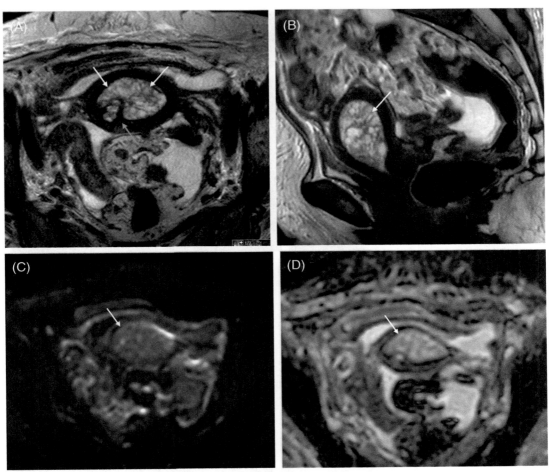

FIG. 17.27 **Endometrial polyp in a 60-year-old woman.** Axial oblique T2-WI (A) and sagittal T2WI (B) show a uterine intracavitary mass with an hypointense central fibrous core (A, orange arrow) and multiple internal cysts with high signal intensity (A and B, white arrows), findings that are in support of an endometrial polyp. The endometrial polyp has low signal intensity on DWI (C, arrow) and high signal intensity on the corresponding ADC map (D, arrow).

should not be performed during the menstruation to avoid this pitfall. In contrast, JZ is not clearly depicted during premenarche and menopause.[79]

- Uterine contractions: transient myometrial contractions give rise to focal bands of low T2 SI perpendicular to JZ or to apparent focal thickening of the JZ that can mimic adenomyosis (Fig. 17.25).[77]
- Leiomyoma: the association with uterine leiomyomas makes JZ measurement more difficult or impossible.[76] Traditionally, adenomyoma presents as a low T2 SI mass with ill-defined borders, minimal mass effect, and multiple bright foci. In contrast, leiomyoma is a low T2 SI mass with well-defined borders, adjacent mass effect and large vessels surrounding the mass.[77]
- Endometrial cancer: the evaluation of the true degree of myometrial invasion by tumor can be challenging with the coexistence of adenomyosis because it may be responsible of a pseudo-widening of endometrium.[77] Furthermore, adenomyosis increases the surface area of interface between tumor and myometrium and facilitates myometrial infiltration.[80] DWI is useful to evaluate the real depth of myometrial invasion, because tumor restricts to diffusion, whereas adenomyosis does not (Fig. 17.32).[77]

17.4.1.3 *Endometrial benign disease*

Endometrial benign abnormalities (endometrial hyperplasia and polyps) are first evaluated with ultrasound and the diagnosis is usually confirmed by endometrial cytology, biopsy and curettage. MRI should be considered when ultrasound is unconclusive and if endometrial sampling fails.[81]

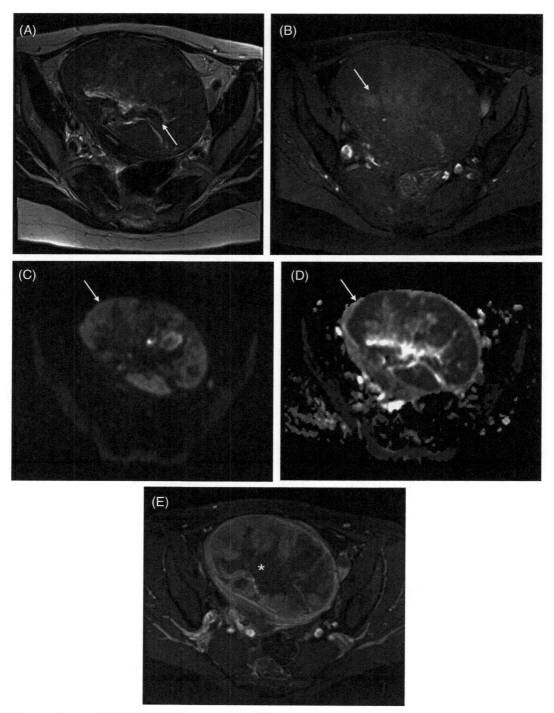

FIG. 17.28   Leiomyosarcoma. Axial T2-WI (A) shows a myometrial mass with dark areas (arrow) and nodular borders. Hemorrhage is seen on axial T1-WI with fat suppression (B, arrow). Axial DWI (C) shows high signal intensity (arrow) that corresponds to low signal intensity areas on ADC map (D, arrow). Axial postcontrast T1-WI with fat suppression (E) shows heterogeneous enhancement with central necrosis (asterisk). These combined features are suggestive of leiomyosarcoma.

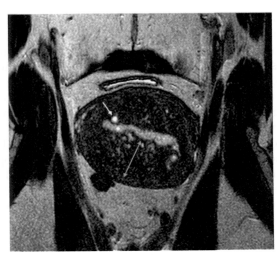

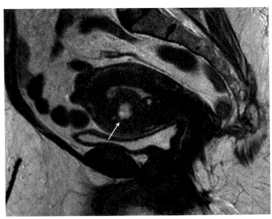

FIG. 17.29 **Adenomyosis in a 54-year-old-woman.** Axial oblique T2-WI shows the classic features of adenomyosis: thickness of the junctional zone (orange arrow) and multiple foci with high T2 signal intensity (white arrow).

FIG. 17.30 **Cystic adenomyoma.** Sagittal T2-WI shows diffuse thickening of the junctional zone and a single intramural focus of high signal intensity in the anterior myometrium (arrow) suggestive of cystic adenomyosis.

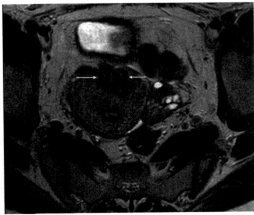

FIG. 17.31 **External Adenomyosis in a 30-year-old woman.** Axial oblique T2-WI shows a subserosal pseudo-mass with a low T2 SI in the outer part of the anterior myometrium not affecting the junctional zone (arrows). The finding is suggestive of external adenomyosis.

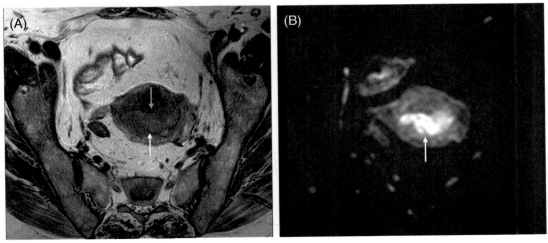

FIG. 17.32 **Pseudowidening of the junctional zone coexisting with endometrial cancer.** Axial oblique T2-WI (A) shows an intermediate T2 signal within the endometrial cavity (white arrow) with diffuse thickening of the junctional zone bulging in the endometrial cavity (orange arrow). On DWI (B) signal hyperintensity is solely seen at the level of the intermediate T2 signal corresponding with the endometrial tumor (arrow); no areas of restricted diffusion are detected within the junctional zone. DWI is very helpful to delineate the cancer.

Endometrial hyperplasia: The incidence of endometrial hyperplasia rises with age and can represent a cause of abnormal bleeding during postmenopausal period. On MR imaging, endometrial hyperplasia appears as thickening of the endometrial strip (>5 mm in women with postmenopausal bleeding) that may be isointense or hypointense to the normal endometrium on T2-WI.[80,82] This appearance is not specific, and any endometrial abnormalities should lead to biopsy if there is a clinical suspicion of malignancy.[83] However, the addition of DWI sequences in the MR examination has improved the sensitivity, specificity and accuracy for the diagnosis of endometrial pathologies, providing useful information to differentiate benign from malignant lesions.[84] Malignant lesions have a high cellularity and are expected to have lower ADC values than benign lesions.[85]

Endometrial polyps: Endometrial polyps are a common cause of abnormal bleeding during postmenopausal age and are more frequently seen in patients that receive tamoxifen therapy. On MR imaging, endometrial polyps appear as a low or intermediate T2-SI intracavitary masses with a central fibrous core and sometimes with high SI foci (internal cyst).[81,83,86] Pedunculated polyps may show a visible stalk. After administration of contrast media, polyps have a strong and early enhancement, whereas on DWI sequence they do not restrict and show a high ADC value (Fig. 17.27C–D).[80]

Pitfall to avoid on MRI:

- Endometrial cancer: In contrast to endometrial cancer, endometrial polyps do not invade the myometrium and do not show internal necrosis. On DWI sequence benign endometrial lesion does not restrict to diffusion, whereas tumor does. Moreover, some authors found that no overlap in ADC values was present between endometrial cancer and normal endometrium, suggesting an ADC value threshold of 1.05×10^{-3} mm^2/s.[87] This information is particularly relevant when endometrial biopsy is not feasible or is inconclusive.
- Submucosal leiomyoma: submucosal leiomyoma may be difficult to differentiate from broad-based polyps, but generally leiomyomas have lower T2 SI (Fig. 17.26).[80]
- Polypoid adenomyomas or adenomyomatous polyp: polypoid adenomyomas usually show a predominant cystic component, whereas endometrial polyps have more frequently the predominance of solid component. If the polypoid lesion shows cysts, hemorrhage, and myometrial invasion, it is highly likely to be a polypoid adenomyomas.[86]

17.4.1.4 *Mullerian duct anomalies*

Many female genital tract anomalies involve the uterus. The congenital malformations of the uterus (also known as Mullerian duct anomalies) are considered an uncommon cause of infertility. A radiological description of these rare pathologies is beyond the scope of this chapter; this topic will be covered extensively in the "MRI of Female Infertility" chapter. However, it should be kept in mind that MR imaging has the highest diagnostic accuracy in the characterization of uterine anomalies, providing detailed information especially in the study of the external profile of the uterine fundus and the cavity shape, and it also allows tissue characterization of the possible uterine septa (Fig. 17.33).[7] The uterine malformations may be associated with anomalies of cervix and vagina, malformations of the ovaries and urinary tract system. The MR imaging protocol should include: (1) multiplanar T2-W acquisitions with planes oriented along

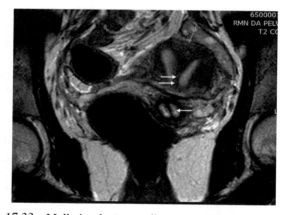

FIG. 17.33   **Mullerian duct anomalies—septate uterus.** T2-WI shows a normal external uterine contour (orange arrow). The hypointense fibrous septum originates from the isointense muscular septum (white double arrows) and extends into the cervical os (white single arrow).

uterine axis, (2) T1-W fat sat sequences to detect blood products and evaluate the presence of hematometra and hematocolpos, and (3) coronal T2-W sequence with large field of view (FOV) to evaluate the presence, position, and morphology of the kidneys (Fig. 17.34).[7]

17.4.2 Nonovarian benign cystic lesions: pelvic space-based approach

Cystic lesions of the female pelvis are common and frequently originated from ovaries. However, it is important to consider also the nonovarian cystic lesions that may mimic those of the ovaries, because a misdiagnosis can greatly affect the patient management.[45] A cystic pelvic lesion can be considered nonovarian when it is separated from the

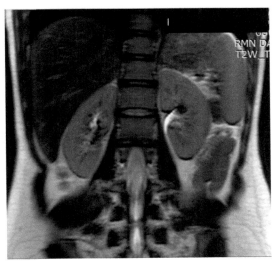

FIG. 17.34 **Mullerian duct anomalies.** Coronal T2-WI with large FOV should be performed to evaluate the presence, position, and morphology of the kidneys.

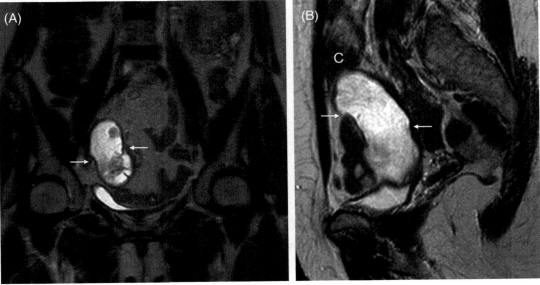

FIG. 17.35 **Low-grade appendiceal mucinous neoplasms.** Coronal T2-WI (A) and sagittal T2-WI (B) show a vertically oriented tubular fluid-filled structure with thin wall (arrows) located in the right lower abdominal quadrant, consistent with a mucocele of the appendix, which was confirmed histologically. C = cecum.

ovaries. If a nonovarian cystic lesion is detected on MRI, the first step of diagnostic algorithm is the definition of its intraperitoneal or extraperitoneal location.[24]

17.4.2.1 *Intraperitoneal nonovarian benign cystic lesions*

Intraperitoneal nonovarian cystic pathologies include lesions originating from the bowel (mucocele of appendix) or from the peritoneal cavity (peritoneal inclusion cyst, paraovarian cyst, canal of Nuck cyst).

Mucocele of the appendix: Mucocele of the appendix is a rare condition defined as a cystic dilatation of the appendiceal lumen caused by an accumulation of mucin.[88] It can mimic an ovarian cystic lesion especially when the appendix is abnormally located in the pelvis (Fig. 17.35). Preoperative diagnosis is crucial to avoid rupture at surgery and potential subsequent development of pseudomyxoma peritonei.[45,89] MRI finding is high T2 SI tubular lesion connected to the cecum. Irregular border thickness should raise suspicion for malignant degeneration.[24]

Peritoneal inclusion cyst: Peritoneal inclusion cysts are non-neoplastic reactive proliferations of mesothelial cells in response to a peritoneal insult. History of previous surgery, trauma, pelvic inflammatory disease, and endometriosis

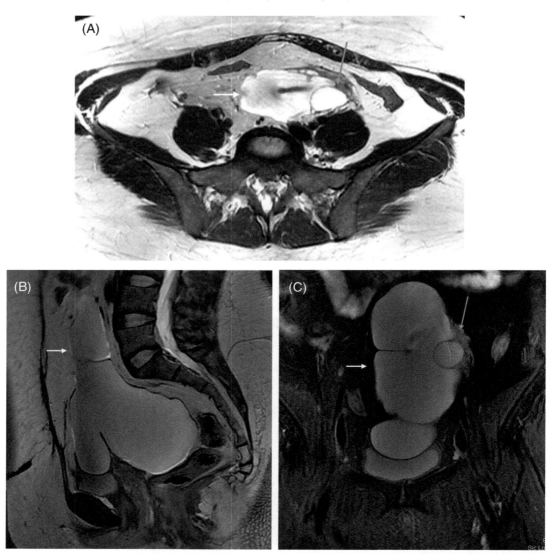

FIG. 17.36   **Left peritoneal inclusion cyst.** Axial T2-WI (A), sagittal T2-WI (B) and coronal T2-WI with fat suppression (C) show a large cystic lesion (white arrows) surrounding the left ovary (orange arrows). The cyst conforms to the shape of the peritoneal cavity because it lacks a true wall.

are known risk factors for the development of peritoneal inclusion cysts. This type of cystic lesion occurs almost exclusively in premenopausal women with active ovaries, pelvic adhesions, and impaired absorption of peritoneal fluid.[90] At imaging, peritoneal inclusion cyst appears as a unilocular or multilocular cyst surrounding the ovary and demonstrates a high T2 SI and a low T1 SI with no solid tissue. The ovary can be entrapped within the cyst and appears like a "spider in a web." Although the ovary may be distorted, it is normal and should not be mistaken with a solid nodular portion of the lesion. The peritoneal inclusion cyst conforms to the shape of the peritoneal cavity because the cyst lacks a true wall and has margins formed by adhesions and adjacent organs (Fig. 17.36).[45,90] Peritoneal inclusion cyst can simulate dilated tube and paraovarian cyst.

Paraovarian cyst: Paraovarian cysts arise in the broad ligament and are usually simple unilocular cysts (Fig. 17.13).[44] Paraovarian cysts are adjacent to but separate from the ovary, while peritoneal inclusion cysts surround the ovary.[24]

Endosalpingiosis: Endosalpingiosis is a benign and rare disease characterized by the presence of glands lined by benign tubal type of epithelium outside the fallopian tube.[91] At imaging, endosalpingiosis usually appears as a multicystic mass. The cystic lesions are commonly located on the surface of the female pelvic organs and in the cul-de-sac. Additionally, they can also occur on the surface of the bladder, peritoneum, lymph nodes and skin.[92] Endosalpingiosis is considered part of the spectrum of peritoneal serous lesions, often coexisting with borderline or serous ovarian tumors. Differential diagnoses include uterine subserosal leiomyoma with cystic degeneration, ovarian cystic tumors, and peritoneal cystic tumors, such as multicystic mesothelioma.[91]

Canal of Nuck cyst: The cyst of the canal of Nuck, also called female hydrocele, is a rare condition. The canal of Nuck originates from a small protrusion of parietal peritoneum through the inguinal ring into the inguinal canal, accompanying the round ligament of the uterus to the labium majus. Failure of obliteration of this canal can result in an indirect inguinal hernia or a hydrocele of the canal of Nuck.[93] At imaging, the cyst of the canal of Nuck appears as a thin-walled fluid collection with a high T2 SI and a low T1 SI.[94] The differential diagnosis list includes not only inguinal hernia, but also enlarge lymph nodes and soft tissue inguinal lesions (lipoma, leiomyoma, endometriosis).

17.4.2.2 *Extraperitoneal benign cystic lesions*

A pelvic cystic lesion located away from the peritoneum should be considered extraperitoneal. If the mass is extraperitoneal in location, it is useful to determine the pelvic compartment where the lesion is situated. The pelvic extraperitoneum is divided in three compartments: anterior, middle, and posterior. These compartments include respectively, the prevesical and perivesical spaces anteriorly, the perirectal and retrorectal spaces posteriorly, and uterus, cervix, and vagina in the middle.

- **Anterior compartment**
  Urachal cyst: Urachal cyst is the most frequent congenital urachal anomalies. The urachus is a midline tubular structure in the prevesical space that extends from the umbilicus to the anterior dome of the bladder. A urachal cyst develops when the urachus closes at both the umbilicus and the bladder ends while an intervening portion remains patent. It is usually asymptomatic until complicated by an infection or bleeding. On imaging, it appears as a fluid-filled cystic lesion (Fig. 17.37); the wall thickening is a sign of superinfection.[95]

- **Middle compartment**
  Nabothian cyst: The Nabothian cysts are retention cysts of the cervical glands. At MR imaging, they appear as a single or multiple cysts in the cervical fibrous stroma showing a high T2 SI (Fig. 17.38), a low T1 SI, and no contrast enhancement.[96]
  Gartner duct cyst: The Gartner cysts are embryologic cysts originating from the residual wolffian (mesonephric) duct remnant. The typical location of this vaginal cyst is along the anterolateral wall of the vagina above the level of the most inferior aspect of the pubic symphysis. The cyst is generally solitary and less than 2 cm in diameter and can show septa. At MR imaging, this vaginal cyst shows a high T2 SI if contains simple fluid or a low T2 SI and a high T1 SI if contains hemorrhagic or proteinaceous fluid (Fig. 17.39).[97]

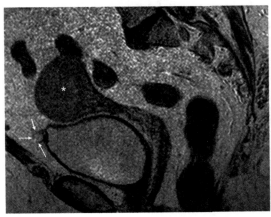

FIG. 17.37   **Urachal cyst in a 74-year-old woman with endometrial cancer.** Sagittal T2-WI demonstrate a fluid-filled structure (arrows) at the midline lower abdomen immediately above the anterosuperior aspect of the bladder, consistent with a urachal cyst. The intermediate T2 signal intensity within the endometrial cavity (asterisk) corresponds to endometrial cancer.

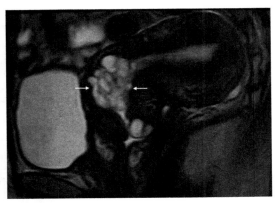

FIG. 17.38   **Nabothian cysts.** Sagittal T2-WI show a retroverted uterus and multiple cysts in the cervical fibrous stroma (arrows) that are consistent with nabothian cysts.

Bartholin gland cyst: The Bartholin's cysts arise from the duct system of Bartholin's glands. The cysts are situated in the posterolateral inferior third of the vagina medial to the labia minora and at or below the level of the pubic symphysis. The cysts are usually unilocular and demonstrate at imaging a high T2 SI and a variable T1 SI depending on their contents (Fig. 17.40).[96,97]

Other less frequent cystic lesions situated in the middle comportment of the pelvic extraperitoneum may affect the uterus, as cystic adenomyoma and cystic degeneration of leiomyoma. Cystic adenomyoma usually presents a hemorrhagic content, while cystic leiomyoma is characterized by simple fluid cystic areas.

- **Posterior compartment**

The posterior compartment includes the perirectal space and the retrorectal space. The perirectal space contains the rectum and the mesorectal fat and is bounded by the mesorectal fascia. The pathologies located in the perirectal space are usually rectal tumors, with adenocarcinoma of the rectum being the most frequent. The retrorectal space is a virtual area between the mesorectal fascia anteriorly and the presacral fascia posteriorly and may be involved by rare tumors and tumor mimics.

We will focus on benign non-neoplastic cystic lesions of the retrorectal space, using a stepwise approach for the lesion characterization, as proposed by Nougaret et al.[24]

- The best tip to retrorectal location of a mass is the anterior dislocation of the rectum and the mesorectal space, easily detected on sagittal images.

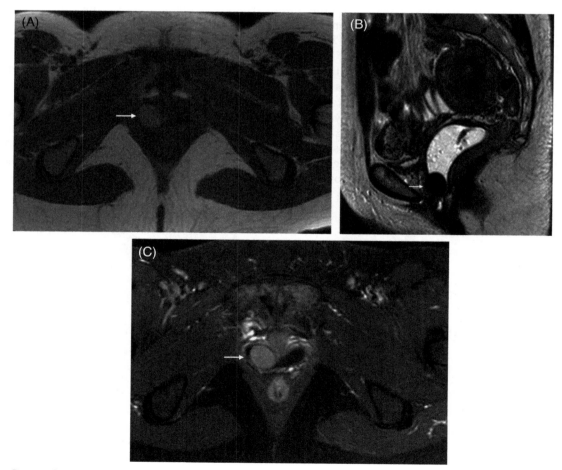

FIG. 17.39   Gartner duct cyst. Axial T1-WI (A), sagittal T2-WI (B) and axial postcontrast T1-WI with fat suppression (C) demonstrate a solitary cystic structure along the right antero-lateral wall of the vagina (arrow) consistent with Gartner duct cyst. The cyst contains hemorrhagic/proteinaceous fluid with high T1 signal intensity (A and C) and low T2 signal intensity (B); enhancement after contrast media administration is absent (C).

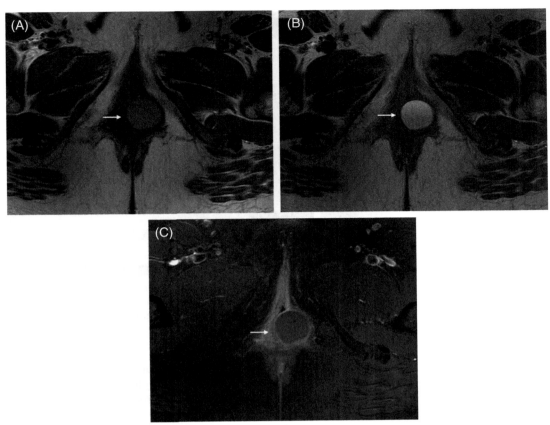

FIG. 17.40 Bartholin gland cyst. Axial T1-WI (A), axial T2-WI (B), axial postcontrast T1-WI with fat suppression (C) demonstrate a solitary cystic lesion in the posterolateral inferior third of the vagina medial to the labia minora (arrow), consistent with Bartholin gland cyst. The cyst has low T1-SI (A), high T2-SI (B), and no enhancement after contrast media administration (C).

- If the retrorectal mass has *high SI on T1-W images*, one should distinguish between a fat-containing or a hemorrhagic lesion. Signal loss after fat saturation is in relation to the presence of macroscopic fat (teratoma), while if the signal remains high is suggestive of hemorrhage content (endometriosis).
  Teratoma: Teratoma is a type of developmental cyst that contains fat, sebum, calcification, and soft tissue from dermoid plugs. At MR imaging, the signal drop on fat suppressed images is pathognomonic.[98]
  Endometriosis: Deep endometriosis may involve the retrorectal space and can affect splanchnic and sacral nerves. It appears as a low T2 SI fibrotic tissue with spicules and internal cystic areas with high SI on fat suppressed T1-W images.[99]
- If the retrorectal mass has *low SI on T1-W images*, one should evaluate the T2 SI and morphology to distinguish between cystic (high T2 SI) and solid (low T2 SI) lesions. The most common benign non-neoplastic lesions with low T1 SI are cystic. In the differential diagnosis of retrorectal cystic masses, the unilocular or multilocular characteristic is important. Among the retrorectal cystic lesions, rectal duplication cyst, epidermoid cyst, and anterior meningocele are usually unilocular, while tailgut cyst is more frequently multilocular.
  Rectal duplication cyst: Duplication cysts are uncommon congenital malformations, usually discovered in childhood. They generally appear as spherical or elongated fluid-filled cyst, more frequently found posterior to the rectum or anus.[100]
  Epidermoid cyst: Epidermoid cyst is a rare congenital lesion of ectodermal origin, generally seen in women during reproductive age. At MR imaging, they appear as unilocular thin-walled cysts with a low T1 SI and a high T2 SI and show restricted diffusion. T2 hypointense foci may be detected within the lesion due to the presence of keratin.[101]

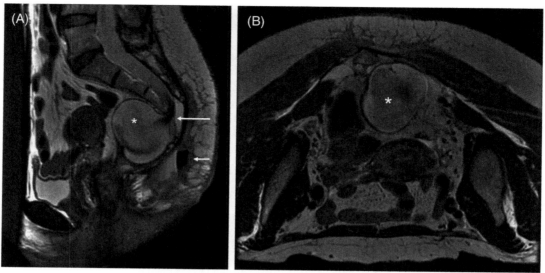

FIG. 17.41   **Anterior presacral meningocele in a female patient with sacrococcygeal malformation.** Sagittal T2-WI (A) and axial T2-WI (B) show a cystic mass in the presacral space (asterisks) that communicates with the thecal sac as indicated by the signal loss area resulting from cerebrospinal fluid turbulent flow (A, long arrow). Also note the presence of a subcutaneous coccygeal abscess (A, short arrow). *Case courtesy of Dr. Marco Panfili, Fondazione Policlinico Universitario Agostino Gemelli IRCCS, Rome, Italy.*

Anterior presacral meningocele: Meningocele is a rare congenital disorder due to herniation of cerebrospinal fluid filled sac lined by dura and arachnoid mater. The anterior meningocele is almost always presacral in location and is associated with sacral defect. At MRI, it is helpful to look for a sacral congenital defect that is associated with an unilocular well-defined cyst communicating with the thecal sac (Fig. 17.41).[102]

Tailgut cyst: Tailgut cyst or retrorectal cystic hamartoma is a rare congenital disease that arise from vestiges of an embryonic hindgut. It is more common in women and usually presents in middle age. Tailgut cyst is a thin walled multiloculated cystic mass filled with mucoid material.[103] On MR imaging, it appears as a multilocular cystic lesion with small cysts clustered together and adherent to the main cyst (honeycomb pattern), with a high T2 SI and a variable T1 SI due to protein and mucin content (Fig. 17.42).[103,104] Malignant change within the cyst is suspected if cystic lesion shows irregular wall thickening or nodular soft tissue with enhancement after contrast media administration.[103]

17.4.3 Deep endometriosis (DE)

Deep endometriosis affects about 20% of women with pelvic endometriosis and is a cause of pain and infertility. DE is defined as fibrous/muscular infiltration of organs and structures containing endometrial tissue below the peritoneum.[105] MRI is recommended as a second-line imaging modality in the preoperative workup of DE.[6] The deeply endometriotic lesions may often appear as a solid tumorlike mass with associated fibrosis and have signal intensity like the smooth muscle with a low T2 SI and an intermediate T1 SI; cystic areas—with or without hemorrhagic content—can be present.[60] DE may involve the posterior pelvic compartment (torus uterinus; utero-sacral ligaments; recto-vaginal septum; pouch of Douglas; recto-sigmoid junction), the anterior pelvic compartment (bladder and round ligaments) and the lateral pelvic compartment (parametrium and ureters). In this chapter we will cover the key imaging features of DE, but an extensive description of this topic will be found in the "MRI of Endometriosis" chapter.

17.4.3.1 *DE of posterior pelvic compartment*

Retrocervical space: The retrocervical space is commonly affected by deep infiltrating endometriosis and is frequently associated with vaginal or intestinal lesions.[60] The retrocervical space includes the torus uterinus and the utero-sacral ligaments. The torus uterinus is involved by endometriosis when there is a mass or thickening in the upper midportion of the posterior cervix.[105] The involvement of the utero-sacral ligaments is present when there is a nodular

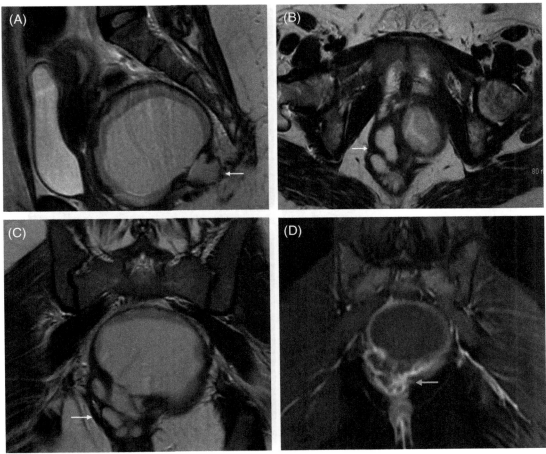

FIG. 17.42 **Tailgut cyst.** Sagittal T2-WI (A), axial T2-WI (B), and coronal T2-WI (C) show a presacral multicystic lesion with honeycomb pattern (white arrows) consistent with a tailgut cyst. The fat saturated postcontrast T1-WI (D) shows irregular wall thickening with enhancement (orange arrow).

mass with a regular or stellate margin close to the cervical utero-sacral insertion or when the ligament shows diffuse or localized fibrotic thickening (Fig. 17.43).

Recto-vaginal space: The recto-vaginal space is a region between the posterior vaginal wall and the anterior rectal wall below the peritoneum. The inferior two-third of this space is the recto-vaginal septum that is rarely affected by endometriosis.[60] Involvement by endometriosis appears as a nodular mass in the recto-vaginal septum.

Vagina: The vaginal endometriosis has a variable appearance from thickening of the superior one-third of the posterior vaginal wall to large polypoid mass that protrudes into the posterior vaginal fornix.[60]

Recto-sigmoid: Intestinal endometriosis occurs in 12–37% of patients and is associated with a severe and multifocal disease.[60] The most frequently affected areas are rectum and recto-sigmoid junction, and the intestinal involvement usually is multifocal. The typical imaging appearance of intestinal endometriosis is a solid nodule with a low T2 SI and an irregular margin attached to the intestinal wall (Fig. 17.44).

17.4.3.2 *DE of anterior pelvic compartment*

Bladder: Nodular endometriotic lesions are usually located at the level of vescico-uterine pouch with possible extension through the bladder wall involving muscular or mucosal layer (Fig. 17.45).[105]

Round ligament: Round ligament is affected by endometriosis if show a fibrotic thickening (usually >1 cm) with regular or irregular margins.[105]

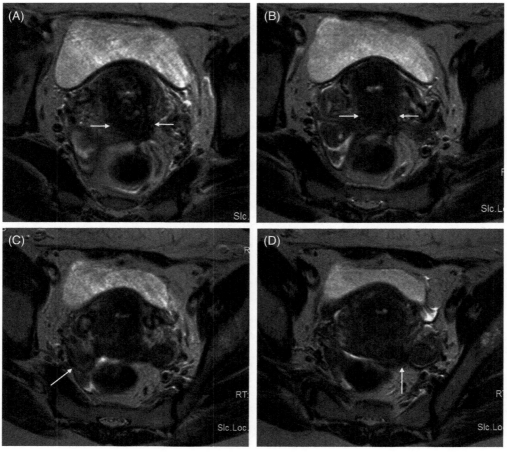

FIG. 17.43   Retrocervical endometriosis. Axial T2-WI (A–D) show a hypointense pseudo-mass involving the torus uterinus (arrows, A and B) and nodular thickening of the utero-sacral ligaments (arrows, C and D), findings that are consistent with retrocervical endometriosis.

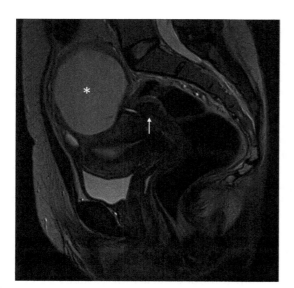

FIG. 17.44   Recto-sigmoid endometriosis. Sagittal T2-WI shows a solid hypointense nodule attached to the anterior wall of the recto-sigmoid junction (arrow). The hyperintense left ovarian cyst is consistent with endometrioma (asterisk).

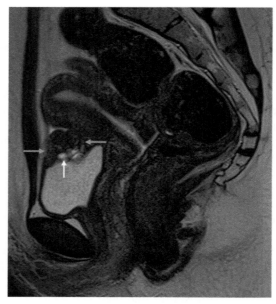

FIG. 17.45   Endometriosis of the vescico-uterine pouch. Sagittal T2-WI shows irregular thickening of the upper external aspect of the bladder wall (orange arrow) that partially obliterates the vescico-uterine recesses. Tiny hyperintense foci (white arrow) are also seen.

17.4.3.3 *DE of lateral pelvic compartment*

Parametrium: solid nodular endometriotic parametrial lesions show spiculated margins and a low T2SI in the paracervical region and may cause ureteral infiltration/dilatation.[105]

17.5 Conclusion

MRI can play a crucial role in assessment and appropriate management of benign female pelvic pathologies. An MRI examination should be usually performed when the pelvic ultrasound is not conclusive and in the preoperative work-up. Knowledge of MRI-related normal findings and key imaging features of common benign female pelvic diseases can expect to aid the early identification of pelvic pathologies.

References

1. Nougaret S, Cunha TM, Benadla N, Neron M, Robbins JB. Benign uterine disease: the added role of imaging. *Obstet Gynecol Clin North Am.* 2021;48(1):193–214.
2. Patel VH, Somers S. MR imaging of the female pelvis: current perspectives and review of genital tract congenital anomalies, and benign and malignant diseases. *Crit Rev Diagn Imaging.* 1997;38(5):417–499.
3. Sheikh-Sarraf M, Nougaret S, Forstner R, Kubik-Huch RA. Patient preparation and image quality in female pelvic MRI: recommendations revisited. *Eur Radiol.* 2020;30(10):5374–5383.
4. Huang SY, Seethamraju RT, Patel P, Hahn PF, Kirsch JE, Guimaraes AR. Body MR imaging: Artifacts, k-Space, and solutions. *Radiographics.* 2015;35(5):1439–1460.
5. Kubik-Huch RA, Weston M, Nougaret S, et al. European Society of Urogenital Radiology (ESUR) guidelines: MR imaging of leiomyomas. *Eur Radiol.* 2018;28(2018):3125–3137.
6. Bazot M, Bharwani N, Huchon C, et al. European society of urogenital radiology (ESUR) guidelines: MR imaging of pelvic endometriosis. *Eur Radiol.* 2017;27(7):2765–2775.
7. Maciel C, Bharwani N, Kubik-Huch RA, et al. MRI of female genital tract congenital anomalies: European Society of Urogenital Radiology (ESUR) guidelines. *Eur Radiol.* 2020;30:4272–4283.
8. Bazot M, Kermarrec E, Benifallah S, Daraï E. MRI of intestinal endometriosis. *Best Pract Res Clin Obstet Gynaecol.* 2021;71:51–63.
9. Canellas R, Rosenkrantz AB, Taouli B, et al. Abbreviated MRI protocols for the abdomen. *Radiographics.* 2019;39(3):744–758.
10. Proscia N, Jaffe TA, Neville AM, Wang CL, Dale BM, Merkle EM. MRI of the pelvis in women: 3D versus 2D T2-weighted technique. *AJR Am J Roentgenol.* 2010;195(1):254–259.
11. Manganaro L, Lakhman Y, Bharwani N, et al. Staging, recurrence and follow-up of uterine cervical cancer using MRI: Updated Guidelines of the European Society of Urogenital Radiology after revised FIGO staging 2018. *Eur Radiol.* 2021;31(10):7802–7816.
12. Nougaret S, Tirumani SH, Addley H, Pandey H, Sala E, Reinhold C. Pearls and pitfalls in MRI of gynecologic malignancy with diffusion-weighted technique. *AJR Am J Roentgenol.* 2013;200(2):261–276.
13. Lum M, Tsiouris AJ. MRI safety considerations during pregnancy. *Clin Imaging.* 2020;62:69–75.
14. Gui B, Cambi F, Micco M, et al. MRI in pregnant patients with suspected abdominal and pelvic cancer: a practical guide for radiologists. *Diagn Interv Radiol.* 2020;26(3):183–192.
15. Safety EPMR, E K, Barkovich AJ, et al. ACR guidance document on MR safe practices: 2013. *J Magn Reson Imaging.* 2013;37(3):501–530.
16. Tsai LL, Grant AK, Mortele KJ, Kung JW, Smith MP. A practical guide to MR imaging safety: what radiologists need to know. *Radiographics.* 2015;35(6):1722–1737.
17. Leyendecker JR, Gorengaut V, Brown JJ. MR imaging of maternal diseases of the abdomen and pelvis during pregnancy and the immediate postpartum period. *Radiographics.* 2004;24(5):1301–1316.
18. Birchard KR, Brown MA, Hyslop WB, Firat Z, Semelka RC. MRI of acute abdominal and pelvic pain in pregnant patients. *AJR Am J Roentgenol.* 2005;184(2):452–458.
19. Park SB, Lee JB. MRI features of ovarian cystic lesions. *J Magn Reson Imaging.* 2014;40(3):503–515.
20. Timmerman D, Van Calster B, Testa A, et al. Predicting the risk of malignancy in adnexal masses based on the Simple Rules from the International Ovarian Tumor Analysis group. *Am J Obstet Gynecol.* 2016;214(4):424–437.
21. Sadowski EA, Paroder V, Patel-Lippmann K, et al. Indeterminate adnexal cysts at US: prevalence and characteristics of ovarian cancer. *Radiology.* 2018;287(3):1041–1049.
22. Reinhold C, Rockall A, Sadowski EA, et al. Ovarian-adnexal reporting lexicon for MRI: a white paper of the ACR Ovarian-Adnexal Reporting and Data Systems MRI Committee. *J Am Coll Radiol.* 2021;18(5):713–729.
23. Sala EJ, Atri M. Magnetic resonance imaging of benign adnexal disease. *Top Magn Reson Imaging.* 2003;14(4):305–327.
24. Nougaret S, Nikolovski I, Paroder V, et al. MRI of tumors and tumor mimics in the female pelvis: anatomic pelvic space-based approach. *Radiographics.* 2019;39(4):1205–1229.
25. Oliveira JD, Cunha TM, Tereso A. Tumors of the broad ligament: what and when to suspect such rare location. *Radiol Bras.* 2020;53(5):349–355.
26. Lee JH, Jeong YK, Park JK, Hwang JC. Ovarian vascular pedicle" sign revealing organ of origin of a pelvic mass lesion on helical CT. *AJR Am J Roentgenol.* 2003;181(1):131–137.
27. Saksouk FA, Johnson SC. Recognition of the ovaries and ovarian origin of pelvic masses with CT. *Radiographics.* 2004;24(Suppl 1):S133–S146.
28. Nishino M, Hayakawa K, Minami M, Yamamoto A, Ueda H, Takasu K. Primary retroperitoneal neoplasms: CT and MR imaging findings with anatomic and pathologic diagnostic clues. *Radiographics.* 2003;23(1):45–57.

29. Tereso A, Oliveira J, Cunha TM. Solitary fibrous tumor of the female pelvis: clues to the radiological diagnosis. *Int J Med Sci Clin Invent.* 2018;6(10):4608–4611.

30. Horta M, Cunha MT. Pitfalls in imaging of female pelvic masses. *Curr Radiol Rep.* 2017;5:53.

31. Dionisio T, Veloso Gomes F, Cunha TM. Non-ovarian pelvic masses: key concepts and useful clues to the radiologist. Poster presented at: European Congress of Radiology (ECR); March 6–10, 2014; Vienna, Austria.

32. Thorek P. Chapter 31: Pelvic viscera. In: Thorek P, ed. *Anatomy in Surgery.* 3rd ed.: Springer; 1985:578–608.

33. Langer JE, Oliver ER, Lev-Toaff AS, Coleman BG. Imaging of the female pelvis through the life cycle. *Radiographics.* 2012;32(6):1575–1597.

34. Hauth EA, Jaeger HJ, Libera H, Lange S, Forsting M. Magnetic resonance imaging of the ovaries of healthy women: determination of normal values. *Acta Radiol.* 2006;47(9):986–992.

35. Outwater EK, Mitchell DG. Normal ovaries and functional cysts: MR appearance. *Radiology.* 1996;198(2):397–402.

36. Duarte AL, Dias JL, Cunha TM. Pitfalls of diffusion-weighted imaging of the female pelvis. *Radiol Bras.* 2018;51(1):37–44.

37. Agostinho L, Horta M, Salvador JC, Cunha TM. Benign ovarian lesions with restricted diffusion. *Radiol Bras.* 2019;52(2):106–111.

38. Togashi K. MR imaging of the ovaries: normal appearance and benign disease. *Radiol Clin North Am.* 2003;41(4):799–811.

39. Outwater EK, Talerman A, Dunton C. Normal adnexa uteri specimens: anatomic basis of MR imaging features. *Radiology.* 1996; 201(3):751–755.

40. Andreotti RF, Timmerman D, Strachowski LM, et al. O-RADS US risk stratification and management system: a consensus guideline from the ACR Ovarian-Adnexal Reporting and Data System Committee. *Radiology.* 2020;294(1):168–185.

41. Levine D, Patel MD, Suh-Burgmann EJ, et al. Simple adnexal cysts: SRU Consensus Conference update on follow-up and reporting. *Radiology.* 2019;293(2):359–371.

42. Jha P, Shekhar M, Goldstein R, Morgan T, Poder L. Size threshold for follow-up of postmenopausal adnexal cysts: 1 cm versus 3 cm. *Abdom Radiol (NY).* 2020;45(10):3213–3217.

43. Kanso HN, Hachem K, Aoun NJ, Haddad-Zebouni S, Klein-Tomb L, Atallah D, Buy JN, Ghossain MA. Variable MR findings in ovarian functional hemorrhagic cysts. *J Magn Reson Imaging.* 2006;24(2):356–361.

44. Kishimoto K, Ito K, Awaya H, Matsunaga N, Outwater EK, Siegelman ES. Paraovarian cyst: MR imaging features. *Abdom Imaging.* 2002;27(6):685–689.

45. Moyle PL, Kataoka MY, Nakai A, Takahata A, Reinhold C, Sala E. Nonovarian cystic lesions of the pelvis. *Radiographics.* 2010;30(4):921–938.

46. Kim JS, Woo SK, Suh SJ, Morettin LB. Sonographic diagnosis of paraovarian cysts: value of detecting a separate ipsilateral ovary. *AJR Am J Roentgenol.* 1995;164(6):1441–1444.

47. Phy J, Foong S, Session D, Thornhill A, Tummon I, Dumesic D. Transvaginal ultrasound detection of multifollicular ovaries in non-hirsute ovulatory women. *Ultrasound Obstet Gynecol.* 2004;23(2):183–187.

48. Rothenberg SS, Beverley R, Barnard E, Baradaran-Shoraka M, Sanfilippo JS. Polycystic ovary syndrome in adolescents. *Best Pract Res Clin Obstet Gynaecol.* 2018;48:103–114.

49. Badeeb A, Brook A, Lee KS. Dark cortical rim: an MRI feature of polycystic ovarian syndrome. *Abdom Radiol (NY).* 2021;46(3):1148–1156.

50. Telischak NA, Yeh BM, Joe BN, Westphalen AC, Poder L, Coakley FV. MRI of adnexal masses in pregnancy. *AJR Am J Roentgenol.* 2008;191(2):364–370.

51. Takeuchi M, Matsuzaki K, Nishitani H. Manifestations of the female reproductive organs on MR images: changes induced by various physiologic states. *Radiographics.* 2010;30(4):1147.

52. Baron KT, Babagbemi KT, Arleo EK, Asrani AV, Troiano RN. Emergent complications of assisted reproduction: expecting the unexpected. *Radiographics.* 2013;33(1):229–244.

53. Chaverri AP, Solis BEA, Paulín FD, Cárdenas JEG. Hyperreactio luteinalis and hypothyroidism: a case report. *Case Rep Womens Health.* 2018;21:e00094.

54. Kim MY, Rha SE, Oh SN, et al. MR imaging findings of hydrosalpinx: a comprehensive review. *Radiographics.* 2009;29(2):495–507.

55. Outwater EK, Siegelman ES, Chiowanich P, Kilger AM, Dunton CJ, Talerman A. Dilated fallopian tubes: MR imaging characteristics. *Radiology.* 1998;208(2):463–469.

56. Tukeva TA, Aronen HJ, Karjalainen PT, Molander P, Paavonen T, Paavonen J. MR imaging in pelvic inflammatory disease: comparison with laparoscopy and US. *Radiology.* 1999 Jan;210(1):209–216.

57. Protopapas AG, Diakomanolis ES, Milingos SD, et al. Tubo-ovarian abscesses in postmenopausal women: gynecological malignancy until proven otherwise? *Eur J Obstet Gynecol Reprod Biol.* 2004;114(2):203–209.

58. Unal O, Koparan HI, Avcu S, Kalender AM, Kisli E. The diagnostic value of diffusion-weighted magnetic resonance imaging in soft tissue abscesses. *Eur J Radiol.* 2011;77(3):490–494.

59. David A, Rockall A. Acute and chronic pelvic pain disorders. In: Forstner R, Cunha TM, Hamm B, eds. *MRI and CT of the Female Pelvis.* 2nd ed.: Springer; 2019:381–405.

60. Chamié LP, Blasbalg R, Pereira RM, Warmbrand G, Serafini PC. Findings of pelvic endometriosis at transvaginal US, MR imaging, and laparoscopy. *Radiographics.* 2011;31(4):E77–100.

61. Khashper A, Addley HC, Abourokbah N, Nougaret S, Sala E, Reinhold C. T2-hypointense adnexal lesions: an imaging algorithm. *Radiographics.* 2020;40(4):1200.

62. Dias JL, Veloso Gomes F, Lucas R, Cunha TM. The shading sign: is it exclusive of endometriomas? *Abdom Imaging.* 2015;40(7):2566–2572.

63. Corwin MT, Gerscovich EO, Lamba R, Wilson M, McGahan JP. Differentiation of ovarian endometriomas from hemorrhagic cysts at MR imaging: utility of the T2 dark spot sign. *Radiology.* 2014;271(1):126–132.

64. Dawood MT, Naik M, Bharwani N, Sudderuddin SA, Rockall AG, Stewart VR. Adnexal torsion: review of radiologic appearances. *Radiographics.* 2021;41(2):609–624.

65. Dahmoush H, Anupindi SA, Pawel BR, Chauvin NA. Multimodality imaging findings of massive ovarian edema in children. *Pediatr Radiol.* 2017;47(5):576–583.

66. Srisajjakul S, Prapaisilp P, Bangchokdee S. Magnetic resonance imaging in tubal and non-tubal ectopic pregnancy. *Eur J Radiol.* 2017;93:76–89.

67. Io S, Hasegawa M, Koyama T. A case of ovarian pregnancy diagnosed by MRI. *Case Rep Obstet Gynecol.* 2015;2015:143031.

68. Revzin MV, Mathur M, Dave HB, Macer ML, Spektor M. Pelvic inflammatory disease: multimodality imaging approach with clinical-pathologic correlation. *Radiographics.* 2016;36(5):1579–1596.

69. Behr SC, Courtier JL, Qayyum A. Imaging of Müllerian duct anomalies. *Radiographics.* 2012;32(6):E233–E250.

70. Deshmukh SP, Gonsalves CF, Guglielmo FF, Mitchell DG. Role of MR imaging of uterine leiomyomas before and after embolization. *Radiographics.* 2012;32(6):E251–E281.

71. Munro MG, Critchley HO, Broder MS, Fraser ISFIGO Working Group on Menstrual Disorders. FIGO classification system (PALM-COEIN) for causes of abnormal uterine bleeding in nongravid women of reproductive age. *Int J Gynaecol Obstet.* 2011;113(1):3–13.

72. Reiter MJ, Schwope RB, Lisanti CJ, Banks NB. Can a T2 hyperintense rim sign differentiate uterine leiomyomas from other solid adnexal masses? *Abdom Imaging.* 2015;40(8):3182–3190.

73. Abdel Wahab C, Jannot AS, Bonaffini PA, et al. Diagnostic algorithm to differentiate benign atypical leiomyomas from malignant uterine sarcomas with diffusion-weighted MRI. *Radiology.* 2020;297(2):361–371.

74. Lakhman Y, Veeraraghavan H, Chaim J, et al. Differentiation of uterine leiomyosarcoma from atypical leiomyoma: diagnostic accuracy of qualitative MR imaging features and feasibility of texture analysis. *Eur Radiol.* 2017;27(7):2903–2915.

75. Kobayashi H, Matsubara S. A classification proposal for adenomyosis based on magnetic resonance imaging. *Gynecol Obstet Invest.* 2020;85(2):118–126.

76. Bazot M, Daraï E. Role of transvaginal sonography and magnetic resonance imaging in the diagnosis of uterine adenomyosis. *Fertil Steril.* 2018;109(3):389–397.

77. Nougaret S, Sbarra M, Robbins J. Imaging spectrum of benign uterine disease and treatment options. *Radiol Clin North Am.* 2020;58(2):239–256.

78. Tamai K, Togashi K, Ito T, Morisawa N, Fujiwara T, Koyama T. MR imaging findings of adenomyosis: correlation with histopathologic features and diagnostic pitfalls. *Radiographics.* 2005;25(1):21–40.

79. Brosens JJ, de Souza NM, Barker FG. Uterine junctional zone: function and disease. *Lancet.* 1995;346(8974):558–560.

80. Sudderuddin S, Helbren E, Telesca M, Williamson R, Rockall A. MRI appearances of benign uterine disease. *Clin Radiol.* 2014; 69(11):1095–1104.

81. Hase S, Mitsumori A, Inai R, et al. Endometrial polyps: MR imaging features. *Acta Med Okayama.* 2012;66(6):475–485.

82. Dreisler E, Sorensen SS, Ibsen PH, Lose G. Value of endometrial thickness measurement for diagnosing focal intrauterine pathology in women without abnormal uterine bleeding. *Ultrasound Obstet Gynecol.* 2009;33(3):344–348.

83. Nalaboff KM, Pellerito JS, Ben-Levi E. Imaging the endometrium: disease and normal variants. *Radiographics.* 2001;21(6):1409–1424.

84. Fujii S, Matsusue E, Kigawa J, et al. Diagnostic accuracy of the apparent diffusion coefficient in differentiating benign from malignant uterine endometrial cavity lesions: initial results. *Eur Radiol.* 2008;18(2):384–389.

85. Bharwani N, Miquel ME, Sahdev A, et al. Diffusion-weighted imaging in the assessment of tumour grade in endometrial cancer. *Br J Radiol.* 2011;84(1007):997–1004.

86. Kawaguchi M, Kato H, Suzui N, et al. MR imaging findings differentiating uterine submucosal polypoid adenomyomas from endometrial polyps. *Br J Radiol.* 2019;92(1095):20180430.

87. Rechichi G, Galimberti S, Signorelli M, et al. Endometrial cancer: correlation of apparent diffusion coefficient with tumor grade, depth of myometrial invasion, and presence of lymph node metastases. *AJR Am J Roentgenol.* 2011;197(1):256–262.

88. Honnef I, Moschopulos M, Roeren T. Appendiceal mucinous cystadenoma. *Radiographics.* 2008;28(5):1524–1527.

89. Fonseca C, Carvalho S, Cunha TM, Gil RT, Abecasis N. The many faces of pseudomyxoma peritonei: a radiological review based on 30 cases. *Radiol Bras.* 2019;52(6):372–377.

90. Jain KA. Imaging of peritoneal inclusion cysts. *AJR Am J Roentgenol.* 2000;174(6):1559–1563.

91. Fujii S, Inoue C, Mukuda N, et al. Magnetic resonance imaging findings of endosalpingiosis: a case report. *Acta Radiol Open.* 2021;10(6):20584601211022504.

92. Ong NCS, Maher PJ, Pyman JM, Readman E, Endosalpingiosis GS. an unrecognized condition: report and literature review. *Gynecol Surg SpringerOpen.* 2004;1(1):11–14.

93. Hosseinzadeh K, Heller MT, Houshmand G. Imaging of the female perineum in adults. *Radiographics.* 2012;32(4):E129–E168.

94. Ozel A, Kirdar O, Halefoglu AM, Erturk SM, Karpat Z, Lo Russo G, Maldur V, Cantisani V. Cysts of the canal of Nuck: ultrasound and magnetic resonance imaging findings. *J Ultrasound.* 2009;12(3):125–127.

95. Yu JS, Kim KW, Lee HJ, Lee YJ, Yoon CS, Kim MJ. Urachal remnant diseases: spectrum of CT and US findings. *Radiographics.* 2001;21(2):451–461.

96. Kier R. Nonovarian gynecologic cysts: MR imaging findings. *AJR Am J Roentgenol.* 1992;158(6):1265–1269.

97. Chaudhari VV, Patel MK, Douek M, Raman SS. MR imaging and US of female urethral and periurethral disease. *Radiographics.* 2010;30(7):1857–1874.

98. Patel N, Maturen KE, Kaza RK, Gandikota G, Al-Hawary MM, Wasnik AP. Imaging of presacral masses: a multidisciplinary approach. *Br J Radiol.* 2016;89(1061):20150698.

99. Chamié LP, Ribeiro D, Tiferes DA, Macedo Neto AC, Serafini PC. Atypical sites of deeply infiltrative endometriosis: clinical characteristics and imaging findings. *Radiographics.* 2018;38(1):309–328.

100. Kim H, Kim JH, Lim JS, et al. MRI findings of rectal submucosal tumors. *Korean J Radiol.* 2011;12(4):487–498.

101. Alvi MI, Mubarak F, Khandwala K, Barakzai MD, Memon A. A rare case of presacral epidermoid cyst in an adult male: emphasis on diffusion weighted magnetic resonance sequences in preoperative imaging. *Cureus.* 2018;10(1):e2050.

102. Kumar J, Afsal M, Garg A. Imaging spectrum of spinal dysraphism on magnetic resonance: a pictorial review. *World J Radiol.* 2017;9(4):178–190.

103. Yang DM, Park CH, Jin W, et al. Tailgut cyst: MRI evaluation. *AJR Am J Roentgenol.* 2005;184(5):1519–1523.

104. Shetty AS, Loch R, Yoo N, Mellnick V, Fowler K, Narra V. Imaging of tailgut cysts. *Abdom Imaging.* 2015;40(7):2783–2795.

105. Bazot M, Daraï E. Diagnosis of deep endometriosis: clinical examination, ultrasonography, magnetic resonance imaging, and other techniques. *Fertil Steril.* 2017;108(6):886–894.

18

MRI of ovarian tumors

Luke Ginocchio[a], Krishna Shanbhogue[a], Lokesh Khanna[b],
Venkata S. Katabathina[b], Srinivasa R. Prasad[c]

[a]Department of Radiology, NYU Langone Health, Grossman School of Medicine, New York, NY
[b]Department of Radiology, University of Texas Health Science Center, San Antonio [c]Department of
Radiology, MD Anderson Cancer Center, Houston, TX, United States

18.1 Introduction

Ovarian masses present a real diagnostic dilemma. Although functional or benign cysts and tumors constitute a vast majority of ovarian masses, ovarian cancer (3% of all cancers in women) remains the second most common gynecologic malignancy and the fifth leading cause of death from cancer in women in the United States.[1] Based on histogenesis and histopathology, ovarian tumors are divided into four major categories: epithelial, germ cell, sex cord–stromal, and metastases. While nonepithelial and benign tumors such as mature teratomas commonly occur in younger patients (20–45 years), epithelial cancers predominate in older patients (45–65 years). Epithelial carcinomas (90% of all ovarian cancers) comprise the most lethal gynecological cancers, with most patients manifesting advanced disease at presentation. High-grade serous carcinoma, constituting 70% of ovarian cancers, accounts for 90% of cancer deaths.[2] There are various epidemiologic, genetic, and lifestyle risk factors for ovarian cancer, including nulliparity, early menopause, gonadal dysgenesis, family history, BRCA1/BRCA2 mutations, Lynch syndrome (LS), smoking, or previous history of breast, endometrial, or colon cancer. In contrast, oral contraceptive use and breastfeeding are protective factors.

In addition to assessing a patient's clinical history and risk factors as described above, serological tests are frequently obtained to evaluate a patient who is either at high risk for ovarian cancer or has a known ovarian mass. The most common serological marker for ovarian cancer is CA-125,[3] elevated in most ovarian malignancies (~80% in general). However, some mucinous and germ cell tumors may not secrete this marker. An additional marker that can be used to assess ovarian cancer is AFP, which may be elevated with immature ovarian teratomas (~50% of cases) and ovarian yolk sac tumors. Finally, β-human chorionic gonadotropin (hCG) may be elevated in a small number of dysgerminomas.

A multimodality approach, including clinical examination, imaging, and serological tests, is essential to detect malignant masses at an early stage. In the setting of normal serum CA-125 assay, endovaginal US, and clinical pelvic examination, the diagnosis of ovarian cancer is virtually excluded. Determination of suspicion for malignancy is critical and is based mainly on imaging morphology. Transvaginal ultrasound (TVUS) is often the initial imaging modality of choice, owing to it being readily available and having a high negative predictive value. It helps stratify masses as either low-risk or high-risk, with high-risk ultrasound features including nonfatty solid vascular tissue, thick septations, and papillary projections.

18.2 Role of MRI in evaluating adnexal masses

MRI is an excellent imaging modality for accurate lesion characterization, particularly in cases of equivocal or non-diagnostic ultrasound findings. The main advantages of MRI are high contrast resolution with excellent soft tissue contrast as well as lack of ionizing radiation exposure and the need for iodinated contrast agents, which is particularly important in young women. On MR imaging, ovarian masses may be broadly categorized into hemorrhagic, fatty, fibrous, cystic, or soft tissue masses.[4] The ability to detect these additional features allows for categorizing certain masses, such as mature cystic teratomas, cysts, endometriomas, leiomyomas, and fibromas, to be diagnosed on imaging alone without the need for histopathologic sampling.[5] MR imaging findings of a plethora of ovarian masses will be discussed in this chapter.

18.3 Pelvic MRI technique

While specific acquisition sequences and total scan time can vary by manufacturer, patient compliance, and the clinical scenario, images must be obtained in at least two planes for adequate pelvic MR imaging evaluation. For pelvic anatomy and tissue characterization, acquisition of both T1- and T2-weighted images is critical. Use of a small field of view, high-resolution matrix, and thin section imaging facilitates depiction of detailed internal architecture of tumors. Additional fat-saturated T1-weighted images can help differentiate fatty and hemorrhagic masses.[6] Diffusion-weighted images using high b-value as well as ADC maps allow distinction of malignant from benign ovarian tumors. These images are also invaluable in assessing treatment response to a plethora of therapeutic options. Gadolinium-enhanced T1-weighted images can help further characterize the internal architecture of cystic lesions and improve the identification of peritoneal implants.[7] Compilation of dynamic contrast enhancement curves is extremely useful for the assessment of malignant tumors.

18.4 Ovarian tumors

Primary ovarian neoplasms are mainly classified into three categories based on pathology: epithelial, germ cell, and sex cord–stromal tumors. Additionally, ovary is a common site for metastatic disease.

18.4.1 Ovarian epithelial tumors

Ovarian epithelial tumors, the most common ovarian neoplasms, are categorized into benign, borderline, and malignant subtypes based on pathological features and biological behavior. Despite a putative origin from a monotonous surface epithelium (peritoneum), ovarian epithelial cancers show remarkable histological diversity with serous, endometrioid, clear cell, mucinous, and transitional subtypes recapitulating Mullerian epithelia of the fallopian tube, uterus, vagina, and ureteral bud, respectively. Most hereditary and sporadic high-grade serous carcinomas, the most common subtype contributing to two-thirds of deaths from ovarian cancer, arise from genetically unstable microscopic precursors in the fallopian tube (serous tubal intraepithelial carcinomas and p53 signatures) and demonstrate rapid, transcoelomic spread with advanced disease at presentation. Low-grade endometrioid and clear cell carcinomas comprise 20% of cancers, develop against the background of endometriosis and portend a favorable prognosis. A subset of clear cell and endometrioid cancers arise from cystadenofibromas. Most low-grade serous cancers develop from benign and borderline serous neoplasms. High-grade serous, low-grade serous, clear cell, and endometrioid cancers show mutually exclusive, predominant *p53*, *BRAF/KRAS*, *PIK3CA*, and *PTEN* mutations, respectively. While high-grade serous cancers show exquisite responsiveness to platinum-based chemotherapy, low-grade serous, mucinous, and clear cell carcinomas are remarkably platinum-resistant.

18.4.2 Ovarian serous tumors

Ovarian serous cystadenomas account for approximately 60% of ovarian serous tumors.[8] They are generally asymptomatic and occur in the fourth to fifth decade of life. They can be bilateral in approximately 15% of cases. On MR imaging, these appear as T1 hypointense, T2 hyperintense lesions without enhancing components[9] (Fig. 18.1). Cyst wall enhancement can be occasionally seen.

Ovarian borderline serous carcinomas have a peak age of presentation of 45 years of age and characteristically have papillary projections. A unique feature of ovarian borderline serous cystadenomas is the noninvasive behavior of extraovarian tumor implants in the advanced stages of the disease.[10] MR imaging features of borderline tumors can overlap with cystadenomas as well as cystadenocarcinoma. These include enhancing internal septations and enhancing papillary projections (Fig. 18.2). Solid enhancing components typical of serous cystadenocarcinoma are rare.

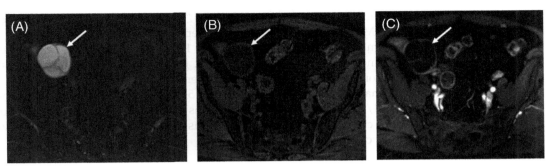

FIG. 18.1 **Serous cystadenoma.** Axial T2-weighted image (A) and axial fat-suppressed T1-weighted image (B) demonstrates a T2 hyperintense, T1 hypointense lesion in the right adnexa with multiple thin septations. Axial contrast-enhanced T1-weighted image (C) demonstrates enhancement of the wall and septae.

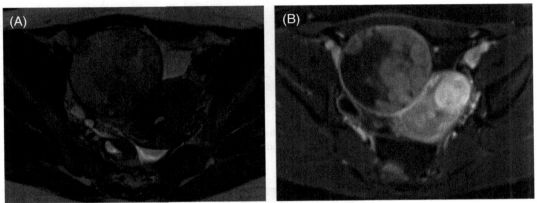

FIG. 18.2 **Serous borderline neoplasm.** Axial T2-weighted image (A) and axial contrast-enhanced T1-weighted image (B) demonstrates a complex right ovarian mass with solid and cystic components.

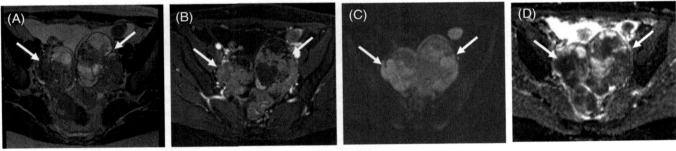

FIG. 18.3 **Serous cystadenocarcinoma.** Axial T2-weighted image (A) demonstrates bilateral complex sold and cystic ovarian masses, with T2 intermediate signal within the solid component. The solid components demonstrate avid enhancement on axial contrast-enhanced T1-weighted image (B), high signal on diffusion-weighted images (C) and corresponding low signal on ADC maps (D).

Ovarian cystadenocarcinoma is the most common type of ovarian malignancy with a peak incidence in the sixth to seventh decade of life.[11] MR imaging demonstrates heterogeneous signal intensity on T1- and T2-weighted images representing cystic and solid components. The solid portion demonstrates intermediate T2 signal, diffusion restriction, and enhancement (Fig. 18.3). Psammomatous calcifications are more commonly found in low-grade serous carcinomas than in high-grade cancers.

18.4.3 Ovarian mucinous tumors

Ovarian mucinous cystadenomas account for approximately 80% of ovarian mucinous tumors.[8] They are generally asymptomatic and occur in the fourth to sixth decade of life. They are rarely bilateral (approximately 2–5% of cases). Mural calcification is more common than in serous tumors.[12] On MR imaging, mucinous cystadenomas typically appear as multiloculated cysts with variable signal intensity within the "locules" due to areas of differing viscosity ("stained glass appearance") (Fig. 18.4). Mild wall enhancement and septal enhancement can be seen.

Ovarian borderline mucinous carcinomas account for approximately 10–15% of ovarian mucinous tumors. There are two subtypes: intestinal (most common) and Mullerian.[13] On MR imaging, these are indistinguishable from mucinous cystadenomas; they may demonstrate septal or wall enhancement (Fig. 18.5).

Ovarian mucinous cystadenocarcinomas account for approximately 5–10% of ovarian mucinous tumors. Generally, the greater the proportion of solid/nodular, nonfatty, nonfibrous tissue is the most powerful predictor of malignancy.[11] On MR imaging, mucinous cystadenocarcinoma appears as a multiloculated cystic lesion with enhancing septations, mural nodules, and solid components (Fig. 18.6).

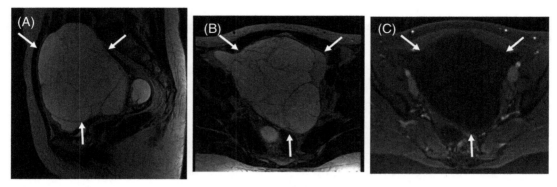

FIG. 18.4   Mucinous cystadenoma. Sagittal (A) and axial T2-weighted images (B) and axial T1-weighted contrast-enhanced image (C) demonstrates a large multiseptate pelvic mass with thin enhancing septae and enhancing wall. No solid components or mural nodules were seen.

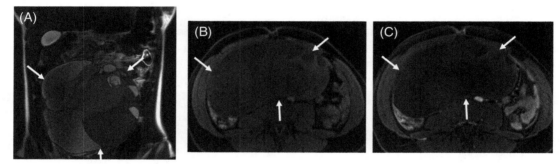

FIG. 18.5   Mucinous borderline neoplasm. Coronal T2-weighted image (A) and axial T1-weighted image (B) demonstrates a large septated pelvic mass, with variable T2 and T1 signal intensity within the different locules, characteristic of mucinous cystic neoplasm. Axial contrast-enhanced T1-weighted image (C) demonstrates enhancement within the septae. No solid components or mural nodules were seen.

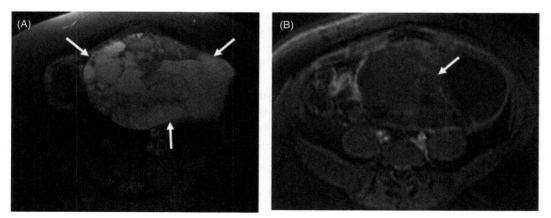

FIG. 18.6   Mucinous cystadenocarcinoma. Axial T2-weighted image (A) demonstrates a large septated pelvic mass, with variable T2 and T1 signal intensity within the different locules, characteristic of mucinous cystic neoplasm. Axial contrast-enhanced T1-weighted image (B) demonstrates multiple enhancing septae and solid enhancing component (arrow in B).

18.4.4 Endometrioid tumors

Endometrioid tumors are often malignant and invasive and account for 8–15% of all ovarian carcinomas.[14] They are the most common malignant neoplasm arising within an endometrioma. High risk factors for malignant transformation include larger size of endometriomas and long duration of endometriosis. Histologically, endometrioid tumors are characterized by the appearance of tubular glands and appear similar to the endometrium. Synchronous endometrial carcinoma or endometrial hyperplasia may be seen in approximately 33% of cases. On imaging, they are often complex nonspecific solid-cystic masses and found associated with endometriosis. On MR imaging, these tumors demonstrate variable signal intensity on T1-weighted images and often demonstrate T2 hypointense signal within the wall, with occasional T2 shading[15] (Fig. 18.7). Heterogeneous, variable enhancement is seen following the administration of gadolinium.

18.4.5 Clear cell tumors

Clear cell ovarian carcinomas account for approximately 2–5% of ovarian carcinomas and have a mean age of presentation of 55 years. In 25% of cases, clear cell carcinomas develop in patients with endometriosis.[16] On imaging, these often appear as a unilocular or large cyst with one or more solid nodular protrusions. These lesions demonstrate variable signal intensity on T1- and T2-weighted images. Enhancing solid component or mural nodule within an endometrioma should raise concern for clear cell carcinoma developing within an endometrioma (Fig. 18.8).

18.4.6 Brenner tumors

Brenner tumors account for approximately 3% of ovarian epithelial neoplasms, with a peak incidence of the fifth to seventh decade of life. In 30% of cases, they are associated with another epithelial ovarian neoplasm of either the ipsilateral or contralateral ovary. Histologically, they appear as transitional cells covered by fibrous stroma.[17] MR imaging features include hypointense T1 and T2 signal with low-level enhancement following administration of gadolinium (Fig. 18.9).

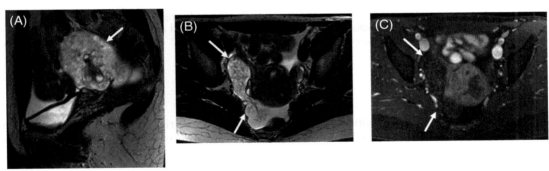

FIG. 18.7   Endometroid neoplasm. Sagittal (A) and axial (B) T2-weighted images demonstrates a well-circumscribed T2 hyperintense right adnexal lesion involving the right ovary with multiple small foci of T2 hypointense signal within. Axial contrast-enhanced T1-weighted image (C) demonstrates heterogeneous enhancing nodular components within the lesion.

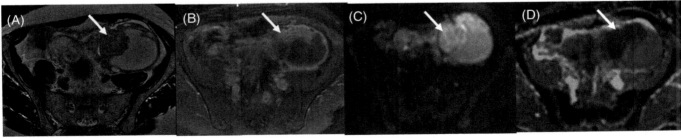

FIG. 18.8   Clear cell carcinoma arising within an endometrioma. Axial T2-weighted image (A) and axial T1-weighted contrast-enhanced image (B) demonstrate a cystic left adnexal mass with solid enhancing component anteriorly (arrow). The solid component demonstrates high signal on diffusion-weighted images (C) and corresponding low signal on ADC maps (D).

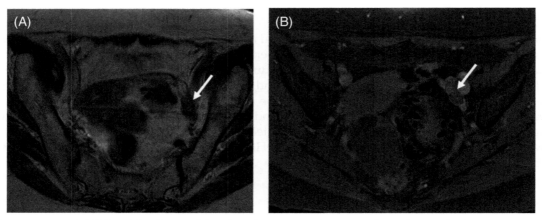

FIG. 18.9   **Brenner tumor.** Axial T2-weighted image (A) and axial T1-weighted contrast-enhanced image (B) demonstrate a solid T2 hypointense mass in the left ovary with moderate enhancement.

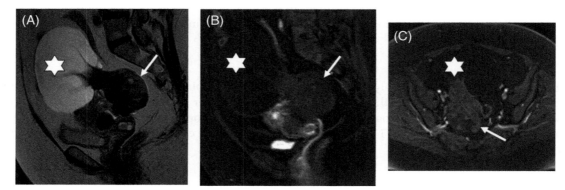

FIG. 18.10   **Cystadenofibroma.** Sagittal T2-weighted image (A) demonstrates a complex right adnexal mass with T2 hyperintense anterior component (asterisk) and T2 hypointense posterior component (white arrow). Sagittal (B) and axial (C) contrast-enhanced T1-weighted images demonstrate no internal enhancement within the anterior cystic component ("cystadenoma" component) and moderate enhancement in the posterior component ("fibroma" component).

18.4.7   Cystadenofibromas

Ovarian cystadenofibromas are relatively uncommon benign epithelial ovarian neoplasms with a dominant fibrous component and represent approximately 1.7% of all benign ovarian tumors.[18] These can be bilateral in approximately 15% of cases. On MR imaging, these appear as either pure cystic or complex cystic lesions with solid components in a nodular or trabecular pattern. On T2-weighted images, these appear hyperintense (cystic portions), with interspersed hypointense areas representing the fibrous portions (Fig. 18.10). The fibrous component enhances simulating cystadenocarcinoma.

18.4.8   Rare epithelial tumors

Squamous cell carcinomas of the ovary are extremely rare tumors that usually arise within a mature cystic ovarian teratoma, with a mean age of diagnosis of 55 years.[19] MR imaging features are variable with no specific features; a large solid component, especially if irregular or with the suggestion of tissue infiltration within a dermoid cyst, should raise concern for squamous cell carcinomas arising within a dermoid cyst. Ovarian fibrosarcomas are fibrous tumors with high mitotic figures, which may arise de novo or from an ovarian fibroma.[20] On MR imaging, these lesions demonstrate variable signal intensity with no specific features. Fibrosarcoma usually presents as a large unilateral ovarian heterogeneous solid mass with frequent areas of hemorrhage and cystic degeneration. Undifferentiated carcinomas are a rare type of malignant ovarian epithelial tumors, which account for approximately 4% of ovarian cancers[21] and exhibit no specific MR imaging features enabling their differentiation from other malignant ovarian neoplasms.

18.4.9 Germ cell ovarian tumors

Germ cell ovarian tumors include teratoma (mature cystic teratoma, immature teratoma, struma ovarii, and carcinoid), dysgerminoma, yolk sac tumor, embryonal carcinoma, choriocarcinoma, and malignant mixed germ cell tumor.

18.4.10 Ovarian teratoma

Mature cystic ovarian teratomas are the most common ovarian neoplasms (accounting for 15% of tumors), which contain elements from at least two of the three germ cell layers. They may contain skin, hair follicles, sweat glands, sebum, blood, fat, bone, nails, teeth, cartilage, or thyroid tissue and may be bilateral in 10–15% of cases. The peak age of incidence is 30 years.[22] Complications include ovarian torsion, rupture, malignant transformation (into squamous cell carcinoma), infection, autoimmune hemolytic anemia, or rarely limbic encephalitis.[23] On MR imaging, the teratomas are diagnosed by the presence of macroscopic fat which is hyperintense on non–fat-suppressed T1WI with loss of signal on fat-suppressed T1WI. Occasionally, the teratomas may show intravoxel fat with signal drop on opposed phase T1WI without visible bulk fat on frequency selective fat-suppressed sequences. On T2WI, cystic component of teratomas is usually hyperintense; may contain fluid–fluid levels. No enhancing components are usually seen on contrast-enhanced T1WI (Fig. 18.11). The Rokitansky protuberance may however occasionally show enhancement. An uncommon but pathognomonic imaging feature of dermoid cyst is that of a large cyst with multiple small spherical structures floating within the cyst ("floating ball" sign) (Fig. 18.12). The spherules represent aggregates of sebaceous materials and are composed of variable proportions of kertain, fibrin, hemosiderin, hair, and fat. Any larger enhancing solid component within a dermoid cyst should raise concern for malignant transformation which is fortunately very rare.

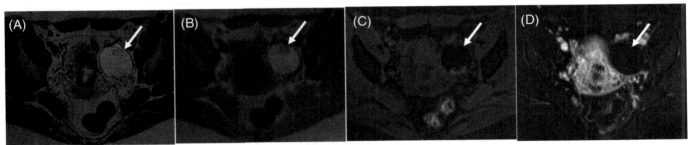

FIG. 18.11 **Mature cystic teratoma.** Axial T2-weighted image (A) and an axial T1-weighted non–fat-suppressed image (B) demonstrate a left ovarian lesion with T2 hyperintense signal, and T1 hyperintense signal. Axial T1-weighted fat-suppressed image (C) demonstrates diffuse signal drop compatible with bulk fat. Axial contrast-enhanced T1-weighted image (D) demonstrates no internal enhancement.

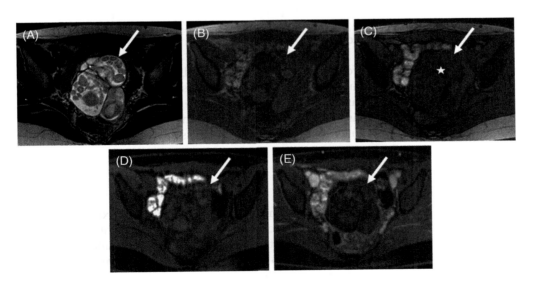

FIG. 18.12 **Mature cystic teratoma with "floating ball" sign.** Axial T2-weighted image (A), axial T1-weighted in-phase (B), and opposed phase (c) demonstrate a large left ovarian lesion with multiple spherical structures floating within a larger cyst. The smaller spherical structures are hyperintense on in-phase image (B) but demonstrate no bulk fat on fat-suppressed T1-weighted image (D). There is signal loss on opposed phase T1-weighted image with the dermoid cyst between in the floating spherical structures, a finding occasionally seen with dermoid cyst (intravoxel fat, asterisk in C). Axial contrast-enhanced T1-weighted image (E) no enhancing solid components.

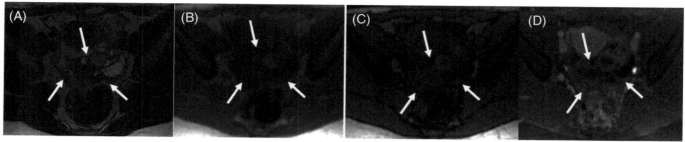

FIG. 18.13   Immature teratoma. Axial T2-weighted image (A) demonstrates a right adnexal mass with T2 intermediate signal and ill-defined infiltrative margins. Axial T1-weighted in-phase (B) and opposed phase (C) images demonstrate signal drop on out of phase sequences. Axial contrast-enhanced T1-weighted image (C) demonstrates moderate heterogeneous enhancement with infiltrative margins.

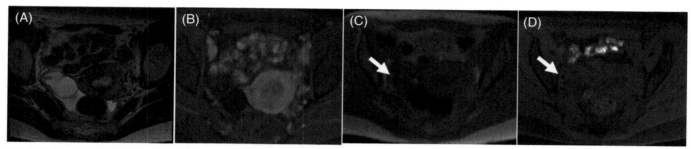

FIG. 18.14   Struma ovarii. Axial T2-weighted image (A) and axial T1-weighted contrast-enhanced image (B) demonstrate a cystic right adnexal mass with few enhancing septae and a small enhancing mural nodule anteriorly. A small focus of bulk fat was seen within this lesion with hyperintense T1 signal on axial T1-weighted image (C) with signal drop on axial fat-suppressed T1-weighted image (arrow in D).

Immature ovarian teratomas are relatively uncommon, representing less than 1% of ovarian teratomas, and often occur in the first two decades of life.[22] They are characterized by the presence of immature or embryonic tissue, in addition to mature tissue elements. They may occur in the presence of an ipsilateral mature cystic teratoma (25% of cases) or a contralateral immature cystic teratoma (10% of cases). MR imaging features include a prominent solid component containing calcifications and interspersed small foci of fat (Fig. 18.13). Areas of hemorrhage may also be seen.[24]

Struma ovarii tumors are a subtype of ovarian teratomas composed predominantly of thyroid tissue (3% of mature cystic teratomas). Approximately 5–8% of cases may be complicated by thyrotoxicosis.[25] On MR imaging, struma ovarii appears as a multiloculated cystic mass with solid components (Fig. 18.14). Cystic spaces within the struma may demonstrate variable T1/T2 signal due to the presence of viscous colloid (T1 hyperintense, T2 hypointense). Solid portions may enhance following administration of contrast. A nonfunctioning struma ovarii cannot be differentiated from other complex cystic ovarian masses.

Ovarian neuroendocrine tumors are rare, accounting for approximately 0.3% of all ovarian tumors.[26] Primary carcinoid tumors are usually unilateral and may present as solid nodules within a cystic teratoma or a pure solid hypervascular mass. At imaging, hypervascular solid mass is seen, which may have nonenhancing areas and is usually indistinguishable from other solid ovarian neoplasms (Fig. 18.15). On T2WI, hyperintense signal suggests a mucinous carcinoid tumor.[27] Metastatic carcinoids are usually bilateral with and associated with the peritoneal disease.

18.4.11 Other ovarian germ cell tumors

Ovarian dysgerminomas are the most common malignant germ cell tumors and account for approximately 1% of all ovarian neoplasms,[28] with a peak incidence in the second to third decade of life. They are thought to arise from primordial germ cells and are considered the ovarian counterpart of testicular seminomas. Approximately 10–17% of cases can be bilateral. On MR imaging, dysgerminomas appear as solid lesions, which are hypointense on T2-weighted images with isointense septae, iso- to hypointense on T1WI, and demonstrate variable enhancement (Fig. 18.16).

Ovarian yolk sac tumors are rare malignant ovarian germ cell tumors that usually occur in the second decade of life and are the most common malignant germ cell tumor of the ovary in children.[29] No specific MR imaging findings

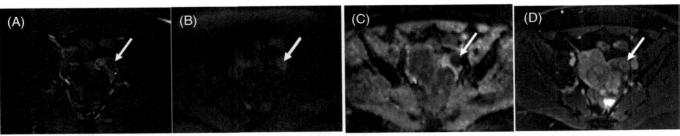

FIG. 18.15 Ovarian carcinoid. Axial T2-weighted image (A), and axial diffusion-weighted image (B), ADC map (C), and axial T1-weighted contrast-enhanced image (D) demonstrate a solid T2 hypointense mass in the left ovary with diffusion restriction and avid enhancement.

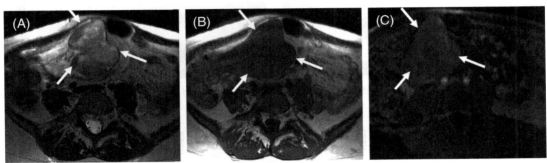

FIG. 18.16 Dysgerminoma. Axial T2-weighted image (A) demonstrates a well-circumscribed lobulated solid pelvic mass with heterogeneous iso- to hyperintense signal on T2-weighted images. Axial T1-weighted non–fat-suppressed image (B) demonstrates isointense T1 signal. Axial contrast-enhanced T1-weighted image (C) demonstrates moderate homogeneous enhancement.

have been described. T1 hyperintense areas representing foci of hemorrhage may be seen within these tumors. Embryonal carcinomas are rare, malignant ovarian germ cell tumors are seen primarily in children, often mixed with other malignant germ cell tumor types. Precocious puberty or menstrual irregularity occurs in 60% of patients[30] and may have elevated β-hCG and/or AFP. On imaging, these appear as predominantly solid lesions with no specific imaging features. Choriocarcinoma is a rare ovarian germ cell tumor, accounting for <1% of ovarian tumors, arising from placental trophoblastic elements. Primary ovarian choriocarcinoma (nongestational ovarian choriocarcinoma) arises presumably from a germ cell and is extremely rare.[26] Serum β-hCG levels are often elevated. On MR imaging, choriocarcinoma appears as heterogeneous vascular solid tumors with cystic, hemorrhagic, and necrotic areas (Fig. 18.17). Malignant mixed germ cell tumors are rare ovarian germ cell tumors, which generally occur in adolescent women of reproductive age.[31]

18.4.12 Sex cord/stromal ovarian tumors

Sex cord–stromal ovarian tumors are classified into pure stromal, pure sex cord, and mixed stromal–sex cord tumors. They include fibroma, thecoma, fibrothecoma, sclerosing stromal tumor, Sertoli–Leydig tumor, granulosa cell tumor, and small cell carcinoma.

18.4.13 Ovarian fibroma and thecoma

Fibromas are the most common ovarian sex cord tumors, accounting for approximately 4% of all ovarian neoplasms. They frequently occur in middle-aged women. Fibromas have very few, if any, thecal cells and no estrogen activity. There is an association with Meigs syndrome (ovarian fibroma, ascites, pleural effusion) and 75% of patients with nevoid basal cell carcinoma syndrome.[32] Fibromas typically appear moderately hypointense compared to uterine myometrium and iso to mildly hyperintense to iliopsoas muscle on T2W images. On T1-weighted images, fibromas are iso to mildly hypointense and show mild homogeneous contrast enhancement[33] (Fig. 18.18). A thin T2 hypointense, enhancing pseudocapsule may be seen, which is composed of loose fibroconnective tissue. Central and peripheral degenerative changes may be seen, which appear T2 hyperintense and hypoenhancing compared to solid components.[33] Larger tumors (>6 cm) are more likely to show pseudocapsule, degenerative changes, peripheral

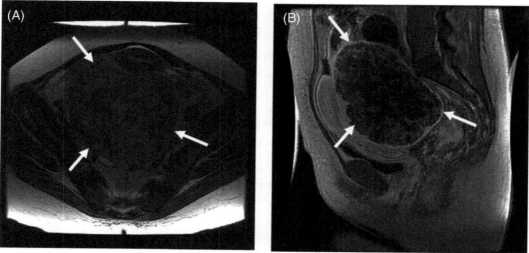

FIG. 18.17 **Choriocarcinoma.** Axial T2-weighted image (A) and sagittal T1-weighted contrast-enhanced image (B) demonstrate a solid heterogeneously enhancing ovarian mass.

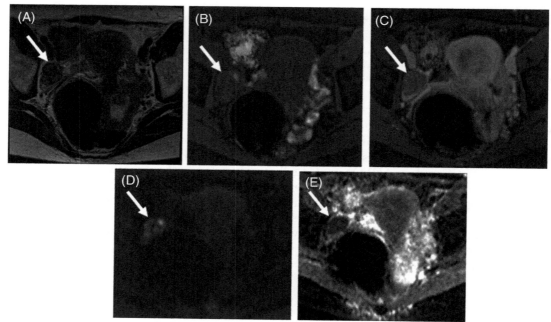

FIG. 18.18 **Ovarian fibroma.** Axial T2-weighted image (A) and axial T1-weighted fat-suppressed image (B) demonstrate a solid right ovarian mass with T2 hypointense signal and T1 isointense signal. Moderate homogeneous enhancement is seen on axial contrast-enhanced T1-weighted image (C). Diffusion-weighted image (D) and ADC Map (E) demonstrate diffusion restriction, a finding occasionally seen with fibroma.

subcapsular cystic areas, heterogeneous T2 signal, and heterogeneous enhancement. The normal ipsilateral ovary is seen in many cases, especially in premenopausal females, and shows normal contour with tumor arising from the periphery and predominantly exophytic.[34] Centrally located tumors may show peripheral cystic areas representing ovarian follicles.

Thecomas are rare ovarian sex cord tumors, accounting for approximately 0.5–1% of all ovarian neoplasms. They most frequently occur in postmenopausal women.[35] Tumors secrete estrogen, and in 60% of cases, have associated uterine bleeding. In addition, >20% have concurrent endometrial carcinoma. Thecomas are typically unilateral solid masses, appear homogeneously isointense to myometrium on T1WI, showing iso- to hyperintense signal on T2WI (Fig. 18.19). Relatively, low-grade enhancement is seen on postcontrast images.[36] Most thecomas occur in combination with fibrous components and are termed fibrothecomas.[36,37] MRI signal may vary depending upon the proportion

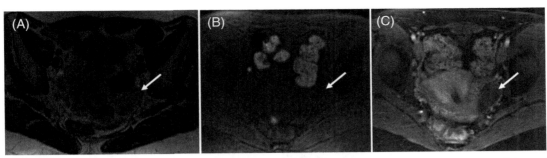

FIG. 18.19 **Thecoma.** Axial T2-weighted image (A) and axial T1-weighted fat-suppressed image (B) demonstrate a left ovarian lesion with T2 intermediate signal, and T1 isointense signal. Axial contrast-enhanced T1-weighted image (C) demonstrates low-level homogeneous enhancement.

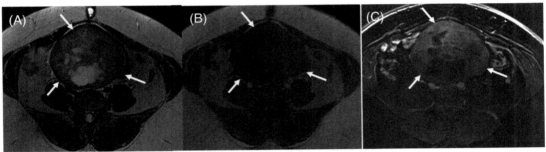

FIG. 18.20 **Fibrothecoma.** Axial T2-weighted image (A) and axial T1-weighted non–fat-suppressed image (B) demonstrate a heterogeneous well-circumscribed midline lower abdominal/pelvic lesion with foci of increased T2 signal. Axial contrast-enhanced T1-weighted image (C) demonstrates moderate heterogeneous internal enhancement.

of fibrous and cellular components (Fig. 18.20). Low signal on T1 and T2W images may be seen owing to abundant fibrous stroma.[37] Larger tumors show variable high T2 signals owing to edema and cystic degeneration.[37] Delayed enhancement may be seen due to fibrous component.[38] Enlargement of the uterus and hyperintense signal of the endocervical glands may be seen. These tumors are usually benign and carry a good prognosis. Fibromas/fibroth-ecomas show significantly less enhancement than myometrium and leiomyomas, which can be used as a differen-tiating feature on dynamic contrast-enhanced MRI.[33]

18.4.14 Other sex cord–stromal ovarian tumors

Sclerosing stromal tumors are rare sex cord tumors, which most frequently occur in young women with a peak incidence in the second to third decades of life. On histology, they are characterized by cellular heterogeneity, prominent vasculature, and a pseudolobular appearance composed of cellular and hypocellular areas.[39] On MR imaging,[40] sclerosing stromal tumors typically appear as multilocular cystic lesions with irregularly thickened septa and tumor walls, and the solid portions may exhibit isointense signal on T2-weighted images with intense enhance-ment following administration of gadolinium (Fig. 18.21).

Sertoli–Leydig cell tumors are rare ovarian sex cord tumors, which account for approximately 0.5% of all ovarian tumors, with an average age of presentation of 14 years. In approximately 30% of cases, the tumors are hormonally active, producing androgens, and patients have virilization symptoms. On MR imaging, these appear as solid lesions with heterogeneous hypointense T2 signal and variable enhancement depending on the fibrous content. On MRI, the solid component appears as lobulated mass, iso- to hypointense to adjacent myometrium on T1, low to inter-mediate signal intensity on T2, depending upon the amount of fibrous stroma (Fig. 18.22). Cystic components appear hyperintense on the T2-weighted image, may show irregularly thickened wall and septations.[41,42] Solid components show intense and heterogeneous enhancement is seen on postcontrast-enhanced images.[43,44] Fibrous stroma shows gradual and concentric enhancement. Infiltration into surrounding organs, such as uterus or bowel, lymphadenopa-thy, and ascites are usually not seen. Most are benign, low-grade tumors with a good prognosis.[45]

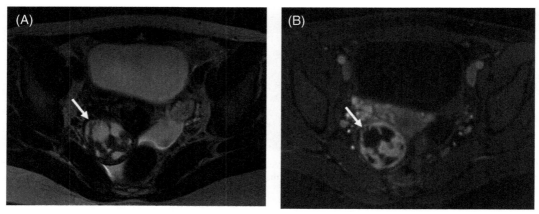

FIG. 18.21   Sclerosing stromal tumor. Axial T2-weighted image (A) demonstrates a well-circumscribed left adnexal mass with solid (isointense) and cystic (hyperintense) components. Axial contrast-enhanced T1-weighted image (B) demonstrates avid enhancement within the solid components.

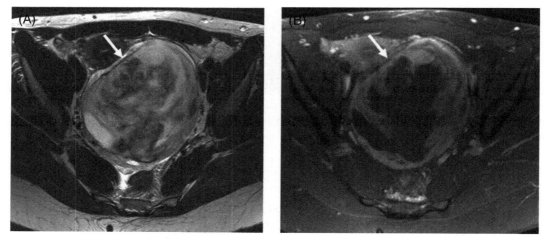

FIG. 18.22   Sertoli–Leydig cell tumor. Axial T2-weighted image (A) demonstrates a well-circumscribed solid pelvic mass with heterogeneous, predominantly hyperintense signal on T2-weighted images. Axial contrast-enhanced T1-weighted image (B) demonstrates moderate heterogeneous enhancement with large central areas of nonenhancement.

Leydig cell tumors comprise a rare group of ovarian neoplasms, a subtype of steroid cell tumors. They are usually solid masses appearing hyperintense on T1 and T2W images due to abundant lipid. Signal intensity on T2W images can vary depending upon the amount of fibrous stroma. Intense contrast enhancement is seen with gadolinium-based contrast agents.

Granulosa cell tumors are ovarian sex cord tumors, which account for 8% of all ovarian tumors, and contain combinations of sex cord and stromal components of the developing gonad, most commonly occurring in postmenopausal women.[46] They are the pure sex cord, low-grade malignant tumors, comprising less than 5% of malignant ovarian neoplasms.[43,47] Adult type (AGCT) is seen in middle-aged and postmenopausal females and is much more common than juvenile type (JGCT), seen in females younger than 30 years age.[36] They can be associated with endometrial hyperplasia, endometrial polyps, endometrial carcinoma, or Maffucci syndrome (in juvenile granulosa cell tumors). These tumors present as predominantly unilateral, purely solid, or complex multilocular cystic masses, showing multiple internal septae, giving a sponge-like appearance on MRI[36,38,43] (Fig. 18.23). On T2WI, cystic areas appear hyperintense with fluid–fluid levels, hemorrhagic fluid appearing hyperintense on T1W images.[48] Solid components appear T1 and T2 isointense, with thick septations appearing hypointense and show intense enhancement on contrast-enhanced images.[43,48] Solid tumors can appear heterogeneous due to areas of hemorrhage, infarction, and fibrosis. Tumors demonstrate a low proclivity for the peritoneal spread at the time of diagnosis. The majority (approximately 80%) of GCTs show concomitant endometrial abnormalities, including hyperplasia, with endometrial cancer seen in 10% cases.[49] Fibroids with red degeneration may be seen secondary to hyperestrogenism. Overall

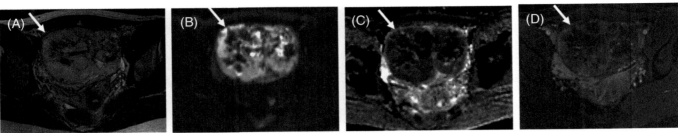

FIG. 18.23 Granulosa cell tumor. Axial T2-weighted image (A) demonstrates a well-circumscribed solid pelvic mass with heterogeneous, predominantly intermediate signal on T2-weighted images. Axial diffusion-weighted image (B) and corresponding ADC map image (C) demonstrate diffuse diffusion restriction with high signal on diffusion-weighted images and low signal on ADC map. Axial contrast-enhanced T1-weighted image (D) demonstrates moderate heterogeneous enhancement.

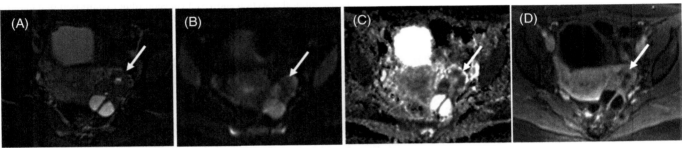

FIG. 18.24 Metastatses from colon cancer. Axial T2-weighted image (A) demonstrates a well-circumscribed lobulated solid left adnexal mass with heterogeneous iso- to hyperintense signal on T2-weighted images. Axial diffusion-weighted image (B) and ADC map (C) demonstrate heterogeneous diffusion restriction. Axial contrast-enhanced T1-weighted image (D) demonstrates heterogeneous avid enhancement.

prognosis is good due to the low malignant potential of most GCTs. JGCTs have a better prognosis than AGCTs; however, they show increased chances of recurrence and are more often associated with endometrial and breast cancer.

Small cell carcinoma of the hypercalcemic type is a rare type of malignant tumor characterized by symptomatic hypercalcemia. Limited characteristic imaging information is available for these tumors.

18.4.15 Metastatses

Ovary is the most common site of metastasis within the gynecological tract. Ovarian metastases (3–30% of ovarian cancers) may occur synchronously or metachronously with the primary malignancy and are commonly bilateral. Colorectal adenocarcinoma is the most common primary cancer that metastasizes to the ovaries. Other primary tumors with ovarian metastases include breast cancer, gastrointestinal tract cancers, pancreatobiliary cancers, and lung cancers. Metastatses commonly involve the ovarian surface or cortex and the hilum. Krukenberg tumors refer to signet ring cell metastases that usually originate in the gastrointestinal tract, most commonly from the stomach; dissemination is either by transperitoneal or hematogenous routes. Average age of presentation is 45 years.[50] On MR imaging, Krukenberg tumors typically appear as predominantly solid bilateral ovarian masses with T1 hypointense and T2 hyperintense signal from mucin production (Fig. 18.24). The solid portion often demonstrates marked enhancement. Ovarian metastases comprise stage IV disease, are relatively refractory to chemotherapy and portend poor prognosis.

18.4.16 Miscellaneous ovarian tumors

Additional ovarian tumors that do not fit into the previously mentioned pathologic categories include collision tumor, carcinosarcoma, and lymphomas. Collision tumors occur when there are two adjacent but histologically distinct tumors in a single ovary with no histologic admixture at the interface, most commonly an ovarian teratoma and an ovarian cystadenoma[51] (Fig. 18.25). Carcinosarcoma is a rare mixed ovarian tumor with both epithelial and stromal components, accounting for less than 1% of all ovarian cancers, and with a peak incidence in the sixth to

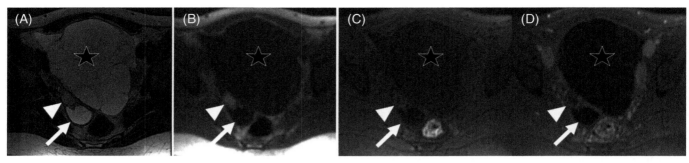

FIG. 18.25 **Collision tumor.** Axial T2-weighted image (A), axial T1-weighted non–fat-suppressed image (B), and axial T1-weighted fat-suppressed image (C) demonstrate a complex right ovarian lesion with a cystic component posteriorly (arrows) and bulk fat anteriorly (arrowhead). The anterior component demonstrates no internal enhancement on T1-weighted contrast-enhanced image (D), while the posterior component demonstrates enhancement of the wall and internal septations. Surgical resection showed a collision tumor comprised of a mature teratoma (anteriorly) and mucinous cystadenoma (posteriorly). The patient also had a large mucinous cystadenoma arising from the left ovary (asterisk).

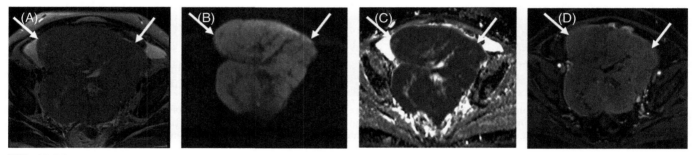

FIG. 18.26 **Ovarian lymphoma.** Axial T2-weighted image (A) demonstrates solid bilateral ovarian mass lesions with T2 intermediate signal. Diffusion-weighted image (B) and ADC map image (C) demonstrate intense diffusion restriction. Axial T1-weighted contrast-enhanced image (D) demonstrates moderate diffuse internal enhancement.

eighth decade of life. MR imaging features are nonspecific, and it is not possible to differentiate carcinosarcomas from other ovarian neoplasms on imaging. Primary ovarian lymphoma accounts for approximately 1.5% of all ovarian tumors, with non-Hodgkin lymphoma being the most common subtype. On MR imaging, these appear as solid mass lesions with intermediate T2 signal and isointense to hypointense T1 signal (Fig. 18.26). Marked diffusion restriction is typical. Enhancement is variable but usually homogeneous and intense.

18.5 Hereditary ovarian tumor syndromes

A diverse group of hereditary cancer syndromes predisposes to the development of bilateral, multifocal distinctive ovarian tumor subtypes.[52] Hereditary ovarian epithelial cancers comprise 10–15% of all ovarian cancers. Radiologists may be the first physician to identify hereditary syndromes based on diagnosing specific ovarian and extraovarian tumors in sporadic cases and familial clusters.[52,53] Hereditary breast and ovarian cancer (HBOC)/*BRCA* syndromes are exclusively associated with high-grade serous carcinomas, while LS patients predominantly develop endometrioid subtypes of ovarian and endometrial carcinomas.[52,54] *BRCA* syndromes and LS account for 65–85% and 10–15% of hereditary epithelial cancers, respectively.[52] Rare syndromes such as Peutz–Jeghers, DICER1, von Hippel–Lindau (VHL), and Gorlin syndromes are associated with sex cord–stromal tumor, Sertoli–Leydig cell tumor, steroid cell tumor, and fibromas, respectively (Table 18.1).[52]

Most *BRCA*-associated serous carcinomas are hypothesized to arise from microscopic precursors within the fimbrial portion of the fallopian tube and due to mutations of BRCA1 and BRCA2 genes.[53] On MRI, ovarian tumors mimic sporadic counterparts and manifests as heterogneosuly enhancing solid/cystic masses with variable degrees of hemorrhage and degeneration.[52,53]

TABLE 18.1 Hereditary ovarian tumor syndromes.

Syndrome	Ovarian tumors	Associated malignancies
BRCA syndromes	High-grade serous carcinomas	Female/male breast, uterus, colon, pancreas, and prostate
Lynch syndrome	Nonserous ovarian epithelial cancers, commonly endometrioid	Colorectal, endometrial, renal pelvic–ureteric, gastric, small bowel, and hepatobiliary
Peutz–Jeghers syndrome	Sex cord–stromal tumors with annular tubules, Sertoli cell tumor and mucinous tumors	Pancreas, GI tract, breast, and cervix
DICER1 syndrome	Sertoli–Leydig cell tumors	Pediatric pleuropulmonary blastomas, cystic nephroma and cervix sarcomas
von Hippel–Lindau syndrome	Ovarian steroid cell tumor and papillary cystadenoma of the broad ligament	Retinal/CNS hemangioblastomas, renal cancers, pheochromocytomas, and pancreatic neuroendocrine tumors
Gorlin syndrome	Ovarian fibromas	Basal cell carcinomas, pediatric medulloblastomas, and skeletal abnormalities

LS is characterized by an increased risk of predisposition to colorectal cancers, endometrial cancer, ovarian cancer, and other solid tumors, including urothelial carcinoma.[52,54] Approximately 50–60% of LS patients manifest initially with gynecological cancer. Ovarian cancers in LS occur 15–20 years earlier than sporadic cancers and about 80% of LS-associated ovarian cancers are of the nonserous type and mimic sporadic counterparts on MRI.[52,54]

18.6 Ovarian tumors with clinical syndromes

Due to hormonal overproduction, functional ovarian neoplasms can present with unique clinical syndromes.[26] Hyperandrogenism and hyperestrogenism are the two most common clinical syndromes associated with ovarian tumors.[26] Other uncommon endocrine and nonendocrine clinical syndromes associated with ovarian neoplasms include excessive production of hCG, carcinoid syndrome, hyperthyroidism, Meigs and pseudo-Meigs syndrome, and paraneoplastic syndromes (Table 18.2).[26]

TABLE 18.2 Ovarian tumors with clinical syndromes.

Clinical syndrome	Ovarian tumors
Hyperandrogenism	Sertoli–Leydig cell and Leydig cell tumors—Common Teratoma, choriocarcinoma, metastases, and Sertoli cell tumors—Uncommon
Hyperestrogenism	Granulosa cell tumors, thecomas, and mucinous cystadenoma—Common Teratoma, Brenner tumor, choriocarcinoma, and stromal luteoma—Uncommon
Excessive hCG	Choriocarcinoma and dysgerminoma
Carcinoid syndrome	Ovarian carcinoids
Hyperthyroidism	Struma ovarii
Meigs syndrome	Fibromas, fibrothecomas, granulosa cell tumor, and Brenner tumor
Pseudo-Meigs syndrome	Teratoma, mucinous cystadenoma, and metastases
Cushing's Syndrome	Steroid cell tumors
Paraneoplastic syndromes: Hemolytic anemia and limbic encephalitis Dermatomyositis, cerebellar degeneration, polyneuritis, and acanthosis	Mature teratoma Epithelial tumors

Hyperandrogenism is a virilization syndrome characterized by a male-pattern of baldness, deepening of the voice, clitoromegaly, and increased muscle mass. Sertoli–Leydig cell tumors and Leydig cell tumors are the most common tumors with hyperandrogenism; ovarian metastases from GI tract neuroendocrine tumors, teratomas, choriocarcinoma, and Sertoli cell tumors also may cause the syndrome.[26,38]

Hyperestrogenism results from increased estrogen production and can result in morphologic changes in the uterus, including endometrial thickening, which can cause amenorrhea to excessive menstrual bleeding in premenopausal females. Breast tenderness and postmenopausal bleeding can be seen in older women.[38,55] There is an increased risk of uterine cancer, which is usually endometrioid adenocarcinoma and breast cancer.[56,57] Premenarchal girls present with isosexual precocity and are characterized by the development of breasts, appearance of axillary and pubic hair, stimulation of sex organs, and irregular uterine bleeding.[55] While granulosa cell tumors and thecomas are sex cord–stromal tumors associated with hyperestrogenism, mucinous cystadenoma is the epithelial tumor associated with hyperestrogenism.[38] Uncommon causes of hyperestrogenism include teratoma, Brenner tumor, choriocarcinoma, and stromal luteoma.[26] In addition to the primary ovarian mass, endometrial thickening/abnormally increased endometrial signal intensity, and thickened myometrium are common findings on MRI.[36]

Nongestational choriocarcinoma with excessive production of hCG may present with isosexual precocity in premenarchal patients and demonstrate theca lutein cysts in the contralateral ovary.[26] Ovarian carcinoid tumors comprise of monodermal teratomas, containing components of well-differentiated neuroendocrine cells; they may present with systemic carcinoid syndrome, characterized by diarrhea, tachycardia, dyspnea, and skin flushing.[37] Struma ovarii is the most common monodermal teratoma, composed of colloid-filled acini, a characteristic feature of mature functioning thyroid tissue and can cause hyperthyroidism.[27]

Meigs syndrome is characterized by ascites and pleural effusion accompanied by a benign ovarian tumor, classically fibroma, others being fibrothecoma, granulosa cell tumor, and Brenner tumor.[58] Pseudo-Meigs syndrome refers to hydrothorax and ascites associated with other ovarian tumors, including struma ovarii, mucinous cystadenoma, mature teratomas, uterine leiomyomas, and ovarian metastatic tumors.[58] Rarely, steroid cell tumors can be associated with Cushing's syndrome.[43,59,60]

While paraneoplastic syndromes such as autoimmune hemolytic anemia and immune mediated limbic encephalitis are associated with mature teratoma, patients with epithelial ovarian tumors may rarely present with dermatomyositis, cerebellar degeneration, polyneuritis, acanthosis, and nephrotic syndrome.[26]

18.6.1 Adnexal mass: MRI pattern-based approach

Most adnexal and ovarian lesions manifest as variegated cystic masses. Paraovarian cystic lesions can be distinguished from ovarian lesions by properly identifying the site of origin and recognizing the anatomic relationship between the gonadal vessels and the cysts. Tubo-ovarian abscesses, hydrosalpinx, hemorrhagic cysts, and endometriosis must be differentiated from ovarian neoplasms because of considerable changes in patient management and prognosis. Tubo-ovarian abscesses appear as complex, multilocular cystic lesions that may be unilateral or bilateral; associated inflammatory stranding strongly suggests the diagnosis. A confident diagnosis can usually be made based on imaging findings in conjunction with clinical and laboratory findings. Temporal changes in size and morphology following antibiotics are also a helpful feature. Pathological and microbiological analyses of "cyst fluid" clinch the diagnosis. Multiplanar demonstration of a cystic lesion in a tubular configuration with "mucosal folds" suggests the diagnosis of a hydrosalpinx. On MR imaging, hemorrhagic cysts and endometriomas display high signal intensity on T1-weighted images. While hemorrhagic cysts show variable signal intensity on T2-weighted images, endometriomas typically exhibit characteristic T2 shading. Postcontrast images, particularly subtraction images, are invaluable for the assessment of clear cell and endometrioid subtypes of ovarian cancer that develop against background of endometriosis.

Most primary ovarian neoplasms appear as cystic masses of varying complexities. Functional ovarian cysts must be differentiated from neoplastic cysts. The diagnosis of corpus luteal cysts and theca lutein cysts (multiple, large cysts in gestational trophoblastic disease) can be made based on clinical and laboratory data. While unilocular ovarian cysts suggest serous cystadenomas, mucinous cystadenomas, and borderline tumors commonly manifest as multilocular cystic masses. Multiple locules in mucinous tumors demonstrate fluids of varying signal intensities on T1- and T2-weighted images. MRI is extremely valuable in the assessment of ovarian malignancies that typically appear as complex cystic masses with solid components. While T2-weighted MRI exquisitely demonstrates septations of multilocular, complex cystic ovarian masses, postcontrast images depict enhancing mural nodules, particularly on subtraction images.

The presence of macroscopic fat is virtually diagnostic of ovarian teratomas. While foci of macroscopic fat is admixed with diffusely infiltrative soft tissue components in immature teratomas, the finding of marked tissue heterogeneity (cystic changes, macroscopic fat, and calcifications) including Rokitansky protuberance is pathognomonic for mature teratomas. MRI plays a critical role in the diagnosis and differentiation of different types of teratomas by definitively identifying macroscopic fat. On frequency selective chemical fat suppression, there is significant, subjective signal loss within fat-containing foci. Also, "India ink" artifact on opposed phase T1-weighted gradient echo images, due to chemical shift artifact at the interface between fat and adjacent structures, can be identified. Presence of an enhancing soft tissue component within a pre-existing teratoma may imply malignant transformation.

Demonstration of low signal intensity masses on T2-weighted images that show minimal contrast enhancement is a typical feature of tumors with significant "fibrous" content; fibromas and cystadenofibromas are prototype examples. However fibromas may have variable MRI characteristics due to either myxoid changes or varying cellularity (cellular fibromas).

The following section outlines the MRI patterns of ovarian lesions, with an algorithmic approach to categorizing specific tumors.

18.7 Synopsis of MRI patterns of ovarian lesions and neoplasms

Unilocular cyst	Complex multilocular cyst	Mixed cystic and solid masses	Fatty masses	Solid masses
Functional cyst	Endometriosis	Epithelial ovarian carcinomas	Mature teratoma	Brenner tumor
Hydrosalpinx	Mucinous cystadenoma	Metastatses	Immature teratoma	Metastatses
Serous Cystadenoma or cystadenofibroma	Borderline ovarian tumors	Nonepithelial ovarian tumors	Malignant teratoma	Sex cord stromal tumors such as fibromas, fibrothecomas, Sertoli–Leydig tumors
Paraovarian cyst	Metastatses			Lymphoma

18.8 MRI pattern-based categorization of ovarian tumors

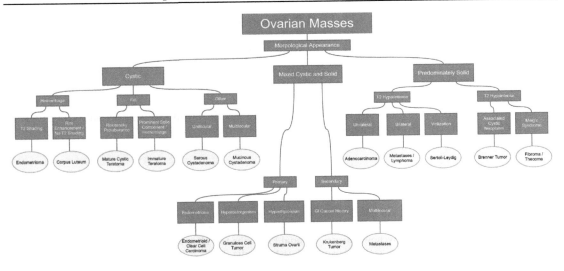

18.9 O-RADS MRI

Ovarian Adnexal Reporting Data System Magnetic Resonance Imaging (O-RADS MRI) is a five-point MRI findings-based scoring system for the characterization of adnexal masses that are indeterminate at US and helps to risk-stratify malignant versus benign masses.[61,62] There are five categories in O-RADS MRI system (one to five) that indicate normal to high risk of malignancy (Table 18.3).[61,62] This system has been validated in a large prospective study and found to have a potential to avoid unnecessary surgeries, preserve fertility, and guide complete oncologic surgeries.[62]

TABLE 18.3 O-RADS MRI risk scoring system.

O-RADS MRI score	Risk category	MRI findings/lesions
0	Incomplete evaluation	N/A
1	Normal ovaries	No ovarian lesion Follicle/simple cyst <3 cm in premenopausal women Corpus luteum Hemorrhagic cyst <3 cm in premenopausal women
2	Almost certainly benign (<0.5% malignancy risk)	Unilocular cyst without enhancement: Simple/endometriotic cysts Macroscopic fat-containing mass: Teratoma Hydrosalpinx with simple fluid Paraovarian cyst Peritoneal inclusion cyst Solid enhancing lesions with dark T2 and dark DWI: fibroma, fibrothecomas and Brenner tumor
3	Low risk (5% malignancy risk)	Unilocular cyst with hemorrhagic/proteinaceous fluid and no solid tissue Multilocular cyst without solid components Solid tissue (excluding T2 dark and DWI dark) with low-risk time intensity curve on DCE-MRI
4	Intermediate risk (50% malignancy risk)	Solid tissue (excluding T2 dark and DWI dark) with intermediate-risk time intensity curve on DCE-MRI If DCE-MRI is not available, solid tissue enhancing less than or same as myometrium at 30–40-second postcontrast images on non-DCE MRI
5	High risk (90% malignancy risk)	Solid tissue with high-risk time intensity curve on DCE-MRI If DCE-MRI is not available, solid tissue enhancing more than myometrium at 30–40-second postcontrast images on non-DCE MRI Ascites, peritoneal/omental nodules

18.10 Summary

There is a rich diversity of benign and malignant ovarian neoplasms with characteristic histopathology, genetics, tumor pathways, biological behavior, and prognosis. It is imperative to distinguish non-neoplastic lesions from tumors and to differentiate benign from malignant neoplasms by noninvasive methods. Recent advances in MRI technology allow multiparametric assessment of a multitude of ovarian neoplasms. MRI is an excellent problem-solving modality with superior contrast resolution and tissue distinction that allows accurate diagnosis, localization, staging, and characterization of adnexal masses and provides a useful roadmap to surgeons. MRI pattern-based diagnosis in conjunction with laboratory and clinical data allows optimal patient management.

References

1. Testa U, Petrucci E, Pasquini L, Castelli G, Pelosi E. Ovarian cancers: genetic abnormalities, tumor heterogeneity and progression, clonal evolution and cancer stem cells. *Medicines (Basel, Switzerland)*. 2018;5(1):16. doi: 10.3390/medicines5010016. PMID: 29389895.
2. Mondal SK, Banyopadhyay R, Nag DR, Roychowdhury S, Mondal PK, Sinha SK. Histologic pattern, bilaterality and clinical evaluation of 957 ovarian neoplasms: a 10-year study in a tertiary hospital of eastern india. *J Cancer Res Ther*. 2011;7(4):433–437.
3. Zanaboni F, Vergadoro F, Presti M, Gallotti P, Lombardi F, Bolis G. Tumor antigen Ca 125 as a marker of ovarian epithelial carcinoma. *Gynecol Oncol*. 1987;28(1):61–67.
4. Siegelman ES, Outwater EK. Tissue characterization in the female pelvis by means of MR imaging. *Radiology*. 1999;212(1):5–18.
5. Troiano RN, McCarthy S. Magnetic resonance imaging evaluation of adnexal masses. *Semin Ultrasound CT MR*. 1994;15(1):38–48.
6. Outwater EK, Mitchell DG. Magnetic resonance imaging techniques in the pelvis. *Magn Reson Imaging Clin N Am*. 1994;2(2):161–188.
7. Stevens SK, Hricak H, Stern JL. Ovarian lesions: detection and characterization with gadolinium-enhanced MR imaging at 1.5 T. *Radiology*. 1991;181(2):481–488.
8. Jung SE, Lee JM, Rha SE, Byun JY, Jung JI, Hahn ST. CT and MR imaging of ovarian tumors with emphasis on differential diagnosis. *Radiographics*. 2002;22(6):1305–1325.

9. Imaoka I, Wada A, Kaji Y, et al. Developing an mr imaging strategy for diagnosis of ovarian masses. *Radiographics*. 2006;26(5):1431–1448.

10. Seidman JD, Kurman RJ. Ovarian serous borderline tumors: a critical review of the literature with emphasis on prognostic indicators. *Hum Pathol*. 2000;31(5):539–557.

11. Jeong YY, Outwater EK, Kang HK. Imaging evaluation of ovarian masses. *Radiographics*. 2000;20(5):1445–1470.

12. Okada S, Ohaki Y, Inoue K, et al. Calcifications in mucinous and serous cystic ovarian tumors. *J Nippon Med School = Nippon Ika Daigaku zasshi*. 2005;72(1):29–33.

13. Hart WR. Mucinous tumors of the ovary: a review. *Int J Gynecol Pathol*. 2005;24(1):4–25.

14. Wagner BJ, Buck JL, Seidman JD, McCabe KM. From the archives of the AFIP. Ovarian epithelial neoplasms: radiologic-pathologic correlation. *Radiographics*. 1994;14(6):1351–1374; quiz 1375-1356.

15. Kinoshita T, Ishii K, Naganuma H, Higashiiwai H. MR findings of ovarian tumours with cystic components. *Br J Radiol*. 2000;73(867):333–339.

16. Ghossain MA, Buy JN, Lignères C, et al. Epithelial tumors of the ovary: comparison of mr and ct findings. *Radiology*. 1991;181(3):863–870.

17. Cuatrecasas M, Catasus L, Palacios J, Prat J. Transitional cell tumors of the ovary: a comparative clinicopathologic, immunohistochemical, and molecular genetic analysis of brenner tumors and transitional cell carcinomas. *Am J Surg Pathol*. 2009;33(4):556–567.

18. Cho SM, Byun JY, Rha SE, et al. CT and MRI findings of cystadenofibromas of the ovary. *Eur Radiol*. 2004;14(5):798–804.

19. Chiang AJ, La V, Peng J, Yu KJ, Teng NN. Squamous cell carcinoma arising from mature cystic teratoma of the ovary. *Int J Gynecol Cancer*. 2011;21(3):466–474.

20. Kaku S, Takeshima N, Akiyama F, Furuta R, Hirai Y, Takizawa K. A unique fibrous tumor of the ovary: fibrosarcoma or mitotically active cellular fibroma? *Anticancer Res*. 2007;27(6c):4365–4369.

21. Kawamoto S, Urban BA, Fishman EK. CT of epithelial ovarian tumors. *Radiographics*. 1999;19 Spec No:S85-S102; quiz S263-104.

22. Outwater EK, Siegelman ES, Hunt JL. Ovarian teratomas: tumor types and imaging characteristics. *Radiographics*. 2001;21(2):475–490.

23. Acién P, Ruiz-Maciá E, Acién M, Martín-Estefanía C. Mature ovarian teratoma-associated limbic encephalitis. *J Obstet Gynaecol*. 2015;35(3):317–319.

24. Saba L, Guerriero S, Sulcis R, Virgilio B, Melis G, Mallarini G. Mature and immature ovarian teratomas: CT, US and MR imaging characteristics. *Eur J Radiol*. 2009;72(3):454–463.

25. Park SB, Kim JK, Kim KR, Cho KS. Imaging findings of complications and unusual manifestations of ovarian teratomas. *Radiographics*. 2008;28(4):969–983.

26. Shanbhogue AK, Shanbhogue DK, Prasad SR, Surabhi VR, Fasih N, Menias CO. Clinical syndromes associated with ovarian neoplasms: a comprehensive review. *Radiographics*. 2010;30(4):903–919.

27. Outwater EK, Siegelman ES, Hunt JL. Ovarian teratomas: tumor types and imaging characteristics. *Radiographics*. 2001;21(2):475–490.

28. Tanaka YO, Kurosaki Y, Nishida M, et al. Ovarian dysgerminoma: MR and CT appearance. *J Comput Assist Tomogr*. 1994;18(3):443–448.

29. Levitin A, Haller KD, Cohen HL, Zinn DL, O'Connor MT. Endodermal sinus tumor of the ovary: imaging evaluation. *AJR Am J Roentgenol*. 1996;167(3):791–793.

30. Kurman RJ, Norris HJ. Embryonal carcinoma of the ovary: a clinicopathologic entity distinct from endodermal sinus tumor resembling embryonal carcinoma of the adult testis. *Cancer*. 1976;38(6):2420–2433.

31. Moniaga NC, Randall LM. Malignant mixed ovarian germ cell tumor with embryonal component. *J Pediatr Adolesc Gynecol*. 2011;24(1):e1–e3.

32. Fonseca RB, Grzeszczak EF. Case 128: bilateral ovarian fibromas in nevoid basal cell carcinoma syndrome. *Radiology*. 2008;246(1):318–321.

33. Shinagare AB, Meylaerts LJ, Laury AR, Mortele KJ. MRI features of ovarian fibroma and fibrothecoma with histopathologic correlation. *Am J Roentgenol*. 2012;198(3):W296–W303.

34. Oh S, Rha S, Byun J, et al. MRI features of ovarian fibromas: emphasis on their relationship to the ovary. *Clin Radiol*. 2008;63(5):529–535.

35. Young RH. Ovarian sex cord-stromal tumours and their mimics. *Pathology (Phila)*. 2018;50(1):5–15.

36. Horta M, Cunha TM. Sex cord-stromal tumors of the ovary: a comprehensive review and update for radiologists. *Diagn Interv Radiol*. 2015;21(4):277–286.

37. Tanaka YO, Saida TS, Minami R, et al. MR findings of ovarian tumors with hormonal activity, with emphasis on tumors other than sex cord-stromal tumors. *Eur J Radiol*. 2007;62(3):317–327.

38. Tanaka YO, Tsunoda H, Kitagawa Y, Ueno T, Yoshikawa H, Saida Y. Functioning ovarian tumors: direct and indirect findings at mr imaging. *Radiographics*. 2004;24(suppl_1):S147–S166.

39. Stylianidou A, Varras M, Akrivis C, Fylaktidou A, Stefanaki S, Antoniou N. Sclerosing stromal tumor of the ovary: a case report and review of the literature. *Eur J Gynaecol Oncol*. 2001;22(4):300–304.

40. Joja I, Okuno K, Tsunoda M, et al. Sclerosing stromal tumor of the ovary: US, MR, and dynamic mr findings. *J Comput Assist Tomogr*. 2001;25(2):201–206.

41. Chen J, Liu Y, Zhang Y, Wang Y, Chen X, Wang Z. Imaging, clinical, and pathologic findings of Sertoli-Leydig cell tumors. *Sci Prog*. 2021;104(2): 00368504211009668.

42. Cai S-Q, Zhao S-H, Qiang J-W, Zhang G-F, Wang X-Z, Wang L. Ovarian Sertoli–Leydig cell tumors: mri findings and pathological correlation. *J Ovarian Res*. 2013;6(1):73.

43. Jung SE, Rha SE, Lee JM, et al. CT and MRI findings of sex cord–stromal tumor of the ovary. *Am J Roentgenol*. 2005;185(1):207–215.

44. Foti PV, Attinà G, Spadola S, et al. MR imaging of ovarian masses: classification and differential diagnosis. *Insights Imaging*. 2016;7(1):21–41.

45. Heo SH, Kim JW, Shin SS, et al. Review of ovarian tumors in children and adolescents: radiologic-pathologic correlation. *Radiographics*. 2014;34(7):2039–2055.

46. Khosla D, Dimri K, Pandey AK, Mahajan R, Trehan R. Ovarian granulosa cell tumor: clinical features, treatment, outcome, and prognostic factors. *North Am J Med Sci*. 2014;6(3):133–138.

47. Horta M, Cunha TM. Sex cord-stromal tumors of the ovary: a comprehensive review and update for radiologists. *Diagn Intervent Radiol*. 2015;21(4):277.

48. Gittleman AM, Price AP, Coren C, Akhtar M, Donovan V, Katz DS. Radiology–pathology conference: juvenile granulosa cell tumor. *Clin Imaging.* 2003;27(4):221–224.
49. Schumer ST, Cannistra SA. Granulosa cell tumor of the ovary. *J Clin Oncol.* 2003;21(6):1180–1189.
50. Ha HK, Baek SY, Kim SH, Kim HH, Chung EC, Yeon KM. Krukenberg's tumor of the ovary: MR imaging features. *AJR Am J Roentgenol.* 1995;164(6):1435–1439.
51. Kim SH, Kim YJ, Park BK, Cho JY, Kim BH, Byun JY. Collision tumors of the ovary associated with teratoma: clues to the correct preoperative diagnosis. *J Comput Assist Tomogr.* 1999;23(6):929–933.
52. Shanbhogue KP, Prasad AS, Ucisik-Keser FE, Katabathina VS, Morani AC. Hereditary ovarian tumour syndromes: current update on genetics and imaging. *Clin Radiol.* 2021;76(4):313. e315-313. e326.
53. Lee MV, Katabathina VS, Bowerson ML, et al. BRCA-associated cancers: role of imaging in screening, diagnosis, and management. *Radiographics.* 2017;37(4):1005–1023.
54. Rothan SM, Menias CO, ElGuindy YM, et al. Imaging of hereditary tumors of the female genital system. *J Comput Assist Tomogr.* 2017;41(3):364–375.
55. Outwater EK, Wagner BJ, Mannion C, McLarney JK, Kim B. Sex cord-stromal and steroid cell tumors of the ovary. *Radiographics.* 1998;18(6):1523–1546.
56. Hammer A, Lauszus FF, Petersen AC. Ovarian granulosa cell tumor and increased risk of breast cancer. *Acta Obstet Gynecol Scand.* 2013;92(12):1422–1425.
57. Rabban JT, Gupta D, Zaloudek CJ, Chen L-m. Synchronous ovarian granulosa cell tumor and uterine serous carcinoma: a rare association of a high-risk endometrial cancer with an estrogenic ovarian tumor. *Gynecol Oncol.* 2006;103(3):1164–1168.
58. Saha S, Robertson M. Meigs' and pseudo-meigs' syndrome. *Australas J Ultrasound Med.* 2012;15(1):29–31.
59. Al Ojaimi EH. Cushing's syndrome due to an ACTH-producing primary ovarian carcinoma. *Hormones (Athens, Greece).* 2014;13(1):140–145.
60. Gupta P, Goyal S, Gonzalez-Mendoza LE, et al. Corticotropin-independent cushing syndrome in a child with an ovarian tumor misdiagnosed as nonclassic congenital adrenal hyperplasia. *Endocr Pract.* 2008;14(7):875–879.
61. Sadowski EA, Maturen KE, Rockall A, et al. Ovary: MRI characterisation and O-RADS MRI. *Br J Radiol.* 2021;94(1125):20210157.
62. Thomassin-Naggara I, Poncelet E, Jalaguier-Coudray A, et al. Ovarian-adnexal reporting data system magnetic resonance imaging (O-RADS MRI) score for risk stratification of sonographically indeterminate adnexal masses. *JAMA Netw Open.* 2020;3(1):e1919896.

19

MRI of female urethra and periurethral pathologies

Jacob Davis[a], Neeraj Lalwani[a], Christine O Menias[b]

[a]Professor of Radiology, Virginia Commonwealth University School of Medicine and Health System, Richmond, VA, United States [b]Department of Radiology, Mayo Clinic in Arizona, Scottsdale, AZ, United States

19.1 Introduction

Evaluation of female urethra remains difficult because of its small size and anatomic location. Most female urethral disorders present with nonspecific symptoms like dysuria, urinary frequency or urgency, recurrent urinary tract infections, and incontinence. Physical examination is often limited and unreliable in distinguishing urethral versus vaginal pathologies. Most of the conventional imagining studies, such as voiding cystourethrography and retrograde double-balloon positive-pressure urethrography are invasive and cannot assess periurethral pathologies. Magnetic resonance imaging (MRI) has become the preferred diagnostic modality for female urethral and periurethral pathologies with its high-resolution multiplanar scanning capability and superior soft tissue contrast resolution.

MRI has the capability to accurately diagnose of a wide spectrum of urethral and periurethral pathologies, and provide a preoperative road map to the surgeons. In this chapter, we describe anatomy and pathologies of the female urethra and periurethral disease.

19.2 Anatomy

The female urethra is a short tubular structure measuring approximately 4–5 cm in length. The urethra arises from the bladder neck at the internal urethral meatus and subsequently courses anteriorly and inferiorly. The external urethral meatus is found anterior/superior to the vagina and posterior/inferior to the clitoris[1] (Fig. 19.1). The pubic symphysis likewise lies anterior to the urethra. Arterial supply is via the vaginal and internal pudendal arteries. Innervation is via hypogastric nerves and the pudendal nerve (S2–S4). Lymphatic drainage for the proximal urethra occurs via iliac, obturator, and peri-aortic lymph nodes. Lymphatic drainage for the distal urethra and urethral meatus occurs via superficial and deep inguinal nodes. Information about lymphatic drainage is important because it allows for targeted investigation when dealing with malignant lesions.

Control and support of the urethra and the urethral sphincters is complex and involves the interplay of multiple muscular and ligamentous structures, namely the pubourethral and urethropelvic (paraurethral, periurethral, and suburethral) ligaments. The internal urethral sphincter (IUS) is located in the neck of the bladder and receives its blood supply from the vaginal artery. The IUS is composed of smooth muscle and controlled predominantly by the autonomic nervous system with input from the parasympathetic nervous system at time of micturition. The external urethral sphincter (EUS), also called the urogenital sphincter,

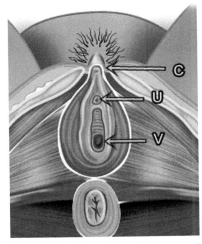

FIG. 19.1 Illustration of the normal external anatomy of the female pelvis. The external urethral meatus (U) is located anterior/superior to the vagina (V) and posterior/inferior to the clitoris (C).

(A)

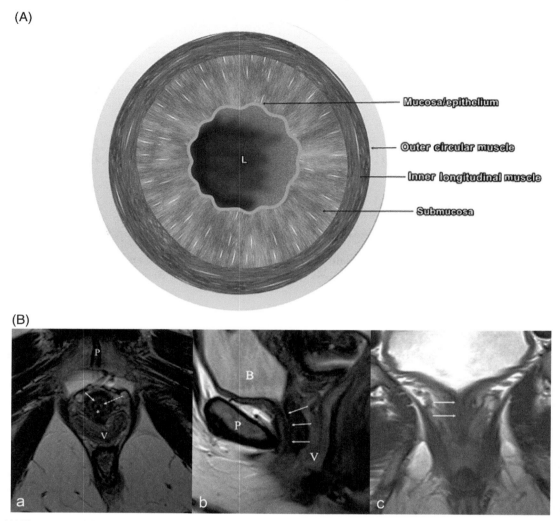

FIG. 19.2 (A) Illustration of the normal cross-sectional anatomy of the female urethra. The female urethra is composed of three layers: collagen-rich outer muscular fibers, elastin-rich submucosa and inner mucosa. The outermost layer is further comprised of an outer circular muscular layer with overlying serosa and an inner longitudinal muscle layer. The submucosal layer is hyperintense on T2WI compared to the muscular and mucosal layers, which gives rise to the characteristic target appearance of the female urethra on axial T2WI. (B) a) Axial T2WI demonstrates the characteristic target appearance of the female urethra. The submucosal layer (dotted arrow) is hyperintense on T2WI compared to the muscular (solid arrow) and mucosal (arrow head) layers. b) Sagittal T2WI also demonstrated the layered appearance of the female urethra extending inferiorly from the bladder (B), posterior to the pubic symphysis (P) and anterior to the vagina (V). c) Coronal T2WI in the same patient.

receives blood supply from the internal pudendal artery, is composed of striated muscle and is innervated by the pudendal nerve. The EUS is composed of three muscles, the circular sphincter urethrae and sphincter urethrovaginalis muscles, and the compressor urethrae muscle, which attaches to the inferior pubic rami. The levator ani, specifically the puborectalis portion, also contributes to urethral closure as the urethra courses through this muscle towards the external orifice.[2,3]

Histologically, the female urethra is composed of three layers: (a) collagen-rich outer muscular fibers, (b) elastin-rich submucosa, and (c) inner mucosa. These distinct layers give rise to the classic "target" appearance of the urethra on axial and sagittal T2WI, as the well-vascularized middle submucosal layer is hyperintense relative to the outer muscular and inner mucosal layers. The outermost layer is further comprised of an outer circular muscular layer with overlying serosa and an inner longitudinal muscle layer. When applicable, a urine-filled urethra will demonstrate a central hyperintense region on axial and sagittal T2WI (Fig. 19.2A and B). The proximal urethra is lined by transitional epithelium. The distal urethra is lined by stratified squamous epithelium. Submucosal mucus-secreting glands are present throughout the urethra with increased concentration in the distal urethra and along its posterolateral aspect. The largest of the glands are known as Skene glands, also called paraurethral glands, and are located in the vestibule of the vulva at the distal aspect of the urethra[1] (Fig. 19.3).

In female patients, the Mullerian/paramesonephric ducts are responsible for formation of the uterus, fallopian tubes and upper one-third of the vagina. The Wolffian/mesonephric ducts are responsible for formation of the internal male reproductive structures, however undergo regression in female patients. Persistent and remnant embryologic structures can mimic true urethral and periurethral pathology.

19.3 MRI technique and protocol

The use of a dedicated MRI protocol for evaluation of the female urethra and periurethral tissues allows for thorough investigation of a large variety of pathologies. Imaging can be performed on either a 1.5 or 3-Tesla machine, although evidence suggests that 3-T machines provide improved resolution of female pelvic structures.[4] Often, a pelvic phased-array coil is used with or without an endoluminal coil (either vaginal or rectal). High resolution, small field of view T2-weighted imaging (T2WI) in axial, coronal, and sagittal planes are essential sequences, particularly in the evaluation of urethral diverticula.[5] Multiplanar imaging permits precise localization of abnormalities. In particular, sagittal imaging allows for localization along the length of the urethra and relative association to the vagina. Coronal imaging allows for comparative visualization of the pelvic floor musculature.

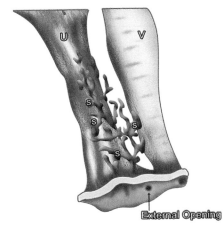

FIG. 19.3 **Illustration of the anatomic relationship of Skene's glands (S) to the urethra (U) and vagina (V).** The external opening of Skene's glands are located in the vestibule of the vagina at the distal aspect of the urethra.

Pre-contrast and post-contrast T1-weighted imaging (T1WI) with fat-suppression are strongly recommended sequences, particularly in the assessment of suspected solid or complicated cystic lesions. The addition of subtraction images permits further detection of subtle enhancement, particularly in regions of already high signal on T1WI, such as hemorrhage and melanin-containing lesions.

Other optional sequences include large field of view, coronal, single shot T2WI for a global view of the lower abdomen and pelvis. A suggested MRI protocol can be seen in Table 19.1.

The use of endovaginal and endorectal coils may improve visualization of urethral diverticula, in particular identifying the diverticular orifice and neck.[6] Functional MRI and MR defecography employ additional sequences to evaluate the pelvic floor, urethral angle and urethral mobility. Please refer to the chapter on MR defecography for more information.

TABLE 19.1 Suggested MRI Protocol for evaluation of the female urethra. Included are essential, recommended and optional sequences for a detailed MRI evaluation of the female urethra.

Essential Sequences	High resolution, thin slice, small field of view, single shot T2WI - urethra a) Axial b) Coronal c) Sagittal Large field of view, single shot T2WI- pelvis a) Axial b) Sagittal
Recommended Sequences	Large field of view, single shot T2WI- abdomen and pelvis a) Coronal Pre-contrast and post-contrast T1WI with fat suppression - pelvis and/or urethra a) Axial b) Coronal c) Sagittal
Optional Sequences	High resolution, small field of view T2WI with fat suppression - urethra a) Axial Large field of view T1WI- pelvis a) Axial Diffusion weighted imaging a) Axial Subtraction imaging

19.4 Classification

Urethral and periurethral pathologies in females can be broadly classified as either cystic or solid, the latter of which is further categorized as benign or malignant.

Cystic pathologies are usually benign. The most common cystic lesions in the female urethral and periurethral region are urethral diverticula, which can be complicated or uncomplicated. Additional considerations include those arising from adjacent periurethral tissue (Skene and Bartholin's gland cysts), or those arising from the vagina (epidermal inclusion cysts) or remnant/residual fetal tissue (Gartner and Mullerian duct cysts).

Solid urethral and periurethral lesions are further classified as benign or malignant. Benign pathologies include leiomyoma, hemangioma, fibroepithelial polyp, caruncle and endometrioma. Malignant pathologies include transitional cell/urothelial cell carcinoma, adenocarcinoma, squamous cell carcinoma, melanoma, and invasion from adjacent pelvic malignancy.

Additional considerations are made for infectious/inflammatory, iatrogenic, and post-traumatic findings.

19.5 Cystic lesions

19.5.1 Urethral diverticulum (UD)

Urethral diverticula comprise the majority of cystic urethral and periurethral masses and accounts for an estimated 80% of urethral and periurethral masses in women.[7] Estimated incidence ranges from 1% to 6% in the general population with predilection for adult females between 20 and 60 with a median age of 40.[4,8]

Symptomatology of UD is vague and nonspecific, which can lead to a delay in diagnosis. In fact, symptoms are often absent with approximately 20% of UD being incidental findings either during imaging or at time of surgery.[4] When present, symptoms are classically described as the "3 D's," namely postvoid dribbling, dysuria and dyspareunia. However, this classical triad is only present collectively in as low as 5% of patients with UD. As high as 27% of patients with UD lack any of the "3 D's."[9] Other symptoms include incontinence, urgency, recurrent urinary tract infection, hematuria or less commonly a palpable mass.[10] In one series that evaluated 79 female patients with periurethral masses, UD was found to represent 100% of nonpalpable masses and 62% of palpable masses.[11]

The pathogenesis of UD is generally considered to be an acquired process which can be iatrogenic (such as repeated instrumentation or postsurgical), infectious/inflammatory or post-traumatic (including birth trauma and mechanical trauma).[12] Regardless of etiology, insult to the submucosal periurethral glands (including Skene glands) can lead to cyst formation. Rupture of these cysts into the urethral lumen leads to formation of UD. These periurethral glands are found in greatest concentration at the distal and posterolateral aspects of the urethra, which corresponds to the most common locations for UD. Because of this, UD can present as a palpable anterior vaginal mass. Rare cases of congenital UD can be seen in the setting of Gartner duct remnants or persistent Mullerian ducts.

On MRI, UD can have a variety of shapes, however are characteristically described as a "saddle-bag" or "horseshoe/C-shaped" periurethral lesion, although other configurations exist. Signal intensity within uncomplicated UD typically follows that of urine (Fig. 19.4A). Fat-suppressed T2W and post-gadolinium imaging can help to visualize a short diverticular neck, the identification of which can help to differentiate UD from other periurethral cystic lesions (Fig. 19.4B). Post-contrast images have additional benefit in assessing for associated complications including infection, calculus formation/retention and malignancy (Fig. 19.4C, D, and E). A stone/calculus will appear as a T2W hypointense structure. Imaging of UD-associated malignancy can vary from subtle wall irregularity to more discrete enhancing mass lesions. The most common malignancy associated with UD is adenocarcinoma (~75%) followed by squamous cell carcinoma (~15%) and urothelial/transitional cell carcinoma (~10%).[13]

Symptomatic urethral diverticula are often managed with diverticulectomy. Recurrent diverticula following surgical excision are more common among those with multiple diverticula, proximal diverticula or those who have had prior urethral procedures.[14] Adverse outcomes include urethral stricture, urethrovaginal fistula, or new stress incontinence. Also, "horseshoe/C-shaped" and circumferential UD are associated with increased risk of recurrence, development of stress incontinence and other adverse outcomes following diverticulectomy.[15,16]

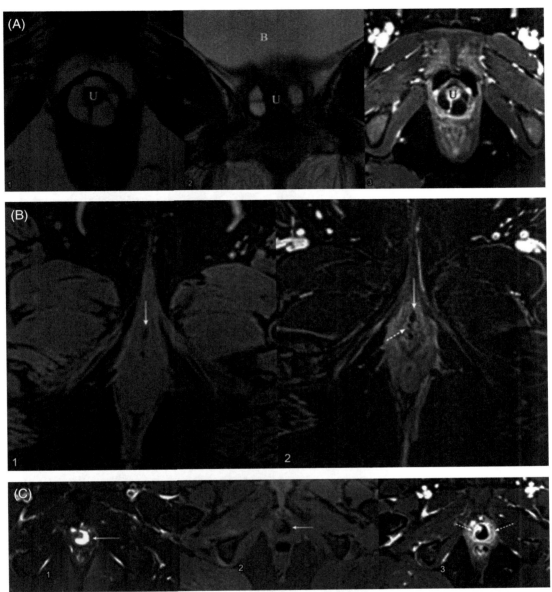

FIG. 19.4 (A) Non-complicated circumferential urethral diverticulum. 1) Axial T2WI demonstrate a T2-hyperintense structure surrounding the urethra (U) consistent with a circumferential urethral diverticulum, which was incidentally noted in a patient undergoing an infectious work-up. The contents of this non-complicated urethral diverticulum follow that of urine found in the bladder (B). 2) Coronal T2WI in the same patient. 3) Axial post-contrast T1WI shows hypointense internal contents without enhancement, consistent with a non-complicated UD. (B) Non-complicated urethral diverticulum with narrow neck. 1) Axial pre-contrast T1WI demonstrates a T1-hypointense structure found posterior to the urethra (solid arrow) consistent with a small urethral diverticulum in a patient with recurrent urinary tract infections and pus per urethra. 2) Axial post-contrast T1WI shows a more conspicuous tract reflecting a narrow diverticular neck. (C) Complicated horseshoe/C-Shaped urethral diverticulum. 1) Axial T2WI demonstrates a C-shaped T2-hyperintense lesion (solid arrows) consistent with a urethral diverticulum. 2) The same lesion is hypointense on T1WI. 3) Axial post-contrast T1WI shows post-gadolinium enhancement (dashed arrows), raising concern for infected UD in a patient with dysuria, difficulty urinating and a palpable mass. (D) Complicated urethral diverticulum with multiple stones. 1) Axial T2WI, 2) Axial T1WI and 3) Sagittal T2WI demonstrate a urethral diverticulum (*) which contains multiple layering T1 and T2-hypointense structures (solid arrows). 4) Note the lack of contrast enhancement on sagittal post-contrast T1WI, consistent with stone/calculus in a patient with dysuria and palpable mass. U: urethra; B: bladder. (E) Complicated urethral diverticulum with clear cell adenocarcinoma. 1) Axial T2WI and 2) Coronal T2WI demonstrate a large T2-hyperintense structure surrounding the urethra (dashed arrow) consistent with urethral diverticulum in a patient with hematuria. Note the presence of multiple T2-hypointense filling defects within the diverticulum (solid arrows). Post-operative pathology demonstrated clear cell adenocarcinoma. B: bladder.

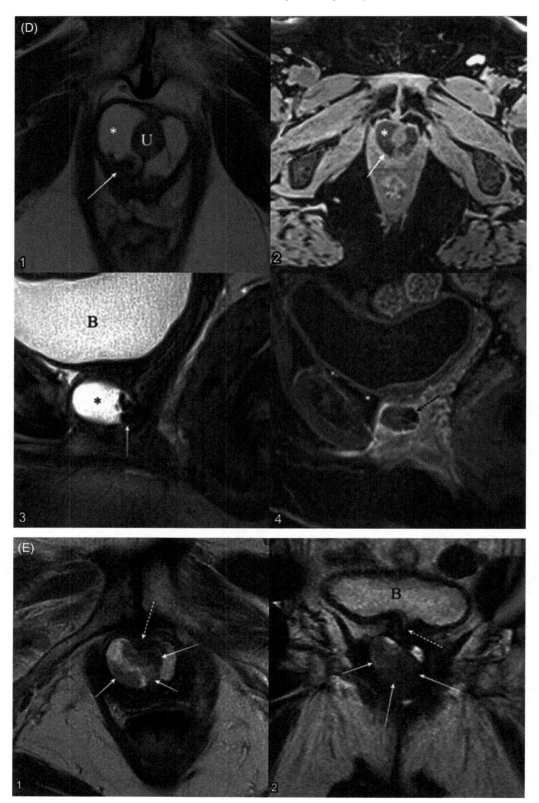

FIG. 19.4 *(Cont.)*

19.5.2 Other cystic periurethral lesions

Additional common cystic periurethral lesions arise from periurethral tissue, the vagina, or persistent/remnant fetal tissue. These pathologies can often be differentiated by their characteristic locations (Table 19.2 and Fig. 19.5). MRI is an ideal tool to assess these findings and provides detailed information about size and associated complications.

Skene glands (also called paraurethral glands) are paired mucus-secreting glands located in the vestibule of the vulva. They are the largest and distal-most of the submucosal glands associated with the urethra and empty lateral to external urethral meatus below the level of the pubic symphysis. Because they are not contiguous with the urethra, there is no discernible connection to the urethra. They classically demonstrate a "tear drop" appearance on sagittal images. Skene's gland cysts become symptomatic when larger than 2 cm in size as they may exhibit mass effect on the adjacent urethra.[17] As with other cysts, they appear hypointense on T1WI, hyperintense on T2WI and do not enhance on post-contrast images. When inflamed, they can become obstructed leading to superimposed infection and abscess formation[18,19] (Fig. 19.6A and B).

Bartholin glands (also called greater vestibular glands) are small, paired glands and function primarily to lubricate the vagina. Bartholin gland cysts are located in the vulva at the level of the labia minora, inferior to the vagina, and below the level of the pubic symphysis. Each gland drains through a 2–2.5 cm long duct that empties into the vestibule at approximately 4–8 o'clock.[20,21] As with Skene gland cysts, there is no discernible connection

TABLE 19.2 Comparison of cystic urethral and peri-urethral lesions (excluding urethral diverticula). Special attention to locations and anatomic relationships is critical for accurate identification of the variety of cystic lesions that are associated with the female urethra.

Other Cystic Urethral and Periurethral Lesion

Lesion	Location	Etiology	Other
Skene gland cyst	Distal/anterior urethra; lateral to external urethral meatus	Dilated distal paraurethral glands	Not connected to urethra; can become infected
Bartholin gland cyst	Vulva; inferior to vagina and below pubic symphysis	Dilated greater vestibular glands	Not connected to urethra; can become infected
Epidermal inclusion cyst	Lower, posterior or lateral vaginal wall	Post-traumatic, post-surgical	-
Mullerian duct cyst	Anterolateral vaginal wall	Persistent Mullerian duct	-
Gartner duct cyst	Anterior, superior vagina; at or above pubic symphysis	Dilated Wolffian duct remnant	Associated with other urogenital anomalies

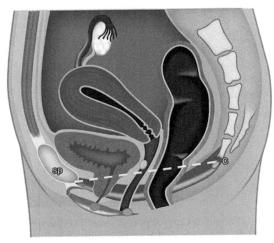

FIG. 19.5 **Illustration demonstrating the anatomic relationship of common cystic urethral and periurethral lesions.** Skene's gland cysts (blue) are found at the level of the external urethral meatus. Bartholin's gland cysts (green) are found at the level of the vulva, inferior to the vagina and below the pubic symphysis. Gartner's duct cysts (yellow) are found in the anterior or superior vagina above the pubic symphysis. Dotted line: pubococcygeal line; Sp: pubis symphysis; C: coccyx.

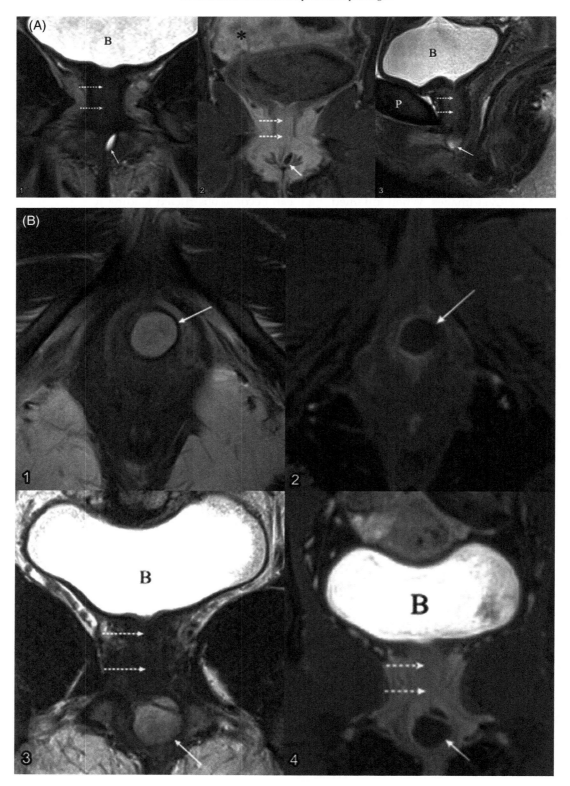

FIG. 19.6 (A) Skene's gland cyst. 1) Coronal T2WI and 2) Coronal post-contrast T1WI demonstrate a T2-hyperintense, T1-hypointense, non-enhancing lesion (solid arrows) along the distal left urethra (dashed arrows), consistent with a Skene gland cyst. 3) Sagittal T2WI also localizes the lesion to the distal urethra, anterior to the vagina. Also present is uterine leiomyoma (*). B: bladder; P: pubic symphysis. (B) Skene's gland cyst. 1) Axial T2WI and 2) Axial post-contrast T1WI demonstrate a T2-hyperintense, T1-hypointense, non-enhancing lesion with internal septation (solid arrows) adjacent to the urethra (dashed arrows). 3) Coronal T2WI and 4) Coronal T1WI localize the lesion to the left of the distal urethra. This is consistent with a Skene gland cyst. B: bladder.

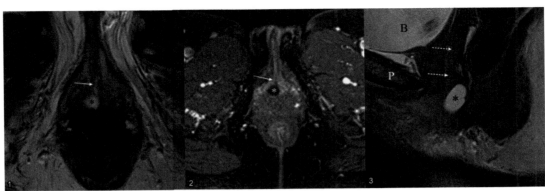

FIG. 19.7   Bartholin's gland cyst. 1) Axial T2WI and 2) Axial post-contrast T1WI demonstrate a T2-hyperintense, T1-hypointense lesion (*) in the peri-urethral region with discernable neck (solid arrow). Sagittal T2WI (3) demonstrate the same lesion along the distal vagina (dashed arrows) below the level of the pubic symphysis (P). This is consistent with a Bartholin gland cyst in a patient with a palpable, fluctuant vaginal mass. B: bladder.

to the urethra. Bartholin gland cysts are frequently asymptomatic and may be seen in up to 3% of the female population.[18,22] Complicated Bartholin gland cysts may be infected, develop an abscess, or undergo malignant transformation. Uncomplicated Bartholin gland cysts appear hypointense on T1WI, hyperintense on T2WI, and do not enhance on post-contrast images (Fig. 19.7). T1-hyperintensity may represent internal hemorrhage or high proteinaceous content. Infected cysts may show adjacent fat stranding and inflammation. Malignant transformation may demonstrate mural nodularity, enhancing solid component, or replacement with a solid/solid-cystic mass.

Epidermal inclusion cysts, particularly those arising from the vagina, are the most common acquired cystic lesion of the vagina. They are typically located at the lower posterior or lateral vaginal wall at the site of prior surgery or trauma, including birth trauma.[23] Epidermal inclusions cysts are lined with stratified squamous epithelium and often remain symptomatic. Inclusion cysts can mimic other cystic periurethral lesions and correlation with clinical history can help differentiate epidermal inclusion cysts from the other pathologies (Fig. 19.8). Symptomatic epidermal cysts are surgically marsupialized.[24]

Persistent/remnant fetal structures can also lead to cystic periurethral lesions. Mullerian duct cysts are found in the anterolateral vaginal wall. These cysts represent remnants of the Mullerian/paramesonephric ducts. Gartner duct cyst represent dilated Wolffian/mesonephric duct remnants, and their presence should prompt further evaluation for additional urogenital anomalies such as ectopic ureteral insertion, renal agenesis, or renal hypoplasia. Gartner duct cysts are classically found in the superior, anterior wall of the vagina above the level of the inferior

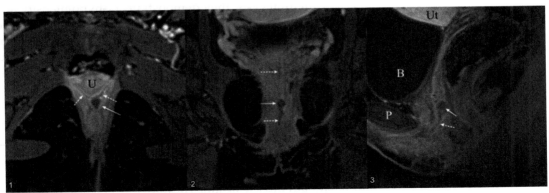

FIG. 19.8   Epidermoid inclusion cyst. 1) Axial post-contrast T1WI, 2) Coronal post-contrast T1WI and 3) Sagittal post-contrast T1WI demonstrate a T1-hypointense, non-enhancing lesion (solid arrow) along the posterior wall of the vagina (dashed arrows) consistent with an epidermoid inclusion cyst. U: urethra; Ut: uterus; B: bladder; P; pubic symphysis.

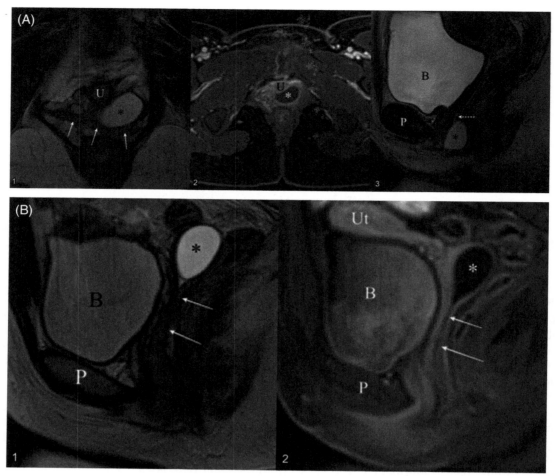

FIG. 19.9 (A) Mullerian duct cyst. 1) Axial T2WI and 2) Axial post-contrast T1WI demonstrate a T2-hyperintense, T1-hypointense, non-enhancing lesion (*) between the urethra (U) and anterior aspect of the vagina (solid arrows). 3) Sagittal T2WI shows the lesion along the distal aspect of the vagina, posterior to the urethra. Also present is a discernible neck (dashed arrows). Post-operative pathology demonstrated a benign Mullerian cyst in a patient with a palpable sub-urethral mass. B: bladder; P: pubic symphysis. (B) Gartner duct cyst. 1) Sagittal T2WI and 2) Sagittal post-contrast T1WI demonstrate a T2-hyperintense, T1-hypointense, non-enhancing lesion (*) along the superior aspect of the vagina (solid arrows) above the level of the pubic symphysis (P). This is consistent with a Gartner duct cyst in a patient with pelvic exam showing a "dark soft tissue mass obstructing the cervix" and ultrasound demonstrating a vaginal cyst. Ut: uterus; B: bladder.

aspect of the pubic symphysis. As with other periurethral cysts, they demonstrate T1-hypointensity and T2-hyperintensity. Occasional T1-hyperintensity can be seen in the setting of hemorrhage or proteinaceous material. Localizing Mullerian and Gartner duct cyst to the anterior-superior wall of the vagina and separate from the urethra is critical as Mullerian and Gartner duct cysts may closely mimic urethral diverticula. Differentiating Mullerian and Gartner duct cysts is of little importance due to the fact they are often asymptomatic and are managed similarly if they are in fact symptomatic[23,25] (Fig. 19.9A and B).

19.6 Solid lesions

19.6.1 Benign

Urethral leiomyoma is a rare, benign tumor of smooth muscle origin. They are most common in reproductive age women and may regress after menopause. When present, symptoms can include palpable mass, hematuria, dyspareunia, and difficulty with urination. Findings on MRI include low to intermediate signal intensity on both

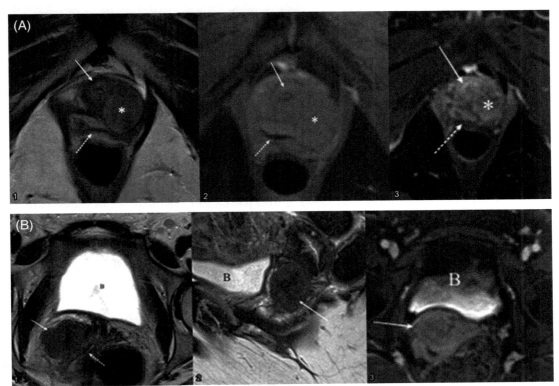

FIG. 19.10 (A) Urethral leiomyoma. 1) Axial T2WI demonstrates a T2-isointense lesion (*) to the left of the urethra (solid arrow) and anterior to the vagina (dashed arrow) in a patient with a palpable periurethral mass. 2) Axial pre-contrast T1WI and 3) Axial post-contrast T1WI demonstrate heterogenous enhancement. The lesion was biopsied with pathology showing a benign periurethral leiomyoma. Note the normal target appearance of the urethra. (B) Vaginal leiomyoma. 1) Axial T2WI and 2) Sagittal T2WI demonstrate a T2-hypointense lesion (solid arrow) on the right aspect of the vagina (dashed arrow). 3) Axial post-contrast T1WI shows heterogenous enhancement, consistent with a vaginal leiomyoma in a patient with a palpable vaginal wall mass.

T1WI and T2WI with homogenous enhancement (Fig. 19.10A). However, leiomyomas with degeneration may show a variable appearance with hyperintensity on T1WI and T2WI; therefore post-contrast enhancement plays a key role in differentiating leiomyoma from other pathologies. Leiomyomas are common throughout the female genitourinary tract, and those arising from adjacent structures, such as the vagina, can mimic those of urethral origin (Fig. 19.10B). Close attention to regional anatomy and associated fat planes can help to differentiate the origin.[26,27]

Hemangiomas are benign vascular neoplasms which, in rare circumstances, can occur in the urinary tract. They are more common in males than females. Symptoms can include hematuria or bloody urethral discharge. Imaging findings are not well established due to an overall low number of case reports, but usually follow the signal characteristics of any adjacent low-flow vascular structures. They are often associated with congenital syndromes that cause hemangiomatosis, such as Sturge-Weber and Klippel-Trenaunay[28] (Fig. 19.11).

Urethral caruncles are benign lesions caused by distal urethral prolapse and are commonly observed along the posterior margin of the external urethral meatus in hypoestrogenic postmenopausal women.[29] Histologically, the caruncles are made up of hyperplastic squamous epithelium, fibrotic and inflammatory tissue. Most are asymptomatic but can occasionally cause pain and hematuria. They appear as soft exophytic lesion with low signal on T1WI and high signal on T2WI. The treatment is often conservative with sitz baths and the application of vaginal creams and topical estrogen.[30]

Fibroepithelial polyps are another example of benign urethral lesions, although they are more common in young male patients. These lesions demonstrate intense post-gadolinium enhancement.[31]

Extra-pelvic endometriosis involves the urinary tract in as high as 12% of cases with the bladder representing the most common location. Endometriosis in the urethra has been reported in 2% of cases with urinary tract

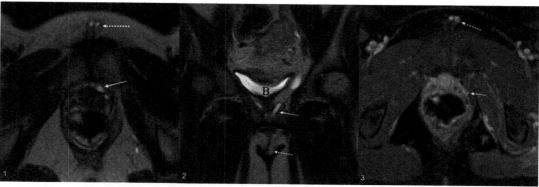

FIG. 19.11   Periurethral hemangioma. 1) Axial T2WI and 2) Coronal T2WI demonstrate multiple T2-hyperintense lesions in the left labia (dashed arrow) and left anterior periurethral region (solid arrow). 3) Axial post-contrast T1WI show similar enhancement characteristics to adjacent vessels. Findings are consistent with multiple hemangiomas in a patient with Klippel-Trenaunay Syndrome. B: bladder.

involvement.[32] Characteristic imaging findings include high signal on T1WI and low to intermediate signal on T2WI.[32,33] Pelvic endometriosis is discussed at length in a separate chapter.

19.6.2 Malignant

Primary urethral carcinoma occurs more often in men and accounts for as low as 0.02% of malignancies in females.[34] Prevalence increases with age, and women may present with bleeding, palpable mass, or obstructive symptoms. The reported distribution of histologic subtypes varies with urothelial/transitional call carcinoma representing 24.9–45%, squamous cell carcinoma representing 19–25.4% and adenocarcinoma representing 29–46.7% of primary urethral carcinomas.[35,36] Some reported risk factors of urethral carcinoma include chronic inflammation, frequent catheterization, HPV infection, smoking, or presence of urethral diverticula.[37]

Less common malignancies such as melanoma may also arise in the urethra. Primary malignant melanoma of the urethra represents approximately 0.2% of all malignant melanomas and is up to three times more common in women than in men. Primary malignant melanoma of the female urethra is usually situated at the external urethral meatus or along the distal urethra.[38] The urethra can also be involved by malignancies from nearby structures.

Primary urethral carcinoma can be differentiated based on their location along the course of the urethra (Table 19.3). Distal/anterior lesions are located in the distal third of the urethra, and proximal/posterior lesions are found in the proximal two thirds. In keeping with histology of the urethra, urothelial/transitional cell carcinoma and

TABLE 19.3   A comparison of primary urethral malignancy by location. In keeping with histology of the urethra, urothelial/transitional cell carcinoma and adenocarcinoma are often found in the proximal/posterior urethra, and squamous cell carcinoma is found in the distal/anterior urethra and urethral meatus. Distal/anterior lesions tend to present earlier and have a better prognosis, which may in part be due to their increased likelihood of being detected on physical exam and relative resectability compared to proximal/posterior lesions. Attention to lymphatic involvement can also assist with localizing malignancies.

Primary Urethral Malignancy	
Proximal/Posterior	**Distal/Anterior**
Proximal 2/3	Distal 1/3 + urethral meatus
Transitional cell/urothelial carcinoma, adenocarcinoma	Squamous cell carcinoma
Iliac, obturator and peri-aortic lymph nodes	Superficial and deep inguinal lymph nodes
Presents later	Presents earlier
Worse prognosis	Better prognosis

adenocarcinoma are often found in the proximal/posterior urethra, and squamous cell carcinoma is found in the distal/anterior urethra and urethral meatus. Distal/anterior lesions tend to present earlier and have a better prognosis, which may in part be due to their increased likelihood of being detected on physical exam and relative resectability compared to proximal/posterior lesions.[39]

Classic MRI findings of urethral malignancies includes low signal on T1WI, high signal on T2WI and heterogenous post-gadolinium enhancement[19] (Fig. 19.12A and B). Melanoma, however, demonstrates characteristic slightly increased signal on T1WI (Fig. 19.12C). Special attention must be paid to depth of involvement, local invasion and distal metastases, as these are important prognostic factors for staging. Depending on the location, primary urethral malignancies can invade the vagina, bladder and even the pubic symphysis. When present, nodal metastases for malignancies of the proximal urethra include iliac, obturator and peri-aortic lymph nodes, whereas superficial and deep inguinal nodes are involved with distal urethral malignancies.[40]

19.7 Miscellaneous

Assorted additional pathologies affect the urethra and are readily evaluated with MRI. As with any part of the urinary tract, the urethra can become infected or inflamed. Edema secondary to urethritis will classically appear as increased signal on T2WI (Fig. 19.13A). Prior infection is just one of many etiologies which can lead to urethral stricture and fibrosis. The list also includes trauma, surgical intervention, radiation, and chronic or frequent catheterization[41] (Fig. 19.13B).

Urethral fistulas can be classified as urethrovaginal, rectourethral and urethroperineal. The underlying pathologies may include Crohn's disease, Behçet disease, or iatrogenic complications such as those following urethral diverticulectomy or vaginal surgery (Fig. 19.13C). Urethral fistulas can also be evaluated with fluoroscopic studies.

The urethra can also be involved by masses and malignancies from adjacent structures such as the vagina, labia, vulva, clitoris, and pubic symphysis. Squamous cell carcinoma (SCC) is the predominant primary malignancy of the external female genital tract accounting for 86% of primary vulvar malignancy and 90% of primary vaginal malignancy.[42] As with urethral malignancy, MRI plays a critical role in the assessment and staging of vaginal and vulvar malignancy. Direct invasion/involvement of the urethra can often occur when locally aggressive SCC is present.[43] Characteristic imaging findings of SCC on MRI include intermediate signal on T2WI, low signal on T1WI and post-contrast enhancement (Fig. 19.14A). Additional primary vaginal malignancies include melanoma and sarcoma. Primary melanoma shows a predilection for the lower vagina, whereas sarcoma often involves the upper vagina.[44]

The urethra is rarely a site of metastatic involvement. The vagina, however, is a common site of metastatic disease with sources including bladder, rectum, and cervix. In some cases, vaginal metastases can mimic urethral and periurethral pathology. An example of this is the so-called "cervical drop metastasis"[45] (Fig. 19.14B).

The clitoris lies in close proximity to the external urethral orifice, and as such, can mimic urethral and periurethral pathologies. It serves as a site for malignancy, including squamous cell carcinoma and sarcoma, or post-traumatic findings, such as hematomas and epidermal inclusion cysts[46] (Fig. 19.15).

The pubic symphysis may be a source of degenerative or post-traumatic pseudocysts, also known as subpubic cartilaginous pseudocysts. When large, these lesions can lead to urinary symptoms or present as a palpable vaginal or vulvar mass. MRI will demonstrate a T2-hyperintense lesion with a characteristic broad-based origin the pubic symphysis and possible mass effect on the anterior urethra.[47]

A variety of highly specialized surgical and procedural interventions exist for the management of pelvic floor prolapse and urinary incontinence. These range from reconstruction urethroplasty to insertion of supportive slings and meshes (Fig. 19.16A) to injection of bulking agents, including but not limited to collagen and calcium hydroxylapatite (Coaptite). Recently injected periurethral collagen may mimic a urethral diverticulum on T2WI due to the high water content, however over time will become hypointense on T1WI and T2WI as water is resorbed. Collagen is nonenhancing on post-contrast imaging (Fig. 19.16B). Due to the calcium component, Coaptite will appear hypointense on T1WI and T2WI and does not enhance on post-contrast imaging[48] (Fig. 19.16C). Awareness of prior interventions is essential to avoid misdiagnosis.

Functional MRI (fMRI) provides additional benefit in the assessment of urethral hypermobility and intrinsic sphincter deficiency. Dynamic imaging allows for special attention to urethral angle, bladder descent, sphincter integrity, and the complex interplay of periurethral ligaments.[49] Please refer to the chapter on MR defecography for more information.

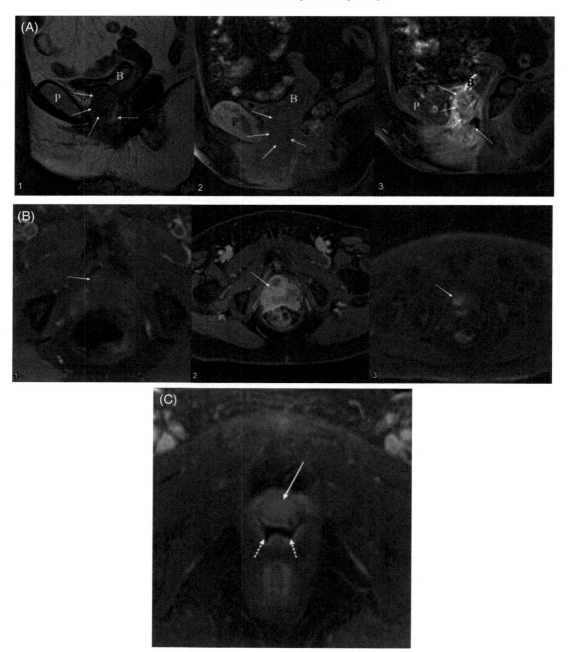

FIG. 19.12 (A) Primary urethral malignancy (squamous cell carcinoma). 1) Sagittal T2WI demonstrate a T2-hypointense urethral mass (solid arrows) spanning from the neck of the bladder (B) to the distal urethra. 2) Sagittal pre-contrast T1W1 and 2) Sagittal post-contrast T1WI shows avid enhancement. Also present is a urethrovaginal fistula (dotted arrow). Not pictured is an enlarged, enhancing left inguinal lymph node. Post-operative pathology demonstrated squamous cell carcinoma of the urethra. P: pubic symphysis. (B) Primary urethral malignancy (urothe-lial/transitional cell carcinoma). 1) Axial pre-contrast T1WI and 2) Axial post-contrast T1WI demonstrate an enhancing mass in the proximal urethra in a patient with hematuria. 3) The mass demonstrates restricted diffusion on diffusion weighted imaging. Post-operative pathology demonstrated urothelial/transitional cell carcinoma which also extended into the bladder neck. (C) Primary urethral malignancy (melanoma) 1) Axial post-contrast T1WI demonstrates an enhancing, expansile lesion (solid arrow) in the distal urethra, anterior to the vagina (dashed arrows). The lesion demonstrated heterogenous T2 signal. Post-operative pathology demonstrated primary urethral melanoma.

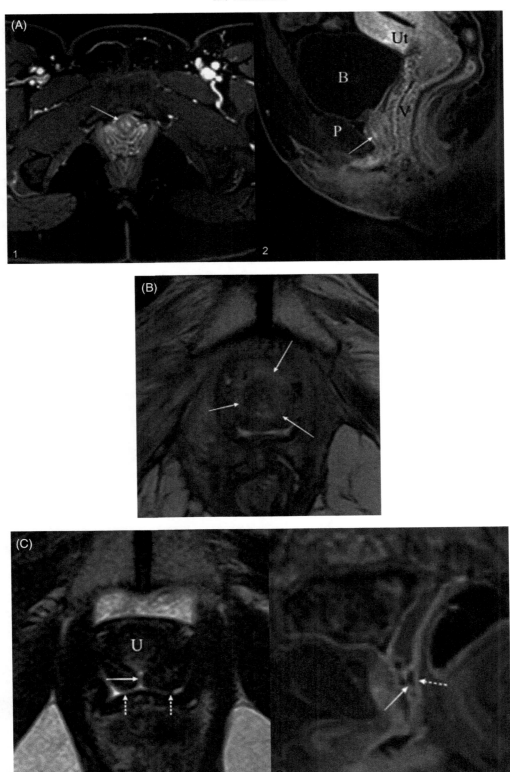

FIG. 19.13 (A) Urethritis. 1) Axial post-contrast T1WI and 2) Sagittal post-contrast T1WI demonstrate enhancing urethral mucosa (solid arrow) suggesting infection/inflammation in a patient with recurrent UTIs and pus per urethra. Ut: uterus; V: vagina; B: bladder; P: pubic symphysis. (B) Urethral fibrosis. 1) Axial T2WI demonstrates ill-defined urethral margins with surrounding T2-hyperintensity (arrows) in a patient with remote history of both cervical and vaginal cancer treated with radiation therapy. Findings are suggestive of post-radiation changes and fibrosis. This patient also has a urethrovaginal fistula which is not pictured. (C) Urethrovaginal fistula. 1) Axial T2WI demonstrates a fistulous connection (solid arrow) between the urethra (U) and vagina (dashed arrows) in a patient with incontinence and malodorous urine following urethral diverticulectomy. 2) Sagittal post-contrast T1WI localizes the fistula to the mid-urethra.

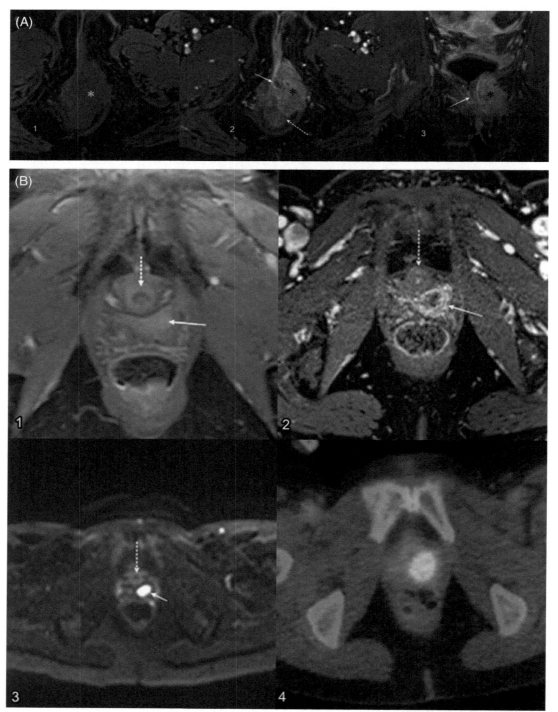

FIG. 19.14 (A) Vulvar malignancy. 1) Axial pre-contrast T1WI and 2) Axial post-contrast T1WI demonstrate an enhancing left vulvar mass (*) with invasion/involvement of an ill-defined posterior urethra (solid arrow) in a patient with recurrent vulvar squamous cell carcinoma. The lower rectum is also involved (dotted arrow). 3) Coronal post-contrast T1WI shows involvement and mass effect on the adjacent urethra. (B) Periurethral malignancy (cervical "drop metastasis"). 1) Axial pre-contrast T1WI and 2) Axial post-contrast T1WI demonstrate an enhancing lesion (solid arrow) along the left posterior aspect of the urethra (dashed arrow) in a patient with a tender urethral mass. 3) The lesion demonstrates diffusion restriction on diffusion weighted imaging. 4) The lesions demonstrates hypermetabolic activity on FDG PET-CT. Post-operative pathology showed adenocarcinoma with specialty staining noting an endocervical origin. This is suggestive of the so-called "cervical drop metastasis". Note the normal target appearance of the urethra.

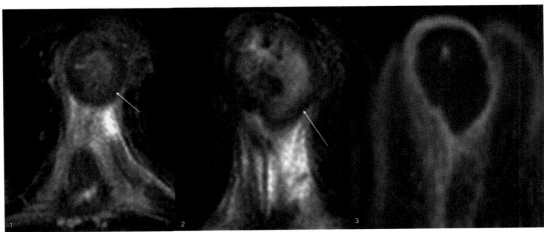

FIG. 19.15 Clitoral hematoma. 1,2) Axial T2WI demonstrates an irregular and well-circumscribed lesions with heterogenous T2 signal (solid arrow). 3) Axial post-contrast T1WI demonstrates no enhancement. Findings are consistent with a clitoral hematoma in a patient with swelling following sexual intercourse.

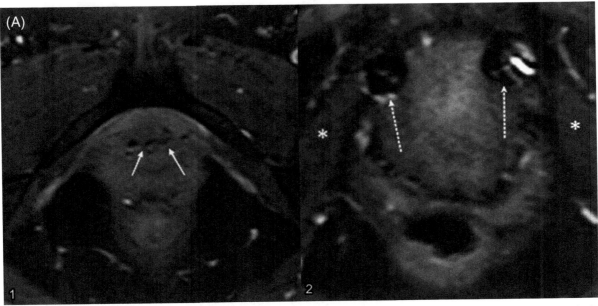

FIG. 19.16 (A) Retropubic mid-urethral sling. 1) Axial T1WI at the level of the mid-urethra demonstrates susceptibility artifact (solid arrows) posterior to the mid-urethra in a patient with a stress urinary incontinence status post retropubic mid-urethral sling. 4) Axial T1WI at the level of the bladder neck demonstrates additional foci of susceptibility artifact (dashed arrows) along the posterior aspect of the pubic rami (*), which are common sites for anchoring the sling. (B) Collagen injection. 1) Axial post-contrast T1WI and 2) Axial T2WI demonstrate a well-circumscribed, non-enhancing, T2-intermediate lesion (solid arrows) surrounding the proximal urethra (dotted arrow) in a patient with stress urinary incontinence status post collagen injection. 3) Coronal post-contrast T1WI and 4) Coronal T2WI localize the injection to the base of the bladder. B: bladder. (C) Calcium hydroxylapatite/Coaptite injection. 1) Sagittal T2WI and 2) Coronal T2WI demonstrate a large urethral diverticulum (*) with visible neck (dotted arrow) containing multiple T2-hypointense, non-enhancing filling defects (solid arrows). Findings are consistent with prior calcium hydroxylapatite (Coaptite) injection in a patient with incontinence and urgency. B: bladder; P: pubic symphysis.

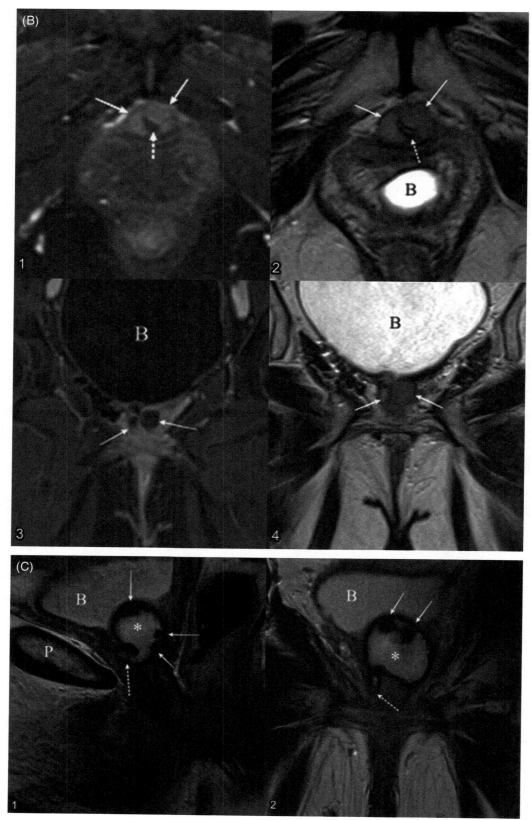

FIG. 19.16   *(Cont.)*

19.7.1 Pearls and pitfalls

Important teaching points with pertinent pearls and pitfalls are summarized in the box below.

Pearls and pitfalls

The proximal (posterior) two thirds and distal (anterior) one third of the urethra shows different histology. The distal urethra is bordered by stratified squamous cells that become transitional cell as the bladder is approached.

Lymphatic drainage for the proximal urethra occurs via iliac, obturator, and peri-aortic lymph nodes. Lymphatic drainage for the distal urethra and urethral meatus occurs via superficial and deep inguinal nodes.

Urethral diverticula make up the majority (80%) of urethral and periurethral cystic masses in females.

Urethral diverticulum classically appears as a "saddle-bag" or "horseshoe/C-shaped" periurethral lesion.

Visualization of the neck communicating with the urethral lumen confirms the diagnosis of urethral diverticulum, which may otherwise mimic periurethral gland cyst on imaging.
Fat-suppressed T2W and post-gadolinium imaging can help to visualize a short diverticular neck.

Post-contrast images can help evaluate complications like infection and malignancy in urethral diverticula and periurethral cysts.

Skene gland cysts classically demonstrate a "tear drop" appearance on sagittal images near the anterior (distal) urethra.

Bartholin gland cysts are located in the vulva (inferior to the vagina) and below the level of the pubic symphysis. Whereas the Gartner's duct cysts are situated along the anterior wall of the vagina above the pubic symphysis.

Primary urethral carcinoma accounts for as low as 0.02% of malignancies in females.

Urothelial/transitional cell carcinoma and adenocarcinoma are often found in the proximal (posterior) 2/3 of the urethra, and squamous cell carcinoma is found in the distal (anterior) 1/3 of the urethra.

Lymph node metastasis follows the respective lymphatic drainages. A malignancy from the proximal urethra involves iliac, obturator and peri-aortic lymph nodes, whereas superficial and deep inguinal nodes are involved with distal urethral malignancies.

Newly injected periurethral collagen can mimic urethral diverticula on T2W images. Though, it gradually becomes T1W/T2W hypointense as water is resorbed.

Coaptite injection may appear hypointense on T1W/T2W images due to its calcium content and does not enhance on post-contrast sequences.

19.8 Conclusion

Familiarity with female urethral and periurethral pathologies, both benign and malignant, and their characteristic imaging findings is essential for accurate classification and diagnosis. MRI plays a critical role in providing a detailed and thorough assessment of the otherwise complex female pelvis and often vague symptom profile.

References

1. Ryu J-ah, Kim B. MR imaging of the male and female urethra. *Radiographics*. 2001;21(5):1169–1185.
2. Sam P, Jiang J, LaGrange CA. *Anatomy, Abdomen and Pelvis, Sphincter Urethrae*: StatPearls; 2021.
3. Jung J, Ahn HK, Huh Y. Clinical and functional anatomy of the urethral sphincter. *Int Neurourol J*. 2012;16(3):102–106.
4. Kataoka M, Kido A, Koyama T, et al. MRI of the female pelvis at 3T compared to 1.5T: evaluation on high-resolution T2-weighted and HASTE images. *J Magn Reson Imaging*. 2007;25(3):527–534.
5. Chou C-P, Levenson RB, Elsayes KM, et al. Imaging of female urethral diverticulum: an update. *Radiographics*. 2008;28(7):1917–1930.
6. Blander DS, Rovner ES, Schnall MD, et al. Endoluminal magnetic resonance imaging in the evaluation of urethral diverticula in women. *Urology*. 2001;57(4):660–665.
7. Greiman AK, Rolef J, Rovner ES. Urethral diverticulum: a systematic review. *Arab J Urol*. 2019;17(1):49–57.
8. Di Gregorio M, Lorge F, Dupont M, de Morais CCFP, Nascimento LC, et al. Female urethral diverticulum: diagnosis, treatment and outcome. *Gynecol Obstet (Sunnyvale)*. 2016;6:374.
9. Baradaran N, Chiles LR, Freilich DA, Rames RA, Cox L, Rovner ES. Female urethral diverticula in the contemporary era: is the classic triad of the "3DS" still relevant? *Urology*. 2016;94:53–56.
10. Pincus JB, Laudano M, Leegant A, Downing K. Female urethral diverticula: diagnosis, pathology, and surgical outcomes at an academic, Urban Medical Center. *Urology*. 2019;128:42–46.
11. Blaivas JG, Flisser AJ, Bleustein CB, Panagopoulos G. Periurethral masses: etiology and diagnosis in a large series of women. *Obstet Gynecol*. 2004;103:842–847.
12. Goepel C, Szakacs M, Farkas B. Management of female urethral diverticulum. *J Gynecol Women's Health*. 2018;10(2):555785.

13. O'Connor E, Iatropoulou D, Hashimoto S, Takahashi S, Ho DH, Greenwell T. Urethral diverticulum carcinoma in females-a case series and review of the English and Japanese literature. *Transl Androl Urol.* 2018;7(4):703–729.

14. Zhou L, Luo DY, Feng SJ, et al. Risk factors for recurrence in female urethral diverticulectomy: a retrospective study of 66 patients. *World J Urol.* 2017;35(1):139–144.

15. Han DH, Jeong YS, Choo MS, Lee KS. Outcomes of surgery of female urethral diverticula classified using magnetic resonance imaging. *Eur Urol.* 2007;51(6):1664–1670.

16. Malde S, Naaseri S, Kavia R, et al. Preliminary report on the effect of urethral diverticulum magnetic resonance imaging configuration on the incidence of new onset urodynamic stress urinary incontinence following excision. *Urol Ann.* 2017;9(4):321–323.

17. Köse O, Aydemir H, Metin O, Budak S, Sonbahar A, Adsan O. Experiences with the management of paraurethral cysts in adult women. *Cent Eur J Urol.* 2014;66(4):477–480.

18. Tubay M, Hostetler V, Tujo C, Rezvani M, Shaaban A. Resident and fellow education feature what is that cyst? Common cystic lesions of the female lower genitourinary tract. *Radiographics.* 2014;34(2):427–428.

19. Chaudhari VV, Patel MK, Douek M, Raman SS. MR imaging and US of female urethral and periurethral disease. *Radiographics.* 2010;30:1857–1874.

20. Govan AD, Hodge C, Callander R. Gynaecology Illustrated. 3d ed. New York: Churchill Livingstone; 1985:195–196.

21. Hill DA, Lense JJ. Office management of Bartholin gland cysts and abscesses. *Am Fam Physician.* 1998;57:1611–6.1619–20.

22. Berger MB, Betschart C, Khandwala N, DeLancey JO, Haefner HK. Incidental Bartholin gland cysts identified on pelvic magnetic resonance imaging. *Obstet Gynecol.* 2012;120(4):798–802.

23. Prasad SR, Menias CO, Narra VR, et al. Cross-sectional imaging of the female urethra: technique and results. *Radiographics.* 2005;25(3):749–761.

24. Mubiayi N, Inguenault C, Crépin G, Cosson M. Epithelial inclusion cyst formation after buried vaginal mucosa: diagnosis and management. *Gynecol Obstet Fertil.* 2003;31(12):1013–1017.

25. Tiwari U, Relia N, Shailesh F, Kaushik C. Gartner duct cyst: CT and MRI findings. *J Obstet Gynaecol India.* 2014;64(Suppl 1):150–151.

26. Del Gaizo A, Silva AC, Lam-Himlin DM, Allen BC, Leyendecker J, Kawashima A. Magnetic resonance imaging of solid urethral and peri-urethral lesions. *Insights Imaging.* 2013;4(4):461–469.

27. N Beng Kwang, Naidu A, Yahaya A, Pei Shan L. Urethral leiomyoma: a rare clinical entity. *Case Rep Surg.* 2016;2016:6037104.

28. Regragui S, Slaoui A, Karmouni T, El Khader K, Koutani A, Attya AI. Urethral hemangioma: case report and review of the literature. *Pan Afr Med J.* 2016;23:96.

29. Conces MR, Williamson SR, Montironi R, Lopez-Beltran A, Scarpelli M, Cheng L. Urethral caruncle: clinicopathologic features of 41 cases. *Hum Pathol.* 2012;43(9):1400–1404.

30. Tomita H, Takeyama N, Hayashi T, et al. Magnetic resonance imaging of a urethral caruncle and the pathologic correlation: a report of 3 cases. *J Comput Assist Tomogr.* 2017;41(6):962–964.

31. Patheyar V, Venkatesh SK, Siew EPY, Consiglieri DT, Putti T. MR imaging features of fibroepithelial ureteral polyp in a patient with dupli-cated upper urinary tract. *Singapore Med J.* 2011;52(3):e45.

32. Leonardi M, Espada M, Kho RM, et al. Endometriosis and the urinary tract: from diagnosis to surgical treatment. *Diagnostics (Basel).* 2020;10(10):771.

33. Bazot M, Lafont C, Rouzier R, Roseau G, Thomassin-Naggara I, Daraï E. Diagnostic accuracy of physical examination, transvaginal sonog-raphy, rectal endoscopic sonography, and magnetic resonance imaging to diagnose deep infiltrating endometriosis. *Fertil Steril.* 2009;92(6):1825–1833.

34. Carvalho Neto J, de, Leão SC, Fakhouri R, Gurgel R, Dias JM, Vieira NF. Adenocarcinoma of the female urethra: a case report. *J Bras Patol Med Lab.* 2016;52(4).

35. Derksen JW, Visser O, de la Rivière GB, Meuleman EJ, Heldeweg EA, Lagerveld BW. Primary urethral carcinoma in females: an epidemio-logic study on demographic factors, histological types, tumour stage and survival. *World J Urol.* 2013;31(1):147–153.

36. Aleksic I, Rais-Bahrami S, Daugherty M, Agarwal PK, Vourganti S, Bratslavsky G. Primary urethral carcinoma: a surveillance, epidemiology, and end results data analysis identifying predictors of cancer-specific survival. *Urol Ann.* 2018;10(2):170–174.

37. Janisch F, Abufaraj M, Fajkovic H, et al. Current disease management of primary urethral carcinoma. *Eur Urol Focus.* 2019;5(5):722–734.

38. Bhutani N, Kajal P, Pawar D. Primary malignant melanoma of the female urethra: report of a rare neoplasm of the urinary tract. *Int J Surg Case Rep.* 2017;41:319–322.

39. Farrell MR, Xu JT, Vanni AJ. Current perspectives on the diagnosis and management of primary urethral cancer: a systematic review. *Res Rep Urol.* 2021;13:325–334.

40. Siosaki MD, Machado RD, Souza AT, et al. Primary proximal urethral adenocarcinoma: case report and brief review. *Can Urol Assoc J.* 2013;7(7-8):E499–E501.

41. de Toledo IA, DeLong J. Female urethral stricture: techniques for reconstruction. *Plast Aesthet Res.* 2022;9:5.

42. Prat J, Mutch DG. Pathology of cancers of the female genital tract including molecular pathology. *Int J Gynaecol Obstet.* 2018;143(Suppl 2): 93–108.

43. Serrado MA, Horta M, Cunha TM. State of the art in vulvar cancer imaging. *Radiol Bras.* 2019;52(5):316–324.

44. Parikh JH, Barton DP, Ind TE, Sohaib SA. MR imaging features of vaginal malignancies. *Radiographics.* 2008;28(1):49–63.

45. Otero-García MM, Mesa-Álvarez A, Nikolic O, et al. Role of MRI in staging and follow-up of endometrial and cervical cancer: pitfalls and mimickers. *Insights Imaging.* 2019;10(1):19.

46. Agarwal MD, Resnick EL, Mhuircheartaigh JN, Mortele KJ. MR imaging of the female perineum: clitoris, labia, and introitus. *Magn Reson Imaging Clin N Am.* 2017;25(3):435–455.

47. Kim CE, Beasley HS. MRI diagnosis of subpubic cartilaginous cyst. *AJR Am J Roentgenol.* 2004;182(1):144–146.

48. Khatri G, Carmel ME, Bailey AA, et al. (2016). Postoperative imaging after surgical repair for pelvic floor dysfunction. *Radiographics.* 2016;36(4):1233–1256.

49. Macura KJ, Thompson RE, Bluemke DA, Genadry R. Magnetic resonance imaging in assessment of stress urinary incontinence in women: parameters differentiating urethral hypermobility and intrinsic sphincter deficiency. *World J Radiol.* 2015;7(11):394–404.

20

MRI of fetus

Gregory Vorona, Jacqueline Urbine

Department of Radiology, Children's Hospital of Richmond, Virginia Commonwealth University
Health System, Richmond, VA, United States

20.1 Introduction

Ultrasound of the fetus remains the primary imaging modality of prenatal screening and diagnosis and it will continue to be the first-line imaging modality due to its lower cost, wide availability, and convenience.[1] The purpose of fetal magnetic resonance imaging (MRI) is to confirm, and to further assess, a suspected finding that was identified on prenatal ultrasound.[2–4] This is in part due to MRI's superior soft tissue contrast relative to ultrasound, as well as its ability to acquire images in true anatomic planes.[1] MRI also is generally not as affected by factors that can significantly limit the sonographic evaluation of fetal structures including oligohydramnios, maternal body habitus, overlying gas/bone, fetal lie, and decent of the fetal head into the maternal pelvis.[2,4]

20.2 Technique

20.2.1 Standardization, accreditation, and guidelines

- There are standards and accreditation processes for fetal/obstetrical ultrasound through both the American Institute of Medicine and the American College of Radiology (ACR).[5,6] This standardization is helpful in ensuring a baseline level of uniformity and quality in obstetrical ultrasounds performed across multiple and diverse sites.
- No similar standardization or accreditation process currently exists, however, for fetal MR. Rather, the ACR and the Society for Pediatric Radiology (SPR) have jointly developed a set of "practice parameters" to help guide centers on when and how to best perform fetal MR.[2]
- The International Society of Ultrasound in Obstetrics and Gynecology (ISUOG) also published a set of guidelines on performing fetal MR in 2017, based on a survey of practices conducted by ISUOG in 2014.[3]
- As a result, there is more heterogenicity in the way that fetal MR is currently implemented compared with obstetrical ultrasound.[7]
- Although fetal MRI may be technically accessible at many medical centers, it requires dedicated knowledge and experience both from the interpreting radiologist and from the MRI technologist to perform adequately.[1,2]

20.2.2 Timing of a fetal MR study

- The optimal timing of a given fetal MRI study is multifactorial, and studies are generally not performed before 18 weeks of gestational age (GA) as studies that are performed prior to this time can give limited diagnostic information due to the small fetal size and due to fetal motion.[2,4]
- If there is a suspected fetal anomaly identified by ultrasound that causes the parents to consider termination, the timing of the fetal MR can be influenced by the local legislation dictating the legal gestational age for abortion.

- If the fetus has a suspected abnormality that may make it a candidate for attempted intra-uterine repair, the timing fetal MR can be determined by the timing of the surgery. For example, intra-uterine myelomeningocele repair is generally performed prior to 26 weeks GA, so fetal MR will be performed prior to 26 GA in these patients to assess surgical candidacy.[4] In cases of a fetal neck mass (i.e., lymphatic malformation or cervical teratoma), a fetal MR may be delayed until later in pregnancy to allow better evaluation of the relationship of the mass with the fetal airway in order to assess the utility for delivery via the Ex Utero Intrapartum Treatment (EXIT) procedure if the fetal airway appears compromised.[4,8]

20.2.3 Patient preparation

- Consent: There is currently no national guidelines or mandate that requires informed consent be obtained before a fetal MRI study.[1,2] A recent survey of sites performing fetal MRI in North America indicated that many centers never obtain written consent (45%) or only sometimes obtained consent (9%).[7] At our center, we routinely obtain written consent from the mother.
- Fasting: It is controversial if maternal fasting prior to the examination significantly impacts fetal motion during the study. The joint ACR-SPR practice parameter in performing fetal MR offers no specific guidance on this practice.[2] In the survey cited above about half of the responding centers (49%) provide no specific pretesting fasting instructions, while some (19%) request that the patient avoid caffeine before scanning.[7] A 2019 study prospectively surveyed patients undergoing fetal MR in 228 encounters for their dietary behaviors before the study, and the authors did not identify any general significant difference in the motion scores between fasting and nonfasting patients.[9] Our current practice is to request that the patient refrain from caffeinated beverages the morning before the examination, and that she avoids sugary drinks (i.e., juice and soda) for three hours before the start of her examination.
- Sedation and maternal anxiety: Maternal sedation is not necessary in the vast majority of contemporary fetal MR cases.[2] At our center, patients have only rarely been given sedatives prior to fetal MR due to concerns of maternal anxiety, and this medication has been prescribed by the referring clinician. We have also found the use of MRI-compatible movie goggles (Resonance Technology Inc, Northridge CA) very helpful in mitigating maternal anxiety during studies, although we have noticed that if the wiring is left in the field of view, it can produce some artifacts that are easily avoidable by having the wire come the other way through the bore.
- Preprocedural counseling and prep: Before positioning the mother, we regularly advise the patient that the study may take 30 minutes or more depending upon fetal motion. The mother is routinely asked to use the restroom and empty her bladder prior to the immediate start of the study.
- Patient positioning: We usually try to position the patient supinely, although if it looks like she will be uncomfortable or if she is the third trimester, we will position the patient in the left lateral decubitus position (to avoid compression of the inferior vena cava). We will regularly place a pillow between the patient's legs. When the patient is imaged in the supine position, we usually will use a single multichannel body coil for anterior coverage and the spine coils built into the table for posterior coverage, although we will use two anterior body coils depending upon patient body habitus and positioning. Any accompanying partner can be present in the MRI suite so long as they go through our standard MRI screening. Hearing protection is performed with earplugs or headphones.

20.2.4 Technique

20.2.4.1 Overview

- To perform fetal MR successfully, there has to be a balance between rapid image acquisition and the image quality, given the significant fetal motion and maternal respiration during the study.[10] The positioning of the fetus can change rapidly (and unexpectedly) during a study, and it is paramount that the most recently acquired images are used to plan the following sequences.[4] Although the specific sequences and imaging planes that are used to assess a given suspected fetal anomaly will vary depending upon the part of the fetal body being evaluated as well as the center, there are certain core sequences that are used by most centers that will be briefly reviewed below (Fig. 20.1).[2,4,10–14]

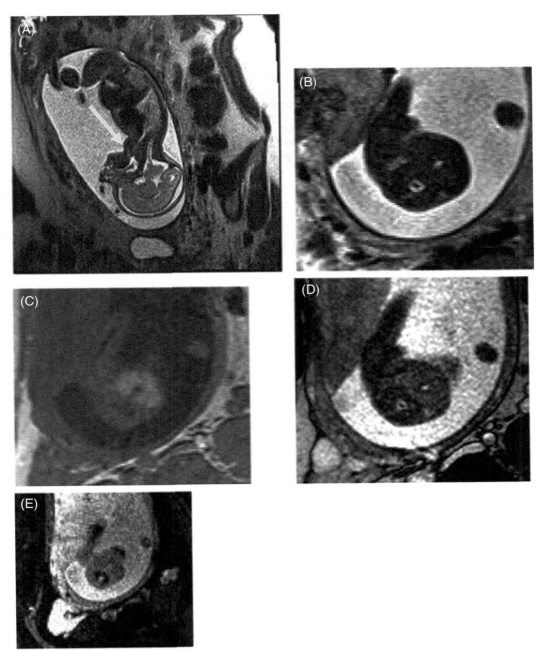

FIG. 20.1   24-week fetus with a neck mass identified by ultrasound. Study performed at 1.5T. Sagittal ssFSE (A) image demonstrating the neck "mass" approximating the cervical trachea. Axial ssFSE (B), spoiled gradient echo T1 (C), ssbGE (D), and apparent diffusion weighted (E) images demonstrate that it follows the expected signal characteristics of thyroid tissue on all sequences, reflecting a fetal goiter.

20.2.4.2 Sequences

Sequence	Vendor names	Weighting	Advantages	Disadvantages
Single shot fast spin echo (ssFSE)	• Siemens: half-Fourier acquisition single-shot turbo-spin echo imaging (HASTE) • General Electric (GE): single-shot fast spin-echo (SSFSE) • Phillips Healthcare: single-shot turbo spin echo (TSE)[10]	T2	• Backbone of most fetal MR protocols.[4,10,12] • Each image is acquired in one to two seconds. • If the fetus moves, only the imaged slice(s) in which the fetus moved will be detrimentally affected.	Long echo trains cause blurring in the phase direction, although this may be mitigated by the use of parallel imaging.[12,15]

Sequence	Vendor names	Weighting	Advantages	Disadvantages
Steady-state balanced gradient echo sequences (ssbGE).	• Siemens: true fast imaging with steady state precession (TrueFISP) • GE: fasting imaging employing steady-state acquisition (FIESTA) • Phillips: balanced fast field echo (bFFE)[10]	• Based on the ratio of T1 to T2. • As a result, signal from muscle and other tissues generally appears dark but liquids and fat appear bright.[12,13,16]	• These sequences are faster, and are less susceptible to fetal motion, compared with the ssFSE sequences.[12] • Some centers have found the ssbGE sequences useful when attempting to evaluate smaller intracranial structures outlined by fluid including the cranial nerves, basal cistern anatomy, inner ear, cerebellar cortex, and vermian lobules.[11]	• There is little contrast between the components of the brain, and some centers only perform with fetal MR neuroimaging when there is persistent fetal movement that significantly degrades the ssFSE sequences.[12] • Susceptible to "banding" artifacts attributable to nonuniformity in the main (B0) magnetic field, which result in band-like signal loss typically at the edges of the FOV and near air/tissue interfaces.[10,12]
Spoiled gradient echo T1-weighted	• Siemens: fast low-angle shot (FLASH) • GE: spoiled gradient echo (SPGR) • Phillips: fast field echo (T1-FFE)[10]	T1	Evaluation of structures that demonstrate intrinsic T1 shortening including the pituitary gland, thyroid gland, liver, fat, meconium, hemorrhage, and calcification.[2,4,11,13]	• Prone to artifact from motion compared with other sequences due to their longer acquisition times.[12] • It has been reported that these sequences should be preferentially performed during maternal breath hold to attempt to mitigate the associated motion artifact.[4,11]
Diffusion weighted imaging (DWI)		DWI	Evaluation of ischemia.[11,12,17]	• As these are usually echo planar images, they are particularly prone to distortion and artifact.

20.2.4.3 Fetal MRI at 3.0T?

- Although most fetal MR is performed at 1.5T, there is growing interest in performing fetal MR at 3T as the higher field strength has the potential to significantly improve image quality. As of 2018, approximately a quarter of fetal imaging centers in North America were reporting the use of 3.0T magnets in routine clinical practice for fetal MR.[7] Performing fetal MR at 3T results in a theoretically doubling of the SNR compared with 1.5T, although in reality the signal gain realized is slightly less than this.[10] In theory the additional signal can be used to obtain better spatial resolution, decrease the amount of noise, decrease the image acquisition time, image at thinner slices, or a combination of these.[3,10,18–21] In our practice we have found that imaging at 3T can be particularly helpful when performing fetal neuroimaging as the extra signal generally gives us additional latitude in decreasing the size of our FOV to better evaluate small intracranial structures, without producing a significant noise penalty (Fig. 20.2). It also allows us to routinely and effectively perform fetal MR imaging at 2–3 mm slices.
- A general trend reported in the literature is that 3.0T fetal MR studies take longer to perform compared with 1.5T studies. One possible reason for this may be the adjustments made by the MRI software to mitigate the SAR, such as increasing the number of slices and/or the TR.[21–24] The longer acquisition time in theory can also make these 3.0T images more susceptible to fetal motion.[21]
- Successful fetal MR imaging at 3.0T is generally more challenging compared with at 1.5T because of additional SAR concerns (discussed later) and because of some exaggerated artifacts that can significantly degrade image quality. Of the latter, artifacts relating to inhomogeneity of the radiofrequency (RF) field, also known as the B1 field, are substantial barriers to 3.0T fetal imaging.[1,10,21] One of the major contributing artifacts is referred to as "dielectric artifact" or "standing wave artifact" and occurs because the wavelength of the RF/B1 transmission field at 3.0T decreases relative to 1.5T. At 1.5T the RF wavelength is approximately 52 cm in soft tissue, and at

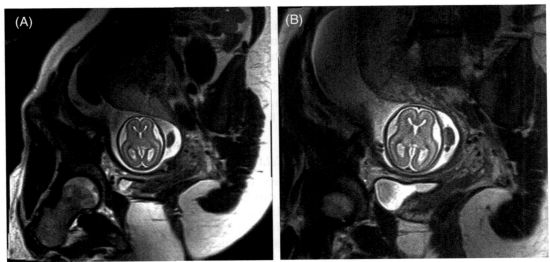

FIG. 20.2 Axial images of a 21-week fetus performed on a 3T unit through the level of the atria using a normal large FOV (A) and a smaller FOV (B). Not how modestly decreasing the FOV on the 3T unit has no significant detrimental impact on noise. Both sets of images were performed at 3 mm intervals.

3.0T it is approximately 26 cm, where in the latter situation it approaches the size of many adults.[10,18,25] As a result, at 3.0T the RF energy emanating from the body transmit coil from different directions that propagates through the mother and fetus can create areas of constructive and destructive interface.[25] An additional cause for the RF/B1 field inhomogeneity relates to areas of relative high conductivity corresponding to diminished RF/B1 field penetration. Although this artifact has been traditionally associated in patients with ascites at 3.0T, the same phenomenon can occur as a result of amniotic fluid, and can be particularly conspicuous and problematic in patients with polyhydramnios.[21,23,25]

- Mitigating the exaggerated artifacts encountered during fetal imaging at 3.0T described above have proved challenging. One initial strategy that has been utilized by some centers is the use of dielectric "pads" or "pillows." These pads can both improve the propagation of the RF/B1 field through improved impedance-matching and by changing the geometry of the patient, and the image quality generally increases with their use. However, these pads can be large and heavy, and are dependent upon adequate positioning that can be uncertain and uncomfortable for the patient.[10,25,26] A newer technological development from some vendors that has been very helpful are multi-channel transmission body coils, which are able to improve RF/B1 field homogeneity through active RF shimming.[10,18,21,25]
- It is worth noting that ISUOG in their 2017 "Practice Guidelines: performance of fetal magnetic resonance imaging" described performing fetal MR at 3T as "...currently not recommended for in-vivo fetal imaging," at that time.[3] This elicited a response from members on the Society for Pediatric Radiology Fetal Imaging Committee, which was subsequently published in the in the same journal, that expressed their disagreement with this statement. In this response they also requested the ISUOG panel consider retracting the statement, given the "proven advantages of 3-T MRI...for fetuses in the second and third trimesters of pregnancy."[19]

20.2.5 Safety

Specific risks to the fetus during MRI studies can be divided into three main categories: biological effects of the static (B0) magnetic field (1.5T or 3.0T), the RF/B1 field, and acoustic injury. Risks to the fetus associated with the use of intravenous gadolinium-based contrast agents will not be discussed, as MR contrast agents should not be routinely administered in fetal MRI studies.[2,27]

20.2.5.1 *Risk from the static (B0) magnetic field*

- Multiple retrospective studies of children who have been exposed to MRI in utero provide reassurance that the risk of teratogenesis and/or miscarriage is extremely low and likely negligible.[27–29] One of the most comprehensive studies to address this concern retrospectively reviewed and compared the outcome of 5654

pregnancies in which the mother underwent MRI in Ontario during the first trimester of pregnancy (weeks 2 to 14) from 2003 to 2015, with 1,418,451 pregnancies in Ontario during the same time without any MRI exposure. When the authors incorporated maternal comorbidities into their analysis (i.e., diabetes, substance abuse, chronic hypertension, etc.), they found that maternal MRI in the first trimester was not associated with a higher risk of stillbirth or neonatal death. Live-born children in the study were followed for a median of 3.6 years and the authors did not identify a significantly higher rate of congenital abnormalities, neoplasm, hearing loss, or vision loss in the overall exposed group during this time.
- There is also evidence that exposure of a fetus to MRI has no significant impact on subsequent long-term neurodevelopmental outcome.[30]

20.2.5.2 Risk from energy deposition from the RF/B1 field

- Each excitation and refocusing RF pulse of a MRI sequence deposits energy into the patient, which is converted to heat.[22] As elevated maternal temperature can have a deleterious effect on embryogenesis, particularly as the fetus has a limited capacity to regulate its own temperature.[22,27,31,32]
- All commercially available MRI systems have safety limits programmed into the pulse sequence to ensure that they stay within the International Electrotechnical Commission (IEC) and US Food and Drug Administration (FDA) guidelines, particularly the dictated specific absorption rate (SAR) and whole-body heating safety guidelines. These guidelines dictate a "normal" mode that is suitable for all patients of an exposure to a whole-body SAR of 2 watts/kg or an elevation in body temperature of less than 0.5°C.[33,34] These limits can be increased to 4 watts/kg and 1.0° whole-body heating in a "first-level" controlled mode under medical supervision.[22,33] The IEC limits pregnant human subjects exposure to a whole-body SAR of 2 watts/kg or a temperature increase of less than 0.5°C over a 30 minute period.[34] Additionally, the International Commission on Non-Ionizing Radiation Protection (ICNIRP) 2004 guidelines state that the body temperature of a pregnant patients should not rise >0.5°C and the temperature of the fetus should not exceed 38°C.[21,35]
- The specific energy dose (SED) is another method used to estimate patient heating, and is a measurement of the cumulative absorbed energy dose during the study. It is expressed as Joules absorbed per kilogram patient weight (J/kg), and the IEC has set SED limit of less than 14,000 J/kg per MRI examination on a first-level controlled MRI study.[22,36]
- In practice, RF tissue heating during a MRI examination is heterogenous, and in pregnant women believed to predominately occur at the periphery of the body and be minimal at the center where the fetus is located.[27] There is no noninvasive way to measure fetal tissue heating.[22] Simulation studies have indicated that the average SAR in the fetus is generally much lower than SAR in the mother.[29,37–39]
- A recent study generated realistic anatomic models of pregnant woman using segmented fetal MRI study images, and used software to estimate SAR amount and distribution at a simulated RF transmit frequency of 3T examinations. It found that maternal positing and fetal rotation could also significantly impact fetal SAR amount, and that SAR deposition was lowest when the mother was in the left lateral decubitus position and when the mother had her arms down at her sides (as the RF power deposition was distributed over a larger volume). It also indicated that although was a positive correlation between maternal BMI and maternal SAR values, that the authors did not identify a correlation between maternal BMI and SAR values in the fetus.[39]

20.2.5.3 Is there additional heating risk when fetal MR is performed at 3T?

- Patient heating/SAR deposition is of greater concern at higher fields strengths (3T) compared with 1.5.[39] The SAR increases with field strength, so that using equivalent parameters there is an approximate 4-fold increase in SAR at 3.0T compared with 1.5T.[22,24]
- The most comprehensive study available at the time of this writing addressing the concern for fetal SAR at 3.0T was a retrospective comparison of 2784 fetal MR studies performed at 1.5T and 463 fetal MR studies performed at 3.0T from a single large pediatric center. The authors found that the 3.0T sequences collectively showed a higher mean SAR compared with the 1.5T studies (1.14 W/kg compared with 1.09 W/kg, respectively), but that these values were statistically equivalent. Similarly, the authors found that the overall accumulated SED per study (1.5T: 965 J/kg; 3.0T: 996 J/kg) were also statistically equivalent. The authors reported that 99.9% of the studies that were reviewed had a SAR of 2 W/kg or less, which again is the upper limit for MRI under normal operating mode.[22]
- It is interesting to mention that there has been at least one report of a lower whole-body SAR value, as reported by the MRI console, when fetal MR is performed at 3.0T compared with 1.5T. In this study twelve

pregnant patients prospectively underwent both 1.5T and 3.0T fetal MR examinations, and the authors reported mean SAR values of 1.6 watts/kg and 0.6 watts/kg, respectively. Of note the 3.0T ssFSE sequence was modified to decrease SAR by using a longer TR, a longer RF pulse duration, and a hyperecho option. The 1.5T and 3.0T studies were also done on platforms from different vendors.[20]

20.2.5.4 *Risk from acoustic noise*

- Fluctuating current within the gradient coils interacts with the static magnetic field (B0) to produce strong Lorentz forces in the coils, and these vibrations create loud acoustic noise that is up to 140 dB (the maximum which is allowed by the FDA). Although the mother has ear protection in the MR environment, the fetus does not, and there is a potential concern for resulting hearing loss in the fetus.[27] The American Academy of Pediatrics (AAP) recommends an upper limit of acoustic noise exposure to be 90 dB for children, with the risk for permanent hearing loss increasing above this level.[40] Human fetuses have been shown to react to noises outside the mother as early as 19 or 20 weeks of gestation.[41]
- Multiple studies of children exposed prenatally to MR, both at 1.5T and 3.0T, have showed no definitive increased risk of hearing loss or impairment relative to the population.[28,29,42,43] This may in part reflect the acoustic attenuation of sound by the gravid abdomen, which is estimated to up to 30 dB.[44–46]

20.2.5.5 *Summary regarding fetal risk of MRI*

- The most recent revision (2020) of a practice parameter developed jointly by the American College of Radiology (ACR) and the Society for Pediatric Radiology outlining the safe and optimal performance of fetal magnetic resonance imaging states: "At this stage, the preponderance of research studies have failed to discover any reproducible harmful effects of exposure of the mother or developing fetus to the 3T or weaker magnetic fields used in the routine clinical MRI process. However, far less is known about the potential effects, if any, of the time-varying gradient and/or radiofrequency magnetic fields used during actual scanning… These theoretical risks should be carefully balanced against the potential benefits to the patient undergoing an MR examination."[2]

20.2.6 Indications

In the following section, some of the general and most common uses of fetal MR will be briefly reviewed. A comprehensive and exhaustive discussion of all of the potential uses of fetal MRI is beyond the scope of this chapter. If the reader is interested to learn more about how to further interpret fetal MR, many helpful publications are available that specifically discuss how to perform and interpret tailored fetal MR studies.[4,11–14,17,47–51]

20.2.7 Interpretation

20.2.7.1 Evaluation of fetal CNS pathology

20.2.7.1.1 Background

One of the primary strengths of fetal MRI has been to improve the diagnostic accuracy of suspected fetal brain anomalies. This is exemplified in the 2017 ISUOG Practice Guidelines in that five of the top six indications for fetal MRI examinations per their survey respondents involve suspected central nervous system anomalies including "posterior fossa anomaly," "corpus callosal anomaly," "microcephaly," "apparently isolated ventriculomegaly," and "neural tube defect."[3] The added value of fetal MR in cases of suspected fetal CNS anomalies has been established through multiple retrospective reviews as well as at least one large prospective, multicenter cohort study.[12,47,52,53]

20.2.7.1.2 Normal anatomy/development

In order to accurately interpret fetal brain MRI, the radiologist should be familiar with the normal developing brain anatomy. As the state of fetal brain development evolves over the developing pregnancy, knowledge of the estimated fetal gestational age is essential for accurate interpretation.[54] At our center, the MRI technologist is instructed to ask the mother her estimated gestational age prior to beginning the study, and the technologist records this information in our electronic medical record.

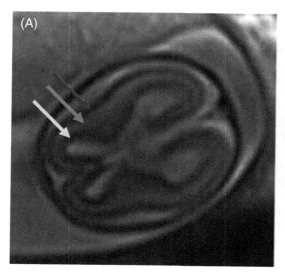 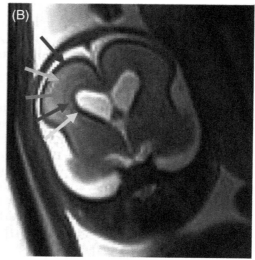

FIG. 20.3   Axial ssFSE fetal MR image through the brain of an 18-week fetus obtained on a 1.5 unit demonstrating the three-layer pattern: germinal matrix (yellow arrow), intermediate zone (green arrow), and cortical plate (purple arrow). Coronal ssFSE fetal MR through the brain of a 23-week fetus obtained on a 3.0T unit demonstrating the five-later pattern: the ventricular zone and subventricular zone constituting the germinal matrix (yellow arow), the periventricular-rich zone or cell sparse layer (brown arrow), the intermediate zone (green arrow), the subplate (orange arrow), and the cortical plate (purple arrow).

The development of the cortex of the cerebral hemispheres starts as early as 8–10 weeks, with neurons and glia proliferating at the ventricular surface of the brain in the region of the germinal matrixes. Neuronal cells subsequently migrate through the fetal cerebral hemisphere using the radial glial cells as scaffolding.[11] The germinal matrix early in gestation essentially surrounds the lateral ventricles, and its size and extent decreases dramatically after approximately 25 weeks of gestation.[55] As a result of development, the fetal brain parenchyma signal changes as the fetus matures. At fewer than approximately 20 weeks of gestation, the fetal brain demonstrates three dominant layers (from inner to outer): the germinal matrix (T2 hypointense), the intermediate layer (T2 hyperintense), and the cortical plate (T2 hypointense). Between approximately 20 and 28 weeks the fetal brain demonstrates five dominant layers (from inner to outer): the ventricular zone and subventricular zone constituting the germinal matrix (T2 hypointense), the periventricular-rich zone or cell sparse layer (T2 hyperintense), the intermediate zone (T2 hypointense), the subplate (T2 hyperintense), and the cortical plate (T2 hypointense) (Fig. 20.3).[12,47]

Regarding myelination, T1 hyperintense signal can first be seen in the tegmentum of the pons at approximately 23 weeks, and within the posterior limb of the internal capsule from approximately 31 weeks.[47,56]

Cortical sulcation occurs in a predictable pattern in normal fetuses, which can help with the dating of the pregnancy when this is uncertain. In general, the major sulci which we found helpful to specifically evaluation at our center to assess appropriate fetal sulcation include: the parieto-occipital fissure (22–23 weeks), the calcarine sulcus (24–25 weeks), the central sulcus (26 weeks), the precentral sulcus (27 weeks), the postcentral sulcus (28 weeks), the superior frontal sulcus (29 weeks), and the inferior temporal sulcus (32 weeks) (Fig. 20.4).[11,47,54]

Biometry is also an important component of brain development to assess during a MR study of the fetal brain.[47] Between 20 and 40 weeks of gestational age, the brain structures undergo accelerated growth, and comparison of the size of these structures relative to normative values is critical to confirm age-appropriate development.[11] There are normative reference values published in the literature, with data from one used to create a free centile calculator available online at the time of this writing.[57,58]

20.2.7.1.3 Ventriculomegaly

The leading indication for fetal CNS imaging is ventriculomegaly, which is defined as an atrial width >10 mm. It is considered mild if the atrial size is 10–12 mm, moderate between 12 mm and 15 mm, and severe if greater than 15 mm.[11,47,59] Interestingly, the atrial width should not vary significantly with fetal age, and the atrial width should remain near-constant throughout the second and third trimesters. The third ventricle should not exceed 4 mm in diameter.[47] Asymmetry of normal-sized (<10 mm) ventricles is not uncommon, and isolated lateral ventricular asymmetry does not appear to be associated with an adverse neurological outcome.[60]

Measurements of the atria can be performed in either the axial or coronal plane. Axial measurements are obtained at the level of the thalami, and coronal measurements are performed at the level of the choroid plexus (Fig. 20.5).

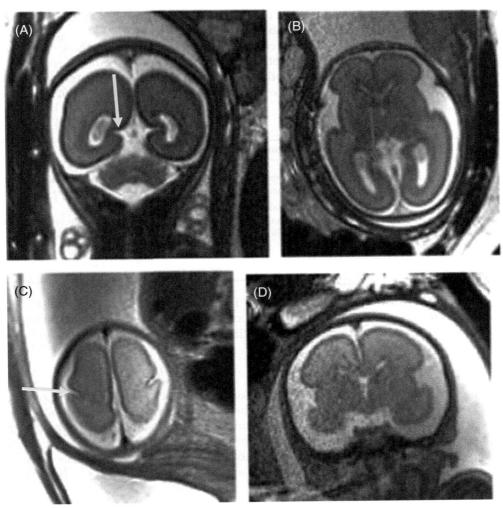

FIG. 20.4 Coronal (A) and axial (B) ssbGE fetal MR image through the calcarine fissures (yellow arrow) of parieto-occipital fissures (purple arrow) of a 25-week fetus. Axial ssFSE (C) through the vertex of the brain in a 27-week fetus demonstrating the central sulcus (yellow arrow), with a coronal ssbGE image in the same fetus (D) demonstrating the absence of frontal sulci. All images were obtained on a 3T unit.

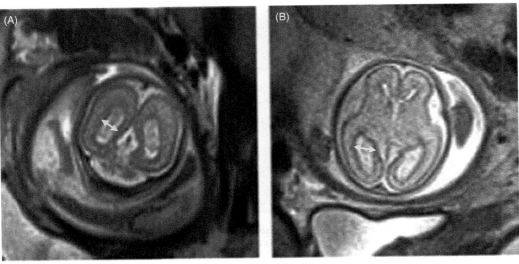

FIG. 20.5 Measurements of atrial size on representative coronal (A) axial (B) ssFSE images of a 21-week fetus obtained on a 3T MRI unit.

There is general concordance between measurements obtained between ultrasound and MRI, although the coronal MR measurements have been shown to be more reliably concordant.[60,61]

Although there are a multitude of etiologies that can result in fetal ventriculomegaly, the mechanisms can be broadly grouped into obstructive and nonobstructive etiologies. Obstructive ventriculomegaly can result from either a defect in CSF circulation (Fig. 20.6) or in CSF resorption, also referred to as noncommunicating and communicating obstructive ventriculomegaly, respectively.[60] Some representative etiologies of fetal ventriculomegaly are outlined in the followed chart:

Causes of fetal ventriculomegaly:

Obstructive, noncommunicating	Obstructive, communicating	Nonobstructive
Aqueductal stenosis • X-linked hydrocephalus (L1CAM mutation) • Rhombencephalosynapsis Malformations obstructing CSF flow • Dandy Walker malformation • Chiari II malformation Intraventricular hemorrhage	Subarachnoid scarring • Subarachnoid hemorrhage Elevated intracranial venous sinus pressure • Vein of Galen malformation • Dural sinus malformation	CSF overproduction • Choroid plexus lesion Malformations • Agenesis or dysgenesis of the corpus callosum Ex-vacuo dilation • Vascular/ischemic injury

In addition identifying and further assessing the cause for fetal ventriculomegaly, fetal MR has also demonstrated value in detecting additional anomalies in 5–50% of seemingly isolated ventriculomegaly identified by ultrasound.[60,62,63] In cases of severe ventriculomegaly, additional CNS anomalies have been reported in 50–85% of cases.[60]

20.2.7.1.4 Commissuration defects

The process of "commissuration" occurs until 18–19 weeks, and reflects the growth of axonal fibers across the midline in order to connect homologous parts of the cerebral hemispheres. The largest commissural tract in the human brain is the corpus callosum.[12] The corpus callosum generally acquires its final shape by approximately 20 weeks, although maturation and growth will continue throughout postnatal life.[11,64]

The corpus callosum can be absent (agenesis), partially absent/foreshortened (hypogenesis), or abnormally thin (hypoplastic). In practice, the term dysgenesis can be used as it is sometimes difficult to differentiate hypogenesis

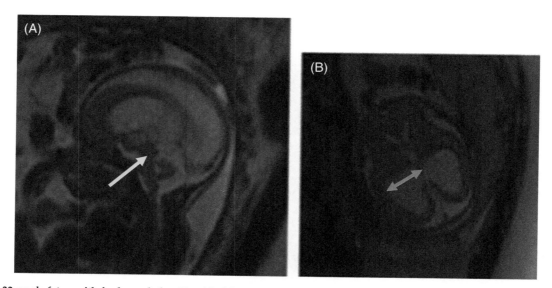

FIG. 20.6   22-week fetus with hydrocephalus identified by ultrasound. Sagittal (A) and axial (B) ssFSE images obtained on a 1.5T unit through the fetal brain demonstrate severe hydrocephalus, with the atria each measuring 18 mm in diameter (green arrow). The cerebral aqueduct should be T2 hyperintense but is not visualized (yellow), and the posterior fossa structures appear otherwise normal, in this fetus with aqueductal stenosis.

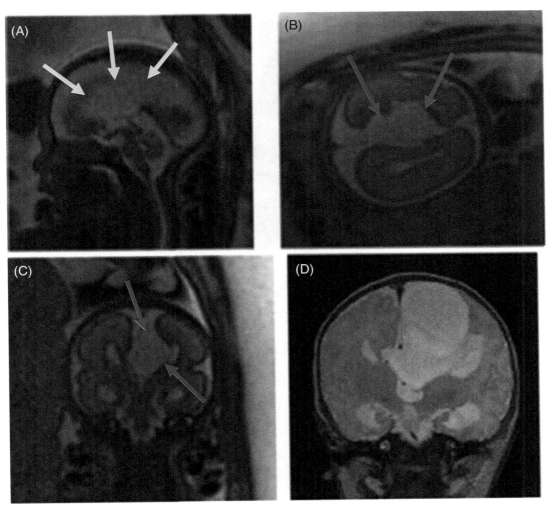

FIG. 20.7   **27-week fetus with suspected midline anomaly identified by ultrasound.** Sagittal (A), axial (B), and coronal (C) ssFSE images from a 1.5T unit demonstrated complete absence of the corpus callosum (yellow arrows) as well as a midline cyst (purple arrows). A coronal T2 image (D) obtained during the immediate postnatal period confirmed these findings.

from hypoplasia.[65] Fetuses with suspected callosal dysgenesis are typically identified on routine screening ultrasound after the cavum septum pellucidum is not visualized, particularly if there is also dilation of the ventricular atria and occipital horns, as the ultrasound diagnosis of agenesis of the corpus callosum (ACC) relies on identifying these indirect signs.[11,65] Unlike ultrasound, fetal MRI can directly visualize the corpus callosum, which may account for the reported 20% of cases of suspected callosal abnormality identified by ultrasound in which fetal MRI reveals a normal corpus callosum.[11,66]

Imaging findings on fetal MRI in cases of ACC include the lack of an identifiable corpus callosum, parallel lateral ventricles, coplocephaly, and a high-riding third ventricle.[17] Relatively common associated malformations that can be identified by fetal MRI include interhemispheric cysts (14–30%) (Fig. 20.7) and lipomas (3%).[65] Fetal MR can also be very helpful due detect additional CNS anomalies which are not commonly seen on ultrasound and which can significantly impact prognosis including abnormal sulcation, posterior fossa abnormalities, periventricular nodular heterotopia, and parenchymal hemorrhage/injury.[11]

20.2.7.1.5 Ventral induction anomalies

Holoprosencephaly (HPE) is a group of disorders that result from failure of hemispheric cleavage, specifically in that there is incomplete partitioning of the telencephalic vesicles into two separate hemispheres along with the

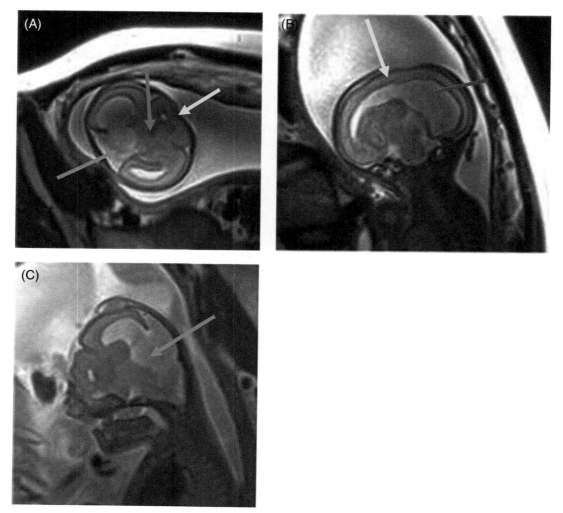

FIG. 20.8   23-week fetus with abnormal brain architecture and absent orbits identified on ultrasound. Axial (A), coronal (B), and sagittal (C) ssFSE images obtained on a 3T unit demonstrate anomalous hemispheric fusion involving both the cerebral mantle (yellow arrow) and deep gray matter structures (blue arrow), a monoventricle (purple arrow), and a dorsal midline cyst (green arrow) in this fetus with alobar holoprosencephaly.

inappropriate development of the interhemispheric fissure and falx cerebri.[65,67] HPE constitutes a continuum of brain malformations including alobar, semilobar, and lobar HPE types.[67]

Alobar HPE is the most severe form of HPE, in which there is complete failure of the telencephalic vesicles to cleave/separate, resulting in a single midline forebrain with a primitive vesicle. This can be accompanied by a large dorsal cyst as well as severe facial malformations/defects. Fetal MR usually does not add much to the US findings in cases of alobar HPE, as by the time of the second trimester scan the diagnosis of alobar HPE should be unequivocable.[67] However, in our experience, parents regularly pursue a confirmatory fetal MR study prior to 24 weeks of gestation if termination is being considered (Fig. 20.8).

Differentiating the semilobar (Fig. 20.9) and lobar variants of HPE can be much more challenging, particularly as there is no simple distinction between these variants, with the exact definitions varying between authors.[65] It is generally accepted that lobar HPE shows greater than fifty percent formation of the corpus callosum and presence of the both the frontal and temporal horns.[68] The thalami should also be separated in lobar HPE, with possible fusion of the deep gray matter structures only within the rostral frontal lobes. In cases of lobar HPE, the septum pellucidum is often absent.[67]

Septo-optic dysplasia (SOD) has typically been included under the spectrum of the disorders of ventral induction, presumably since it can also involve absence of the septum pellucidum, although there is increasing recognition

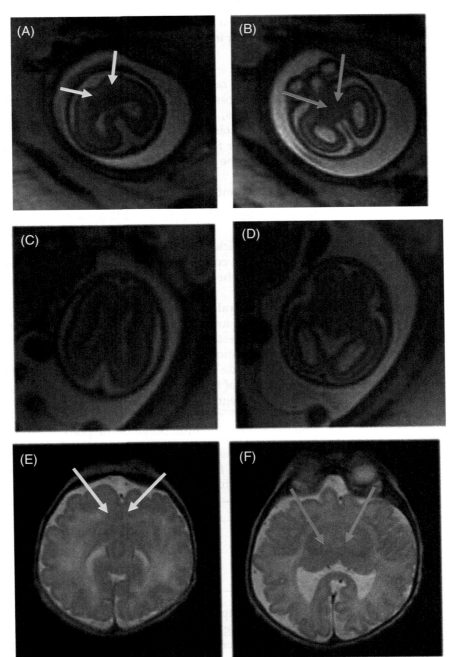

FIG. 20.9   20-week twin gestation in which the cavum septum pellucidum was not visualized in one of the twins. Axial images obtained on a 1.5T scanner through the abnormal twin (A and B) compared with the normal twin (C and D) demonstrate anomalous midline anterior fusion of the cerebral hemispheres in the affected twin (yellow arrows), including the basal ganglia and thalami (red arrows). These findings were confirmed postnatally at 3 days of life (E and F).

that this shared classification with HPE may be erroneous as there are not usually other abnormalities that are typically associated with anomalies of hemispheric cleavage.[65] SOD classically involves a combination of (1) optic nerve hypoplasia, (2) pituitary hypofunction, and (3) midline brain abnormalities including dysgenesis of the septum pellucidum and/or corpus callosum, and hypoplasia of the brainstem and/or vermis.[67] Although challenging, assessment of the fetal optic nerves can be performed, particularly when the study is done later in gestation and on 3T equipment.[65] In our experience, fetal MR has added value in cases of suspected SOD by detecting associated schizencephaly or polymicrogyria, which can be present in up to half of cases of SOD.[69]

20.2.7.1.6 Posterior fossa malformations

The cerebellum and brainstem are vulnerable to a wide range of disruptions and destructions, which can be challenging to assess with ultrasound due to the progressive ossification of the skull base.[11,70] Conversely, fetal MR allows for direction visualization of the cerebellar hemispheres, vermis, and brainstem in three orthogonal planes with satisfactory anatomic detail.[11] However, in many circumstances, postnatal MRI follow-up is still advisable.[71] The key determinants of outcome in the assessment of posterior fossa anomalies include the degree of hypoplasia in the cerebellum, the size and configuration of the vermis, the degree of brainstem development, and the presence of other associated anomalies.[72]

In our assessment of the fetal posterior fossa, important anatomic landmarks that we specifically assess include:

- The major vermian landmarks should be present by 18–21 weeks, including the fastigial point and the primary fissure.[70,72]
- The cerebellar vermis usually covers the fourth ventricle by 20 weeks.[70]
- The diameter of the cerebellum and height of vermis, comparing them to the expected biometry for the fetal age, noting that during the second trimester usually the transverse cerebellar diameter in millimeters is about equal to the gestational age in weeks.[70]
- The degree of vermian lobulation noting that in general the prepyramidal fissure is seen at 21 weeks, the secondary fissure is seen at 24 weeks, and all fissures are usually visible of 27 weeks. The implication of this pattern of development is that prior to 27 weeks of gestation, it may be difficult to accurately determine if the pattern of vermian lobulation is appropriate for gestational age.[72]
- As the cerebellum and vermis develop, the angle made between the vermis and brainstem ("tegmento-vermian angle") gradually decreases, referred to as "closure" of the fourth ventricle. The normal tegmento-vermian angle has been to be reported to be less than 10–18 degrees, with values of greater than 40 degrees typically associated with cystic posterior fossa malformations.[70,72]
- The morphology of the brainstem, including the normal ventral bulge of the pons.

Posterior fossa malformations can be very broadly categorized into two main categories: those with increased cerebrospinal fluid (CSF) and those with decreased CSF fluid spaces within the posterior fossa.[70] Representative etiologies are listed in the chart below, and some will be further discussed:

Increased posterior fossa CSF space	Decreased posterior fossa CSF space
- Dandy Walker malformation - Vermian hypoplasia/vermian dysplasia - Blake pouch remnant - Mega cisterna magna - Arachnoid cyst	- Chiari II malformation

The classic Dandy Walker malformation (DWM) comprises vermian hypoplasia, dilation of Blake's pouch (a normal, temporary, embryonic membranous out-pocketing of the posteroinferior fourth ventricle that should fenestrate and becomes the foramen of Magendie), and cystic enlargement of the posterior fossa. Hydrocephalus is also commonly another finding, although it is not necessary to make the diagnosis on fetal MR as it can develop after birth.[72] The vermis is usually also elevated and upwardly rotated, with a tegmento-vermian angle of over 40 degrees (Fig. 20.10). DWM can be isolated or occur in association wither other CNS abnormalities is approximately 50–60% of cases.[73]

The terms "vermian hypoplasia" and "vermian dysplasia" are used to reflect a small cerebellar vermis for the fetal gestational age, usually with some degree of superior rotation or elevation of the vermis, but without enlargement of the posterior fossa (Fig. 20.11). These terms are increasingly be used to replace prior nomenclature including "Dandy-Walker variant" and "inferior vermian hypoplasia."[70,72] Indeed, the current understanding of vermian development indicates that the inferior aspect of the vermis (lobules IX and X) develops around 16 weeks compared with the mid-aspect of the vermis (lobules VI and VII) which develops later in gestation.[70,74] It is important to note that in some instances the vermis may appear malrotated and mildly hypoplastic during early second trimester imaging (around 21 weeks), with normalization of vermian size and positioning on subsequent imaging performed later in pregnancy or postnatally (Fig. 20.12). This phenomenon has been describe as "delayed rotation of the

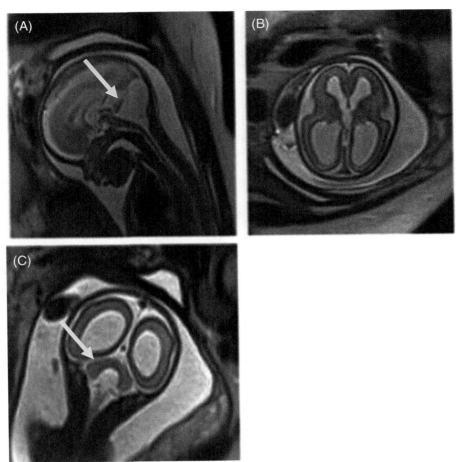

FIG. 20.10 **25-week fetus with suspected posterior fossa malformation.** Axial ssFSE (A) demonstrates a dimunitive, malrotated vermis (arrow) and cystic dilation of the posterior fossa. Axial ssFSE (B) demonstrates supratentorial ventriculomegaly. Coronal SSFE (C) demonstrates small, splayed cerebellar hemispheres (arrow).

cerebellar vermis," and is believed to relate to physiologically delayed fenestration of Blake's pouch (Fig. 20.13).[75] It may be as a result of this phenomenon that it has been reported that a second-trimester diagnosis of inferior vermian hypoplasia is confirmed postnatally in only 68 percent of cases.[75,76]

The term "Chiari II malformation" can include multiple intracranial anomalies in the setting of an open neural tube defect (myelomeningocele or myelocele), with the usual major findings including a small posterior fossa with descent of cerebellar tissues and resulting hydrocephalus (Fig. 20.14). There may also be indentation of the frontal bones ("lemon-shaped cranium") as well as atypical curvature of the cerebellum ("banana" sign).[70] Given the potential for fetal surgery in some patients with an open neural tube defect detected prenatally, a grading scheme has been proposed for surgical candidacy: grade 1: patient fourth ventricle and cisterna magna, grade 2: effaced fourth ventricle and patent cisterna magna, grade 3: effacement of both the cisterna magna and fourth ventricle. Using this system, grades 2 and 3 are potential candidates for fetal surgery, with grade 3 being the best candidate. Fetal MR can also be useful to assess for potential surgical exclusion criteria including the absence of hindbrain herniation, additional intracranial abnormalities not explained by an open spinal dysraphism, the upper level of the defect being higher than T1 or lower than S1, kyphosis >30 degrees, and/or any other fetal anomaly not explain by the open spinal dysraphism.[77]

20.2.7.1.7 Malformations of cortical development (MCD)

The development of the cortex begins within neurons and glia proliferating at the ventricular surface of the brain in the region of the germinal matrix as early as 8–10 weeks, which subsequent migration of these cells through

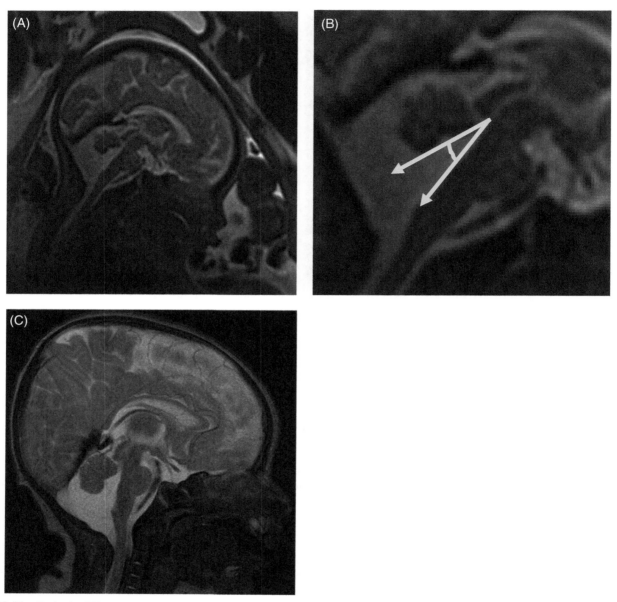

FIG. 20.11 Sagittal ssFSE images obtained on a 1.5T unit through the brain (A) and posterior fossa (B) of a 32-week fetuses with concern for Dandy-Walker malformation by ultrasound. The tegmento-vermian angle is >20 degrees (yellow arrows, and the vermis appears mildly hypoplastic. Sagittal T2 image (C) through the brain shortly after birth at term demonstrates similar findings in this patient with vermian hypoplasia/dysplasia.

the cerebral hemispheres including along the radial glial fibers. The cells then organize on the surface of the hemispheres to become the cerebral cortex. An aberration of any of these processes (proliferation, migration, and/or cortical organization) can result in a spectrum of developmental structural brain abnormalities.[12] Among all possible brain malformations detected by prenatal imaging, MCD have been described as being the most difficult (and at times impossible) to detect with ultrasound. As such, fetal MRI offers clear advantages over fetal ultrasound.[11]

Representative types of MCD identifiable on fetal MR can include polymicrogyria (excessive sulcation), schizencephaly (abnormally deep sulci) (Fig. 20.15), lissencephaly (inadequate sulcation for the fetal gestational age), and gray matter heterotopia (abnormal migration).[17] Polymicrogyria most commonly affects the perisylvian regions and can be identified as areas of unusual gyral frequency as well as irregularity, sometimes with enlargement of the overlying extra-axial space.[65] Schizencephaly, particularly when "open-lip," appears as clefts extending through the cerebral mantle allowing continuity of the extra-axial CSF space with the lateral ventricle.[60] With lissencephaly/

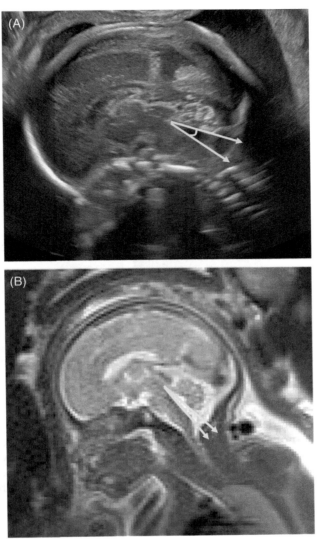

FIG. 20.12 Sagittal sonographic image (A) through the posterior fossa of a 21-week fetus demonstrates mild malrotation/elevation of the vermis, which appears subjectively diminutive. The tegmento-vermian angle is almost 20 degrees. Sagittal fetal MR image through the same area on a 3T unit at almost 25 weeks (B) demonstrates normal size of the vermis, as well as a tegmento-vermian angle of less than 10 degrees in this fetus with delayed rotation of the vermis.

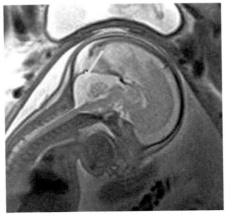

FIG. 20.13 Sagittal fetal MR through the posterior fossa of a 27-week fetus performed on a 3T unit demonstrate a prominent retrocerebellar CSF space/a "mega cisterna magna" (yellow arrow), noting that the vermis appears fully formed and that the tegmento-vermian angle is within normal limits. This is hypothesized to also potentially result from the delayed fenestration of Blake's pouch.

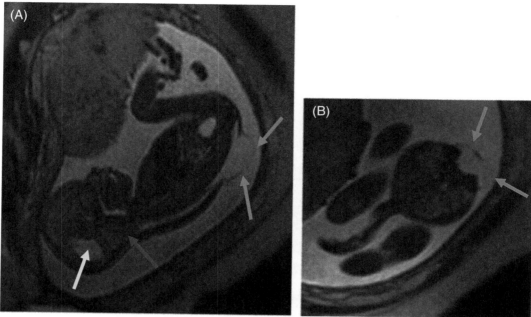

FIG. 20.14   Sagittal ssSFE image obtained on a 1.5T unit through the brain and spine (A) of a 21-week fetus with suspected myelomeningocele. There are the typical fetal findings of a Chiari II malformation including effacement of the extra-axial space, ventriculomegaly (yellow arrow), and a small/crowded posterior fossa (purple arrow). The myelomeningocele sac/neural placode is seen demonstrated on both sagittal and axial (B) images (green arrows).

pachygyria, fetal MR shows varying degrees of simplification of the gyral pattern relative to the fetal gestational age, occasionally with a thick band of arrested neurons within the developing white matter. It can be very difficult to confidently and accurately diagnosis in the early second trimester when primary sulcation is in its early stages and the majority of the brain surface is normally smooth. Gray matter heterotopia is classified based on its location including periventricular/subependymal, subcortical, and transmantle. Of these, the periventricular/subependymal subtype is the most commonly encountered on fetal MR and appears as nodules isointense to gray matter along the margins of the lateral ventricles.[65]

20.2.7.2 Evaluation of fetal face and neck pathology

20.2.7.2.1 Background

Fetal MRI can provide additional useful information in the setting of suspected fetal head and neck anomalies, attributable to its superior soft tissue contrast relative to ultrasound, and due to potential suboptimal fetal positioning and shadowing artifacts from bone during sonographic evaluation.[49] Fetal MRI can also be useful in providing additional characterization of suspected fetal head and neck masses including vascular tumors, low-flow vascular malformations, and teratoma.[48] In some of these cases fetal MRI can provide significant value in delivery planning when there is questionable fetal airway compromise, in that when there is concern for potential compromise, delivery via an EXIT procedure should be anticipated.[8,49] The purpose of the EXIT procedure is to secure the fetal airway immediately prior to complete fetal delivery, while the fetus is still connected to the uteroplacental circulation. The criteria for EXIT procedure can include the diagnosis of teratoma, a mass greater than 5 cm, polyhydramnios or the absence of gastric fluid, and/or signs of intrinsic airway obstruction such as hyperexpanded lungs or a flattened diaphragm.[49]

20.2.7.2.2 Cystic head and neck masses

Low-flow vascular malformations reflect mass-like lesions comprised of anomalous venous and/or lymphatic channels, and are most common in the head and neck. Predominately lymphatic lesions are often detected prenatally while predominately venous lesions are usually detected later in life. A recently introduced classification system for lymphatic malformations that can be applied to prenatal MRI includes four distinct types: type 1 lesions are cystic with multiple thin and/or thick septations, type 2 lesions are predominately cystic with no more than three septa-

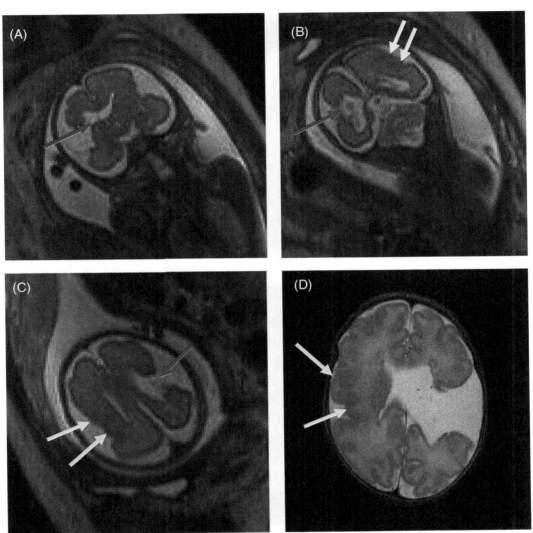

FIG. 20.15 Coronal (A and B) and axial (C) ssSFE images obtained on a 1.5T unit through the brain of a 29-week fetus with concern for "fusion of the frontal horns" on prenatal ultrasound. The images demonstrate a large CSF-filled cleft extending through the left cerebral hemisphere compatible with open-lipped schizencephaly (purple arrows), as well as abnormal thickening and irregularly of a region of cortical plate within the contralateral hemisphere (yellow arrows). Postnatal axial T2 image (D) confirmed the left schizencephalic cleft, as well as the right-sided perisylvian polymicrogyria (yellow arrows).

tions, type 3 lesions are purely cystic, and type 4 are solid and cystic with at least a thirty percent solid part. The majority of prenatally diagnosed lymphatic malformations are type 1 or 2.[48] Fetal MR imaging can be very useful in these cases to evaluate the relationship of the malformation to the great vessels and trachea, particularly to assess for airway patency. The lesions typically are intermediate to low signal on T1 and high signal on T2, and routinely infiltrate across the tissue planes and between vessels (Fig. 20.16).[49]

The head and neck region is the second most common site for teratoma, after the sacrococcygeal region. They usually present as anterior neck masses with resulting neck hyperextension, but can also occur within the oral or nasal cavity. On fetal MR these lesions usually demonstrate mixed signal intensity including both solid and cystic components, as well as possible areas of calcification and/or hemorrhage.[49] Although the detection of intralesional calcification was once considered to be pathognomonic for teratoma, it is now understood that some lymphatic malformations (particularly type 4) can contain phleboliths that simulate tumoral calcification on MRI.[48] As with lymphatic malformations, evaluation of the fetal airway is particularly important to assess the need for a possible EXIT procedure. It should be noted that lymphatic malformations, hemangiomas, and teratomas can in some circumstances be indistinguishable on MR imaging unless fat is identified within the

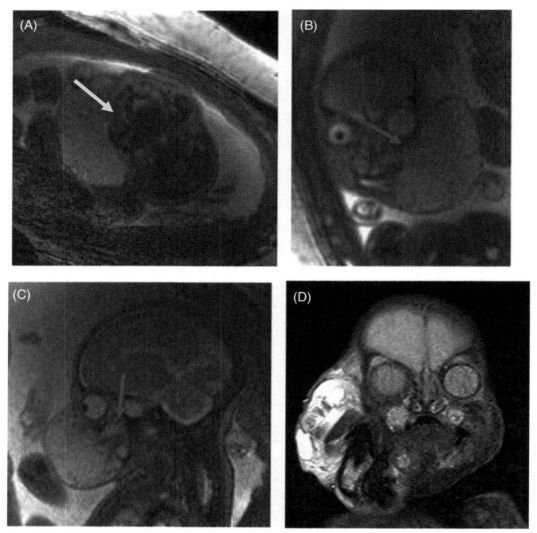

FIG. 20.16   Axial (A), coronal (B), and sagittal (C) ssbGE images obtained on a 3.0T unit through the face of a 26-week fetus demonstrate a lobulated, infiltrative, multi-loculated cystic lesion involving right face and neck. The lesion approximates the right aspect of the maxilla (yellow arrow) and deep neck space (purple arrow). Coronal STIR sequence of the face (D) done at 1 week of life after partial embolization of the facial and neck lymphatic anomaly.

lesion to indicate teratoma; as such an additional fat-suppressed MR pulse signal can be particularly helpful for confirmation.[49]

20.2.7.3 Evaluation of fetal body pathology

20.2.7.3.1 Overview

Although ultrasound is still the gold standard for the assessment of fetal body malformations, MRI has gained great prominence in recent years. In situations in which ultrasound has low sensitivity, such as maternal obesity, abdominal scarring, and oligohydramnios, MRI has proven to be a safe and accurate method.[78] As discussed previously, there is generally less artifact when these studies are performed at 1.5T. The following is an overview of fetal anomalies that are seen in the chest, abdomen, and pelvis by MRI, with postnatal imaging findings as available.

20.2.7.3.2 Congenital thoracic anomalies

The most commonly encountered congenital thoracic anomalies are classified into three broad categories: bronchopulmonary (lung bud) anomalies, vascular anomalies, and combined lung and vascular anomalies.[79] Congenital pulmonary airway malformations (CPAMs) and bronchial atresia fall into the category of bronchopulmonary anomalies.

Vascular abnormalities may accompany bronchopulmonary abnormalities in some cases, creating a hybrid lesion.[80] At imaging evaluation of any fetal chest mass, it is important to note the presence of hydrops, the presence or absence of a systemic arterial supply, mass effect on the mediastinum, and other associated organ system anomalies.

Only three types of CPAMs are distinguished at imaging: large cyst CPAM (type I) and small cyst CPAM (type II), which constitute macrocystic CPAMs; and microcystic or solid type (type III) lesions, which have cysts that are smaller than 5 mm in diameter, with no discernible cystic spaces (Fig. 20.17).[80]

Bronchial atresia is a rare anomaly resulting from focal obliteration of a segmental, subsegmental, or lobar bronchus.[81] The bronchi distal to the stenosis are dilated and filled with mucus, with mild hyperinflation of the adjacent lung due to collateral air drift. In bronchial atresia, the airway is occluded and usually distended on MRI rather than narrowed (Fig. 20.18).[80]

In addition to primary cystic lesions of the thorax, partial absence of the diaphragm in the setting of congenital diaphragmatic hernia (CDH) can also result in cystic-appearing lung lesions at fetal ultrasound. Ultrasound is used to initially diagnosis CDH and to calculate of lung-to-head ratio (LHR),[82] while fetal MRI has demonstrated utility in categorizing the type of hernia on the basis of its location as well as the contents of the hernia and the effect of these contents on adjacent structures, all of which is vital for surgical planning (Fig. 20.19).[80] Ideally, fetal MRI is performed in the 2nd trimester in cases of CDH, in order to best predict antenatal morbidity and mortality.[83]

Tracheoesophageal anomalies straddle both the fetal chest and abdomen, depending on the type of congenital malformation (Fig. 20.20).

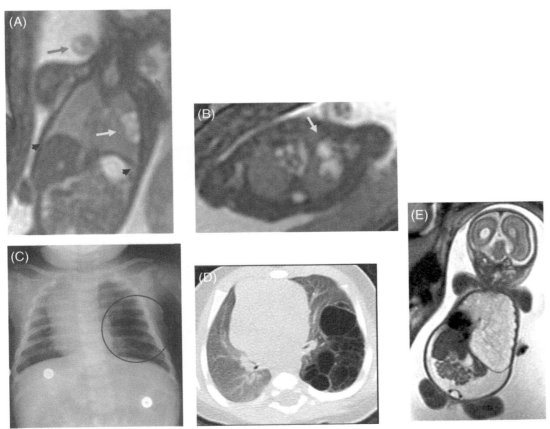

FIG. 20.17 Coronal (A) and axial (B) T2-weighted imaging at 1.5T through the fetal body of this 20-week singleton fetus demonstrates a cluster of hyperintense small cysts (<1.5 cm) in the lateral aspect of the left hemithorax (yellow arrows) with intact diaphragm (purple arrows), consistent with congenital pulmonary airway malformations (CPAMs). Note the nuchal cord (green arrows). Postnatal chest radiograph (C) and axial contrast-enhanced chest CT (D) demonstrate the Type II CPAM to be located in the left lower lobe (purple circle), with subsequent mass effect on the mediastinum. A coronal T2-weighted image at 1.5T in a different 18-week fetus (E) demonstrates a massive, nonsurvivable left sided CPAM with fetal ascites and polyhydramnios and associated ascites.

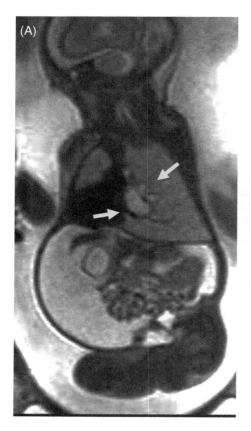

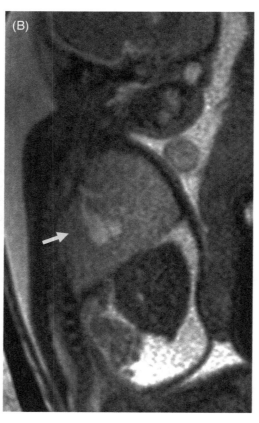

FIG. 20.18 Coronal (A) and sagittal (B) T2-weighted imaging at 1.5T through the fetal body of this 19-week singleton fetus demonstrates round and branching dilated tubular structures in the perihilar region consistent with bronchial atresia (yellow arrows). Additionally, there is fetal ascites and polyhydramnios.

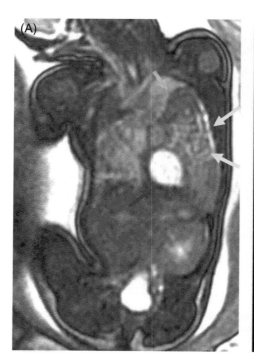

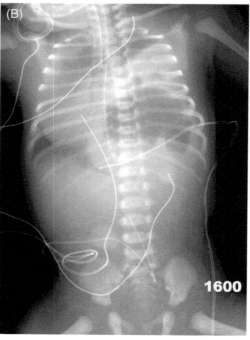

FIG. 20.19 Coronal HASTE (A) T2-weighted imaging at 1.5T through the fetal body of this 34-week singleton fetus demonstrates absence of the left hemidiaphragm with subsequent herniation of the fluid-filled stomach bubble (purple arrow), spleen (orange arrow), and multiple loops of bowel (yellow arrows) into the left hemithorax, consistent with congenital diaphragmatic hernia (CDH). Postnatal radiograph of the chest and abdomen (B) demonstrates similar findings with marked mediastinal shift to the right and low right lung volumes.

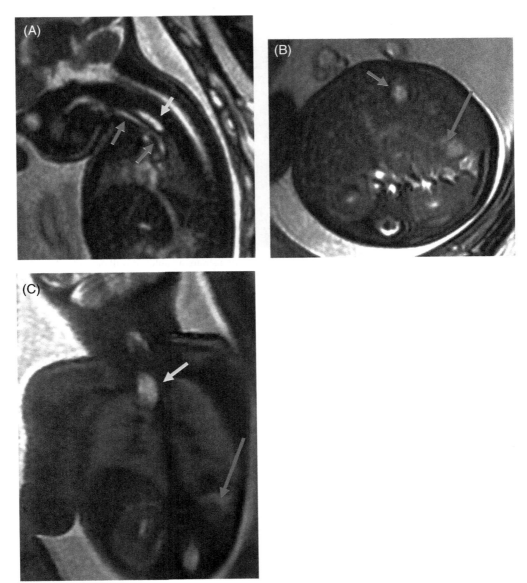

FIG. 20.20 T2 HASTE sequences from a fetal MR at 1.5T in a 20-week singleton fetus demonstrates a fluid-filled esophageal pouch (A and C, yellow arrow) separate from the fluid-filled trachea (A, red arrow) as well as absence of the expected left upper quadrant stomach bubble (B and C, **blue** arrow), in keeping with a proximal esophageal atresia without a tracheoesophageal fistula (TEF) (Type A TEF). Notice the fluid-filled gallbladder in B (red arrow). *Courtesy of J. Shah.*

20.2.7.3.3 Fetal abdominal and pelvic anomalies

When evaluating malformations of the fetal abdominal wall, MRI is used in the prognostic evaluation of intestinal atresia, gastroschisis, and omphalocele complications.[84] MRI is a more accurate method than is ultrasound for the characterization of the pelvic and abdominal extent of sacrococcygeal tumors,[85] as well as providing more information on the compression of adjacent organs.[78]

Omphalocele, a defect of the anterior abdominal wall which is encapsulated by the parietal peritoneum, occurs in 1/4000 live births and is accompanied by other malformations in 72% of cases (Fig. 20.21).[78]

Gastroschisis, a rare anomaly characterized by the herniation of the abdominal contents through a defect in the periumbilical abdominal wall on the right, occurs without an associated hernia sac, such that the abdominal contents are in direct contact with the amniotic fluid (Fig. 20.22). Gastroschisis, which can be accompanied by other

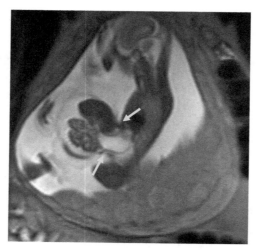

FIG. 20.21 Sagittal T2 HASTE image at 1.5T in a 19-week singleton fetus demonstrates an anterior wall defect (yellow arrows) that is encapsulated, consistent with omphalocele. Note that the herniation sac contains liver, stomach, bowel loops, and ascitic fluid. *Courtesy of M. Halverson.*

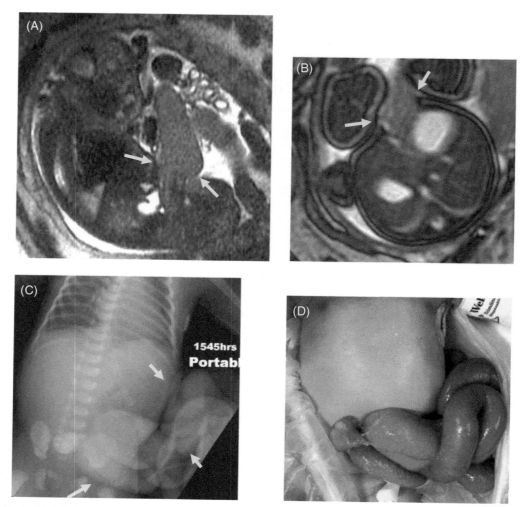

FIG. 20.22 Sagittal SSFSE (A) and axial HASTE (B) T2-weighted imaging at 1.5T through the fetal body of this 36-week singleton fetus demonstrates an anterior abdominal wall full-thickness defect lateral to the midline through which bowel herniates (yellow arrows), consistent with gastroschisis. A postnatal abdominal radiograph (C) demonstrates similar findings with a paucity of intra-abdominal bowel gas in the right hemiabdomen and loops of bowel, not in a sac, extending to the left, external to the patient (yellow arrows). Preoperative photo of the neonate's anterior abdominal wall demonstrates similar findings (D).

malformations in 19–31% of cases, presents complications, such as intestinal obstruction, perforation, peritonitis, necrotizing enterocolitis, short bowel syndrome, and fistulas.[78]

Renal anomalies can also be further evaluated by fetal MRI as any structural or functional defects in the fetal urinary tract can result in a substantial reduction of amniotic fluid volume (oligohydramnios or anhydramnios), which, in turn, can cause fetal pulmonary hypoplasia, as well as abnormal development of several other fetal structures.[86] Multicystic dysplastic kidney (MCDK) is among the most common causes of end-stage renal disease and renal failure in the neonate; however, the prognosis of unilateral MCDK is excellent, with natural involution of the affected kidney and development of compensatory hypertrophy of the contralateral kidney. But, nevertheless, MCDK can be fatal when it involves both kidneys (Fig. 20.23).[86]

Sacrococcygeal and pelvic anomalies can be confusing to evaluate in the fetus as many structures appear to overlap in such a small space. Given meconium's high T1 signal, fetal MRI allows for better evaluation of the adjacent colon in any cases of abdominal or pelvic mass. Additionally, hemorrhage into the tumor can be

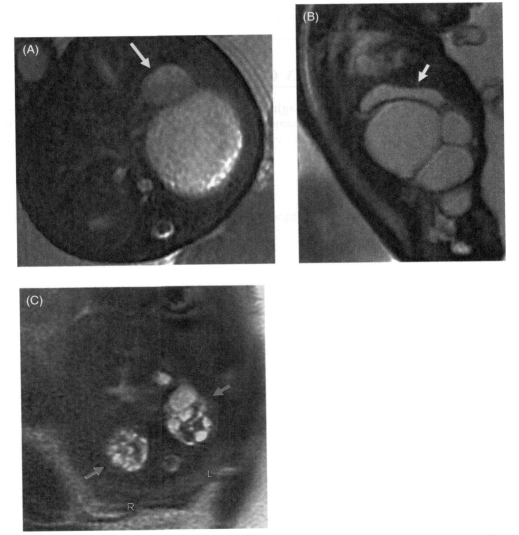

FIG. 20.23   Axial (A) and sagittal (B) T2 HASTE fetal MR at 1.5T in a 21-week singleton fetus demonstrates a left-sided multicystic structure centered in the retroperitoneum with no normal intervening renal parenchyma, in keeping with unilateral, left-sided MCDK. Note the mass effect on the stomach bubble (yellow arrow). Axial T2 HASTE imaging of a different 18-week singleton fetus (C) demonstrates bilateral multicystic structures replacing the expected kidneys (red arrows) with associated anhydramnios, consistent with a nonsurvivable bilateral MCDK. *Courtesy of J. Shah.*

evaluated at fetal MRI,[85] utilizing T1 and EPI sequences. Finally, using MRI in conjunction with fetal ultrasound can help the pediatric surgeons to better visualize the proper postnatal approach in the resection of abdominal and pelvic fetal masses,[85] which leads to expedient surgical treatment as well as improved patient outcome (Figs. 20.24-20.28).

Pearls and pitfalls

- Make sure that mom has voided and is comfortable on the MRI table, which may result in a slightly obliqued configuration of the maternal abdomen and pelvis, prior to starting the exam.

- Review large FOV images in all 3 planes to assess for fetal number, volume of amniotic fluid, state of cervix, location of placenta, and any maternal abnormalities.

- Perform imaging of suspected fetal abnormality first as mom may become uncomfortable during the exam, triggering an early end to the study.

- Make sure that the radiologist is reviewing the study in real-time, either at the console with the MRI technologist or remotely, such that adjustments can be made quickly.

- Utilization of a dictation template is generally preferred by referring clinicians.

- Always include the expected fetal age in the report.

- Communicate any critical findings to the referring clinician/consulting colleagues expeditiously, in the interest of optimizing parental and referring provider awareness and decision making.

20.3 Conclusion

Although fetal ultrasound remains the primary imaging modality of prenatal screening and diagnosis, the utility of fetal MRI in confirming and further assessing some suspected findings has been established. With continued improvements in software and hardware by the MR vendors, its role in prenatal diagnosis will likely continue to evolve.

Acknowledgements

We would like to express our appreciation to Dr. Jignesh Shah and Dr. Mark Halverson for the images that they contributed to our chapter.

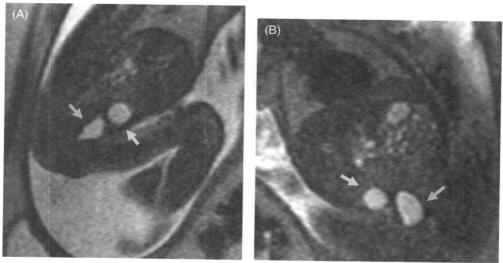

FIG. 20.24   Sagittal (A) and coronal (B) T2 HASTE MRI images at 1.5T in a 19-week singleton fetus demonstrate a hyperintense cystic structure (yellow arrow) in the right lower quadrant, separate from the bladder (orange arrow). At postnatal surgery, this was found to be a duplication cyst. *Courtesy of M. Halverson.*

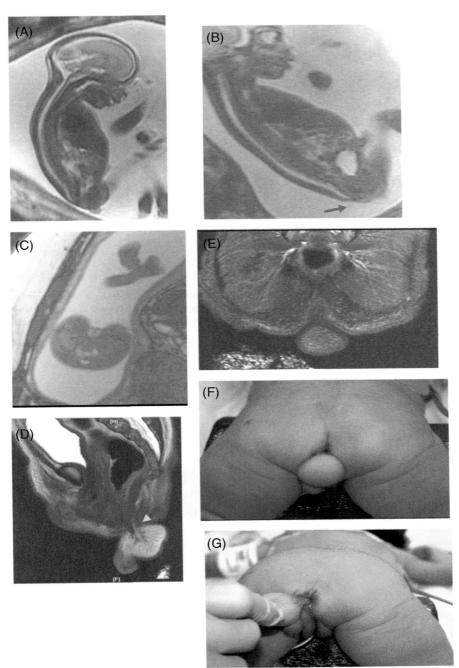

FIG. 20.25 Fetal MRI performed at 1.5T (A–C) on a 22-week singleton fetus demonstrates an exophytic structure (yellow arrow) extending from the perineal region on this sagittal T2 HASTE sequence (A), somewhat posterior to the expected location of a scrotal sac. Sagittal T2 SSFSE (B) demonstrates that the sacrum is normally formed (blue arrow), making a sacrococcygeal teratoma unlikely. A normal-appearing labia (red arrow) is demonstrated on axial T2 SSFSE (C), excluding ambiguous genitalia. Postnatal T2-weighted MRI in sagittal and axial planes (D and E, respectively) demonstrates a vascular pedicle (yellow arrow) supplying the exophytic rounded mass, noting a normal appearance of the remainder of the sacrum, coccyx, and perineal structures. Intraoperative pictures (F and G) show a similar gross appearance of this perineal hamartoma.

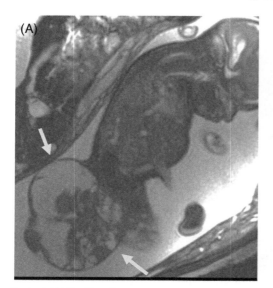

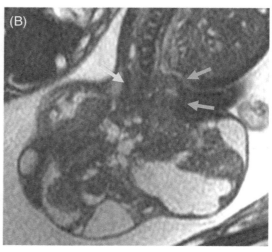

FIG. 20.26 Sagittal (A) T2 TRUFI MR image at 1.5T in this 20-week singleton fetus demonstrates a heterogeneous, partially exophytic mass (yellow arrows) extending from the sacral region, in keeping with a sacrococcygeal teratoma. Zoomed in sagittal image (B), shows abrupt cut-off of the sacrum (yellow arrow) as well as an intrapelvic component of the mass (orange arrows), indicating a Type II sacrococcygeal teratoma which was confirmed at postnatal excision. *Courtesy of J. Shah.*

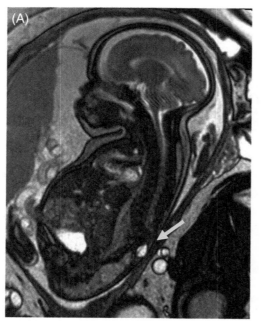

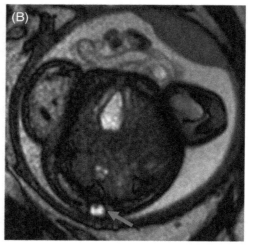

FIG. 20.27 Sagittal (A) and axial (B) T2-weighted sequences obtained at 1.5T on a 32-week singleton fetus demonstrates sacral agenesis with abrupt cut-off of the lumbar spine with cystic-appearing spinal dysraphism (yellow arrow) and probable tethering of the spinal cord (red arrow) (note the T2 hyperintense bladder anteriorly).

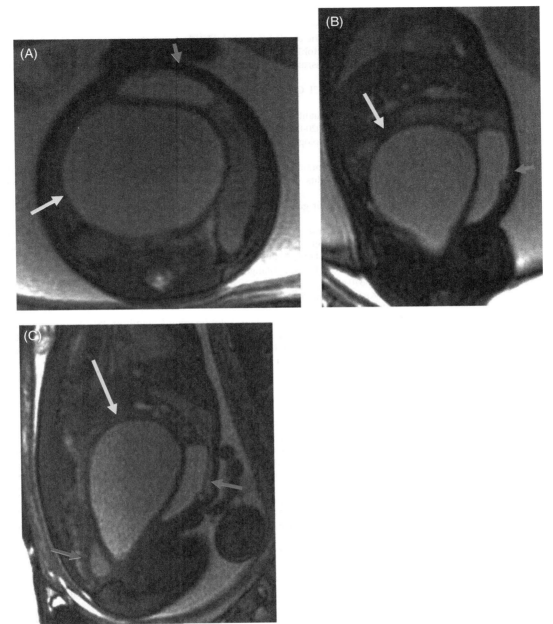

FIG. 20.28 Multiplanar T2 HASTE fetal MR at 1.5T in a 20-week singleton female fetus demonstrates a large cystic structure (yellow arrows) centered in the pelvis which displaces the bladder anteriorly (red arrows) and the rectum posteriorly (blue arrow). At postnatal exam, this was found to be hematometrocolpos. *Courtesy of J. Shah.*

References

1. Plunk MR, Chapman T. The fundamentals of fetal MR imaging: part 1. *Curr Probl Diagn Radiol.* 2014;43(6):331–346. doi:10.1067/j.cpradiol.2014.05.014.
2. ACR-SPR Practice Parameter for the Safe and Optimal Performance of Fetal Magnetic Resonance Imaging (MRI). 2020, https://www.acr.org/-/media/ACR/Files/Practice-Parameters/mr-fetal.pdf.
3. Prayer D, Malinger G, Brugger PC, et al. ISUOG practice guidelines: performance of fetal magnetic resonance imaging. *Ultrasound Obstet Gynecol.* 2017;49(5):671–680. doi:10.1002/uog.17412.
4. Aertsen M, Diogo MC, Dymarkowski S, Deprest J, Prayer D. Fetal MRI for dummies: what the fetal medicine specialist should know about acquisitions and sequences. *Prenat Diagn.* 2020;40(1):6–17. doi:10.1002/pd.5579.
5. The American Institute of Ultrasound in Medicine. Standards and Guidelines for the Accreditation of Ultrasound Practices. 2020. https://www.aium.org/officialstatements/26

6. The American College of Radiology. Exam Requirements: Obstetrical Ultrasound. 2021. https://accreditationsupport.acr.org/support/solutions/articles/11000062865-exam-requirements-obstetrical-ultrasound-revised-2-24-2021-

7. Chapman T, Alazraki AL, Eklund MJ. A survey of pediatric diagnostic radiologists in North America: current practices in fetal magnetic resonance imaging. *Pediatr Radiol.* 2018;48(13):1924–1935. doi:10.1007/s00247-018-4236-3.

8. Levine D. Timing of MRI in pregnancy, repeat exams, access, and physician qualifications. *Semin Perinatol.* 2013;37(5):340–344. doi:10.1053/j.semperi.2013.06.011.

9. Yen CJ, Mehollin-Ray AR, Bernardo F, Zhang W, Cassady CI. Correlation between maternal meal and fetal motion during fetal MRI. *Pediatr Radiol.* 2019;49(1):46–50. doi:10.1007/s00247-018-4254-1.

10. Machado-Rivas F, Jaimes C, Kirsch JE, Gee MS. Image-quality optimization and artifact reduction in fetal magnetic resonance imaging. *Pediatr Radiol.* 2020;50(13):1830–1838. doi:10.1007/s00247-020-04672-7.

11. Moltoni G, Talenti G, Righini A. Brain fetal neuroradiology: a beginner's guide. *Transl Pediatr.* 2021;10(4):1065–1077. doi:10.21037/tp-20-293.

12. Jarvis DA, Griffiths PD. Current state of MRI of the fetal brain in utero. *J Magn Reson Imaging.* 2019;49(3):632–646. doi:10.1002/jmri.26316.

13. Manganaro L, Antonelli A, Bernardo S, et al. Highlights on MRI of the fetal body. *Radiol Med.* 2018;123(4):271–285. doi:10.1007/s11547-017-0834-7.

14. Furey EA, Bailey AA, Twickler DM. Fetal MR imaging of gastrointestinal abnormalities. *Radiographics.* 2016;36(3):904–917. doi:10.1148/rg.2016150109.

15. Li Y, Zhang X. Advanced MR imaging technologies in fetuses. *OMICS J Radiol.* 2012;1(4):e113. doi:10.4172/2167-7964.1000e113.

16. Chavhan GB, Babyn PS, Jankharia BG, Cheng HLM, Shroff MM. Steady-state MR imaging sequences: physics, classification, and clinical applications. *Radiographics.* 2008;28(4):1147–1160. doi:10.1148/rg.284075031.

17. Masselli G, Vaccaro Notte MR, Zacharzewska-Gondek A, Laghi F, Manganaro L, Brunelli R. Fetal MRI of CNS abnormalities. *Clin Radiol.* 2020;75(8). doi:10.1016/j.crad.2020.03.035 640.e1-640.e11.

18. Huang SY, Seethamraju RT, Patel P, Hahn PF, Kirsch JE, Guimaraes AR. Body MR imaging: artifacts, k-space, and solutions. *Radiographics.* 2015;35(5):1439–1460. doi:10.1148/rg.2015140289.

19. Barth R, Victoria T, Kline-Fath B, Estroff J, Society for Pediatric Radiology Fetal Imaging Committee. ISUOG guidelines for fetal MRI: a response to 3-T fetal imaging and limited fetal exams. *Ultrasound Obstet Gynecol.* 2017;50(6):804–805. doi:10.1002/uog.18946.

20. Krishnamurthy U, Neelavalli J, Mody S, et al. MR imaging of the fetal brain at 1.5T and 3.0T field strengths: comparing specific absorption rate (SAR) and image quality. *J Perinat Med.* 2015;43(2):209–220. doi:10.1515/jpm-2014-0268.

21. Weisstanner C, Gruber GM, Brugger PC, et al. Fetal MRI at 3T-ready for routine use? *Br J Radiol.* 2017;90(1069):20160362. doi:10.1259/bjr.20160362.

22. Barrera CA, Francavilla ML, Serai SD, et al. Specific absorption rate and specific energy dose: Comparison of 1.5-T versus 3.0-T Fetal MRI. *Radiology.* 2020;295(3):664–674. doi:10.1148/radiol.2020191550.

23. Nagaraj UD, Calvo-Garcia MA, Merrow AC, Zhang B, Tkach JA, Kline-Fath BM. Utilization of 3-T fetal magnetic resonance imaging in clinical practice: a single-institution experience. *Pediatr Radiol.* 2021;51(10):1798-1808. doi:10.1007/s00247-021-05087-8.

24. da Silva NA, Vassallo J, Sarian LO, Cognard C, Sevely A. Magnetic resonance imaging of the fetal brain at 3 Tesla: preliminary experience from a single series. *Medicine (Baltimore).* 2018;97(40):e12602. doi:10.1097/MD.0000000000012602.

25. Brink WM, Gulani V, Webb AG. Clinical applications of dual-channel transmit MRI: a review. *J Magn Reson Imaging.* 2015;42(4):855–869. doi:10.1002/jmri.24791.

26. Victoria T., Jaramillo D., Roberts T., et al. Fetal magnetic resonance imaging: jumping from 1.5 to 3 Tesla (preliminary experience). Pediatric Radiology. 2014; 44(4): 376-86. https://pubmed.ncbi.nlm.nih.gov/24671739/.

27. Little JT, Bookwalter CA. Magnetic resonance safety: pregnancy and lactation. *Magn Reson Imaging Clin N Am.* 2020;28(4):509–516. doi:10.1016/j.mric.2020.06.002.

28. Chartier AL, Bouvier MJ, McPherson DR, Stepenosky JE, Taysom DA, Marks RM. The safety of maternal and fetal MRI at 3 T. *AJR Am J Roentgenol.* 2019;213(5):1170–1173. doi:10.2214/AJR.19.21400.

29. Chansakul T, Young GS. Neuroimaging in pregnant women. *Semin Neurol.* 2017;37(6):712–723. doi:10.1055/s-0037-1608939.

30. Zvi E, Shemer A, Toussia-Cohen S, et al. Fetal exposure to MR imaging: long-term neurodevelopmental outcome. *AJNR Am J Neuroradiol.* 2020;41(11):1989–1992. doi:10.3174/ajnr.A6771.

31. Chambers CD, Johnson KA, Dick LM, Felix RJ, Jones KL. Maternal fever and birth outcome: a prospective study. *Teratology.* 1998;58(6):251–257. doi:10.1002/(SICI)1096-9926(199812)58:6<251::AID-TERA6>3.0.CO;2-L.

32. Moretti ME, Bar-Oz B, Fried S, Koren G. Maternal hyperthermia and the risk for neural tube defects in offspring: systematic review and meta-analysis. *Epidemiology.* 2005;16(2):216–219. doi:10.1097/01.ede.0000152903.55579.15.

33. Zaremba L. FDA Guidelines for Magnetic Resonance Safety. https://www.aapm.org/meetings/02AM/pdf/8356-48054.pdf

34. International ElectrotechnicalCommission. Medical electrical Equipment-Part 2-33: Particular Requirements for the Basic Safety and Essential Performance of Magnetic Resonance Equipment for Medical Diagnosis. IEC 60601-2-33. Ed. 3. 2010, https://webstore.iec.ch/publication/22705.

35. International Commission on Non-Ionizing Radiation Protection. Medical magnetic resonance (MR) procedures: protection of patients. *Health Phys.* 2004;87(2):197–216. doi:10.1097/00004032-200408000-00008.

36. International Electrotechnical Commission. International standard, medical equipment – part 2: particular requirements for the safety of magnetic resonance equipment for medical diagnosis. 2002, https://webstore.iec.ch/publication/2647.

37. Hand JW, Li Y, Thomas EL, Rutherford MA, Hajnal JV. Prediction of specific absorption rate in mother and fetus associated with MRI examinations during pregnancy. *Magn Reson Med.* 2006;55(4):883–893. doi:10.1002/mrm.20824.

38. Gowland PA, De Wilde J. Temperature increase in the fetus due to radio frequency exposure during magnetic resonance scanning. *Phys Med Biol.* 2008;53(21):L15–L18. doi:10.1088/0031-9155/53/21/L01.

39. Abaci Turk E, Yetisir F, Adalsteinsson E, et al. Individual variation in simulated fetal SAR assessed in multiple body models. *Magn Reson Med.* 2020;83(4):1418–1428. doi:10.1002/mrm.28006.

40. Tirada N, Dreizin D, Khati NJ, Akin EA, Zeman RK. Imaging pregnant and lactating patients. *Radiographics*. 2015;35(6):1751–1765. doi:10.1148/rg.2015150031.

41. Hepper PG, Shahidullah BS. Development of fetal hearing. *Arch Dis Child Fetal Neonatal Ed*. 1994;71(2):F81–F87. doi:10.1136/fn.71.2.f81.

42. Reeves MJ, Brandreth M, Whitby EH, et al. Neonatal cochlear function: measurement after exposure to acoustic noise during in utero MR imaging. *Radiology*. 2010;257(3):802–809. doi:10.1148/radiol.10092366.

43. Strizek B, Jani JC, Mucyo E, et al. Safety of MR imaging at 1.5 T in fetuses: a retrospective case-control study of birth weights and the effects of acoustic noise. *Radiology*. 2015;275(2):530–537. doi:10.1148/radiol.14141382.

44. Glover P, Hykin J, Gowland P, Wright J, Johnson I, Mansfield P. An assessment of the intrauterine sound intensity level during obstetric echo-planar magnetic resonance imaging. *Br J Radiol*. 1995;68(814):1090–1094. doi:10.1259/0007-1285-68-814-1090.

45. Gerhardt KJ, Abrams RM. Fetal hearing: characterization of the stimulus and response. *Semin Perinatol*. 1996;20(1):11–20. doi:10.1016/s0146-0005(96)80053-x.

46. McJury M, Shellock FG. Auditory noise associated with MR procedures: a review. *J Magn Reson Imaging*. 2000;12(1):37–45. doi:10.1002/1522-2586(200007)12:1<37::aid-jmri5>3.0.co;2-i.

47. Coblentz AC, Teixeira SR, Mirsky DM, Johnson AM, Feygin T, Victoria T. How to read a fetal magnetic resonance image 101. *Pediatr Radiol*. 2020;50(13):1810–1829. doi:10.1007/s00247-020-04768-0.

48. Feygin T, Khalek N, Moldenhauer JS. Fetal brain, head, and neck tumors: prenatal imaging and management. *Prenat Diagn*. 2020;40(10):1203–1219. doi:10.1002/pd.5722.

49. Nagarajan M, Sharbidre KG, Bhabad SH, Byrd SE. MR imaging of the fetal face: comprehensive review. *Radiographics*. 2018;38(3):962–980. doi:10.1148/rg.2018170142.

50. Werner H, Nogueira R, Lobo Lopes FPP. MR imaging of fetal musculoskeletal disorders. *Magn Reson Imaging Clin N Am*. 2018;26(4):631–644. doi:10.1016/j.mric.2018.06.011.

51. Victoria T, Johnson AM, Moldenhauer JS, Hedrick HL, Flake AW, Adzick NS. Imaging of fetal tumors and other dysplastic lesions: a review with emphasis on MR imaging. *Prenat Diagn*. 2020;40(1):84–99. doi:10.1002/pd.5630.

52. van Doorn M, Oude Rengerink K, Newsum EA, Reneman L, Majoie CB, Pajkrt E. Added value of fetal MRI in fetuses with suspected brain abnormalities on neurosonography: a systematic review and meta-analysis. *J Matern Fetal Neonatal Med*. 2016;29(18):2949–2961. doi:10.3109/14767058.2015.1109621.

53. Jarvis D, Mooney C, Cohen J, et al. A systematic review and meta-analysis to determine the contribution of MR imaging to the diagnosis of foetal brain abnormalities In Utero. *Eur Radiol*. 2017;27(6):2367–2380. doi:10.1007/s00330-016-4563-4.

54. Saleem SN. Fetal MRI: an approach to practice: a review. *J Adv Res*. 2014;5(5):507–523. doi:10.1016/j.jare.2013.06.001.

55. Vasung L, Lepage C, Radoš M, et al. Quantitative and qualitative analysis of transient fetal compartments during prenatal human brain development. *Front Neuroanat*. 2016;10:11. doi:10.3389/fnana.2016.00011.

56. Girard N, Raybaud C, Poncet M. In vivo MR study of brain maturation in normal fetuses. *AJNR Am J Neuroradiol*. 1995;16(2):407–413.

57. Kyriakopoulou V, Vatansever D, Davidson A, et al. Normative biometry of the fetal brain using magnetic resonance imaging. *Brain Struct Funct*. 2017;222(5):2295–2307. doi:10.1007/s00429-016-1342-6.

58. Conte G, Milani S, Palumbo G, et al. Prenatal brain MR imaging: reference linear biometric centiles between 20 and 24 gestational weeks. *AJNR Am J Neuroradiol*. 2018;39(5):963–967. doi:10.3174/ajnr.A5574.

59. Scelsa B, Rustico M, Righini A, et al. Mild ventriculomegaly from fetal consultation to neurodevelopmental assessment: a single center experience and review of the literature. *Eur J Paediatr Neurol*. 2018;22(6):919–928. doi:10.1016/j.ejpn.2018.04.001.

60. Mirsky DM, Stence NV, Powers AM, Dingman AL, Neuberger I. Imaging of fetal ventriculomegaly. *Pediatr Radiol*. 2020;50(13):1948–1958. doi:10.1007/s00247-020-04880-1.

61. Garel C, Luton D, Oury JF, Gressens P. Ventricular dilatations. *Childs Nerv Syst*. 2003;19(7-8):517–523. doi:10.1007/s00381-003-0795-0.

62. ENSO Working Group. Role of prenatal magnetic resonance imaging in fetuses with isolated mild or moderate ventriculomegaly in the era of neurosonography: international multicenter study. *Ultrasound Obstet Gynecol*. 2020;56(3):340–347. doi:10.1002/uog.21974.

63. Griffiths PD, Bradburn M, Campbell MJ, et al. Use of MRI in the diagnosis of fetal brain abnormalities in utero (MERIDIAN): a multicentre, prospective cohort study. *Lancet*. 2017;389(10068):538–546. doi:10.1016/S0140-6736(16)31723-8.

64. Craven I, Bradburn MJ, Griffiths PD. Antenatal diagnosis of agenesis of the corpus callosum. *Clin Radiol*. 2015;70(3):248–253. doi:10.1016/j.crad.2014.11.004.

65. Choi JJ, Yang E, Soul JS, Jaimes C. Fetal magnetic resonance imaging: supratentorial brain malformations. *Pediatr Radiol*. 2020;50(13):1934–1947. doi:10.1007/s00247-020-04696-z.

66. Glenn OA, Goldstein RB, Li KC, et al. Fetal magnetic resonance imaging in the evaluation of fetuses referred for sonographically suspected abnormalities of the corpus callosum. *J Ultrasound Med*. 2005;24(6):791–804. doi:10.7863/jum.2005.24.6.791.

67. Calloni SF, Caschera L, Triulzi FM. Disorders of ventral induction/spectrum of holoprosencephaly. *Neuroimaging Clin N Am*. 2019;29(3):411–421. doi:10.1016/j.nic.2019.03.003.

68. Yang E, Chu WCW, Lee EY. A practical approach to supratentorial brain malformations: what radiologists should know. *Radiol Clin North Am*. 2017;55(4):609–627. doi:10.1016/j.rcl.2017.02.005.

69. Miller SP, Shevell MI, Patenaude Y, Poulin C, O'Gorman AM. Septo-optic dysplasia plus: a spectrum of malformations of cortical development. *Neurology*. 2000;54(8):1701–1703. doi:10.1212/wnl.54.8.1701.

70. Miller E, Orman G, Huisman TAGM. Fetal MRI assessment of posterior fossa anomalies: a review. *J Neuroimaging*. 2021;31(4):620–640. doi:10.1111/jon.12871.

71. Limperopoulos C, Robertson RL, Khwaja OS, et al. How accurately does current fetal imaging identify posterior fossa anomalies? *AJR Am J Roentgenol*. 2008;190(6):1637–1643. doi:10.2214/AJR.07.3036.

72. Robinson AJ, Ederies MA. Diagnostic imaging of posterior fossa anomalies in the fetus. *Semin Fetal Neonatal Med*. 2016;21(5):312–320. doi:10.1016/j.siny.2016.04.007.

73. D'Antonio F, Khalil A, Garel C, et al. Systematic review and meta-analysis of isolated posterior fossa malformations on prenatal ultrasound imaging (part 1): nomenclature, diagnostic accuracy and associated anomalies. *Ultrasound Obstet Gynecol*. 2016;47(6):690–697. doi:10.1002/uog.14900.

74. Robinson AJ. Inferior vermian hypoplasia—preconception, misconception. *Ultrasound Obstet Gynecol*. 2014;43(2):123–136. doi:10.1002/uog.13296.

75. Pinto J, Paladini D, Severino M, et al. Delayed rotation of the cerebellar vermis: a pitfall in early second-trimester fetal magnetic resonance imaging. *Ultrasound Obstet Gynecol*. 2016;48(1):121–124. doi:10.1002/uog.15782.

76. Ghi T, Contro E, De Musso F, et al. Normal morphometry of fetal posterior fossa at midtrimester: brainstem-tentorium angle and brainstem-vermis angle. *Prenat Diagn*. 2012;32(5):440–443. doi:10.1002/pd.3834.

77. Nagaraj UD, Kline-Fath BM. Imaging of open spinal dysraphisms in the era of prenatal surgery. *Pediatr Radiol*. 2020;50(13):1988–1998. doi:10.1007/s00247-020-04734-w.

78. Matos APP, Duarte L de B, Castro PT, Daltro P, Werner Júnior H, Araujo Júnior E. Evaluation of the fetal abdomen by magnetic resonance imaging. Part 2: abdominal wall defects and tumors. *Radiol Bras*. 2018;51(3):187–192. doi:10.1590/0100-3984.2016.0142.

79. Zylak CJ, Eyler WR, Spizarny DL, Stone CH. Developmental lung anomalies in the adult: radiologic-pathologic correlation. *Radiographics*. 2002;22 Spec No:S25–S43. doi:10.1148/radiographics.22.suppl_1.g02oc26s25.

80. Biyyam DR, Chapman T, Ferguson MR, Deutsch G, Dighe MK. Congenital lung abnormalities: embryologic features, prenatal diagnosis, and postnatal radiologic-pathologic correlation. *Radiographics*. 2010;30(6):1721–1738. doi:10.1148/rg.306105508.

81. Langston C. New concepts in the pathology of congenital lung malformations. *Semin Pediatr Surg*. 2003;12(1):17–37. doi:10.1053/spsu.2003.00001.

82. Mehollin-Ray AR, Cassady CI, Cass DL, Olutoye OO. Fetal MR imaging of congenital diaphragmatic hernia. *Radiographics*. 2012;32(4):1067–1084. doi:10.1148/rg.324115155.

83. Style CC, Mehollin-Ray AR, Verla MA, et al. Timing of prenatal magnetic resonance imaging in the assessment of congenital diaphragmatic hernia. *Fetal Diagn Ther*. 2020;47(3):205–213. doi:10.1159/000501556.

84. Nakagawa M, Hara M, Shibamoto Y. MRI findings in fetuses with an abdominal wall defect: gastroschisis, omphalocele, and cloacal exstrophy. *Jpn J Radiol*. 2013;31(3):153–159. doi:10.1007/s11604-012-0163-7.

85. Danzer E, Hubbard AM, Hedrick HL, et al. Diagnosis and characterization of fetal sacrococcygeal teratoma with prenatal MRI. *AJR Am J Roentgenol*. 2006;187(4):W350–W356. doi:10.2214/AJR.05.0152.

86. Mileto A, Itani M, Katz DS, et al. Fetal urinary tract anomalies: review of pathophysiology, imaging, and management. *AJR Am J Roentgenol*. 2018;210(5):1010–1021. doi:10.2214/AJR.17.18371.

Index

Page numbers followed by "*f*" and "*t*" indicate, figures and tables respectively.